THE 8th DAY OF HUNGER STRIKE

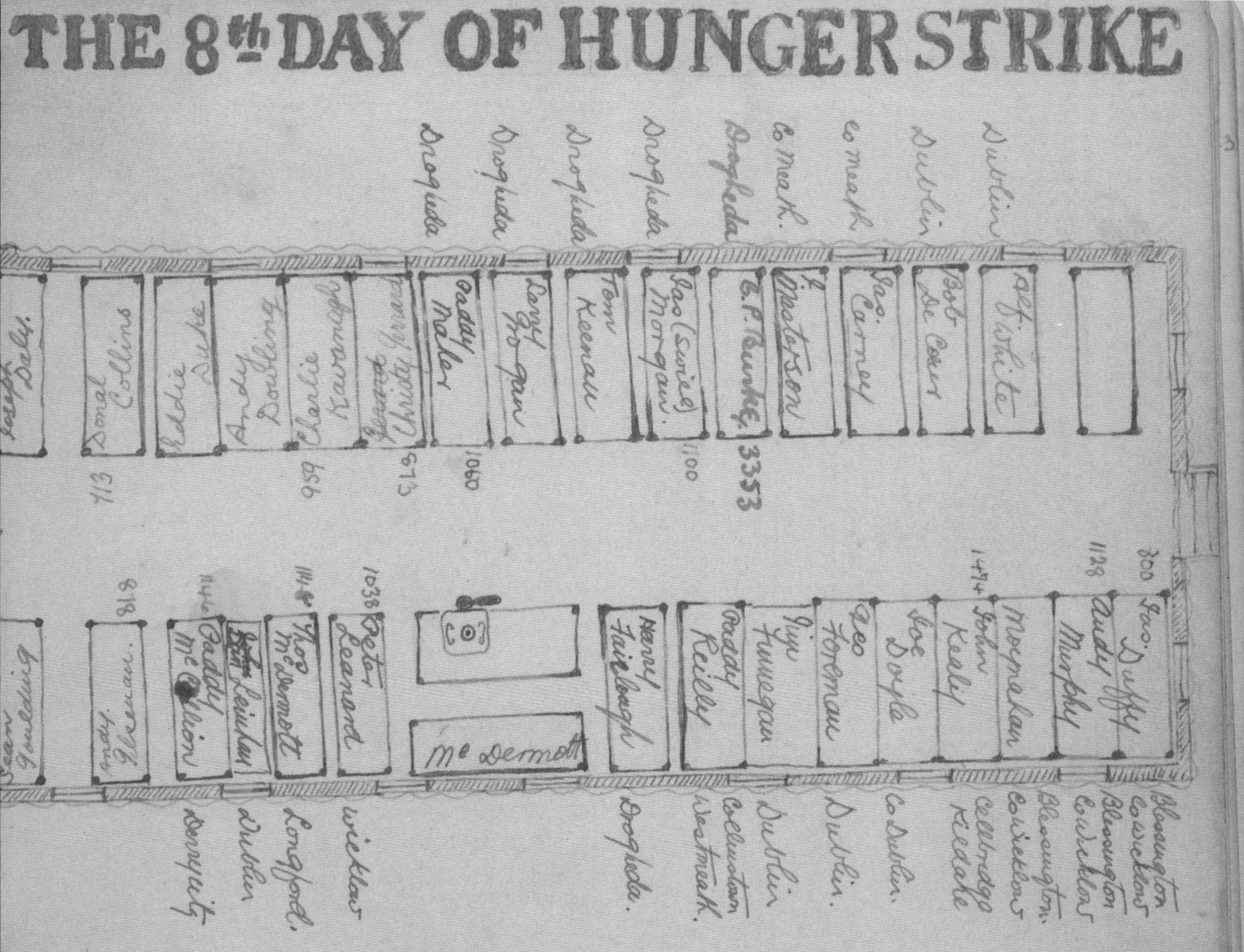

Pages from the prison autograph book belonging to IRA Volunteer Seán Sharkey who was interned in Tintown No. 3, The Curragh, County Kildare during the Irish Civil War. This diagram of the layout of one of the 'huts' in the sprawling Tintown internment camp includes the names and native counties of the republican prisoners on the eighth day of a hunger strike in the autumn of 1923. Often considered the final act of the Civil War, the mass hunger strike of October–November 1923, which began in Mountjoy Gaol and involved an estimated 8,000 prisoners across Ireland at its height, ended following the deaths of Cork Volunteer Denis Barry (interned in Newbridge) on 20 November at the Curragh Military Hospital and Cavan-born Andy Sullivan (interned in Mountjoy) on 23 November. [Image: Seán Sharkey Collection, courtesy of Neil Sharkey, Tipperary Studies, Tipperary County Council]

Atlas of the Irish Civil War

NEW PERSPECTIVES

Cover image (left) Seán Keating, *An Allegory* (1924). Known for his politicised paintings in support of Irish nationalism between 1916 and 1922, the internecine violence of the post-Treaty Civil War (1922–3) ensured that the artist would repudiate violence for the rest of his life. In later years he wrote: 'I used to feel strongly about things between 1916 and 22, but the situation after 1922 was so heartbreaking that I thought no more about it.' Yet, he did think more about it, and in spite of the fact that Keating's post-1923 paintings remained politicised, democratic, confrontational, critical and, at times, even subversive, the Civil War taught him that violence was not the way forward. *An Allegory* was the artist's first major post-Civil War painting, the title of which denoted for his viewers, then and now, how he wanted the painting to be understood. Composed as a series of three vignettes in the foreground, Keating's architectural background is equally important to his metaphorical intention, so that the painting may be 'read' from side to side, as well as from back to front. The building is Woodtown House, a classical bow-ended mansion at the foot of the Dublin Mountains, in which Keating and his wife, May, had been renting rooms since 1921. In *An Allegory* the classical balance of the house has been ruined, the implication being that social order was in disarray. Two men, one a religious figure, the other an archetypal businessman figure who, coincidentally or not, bears a resemblance to unionist leader Edward Carson, stand in conversation to the left of the foreground. One rolls his thumbs, the other rests on his stick, as if indifferent to the scene. In the middle, seated beneath an ancient tree, May Keating is the model for worn-out Mother Ireland, the nascent post-Civil War baby at her breast. Keating, then aged thirty-five, but weary and aged with heartbreak, lies against the base of the tree, while two men from either side of the Civil War divide dig a grave among the knotty, complicated roots in which to bury their differences in the tricolour-draped coffin. The artist's aim was to paint an image that visually called a halt to violence. It was now time to move on, and to begin to build the state that had been imagined for so long. *An Allegory* was exhibited first in the Carnegie Institute in Pittsburgh (1925), and then in the Carnegie International in New York (1926), where it would have had great appeal to the large Irish-American population. The painting was returned to Ireland and shown in the Munster Arts Club in 1926, before being sent to the Royal Academy in London in 1927, followed by the Royal Scottish Academy in 1928. [Text: Dr Éimear O'Connor / Image: courtesy of the National Gallery of Ireland © Estate of Seán Keating, IVARO Dublin, 2023 / See Éimear O'Connor, *Seán Keating: Art, politics and building the Irish Nation* (Newbridge, 2013)]

Fig. 2 (right) Seán Keating, Study for *An Allegory*, *c.*1921–4. [Source: private collection. Reproduced with kind permission of the owner. © Estate of Seán Keating, IVARO Dublin, 2023]

Atlas of the Irish Civil War

NEW PERSPECTIVES

Editors: Hélène O'Keeffe, John Crowley, Donal Ó Drisceoil, John Borgonovo and Mike Murphy

Produced in partnership with the National Library of Ireland and with support from the Department of Tourism, Culture, Arts, Gaeltacht, Sport and Media

Irish Civil War Fatalities Index: Andy Bielenberg and John Dorney

Production Editor: Maria O'Donovan

First published in 2024 by
Cork University Press
Boole Library
University College Cork
T12 ND89
Ireland

Reprinted 2024

Library of Congress Control Number: 2024941916

Distribution in the USA Longleaf Services, Chapel Hill, NC, USA.

ISBN: 9781782055921

Book Design and typesetting: Anú Design, Tara

Printed in Italy by Printer Trento

College of
Arts, Celtic Studies & Social Sciences

Tailte Éireann
Clárúchán, Luacháil, Suirbhéireacht
Registration, Valuation, Surveying

Contents

Section 10

List of Contributors

Síobhra Aiken is a Lecturer in the Department of Irish and Celtic Studies at Queen's University Belfast. She is the author of the prize-winning *Spiritual Wounds: Trauma, testimony and the Irish Civil War* (2022).

Daniel Ayiotis is a historian and archivist. He is a commandant in the Irish army and since 2017 has served as officer commanding and director of the Irish Military Archives.

Andy Bielenberg is a Senior Lecturer in the School of History, University College Cork. He has published extensively on revolutionary Ireland and is Principal Investigator for the government of Ireland-funded Irish Civil War Fatalities Project (2024).

James Bonsall is an archaeologist and director of Fourth Dimension Prospection in Sligo. He is a co-author of *The Six: The lives and memorialisation of Sligo's Noble Six* (2022).

Lia Brazil is a research fellow at Nuffield College, University of Oxford. She is currently working on a book on the history of international law and humanitarian relief in Ireland and South Africa.

Joanna Brück is Full Professor of Archaeology, University College Dublin and Principal Investigator on the Irish Research Council-funded project Archaeology of the Irish Revolution. She co-edited the volume *Making 1916: Material and visual culture of the Easter Rising* (2015).

Sarah-Anne Buckley is Associate Professor in History and Vice-Dean for Equality, Diversity and Inclusion for the College of Arts, Social Sciences and Celtic Studies, University of Galway. She is Co-principal Investigator of the Tuam Oral History Project and co-author of the *Old Ireland in Colour* series.

Edward Burke is Assistant Professor in the History of War Since 1945 at the School of History, University College Dublin. His publications include *Ulster's Lost Counties: Loyalism and paramilitarism since 1920* (2024).

Noel Carolan is a PhD student and Irish Research Council-funded scholar at Dublin City University. His research focuses on food supplies in Ireland during the early twentieth century.

Ciara Chambers is a Senior Lecturer and Head of Department of Film and Screen Media, University College Cork. Her publications include *Ireland and the Newsreels* (2012) and *Researching Newsreels* (2018).

Cécile Chemin is Senior Archivist at the Irish Military Archives, and Director of the Military Service (1916–23) Pensions Collection Project.

Linda Connolly is Professor of Sociology and Director of Maynooth University Social Sciences Institute. She edited *Women and the Irish Revolution, 1917–1923: Feminism, activism, violence* (2020).

Catriona Crowe is an archivist and historian. She is a member of the Royal Irish Academy, former Head of Special Collections at the National Archives of Ireland and co-editor of the volume *'A very hard struggle': Lives in the Military Service Pensions Collection* (2023).

Brian Crowley is the Collections Curator at the Kilmainham Gaol Museum. A former director of the Irish Museums Association, he is author of *Patrick Pearse: A life in pictures* (2013).

Robert Delaney is a military historian and sergeant armament artificer in the Irish Defence Forces. He received an MLitt from Maynooth University for his study of the 18-pounder in Irish service, 1922–42.

Gabriel Doherty lectures at the School of History, University College Cork. His publications include the co-edited volume *Michael Collins and the Making of the Irish State* (2006) and (co-written) *Terence MacSwiney: Caught in the living flame* (2022).

Anne Dolan is Associate Professor in Modern Irish History, Trinity College Dublin. Her publications include *Commemorating the Irish Civil War: History and memory, 1923–2000* (2003) and (co-written) *Days in the Life: Reading the Michael Collins Diaries, 1918–1922* (2022).

Terence Dooley is Professor of History and Director of the Centre for the Study of Historic Irish Houses and Estates, Maynooth University. His books include *Burning the Big House: The story of the Irish country house in a time of war and revolution* (2022).

Michael Doorley is Associate Lecturer in History, Politics and International Relations at the Open University. His many publications on the Irish revolution in the United States include the biography *Justice Daniel Cohalan, 1865–1946: American patriot and Irish-American nationalist* (2019).

Theo Dorgan is a poet and broadcaster. A member of Aosdána and former Director of Poetry Ireland, he is the author of numerous poetry collections and non-fiction works, and co-editor of *Revising the Rising* (1991).

John Dorney is a research assistant with the Irish Civil War Fatalities Project. He is the author of *The Civil War in Dublin: The fight for the Irish capital, 1922–1923* (2017).

Marion Dowd lectures in Prehistoric Archaeology at the Atlantic Technological Institute. Her publications include *The Archaeology of Caves in Ireland* (2015) and the co-written *The Six: The lives and memorialisation of Sligo's Noble Six* (2022).

Hilary Dully is a writer, documentary filmmaker and the editor of Máire Comerford's memoir, *On Dangerous Ground: A memoir of the Irish revolution* (2021).

Lindsey Earner-Byrne is Professor of Contemporary Irish History, Trinity College Dublin. Her publications include *Letters of the Catholic Poor: Poverty in independent Ireland, 1920–1940* (2017) and (with Diane Urquhart) *The Irish Abortion Journey, 1920–2018* (2019).

Seán Enright is a Circuit Court judge and a legal historian of the Irish revolutionary period. His published works include *The Irish Civil War: Law, execution and atrocity* (2019; 2022).

Bryce Evans is Professor of Modern World History, Liverpool Hope University. He is the author of *Feeding the People in Wartime Britain* (2022) and co-author, with Stephen Kelly, of *Frank Aiken: Nationalist and internationalist* (2014).

Frank Fagan is a psychotherapist and historian with an MA in Local History from University College Cork. He has a particular interest in the legacy and aftermath of the Civil War in County Sligo.

Diarmaid Ferriter is Professor of Modern Irish History, University College Dublin. He has published widely on the social, political and cultural history of twentieth-century Ireland. His most recent work is *Between Two Hells: The Irish Civil War* (2021).

John FitzGerald is Adjunct Professor of English and former Director of Information Services and University Librarian at University College Cork. His second collection of poetry, *Long Distance*, was published in 2024.

John Gibney is Assistant Editor with the Royal Irish Academy's Documents on Irish Foreign Policy programme. He is the co-author of *The Handover: Dublin Castle and the British withdrawal from Ireland, 1922* (2022) and *On an Equal Footing with All: Ireland at the League of Nations 1923–1946* (2023).

Liz Gillis is a historian, broadcaster and author from the Liberties in Dublin. Her books include *The Fall of Dublin* (2011) and *The Hales Brothers and the Irish Revolution* (2016).

Lisa Godson is a cultural historian and curator and is currently a Visiting Research Fellow at the School of Architecture, Planning & Environmental Policy, University College Dublin. She co-authored *Making 1916: Material and visual culture of the Easter Rising* (2015) and *Uniform: Clothing and discipline in the modern world* (2019).

Adrian Grant is a Lecturer in Policy at the School of Applied Social and Policy Sciences, Ulster University. He is the author of *Irish Socialist Republicanism, 1909–36* (2012) and *The Irish Revolution: Derry, 1912–23* (2018).

Joshua Griffith is a student of the BA in Animation, Visual Effects and Motion Design at MTU (Kerry Campus). He works across a range of visual media and disciplines, from illustration to animation, and 3D modelling to VR.

Brian Hanley is Assistant Professor of Twentieth Century Irish History, Trinity College Dublin. He has written widely on Irish republicanism and radicalism, including, most recently, *Republicanism, Crime and Paramilitary Policing in Ireland, 1916–2020* (2022).

Gerard Hanley is a research fellow at the School of History and Geography, Dublin City University. He is co-author, with Daithí Ó Corráin, of *Cathal Brugha: 'An indomitable spirit'* (2022) and author of *Workers, Politics and Labour Relations in Independent Ireland, 1922–46* (2024).

Aidan Harte is an archaeologist at the School of Archaeology, University College Dublin. He is senior researcher for the Irish Research Council-funded project Archaeology of the Irish Revolution, led by Professor Joanna Brück.

Brian Hughes lectures in History at Mary Immaculate College, Limerick. He is the author of *Defying the IRA? Intimidation, coercion and communities during the Irish revolution* (2016) and co-editor of *Southern Irish Loyalism, 1912–1949* (2020).

Heather Jones is Professor of Modern and Contemporary European History, University College London. She is the author of *Violence Against Prisoners of War in the First World War: Britain, France and Germany, 1914–1920* (2011) and *For King and Country: The British monarchy and the First World War* (2021).

Lar Joye is Port Heritage Director at Dublin Port. A historian, curator and film archivist, he previously curated the award-winning exhibition *Soldiers and Chiefs: The Irish at war at home and abroad from 1550 to the present day* at the National Museum of Ireland at Collins Barracks.

Stephen Kelly is Head of History, Politics and International Relations and Professor of Modern Irish History, Liverpool Hope University. His most recent publication is *Gerald Boland, 1885–1973: A life* (2024).

Ian Keneally is an author, historian and documentary maker. He was Historian in Residence for County Westmeath, 2020–3, and author of, among other publications, *Courage and Conflict: Forgotten stories of the Irish at war* (2009).

Michael Kennedy is Executive Editor of the Royal Irish Academy's Documents on Irish Foreign Policy (DIFP) series and head of the DIFP series. He is co-author of *Ireland: A voice among the nations* (2019) and *On an Equal Footing with All: Ireland at the League of Nations, 1923–1946* (2023).

Eoin Kinsella is managing editor of the Royal Irish Academy's *Dictionary of Irish Biography*. His books include *The Irish Defence Forces, 1922–2022: Servants of the nation* (2023) and *The Irish Dental Association: A centenary history* (2023).

Heather Laird is a Senior Lecturer in the Department of English, University College Cork. Her publications include *Subversive Law in Ireland, 1879–1920* (2005) and *Commemoration* (2018), which reimagines commemoration and promotes new thinking on the Irish revolution.

Leeann Lane is Associate Professor in the School of History and Geography, Dublin City University. Her biography *Dorothy Macardle* was published in 2019, and she is currently working on a book on Mary MacSwiney.

Donnacha Seán Lucey is a historian and Research Manager in the College of Business and Law, University College Cork. He is the author of *The End of the Irish Poor Law? Welfare and healthcare reform in revolutionary and independent Ireland* (2015).

Mary MacDiarmada is a research fellow at the School of History and Geography, Dublin City University. She is the author of *Art O'Brien and Irish Nationalism in London, 1900–1925* (2020).

Emily Mark-Fitzgerald is Associate Professor in the School of Art History and Cultural Policy, University College Dublin. Her publications include *Commemorating the Irish Famine: Memory and the monument* (2013).

Ann Matthews is a historian and playwright. Her books include *Renegades: Irish republican women, 1900–1922* (2010) and *Dissidents: Irish republican women, 1923–1941* (2012).

Laura McAtackney is a Professor in the Radical Humanities Laboratory and Archaeology, University College Cork. Her research centres on contemporary archaeology, especially intersections with conflict, institutions, colonialism and gender.

Brian McCarthy is a career guidance counsellor and has a PhD in History from University College Dublin. He is the author of *The Civic Guard Mutiny* (2012).

Pat McCarthy is a Research Associate in the School of History and Geography, Dublin City University. He is the author of *The Irish Revolution, 1912–23: Waterford* (2015), and holds a PhD from University College Dublin.

David McCullagh is a journalist, author and historian. His books include the two-volume biography of Éamon de Valera, *De Valera: Rise, 1882–1932* (2017) and *De Valera: Rule, 1932–1975* (2018).

Ailbhe McDaid is an Assistant Professor in English Language and Literature, Mary Immaculate College, Limerick. Her publications include '"When we've licked the wounds of history": Literary representations of women's experiences of the War of Independence and Civil War', in Linda Connolly (ed.), *Women and the Irish Revolution, 1917–1923: Feminism, activism, violence* (2020).

Fearghal McGarry is a Professor of History, Queen's University Belfast and a member of the Royal Irish Academy. His most recent book is the co-edited *The Irish Revolution: A global history* (2022).

Owen McGee is a historian and author. His books include *The IRB: The Irish Republican Brotherhood, from the Land League to Sinn Féin* (2005) and *Arthur Griffith* (2015).

Claire McGing is an EDI manager at the Institute of Art, Design + Technology, Dún Laoghaire. Her most recent publication is 'Without distinction of their sex': The roles of women in the 1923 general election', in Elaine Callinan, Mel Farrell and Thomas Tormey (eds), *Vying for Victory: The 1923 general election in the Irish Free State* (2023).

Tony McGrath is a historian and chartered quantity surveyor, based in Cork. His website 'Reading the Signs' (https://readingthesigns.weebly.com) identifies and locates memorials and related road signs across Ireland.

Ronan McGreevy is an *Irish Times* journalist and historian. His most recent book is *Great Hatred: The assassination of Field Marshal Sir Henry Wilson MP* (2022).

Anne-Marie McInerney is a librarian at Dublin City Library and Archive. She received a PhD from Trinity College Dublin in 2014 for a thesis on the internment of anti-Treaty IRA members in the Irish Free State, 1922–4.

Jason McKevitt is a teacher based in Mullingar who researches military and social history.

Ciara Meehan is a Professor and the Dean of Students, University of Galway. Her publications include *The Cosgrave Party: A history of Cumann na nGaedheal, 1923–1933* (2010).

Conor Morrissey is a Senior Lecturer in British/Irish History, King's College, London. He is the author of *Protestant Nationalists in Ireland, 1900–1923* (2019).

Terry Moylan is a writer on Irish traditional music, dance and song. His books include *The Indignant Muse: Poetry and songs of the Irish revolution* (2016).

Robert Mulraney teaches Archaeology at the Institute of Technology, Sligo. He is a co-author of *The Six: The lives and memorialisation of Sligo's Noble Six* (2022).

Conor Mulvagh is an Associate Professor in Irish History, University College Dublin. He is the author of *The Irish Parliamentary Party at Westminster, 1900–18* (2016).

Gary Murphy is Professor of Politics in the School of Law and Government, Dublin City University. His most recent book is *Haughey* (2021).

William Murphy is Associate Professor in History in the School of History and Geography, Dublin City University. He is the co-author with Anne Dolan of *Days in the Life: Reading the Michael Collins diaries, 1918–1922* (2022).

Niall Murray is a historian and a PhD candidate at the School of History, University College Cork. He is also a member of the Irish Research Council-funded Archaeology of the Irish Revolution project team at the School of Archaeology, University College Dublin.

Daithí Ó Corráin is Associate Professor in History in the School of History and Geography, Dublin City University. He recently co-wrote *Cathal Brugha: 'An indomitable spirit'* (2022) with Gerard Hanley.

Micheál Ó Fathartaigh is a Lecturer at the Dublin Business School and committee member of the Social Sciences Research Centre, University of Galway. He is the co-author with Liam Weeks of *Birth of a State: The Anglo-Irish Treaty* (2021).

Aaron Ó Maonaigh is a historian and secondary school teacher whose research and publications focus on sport during the Irish revolution, 1912–23, and on County Wexford during the Irish Civil War.

Pádraig Óg Ó Ruairc has written several books about the Irish revolution, most recently *The Disappeared: Forced disappearance in Ireland, 1798–1998* (2024).

Paul O'Brien is a writer and journalist, and author of *Sean O'Casey: Political activist and writer* (2023).

John O'Callaghan is a Lecturer at the Atlantic Technological University, Sligo. His books include *The Battle for Kilmallock* (Cork, 2011) and *The Irish Revolution, 1912–23: Limerick* (2018).

Liam O'Callaghan is Associate Professor in the Department of Sport and PE/Sport Psychology, Liverpool Hope University. His publications include *Rugby in Munster: A social and cultural history* (2011).

Helen O'Carroll is a historian and curator of Kerry County Museum. She was awarded the Kerry Heritage Award in 2018.

Éimear O'Connor is Director of Galleries and Access at the National Museum of Ireland. She is the author of *Seán Keating: Art, politics and building the nation* (2013).

Emmet O'Connor is a Senior Lecturer in History, University of Ulster, who has published widely on labour history. He is Honorary President of the Irish Labour History Society. His most recent book is *Rotten Prod: The unlikely career of Dongaree Baird* (2022).

Rory O'Dywer lectures in the School of History, University College Cork. His publications include *The Eucharistic Congress, Dublin, 1932* (2009).

Owen O'Shea is a historian and author of several books on his native Kerry, including *No Middle Path: The Civil War in Kerry* (2023).

Charlie Roche is a geographer and cartographer at MobileGIS who works closely with the Geography Department at University College Cork. He has mapped many of the Atlas of the Irish Revolution Project digital outreach initiatives, including the recent Irish Civil War Fatalities Project.

Gerard Shannon is a historian from Skerries, County Dublin. He is the author of *Liam Lynch: To declare a republic* (2023).

Justin Dolan Stover is Associate Professor in the Department of History, Idaho State University. His most recent book is *Enduring Ruin: Environmental destruction during the Irish revolution* (2022).

Ciarán Wallace is Keeper of the Virtual Record Treasury of Ireland. He has worked on numerous digital humanities projects, holds a PhD in History from Trinity College Dublin, and has published on Dublin's social and cultural history.

Eoin Swithin Walsh is a historian and author of *Kilkenny: In times of revolution, 1900–1923* (2019). He holds an MA in Modern Irish History from University College Dublin.

Margaret Ward is Honorary Senior Lecturer in History, Queen's University Belfast. Her pioneering book *Unmanageable Revolutionaries: Women and Irish nationalism* was republished in an updated and revised edition in 2021.

Liam Weeks is a Senior Lecturer in the Department of Government and Law, University College Cork. He is the co-author, with Mícheál Ó Fathartaigh, of *Birth of a State: The Anglo-Irish Treaty* (2021).

Gerry White has written extensively on Irish military history from 1913–23. His books include the co-authored *The Barracks: A history of Victoria/Collins Barracks* (1997) and *Irish Volunteer Soldier, 1913–1923* (2003).

Pádraig Yeates is a labour and social historian and journalist. His publications include *A City in Civil War: Dublin, 1921–24* (2015).

Foreword

by President Michael D. Higgins

This is a work that was necessary and will be welcomed as going a long way to fill a significant gap in Irish historiography.

The events of the period covered by this important new contribution to the historiography of the Irish Civil War are among the most important in modern Irish history – not only in terms of how they occurred and the consequences that followed, but in what they tell us about the assumptions they carried, about the changing perceptions of the balance between political possibilities and military action, of the importance of land and the impact of the graziers' expansion which created tensions that came to the fore in the period, a period influenced, too, as to tentativeness in terms of the future hold of empires and the force of a mythic dream of independence.

The Civil War was not inevitable. The violence that was waged as part of Ireland's Civil War in 1922–3, and the bitterness and exclusion of its outcome, were an appalling human tragedy for so many Irish families. Its legacies were manifold and harmful and would remain so for succeeding generations, leaving the wounds of the war and the hurt of exclusion unhealed for decades. Its aftermath constituted a bitter remnant that stained Irish society, casting dark shadows of real and imagined versions of military successes and losses that in their narrowness prevented social egalitarianism and impeded cohesion.

A century on, partly as a result of the important work to which we give the title 'ethical recall', in its most hopeful and inclusive sense, we are now perhaps in a better position to seek to speak to the fullness of the experience of the period, drawing on existing and new scholarship, allowing excluded or neglected narratives some space, and doing so with courage and inclusivity. For all these reasons, I so welcome this latest contribution to the historiography, *Atlas of the Irish Civil War: New perspectives*, from University College Cork scholars Dr Hélène O'Keeffe, Dr John Crowley, Dr Donal Ó Drisceoil, Dr John Borgonovo and Mr Mike Murphy.

We have long been aware that the Civil War cost the lives of many well-known public figures; other lives lost are perhaps lesser known but should not be forgotten, nor should the livelihoods destroyed, or those driven into poverty or exile. By including an Irish Civil War Fatalities Index of all the combatant and civilian fatalities of the Civil War, the *Atlas* provides the first ever full listing of all those who died. It constitutes a fitting tribute and a most worthwhile exercise in ethical remembrance.

We all must recognise the atrocities of the Civil War for what they meant to both sides – cruel, vicious and at times informed by vengeance concentrated in a short period – but we cannot neglect context, recognising, too, the role that empire played in not only denying independence, which had received the vote of the people, but also how it sought to inflict humiliation, and pursued a particular undisciplined form of warfare in 1919–21 that impacted on civilians and civilian infrastructure; it also provoked civil war through its demands and impositions.

Among the greatest omissions in our consideration to date is the very limited space that has been granted to those who sought peace or to end the conflict. Such people were aware of what had been lost and of the needless suffering that ensued when the British government refused to accept the will of the people as expressed freely and overwhelmingly in the election of 1918. They knew that conscription drew the greatest cost from the poorest and the working class.

Peace efforts continued into the Civil War period, including those led by Tom Johnson and the Labour and trade union movement on an all-island basis. Such efforts included the threat of the Labour Party to remove its seventeen members from the Dáil in an effort to end the drift to militarism and, on 23 April 1922, the Irish Congress of Trade Unions, led by Johnson, called a one-day general strike titled 'End the Militarism'. This general strike resulted in what the *Irish Times* called the 'complete paralysis of all the nerves of industrial, commercial and social life'.

Much more important than any such description was that an anxiety for peace represented the demands of a weary people who had suffered the 1918 flu pandemic, the War of Independence and now a conflict between fellow comrades. This was experienced directly and generationally in my own family.

At the parliamentary level the Labour Party was offering the only official opposition to the Provisional Government, while its members worked at times under death threats from anti-Treaty forces. Labour stood apart from the aggression, arguing that it was time the gun was taken out of politics following four years of brutal conflict. Publicly and in parliament, it opposed the extrajudicial killings undertaken by the state.

Militarism, including militant nationalism with its narrow focus, can too easily ride roughshod over workers' rights, a point well known to trade unionists who had called general strikes on no less than three occasions over the course of the independence struggle. Later narratives would comprehensively ignore these efforts at achieving peace. There was in heroic commemoration a strut to the gun that the peace proposals were seen to lack.

I am glad that this volume provides important perspectives on gender. Female republican military activity was highly visible and widely publicised throughout the Civil War, and Cumann na mBan would assume greater military responsibilities than it had during the War of Independence, thereby transgressing gender boundaries and confounding some male republican leaders' efforts after the war to reclaim their narrowly defined respectability and masculinity.

The aftermath of the Civil War led to a 1920s and 1930s which saw many other lives so damaged that recovery was impossible and emancipation barely a dream. The aftermath for some republicans included involuntary emigration or, for those without land or security, enforced poverty at home and repression for many. The pension administration was handled in an insensitive, even cruel, way, as an uncaring bureaucracy, which harassed even the most abject of the poorest of the poor. Such an approach revealed a consensus on property, Church and the importance of only helping the 'deserving', morally approved poorest.

These decades, the embryonic period of the newly independent Irish state, would reveal how fully faded now was any vision, such as was contained in the Democratic Programme of the First Dáil, for an inclusive, egalitarian state, had it ever existed, nor would the remaining fingers of empire allow any such egalitarian tendencies to emerge.

Such egalitarian tendencies – always a weak light within the nationalist movement – would be quelled by the strident tones of a nationalism that would ape so much of empire's assumptions. While it displaced the formal version of the previous colonial authority, it mimicked it with a new but similar version that bore newly honed versions of more localised authoritarian tendencies, ones with strong clericalist leanings.

Competing forms of exclusion of the 'Other' – be it religious, professional, economic or social – vied for space and prevailed. 'Bolshevism' was the term of abuse fired at workers at home or abroad, be it from pulpits or conservative politicians who together would now act as gatekeepers to the professions for lay and clerical generations to come.

Some themes of social class, until quite recently an area comprehensively neglected in the historiography of the period, are such a welcome inclusion in this book. The pervasiveness of class distinction would become a defining feature of the decades that followed the Civil War. Anti-intellectualism was rampant, as was sectarianism, reinforcing divisions, toxicity and notions of 'the Other'.

The fresh perspectives contained in this *Atlas* on the military and political history of the Civil War, the new insights into regional, national and, indeed, international aspects that stood behind the war – all of this is so welcome.

In addition to gender and class, the explorations of propaganda, trauma, culture and labour are also important contributions to the historiography, while the more than 400 photographs and archival documents, as well as newly created maps, tables and charts reprinted herein provide fresh and vivid illustrations of the war that detail and contextualise combatant and civilian fatalities over the eleven months from June 1922 to May 1923.

The photographs in particular tell us so much. The youth of the Volunteers is so striking, but so, too, is their dress. The gap between their form of dress, with their shirts and braces-supported trousers, the occasional cap, versus the later photographs of those hatted and suited representatives sent to London, or delegated later to Dublin to debate the Treaty, is striking.

It is interesting to ask what proportion of those who took part in the War of Independence or the Civil War were indentured to the trades. This is a significant gap that remains, as does the significance of position in the family. I cannot help asking how many among them became proprietors of a farm? How did they, as siblings or neighbours in the future, react to their having been divided, not only by sides taken, but in terms of prospects for the future? All of these issues serve as background to the 1923 Land Act and the 1924 Commission on Agriculture and the consequences of the difference between its majority and minority reports. Land for the landless gave way to the graziers, the cattle economy. Strong farmers united to face the agricultural labourer.

In the moment of the photos of the flying columns, they are united, both in circumstance and purpose as well as dress. Yet this bonding will not last, and when their stories are recovered, when the Civil War ends, they will tell of more than a great scattering. They will give evidence of the consequences of an inheritance pattern as to land that required not only a scattering, but of lives with different roles. Life as a non-emigrating relative – usually a woman in the statistics – a 'relative assisting', would be a lesser life than proprietorship. A room in the house and seat in the car to Mass was a common provision in wills.

The release of the Land Commission papers will make so much good scholarship possible, allowing the reconstruction, for example, of the experience of those, such as my own father, who were incarcerated during the Civil War. We have two diaries, but as to weekly parcels, the circumstance of release, how it was done – little. I have written elsewhere of how those released from prison were often targets – names to be submitted to the special anti-land-agitator force, the Special Infantry Corps.

Our past on this island is one that is replete with lost opportunities for peace, for reconciliation from old exclusionary versions of the 'Other'. A century on, we now have an opportunity to achieve different inclusive versions of ourselves and others, and to construct a bright, even emancipatory future for all who want to call this island home, with our diverse histories and memories all respectfully taken into account. The new good history that fills the gaps has but one objective surely: to tell the truth as you see it. What the response may be is history for another day.

All of this new, brave, inclusive history facilitates a shared future that offers hope and capacity for facing new challenges, none greater than delivering a new symmetry of ecology, economy and society, projects towards which we may work together, to which we might all be united: a shared island at peace, one that proudly demonstrates its values of inclusivity, diversity, equality and possibility.

Acknowledgements

The *Atlas of the Irish Civil War: New perspectives* was born out of an eight-week public lecture series organised by the Atlas of the Irish Revolution research team, University College Cork (UCC) in partnership with the National Library of Ireland (NLI) in the autumn of 2022. The NLI has been a generous and supportive partner during the production of this and earlier volumes in the Cork University Press Atlas series, and a vital collaborator in a series of map-based, public outreach projects since 2016. We are very grateful to Director Audrey Whitty and the dedicated staff at the NLI. The support of Bríd O'Sullivan, the NLI's Head of Learning and Outreach, was essential in providing a public platform to discuss the latest research on the Irish Civil War and facilitating access to the NLI's rich archive of Civil War-related material. We are also enormously grateful to Bernadette Metcalfe and James Harte at the NLI, who answered our requests for almost 200 of the images and documents presented here.

This new volume represents the second strand of the two-strand Mapping the Irish Civil War research and public engagement project, funded by the Department of Tourism, Culture, Arts, Gaeltacht, Sport and Media under the Decade of Centenaries Programme 2023. The first strand – the Irish Civil War Fatalities Project – was launched by Minister Catherine Martin TD on 29 March 2024, and the findings of that project are presented as a central chapter in this volume. The support of Rónán Whelan and his colleagues in the Commemorations Unit of the Department of Tourism, Culture, Arts, Gaeltacht, Sport and Media, and the members of the Expert Advisory Group on Centenary Commemorations, who saw such potential in the proposal for the two-strand project, is also deeply appreciated. The editors would also like to acknowledge the work of Charlie Roche (MobileGIS), who developed the interactive map of Civil War fatalities during the first phase of this project, and of Neil Leyden, RTÉ Digital, and Anna Carey, who helped to facilitate wide public access to the project.

This ambitious production benefited from the generous support of colleagues at all levels in UCC. The editors wish to thank President John O'Halloran for his support to both the School of History and the Department of Geography in realising this latest addition to the landmark Atlas series. We especially want to acknowledge the encouragement and support of UCC's College of Arts, Celtic Studies and Social Sciences (CACSSS), in particular the Head of College Professor Chris Williams, an accomplished historian and a champion of interdisciplinary research, outreach in the humanities and the Atlas of the Irish Revolution project. His sudden loss in March 2024 was a blow to our editorial team and to the entire university community. We are also greatly indebted to the following among the university staff: Conor Delaney (CACSSS), Dr Hiram Morgan (School of History), Dr Fiona Cawkwell (School of the Human Environment), Dr Denis Linehan (Department of Geography), Crónán Ó Doibhlin (Head of Collections, UCC Library), Emma Horgan (Archivist, UCC Library), Professor John Cryan (Vice President for Research and Innovation) and John FitzGerald (Adjunct Professor of English).

We are also immensely grateful to the following individuals and institutions: Dr Orlaith McBride, Director, and Zoë Reid, Keeper of Public Services and Collections, National Archives of Ireland; Maeve Sikora and Clare McNamara, National Museum of Ireland; Philip Roe, Registrar, Dublin City Gallery The Hugh Lane; Shay Cody, President, Irish Labour History Society; Kate Manning, Principal Archivist, University College Dublin Archives; Jennifer Doyle, The Library of Trinity College Dublin Collections; Commandant Daniel Ayiotis, Officer-in-Charge, Irish Military Archives; Anne Marie Forbes, The Jackie Clarke Collection; Razib Chatterjee, RTÉ Archives; John O'Mahony and Jim Coughlan, Irish Examiner Archives; James Grange Osborne, Independent Newspapers (Ireland) Ltd; Bruce Stewart and Ricorso; National Museums Northern Ireland; Rory Griffiths, Archive Coordinator, British Pathé Ltd; Stuart A. Rose Manuscript, Archives, & Rare Book Library, Emory University; Aisling Doyle, Archivist, ESB; Ailbe van der Heide, National Folklore Collection, UCD; Linda Murphy, Gill Books; the Hesburgh Libraries of the University of Notre Dame; Chris Walsh, IVARO; Michelle Bourke, Whyte's Auctioneers; Lisa Burke, Tyrone Productions; Gormleys Fine Art; Aileen Mooney and Anne O'Neill, An Post; Adam's Auctioneers; Jason Kiernan, Senior Digital Communications Manager, Houses of the Oireachtas Service; Philip Devine, IFI Irish Film Archive; Lisa McElligott, Munster Technological University, and Dr Eimear Purcell, National University of Ireland. We would also like to thank Daniel O'Connell, Tailte Éireann. We acknowledge and are grateful for permission to reproduce maps under © Tailte Éireann, copyright permit no. MP 003224.

The editors are especially indebted to Dr Brian Kirby, Provincial Archivist, Irish Capuchin Archives; Cécile Chemin, Senior Archivist, Irish Military Archives; Niamh O'Brien, National Gallery of Ireland, and Brian Crowley, Curator of Collections, Kilmainham

Gaol Museum/OPW, for their time, care and expertise in helping to source some of the rarest and most striking imagery for this new atlas.

Depicting the variety of personal and communal experiences of the Civil War at local level though imagery and archival documents was made possible by the generous contributions from city and county archives, libraries and museums. We are very grateful to the following: Dan Breen, Cork Public Museum; Brian McGee, Cork City and County Archives; Pat Bracken, Tipperary County Library; Mary Guinan Darmody, Tipperary Studies; Niamh Brennan, Donegal County Archives; Fionnuala Parfrey, Dublin City Archives; Archbishop Dermot Farrell and the Dublin Diocesan Archives; Patricia Corish and David Power, South Dublin Libraries; Sarah Hayes-Hickey, Limerick Archives; Matthew Potter, Limerick Museum; Lorraine McCann, Louth County Archives; William Fraher, Waterford County Museum; Michael Cannady, The Museum of the Irish Revolution; Cailín Gallagher, Westmeath County Library; Orla Connaughton, Offaly Archives; Meath County Archive; County Monaghan Museum; Helen O'Carroll, Kerry County Museum; and Tom Donovan, the *Old Limerick Journal*. With thanks also to Dermot McMonagle for sharing his in-depth knowledge of Ballyconnell.

The editors would also like to acknowledge the generosity of those who gave permission to publish rare images and documents from private or family collections. With thanks in particular to Edel Doherty and the Doherty family of Currinara, Foxford, County Mayo for their permission to reproduce photographs of Margaret Doherty and the Doherty family, and to Eleanor Hooker for the image of Eileen Mary Warburton Biggs (née Robinson). To Miriam and Hilary Jones and Rosaleen Monaghan, who gave permission to print the last letters, written on the eve of their executions, by Luke Burke and Colum Kelly respectively. Special thanks also to Philip McConway for his assistance. We are also very grateful to Frank Fagan, a historian and contributor to this volume, who generously supplied a selection of images from his private collection and helped to source several others. With thanks also to the Delahunty family; the Comerford family; the Roache family; Joe Mellett; Pádraig Kilgannon, Plunkett Doherty and Aidan Marren for supplying original photographs from their family collections. Gratitude is also due to Mary Gallagher, John Fitzgerald, Cormac O'Malley, Róisín Crowley, Tadhg Crowley and Neil Sharkey for providing permission to reproduce archival images and documents donated by them or their families to local and national institutions. Thanks also to Mary Ahern.

Section 9 of this volume, which considers the legacies of the Irish Civil War, was significantly enriched by the generous donation of original artwork by Debbie Chapman, Orla de Brí, Joshua Griffith, Garreth Joyce, Hughie O'Donoghue and Mick O'Dea, and poetry by Victoria Kennefick. Original photography was kindly provided by Ros Kavanagh, Michael Reynolds, Aidan Harte, Robert Mulraney, John Crowley and Gerard Hore.

Like previous atlases, the production of this volume was conducted in a spirit of collaboration and the editors wish to sincerely thank all those directly involved in that process. First and foremost, our eighty-nine contributors, whose chapters, case studies and short essays add considerably to our knowledge of the Irish Civil War, and who engaged with the editorial process with such enthusiasm and generosity. Numerous contributors helped in additional, various ways, including sourcing and securing permission for images, and providing data for, and reviewing, maps. With special thanks in this regard to John Dorney, Andy Bielenberg, Frank Fagan, Ian Keneally, Helen O'Carroll, Anne Matthews, Linda Connolly, Michael Doorley, Michael Kennedy, Margaret Ward, John Gibney, Eoin Kinsella, Justin Dolan Stover, Tony McGrath, Brian McCarthy, Ciarán Wallace, Pat McCarthy, Laura McAtackney, Éimear O'Connor, Donnacha Seán Lucey, Terence Dooley, John O'Callaghan, John Fitzgerald, Hillary Dully, Rob Delaney, Edward Burke and Eoin Swithin Walsh.

On a personal note, we would like to express our gratitude to our families for their advice, encouragement and admirable forbearance during the production process: heartfelt thanks to Barra Vernon, Maurice, Jane, Claire and David O'Keeffe; to Jer, Anne, Ciarán and Martin Crowley, and Kevin, Margaret, Eoin, Joe and Paul Crowley for all their support and hospitality; to Ethan, Neil and Aoife Murphy, and especially Cailíosa Murphy for her oversight and advice; to Orla McDonnell; and to all the Borgonovos in the United States.

The ambition of the Atlas of the Irish Revolution research team could not have been realised without the dedicated team at Cork University Press. We would like to extend our particular thanks to commissioning editor and production editor Maria O'Donovan for her oversight, guidance and patience. She has been an essential collaborator in the production of the trilogy of key works on Irish history that began with the publication of the *Atlas of the Great Irish Famine* in 2012 and culminates with this new *Atlas of the Irish Civil War*. Thanks also to Sinéad Neville for her support at the press, to Maureen Fitzgerald for helping us navigate the complex world of rights and permissions, to James Ryan who copyedited the text, to Dominic Carroll and Claire Fitzgerald for their vigilant proofreading, and to Karen Carty for her elegant design. Finally, we would like to thank Mark O'Sullivan at Áras an Uachtaráin, and especially President Michael D. Higgins, who did us the great honour of contributing the foreword.

Fig. 1 A barefoot boy holding a sword salvaged from Victoria (now Collins) Barracks, Cork city, *c.*8 August 1922. When the National Army captured Cork city, the retreating IRA set fire to the structures within the massive Victoria Barracks complex on Old Youghal Road. Residents from some of Cork's poorest neighbourhoods descended on the smouldering ruins to salvage anything of value. Looting of abandoned and damaged property occurred in many areas throughout the Civil War. [Image: National Library of Ireland, NLI HOGW 24]

Introduction

A search for traces of the Irish Civil War (1922–3) in the National Library of Ireland's vast collection leads inevitably to the catalogue of sepia images captured by Cork-born freelance photographer and British army veteran William David (W.D.) Hogan. Sanctioned by the new National Army in a climate of strict military censorship and acquired by the National Library between 1995 and 2007, Hogan's gelatin silver prints of uniformed soldiers, political rallies and state funerals have become a defining visual reference point for that tumultuous period in Irish history. Unusual in a collection that focuses primarily on the progress of the war from the Free State perspective is a photograph of a solitary child. Barefoot, he holds aloft a sword salvaged from the ruins of Victoria (now Collins) Barracks in Cork city after it was burned by the retreating IRA garrison in August 1922. The composition is simple, the subject modest, but the image is powerfully evocative of the social, political and, indeed, cultural context of Ireland in the midst of civil war. The ceremonial sabre, abandoned by an officer of the evacuating British army, speaks to the surprising speed of the regime change that followed the ratification of the Anglo-Irish Treaty. Shouldered by a child, the weapon is a potent metaphor for the steady militarisation of Irish society after 1913 and the normalisation of political violence for a generation born into war. The sabre is also suggestive of the continued British influence on events in Ireland during 1922 and for decades afterwards, and the ruined backdrop is a reminder of the widescale physical damage wrought by the Civil War. The boy's frayed hat and bare feet testify to the extreme poverty of Ireland's working class in the face of economic depression and high unemployment, which forced families to hunt for salvage in the wreckage and many of their sons to don the green serge uniform of the new National Army. Shawled and indistinct at the edge of the frame, the woman and girl are representative of the many, still untold stories of female experience during the Irish revolution, and the underexplored intergenerational impact of those formative years.

The photograph, stamped inadvertently with the photographer's fingerprint, is an appropriate image with which to open this new volume, which seeks to address a conflict described by many Civil War veterans as 'best forgotten'.[1] Produced in partnership with the National Library of Ireland in the final year of the Decade of Centenaries, 2012–23, the *Atlas of the Irish Civil War: New perspectives* is a timely forum for engaging with current debates and asking new questions about the conflict – questions inspired by commemorative activity, access to new sources and data, and the emergence of new directions in Civil War scholarship.

Civil War in Ireland

The Irish Civil War erupted during a period of extreme global upheaval. Exhausted by four years of international war, European powers were unable to control the restless people within their own borders. Regimes fell, empires broke up and states fought for new territories. Revolutions and civil wars raged across central and eastern Europe, the Middle East and central Asia. Ireland had been rocked by consecutive political crises since 1912: a near civil war between nationalists and unionists during the Home Rule Crisis; Ireland's contested participation in the First World War; the 1916 Easter Rising; the influenza pandemic of 1918–19; the War of Independence of 1919–21; and sectarian violence in what became Northern Ireland, especially during 1920 and 1922.

The immediate context of Ireland's internecine conflict was an intense campaign to secure national independence. Enjoying popular support, this mass movement of primarily young Catholic men and women of limited social standing had supplanted the comfortable Irish political establishment by 1918. During the next two years it deployed widespread and imaginative civil disobedience, sophisticated international propaganda and pioneering guerrilla warfare tactics to paralyse British governance in Ireland by July of 1921. With neither side able to secure an outright military victory, the British government agreed to a truce with Dáil Éireann, the illegal, secessionist parliament of the self-declared Irish Republic. Subsequent peace negotiations produced a settlement that ultimately shattered the independence movement and created the conditions for a civil war fought between June 1922 and May 1923.

The Irish Civil War was not as bloody as other civil wars fought during this same period. Ireland did not experience years of regionalised faction fighting, as occurred in Mexico and China. There were not the clear class divisions seen in Russia and Finland. Ireland did not become a proxy battlefront for neighbouring states, as in the Balkan borderlands. The Irish Civil War was not fought along religious or ethnic lines, as in Turkey or Upper Silesia. There were no battles between supporters and opponents of the

COPY.

OGLAIGH NA h-EIREANN.

HEADQUARTERS,
1st. SOUTHERN DIVISION.
10/12/21.

1.

At a meeting of Divisional Staff Officers and all Brigade Commandants of 1st. Southern Division, held in Cork on Saturday, December 10th., the following resolution was unanimously adopted, to be forwarded to the Chief of Staff, with a request that it be transmitted to the Cabinet:-

" The Treaty as it is drafted is not acceptable to us "as representing the Army in the 1st. Divisional Area, and "we urge its rejection by the Government."

The following points in the principal paragraphs of the Treaty, are those to which we object, and the notes appended under each paragraph contain the views which we suggest should be substituted for them.

PARAGRAPH 1 of TREATY.

(a) There is at present no Commonwealth of Nations. Should such be established, it must be a Commonwealth of Free Nations.

(b). It is on the basis of (a) above that our suggestions are put forward.

Gt. Britain to be included with other Nations in the Commonwealth of Nations when such is established, thus putting all Nations in Commonwealth on a basis of equality. It is pointed out that if this is accepted by Gt. Britain she could not continue to coerce India and Egypt.

PARAGRAPH 2 OF TREATY.

Paragraph 1 as outlined above will automatically eliminate paragraph 2 of the Treaty.

2.

PARAGRAPH 3 OF TREATY :

(a). A representative of the Crown in Ireland is not acceptable, ~~IN IRELAND~~ but a representative of the Commonwealth of Nations, appointed by the Irish Government, to represent the Executive of Commonwealth of Nations, would be acceptable.

(b). OATH. " .... will be faithful to Executive Body of Commonwealth of Nations ....." to be substituted for ...... " faithful to King George V etc."

PARAGRAPH 6 of TREATY.

A free Ireland presupposes all her Ports and Harbours to be under her own control. Arrangements to be made for the taking over our own Coastal Defences before Treaty is ratified.

PARAGRAPHS 11 to 16 OF TREATY (inclusive).

Partition is not acceptable in any form.

SIGNED:

Staff 1st. Southern Div.	Liam O'Loingsig	Commdt.
	Liam Deireac	Adjt.
	Seosam O'Concubair	Q.M.
	Foinin O'Donnocada	I/O.
Cork Brigades	Sean O' [handwritten signature]	Commdt.
	Seo C. Paor	Commdt.
	Sean O'hIarlan	Commdt
	Sean O'Maolain	Commdt.
	Gibbar De Ros	Commdt.
Kerry Brigades	Amlaoib Ua Murcada.	Commdt.
	Sean Ua Ris	Commdt.
	Diarmuid O'Riogbaildain.	Commdt.

3.

West Limerick Brigade	Gearoid Macamlaoib	Commdt.
Waterford Brigade.	Padraig O'Faolain	Commdt.

Fig. 2 Copy of a statement by officers of the 1st Southern Division rejecting the Treaty, 10 December 1921. During 1921–2 it was generally believed that the IRA functioned as a hierarchical military organisation dominated by Michael Collins and IRA Chief of Staff Richard Mulcahy. In reality, the army operated in a decentralised manner, and was locally governed by its (mainly) elected leadership who exercised collective decision-making. Yet prior to the signing of the Treaty, the Dáil Cabinet did not consult the IRA's provincial leadership, including those commanding the formidable 1st Southern Division comprised of ten IRA brigades in counties Cork, Kerry, Waterford and west Limerick. During the week between the signing of the Treaty and the opening of the Dáil debates on 14 December, the 1st Southern Division's senior officers gathered, discussed and then transmitted their polite but firm opposition to the Treaty: 'we urge its rejection by the government'. They did so on their own initiative, without meaningful consultation with leaders of other provincial units. The 1st Southern's counter-proposals asserted Ireland's equal status within any commonwealth of nations (to be renamed, the officers suggested, the 'Commonwealth of Free Nations'), assumed control of Irish coastal defences, and maintained the island's territorial unity ('partition is not acceptable in any form'). Compromise alternatives to the clauses in the Treaty that provided for a governor general and an oath of allegiance were advanced. The Munstermen also opposed British coercion of India and Egypt, signalling their willingness to join a co-equal commonwealth of nations but not an empire of states controlled by Britain. The Irish Cabinet did not respond formally to the 1st Southern Division statement, but Collins and Mulcahy did reach out to the officers through the Irish Republican Brotherhood. Ultimately, the 1st Southern Division's three senior officers (Liam Lynch, Liam Deasy and Florrie O'Donoghue) attended some of the Dáil debates, which did little to soften their opposition to the Treaty. Their Treaty opposition (and that of their subordinate officers) signalled profound and potentially dangerous dissatisfaction within the IRA. Military opposition to the Anglo-Irish Treaty continued to grow in the ensuing weeks, as provincial unit leaders quietly prepared to repudiate government control and defend the sovereign self-declared Irish Republic to which they had sworn allegiance in 1919. The adoption of this policy at an army convention held in Dublin's Mansion House during March 1922 created the conditions for an open and ultimately deadly split between Treaty opponents and supporters. [Document: National Library of Ireland, Florence O'Donoghue Papers, MS 31,239]

old regime, as happened in Germany and Hungary. The Irish Civil War was not fought over property or capitalism, though there was a class dimension at work, with the Free State representing what might be referred to as the Irish establishment. The two opposing groups of combatants in Ireland were largely Catholic nationalists with broadly similar cultural identities. Their war was, in many ways, limited and self-contained. There were no large-scale brutal massacres or mass expulsions of civilians; deadly violence did not linger long after the conflict's end in mid-1923. Instead, the Irish Free State quickly established itself and emerged as a relatively peaceful, democratic and demilitarised society.

So why was the war fought? Was it a war between irreconcilables and pragmatists? Of imperialists against republicans? A battle between the forces of democracy and anarchy? The Irish Civil War was caused by the ratification of the Anglo-Irish Treaty by the separatist republican parliament, Dáil Éireann, in January 1922. The Treaty created a twenty-six county Irish Free State with dominion status, situated within the British Empire (later termed the British Commonwealth of Nations). Ireland's other six counties comprised the unionist-dominated polity of Northern Ireland, created by the Government of Ireland Act in December 1920, which had come into official existence in May 1921. The proposed 'Irish Free State' fell far short of the self-declared republic established in January 1919 but, according to the 'stepping stone' philosophy of Treaty signatory, Michael Collins, it provided the freedom to achieve freedom – to win full independence incrementally. While nationalists of all types opposed partition and assumed the border as then established would be temporary, they had no real strategy to defeat Northern unionists who were well-armed and willing to fight to remain in the United Kingdom. Indeed, the Civil War offered an opportunity to the unionist rulers of the newly created Northern Ireland to consolidate their power. Rather than the partition of the island, as has often been emphasised by post-independence republicans, the 1922 split in the nationalist movement was primarily over the new Irish Free State's status as a crown dominion within the British Empire. 'The burning issue', as Ronan Fanning notes, 'was sovereignty, not unity', and the Civil War was very much a twenty-six-county conflict.[2]

A threat to empire

While the United Kingdom governed herself democratically, most of her colonial subjects had no voice in their own affairs. Because the Irish independence struggle threatened the British Empire

Fig. 3 Constance Markievicz TD (left) and Dr Kathleen Lynn about to attend a Dáil debate on the Treaty at the National University buildings, Earlsfort Terrace, Dublin. The debates were held in public and private sessions between 14 December 1921 and 7 January 1922. [Image: National Library of Ireland, INDEXMB1]

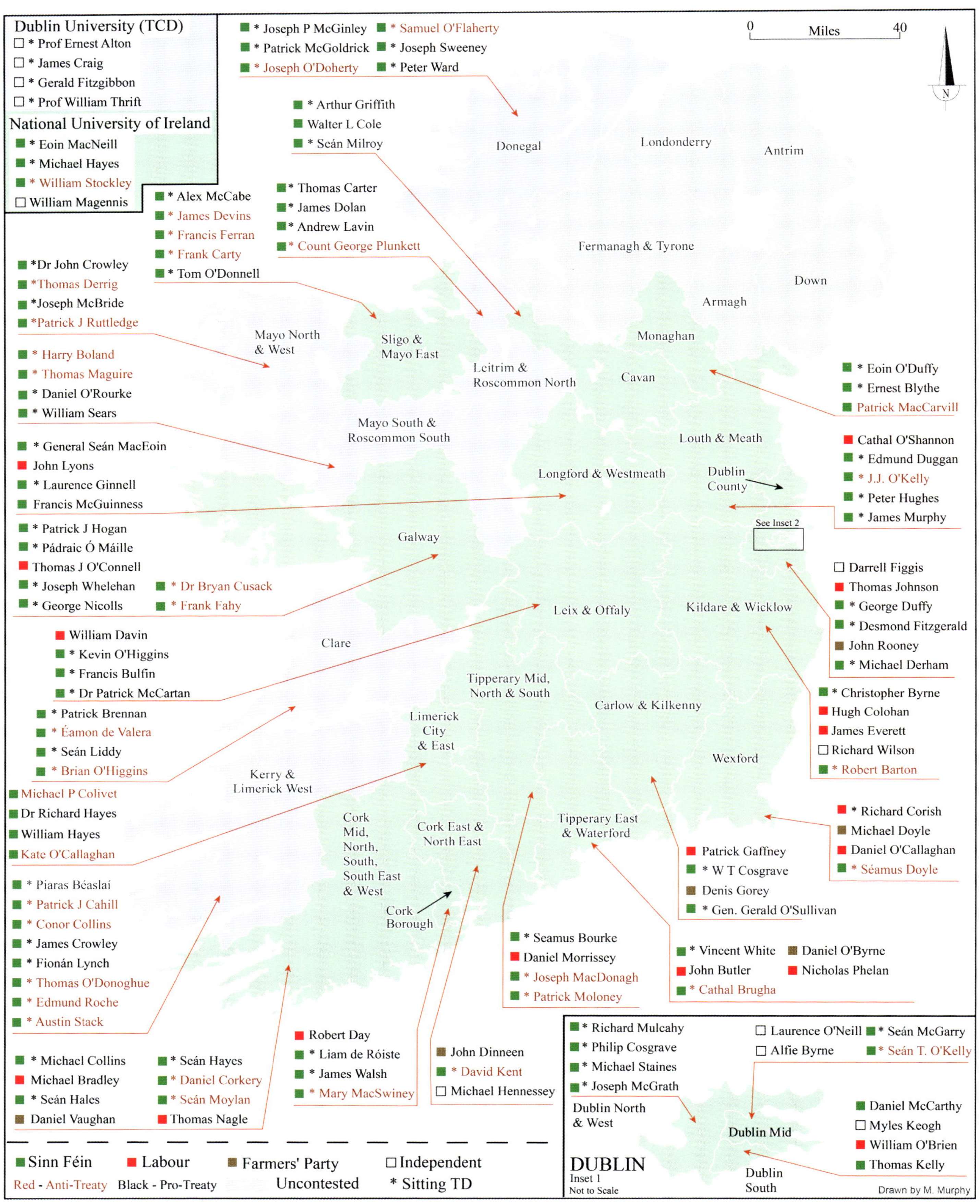

Dublin University (TCD)
* Prof Ernest Alton
* James Craig
* Gerald Fitzgibbon
* Prof William Thrift
National University of Ireland
* Eoin MacNeill
* Michael Hayes
* William Stockley
William Magennis
* Joseph P McGinley
* Samuel O'Flaherty
* Patrick McGoldrick
* Joseph Sweeney
* Joseph O'Doherty
* Peter Ward
0 Miles 40
N
* Arthur Griffith
Walter L Cole
* Seán Milroy
Donegal
Londonderry
Antrim
* Alex McCabe
* James Devins
* Francis Ferran
* Frank Carty
* Tom O'Donnell
* Thomas Carter
* James Dolan
* Andrew Lavin
* Count George Plunkett
Fermanagh & Tyrone
*Dr John Crowley
*Thomas Derrig
*Joseph McBride
*Patrick J Ruttledge
Down
Armagh
Mayo North & West
Sligo & Mayo East
Monaghan
Leitrim & Roscommon North
Cavan
* Harry Boland
* Thomas Maguire
* Daniel O'Rourke
* William Sears
* Eoin O'Duffy
* Ernest Blythe
Patrick MacCarvill
Mayo South & Roscommon South
Louth & Meath
* General Seán MacEoin
John Lyons
* Laurence Ginnell
Francis McGuinness
Cathal O'Shannon
* Edmund Duggan
* J.J. O'Kelly
* Peter Hughes
* James Murphy
Longford & Westmeath
Dublin County
See Inset 2
* Patrick J Hogan
* Pádraic Ó Máille
Thomas J O'Connell
* Joseph Whelehan
* George Nicolls
* Dr Bryan Cusack
* Frank Fahy
Galway
Darrell Figgis
Thomas Johnson
* George Duffy
* Desmond Fitzgerald
John Rooney
* Michael Derham
Leix & Offaly
Kildare & Wicklow
William Davin
* Kevin O'Higgins
* Francis Bulfin
* Dr Patrick McCartan
Clare
Tipperary Mid, North & South
Carlow & Kilkenny
* Christopher Byrne
Hugh Colohan
James Everett
Richard Wilson
* Robert Barton
* Patrick Brennan
* Éamon de Valera
* Seán Liddy
* Brian O'Higgins
Limerick City & East
Wexford
Kerry & Limerick West
Michael P Colivet
Dr Richard Hayes
William Hayes
Kate O'Callaghan
Cork Mid, North, South, South East & West
Cork East & North East
Tipperary East & Waterford
* Richard Corish
Michael Doyle
Daniel O'Callaghan
* Séamus Doyle
Patrick Gaffney
* W T Cosgrave
Denis Gorey
* Gen. Gerald O'Sullivan
* Piaras Béaslaí
* Patrick J Cahill
* Conor Collins
* James Crowley
* Fionán Lynch
* Thomas O'Donoghue
* Edmund Roche
* Austin Stack
Cork Borough
* Seamus Bourke
Daniel Morrissey
* Joseph MacDonagh
* Patrick Moloney
* Vincent White
Daniel O'Byrne
John Butler
Nicholas Phelan
* Cathal Brugha
Robert Day
* Liam de Róiste
* James Walsh
* Mary MacSwiney
John Dinneen
* David Kent
Michael Hennessey
* Richard Mulcahy
* Philip Cosgrave
* Michael Staines
* Joseph McGrath
Laurence O'Neill
Alfie Byrne
* Seán McGarry
* Seán T. O'Kelly
* Michael Collins
Michael Bradley
* Seán Hales
Daniel Vaughan
* Seán Hayes
* Daniel Corkery
* Seán Moylan
Thomas Nagle
Dublin North & West
Dublin Mid
Daniel McCarthy
Myles Keogh
William O'Brien
Thomas Kelly
Sinn Féin
Labour
Farmers' Party
Independent
Red - Anti-Treaty
Black - Pro-Treaty
Uncontested
* Sitting TD
DUBLIN
Inset 1
Not to Scale
Dublin South
Drawn by M. Murphy

Fig. 4 (opposite) Map showing the candidates returned for each constituency in the June 1922 general election in order of the seats won. Party affiliation (if any) and whether the candidate was a sitting TD is indicated, as well as the pro- or anti-Treaty stance taken by Sinn Féin 'panel' candidates. To facilitate an election in the face of potential anti-Treaty sabotage, to avoid widening the split in Sinn Féin, and to maintain that party's dominance, an electoral pact was agreed on 18 May 1922. A panel of Sinn Féin candidates would stand in proportion to the respective existing strengths of the pro- and anti-Treaty sides in the Dáil. After the election a 'coalition' Cabinet would be formed. Of the 124 Sinn Féin TDs in the Second Dáil, 118 were reselected as candidates. Two pro-Treaty TDs had died, Richard Corish stood for Labour, Paul Gilligan in Cavan was replaced by pro-Treaty candidate Walter Cole, and Frank Drohan in Waterford-East Tipperary had resigned his seat. Dan Breen (anti-Treaty) stood in Drohan's place as the sole 'joint panel' candidate, but failed to be elected, despite, as he put it, having 'succeeded in inducing the Farmers' candidates to withdraw'. In Monaghan Seán MacEntee was replaced by Patrick McCarvill, apparently due to MacEntee's broken promise to resign rather than vote against the Treaty. Only two female candidates ran in 1922: Kathleen O'Callaghan (unopposed) and Mary MacSwiney, both anti-Treaty, and both returned to the Third Dáil from which they abstained. Sinn Féin TDs retained their thirty-four seats in the seven uncontested constituencies in the west, and won sixty of the ninety seats the party was forced to contest, securing 73 per cent of the seats overall. Anti-Treaty TDs, however, performed more poorly than pro-Treaty candidates, with twenty-two incumbents from that camp losing their seats. They outperformed the pro-Treaty candidates only in poorer Connacht constituencies (a pattern replicated in the August 1923 general election) and suffered their greatest losses in Leinster, claiming only five of the forty-four seats. Though complex and untested at national level in 1922 (the 1921 election was uncontested in the South), the new system of proportional representation – single transferable vote – was successfully employed. With anti-Treatyites winning just under 22 per cent of first-preference votes and failing to top the poll in any constituency, the election demonstrated a clear, if not 'ringing', endorsement of the Treaty by the 62.5 per cent of the electorate that turned out to vote on 16 June. The results in 1922 testify more than anything else to the electorate's desire for peace and stable government after more than a decade of war and revolution. The twenty-four seats in total secured by the Labour Party (seventeen) and the newly formed Farmers' Party (seven), both supportive of the Treaty (though Labour remained nominally neutral on the subject), and their combined first-preference vote of over 40 per cent, also indicates a significant concern with socio-economic issues among the electorate despite the dominance of the Treaty issue. A proportion of their votes, however, were likely 'lent' by voters who wished simply to oppose Sinn Féin, including former Irish Parliamentary Party diehards. Labour performed best in the trade union urban centres of Dublin and Cork and those areas of Leinster and Munster where the Irish Transport and General Workers' Union had established a strong base through the organisation of agricultural labourers since 1918. Although some Farmers' Party candidates bowed to intimidation and withdrew before the contest, it performed well in the large-farm districts of south Leinster and north and east Munster. Independents won a further ten seats (including the four unopposed seats in the Dublin University constituency). Though the election was followed quickly by civil war, it represented, as Bill Kissane notes, 'Ireland's commitment to democratic principles'. [Updated version of a map first published in the *Atlas of the Irish Revolution* (Cork, 2017) / Sources: B. Walker, *Parliamentary Election Results in Ireland, 1918–1922* (Dublin, 1992); contemporary newspaper reports; and M. Gallagher, 'The Pact General Election of 1922', *Irish Historical Studies*, vol. xxii, no. 84, September 1979, pp. 404–21; quotations: Dan Breen, *My Fight for Irish Freedom* (Tralee, 1964), p. 168; Bill Kissane, 'The 1922 "Pact" Election', Civil War Project, UCC and RTÉ, rte.ie/history, June 2022]

by inspiring colonised people in places like India and Egypt, the British government insisted that the Irish Free State remain within the empire. The partition of Ireland negated any suggestion that the imperial status of the proposed 'Free State' was needed to satisfy Ulster unionists. The Treaty's oath of allegiance ensured that no internal compromise could paper over the fact that the Free State's sovereignty came from the British crown rather than the Irish people. During fifteen days of rancorous Dáil debates straddling the Christmas break in December 1921, pro- and anti-Treaty Sinn Féin TDs marshalled their arguments regarding the settlement's strengths and weaknesses. The real question was whether the differences were worth risking renewed war with an empire that controlled nearly one quarter of the world's population. Pragmatism was a major element in the strong public and political support for the Treaty. The British influence in shaping events in Ireland did not end with the signing of the Treaty on 6 December 1921 or the symbolic 'surrender' of Dublin Castle, the centre of British administration in Ireland, on 16 January 1922. While the evacuation of British troops began almost immediately after the Dáil's narrow acceptance of the Treaty, the threat of British intervention was ever present throughout the ensuing six-month crisis. For the Provisional Government, in which administrative power had been vested pending a general election, further and even more dangerous pressure came from the majority within the Irish Republican Army (IRA) who bitterly opposed the Treaty.

From the outset, influential elements of Irish civil society strongly supported the Treaty, particularly the Catholic Church, newspapers, the business community and constitutional nationalists. Others feared their intervention could undermine national unity. Across Ireland there was little appetite for a civil war. Cumann na mBan, the republican women's organisation, was the first branch of the independence movement to openly split, with most members rejecting the Treaty at a convention on 5 February 1922. With an estimated 70–5 per cent of the organisation opposing the agreement with Britain, the IRA was next. At a convention in Dublin's Mansion House on 26 March, anti-Treaty officers repudiated Dáil Eireann's control of the IRA, established a new army executive, and vowed to defend the Irish Republic from the new Irish Free State.

During this period of constitutionally ambiguous dual authority, when Michael Collins's Provisional Government operated in tandem with the pro-Treaty ministry of the undissolved Second Dáil, many good-faith efforts were made to close the breaches in the independence movement's political and military wings.[3] In April trade unionists voiced their opposition to a threatened civil war by holding a one-day general strike against militarism and strove to find a workable solution to the Treaty split right up to the outbreak of armed conflict. The Irish Labour Party and Trade Union Congress was officially neutral but de facto pro-Treaty; keeping Labour on board was crucial to the pro-Treatyites in the battle for legitimacy. A women's peace movement also attempted to bridge the widening rift between the rival sides. As evinced by extensive army-unity negotiations, both sides of the IRA's Treaty divide recognised the danger and undesirability of war. But many had difficulty envisioning an armed conflict between former comrades, believing, like Dublin Volunteer Joseph Lawless, that 'the patriotic fervour that pervaded the national movement

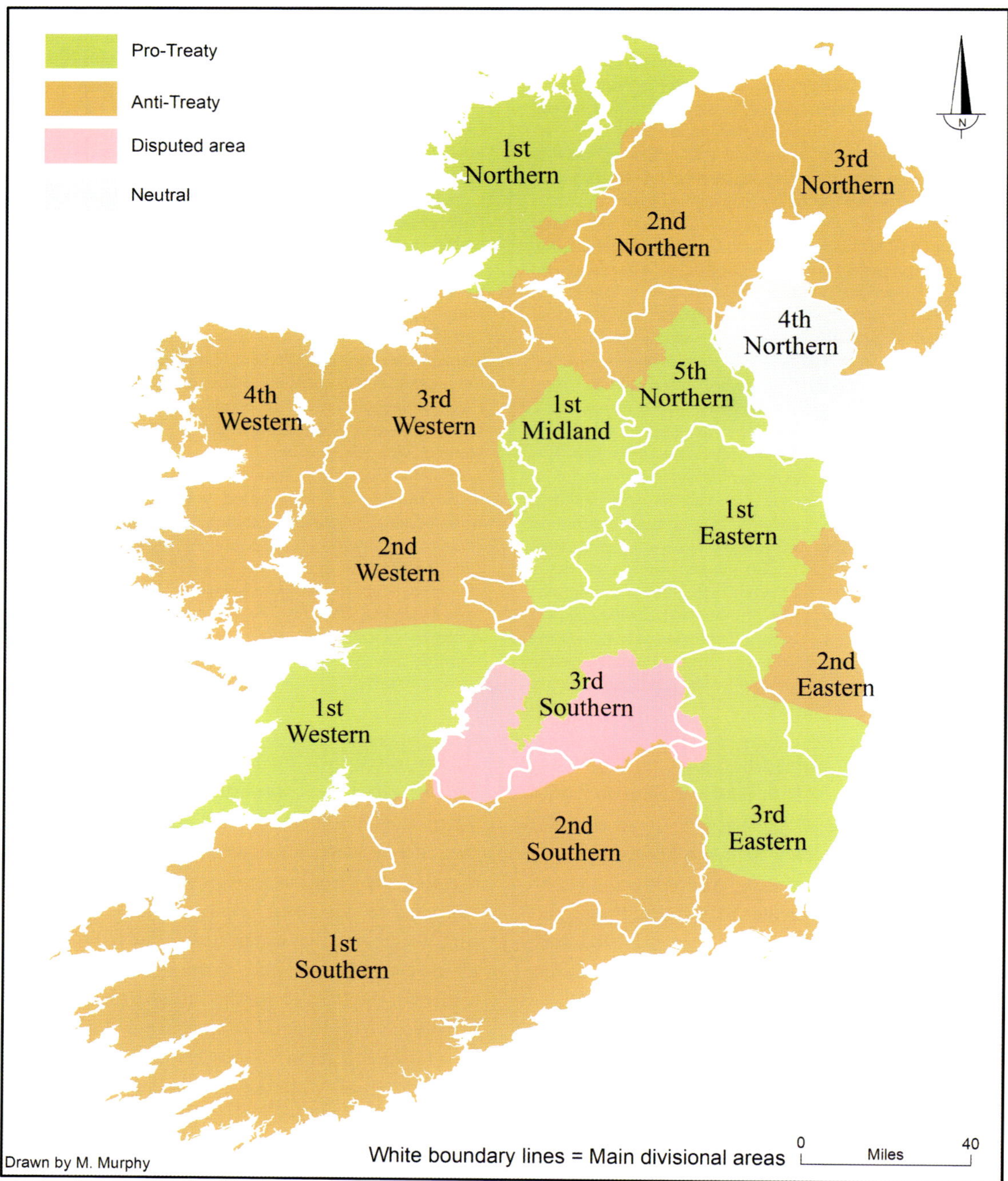

Fig. 5 Map showing stances taken by IRA divisions on the issue of the Anglo-Irish Treaty in the spring of 1922. Out of sixteen divisions, seven remained loyal to the pro-Treaty general headquarters (GHQ). A number of those divisions located in Leinster were among the poorest performing in the IRA, but others in Clare (particularly parts of the county controlled by Michael Brennan), Longford (under the influence of Seán Mac Eoin) and a strong minority of the Dublin No. 1 Brigade were among the most active units of the pre-Truce IRA. The two largest divisions – the 1st and 2nd Southern divisions under Liam Lynch and Ernie O'Malley respectively, which contained the IRA's most formidable units and over 40 per cent of the army's personnel – were anti-Treaty (although the latter and the 3rd Southern Division contained significant pro-Treaty units; see 'Disputed area'). Divisions in Connacht, which saw more limited military action during the War of Independence, also opposed the Treaty and, during the Civil War, provided some of the most determined armed resistance to the Free State. The Treaty shadings presented here are not precisely matched to the divisional areas. This is to indicate that not all subordinate units and rank-and-file members within a division supported its stance on the Treaty. Some areas became hostile to their brigade and/or divisional headquarters. Frank Aiken and his 4th Northern Division were neutral before and at the outset of the Civil War before joining the republican forces. The rapid crown forces evacuation in early 1922, and the agreement that all vacated barracks would be occupied by local IRA units regardless of their stance on the Treaty, meant that, by the spring, anti-Treaty units controlled much of the country. Beyond Clare the vacated British army barracks in Listowel, County Kerry, and Skibbereen, County Cork, were the only ones in southern Munster occupied by Volunteers loyal to the Provisional Government. At the opening of the Civil War the anti-Treaty IRA had the advantage numerically (though not in arms), but failures in organisation and strategy meant that it lost the initiative to a burgeoning, centrally controlled and well-equipped, if largely untrained, National Army. [Updated version of a map first published in the *Atlas of the Irish Revolution* (Cork, 2017)]

through the war years would not permit partisan rancour to go to the length of actual war'.[4] Such failures of imagination are common before civil wars, but the main protagonists did not sleepwalk into armed conflict. Political positions grew ever more hardened and entrenched, aided by the increasingly bitter propaganda war.

Each side argued domestically and internationally that their cause enjoyed legitimacy. For republicans the conflict was about opposing an imperial entity foisted upon Ireland by the British government; their Free State opponents were regarded as tools of British imperialism. For Free State supporters the war was fought in defence of a government that enjoyed clear popular support, as seen in the results of the June 1922 general election; their republican opponents were mutineers against a lawful government, or 'irregulars', a highly loaded term that formed part of an arsenal of propagandist terminology used by both sides. The continued deployment of such labels in the discourse of Free State politics was part of the continuation of the Civil War by other means.

A 'republic with a thin veneer'

Efforts to reunite the pro- and anti-Treaty factions in the spring of 1922 ended in failure. The anti-Treaty IRA threatened the operations of the new Provisional Government and raised tensions further by occupying the Four Courts (the headquarters of Ireland's judiciary) and other prominent buildings in the capital.

The civilian administration delayed dealing decisively with old

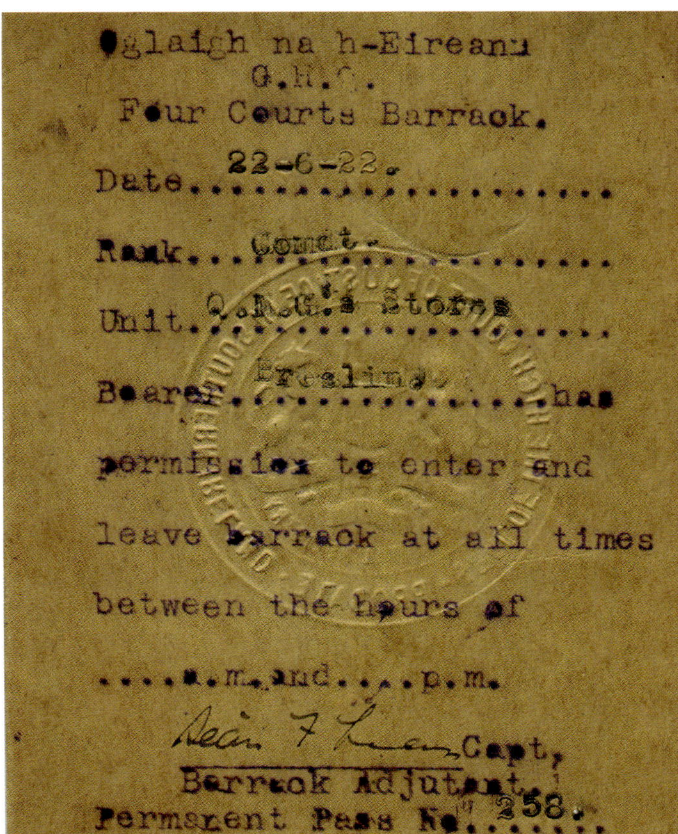

Óglaigh na h-Eireann
G.H.Q.
Four Courts Barrack.
Date 22-6-22.
Rank Comdt.
Unit Q.M.G.'s Stores
Bearer Breslin has permission to enter and leave barrack at all times between the hours of ....a.m. and ....p.m.
Capt,
Barrack Adjutant.
Permanent Pass No. 258.

Fig. 6 Pass, dated 22 June 1922, signed by Seán Lemass (later Taoiseach) in his role as barracks adjutant at the Four Courts. The eighteenth-century Four Courts building on Inns Quay is closely associated in the collective memory with the Civil War, but the residential streets around that notable symbol of British law and order also witnessed some of the most brutal and chaotic fighting of the 1916 Rising. Home to the Public Record Office of Ireland, the Land Registry Offices and the administrative centre of the Irish judiciary, the Four Courts complex was occupied again in April 1922 by approximately 200 republicans in open defiance of the Provisional Government. It served as both garrison and national headquarters for the anti-Treaty IRA executive led by Rory O'Connor, Liam Lynch, Liam Mellows and Joe McKelvey. This pass was issued to Peadar Breslin (who would be fatally wounded during an escape attempt from Mountjoy Gaol on 10 October 1922) and granted him access to the anti-Treaty IRA garrison during its occupation. The reverse side shows an anti-counterfeiting device utilising an embossed seal, which carries the royal crest surrounded by the legend 'Probate Seal of the High Court of Justice in Southern Ireland'. Tensions had escalated among the anti-Treaty IRA (hereafter IRA) in mid-June following the publication of the Free State constitution, which fell far short of republican aspirations, and the general election delivered a pro-Treaty majority. On 18 June, when the IRA met at a convention in Dublin's Mansion House to consider an 'army reunification' proposal, Liam Lynch and the moderate officers of his 1st Southern Division split with the hard-line delegates who opposed any agreement with the Provisional Government. Led by Mellows and O'Connor, the IRA's militant wing returned to the Four Courts, locked out Lynch and his supporters, and replaced Lynch as chief of staff with Joe McKelvey of Belfast (Lynch and his officers relocated to the nearby Clarence Hotel). The situation deteriorated further when, on 22 June, IRA gunmen in London assassinated Sir Henry Wilson, apparently on their own initiative. The British Cabinet blamed the Four Courts executive and demanded an immediate response from the Provisional Government against the 'irregular elements of the IRA' in 'open rebellion in the heart of Dublin'. When members of the Four Courts garrison arrested National Army general J.J. 'Ginger' O'Connell on 27 June, a convenient pretext was provided for an attack. [Image: Breslin Collection, South Dublin Libraries / Quotation: David Lloyd George to Michael Collins, 22 June 1922, National Archives UK, CAB/23/30]

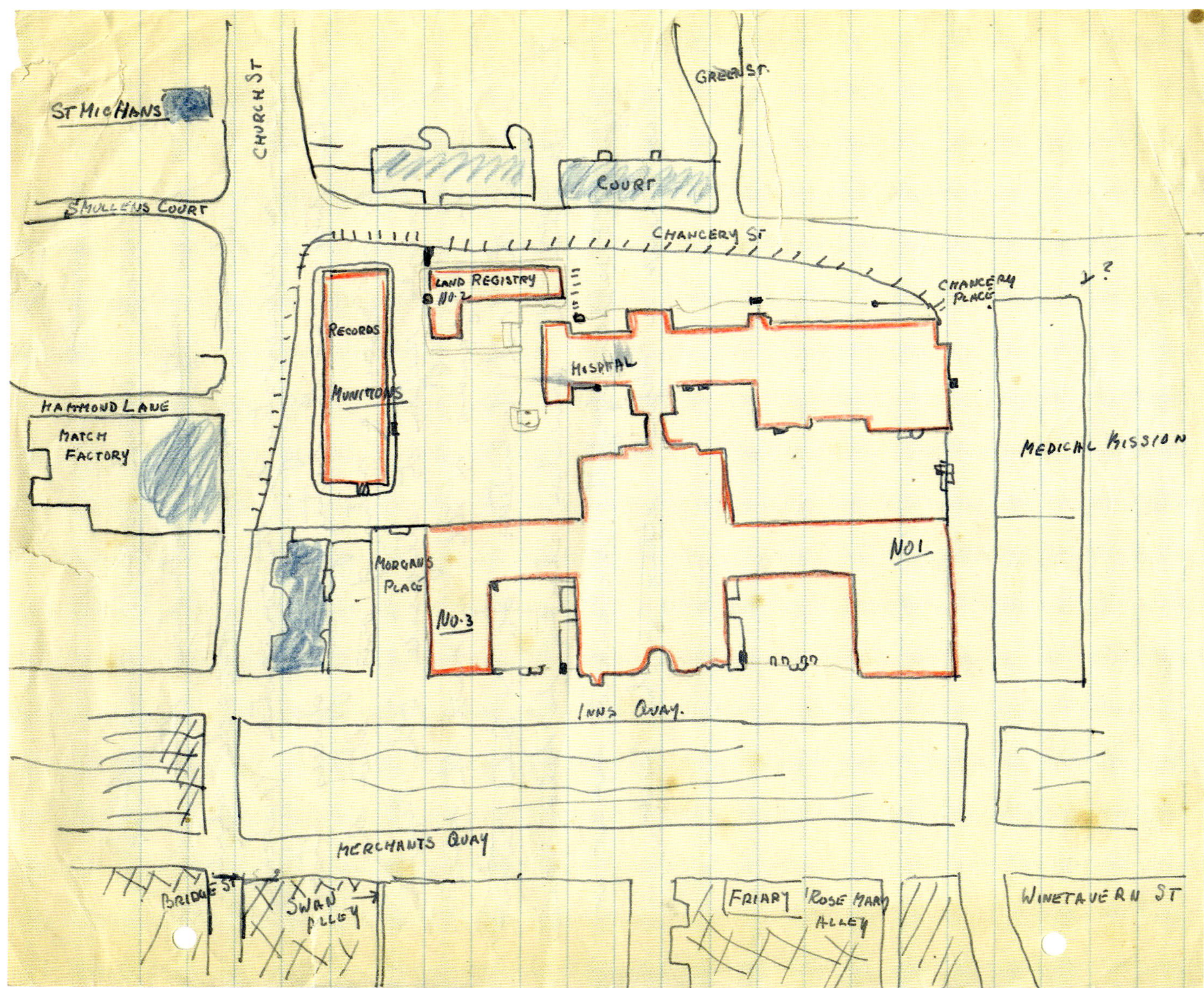

Fig. 7 Included in the papers of Ernie O'Malley, deposited in UCD Archives by his son, Cormac O'Malley, in 1974, is this sketch depicting the area around Dublin's Four Courts on the north side of the River Liffey. O'Malley, who was a member of the Four Courts garrison, delineated in red the areas of the complex occupied by the anti-Treaty forces. Offices in the solicitors' block were designated IRA executive headquarters, where planning proceeded in the spring to continue enforcement of the Belfast boycott, import arms, commandeer supplies and mount a joint IRA offensive in Northern Ireland. The more isolated Public Record Office of Ireland (PROI) was chosen for munitions production and the storage of land mines. Despite having occupied the building for more than two months, the IRA executive did little to prepare for an attack. Tunnelling between the buildings in the complex remained incomplete, provisions were low, and O'Malley, who had unsuccessfully argued for the placement of snipers around the complex, described their defences as 'hopeless'. Anticipating the attack, Quartermaster General Liam Mellows ordered the removal of documents and cash to the Capuchin Friary in Church Street, while the garrison commander, Paddy O'Brien, attempted to organise the approximately 180 Volunteers scattered throughout the complex. The orderlies section, staffed by Na Fianna Éireann, was in the PROI, while the headquarters block was at the rear of the courts, both isolated from the central building. National Army soldiers surrounded the Four Courts on the night of Tuesday 27 June. They occupied the Medical Mission and the Four Courts Hotel, covering both flanks of the courts and the Bridewell prison to the rear. Snipers were placed in the tower of St Michan's church and Jameson Distillery in Smithfield. and two 18-pounder field guns positioned on the opposite side of the Liffey. Early on Wednesday 28 June, upon the expiration of Collins's ultimatum to the IRA garrison to surrender or be attacked, the National Army opened fire on the building. After two days of relentless rifle and artillery fire, two breaches were opened in the walls, one in the PROI and one in the north wing. An infantry assault, followed by close-quarter fighting, led to the deaths of four men, two on each side, before the PROI was taken on Friday morning. Just after midday on 30 June an explosion in the PROI sent plumes of smoke into the Dublin skyline. Resigned to surrender, the anti-Treaty Volunteers marched out onto Chancery Street and down the quays, led by Rory O'Connor, Liam Mellows and Ernie O'Malley. The explosion marked the end of the Battle of the Four Courts, but the Civil War had just begun. [Document: Papers of Ernie O'Malley P17a/304, UCDAD / Quotations: David Lloyd George to Michael Collins, 22 June 1922, National Archives UK, CAB/23/30; Ernie O'Malley, *The Singing Flame* (Dublin, 1992), p. 91 / See also Michael Fewer, *Battle of the Four Courts: The first three days of the Irish Civil War* (London, 2018)]

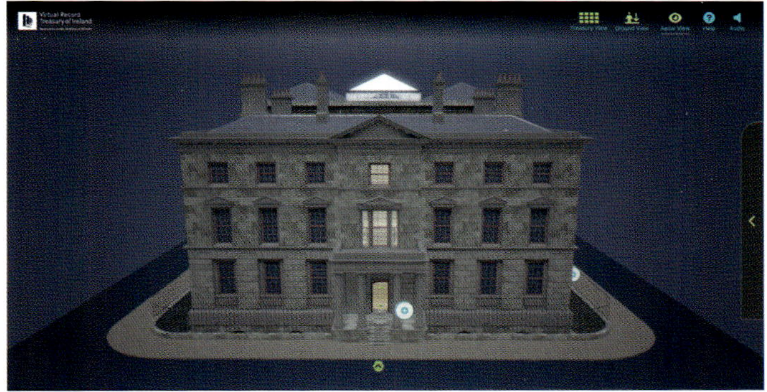

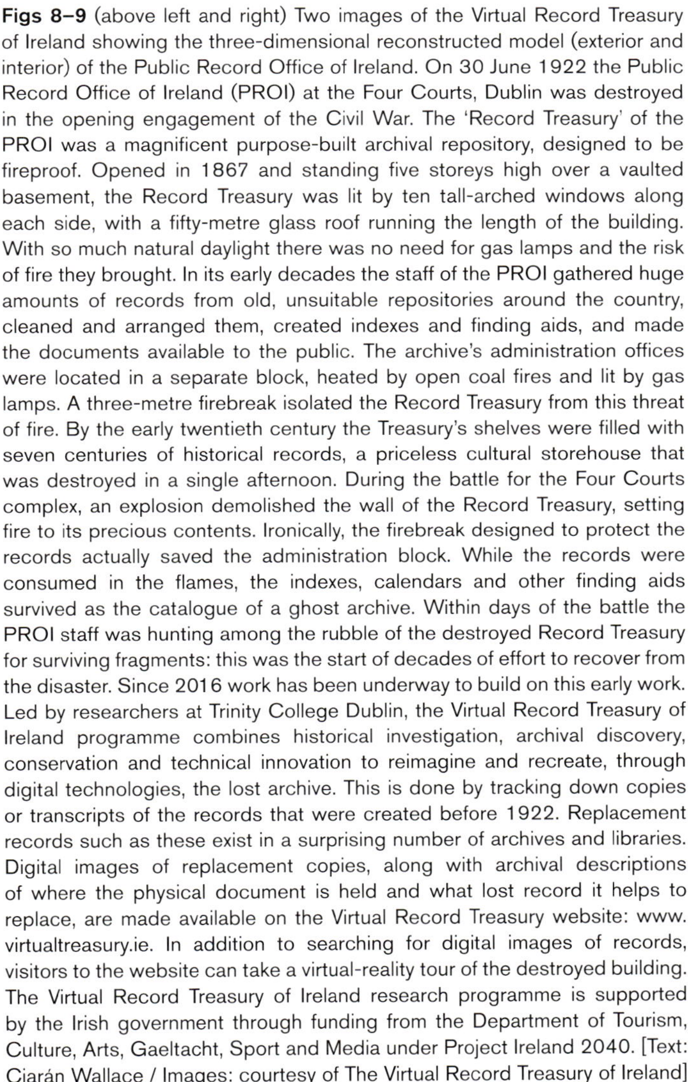

Figs 8–9 (above left and right) Two images of the Virtual Record Treasury of Ireland showing the three-dimensional reconstructed model (exterior and interior) of the Public Record Office of Ireland. On 30 June 1922 the Public Record Office of Ireland (PROI) at the Four Courts, Dublin was destroyed in the opening engagement of the Civil War. The 'Record Treasury' of the PROI was a magnificent purpose-built archival repository, designed to be fireproof. Opened in 1867 and standing five storeys high over a vaulted basement, the Record Treasury was lit by ten tall-arched windows along each side, with a fifty-metre glass roof running the length of the building. With so much natural daylight there was no need for gas lamps and the risk of fire they brought. In its early decades the staff of the PROI gathered huge amounts of records from old, unsuitable repositories around the country, cleaned and arranged them, created indexes and finding aids, and made the documents available to the public. The archive's administration offices were located in a separate block, heated by open coal fires and lit by gas lamps. A three-metre firebreak isolated the Record Treasury from this threat of fire. By the early twentieth century the Treasury's shelves were filled with seven centuries of historical records, a priceless cultural storehouse that was destroyed in a single afternoon. During the battle for the Four Courts complex, an explosion demolished the wall of the Record Treasury, setting fire to its precious contents. Ironically, the firebreak designed to protect the records actually saved the administration block. While the records were consumed in the flames, the indexes, calendars and other finding aids survived as the catalogue of a ghost archive. Within days of the battle the PROI staff was hunting among the rubble of the destroyed Record Treasury for surviving fragments: this was the start of decades of effort to recover from the disaster. Since 2016 work has been underway to build on this early work. Led by researchers at Trinity College Dublin, the Virtual Record Treasury of Ireland programme combines historical investigation, archival discovery, conservation and technical innovation to reimagine and recreate, through digital technologies, the lost archive. This is done by tracking down copies or transcripts of the records that were created before 1922. Replacement records such as these exist in a surprising number of archives and libraries. Digital images of replacement copies, along with archival descriptions of where the physical document is held and what lost record it helps to replace, are made available on the Virtual Record Treasury website: www.virtualtreasury.ie. In addition to searching for digital images of records, visitors to the website can take a virtual-reality tour of the destroyed building. The Virtual Record Treasury of Ireland research programme is supported by the Irish government through funding from the Department of Tourism, Culture, Arts, Gaeltacht, Sport and Media under Project Ireland 2040. [Text: Ciarán Wallace / Images: courtesy of The Virtual Record Treasury of Ireland]

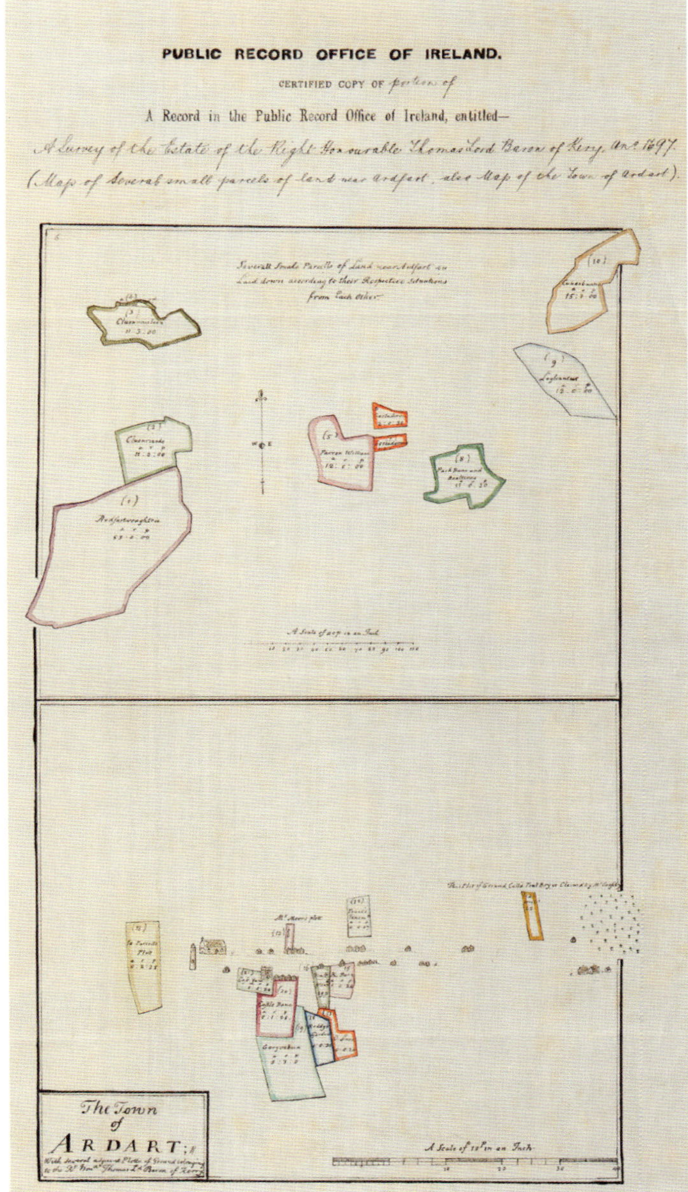

Fig. 10 (right) Map of the town of Ardart [Ardfert], County Kerry from Henry Pratt's 1697 survey of the estate of Thomas [Fitzmaurice], Lord Kerry. In 1915 M.J. Byrne, a solicitor in Listowel, County Kerry, presented an important set of early estate maps to the Public Record Office of Ireland (PROI). The originals were destroyed in the fire. Fortunately, copies of maps like this one, with their official PROI verification, survive in the Boole Library, University College Cork. Digital images of similar maps can now be viewed online. Through the generosity of the Boole Library and many other partners around Ireland and internationally, the Virtual Record Treasury is democratising access to these invaluable records. [Text: Ciarán Wallace / Image: courtesy of The Virtual Record Treasury of Ireland and Boole Library UCC, U 121/1]

colleagues, drawing the ire of the British government. However, this allowed the Provisional Government time to consolidate power, explore avenues for reconciliation, and build up the new National Army, provided for under Article 8 of the Treaty and formed around a nucleus of pro-Treaty units of the IRA loyal to Collins and Minister for Defence Richard Mulcahy. By May hopes of averting civil war balanced on a precarious election pact signed by the two rival wings of Sinn Féin, through their two political leaders Michael Collins (pro-Treaty) and Éamon de Valera (anti-Treaty). The formation of a post-election coalition government was predicated on the promise of a compromise constitution that, by eliding reference to the crown, would reconcile republican aspirations with the terms of the Treaty. On 27 May the British predictably rejected Collins's constitution, which provided for, in Lloyd George's words, 'a republic with a thin veneer', and a revised draft, reinstating the primacy of the oath of fidelity, was reluctantly approved by the Provisional Government Cabinet on 12 June.[5] The text of the Constitution of the Irish Free State appeared in morning newspapers four days later, as the electorate cast their votes in a general election that delivered a pro-Treaty Sinn Féin majority. Facing continued opposition to its legitimacy, and the immediate threat of British intervention following the assassination of Field Marshal Sir Henry Wilson in London, the Provisional Government authorised an artillery assault on Dublin's Four Courts on 28 June. A three-day siege ended with massive explosions that destroyed most of the priceless records and manuscripts in the Public Records Office of Ireland and caused the surrender of the IRA garrison.

The Battle for Dublin, described as a brutally ironic reenactment of 1916, had ended by 5 July after IRA and Cumann na mBan combatants surrendered to Free State forces in the smouldering city centre.[6] In its aftermath, Oscar Traynor, officer commanding the Dublin Brigade, issued a message to embolden the broken ranks of the 'Army of the Irish Republic'. He pointedly invoked Ireland's 'apostolic succession' of separatist martyrs augmented on 5 July by Cathal Brugha's fatal last stand in Sackville (O'Connell) Street.

> Those who would make us bend the knee to England's king have suffered severely, and they will now know that they will not be permitted to destroy the Republic or surrender our national independence with impunity. We can now at once revert to the tactics which made us invincible formerly, and which can now equally ensure that the Republic of Tone and Emmet, of Pearse and Connolly, of MacSwiney and Barry, of McKee and Clancy and of Cathal Brugha will not be supplanted by an alien monarchy.[7]

Fig. 11 Public Record Office of Ireland Search Room, destroyed during the Battle of the Four Courts in 1922. [Image: Part of the Independent Newspapers Ireland/NLI Collection, INDH203]

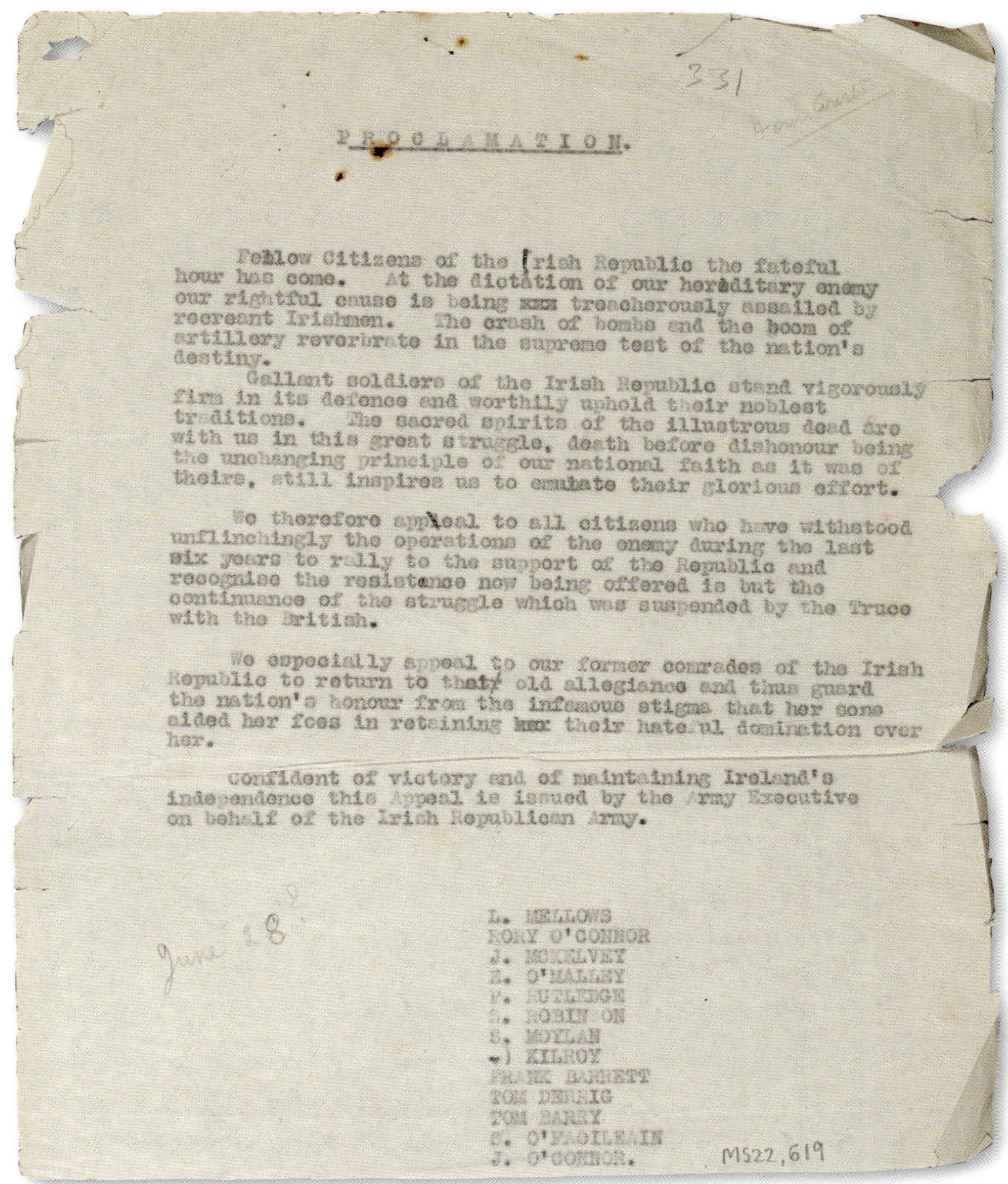

331

P R O C L A M A T I O N.

Fellow Citizens of the Irish Republic the fateful hour has come. At the dictation of our hereditary enemy our rightful cause is being xxx treacherously assailed by recreant Irishmen. The crash of bombs and the boom of artillery reverbrate in the supreme test of the nation's destiny.

Gallant soldiers of the Irish Republic stand vigorously firm in its defence and worthily uphold their noblest traditions. The sacred spirits of the illustrous dead are with us in this great struggle, death before dishonour being the unchanging principle of our national faith as it was of theirs, still inspires us to emulate their glorious effort.

We therefore appeal to all citizens who have withstood unflinchingly the operations of the enemy during the last six years to rally to the support of the Republic and recognise the resistance now being offered is but the continuance of the struggle which was suspended by the Truce with the British.

We especially appeal to our former comrades of the Irish Republic to return to their old allegiance and thus guard the nation's honour from the infamous stigma that her sons aided her foes in retaining xxx their hateful domination over her.

Confident of victory and of maintaining Ireland's independence this Appeal is issued by the Army Executive on behalf of the Irish Republican Army.

June 28

L. MELLOWS
RORY O'CONNOR
J. McKELVEY
E. O'MALLEY
P. RUTLEDGE
S. ROBINSON
S. MOYLAN
J. KILROY
FRANK BARRETT
TOM DERRIG
TOM BARRY
S. O'FAOILEAIN
J. O'CONNOR.

MS22,619

Fig. 12 Proclamation issued by the anti-Treaty forces in Dublin, 28 June 1922. [Document: National Library of Ireland, Kathleen McKenna Napoli Papers, MS 22,619]

The depiction of the fight by anti-Treaty polemicists as the newest phase in the struggle against Ireland's 'hereditary enemy' was affirmed, during and after the Civil War, by republican balladeers and propagandists, on prison walls and in prison autograph books, and in commemorative rhetoric.[8] Heirs to the same separatist tradition, supporters of the Free State emphasised the irresponsibility, anarchism and unpatriotic ruffianism of the anti-Treaty campaign, and expressed horror at 'the cruel spectacle of men calling themselves Irishmen casting a shadow upon our patriot dead'.[9] The message, carefully mediated by the pro-Treaty press, was that historic sacrifices had been vindicated by the creation of a democratic Irish Free State.

Any hope that the fighting would be confined to Dublin was dashed as combat broke out across the country. Both sides rushed to mobilise fighters. The Free State's National Army grew from an estimated 8,000 men at the outset of the Civil War to just over 30,000 in August 1922 and almost 55,000 by the spring of 1923. The IRA had a nominal strength of almost 90,000 in July 1922, though most members were unarmed, and thousands dropped out as the conflict progressed. At least 15,000 Cumann na mBan members initially took the anti-Treaty side, and about 400 female republicans were eventually jailed. Membership figures for the much smaller pro-Treaty women's organisation, Cumann na Saoirse, awaits further research. Another, less recognised faction were the thousands of War of Independence veterans who refused to participate in the Civil War. Between ten and twenty thousand later joined the Neutral IRA, a patriotic peace organisation founded in December 1922. Many felt as Neutral IRA leader Florrie O'Donoghue did when,

Fig. 13 The ruins of the Granville Hotel on Dublin's Sackville (O'Connell) Street. When the bombardment of the Four Courts commenced on 28 June, the IRA's Dublin Brigade, under Oscar Traynor, occupied a number of positions in central Dublin. Although driven from Flower Hall on 28 June, they secured fourteen buildings on the east side of Sackville Street, known as 'The Block', as well as the YMCA building on the opposite side of the street, the tramway office at the corner with Cathedral Street, St Thomas's church at the rear of 'The Block', Hughes and Moran's hotels in Gardiner Street/Talbot Street, and positions in Blackhall Place, D'Olier Street and Aungier Street. The National Army set up command on the west side of Sackville Street, severing any connection with the Four Courts, which fell on 30 June. The National Army then concentrated on Traynor's positions, taking over Amiens Street Station and the railway bridge covering Hughes and Moran's, and driving out IRA garrisons until it reached Sackville Street. Three armoured cars and an 18-pounder field gun were deployed against 'The Block', and on 3 July Traynor ordered the evacuation of most of the garrison from the Gresham Hotel. A small force commanded by Cathal Brugha remained as a rearguard. Over the next three days the complex was bombarded, but Brugha refused Traynor's advice to surrender. By Wednesday the small garrison had retreated to the last tenable position, the Granville Hotel. When shell fire from the 18-pounder set the building aflame, Brugha ordered his garrison to surrender. That evening Brugha emerged from the burning hotel. Called on to surrender, he refused and was fatally wounded. [Image: Part of the Independent Newspapers Ireland/NLI Collection]

in July 1922, he penned his resignation letter to Liam Lynch: 'My judgement convinces me that out of Civil War will come, not the Republic, or unity, or freedom, or peace but a prolonged struggle in which the best elements in the country will be annihilated or overborne. In no circumstances could I be part of a conflict which would bring about such deplorable results'.[10]

Violence soon visited every county in the Free State, which helped to ensure the Civil War's deep and indelible mark on the country's collective memory. During the conventional phase of fighting (June–August 1922), the National Army battled the IRA in cities and towns across the country. Though hastily recruited and largely untrained, the centrally controlled National Army, well equipped with British armoured cars and artillery, quickly gained the upper hand. After just seven weeks and a series of decisive amphibious landings on the south and west coasts, it had forced the IRA from urban centres and deeper into the countryside.

The deaths of Michael Collins and Arthur Griffith within ten days of each other in August 1922 heralded the onset of the Civil War's next phase, characterised by the IRA's campaign of guerrilla warfare and economic sabotage intended to undermine the institutions of the Free State. For a few months the IRA rendered parts of Ireland ungovernable. Much of the Free State's popular support depended on its promise to resume basic services and to provide enough security to steady the economy. William T. Cosgrave's administration delivered a measure of normal governance but struggled to fulfil all its functions and obligations. On the other side, though, the anti-Treaty movement made little effort to create an effective counter-state, such as that presided over by Dáil Éireann from 1919 to 1921. While Éamon de Valera led a shadow executive under the authority of the defunct Second Dáil, it failed 'the crucial legitimacy test'.[11] Those desiring the return of peace, law and order, looked to the Free State and increasingly blamed the IRA for ongoing national dysfunction.

The IRA was progressively ground down by the better-armed and better-organised National Army. Beyond the Free State's greater numerical strength, the republican rank and file were demoralised by growing popular opposition to continued war, excommunication by the Catholic Church in October 1922, and the passage of the Army (Special Powers) Resolution in September 1922, which provided for mass internment, military courts and capital punishment for a variety of offences. The IRA chief of staff, Liam Lynch, responded to the first executions in November with a general order for IRA operations

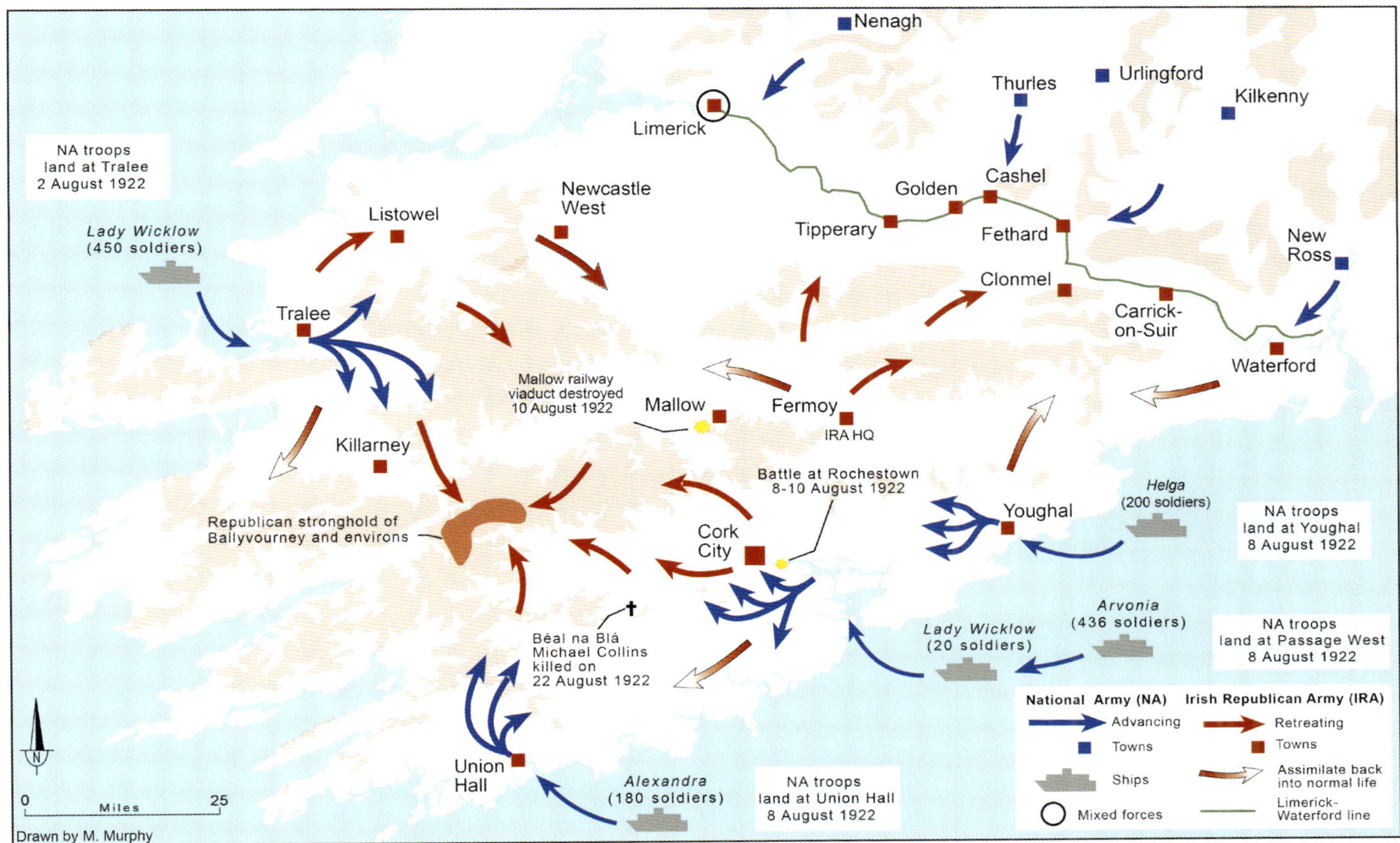

Fig. 14 The Battle for Munster, July–August 1922. During late July and early August, the National Army (NA) and the IRA fought a series of engagements across the province of Munster. At the outset of the Civil War, republican forces cleared the NA from much of the province and held a defensive line anchored by the cities of Limerick in the west and Waterford in the east. The loosely organised IRA 'field army' was comprised of numerous individual brigade and battalion columns, each usually numbering between twenty-five and fifty fighters. It faced rapidly growing NA forces that were well armed with artillery and armoured vehicles. The NA won a critical victory during the ten-day battle of Limerick, which ended on 21 July. On the other end of the line the NA overcame weaker IRA resistance and captured Waterford city, also on 21 July. During the next two weeks the NA methodically pushed the republicans back in counties Tipperary, Limerick and Waterford, capturing the towns of Carrick-on-Suir and Clonmel in the process. The most intense fighting occurred during the two-week battle of Kilmallock, which extended into the nearby villages of Bruff and Bruree. The combat there varied from artillery and infantry attacks on primitive defences to fluid counter-attacks carried out by lorry-borne troops supported by armoured cars. The republicans, commanded by Liam Deasy, fought against a large but inexperienced NA force led by Eoin O'Duffy and W.R.E. Murphy. Republican positions broke after the NA conducted surprise amphibious landings in counties Kerry and Cork in early August. Although the IRA had anticipated a seaborne assault, and garrisoned coastal ports and destroyed some docking facilities, their flimsy defences were no match for determined NA troops. Government forces arriving at Fenit, County Kerry captured Tralee after a brief fight on 2 August. A more ambitious assault occurred on 8 August, when Emmet Dalton organised three simultaneous landings of Free State troops at Youghal, Union Hall and Passage West in County Cork. The NA brushed aside light republican resistance at Youghal and Union Hall, but faced much more determined opposition while trying to seize Cork city. During the three-day 'Battle of Douglas' on the city's outskirts, hundreds of troops faced each other, though once again Free State artillery and armoured cars proved decisive. The republicans evacuated Cork and fell back to the mountainous area around Ballyvourney, west of Macroom. The Limerick/Waterford line collapsed completely, as many of its front-line units scrambled to contest the NA's amphibious offensive behind them. While Emmet Dalton's forces pushed aggressively inland across County Cork, Eoin O'Duffy's men around Kilmallock moved south with less urgency. Scattered IRA resistance and road and railway sabotage bought the republicans critical time. IRA commander Liam Lynch managed to disperse his small 'field army' before it could be captured by converging NA forces. Though the Free State won a decisive victory, it failed to destroy republican resistance. When Lynch ordered a resumption of guerrilla tactics in mid-August, he was able to mobilise enough seasoned IRA fighters to make much of the province ungovernable. One of the republicans' first guerrilla successes had immense political ramifications, when the IRA ambushed the Free State Commander in Chief Michael Collins's convoy at Béal na Blá on 22 August. With the death of Collins, both sides recognised that, though the Battle for Munster was over, it had been replaced by a guerrilla war that would last considerably longer. [Updated version of a map first published in the *Atlas of the Irish Revolution* (Cork, 2017)]

Fig. 15 IRA South Tipperary Brigade in a charabanc on Main Street, Graiguenamangh, County Kilkenny, July 1922. [Image: The Anvil Books Collection, Dún Laoghaire–Rathdown Local Studies Department]

against the 'enemy'. These included shooting on sight those TDs who had supported the 'Murder Bill' and burning the offices and homes of leaders and prominent associates of the new state. Tension mounted in Dublin in the first week of December. Ministers slept on mattresses in heavily fortified government buildings, trains destined for the capital were searched, and commentators feared possible IRA violence at the formal inauguration of the Free State on 6 December – the first anniversary of the signing of the Treaty. However, with minimal fanfare, the new dominion state, underpinned by the Irish Free State constitution, formally came into being. It was described by the *Cork Examiner* as an 'epoch-making day in the story of Ireland', when 'her freedom was born, and she became a nation among the nations of the world'.[12] Yet such soaring rhetoric could not match the grim reality of continued fratricide. On 7 December the IRA assassinated pro-Treaty TD Seán Hales. Within twenty-four hours the Free State Cabinet sanctioned the extrajudicial 'reprisal' executions of four prominent republican prisoners, Rory O'Connor, Liam Mellows, Joe McKelvey and Dick Barrett.

Outmanned, outgunned, ostracised by the Catholic Church and abandoned by most of the people, the IRA became increasingly desperate in early 1923. Internment camps, army barracks and civilian prisons strained to accommodate almost 13,000 republican internees. There appeared to be no hope for an anti-Treaty military victory over the Free State. The Civil War ended on 24 May not with a negotiated peace but with a dump-arms order issued by IRA Chief of Staff Frank Aiken, successor to Liam Lynch, who was fatally wounded in Tipperary on 10 April. In May Éamon de Valera directed the 'Legion' of the IRA 'Rearguard' to temporarily cede military victory to 'those who ha[d] destroyed the Republic', and declared that 'other means must be found to safeguard the nation's right'. The nation's right, de Valera would argue after his release from Kilmainham Gaol in 1924, was best safeguarded by participating in conventional electoral politics.

Righteousness of their cause

For the most part, those who participated in the Civil War believed in the righteousness of their cause. Neither side, however, exerted sufficient control over its rank and file, and both armies were guilty of gross misconduct, including some long-occluded incidents of gender-based and sexual violence. New research by Andy Bielenberg and John Dorney suggests that the National Army was responsible for the deaths of at least 157 prisoners, both in official executions and unofficial roadside killings, between 28 June 1922 and 24 March 1923. Events in County Kerry in March 1923 and the controversial and brutal killings of teenage republicans in Dublin in August and October 1922 are seared on the collective memory of the conflict. Property was regularly commandeered or set alight, food supplies disrupted, and the republicans' destruction of bridges, roads and railways severely impacted commercial and everyday life. New enmities were forged, but old scores were also settled at local level, where land disputes with origins in the nineteenth century were infused with a fresh intensity. While the scale and nature of agrarian unrest at local level awaits further research, Section 3 in this volume explores the government's responses to the simultaneous surges in agrarianism, ordinary criminality and labour militancy that seemed to herald a collapse in social order in 1922, and the lasting associations formed between the 'defence of private property rights and the defence of the fledgling state'.[13]

Following the Civil War the Irish Free State stabilised quickly. Prisons were emptied after a short-lived and demoralising mass hunger strike in the autumn of 1923, and an amnesty declared. For W.T. Cosgrave's Cumann na nGaedheal government, admission to the League of Nations in September 1923 was an important symbolic step by the nascent Irish Free State in asserting its own legitimacy and sovereignty. Disorganisation and disillusionment, however, prevailed among Civil War IRA veterans, many of whom had served prison terms or otherwise suffered from the long-term physical and psychological consequences of their activism. Barred from civil service posts in an inhospitable Free State and unwilling to remain under the jurisdiction of the twenty-six-county dominion, several thousand republicans left for Britain and the United States in the 1920s. These communities of republican 'wild geese' watched bitterly from a distance as the island's northern frontier remained unchanged after the collapse of the Boundary Commission in November 1925.[14] The reorganised IRA did not resume its armed attacks against the state during the interwar period. Many in the anti-Treaty movement followed the parliamentary path with the new Fianna Fáil party, which recast the 'odious oath' as an 'empty formula' and entered Dáil Éireann in 1927. However, the shadow of the Civil War hung over many areas of life and governance. The state's execution policy left a bitter legacy, families and friendships were fractured, and the scarred Free State government engaged in what Anne Dolan called a 'frenzy of respectability'.[15] Puritanical and paternalistic, Cumann na nGaedheal was 'firm with its opponents, careful with its money and hard on those who needed its kindness most'.[16] The Free State's treatment of farm labourers and postal strikers during the Civil War also left its mark. As Gerard Hanley points out, 'for the next decade

Fig. 16 This photograph, first printed in the *Illustrated London News*, 15 July 1922, captures the aftermath of fierce fighting between the National Army and the IRA in Dublin during the first week of July 1922, culminating in 'the surrender of the rebels' on 5 July. A smiling soldier, 'protecting' a postbox surrounded by debris, poses for a photographer. Visible beneath each letter-box slot are the initials SE, for Saorstát Éireann (the Irish Free State); a sign on the railing beneath reads 'An Post' (simply indicating 'the post') in an Irish script. As the national postal service (formerly the Department of Posts and Telegraphs) did not adopt the An Post nomenclature until 1984, these additions to the letterboxes refer to the reclamation of Irish postal insignia and enhanced use of the Irish language as part of the new project of state building. Official control of the national postal service passed to the Free State on 1 April 1922, but, in practice, collaboration with the British Post Office proved a necessity during the transitional period, especially during the chaos of the Civil War. The photograph was one of three images illustrating the article 'Dublin's Finest Street a Wreck: Twice Destroyed in Six Years' (credited to Topical [Topical Press Agency] and INA). The first, leading, image provides a panoramic view from atop Nelson's Pillar, as a large crowd is held back from the still-smouldering ruins along the eastern side of Sackville (O'Connell) Street, including the tramway office, Hammam Hotel and the Granville Hotel; a second detailed shot shows the near-total obliteration of the Gresham Hotel. This photograph outside the post office carries the caption, 'After the surrender of the rebels: Irish Free State soldiers guarding a letter-box outside the General Post Office in Sackville Street'. It was taken at the site of the temporary GPO on 16 Upper Sackville (O'Connell) Street, next door to the heavily damaged Granville Hotel, as the original GPO (mostly destroyed, except for its facade, in 1916) was not reopened until 1929. Post offices and mail trains served as republican targets, with the aim of disrupting or intercepting communications and raiding stocks of cash, stamps and postal orders. By the 1920s the *Illustrated London News* had almost completely shifted away from wood engraving to direct photomechanical reproductions of arresting photographs such as this one. This weekly edition also featured a large photograph of the republican commandant Cathal Brugha's funeral cortège passing by the ruins of the Granville Hotel on 10 July, close to where he had been fatally shot five days earlier; and, in a tragic foreshadowing of continued violence, included a feature on the marriage of Edwina Ashley to Lord Louis Mountbatten, who, over a century later, was assassinated by the Provisional IRA in County Sligo on 27 August 1979, when he was seventy-nine years old. [Text: Emily Mark-Fitzgerald / Image: courtesy of Dún Laoghaire-Rathdown County Council Library Service / See also C.I. Dulin, *Ireland's Transition: The postal history of the transitional period, 1922–1925* (Dublin, 1992)]

THE COST.

MR. RORY O'CONNOR

when asked who would pay replied:

"THE IRISH PEOPLE WILL PAY"

The cost now upwards of £20,000,000

is mounting daily as the WANTON DESTRUCTION goes on.

DESTRUCTION which confers no Military Advantage whatsoever. DESTRUCTION which will have to be paid for. DESTRUCTION which will eat up the money which could have been better spent.

LOOK AROUND YOU! 21,000 FAMILIES in Dublin alone, HAVE TO LIVE IN SINGLE ROOMS.

A DOZEN HUMAN BEINGS have in many cases to live and sleep in a single filthy apartment.

SEE in every town the rotten slums in which workers have TO LIVE AND REAR THEIR CHILDREN.

SEE the diseased and rickety children of the poor, the result of starvation and rotten surroundings.

SEE THE HOVELS on the countryside, and the rocky patches which good citizens of Ireland have to try to till.

Then Think of This:

That for the first time there was in power an Irish Government with THE SCHEMES, THE WILL AND THE WAY to provide

DECENT DWELLINGS
DECENT FARMS
DECENT LIVELIHOODS

But the Rants who armed for War and still more War insisted on having their way.

Fig. 17 (above) A pro-Free State leaflet headed 'The Cost'. Using a reported throwaway comment from anti-Treaty IRA leader Rory O'Connor in answer to a journalist's question about who would bear the cost of conflict, this leaflet details the escalating costs of the IRA's campaign of destruction, and suggests that what would prevent the Free State from providing decent housing, farms and livelihoods to the Irish poor was the continuing costs of the war being waged by 'the Rants'. [Document: Kilmainham Gaol Museum 20NO-1D11-11-200]

Fig. 18 (opposite) Map of damaged bridges (post-Truce) in north Cork. The impact of the War of Independence and Civil War on civilian life is well illustrated by visualising the extent of damage to road and rail infrastructure caused by military actions. In north County Cork at the end of 1924, almost 200 bridges remained damaged as a result of military operations over the previous four years. Over eighteen months after the Civil War ended, local authorities had only fully repaired fewer than thirty of the bridges damaged in the area since April 1920. Most damage occurred during the War of Independence, particularly during periods of intense IRA activity. The spring 1920 campaign of RIC barracks attacks and a spring/summer 1921 resurgence in ambushes on crown forces contributed significantly to the destruction or damage of 137 bridges in north Cork before the July 1921 Truce. But the concentration of military activity around the Cork–Limerick border in the early months of the Civil War is evident from the devastation to transport infrastructure in surrounding districts. Cork County Council staff estimated that thirty-nine bridges were damaged across its northern divisional area in August 1922 alone – over one third of the 105 recorded post-Truce incidents that left such structures in dangerous or unusable condition (only these post-Truce incidents are shown on the map). This coincided with the mass retreat of anti-Treaty IRA fighters from east Limerick into County Cork and neighbouring parts of County Kerry after weeks of line fighting against National Army forces around Kilmallock, Bruree and Bruff through early August. As they continued through the Charleville, Mallow, Mitchelstown and Fermoy districts, IRA units slowed their enemy's pursuit by destroying bridges in their wake. But the number of damaged bridges reflects more than just the intensity of the fighting; it also underlines its impact on civilian life. The IRA deliberately targeted road bottlenecks to isolate enemy garrisons, disrupt easy movement between towns, and protect meeting and hiding places. In the case of twenty-five bridges in north Cork, repairs were still ongoing – or had not yet even begun – to damage inflicted during the War of Independence. Three bridges damaged or blown up in April 1920 within a few miles of the village of Ballyhea, between Charleville and Buttevant, were still unusable when they were damaged again in August 1922. One crossed the Awbeg River close to Ballyhea Creamery, to which access for local suppliers was further restricted by long-standing damage to another bridge a half-mile away. Attacks on bridges between Fermoy and Mitchelstown in November 1922 likely reflected IRA efforts to disrupt National Army transport from nearby Kilworth and Mountain Barracks during the Civil War's guerrilla phase. Around the Knockmealdown Mountains and into neighbouring areas of counties Tipperary and Waterford, where Liam Lynch regularly convened the IRA executive in early 1923, military movement was hindered by continued attacks on bridges in north-east County Cork in the same months. The economic and social consequences of damaged roads and bridges for local residents probably contributed to enthusiasm for the pro-Treaty cause. Impeded access to country markets, fairs and other income sources through damaged road and rail networks had seemed at an end during the Truce of July 1921. However, by the end of 1924 outstanding repair costs had reached almost £45,000 in north Cork. Hard-pressed local ratepayers feared the costs would be recouped through increased charges. Fortunately for them, local authorities became eligible for reimbursement from the Free State government under the Damage to Property (Compensation) Act 1923, which finally began the reconstruction process. [Text: Niall Murray / Map source: 'Cork County Northern Division, Return of Damaged Bridges', 17 December 1924, by R. F. O'Connor, county surveyor, Cork County Council northern division, CC/SR/F/001, Cork City and County Archives / Sources: John O'Callaghan, *The Battle for Kilmallock* (Cork, 2022); Gerard Shannon, *Liam Lynch: To declare a republic* (Newbridge, 2023), pp. 256–9; Florence O'Donoghue, *No Other Law: The story of Liam Lynch and the Irish Republican Army, 1916–1923* (Dublin, 1954), pp. 299–303]

Cumann na nGaedheal viewed labour relations and labour unrest only through the prism of the Civil War. A disregard for labour relations, an intolerance of labour unrest and ambivalence towards workers' conditions and the plight of the unemployed became the order of the day.'[17] Even after Ireland secured sovereign independence, Civil War divisions and embedded enmities persisted within communities. These were most publicly evident in the independent state's two main political parties, pro-Treaty Cumann na nGaedheal (rebranded as Fine Gael, in an amalgamation with the National Guard, or Blueshirts, and the National Centre Party in 1933) and the anti-Treaty Fianna Fáil (founded after a split with Sinn Féin in 1926). Memory of the war remained vivid, but it was carefully navigated. Intercommunal boundaries over the Treaty were generally respected, and only started to fade in recent decades.

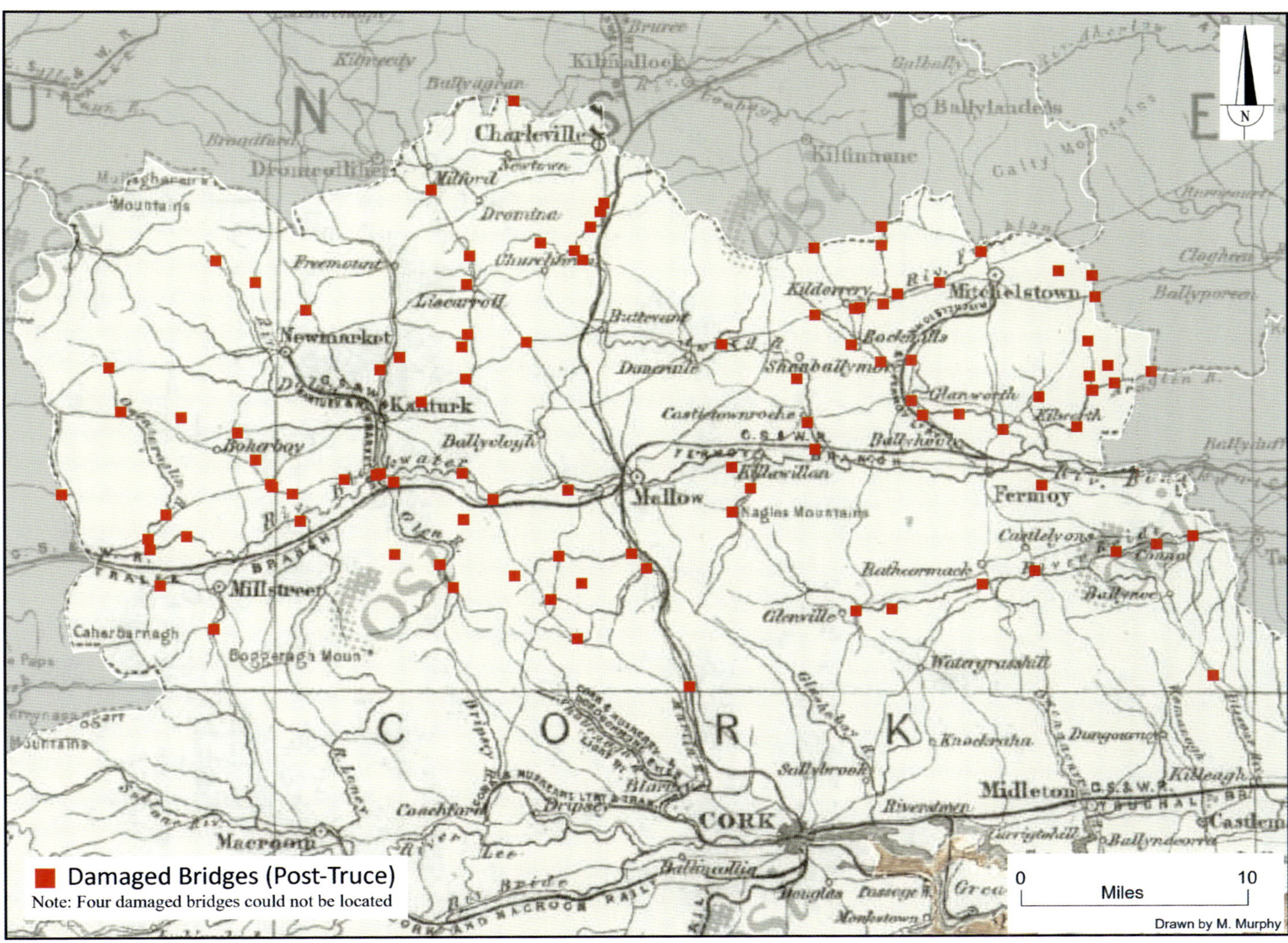

Commemorating the 'dead who died for Ireland' between 1916 and 1923 was an effective means for defeated republicans to register opposition to the 'illegitimate' Free State and its chiefs, refill its depleted ranks, and claim a moral victory in a militarily ceded civil war. Yet the government showed little appetite for official commemorations and memorials to the Irish revolution's (anti-) climactic final phase. There was also a reluctance by many veterans to speak openly about the Civil War in the context of what Síobhra Aiken has called a 'state promoted and societally-endorsed "amnesia"'.[18] Aiken's recent study of 'traumatic silence' and the 'silence breakers' – those architects of a 'counter-memory' evinced in fictionalised testimonies and popular narratives in the decades after the Civil War – challenges the idea that a 'veil of silence' was drawn around that conflict.[19] Within communities of veterans the Civil War remained a live issue for generations; but it was usually discussed quietly, in private, in part to avoid passing the conflict's pain and anger on to their children.[20] As Máire MacSwiney Brugha explained in 2009, 'The generation that goes through a civil war should not impose it on the next generation. They should be allowed to make their own decisions and to do their own thinking.'[21] Nonetheless, memories of the Civil War lived on in many families through oral narratives and, in many cases, such oral testimony is the only surviving evidence of the emotional and physical impacts of the Civil War and its fraught afterlife. Memory, as Pierre Nora observed, also 'takes root in the concrete, in spaces, gestures, images, and objects', which is apparent in the many different images presented in this new *Atlas*.[22]

Emerging scholarship

For those scholars working on the Irish Civil War, the Decade of Centenaries has brought public attention to a neglected topic. Curiosity about this war is evident across the island and beyond. The Atlas of the Irish Revolution research team in University College Cork coordinated several public engagement projects in 2022 to mark the centenary of the Irish Civil War. Of particular relevance was a public history project in partnership with RTÉ Digital, a public lecture series in collaboration with the National Library of Ireland, and the four-day Irish Civil War National Conference at UCC, organised with the Department of Tourism, Culture, Arts, Gaeltacht, Sports and Media. These projects invited contributions from a range of Civil War scholars, and ultimately demonstrated

Fig. 19 Mallow railway bridge photographed after its destruction by the IRA on 8 August 1922. [Image: Courtesy of the Irish Examiner Archive]

the burgeoning scholarship in the field and the potential for an atlas of the Irish Civil War.

Organised into ten thematic sections, this new volume builds on the *Atlas of the Irish Revolution* published in 2017. That landmark publication sought to illuminate the multiplicity of military, political, economic, social, demographic and cultural phenomena in the pivotal years from the beginning of the Home Rule Crisis in 1912 to the end of the Civil War in 1923. The focus on national and international dimensions was combined with family, street-level, local, county, regional and provincial studies to uncover the multifaceted dynamics at play during the 1912–23 period. While the *Atlas of the Irish Revolution* benefited from archival releases and the flowering of new research in the first half of Ireland's commemorative decade, the volume's relatively brief treatment of the Civil War anticipated the emergence of new scholarship in that decade's closing years. Underpinned by the same guiding principles and viewed through a similar cartographic lens, this complementary volume introduces fresh perspectives on how the Civil War battle lines were drawn and crossed, and how the conflict was perceived, presented and remembered. It also foregrounds the international, gender and labour dimensions of the intra-nationalist war that marked the birth of the new state. The *Atlas of the Irish Civil War: New perspectives* showcases the fruits of new research by more than ninety scholars whose work has pushed Civil War historiography beyond simplistic dichotomies, the study of key protagonists and basic chronologies of armed conflict, and arrived at more nuanced and inclusive treatments of that complex period.

In the seven years since the publication of the *Atlas of the Irish Revolution*, scholars have reaped the benefits of newly released archival sources, such as the civilian compensation files in the National Archives of Ireland and the Military Service Pensions Collection (MSPC) in the Irish Military Archives. This material has facilitated wider and deeper consideration of the high price paid by so many Irish women and children for the new Free State and the struggle for survival long after the guns were silenced. New pathways of enquiry have opened into the military history of the Civil War at local level, as demonstrated in Section 2 of this volume, and the MSPC in particular has bolstered our understanding of the backgrounds and social profiles of the combatants and their dependants, of lives heavily influenced by contemporary social mores, and the bitter afterlife of the eleven-month conflict. Evidence from other, often neglected, sources like material culture, balladry, oral history, poetry, family archives and testimonial fiction has also helped to infuse the monochrome historical record with the colour of personal and local, lived experience. Consistent with the interdisciplinarity of the *Atlas of the Irish Revolution*, contributors from the fields of geography, history, art history, archaeology, memory studies, political science, literary and gender studies marshal these and more traditional sources to examine the Civil War through new analytical frameworks.

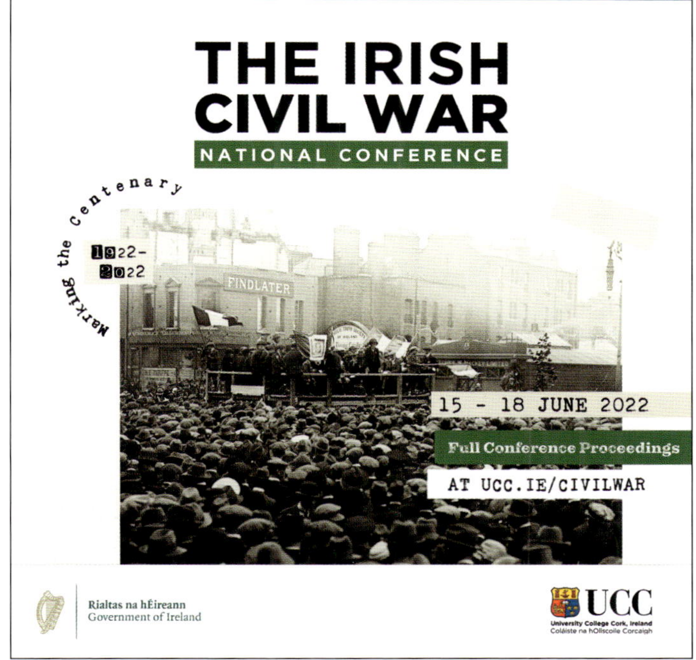

Fig. 20 (left) Poster advertising visits to the Shannon hydroelectric scheme – 'this Mighty Project in the making', *c.*1928. One of the major infrastructure projects embarked on by the Free State was the Shannon hydroelectric scheme, which began in 1925 and was completed by 1929. The dam and power plant at Ardnacrusha in County Clare quickly became a symbol of the Free State's economic ambitions, signifying its modernity to the outside world. The scheme was a challenging engineering feat, and such was its scale and grandeur that it became an attraction in its own right to thousands of curious visitors. The German company Siemens was contracted to complete the project, with the artist Seán Keating, on his own initiative, also capturing in paint the scheme's progress, its historic nature and its symbolism. Keating was heavily invested in the latter, believing that the project represented Ireland's economic future. His allegorical painting *Night's Candles Are Burnt Out* represents an old and new Ireland, the Shannon scheme constituting a future full of vision and hope, the other Ireland personified by characters embodying its conservative values (see pp. 382–3). Ironically, the project itself was marred during its 'making' by the treatment of the workers and the forty-seven who died during its construction and 'related accidents'. [Image: © ESB Archives / Source: Gerard Hanley, *Workers, Politics and Labour Relations in Independent Ireland, 1922–46* (Dublin, 2024), p. 64]

Fig. 21 (above) Promotional graphic for the Irish Civil War National Conference at University College Cork (UCC), 15–18 June 2022. This four-day national conference was one of the principal events in the state's Decade of Centenaries programme in 2022, and the largest academic gathering of the Decade of Centenaries cycle (2012–23). Over 130 national and international scholars, many of whom are contributors to this volume, gathered in UCC to explore the political, social, cultural, military and economic dimensions of the Irish Civil War. The event demonstrated intense public interest in the conflict. Over four days an estimated 2,000 people attended either the academic proceedings or one of the many commemorative public events held across Cork city centre in partnership with various local cultural institutions. Supported with funding from the Department of Tourism, Culture, Arts, Gaeltacht, Sport and Media (with additional support from Cork City Council and Cork County Council), proceedings were open to the public, live-streamed and recorded for viewing in collaboration with RTE.ie. The UCC conference organising committee was chaired by the late Professor Chris Williams, and included Mervyn O'Driscoll, John Borgonovo, Hélène O'Keeffe, Niamh Sweeney and Eugenie Hanley. The full conference proceedings, including the opening address by An Taoiseach Micheál Martin, are available to view at ucc.ie/civilwar.

The thirteen core chapters, twenty case studies and numerous caption essays by a range of established and emerging scholars are complemented by over forty maps, reflecting the most recent research. Maps have a unique power to capture both the temporal and spatial dimensions of the conflict, and its military, political, social and economic impacts. The wide-angle cartographic lens can capture national and international patterns and trends; but, as the focus narrows, it also allows for more intimate portrayals of events on the ground, sometimes confirming but occasionally challenging the received narratives of the Irish Civil War. One example is the map depicting Ann Matthews's research into the places of arrest of female internees during the Civil War. Her findings, gleaned from diverse archival sources, revise the traditionally accepted number of women imprisoned during the conflict. Maps based on Justin Dolan Stover's research into the compensation files in the National Archives of Ireland capture both the scale and local intensity of politically motivated infrastructural damage and the impact of renewed agrarianism in the law-and-order vacuum created by the

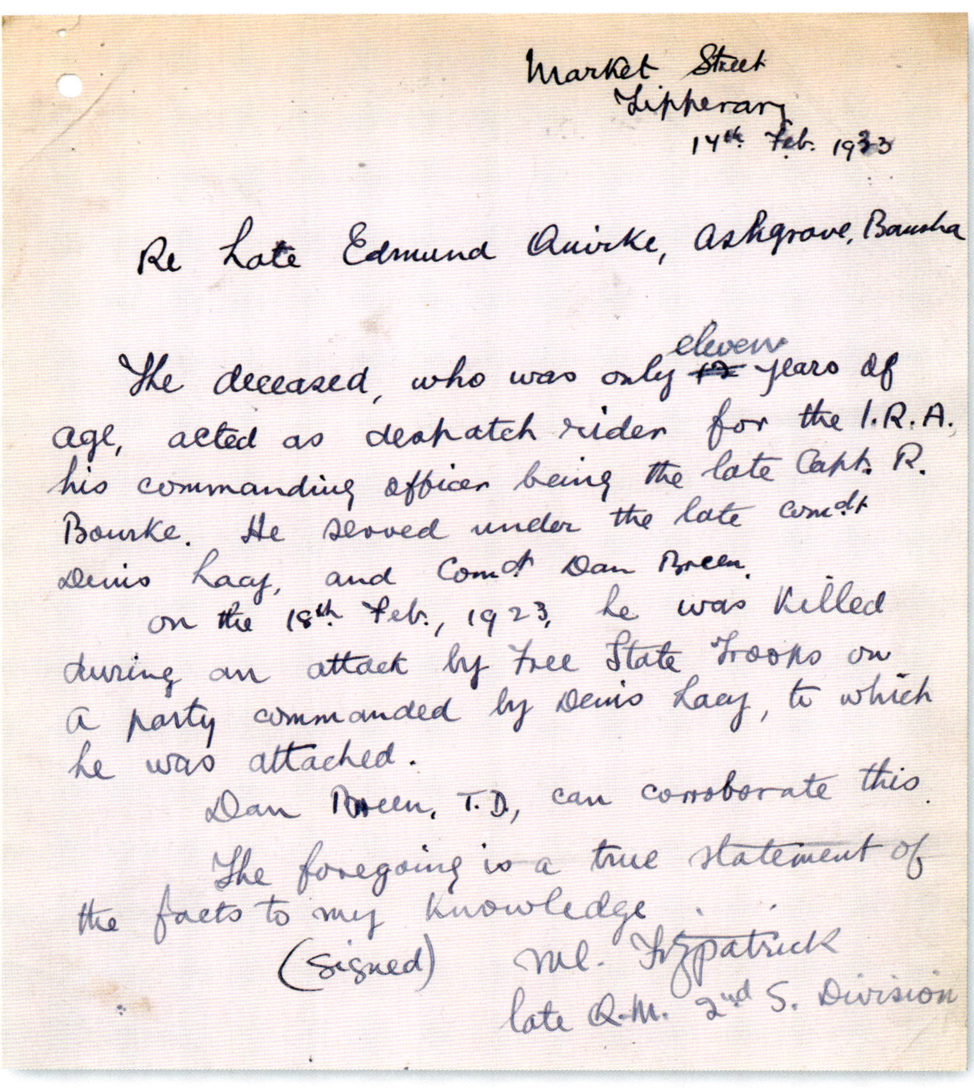

Market Street
Tipperary
14th Feb. 1933

Re Late Edmund Quirke, Ashgrove, Bansha

The deceased, who was only eleven years of age, acted as despatch rider for the I.R.A. his commanding officer being the late Capt. R. Bourke. He served under the late Comdt Denis Lacy, and Comdt Dan Breen.

On the 18th Feb., 1923, he was killed during an attack by Free State Troops on a party commanded by Denis Lacy, to which he was attached.

Dan Breen, T.D., can corroborate this.

The foregoing is a true statement of the facts to my knowledge.

(Signed) Ml. Fitzpatrick
late Q.M. 2nd S. Division

Fig. 22 Letter from Michael Fitzpatrick, former quartermaster of the 2nd Southern Division, in support of James Quirke's ultimately unsuccessful application for a military service pension for his late son, Edmund Quirke. Ten-year-old Quirke was classified as an IRA dispatch rider and 'intelligence officer' for pension purposes, but he was simply in the wrong place at the wrong time on 18 February 1923. He received a fatal gunshot wound to the head during an engagement between Free State forces and Denis Lacey's IRA active service unit billeted at Quirke's farmhouse at Ashgrove, near Bansha in County Tipperary. It remains unclear, however, which side fired the fatal shot. According to new research by Andy Bielenberg and John Dorney, Quirke was one of twenty-seven Civil War fatalities (eleven girls and sixteen boys) aged under fifteen (see p. 218). [Document: MSPC DP3369 / Image: courtesy of Military Archives/MSPC Project]

evacuation of the British forces. The cartographic representation of singular incidents and engagements – like the movements of the 'Sliabh na mBan' armoured car after it was captured by republican forces in west Cork in December 1922 and the IRA attack on Ballyconnell, County Cavan in early 1923 – is based primarily on detailed new research at local level.

Perhaps most significant is the selection of maps based on Andy Bielenberg and John Dorney's Irish Civil War Fatalities Project.[23] They offer significant new insights into the geography of conflict-related fatalities in Ireland between the opening shots of the Civil War on 28 June 1922 and the ceasefire and dump-arms order on 24 May 1923. Moving beyond the varying estimates proffered by historians over many decades, Bielenberg and Dorney's research enumerates for the first time all civilian and combatant deaths during the Civil War, while also providing information on the date and location of each fatality, previous military service, if any, age, occupation and county of origin. These additional details allow for a unique social survey of the Civil War dead and the temporal and spatial patterns of the fatalities. The new fatalities maps fill in significant gaps in the historical record, underscore the necessity for more in-depth local research, and invite more discerning and nuanced responses. Taken together, these new research findings will influence how the Civil War is understood and interpreted long after the end of the Decade of Centenaries. In naming the dead the Irish Civil War Fatalities Project continues a process of recovery more than a century after the end of the conflict, and the full list of Civil War fatalities, in Section 10 of this volume, is a timely and necessary memorial to those men and women, civilians and combatants, killed during the war.

In his 'Machnamh 100' Civil War seminar, President Michael D. Higgins emphasised the importance of 'the view from below', the 'people's history of the time in question'.[24] This volume seeks to follow his advice by exploring the significance of the everyday – the lived experience of the Irish Civil War. What was life like for those bystanders swept up in struggle? What was the experience of those whose property was confiscated or destroyed, those whose livelihoods were threatened by disrupted communications and torn-up roads, those who simply tried to get on with life against

Fig. 23 Colum Kelly's letter to his mother Rose written the day before his execution by the National Army at Birr Castle on the morning of 26 January 1923. A native of Tullamore, Kelly was twenty-two years of age. William Conroy, aged eighteen, and Patrick Cunningham, twenty, were tied to chairs and executed alongside him for alleged armed robberies. The poignancy of his final farewell speaks to the tragedy of civil war: 'Tell my uncle Tommy and his Mrs I am bidding them the last fairwell [*sic*] and the children also. Tell them to pray for me and I will do the same for them in heaven. We got the Priest and all the rites of the Church and am dying a Happy Death. Tell my uncle Jimmy I bid him goodbye. We will be shot in Birr Castle in the morning at 8 o'clock'. [Document: courtesy of Rosaleen Monaghan]

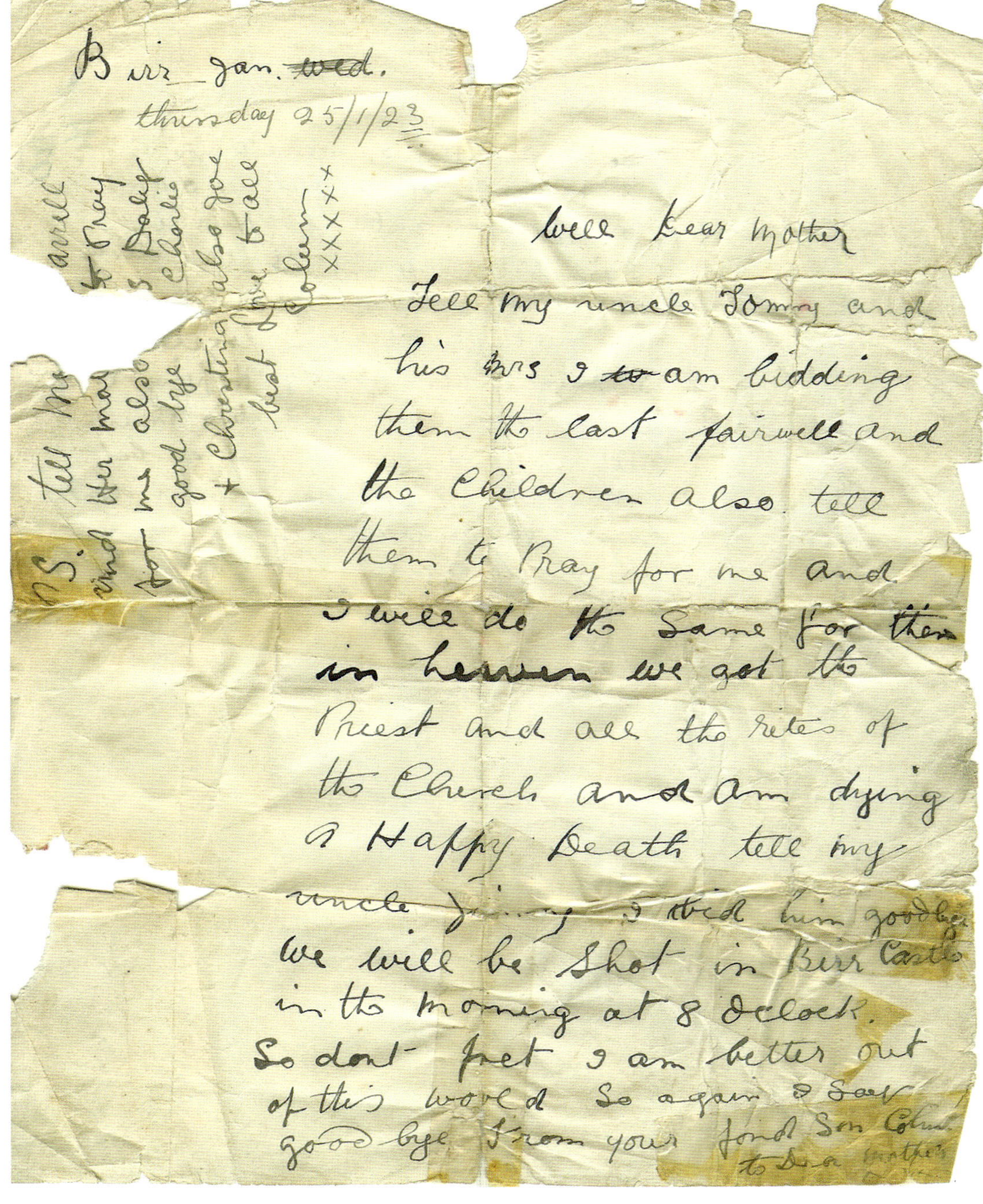

Birr Jan. ~~wed.~~
thursday 25/1/23

Well Dear Mother
Tell my uncle Tommy and his Mrs I ~~to~~ am bidding them the last fairwell and the Children also tell them to Pray for me and I will do the Same for them in heaven we got the Priest and all the rites of the Church and am dying a Happy Death tell my uncle Jimmy I bid him goodbye We will be Shot in Birr Castle in the morning at 8 Oclock. So dont fret I am better out of this world So again I Say good bye from your fond Son Colum
to Dear mother

the backdrop of political violence? The visualisation of the Civil War in this book sets out to capture that human dimension partly through letters, autograph books and diary entries. These archival documents are often poignant in their intimacy and revelatory of the writers' preoccupations with everything from politics and ideology to the bread-and-butter issues facing so many families in 1922 and 1923.

Government and military reports and memoranda provide insights into the deeply held convictions that sparked and perpetuated the eleven-month Civil War. They also address the often-neglected efforts to reconcile the two sides in the months before the outbreak of hostilities. Material culture, graffiti assemblages, portraiture, photographs, propaganda materials and cartoons have their own stories to tell about the how the conflict was perceived, interpreted and represented. These rare, and in many cases previously unpublished, images and documents open a window onto the past, capturing moments as they happened and phenomena that do not lend themselves easily to mapping. The pro-Treaty TD and diarist Liam de Róiste, for example, wrote of the calmness of the people in Cork city on the day after the Four Courts attack, not only because of the assumption that the 'business' would soon be over, but also because of the 'many episodes we have lived through during the past six or seven years. Our senses of wonder and surprises are dulled or deadened. To

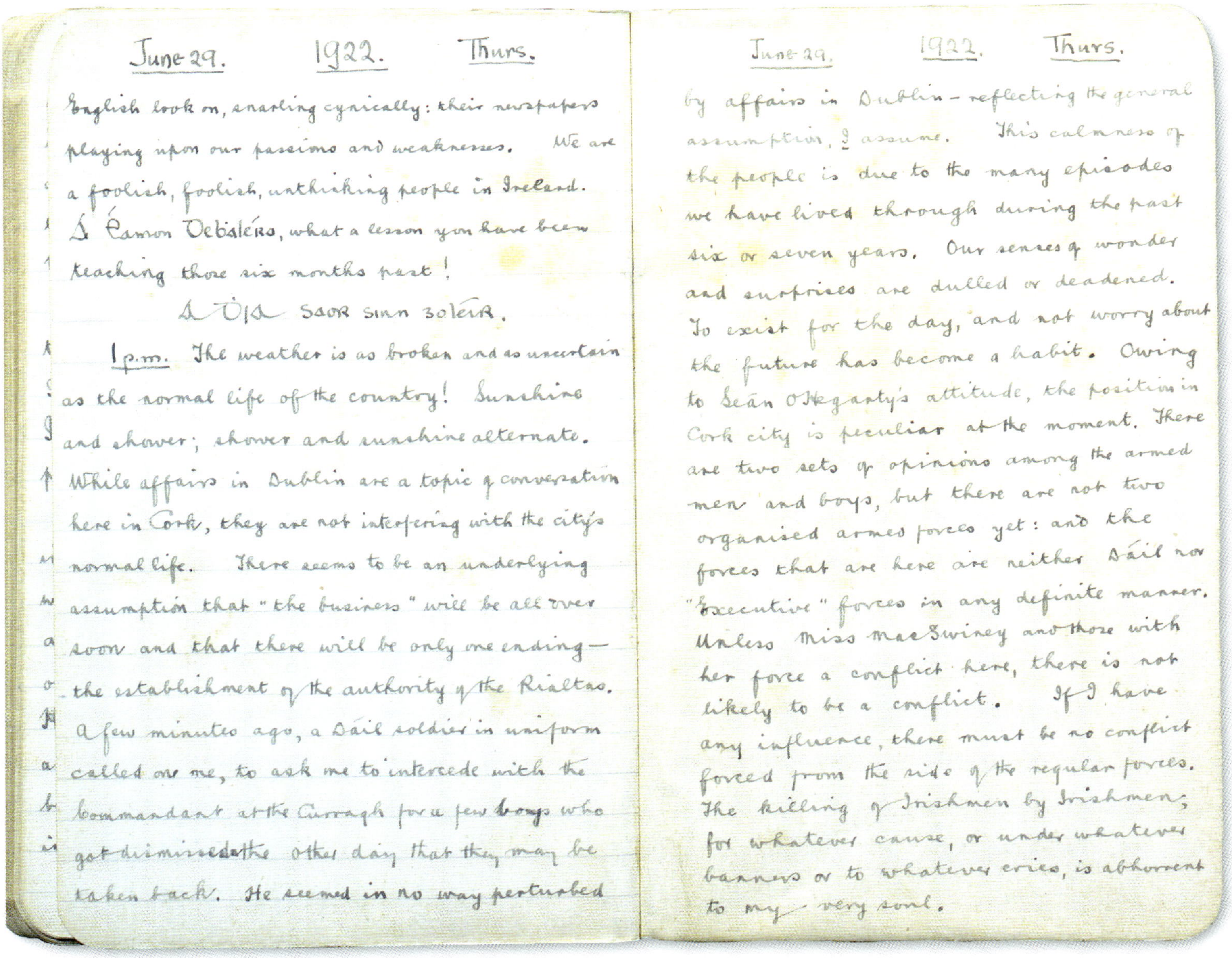

June 29. 1922. Thurs.

English look on, snarling cynically: their newspapers playing upon our passions and weaknesses. We are a foolish, foolish, unthinking people in Ireland.

A Éamon DeValera, what a lesson you have been teaching those six months past!

A Dhia saor sinn goléir.

1 p.m. The weather is as broken and as uncertain as the normal life of the country! Sunshine and shower; shower and sunshine alternate. While affairs in Dublin are a topic of conversation here in Cork, they are not interfering with the city's normal life. There seems to be an underlying assumption that "the business" will be all over soon and that there will be only one ending – the establishment of the authority of the Rialtas. A few minutes ago, a Dáil soldier in uniform called on me, to ask me to intercede with the Commandant at the Curragh for a few boys who got dismissed the other day that they may be taken back. He seemed in no way perturbed

June 29. 1922. Thurs.

by affairs in Dublin – reflecting the general assumption, I assume. This calmness of the people is due to the many episodes we have lived through during the past six or seven years. Our senses of wonder and surprises are dulled or deadened. To exist for the day, and not worry about the future has become a habit. Owing to Seán O'Hegarty's attitude, the position in Cork city is peculiar at the moment. There are two sets of opinions among the armed men and boys, but there are not two organised armed forces yet: and the forces that are here are neither Dáil nor "Executive" forces in any definite manner. Unless Miss MacSwiney and those with her force a conflict here, there is not likely to be a conflict. If I have any influence, there must be no conflict forced from the side of the regular forces. The killing of Irishmen by Irishmen; for whatever cause, or under whatever banners or to whatever cries, is abhorrent to my very soul.

Fig. 24 Extract from the diary of Liam de Róiste (1882–1959), 29 June 1922. An astute observer of events, de Róiste was a central figure in cultural and political circles in Cork city by 1922. By the time of his election to the First Dáil in December 1918, he had assumed leadership roles in the Cork Industrial Development Association and the Cork branches of the Gaelic League, the Celtic Literary Society and Sinn Féin. His early diaries, preserved with his papers in Cork City and County Archives and partially digitised during the Decade of Centenaries, capture the exciting cultural ferment in early twentieth-century urban Ireland, and the restlessness among advanced nationalists like de Róiste and his friend Terence MacSwiney for sweeping political and social change. De Róiste kept his parliamentary seat in the 1921 general election and, as deputy speaker in Dáil Éireann, presided over many of the debates on the Anglo-Irish Treaty in Earlsfort Terrace, before casting his vote in favour of the agreement. The diary entries during this period, when de Róiste also served as an alderman on Cork Corporation, provide not only powerful pen pictures of key protagonists and insights into the local dynamics of the Treaty split, but also access to real-time, personal reactions to unfolding events. De Róiste, for example, was involved in the unsuccessful efforts to reconcile the opposing Sinn Féin camps in the months before the outbreak of the Civil War. He was elected to the Third Dáil in the June 1922 election – the pro-Treaty majority, he suggested in his diary on 17 June, was 'the people's answer to revolver rule, Dáil talk, [and] machine-made politics'. Just under a fortnight later, the civil war long feared by the Cork TD was precipitated by the Provisional Government's attack on the Four Courts. 'The killing of Irishmen by Irishmen', wrote de Róiste on 29 June, 'for whatever cause, or under whatever banners or to whatever cries, is abhorrent to my very soul'. He did not contest the August 1923 election, but stood unsuccessfully as a Cumann na nGaedheal candidate in 1927. He continued to study, write and lecture on Irish history and culture until his death on 15 May 1959. [Document: Cork City and County Archives] exist for the day, and not worry about the future has become a habit.'[25] The maps, images and documents are captioned with short essays by members of the editorial team or, where indicated, invited scholars, who analyse and contextualise the content and, in many cases, elaborate on personalities or themes alluded to in the main contributions.

Opening the Irish Civil War National Conference at University College Cork in June 2022, Taoiseach Micheál Martin drew on his own family experience, broadly representative of families across Ireland, when he asserted that: 'Those most touched by the Civil War were the people least likely to talk about it … Nationally, we have never stopped talking about the Civil War, but we have done too little to try to understand it. The questions we ask, the lenses which we apply when reviewing it, have remained largely unchanged.'[26] Like the conference, which brought together 130 scholars over four days to share their research, and the large-scale, collaborative public history and documentary projects coordinated by UCC's Atlas of the Irish Revolution team during the Decade of Centenaries, this volume seeks to widen and deepen the interrogative lens.[27] It does not purport to offer a sense of closure, nor an agreed narrative, nor an official history. Instead, it allows for a diversity of views and perspectives grounded in original scholarship, academic rigour and archival discovery. The history of the Irish Civil War is still being written. This is the latest contribution to that process.

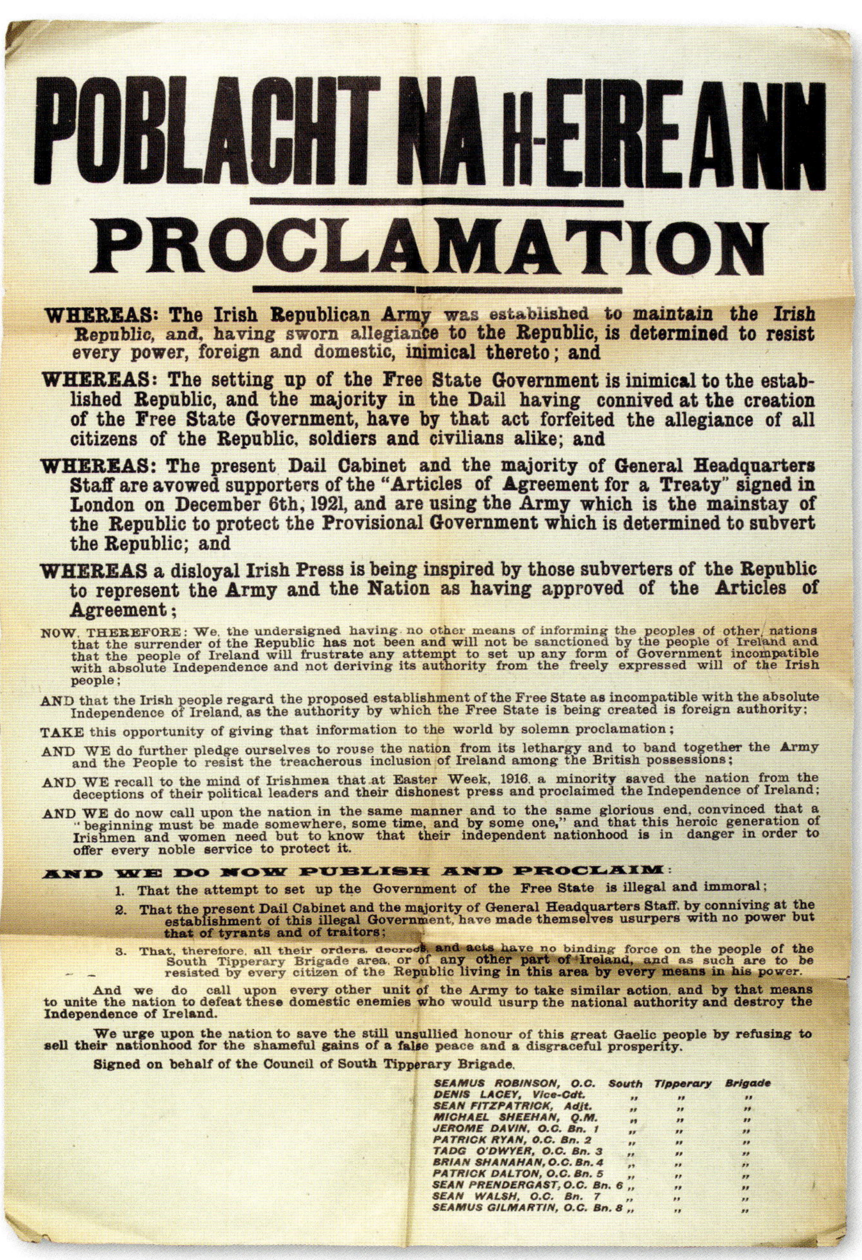

POBLACHT NA H-EIREANN

PROCLAMATION

WHEREAS: The Irish Republican Army was established to maintain the Irish Republic, and, having sworn allegiance to the Republic, is determined to resist every power, foreign and domestic, inimical thereto; and

WHEREAS: The setting up of the Free State Government is inimical to the established Republic, and the majority in the Dail having connived at the creation of the Free State Government, have by that act forfeited the allegiance of all citizens of the Republic, soldiers and civilians alike; and

WHEREAS: The present Dail Cabinet and the majority of General Headquarters Staff are avowed supporters of the "Articles of Agreement for a Treaty" signed in London on December 6th, 1921, and are using the Army which is the mainstay of the Republic to protect the Provisional Government which is determined to subvert the Republic; and

WHEREAS a disloyal Irish Press is being inspired by those subverters of the Republic to represent the Army and the Nation as having approved of the Articles of Agreement;

NOW, THEREFORE: We, the undersigned having no other means of informing the peoples of other nations that the surrender of the Republic has not been and will not be sanctioned by the people of Ireland and that the people of Ireland will frustrate any attempt to set up any form of Government incompatible with absolute Independence and not deriving its authority from the freely expressed will of the Irish people;

AND that the Irish people regard the proposed establishment of the Free State as incompatible with the absolute Independence of Ireland, as the authority by which the Free State is being created is foreign authority;

TAKE this opportunity of giving that information to the world by solemn proclamation;

AND WE do further pledge ourselves to rouse the nation from its lethargy and to band together the Army and the People to resist the treacherous inclusion of Ireland among the British possessions;

AND WE recall to the mind of Irishmen that at Easter Week, 1916, a minority saved the nation from the deceptions of their political leaders and their dishonest press and proclaimed the Independence of Ireland;

AND WE do now call upon the nation in the same manner and to the same glorious end, convinced that a "beginning must be made somewhere, some time, and by some one," and that this heroic generation of Irishmen and women need but to know that their independent nationhood is in danger in order to offer every noble service to protect it.

AND WE DO NOW PUBLISH AND PROCLAIM:

1. That the attempt to set up the Government of the Free State is illegal and immoral;
2. That the present Dail Cabinet and the majority of General Headquarters Staff, by conniving at the establishment of this illegal Government, have made themselves usurpers with no power but that of tyrants and of traitors;
3. That, therefore, all their orders, decrees, and acts have no binding force on the people of the South Tipperary Brigade area, or of any other part of Ireland, and as such are to be resisted by every citizen of the Republic living in this area by every means in his power.

And we do call upon every other unit of the Army to take similar action, and by that means to unite the nation to defeat these domestic enemies who would usurp the national authority and destroy the Independence of Ireland.

We urge upon the nation to save the still unsullied honour of this great Gaelic people by refusing to sell their nationhood for the shameful gains of a false peace and a disgraceful prosperity.

Signed on behalf of the Council of South Tipperary Brigade.

SEAMUS ROBINSON, O.C.	South	Tipperary	Brigade
DENIS LACEY, Vice-Cdt.	"	"	"
SEAN FITZPATRICK, Adjt.	"	"	"
MICHAEL SHEEHAN, Q.M.	"	"	"
JEROME DAVIN, O.C. Bn. 1	"	"	"
PATRICK RYAN, O.C. Bn. 2	"	"	"
TADG O'DWYER, O.C. Bn. 3	"	"	"
BRIAN SHANAHAN, O.C. Bn. 4	"	"	"
PATRICK DALTON, O.C. Bn. 5	"	"	"
SEAN PRENDERGAST, O.C. Bn. 6	"	"	"
SEAN WALSH, O.C. Bn. 7	"	"	"
SEAMUS GILMARTIN, O.C. Bn. 8	"	"	"

Fig. 25 Anti-Treaty proclamation by the council of the IRA South Tipperary Brigade pledging to fight against the Treaty and its supporters, who 'are to be resisted by every citizen of the Republic'. [Document: National Library of Ireland, Erskine Childers Papers, MS 48,085/2]

Arthur Griffith (far right) with members of the Irish Treaty delegation, including George Gavan Duffy, Robert Barton and Erskine Childers, on the return trip from London after signing the Anglo-Irish Treaty on 6 December 1921. [Image: National Library of Ireland, HOG3]

SECTION 1

Before the War

Fig. 1 Map showing the extent of the British Empire in the early 1920s. By the end of September 1923, with the inclusion of Mandatory Palestine, the British Empire was at its greatest geographical extent, covering one fifth of the world's land mass and embracing a population of *c.* 460 million. While the First World War and its aftermath had witnessed the break-up of the Russian, Ottoman, German and Austro-Hungarian empires, Wilsonian ideas of self-determination and the founding of the League of Nations posed a threat to the British Empire. Britain's increasing military commitments in the post-war years and the rise of anti-colonial nationalism underscored the real threat of imperial overstretch. The Anglo-Irish Treaty from a British perspective was, then, largely framed by the pivotal question of empire and Ireland's place within it. To that extent, the Treaty was seen as a template for imperial reform that could later be adopted in its other troublesome territories.

CHAPTER 1

The Treaty and the Irish Civil War: British perspectives

Heather Jones

The Irish Civil War posed significant security, economic and cultural questions for Britain and its empire. Yet we still know too little about how the British government and general public reacted to it. There has been much more historiographical focus on British military and political decision-making and public opinion during the War of Independence (1919–21), and while, in recent decades, new publications have begun to address the imbalance, research into British perspectives on the conflict remains limited.[1]

By late 1921 there was consensus in Britain on a number of points regarding Ireland. There was an intense desire to remove the Irish question completely from British politics, with a hoped-for successful settlement in Ireland through partition and the Anglo-Irish Treaty of 6 December 1921. Ireland was seen as having negatively dominated British politics since 1912. Not only was political violence in Ireland considered damaging to Britain's international reputation, but it tied up economic and military resources, which, post-war, the majority of British politicians and public believed, needed to be turned towards domestic British issues, such as the threat from militant socialism, fears of Bolshevism within Britain, the Glasgow radical strike wave, and the need for welfare reforms to mollify First World War veterans and create the promised 'homes fit for heroes'.

However, the issues at stake in the Irish Civil War also varied widely for different groups within British society. The initial reaction to the Anglo-Irish Treaty revealed serious political divisions. The Liberal Party, traditionally supportive of Irish Home Rule, had split during the First World War into Coalition Liberals and Independent Liberals, and this bitter division had greatly weakened liberalism as a force in British politics. By December 1921 Coalition Liberal leader David Lloyd George only remained as British prime minister due to the support of the Conservative (Tory) Party. The Liberal Party's agenda by December 1921 was to find a treaty settlement for Ireland acceptable to the Tories so that they would not bring down the government over it. Ultimately, the Tories only grudgingly accepted the Anglo-Irish Treaty, with a significant party minority – known as the diehards – opposed, believing it gave in to insurgents and set a dangerous precedent for the empire. The Tory party leader, Austen Chamberlain, feared that these diehards would use his role as negotiator and signatory to the Treaty to challenge his leadership.[2] For the majority of the party, however, keen to jettison coalition government for single-party Tory rule, the Treaty presented an opportunity to play politics and try to bring down Lloyd George.

In contrast, the vast majority of sympathisers with Irish nationalism in British political circles enthusiastically supported the Treaty. The British Parliamentary Labour Party – whose views on the Treaty have been the subject of recent work by Ivan Gibbons – was keen to position itself as a party capable of government and of managing British interests on the international stage, part of its effort to disassociate itself from radical manifestations of socialism on the continent, particularly from Bolshevism.[3] For this reason, Labour, which had openly opposed the British government's policies on Ireland during the War of Independence, now supported the Treaty as part of a policy of proving its moderation to British voters. The British Trades Union Congress likewise backed the Treaty.

Serious divisions

This alienated the mainstream British labour movement from the largest Irish nationalist diaspora organisation in Britain, the Irish Self-Determination League (ISDL), which decided to support the anti-Treaty cause.[4] However, even at its height in summer 1921, when the ISDL had 300 branches across Britain, its membership of 38,726 represented just over 2 per cent of Britain's 1.5 million Irish diasporic population, making it difficult to assess how representative it was of wider diaspora views on the Civil War, and suggesting that much of the diaspora did not become directly involved in political activism.[5] In fact, while we have some excellent research on the diaspora's attitudes during the War of Independence, far less is known about how the Civil War impacted upon the Irish in Britain, both unionist and nationalist.[6] However, during the War of Independence, there was 'an extended campaign of IRA incendiary attacks' in British cities and clandestine IRA arms trading with British criminal gangs and communists.[7] Some of these pre-existing networks continued to exist into the Civil War period.

The make-up of the diaspora in Britain was also affected by the Civil War. The signing of the Treaty and withdrawal of British military and administrative personnel led to a wave of migration to

Fig. 2 Art O'Brien (seated, left) with (l-r) Harry Boland, George Gavan Duffy and Seán T. O'Kelly at the Irish Race Convention in Paris, 21–28 January 1922. O'Brien, a stalwart advocate of Irish culture and nationalism in London since 1900, was appointed Dáil Éireann's envoy to London in 1919. He ran a vibrant propaganda campaign in support of the War of Independence, and established the Irish Self-Determination League of Great Britain, which, by early 1921, numbered 38,726 members in over 200 branches. He vehemently rejected the Treaty, however, despite a very close friendship and working relationship with Michael Collins. His last 'diplomatic outing' was to the Irish Race Convention in Paris in January 1922. He is seen in this photograph with fellow anti-Treatyites Harry Boland and Seán T. O'Kelly, and George Gavan Duffy, who was a signatory of the Treaty. In April 1922 Gavan Duffy, now minister for foreign affairs, sacked O'Brien from his position as London envoy. O'Brien then became 'de Valera's man in London' and launched a propaganda campaign in favour of 'the Republic'. He regularly opined that Collins and Griffith were 'acting dictatorially and as a law unto themselves'. Correspondence between de Valera and O'Brien during this period shows that de Valera still hoped that world opinion could be swayed in favour of a republic and that he would be invited once again to negotiate in London. O'Brien organised and funded republican envoys in Paris (Leopold Kerney), Genoa/Rome (Donal Hales) and the United States (Laurence Ginnell). O'Brien was also actively involved in channelling money from the United States through London to Dublin in support of republicans during late 1922 and early 1923. At a meeting in Bermondsey on 21 January 1923, O'Brien was introduced as 'the deputy of President de Valera'. One speaker referred to Collins as 'Churchill's chum', while all present vowed to do all in their power to achieve a republic. The Home Office reported that O'Brien was using weekly meetings of the Gaelic League of London at the Minerva Café in Holborn as a cover for meeting Irish extremists. An Irish Republican Prisoners' Fund was established with the actual remit of supporting anti-Treaty soldiers in Ireland. O'Brien briefed sympathetic MPs to ask questions in the House of Commons, particularly in relation to the execution without trial of republican prisoners, asking why the British government did not intervene. He also prepared a dossier on Free State executions for the International Red Cross at de Valera's request. In the early hours of 11 March 1923, however, O'Brien was one of around a hundred suspected republican activists rounded up by the British authorities and deported to Mountjoy Gaol in Dublin, with the cooperation of the Free State government. O'Brien successfully challenged his deportation in a case taken in London, where it was deemed illegal to have deported British subjects to another jurisdiction. In May 1923 all the deportees were sent back to Britain and were eventually compensated for their ordeal. Ironically, O'Brien's case had confirmed the status of the Free State as a separate entity to the British state. His freedom was short-lived as he was arrested again and convicted of sedition at the Old Bailey in London. He was sentenced to two years in prison in July 1923, thus ending his anti-Treaty activities. [Text: Mary MacDiarmada / Image: National Library of Ireland, Kathleen McKenna-Napoli Photographic Collection, NPA MKN3]

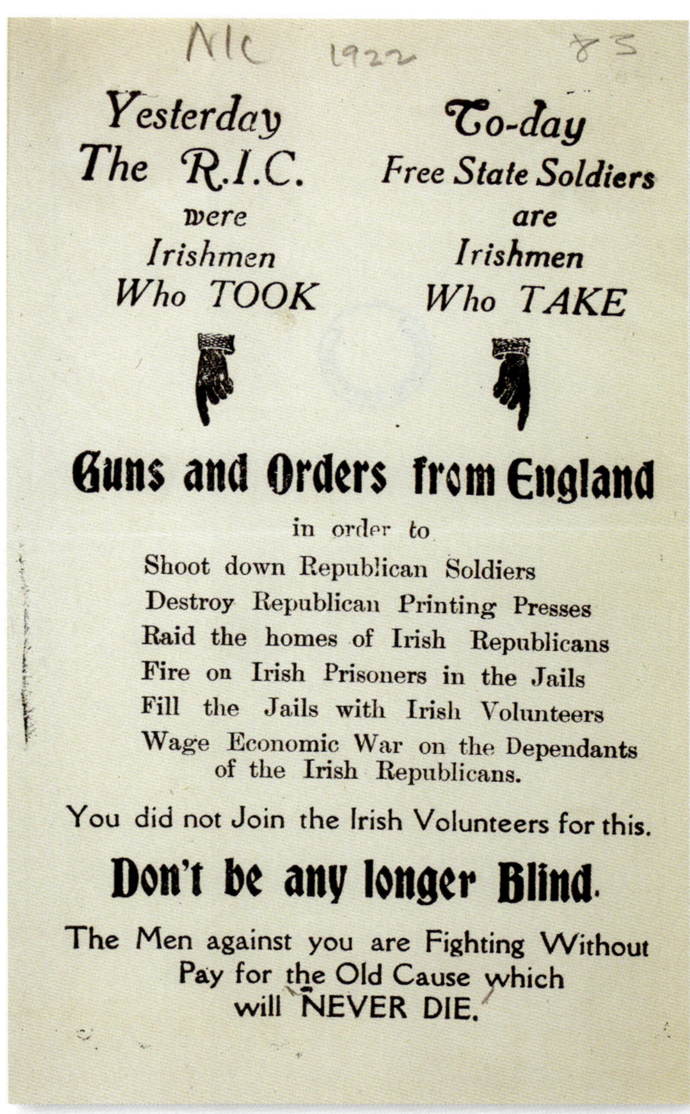
Yesterday The R.I.C. were Irishmen Who TOOK

To-day Free State Soldiers are Irishmen Who TAKE

Guns and Orders from England

in order to

Shoot down Republican Soldiers

Destroy Republican Printing Presses

Raid the homes of Irish Republicans

Fire on Irish Prisoners in the Jails

Fill the Jails with Irish Volunteers

Wage Economic War on the Dependants of the Irish Republicans.

You did not Join the Irish Volunteers for this.

Don't be any longer Blind.

The Men against you are Fighting Without Pay for the Old Cause which will NEVER DIE.

Fig. 3 Republican handbill addressed to former IRA Volunteers serving in the National Army. It compares them to the Royal Irish Constabulary members who took 'guns and orders from England', and contrasts them to their anti-Treaty foes who were 'Fighting Without Pay for the Old Cause'. [Document: National Library of Ireland, D143]

Britain, largely of personnel from Britain who had been employed in Ireland and also of a number of Irish employees and their families, including many former Royal Irish Constabulary (RIC) men. The violence in spring 1922 in the newly created Northern Ireland saw migration to Britain by refugees fleeing the violence. Catholic refugees from Belfast went to Glasgow and Liverpool. The Bandon Valley killings of April 1922 saw a wave of loyalist refugees from west Cork flee to Britain. In total in the spring of 1922 'perhaps as many as 20,000 people, some with their entire families', arrived in Britain from Ireland and 'were given refugee status'.[8] Socio-economic factors in the Civil War also drove migration: the war was accompanied by local level agrarian violence and cattle rustling, which led many of those targeted and intimidated to sell up and move elsewhere, including Britain, while the anti-Treaty arson campaign against big houses saw some of their staff also migrate to Britain for new work in the wake of a house burning. Finally, after the Civil War ended, some on the anti-Treaty side migrated to Britain to start a new life, following the humiliation of defeat. The process of migration was also not always permanent. Many made use of pre-established kinship networks across Britain from previous generations of emigration to spend some time abroad while waiting to see if political volatility subsided in Ireland.

Further research is needed on how those who left Ireland for Britain in 1922–3 impacted on wider public opinion and political attitudes in Britain. Some new Irish refugee communities, such as former RIC men who settled in Letchworth, appear to have generally kept away from political activism.[9] In contrast, some active lobby groups, such as the newly formed Southern Irish Loyalist Relief Association, supported Irish refugees from pro-British backgrounds in this period. Its supporters included MPs and peers drawn mainly from the right wing of the Tory Party and from Anglo-Irish elites, many of whom rejected the Treaty as a British sell-out of Southern unionists, and who lobbied for more support for loyalists who had remained in the Irish Free State during the Civil War.

Irish connections

Personal connections with Ireland helped drive a range of different political views in Britain on the Treaty and subsequent Civil War. Winston Churchill, secretary of state for the colonies in 1922, had spent part of his childhood in Dublin and was an ardent supporter of the Treaty he had negotiated and signed.[10] In contrast, Andrew Bonar Law, who would be reappointed leader of the Tory party in October 1922, came from an Ulster unionist family and only very reluctantly endorsed the Treaty in parliament in December 1921. Influential figures such as the two powerful press-baron brothers, Alfred Harmsworth, who became Lord Northcliffe, and Harold Harmsworth, who became Lord Rothermere, also had close Irish connections – their mother was an Ulster unionist from County Down, and Alfred, who was born in Ireland, maintained contact with relatives and owned a property there.[11] Lord Northcliffe kept in close touch with the Treaty negotiations, warning against a British 'government surrender' but also supporting partition, coupled with greater autonomy for the South, as a solution that would benefit 'the empire, Anglo-American relations and Ireland in that order'.[12]

The Treaty and the British parliament

The divisions among British politicians regarding the Anglo-Irish Treaty remain surprisingly under-researched. As parliamentary historian David Torrance points out: 'Despite its significance to the history of the United Kingdom, the Anglo-Irish Treaty [...] has had remarkably little attention from historians and constitutional scholars' and the British parliamentary debates on the Treaty have been 'especially neglected'.[13] Article 18 of the Anglo-Irish Treaty stated that its provisions required approval by parliaments in both the UK and Ireland. The reality was, however, that getting the Treaty

Fig. 4 Portrait of Winston Churchill (1874–1965) by John Lavery (1915). Churchill's political life encompassed two world wars and spanned more than half a century. It began with his election, at twenty-five, to the House of Commons in 1900 and ended with his resignation from the premiership in 1955. His long relationship with Ireland has been described as complex, even capricious, but his support for Home Rule as a prominent Liberal between 1905 and 1915, his hardline response to IRA insurgency after 1916, his ardent defence of the Treaty and scorn for Irish neutrality during the Second World War were all driven by the same desire to secure Britain's international and imperial security. Something of his formidability, his clear-eyed confidence, even the inclination towards bombast noted by Michael Collins during the Treaty negotiations is captured in this portrait by Belfast-born Sir John Lavery (knighted in 1918). The painting also hints at the familiarity between subject and artist, the London neighbours who socialised together and shared an affinity for art. Indeed, Lavery and his wife Hazel encouraged Churchill's own artistic efforts during a period of political and personal uncertainty following the disastrous 1915 naval assault on the Dardanelles for which, as First Lord of the Admiralty, he was widely held responsible and forced to resign. After a short stint fighting on the Western Front, Churchill returned to government as minister of munitions in 1917. In January 1919 he was appointed secretary of war and minister of the air in Lloyd George's coalition government and, during the War of Independence, advocated a strong British stand against the IRA, which he condemned as a 'gang of squalid murderers'. As secretary of state for the colonies and chairman of the Cabinet commission on Irish affairs, Churchill played a leading role in the Treaty negotiations in London. He described the resulting agreement 'not as a humiliation' but as 'a great and peculiar manifestation of British genius'. Tied to the Treaty not only on principle but also politically as one of its key architects, Churchill spoke resolutely in support of the Free State Bill as it was piloted through the House of Commons. He offered encouragement and military support to the Provisional Government to ensure the enforcement of the Treaty, but became increasingly critical of Collins's inaction against the 'irregulars, hooligans [and] Bolsheviks of the IRA'. Unless the Provisional Government ended the occupation of the Four Courts, Churchill told the House of Commons on 26 June 1922, the British government would consider the Treaty violated and would assume 'full liberty of action'. Collins railed against the ultimatum, which undermined the autonomy of the Free State government, but believed that action was necessary. The attack on the Four Courts on 28 June represented a triumph for Churchill's intractability on the Treaty but, as Paul Bew writes, he once again 'underestimated the strength of anti-British sentiment in nationalist Ireland'. [Painting: Collection & image © Hugh Lane Gallery – Lady Lavery Memorial bequest through Sir John Lavery, 1935 / See Paul Bew, *Churchill and Ireland* (Oxford, 2016)]

through parliament was a major challenge for David Lloyd George, who had already faced down a motion put forward by Tory diehards condemning the Treaty negotiations in the House of Commons in October 1921. Peers in the House of Lords were also divided on the Treaty. Ultimately, Lloyd George made three key strategic moves to ensure its passage. First, the Treaty was presented to parliament for approval, unusually, through a king's speech by King George V to both houses on 14 December 1921, which opened a special session of parliament solely dedicated to the Treaty. Both houses were then asked to approve the Treaty by voting in favour of the text of a 'humble address' in reply to the king's speech. The proposed text of the humble address endorsed the Treaty's articles of agreement, stating that parliament was ready to 'confirm and ratify them' and congratulated the king on his role in reconciliation.[14] This use of the monarchy undermined Treaty opposition. George V was immensely popular following his leadership role during the First World War and the Tory party was infused with monarchist beliefs.[15] The humble address, which combined approving the Treaty with congratulating the king, implied that to reject the Treaty was to reject the king's own endeavours for peace. Moreover, a proposed humble address text was a parliamentary juggernaut that was extremely difficult to stop. There were numerous strident speeches in opposition to the Treaty in the long debates that followed in both houses on 15 and 16 December 1921. Sir Frederick Banbury MP declared in the Commons that 'we cannot make a Treaty with Yorkshire and how can we make a Treaty with Ireland?', while Lord Sydenham in the Lords stated that the Treaty was a 'stupendous surrender' and 'nebulous'.[16] However, preventing it being accepted by parliament required full agreement on an alternative wording in the proposed text of a humble address to the king. This procedure was much more difficult than simply mobilising opponents to vote against the Treaty would have been in a direct, straight vote for or against the Treaty itself. This difficulty was clear when attempts were made in both the House of Commons, by Col. John Gretton MP, and the House of Lords, by the Duke of Northumberland, to get the text of parliament's humble address to the king, approving the Treaty, amended.[17] Both Gretton and Northumberland's efforts were similarly worded. The Duke of Northumberland sought to add the following:

> But we humbly represent to Your Majesty that this House regrets that the settlement of the Government of Ireland indicated in the gracious Speech from the Throne would involve the surrender of the rights of the Crown in Ireland, give power to establish an independent Irish Army and Navy, would require further sacrifices from Ulster, and would not safeguard the rights of the loyalist population in Southern Ireland.[18]

Both amendment attempts failed.

Second, the prime minister emphasised King George V's strong personal support for the Treaty. In the king's speech to parliament the sovereign spoke of his 'heartfelt joy' on learning of the agreement and his 'earnest hope' that the Treaty would end

Fig. 5 Republican handbill with a drawing of the Royal Irish Constabulary cap badge. The badge contained an Irish harp capped by the British crown. It was also worn by the Black and Tans. [Image: National Library of Ireland, EPH B8]

'the strife of centuries'.[19] Lloyd George's final shrewd move was the decision that the British parliament would be promised a further vote on the process – the vote to approve the Anglo-Irish Treaty in December 1921 would be followed by a later vote to approve the constitution of the Irish Free State after a draft had been agreed, which would complete the final ratification of the Treaty. This reassured moderates because it suggested a further degree of control on how the Treaty terms would be later implemented in Ireland.

After several days of debate, both houses of parliament voted to present the unamended proposed humble address to the king, approving the Treaty: the Commons on 16 December by 401 to 58 and the Lords by 166 to 47 on 19 December. The Treaty was thereby approved, and the king prorogued the specially convened session of parliament. On 31 March 1922 parliament then passed the Irish Free State Agreement Act, which gave the Treaty the force of law and provided measures to give effect to the agreement, creating the British legal framework for the full transfer of government power from Westminster to Dublin.

Free State: a successful blueprint?

Following parliament's approval of the Treaty, the pro-Treaty majority consolidated its position. By the spring of 1922 British politicians like Winston Churchill were heavily invested in making the Treaty a success. There was never just 'one' uniform British perspective on the Irish Civil War, but between January and July 1922 an overall pro-Treaty consensus had clearly emerged. Central to this consensus was the idea that the Treaty represented a model of imperial reform: it piloted experimental innovations to dominion status that could later be applied to other problematic imperial territories with militant nationalist movements, such as Egypt or India. There was optimism in early 1922 that the Free State might provide a successful blueprint for the interwar imperial reforms believed necessary in the wake of the changes brought by the First World War, the rise of Wilsonian ideas of self-determination, and the establishment of the League of Nations.

Imperial thinking was absolutely central to how the British negotiated the Treaty, and to their own identity and polity. For the negotiators Britain was the fulcrum of a global British world, and they believed that an imperial, transnational British identity was shared across its empire. The First World War had strained this system, triggering wartime resentment of British government control in the so-called 'white dominions' of Australia, Canada, Newfoundland, New Zealand and South Africa, and over how their menfolk were deployed on the war fronts. Dominions were a relatively recent pre-war idea – most had only come into existence after 1900; only Canada was older. They had their own democratically elected parliaments, but they had no independent foreign policy or army before 1914, and were automatically drawn into a global conflict when London declared war on Germany in August 1914. Their men went to fight not as independent national armies but as corps within the existing British army. By 1917, under pressure from dominion prime ministers, Lloyd George had created the Imperial War Cabinet, which operated alongside the British War Cabinet and, at which, the dominions had a say in how the war effort was being run. But it was clear by the end of the war that the dominions were collectively bargaining for greater independence and reform – something that finally came in 1926 with the Balfour Declaration.

For Britain the Anglo-Irish Treaty piloted a settlement that would model a new, more independent dominion status. The Irish Free State was to be the first dominion to have its own independent national army, while also remaining part of the British imperial world. At the point when the Treaty was signed, no dominion in the empire had separate nationality status – all dominion populations were legally 'British subjects' of the British crown under international law. This status was described during the Dáil Treaty debates as a 'common citizenship' with Britain, much to the chagrin of Irish anti-Treaty figures.[20] The Free State constitution broke with the Treaty, and with dominion norms, by creating a separate Irish nationality intended to undermine the British-subject status that the Treaty preserved.

Imperial reformers in London sincerely believed that dominion status needed to be revised for the 1920s. In future, they planned, dominions would be united to Britain solely through their relationship with the British crown – a monarchist loyalty and identity to be retained in perpetuity – while their political direct ties to Westminster and Whitehall were to be gradually reformed and dismantled in favour of increased self-government. This was why the oath of allegiance in the Anglo-Irish Treaty mattered to the British. It signified this common allegiance to the crown and shared imperial British identity, which were to remain for what were envisaged as more independent dominion states within the empire.

Allegiance to the king and imperial 'consent'

For Lloyd George allegiance to the king was the principle 'upon which the whole fabric of the Empire and every constitution within it are based'.[21] All parliamentarians across the empire took an oath of allegiance to the crown. A republic would, therefore, destroy the Anglo-Irish Treaty as a policy innovation model for imperial dominion reform. Many British political figures also hoped that, in the long term, the Treaty would see the new Northern Ireland merge into the Free State to form one all-island dominion within the British Empire, with potential for the Northern Ireland parliament surviving as a federal parliament in a united Ireland. For example, Churchill, in the House of Commons in June 1922, referred to Northern Ireland coming 'into a Dublin Parliament […] as I trust some day she may – of her own free will'.[22]

The Treaty was also an experiment in interwar ideas of imperial 'consent'. Following the First World War the international political climate around empire had changed with the foundation of the League of Nations and agreement that Germany's former colonies could only be administered by Britain and France as postwar mandates until they were ready for full independence, rather than as traditional colonies. British interwar imperial reforms were partly a response to this shift in international attitudes to empire. By 1921 the term 'Commonwealth', rather than 'Empire', was increasingly used, and it was referred to as a British 'family' of nations who had chosen to be together under British stewardship, bound by a shared loyalty to the British crown – an arrangement, Britain claimed, to which they consented. Of course, this was all propaganda – coercion, violence and racial discrimination were used to sustain British rule in multiple territories across the empire. However, the idea that an empire 'by consent', some kind of democratic empire, could emerge in the post-war period was firmly promoted by imperial reformers. This was one reason why the British government was so keen that there should be a general election in the new Free State in 1922 – and why it was so concerned when it was delayed after the spring deal between Collins and de Valera. Elections that produced

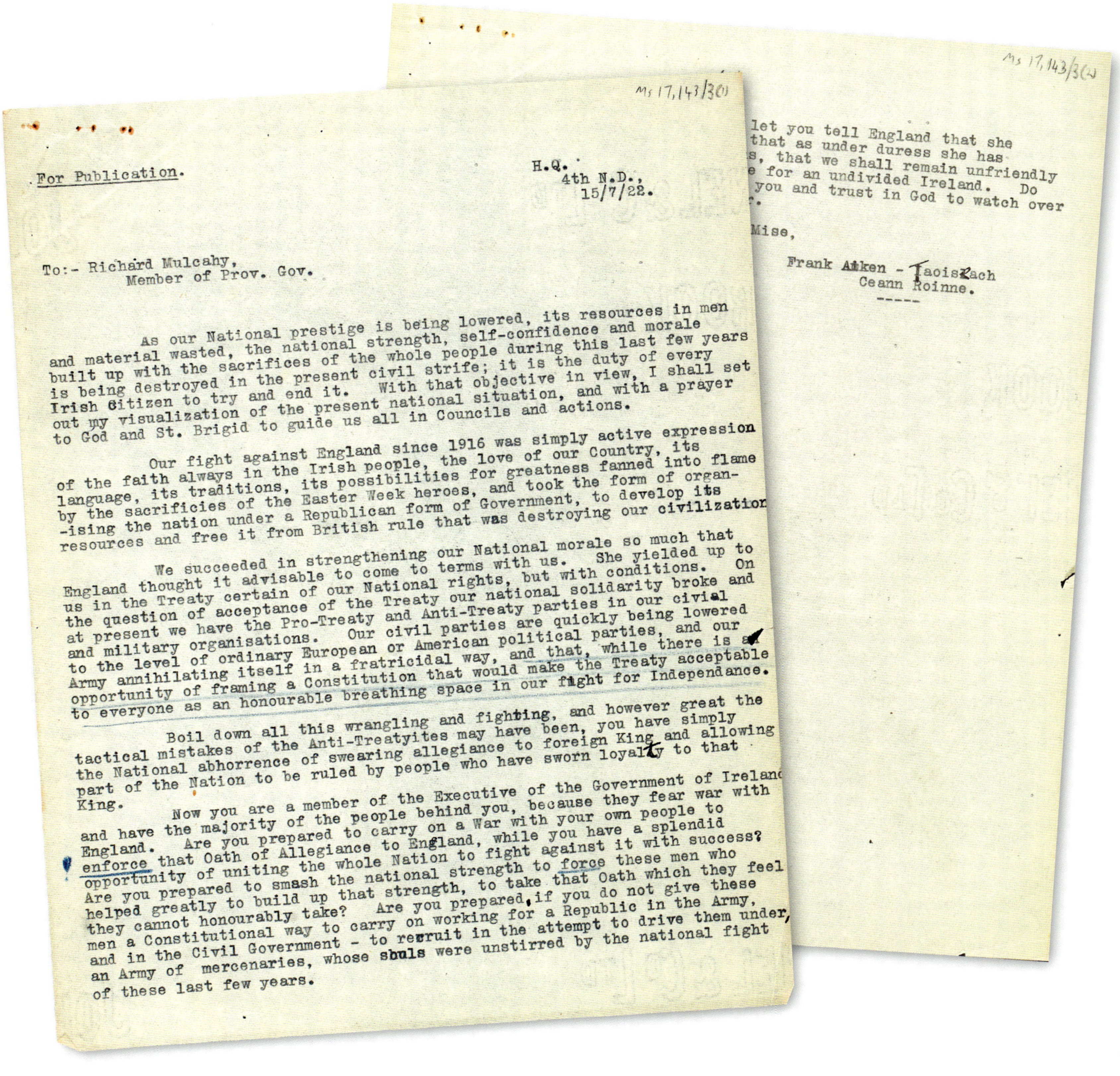

Ms 17,143/3(1)

For Publication.

H.Q.
4th N.D.,
15/7/22.

To:- Richard Mulcahy,
Member of Prov. Gov.

As our National prestige is being lowered, its resources in men and material wasted, the national strength, self-confidence and morale built up with the sacrifices of the whole people during this last few years is being destroyed in the present civil strife; it is the duty of every Irish Citizen to try and end it. With that objective in view, I shall set out my visualization of the present national situation, and with a prayer to God and St. Brigid to guide us all in Councils and actions.

Our fight against England since 1916 was simply active expression of the faith always in the Irish people, the love of our Country, its language, its traditions, its possibilities for greatness fanned into flame by the sacrificies of the Easter Week heroes, and took the form of organ- -ising the nation under a Republican form of Government, to develop its resources and free it from British rule that was destroying our civilization

We succeeded in strengthening our National morale so much that England thought it advisable to come to terms with us. She yielded up to us in the Treaty certain of our National rights, but with conditions. On the question of acceptance of the Treaty our national solidarity broke and at present we have the Pro-Treaty and Anti-Treaty parties in our civial and military organisations. Our civil parties are quickly being lowered to the level of ordinary European or American political parties, and our Army annihilating itself in a fratricidal way, and that, while there is a opportunity of framing a Constitution that would make the Treaty acceptable to everyone as an honourable breathing space in our fight for Independance.

Boil down all this wrangling and fighting, and however great the tactical mistakes of the Anti-Treatyites may have been, you have simply the National abhorrence of swearing allegiance to foreign King and allowing part of the Nation to be ruled by people who have sworn loyalty to that King.

Now you are a member of the Executive of the Government of Ireland and have the majority of the people behind you, because they fear war with England. Are you prepared to carry on a War with your own people to enforce that Oath of Allegiance to England, while you have a splendid opportunity of uniting the whole Nation to fight against it with success? Are you prepared to smash the national strength to force these men who helped greatly to build up that strength, to take that Oath which they feel they cannot honourably take? Are you prepared, if you do not give these men a Constitutional way to carry on working for a Republic in the Army, and in the Civil Government - to recruit in the attempt to drive them under, an Army of mercenaries, whose souls were unstirred by the national fight of these last few years.

Ms 17,143/3(2)

let you tell England that she
that as under duress she has
s, that we shall remain unfriendly
e for an undivided Ireland. Do
you and trust in God to watch over
r.

Mise,

Frank Aiken - Taoiseach
Ceann Roinne.

Fig. 6 In this letter to Richard Mulcahy, dated 15 July 1922, Frank Aiken highlights the centrality of the oath of fidelity to republican opposition to the Treaty and the Free State government. Aiken, commander of the IRA's 4th Northern Division, had taken a neutral stance during the IRA split. He remained under the Dáil's Ministry of Defence until he refused, when pressed, to endorse the Provisional Government. His base in Dundalk was captured by the pro-Treaty 5th Northern Division one day after the letter was written. All the 'wrangling and fighting', Aiken wrote to Mulcahy, could be boiled down to the 'National abhorrence of swearing allegiance to [a] foreign King and allowing part of the Nation to be ruled by people who have sworn loyalty to that King'. [Document: National Library of Ireland, Thomas Johnson Papers, MS 17,143/3]

Fig. 7 A Constance Markievicz caricature of Treaty signatory Arthur Griffith, atop dead and wounded civilians, waving the Union Jack and leading Ireland 'into the Empire'. [Image: National Library of Ireland, PD 3076 TX 13]

a majority vote in support of the Treaty would symbolise Ireland's democratic acceptance of dominion status. This also explains the Irish anti-Treaty argument that to accept the Treaty was to consent to the British Empire, an objection that surfaced repeatedly during the Dáil Treaty debates.[23] Seamus (James) Lennon TD, for example, declared on 7 January 1922 that: 'I will not vote or cast my vote to bring the citizens of the Irish Republic whom I represent, to bring these men into the British Empire'.[24]

Implementing the Treaty in full

For all these reasons – in particular, to showcase imperial consent and model dominion innovations – the need to implement the Treaty in full determined British views of the Irish Civil War. British elites understood Ireland in 1922 overwhelmingly through the prism of one political policy – the Treaty. It tied Ireland to central questions of empire and of upholding international law, as the Treaty was regarded as an international agreement, and to theoretical constitutional issues regarding nationality and monarchy for the British government. This helps to explain the considerable British investment in trying to implement and preserve the Treaty settlement in the spring and summer of 1922 when it came under threat from the Irish anti-Treaty movement. The continued existence of the IRA was also seen as an ongoing security threat to the new Northern Ireland.

However, Britain was limited in what it could do to enforce the Treaty as the slide into civil war accelerated. Sending British troops into the Free State area was politically unworkable. It would undermine the Free State's claim to independence, damaging its popularity in Ireland. It would also play into anti-Treaty strategy, which was to rerun the Easter Rising by occupying central Dublin buildings in 1922, hoping that a British attack to enforce the Treaty would reunite the IRA in a renewed campaign against the British and destroy the Treaty settlement. Sending in British troops would also badly damage British propaganda claims that the Treaty was an example of a population consenting freely to being part of the British Empire and of post-war self-determination.[25] These constraints became very clear when Sir Henry Wilson was assassinated in London by Irish nationalists in June 1922. An apoplectic Winston Churchill blamed the anti-Treaty IRA and believed it imperative that the Free State act against the anti-Treaty occupation of the Four Courts, seriously threatening to use British force to do so if the Provisional Government would not act. However, the impossibility of sending in British forces was made clear to him and to the British Cabinet by Nevil Macready, the general commanding British forces in Ireland, who correctly realised that a British attack would jeopardise the majority Irish public support for the Treaty evinced in the general election of 16 June and that, given the phased withdrawal of British troops since January 1922, any reoccupation would have been very difficult. The war-weary British public was also largely in favour of the demobilisation of troops and the reduction of British overseas military commitments, while the Treasury was driving army cuts to offset Britain's substantial First World War debts. There was a serious problem of imperial military overstretch, with British forces involved in, among other commitments, occupying the German Rhineland, violently suppressing uprisings in Britain's new mandate territories of Iraq and Palestine, and militarily supporting the Whites in the Russian Civil War. Harry Boland TD accurately foresaw that imperial military overstretch would prevent Britain enforcing the Treaty militarily, telling the Dáil on 7 January 1922 that, 'while I am casting my vote prepared for war, [...] I am convinced that there can be no war in Ireland. Allenby requires ninety thousand men in Egypt; India is in flames [...]'.[26]

Moreover, dominion independence was a deeply fraught issue in the British Empire in 1922, this made clear when, in September, the dominions refused to automatically go to war at Britain's behest to enforce Turkish compliance with the Treaty of Sèvres. Known as the Chanak Crisis, this was the final of a series of crises (another was Lloyd George's brazen sale of honours) that ultimately ended Lloyd George's premiership.[27] If the dominions were against militarily enforcing a peace treaty on Turkey, it was evident they would be outraged if Britain used force to make a fellow dominion – the Irish Free State – comply with its.

Fig. 8 Sir Henry Wilson (far right) at the 1918 Inter-Allied Conference at Versailles. Field Marshal Sir Henry Wilson was born in 1864 in Dublin and brought up on the Currygane estate near Ballinalee, County Longford. The Wilsons were a strongly unionist family with roots in County Antrim. Wilson made an undistinguished start to his military career, failing the entrance examinations for Sandhurst and Woolwich multiple times, before earning a commission through the Longford militia and the Royal Irish Regiment. He rose through the ranks, becoming the director of military operations before the First World War. An ardent southern unionist, he was involved behind the scenes in the Curragh incident in 1914 when Anglo-Irish officers threatened to resign their commissions if they were forced to march on Ulster. He earned the enmity of the then British prime minister, Herbert Asquith, but his fortunes changed when David Lloyd George succeeded Asquith in December 1916. In February 1918 Wilson was appointed Chief of the Imperial General Staff (CIGS), the head of the British army. He advocated for British deference to the combined Allied command under his friend Marshal Ferdinand Foch, which eventually won the war in November 1918. Wilson was fêted as one of the men responsible for the Allied victory, and he was part of the British delegation at the peace talks at Versailles in 1919. In that year he was appointed as the youngest British field marshal since Wellington. It was a role he retained during the War of Independence. Wilson fell out with the British government over its policy on Ireland. He believed that the 'murder gang', as he called Sinn Féin and the IRA, should be crushed by saturating the Irish countrywide with troops – a policy that was deemed politically impossible by the British government. Wilson opposed the Anglo-Irish Treaty that established the Free State. In February 1922 he retired as CIGS and, within days, was elected unopposed as an Ulster Unionist MP for the constituency of North Down. A month later he was appointed the military advisor to the Northern government of Sir James Craig. Wilson was blamed for the excesses of the B Specials and the newly established RUC in the North, and quickly became a hate figure within Irish nationalism. Though he preached moderation in private, Wilson made many inflammatory speeches as an MP, exhorting the British government to invade the South and restore order. Wilson was assassinated on the doorstep of his London home by two British-born Irish nationalists and World War One veterans Reggie Dunne and Joe O'Sullivan on 22 June 1922. The British government blamed the anti-Treaty rebels then occupying the Four Courts. This was an erroneous assumption. In *Great Hatred: The assassination of Field Marshal Sir Henry Wilson MP*, I set out why I believe Michael Collins was ultimately responsible for Wilson's death. Nevertheless, the British government ultimatum to the Provisional Government that it deal with the anti-Treaty rebels led to the civil war that broke out on 28 June when the National Army shelled the Four Courts using borrowed British guns. Wilson was buried in the crypt of St Paul's. His diaries, posthumously published by his friend Major General Sir Charles Callwell in 1927, damned him as an intriguer and gossiper, and his reputation did not recover. [Text: Ronan McGreevy / Image: First World War Official Photographs Collection, National Library of Scotland]

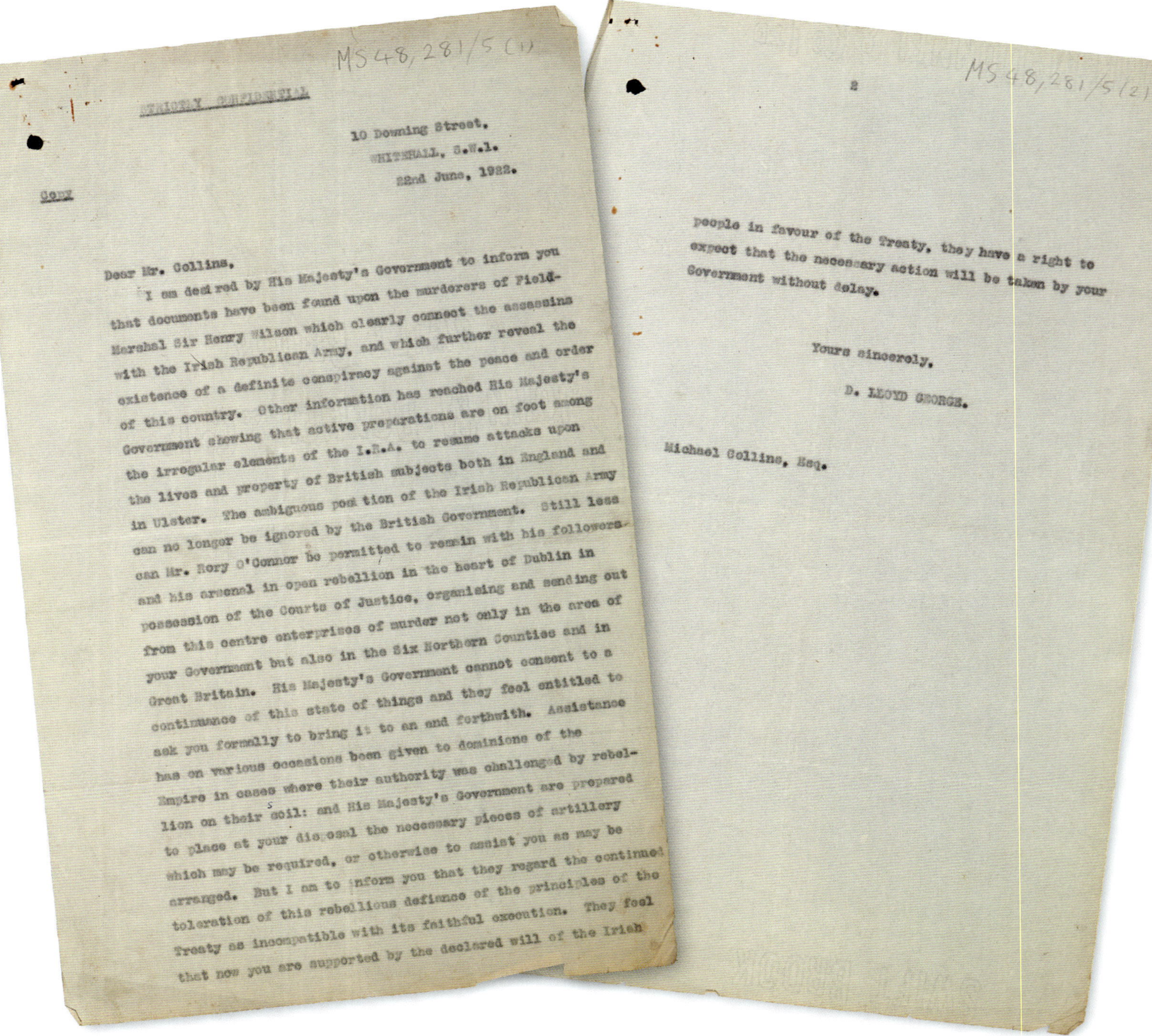

MS48,281/5(1)

STRICTLY CONFIDENTIAL

10 Downing Street,
WHITEHALL, S.W.1.
22nd June, 1922.

Copy

Dear Mr. Collins,

I am desired by His Majesty's Government to inform you that documents have been found upon the murderers of Field-Marshal Sir Henry Wilson which clearly connect the assassins with the Irish Republican Army, and which further reveal the existence of a definite conspiracy against the peace and order of this country. Other information has reached His Majesty's Government showing that active preparations are on foot among the irregular elements of the I.R.A. to resume attacks upon the lives and property of British subjects both in England and in Ulster. The ambiguous position of the Irish Republican Army can no longer be ignored by the British Government. Still less can Mr. Rory O'Connor be permitted to remain with his followers and his arsenal in open rebellion in the heart of Dublin in possession of the Courts of Justice, organising and sending out from this centre enterprises of murder not only in the area of your Government but also in the Six Northern Counties and in Great Britain. His Majesty's Government cannot consent to a continuance of this state of things and they feel entitled to ask you formally to bring it to an end forthwith. Assistance has on various occasions been given to dominions of the Empire in cases where their authority was challenged by rebellion on their soil: and His Majesty's Government are prepared to place at your disposal the necessary pieces of artillery which may be required, or otherwise to assist you as may be arranged. But I am to inform you that they regard the continued toleration of this rebellious defiance of the principles of the Treaty as incompatible with its faithful execution. They feel that now you are supported by the declared will of the Irish

MS48,281/5(2)

2

people in favour of the Treaty, they have a right to expect that the necessary action will be taken by your Government without delay.

Yours sincerely,

D. LLOYD GEORGE.

Michael Collins, Esq.

Fig. 9 Copy of a letter from David Lloyd George to Michael Collins, 22 June 1922, regarding the assassination of Sir Henry Wilson and the activities of the IRA. [Document: National Library of Ireland, Eoin O'Duffy Papers, MS 48,281/5]

Limited leverage

For all these reasons, the British government had very limited leverage by summer 1922, but what it had it used effectively. It threatened the Provisional Government with war if it did not act against the Four Courts; delayed the ongoing evacuation of British troops from the Free State area; and offered the Free State authorities arms to tackle the anti-Treaty militants themselves. A draft letter from Lloyd George to Michael Collins on 22 June 1922 stated that the latter was to be offered any military help necessary.[28] Unable to send troops, Britain's most important role in the Irish Civil War was to equip the Free State with arms, predominantly heavy artillery guns, machine guns and munitions, to help build up the new National Army, which was heavily outnumbered by the anti-Treaty IRA when the Civil War began with the shelling of the Four Courts on 28 June. On 4 July the British government even agreed to supply the Provisional Government with ammunition containing 'lachrymatory and other similar gas' 'for use against the rebels'; however, the War Office intervened, stating that the use of gas would be illegal under international law.[29] Clearly concerned

Fig. 10 (right) 'When England Gave the Orders'. This anti-Treaty ballad emphasised a central theme of republican Civil War propaganda: Michael Collins and the Free State were acting on the orders and in the interests of the British state. [Document: OLS Samuels, box 5, no. 167, The Board of Trinity College Dublin]

Fig. 11 (below) An 18-pound field gun in Dublin in July 1922. During the conventional phase of fighting, the National Army enjoyed an overwhelming firepower superiority over the IRA, particularly in terms of field artillery and armoured vehicles supplied by the British government. Here, during the Battle for Dublin, Free State troops and their 18-pound field gun shell 'The Block' from the corner of Henry Steet and Sackville Street. Artillery detonations eventually caused fires in the interconnected republican-occupied buildings, which led the republican garrison to flee or surrender. National Army soldiers often decorated their vehicles with names and/or messages. The front of the armoured lorry offers a comic message, 'For God's Sake, Aim Straight'. On the vehicle's side reads a more serious 'We have no time for Trucers', which is a warning to IRA members who were not involved in the War of Independence and may have recently joined the republican forces. [Image: courtesy of Dún Laoghaire-Rathdown County Council Library Service]

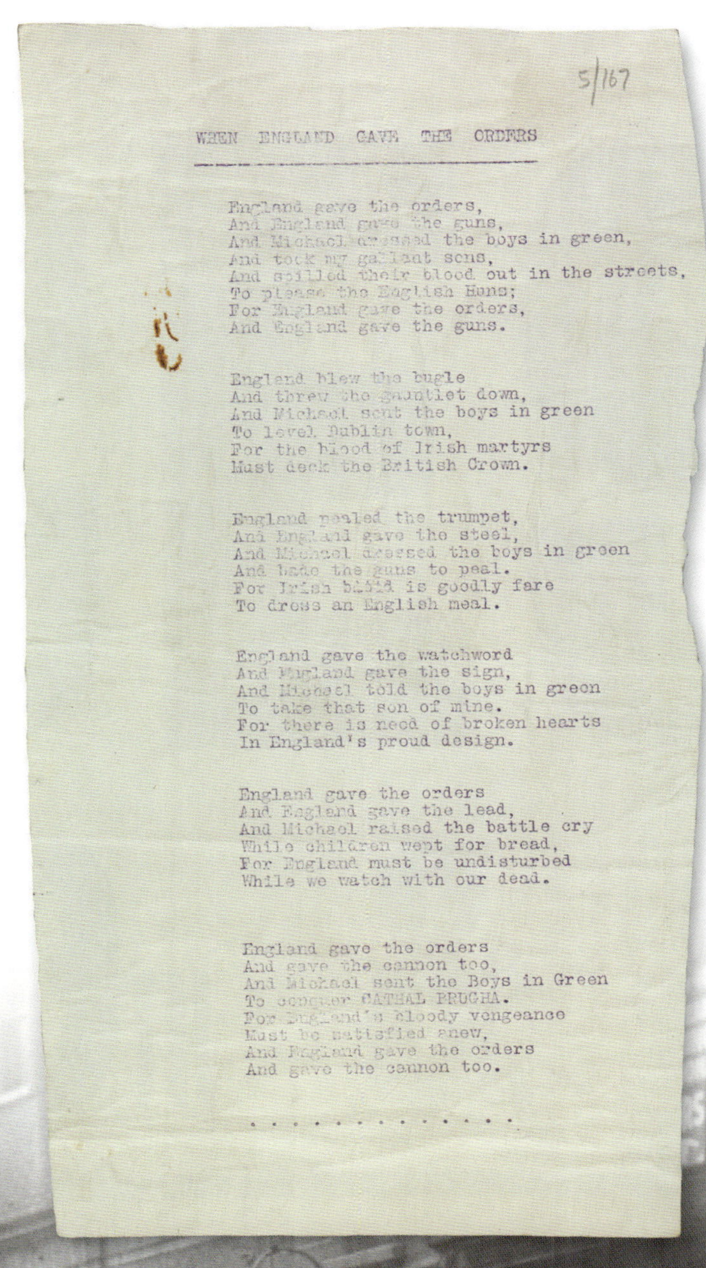

5/167

WHEN ENGLAND GAVE THE ORDERS

England gave the orders,
And England gave the guns,
And Michael [illegible] the boys in green,
And took my gallant sons,
And spilled their blood out in the streets,
To please the English Huns;
For England gave the orders,
And England gave the guns.

England blew the bugle
And threw the gauntlet down,
And Michael sent the boys in green
To level Dublin town,
For the blood of Irish martyrs
Must deck the British Crown.

England pealed the trumpet,
And England gave the steel,
And Michael dressed the boys in green
And bade the guns to peal.
For Irish blood is goodly fare
To dress an English meal.

England gave the watchword
And England gave the sign,
And Michael told the boys in green
To take that son of mine.
For there is need of broken hearts
In England's proud design.

England gave the orders
And England gave the lead,
And Michael raised the battle cry
While children wept for bread,
For England must be undisturbed
While we watch with our dead.

England gave the orders
And gave the cannon too,
And Michael sent the Boys in Green
To conquer CATHAL BRUGHA.
For England's bloody vengeance
Must be satisfied anew,
And England gave the orders
And gave the cannon too.

. . . .

about Britain's international reputation, the War Office also emphasised that 'what has been going on in Dublin is not war' but mere political unrest.[30] The consignment of gas grenades that had already reached Dublin was disposed of by being thrown into the sea.[31]

Lessons had been learned. The War Office was keen for the Free State authorities to do any fighting required to suppress the anti-Treaty side, thereby sparing Britain the kinds of reputational damage it had incurred from the use of reprisals in the War of Independence. This policy of arming proxies to fight in Ireland was also followed with regard to the new Northern Ireland, where, with the exception of the Pettigo and Beleek incident, Britain avoided direct intervention using the British army. It relied instead on supplying arms and money to Sir James Craig to defend the

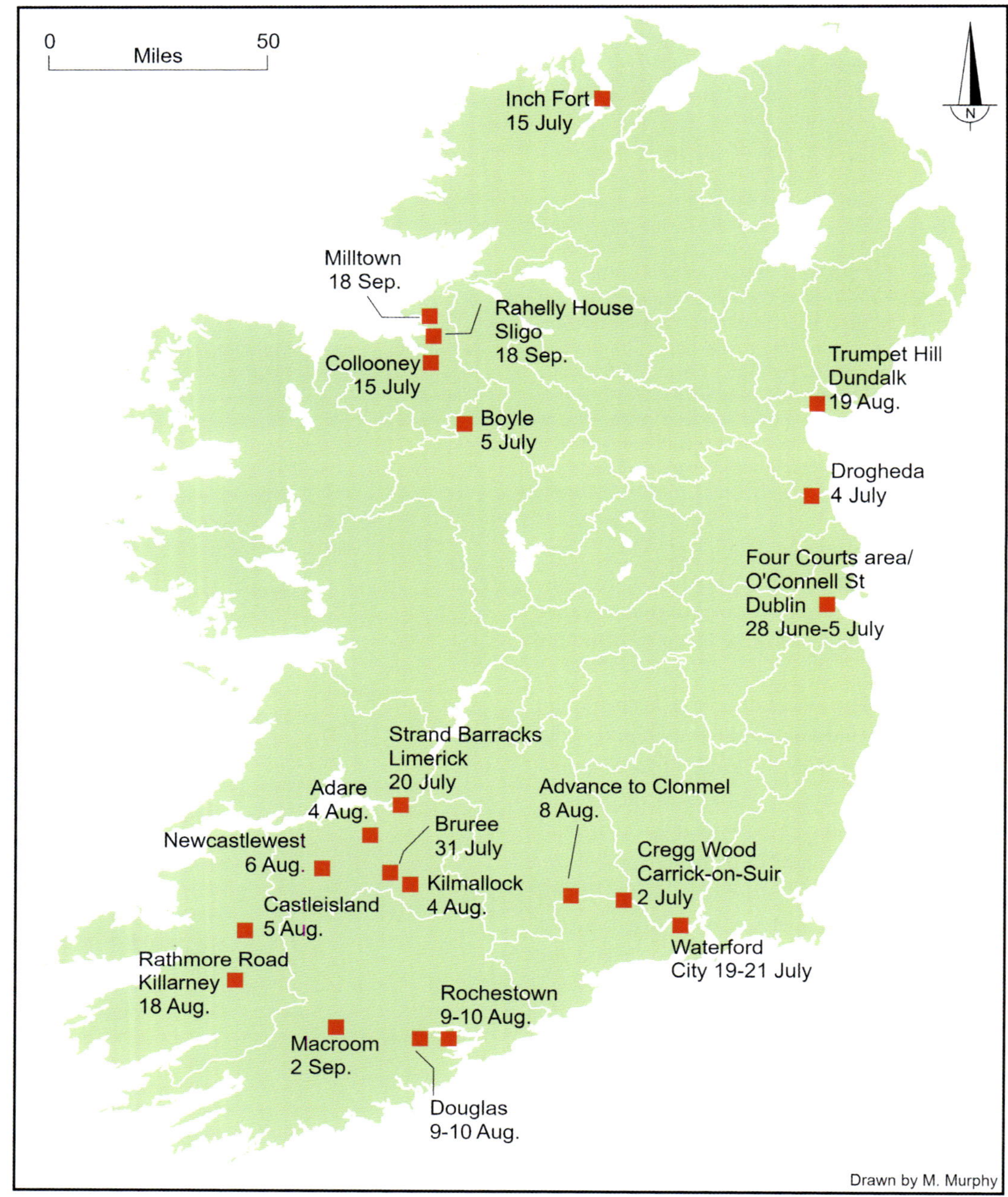

Fig. 12 Map showing the locations were artillery was used during the Civil War. During the battle for the Four Courts, the deployment of the 18-pound field gun was rudimentary, even crude, and plenty of mistakes were made by National Army 'gunners' who knew very little about artillery. It was hoped initially that the bombardment would make the defending garrison surrender but, in due course, the artillery pieces were used to breach the walls of the complex to allow the infantry to storm in (Fig. 13). This type of action was repeated, though on a smaller scale, against republican positions in Millmount in Drogheda and the Strand Barracks in Limerick. Nine 18-pounders were deployed across the country during the early months of the war, and gunnery improved as the Provisional Government's 'call to arms' brought retired or demobbed Royal Artillery personnel into the army. Waterford was the only city to be shelled, when anti-Treaty strongholds were targeted before the Free State infantry assault. Elsewhere, the field gun was often attached to the National Army column as it advanced into republican-held territory. In this role the gun was a support weapon to be used by the infantry commander when stiff resistance like the anti-Treaty machine-gun position was encountered. Some commanders made better use of their guns than others. Commandant-General John Prout followed British *Field Service Regulations* by positioning the 18-pounder at the rear of the advance guard when his column left Waterford for Clonmel. From this position it was brought into action without difficulty when a republican machine-gunner attacked his flank. In west Limerick, Brigadier Tom Keogh refined a combined-arms strategy deploying the 18-pounder, the armoured car and the infantry in a coordinated way to take the towns of Adare, Rathkeale and Newcastle West. The guns were sometimes attached to smaller military convoys, and in Kerry an 18-pounder was used to fend off an ambush. On all these occasions a couple of shells were all that was required to make republicans withdraw. Two types of ammunition were used: high-explosive shells and shrapnel shells. The most conventional deployment of a field gun was during the battle for Kilmallock. The artillery piece used there may have been fitted with a sight, and targets were indicated by an observer on the battlefield using signalling flags. Generally, the 18-pounders were towed by a Lancia armoured car or by a commandeered civilian lorry, though for longer journeys they were carried portée style in the back of a lorry. [Text: Robert Delaney / Source: Robert Delaney, 'The 18-pounder field gun in Irish service, 1922–1942' unpublished M.Litt thesis, Department of History, Maynooth University, July 2022]

Fig. 13 A view of the west wing of the Four Courts from Merchant's Quay. [Image: Reproduced by kind permission of UCD Archives. Desmond FitzGerald Photographs, P80/PH/31]

new Northern Ireland regime using locally mobilised police and paramilitary police forces. This policy brought its own problems, with Churchill decrying in parliament in June 1922 the uses to which some of the weaponry was put: what he termed the 'vile' sectarian violence in Northern Ireland by Protestants against Catholics.[32]

As the twenty-six counties descended into full-blown civil war, Britain's disappointment with the situation grew. The Treaty looked more and more like a failed policy by autumn 1922. There was consternation in London political circles in August when Arthur Griffith and Michael Collins, both Treaty signatories, died within days of each other, because these two men were viewed as pivotal figures in ensuring the Treaty settlement survived. This was followed by considerable relief among British elites at discovering that the new head of the Provisional Government, W.T. Cosgrave, was an effective and reliable organiser, a stickler for legal detail who would implement the Treaty in full. Indeed, by January 1923 key Whitehall advisor to the prime minister on Ireland, Thomas Jones, noted approvingly the publication in the press of a 'satisfactory' message from Cosgrave criticising the anti-Treaty forces.[33] Collins's death received wall-to-wall coverage in Britain and marked the highpoint of British public interest in the Irish Civil War. Collins had a certain mystique for the British press, which had romanticised him as a handsome, glamorous gunman-turned-politician during the Treaty negotiations, famous to British audiences. W.T. Cosgrave, in contrast, was far less well known and never drew the same British press attention to Irish issues.[34]

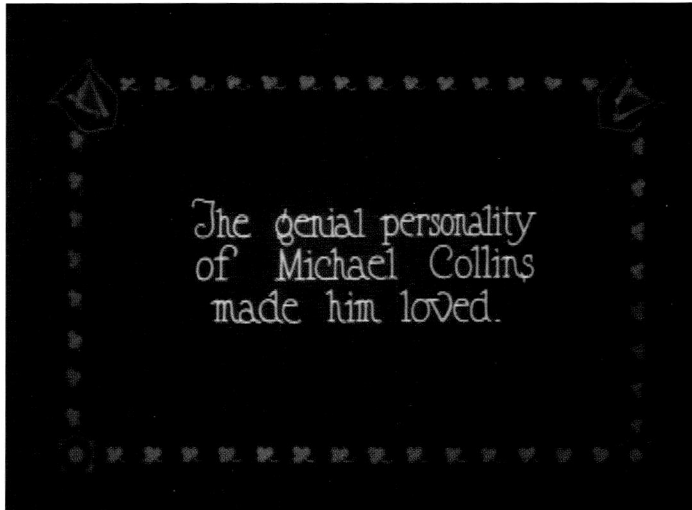

Figs 14 and 15 Two stills taken from the newsreel 'In Memory of Michael Collins' (1922). At a debate in the London School of Economics in May 1923, G.K. Chesterton used the treatment of Michael Collins to make a point about the fickle nature of the British press: 'Did the British public learn anything from the press about the extraordinary events that caused the change of front towards Ireland? All the press did was to call Michael Collins a murderous assassin on the Monday and a noble national hero on the Tuesday.' In many respects Chesterton had a point. In 1920 and 1921 Collins had become a way for the British press to explain the troubles in Ireland to their readers. Just as Pancho Villa became shorthand for the Mexican Revolution in American newspapers, Collins gave what was happening in Ireland a name. Through the early months of 1921 Collins was reported everywhere and behind everything; he was 'the chief of the "gun men"', 'the "Moriarty" of the Irish Republican Brotherhood', 'the bad man of Ireland', even the 'MOST "WANTED" MAN IN THE WORLD'. And in its own way this did the British government some service. The more 'elusive' he became, the more plausible it seemed that this 'genius of fighting Ireland' had not been caught. But when it came to the prospect of negotiating a peace, when it became more likely that the 'chief of the criminal guerilla [*sic*]' might be someone the British government would have to reckon with, the Collins to be found in the British press began to change. As early as March 1921 the *Manchester Guardian* suggested that 'when the horror and the misery of the present years are forgotten' between Britain and Ireland, tales of Collins's adventures would make for 'episodes of high romance as realistic as anything in Dumas and Stevenson'. By 11 October 1921, when negotiations opened, the *Daily Mail*'s editorial described him as 'jovial Mr Collins', as 'a very conservative outlaw'. Apparently, the 'fighter has become friend'. This shape-shifting Collins was a creature of a thoroughly modern British media, projecting him to a mass audience. In 1921 the *Daily Mirror* was read in over one million homes, the *Daily Mail* in nearly two million. Close to two million families took their Sunday helping of scandal from the *News of the World*, and reports of Collins were devoured by that appetite for sensation that spread out from the national newspapers to every corner of the regional press. As the 1910s became the 1920s, cinema admissions in Britain had reached an estimated 600 million annually. And once Collins travelled to London, he became a newsreel feature, too, both adding to his fame and affecting its texture. In the months that followed the signing of the Treaty, the British media largely reflected the reactions of the British government to Collins's intentions and actions as head of the new Provisional Government. While the *Morning Post* remained steadfast in its disgust that such a figure was tolerated, while gossip columns mused about his wedding plans, when Collins disappointed London whether with drafts of the constitution or his apparent unwillingness to deal with the anti-Treaty IRA, he was promptly criticised. In February 1922 the *Daily Mirror* complained that he now had none of the power he 'possessed as the "mystery" leader of a desperate guerrilla war'; 'he has a sadly diminished influence as a peaceful and prosaic Minister'. He was deemed 'pigeon-livered', 'powerless' because of the de Valera pact. Only with the first photograph of him in uniform, with the firing on the Four Courts, did he become 'the "Big Fella"' once again, the 'Idol of his Troops'. And when he died much of the media seemed to mourn. Taken from a British Pathé newsreel, this image and inter-title suggests the 'pistol king of Ireland' was no more. [Text: Anne Dolan and William Murphy / Stills: Courtesy of British Pathé / Sources: *Manchester Guardian*, 16 May 1923; Nancy Brandt, 'Pancho Villa: The making of a modern legend', *The Americas*, vol. 21, no. 2, 1964; *Western Gazette*, 29 April 1921; *Yorkshire Post*, 11 October 1920; *Daily Express*, 17 March 1921; *Dundee Evening Telegraph*, 31 March 1921; *Sunday Express*, 9 October 1921, 27 February 1921; *Observer*, 12 December 1920; *Manchester Guardian*, 29 March 1921; *Daily Mail*, 11 October 1921; *Edinburgh Evening News*, 10 December 1921; Adrian Bingham, *Family Newspapers? Sex, private life, and the British popular press, 1918–1978* (Oxford, 2009), pp. 19–22; Trevor Griffiths, 'Quantifying an "Essential Social Habit": The entertainment tax and cinema going in Britain, 1916–1934', *Film History*, vol. 31, no. 1, 2019, p. 14]

Dwindling interest

British political and press attention to Ireland dwindled by autumn 1922 because of more pressing global and domestic issues and because, once the Civil War's conventional phase ended, most were convinced that a Free State military victory was imminent. Violence in Northern Ireland, which had drawn British political and public attention to Ireland in the first half of 1922, also dramatically reduced during the Civil War. Moreover, a dearth of British reporters on the ground in Ireland meant that Civil War news was intermittent and unevenly focused on Dublin and on pro-Treaty views. British politicians had little appetite for any British political engagement with anti-Treaty forces or their arguments, which were marginalised in much of the British press as incoherent and ideological, and London's political intelligence was derived mostly from the Free State government and Southern unionist interlocutors.

By October 1922 British domestic politics entered a phase of turmoil that left little energy for following events in Ireland. Following the Chanak Crisis, on 19 October at the Carlton Club the Tory party voted decisively, against the advice of its leader, to reject continuing to support the coalition government led by Lloyd

George, who immediately resigned. The subsequent upheaval saw key figures involved in the Irish settlement, including Lloyd George and Churchill, gone from power. Bonar Law became the new Tory party leader and prime minister on 23 October and called a general election for 15 November 1922.[35] Election programmes focused overwhelmingly on domestic socio-economic issues, the League of Nations and the Treaty of Versailles, while the Anglo-Irish Treaty and Irish Civil War featured little, even though this was the first occasion that the public in Britain could give its verdict at the ballot box on partition and on the Treaty.[36]

There was, however, one final moment of reckoning in Britain with the Anglo-Irish Treaty that makes clear British disappointment with the Treaty and the Irish Civil War. In November 1922 the British parliament met, as required, to vote to enact the new Irish Free State constitution and give it legal force throughout the empire. The contrast with the pro-Treaty optimism of December 1921 and spring 1922 could not be clearer. When, on 20 November 1922, the House of Commons assembled for a three-week session to pass the Irish Free State Bill enacting the constitutional arrangements of the Treaty and completing its ratification, there was already a majority of voices arguing that, for Britain, the Anglo-Irish Treaty had turned out to be a failure. But there were no alternatives; they could not undo the Treaty militarily or politically. As new Prime Minister Andrew Bonar Law stated on 27 November, the Irish 'have got to work it out for themselves'.[37] Even rejecting the proposed Irish Free State constitution was not an option: the Provisional Government would cease to be legal unless the House of Commons passed its approval of the Irish Free State Bill by 6 December 1922, and this left no time for major amendments.[38] It was still in Britain's interest that the pro-Treatyites win the Irish Civil War because an anti-Treaty regime would be a greater threat to Northern Ireland and to Britain's monarchist empire, by inspiring similar nationalist movements elsewhere. Hence, the bill had to be rushed through.

British disappointment

Figures such as Lord Birkenhead (F.E. Smith), who had signed the Treaty for the British side, tried to defend it, claiming that more time was needed before judgement was passed on it, but the overall mood was one of disappointment. This came from the left as well

27

WOULD ENGLAND GO TO WAR?

Lord Birkenhead Says Not

SPEAKING IN THE BRITISH HOUSE OF LORDS ON JULY 23rd, 1923, LORD BIRKENHEAD SAID IN REFERENCE TO THE TREATY:

" If a settlement had not been arrived at there would have been at least 100,000 armed men in Ireland to maintain the only alternative system to the Treaty. The War Office estimate was that 200,000 men would have been required for Ireland alone—and that was a moderate calculation. Parliament would not have granted you the money, and the country would not have given you the volunteers "

SO LLOYD GEORGE'S THREAT OF IMMEDIATE AND TERRIBLE WAR WAS ALL BLUFF.

Figs 16 and 17 (left) Lord Birkenhead, photographed by the *Daily Mirror* [n.d.]. Frederick Edwin Smith (1872–1930), the 1st Earl of Birkenhead, was the Lord Chancellor (1919–22) and one of the British signatories to the Anglo-Irish Treaty of 1922. (right) Republican handbill quoting Lord Birkenhead's statement in the House of Lords, 23 July 1923. The statement was to the effect that Britain would have needed to at least double its number of troops in Ireland had the Treaty not been signed, and the cost of such a deployment would not have been acceptable to parliament. The handbill draws the obvious conclusion that Lloyd George's threat of 'immediate and terrible war' in the event of the Irish delegation not signing 'was all bluff'. [Image: National Library of Ireland, NPA BIR. Document: National Library of Ireland, pamphlet volume D549] as the right. Communist MP Shapurji Saklatvala presented the argument that the Treaty was the product of British coercion:

> it was distinctly understood between my electors and myself that they did not wish me to back up a Treaty which was based upon coercion, and was signed under duress. [...] Hon. Members on all sides of the House have written and spoken in unmistakable terms in expressing their views that the unfortunate part of the Treaty was that the signatures were obtained under duress.[39]

Bonar Law admitted that the Free State constitution contained 'expressions as to the meaning of Dominion status which they would rather not see in', while Labour MP Ramsay MacDonald noted that the Treaty set a dangerous precedent for the other dominions and their constitutional relationship with Britain, which had always been 'organic rather than legal', and not clarified in writing, a direct result of Britain's unwritten constitution.[40] Indeed, as historian Deborah Lavin points out, dominion status itself had been meant to stay 'undefined, and seemed indefinable' after the dominion prime ministers had 'rejected a written constitution in the Imperial Conference of 1921'.[41] Ramsay MacDonald added his hope that 'the phrases that, of necessity I think, have had to be used in this Bill may be allowed to remain there and may not be taken out of it in another place'.[42] In other words he wished that the Irish Free State model might not spread to the other dominions. There was also objection to Article 3 of the new Free State constitution, which introduced the principle of an independent Irish national citizenship. No other dominion had this in November 1922. The Treaty settlement was no longer a pilot for the dominions' future within the empire, but a threat to it. Michael Collins's failed attempts earlier in the year to convince the British to accept a Free State constitution that went beyond the terms of the Treaty had the knock-on effect of delaying the finalisation of the constitution text, forcing the Commons to rush its debates and to accept elements within it that went against British policies on what powers a dominion could have.

Questioning Free State policies

There was disappointment regarding the security situation, too. Some MPs were concerned about the security threat posed by a large and well-armed Irish National Army next door to Britain.[43] Diehard Tory MP Col. Gretton even claimed that the British press had begun to self-censor and avoid detailed reporting of the violence of the Irish Civil War because it might damage British public support for the Treaty, undermine the British political figures who had agreed it, and even stir up unwanted public demands for British intervention.[44] Concerns were also aired about the Free State's draconian execution policy, highlighting further British disappointment with the Treaty outcome. The execution of Erskine Childers on 24 November 1922 coincided with the aforementioned Commons debate, and the fact that Childers had been killed for possessing a pistol gifted to him by Michael Collins was widely reported in the British press – one of the few Civil War stories covered extensively in Britain in this phase of the conflict. Labour politician Keir Hardie asked on 30 November 1922 if the British government had made 'any representations to the Irish Free State Government to prevent the execution of Erskine Childers and his four colleagues; and whether His Majesty's Government will make representations to prevent further executions of war prisoners in Ireland'.[45] The British government, however, affirmed it would not intervene in any way with Free State decisions on executions.[46] If it did it could have undermined the Free State's claims to independence. Yet this response also reflected a sense in the Commons that Britain had no moral authority to instruct the Free State government given its own discredited reprisals policy in the War of Independence: when Col. Gretton outlined examples of republican and Free State Civil War violence, he was heckled in parliament by other MPs with 'The Black and Tans did that'.[47] By March 1923 there were even questions in the Commons about whether it was right to deport those associated with anti-Treaty activity in Britain – in particular the buying of arms and gunrunning – to Irish Free State custody given the Free State's mistreatment of prisoners.[48] The British government's reply again reflected lessons learned from the War of Independence: it stated that holding anti-Treaty supporters in British jails risked making martyrs of them.[49] However, for some on the British far right the Free State's ruthlessness offered a model. In October 1922, the month of Mussolini's march on Rome, the British journal *The Nation* remarked that 'Ireland's failure strengthens the cause of those who believe in strong imperial government rather than democracy', another example of perceptions that the Treaty had failed for Britain.[50]

By spring 1923 the Irish Civil War aroused little debate in the British press or politics. Bonar Law had strong feelings on Ireland but was terminally ill with throat cancer and by April 1923 had been sent to the Mediterranean to recuperate, leaving Foreign Secretary Lord George Curzon holding the fort.[51] Busy with negotiations with Turkey for the Treaty of Lausanne, Curzon had little room for focusing on the Irish Civil War. Until Bonar Law resigned in May 1923, this was a lame-duck government. Moreover, the fifty or so Tory MP diehards were, by 1923, largely silenced, having lost the votes on both approval of the Treaty in December 1921 and on passing the Irish Free State constitution and final ratification in 1922. Even the Tory party name was shifting – the Conservative and Unionist Party had often been referred to in Britain as the Unionist Party; now, symbolically, the name Conservative returned to dominance, reflecting the diminished importance of connections to the island of Ireland in British politics.[52]

Disengagement

By the spring of 1923 it was clear that an emotional disengagement from Ireland had occurred. In contrast to the spring of 1922, when refugees from Ireland were championed by Henry Wilson, or June 1922, when Winston Churchill could threaten the resumption of war in Ireland, there was little British reaction in May 1923 when

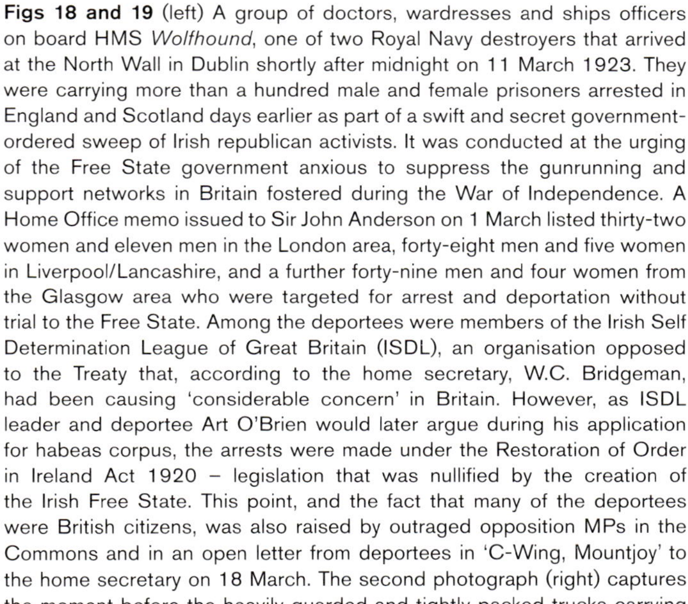

Figs 18 and 19 (left) A group of doctors, wardresses and ships officers on board HMS *Wolfhound*, one of two Royal Navy destroyers that arrived at the North Wall in Dublin shortly after midnight on 11 March 1923. They were carrying more than a hundred male and female prisoners arrested in England and Scotland days earlier as part of a swift and secret government-ordered sweep of Irish republican activists. It was conducted at the urging of the Free State government anxious to suppress the gunrunning and support networks in Britain fostered during the War of Independence. A Home Office memo issued to Sir John Anderson on 1 March listed thirty-two women and eleven men in the London area, forty-eight men and five women in Liverpool/Lancashire, and a further forty-nine men and four women from the Glasgow area who were targeted for arrest and deportation without trial to the Free State. Among the deportees were members of the Irish Self Determination League of Great Britain (ISDL), an organisation opposed to the Treaty that, according to the home secretary, W.C. Bridgeman, had been causing 'considerable concern' in Britain. However, as ISDL leader and deportee Art O'Brien would later argue during his application for habeas corpus, the arrests were made under the Restoration of Order in Ireland Act 1920 – legislation that was nullified by the creation of the Irish Free State. This point, and the fact that many of the deportees were British citizens, was also raised by outraged opposition MPs in the Commons and in an open letter from deportees in 'C-Wing, Mountjoy' to the home secretary on 18 March. The second photograph (right) captures the moment before the heavily guarded and tightly packed trucks carrying male deportees departed with an armoured-car escort for Mountjoy Gaol. Various allegations of ill-treatment, 'petty tyrannies and indignities' arose during their two-month internment, most notably accusations of torture in Mountjoy's basement cells. The Irish administration refuted claims reported by British newspapers in mid-May that prisoners were suspended 'seven feet from the ground' and left 'for five hours hanging by their hands'. One deportee, Kathleen Brookes, alleged that 'Deputy Governor Mr O'Keefe visited the women's cell at midnight. He was under the influence of drink, and had with him eight or nine soldiers. Torches were flashed and revolvers brandished in the women's faces and generally there was a terrible scene'. Their internment lasted until 17 May 1923, when ninety were released and returned to Britain on board the *Lady Wicklow*. The deportees subsequently sought compensation on the basis that their arrests had been illegal. The Irish Deportees Compensation Tribunal convened by the British government examined the cases, deemed the detention illegal, and awarded damages to the men and women involved, including Kathleen Brookes, who received £562. [Text: Anne-Marie MacInerney / Images: courtesy of whytes.com / Sources: W.C. Bridgeman to Attorney General, 31 January 1923, HO / 144/3746, NAUK; Result of discussion with Capt. Parker of the Admiralty, 4 March 1923, HO/144/3746, NAUK; Home Office to Sir John Anderson, 1 March 1923, HO/144/3746, NAUK; Open letter from the Irish deportees from England Committee to W.C. Bridgeman, in the Home Office, Whitehall, 18 March 1923, EPH E199, NLI; *Irish Times*, 18 May 1923, *Manchester Guardian*, 18 and 19 May 1923, 16 October 1923]

the Irish Civil War petered out. In 1922 Ireland had become entirely associated with one policy – the Treaty gamble. Britain had devoted huge amounts of political energy to it while its success still hung in the balance in the first half of the year, but once the Free State was officially established in December 1922, and mired in bitter civil war, Britain saw no other option but to rapidly disengage.

The Irish Civil War bitterly disappointed Britain's high hopes for the 1921 Anglo-Irish Treaty. But British hopes had always greatly overestimated the ideological commitment to the Treaty dominion settlement on the Irish pro-Treaty side, most of whom viewed it merely as an inconvenient prelude to fuller independence. The British, in contrast, had genuinely thought the Treaty would ensure a cultural loyalty to Britain among Free State nationalists, now granted their own dominion. This was always unrealistic. But the Civil War violence triggered by the Treaty undermined the idea that it could offer a successful model for imperial reform elsewhere. The Civil War also exposed the limits of British military and political power to directly enforce an international treaty settlement that part of a population rejected. The need to support the Free State government through civil war also meant Britain had to accept a Free State constitution that went far further than it had anticipated in redefining dominion status, one that undermined the very legal and political concept of 'dominion'.

With a significant section of the population still supporting the anti-Treaty position after the end of the Civil War, Free State politicians continued to distance themselves as much as possible from association with the Treaty per se and to emphasise it as merely a means to a separatist end. The all-island Irish dominion within the British Empire that the British had hoped for never came into existence – sectarian violence in Northern Ireland had

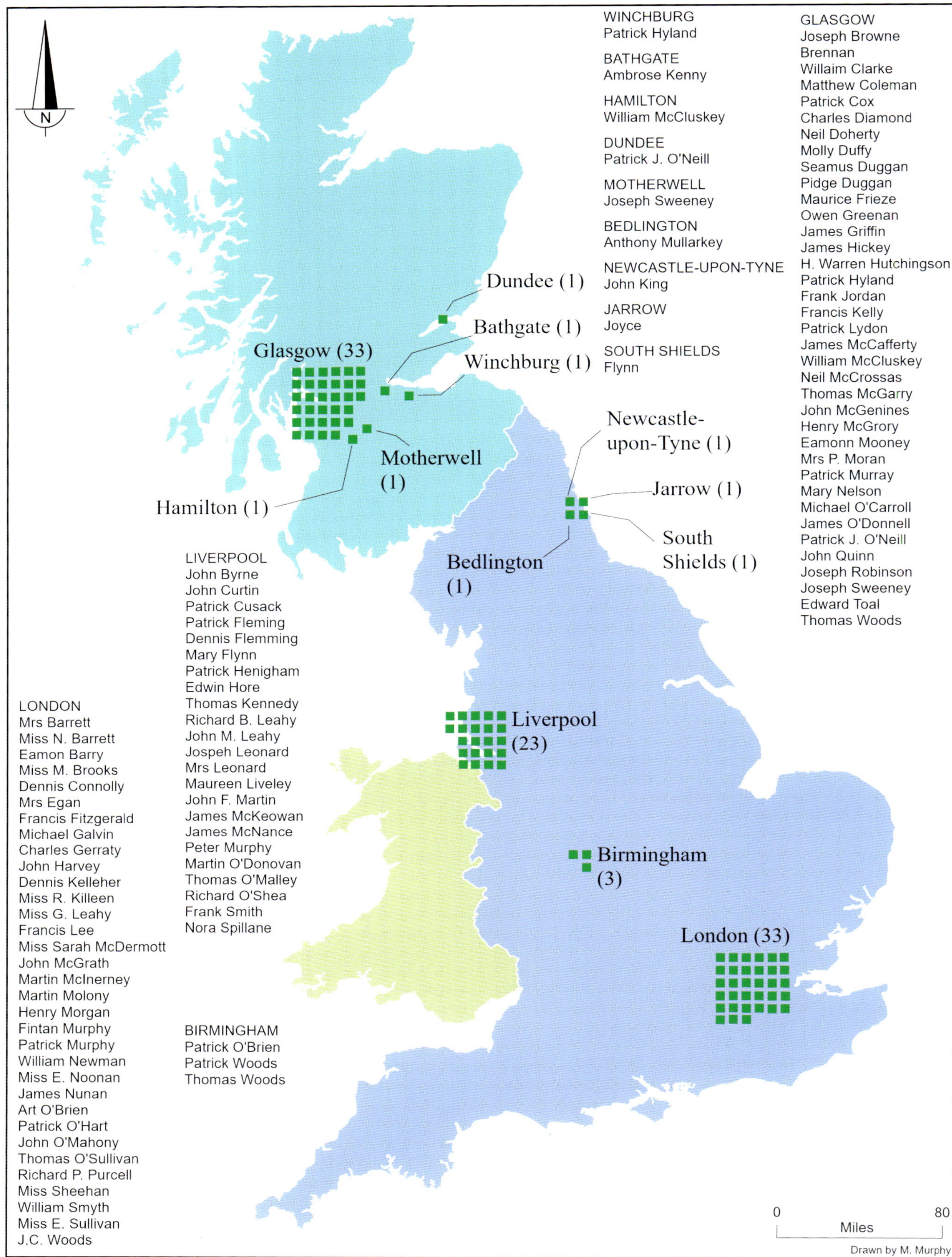

Fig. 20 Names and locations of arrest of deportees from Britain, March 1923. [Source: National Library of Ireland, Art Ó Briain Papers, MS 8,432/37]

18

LLOYD GEORGE

Speaking with reference to the Irish men and women arrested in England and deported to Ireland, said on March 28th, 1923:

"The Home Secretary was bound to take stern action to help *those who are fighting the battle of the British Empire and the connection of Ireland with this country*"

Why should you Irish people pay in blood and men and money for the battle of the British Empire?

Fig. 21 (above left) Sinn Féin propaganda leaflet highlighting a statement by David Lloyd George in the House of Commons on 28 March 1923. The comment, made in the context of a debate on the deportees to Ireland, implied that the Free State government was 'fighting the battle of the British Empire'. [Document: National Library of Ireland, pamphlet volume D549]

Fig. 22 (above right) Republican handbill issued after the Battle for Dublin, June/July 1922. The handbill shows 'What the Treaty Gives You' (British-supported destruction of the republic) and sarcastically asks if this was what was meant by a 'Vote for the Treaty and Peace', as suggested by the pro-Treatyites after the 16 June general election. The cartoon later appeared on the cover of the 9 December issue of *Poblacht na hÉireann* (Scottish edition), with 'Vote for the Treaty and Peace' replaced by 'A Charter of Freedom!'. [Image: National Library of Ireland, EPH D161]

worsened in spring 1922 following the Treaty – and partition continued. Referring to the Anglo-Irish Treaty and partition in the 1930s, Churchill stated: 'All this policy still lies in controversy, and bitter have been the disappointments of those who signed the Treaty.'[53] This included him. Yet, for all the contemporary professions of British disappointment with the Treaty's failures and the Irish Civil War, it is worth remembering that Britain's preferred side – the Irish Free State – still won. The Irish Civil War may have accelerated a much deeper and more rapid break with Ireland than Britain had hoped for when it agreed the Treaty in December 1921 but, ironically, this was what would also allow Britain to so rapidly disengage from Irish politics in 1923.

But this disengagement came at a high cost. The very dominion status that the Treaty had pioneered, of greater autonomy within the empire, became a means to ultimately dismantle the Treaty itself and the empire. At the 1926 Imperial Conference, the Irish Free State worked together with other dominions, particularly Canada and South Africa, to obtain the conference's Balfour Declaration, which declared the dominions autonomous and equal communities within the British Empire. Further international reform of dominion status followed: the 1931 Statute of Westminster allowed dominions full legislative independence in all internal affairs and, crucially, the right to repeal earlier Westminster legislation: this opened the door to Éamon de Valera's reforms of the 1930s, which included replacing the 1922 Free State constitution with his 1937 one, which nullified much of the Anglo-Irish Treaty. Far from saving the British Empire, the Anglo-Irish Treaty provided a template to dominions for dismantling it. This potential outcome was already clearly visible in the political debates and propaganda that drove the Irish Civil War, but by 1923 very few in Britain were paying attention.

CASE STUDY

The Treaty Debates and the Irish Civil War

Liam Weeks and Mícheál Ó Fathartaigh

The Dáil debates over the Anglo-Irish Treaty in December 1921 and January 1922 represent a landmark moment in the Irish revolutionary period; first, because the debates culminated in a vote to accept a Treaty that created the Irish Free State and, second, because they marked the collapse of the façade of Sinn Féin unity. The seeds of any civil conflict are usually sown well in advance, and the Irish case was no different. Founded, in its first iteration, by Arthur Griffith in 1905–7 to unite the broad church of Irish separatism and reconstituted with a clearly defined republican agenda in the wake of the Easter Rising, Sinn Féin had always counted both moderates and extremists among its membership. The republican party swept the board at the 1918 general election, and on 21 January 1919 the twenty-eight deputies still at liberty declared a sovereign Irish republic and established a secessionist parliament, Dáil Éireann.

Less than three years later, 124 Sinn Féin candidates were returned unopposed to the Parliament of Southern Ireland, one of two new polities created by the Government Ireland Act 1920. Unwilling to recognise the new political entity, Sinn Féin used the election as the basis for forming the Second Dáil. Within months the apparently monolithic party was deeply split by the Treaty, which created a twenty-six county Free State with dominion status in the British Commonwealth. Certainly, it offered far more than the Government of Ireland Act, but fell far short of the hoped-for republic. Despite the 'stepping stone' philosophy of Treaty signatory Michael Collins, many hardline republican TDs were unwilling to accept its provisions for an oath of fidelity to the British Crown, a resident governor general and, in the clause promising a Boundary Commission, the recognition, as Gavin Foster writes, 'of some sort of permanent partition'.[1]

The debates

The debates, held in public and private sessions, began on 14 December 1921 and continued, with a break for Christmas, until the decisive vote on 7 January 1922. Unlike the Parliament of Southern

Fig. 1 Arthur Griffith (centre) with Kevin O'Higgins (left) and William T. Cosgrave in Dublin, 1922. [Image: National Library of Ireland, Hogan-Wilson Collection, HOGW 31]

Fig. 2 Kathleen O'Callaghan (second from right) with (l-r) Kathleen Clarke, Countess Markievicz and Margaret Pearse at the Mansion House in Dublin, July 1921. Kathleen (Kate) O'Callaghan (née Murphy) (1885–1961) was a Sinn Féin politician, educator and campaigner for women's rights. Born into a separatist family in Crossmahon, Bandon, County Cork, she received her formal education in Dublin and Cambridge. In 1912 she succeeded her late sister as a lecturer in education at Mary Immaculate College of Education, a position she held until her marriage to Michael O'Callaghan in 1914. A founding member of the Limerick branches of the Gaelic League and Cumann na mBan, O'Callaghan played a distinguished role in nationalist and charitable circles in Limerick. Personal tragedy struck on 7 March 1921 when her husband, the former republican mayor of Limerick, was shot dead in their home, likely by British forces. O'Callaghan refused to attend the military inquest into the killing, replying that she would only appear at an inquest run by her own countrymen. Two months later she was elected unopposed to the Second Dáil as Sinn Féin TD for Limerick City-Limerick East. Like the other five female TDs elected in May 1921, O'Callaghan was trenchantly opposed to the Treaty. They claimed to 'know the women of Ireland' when speaking against its terms during the Treaty debates, but Mary MacSwiney, Kate O'Callaghan, Kathleen Clarke and Margaret Pearse, close relatives of recent republican 'martyrs', also understood the powerful symbolism of their personal grief. 'We paid a big price for the Treaty', O'Callaghan claimed, 'and for my right to stand here'. Castigated by pro-Treaty TDs for 'rattling the bones of the dead', O'Callaghan asserted the agency of the female deputies, the 'women of character' who would 'vote for principle, not for expediency'. In the aftermath of the Sinn Féin split, in March 1922, O'Callaghan put forward a Dáil motion to enfranchise all women at the 1922 general election. As a suffragist she argued that it was an 'injustice' to restrict voting rights to women over the age of thirty. With political support coming entirely from anti-Treaty TDs, O'Callaghan was accused of trying to 'torpedo' the Treaty. The vote was defeated on predictable lines (thirty-eight in favour, forty-seven against). Citing practical challenges with the electoral register to defend the pro-Treaty majority decision, Arthur Griffith pledged that his government would prepare to enfranchise all women voters after the 1922 election. Article 14 of the constitution of the Irish Free State, which came into effect in December 1922, finally granted suffrage to all women on equal terms with men. Only two female TDs were returned in the 'pact' general election of 1922: Kathleen O'Callaghan (unopposed) and Mary MacSwiney. They boycotted the Third Dáil along with other anti-Treaty TDs. During the Civil War Éamon de Valera named O'Callaghan to the republican 'council of state', which was intended to provide civil legitimacy to the anti-Treaty movement. In April 1923 O'Callaghan was arrested and imprisoned in Kilmainham Gaol, where she participated in a hunger strike. She lost her Dáil seat in the 1923 general election, and never again ran for public office. She returned to a post at Mary Immaculate College between 1924 and 1928 and, in her post-parliamentary life, was active in arts and cultural endeavours in Limerick. In 1937 she opposed the new constitution, partly because of the articles relating to the position of women, which she regarded as a betrayal of the 1916 Proclamation. [Text: Claire McGing / Image: National Library of Ireland, HOGW 151 / Sources: Maedhbh McNamara and Paschal Mooney, *Women in Parliament – Ireland: 1918–2000* (Dublin, 2000), p. 82; Marie Coleman, 'Kate (Kathleen) O'Callaghan', *Dictionary of Irish Biography*, https://doi.org/10.3318/dib.006544.v1; see also Claire McGing, 'Women's Political Representation in Dáil Éireann in Revolutionary and Post-revolutionary Ireland', in Linda Connolly (ed.), *Women and the Irish Revolution* (Kildare, 2020), p. 89]

Ireland, which met for its first and only time in Dublin's Mansion House on 14 July to formally approve the Treaty, the British government did not recognise the Second Dáil, and its decision, therefore, did not have any legal basis. But the symbolism of the Dáil debates and the vote on the Treaty was highly significant. The debates in Earlsfort Terrace, closely followed by the press, also represented one of the few times that the members of the Second Dáil assembled in one place. Formed against the backdrop of the War of Independence, during which many of its members were imprisoned or on the run, the parliament had met on just twenty-one occasions since May 1921.

Much was discussed during those fifteen days of debate (amounting to over 440,000 words), but many TDs contributed very little. In fact six was the average number of contributions per deputy, and twenty-four TDs did not utter a single word. The Dáil president, Éamon de Valera, spoke most frequently (334 contributions), followed by plenipotentiaries Michael Collins (203) and Arthur Griffith (193). Among the female TDs, Countess Markievicz (57) and Mary MacSwiney (74) were the most vocal; the other four female deputies, Kathleen Clarke, Dr Ada English, Kathleen O'Callaghan and Margaret Pearse, made a combined total of twenty contributions.

The silence of some of the deputies during the high-profile debates might be attributable to a lack of confidence in their oratorical skills. Many had been handpicked by Michael Collins and Harry Boland in 1921, and oratory was not high on the list of priorities for parliamentary candidature. It may also be explained by their inexperience in parliament and their dearth of knowledge concerning the Treaty negotiations in London. The terms of the Treaty had come as a shock to many TDs buoyed by the jubilation of the July Truce and convinced that a greater measure of independence was at hand. For them compromise on key issues such as the oath of fidelity was unacceptable, and so the temporary parliamentary chambers in University College Dublin (now the National Concert Hall) became the scene for a clash between what Michael Laffan called 'purists and pragmatists'.[2]

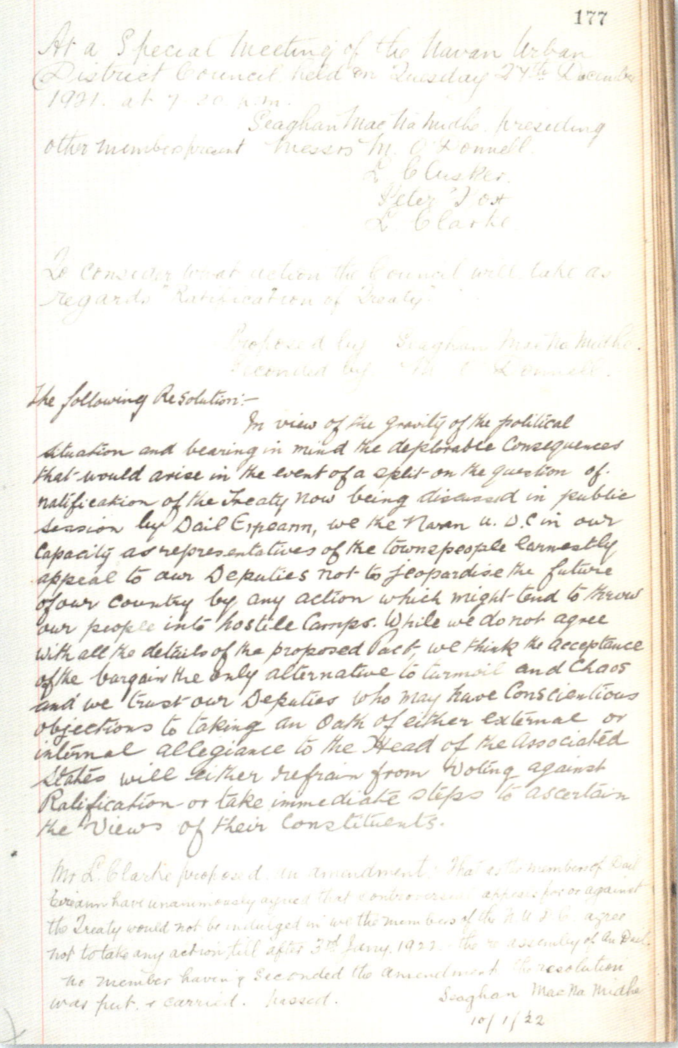

177

At a Special Meeting of the Navan Urban District Council held on Tuesday 27th December 1921. at 7.30 p.m.
Seaghan Mac Na Midhe presiding
other members present Messrs M. O'Donnell
L. Clusker
Peter Fox
L. Clarke

To consider what action the Council will take as regards "Ratification of Treaty".

Proposed by Seaghan Mac Na Midhe.
Seconded by M. O'Donnell.

The following Resolution:–
In view of the gravity of the political situation and bearing in mind the deplorable consequences that would arise in the event of a split on the question of ratification of the Treaty now being discussed in public session by Dail Eireann, we the Navan U.D.C in our capacity as representatives of the townspeople earnestly appeal to our Deputies not to jeopardise the future of our country by any action which might tend to throw our people into hostile camps. While we do not agree with all the details of the proposed Pact, we think the acceptance of the bargain the only alternative to turmoil and chaos and we trust our Deputies who may have conscientious objections to taking an Oath of either external or internal allegiance to the Head of the Associated States will either refrain from voting against Ratification or take immediate steps to ascertain the views of their constituents.

Mr L. Clarke proposed an amendment: That as the members of Dail Eireann have unanimously agreed that controversial appeals for or against the Treaty would not be indulged in we the members of the N.U.D.C. agree not to take any action till after 3rd Jany. 1922 the re assembly of An Dail. No member having seconded the amendment the resolution was put & carried. passed.

Seaghan Mac Na Midhe
10/1/22

Fig. 3 Resolution proposed by Seaghan Mac Na Midhe, Navan Urban District Council, 27 December 1921 urging local parliamentary representatives to consider the consequences of voting against ratification of the Treaty, 'the only alternative to turmoil and chaos'. [Document: courtesy of Meath County Archive. See also Tom French (ed.), *Curraghtown July 1922* (2022)]

Extreme bitterness

From the beginning, the debates were marked by extreme bitterness and an ideological polarisation that would become more entrenched in the months before the outbreak of military conflict. In a recent study we applied a range of statistical tools that treat words as data to the text of the Treaty debates to determine the primary points of difference between the pro- and anti-Treaty factions.[3] We considered not only the content of the contributions from both sides, but also the tone and complexity of the language, and the policy preferences and backgrounds of the deputies. The findings ran contrary to expectations, because in all the categories examined the anti-Treaty deputies did not differ significantly from those who supported the settlement. In fact the results suggest that, regardless of how they voted on 7 January 1922, most TDs were negatively disposed towards the Treaty as a final settlement and used relatively straightforward language in comparison to contemporary debates in the British House of Commons. Furthermore, there was no clear parallel between a TD's stance on the Treaty and their age, occupation or level of education. The most frequently used words, indicating the deputies' preoccupation with the role of the British king in the proposed Free State, were 'Treaty' (1,704 mentions), 'people' (1,404), 'Ireland' (1,247), 'Irish' (1,112), 'country' (634), 'republic' (604) and 'British' (593).

It is also worth considering what was not said during the debates. Most significantly, the question of partition was largely ignored. While Ulster was mentioned 101 times, the newly created Northern Ireland jurisdiction was referred to only twenty-five times, 'the border' twice and 'partition' twenty-six times. Protestant(s) were not mentioned at all, while the words 'unionist' and 'unionism' were used thirty-six times in total. The neglect can be explained by the sense that, given the Treaty's loosely worded provision for the establishment of a commission to decide on the boundary of Northern Ireland 'in accordance with the wishes of the inhabitants', dialogue on the border could be postponed. Interestingly, the Boundary Commission was invoked just once, by Mayo North and West TD Thomas Derrig, and Seán MacEntee was the only TD to state explicitly that partition was the reason for his opposition to the Treaty. Only five of the twenty-one TDs representing border constituencies voted against the Treaty.

Also interesting was the relative neglect of the economy and industry. The Treaty imposed substantial financial obligations on the new state, including liability for a portion of Britain's war debt, but the economy was referenced only fifty-four times and industry only thirteen. Many assumed that the Boundary Commission would render the Northern jurisdiction economically unviable, and few TDs were prepared to discuss the implications of dominion status for the new state's fledgling economy. Ultimately, nationalism took precedence over fiscal concerns. The quantitative analysis of the text of the debates by these authors reveals little about the fatal split in Sinn Féin that was to emerge, but it does establish that, in the winter of 1921–2, the fault lines were not, as has been widely asserted, based on partition, class or the influence of 'extreme' or 'hysterical' female deputies.

The split

Considering the broad agreement among Sinn Féin deputies on questions of policy, the reasons for the devastating rupture in Sinn Féin must be sought elsewhere. The vote in favour of the Treaty on 7 January 1922 was taken immediately after the Christmas break, during which deputies had returned to their constituencies and were influenced by the pervasive desire for peace after seven years of war and revolution. During the subsequent debates several TDs referred explicitly to how this widely expressed desire for peace overrode their own opposition to the Treaty, and it must have provided clarity for others who were undecided. In one extreme example of local influence, Waterford-Tipperary East TD Frank Drohan resigned his seat two days before the vote 'due to a conflict of position between his rejection of the Treaty and his constituents' support for it'.[4] Those TDs more resistant to the calls for peace at constituency level, and accused of lacking a democratic sensibility, invoked the established mandate for the republic proclaimed in 1916. Carlow-Kilkenny TD Edward Aylward, for example, remained resolute: 'I was elected a Republican to uphold the Republic of Ireland, and I shall do that to the best of my ability. Should my constituents change their mind then they can remove me at the next election.'[5] The vote, sixty-four votes to fifty-seven in favour of the Treaty, was a sounding of Dáil sentiment taken at a particular moment. Given the initial fluidity of some TDs' positions, the result may have been different, as Mayo South-Roscommon South TD Dan O'Rourke told the Dáil, if it had been taken before Christmas. It is also worth noting that, because many of the deputies of the Second Dáil had been nominated rather than elected to their seats in 1921, they were not as representative of the Irish population as

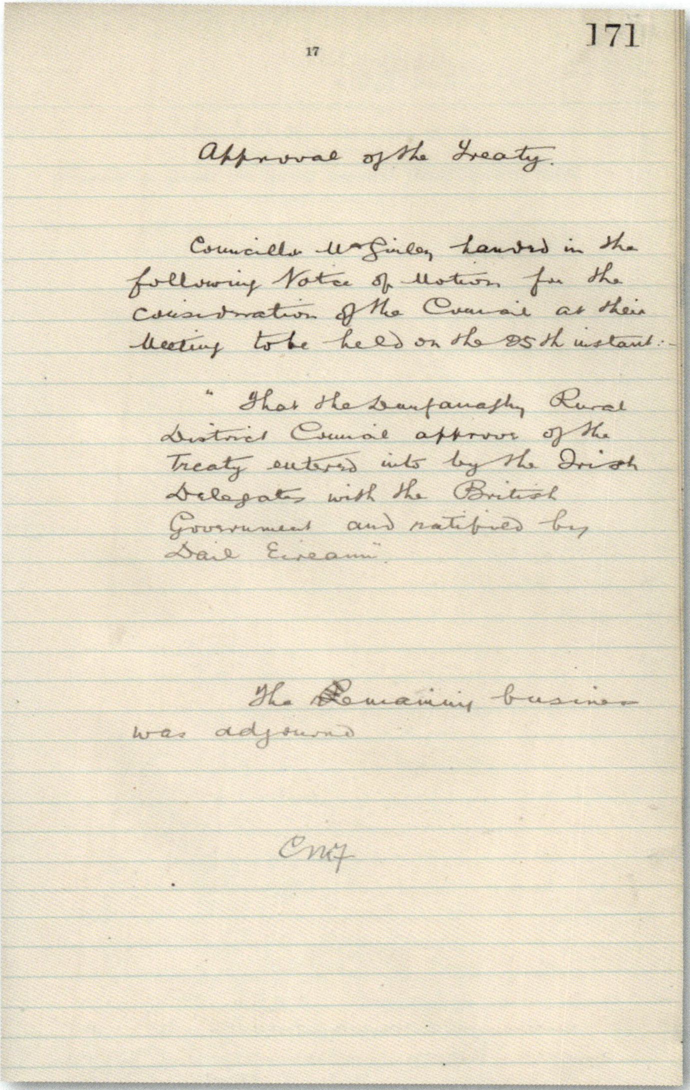
171

17

Approval of the Treaty.

Councillor McGinley handed in the following Notice of Motion for the consideration of the Council at their Meeting to be held on the 25th instant:-

"That the Dunfanaghy Rural District Council approve of the Treaty entered into by the Irish Delegates with the British Government and ratified by Dail Eireann."

The Remaining business was adjourned

Fig. 4 Motion proposing 'Approval of the Treaty', Dunfanaghy Rural District Council, County Donegal, February 1922. The Treaty split manifested itself differently within elected local government bodies across the Free State. Many county councils, urban district councils, rural district councils, poor law guardians, and other authorities debated their Treaty stance. While the national question galvanised many representatives from Sinn Féin and constitutional nationalist parties, others, particularly those representing labour, farmer and commercial parties, emphasised the need for local stability. Some public bodies endorsed the Treaty in clear and striking language. Others offered more muted or ambiguous statements, typically calling for national unity and deference to Dáil Éireann. Still other bodies took no action at all, seemingly to sidestep internal divisions that might worsen tense situations in their communities. [Document: courtesy of Donegal County Archives]

a democratically elected parliament. It was certainly more radical, with 47 per cent of TDs voting against the Treaty on 7 January. In contrast, 98.5 per cent of public bodies endorsed the Treaty, with 78 per cent of the electorate voting for pro-Treaty panel candidates in the June election.

The rift within Sinn Féin widened after de Valera, narrowly defeated in his bid to retain the presidency, led the anti-Treaty TDs out of the Dáil on 10 January. They returned for the subsequent sitting on 28 February and, in an effort to present a united front and

1921
LONDON
DEC 6
Mór an
sníom do
rongad ann .i.
fionġal ar ṫu
at de danann,
agus is fada bias
fionġal aga dé
anam an-éir
inn da éis.
Oide Ċloinn
Tuireann
Na curu
ata taith-
mechta la
feine:
cuir indlisteċa...
Beim naillech
nad nertad
tuatha.
Senchus mor
Contracts which are
Dissolved by the
FENI.....
Taking an Oath
which the
country
does not
confirm

Fig. 5 (opposite) The Treaty page from Art O'Murnaghan's highly ornate and impressive *Leabhar na hAiséirighe / The Book of the Resurrection* was one of twenty-seven vellum pages commemorating the struggle for Irish independence and took from 1924 to 1951 to complete. Born in Southampton to an Irish father and a Welsh mother, O'Murnaghan attended a local grammar school, winning a scholarship to Cambridge University, which he did not take up. He spent a period as an apprentice chemist and was later employed in the Carnegie Public Library in Southampton. A keen and self-taught artist, he moved to Dublin in 1898, where he obtained work designing wallpaper. Inspired by the cultural revival, he befriended leading lights such as Douglas Hyde and Arthur Griffith, creating designs for the Gaelic League and contributing articles and drawings to Griffith's weekly journal, *The United Irishman* ('established to promote the principles of Wolfe Tone and Thomas Davis'), which had its offices on Fownes Street. Throughout this period O'Murnaghan was developing his own artistic style, drawing inspiration primarily from insular art and, in particular, the illuminated manuscripts crafted in the medieval monasteries. Other influences derived from his interest in oriental art and eastern mysticism. When O'Murnaghan was chosen by the Irish Republican Memorial Committee in 1922 to create a commemorative manuscript, he considered it his 'life's mission and masterpiece'. It was labour-intensive work, with O'Murnaghan constantly battling a lack of funds. The project was interrupted on several occasions, with O'Murnaghan leaving the work and then coming back as financial circumstances allowed. He later found a patron in the Tyrone-born and US-based republican Joseph McGarrity (1874–1940), who supported him in his endeavours (Fig. 6). Constantly under pressure to deliver, O'Murnaghan explained to McGarrity, in a letter dated 15 May 1938, the need for continued patience given the unique undertaking: 'It would be a fatal thing however, for the artist of such a historic and unique work as that which it has come to my lot to be the man who is to create it, if he dared to allow his mind to be caught up in that most destructive disturbance of rhythm, of balance, of inward certainty of success – an anxious mind'. The content of the individual pages was also a matter of contention. Máire Comerford, writing earlier to McGarrity, was clear that the memorial committee's intention was to enshrine only 'the names of those who fell for the absolute independence of Ireland, and no others'. [Image: © National Museum of Ireland / Document: National Library of Ireland, MS 17,475/7 / See Peter Figgis, 'Remembering Art of Murnaghan', *Irish Arts Review*, vol. 2, no. 4, 1985, pp. 41–4, and Andrew O'Brien and Linde Lunney, 'O'Murnaghan, Arthur Walter', *Dictionary of Irish Biography*, 2009, https://doi.org/10.3318/dib.006913.v1]

Fig. 6 (below) The second page of a four-page letter from Art O'Murnaghan to Joseph McGarrity, dated 15 May 1938, in which the artist describes how the vellum work is progressing in his new, elevated, well-lit studio in a house off St Stephen's Green in Dublin. [Document: National Library of Ireland, Joseph McGarrity Papers, Ms 17,475/7]

avoid a descent into civil war, participated in negotiations for a 'pact election' in June. On 2 March the Second Dáil ratified an agreement reached at the Sinn Féin ard fheis in February that the elections, required under the terms of the Treaty, would be postponed for three months. It also agreed that a new constitution would be put to the people while the Dáil, under Arthur Griffith's presidency, would continue to function as a parallel administration to the Provisional Government under the chairmanship of Michael Collins.[6] Intended as a temporary measure, but prolonged by the outbreak of civil war, the constitutionally ambiguous system of dual authority in the twenty-six counties remained in place until the Third Dáil, elected in June 1922, finally met in September 1922.

The impact of the Civil War and the creation of the Irish state

What can be described as the 'arbitrary split' in Sinn Féin over the terms of the Treaty in Earlsfort Terrace was sealed in blood during the eleven-month Civil War. With the onset of military conflict, ideological positions on the Treaty hardened and determined the course of the TDs' public lives thereafter. Working within the terms of the Treaty, the pro-Treatyites, reconstituted as Cumann na nGaedheal in advance of the August 1923 general election, were determined to put in place the economic, social and political foundations of the new state. In opposition anti-Treaty Sinn Féin and, later, Fianna Fáil remained resolutely republican, dedicated to securing the 'political independence of a united Ireland as a republic'. Those seeking the roots of Ireland's two-party system in the Treaty debates, however, might be surprised at the mutable nature of deputies' positions in the winter of 1921–2. Until civil war consolidated their positions, there remained the possibility of compromise.

2

My dear Joe, I understand with the greatest sympathy, the anxiety of the Committee for speed, and all my best energies are used in building up the pages as I get on to them. It would be a fatal thing however, for the artist of such a historic and unique work as that which it has come to my lot to be the man who is to create it, if he dared to allow his mind to be caught up in that most destructive disturbance of rhythm, of balance, of inward certainty of success —— an anxious mind.

I don't mind confiding to you, but, forty years of struggling married life – hoping someday for some certainty of outlook for me and mine — the only result to-day is the same conditions as all along. If any man might be anxious for the future, one with my prospects should be — but – if I dwell on them for ten minutes – what would happen to the joyous colour and rich ornament and great ideas of Ireland of the future. No my dear Joe —— anxiety and impatience (however slight) are not for me. Possibly some of my own family think I do not care —— I do, but I think and work in the NOW, and, as somebody said, "Work as if I would live for ever".

All those years have made me what I am —— we are all at every moment, the being resulting from all our nights and days — and, you and I may rejoice that we are together giving something to Ireland of all the to-morrows, that will be the admiration of all who see or hear of The Book.

God bless you, Joe, and your wife, and your family. I'm looking forward to seeing your face soon — I want to know your letter, to have a free hour or two out in the country where we could talk. Must close now and get on collecting

Fig. 1 *Portrait of Arthur Griffith* (*c.* 1920), oil on canvas, by Lily Williams. [Painting: Collection & image © Hugh Lane Gallery]

Arthur Griffith

Owen McGee

Arthur Griffith (1871–1922) was a Dubliner who worked as a printer and then as a self-employed review editor. As the author of *Sinn Féin Policy* (1906), he provided the blueprint for the formation of the First Dáil in 1919. Personally shy, he considered himself unsuited to lead a political party and so was happy to concede the leadership of Sinn Féin to Éamon de Valera in October 1917. During the latter's American tour (June 1919–December 1920), Griffith served as acting president of the Dáil. In July 1921, after eight months in prison, he was appointed minister for foreign affairs. As a result he led the Irish delegation of plenipotentiaries to London that October intent that, if negotiations broke down, that it would be on the issue of partition rather than the crown. In the aftermath of the Treaty vote he was adamant that the Dáil must be considered as a functioning parliament that was supported by a civil administration. He defended this position by arguing that the formation of the parallel administration demanded by the Treaty – the establishment of a Provisional Government – would serve to augment, rather than deplete, the Dáil's authority owing to the incomplete authority of the republican administration to date and a right of the Dáil to direct both administrations. Elected president of the Third Dáil after de Valera's narrow defeat in January 1922, Griffith appointed key personnel in the Provisional Government.

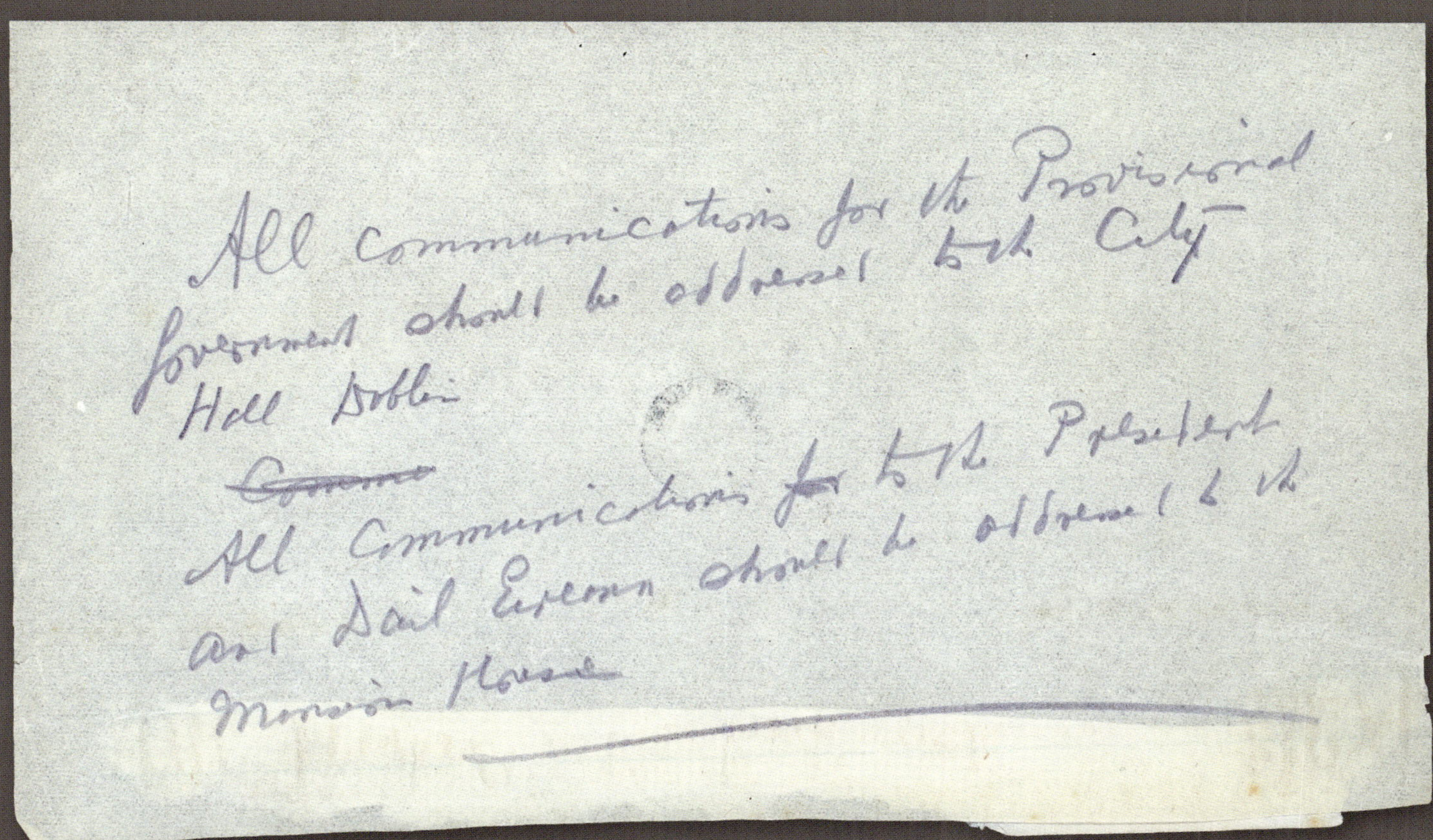

All communications for the Provisional Government should be addresed to the City Hall Dublin

~~Commu~~

All Communications ~~for~~ to the President and Dáil Eireann should be addresed to the Mansion House

Fig. 2 This simple handwritten note by Arthur Griffith clarifying the addresses to which communications were to be sent highlights the blurred lines between the parallel pro-Treaty Cabinets in early 1922. Michael Collins and his Cabinet took up temporary residence in Dublin's City Hall while Dáil Éireann ministers continued to conduct business from the Mansion House. Confusion about the duplicate ministries and their respective powers was demonstrated during angry Dáil exchanges in the spring. Some anti-Treaty TDs were furious that the Dáil departments were being 'absolutely subverted' by those of the Provisional Government, and members of the Dáil Cabinet were responding to their correspondence as 'Ministers of the Provisional Government'. [Document: National Library of Ireland, Kathleen McKenna Napoli Papers, Ms 22,752/ Quotation: *Dáil Debates*, vol. T, no. 1, 28 Feb. 1922]

For the most part these matched the ministry of his new Dáil Cabinet, with the notable exception of the presidency, defence and foreign affairs portfolios, which were retained by the Dáil alone. This claim to executive authority reflected Griffith's belief that London would not retain extensive powers of veto. However, he received several rude awakenings.

In late January a Dáil Cabinet sub-committee under Griffith's chairmanship attempted to bring both Dublin Castle's local government board and management of the Post Office Savings Bank under the authority of the Dáil's existing administration. The British government promptly called him to London to explain that this was not allowed. On presenting a draft constitution to the British Cabinet in early March, Griffith claimed for Dublin full powers of fiscal autonomy as well as rights to make diplomatic appointments. London withheld a definite response until early June, when David Lloyd George explained to an incredulous Griffith that such powers were not extended to British dominions. Griffith expected that the dual role of his finance minister, Michael Collins, as chairman of the Provisional Government could guarantee the full cooperation of the country's financial institutions with the Dáil's directives. However, the banks soon made it clear that they would only be prepared to cooperate with civil service transfers from London that had been approved by the British government, and would not take directives from politicians. This had a direct bearing on Griffith's political plan for the formation of a new National Army. Shortly before his death that August, Griffith gave voice to a founding claim of the Irish Free State government in waiting: it was a parliamentary democracy, validated by a popular vote, and therefore its efforts to found its own National Army merited full support. Between February and April Griffith's Cabinet drafted legislation to grant all IRA personnel that had sworn allegiance to the Dáil in the past, pensions or generous salaries if they became members of either the new army or police force. Knowing that the IRA was split, Griffith wanted to postpone all IRA conventions until these policies could be implemented and, in the meantime, supported all efforts to negotiate army unity provided that authority was retained by the Dáil's defence ministry. Upon the outbreak of civil war in late June, Michael Collins requested the authority of Griffith to assume command of the National Army, which was still nominally pledged to attaining army unity. However, it would soon be financed by banking authorities that did not share this aspiration. As such, Griffith died with his political plans for the Irish Free State largely in ruins: neither fiscal autonomy nor army, nor, indeed, national, unity had been attained. His most significant achievement in 1922 was to resist all pressure from London, Irish unionists and bankers to give the unelected Free State Senate constitutional powers of veto over Dáil legislation. This legislative freedom of the Dáil, exercised from December 1922, was the constitutional basis upon which the Free State could strive to live up to its founding ideals.

Fig. 3 (above left) Arthur Griffith and Michael Collins arriving at St Mel's Cathedral in Longford on 21 June 1922 for the wedding of Alice Cooney and Seán Mac Eoin, TD for Longford-Westmeath and GOC Western Command. [Image: National Library of Ireland, Arthur Griffith Papers, MS 49,530/27/7]

Fig. 4 (opposite) Funeral of Arthur Griffith in Glasnevin Cemetery, 16 August 1922. Griffith died suddenly of a cerebral haemorrhage on 12 August 1922 aged just fifty-one. It was a heavy blow to the pro-Treaty government, which had benefited from Griffith's well-honed political and communications skills. Founder of Sinn Féin fifteen years earlier, Griffith was perceived as an elder statesman even by the anti-Treaty side. The imprisoned Seán T. O'Kelly wrote to Griffith's widow, Maud: 'Future generations of Irish men and women shall draw inspiration [from] a truly patriotic son whose political philosophy so eloquently taught, and whose long years of toil and sacrifice brought the present generation of Irishmen from their knees to their feet, and rekindled in their hearts the almost extinct flame of liberty.' In a magnanimous tribute to the man who had recently condemned him as a 'damned Englishman', anti-Treaty propaganda supremo Erskine Childers wrote in *Poblacht na hÉireann*: 'Deep and impassable as [is] the gulf that in recent months has divided us from Arthur Griffith, we join today in mourning the death of a great Irishman.' After High Mass in Dublin's Pro-Cathedral on 16 August 1922, Griffith's tricolour-draped coffin was buried in Glasnevin Cemetery. Maud Griffith chose (and paid for) a memorial featuring a broken column to mark his modest grave. [Image: National Library of Ireland, Keogh Photographic Collection, Ke 170 / Quotations: cited in Seán Ó Lúing, *Art Ó Gríofa* (Dublin, 1953), p. 403; *Poblacht na hÉireann*, 14 August 1922]

Fig. 5 (right) Draft proclamation, handwritten by Arthur Griffith in late July 1922, delaying the first meeting of the Third Dáil until 12 August. This was the third of five prorogations before the parliament, which was elected on 16 June and due to assemble for the first time on 1 July, finally met on 9 September 1922. Continued postponements during this period meant that the Civil War was being prosecuted by a government acting without parliamentary sanction, which caused anti-Treaty opponents to denounce the regime as a military dictatorship. This third delay, wrote Griffith, was necessary to 'complete the work of restoring order and the security of life and property, which is [parliament's] prime duty'. Furthermore, the government did not want to 'interrupt […] the vital and primal work' of the twenty-one pro-Treaty TDs serving in the National Army and 'actively engaged in the work of delivering the people from this dastardly oppression and making Ireland safe for democracy'. On 24 July, less than a week before the proclamation was issued, a meeting of nine neutral pro- and anti-Treaty TDs in Cork had called on the Provisional Government to summon the Third Dáil so that it could pass a motion demanding a ceasefire. Additional peace meetings were held in different Munster towns during the same period. Ultimately, the triumph of the National Army in the conventional phase of fighting put an end to the peace movement, and the government's legitimacy was protected when the Third Dáil finally gathered on 9 September. The new government which then formed did not include the two dominant pro-Treaty leaders Michael Collins and Arthur Griffith, who had died just weeks before. [Document: National Library of Ireland, Kathleen McKenna Napoli Papers, MS 22,764]

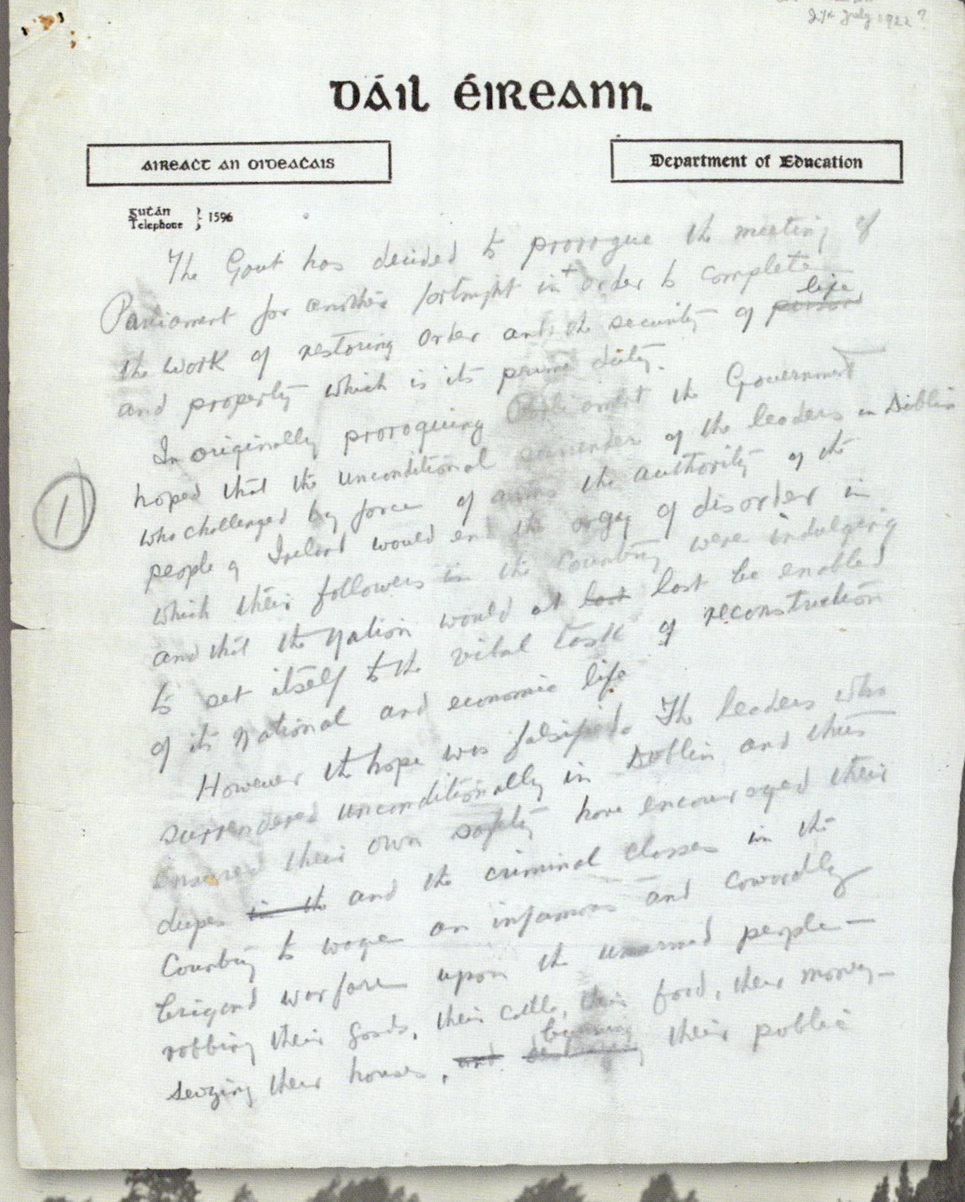

CASE STUDY

Military Dress and the Irish Civil War

Lisa Godson

On 1 February 1922 a small contingent of troops marched from the Phoenix Park through Dublin city centre to formally accept the handover of Beggars Bush Barracks from the British military. These soldiers were the first of the nascent Irish army to be clad in a newly designed uniform, broadly based on that of the Irish Volunteers, and cheering crowds made their parade an 'occasion of a popular demonstration'.[1] Although fewer than fifty soldiers participated, their appearance was heralded as representing a valorous past and a patriotic future. A few days earlier, the *Freeman's Journal* predicted that 'Irish soldiers in the national uniform' would 'soon be seen

Fig. 1 (below) Wearing new uniforms, soldiers of the Dublin Guards march through the streets of Dublin behind Captain Paddy O'Daly and the Fintan Lalor Pipe Band on their way to take over Beggars Bush Barracks, 1 February 1922. They were resplendent in greyish-green uniform with dark-blue facings, Sam Browne belts, peaked caps, brown leather leggings, rifles and burnished bayonets. The uniforms and accoutrements communicated that the soldiers were part of a 'regular' army of a recognised government, with small style alterations visually differentiating them from their British army predecessors. 'From a spectacular point of view', the *Irish Times* reported, 'the taking over of the barracks [the former headquarters of the Auxiliary Division of the Royal Irish Constabulary] was more impressive than the "surrender" of Dublin Castle' on 16 January. [Image: National Library of Ireland, NPA CIVP5/ Quotation: *Irish Times*, 2 February 1922]

in the streets of our cities or marching through the countryside of the land they have freed'. The newspaper reported that, before long, 'Ireland's wonderful unseen army' would emerge into view 'as an organised military force', emphasising their future visuality and visibility as materialised through uniform.[2]

Newspapers outlined the preparations that were being put in place so that those guerrilla fighters who had won the War of Independence from the shadows could now be seen as a national army in the open. It was reported that orders had gone out to Irish mills for 'the well-known grey-green cloth'[3] and to Drogheda and Cork for lining, as well as to a Dublin firm for buttons, and that all equipment would be of native manufacture so that 'the Irish soldier, from head, to foot' would be 'encased in Irish material'.[4] In a nod to a fabled London *Times* editorial of the 1840s, the *Freeman's* correspondent wrote that 'the day at last has come when the khaki coats will be rarer in Ireland than the "red Indian on the shores of Manhattan"', to be displaced by high-collared 'jackets green' with 'IV' (Irish Volunteer) buttons and 'FF' (Fianna Fáil) badges on soft-crowned caps.[5]

Fig. 2 National Army major-general's tunic worn by Professor James Hogan. Born to a prominent family in Galway (his brother, Patrick, was future minister of agriculture), James Hogan was a diligent student of early modern Irish history at University College Dublin, who managed to simultaneously undertake very active IRA service during the War of Independence. He was a prominent fighter in Michael Brennan's East Clare flying column, even after his appointment to the chair of history at University College Cork (UCC) in 1920 at the tender age of twenty-two. Taking leave from UCC, Hogan supported the Treaty and acted as a Free State government advisor in early 1922. At the outbreak of the Civil War he assumed senior administrative posts at National Army general headquarters in Dublin. He was then promoted to National Army director of intelligence with the rank of major-general. Hogan left the army in August 1923 and took up his professorial duties at UCC. During the 1930s he was a founding member of the Army Comrades' Association and was active in the Blueshirt movement until 1934, when he resigned out of disgust with General Eoin O'Duffy's leadership. His former student, historian Dr Margaret MacCurtain, noted that Hogan was appalled by the 1922 destruction of the Public Record Office in the Four Courts, and responded by working to establish the Irish Manuscripts Commission and the journal *Analecta Hibernica*, which he edited from 1930 until his death in 1963. He later served on the Bureau of Military History advisory committee, which played such a critical role in protecting the records of revolutionary Ireland. [Image: Cork Public Museum / See Margaret MacCurtain, 'James Hogan', *Dictionary of Irish Biography*, https://doi.org/10.3318/dib.004049.v1; and Donnchadh Ó Corráin (ed.), *James Hogan: Revolutionary, historian and political scientist* (Dublin, 2001)]

Uniformly clad

The expectation that a uniformly clad army could mobilise and march untrammelled through the land was upended by the Civil War. Despite early optimism the supply of standard kit was sluggish during the volatile months leading up to the conflict. Throughout the spring of 1922, officers were fitted out by military and equestrian tailors such as Callaghan's of Dublin; as in other armies, leaders were granted greater individualism than the rank and file. The list of kit issued in May 1922 suggests little difference between ranks in the components of the uniform, although the quartermaster general specified that officers be equipped with Sam Browne belts and slacks as well as breeches.[6] Hierarchy was both visible and felt on the body through fabric, as officer dress was made of whipcord, a durable but comfortable worsted, whereas lower ranks wore thick and rough serge nicknamed 'bull's wool'.[7]

National values

Formal communications warned soldiers that their uniforms conveyed national values and would help them win the loyalty of the populace. An article in the army journal *An t-Óglach* commented on growing divisions in the army: 'Whether on or off duty our officers and men must ever keep in mind the uniform they wear, and by word or act do nothing to lessen its respect in the minds of the people'.[8] This was typical of contemporary discourse about military dress: that when a citizen submitted to be uniformed as a soldier, they became representative of the nation and their new dress both inculcated and required greater discipline of the body and character.[9] Ultimately, uniform validated state violence.

The rapid increase in recruits during the Civil War led to an even worse crisis in supply from Irish manufacturers, just as it became most vital to Free State leaders that the army be recognised as the nation's only patriotic and legitimate combatants. Local manufacturers found it difficult to meet demand and the government was unwilling to advance money to enable an expansion in production. The Irish Tailors' and Tailoresses' Union wrote that, despite the availability of tailors and supply orders in factories, there was 'no room or plant machinery' to accommodate further workers.[10] To augment

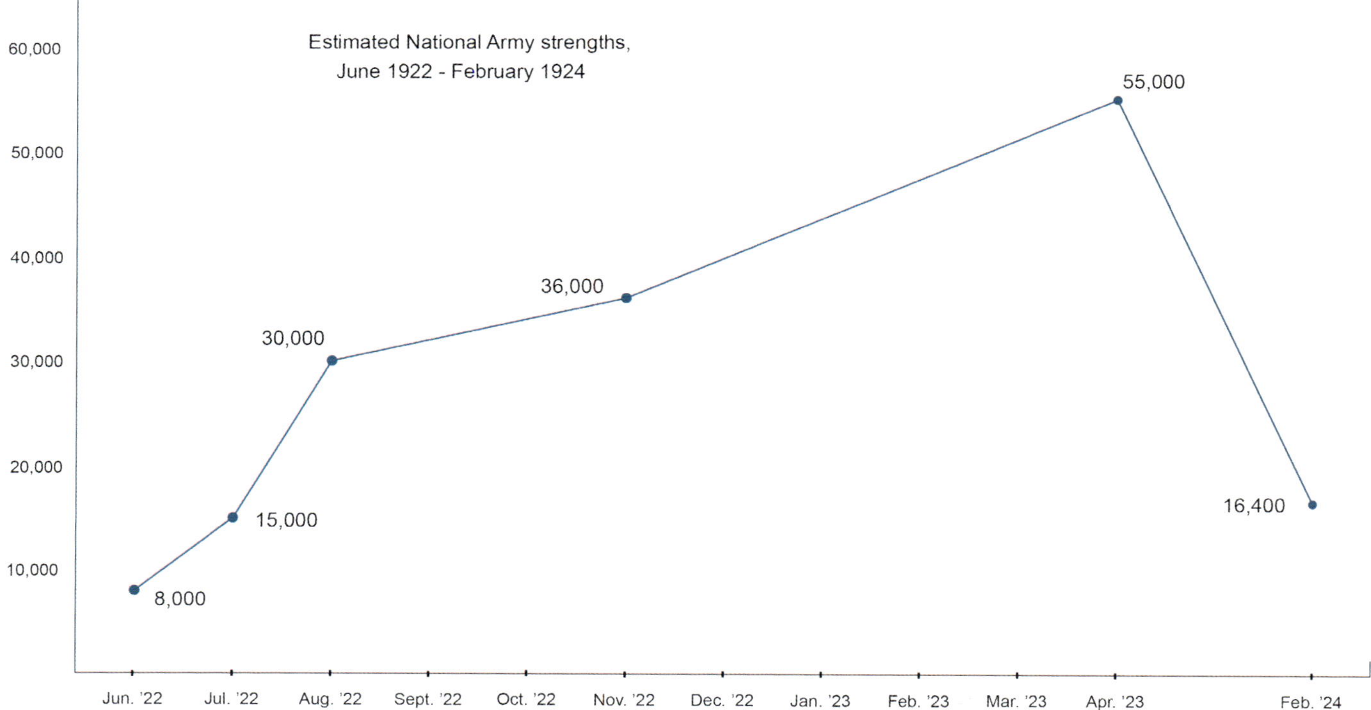

Fig. 3 Graph showing the growth of the National Army, February 1922–April 1923. The armed forces of the Irish Free State were formally brought into existence by the provision of public funds on 1 February 1922. Recruiting for what became known as the National Army opened that month in Beggars Bush Barracks. It is not possible to establish precisely how many men signed up between February 1922 and the start of the Civil War at the end of June. The split within the IRA naturally complicated recruitment efforts, while formal records of enlistment were not preserved (apart from a ledger containing the names and addresses of *c.* 3,000 men who passed through the Curragh Camp between February and July 1922). General Seán Mac Mahon recalled in 1924 that when the Civil War began there were approximately 8,000 men in the National Army (Michael Hopkinson later placed the figure at 9,200). Fewer than 6,000 were armed, and fewer again had received uniforms or training. With Dublin secured in the first week of July, and facing the prospect of an internecine struggle, the Provisional Government approved an establishment of 35,000 men for the National Army. On 6 July a 'national call to arms' was issued – crowds of young men eager to sign up were reported at each of the Dublin recruiting stations over the following days. Enlistment escalated rapidly over the ensuing weeks and by 5 August the army's strength stood at just over 30,000 (15,000 regulars and 15,700 reserves). Such rapid recruitment was even more notable for the fact that the army had no fabric of organisation in – and was therefore unable to recruit from – large parts of the country, including most of Munster, as well as Sligo, Mayo, Leitrim, Louth, Offaly and south Wexford. The success of the 'national call to arms' brought logistical headaches. New recruits received basic training at best, while record keeping was haphazard. Major General Seán MacEoin, GOC Western Command, admitted in early August that he was uncertain as to the whereabouts of as many as 1,000 men who were nominally under his command. Efficient administration of an army whose exact numbers and distributions were unknown was next to impossible. In September 1922 the paymaster at Wellington Barracks (later renamed Griffith Barracks) told the Army Finance Office that he was forced to issue pay based on the word of individual soldiers as to the date of their last payment. A census of all National Army personnel was carried out on 12 and 13 November 1922, which formed the basis of subsequent payroll and other army records (Fig. 4). It revealed that there were then just over 36,000 personnel in uniform. Enlistment was paused on 15 November but reopened two weeks later at Pearse Street recruiting depot, Dublin – the first time that the process was centrally controlled. From this point onwards recruits typically enlisted for six months and recruitment remained open until the end of April 1923. Personnel numbers then stood at between 52,000 and 55,000 (previous estimates for the National Army's strength at the end of the war have been as high as 60,000). Targeting a reduction of at least 30,000 across all ranks by March 1924, the National Army's general staff began planning for mass demobilisation – a difficult process that saw thousands added to the unemployed and was a major factor in the short-lived army mutiny crisis of March 1924 (see p. 362). [Text: Eoin Kinsella / See also 'Memorandum on the development of the defence forces in the period 1923–1927', General Staff Reports, HS/A/0876, Irish Military Archives]

inadequate local supply, fabric was purchased from the British Army Disposals Board, dyed and made up in Schneider's garment factory in Whitechapel (east London), which had been involved in British-uniform production during the First World War.[11]

The wearing of Irish army uniform during the Civil War communicated allegiance in seemingly unambiguous terms, but the use of dress by anti-Treaty combatants was multifaceted. On the one hand, 'irregulars' came to be iconicised clad in trench coats and soft caps, thus continuing the flying column fashion style common in the War of Independence. Trench coats were frequently mentioned in reports of the discovery of caches of equipment and weapons.[12] But clothing was also used to denote status, to hide guerrilla fighters' identities, and for republican women to fulfil military roles. Ernie O'Malley was deeply sensitive to appearance,

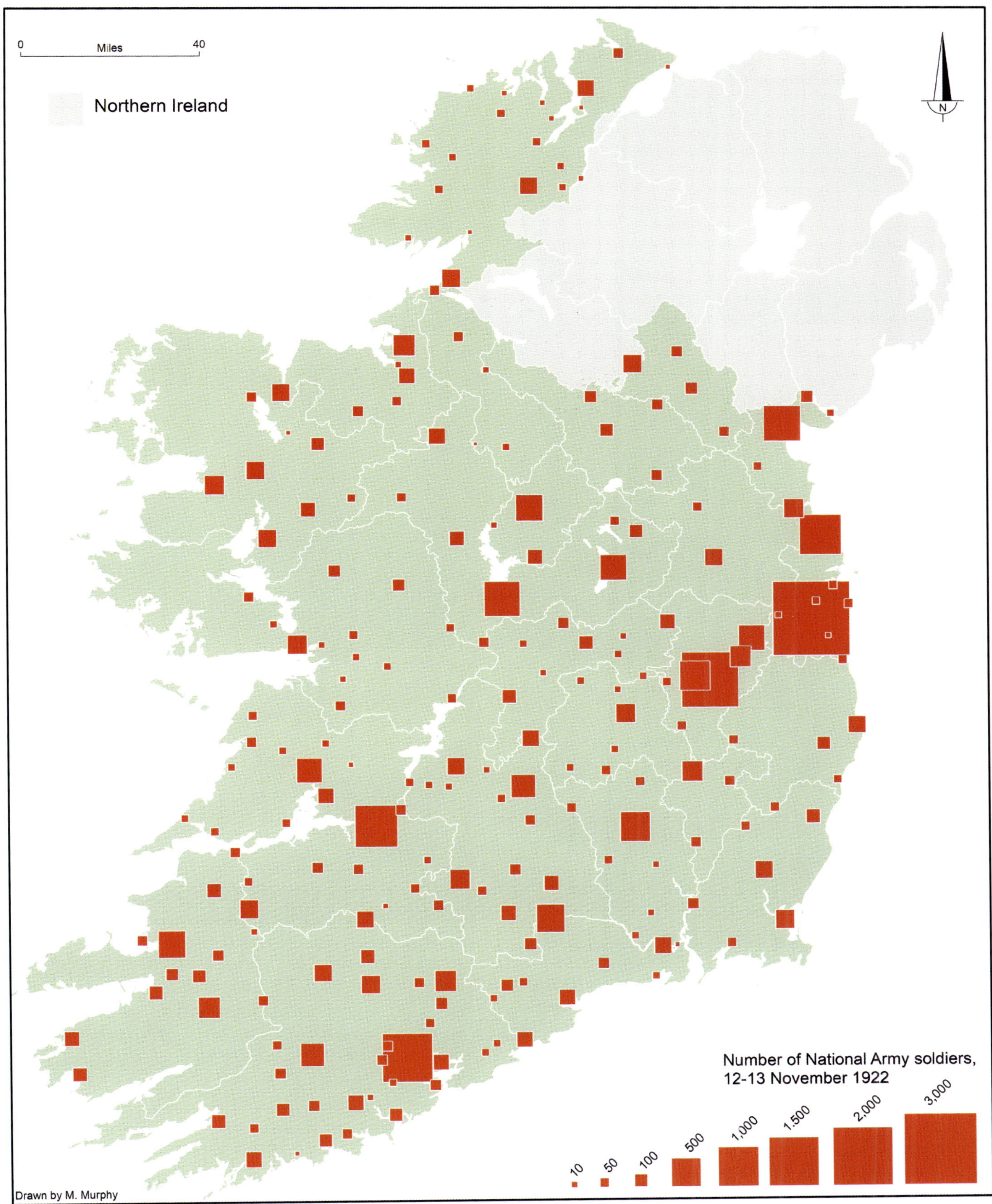

Fig. 4 Map showing the location and strength of the National Army across the Free State area, 12–13 November 1922, the date of the army census. [Updated version of a map first published in the *Atlas of the Irish Revolution* (Cork, 2017) / Source: Irish Military Archives, National Army census, 12–13 November 1922]

Fig. 5 National Army Recruiting Office, Pearse Street, Dublin. [Image: National Library of Ireland, HOG115]

and his Civil War memoir *The Singing Flame* offers particularly rich material on clothing. He tells how Nell Humphreys persuaded him that his clothes were 'unbecoming to an Assistant Chief of Staff'. This led to O'Malley being fitted for a smart suit despite this delaying his departure on service by some days.[13] He details many instances of dress being used for disguise, such as when Austin Stack appeared as a Protestant minister 'in a peppery grey suit' or how various uniforms were smuggled into jails to help prisoners to escape.[14] And, just as O'Malley had dressed up in his Dublin Fusilier brother's uniform to acquire arms in 1917, there were instances of anti-Treaty IRA forces stealing National Army uniforms to wear while undertaking raids, such as in Fermoy in February 1923.[15] Perhaps most strikingly, O'Malley describes scenes at Glasnevin cemetery in autumn 1922, where 'soldiers in green uniforms marched […] after bands playing the Dead March, following their dead', in a reference to state management of funerary rituals, but 'our men were buried quietly' save for 'Cumann na mBan girls in uniform' who 'fired a volley over the graves'.[16]

Most histories of military uniforms emphasise their role in shaping modern masculinity. However, the conspicuousness of armed and uniformed women and the relationship of Irish nationalists to dress throughout the entire revolutionary period suggests that far more complex forces were also at play.

Fig. 6 Uniformed members of Cumann na mBan at the funeral of Cathal Brugha (1874–1922) at Glasnevin Cemetery, 10 July 1922. Dáil Éireann minister for defence during the War of Independence and a fierce opponent of the Treaty, Brugha, who fought in the IRA 'Block' on Upper Sackville (O'Connell) Street during the Battle of Dublin, was the first high-profile fatality of the Civil War (see p. 411). Seán T. O'Kelly (left) and Ciaran McMenamy from Armagh shouldered the tricolour-draped coffin and, at the request of Brugha's widow Caitlín, 'only the women of the Republican Movement' formed the guard of honour. The woman at the front of the photograph wears a fedora hat and a Cumann na mBan tunic with tie and Sam Browne belt. Her masculine fashion style speaks to a growing militarisation of the republican women's organisation during the Civil War, as members assumed many duties previously carried out by IRA members. Cumann na mBan became the public face of militant republicanism during a period when IRA units were unable to attend funerals. Republican women assumed marshalling and processional duties at the spectacle funerals of prominent anti-Treaty leaders like Brugha, Harry Boland and Liam Lynch, as well as at those of numerous ordinary Volunteers. [Image: Cashman Collection © RTÉ Archives, 0505/101/ See John Borgonovo, 'Cumann na mBan, Martial Women and the Irish Civil War, 1922–1923', in Linda Connolly (ed), *Women and the Irish Revolution* (Newbridge, 2020)]

Fig. 1 Royal Irish Constabulary uniforms being dumped outside Dublin Castle during the evacuation, 17 August 1922. [Image: Cashman Collection © RTÉ Archives, 0505/064]

Disbandment of the Royal Irish Constabulary

Brian Hughes

In January 1922 it was announced that the Royal Irish Constabulary (RIC) would be disbanded. Easily overlooked as Ireland moved towards and beyond the outbreak of the Civil War, this was nonetheless a significant enough process in the wider context of the Irish revolution. Indeed, in April 1922 the *Cork Examiner* pointed to disbandment of the RIC and Auxiliary Division and the commitment to withdraw the military from Ireland as victories for the Anglo-Irish Treaty and evidence that the British government was 'carrying out their part of the contract'. The entire Auxiliary Division had departed Ireland by 24 January 1922 (though were paid in full until the end of March). Members of the regular RIC in the twenty-six counties that became the Irish Free State, which included the 'Black and Tans' recruited mostly from Britain from early 1920, were first transferred to larger centres before being released in a staggered fashion in groups of thirty or forty. British recruits generally went first, and all were reported to have left Ireland by mid-March. The disbandment of all remaining Irish-born members was due to be completed at the end of March, but ultimately took longer. The RIC had completely evacuated Limerick city in February 1922, for instance, while barracks in Cork city were not handed over until 12 and 13 April. The process had been suspended and then resumed at a slower pace in early April following concerns for the safety and family arrangements of disbanded men. None of the worst predictions came to pass, but fourteen serving and at least fifteen disbanded RIC were killed in 1922 in the twenty-six counties. Many more suffered threats and intimidation of various kinds. By May 1922 there were just under 2,000 men remaining in four centres in Southern Ireland. Disbandment of the force in Northern Ireland, which had been officially delayed, also began in May and the Royal Ulster Constabulary was founded on 1 June 1922. A contingent of RIC remained in Dublin over the summer, at Ship Street and Dublin Castle as a Castle Guard Company and Castle Clerical Company, and at Gormanston Camp to the north of the city. The final disbandment was completed in late August 1922. On 17 August Michael Staines led members of the new Civic Guard into Dublin Castle to take over policing duties in the traditional seat of British administration in Ireland. But there was no direct handover, and it was an informal and largely underwhelming affair. Only about sixty or seventy of the Civic Guard were said to be in uniform and, by the time they arrived, the RIC had already made its quiet exit in cabs and hackney cars. The *Irish Times* suggested that many of the

Fig. 2 (left) Royal Irish Constabulary officers outside a shop on St Patrick's Street, Cork city, 1921. [Image: National Library of Ireland, HOGW 52]

Fig. 3 (below left) Members of the Royal Irish Constabulary during one of the last inspection parades in Cork city, 1922. [Image: National Library of Ireland, HOGW 109]

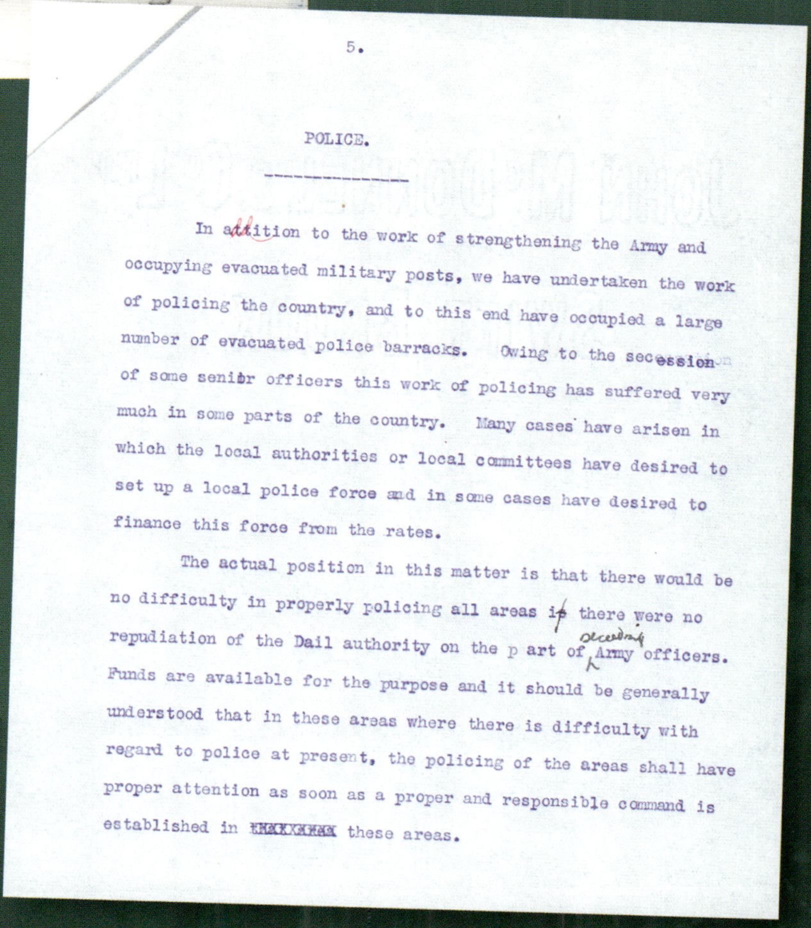

onlookers 'regarded the proceedings with a feeling of regret at the passing of what was admittedly the finest police force in the world', while the *Irish Independent* preferred to focus on the cheering crowds that greeted the Civic Guard as it marched to the Castle. At the end of the month the last remaining RIC left Gormanston. An order of council, signed by the Lord Lieutenant of Ireland, announced 31 August 1922 as the official date of disbandment. The Dublin Metropolitan Police survived, rebranded with new cap badges, until it was folded into An Garda Síochána in 1925.

[Text: Brian Hughes / Sources: *Cork Examiner*, 8, 13, 14 Apr. 1922; *Irish Times*, 14, 25 Jan., 16 Mar., 6 Apr., 11 May, 18 July, 18 Aug. 1922; *Irish Independent*, 18 Aug. 1922; *Weekly Irish Times*, 2 Sept. 1922; Donal J. O'Sullivan, *The Irish Constabularies 1822–1922: A century of policing in Ireland* (Kerry, 1990), p. 369; Richard Abbott, *Police Casualties in Ireland, 1919–1922* (Cork, revised edn 2019), pp. 275–91; John Reynolds, *46 Dead Men: The Royal Irish Constabulary in County Tipperary, 1919–1922* (Cork, 2016), p. 159; Brian Hughes, *Defying the IRA? Intimidation, coercion, and communities during the Irish Revolution* (Liverpool, 2016), pp. 192–202]

5.

POLICE.

In addition to the work of strengthening the Army and occupying evacuated military posts, we have undertaken the work of policing the country, and to this end have occupied a large number of evacuated police barracks. Owing to the secession of some senior officers this work of policing has suffered very much in some parts of the country. Many cases have arisen in which the local authorities or local committees have desired to set up a local police force and in some cases have desired to finance this force from the rates.

The actual position in this matter is that there would be no difficulty in properly policing all areas if there were no repudiation of the Dail authority on the p art of seceding Army officers. Funds are available for the purpose and it should be generally understood that in these areas where there is difficulty with regard to police at present, the policing of the areas shall have proper attention as soon as a proper and responsible command is established in XXXXXXXX these areas.

Fig. 4 (above) Memorandum from General Richard Mulcahy, 26 April 1922, regarding procedures to be followed under the terms of the Treaty in handing over military and police posts after the evacuation of the British army and the RIC. In early 1922 the Provisional Government agreed that all evacuated barracks would be occupied by local IRA units, regardless of their stance on the Treaty. The result was that, by the spring, numerous military barracks in Connacht and Munster – as well as the Four Courts in Dublin – were in the hands of the anti-Treaty IRA, unprepared to accept Mulcahy's authority or recognise the legitimacy of the Provisional Government. The last page of the memorandum, reproduced here, deals with the difficulties involved in filling the policing vacuum in anti-Treaty areas of the country. [Document: National Library of Ireland, Kathleen McKenna Napoli Papers, MS 22,808/3]

A jaunting car carefully negotiates a temporary repair to a road damaged during the Civil War. [Image: National Library of Ireland, HOGW 28]

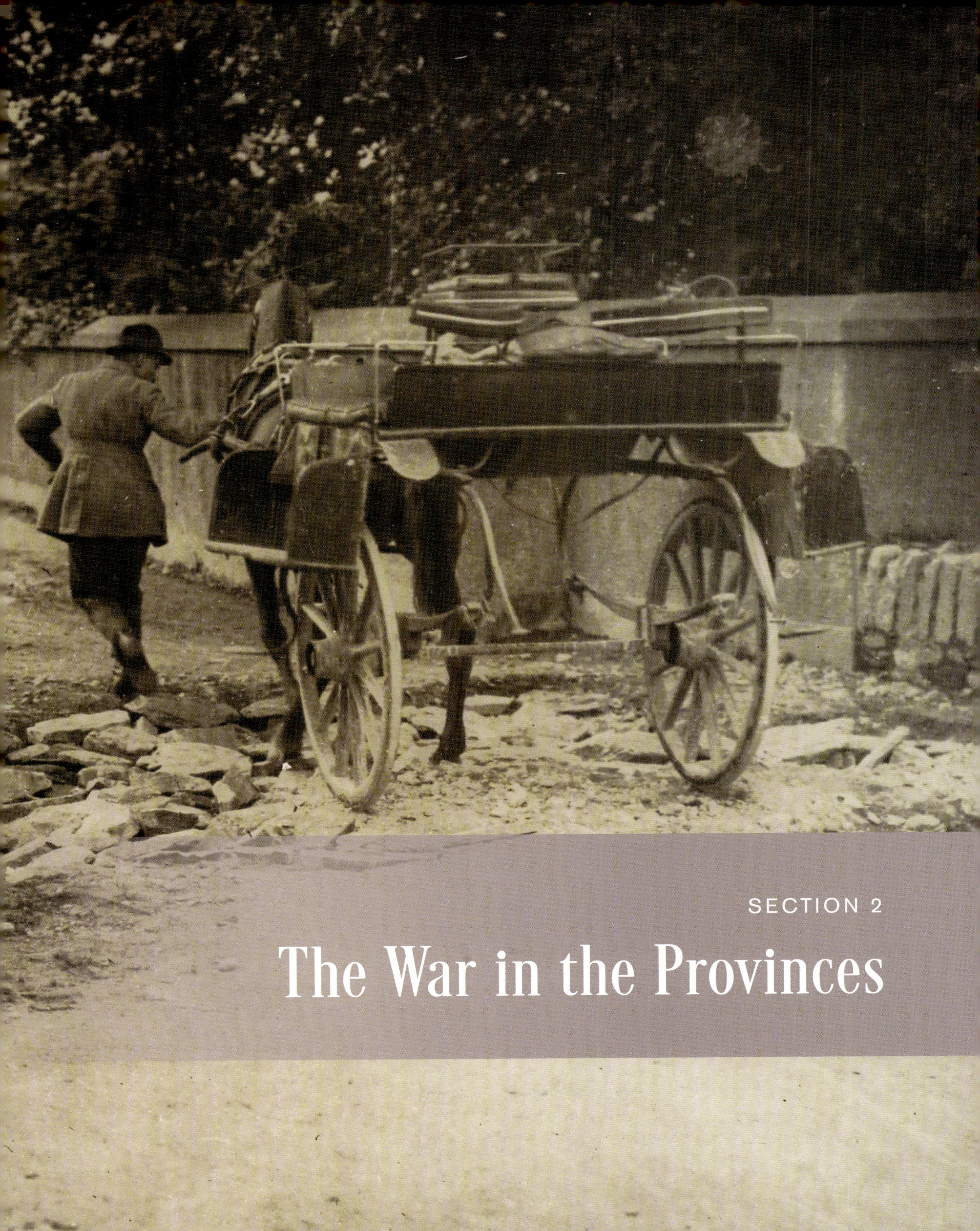

SECTION 2

The War in the Provinces

Fig. 1 A field ambulance arriving in the village of Bruff, County Limerick, late July 1922. [Image: National Library of Ireland, Hogan Photographic Collection, HOG111]

CHAPTER 2

The Irish Civil War in Provincial Ireland: Landscapes, communities and localised conflict

John Borgonovo

Like the Irish War of Independence, the Irish Civil War varied regionally, affected communities differently, and intensified and weakened at separate times. People experienced the Civil War in multiple ways, yet all felt its disruptive and often traumatic impacts. In early 1922 the independence movement split over the terms of the Anglo-Irish Treaty, which established the Irish Free State administered initially by a Provisional Government. The Free State's National Army was established within Dublin during those first months. Its foundations rested on clear pro-Treaty sentiments across most of Leinster, boosted by enthusiastic endorsements from the Catholic hierarchy, nearly every newspaper in the new Free State, and other influential elements of Irish civil society.[1] The National Army secured critical support from a few of the IRA's prominent units, most notably in Longford, Donegal, east Clare and east Limerick. It also leveraged the military expertise brought by Dublin-based officers and staff from the IRA's General Headquarters, who generally adhered to the Free State.[2]

Communal governance

Much of the IRA and Cumann na mBan opposed the Treaty, including large and experienced fighting units in Connacht and Munster. At all organisational levels the IRA had governed itself democratically through elected leaders who exercised collective decision-making. That structure played out in the Treaty split, as unit members (in companies, battalions and brigades) often determined their stance collectively. As can be expected, any group decision on the Treaty created its own dynamics, manifesting as individual defections to the other side or withdrawal from the IRA altogether.[3] Potential flashpoints emerged from January to March 1922 during the rapid evacuation of the British army and the disbandment of the Royal Irish Constabulary (RIC). To avoid armed clashes over control of the abandoned barracks, an agreement was reached between anti-Treaty IRA and the National Army (and some pro-Treaty IRA units) that the local IRA unit would take charge of any garrison in its territory, regardless of its attitude towards the Treaty.

Figs 2 and 3 The departure by sea of British troops from Ireland in 1922. [Images: courtesy of Kilmainham Gaol Museum/OPW]

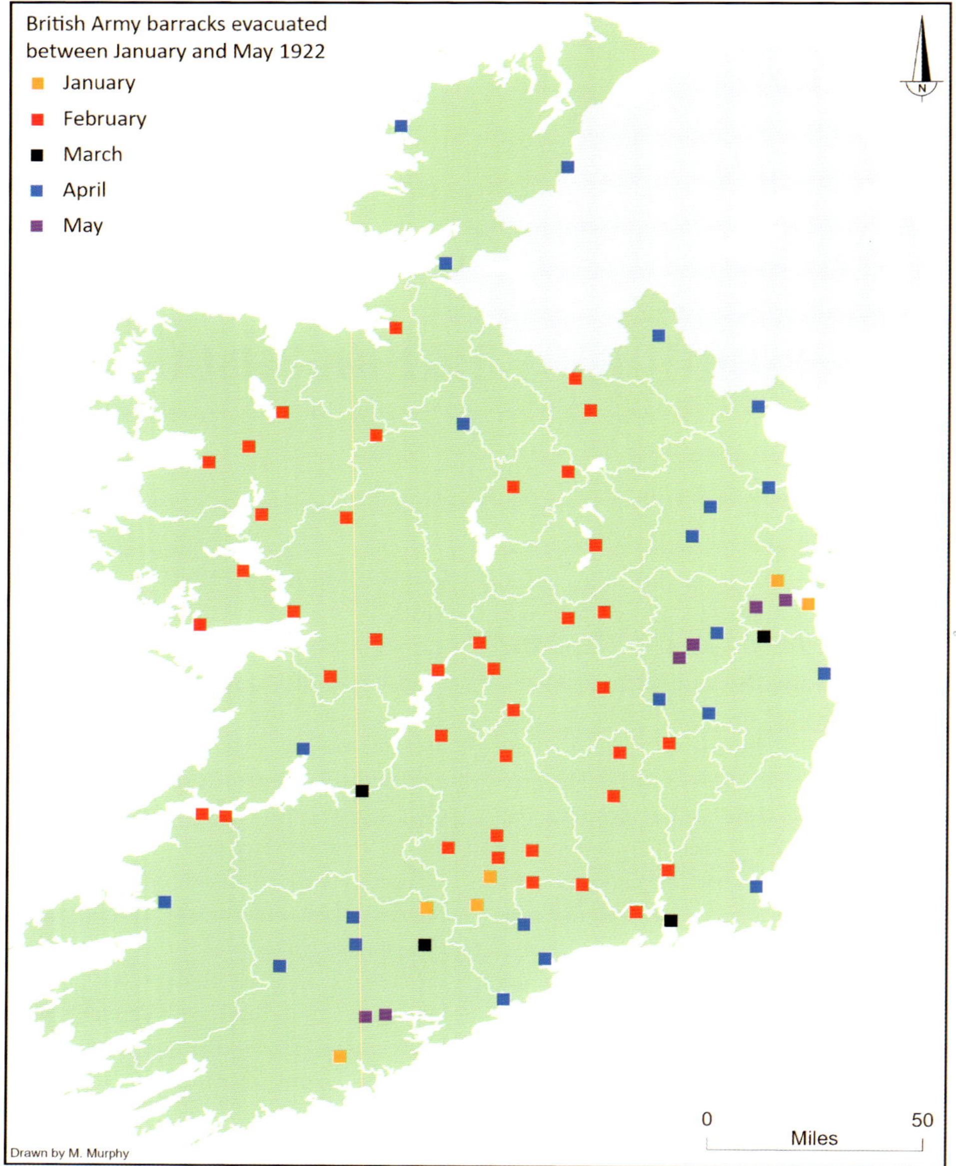

Fig. 4 Map indicating the pattern of the British military withdrawal from 'Southern' Ireland in the early months of 1922. Immediately after the appointment of the Provisional Government of Ireland in January 1922, British forces began to evacuate the twenty-six counties that were to become the Irish Free State. By the end of January troops were departing from Ireland by sea on almost a daily basis, with many earmarked for service in Europe or across the British Empire. Barracks began to be evacuated in Leinster and Munster, with the process accelerating in February as the British rapidly withdrew from military installations across Connacht, much of the midlands and the south-east. The British government intended to withdraw its forces as quickly as was practicable. It viewed their departure as a tangible statement of political intent, but was also wary of being dragged into any burgeoning conflict in Ireland. Furthermore, because British commanders were confident that they could reoccupy the twenty-six counties rapidly if the political situation, in British eyes, required them to do so, there was no need to maintain a substantial military presence, especially as the capabilities of the remaining garrison were weakened by the evacuation. The British abandoned Connacht, Munster and Leinster in turn: by mid-February virtually no troops were left west of the Shannon and, by the end of March, the interior of Munster was fully evacuated. The logistics involved in the withdrawal were enormous. Thousands of tons of supplies and equipment had to be secured against a backdrop of intermittent attacks and unrest, though some of this material was transferred to the new governments in Belfast and Dublin. The departures of British units were usually conducted with military ceremonials and often accompanied by sales of unwanted material. The British also noted that their departure was occasionally met with apprehension by some of the inhabitants in garrison towns. This was presumably rooted to some degree in political loyalties, but the British military had been a fixture of Irish life for centuries and was woven into the socio-economic fabric of towns and cities across the island. Now this was ending, the withdrawal was bound to have an impact on everyday life. By the end of May the evacuation was effectively over. The Royal Air Force had departed from the aerodrome at Baldonnell, the barracks at Naas, the Curragh and Portobello were handed over to the Provisional Government, and the final British detachments in Youghal, Ballincollig, Cork and Cobh (Queenstown) were withdrawn. On 25 May the Naval Command, Western Approaches was abolished, but the British government had already been informed that, as of 18 May, virtually all British troops had been evacuated from the twenty-six counties. The exceptions were those stationed in the coastal garrisons specified by the Treaty or clustered in the 'Dublin District', where substantial British forces were retained as a precaution until the Irish Free State was officially established in December 1922. After a presence that had lasted for centuries, the British military withdrawal from 'Southern' Ireland was completed in a matter of months. [Text and map data: John Gibney]

This left anti-Treaty forces in control of much of the country beyond Leinster. However, the British abandonment of hundreds of police stations and prominent army barracks and depots also bolstered the Provisional Government, as it demonstrated clearly to residents that the Treaty had essentially ended the British military presence in their locale and thus fundamentally altered Anglo-Irish relations.

As the country slid towards civil war during April and May, the IRA retained undisputed governmental authority in many parts of the country. However, no effective police force was available, and the IRA remained largely a part-time organisation. Throughout this period agrarian agitation spiked in many rural areas, and opportunistic property crime occurred in towns and cities. Thousands of Catholic refugees fled south to escape sectarian violence in the Six Counties (particularly Belfast). This contributed to fears of a broad religious conflict across the entire island, which intensified following the IRA's killing of thirteen Protestants in the area around Bandon, County Cork in late April. Militant and sometime aggressive strikes by trade unions were highly visible during this period and included a number of red-flagged 'workers' soviets'. After the anti-Treaty IRA repudiated Dáil Éireann in March 1922, local units no longer received government financial assistance (such payments were made after the British evacuation). To offset these losses, the anti-Treaty IRA raided banks throughout provincial Ireland and commandeered supplies from merchants in their communities. Taken together, this activity unsettled communities across the Free State, and increased public desire for the stable governance promised by Treaty supporters.

Fig. 5 Cork No. 1 Brigade IRA after its takeover of Victoria Barracks. There was an air of expectation in Cork on the morning of 18 May 1922 as, later that day, in an historic event for the city, the British army would evacuate Victoria Barracks. In an elevated position north of the city and with accommodation for over 2,000 troops, the barracks, first occupied by the British army in 1806, was the largest military installation in Munster and the headquarters of the army's 6th Division. The evacuation presented the Provisional Government with a problem. The city was a stronghold of Seán O'Hegarty's formidable Cork No. 1 Brigade anti-Treaty IRA, but the British army would only hand over its military installations to the pro-Treaty National Army. It was expected that O'Hegarty's brigade would resist any attempt by the National Army to move into Cork. Though vocally anti-Treaty, O'Hegarty sought to avoid civil war, meeting with the minister for defence, Richard Mulcahy, to discuss possibilities for a peaceful handover. Eventually, they reached an agreement whereby the barracks would be 'officially' taken over by National Army Captain Hugh MacNeill (nephew of Eoin MacNeill) representing the Provisional Government, who would then immediately hand it over to O'Hegarty's men after the British departed. Cork No. 1 Brigade agreed to maintain law and order; ensure an unhindered general election; support army reunification in the spirit of the Army Documents and meet routine administrative requirements of National Army general headquarters. For its part the National Army would pay debts incurred by the brigade and supply the IRA garrison with rations. The agreement in place, MacNeill arrived at the gate on Rathmore Road accompanied by an advance party of Cork No. 1 Brigade at 5 p.m on 18 May. He was met by Captain J.G. Magahy of the Royal Engineers and taken on an inspection of the barracks, during which MacNeill protested that the flagpole, now stripped of the Union Jack, was being cut down. Despite an officer's reassurance that this was customary when evacuating a barracks, the National Army captain heard another soldier mutter that it would be 'unbecoming' for the pole to fly a rebel flag. By the time MacNeill had completed his inspection at 6.30 p.m., the British garrison had formed up on the barracks square while hundreds of Cork residents had gathered outside the main gate on the Old Youghal Road to witness their departure. Finally, at 7 p.m., the order was given to 'move out'. Many in the crowd cheered as the soldiers marched out of the gate down to Custom House Quay, where the SS *Classic* would take them back to Britain. As the last column passed through the gate, Captain Magahy handed the keys of the barracks to Hugh MacNeill, a small act that marked the end of an era. Within an hour 200 IRA men led by Seán O'Hegarty and the Volunteer Pipe Band and including Seán Murray, selected as the new commanding officer of the barracks, marched through the main gate. The new era of peace hoped for by the assembled crowd was not to be. Within five weeks Ireland was plunged into civil war. There would be no peaceful handover in August 1922 when the evacuating IRA garrison put the barracks to the torch. O'Hegarty, a founding member of the Neutral IRA, was not among them. [Text: Gerry White / Image: courtesy of the Irish Examiner Archive / See *Cork Examiner*, 19 May 1922; Dan Harvey and Gerry White, *The Barracks: A history of Victoria/Collins Barracks* (Cork, 1997), p. 247]

Fig. 6 The Royal Navy arms ship the *Upnor* at the pier in Ballycotton, County Cork, 29 March 1922. The IRA's capture of the *Upnor* was among the most spectacular republican coups of the revolutionary period, involving hundreds of IRA Volunteers. It also had a significant impact on the balance of military power prior to the Irish Civil War. As the British police and military evacuated Ireland in early 1922, their assorted small arms were deposited at the Haulbowline Royal Navy base in Cork Harbour. The weapons were to be transported to the Royal Navy magazine at Devonport (Plymouth) by a special arms steamer, the *Upnor*. As the arms were slowly loaded, an IRA member working at Haulbowline notified his superiors in the IRA's Cork No. 1 Brigade, a unit that, during the War of Independence, had built a reputation for audaciousness and sound intelligence. At midday on 29 March 1922 the *Upnor* departed Haulbowline bound for Plymouth. In Cobh, after an unexpected delay (a tug targeted for hijacking had unexpectedly left port), a well-armed IRA party, along with a small gang of IRA Volunteers and sympathisers with seagoing experience, quietly boarded the tug *Warrior*, made prisoners of her crew, and slipped out of the harbour past two British coastal forts (named Camden and Carlisle) and the Spike Island fort. *Warrior* pursued the *Upnor* for 130 kilometres (80 miles), before finally overtaking the laden steamer late in the afternoon. *Warrior* flew a stolen King's Harbour Master's flag, while an IRA Volunteer, dressed in a Royal Navy jumper, stood on deck waving an official Royal Navy message envelope (also stolen). He called to the *Upnor* that he was carrying an important dispatch from Admiralty headquarters, and to send over a small boat to collect it. The *Upnor* captain complied, but when his small party rowed over to the tug, IRA Volunteers emerged from hiding, captured the crew, and used the boat to return to, and swarm onto, the *Upnor*. Having made prisoners of the crew, IRA replacements boarded, taking control of the ship. The two vessels then made for the small port of Ballycotton, about 30 kilometres (*c.* 19 miles) east of Cork Harbour. There, IRA Volunteers waited in an estimated seventy-seven lorries commandeered from businesses around Cork. Elsewhere, IRA teams blocked roads, cut telephone and telegraph lines, and even seized the Roches Point lighthouse to hinder British communications and reinforcements. When the *Upnor* finally docked, hundreds of crates of weapons, ammunition, and explosives were quickly removed, loaded onto lorries, and driven to prearranged arms dumps around Cork. Historian Tom Mahon estimates that the haul amounted to at least forty machine guns, 700 pistols, 1,000 rifles, and 200,000 rounds of ammunition, along with significant amounts of high explosives and grenades. The captured arms dramatically improved the anti-Treaty IRA's armaments in Munster, making those units much more militarily formidable and ultimately allowing them to field dozens of new flying columns in the ensuing Civil War. Beyond displaying the Cork No. 1 Brigade's skilful and precise planning, the capture of the *Upnor* also humiliated the Provisional Government, the Royal Navy and the British government. In a report to the Cabinet, Colonial Secretary Winston Churchill fumed: 'There is no doubt that the Irish have a genius for conspiracy rather than for government. The government is feeble, apologetic, expostulatory: the conspirators active, audacious and utterly shameless' (quoted by Tom Mahon). [Image: Cork Public Museum / See Tom Mahon, *The Ballycotton Job: An incredible true story of IRA pirates* (Cork, 2022). See also John Borgonovo, *The Battle for Cork: July–August 1922* (Cork, 2011)]

The conventional phase: June–August 1922

Armed hostilities erupted on 28 June in Dublin when the National Army attacked and later captured the anti-Treaty IRA (hereafter IRA) executive headquarters in the Four Courts complex. Victory over the IRA in Dublin a few days later allowed the Free State government to function in the capital without serious hindrance and to build up its military strength there for the duration of the war. Dublin was also connected to two important regional National Army bases, at Athlone and the Curragh, which provided launching pads for subsequent Free State advances into Connacht and Munster. The Free State leadership was unified and dominated by a singular political/military figure, 'Commander-in-Chief' Michael Collins. He exercised effective command and control over the National Army and the civilian government. The National Army operated on internal lines and could shift forces to reinforce units facing republican resistance. The British government had also handed over an abundance of weaponry, including automatic weapons and field artillery. The inclusion of scores of British lorries and armoured cars enabled the Free State forces to concentrate, move rapidly and advance on multiple fronts.

After relocating from Dublin to Cork, IRA Chief of Staff Liam Lynch formed what can be called the IRA 'Field Army', comprised of between 3,000 and 4,000 relatively experienced and well-armed fighters in Munster, supported by tens of thousands of unarmed IRA Volunteers and Cumann na mBan members.[4] This force consolidated its hold over most of the province of Munster, but it could not reinforce other areas of significant anti-Treaty resistance, particularly in Mayo, Sligo and Wexford. The IRA was also mobile, though the 'Field Army's' flat and decentralised structure hindered close coordination and left many units essentially on their own. Powerful republican columns located in Cork, Kerry and Tipperary preferred to operate in their home territories, while republican leaders remained divided over war strategy. Important IRA units were still debating whether to participate in the Civil War well into July 1922.

During the 'conventional' phase of fighting (July to mid-August 1922), both sides fought in the relative open. Over the next six or seven weeks, the National Army drove the IRA from urban Ireland, as it pushed through republican territory towards the western and southern coasts. In July the National Army forced the IRA out of most of Leinster, and from major towns in Connacht. There were several relatively large clashes involving hundreds of troops in Wexford, Tipperary, Limerick, Waterford, Mayo and Sligo. Large republican and National Army formations manoeuvred around places like Blessington, Enniscorthy, New Ross, Urlingford, Ferns and Thomastown. Guerrilla-style skirmishing occurred near towns such as Birr, Tullamore, Roscrea and Nenagh. Some market towns experienced urban warfare, which paralysed their local economies. For example, Sligo town saw repeated gun battles over a few weeks, while Enniscorthy, Tipperary town and Carrick-on-Suir experienced multiple days of fighting. The National Army shelled republican positions in Boyle, while the IRA captured a pro-Treaty IRA garrison in Skibbereen with a recycled cannon. Collooney (County Sligo)

Fig. 7 National Army (NA) soldiers, including General Frank Thornton (on the right in the front row), standing beside two Rolls-Royce armoured cars. 'The Fighting 2nd' still bears its British registration, 1043 CK. In response to escalating IRA activity in late 1920, the crown forces increased their mobility and protected their vehicles by using Lancia armoured trucks and Peerless and Rolls-Royce armoured cars. Between January 1922 and August 1923, over 1,143 motor vehicles were handed over to the new National Army. Among them were 111 one-and-a-half-ton Lancia armoured trucks, which had a maximum speed of about 34 mph and could carry up to ten soldiers and a Lewis machine gun. They were used by the NA as personnel carriers and to transport 18-pound artillery guns. Some had wire-mesh cages to protect them from grenades, but they were not invincible to attack, and the addition of heavy armour shortened their working lifespan. Other armoured Lancia trucks were handed over to the newly formed Royal Ulster Constabulary, and one is preserved in the National Museums of Northern Ireland. The Rolls-Royce (1920 pattern) armoured car, built on the civilian Silver Ghost chassis and weighing 3.8 tons, was armed with a .303 Vickers machine gun and carried a four-man crew. Equipped with pneumatic tyres and an engine regarded as quiet by 1922 standards, it could reach a speed of 20 mph on country roads. By 1921 the British army in Ireland had thirty-one of these vehicles, and later handed over thirteen to the NA. At six tons and built on an American Peerless truck chassis, the Peerless armoured car was much heavier and slower than the Rolls-Royce. With a maximum speed of only 18 mph, they were restricted to maintained rural roads and urban areas. Two, for example, were shipped to Cork city. They did pack a punch, however. A crew of five had access to two turrets housing French Hotchkiss machine guns and over 3,500 rounds of ammunition. Only seven of the seventy Peerless armoured cars in Ireland at the time of the Truce were transferred to the NA. Clearly, the British government was willing to hand over what it considered a sufficient number of armoured vehicles and field artillery to suppress the IRA, but not enough to be dangerous to the British army in any future war. The armoured vehicles gave the NA a key advantage over the poorly equipped IRA, but there was a constant shortage of qualified drivers and mechanics, and the unforgiving rural roads rendered many vehicles unserviceable. The IRA's Cork No. 1 Brigade built three armoured cars onto civilian chassis, and other IRA units captured Free State armoured cars. The 'Muntineer' was captured by the IRA in May 1922 and destroyed during the attack on the Four Courts, and the 'Balinalee' and 'Sliabh na mBan' ('Slievenamon') fell into IRA hands later in 1922, briefly wreaking havoc in their locales before their recapture (see pp. 62–3). Finally, the 'Moon Car', a Rolls-Royce Silver Ghost seized by the IRA from the Clark family in Cork and fitted with armour and Lewis guns, was used during the Civil War and afterwards, most notably in an IRA attack on Royal Navy sailors and a warship in 1924 at the Treaty port of Cobh. It was buried afterwards but recovered decades later and is now preserved in the National Museum of Ireland. [Text: Lar Joye / Image: National Library of Ireland, HOG65]

changed hands multiple times, as did Clifden, Ballina, Dundalk and Kenmare. These were major events in the history of these localities causing significant disruption to daily life.

In those early weeks, much attention rested on the so-called 'Munster Republic', where thousands of National Army troops faced a force of armed IRA fighters about half their number protecting a republican defensive 'line'. A week-long battle rocked Limerick city, while clashes in and around Carrick-on-Suir and Waterford city likewise lasted for nearly a week. Probably the most intense combat occurred in the Kilmallock-Bruff-Bruree area, as about 2,000 Free State troops clashed with about 1,000 IRA fighters.[5] Possessing far superior firepower, the National Army succeeded on all fronts, even when it came up against stubborn republican resistance. Surprise Free State amphibious landings in

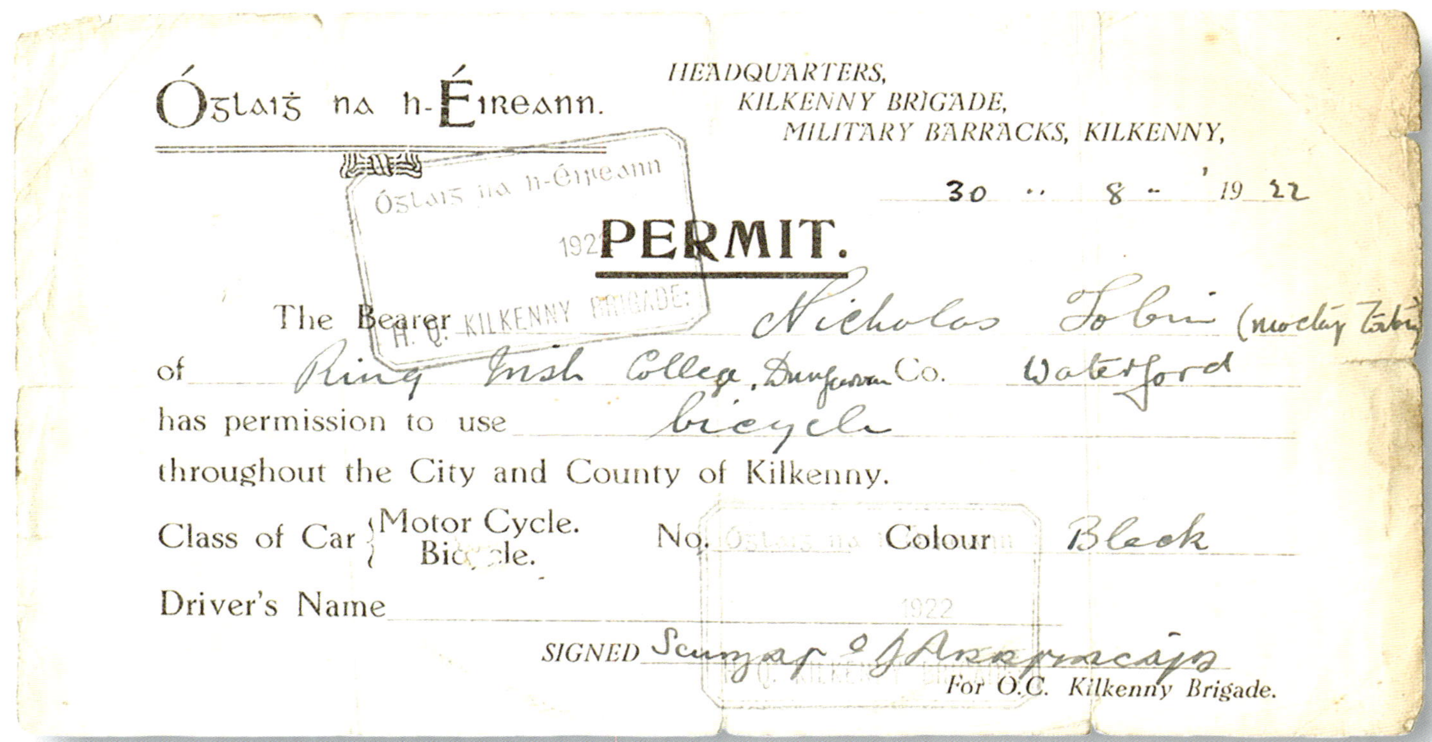

Óglaiġ na h-Éireann.

HEADQUARTERS,
KILKENNY BRIGADE,
MILITARY BARRACKS, KILKENNY,

30 .. 8 .. 1922

PERMIT.

The Bearer Nicholas Tobin (Nioclás Tóibín)
of Ring Irish College, Dungarvan Co. Waterford
has permission to use bicycle
throughout the City and County of Kilkenny.
Class of Car {Motor Cycle. Bicycle. No. Colour Black
Driver's Name
SIGNED [illegible]
For O.C. Kilkenny Brigade.

Óglaiġ na h-Éireann 1922 H.Q. KILKENNY BRIGADE.

Fig. 8 Permit for the use of a bicycle in Kilkenny city and county issued by IRA Headquarters, Kilkenny Brigade, Military Barracks, Kilkenny on 30 August 1922 to Nicholas Tobin (Nioclás Tóibín), a teacher at the Irish college in Ring, County Waterford and a noted Irish-language scholar, poet and prose writer. In early May 1922, prior to the outbreak of the Civil War in Dublin, Kilkenny had witnessed an outbreak of hostilities between the anti-Treaty IRA and Free State forces, resulting in the former occupying several prominent buildings across the city. There were no fatalities during the two-day engagement that ultimately saw the National Army quickly regain control of the city, but more than twenty people were wounded. Large numbers of IRA and Cumann na mBan members were detained, but were subsequently released following peace negotiations in Dublin. During the early conventional phase of the Civil War, there was a series of engagements at Callan, Thomastown and Mullinavat as the National Army sought to exert its control across the county, with the city becoming increasingly important militarily in the south-east as a National Army stronghold in the battle for the 'Munster Republic'. For a teacher like Tobin, however, life went on despite the ensuing turmoil and daily inconveniences, and the permit for the use of the bicycle – which was the principal mode of transport for many people at the time – was a simple necessity. Later in the year he married Siobhán Jennings, who was the matron in Ring College. [Image: courtesy of Whyte's Auctioneers / See Eoin Swithin Walsh, *Kilkenny: In times of revolution, 1900–1923* (Dublin, 2018) pp. 179–98]

county Kerry (Fenit and Tarbert) on 3 August and county Cork (Passage West, Youghal and Union Hall) on 8 August broke the back of conventional republican resistance in Munster (see p. xxix). The Civil War soon transitioned into its much longer and more contested guerrilla phases.

The spectacle of warfare can be compelling to participants and bystanders alike. In different communities the conventional phase produced striking moments that were long remembered. Soldiers sometimes numbering in their hundreds moved along the highways and byways, often accompanied by loud armoured cars and lines of heavy lorries. Rifle and machine-gun fire echoed across the landscape, while the less familiar booms of artillery were also occasionally heard. The IRA and the National Army set up headquarters and defensive positions in towns, ports, bridges, villages and crossroads across provincial Ireland. Armed units from both sides occupied major local landmarks, such as army and police barracks, hotels, workhouses, manor estates, factories, coastguard stations, schools, railway stations and the occasional castle. These headquarters and defensive fortifications often became a hub of activity during combat operations, and curious residents sometimes gathered to watch the fraught comings and goings. Certain barracks or reinforced buildings were first occupied by the crown forces in 1920–1, then taken over by the IRA in 1922, and finally captured and used by the National Army a few months later. Shops, estates and large farms were often targeted for commandeering by passing troops (particularly the IRA), while military medical units (on both sides) and local doctors and nurses treated the wounded in temporary first aid stations, hospitals, convalescent homes and doctors' surgeries. Local priests were often called to administer the last rites or celebrate funeral Masses. Even in quiet areas that escaped major clashes, residents witnessed remarkable scenes of troop movements, occupied buildings, commandeered property, food shortages, burning structures and blocked roads.

Perhaps best remembered was the IRA destruction carried out at the close of the conventional phase. IRA Volunteers retreating from towns and cities seized goods and vehicles that they could hide in their remote guerrilla bases, and then burned, destroyed or damaged remaining items deemed useful to the National Army.

Fig. 9 (right) Three soldiers and four civilians pose in a breach blasted in the wall of Strand Barracks by National Army artillery. The battle for Limerick city started on 11 July 1922. A week of sniping, running street battles and dramatic but ineffective raids by armoured cars on fortified positions resulted in stalemate. Then, on 19 July, a National Army 18-pound field gun entered the fray. It shelled the IRA-occupied Strand Barracks on 20 July, blowing the front gate away and forging a breach that was apparently large enough to admit a horse and cart. When a second barrage reduced the four-foot-thick stone walls to 'a palsied pile, a grim tribute to the accuracy of the national artillery', the barracks surrendered. The gun's next target, the Castle Barracks, was soon ablaze. While the thirteenth-century structure was saved, it remains unclear whether the fire was caused by shelling or republican arson. Acknowledging its powerlessness against artillery, and to deprive the National Army of accommodation and operational bases, the retreating IRA used petrol and paraffin to burn the Ordnance Barracks and New Barracks. *Sgéala Chatha Luimnighe* (*Limerick War News*) reported, 'all night [20–21 July] the city was illuminated by the flames [...] The destruction is enormous'. The Ordnance Barracks was gutted. The blocks on three sides of the New Barracks square were razed, as were the officers' mess, the church, the gymnasium, and the hospital. An explosion, caused either by mines or a broken gas main, rained stone, bricks and other debris on nearby civilian homes. Locals salvaged food and looted anything manageable, thousands evacuated, commerce ground to a halt, the rail and mail services ceased and there were no newspapers, apart from propaganda sheets. The ten-day battle in the densely populated city centre caused the fatal wounding of almost as many civilians (eleven) as combatants (seven National Army, three IRA and one member of Na Fianna). In September 1922, compensation claims for £195,000 relating to the battle for Limerick were lodged under the Malicious Injuries Act. By late 1923 there were more than 600 such applications from the city and 1,000 from the county. The majority ranged from 30s to £250 and covered 'loss of profit, consequential losses, destruction of property, loss of house accommodation, loss of clothing etc'. Many complaints concerned IRA commandeering of tobacco and foodstuffs. Several big businesses – chief among them bacon factories (Denny's, Masterson's and Shaw's), dairy producers (Cleeve's) and mills (Bannatyne's and Cannock's) – claimed over £1,000 each. The highest individual claim came from the Community of the Convent of Mercy for nearly £24,000 in respect of the Ordnance Barracks. Some uncompromising opponents of the Treaty and Free State proved more flexible about personal economic recovery: Madge Daly, whose bakery provisioned the city's IRA, claimed £2,250 for damage to its premises. [Text: John O'Callaghan / Image: courtesy of Dr Matthew Potter, Curator Limerick Museum / Sources: *Irish Times*, 23 July 1922, *Sgéala Chatha Luimnighe* (*Limerick War News*), 21 July 1922, *Cork Examiner*, 25 Sept. 1922, *Limerick Leader*, 7 Nov. 1923]

Fig. 10 (below) This photograph captures a moment after the IRA withdrawal and the burning of the Ordnance Barracks. Looking along Mulgrave Street to the barracks entrance at the left, between the entrance and the three youths facing the camera, is a cart laden with wood; on the extreme right is a man sitting on the shafts of a horse and cart laden with what appears to be a cast-iron stove and a machine with a large wheel handle. [Text: John O'Callaghan / Image: courtesy of Dr Matthew Potter, Curator Limerick Museum]

Scores of former RIC barracks were set alight, while equipment was stripped from British army bases before the buildings were burned. These included major landmarks in garrison towns like Birr, Cahir, Castlebar, Clonmel, Fermoy, Mallow and Tralee. Civilian looting often preceded or followed the arson. Such destruction also signalled to the local population that their long-time economic engine – the British army – was indeed gone and would not return. Along the republican-held coastline, coastguard stations were likewise torched, while some piers and quays were damaged or destroyed to prevent landings by the National Army, denying coastal communities their economic lifeline. To disrupt Free State movement, the IRA cut telephone and telegraph lines and wrecked their exchanges. The republicans systematically hindered movement on roads, bridges and railways with trenches, downed trees and collapsed spans. The sabotage of communications infrastructure and burning of so many buildings during the IRA retreat from urban Ireland was

Fig. 11 (above) A woman and girl salvage wood from Victoria (now Collins) Barracks in Cork city after it was destroyed by fire in August 1922. Retreating IRA forces methodically destroyed military and police barracks and other structures with possible military utility as they withdrew from villages, towns and cities during July and August 1922. Once the IRA departed, civilians often descended to gather abandoned items they deemed useful, from timber and wiring to furniture and tableware. Sometimes they risked the dangers posed by burning structures and, on occasion, tried to empty buildings they knew the IRA had selected for destruction even before the fires were set. This kind of opportunistic looting by the urban poor was broadly condemned, and often perceived by the Irish establishment as indicative of a dangerous decline of moral standards during the revolutionary period. [Image: National Library of Ireland, HOGW 140]

Fig. 12 Smoke billowing from the courthouse, Swinford, County Mayo, August 1922. [Image: reproduced with the kind permission of Joe Mellett, Swinford, grandson of Joseph A. Mellett, who took the original photograph]

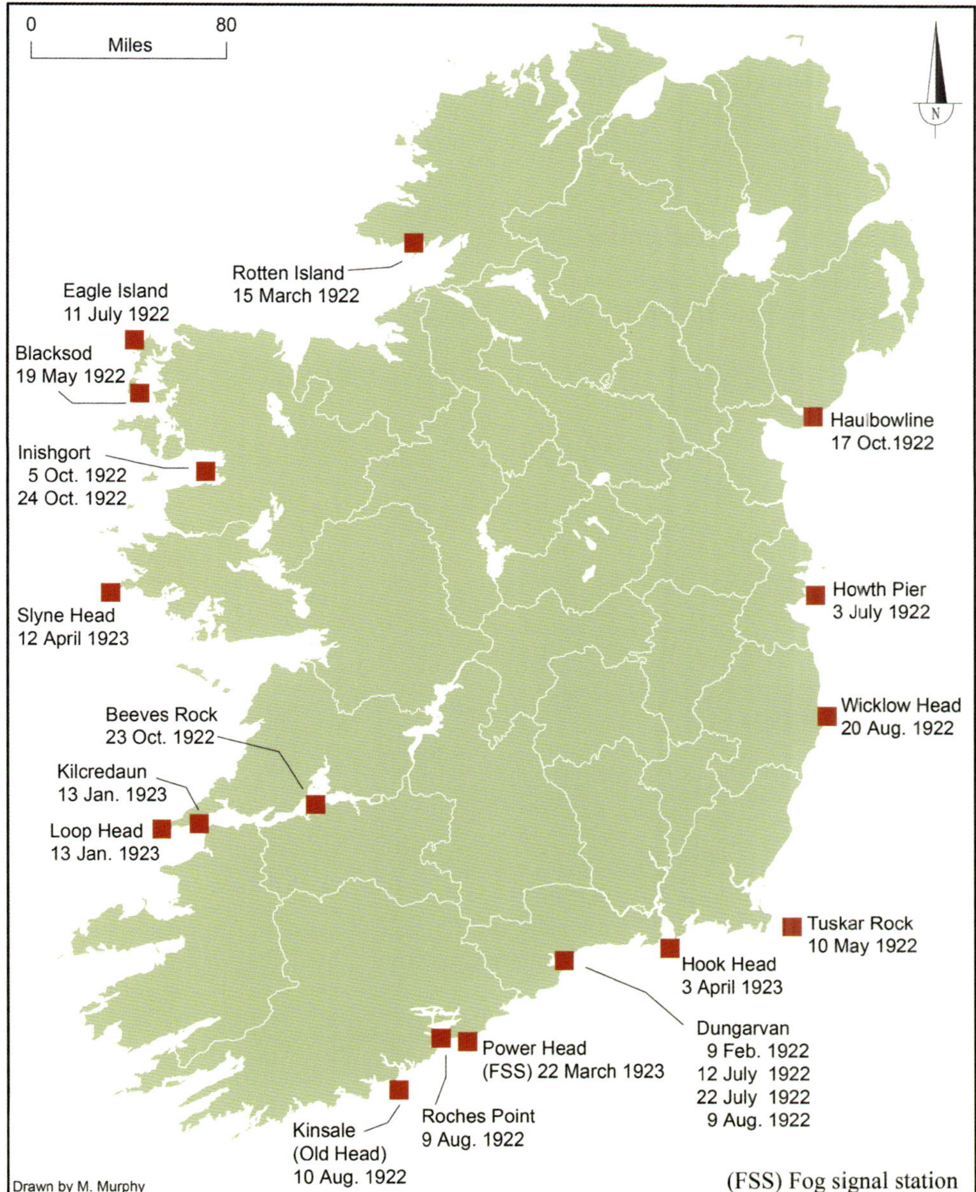

Fig. 13 Map showing raids on lighthouses during the Civil War. During the War of Independence the IRA conducted a systematic campaign of raids on lighthouses and fog-signal stations, seeking equipment such as telescopes and signalling lamps and, above all, explosives. A February 1920 review of the stock of explosives held by Irish Lights (Ireland's lighthouse authority) illustrated the potential bounty available: more than twenty-one tons of gun cotton were stored around the coast for use in fog signals – vital elements in the coastal network of aids to navigation. Vast quantities were stolen by the IRA in 1920 and 1921. By the end of 1921 Irish Lights had taken the drastic step of transferring most of its explosives away from remote and vulnerable lighthouses and fog-signal stations. Navigating the coast became increasingly difficult and dangerous, with fog signalling suspended at several hazardous locations. The Anglo-Irish Treaty brought little relief. When Dungarvan and Rotten Island lighthouses were raided in February and March 1922 by men claiming to be from the IRA, there was confusion at Irish Lights headquarters. Were they dispatched by the Provisional Government? In fact, the raids warned of the emerging Treaty split. Between February 1922 and April 1923 there were twenty-two raids (or similar incidents) at eighteen different lighthouses and fog-signal stations. The frequency of raids intensified when the simmering tensions of early 1922 boiled over into civil war. From the very outset of the Civil War, lighthouses had made poor targets when compared to similar raids during the War of Independence. Irish Lights had learned the hard lessons of 1920–1. Fog signals remained inactive, and explosives were now stored more securely. As a result Civil War raids yielded little tangible reward. The only raid of the Civil War to successfully secure explosives took place in early April 1923 at Hook Lighthouse in Wexford. The 'bounty' was, however, just fourteen detonators and two cotton-powder charges – a paltry haul compared to the thousands of detonators and explosive charges stolen from Irish Lights in 1920 and 1921. The ultimate failure of the IRA's lighthouse campaign can be seen in the Civil War's final raid, at the Slayne Head lighthouse in County Galway on 12 April 1923, a month before the IRA unilaterally declared a ceasefire. The IRA left the lighthouse with a single telescope, dealing yet another disappointment to the demoralised republicans. [Text: Eoin Kinsella / Sources: Eoin Kinsella, 'Safety at Sea Through War and Upheaval, Irish Lights, 1911–1923 Exhibition', Commissioners of Irish Lights, 2016; 'The Commissioners of Irish Lights and IRA Raids on Lighthouses during the War of Independence', RTÉ Century Ireland: https://www.rte.ie/centuryireland/index.php/articles/the-commissioners-of-irish-lights-and-ira-raids-on-lighthouses. See also John Borgonovo 'The Heritage of the Revolution: Coastal legacies', in R. Devoy, V. Cummins, B. Brunt, D. Barlett and S. Kandrot (eds), *The Coastal Atlas of Ireland* (Cork, 2021), pp. 314–18]

often locally unpopular. To some residents, destruction in their locale confirmed tropes used in Free State propaganda, which depicted militant republicans as irrational, savage, primitive and anarchic.[6] While destruction and disruption may have been militarily justifiable to the IRA, it politically damaged the broader anti-Treaty movement.

The early guerrilla phase: September–December 1922

Now located in the rural hinterlands, the IRA waged a guerrilla campaign against government forces, which lasted from mid-August 1922 to May 1923. Andy Bielenberg's fatalities project has shown clear delineations in casualty counts during an 'early guerrilla phase' (September–December 1922), and a 'late guerrilla phase' (January–May 1923).[7] As in the War of Independence, armed republican resistance during both guerrilla phases was decentralised, with each IRA brigade and locality fighting its own, separate war. The IRA at this point was far better armed than it had been during the Anglo-Irish War, particularly in rifles, ammunition, machine guns and newly developed land mines. Republican flying columns were more experienced and lethal, as most guerrilla fighters were also

COPY REPORT FROM I/O.SWINFORD.

I₁₁th November 1922

On the 7th inst., 20-25 Irregulars made a sweep on the town (Charlestown) and raided principal business houses taking boots, drapery, tobacco and cigarettes etc., all armed with rifles; Guard of men on roads leading to Ballaghadereed and Swinford while the raid was in progress. All the men were of Carthy's Column and came from Aclare direction.

Section of II Irregulars always in Curry (Co. Sligo)

NAMES

Two Duffys, J. McGwynn, Regan and Graham (Broher Village) McGwynn (Fuel Village) P. Brennan, T. Brennan and Capt. Brennan (Curry)

Leave rifles occasionally in P. Marren's Curry when attending Mass in Curry Church. Sleep very often in John Marren's and Biddy Marren's (Montua Village)

3 or 4 unarmed Irregulars visited Charlestown on the I2th inst., at night. Also on the night of the I3th inst. Among then was T. McCarrick, Tubbercurry.

East Mayo crowd divided into sections 6 men and sect, leader in each. Two Columns P. Mc.Dermott O/C of one and P. Fitzpatrick O/C of the other. Once sect. of 7 men in Castleduff (Carracastle District)

Night of I4th inst. Charlestown Hibernian Bank was set on fire by Irregulars and destroyed 9.30 p.m. I2-I4 descended on the town in twos and threes. All from Cloonaughill and Curry Districts (Co. Sligo) Pickets placed on roads leading from town and immediately the work of destruction commenced. Armed with Revolvers no rifles at all. There was no responsible leader of the crown (at all) Charlestown has suffered severely at the hands of the Irregulars and Comdt. Comdt. Egan has pointed out the necessity of having a Garrison stationed there.

Fig. 15 (left) Report of Swinford National Army intelligence officer detailing IRA activity in Mayo and Sligo, 10 November 1922. Numerous IRA columns moved about Mayo and Sligo throughout the final months of 1922. Here, the intelligence officer records IRA depredations in the village of Charlestown, County Mayo, about 12 kilometres west of Swinford, nearly astride the Mayo/Sligo boundary. The officer mentions four separate IRA raids on Charlestown in one week and suggests that a National Army garrison should be stationed in the village. The report identifies many of the visiting IRA Volunteers and their hidden bases and sleeping places. The level of detail suggests that significant information about the IRA flowed from the local population to the National Army. [Document: National Library of Ireland, Ernie O'Malley Papers, MS 10,973/7/20] veterans of the War of Independence and the conventional fighting. The republican women's organisation Cumann na mBan was more closely integrated into the IRA's support and logistical network.[8] However, significant stresses could now be felt within most IRA units. Leaders and active members across the organisation suffered heavily from arrests during the war's first weeks. Thousands of demoralised rank-and-file Volunteers abandoned the struggle following the collapse of conventional resistance. A devoted republican core continued with the guerrilla campaign, though with lower morale, far fewer personnel, weakened civilian support, and fewer material resources at their disposal.

The National Army expanded rapidly throughout the summer and autumn, and ultimately numbered 55,000 soldiers by early 1923.[9] Many had previously served with the British army during the First World War, and their combat experience and technical expertise helped to professionalise the army. Others were IRA veterans of the War of Independence, while some had no prior military service at all. Recruits enlisted for patriotic reasons and a sense of adventure, but also out of economic necessity. The Civil War took place amid a deep post-war recession in Britain and Ireland, which made a soldier's steady pay enticing. The National Army had little difficulty filling its ranks; when troops entered towns and cities, they typically carried hundreds of extra rifles to arm new recruits on the spot.[10]

National Army soldiers sometimes served in their home locale, where they knew the geography, could identify active republicans, and could locate safe houses and other hideouts critical to the IRA's survival. On the other side, IRA guerrillas could likewise name individual enemies from their locality and place them and their families. Such familiarity raised communal tensions and introduced a disturbing intimacy to the conflict. Much of the National Army officer corps had served with the IRA during the 1919–21 conflict, and thus understood guerrilla warfare. Ordinary Free State soldiers posted outside their home areas recognised basic Irish social, cultural and political norms and nuances. Overall, the Free State forces posted to a community enjoyed crucial local knowledge about the place and its people that British counter-insurgency forces had lacked in 1920–1.

The constant presence of National Army troops in communities of all sizes was yet another element of provincial Ireland's lived experience of civil war. Cities, towns and even villages became highly militarised environments, where Free State soldiers were visible and active. They manned roadblocks, undertook foot and lorry patrols, and protected banks, jails, courthouses and other government buildings. Many areas remained under night-time curfews, and civilians required military permits to use automobiles and even bicycles. The National Army was widely dispersed. Some garrisons numbered fewer than a dozen soldiers, while others dominated the countryside. For example, in November 1922 387 National Army soldiers were posted in Mullingar, 271 in Killarney, 253 in Sligo town, 252 in Charleville, 193 in Wexford town, 165 in Portlaoise, 131 in Cahir, and 118 in Roscommon town. Scores of small garrisons appeared in villages like Galbally, Kilkee, Bundoran, Killybegs, Tramore, Woodford and Rathdrum.[11] In some towns troops were housed in private homes, which added another domestic element to their local presence.

Free State military discipline varied. In certain areas troops were relatively well integrated with residents and brought a welcome boost to the economy. In other places troops were poorly controlled, badly trained and often associated with drunkenness

Fig. 16 (below) D Company, 1st Battalion, Dublin Guards. In the first months of 1922 the National Army emerged as a force loyal to the Provisional Government and separate from the IRA. Initially, its most prominent and formidable unit was the 'Irish Guards' (known as the Dublin Guards), which was raised primarily from Dublin IRA veterans active in the War of Independence and often officered by former members of Michael Collins's 'Squad'. The 'Guards' retained an elite status owing to members' distinguished fighting records in the War of Independence and their close connection to Collins. During the conventional phase of the Civil War, the Dublin Guards were frequently deployed to help bolster less reliable units, particularly during dangerous amphibious operations. In 1923 some of the unit's officers were implicated in the unauthorised killing of prisoners across County Kerry. [Image: reproduced by kind permission of UCD Archives. Desmond FitzGerald Photographs: P80/PH/161]

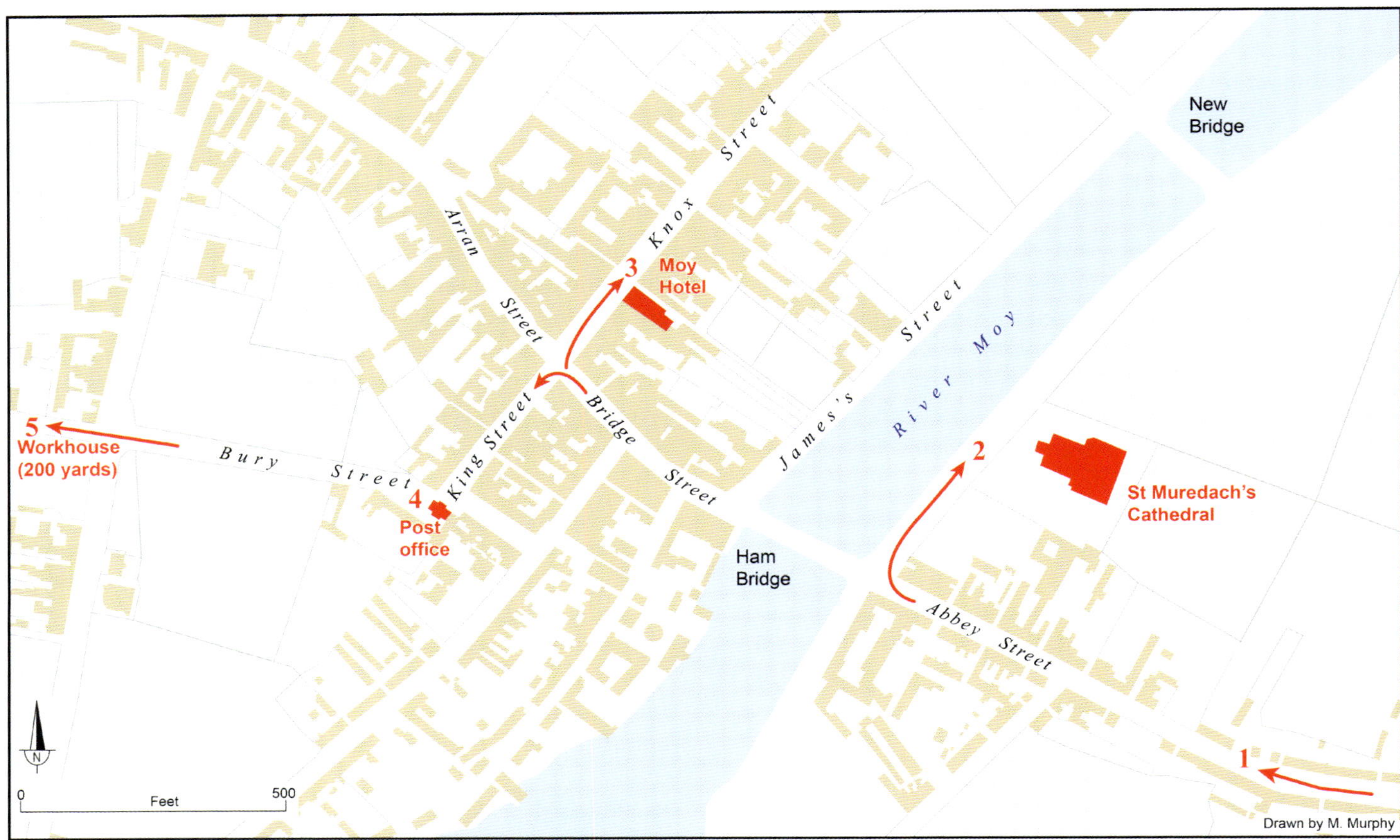

1. From their base in Bonniconlon (six miles north of Ballina), a large force of about 200 IRA Volunteers, commanded by General Michael Kilroy and accompanied by the captured armoured car 'Ballinalee', approached a National Army checkpoint at the entrance to the town. In the exchange between the IRA and the sentries, Private Thomas Lackey of the National Army was wounded, and twenty-two-year-old medical student Constance Tynan received a fatal gunshot wound to the chest.

2. The attacking party now divided into sections. One surrounded St Muredach's Cathedral, where thirty-four National Army soldiers were attending the month's mind requiem Mass for Lieut. Patrick Moran. After a standoff that involved the intervention of parish priest Fr Greany, the National Army soldiers surrendered and handed over their weapons.

3. Another section headed for the hotel, where National Army officers were billeted, and gained entry through the rear of the building. The officers exited onto Knox Street, where they were captured by the IRA.

4. The main attacking party followed the 'Ballinalee' into King Street and came to a halt outside the post office, which also served as a National Army observation post. A landmine planted in the porch exploded at 11.30 a.m., shattering panes of glass in King Street and stopping the post office clock. The National Army defenders surrendered.

5. Having secured the town, the IRA turned its attention to the workhouse, which served as the National Army's main barracks and a detention centre for republicans. The 'Ballinalee' continued up Bury Street to the workhouse where, during an exchange of fire, twenty-six-year-old civilian Malachy Geraghty was killed. The IRA freed the republican prisoners and departed that evening with the National Army garrison's weapons, ammunition and fuel.

Fig. 17 The capture of Ballina, 12 September 1922. The formidable anti-Treaty forces in County Mayo displayed their lethality in the summer and autumn of 1922. Their leader, Michael Kilroy, was a coachbuilder/blacksmith and a prominent guerrilla commander during the War of Independence. By the beginning of the Civil War, Kilroy commanded the IRA's 4th Western Division and served on the IRA executive. During the first months of fighting, he and his experienced west Mayo fighters sallied forth across the county, venturing as far as Sligo to bolster republican resistance there. In early September Kilroy and the Mayo IRA achieved probably their most impressive victory of the Civil War when they captured the entire National Army garrison at Ballina. On this occasion they were buttressed by the celebrated IRA armoured car the 'Ballinalee' (captured from the National Army), which had been driven over from Sligo to join the attack. According to the Military Service Pensions Collection testimony of IRA officer P.J. Ruttledge, a Cumann na mBan member ('Miss Clarke') came out from Ballina and warned the approaching IRA forces on the night of 11 September that they were expected by the National Army that night. They then rescheduled the attack for late the following morning and surprised the tired garrison. Beyond capturing the arms of over 100 National Army soldiers (who were then set free), the IRA also commandeered food, clothing and cash from the Bank of Ireland, before retreating safely back into the hills. On 29 October Kilroy's troops achieved another coup when they seized Clifden, County Galway and captured its garrison of eighty-nine National Army soldiers. However, on 25 November 1922 sweeping Free State forces cornered and captured Kilroy and much of his flying column near Newport, County Mayo. By that time, the 'Ballinalee' was already out of the war, having been captured in late September by the National Army in north Sligo near Benbullen during an operation that also resulted in the controversial death of six IRA fighters (known as 'the noble six'). Michael Kilroy emerged from the Civil War as a TD for the Mayo South constituency, which he represented until 1937, first for Sinn Féin and then for Fianna Fáil. His IRA subordinate P.J. Ruttledge served in the Dáil from 1921 to 1951 and was a Cabinet minister in several Fianna Fáil governments, including a six-year stint as minister for justice. [Map data and text: Frank Fagan]

Fig. 18 A rare photograph of Sligo republicans during the Civil War. Sitting second from the left in the front row and holding a rifle is the divisional adjutant, Brian MacNeill, the twenty-two-year-old son of Provisional Government minister Eoin MacNeill, who was shot, reputedly after surrendering, on or near Benbulben Mountain on 20 September 1922. Harry Doherty, whose brother kept the photograph, is standing at the back on the right. [Image: courtesy of Plunkett Doherty]

and casual violence. Gemma Clark has written about common forms of 'ordinary violence' in the Civil War, focusing primarily on republican and unidentified perpetrators.[12] Linda Connolly's research has illuminated acts of rape and other sexual and gendered violence committed by both National Army and IRA troops.[13] Extensive evidence found within both contemporary and subsequent documentation shows widespread National Army abuse of republican prisoners, particularly beatings and torture.[14] More study is needed to fully understand this and other forms of state violence experienced by communities during the Civil War. It appears that collective punishment of entire communities by state forces was much rarer in the Civil War than in the Irish War of Independence, though this conclusion is tentative and requires more in-depth research.

Republicans reorganised after their conventional-phase defeat and enjoyed limited guerrilla success in late 1922. This was most evident in counties Sligo, Mayo, Wexford, Tipperary, Cork and Kerry, where much of the hinterland was undisturbed by the National Army. New IRA flying columns also operated in areas that had largely been quiet during the War of Independence, such as counties Wicklow, Leitrim, Kildare, Kilkenny and Carlow. During the autumn IRA Volunteers emerged from their hideouts to stage large-scale attacks on isolated National Army garrisons. They struck major market towns such as Macroom, Sligo, Kenmare, Callan, Clifden, Carrick-on-Suir, Dromahair, Bantry, Ballina and Millstreet. For residents these battles engulfed their urban areas, occasionally for days. Invading republican forces sometimes numbered in the hundreds and captured and disarmed entire Free State garrisons before retreating. However, other republican attacks were driven off and, even when successful, IRA victories were rarely followed up. In areas where the IRA remained formidable, guerrilla resistance was patchy, and flared up and receded with little warning.

Disrupted landscape

Historian John Dorney has identified the IRA's primary military strategy as preventing the Free State government from functioning, and bankrupting the new state by disrupting the economy, preventing the collection of tax and revenue, and forcing massive public spending on defence.[15] Throughout the autumn and early-winter months of 1922, the IRA cut down telegraph and telephone lines to disrupt communications, and damaged roads, bridges and railways to slow Free State troop movements. During this campaign against infrastructure, republicans carried out thousands of individual acts of sabotage across the country, with particular

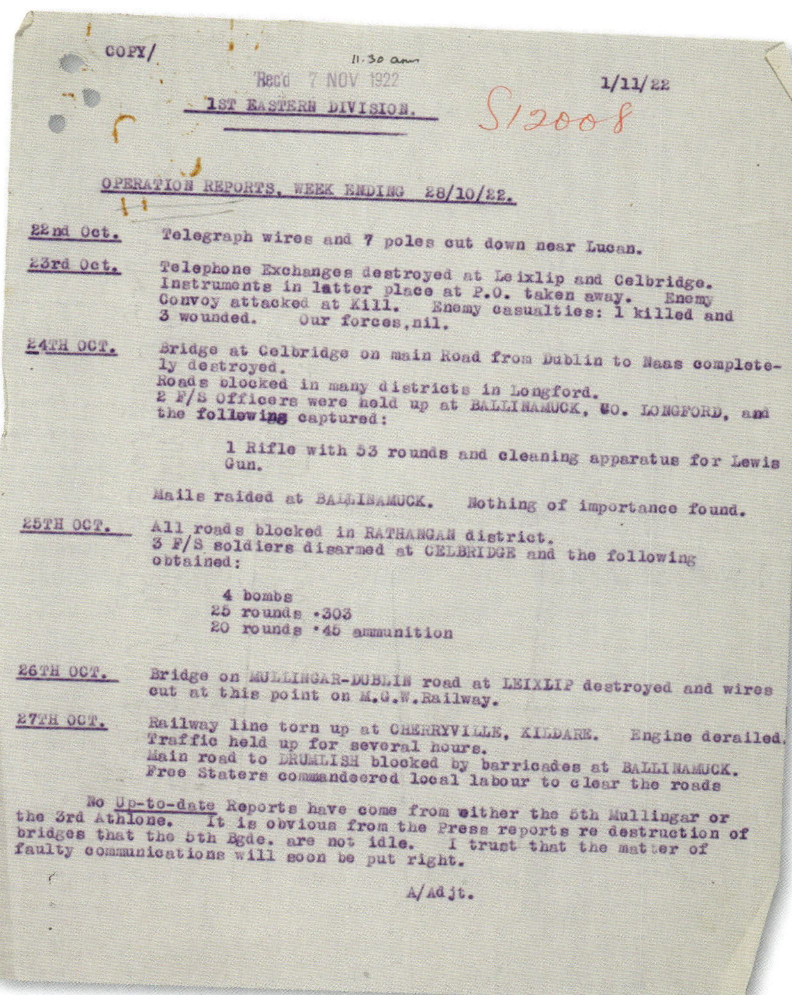

COPY/

11.30 am

Rec'd 7 NOV 1922

1/11/22

1ST EASTERN DIVISION.

S12008

OPERATION REPORTS, WEEK ENDING 28/10/22.

22nd Oct. Telegraph wires and 7 poles cut down near Lucan.

23rd Oct. Telephone Exchanges destroyed at Leixlip and Celbridge. Instruments in latter place at P.O. taken away. Enemy Convoy attacked at Kill. Enemy casualties: 1 killed and 3 wounded. Our forces,nil.

24TH OCT. Bridge at Celbridge on main Road from Dublin to Naas completely destroyed.
Roads blocked in many districts in Longford.
2 F/S Officers were held up at BALLINAMUCK, CO. LONGFORD, and the following captured:

1 Rifle with 53 rounds and cleaning apparatus for Lewis Gun.

Mails raided at BALLINAMUCK. Nothing of importance found.

25TH OCT. All roads blocked in RATHANGAN district.
3 F/S soldiers disarmed at CELBRIDGE and the following obtained:

4 bombs
25 rounds ·303
20 rounds ·45 ammunition

26TH OCT. Bridge on MULLINGAR-DUBLIN road at LEIXLIP destroyed and wires cut at this point on M.G.W.Railway.

27TH OCT. Railway line torn up at CHERRYVILLE, KILDARE. Engine derailed. Traffic held up for several hours.
Main road to DRUMLISH blocked by barricades at BALLINAMUCK.
Free Staters commandeered local labour to clear the roads

No Up-to-date Reports have come from either the 5th Mullingar or the 3rd Athlone. It is obvious from the Press reports re destruction of bridges that the 5th Bgde. are not idle. I trust that the matter of faulty communications will soon be put right.

A/Adjt.

Fig. 19 Weekly operations report of the IRA's 1st Eastern Division, 28 October 1922. The IRA maintained detailed records of its various units and activities up until the end of the Civil War, such as this document emanating from the headquarters of the 1st Eastern Division, which encompassed units in Leinster. This report during the war's early guerrilla phase outlines a number of IRA attacks on roads and infrastructure, as well as on National Army troops, in counties Kildare, Longford and Dublin during a single week. While there were comparatively few deaths in those areas during the Civil War, the civilian population experienced ongoing disruptions and sabotage, as noted here. The IRA's release of captured National Army soldiers on two occasions also suggests that not all participants in the conflict were eager to kill their former comrades. [Document: National Library of Ireland, Ernie O'Malley Papers, MS 10,973/11/39] focus on road, rail, telegraph and phone networks. The IRA effort dislocated trade, hurt commerce, inconvenienced travellers and isolated towns and villages. Yet such disruptions further undermined republicans' legitimacy within the community and set the stage for growing public support for the Free State's attempts to introduce governance into areas where lawlessness had reigned for months.

Republican guerrillas utilised their landscape whenever possible. In agricultural areas, friendly farmers constructed underground dugouts as hiding places, often in barns and outhouses. The IRA often relocated to remote bogs and mountainous areas, which were difficult for the National Army to access. Marion Dowd has written about the republicans' use of caves as hideouts and arms dumps. On rivers and in coastal areas, the IRA moved about in small boats and often sheltered on islands or isolated shorelines. Certain IRA units took to the high seas, and hijacked or attempted to hijack passing freight steamers, to seize anything useful in their hulls. On inland waterways, canal boats were held up and ransacked.[16] Fighters and fugitives usually moved around at night, using a variety of methods, from bicycles and pony and traps, to automobiles and motorcycles. They walked immense distances, often in the cold and rain. By this stage less assistance was forthcoming from the civilian population. Local clerical denunciations mounted following the Catholic hierarchy's excommunication of IRA fighters in October 1922. Food was scarcer, messages became more difficult to deliver, and overall living conditions deteriorated for hidden guerrillas.

While historians have generally emphasised the failings of the republican military campaign during this period, Free State progress was not entirely clear even to government leaders at the time. Since the IRA organisation was largely opaque, many assumed IRA resistance could continue indefinitely, and thus destabilise and potentially defeat the Free State over the long term. The government feared ongoing state disfunction would demoralise its supporters and even validate British imperial racial stereotypes of the Irish as inherently incapable of orderly self-government. Desperate to end the fighting, in November 1922 the Provisional Government took the drastic step of executing IRA prisoners captured in possession of arms. The implementation of such an extreme measure showed the government's (particularly the National Army's) deep concerns about ongoing IRA resistance. It was not then clear, however, that the republican war effort was slowly unravelling under sustained National Army pressure.

Fig. 20 (opposite) Map based on civilian compensation claims under the Damage to Property (Compensation) Act 1923 for counties Cork, Kerry, Limerick and Clare. Damage to urban and rural spaces was widespread throughout the Irish revolution. Destruction during the Civil War occurred on different scales, affecting public and personal spaces, and civic and private property. Examining what was destroyed, where and when, helps us to understand the nature and pace of the Civil War at local, regional and national levels. Examining returns from the Damage to Property (Compensation) Act 1923 for the counties of Cork, Kerry, Limerick, Clare and Sligo (some of the first records in the collection to be processed and released) shows that damage to Irish environments occurred as a result of military actions, but also for other reasons. Free State and republican forces trenched and barricaded roads and destroyed bridges to affect mobility in an area, which often impacted on private property. Locals submitted claims for damage to bicycles, motorbikes, cars, and horses and carts, which fell into newly opened trenches along familiar roads. The destruction of bridges resulted in horses and other livestock falling from compromised structures and being injured; in some cases animals drowned in the water below. In other instances debris from a destroyed bridge clogged the waterway below, causing bordering lands to flood, which, in turn, ruined crops and washed away fencing. Inhabitants evaded blocked roads and fallen bridges by carving their own passages through adjacent lands, which then sunk and flooded under the weight and regularity of new traffic. When it came to road blocking, the use of trees was particularly common. Claimants who listed trees destroyed on their property commonly claimed that cross-cut saws and axes were missing from barns and outhouses. It was not unusual for a single property to experience multiple incidents of tree destruction, or for hundreds of trees to be cut in a single instance. While both Free State and republican forces cut trees for use as road barricades – a common practice during the War of Independence as well – they were also destroyed for other reasons. For instance, foreign species of ornamental trees on landed estates were often destroyed as anti-colonial demonstrations, cut or burned with no intention of using them for road blocking. In other cases timber was cut and looted as it brought a good price in a scarce market. Some claimants provided detailed accounts of the trees they had lost, citing the number, species and trunk diameters in order to convey the extent of damage and to secure maximum compensation. Property and boundaries were violated in other ways. In many places stone walls were demolished and the debris thrown on roads to impede traffic or repurposed to form barricades. But their destruction – as well as that of other fences, gates and boundary markers – evidenced deeper social upheaval. Political unrest and military conflict in Ireland created a vacuum in public order that permitted agrarian unrest to resurface. Portions of walls and fences along grazing fields were thrown down and livestock driven off lands as protests against large landowners, grazing farmers and the alleged inequitable distribution of land. According to claimants, motivations for such destructive acts ranged from disputes over previous land purchases to arguments over grazing rights to outright intimidation. Damage to farmland, field equipment and crops was also prevalent. Multiple accounts detail the amount of cut turf, measured in creel baskets, broken up, scattered or thrown back into the bog. Sabotage in the form of meadow spiking damaged field implements and machinery, injured livestock and complicated the harvest. Hay and other crops were frequent targets for burning. Of all the methods of environmental destruction during the Irish Civil War, fire was perhaps the most versatile. Fire, both as a by-product of conflict and a tool for sabotage and intimidation, consumed a variety of objects in both the natural and built environments. As a means of controlling space, incendiarism destroyed dwelling houses, workshops and their contents, and was particularly politicised in the widespread destruction of 'big houses' throughout the country. [Text and map data: Justin Dolan Stover]

The late guerrilla phase (January–May 1923)

The republicans lacked an unarmed wing to their movement that would concentrate on issues arising from their disruption of local governance, courts, policing and land transfers. Though Sinn Féin and Dáil Éireann had created a vibrant republican civil administration during the War of Independence, similar non-violent resistance was neglected by the IRA, which concentrated primarily on the military campaign. Anti-Treaty TDs from the Second Dáil established a nominal republican Cabinet headed by 'President' Éamon de Valera, but it did not function or govern, and, according to Charles Townshend, 'had an air of unreality'.[17] Republicans never developed a robust propaganda arm, in sharp contrast to the Free State government. While Cumann na mBan attempted to fill this vacuum by covertly producing and distributing propaganda sheets (and posters and slogans painted on walls at night), its depleted

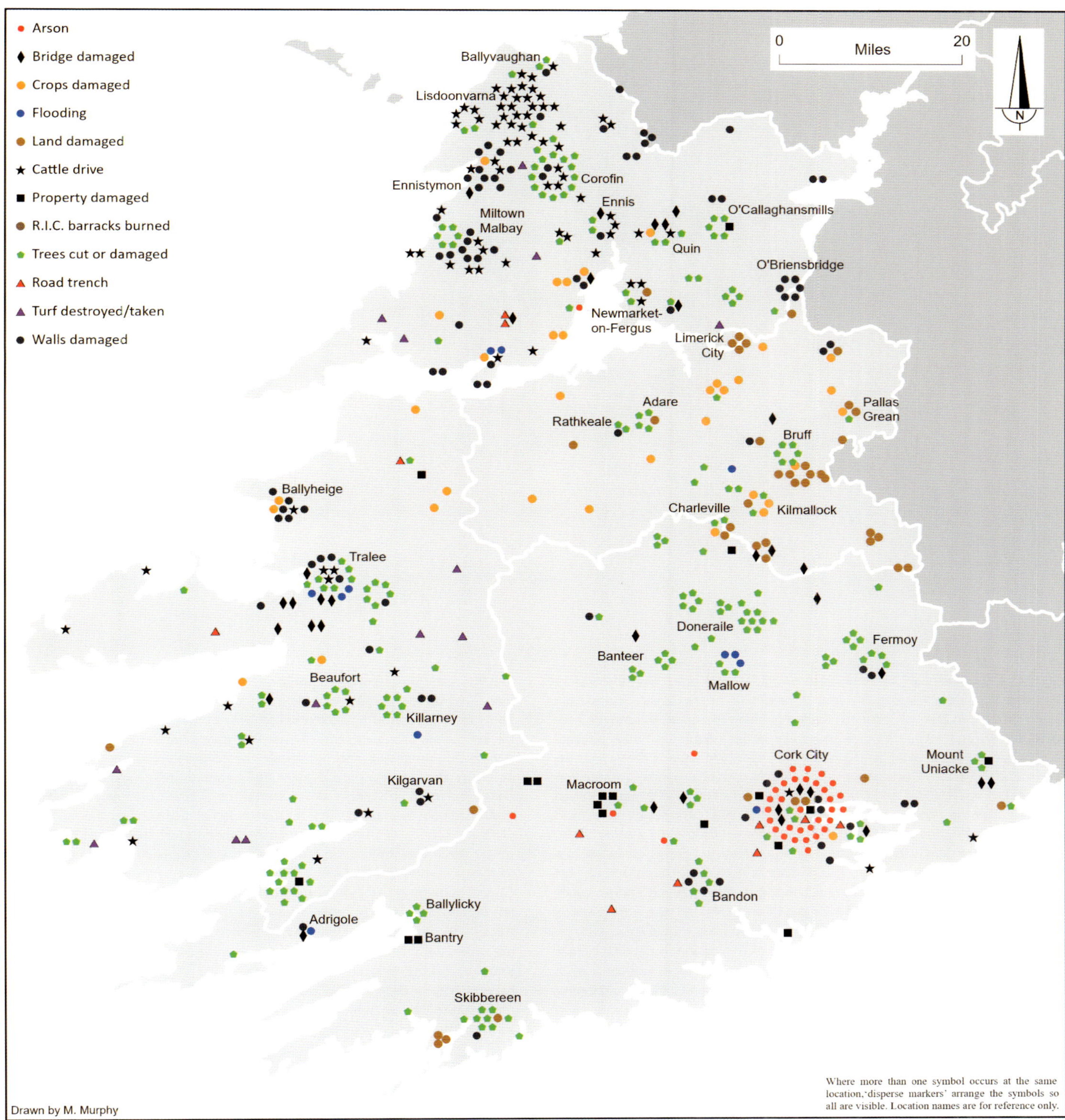

members were also increasingly diverted into a direct military role.[18] The republicans' lack of urgency about winning public support contributed to the IRA's rapid decline in the new year.

The National Army, as Gareth Prendergast has explained, focused on increasing the Free State's governing and economic capabilities.[19] By repairing communal infrastructure, reviving the economy, returning the state's rule of law and ending republican disruptions to ordinary life, the Free State forces hoped to starve the IRA of popular support. For example, amid widespread IRA interference and destruction with the railway network, the National Army created the Railway Protection, Repair and Maintenance Corps in September 1922. This unit of ordinary soldiers and mechanical, engineering and technical specialists maintained railway lines, stations and rolling stock and protected them from continuous IRA sabotage attacks. It also established fifty block houses to guard vulnerable sections of track. The development of

Fig. 21 Commissioner Michael Staines TD (right) and Superintendent Matthias McCarthy leading the first detachment of the Civic Guard from Dame Street into Dublin Castle to assume policing responsibilities in the new state, 17 August 1922. Six months earlier, in early February 1922, Michael Collins had set about establishing a new police force to replace the soon to be disbanded Royal Irish Constabulary (RIC). He formed an organising committee of hand-picked IRA, RIC and Dublin Metropolitan Police (DMP) men who had served Collins in various capacities during the War of Independence and tasked them with providing a blueprint for the force within three weeks. Under the chairmanship of Staines, the committee understood the significance of a national police force, a 'people's guard' distinct from its predecessor, as part of the Provisional Government's state building and legitimising efforts. While the centralised structure of the RIC would be maintained, the armed ranks, uniformed in blue rather than RIC green, would be filled almost exclusively by former IRA men in recognition of their years of service in the national cause. Once the Royal Dublin Society (RDS) in Ballsbridge was acquired as a temporary headquarters, another committee member, East Clare TD and former IRA commander Patrick Brennan assumed responsibility for recruitment and training. To qualify for service, recruits had to be aged between nineteen and twenty-seven, unmarried, literate, at least five feet nine inches in height with an average chest measurement of thirty-six inches. Successful applicants were issued with registered numbers, including some former policemen given preference if they had been dismissed from the RIC or had resigned for 'conscientious or patriotic motives'. In the politically polarised climate of early 1922, newspaper advertising was avoided, and recruits were selected on the basis of recommendations by IRA brigade officers. Brennan's central role, and the support of Superintendent Seán Liddy, another Clare TD and former IRA brigade officer, explains the disproportionate number of recruits arriving from Clare and neighbouring counties Limerick and Galway in the first wave of recruitment (Fig. 22). Brennan later recorded how anti-Treaty IRA opposition to the work of his appointment officers in counties like Cork, Kerry and Mayo negatively affected recruitment. On 25 April the Civic Guard headquarters was transferred to the recently vacated Kildare Barracks, where training continued until the announcement in early May that the majority of commissioned ranks would be awarded to former RIC men. Outraged recruits, including an influential anti-Treaty faction under Thomas Daly, issued an ultimatum to Staines on 15 May. They demanded the immediate expulsion of the five ex-RIC men and threatened drastic action if their demands were not met. When the commissioner sought to exert his authority at a general parade, over 900 recruits broke ranks, took up arms and refused to recognise the authority of Staines and his headquarters staff. Staines evacuated Kildare with most of his senior officers and, on Collins's orders, set up an alternative headquarters in Dublin. The stand-off between the Provisional Government and its police force was brought to a head when the Kildare armoury was raided by members of the Four Courts garrison on 18 June and defused a week later when Collins promised an inquiry into what became known as the Civic Guard 'mutiny'. On 18 August, the day after Staines led 380 civic guards into Dublin Castle, the executive council accepted the recommendations of the Commission of Enquiry: elected deputies like Staines and Brennan would be ineligible for service and, in order to win public confidence, the Civic Guard would be reconstituted as an unarmed, strictly non-political police force. Less than a month later, thirty-year-old Eoin O'Duffy, former National Army chief of staff, succeeded Staines as commissioner. The charismatic O'Duffy proved an effective leader, restoring discipline, formalising duties and instilling a moral and nationalist ethos in the Civic Guard. Concerned that 'every county in the state should have representation in the Guard', he also temporarily suspended recruitment from Clare, Limerick and Galway, the area described during the mutiny inquiry as 'Brennan's sphere of influence'. After the first detachments were deployed from September 1922, the IRA employed intimidatory tactics rather than violent physical attacks against the unarmed force. Harry Phelan, shot by the IRA in Mullinahone, County Tipperary on 14 November 1922, was the only member of the Civic Guard to die on duty during the Civil War. The Civic Guard was renamed An Garda Síochána (the Guardians of the Peace) and given legislative authority in August 1923. [Text: Brian McCarthy / Image: Cashman Collection © RTÉ Archives, 0505/068/ See also Evidence of Patrick Brennan, 21 July 1922, in Minutes of Evidence to Mutiny Enquiry; Brian McCarthy, *The Civic Guard Mutiny* (Cork, 2012)]

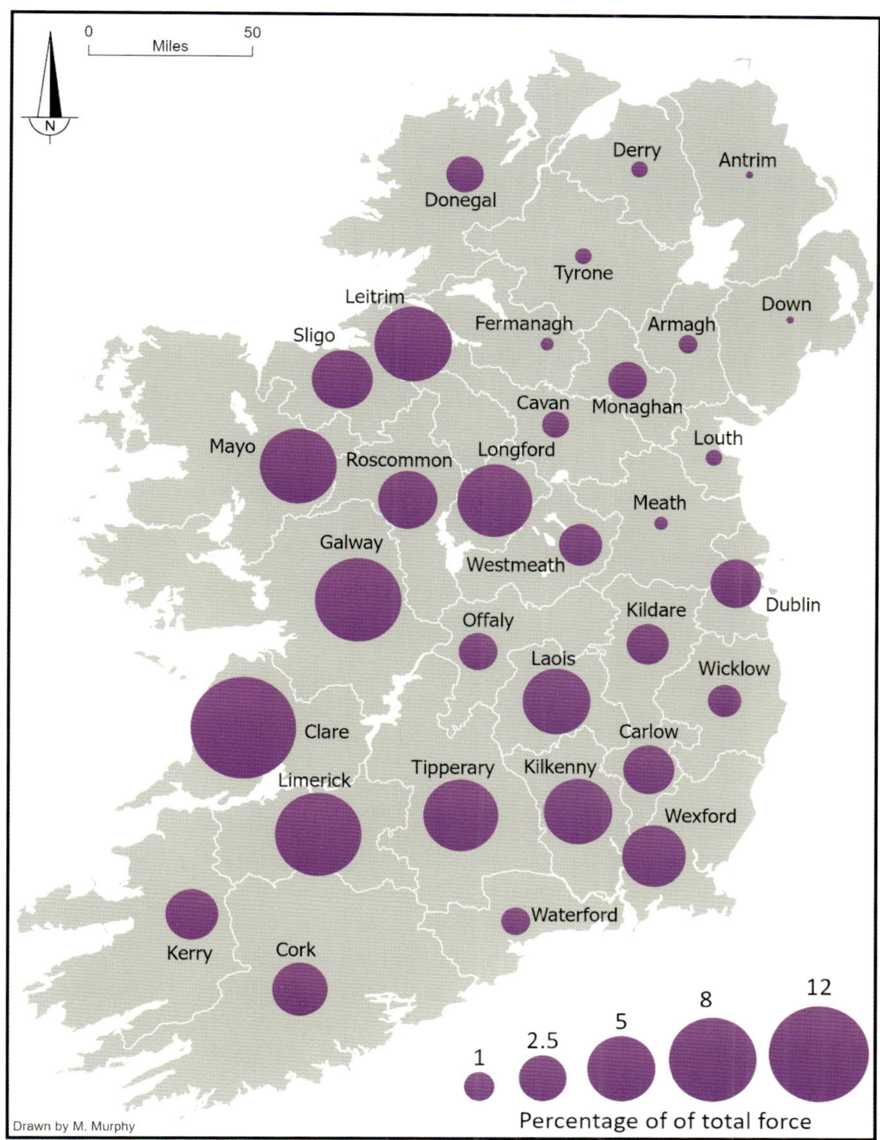

Fig. 22 Map: County of origin of Civic Guard recruits, February–May 1922. [Source: Civic Guard (Garda Síochána) Temporary Register, UCD. See also Liam McNiffe, *A History of the Garda Síochána* (Dublin, 1997), p. 36]

the Railway Corps underscores the priority the Free State authorities placed on normalisation and economic stability, which, in many ways, depended on the continued operation of Ireland's extensive railway network.[20]

Government investment in law and order also began to pay dividends. Throughout the revolutionary period local communities experienced periodic surges in ordinary crime, particularly at times when the police were besieged or absent. IRA policing efforts were haphazard and not always effective, particularly following the disbandment of the RIC and the British withdrawal from the Free State in early 1922.[21] The Provisional Government initially prioritised the creation of its new police force, the Civic Guard, but faced a serious setback when its first recruiting class mutinied in Kildare Barracks during May 1922.[22] The new force slowly recovered and then expanded during the rest of the year, opening scores of new stations in late 1922. By the end of the year nearly 2,000 guards had been deployed to roughly 200 stations across the country.[23] Momentum continued into 1923 as the unarmed force brought some stability to local communities without further inflaming tensions with anti-Treaty forces.

Outside the towns agrarian disorder had surged after the rapid British withdrawal in early 1922, and included threats, land seizures, cattle driving and other forms of agrarian harassment. This 'new Ranch War' (as described by James Donnelly) echoed similar outbreaks that struck rural Ireland in 1918 and 1920, and often targeted graziers operating on the eleven-month system and holdings controlled by the Congested Districts Board.[24] Agrarianism was seen by the Free State government as a danger that could spark wider class and social conflict. As Heather Laird explained: 'A connection was made between land seizures and anti-Treaty "irregularism", and a corresponding link forged between the defence of private property rights and the defence of the fledgling state.'[25]

In this unstable rural environment, the National Army organised a new unit known as the Special Infantry Corps (SIC) in January 1923. It eventually numbered about 4,000 troops and was deployed in areas experiencing social disorder, particularly relating to agrarian and industrial unrest.[26] As Gavin Foster explained: '[B]lurring the line between a conventional military force and professional civilianized constabulary, the SIC's origins and activities offer a window on the complex dynamics of disorder and violence during and immediately following the civil war.'[27] The SIC supported the Free State agricultural elite and sided with employers against militant trade unions during strikes. Foster points out that the SIC even sought to curtail *poitín* consumption because the Free State's metropolitan elite considered it representative of rural Ireland's disreputable character traits, particularly its lack of deference to state authority and ordinary law and order.[28]

Meanwhile, the National Army continued to diminish IRA units through raids, patrols and arrests, putting fighting groups on the defensive and driving them deeper into the hinterland. Remote republican strongholds such as the Ox Mountains in Sligo, the Glen of Aherlow in Tipperary, Gougane Barra in west Cork, the Iveragh Peninsula in Kerry, Kyle townland in south Wexford, and the Knockmealdown Mountains in Tipperary and Waterford were subjected to large-scale National Army sweeps and continuous raids. By this stage republican guerrillas primarily focused on

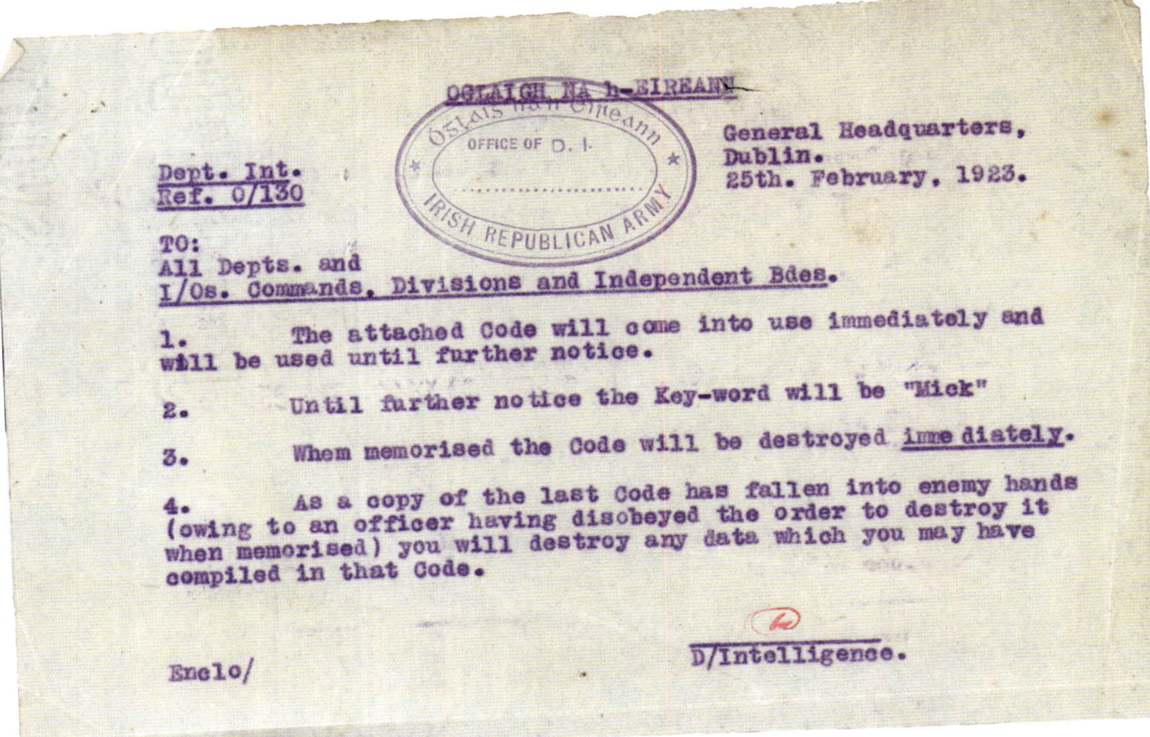

ÓGLAIGH NA h-ÉIREANN

OFFICE OF D. I.
IRISH REPUBLICAN ARMY

Dept. Int.
Ref. O/130

General Headquarters,
Dublin.
25th. February, 1923.

TO:
All Depts. and
I/Os. Commands, Divisions and Independent Bdes.

1. The attached Code will come into use immediately and will be used until further notice.

2. Until further notice the Key-word will be "Mick"

3. Whem memorised the Code will be destroyed imme diately.

4. As a copy of the last Code has fallen into enemy hands (owing to an officer having disobeyed the order to destroy it when memorised) you will destroy any data which you may have compiled in that Code.

Enclo/

D/Intelligence.

Fig. 23 IRA code cover sheet, 25 February 1923. The IRA communicated via written messages carried by a network of couriers. Much of this communication work was managed and undertaken by members of Cumann na mBan. Some of these messages were coded to mitigate against the disclosure of sensitive information should they fall into enemy hands. The National Army had much more secure communications, including wireless (radio) transmitters and receivers in its important headquarters. In smaller garrisons the National Army could depend on messenger couriers arriving by motor car, motorcycle, train and even, on occasion, airplane. [Document: from Joe Barrett (Clare) Intelligence files. Reproduced courtesy of Clare County Archives, with thanks to the Barrett and Sheehan families]

survival rather than disrupting Free State governance. Their public support continued to dry up, leaving the remaining IRA guerrillas isolated and vulnerable to the National Army's onslaught.

The Free State government ruthlessly prosecuted the war and wore down IRA forces during these final months. Despite a republican counter-reprisal arson campaign in February 1923, government executions continued both officially and unofficially. In March the National Army in Kerry killed dozens of IRA prisoners in shocking circumstances. In other areas state executions acted as clear reprisals for IRA resistance, such as the executions by firing squad of IRA leader Charlie Daly and three of his comrades in Drumboe Castle in Donegal on 14 March 1923.[29] It should be emphasised that official government-authorised executions were carried out across the country, in at least seventeen different towns/counties beyond Dublin. Seán Enright argues that this appears to have been a deliberate policy to spread responsibility for the controversial policy across major military command districts. Each execution made its own ripple in its immediate locale. Scores of prisoners were killed in custody and their corpses frequently dumped on the roadside. Such killings became deeply embedded in the republican collective memory and bred recriminations that lasted generations.

After the National Army captured the IRA deputy chief of staff, Liam Deasy, on 15 January 1923 and sentenced him to death, Deasy issued a public statement calling the IRA campaign futile and asking republicans to lay down their arms. IRA prisoners in Limerick, Clonmel and Cork prisons also appealed to the IRA leadership to end the conflict. The demoralised and dissenting prisoners were saying out loud what many republican leaders and rank and file thought privately – that armed resistance no longer offered republicans a feasible way to defeat the Treaty.

Free State victory and republican defeat

By this stage roughly 13,000 IRA Volunteers and about 400 republican women were imprisoned. Most were eventually transferred to major army camps and prisons in the Curragh and Dublin. But many also filled county jails in places like Cork, Kilkenny, Limerick, Sligo and Tralee. Most local National Army garrisons had their own facilities for captured republicans and civilians detained for questioning. Thus, imprisonment became part of the local experience of civil war, while in many areas humanitarian assistance for republican prisoners became one of the last visible manifestations of support for the anti-Treaty cause.

Throughout these final months thousands of anti-Treaty republicans went into hiding, dropped out of the movement or left the country entirely. Many IRA units ceased to function, and most others could no longer effectively resist the National Army. Facing the disintegration of its remaining forces, the IRA executive called a unilateral ceasefire on 30 April 1923. The following month the IRA dumped arms without formally surrendering to the Free State government. Though the killing and unrest continued on a reduced scale for months (and even years), opposition to the Treaty eventually moved to the parliamentary arena, where republicans ultimately found success.

At the end of the Civil War Irish society was highly militarised. In excess of 250,000 men and women had served in various armed (and unarmed) forces during the First World War, the War

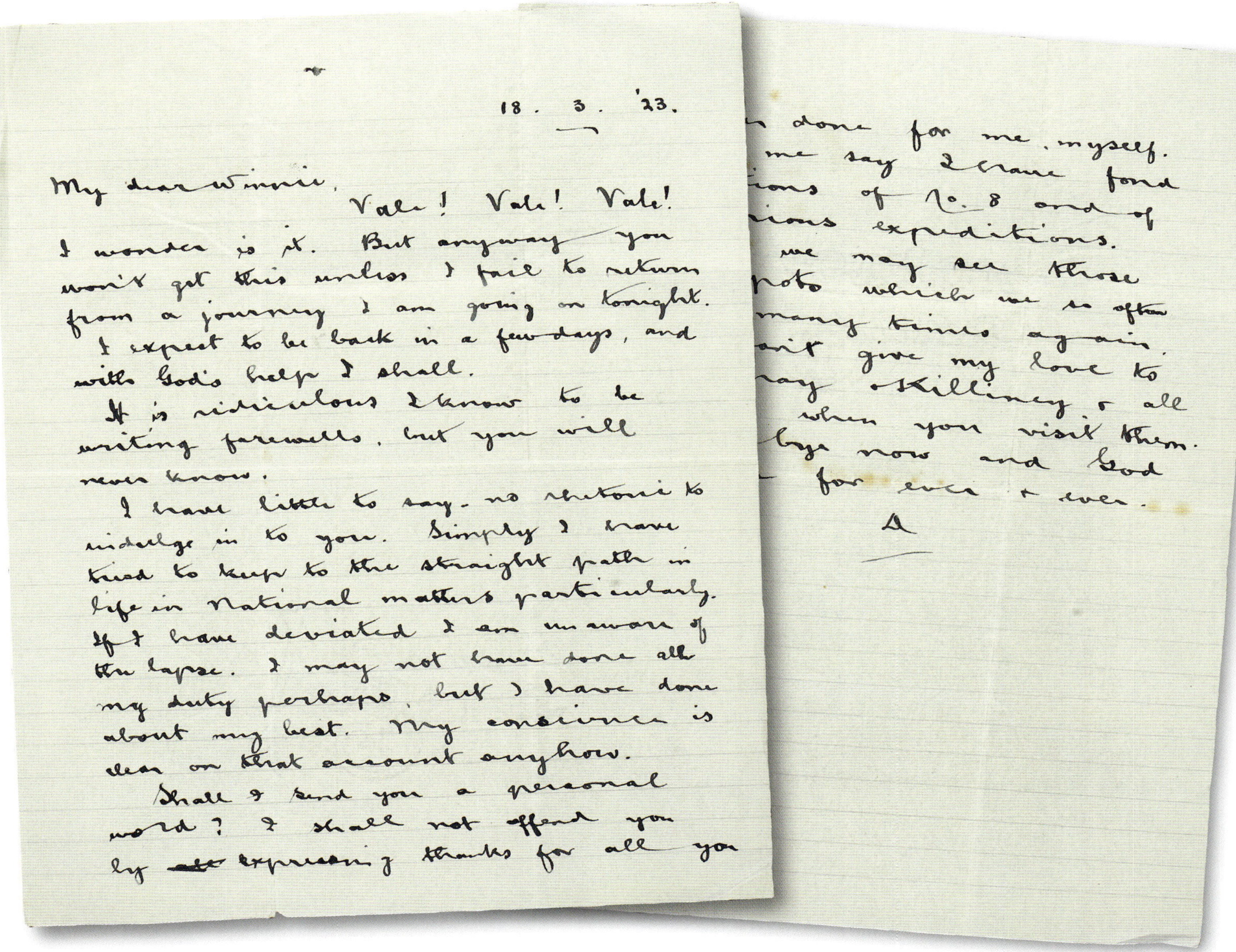

18. 3. '23.

My dear Winnie,

Vale! Vale! Vale!

I wonder is it. But anyway you won't get this unless I fail to return from a journey I am going on tonight.

I expect to be back in a few days, and with God's help I shall.

It is ridiculous I know to be writing farewells, but you will never know.

I have little to say - no rhetoric to indulge in to you. Simply I have tried to keep to the straight path in life in National matters particularly. If I have deviated I am unaware of the lapse. I may not have done all my duty perhaps, but I have done about my best. My conscience is clear on that account anyhow.

Shall I send you a personal word? I shall not offend you by ~~all~~ expressing thanks for all you

... done for me, myself.
... me say I crave fond
... ions of No. 8 and of
... ions expeditions.
... we may see those
... oto which we so often
... many times again.
... ait give my love to
... ay Killiney & all
... when you visit them.
... bye now and God
... for ever & ever.

A

Fig. 24 Letter from Austin Stack (1879–1929) to his future wife Winifred Gordon, 18 March 1923. At the time of writing, the Civil War was reaching a by now almost inevitable denouement, as Free State forces were circling in on the IRA leadership. In that context meetings of the army executive were difficult to organise and frequently disrupted by National Army search parties. At the end of March the army executive finally met at the Nire Valley in the Comeragh Mountains in County Waterford, where peace moves were discussed. Stack, the minister for finance in the republican government, was aware of the impending danger when he wrote to Winifred, 'It is ridiculous I know to be writing farewells, but you will never know'. Stack was resolute to the end in his defence of the republic; to him it was a matter of honour and principle: 'I have tried to keep to the straight path in life in national matters particularly. If I have deviated I am unaware of the lapse. I may not have done all my duty perhaps, but I have done about my best. My conscience is clear on that account anyhow'. In early April the encroaching National Army captured and wounded the IRA adjutant general, Tom Derrig, while the chief of staff, General Liam Lynch, was shot in the Knockmealdown Mountains and later died. Stack was also subsequently captured. [Document: National Library of Ireland, Austin Stack Papers, MS 22,398/11. See David McCullagh, *De Valera: Rise, 1882–1932* (Dublin, 2017), p. 314]

of Independence and the Civil War. Within every community in Ireland, veterans of different conflicts were present, known and visible. Their neighbours had to adapt to them and learn to accommodate their often-competing political loyalties, their grievances and their injuries, both physical and psychological.

It has become something of a trope to claim the Irish Civil War was not remembered. This is false: the conflict remained a living issue within Irish society for generations. In every city, town and village across the Free State, the Civil War was discussed by both civilians and combatants, particularly among those most directly impacted by events. But they did so quietly and in select company, fearful of reviving divisions with their neighbours or passing poisonous memories on to a new generation. Those who bore witness to the Irish Civil War often required decades to process what they had seen and experienced. For many, even that was not time enough.

The 'Sliabh na mBan' Armoured Car

Niall Murray

The December 1922 IRA attack on a National Army outpost in the mid-Cork village of Ballymakeera was notable for the key role played by the Rolls-Royce armoured car, the 'Sliabh na mBan'. On the night of 2 December National Army driver Jock McPeake, who had changed sides in the Civil War, took the car out of the barracks in Bandon with IRA assistance. On its way to a temporary stopover at Galvin's safe house at Clodagh near Crookstown, the 'Sliabh na mBan' almost certainly drove through the site of the Béal na Blá ambush, where, on 22 August 1922, McPeake had operated the armoured car's mounted machine gun. The IRA planned to use the newly acquired 'Sliabh na mBan' in an attack on Free State forces at Inchigeelagh, so McPeake next drove it to Kealkill, near Bantry, where it was kept overnight. Plans changed when IRA Volunteer Pat Hegarty was arrested with a revolver near Ballymakeera, a village close to the Cork–Kerry border, where around 100 National Army soldiers were billeted. It was likely that Hegarty would be executed if taken to Cork city, so the IRA devised a rescue plan that involved the 'Sliabh na mBan' driving through the early hours of Monday 4 December from Kealkill through Keimaneigh, Ballingeary and Renanirree towards Ballymakeera. IRA gunmen waited on hills north and south of the village. When the armoured car arrived around daybreak, it directed machine-gun fire at homes and businesses on Ballymakeera's single street. Gunfire was focused on the main army billet at the Hibernian Hotel, where Hegarty was being held. Firing also came from hillside riflemen and machine-gunners, and grenades and bombs were thrown by an IRA column that followed the car into the village on foot. The barrage of fire, which made resistance difficult and prevented National Army soldiers reaching their Lancia armoured car, provided cover for IRA rescuers to break into the hotel and liberate Hegarty. The battle lasted at least three hours and resulted in the deaths of local civilian Cornelius O'Leary and National Army Sergeant Thomas Nolan from Carlow town. Two wounded soldiers, Sergeant George McGlynn from County Kildare and Private William McNiece from Westmeath, died later in hospital. After the National Army soldiers surrendered, they were marched west by retreating Kerry IRA members. They were left at Loo Bridge railway station and walked from there to raise the alarm in Killarney. The IRA drove the damaged 'Sliabh na mBan' slowly toward Ballingeary, then to Gougane Barra. The car was hidden at a nearby mountain farm at Derreenlunnig, where several key engine parts were removed to render it inoperable if recaptured. The next day army search parties from Macroom focused efforts to find the 'Sliabh na mBan' on the Ballymakeera and Kilmichael areas. On Saturday 9 December the car was found hidden under furze at Cronin's Derreenlunnig farm. It was towed by the National Army to Macroom and later taken to Cork.

[These maps are adapted from work by Abarta Heritage for Cork County Council in 2022 on the movements of the 'Sliabh na mBan' armoured car around the December 1992 IRA attack on Ballymakeera. Mapping by Sara Nylund, research and text by Tara Clarke and Niall Murray using Landscapes of Revolution methodology developed by Dr Damian Shiels. Further reading: Donal Ó hÉalaithe (ed.), *Memoirs of an Old Warrior: Jamie Moynihan's fight for Irish freedom, 1916–1923* (Cork, 2014), pp. 240–8; Patrick J. Twhoig, *The Dark Secret of Béalnabláth* (Cork, 1991), pp. 216–21; P.J. Kavanagh, 'Carlow Men in Cork Ambush', *Carloviana: Journal of the Old Carlow Society*, vol. ii, no. 27, 1978–9, pp. 4–6.]

Fig. 1 The restored 'Sliabh na mBan' ('Slievenamon') armoured car, currently on display at the Curragh Military Museum. [Image: South Dublin Libraries/ David Power]

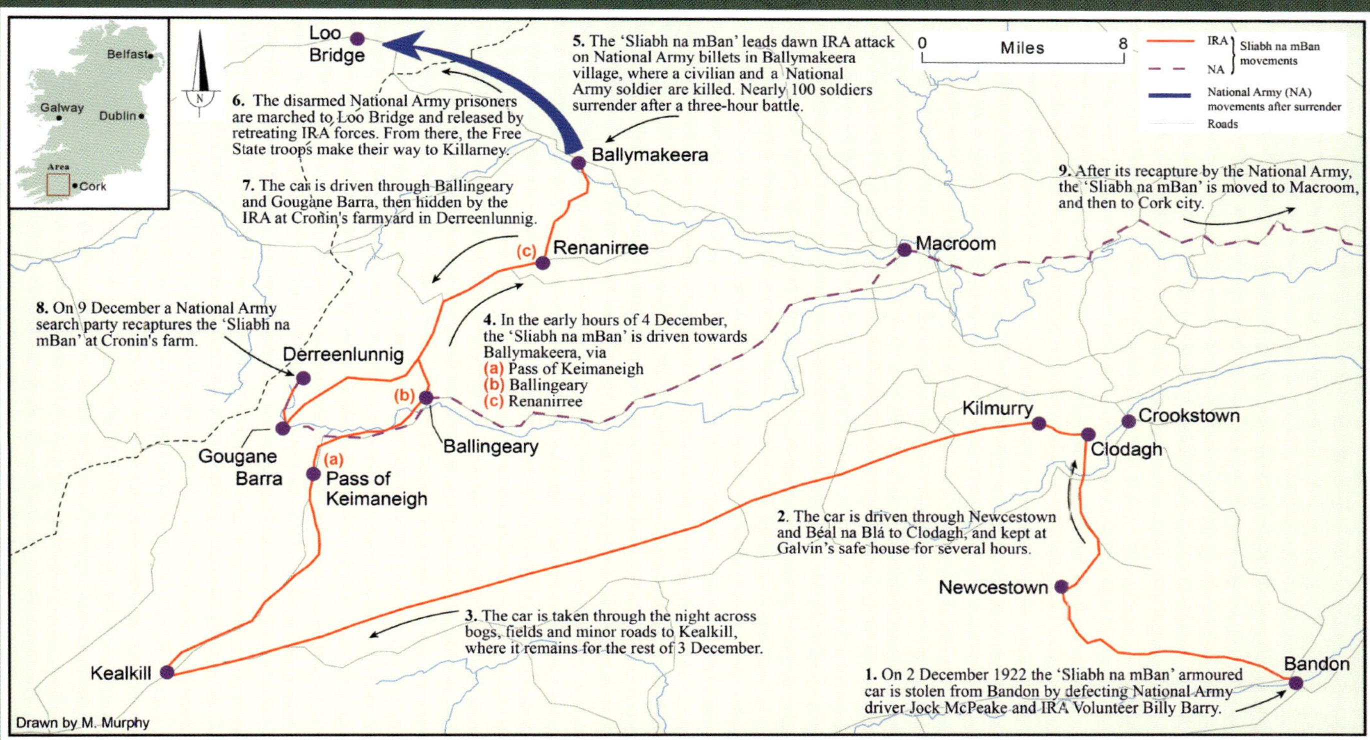

Fig. 2 Movements of the 'Sliabh na mBan' ('Silevenamon') armoured car around west Cork, December 1922.

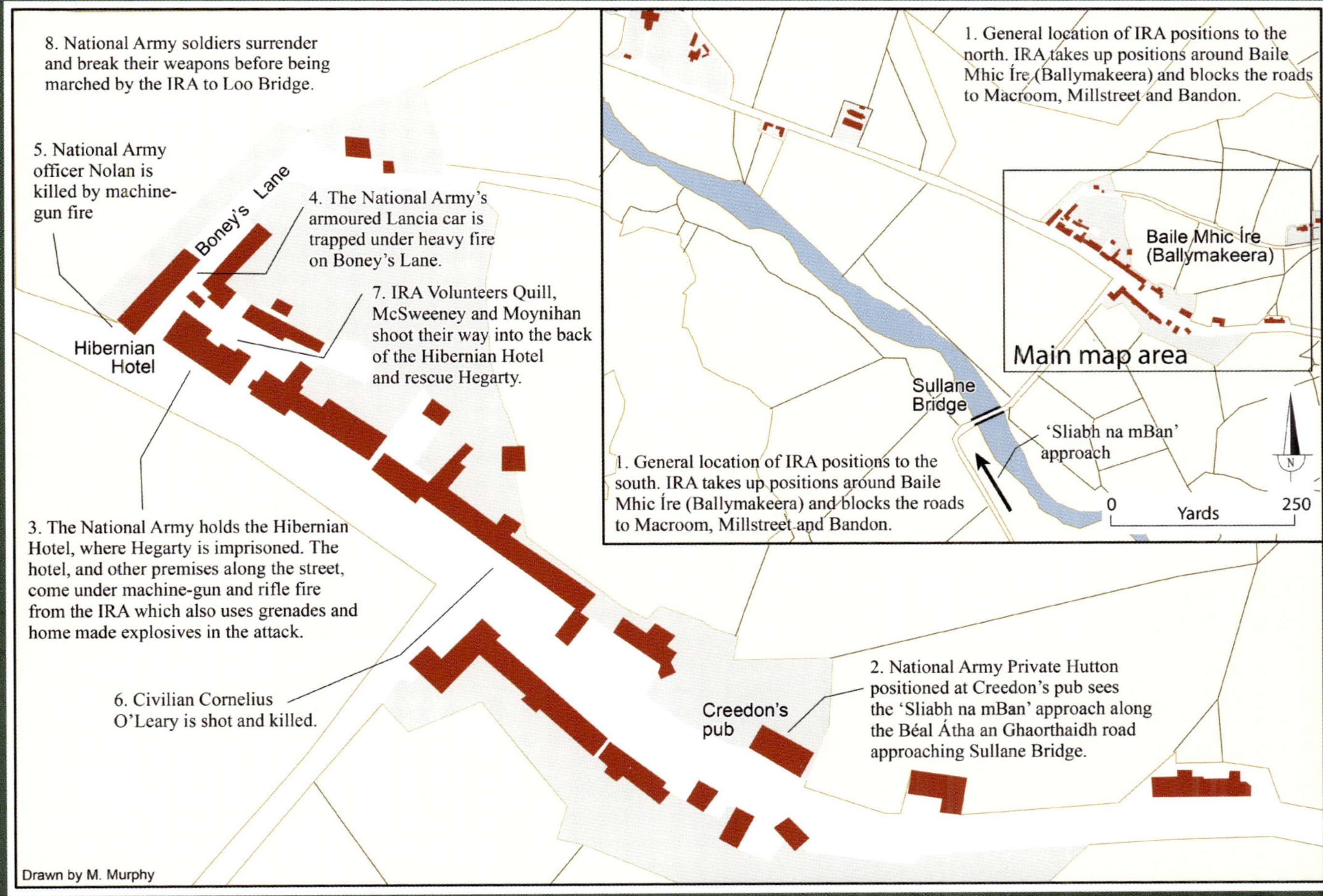

Fig. 3 IRA attack on the village of Ballymakeera, County Cork, 4 December 1922

CASE STUDY

Graffiti at Ash Hill Towers

Aidan Harte, Niall Murray and Joanna Brück

The material remains of the Civil War offer a unique and powerful perspective on the lived experience of the period. They represent a tangible connection with the past, intruding into the present in a way that demands an emotional reckoning, for their physicality calls attention to what – and who – is lost. Here, we discuss the extraordinary graffiti made by soldiers and prisoners at Ash Hill Towers, an eighteenth-century country house just outside Kilmallock, County Limerick.[1]

Ash Hill Towers was unusual in the revolutionary period for being occupied by four different armed forces. It accommodated the local Royal Irish Constabulary after the IRA destroyed its Kilmallock barracks in May 1920, and was in simultaneous use by over 100 members of the British army's Machine Gun Corps during the remainder of the War of Independence.[2] In the Civil War, an anti-Treaty IRA field headquarters was established at Ash Hill Towers during heavy local fighting in July 1922.[3] The house was abandoned in early August 1922 as the IRA fled the advancing National Army, which took over the house and retained control of the Kilmallock area thereafter.

Traces of conflict

Over eighty examples of graffiti survive in the attic rooms of the house, with another nineteen on a wooden door that was removed and is now in an outbuilding. The doors to each room have chains fixed to the outside, evidence of their use as makeshift holding cells.

Fig. 1 Ash Hill Towers, an eighteenth-century country house just outside Kilmallock, County Limerick. [Image: National Library of Ireland, L_ROY_10352]

Most of the graffiti is in pencil, although crayon was also used, and some was simply scratched into the plaster. Names and initials are common, often accompanied by army registration numbers and military ranks. It is perhaps no surprise that the military and political affiliations of those who left the graffiti were a central preoccupation.

Identifying names in the graffiti is not always easy. One reads 'E. Costello Kilfinane Prisoner of War Ash Hill Tower Kilmallock arrested 23.3.1921'. Costello was a Volunteer in Kilfinane Company of the East Limerick Brigade of the IRA; the reason for his arrest in 1921 is unknown, but he was briefly in custody a year earlier for firing at his local RIC barracks.[4] As a prisoner, making a mark was itself a small act of rebellion. Other names cannot be matched to local IRA companies, although the completeness of even the most reliable sources for IRA membership – lists compiled by surviving officers in the mid-1930s to help the Department of Defence verify military service pension claims – is not guaranteed.[5]

Some graffiti evokes the challenges of imprisonment; for example, a makeshift calendar marking off twenty-eight days and, in the same room, the ironic repetition six times of a line from a 1908 song, 'I Stand in the Land of Roses'. Other graffiti may have been created by soldiers stationed at Ash Hill Towers; for example, a list of munitions including 'Thom Rd 330'. This most likely dates to the Civil War when both sides were using Thompson sub-machine guns. Revolvers are depicted in three locations, as well as other images that might reflect the preoccupations of young men waiting for action, including scenes of a gunfight, a boxing match, horses and a bicycle. Scraped into the wall of the corridor is 'IRA [...] _arrison' – left, perhaps, as the anti-Treaty forces withdrew.

Complex histories

There are also several portraits. Some are naturalistic, like, for example, the side profile of a man with a moustache, while others are more cartoon-like. Local tradition suggests that the detailed side profile of a woman wearing a hat, watch and earrings may be of a nurse (Fig. 2). She is shown smoking a cigarette – a mark of female autonomy and defiance of conformity in 1920s Ireland. During the Civil War, anti-Treaty forces used Ash Hill Towers as a field-dressing station. Cumann na mBan personnel there were managed by a qualified nurse and two ambulances were available, possibly commandeered from nearby Kilmallock Workhouse.[6]

The complexity of individual histories is illustrated by the words '7211320 Lance Sgt. M. Duhig, 2nd Roy. Mun. Fus Khartoum SUDAN' in one of the rooms (Fig. 3). Martin Duhig served in the Royal Munster Fusiliers from 1913 until 1922. He was never a member of the IRA, at least according to nominal rolls of local battalions and those for his native Limerick city. This means he was almost certainly in Ash Hill Towers with the National Army,

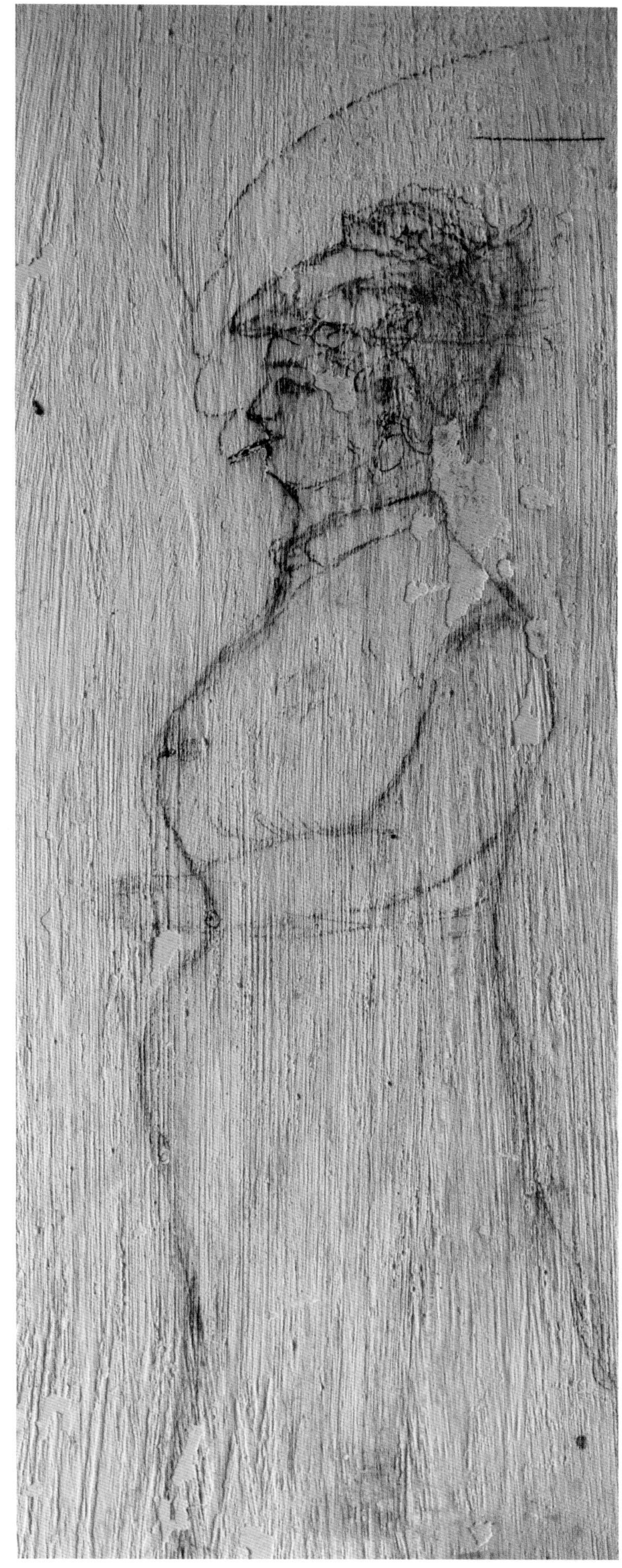

Fig. 2 Graffiti at Ash Hill Towers featuring the side profile of a woman smoking a cigarette. [Image: Aidan Harte]

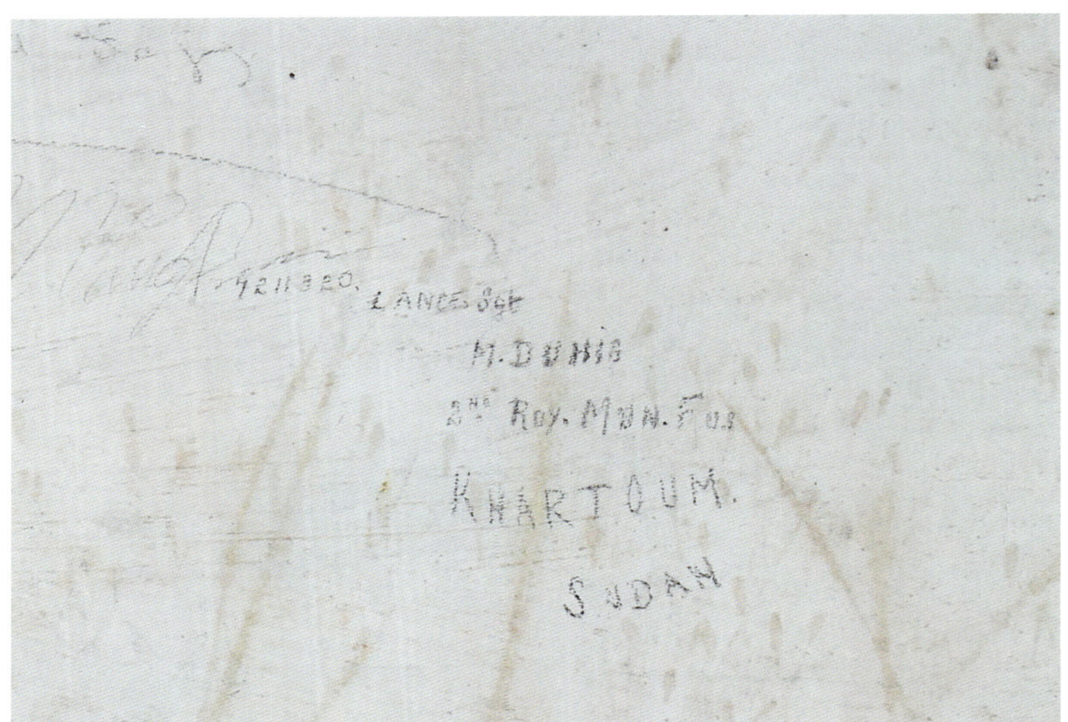

Fig. 3 Graffiti at Ash Hill Towers: '7211320 Lance Sgt. M. Duhig, 2nd Roy. Mun. Fus Khartoum SUDAN'. [Image: Aidan Harte]

Fig. 4 Graffiti at Ash Hill Towers featuring a mounted German cavalry officer. [Image: Aidan Harte]

dating his presence to no earlier than August 1922.[7] He does not appear in the National Army's November 1922 census, telling us that any National Army service was brief;[8] this may be reflected in the affiliation he chose to inscribe on the walls of Ash Hill Towers. Elsewhere, the detailed rendering of a mounted German cavalry officer may have been made by a member of the British military stationed at Ash Hill Towers during the War of Independence or by a member of the anti-Treaty IRA or of the National Army who had previously served in the British army (Fig. 4).

The destruction of big houses throughout the revolutionary period is well documented.[9] In contrast, at Ash Hill Towers the symbolic potential of the big house was drawn on to create new forms of authority in an unstable political landscape. One hundred years later the fragmented narratives of graffiti in a dusty attic leave affective traces of the disruption, ambiguities and human costs of conflict, summoning ghosts banished to the periphery of history.

Fig. 5 (above) National Army soldiers on the main street of Bruff, County Limerick, late July 1922. To impede the southern advance of the National Army after the fall of Limerick City on 21 July 1922, the retreating IRA established a defensive line across south Limerick, centred on Kilmallock. The strategically important, walled market town was the south-western vertex of what became known as the Bruff-Bruree-Kilmallock triangle. Between 20 July and 5 August 1922 this area saw the heaviest continuous fighting of the Civil War. The opening skirmishes in the area went in the republicans' favour, with the IRA taking Bruff (at the triangle's apex) on 21 July after a successful attack on the National Army garrison at the Old Barracks on Main Street. Bruff, however, was soon retaken, and on 30 July the IRA was pushed out of Bruree by about 300 National Army soldiers, supported by two armoured cars. After an IRA counter-attack on Bruree was repulsed on 2 August, General Eoin O'Duffy and his second in command, Major General W.R.E. Murphy, focused on Kilmallock. An experienced First World War officer, Murphy conceived a plan for a deliberate attack on multiple fronts (operation order No. 6), which contrasted with a loose IRA command style. Those problems of what Michael Hopkinson described as 'local particularism' undermined cooperation between the IRA's Cork, Kerry and Limerick brigades around Kilmallock but the National Army commanders, who had been stung by determined republican resistance at Bruff and Bruree, were unaware of this undercurrent of dissension. Eoin O'Duffy believed that 'on the Kilmallock frontier' they would face the 'best fighting material the irregulars [could] muster'. From 3 August, the National Army formed a semi-circular cordon around the town, stretching from Bruree in the west to Riversfield House in the south-west. Headquartered at Ballycullane on the northern outskirts of Kilmallock, the 2,000 men under O'Duffy and Murphy faced an estimated 1,000 IRA Volunteers under Liam Deasy and Seán Moylan, with field headquarters at Ash Hill Towers. Kerry Volunteer Johnny O'Connor later recalled the incongruity of the filthy and exhausted IRA fighters sleeping along the corridors of the Gothic mansion after the evacuation from Limerick city. Frank O'Connor, too, recorded the surrealism of the candlelit hall where the men, with 'rifles slung over their shoulders', were quietly observed by the 'tusked and antlered heads' of the big game trophies mounted on the walls. As historian John O'Callaghan notes, 'the geography of Kilmallock', sitting on the banks of the River Loobagh and surrounded by hills, 'lent itself to a stubborn defence'. This is why Murphy's plan of attack prioritised those elevated positions, which also allowed the National Army 'to maximise its decisive advantage – the 18-pounder gun sited on a hill outside the village of Dromin to the north'. The operation commenced on the morning of 4 August. While heavy IRA rifle and machine-gun fire on the slopes of Kilmallock Hill answered National Army artillery, it proved little more than a delaying action to cover a large-scale IRA evacuation. IRA Volunteers from Cork and Kerry had already started to slip away to defend their southern flank after the National Army landing at Fenit outside Tralee on 2 August. Murphy's men commanded all of the high ground around Kilmallock on 5 August, and were met with only a token resistance when they marched into the town. On 8 August substantial IRA columns from Cork departed the Kilmallock front by commandeered trains, racing to the southern coast to unsuccessfully challenge the National Army's amphibious landings at Passage West, Union Hall and Youghal, thereby further weakening the collapsing IRA defence. The National Army quickly seized Adare, Rathkeale and Newcastle West in the following days. Within two weeks of the capture of Kilmallock, the National Army held every significant urban centre in north Munster, and clasped hands with National Army troops pushing north and east from Cork and Kerry. The line fighting around Kilmallock in late July and early August 1922, involving defined fronts, fortified buildings, artillery positions and even trenches dug at Knocksouna Hill, represented the most classic example of conventional warfare during the Irish Civil War. Better armed, led and organised, the National Army decisively defeated much of the IRA 'field army'. The republicans disbanded, returned to their home areas and prepared to resume the offensive using the guerrilla warfare techniques they had mastered against the crown forces in 1920–1921. [Image: Desmond FitzGerald Photographs, P80/ PH/64. Reproduced by kind permission of UCD Archives / Quotations: Michael Hopkinson, *Green Against Green: The Irish Civil War* (Dublin, 2014) p. 281; *Limerick Chronicle*, 29 July 1922; Cormac K.H. O'Malley and Tim Horgan (eds), *The Men Will Talk to Me: Kerry interviews by Ernie O'Malley* (Cork, 2012), p. 292; Frank O'Connor, *An Only Child* (New York, 1961) pp. 215–6; John O'Callaghan, *The Battle for Kilmallock* (Cork, 2012), pp. 12, 49–50; John O'Callaghan, 'The War for Limerick County', in Seán William Gannon (ed), *'The Inevitable Conflict': Essays on the Civil War in County Limerick* (Limerick, 2022)]

Moore Hall, County Mayo

John Crowley

Fig. 1 (above) Aerial view of the ruins of Moore Hall, located near the village of Carnacon, County Mayo. This 'big house' dates to the late eighteenth century, with the design credited to Waterford-born architect John Roberts. In the early 1900s the house and estate (c.12,500 acres in extent) was owned by the novelist George Augustus Moore, who had inherited it from his father George Henry Moore, a landlord and Catholic MP for County Mayo, who had played a leading role in founding the Catholic Defence Association while also a prominent supporter of the Tenant League. A bitter falling out between George Augustus and his younger brother Maurice over land, finance and religion meant that neither brother resided in Moore Hall at the time of the Civil War. The house was burned on 31 January 1923 by the IRA in reprisal for the executions of republican prisoners, which had totalled thirty-four during that month alone. Operation Order No. 16, which was issued to the officers commanding of all IRA divisions, targeted senators' houses for burning in retaliation for the government's execution policy. While Moore Hall was in the ownership of George Moore, it was targeted principally because of his brother's membership of the Free State Senate. The latter's stance in relation to republican opponents of the Treaty, whom, he claimed, as Daithí Ó Corráin points out, 'were not genuine republicans because they did not attest to the republican ideal of "government by the people for the good of the people"', may also have influenced the attack. Moore joined Fianna Fáil in 1928 and, in the same year, published *British Plunder and Irish Blunder*, a pamphlet on the land-annuities issue that influenced the party's commitment to withhold the payment of the annuities to Britain. The first Fianna Fáil government withheld the payment in 1932, sparking a six-year 'economic war' with Britain, which regarded the annuities as part of the debt the Free State owed under the Treaty. [Image: courtesy of Michael Reynolds / See Daithí Ó Corráin, '"A Most Public Spirited and Unselfish Man": The career and contribution of Colonel Maurice Moore, 1854–1939', *Studia Hibernica*, no. 40 (2014), p. 125; Donal Ó Drisceoil, *Peadar O'Donnell* (Cork, 2001), pp. 48–50]

Fig. 2 Portrait of Colonel Maurice Moore (1854–1939). A professional soldier and veteran of the Boer War, Moore was an Irish-langauge enthusiast and Gaelic League activist and a close ally of the League's founder Douglas Hyde. He was also a strong advocate of the Irish agricultural cooperative movement. A member of the provisional committee of the Irish Volunteers, he left John Redmond's National Volunteers in 1916 when he became dissatisfied with the Irish Parliamentary Party's influence over the military organisation. In the aftermath of the Rising, he lent his support to Sinn Féin. In 1921 he was sent as a Dáil Éireann envoy to South Africa to garner support for Irish independence. He viewed the Treaty as a stepping stone to further freedom, and called into question the republican credentials of those who opposed it. A member of the Free State Senate from its inception in 1922 until its abolition in 1936, he also served in its successor, Seanad Éireann, from 1938 until his death the following year. [Image: National Library of Ireland, POOLE 2797/1]

Telegráfa an Puist.

Ní mór an fuirm seo cur le h-aon fiafrú a déanfar mar geall ar an telegrám so.
(This form must accompany any enquiry respecting this telegram).

Oifig Tosnuighthe, agus Teagaisc Seirbhísí.

Táille le díol } s. d.

Stampa Oifige.

MERRION 1 FE 23 DUBLIN

Belmullet

Sinneadh isteach ar a (Handed in at) } M.

Fachta annso ar a (Received here at) } M.

Go (TO)

1 52 3 30

Col Moore 5 Sea View Terrace
Ailesbury Road Dublin
Moorehall house burned down
last night nothing saved
Reilly

(a) Foghluim Gaedhilg, cabhruig le cleasa na nGaedheal, agus cuiduig le Saothar Gaedhealach. (b) Cuir do chuid airgid i mbanc an Puist. (c) Sealbuig Telefón.

(a) Learn Irish, foster Irish games and support Irish Industries. (b) Put your savings into the Post Office Bank. (c) Instal a Telephone.

(5545) —1,600,000.6-22.A. Thom & Co.,Ltd.,Dublin.

Fig. 3 (top) Moore Hall, Castlebar, County Mayo. [Image National Library of Ireland, L_IMP_3854] **Fig. 4** (above) Telegram sent by James Reilly, land steward, Moore Hall, County Mayo on 1 February 1923 to inform Colonel Maurice Moore that Moore Hall had been burned down and nothing was saved. [Document: National Library of Ireland, Colonel Maurice Moore Papers, MS 8,489/2/8]

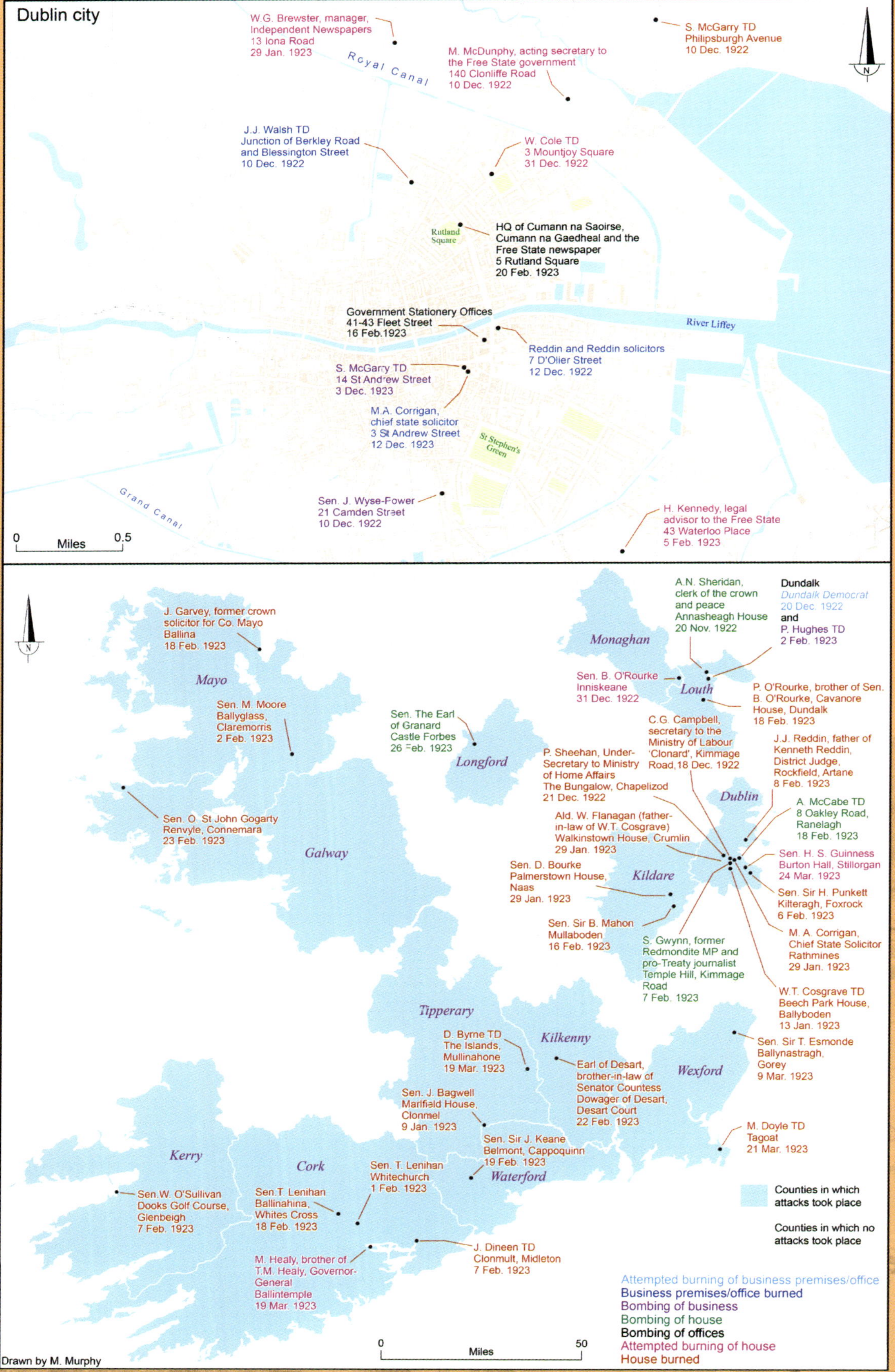

Fig. 5 Map showing the main incidents of IRA attacks (mainly incendiary) on properties of individuals associated with the Free State, December 1922 - March 1923. On 30 November 1922 IRA Chief of Staff Liam Lynch sent instructions for operations against 'the enemy', which included shooting on sight TDs who had voted for the Provisional Government's Army (Special Powers) Resolution and the destruction of residences and offices of those prominently associated with the state. This included the homes of all senators in the newly created Free State upper house, which met for the first time on 11 December 1922. Following the killing of Seán Hales TD and the wounding of Pádraig Ó Maille TD on 7 December, the Free State extrajudicially executed four leading republican prisoners in Mountjoy Gaol, which seemed to act as a deterrent to further attempts on the lives of parliamentarians; the campaign against property, however, began in earnest with the burning of the house of Seán McGarry TD in Dublin, which resulted in the tragic death of his seven-year-old son. [Updated version of a map first published in John Crowley et al. (eds), *Atlas of the Irish Revolution* (Cork, 2017) / Sources: contemporary newspaper reports; Donal O'Sullivan, *The Irish Free State and its Senate* (London, 1940), pp. 99–109]

CASE STUDY

'Small House' Burnings during the Irish Civil War: A County Kilkenny case study

Eoin Swithin Walsh

The literature of revolutionary Ireland usually mentions the burning of more than 300 'big houses' during the War of Independence and the Civil War. That is understandable given the intrinsic architectural and heritage value of the properties and their symbolic resonance in the landscape, but also because the demise of the big house had lasting consequences for local rural economies. Often overlooked in the historiography are the numerous 'small house' burnings perpetrated by both sides during the Civil War. These did not always make the headlines due to the humbler status of the buildings and their occupants. Similar to the big house burnings, the peak of these smaller-scale arson attacks occurred during the Civil War's guerrilla phase, particularly after January 1923. As such, they fit into what Gemma Clark has termed the 'everyday violence' of the Irish Civil War.[1]

While small house burnings were occasionally motivated by long-held agrarian grievances, most were the result of an inhabitant's – or a family's – involvement, or perceived involvement, in some aspect of the conflict. Reminiscent of the reprisal attacks of the War of Independence, the experience was deeply traumatic for the displaced families, particularly for women, children and the elderly, who, unlike the young men who could go on the run, were resident in the houses when they were attacked.

This type of warfare tended to escalate locally as a cycle of burnings and reprisal attacks. For the hard-pressed and under-resourced IRA in early 1923, arson was a cost-efficient and effective way to demonstrate continued resistance to the Irish Free State. The deployment of arson against their republican opponents was more difficult for National Army troops, who were ostensibly ruled by a code of discipline. Yet National Army soldiers still conducted arson attacks, often while dressed in civilian clothes, seemingly driven by a need to strike back at their elusive IRA opponents.

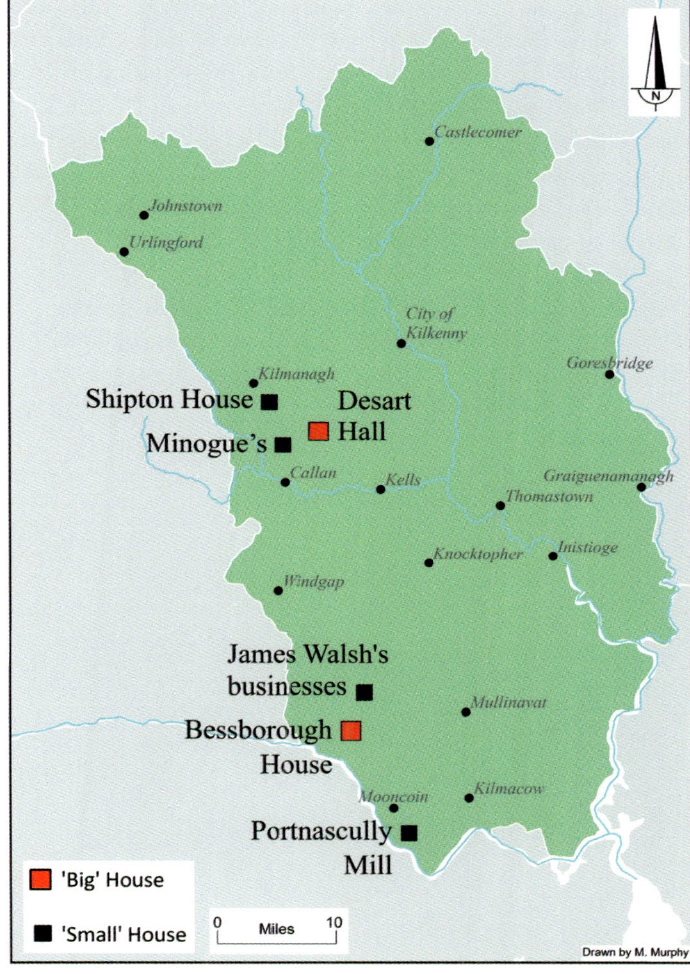

Fig. 1 Map showing the locations of the six 'big' and 'small' houses burned in south Kilkenny between the end of February and the beginning of April 1923, highlighting the reprisal/counter-reprisal nature of arson attacks by the IRA and the National Army. [Map data: Eoin Swithin Walsh]

Small house burnings in County Kilkenny, March–April 1923

An investigation of a three-week period in south County Kilkenny highlights the different elements and repercussions of this type of warfare. Two big house burnings occurred in Kilkenny during late February 1923: Desart Hall in Cuffesgrange and Bessborough House in Piltown. Less than a month later, on 18 March 1923, the home of Dr Daniel Byrne, a Farmers' Party TD living at The Islands, near Mullinahone, was burnt down by the IRA. Byrne may have been targeted as a pro-Treaty member of the Free State parliament; however, the fact that his brother-in-law, Captain Eddie Cuddihy, was a serving National Army officer in the local area, and had previously lived in the house, was a more likely reason for the arson attack. On 20 March the Teehan family home in Kilmanagh – known as Shipton House – was burnt down by Free State soldiers, who also struck the next night in nearby Ballyclovan, burning Richard Minogue's home and grocery business.

Set on 125 acres of farmland, Shipton House had been a crucial IRA meeting place and safehouse during the War of Independence. According to Bill Quirke, officer commanding of the 2nd Southern Division IRA, it was also 'a Field GHQ for a considerable period' during the Civil War.[2] This made the Teehan family a prominent target for local National Army troops, as were the Minogues, who often supplied food and housed fugitive republicans. The head of the Teehan household was fifty-four-year-old Bridget, mother of twelve children, including two daughters, Molly and Kitty, who were leading members of Kilkenny Cumann na mBan. One son, Richard, had been imprisoned after his capture during an IRA ambush in Kilmanagh the previous October. Molly Teehan later recalled the events of 20 March 1923. Local tensions were high after the recent burning of Dr Byrne's house, and Free State forces were alerted to the presence at the Teehan home of the IRA leadership en route to an executive meeting in County Tipperary:

> President [Éamon] De Valera called during [the] night with [Frank] Aiken, Austin Stack, Seany Dowling, Tom Derrig [and] Seany Hyde [...] All the local men were on the run & were it not for our help, the whole crowd could have been captured in a strange countryside. [I] got safe conduct for them & that night, scarcely had the company gone, when the house was raided & burned by armed & masked men.[3]

Fig. 2 Photograph of the home and rebuilt business premises of Kilkenny county councillor, James Walsh, in Templeorum, Piltown, included in the compensation file held in the National Archives of Ireland (photographed circa late 1920s). The building was set alight by an armed IRA party at midnight on Easter Monday 2 April 1923. It was not Walsh's first encounter with the IRA. During the previous months his delivery van was taken and destroyed, and he was also held captive by the IRA for three weeks. [Image: National Archives FIN/COMP/2/10/78. Reproduced by kind permission of the director of the National Archives]

James Walsh, Templeorum

Two weeks after the Shipton burning, at midnight on Easter Monday, 2 April 1923, an IRA party set fire to a dwelling house, grocery and bakery owned by a Kilkenny county councillor, James Walsh, in Templeorum, Piltown.[4] Although his premises was over 30 kilometres (*c.* 19 miles) from Shipton, Walsh was targeted because of his repeated and public denunciation of IRA violence, including at council meetings. Indeed, Walsh had already suffered for his fierce opposition to the anti-Treaty cause. Republicans boycotted his businesses, and he was imprisoned by the IRA for three weeks in 1922. This made him a leading candidate for any reprisal on Free State supporters in the area.[5] He and his wife, Nannie, had eleven children, the youngest just a toddler, so the destruction of their home and businesses (including the stock and contents) caused considerable hardship for the Walsh family. A number of their employees were also faced with unemployment.

Portnascully Mill

The next house burning occurred two nights later, in the neighbouring parish of Mooncoin. This time the target was Portnascully Mill, the family home of Jack 'Na Coille/Culla' Walsh (no relation to James), leader of the 9th Battalion Kilkenny IRA. On the run for many months by April 1923, Walsh was not at home on the night of the reprisal attack. His fifty-five-year-old widowed mother, Mary, later described how she and her daughters were awakened by National Army soldiers in mufti in the early hours of 4 April:

> [N]ine men, all armed with rifles and revolvers and carrying petrol tins entered the yard. I was in bed. I saw the men pumping petrol on the outhouses and I got up and went to the bedroom window. One of the men told me to get up at once and open the door. I refused [...] he drove in the window. My daughter came down and opened the door. One of the men rushed in and ordered us all out [...] We dressed and went out. The men then sprinkled petrol on the chairs and tables and on the children's bed. We went out into the yard and let the cattle [out] into the field. The dwelling house was then set on fire. Bombs must [have] be[en] used as the walls shattered.[6]

Along with the destruction of the five-bedroomed house and outhouses, five tons of valuable hay and five tons of mangolds – winter feed for the livestock – were also destroyed.

Fig. 3 Jack 'Na Coille' Walsh (1894–1967) and Hannie McGrath on their wedding day in July 1946. Jack 'Na Coille' Walsh was officer commanding, 9th Battalion, Kilkenny Brigade IRA during the War of Independence and Civil War. The battalion was headquartered in Mooncoin parish. His family home at Portnascully Mill, Mooncoin was burned by non-uniformed National Army soldiers on 4 April 1923 while he and his brother Ned were on the run. [Image: courtesy of the Delahunty family, Portnascully]

Trauma

Such arson attacks had far-reaching economic consequences for the families, but we should also consider the trauma induced by violent attacks on the family home. It was often the women, children or the elderly who were most exposed and had to face night-time invasions by menacing attackers bent on destruction. Terrorised and fearing possible physical assault, they were forced to watch helplessly as their possessions and keepsakes, and very often their livelihoods, went up in smoke. As Mary McAuliffe, Louise Ryan, Linda Connolly and others have written with reference to the blurred lines between the 'home front' and the 'battle front' during the War of Independence, this type of warfare, centred on the domestic sphere, thrust women and children unwillingly onto the front line. While the Military Service Pensions Collection files include some detail about the nature and financial cost of these attacks, the consequential trauma suffered is not well documented. Indeed, the necessity to relive the event during their required attendance at court to secure compensation must have reinforced the trauma. Mary Walsh's case, following the destruction of Portnascully Mill, went all the way to the High Court after the state appealed the compensation awarded by a lower court because of her son's IRA activities. In that hearing Mary Walsh gave a masterclass in deflection while under cross-examination. She skilfully walked a fine rhetorical line between proving she played no part in helping to 'subvert' the Free State and not undermining the cause for which her children fought.

All the victims of Civil War arson in this Kilkenny case study received some form of modest compensation and their homes were later rebuilt. It is important, when considering the physical destruction wrought by the Civil War, not to neglect these small house burnings, perpetrated by both sides and replicated across the country, nor their impact on families and communities.

Fig. 4 Mary Walsh (standing here beside her mother, Mrs Conway, Tybroughney, Piltown, *c.*1890). Mary was mother of Jack 'Na Coille' and Ned Walsh and was present with her daughters at their home at Portnascully Mill when it was raided and set alight by National Army soldiers on 4 April 1923. This was a reprisal attack for the burning of James Walsh's home and business two nights previously. Some years later Mary Walsh took to the witness stand at the High Court and defended her compensation claim, which the state tried to block. [Image: courtesy of the Delahunty family, Portnascully]

CASE STUDY

Tormore: The strategic use of a cave dugout during Sligo's Civil War

Robert Mulraney, Marion Dowd and James Bonsall

In 1936 a priest arrived at a remote farm in County Sligo. A young Chris Branley joined the priest's small group to visit a cave, unknown to him, on his family land. It was here that the priest, the boy's father and others had spent six weeks on the run in 1922, here that Billy Pilkington 'had promised God that [he] would become a priest if he survived'.[1]

Following a tentative Truce period, the 3rd Western Division under the command of GOC Billy Pilkington sustained a reluctant campaign of engagement with Free State forces. The National Army's ability to successfully buttress Arthur Griffith's election meeting in Sligo town in April 1922 saw the IRA switch to a guerrilla campaign, as county towns fell to the National Army. In July, however, a spectacular divisional ambush on National Army troops at Dooney Rock/Tobernalt, which killed four soldiers, saw the capture of GOC Seán Mac Eoin's 'Ballinalee' armoured car, which was regularly deployed against National Army garrisons that summer.

Retreat from Rahelly

When open conflict in Dublin and Munster had been contained by the National Army in September 1922, thousands of troops, many of whom were seasoned fighters, were transported with heavy armaments to Mayo and Sligo.[2] Billy Pilkington's division fiercely resisted, but was eventually forced to retreat to its base at Rahelly House in north Sligo. On 18 September the National Army captured Rahelly, forcing an evacuation of approximately 120 IRA men, who took refuge in the Dartry Mountains. Six of them were isolated two days later, disarmed and machine-gunned to death by officers acting under the orders of Seán Mac Eoin.[3] Many more men were arrested, while others managed to break through the cordon and retreat into the mountains.[4]

As September turned to October, the *Derry Journal* reported that 'absolute quiet reigns [...] There is no trace of any further irregulars in the neighbourhood of Rahelly or on the mountains'.[5] Over thirty IRA men remained on the run, however, and spent up to six weeks in Tormore Cave, high in the mountains overlooking Glencar Valley, one of the most successfully deployed IRA dugouts in the country.

Excavating Tormore Cave

Following the planned IRA evacuation of Rahelly House, and in extremely poor weather conditions, Billy Pilkington had led a group of approximately thirty men to Tormore Cave. The Sligo IRA possessed a number of cave dugouts in the region, but Tormore

Fig. 1 Former 3rd Western Division IRA leadership at a reunion dinner in Sligo, 1963. (l–r) Peadar Glynn, officer commanding 1st Sligo Brigade active service unit and divisional adjutant; Billy Pilkington, general officer commanding 3rd Western Division, acting quartermaster general IRA executive, and subsequently a Redemptorist priest; and Tom Scanlon, officer commanding 1st Battalion, Sligo town. An intensely committed republican, Pilkington's colleagues remembered how he instructed his men to 'get down on your knees' and pray for the two RIC constables executed in Sligo on Pilkington's orders in 1921. [Image: courtesy of Anne Feehily / Quotation: Ernie O'Malley Notebooks, P17b/133: Tom Deignan, UCDA]

Fig. 2 A group of republicans with the captured Free State armoured car 'Ballinalee'. Seamus Devins TD, who was captured and killed near Benbulben on 20 September 1922, is leaning on the turret. [Image: reproduced by kind permission of Pádraig Kilgannon]

was the most secure, possibly reserved for emergency situations. It had been prepared for occupation prior to the Civil War, likely during the Truce period. A century later a licensed archaeological excavation of the cave took place to investigate the physical evidence left by the men in September 1922.[6]

Accessing the cave involves an awkward scramble up a steep rocky cliff to the entrance (Fig. 3). The dark space of the entrance, making the cave easily spotted from below, was found to have been concealed by a large boulder and roughly mortared walling, rendering it invisible. Beyond the entrance the cave passage slopes down abruptly. Archaeological excavation revealed a series of large, flat limestones carefully set in place to serve as steps. These lead down to the most spacious, sheltered and dry part of the cave. Overall, this western section of the cave passage, measuring six metres by two metres, is comfortably habitable and is where most signs of occupation were found. East of this area the cave becomes damper and colder, finally becoming a constricted and muddy space which closes down at nineteen metres in length.

The main 'occupation space' in Tormore Cave had been deliberately built up and levelled, representing significant efforts to make the internal space more habitable (Fig. 4). The entire floor space was then enclosed by the construction of a U-shaped setting of stones, open at the steps for access. The U-shaped setting, constructed of limestone originating from the cave floor, was bonded with mortar. Within this defined area, a mortar floor had been laid. Subsequent geochemical sampling of the bond material confirmed it as a basic quicklime mortar. Part of the mortared floor was covered with ten flagstones.

The preparation works in this part of the cave passage served to provide an organised workspace for storing, preparing and maintaining objects, such as munitions, explosives and medical supplies. It is likely that its potential for use as a hideout was integral to its design and that, in September 1922, the men seeking refuge took some comfort from the modifications which would have served to define and contain an area that was level, insulated, drier and cleaner than the natural cave.

The U-shaped stone setting had an intentional opening in front of a natural recess in the southern cave wall, which appears to have been a focus for activities. An accumulation of artefacts was recovered from excavation of the soil deposits in this recess, mainly domestic items related to the 1922 occupation – fragments of two ceramic dishes, fish (cod) bones, burnt chicken bones and a fragment of a clay smoking pipe.

Within the wider occupation area, further fragments of the ceramic dishes, a pottery jar typical of those used in rural dwellings, fragments of two billycans and a glass bottle were discovered. These likely originated from local families who supplied food and beverages to the men in hiding. Local memory maintains

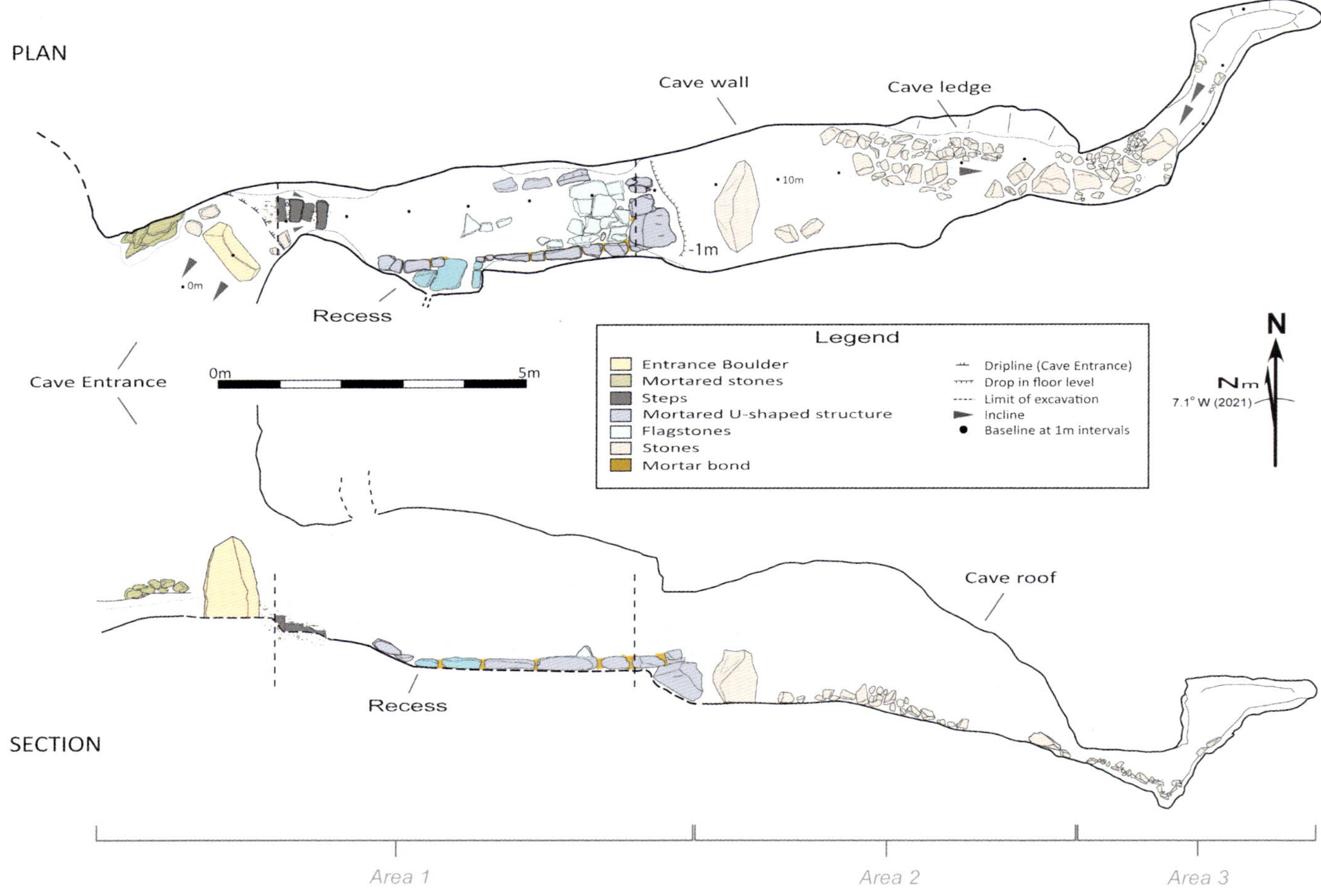

Fig. 3 Survey of Tormore Cave, in plan and section, combining traditional cave survey techniques with excavation drawings, and showing the main constructed features in the cave. [Surveyed and drawn by Robert Mulraney]

that the men did not cook in the cave; food was left out for them. Fragments of a three-legged iron skillet pot were also recovered, and it is suggested that it functioned as a portable toilet, stowed with its lid on at the back of the cave, to be emptied when required.

Other artefacts recovered are more difficult to interpret but include a possible belt buckle and a copper alloy mesh, likely the scrubbing component of a rifle pull-through. Seventeen copper rivets set in iron may have been part of a medical chest or the shrapnel components of an improvised explosive device. A twisted copper wire in a cotton sleeve, with a looped end, likewise suggests something of a more militaristic provenance – perhaps representing the electrical contact of a communications device, such as a field telephone, or of a wet-cell battery.

Severe hardship

The approximately thirty IRA men who endured six weeks in the Tormore Cave dugout undoubtedly suffered severe hardship. The dugout would have been furnished with bedding material, typical of other dugouts, but the historical weather reports and contemporary accounts indicate the weather was particularly cold and wet during the period in question. Local narratives recall that no fires were lit in the cave, a claim supported by the archaeological excavation, although partially burnt turf was recovered from the recess.[7] It is likely, however, that the turf sods may have been used to light the dark cave interior rather than as a heat source.

Surviving confinement

Crucially, the occupation of the cave was wholly dependent on community support, a role played predominantly by women who cooked and transported food while National Army forces patrolled the area. In addition, the fact that Pilkington was able to transfer control of the divisional command during his stay in Tormore Cave is testament to the risky work undertaken by the women who carried his dispatches. It is remembered that local women also provided basic healthcare by treating trench foot, which was a particular issue for the men. Some of the support work was carried out by members of Cumann na mBan, but most was by civilian women.

Pilkington, a figure who commanded much loyalty, likely

Fig. 4 Archaeological planning of the mortar floor and stone walls in Tormore Cave. [Image: courtesy of Robert Mulraney]

maintained military discipline while confined to the cave dugout, setting menial tasks for the men who, aware that six of their comrades had been killed, must have suffered great anger and despair, in addition to their daily frustration at confinement. A particularly pious man, Pilkington was often remembered to have had his men say the rosary before or after 'a job'. It is likely that in the cave the rosary and other prayers were recited multiple times each day to help create a sense of routine and endurance.

By mid-October the National Army's presence in the Glencar Valley was sufficiently reduced that it was felt safe to leave Tormore Cave. The crippling of the division was a temporary one and the IRA resumed its attacks on Free State infrastructure, albeit from a considerably weaker position. As late as March 1923, Liam Lynch anticipated a 'western resurgence under Pilkington'.[8] Following Lynch's death in April, Pilkington was elected to the IRA executive and was involved in the decision to dump arms in May, despite his assertion that 'they could have kept fighting, because they were at their very strongest'.[9]

While nursing a broken collar bone in the Tormore Cave dugout, Billy Pilkington had 'promised God that [he] would become a priest if he survived'. He remained true to this sentiment and, a day after resigning from the executive, on 22 November 1924, he entered the Redemptorist Order in Liverpool. Due to his hard-line republican stance, the Redemptorists in Ireland would not accept him into their own communities. Thereafter, Father William Pilkington, the Tormore men and the cave dugout, which likely saved many men's lives, fell into obscurity except for the fragments retained in local memory and the archaeological footprint within the cave itself.

Liam Lynch

Gerard Shannon

Born outside Anglesboro village in rural Limerick in 1892, Liam Lynch was working as a shop clerk in north Cork in 1916. Radicalised into the republican cause in the aftermath of the Easter Rising, he joined the reorganised Irish Volunteers in Fermoy in 1917. Lynch quickly worked his way up the ranks and was recognised for his dedication and tireless organisational skills. In a letter to his brother Tom in late 1917, he wrote the words most famously associated with him: 'We have declared for an Irish republic and will not live under any other law'. As officer commanding Cork No. 2 Brigade, Lynch emerged as one of the most important guerrilla commanders during the War of Independence, and, as commandant of the 1st Southern Division after April 1921, the most influential IRA officer to publicly oppose the Treaty. Elected chief of staff of the IRA after the army convention in March 1922, Lynch was at first determined to find a compromise with his pro-Treaty opponents. Yet when civil war broke out in June 1922, he travelled south and established a military headquarters in Limerick city. His goal was to hold territory for republicans south of a proposed defensive line between Limerick city and Waterford city (often wrongly referred to as 'the Munster Republic'). However, the collapse of a temporary truce between pro- and anti-Treaty forces in Limerick city in mid-July began the rapid loss of republican territory in the weeks that followed. Lynch would never seriously consider any peace proposals thereafter, whatever the political and military realities. From August 1922 he ordered a return to guerrilla tactics. This is considered one of the few tactical successes of his tenure as chief of staff and resulted in significant ambushes, including, most dramatically, the ambush at Béal na Blá. In response to the execution of republican prisoners by the Free State, he also issued ruthless orders to shoot TDs who voted for the 'Murder Bill'. Yet, beyond the killing of Seán Hales on 7 December,

Fig. 1 (left and below) Front and back of a map of the Tipperary/Waterford border region used by Major General John T. Prout during the National Army operation to track down Liam Lynch and the IRA executive members meeting in the area in April 1923. The arrows indicate the direction of troop sweeps and searches. The location circled in the lower left-hand corner of the map marks the spot where Lynch was shot. [Document: National Library of Ireland, Liam Lynch Papers, MS 36,251/32]

Fig. 2 Photograph of Liam Lynch's body laid out in Clonmel, County Tipperary, April 1923. [Image: National Library of Ireland, Florence O'Donoghue Papers, MS 31,422/3]

MS 36,251/30(1)

Óglaiġ na h-Éireann.
(IRISH REPUBLICAN ARMY)

GENERAL HEADQUARTERS,
DUBLIN

Árd Oifig, Áth Cliath.

6-7-23.

Dept:— C/S.

Ref. No.

A [illegible] a ċara.

I was very glad to hear from you. Liam used often speak of you & we were all delighted when your letter came.

I was with Liam when he was wounded. Six of us altogether were billeted at the foot of the Knockmealdowns near Goatenbridge. The alarm came at 4.am that the Staters were about & we made for the mountains to cross to Mellary.

But it was a much bigger round-up than we expected. There must have been at least 6,000 Staters on the warpath that day. In avoiding one column we ran into another on the mountains. There was a running fight for about twenty minutes, they with rifles & we with revolvers when the firing suddenly ceased. Then a single shot rang out & Liam fell.

We could hardly believe him when he said he was hit. We started to carry him off. saying the act of contrition & he repeating it. He was suffering badly - he was shot through the body-

Fig. 3 (above left) First page of a letter dated 6 July 1923 from IRA chief of staff, Frank Aiken, to Tom Lynch describing Liam Lynch's death. The dramatic circumstances of Lynch's death added to his stature in republican memory. Trying to evade a National Army round-up, Lynch and a small group of senior anti-Treaty generals scrambled along an open mountainside track and engaged in a running gun battle with approaching National Army troops. After Lynch was mortally wounded, he told his comrades to abandon him as he lay in agony. They had only a moment to gather his papers and say a prayer; they fled under heavy gunfire. Beyond the loss of Lynch and its implications for continued anti-Treaty resistance, his colleagues had to reckon with the abandonment of a friend and their own close brush with death. [Document: National Library of Ireland, Liam Lynch Papers, MS 36,251/30]

Fig. 4 (above right) A badge with a photograph and quotation attributed to Liam Lynch, created *c.* 1923 to commemorate Lynch's death. [Image: National Library of Ireland, Heery and Molloy Papers, MS 13,712/2/19]

Lynch's orders were not widely carried out. By early 1923 the anti-Treaty IRA faced considerable military reversals, mass imprisonment and steady demoralisation among all ranks. Despite the continued optimism in his official dispatches, and his dedication to the declared republic, Lynch's letters to his brother reveal that his heart was not in this fraternal conflict: 'The disaster of this war is sinking to my very bones', wrote Lynch in September 1922. 'Who could have dreamt that all our hopes could have been so blighted'. At a secret IRA executive meeting in late March 1923, Lynch's was the deciding vote against a motion to cease military operations, because he hoped to secure artillery pieces from contacts in Europe. Less than three weeks later, while en route to the next executive meeting, he was fatally wounded by a National Army bullet in the Knockmealdown Mountains. As his adjutant, Todd Andrews, later observed, Lynch's 'iron will' had kept the military fighting going, and his death on 10 April was a decisive turning point for the IRA. Fondly remembered by his comrades, Lynch is still widely commemorated, most notably with a sixty-foot round tower built on the site where he was shot – the largest monument to any individual killed during the War of Independence and the Civil War.

Fig. 5 General Liam Lynch Memorial, Knockmealdown Mountains, County Tipperary. Arguably the most impressive memorial to emerge from revolutionary Ireland, it marks the approximate spot where Lynch was mortally wounded by National Army soldiers as he and his party dashed over an exposed hilltop on the Knockmealdown Mountains. Designed by Denis Doyle in the style of a medieval round tower, the fifty-foot structure was financed and constructed largely by anti-Treaty IRA veterans from the immediate area around Knockmealdown. The project began after Fianna Fáil took office in 1932 and was completed in just three years. The estimated 15,000 who attended the unveiling in the rain on 7 April 1935 heard the IRA chief of staff, Moss Twomey, declare that Lynch 'detested the thought of war between Irishmen in England's interest'. Annual commemorations at the Liam Lynch Memorial, the most popular associated with Fianna Fáil, have served a similar public function to that of the Michael Collins commemoration at Béal na Blá for Fine Gael. [Image: National Library of Ireland, Eason Photographic Collection, EAS_4050 / Quotation: *Irish Press*, 8 April 1935]

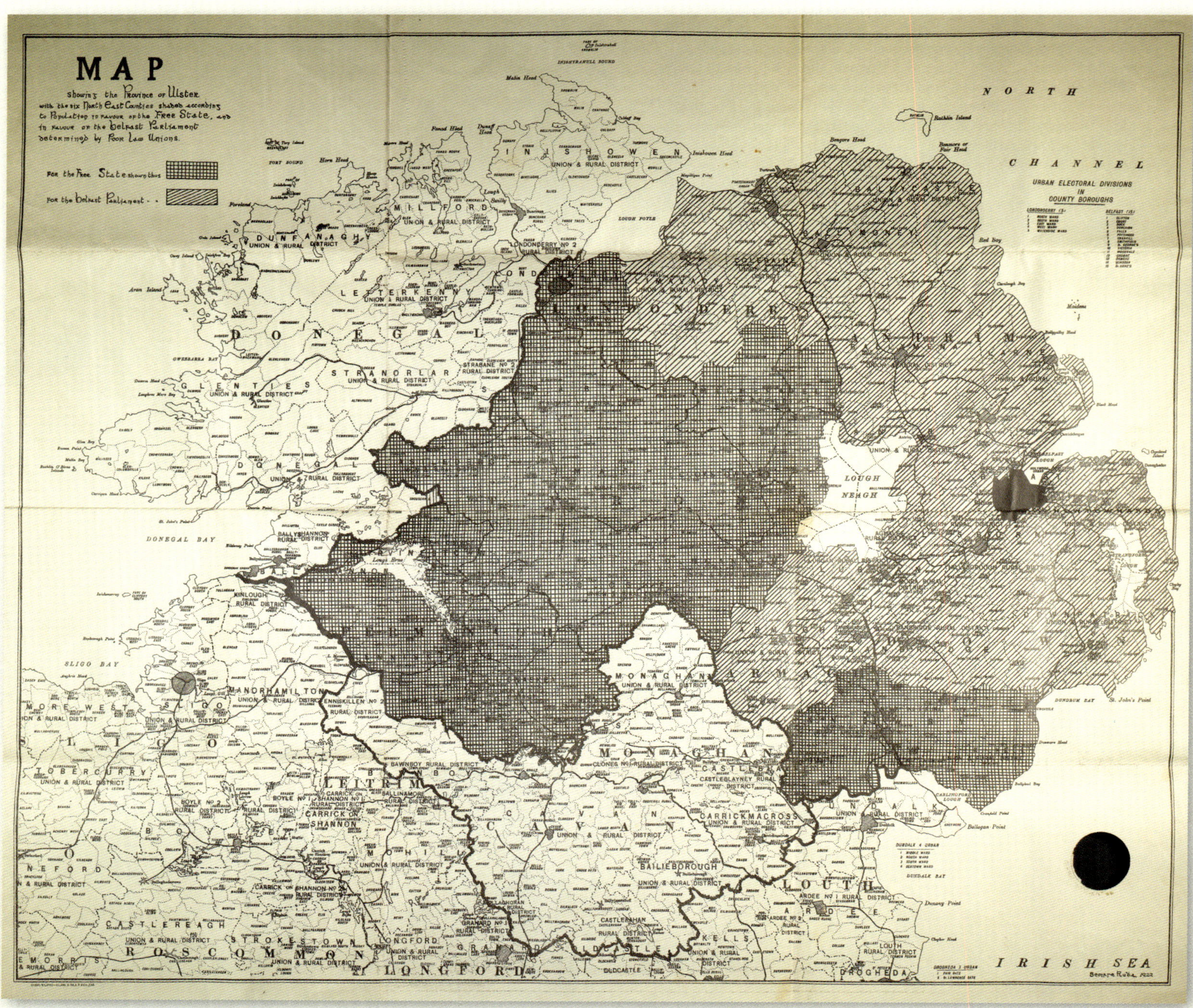

Fig. 1 Map of Irish poor law unions, adapted in 1923 by Seoirse Rudha for the Boundary Commission. The purpose of this map was to support the Free State's claim to territory included in the polity of Northern Ireland created by the 1920 Government of Ireland Act. The lithograph shows the province of Ulster with the six north-eastern counties shaded to indicate areas in which a majority favoured either the 'Free State' or the 'Belfast Parliament'. [Image: National Library of Ireland, Sweetman Papers, MS 47,591/2]

CHAPTER 3

Civil Conflict in Ireland, 1922-3: Political violence and the consolidation of Northern Ireland

Adrian Grant

The Irish Civil War was a twenty-six-county affair, which is in some ways ironic given that ten years earlier Ulster was viewed as a powder keg with the potential to explode into a full-blown civil conflict between unionists and nationalists.[1] The riots and street violence of 1913–14, in particular, were the worst experienced in decades and resulted in the first fatality as a result of political violence in Ireland during the turbulent 1912–23 period.[2] By 1920 the constitutional future of Ireland was no less certain, despite the passage of the Government of Ireland Act that year and the establishment of a Northern Ireland parliament and government in 1921. Ireland was officially partitioned by the act, but few nationalists were willing to accept its finality. Equally, few unionists were content to rest on the laurels provided by an act of the Westminster parliament, which the majority of people in Ireland no longer recognised as having democratic legitimacy. This brew of nationalist expectation and unionist insecurity partially explains the sharp upsurge of violence in parts of the six counties between the summers of 1920 and 1922. This intense prequel to the events of 1922–3 in the North must be explored if one is to fully comprehend the swift and definite consolidation of Northern Ireland in the early 1920s.

The shelling of the Four Courts on 28 June 1922 induced a collective turn-away from the North on the part of the Civil War belligerents. This resulted in the evaporation of the sharpest ends of unionist insecurity and instilled a determination to crack down hard on opposition to partition and the Northern Ireland project. Northern republicans with the inclination to resist lacked the necessary clout to force a Southern rethink on taking the fight to Northern Ireland, while those nationalists who felt armed resistance was now futile waited anxiously for the establishment of the Boundary Commission proposed under the Anglo-Irish Treaty of 1921. Most believed, wrongly as it turned out, that the definitively majority nationalist areas of the six counties would be transferred to the jurisdiction of the Free State.[3] For the Ulster unionists convinced of the merits of a smaller territory than the historic nine-county province of Ulster, the main task at hand was to resist any awarding of land to the South by the Boundary Commission so as to ensure viability. This chapter assesses events and processes in the North of Ireland in this period with a focus on political violence and on how the Northern Ireland government asserted its control over the six counties, and how this assertion impacted on the people and politics of the region in the shadow of the Civil War.

Sectarian tensions and political violence in the North, 1920–22

Early 1920 saw a shift in the conversation about how the 'Ulster question' would be addressed. The British government, not wanting to appear all carrot and no stick, put in motion preparations for a new Home Rule bill in 1919. This would eventually become the Government of Ireland Act, which was largely ignored by nationalist Ireland but was the legislative basis for the establishment of Northern Ireland. A committee, chaired by the former Irish unionist leader Walter Long, put forth recommendations for a new constitutional arrangement, eventually landing in the spring of 1920 on the idea of two unicameral parliaments. Northern Ireland would comprise six counties and Southern Ireland the other twenty-six.[4] Proposals for a jurisdiction comprising the nine counties of Ulster were opposed by the Ulster unionists on the basis that control of such an area, containing the large nationalist populations of Cavan, Donegal and Monaghan, would be too difficult to maintain. For the remainder of the year the legislative basis for the partition of Ireland and the establishment of a six-county Northern Ireland made its way through parliament at Westminster. The nationalist-majority counties of Fermanagh and Tyrone, as well as the city of Derry, were included to maximise the geographical area within the bounds of what could be easily controlled by a perpetual unionist majority.[5]

However, 1920 also saw the introduction of a proportional-representation (PR) electoral system using the single transferable vote for local elections across Ireland. The British government, anticipating further eradication of the moderate nationalist vote

Fig. 2 Poster advertising an election meeting on 8 May 1921 in support of Michael Collins and Francis (Frank) Aiken, the republican candidates for County Armagh. Elections to the parliaments of Northern and Southern Ireland – the two polities created by the Government of Ireland Act (1920) – took place in late May 1921. In the twenty-six counties 124 Sinn Féin candidates, who refused to recognise the new political entity of Southern Ireland, were returned unopposed to the Second Dáil. The elections held on 24 May, under the proportional-representation system, in Ulster's six north-eastern counties, however, proved a disaster for the party, despite an electoral pact with the Irish Parliamentary Party designed to avoid splitting the nationalist vote, a highly resourced campaign, and the optimism of Éamon de Valera, who secured one of Sinn Féin's paltry six seats. Collins, who called on the electors in Armagh to vote 'on the ground that Ireland is one and indivisible, and that she is not to be torn asunder by any act of an English assembly', was elected on the first count. Such assertions did not impress the unionist majority who returned all forty Unionist Party candidates to the fifty-two seat parliament of Northern Ireland, with almost 70 per cent of the first-preference votes. The parliament, with its overwhelmingly unionist membership, was opened by George V on 22 June 1921, after which the British government turned its attention to securing a truce, followed five months later by the Anglo-Irish Treaty. Under Articles 17 and 18 of the Treaty, the members elected to the House of Commons of Southern Ireland in May 1921 – and not Dáil Éireann – were required to approve the Treaty. Sixty-four members of the Parliament of Southern Ireland, including the four unionist MPs for Trinity College, met for the first and final time on 14 January 1922 in the Oak Room of Dublin's Mansion House. They appointed a 'Provisional Government' to which, according to the Treaty, the British would formally hand over 'the powers and machinery requisite for the discharge of its duties'. This interim government, chaired by Michael Collins, was intended to operate until a new parliament, elected by the people, enacted the constitution of the Irish Free State, which was set to come into official existence on 6 December 1922. [Document: National Library of Ireland, EPH F236 / Quotation: *Freeman's Journal*, 21 May 1921]

after the Sinn Féin landslide at the 1918 general election, clearly believed that PR would at least put a halt to the onward march of republicanism.[6] While Sinn Féin continued to demonstrate its dominance of politics, taking the most seats, the more reflective PR system contributed to the rise of Labour into second place, and the maintenance of a significant nationalist party and Southern unionist presence in local government.[7] The new electoral system had a very different effect in the North. The Ulster unionists were opposed to its introduction, mainly due to the threat it posed to their electoral dominance, particularly in west Ulster. This led to a public disagreement between Southern and Northern unionists, with the former vociferously supporting the introduction of PR as a way to maintain representation in Southern councils and place checks on the rise of Sinn Féin. Ulster unionists couched their anti-PR rhetoric in criticisms of the government for using Ireland as an experimental site for new and confusing ideas, which contributed to the image of Ireland as being categorically different from Britain.[8]

Derry City, Fermanagh and Tyrone all returned anti-union majorities, calling into question the legitimacy of the proposed six-county Northern Ireland's western periphery. This represented a challenge to unionist authority and the image of a viable Northern Ireland before the institutions were even finalised on paper. Fermanagh and Tyrone later faced severe difficulties and were eventually disbanded in December 1921 by the Northern Ireland government due to their 'recalcitrance' and declarations of allegiance to Dáil Éireann.[9] Derry City avoided a similar fate by walking the tightrope between the authorities in Belfast and Dublin and declaring formal allegiance to neither.[10] The 1920 local election results caused great upset among unionists on the western fringe of the six-county area, who feared such symbolic events could push the counties into the orbit of a southern jurisdiction, or indeed strengthen calls for thirty-two county settlement.

The January 1920 elections were followed by a significant increase in sectarian tensions in western Ulster. Tensions rose generally in the six counties as the partition question continued to dominate established political discourse. An increase in IRA activity in Southern counties also had an effect on community relations in the North, while some of the actions of the new councils in Derry, Fermanagh and Tyrone provoked angry reactions from unionists. In Derry, for example, the Union flag was removed from the Guildhall as a gesture to demonstrate that the new council would represent all citizens regardless of political background.[11] Such gestures were interpreted by unionists as triumphalist displays in a city where control of public spaces had been a deeply sensitive political issue since the construction of the walled city of Londonderry in the early seventeenth century.

Sectarian tensions increasingly spilled over into violence during the spring of 1920. Then, in the summer, the violence began to spiral. In June 1920 in Derry twenty people (mostly non-combatants) were killed over the course of one week during pitched gun battles between an embryonic resurgent Ulster Volunteer Force and a combined force of IRA and nationalist ex-servicemen.[12] The following month sectarian violence flared in Belfast, starting with shipyard expulsions and escalating to hundreds of deaths over the next two years – right up until the opening weeks of the Civil War taking place on the other side of the border.[13] In late 1920 and early 1921 the embryonic Northern Ireland government began the slow process of building up the infrastructure of a new political entity. There was an early and sustained focus on security, which also fed into the project to create a cross-class unionist alliance that would secure the foundations of the new government. There had long been unionist distrust for and suspicion of the Royal Irish Constabulary (RIC). Many of the ranks and some of the officers in the North were Southern Catholics. Suspicions were aired by some Derry unionists, for example, that the police stationed in the Bogside area turned a blind eye to IRA activity.[14] The IRA had, in fact, attempted to burn the Bogside barracks on numerous occasions and eventually succeeded in doing so. There may have been some truth to the rumours, however, as IRA members remembered being offered guns from the barracks during the violence of June 1920, and some of the police from the barracks offered their resignations on the back of suspicions that their colleagues in other city barracks had acted in concert with loyalists to target nationalists.[15] The complexity of the Northern unionist relationship with the RIC explains in large part the drive to form a definitively 'Ulster' force in the opening years of the 1920s. By late 1920 recruits to the Ulster Special Constabulary (USC) were flowing in. This reserve force, which was overwhelmingly unionist in composition, had multiple effects. It buttressed a strained police force and was able to discourage and combat IRA activity in parts of the North. It provided the Ulster identity in the police so desired by many. It acted as a safety valve, drawing the energy of those who had been involved, or potentially were on the road to involvement, in vigilante-style loyalist violence, and it provided a decent job for the growing number of working-class unemployed in Northern Ireland.[16] The latter benefit contributed to the wider state-building project, giving a potentially disgruntled unionist working class a stake in the Northern Ireland project and clearly defining the enemy of the state as those who would have preferred to come under the jurisdiction of Dublin.

Truce, Treaty and the joint IRA Northern offensive of 1922

Tensions increased further and violence spiralled again during the Truce period and between the signing of the Treaty and the outbreak of the Civil War. This was particularly the case in the spring of 1922 when a joint pro- and anti-Treaty IRA operation escalated action along the border and inside Northern Ireland. There had been a large measure of unionist discontent at the legitimisation of the IRA as a result of the Truce. The USC had been demobilised and IRA members were appointed as Truce liaison officers, working alongside the RIC to monitor activity at a local level. Training camps were established throughout rural parts of the North, where a hugely expanded IRA membership was trained in the use of Thompson sub-machine guns and bomb throwing.[17] Well-known IRA officers,

There is the question of N.E. Ulster. Let us look at the position there.

At the height of our national struggle, against the wishes of the entire Irish people, the British Government passed an Act of Parliament by which our six north-eastern counties were divided off politically from the rest of Ireland. The principle on which that partition rested was that minorities have a right to be protected, and that under a native Irish Government, the lives and liberties of the people in those six counties might be endangered.

But if that claim is made on behalf of Protestants and Orangemen, it must also be allowed on behalf of Catholics and Nationalists, who form a larger minority within the six counties than the population of the six counties is in the population of the whole of Ireland.

Have the lives and liberties of Catholics and Nationalists been safe under the rule of the Belfast Parliament? The Catholics of Belfast form roughly one-third of the population. For the first five months of this year, while 87 Portestants were killed and 177 wounded, 150 Catholics were killed and 288 were wounded. In the three weeks from the 31st May to the 25th June, 28 Catholics were killed and 90 wounded, to 8 Protestants killed and 21 wounded. Since July 1920, 9,000 Catholics have been driven from their employment in Belfast, and 23,500 Catholics have been hunted from their homes. No Protestants have been driven from their employment or their homes.

Since last November they have had their full police and government established in the six counties, with that force and government backed by endless British troops and unlimited British money.

That Government has been established and has been functioning all the time. Yet it is since that Government has been in power

\- 1 -

that that savagery, which was always inclined to break out, and which has been steadily operating since July 1920, has been allowed to run absolutely riot.

And for what purpose? The motive and object are the same as they have always been: the utilisation of the savagery of the Belfast mob for political ends — in an effort to prevent Irish freedom when the possibility of it was foreseen in 1920; in an effort to destroy it since it has come into being.

If they had any stateable political case in favour of Partition, or, rather, in favour of the restoration of the Union which has been their real object, they would state it to the world. But as their object has been to promote anarchy throughout Ireland as a means to get back the Union and their old position of domination, what they do is, not to state an honourable political case, but to turn on their Belfast mob to create an intolerable situation in order to provoke counter feelings and acts resulting in disturbance in the whole of Ireland.

The number of persons killed in the 26 counties between the 6th December and the beginning of June was 46. The number of persons killed in the City of Belfast alone between the first of January and the beginning of June was 275. The 26 counties tells no such story of murder, violence and anarchy as has been revealed daily and nightly in the City of Belfast, carried out unchecked under the eyes of the British Forces.

These figures are of interest in view of advice to us to restore ordered conditions in speeches which were delivered two or three weeks ago in the British House of Commons.

We were not at all deceived by those speeches. We well understood the need of the British Ministry to cover up an awkward political situation — to save their faces with their own die-hards. Bluster is sometimes useful. To blame someone else when you are in a weak position is a effective way of diverting attention.

\- 2 -

Fig. 3 Typescript notes by Michael Collins (n.d., likely early July 1922), mainly concerning the Northern question. As a leading member of the Irish delegation that signed the Treaty, and as the head of the Provisional Government established on foot of its provisions, Collins was keenly aware of the potential for violent disagreement among republicans regarding its terms, and sought ways to prevent it. There are various explanations for this approach: his genuine commitment to the republican ideal of unity; his affection and admiration for many of his erstwhile comrades on the anti-Treaty side; and his belief that the passage of time would either vindicate his 'stepping-stone' approach or (more cynically) afford him the opportunity to recruit and train an army pledged to support the Treaty. Whatever the reasons, both Collins and the anti-Treaty IRA viewed the institutions of Northern Ireland as their common foe and cooperated in plans to attack them in the first half of 1922. The offensive afforded both sides political breathing space in which sincere efforts were made to achieve at least a partial reconciliation. In facilitating an offensive against the North, Collins was playing a dangerous game. When he signed the Treaty he not only recognised the existence of the six-county statelet but accepted its right to opt out of the Irish Free State when it formally came into existence in December 1922. In the opening months of 1922 he met, and concluded agreements with, James Craig, which covered a wide range of contentious matters including the termination of the nationalist Belfast boycott, the return of Catholic workers to the shipyards of the city, reform of the Ulster Special Constabulary and, potentially of greatest significance, changes to the mechanisms of the Boundary Commission. These agreements, however, rang hollow given Collins's efforts to destabilise Northern Ireland and the sectarian violence that was increasingly a feature of life in Belfast in particular. This document illustrates the extent to which duplicity was part of Collins's modus operandi at this time. He publicly disavowed the use of force as a tool to persuade unionists to abandon their opposition to independence but, in private, facilitated it. More fundamentally, he shared with his anti-Treaty opponents the view that British support was emboldening Northern unionist violence and opposition to unity. In this they underestimated the habituated, visceral opposition of that community to 'Dublin rule', even (perhaps especially) where London seemed sympathetic to the suggestion. Given Collins's anti-partition rhetoric and other indications that he retained a shared sensibility with the anti-Treaty camp (including the 'Pact election' agreement and the republican orientation of the draft Free State constitution), members of the British Cabinet had good reason to doubt his bona fides regarding the Treaty by June 1922. The assassination of Henry Wilson afforded them the perfect opportunity to drive a wedge between the two sides of the republican constituency. The consequent threat to use British troops in Dublin to attack the Four Courts was sufficient to not alone trigger the start of the Civil War, but also bring the Northern campaign to a swift, unsuccessful conclusion. [Text: Gabriel Doherty / Document: National Library of Ireland, Kathleen McKenna Napoli Papers, MS 22,774]

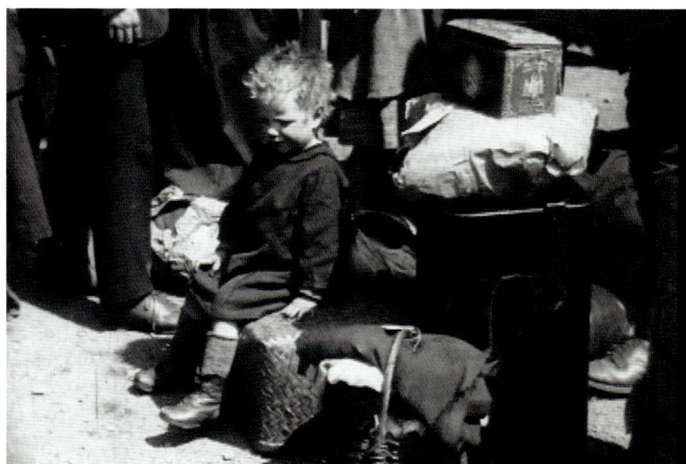

Fig. 4 (above) A still from the newsreel 'Refugees from Ulster' (Pathé, issued 8 June 1922). In November 1920 Joe Devlin MP, speaking in the House of Commons during the third reading of the Government of Ireland Bill, predicted the impact of partition on the minority Catholic community. It would be 'the story of weeping women, hungry children, hunted men, homeless in England, houseless in Ireland'. In just under two years – between July 1920 and June 1922 – 499 people died during intense violence in Belfast, including seventy-eight women and at least twenty-seven children, with Catholics suffering disproportionately. Those known to have republican sympathies were often singled out. Breid McCamphill, a Belfast Cumann na mBan member who later joined the anti-Treaty forces in Dublin, recalled the moment when 'Our house was taken from us [...] furniture and everything we had was put on the street about 5 minutes before curfew and we had to come to Dublin'. According to Maud Gonne MacBride, president of the Dublin Relief Committee, which supported those fleeing from the horrors of anti-Catholic violence often referred to as 'the pogrom', 'every train from the North brought wild-eyed refugees, women half-demented and children sick with terror. They had nowhere to go'. Some were billeted in the Fowler Hall in Parnell Square (which belonged to the Orange Order), where they 'stood in forlorn groups and sat on the bare floors of the spacious rooms'. Many were suffering from injuries. 'It was piteous', Gonne MacBride recalled in 1939, 'to see the maimed children and the nerve-shattered mothers'. Her friend, Charlotte Despard, sister of the former British viceroy, Lord John French, and active in feminist and republican circles, opened her large Dublin home, Roebuck House, to the refugees. Arthur Griffith accused the IRA of deliberately bringing down refugees from the North. This was not the policy of the Provisional Government, which was anxious to demonstrate its ability to establish a system of law and order so that the plebiscite on the boundary promised by Lloyd George could take place as soon as possible. At another meeting Michael Collins urged the relief committee to not encourage refugees and to send back any who were willing to return. He believed Northern Catholics should 'hold their own corner there' until the expected results of the promised plebiscite would 'make a separate Government in the North impossible'. The White Cross, which, since 1921, had been distributing aid to those affected by the conflict, was encouraged to build houses for those whose homes had been destroyed in sectarian attacks. Its expenditure on personal relief in Belfast until 31 August 1922 was £362,356 16*s*1*d*, far greater than payments elsewhere in Ireland, but much less was spent on reconstruction. Difficulties in providing for the influx of Northerners into Dublin led to armed men ordering a number of families 'to billet some Belfast refugees', a threat that was not well received by those targeted in this way. The Southern government claimed it lacked resources to provide either homes or employment to refugees. By the end of 1922 most of them had returned over the border, 'abandoned', as Diarmaid Ferriter writes, 'by all sides'. [Text: Margaret Ward / Image: courtesy of British Pathé / Sources: Joe Devlin, 11 November 1920, *HC Deb.*, vol. 134, col. 1455; With thanks to Kieran Glennon for the fatality figures; MSP34REF20630, Breid (née McCamphill) Dobbyn; Maud Gonne MacBride, 'The Real Case Against Partition', *Capuchin Annual,* 1943; Maud Gonne MacBride, 'When Children Were Marks for Orange Bullets', *Irish Press,* 24 April 1939; *Report of the Irish White Cross to 31 August 1922* (Dublin, 1922), p. 125; Diarmaid Ferriter, *Between Two Hells: The Irish Civil War* (London, 2021), p. 30]

Fig. 5 (below) Burned-out terraced houses in Saunderson Street, Belfast destroyed in rioting on 17 April 1922. [Image: Desmond FitzGerald Photographs. P80/PH/157. Reproduced by kind permission of UCD Archives]

armed and in uniform, attended such camps and strode around nearby urban areas proudly and unmolested by the RIC.[18] Many of these officers were prison escapees who had until recently been on the run. IRA checkpoints were established on rural roads near the training camps, meaning that unionists were regularly stopped and questioned by armed IRA members.[19] In early 1922 this did not result in open confrontation, but left many unionists seething with discontentment. The signing of the Anglo-Irish Treaty with its provision for a Boundary Commission on 6 December 1921 did little to salve unionist insecurity, despite the advances that had been made in terms of laying the foundations of Northern Ireland and greatly expanding its security apparatus.

Such rising tensions were clearly building towards a confrontation between the IRA and either a clutch of vigilante groups or an expanded and remobilised USC. The knock-on effect of this would almost inevitably be broader sectarian violence between unionists and nationalists. As Robert Lynch has shown, the people of Belfast usually experienced the sharpest ends of these ripple effects arising from events elsewhere in Ulster.[20] An exploration of some of the events that precipitated violent confrontations provides some insight into the dynamics of conflict in the North at this time and, indeed, how these impacted on people and politics north and south of the border.

Tensions continued to rise between the IRA and the security forces of the new government, and also between unionists and nationalists more broadly in the months prior to the outbreak of the Civil War. IRA members attempting an escape from Derry Gaol killed a prison warder and a USC member in December 1921 and were sentenced to death. The sentences hung over the politics of North–South relations in early 1922, forming part of the talks between Michael Collins and James Craig that led to the Craig–Collins pacts.[21] Attempts to break the prisoners out to avoid the executions also caused controversy. A group of Monaghan footballers, on their way to Derry for the Ulster final, were arrested and imprisoned on 14 January under charges that they were travelling to the city to stage a jail break, which the armed IRA members of the party probably were.[22] In response Eoin O'Duffy and others organised mass border raids in Fermanagh and Tyrone in mid-February, kidnapping prominent unionists and holding them as bargaining chips to have the footballers released. The forty-odd people kidnapped were taken to various locations across the border, but it is thought that they all ended up in Clones Workhouse at one point. Michael Collins, as was his tactic at this time, pleaded ignorance about the kidnappings while he played the role of statesman in negotiations with James Craig to find peace between North and South. The kidnappings, however, only had the effect of increasing tensions between the IRA and the USC along the border, making everyday life extremely difficult for people in the area. Diplomatic efforts were made in an effort to reduce these tensions, and on 21 February the 'footballers' were released. The IRA then reciprocated by allowing the kidnapped hostages to return home. Despite this, tensions did not ease. Border disputes persisted, while sectarian violence continued to cripple Belfast.[23]

The first Craig–Collins pact was signed in January 1922 and included provision for the end of the Belfast boycott and the facilitated return of expelled workers to the Belfast shipyards. The pact quickly floundered and was never fully implemented amid continuing violence and the acrimony stirred by the border kidnappings.[24] Then followed a serious altercation at Clones, County Monaghan. The 'Clones affray', as it become known, occurred when a group of USC was travelling to Enniskillen on a train that crossed the border into Monaghan. The train stopped and some of the Specials got off to stretch their legs. Word reached the local IRA, who then attacked the Specials at the train station. At the end of the gun battle, four Specials and one IRA member lay dead.[25] The 'Clones affray' reverberated in the politics and sectarian dynamics of the period that followed. Unionists saw it as a ruthless attack on police going about their normal duties, while nationalists saw it as a brazen border incursion by the hated USC, who had no permission to operate south of the border.

After the events at Clones, IRA activity along the border increased. The police build-up at the frontier, already bolstered significantly after the kidnappings, grew even larger and many worried that confrontation between the two sides was inevitable. British troop withdrawals from the Free State were suspended and reinforcements were drafted into Northern Ireland, with the purpose of alleviating Craig's concerns about IRA attacks coming from across the border.[26] Collins was using every tool at his disposal to destabilise Northern Ireland at this time, and the 'Clones affray' and other IRA actions along the border and in Belfast formed part of this wider destabilisation strategy.

Thirty-one people were killed in Belfast in the days following the 'Clones affray' – some in the most brutal circumstances, including children subjected to a bomb attack.[27] Things only got worse in Belfast as the year went on. On 24 March men in police uniforms burst into the McMahon family home in north Belfast and shot all eight male occupants. Five members of the family and their lodger died.[28] Such attacks were interpreted as reprisals for IRA attacks in Belfast, but should also be seen in the context of increased IRA attacks in other parts of Northern Ireland during late March, as well as the significant increase in IRA activity on the southern side of the border between March and early May 1922.

Events in the North drew the focus of Southern republicans and provided a cause around which the opposing IRA factions could unite. Southern IRA officers were sent north to the 1st and 2nd Northern Divisions to organise the envisaged offensive, including Seán Lehane in command of the joint force, with Charlie Daly who had been in the area since 1921 as his deputy. The plan was for the Southern border divisions to 'invade' the six counties and be joined by a 'rising' of the units based inside Northern Ireland in early May.[29] British-supplied Free State arms were exchanged with those of anti-Treaty units, with the latter then sent north to avoid detection lest the involvement of the Free State be detected by the Northern Ireland or British governments. The arms were transported into the North secretly and the operations had the intended effect of keeping the opposing sides on the Treaty divide busy with a common aim and a common enemy. Some Northern

Fig. 6 This photograph, taken in July 1921, shows Dan Hogan seated outside Lough Bawn House in County Monaghan. It was the former residence of Colonel William Tennison, high sheriff of Monaghan, leading county unionist and local commander of the Ulster Volunteer Force, and was used as a 'training camp by the IRA during the Truce' (Dooley, p. 125). While less well known than his brother Michael, who was killed in Croke Park on Bloody Sunday on 21 November 1920, Dan, like others who were heavily involved in the Gaelic Athletic Association (GAA), also played his part in the War of Independence and subsequent Civil War. The Hogan brothers were sons of a strong farmer from Grangemockler, County Tipperary. In 1917, at the age of twenty-two, Dan moved to Clones, County Monaghan to take up employment as a clerk with the Great Northern Railway (GNR) Company. In Clones he befriended Eoin (Owen) O'Duffy, whose great organisational skills had transformed the GAA in Monaghan and Ulster. O'Duffy was equally adept as a Sinn Féin organiser and Irish Volunteer and used the GAA as a recruiting vehicle for the Volunteers in the county. Hogan quickly established himself in the ranks of the IRA, becoming a senior figure in Monaghan during the War of Independence. With O'Duffy he led the attack on Ballytrain Royal Irish Constabulary barracks in February 1920 that marked the real beginning of the war in the county. On 14 January 1922, shortly after the ratification of the Treaty by the Dáil, Hogan, along with several other senior IRA officers, travelled to Derry apparently as members of the Monaghan senior football panel. Fulfilling the fixture with Derry, however, was part of a greater plan to rescue three IRA men facing execution in Derry Gaol, a point of real anger and resentment among republicans. However, as Robert Lynch has detailed, the motorcade was intercepted in Dromore, County Tyrone by the Ulster Special Constabulary (USC), and team members, including Hogan, were arrested. In early February the IRA retaliated by crossing the border and rounding up forty-two local unionists to be held as hostages until the release of Hogan and those imprisoned with him. The situation deteriorated further following a violent confrontation at Clones railway station, which became known as the 'Clones affray'. This incident took place on 11 February 1922 between a party of USC travelling by train to Enniskillen and members of the local IRA. It resulted in the killing of IRA Commandant Matt Fitzpatrick and four USC constables – Robert MacMahon, James Lewis, William McFarland and Sergeant Dougherty – and the wounding of several others. News of the attack on the USC men at Clones and the bullet-ridden and bloodstained carriages rapidly spread and further inflamed sectarian tensions in Belfast. Two days later, amid a new round of bloody Belfast street clashes, one act stood apart: the horrific throwing of a bomb among children playing in Weaver Street. It resulted in the deaths of four girls – Ellen Johnston (eleven), Catherine Kennedy (fifteen), Eliza O'Hanlon (aged eleven) and Rose Anne McNeill (thirteen) – and two women – Maggie Smith (fifty-three) and Mary Owen (forty) – all of whom were Catholic. The Northern Ireland prime minister, Sir James Craig, and unionist newspapers depicted the Weaver Street bombing as largely accidental but triggered by the IRA's seizure of unionist hostages and attacks on the USC at Clones. However, as Nadia Dobrianska has argued, Belfast nationalists challenged Craig's portrayal of the Weaver Street attack and emphasised that the city's Catholic population had been under attack for a week prior to the 'Clones affray'. Amid rising recriminations and angry debates in the House of Commons, backchannel negotiations were opened. Ultimately, on 21 February the Monaghan footballers, including Hogan, were released at the behest of the British government, while the IRA in turn freed many of its unionist hostages. Hogan later played an active part in the Irish Civil War, rising to the rank of major general in the National Army's Eastern Command. When the anti-Treaty IRA captured John Bagwell, the general manager of the GNR, it was Hogan who secured his release by threatening reprisals on IRA prisoners. In the post-Civil War period he was appointed chief of staff of the Defence Forces in 1927, before later resigning and then emigrating to the United States. [Image: courtesy of County Monaghan Museum / Sources: Terence Dooley, *Monaghan: The Irish revolution, 1913–23* (Dublin, 2017), p. 125; Karl O'Hanlon, 'Remembering My Great-Aunt Eliza, Killed in Weaver Street Bombing 100 Years Ago', *Irish Times*, 13 February 2022/ See also Robert Lynch, 'The Clones Affray, 1922 – Massacre or invasion?' *History Ireland*, vol. 12, no. 3, 2004; Nadia Dobrianska, 'The Weaver Street Bombing in Belfast 1922: Violence, politics, and memory', *Irish Historical Studies*, vol. 47, no. 172, November 2023, pp. 259–77]

Copy

12, Leoville St.
Belfast.

18/9/36

To
The Pensions Claims Board,
Griffith Bks. Dublin.

Sir,

With regard to the claim submitted by Miss Eileen O'Boyle, 244, Falls Road, Belfast, I beg to state that I have known her intimately since 1914 and that she has been a tireless worker in the cause of Ireland since the formation of the Belfast Branch of the Cumann na mBan. Her activities comprised visitation of prisoners in Belfast Gaols, the provision of parcels, etc. corresponding with their relatives. When the struggle reached its climax she gave up well paid employment and undertook the carriage of despatches to Dublin, Cavan, Newry, Dundalk, etc. she was to a great extent responsible for keeping open communications between the 3rd, 4th and 5th Northern Divisions and when a column sent from the Belfast Brigade to operate in Co.Cavan her job was to see to the transfer of arms etc during the Civil War period she still continued her activities and was eventually arrested by Colonel Gilmartin interned in Kilmainham and the North Dublin Union. I know that in many cases she was compelled to meet her own expenses and she suffered materially in that she was unable to resume her old employment in a loyalist firm by reason of her political activities, arrest, etc. and the subsequent depression in other firms, rendered it impossible to obtain other employment. I know no other member of the C. na mBan whose record surpasses Miss O'Boyle, who is also known or was known to the Minister for Defence, Mr. F. Aiken, Ex-Capt. Andrew O'Hare, Col. Gilheaney, not to mention the Officers of the old 3rd Northern Division now serving in the National Army.

(Signed) David McGuinness.
Ex-Capt. National Army.
Ex-I.O.3rd Northern Div.

MMcC.

Fig. 7 (opposite page) Reference letter written by David McGuinness in September 1936 in support of Nellie O'Boyle Neeson's successful application for a military service pension. The joint IRA 'Northern offensive' against partition by pro- and anti-Treaty IRA failed dismally. To avoid arrest many republicans fled south to the Curragh. On 22 May 1922 James Craig introduced internment. The IRA and Cumann na mBan were now illegal organisations, and what republicans termed the 'big round-up' began. Winifred Carney, Molly Kerr and Rose Black, all Belfast Cumann na mBan members, were imprisoned in Armagh Gaol for varying lengths of time. Some activists were driven from their homes during the 'pogrom' against Catholics, while others were served with deportation orders and forced to move south. Women had fed, delivered messages and acted as lookouts for the IRA men on the run but, with their disappearance, Cumann na mBan activity in the North focused upon collecting funds for the prisoners and distributing aid to their families. Una MacCrudden testified that 'this was the most difficult time, as so many former friends had become enemies owing to the "Split"'. A few women, however, continued to provide military support to the anti-Treaty forces. Belfast woman Nellie O'Boyle was one of the most active. O'Boyle was one of eleven children. In 1911 she and four of her sisters were living on the Falls Road with their widowed mother, all working as stitchers; a common trade for women while the Belfast linen industry flourished. All spoke Irish as well as English and were active in the Gaelic League. O'Boyle joined Cumann na mBan in 1914: 'I took an oath to the Republic on Cave Hill in company with the late Sean McDermott, Bulmer Hobson and Seamus McKenna [...] Throughout the whole period I stood firm by my oath and never wavered'. In 1920, recognising her abilities, the Belfast IRA seconded O'Boyle into its ranks. During 1921 she was one of a group of Cumann na mBan women who transported a quantity of guns and ammunition to an active service unit (ASU) being formed in Cavan. O'Boyle made five trips and then spent a week in Cavan, taking delivery of arms and carrying dispatches. When the ASU was ambushed at Lapanduff, with one death and the capture of several activists, O'Boyle was sent back to identify the dead man, make funeral arrangements, and contact the three men on the run. With the failure of the Northern offensive, weaponry (other than for defence purposes) was no longer required in Belfast. With the start of the Civil War O'Boyle carried large quantities of munitions from Belfast to Anne Street barracks in Dundalk for the use of the Belfast column operating in County Louth. Altogether she made four trips to Dundalk with arms and dispatches. On one occasion she carried dispatches to Derry, but found the men were all on the run. On 3 April 1923 O'Boyle was arrested in Cavan. She spent time in jail in Clones, Kilmainham and the North Dublin Union, before being released that September. She had given up her job while active and the loyalist firm she had worked for refused to re-employ her. She was unable to find another position in the changed circumstances of post-war economic depression. In 1926 she married Henry Neeson, a baker who had not been politically involved. They had one son. Surviving in a highly repressive Northern state, Nellie O'Boyle Neeson concentrated upon the welfare of her family. She died in 1954. She was given a republican funeral in Belfast, her obituary calling this 'a fitting tribute to a gallant and patriotic Irishwoman who sacrificed so much in the sacred cause of Ireland'. [Text: Margaret Ward / Document: MSP34REF11037, Nellie (née O'Boyle) Neeson. Image courtesy of Military Archives/MSPC Project / Sources: MSP34REF27204, Una MacCrudden; family information kindly given by Conor Neeson, grandson of Nellie]

IRA members crossed the border into Donegal to organise and prepare for the 'rising'.[30]

The thinking behind the Northern offensive was to concentrate action on the border and inside Northern Ireland. IRA units on both sides of the border were to take part, spreading the Northern security forces thin on the ground and putting them under more intensive pressure. The proposed offensive, commonly referred to by IRA members as 'The Rising' or the 'May offensive' was planned to commence on 2 or 3 May after a meeting of the Northern divisional commanders. Things began to fall apart almost immediately, however. The 3rd Northern Division, centred on Belfast, requested that action be delayed while it awaited weapons. This was agreed to, but the 2nd Northern Division in south Derry and Tyrone were permitted to proceed. The pro-Treaty divisions on the southern side of the border took no action in support of the 2nd Northern, leaving those in Derry and Tyrone severely exposed.[31] The joint IRA force under Lehane and Daly did rise, however, taking actions that had significant consequences in the weeks leading up to the outbreak of the Civil War. Its attempts to attack Derry city from its northern and southern border hinterlands in Donegal kept the police and army busy for a short time, but did little to achieve the intended effect of the overall offensive.[32]

The 2nd Northern Division attempted to do as much damage as it could in its solo effort. The isolated nature of this action and the gap between what was intended and what actually happened promotes an image of small skirmishes in the area. There were, however, a significant number of attacks on RIC barracks and infrastructural targets spread across a wide area. An eyewitness described viewing the landscape from a distance, saying that 'it reminded me of what one was accustomed to see during the Great War in France. Signals were being exchanged by the Sinn Féiners all along the Sperrins'.[33] Barracks were attacked in Bellaghy, Draperstown and Moneymore, resulting in the death of one police constable and injuries to more.[34] Bridges were blown up, telegraph wires cut, and mills were burned in the predominantly unionist northern part of north County Derry.[35]

The joint IRA 'invasion' of Derry from Donegal took place in the early hours of 4 May. While they were not able to get further than the USC and British army posts on the northern side of the border, there was an atmosphere of large-scale invasion in the dead of night. Over 100 men in lorries and cars, armed with machine guns and rifles, attacked the posts, keeping up a steady engagement for a number of hours.[36] The pro-Treaty units under the command of Joe Sweeney in Donegal did not rise with the joint IRA force, further contributing to the collapse of the offensive.[37] Tensions had been rising between the two groups prior to early May, with the latter being led by anti-Treaty officers and its ranks quickly filling up with men from the six counties who were not entirely welcomed in Donegal.

These tensions boiled over later on the morning of 4 May when the joint IRA force raided a bank in Buncrana, County Donegal. An altercation took place with local pro-Treaty soldiers, which escalated into a firefight in the town's market square. When the shooting stopped, two bystanders (a nine-year-old girl and a nineteen-year-old woman) lay gravely wounded. Both of them later died in hospital.[38] In the afternoon a pro-Treaty detachment was driving through Newtowncunningham and spotted a group of men from the joint IRA force. The circumstances of the event were keenly disputed at the time and after, as neither side was willing to admit to having fired the first shots. In any case, a firefight broke out, resulting in two pro-Treaty forces being shot dead and more wounded.[39] The likelihood of any kind of joint action between

Sweeney's pro-Treaty forces and the joint IRA force in Donegal was non-existent after 4 May. Sweeney had no qualms about attacking their positions rapidly and treating them as an anti-Treaty force after the shelling of the Four Courts on 28 June.[40] This was despite their continued status as a neutral force tasked with concentrating on attacking the six counties, but the events of early May were still forefront in the minds of those in the north-west.

The IRA also carried out actions inside Northern Ireland that had major repercussions, most notably at Ballyronan in south Derry. On 3 May the IRA ambushed and killed a three-man USC patrol in the area, causing outrage and an intense hunt for those who carried out the attack. The IRA members managed to get out of Northern Ireland after spending time hiding on a boat floating in the middle of Lough Neagh.[41] Only weeks earlier, in March, one USC commander in the area noted the existence of a group within the Special Constabulary who advocated killing Catholics in large numbers if IRA actions continued. He doubted if he would be able to control such elements for much longer.[42] Throughout the month of May a series of reprisals attacks on republicans and Catholic civilians took place in the area.

On the morning of 6 May a group of men was ordered out of a house near Dungiven and shot multiple times, before their bodies were dumped in a flax hole. In the early hours of 11 May men wearing police caps entered the McKeown family home in the Ballyronan area. The three sons present in the house were shot in front of their parents, one of them fatally.[43] The assailants were thought to be searching for another brother, Henry McKeown, who was a prominent republican believed to be involved in identifying and targeting special constables in the area.[44] The IRA acted again on 19 May, burning a flax mill in Desertmartin. The USC reacted by burning every known Catholic business and residential premises in the town and firing rounds into pubs and houses. Four local men, a father and his three sons, were among those accused of burning the mill by local USC. They were taken from their home and shot dead at the side of a road outside the town.[45] Another man, an IRA member, was killed in Desertmartin in July, and throughout the summer sectarian tensions and violence continued in the form of threatening letters, arson attacks and the draping of unwanted flags on homes and businesses.[46]

Defeating the Northern IRA

The sharp rise in IRA actions, followed by reprisals and a general state of lawlessness, gave the Northern Ireland government serious cause for concern in May. A turning point came on 22 May when the IRA assassinated the unionist MP William Twaddell in Belfast.[47] Coercive legislation in the form of the Special Powers Act had been passed the previous month and was now invoked to proscribe the IRA and introduce internment without trial, among other measures. This piece of 'emergency legislation' remained on the statute book until the introduction of direct rule in 1972 and had formed one of the central grievances of the civil rights movement in the 1960s.[48] The crackdown on the IRA was immediate and highly effective. The majority of those not picked up and interned within the first twenty-four hours fled across the border to seek refuge and organise to continue the fight from an envisaged Southern sanctuary. An audacious 'invasion' took place in Fermanagh at the end of May when a joint IRA force occupied the village of Belleek. This forced a major battle in the Belleek–Pettigo border area, with the British army using artillery to retake this small corner of Fermanagh. It would be the only significant attack and counter-attack of the period, however.[49] Interned republicans faced desperate circumstances, particularly those held on board the prison ship *Argenta*, where conditions were reportedly terrible. The last of the internees was not released until the end of 1924, by which time the threat from the IRA or the perceived enemy government south of the border had long since evaporated.[50] The principal effect of the Special Powers Act and its vigorous application was that the IRA's war in the North was effectively over as early as June 1922.

Those IRA members who fled across the border did so with the intention of regrouping and joining up with the existing joint IRA structures in an effort to continue undermining the structures of Northern Ireland, and potentially engaging in more assertive and aggressive action. Plans were made for the joint fighting force to regroup and take the fight to the North, right up until the shelling of the Four Courts. It has been contended, however, that this clandestine planning process was more of a means to distract the increasingly fractious pro- and anti-Treaty IRA factions with a common aim, rather than a genuine plan to invade or carry out any kind of major offensive operation north of the border to end partition or protect the nationalist minority.[51] Once hostilities broke out in Dublin on 28 June, the pro-Treaty forces in Donegal moved quickly, interpreting the joint IRA as an enemy force and putting it on the back foot rapidly.[52] Most of the Northerners in the joint force swiftly left on the basis that they had no dog in the Civil War fight, with only a small number remaining to contribute to what was now the anti-Treaty fight in Donegal, led by Lehane and Daly. A large number agreed to join the National Army in an arrangement that guaranteed their neutrality would be respected, that they would not be expected to fight in the Civil War, and that they would be trained exclusively for an envisaged attack on Northern Ireland.[53] Stories of ill-treatment have emerged from this group, some of whom alleged that attempts were made to force them to fight in the Civil War.[54] This neutral force numbered in the region of 800–900 men from across the six counties. More left as the summer months went on, while those remaining on the border in late August were sent to Keane Barracks at the Curragh, ostensibly to train for the future fight against Northern Ireland. Further pressure was placed on them when at the Curragh, and a detachment of those willing was sent to Kerry to fight against the anti-Treaty forces there. It was suggested at the time and since that the real object of this neutral Northerner force at the Curragh was simply to occupy a large group of men who could have potentially become anti-Treaty fighters in the Civil War. Certainly, there does not appear to have been any intention of using them to carry out operations against, or in, Northern Ireland from August 1922 onwards.

Fig. 8 The Belleek–Pettigo triangle, the Northern offensive and Operation Basil. On 18 May the Northern Border Commission – made up of British and National Army liaison officers – visited the County Donegal border village of Pettigo and found the area to be 'very quiet'. The next day the joint National Army/anti-Treaty IRA Northern offensive began with a series of raids and ambushes, particularly in the border areas of Fermanagh and Tyrone. Unlike the Northern IRA, the National Army failed to mobilise in strength; only a few 'regular' soldiers crossed the border – some took up positions in Belleek – possibly due to mounting distrust towards the anti-Treaty forces. Prime Minister Sir James Craig's government ordered the Ulster Special Constabulary (USC) to retake the western side of Lower Lough Erne, also known as the 'Belleek triangle'. On 27 May Fermanagh USC county commandant, Basil Brooke, sent a force made up of sixty-four 'A' and 'B' Specials, by boat to the western shore of the 'triangle', where they took possession of Magherameena Castle, ejecting the local Catholic priest and prominent Sinn Féin supporter Fr Lorcan O'Kieran from his home. Rather than giving up Belleek, the IRA went on the attack; a USC constable, Wexford-born Thomas Rickerby, was killed in an ambush near Belleek Fort on 28 May when USC commanders attempted to send reinforcements. The USC was forced to abandon Magherameena and retreated in small boats to nearby Buck Island, from where it was evacuated on 29 May by a local vessel, *The Pandora*, owned and captained by Hazel Laverton. The geography of west Fermanagh meant that it was almost impossible to defeat the IRA and elements of the National Army unless the British army occupied the hills in Donegal that overlooked Tullyhommon and Belleek and the roads that connected both places to the rest of Fermanagh. The operation to take Pettigo – named 'Basil' – was an entirely British army affair, aside from some borrowed USC lorries and drivers. On Sunday morning, 4 June, two companies each from 1st Battalion, Lincolnshire Regiment and 2nd Battalion, South Staffordshire Regiment, supported by a section of howitzers and five armoured cars, moved quickly to occupy Pettigo and the surrounding area. A USC driver, twenty-year-old Leitrim-native Thomas Dobson, was shot dead by IRA gunfire from Drumharriff Hill, overlooking Pettigo and on the Donegal side of the border. According to the National Army, Pettigo was defended by a force of eighty-six men; fifty-five of these were 'pro-Treaty' (largely, but not exclusively, soldiers drawn from the 1st Northern Division) and the rest anti-Treaty IRA Volunteers. At 1.20 p.m., the British commander of Operation Basil, Colonel Louis Wyatt, ordered the firing of four howitzer rounds on an IRA position on Drumharriff Hill and for flanking parties to take the hills to the south-west and north-east of the village. Three IRA Volunteers, Bernard McKenna, William Kearney and Patrick Flood, were killed on Drumharriff Hill after being outflanked – 'a British Lewis gun catching them in the rear and a bayonet party from the west'. Two more artillery rounds were fired at National Army/IRA positions in Pettigo village itself. At approximately 1.40 p.m. Col. Wyatt ordered a ceasefire and walked up towards the Mill Street bridge in Pettigo accompanied by an armoured car. There he spoke to Lieutenant Hugh Martin, a National Army officer from Derry. Wyatt informed Martin that he and his men had up to 2 p.m. in which to evacuate Pettigo. Captain Michael O'Farrell, a twenty-five-year-old National Army medical officer in command of the garrison at Pettigo, claimed that he agreed to this, but that he and some of his men were fired on and taken prisoner before the time elapsed. The British armoured cars crossed the border, firing at what they reported as 'manned houses'. By 2.15 p.m. Wyatt and his men had taken control of Pettigo, capturing fifteen prisoners, including O'Farrell. A police Lancia car seized by the IRA on 28 May and a Lewis gun were also recovered. A National Army officer, Joseph Murray, recalled that he moved from Ballyshannon with reinforcements towards Pettigo to cover the retreat of the garrison and soldiers. Realising the scale of the British offensive, Murray quickly decided not to contest the British assault any further: 'Joe Sweeney [commander 1st Division, National Army] and I decided that our men would be massacred. We decided to withdraw them [from Belleek]. We knew that if we provoked the British, they would take Ballyshannon.' Only IRA Volunteers remained in Belleek when British soldiers entered the village on 8 June, quickly seizing it and the overlooking fort (in County Donegal) without fatalities on either side. The onset of the Civil War meant that proposals for a future National Army offensive against Northern Ireland were pushed aside. Pettigo was handed over by the British army to a Free State garrison on 9 January 1923 and the fort at Belleek was returned the following year. [Text: Edward Burke / Sources: NAUK: CAB 21/254: Northern Ireland: invasion of, Republican: Memorandum from Major General Cameron, Command. Ulster District, to General Headquarters Ireland, 6 June 1922; Nevil Macready, *Annals of an Interesting Life, Volume 2* (London, 1924), p. 622; PRONI: T/2616/3; Livingstone Papers: Joseph Murray, 16 June 1967; NAUK: CAB 21/254: Memorandum from Major General Cameron, Command. Ulster District, to General Headquarters Ireland, 6 June 1922.; Mervyn Dane, *The Fermanagh 'B' Specials* (Enniskillen, 1970), p. 9.; NAUK: WO 32/9527: Provisional Government of Ireland Committee – Operations in the Pettigo Area: Report by Colonel-Commandant Dan Hogan, 7 June 1922. The Tank Museum, History of 5th Armoured Car Company, 1920–1922: Report on Pettigo and Belleek, June 1922; NAUK: WO 32/9527: Report by Colonel-Commandant Dan Hogan, 7 June 1922: Witness Statement by Lieutenant Hugh Martin; CAB 21/254: Memorandum from Major General Cameron, 6 June 1922; 'Moving on Belleek'. *Belfast Newsletter*, 8 June 1922; PRONI: T/2616/3: Livingstone Papers: Joseph Murray, 16 June 1967]

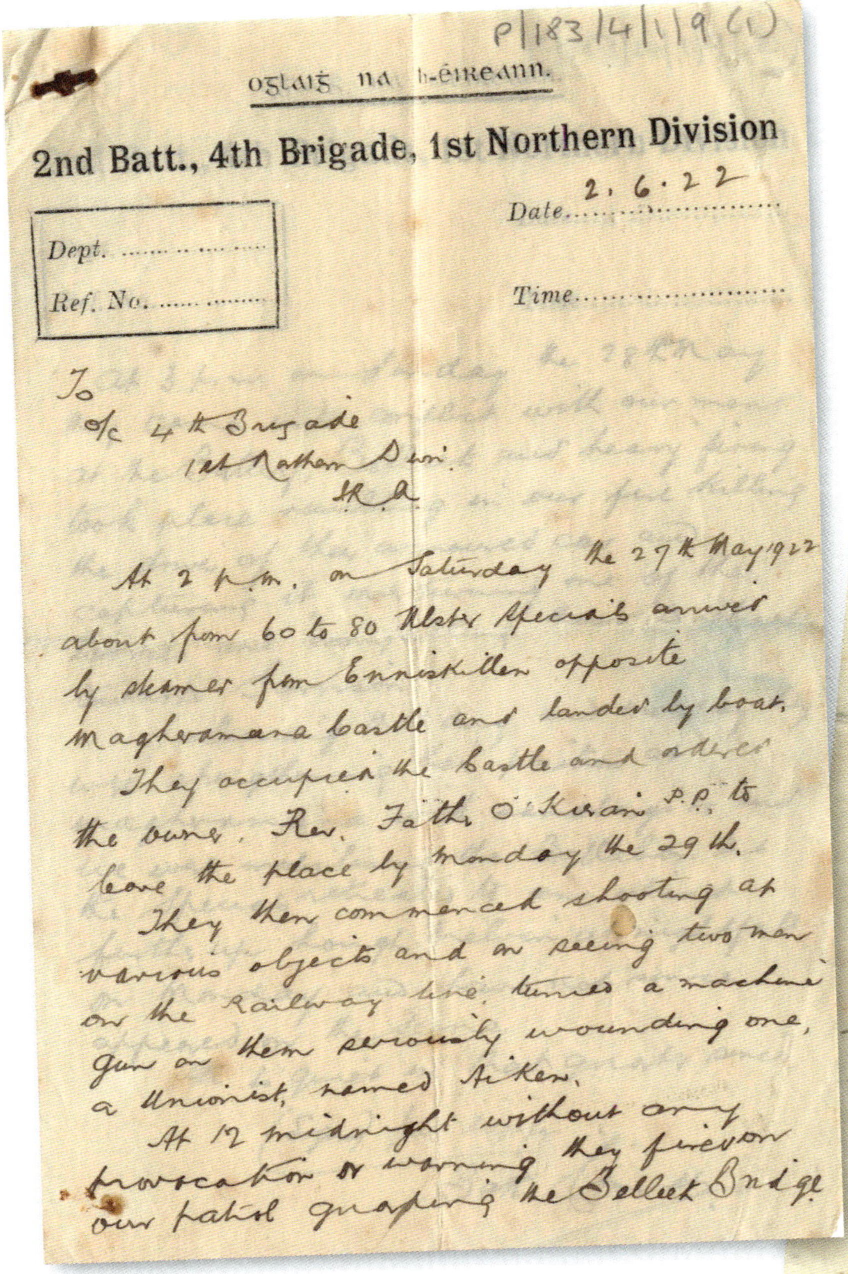

P/183/4/1/9(1)

Óglaiġ na h-Éireann.

2nd Batt., 4th Brigade, 1st Northern Division

Date 2.6.22

Dept. ....

Ref. No. ....

Time............

To
O/c 4th Brigade
1st Northern Divn.
I.R.A.

At 2 p.m. on Saturday the 27th May 1922 about from 60 to 80 Ulster Specials arrived by steamer from Enniskillen opposite Magheramena Castle and landed by boat.

They occupied the Castle and ordered the owner, Rev. Father O'Kieran P.P. to leave the place by Monday the 29th.

They then commenced shooting at various objects and on seeing two men on the Railway line turned a machine gun on them seriously wounding one, a Unionist, named Aiken.

At 12 midnight without any provocation or warning they fired on our patrol guarding the Belleek Bridge

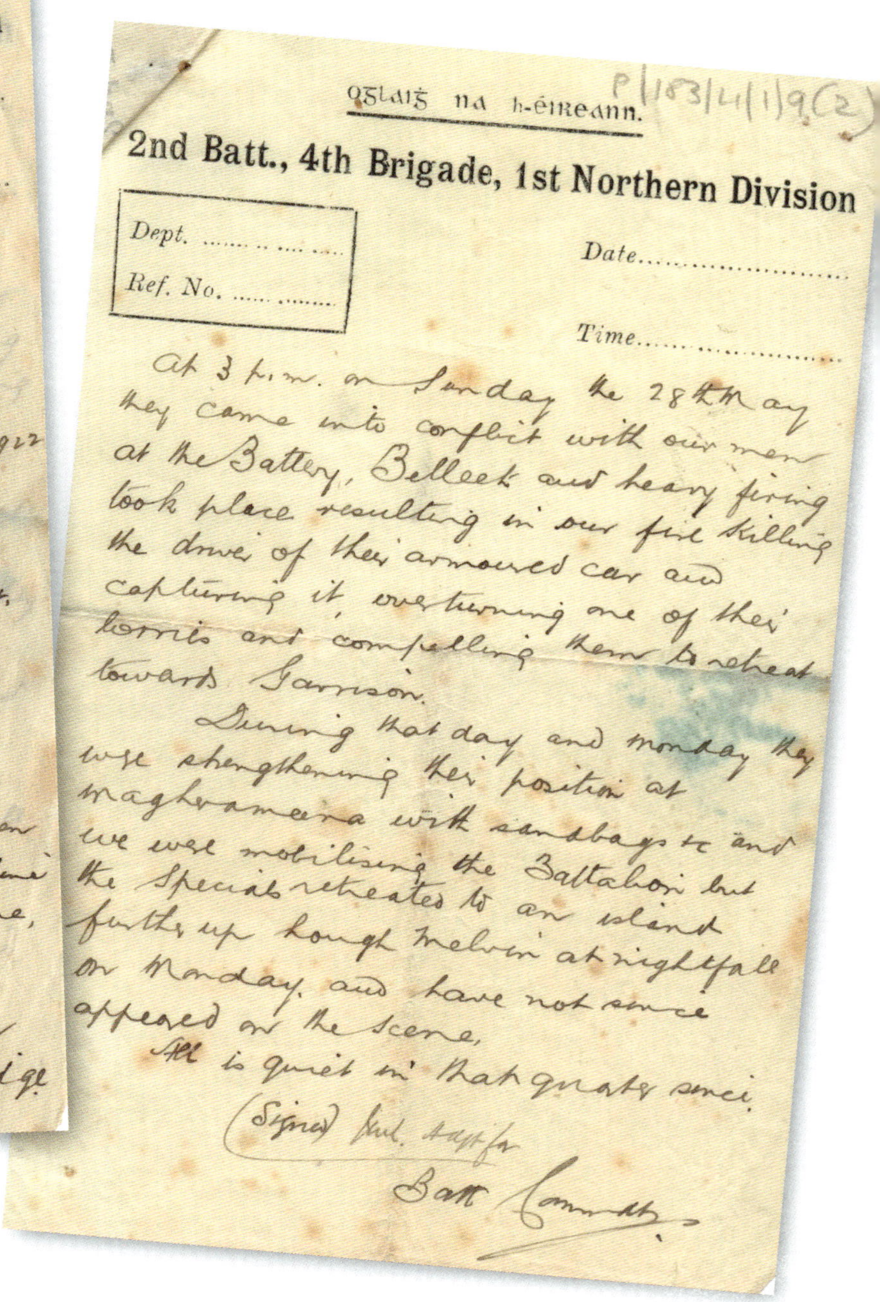

P/183/4/1/9(2)

Óglaiġ na h-Éireann.

2nd Batt., 4th Brigade, 1st Northern Division

Dept. ....

Ref. No. ....

Date............

Time............

At 3 p.m. on Sunday the 28th May they came into conflict with our men at the Battery, Belleek and heavy firing took place resulting in our fire killing the driver of their armoured car and capturing it, overturning one of their lorries and compelling them to retreat towards Garrison.

During that day and Monday they were strengthening their position at Magheramena with sandbags &c and we were mobilising the Battalion but the Specials retreated to an island further up Lough Melvin at nightfall on Monday and have not since appeared on the scene.

All is quiet in that quarter since.

(Signed) Intel. Adjt for
Batt Commdt.

Fig. 9 Dispatch to Joseph Murray, officer commanding 4th Brigade (South-east Donegal), 1st Northern Division IRA, 2 June 1922. From the papers of Joseph Murray (1893–1975), the report from the commandant of the 2nd Battalion covers the events of 27–29 May 1922. He describes a series of fierce engagements between the 'Specials' and the local IRA days before the arrival of the British army. Born in Monaghan and active in the Gaelic Athletic Association and Gaelic League, Murray was a National school teacher who, during the War of Independence, served as an intelligence officer and later vice-officer commanding and adjutant of the 4th Brigade, 1st Northern Division. As Pauric Travers notes, the war in Donegal 'was on a smaller scale than much of the rest of the country'. Donegal experienced a much more intense, if short-lived, Civil War, even though the majority of the local IRA, including Murray, took the pro-Treaty side. Given the county's border location, partition was central to its Civil War experience. The influx of anti-Treaty IRA members from Northern Ireland, backed by seasoned republican fighters from Munster sent north to join the IRA's abortive 'Northern offensive', contributed significantly to a more bitter phase of fighting. As the Civil War petered out in Donegal in October 1922, Joseph Murray joined the new Civic Guard as an inspector. In February 1923 he was transferred to the Dingle District in County Kerry. Promoted to superintendent in 1924, he subsequently served in the Dungarvan, Bailieboro, Westport, Gorey and Killaloe districts before his transfer in 1945 to Cavan Town District, where he served until his retirement in March 1958. [Document: courtesy of Donegal County Archives / See Pauric Travers, *The Irish Revolution, 1912–23: Donegal* (Dublin, 2022)]

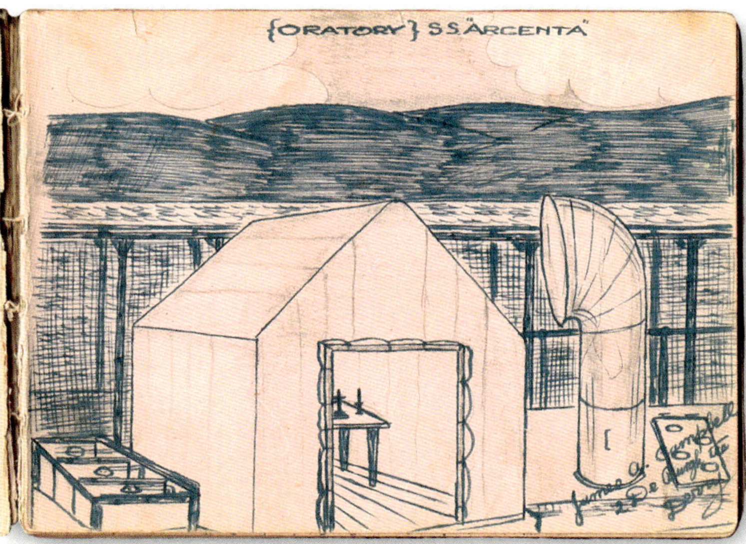

Fig. 10 a–c Pages from internees' autograph books, *Argenta* prison ship, Belfast, 1922–3. The *Argenta* was a US-made wooden steamer, purchased for £3,000 by the Northern Ireland government in May 1922 in anticipation of the introduction of internment. It was refitted as a prison ship at Harland & Wolff shipyard, and received its first internees on 20 June. The *Argenta* was the main site of internment for republicans in Northern Ireland in 1922–3; other jail sites were the Larne (Workhouse) camp, Belfast Prison and Derry Gaol. Up to 345 men (almost half of all internees in Northern Ireland) were held aboard the *Argenta* in cramped conditions, with groups of up to fifty-six men held in steel cages below deck. Conditions were unsanitary and disease was rife. In good weather the internees could exercise and mingle on the ship's deck in daytime. The vessel was initially anchored in Belfast Lough, was moved to Larne Lough in August 1922, and remained in use until January 1924. Just under half the internees on the ship (131) joined the countrywide hunger strike of republican prisoners and internees in October 1923; most were transferred to either Larne Workhouse or Belfast Prison. The remaining 101 internees on the *Argenta* in January 1924 were transferred to Belfast Prison and gradually released, most after agreeing to abide by exclusion orders from some or all of Northern Ireland. [Images a and b: National Library of Ireland, MS 50,137; image c: The 'Oratory' from James Morgan's autograph book, courtesy of whytes.com / See Denise Kleinrichert, *Republican Internment and the Prison Ship* Argenta, *1922* (Dublin, 2001); Seán McConville, *Irish Political Prisoners, 1920–1962* (London, 2014), and Anne-Marie McInerney, 'Internment on the Prison Ship *Argenta*', https://www.theirishstory.com/2020/05/04/internment-on-the-prison-ship-argenta/]

Following the death of Michael Collins on 22 August 1922, the Free State government pursued a policy of pacification in its approach to Northern Ireland. This sealed the fate of the Northern neutrals in the Curragh, with Ernest Blythe taking a particularly negative attitude towards them. At the end of the Civil War he reportedly told them to either join the army or get out. Those who refused to enlist were taken to the border and left to their own devices when they got there. They were immediately interned or heavily surveilled by police for years afterward.[55] Others tried to remake their lives in an extremely hostile environment. One example was John Lafferty, from Magilligan, County Derry. Lafferty fought in the GPO in 1916 with the Kimmage Garrison, continued his activism in his home area during the War of Independence, and fled across the border in May 1922, joining the National Army as a neutral Northerner. When he refused to fight in the Civil War, his superiors attempted to have him imprisoned. He fled and eventually travelled to Dublin to complain to Richard Mulcahy about his treatment. He was again held in custody with no resolution to his problem, and then sent back home in November 1922. Like many others he felt his refusal to choose sides in the South precluded him from accessing employment in the army, gardaí or other public positions. When he got back to the six counties, he attempted to establish a business after struggling to find employment. The business failed in the difficult economic circumstances and the lack of patronage coming from his unionist neighbours. His wife then died, and he had four children to care for.[55] After much pleading he was awarded a military service pension, but felt compelled to emigrate, living out his remaining years in Chicago.

Lafferty was not the only one to leave Northern Ireland out of economic necessity. For some, poor economic circumstance was exacerbated by their political affiliations or previous activities. The push factor in the migration of republican activists was certainly stronger than the pull of their final destinations. But it was not just republicans or active republicans who left – and, indeed, many of them stayed in Northern Ireland after they were released from internment. The post-war economic slump hit hard in

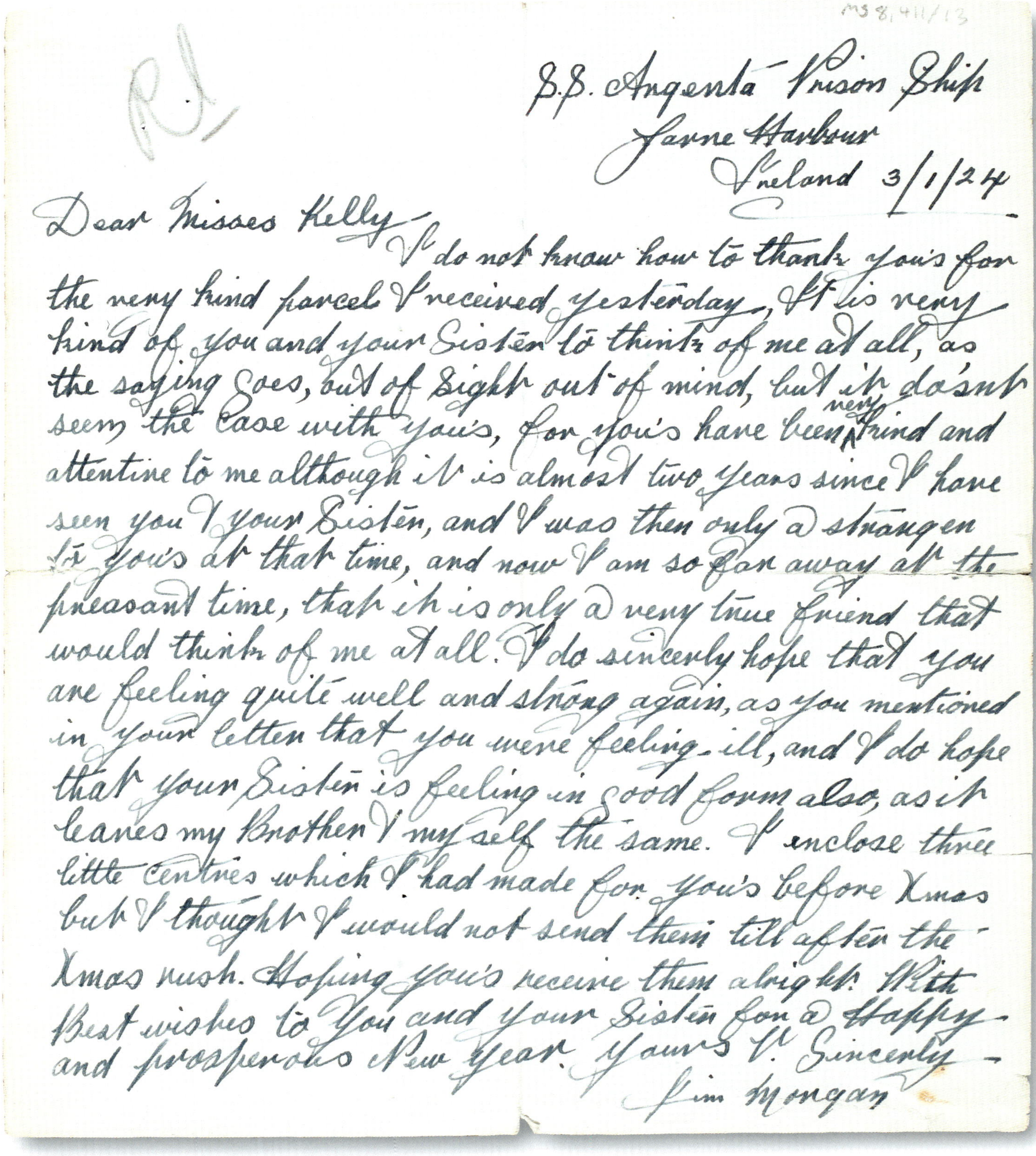

S.S. Argenta Prison Ship
Larne Harbour
Ireland 3/1/24

Dear Misses Kelly
I do not know how to thank you's for the very kind parcel I received yesterday, It is very kind of you and your Sister to think of me at all, as the saying goes, out of sight out of mind, but it do'snt seem the case with you's, for you's have been very kind and attentive to me although it is almost two years since I have seen you & your Sister, and I was then only a stranger to you's at that time, and now I am so far away at the preasant time, that it is only a very true friend that would think of me at all. I do sincerly hope that you are feeling quite well and strong again, as you mentioned in your letter that you were feeling ill, and I do hope that your Sister is feeling in good form also, as it leaves my Brother & my self the same. I enclose three little centres which I had made for you's before Xmas but I thought I would not send them till after the Xmas rush. Hoping you's receive them alright. With Best wishes to You and your Sister for a Happy and prosperous New Year. Your's V. Sincerely
Jim Morgan

Fig. 11 Letter from Jim Morgan, a prisoner on the *Argenta* prison ship, to Kate Kelly, 3 January 1924, thanking her for sending a parcel. [Document: National Library of Ireland, MS 8,411/13]

Figs 12 and 13 (above) Portrait of Ernest Blythe/Earnán de Blaghd (1889–1975) by Ernest Forbes, aka 'Shemus'. (right) First page of Blythe's influential 9 August 1922 memorandum on the Provisional Government's Northern policy. Blythe was an unusual Irish revolutionary, being a Northern Protestant from County Antrim. He moved to Dublin to work in the Department of Agriculture and Technical Instruction in 1905. He was active in the Gaelic League along with Seán O'Casey, who instigated Blythe's admittance to the Irish Republican Brotherhood (IRB) in 1906. He returned north in 1909 to work as a journalist with the unionist *North Down Herald*. He was briefly a member of the Orange Order (1910–12) while continuing his IRB work, including an editorial position with its new paper *Irish Freedom* from 1910. Historian David Fitzpatrick has speculated that there may have been a touch of the 'double agent' about Blythe, seeking 'to enlighten republicans about unionism, and unionists about Irish nationality'. He returned south in 1913, worked as a farm labourer on the Dingle Peninsula to improve his Irish, and threw himself into organisational work with the Irish Volunteers and the IRB. Blythe was imprisoned in Britain following the Easter Rising. After his release he was elected to the Sinn Féin executive in 1917. Elected TD for Monaghan North in the 1918 general election, Blythe was appointed director of trade and commerce in the First Dáil. He opposed the Dáil's Belfast boycott policy, believing it to be counterproductive. He supported the Treaty but disagreed with Michael Collins's subsequent dual Northern policy of 'public conciliation and covert subversion'. His 9 August memorandum (when he was minister for local government) marked a decisive shift in government thinking about the North, and criticised Collins's 'belligerent policy', which proved 'useless for protecting the Catholics or stopping the pogroms'. Blythe argued in the strongest terms that neither military nor economic pressure would result in reunification and, if there was to be any hope of 'getting the Six Counties back', it depended on the 'abandonment of all thought of force on our part'. Amicable relations between the two governments and the adoption of a 'peaceful policy' remained the best strategy 'to prepare the way for a state of feeling which may lead to the unity of Ireland'. His policy suggestions were adopted and set a template for future governments also. Blythe became minister for finance in 1923 and is best remembered for cutting the old-age pension in his first austerity budget. He became vice-president of the Executive Council in 1927 following the assassination of Kevin O'Higgins, and also took on the additional role of minister for posts and telegraphs. He left office with the Cumann na nGaedheal government in 1932 and lost his seat in 1933, after which he served two years as a senator (1934–6). He was an enthusiastic Blueshirt while that movement lasted, after which he drifted from politics, becoming general manager of the Abbey Theatre (1941–67), having been a director since 1935. He continued to take an active part in discussions and debates on the North, opposing anti-partition campaigns and arguing for the deletion of Articles 2 and 3 of the 1937 constitution, which claimed the six counties as part of the 'national territory'. [Memo from the Papers of Ernest Blythe, UCDA P24/70. Reproduced by kind permission of UCD Archives / Image: 'Mr. Ernest Blythe' by Shemus, National Library of Ireland, PD 4309 TX 184 / See Patrick Buckley, 'Ernest Blythe', *Dictionary of Irish Biography*, https://www.dib.ie/biography/blythe-ernest-de-blaghd-earnan-a0753 and David Fitzpatrick, *Ernest Blythe in Ulster: The making of a double agent?* (Cork, 2018), quotes from back-cover blurb and p. 156]

P24/70(2)

POLICY IN REGARD TO THE NORTH-EAST

(1)

The results of the General Election and the still more important results of the offensive against Irregulars put the Government for the first time in a position to decide freely upon its policy in regard to the North-East.

(2)

There is no prospect of bringing about the unification of Ireland within any reasonable period of time by attacking the North East, its forces or Government. Military operations on regular lines are out of the question because of the certainty of active British support. Guerilla operations within the Six Counties can have noe of the success which attended our operations against the British. The fact that the Protestant population (in most places the majority) will everywhere be actively on the side of the Government makes that impossible. The continuance of guerilla warfare on any considerable scale can only mean within a couple of years the total extirpation of the Catholic population of the North East. The events of the past few months make that evident. As soon as possible all military operations on the part of our supporters in or against the North East should be brought to end.

Economic pressure against the North East, gives no greater promise of satisfactory results than military action. The prosperity of the North East depends mainly on (1) Agriculture (2) Shipbuilding (3) Linen. The wholesale distributing trade is quite a minor factor. Nothing that we can do by way of boycott - the economic weapon heretofore in use - will bring the Orange party

1920–1 and the unemployment rate in Northern Ireland fluctuated between 10 and 20 per cent until 1932.[57] Some industries went into terminal decline, and work was extremely scarce for nationalists as well as unionists. Jobs in the USC and newly formed Royal Ulster Constabulary (RUC) provided a safety valve that brought a potentially critical unionist working class into the fold.[58] Those who emphasised a class consciousness to the extent that they felt comfortable critiquing the Unionist Party found themselves identified as the kind of 'rotten Prods' that had been ejected from the Belfast shipyards in 1912 and again in 1920.[59]

The making of Northern Ireland

The story of Northern Ireland in the June 1922 to May 1923 period is one of consolidation and state building. The government cracked down firmly on dissent, while the enemy of its project was distracted with internecine conflict. Victory over the IRA was decisive and was aided by the extrajudicial violence of the security services. People who did not subscribe to the unionist project in the six counties quickly realised that the game was lost and that armed resistance, or reliance on the republican political strategy, were not going to get them far. When the IRA collapsed north of the border, active anti-partition nationalists who remained at home looked to the hope held out by the Boundary Commission. It is difficult to see what other choice they had. The flagship Sinn Féin strategy of non-recognition of Northern institutions was coming apart at the seams, as typified by the Free State ceasing to pay Northern teachers' salaries, thereby forcing them to recognise the Northern Ireland Department of Education.[60] Nationalists in Northern border areas felt they could be delivered into the arms of the Free State, particularly those areas where local government had been in nationalist control since 1920. They believed they had the resources and clout to make the strongest case possible for a favourable revision of the boundary, but the unionist government abolished PR in local elections in 1922 and, when the next elections came about in 1924, those council areas were once again controlled by the Unionist Party on behalf of a unionist minority population.[61] The problems associated with unionist local government in these areas were all too clear less than fifty years later when the next phase of sustained violent conflict in the North commenced.

Creating the ideal Northern Ireland required keeping dissent in its place, so if those who did not fit the ideal image wanted

Fig. 14 'The Fat Boy of the North', *Saturday Herald*, 17 October 1925. Cartoonist Gordon Brewster, referencing 'The Fat Boy' from Charles Dickens's *The Pickwick Papers*, highlights the bloated budget allocatec to the Royal Ulster Constabulary at a time of relative peace in Northern Ireland, in contrast to meagre amounts paid in social welfare at a time of rising unemployment. [Image: National Library of Ireland, PD 2199 TX 424]

to move elsewhere, the government did not strain to convince them to remain. This was clearly demonstrated by the Northern Ireland government's attitude to National Army recruitment agents from the South carrying out their duties in the six counties. These recruitment agents were allowed to carry on their work across Northern Ireland, unless their presence was likely to cause trouble, usually in unionist areas.[62] The secretary at the Ministry of Home Affairs noted in March 1923 that agents operating in Derry were to be accommodated since the majority of those responding to recruitment calls were 'out of works' and 'ne'er do wells' whose loyalty to Northern Ireland was questionable.

When a large group left the city to join the National Army in February 1923, they were individually interviewed by the RUC and USC before they crossed the border. The police commissioner noted that 'most of the men who joined up were drawing out of work Donation at the Labour Exchange and their absence from the City and six Counties should mean a considerable saving of money to the Northern Government'. It was also found that the main motivations for Northern recruitment to the National Army were based on economic factors.[63] Religious affiliation and community identity stood for little if one did not fully subscribe to the unionist project. The 1,685 recruits who crossed the border between April and December 1921 included unemployed unionists from the staunchly loyalist areas of the Shankill, Crumlin and Newtownards Roads in Belfast. The RUC also noted that there was keen interest from the Free State to attract unionist ex-soldiers due to the likelihood that they would be 'far more vigorous in the execution of their duty against the Republicans than those joining from the Free State'.[64]

The Southern republican turn to inward conflict in June 1922 provided the Northern Ireland government with the space it needed to defeat the IRA. This was easily achieved, often with bloody results and little opposition. Collins's parallel strategies of aggression and pacification did not succeed and his priorities lay elsewhere from June to August 1922. Following his death there was little in the way of even a semi-coherent strategy coming from Dublin, and the Northern minority was essentially left to its own devices. The Northern Ireland government had the freedom and space to consolidate its power and continue with the state-building project, albeit with the threat of the Boundary Commission looming and an acute sense of insecurity arising from distrust in the minority population. By the end of the 1920s, after the collapse of the Boundary Commission left the Northern frontier unchanged, Northern Ireland was firmly established, the minority held in check, and any threat of destabilisation coming from the South was entirely rhetorical.

Frank Aiken and the Breakout from Dundalk Gaol

Fig. 1 (above) Frank Aiken (right) photographed in 1926 during a fund-raising tour in the United States. Aiken (1898–1983) was born in south Armagh. Aged sixteen, he joined the Irish Volunteers and, following the Easter Rising, became a Sinn Féin organiser. He was arrested in 1918 for illegal drilling and imprisoned in Belfast. Following his release, and as the War of Independence took hold, Aiken made a name for himself orchestrating daring IRA raids and ambushes in south Armagh and south Down. By March 1921 Aiken had risen to commandant of the 4th Northern Division and, in June of the same year, he meticulously planned the spectacular derailing of the train carrying the cavalry regiment that had escorted George V at the opening of the Northern Ireland parliament. However, it was in the period following the Truce of July 1921 that Aiken really made his name. He opposed the Treaty but initially urged restraint after the Dáil had ratified the deal, assuming a steadfast neutrality he would later apply to foreign policy as minister for the coordination of defensive measures during the 1939–45 Emergency. In a list drawn up in March 1922, Aiken was the only senior IRA officer described as 'non-partisan'. His earnest effort to avoid civil war was reflected in his role in negotiations leading to the electoral pact between Collins and de Valera in May 1922, with Aiken's division taking no part in the series of covert offensives against the Northern state sanctioned by Collins. Aiken was implacably opposed to the formation of what he regarded as the sectarian entity of Northern Ireland. Nonetheless, he was associated with an episode of sectarian violence in the North that tainted his reputation: responding to the gang rape of a heavily pregnant local Catholic woman by a group of Ulster Special constables, Aiken's troops carried out a notorious reprisal in the town of Altnaveigh on 17 June 1922, killing six innocent members of a small Presbyterian community. Meanwhile, his middle-ground position was becoming increasingly untenable as the Civil War intensified, and his eventual refusal, when pressed, to endorse the Provisional Government in Dublin led to his imprisonment in Dundalk Gaol in July 1922. He wasted no time in leading a mass escape of 100 prisoners and responded to what he saw as a double-cross by the Free State minister for defence, Richard Mulcahy, by angrily renouncing his neutrality. His republican colleague, Todd Andrews, called Aiken's subsequent dramatic recapture of Dundalk from Free State forces 'the most spectacularly efficient' IRA operation during the entire Civil War. Yet the Civil War placed this restless guerrilla and his men in a strange limbo: whereas previously they could escape south across the new border, they now found themselves fugitives in both states. Nevertheless, he continued to evade capture and his by-now-established renown led to him being elected successor to Liam Lynch as chief of staff by the IRA's executive in April 1923. Aiken had helped to carry the dying Lynch across the Knockmealdown Mountains before his body was laid down, and now, wearied by war, it would be Aiken who would secure his place in history by issuing the order to 'dump arms' in May 1923. [Text: Bryce Evans / Image: Papers of Frank Aiken, P104/2797. Reproduced by kind permission of UCD Archives]

Today is the first news we got from the outside world, no Newspapers from any quarter

Dundalk
Friday Aug 18th

Dear Jennie
I got your letter & enclosure (£1) safely on Monday morning and will have Masses offered as requested but as you must be aware we had no means of communication either by wire, telephone or post since and I suppose you must think we are dead & buried, but thank God we are all alive and well both in Roden Place and St. Helena and Nellie was here this day & is still on foot, I need not tell you of our experience & all that happened since last Monday, as you will have the true acct in the Democrat before perhaps you get this letter as Pat Watters says the post is going via Holyhead. The worst time we had was on Wednesday night & we spent it mostly in the cellar as the Irregulars were sniping from

Century Tower next door from
Haughey's top windows and
Distillery. We were closed up
6 o/c and at ½ nine Dr. O'Hagan
from the Hospital that
Free State Troops were on the
hill & to send him a
supply of Cigs, as he would
home & Dr. Clarke would
up. Johnnie got home
Frank Byrne's funeral
previously he went there
Frank Henry & Stephen Hueston
said the Troops were in
& attended the funeral
was a great but sad sight
that they were coming in
numbers to Dundalk
expected them in at 10 o/c
to the cellar as from
until morning we were
anxious state, knowing
the first shot from next door
they would shell the Century tower
& we might all be killed but
a deluge of rain came on during
the night and the Troops did not
come in until Morning before

Fig. 2 First two pages of a four page letter written by Esmay Young from Roden Place in Dundalk to her daughter Jeannie Mahony in Drogheda, dated 18 August 1922. It is clear from the letter that she had a great deal of sympathy for the 'valiant soldiers' who were now under attack from National Army troops sent to wrest back control of Dundalk from those in the IRA's 4th Northern Division under the command of Frank Aiken. Aiken's initial neutrality and equivocation vis-à-vis the authority of the Provisional Government had presented the latter with a significant problem, which meant that Louth and especially Dundalk would endure a great deal of turmoil during the ensuing conflict. In an attack beginning on 14 August, Aiken had reclaimed the town from the National Army, which was now intent on taking it back. Young's letter captures the immediacy of war from the point of view of a civilian caught up in the crossfire. She notes the 'Irregulars sniping from the Century Tower next door' as well as the 'rifles left in McDonalds' garden and in Haugheys'' by those fleeing the advancing Free State forces. Confined to a cellar, the fear of being shelled and killed was real. The ferocity of the onslaught meant that familiar streets were largely unrecognisable after the fighting had stopped: 'If you only saw Francis Street, Earl St. and Park St. anything like it. Every window top and bottom were broken and poor Miss Murphy Francis St. and Peter Kieran's ceilings down, furniture and everything down and broken and McManus's as bad and both sides of Earl St. not a safe window, every place boarded up, such a difference in the streets we passed through Wed. morning'. [Document: Louth County Archives, PP00011/006]

Fig. 3 Places of birth of the escapees from Dundalk Gaol, July 1922. The escape of Frank Aiken and other officers of the 4th Northern Division of the IRA from Dundalk Gaol in July 1922 represents one of the most dramatic escape stories in the Civil War period, and (through the circumstances surrounding it) provides a particularly vivid insight into the confused, complex and tragic mix of elements and forces so evident at the beginning of the Civil War. Aiken (chief of staff of the 4th Northern Division) had established his headquarters in Dundalk barracks in April 1922 and, when the Civil War began in late June, his division had attempted to maintain a position of neutrality between the opposing sides, against increasingly impossible odds. Aiken was invited to Portobello Barracks in Dublin for negotiations (beginning 6 July) with General Richard Mulcahy, then serving as both minister for defence and chief of staff of the National Army. At the end of the negotiations Aiken was requested to submit a memorandum summarising the views he had expressed, as soon as possible, to the commander in chief of the National Army (Michael Collins) and the head of the Provisional Government (an ailing Arthur Griffith). Aiken then returned to Dundalk to begin composing the memorandum, but, within a short period of his return, the town was taken over by National Army troops and Aiken was arrested, along with other officers of his division in Dundalk Barracks who refused to declare allegiance to the National Army. Aiken and the other officers who refused to cooperate were then imprisoned in Dundalk Gaol. Various other officers of Aiken's division who were not in Dundalk that night immediately began making an escape plan for their comrades. As it happened, this division (now, by force of circumstance, anti-Treaty) was the most advanced in the use of explosives among any anti-Treaty division. With expert planning (including secret communication with Aiken and 'friendly' warder collusion), a hole, approximately four-feet-square, was blown into the base of the wall of the jail at a carefully agreed time and location, which facilitated the escape of Aiken and approximately 110 other prisoners on 27 July. Escape routes from the town, transport and other logistics were also carefully arranged. It was a master-class jailbreak, though some of the rearguard most prominently involved in planning the escape were arrested that night. Aiken and his men later retook the town of Dundalk from National Army troops on 14 August, though he then immediately resumed his position of extreme reluctance to engage his division in the Civil War. The division essentially went into retreat. Ultimately, it was very appropriate that it was Aiken who, in May 1923, issued the dump-arms order to anti-Treaty forces that paved the way for an end to the Civil War. [Text: Rory O'Dwyer / Source: Dundalk General Register of Prisoners, NAI/PRIS/1/16/1, reproduced in Donal Hall, *Hole in the Wall: Dundalk Jail during the Civil War* (2022)]

CASE STUDY

Protestants and the Irish Civil War

Conor Morrissey

By the early 1920s Protestants in the twenty-six counties that became the Irish Free State found themselves, as with many other European minorities, stranded on the wrong side of a newly drawn border. Enormous attention has been paid to the population decline experienced by Protestants during this time: less interest has been shown in the significant decrease in Protestant political activity in the same period. Franchise expansion, land purchase (which brought an end to gentry influence) and the Ulster orientation of unionism were all long-term trends; Sinn Féin's victory in 1918, the outbreak of the War of Independence, the passing of the Government of Ireland Act and the eruption of sectarian violence in the north-east were more acute, forcing Protestants to devise new forms of representation and communication.

Local meetings held under no political banner became important: during the fraught period of August to September 1920 at least seventeen Protestant regional assemblies took place, at which local communities stated their abhorrence at sectarian attacks in the North and their belief in the tolerance of their Catholic neighbours, and at which they sought to affirm their place in the country generally.[1] By 1922 traditional opposition to

Fig 1. Ernest Blythe, minister for local government, August 1922–October 1923 (see p. 97). [Image: National Library of Ireland, Kathleen McKenna Napoli Papers, NPA MKN26]

Lissiniskey
Nenagh

July 13th 1922

My dear Tom,

Yours of the 10th to hand. I think since the 29th of June we have had no post here. Dreadful things have happened since I wrote you April 25th. I left Rathurbet April 30th & went to Ballygibbon. On May 15th a body of men took forcible possession of 30 acres of land there. They cut trees down, yelled & shouted, drove every workman & domestic servant away,not one has yet returned. We were left with 9 cows to milk,calves & all sorts of fowl, young & old to feed. Over 90 sheep & lambs to care,all the work of the house to do. Well we did it. The sheep were the great trouble,it was the time for them to be dipped,washed & shorn. They could not be dipped or washed but Betty,Lilla & David sheared all the sheep,but we lost a good many on account of the sheep not being dipped. They got full of maggots. It was dreadfull. The cows were easily managed,we all milked them. I got quite good at it I did two night & morning. We just worked all day. On the night of June 14th we had a dreadfull raid starting about 2.30. The raiders smashed every window & the hall door first. We had collected in one room,they rushed into it. David & Betty were badly beaten by them with their clenched fists,Lilla was not so badly beaten & Poll only got one blow on her face,we were in a dark room most of the time,it was hell. I escaped without a blow. Over & over again they held revolvers & shotguns at us & said they would shoot us. They did awful mischief in the house,breaking china & table glass,drank all whiskey & claret. They empted every drawer out on the floor,Oh such a state - the dirty swine - they left the place in. They stole heaps of things, especially belonging to me,one thing was my dressing-case. I got this case together by my tennis prizes,certainly 20 years ago I started this. Every prize I took out in something for my case. Every thing was initialed,dated & where won & at last I got the case itself. I was proud of it. It was my tennis life & it has gone, they took my bicycle,such a good one & several wedding presents,antique buckles belonging to my grandmother,my only watch, between £4 & £5 ,my emerald pendant & gold chain. Oh Tom I am sick when I think of it all. Then the Free Staters had to send a guard of 7 to protect the Youngs,fancy that in a small house. They were there day & night,Guard changed once in 24 hours. We then had to feed them,cook for them,wash up after them & keep their sittingroom,but we drew the line at their bedroom , we left that. On the 19th I got married. Such a wedding,no one would allow me to put it off. I got a grey dress to be married in,late on Sunday night I put it on for the first time to see if it would fit,it did grand,I got it from Peter Robinson's. I had hardly any trousseau & some of the little I had, hadthe raiders had taken. I had no hat. I borrowed one of Betty's,all Lilla's had been taken. We got up before 6 o'clock,I swept & dusted the Guard's sittingroom (I was to be married at 9 o'clock) & then started to bring in the cowsto be milked, of course they had broken out & Lilla & I had a long trudge before we got them; when I got them in the motor was waiting to take me to the church. Lilla & I just roared with laughter,Lilla said:"Oh you do look like a bride". We escaped milking the cows,because I got round two of the guard the previous night by telling them of my wedding,they were as interestd as any woman & offered to milk the cows. It was a saving. We all had a mouthfull of breakfast,I jumped into some clothes,so did the others,we left David at home,you see he had no hat,no boots,the raiders took them & his poor face was a sight after the beating,poor dear. Off I went,when I got to the church the in-laws & a few friends were there,outside of the church,I was kissed by everywoman,by that time the borrowed hat was on the back of my head. Tom gave me away. I did everything wrong,I only thought of my mother,I never listened. We motored away to Greystones,stayed a week there & motored back here. Since then times have been rocky. On the 1st the four Youngs with a small handbag & 3 dogs arrived for shelter. The Free Staters in Nenagh were so hard pressed the had to take their guard; they were afraid of being murdered,so they cleared out leaving everything,even to the poor milch cows. Oh what a happy land is Ireland! The Isle of Saints! That night two men roused us by beating the hall door with a mild request for the motor car. We made no move,they played round the hall door & back gate for an hour & then left. A few nights after we had between 20 & 30 Republicans all round the place,at 12.30 they woke us up & we had to let them in. They billited six on us. Fire had to be lit,food prepared,then blankets & sheets. I thought the sheetes distinctly funny. We had them all night,& for breakfast. On the 8th seven armed Republicans arrived in a motor car,just after dinner. They stayed 3 hours robbing. When they left they took Hubert's moter car & their own piled with our goods also Hubert's bicycle. I soon will have nothing left. Sich a haul. Poor Hubert has no inside clothes & only one suit,no socks or stockings. It is absolutely awful. Out of three handsome sets of brushes,I have not one,not even a comb,or nail brush or clothes brush. I lost rugs,rings,brooches,my riding waterproof cost £8 ,hats , muffler,gloves & several handsome wedding presents,fortunately the big part of them are in the bank. Hubert lost all his watches,£5 & heaps of other things. But we are still alive & I can yet even laugh. Will you be tired with all this? We got the Youngs off on Tuesday by motor to Kingstown, they are now safe in England.

With love

n Your affect.cousin

Gay White

Fig. 2 (opposite page and above) Letter written by Gay White of Lissiniskey House to her cousin Tom detailing an attack on her home during the early months of the Civil War. Lissiniskey was a substantial, three-storey, five-bay property, located 7 kilometres (4.5 miles) from Nenagh town, and was built in the latter decades of the eighteenth century. The Whites were a Protestant family who suffered intimidation, attacks on property, theft and physical violence. The targeting of local Protestant families was so widespread that the Church of Ireland bishop of Killaloe and Clonfert, Thomas Sterling Berry, declared that 'there is scarcely a Protestant family in the district which has escaped molestation'.* White describes a raid on Lissiniskey House that took place on 14 June and the beatings endured by family members: 'we had collected in one room, they rushed into it. David and Betty were badly beaten with the clenched fists. Lilla was not so badly beaten, and Poll only got one blow to her face, we were in a dark room most of the time. It was hell.' She also details how the 'Free Staters had to send a guard of 7 to protect the Youngs', another local family. And yet five days after the raid and amid all the turmoil, Gay White got married: 'no one would allow me to put it off'. Following the wedding and a brief stay in Greystones, the newly married couple returned to Lissiniskey. However, the intimidation continued. On 1 July the four Youngs took shelter in the house after the 'hard pressed' 'Free Staters' were forced to remove their guard. The IRA later billeted 'six on us', while on 8 July seven armed republicans robbed the house and family of even more possessions, including a motor car and bicycle. [Document: courtesy of Offaly Archives, IEOCLP131/2/2/6 / *See Marie Coleman, 'Biggest Impact of Irish Civil War on Protestants Involved Assaults on People and Property', *Irish Times*, 15 May 2023] an independent Ireland had given way to an understanding that political change was coming. Southern Protestants greeted the signing of the Anglo-Irish Treaty with relief. The *Church of Ireland Gazette* stated:

> We have little fear of our fellow-countrymen who will be entrusted with our destinies under the new Free State. We have considerable faith in the inherent sense of justice with which the Irish people are imbued, and believe that the rights and interests of the minority in the South and West of Ireland will be quite safe in the hands of the majority. We are Irish too.[2]

However, cases of violence and intimidation, most notably the killing of thirteen Protestants in west Cork towards the end of April 1922, caused great alarm, and led some to leave the country permanently.[3] It was in this context that the Protestant Convention met in the Mansion House in Dublin on 11 May 1922. The convention passed an apolitical set of resolutions that condemned violence and expressed the hope that Protestants could live in peace with their neighbours.[4] The convention did not form the basis for any political movement; indeed, a desire to avoid too many political entanglements is apparent. The Irish Unionist Alliance and the more moderate Unionist Anti-Partition League ceased operations in 1922; the Irish Dominion League, which might have developed into a vehicle for heterogeneous opinion, had closed the previous year.

Foreboding

It was with a sense of foreboding that most Southern Protestants met the outbreak of civil war. Protestant nationalists inhabited a different political and social sphere; the decisions they made more closely resembled those of Catholic nationalists. Figures such as Erskine Childers, Robert Barton, Albinia Brodrick, or the converts to Catholicism Maud Gonne and Constance Markievicz, may give the impression of uncompromising republicanism among Protestants from a nationalist background. However, there were several high-profile pro-Treatyites, including Ernest Blythe, Darrell Figgis and Alice Stopford Green.

The new National Army was not exclusively Catholic. According to the Free State army census of the night of 12–13 November 1922, there were 251 Protestant servicemen, amounting to 0.76 per cent of a total army strength of 33,210. Of these, 220 have been identified as Irish Protestants, as opposed to British recruits. Anglicans predominated, with 190 men; 82 per cent held the ranks of volunteer or private, although there were about sixteen Irish Protestant officers. Very few had showed nationalist sympathies during the period 1916–21, and the vast majority came from working- and lower-middle-class backgrounds, suggesting economic factors, as well as perhaps a desire to see law and order restored, drove Protestant recruitment. Although they were a small proportion of the army, Protestant servicemen are an early indicator of unobtrusive engagement with the new state.[5]

Cause of decline

Between 1911 and 1926 the Protestant population of the twenty-six-county area fell by 33 per cent. Anglicans, the largest denomination, declined by 34 per cent; the smaller Presbyterian and Methodist Churches lost 29 per cent and 35 per cent respectively.[6] The cause of this fall has proved controversial; however, some consensus has recently emerged. Most agree that the period *c.*1920–3 witnessed the most substantial decline. The 'ethnic cleansing' thesis has few adherents; most scholars argue that revolutionary violence played a smaller role in causing depopulation than did a range of other factors: historians have placed emphasis on voluntary emigration, the closure of British garrisons, low nuptiality and fertility, and the burning of big houses.[7] There is greater emphasis on those who left the country but returned when peace was restored, and on that majority of Protestants who never left at all.[8] Indeed, in May 1923, with the end of the war imminent, the *Gazette* struck a guarded but optimistic tone:

> We must turn our backs resolutely to the past, forgetting the grievances of centuries, facing the future with confidence for the first time in a hundred and twenty years. The dead past must be allowed to bury its dead and there must be no more *post mortems.* The Free State stands now on its own legs.[9]

Fig. 3 The Irish rugby team at Leicester on 10 February 1923 when they were defeated by England in an intense Five Nations rugby match. The Irish Rugby Football Union (IRFU) was founded in 1879 after a merger between the Dublin-based Irish Football Union (founded in 1874) and the Belfast-based Northern Football Union (founded in 1875). In the decades that followed, rugby grew from a game confined to the Protestant upper middle classes to one that cut across sectarian divisions in Ireland. By the 1920s the game commanded the loyalty of significant swathes of the Catholic elite and, in Limerick, enjoyed a working-class following. It was a sport that generated strong fraternal bonds both within and between nations. In that context the IRFU's attitude to partition was quite simple: it ignored it. 'The rugby game [...] recognises no border', the IRFU told Cavan RFC in 1926. The latter, in light of partition, was seeking to affiliate to the Leinster branch. Given that 'the position of the Co. Cavan RFC remains geographically the same as before the Treaty', it was told that it could only become a member of the IRFU by joining the Ulster branch. The IRFU, then, remained stubbornly committed to the game's all-island structure, believing that the game would rise above the political turmoil around it. Ireland's fixture against Wales at Lansdowne Road in 1923, for example, took place in the same week as the atrocity at Ballyseedy, County Kerry. In the days after the match the National Army executed eleven republicans. The Ireland fifteen that took the field against England in the first post-independence international a few weeks earlier was culturally diverse: it included Southern Catholics, Southern Protestants and Northern Protestants. Just to add complexity, the Protestants came from four different sects: Church of Ireland, Presbyterian, Methodist and Unitarian. Assuming a rough alignment between religious affiliation and national loyalty, it is clear that there was no stable idea of what 'Ireland' and 'Irishness' signified in rugby terms; this meant that issues of symbolism were fraught. The IRFU designed its own flag in 1925, and only agreed to fly the tricolour at home fixtures when pressured to do so by the minister for external affairs, Paddy McGilligan, in 1932. 'Amhrán na bhFiann' was played before matches at Lansdowne Road, but purely as a gesture of respect to the host state. It was never played at away fixtures as it was not the team's official anthem (the Irish rugby team did not have one until 1995). These were compromises that had to be made – there was too much to lose, in the eyes of officials, by allowing political events to disrupt the harmony of Irish rugby. The game was not an unblemished beacon of unity: it never shook off its elitism, and Northern Catholics were largely absent from it. That said, rugby still provides a striking example of cross-border cooperation. [Text: Liam O'Callaghan / Image: TopFoto]

A detachment of the National Army's Special Infantry Corps providing protection for farmers in County Waterford during a farm labourers' strike in 1923. [Image: National Library of Ireland, POOLEWP 3123]

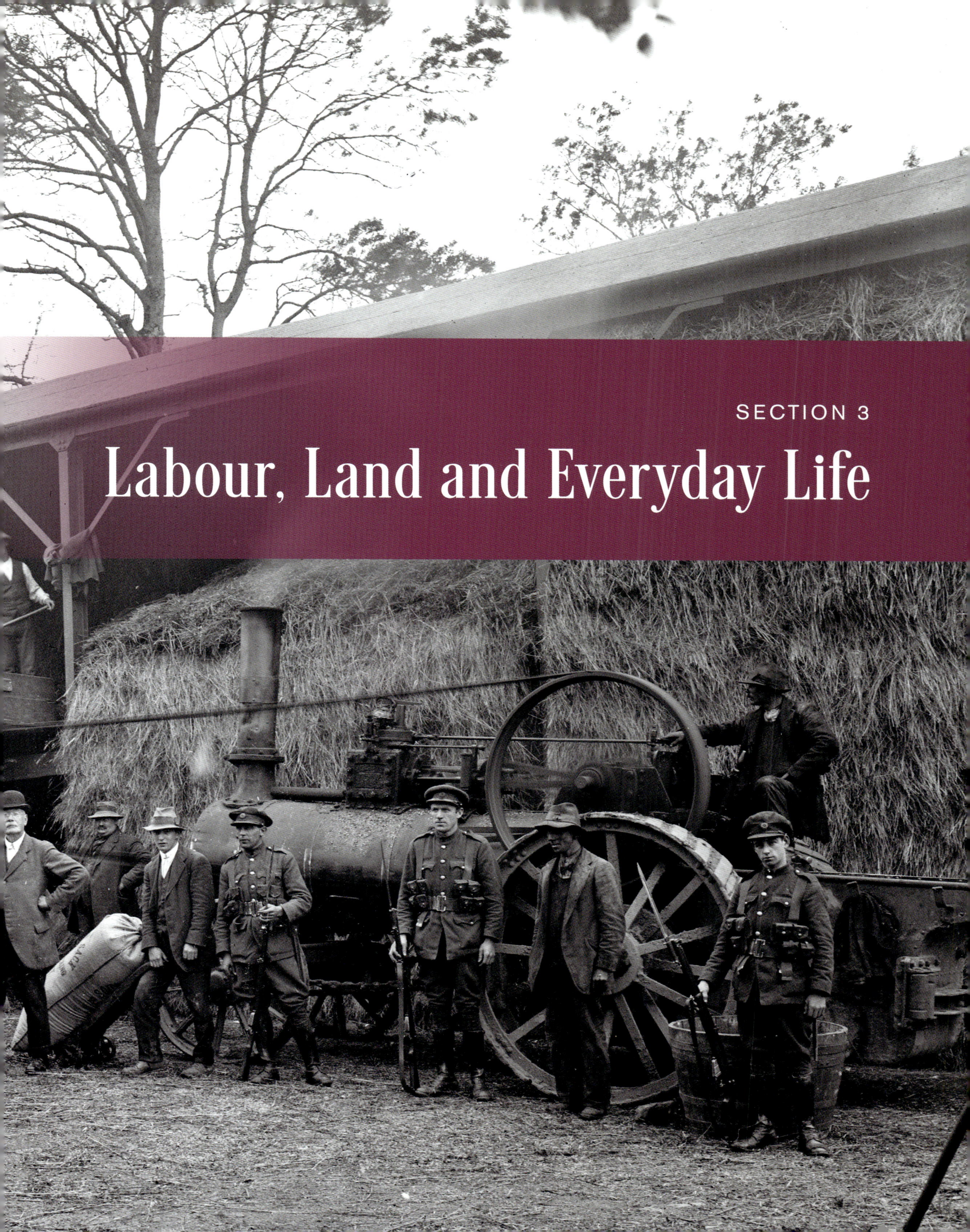

SECTION 3

Labour, Land and Everyday Life

THOMAS JOHNSON
1928

CHAPTER 4

'What the hell do they want a republic for?' Labour, the left and the Irish Civil War

Emmet O'Connor

In July 1922, after Dublin fell to Free State forces, Roddy Connolly hastened to London to meet Mikhail Markovich Borodin. Roddy, son of James, was leader of the Communist Party of Ireland (CPI). Borodin represented the Communist International, or Comintern, in Britain and was responsible for the maintenance of orthodoxy in the Communist Party of Great Britain. A legend in Bolshevik circles for his sharp analysis, he would be appointed Comintern emissary to China and Soviet legate to Sun Yat-sen in 1923.[1] Connolly outlined the far-left view of the crisis: the Civil War was a counter-revolution, instigated by British imperialism; republican resistance would bankrupt the Free State compelling a return of the British and the restoration of revolutionary conditions. Borodin scoffed:

> It is my firm opinion that they will crush the Republicans [...] It is really laughable to fight the Free State on a sentimental plea. They want a Republic. What the hell do they want a Republic for? [...] There are two military sections fighting – one is very strong and the other is very weak. One say Ireland should be fighting for prosperity. The other one is absolutely void of interest in any [such] matters.[2]

Ironically, Borodin had summed up the Irish Labour Party view of the Civil War.

Labour had emerged from the War of Independence in good heart. Thanks to the war economy and the post-war boom, membership of the Irish Labour Party and Trade Union Congress (ILPTUC) stood at nearly 200,000, double the 1917 figure.[3] Thanks to revolutions, at home and abroad, trade union militancy was matched by a confident radicalism. Now Labour expected the Anglo-Irish Treaty to settle the national question and clear the decks for class politics. Its overriding concern in 1922–3 was to heal the divisions over the Treaty and focus on social issues. The project would be complicated by the absence of dedicated political

Fig. 1 (opposite) Thomas Johnson (1872–1963), oil on canvas, by Sarah Cecilia Harrison (1928). Labour leader Johnson was born in Liverpool and moved to Belfast in 1903. As a member of Belfast Trades Council, he worked with both Larkin and Connolly and became founding vice-chairman of the Labour Party in 1912. As president of the Irish Labour Party and Trade Union Congress (ILPTUC) in 1914–16 he opposed recruitment and lost his job in Belfast in 1918 due to his role in the anti-conscription campaign. He moved to Dublin that year and was responsible for drafting the Democratic Programme of the First Dáil in 1919. He was elected TD for Dublin County in the June 1922 general election and, from 1923 to 1927, was leader of the Labour Party in the Dáil. Following the loss of his seat in 1927, he served as a senator from 1928 to 1936. Labour had no presence in the Dáil that voted on the Treaty (having stood aside in the elections of 1918 and 1921) and officially declared its neutrality on the issue. Before the final vote was taken on 7 January, the party devised a strategy aimed at avoiding a damaging schism, involving approval of the Treaty by a Southern Ireland parliament separate from the Dáil, vesting sovereignty in the Dáil, and an oath that would imply allegiance to the constitution, not the king; but it came to nought. Labour's subsequent proposals on socio-economic policy and the nationwide strike against militarism on 24 April likewise failed to influence either side. Labour had sidelined itself politically and was now discovering its impotence. Johnson was among those who privately favoured acceptance of the Treaty and, once the vote had been taken, drafted a statement in his capacity as secretary of the ILPTUC declaring the issue closed, and urging attention to socio-economic reform. This emphasis also informed the party's programme in the June 1922 general election, when it performed remarkably well, with seventeen of its eighteen candidates elected; its vote share would have yielded many more seats had it put forward more candidates. Johnson and other Labour activists, including his wife Marie, made numerous attempts to prevent civil war up to the last minute, but the die was cast. Once war began, Labour could do little, especially as the Dáil was prorogued until September. When it finally met on 9 September, Johnson was elected leader of the parliamentary party and he attempted to perform the role of opposition leader in fraught circumstances. The government was dismissive of Labour efforts to influence the constitution and of its opposition to repressive policies. Republicans likewise ignored Labour's criticisms of their actions and denounced the party for legitimising the Free State. Johnson, given the additional fact of his Englishness, was a frequent target of abuse and threats. When the Third Dáil was dissolved in August 1923, he declared the wish of many 'to blot out of Ireland's history the last 18 or 20 months' but felt proud that Labour had at least contributed to 'the building up of the idea of Parliamentary institutions'. However, in the ensuing general election, Labour's share of the vote was halved, it lost three seats, and Johnson barely held his own seat. [Image: courtesy of the Houses of the Oireachtas / See J. Anthony Gaughan, *Thomas Johnson, 1872–1963: First leader of the Labour Party in Dáil Éireann* (Dublin, 1980)]

WHAT IRISH REPUBLICANS STAND FOR

BY

CONSTANCE DE MARKIEVICZ.

"The conquest of Ireland has meant the social and political servitude of the Irish masses, and therefore the reconquest of Ireland must mean the social as well as the political independence from servitude of every man, woman and child."

—JAMES CONNOLLY.

I offer this little leaflet humbly to the memory of Wolf Tone, of Mitchell, of Lawler, and of James Connolly to whom I am indebted for the faith and the knowledge that inspired it.

Reprinted from *Forward* by courtesy of the Editor.

PRICE — TWOPENCE.

Fig. 2 (opposite) Cover of an eight-page pamphlet by Constance Markievicz, published in Scotland by Civic Press in 1923. The socialist republican polemic, first printed in the left-wing Glasgow-based newspaper *Forward*, casts the 'Free State' as a construction by the imperialist and capitalist British government and its Irish counterparts who were intent on destroying the 'growing movement towards the development of the Co-operative Commonwealth (Worker's Republic) in Ireland'. She depicts the Free State government as opportunistic profiteers and the British-sponsored military campaign as the latest phase in England's eight-century-long mission to impose the 'alien and repugnant' system of feudal capitalism on Ireland. Markievicz's admiration for James Connolly, the international socialist famed for his Marxist interpretation of Irish history, is heavily imprinted on the text. She quotes his idealised allusions to a classless, civilised, egalitarian and democratic Celtic past, which, she insists, inspired the modern republican movement. For Markievicz, 'a civilisation based on Gaelic ideals', with a democratic system of government exemplified by the First Dáil, was Ireland's best hope for the future. The alternative, she argues, under the present system whereby the Westminster system had been merely transferred to Dublin, was 'wage slavery', the continued strangulation of native industry and agriculture under state capitalism and the condemnation of 'their fellow countrymen to starvation, exile and extermination'. She concludes with another quote from Connolly, which she deems an apt description of the Free State government and its 'anti-Labour, militarist' policies: 'The political instruments of today are simply the coercive forces of Capitalist society'. [Document: National Library of Ireland, Thomas Johnson Papers, MS 17,141/20]

structures (the party and Congress were one and the same), weak leadership and internal differences over the Anglo-Irish Treaty. The end of the independence struggle also diminished Labour's political value. The Democratic Programme was merely one of a number of overtures from Sinn Féin to Labour. Dáil Eireann's Department of Labour was virtually the department of the Labour Party. Its job was to keep the labour movement onside, or in benevolent neutrality at least. It was no coincidence that the minister of labour from 1919 to 1922 was Constance Markievicz, former Irish Citizen Army (ICA) officer and an admirer of James Connolly. After the ratification of the Treaty, the Provisional Government invited Tom Johnson to nominate her successor. Johnson, political secretary of the ILPTUC, declined.[4] It would be the last crumb of comfort thrown to Labour by the national revolution. The economic boom had yielded to a slump in August 1920. Food prices fell, industry was affected in 1921 and, by 1922, over 25 per cent of insured workers were unemployed.[5] Employers demanded wage cuts and unions struck to 'hold the harvest'. As an industrial war staggered on in fits and starts from August 1921 to December 1923, the Irish government's attitude towards workers hardened to outright hostility.

Under fire

From the far left, Labour came under fire from socialist republicans, Larkinites, and the CPI. The first two had no formal organisation, though Larkinites were prominent in the Dublin Trades Council, which had split in 1920 when the Irish Transport and General Workers' Union (ITGWU) led the formation of a rival Dublin Workers' Council. Nor had they a programme other than loyalty to the republic or James Larkin and antagonism to William O'Brien, who had succeeded him as ITGWU supremo after Big Jim's flight to America in 1914. O'Brien's dictatorial style and ambition to make the ITGWU the 'One Big Union' generated scattered resentment in the fractious Dublin trade union movement. Always a visceral republican, Larkin denounced the six 'traitors', 'helots' and 'Judases' who signed the 'foul and destructive' Treaty, and suggested they hang themselves from London Bridge.[6] Although he was then mouldering in a New York jail on a charge of 'criminal anarchy', his return to Ireland was expected. The CPI was more marginal again, with some fifty members. Unfazed, Roddy Connolly predicted that the peace talks in London would split Sinn Féin and the anti-Treaty minority would turn to the CPI and Soviet Russia for help.

Workers' attitudes to the Civil War are severely under-researched. Gavin Foster's *The Irish Civil War and Society: Politics, class, and conflict,* the one comprehensive study of its social dimension, is more about Free State and republican perceptions than labour.[7] For reasons that will become apparent, mainstream labour historians have never thought the Civil War an attractive subject. Of course, as Foster notes, the lack of empirical research on class has not discouraged a little library of Marxist or conservative explanations of what the war ought to have been about. Marxists seeking to couple class with revolution have found organised labour an inconvenience. Jackson's British Communist history of Ireland dismissed the 'skilled-labour element and the Labour Party generally' as 'paralyzed by division'.[8] Academic analyses have been shaped by Labour's post-Civil War marginality in Irish politics and presumptions about the conservative nature of the national revolution. Yet the Civil War is very revealing about the Labour Party and trade unions; it was seminal in the evolution of socialist republicanism, and Labour and the left were important to the war in their different ways. Treatyites recognised that keeping Labour within the fold was critical to the regime's legitimacy, and anti-Treatyites turned for aid to the CPI.

Clearing the decks

From December 1921 the ILPTUC undertook a series of peace initiatives. When Dáil Éireann adjourned for Christmas, the executive approached Sinn Féin leaders with ingenious suggestions on how to circumvent the thorny issue of the oath of allegiance. Labour's solution was a constitution vesting sovereignty in Dáil Éireann and an oath that would 'imply allegiance to the constitution'.[9] On 10 January 1922, Labour's first formal deputation to Dáil Éireann urged TDs to concentrate on social issues like the worsening unemployment problem. That same day the Congress executive issued a 'call to action', regretting that it had not been consulted on the Treaty negotiations and affirming that, whatever the outcome, Free State or Republic, it would not be a Workers' Republic, and it was time for Labour to assert itself politically. Labour's urgency was driven by Johnson, who was strongly pro-Treaty and canvassed for it privately while publicly taking a neutral stance, a duplicity that infuriated his critics.[10] Johnson was adept at citing radical reasons for conservative decisions. Purporting to want to clear the way for class struggle, in reality he hankered after constitutional stability and a safe environment for orderly

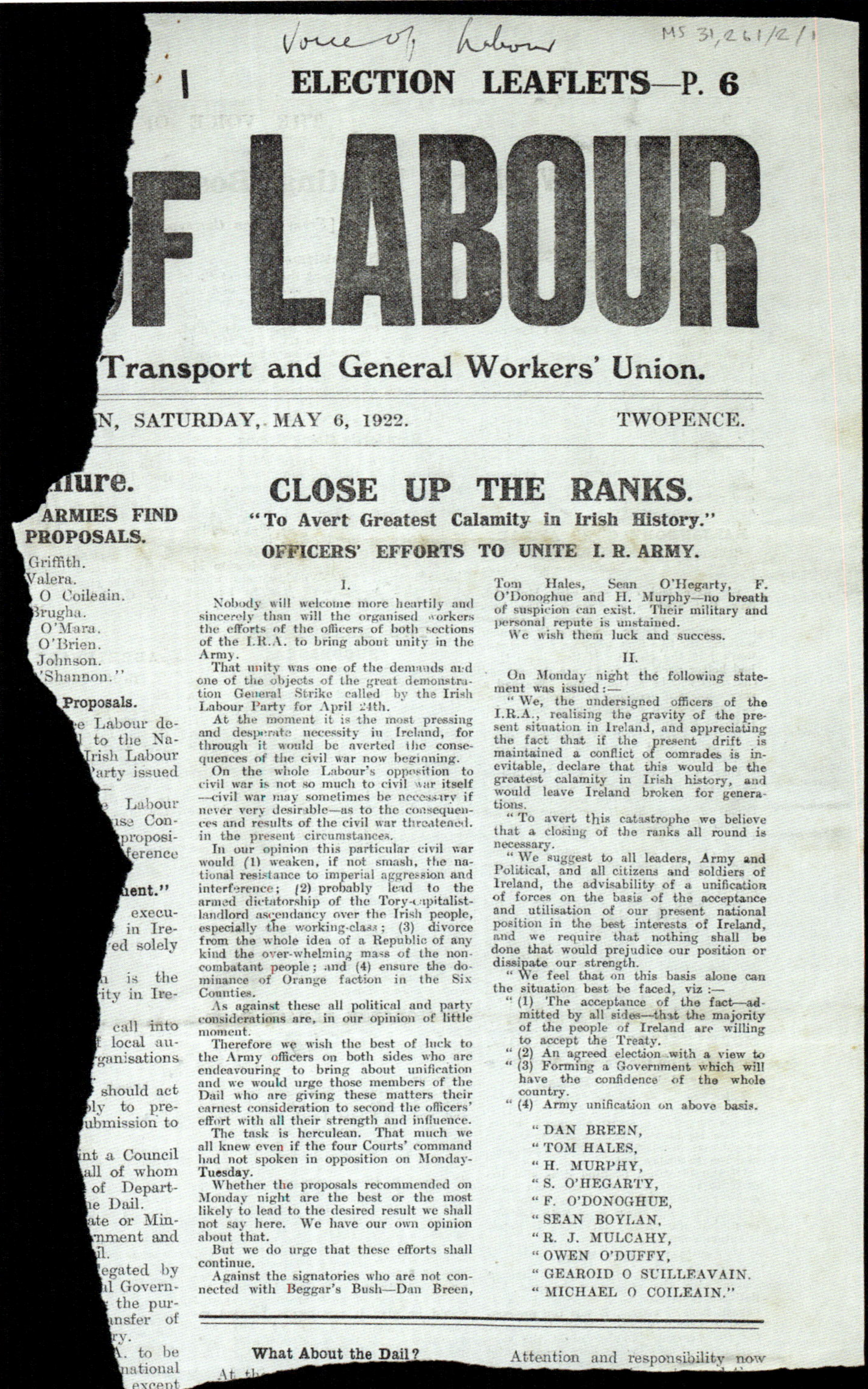

ELECTION LEAFLETS—P. 6

F LABOUR

Transport and General Workers' Union.

N, SATURDAY, MAY 6, 1922. TWOPENCE.

ıılure.

ARMIES FIND PROPOSALS.

Griffith.
Valera.
O Coileain.
Brugha.
O'Mara.
O'Brien.
Johnson.
'Shannon."

Proposals.

e Labour de- / to the Na- / Irish Labour / Party issued / Labour / ise Con- / proposi- / ference

ent."

execu- / in Ire- / ed solely / is the / ity in Ire- / call into / local au- / ganisations / should act / ly to pre- / ubmission to / nt a Council / all of whom / of Depart- / e Dail. / ate or Min- / nment and / il. / egated by / l Govern- / the pur- / nsfer of / ry. / . to be / national / except

CLOSE UP THE RANKS.

"To Avert Greatest Calamity in Irish History."

OFFICERS' EFFORTS TO UNITE I. R. ARMY.

I.

Nobody will welcome more heartily and sincerely than will the organised workers the efforts of the officers of both sections of the I.R.A. to bring about unity in the Army.

That unity was one of the demands and one of the objects of the great demonstration General Strike called by the Irish Labour Party for April 24th.

At the moment it is the most pressing and desperate necessity in Ireland, for through it would be averted the consequences of the civil war now beginning.

On the whole Labour's opposition to civil war is not so much to civil war itself—civil war may sometimes be necessary if never very desirable—as to the consequences and results of the civil war threatened. in the present circumstances.

In our opinion this particular civil war would (1) weaken, if not smash, the national resistance to imperial aggression and interference; (2) probably lead to the armed dictatorship of the Tory-capitalist-landlord ascendancy over the Irish people, especially the working-class; (3) divorce from the whole idea of a Republic of any kind the over-whelming mass of the non-combatant people; and (4) ensure the dominance of Orange faction in the Six Counties.

As against these all political and party considerations are, in our opinion of little moment.

Therefore we wish the best of luck to the Army officers on both sides who are endeavouring to bring about unification and we would urge those members of the Dail who are giving these matters their earnest consideration to second the officers' effort with all their strength and influence.

The task is herculean. That much we all knew even if the four Courts' command had not spoken in opposition on Monday-Tuesday.

Whether the proposals recommended on Monday night are the best or the most likely to lead to the desired result we shall not say here. We have our own opinion about that.

But we do urge that these efforts shall continue.

Against the signatories who are not connected with Beggar's Bush—Dan Breen, Tom Hales, Sean O'Hegarty, F. O'Donoghue and H. Murphy—no breath of suspicion can exist. Their military and personal repute is unstained.

We wish them luck and success.

II.

On Monday night the following statement was issued:—

"We, the undersigned officers of the I.R.A., realising the gravity of the present situation in Ireland, and appreciating the fact that if the present drift is maintained a conflict of comrades is inevitable, declare that this would be the greatest calamity in Irish history, and would leave Ireland broken for generations.

"To avert this catastrophe we believe that a closing of the ranks all round is necessary.

"We suggest to all leaders, Army and Political, and all citizens and soldiers of Ireland, the advisability of a unification of forces on the basis of the acceptance and utilisation of our present national position in the best interests of Ireland, and we require that nothing shall be done that would prejudice our position or dissipate our strength.

"We feel that on this basis alone can the situation best be faced, viz:—

"(1) The acceptance of the fact—admitted by all sides—that the majority of the people of Ireland are willing to accept the Treaty.

"(2) An agreed election with a view to

"(3) Forming a Government which will have the confidence of the whole country.

"(4) Army unification on above basis.

"DAN BREEN,
"TOM HALES,
"H. MURPHY,
"S. O'HEGARTY,
"F. O'DONOGHUE,
"SEAN BOYLAN,
"R. J. MULCAHY,
"OWEN O'DUFFY,
"GEAROID O SUILLEAVAIN.
"MICHAEL O COILEAIN."

What About the Dail?

At th

Attention and responsibility now

Fig. 3 Newspaper cutting from the ITGWU organ, the *Voice of Labour*, 6 May 1922, welcoming the 'Army Officers' initiative to 'close up the ranks'. This initiative saw prominent anti-Treaty IRA leaders appealing for national unity, in the face of impending civil war, which they felt would be catastrophic for the independence movement. Their solution was to create a pro- and anti-Treaty coalition to lead the government and the army, which could then implement the Treaty while maintaining a united front. Cork No. 1 Brigade commander, Seán O'Hegarty, addressed a sitting of Dáil Éireann and warned that civil war would 'leave a print on Ireland and a print in every man's mind that can never be removed; you break the country utterly and destroy any idea of a republic'. The army officers' effort led to the Collins/de Valera pact election and the army unification agreement in June 1922, which briefly offered an alternative to civil war. However, the outbreak of fighting ended all hope of national unity. Most officers who signed the appeal joined the fighting, though O'Hegarty and his colleague Florrie O'Donoghue (adjutant, 1st Southern Division) both took a neutral position, and later established the Neutral IRA organisation, which continued peace efforts into 1923. [Document: National Library of Ireland, Florence O'Donoghue Papers, MS 31,261/2/1]

social democratic politics. The 'call to action' evaded the national question with carefully worded ambiguity, before indulging in the standard class rhetoric of 'the red flag times':

> one more chapter of the still uncompleted story of Ireland's struggle for national freedom has been closed […] responsibility for the government of Ireland will rest in future on the Irish people alone. Henceforward the struggle which you, the workers, must perforce engage in shall be plainly and openly a struggle against capitalism.[11]

A special conference in Dublin's Abbey Theatre on 21 February confirmed by 104–49 votes that Labour would contest the next general election. The ILPTUC executive's motion regretted that the Treaty entailed partition and less than total freedom, condemning both for disappointing national aspirations rather than for their economic implications. Not since James Connolly's death had Labour analysed the national question in socialist terms, opting instead to tail Sinn Féin while avoiding illegality. The motion welcomed the Treaty for putting 'three-fourths of Ireland in a position to govern themselves in respect of ninety-nine hundredths of their individual day to day affairs', and argued that the next election would not be simply about the Treaty but about the constitution and governance of the new state.

Labour candidates would be free to express their own views on the Treaty, provided they accepted the Labour whip. Nothing was said on the oath of allegiance. Those against the motion ranged from delegates who felt politics would divert energies from trade unionism to republicans who argued that, despite its official neutrality, entering Dáil Éireann would make Labour pro-Treaty. There is nothing to suggest that the conference vote was not representative of membership feeling. All unions were divided on the issue, with, usually, sizable minorities against participation. The only one to oppose the motion was the National Union of Vehicle Builders. Its Dublin branches voted 80–50 against, but out of 800 members.[12] It is clear that the vast bulk of trade unionists wanted the Treaty issue settled peacefully and parked for the moment. Almost all delegates to the special conference called for a plebiscite on the Treaty before any elections. Their indifference to anti-Treaty politics mirrored the indifference of republicans to Labour before the outbreak of hostilities. Free Staters were no more accommodating. After Johnson despaired of a plebiscite before the elections, he begged Arthur Griffith for a referendum on polling day, and for prior publication of the proposed Free State constitution. In late March Griffith told him the Cabinet had rejected the referendum idea as likely to confuse the voters. He did promise to publish the draft constitution, but did not do so until the morning of the general election.[13]

Labour also acted directly to thwart the possibility of war. On 10 January 1922 O'Brien enquired of the IRA if working-class Volunteers would be willing to join a 'Workers' Army'.[14] He then tried to bring the 200-strong ICA – scarcely active since Easter Week – under ILPTUC control by incorporating it into the proposed Irish Workers' Army (IWA). O'Brien noted 'very encouraging replies' to the proposal from ITGWU branches in the provinces. The ICA executive agreed in the hope of attracting financial support, and units of the IWA were established. On 11 April the Congress executive issued a statement insisting that sovereignty must lie with Dáil Éireann rather than 'the army [the IRA]'. When the IRA seized the Four Courts on 14 April, Congress arranged further interviews with Sinn Féin leaders, and urged support for the Mansion House Peace Conference. Convened by Archbishop

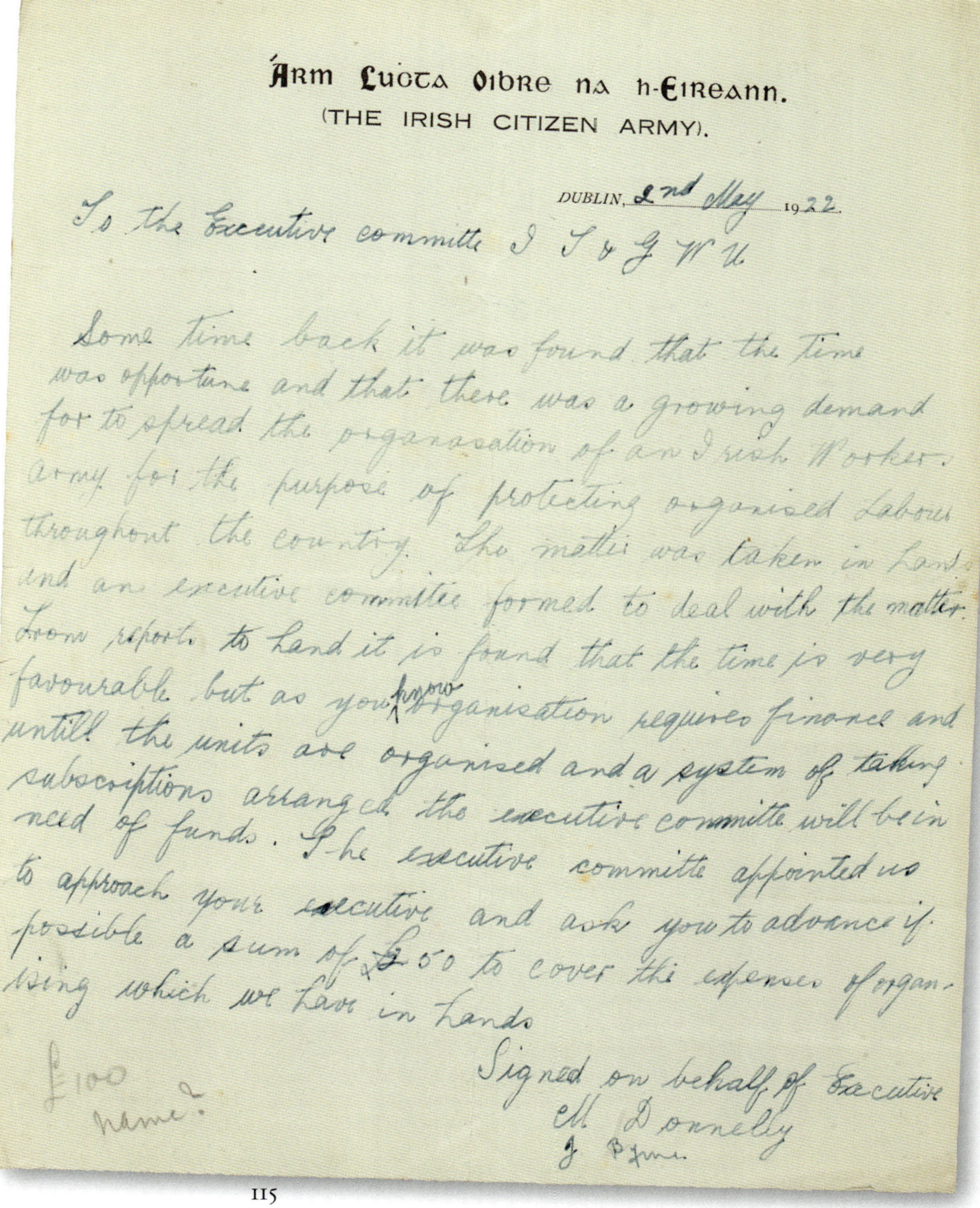

Árm Lucta Oibre na h-Eireann.
(THE IRISH CITIZEN ARMY).

DUBLIN, 2nd May 1922.

To the Executive committe I T & G W U

Some time back it was found that the time was opportune and that there was a growing demand for to spread the organisation of an Irish Worker army for the purpose of protecting organised Labour throughout the country. The matter was taken in hands and an executive committee formed to deal with the matter. From reports to hand it is found that the time is very favourable but as your now organisation requires finance and untill the units are organised and a system of taking subscriptions arranged the executive committe will be in need of funds. The executive committe appointed us to approach your executive and ask you to advance if possible a sum of £250 to cover the expenses of organ-ising which we have in hands

Signed on behalf of Executive
M. Donnelly
J Byrne

£100
name?

Fig. 4 Letter dated 2 May 1922 from Michael Donnelly and John Byrne of the Irish Citizen Army to the Irish Transport and General Workers' Union executive committee, requesting £250 to cover the expense of organising the Irish Workers' Army. [Document: National Library of Ireland, William O'Brien (1881–1968) Papers, MS 15,673/8/17]

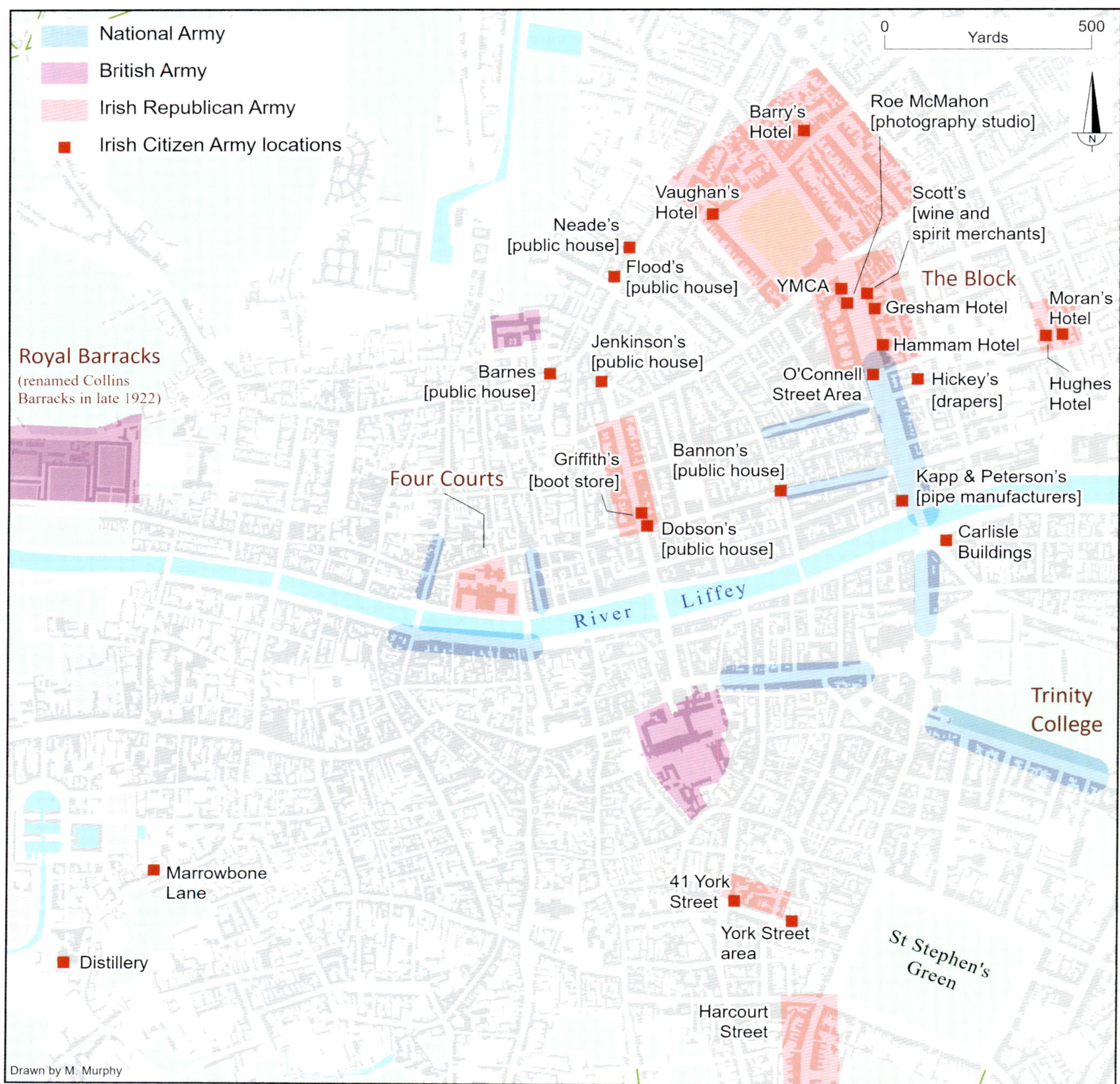

Fig. 5 Map showing the locations occupied by members of the Irish Citizen Army (ICA) during the Battle for Dublin, 28 June–5 July 1922. The ICA, the workers' militia that emerged from the 1913 Lockout, played a significant role in the Easter Rising. Uniquely among military organisations of the period, it included women as well as men, was largely working class in composition, and was closely linked to the Irish Transport and General Workers' Union (ITGWU). Though it remained an independent body, the ICA played only a limited role during the War of Independence, largely as an auxiliary to the IRA. Indeed a number of its Volunteers left to join the larger organisation in this period. However during the Truce it began to recruit again and, though mainly Dublin-based, it did have units in other parts of the country and in Scotland. The Treaty and the looming threat of civil war then combined to split the organisation. A section of the ICA was close politically to the trade union and Labour Party leadership and effectively took a neutral position. In the spring of 1922 they attempted to form a new Irish Workers' Army (IWA), which, while eschewing the conflict over the Treaty, would continue to fight for a workers' republic. In April 1922 the nascent IWA provided armed stewards for a rally during the general strike against militarism. As a result, its organisers were expelled from the ICA, in which the majority took a more distinct anti-Treaty position. The IWA remained close to the ITGWU leadership and, when fighting began in Dublin in June 1922, garrisoned its headquarters in Parnell Square. It remained neutral, however, in the ensuing clashes in the city. In contrast, over 130 ICA members, men and women, took part in the fighting on the anti-Treaty side, joining with the IRA in the clashes with Free State forces around O'Connell Street. A small communist armed group, the 'Red Guard', led by young ICA veteran Roddy Connolly, also took some part in the fighting. Ultimately, over 160 ICA Volunteers (including around thirty women) fought on the anti-Treaty side. They were active into the winter in Dublin, both in the city and in areas in the south of the county. However over fifty of them were imprisoned by late 1922 and the organisation had little independent impact by this stage. At least twenty ICA members (all Easter Rising veterans) joined the National Army. All these divisions within one small organisation illustrate the diversity of opinion and contested nature of the Treaty among the working class itself. [Text: Brian Hanley / Source: Nominal Rolls and Military Service Pension Files, Irish Military Archives]

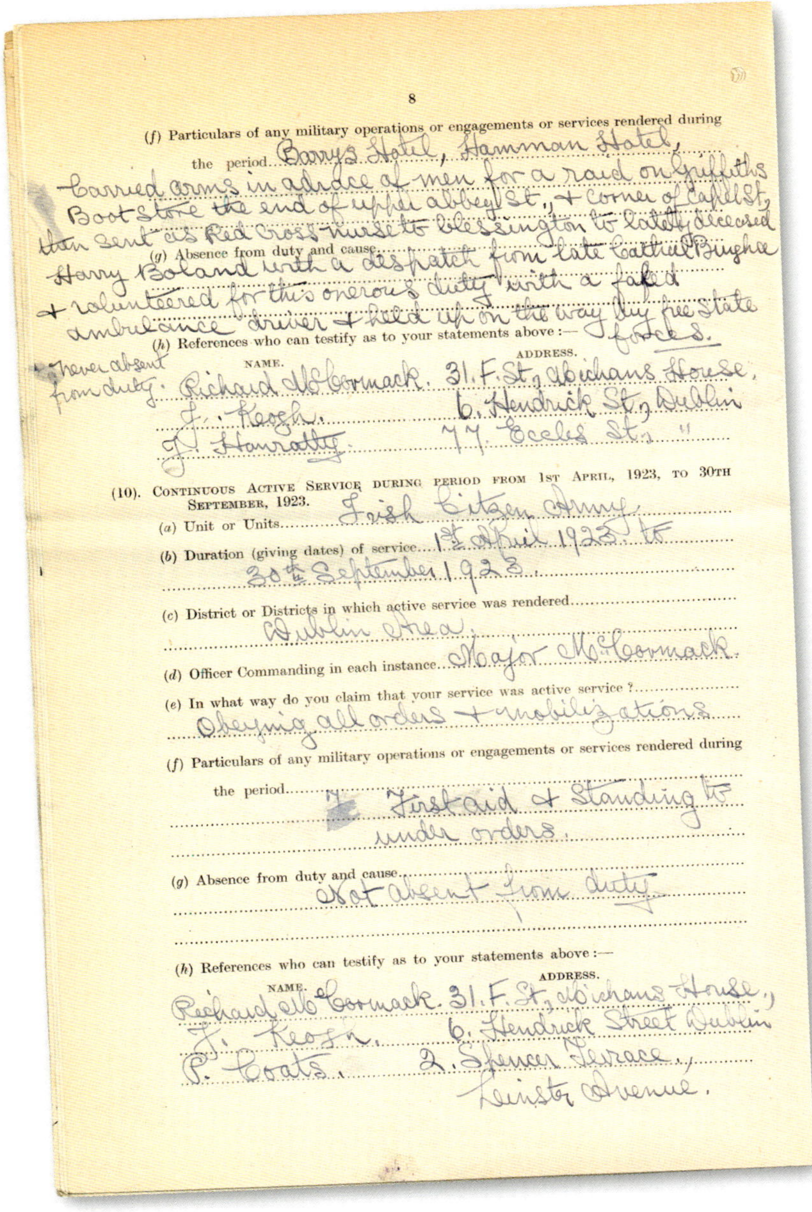

8

(f) Particulars of any military operations or engagements or services rendered during the period. Barrys Hotel, Hamman Hotel, Carried arms in advance of men for a raid on Griffiths Boot store the end of upper abbey St, + corner of Capel St, then sent as Red Cross nurse to Blessington to lately deceased Harry Boland with a despatch from late Cathal Brugha + volunteered for this onerous duty with a fake ambulance driver + held up on the way by free state forces.

(g) Absence from duty and cause. Never absent from duty.

(h) References who can testify as to your statements above:—

NAME.	ADDRESS.
Richard McCormack.	31. F. St, [illegible] House,
J. Keogh.	6. Hendrick St, Dublin
J. Hanratty.	77 Eccles St. "

(10). CONTINUOUS ACTIVE SERVICE DURING PERIOD FROM 1ST APRIL, 1923, TO 30TH SEPTEMBER, 1923.

(a) Unit or Units. Irish Citizen Army

(b) Duration (giving dates) of service. 1st April 1923 to 30th September 1923.

(c) District or Districts in which active service was rendered. Dublin Area.

(d) Officer Commanding in each instance. Major McCormack.

(e) In what way do you claim that your service was active service? Obeying all orders + mobilizations.

(f) Particulars of any military operations or engagements or services rendered during the period. First aid + Standing to under orders.

(g) Absence from duty and cause. Not absent from duty.

(h) References who can testify as to your statements above:—

NAME.	ADDRESS.
Richard McCormack.	31. F. St, [illegible] House,
J. Keogh.	6. Hendrick Street Dublin
P. Coats.	2. Spencer Terrace, Leinster Avenue.

Fig. 6 Hand-written testimony from ICA member Annie Collins about her Civil War service written as part of her unsuccessful application for a military service pension. [Document: MSP34REF1139 / Image courtesy of Military Archives/MSPC Project]

Edward Byrne and the lord mayor of Dublin, the conference brought Griffith, Michael Collins, Éamon de Valera and Cathal Brugha, together with Johnson, O'Brien and Cathal O'Shannon.

The ILPTUC then called a general strike for 24 April, the sixth anniversary of the Easter Rising. General strikes were now a regular tool in the box. Labour had struck against conscription in 1918, for international proletarian solidarity in 1919 and for the release of political prisoners in 1920. In theory the 1922 action was 'against militarism' on both sides, but everyone regarded it as directed against the Four Courts command, and it enjoyed the blessing of the Catholic Church, pro-Treaty and business elements, and the press. It is likely it had the backing of Ulster Protestant workers, because it was successful in places where the 1918–20 strikes were not, such as the Great Northern Railway. Republicans urged workers to boycott rallies in support of the strike. While the ITGWU's *Voice of Labour* boasted 'The stoppage was complete', the far left sneered and the CPI organised three counter-demonstrations against the 'great lockout'.[15] The tensions shattered the fragile IWA. ICA rank and filers had always suspected the IWA initiative as a take-over bid to bring them under ITGWU control, and the deployment of Workers' Army men as marshals during the stoppage led the bulk of Citizen Army men to associate with the IRA, promising Ernie O'Malley that if the Four Courts were attacked, they would defend it. In part they were driven by animosity towards O'Brien.[16] The ICA was no less suspicious of the CPI and stymied all efforts at communist infiltration. Reluctantly, the party decided to form its own 'Red Guard'.[17] A few revolvers were acquired, and ex- Irish Guardsman Liam O'Flaherty provided basic training. Roddy Connolly knew it was a feeble gesture; the IRA, he wrote, was 'Our only hope'.[18]

Labour prolonged the Mansion House Peace Conference and the Sinn Féin factions were eager not to be seen to reject its ten-point peace plan, which essentially involved IRA unity under a common command and acceptance of the supremacy of Dáil Éireann. Griffith and Collins endorsed a plebiscite on the Treaty, but de Valera wanted the elections postponed, ostensibly until a new register of electors was compiled, and the Treaty meanwhile 'left in abeyance'. The conference broke down on 29 April over the question of the elections.[19]

Just eighteen Labour candidates stood in the elections for the Third Dáil on 16 June. Without political branches, the ILPTUC was reliant on trades councils to organise constituency campaigns. Mindful of divided opinions among trade unionists, the executive made no national appeal for funds. The bulk of finance was provided by the ITGWU. Unions with no nominees were reluctant to contribute. It was Labour's first general election and, fearing the consequences of a poor showing, Congress was reluctant to field candidates where it felt there was little hope of success. Another deterrent was the Collins–de Valera pact, announced on 20 May. De Valera hoped the pact would see all Sinn Féin candidates returned unopposed and appealed to other potential candidates not to contest. At least one Labour man withdrew in consequence. Larkin was offered a nomination for North Dublin and declined with customary vehemence. His cable asking 'What of Ulster? Damn politics [...]' was one of the few references in southern Labour circles to the 'pogroms' in Belfast that followed the workplace expulsions of Catholics and 'rotten Prods' in July 1921.[20] The Congress executive was not embarrassed by the growing popular perception of Labour as pro-Treaty, confident that it was in tune with public opinion. O'Brien believed that Collins agreed to the pact only to avoid the IRA disrupting the elections, and Collins repudiated it four days before polling.[21] Seventeen Labour candidates were elected, one narrowly missing a quota. With 21 per cent of the votes cast, the party would certainly have won more seats

Fig. 7 Liam Mellows (1892–1922) delivering the oration at the anti-Treaty IRA commemoration at Wolfe Tone's grave, Bodenstown, County Kildare, 20 June 1922. From 1891, the annual 'pilgrimage' to Bodenstown took place on the Sunday closest to Tone's birthday on 20 June (a practice that has continued to the present day). No gathering occurred in the dying days of the War of Independence in 1921, and the following year the traditional Sunday gathering (on 25 June), organised by the Wolfe Tone Memorial Association, was a pro-Treaty affair, featuring a large body of National Army troops and an oration by P.S. O'Hegarty. Two other commemorations were also held that Sunday by anti-Treaty organisations – one by Na Fianna Éireann, led by Barney Mellows, which was addressed by his brother Liam, and the other by Cumann na mBan, addressed by Áine Ceannt and Constance Markievicz. The anti-Treaty IRA, along with the Irish Citizen Army, had held its own commemoration on the previous Tuesday, 20 June. In an atmosphere of what attendee Todd Andrews called 'approaching doom' (the Civil War began a week later), Margaret Pearse laid a wreath on the grave and Mellows declared that: 'We who meet together on this holy ground do not assemble today to sing the swansong of Irish Republicanism. The Irish Republican movement is not dead. Certain people have taken the road of expediency and descended into hypocrisy to achieve their object but Republicans must not deviate one inch from the straight road [...] Though the outlook is black and the odds against us heavy, we will continue the struggle, believing our cause is just.' Mellows had joined Na Fianna in 1911 and was sworn into the Irish Republican Brotherhood in 1913. In 1914 he was elected to the Irish Volunteers executive, and became an organiser in Galway, where he led attacks on the police in Easter Week 1916. He evaded arrest and escaped to the United States, where he worked with John Devoy on the *Gaelic American*. Mellows was elected to the First Dáil in 1918 while still in the US, where he helped organise a number of tours by Irish republicans, including that of de Valera in 1919–20. He returned to Ireland in October 1920 and joined the IRA general headquarters staff, with responsibility for arms procurement. Mellows was returned unopposed to the Second Dáil in 1921, but lost his seat in the pact election of June 1922, four days before he delivered his Bodenstown speech as a leading member of the Four Courts IRA executive. He was captured in the Four Courts and imprisoned in Mountjoy Gaol, where he organised classes, games and a prison magazine called *The Book of Cells*. A group including socialist trade unionist Peadar O'Donnell and Walter Carpenter of the Communist Party of Ireland formed around Mellows, based in the cell he shared with Joe McKelvey; it held discussions on future policies and tactics. These influenced this piously Catholic Fenian idealist to construct his 'Notes from Mountjoy' – the outline of a socialistic policy for the anti-Treaty movement, which was captured by the authorities and published under red scare headlines in the pro-Treaty press. Along with McKelvey, Rory O'Connor and Dick Barrett, Mellows was executed in Mountjoy on 8 December 1922 in retaliation for the killing of pro-Treaty TD Seán Hales the previous day. His late conversion to socialism, followed by his martyrdom and his exaggerated elevation to the Irish socialist pantheon, first by his comrade Peadar O'Donnell and then his first biographer, the communist C. Desmond Greaves, made Mellows an enduring, if unlikely, icon for the left of the republican movement. [Image: National Library of Ireland, HOGW 197 / See C. Desmond Greaves, *Liam Mellows and the Irish Revolution* (London, 1971); Conor MacNamara (ed.), *Liam Mellows: Soldier of the Irish Republic – selected writings, 1914–1922* (Dublin, 2019); *Cork Examiner*, 22 June 1922; Mario Corrigan, James Durney, Karel Kiely, Kevin Murphy with Kevin O Kelly, *A Timeline of the Civil War in County Kildare, 1922–1924* (Naas, 2022)]

with more candidates. Labour had two advantages in the campaign: it was exceptional in addressing social and economic issues, which it could do credibly thanks to the relative success of trade unions in withstanding employer demands for pay cuts; and it was the main alternative to continued Sinn Féin dictatorship.

Mission to Moscow

When the Civil War started, the divide between Labour and the far left became more pronounced. The ICA joined the Battle for Dublin with a dowry of 3,000 rounds of ammunition for the IRA. The CPI chipped in with its 'Red Guard' of about twelve men. In London, Borodin told Roddy Connolly to present a social programme to the republicans. Connolly had been appealing to republicans repeatedly in the CPI paper, the *Workers' Republic*. On 12 April he told Moscow: 'it is becoming more apparent that the [IRA] controls the entire situation, that the 80,000 armed [IRA] men are the real dominant factor', adding that some members of the IRA executive were calling themselves 'social republicans' and that the 'IRA in large numbers are drifting towards us'. Through leading the IRA, the CPI had the possibility of 'jumping from 200 to 20,000 members in the course of the next six months'.[22]

The IRA did promulgate an agrarian programme on 1 May, instructing local commandants to seize specified land and property for distribution to the people. The manifesto was largely the work of an agrarian radical, P.J. Ruttledge, with the support of O'Malley and Thomas Derrig. It was never applied or championed by anti-Treatyites.[23] Still it seemed to the CPI that events were moving in the right direction. 'Civil War necessary' read the headline in the *Workers' Republic* on 6 May. But by July Connolly was much more doubtful about the republicans. Borodin insisted they proceed, if only for propaganda purposes. Together they drafted a

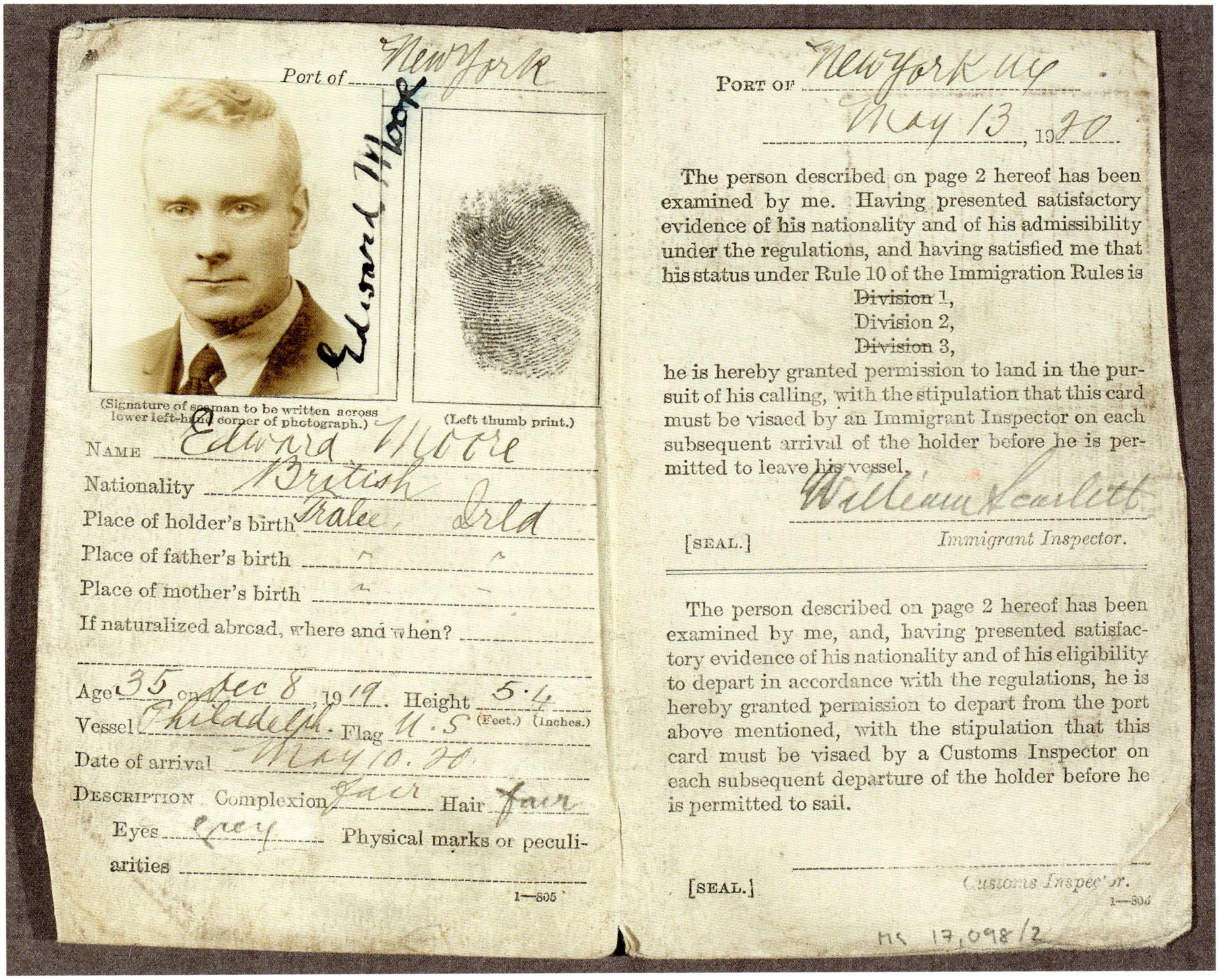
Port of New York

Edward Moore

(Signature of seaman to be written across lower left-hand corner of photograph.)

(Left thumb print.)

Name Edward Moore

Nationality British

Place of holder's birth Tralee, Irld

Place of father's birth

Place of mother's birth

If naturalized abroad, where and when?

Age 35 on Dec 8, 1919. Height 5·4 (Feet.) (Inches.)

Vessel Philadelph. Flag U.S

Date of arrival May 10. 20.

Description Complexion Fair Hair Fair

Eyes Grey Physical marks or peculiarities

1—805

Port of New York NY.

May 13, 1920

The person described on page 2 hereof has been examined by me. Having presented satisfactory evidence of his nationality and of his admissibility under the regulations, and having satisfied me that his status under Rule 10 of the Immigration Rules is

~~Division 1~~,
Division 2,
~~Division 3~~,

he is hereby granted permission to land in the pursuit of his calling, with the stipulation that this card must be visaed by an Immigrant Inspector on each subsequent arrival of the holder before he is permitted to leave his vessel.

William Scarlett

[SEAL.] *Immigrant Inspector.*

The person described on page 2 hereof has been examined by me, and, having presented satisfactory evidence of his nationality and of his eligibility to depart in accordance with the regulations, he is hereby granted permission to depart from the port above mentioned, with the stipulation that this card must be visaed by a Customs Inspector on each subsequent departure of the holder before he is permitted to sail.

[SEAL.] *Customs Inspector.*

1—806

MS 17,098/2

Fig. 8 US alien seaman's identification card for Edward Moore with Liam Mellows's photograph and fingerprint, 13 May 1920. [Image: National Library of Ireland, MS 17,098/2] manifesto demanding state ownership of heavy industry, transport and the banks; land redistribution; an eight-hour working day; joint councils of workers, trade unions and the state to regulate working conditions; municipalisation of public services; rationing of housing and abolition of rents; maintenance for the unemployed at trade union rates; and universal arming of workers.[24] A version appeared in the *Workers' Republic* on 29 July, and the paper adjusted its editorial line to concede that people saw little material advantage in opposing the Free State and to emphasise the need for republicans to 'attract the masses'.

On 26 July Connolly met Liam Lynch in Fermoy. At this stage even O'Malley, acting assistant chief of staff and director of the northern and eastern commands, was unclear as to IRA policy. A day earlier Lynch had written to O'Malley, stating the disastrously defensive and legalistic strategy he would cling to: the IRA would wait for Dáil Éireann to act as the government of the republic, and allow no other government to function; the war would be won by guerrilla tactics.[25] The minutes of Lynch's staff meeting the next day noted: 'Connolly [...] suggested forming a government which would have a democratic policy, in this way Labour could be got behind Republicans. Can get any amount of arms etc if they can be got into the Country.' Lynch directed his staff to get 'a Labour Propaganda Dept working'.[26] In August Borodin's secretary and the chairman of the British party met 'two of the Chiefs of Staff of the IRA' in a Dublin suburb and signed a joint document for submission to their respective executives.[27] The deal envisaged that the IRA would create a new party with a radical programme in return for weapons. On 22 August Connolly was in Berlin ordering the Comintern to provide him with immediate air transport to Moscow. He was definite about the IRA's commitment, less so about the Comintern's.[28]

The communist intervention triggered a left turn in senior republican thinking. With no confidence in Lynch's strategy, O'Malley decided it was essential to create a government with a democratic programme that would 'get the workers'.[29] Liam Mellows's 'Notes from Mountjoy', the fruit of a left republican discussion group in Mountjoy Gaol, urged the IRA to adopt the CPI programme. It would be a seminal document in the canon of socialist republicanism. But it was too little, too late. Perversely, the IRA was at the same time antagonising the ILPTUC with attacks on the railways and warnings that railwaymen assisting the Free State would be legitimate targets.[30] Crucially, Lynch was not convinced, Moscow got cold feet, fearful that military aid to the IRA would jeopardise relations with Britain, and Johnson was never going to ally Labour with the 'irregulars'. The IRA's search for weapons continued, in Germany and from the Russians, but without CPI involvement.

A model toy in a hurricane

From June to September the ILPTUC renewed its quests for peace and directed workers to stay out of the conflict. Johnson, O'Brien and O'Shannon, editor of the *Voice of Labour*, visited the Four Courts, Mountjoy and government offices, pleading for a truce and urging the Provisional Government to shelter families displaced by the fighting. The executive's annual report for 1921–2 blamed the government for its unilateral declaration of war, but also deemed 'the political claims of the Republican Party to be irrational' and condemned their methods of warfare: 'Ambushes in the city streets, the destruction of bridges, railway tracks, and buildings are tantamount to a war upon the people.' A motion to delete these references was defeated 91–35.[31] Above all, Labour pressed the Provisional Government to convene Dáil Éireann. On 27 June it was announced that the Dáil would assemble on 1 July. With the shelling of the Four Courts, Griffith deferred the meeting until 15 July. On 12 July the Provisional Government appointed a war council and postponed the Dáil until 15 August. Clearly, the intention was to get the war sorted first. Labour protested that Free State aggression could have no legitimacy without a convention of Dáil Éireann and eventually threatened to have its TDs resign their seats. Aware of Labour's importance to creating a functioning parliamentary democracy, the Third Dáil finally convened on 9 September.[32] But be careful what you wish for. Reconciling the gritty dynamic of industrial struggle with the shadowboxing of parliamentary politics is tricky at the best of times. An inexperienced team of TDs was taking it on at the worst of times. And their chief was Johnson, a nice man who hated confrontation and did not want to be leader. A poor tactician, he surrendered his trump card from the outset, making it clear he was absolutely committed to stability.

However Johnson came into his element as a parliamentarian. As leader of the official opposition in the formative years to 1927, he played a part as vital to the legislature as the Ceann Comhairle or president, and his devotion to organising the Labour TDs as a coherent force would make him an enduring icon of the party, and one more representative than Connolly or Larkin.[33] As the Redmondite Denis Gwynn detected, his stance was often driven more by personal zeal for peace and order than party policy. Gwynn captured what made him so admired and so vilified: 'He brought to the political development of the Free State that sense of responsibility for popularly elected government that is characteristic of the English "moderate" trade union leader. It is hard to imagine that any Irishman could have filled the position in the same way.'[34]

In addition to sustaining a critique of the government's social and economic policies and holding the army and the Garda Síochána to account, Labour anticipated the work of Fianna Fáil. It tried to remove all references to British institutions from the constitution, minimise the role and status of the Governor-General, prevent the introduction of the Seanad and university representation, and insert elements of the Democratic Programme into the constitution. Unfortunately for Labour, it was not seen to be getting anything in return for propping up the regime and what Johnson regarded as principle and self-sacrifice, others saw as humbug. The government derided his humanitarian criticism of security practices and ignored his efforts to influence the Saorstát constitution, though drafting a constitution was supposed to be the primary concern of the Third Dáil.[35] Larkinites and the CPI were scathing. Even within the ILPTUC there were appeals to withdraw his deputies from Dáil Éireann in protest at the partisan deployment of the National Army

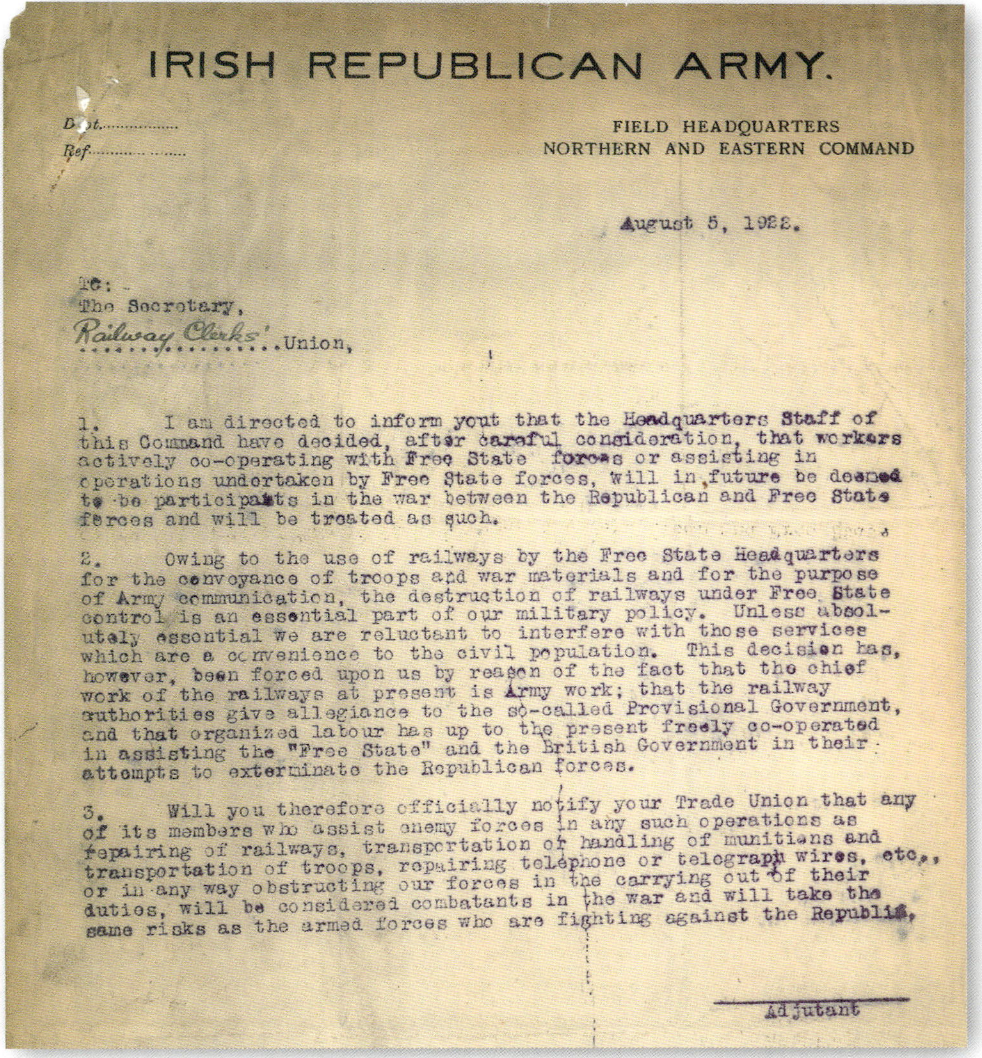

IRISH REPUBLICAN ARMY.

Dept.................

Ref......................

FIELD HEADQUARTERS
NORTHERN AND EASTERN COMMAND

August 5, 1922.

To: -
The Secretary,
Railway Clerks'...Union,

1. I am directed to inform you that the Headquarters Staff of this Command have decided, after careful consideration, that workers actively co-operating with Free State forces or assisting in operations undertaken by Free State forces, will in future be deemed to be participants in the war between the Republican and Free State forces and will be treated as such.

2. Owing to the use of railways by the Free State Headquarters for the conveyance of troops and war materials and for the purpose of Army communication, the destruction of railways under Free State control is an essential part of our military policy. Unless absolutely essential we are reluctant to interfere with those services which are a convenience to the civil population. This decision has, however, been forced upon us by reason of the fact that the chief work of the railways at present is Army work; that the railway authorities give allegiance to the so-called Provisional Government, and that organized labour has up to the present freely co-operated in assisting the "Free State" and the British Government in their attempts to exterminate the Republican forces.

3. Will you therefore officially notify your Trade Union that any of its members who assist enemy forces in any such operations as repairing of railways, transportation of handling of munitions and transportation of troops, repairing telephone or telegraph wires, etc., or in any way obstructing our forces in the carrying out of their duties, will be considered combatants in the war and will take the same risks as the armed forces who are fighting against the Republic.

Adjutant

Fig. 9 Letter from the IRA to Irish Railway Clerks' Union [Association], 5 August 1922. One of the most ingrained memories for those who lived through the Civil War was the near constant disruption to the rail network. From the early weeks of the conflict, the IRA leadership issued orders for the destruction of rail infrastructure across the country. The initial objective was to block, or at least slow down, the movement of National Army troops and equipment. However the 'war on the railways' also greatly affected civilians, dependent on the trains not only for convenient and relatively fast transport between towns and cities, but also for the conveyance of mail, food supplies and the all-important daily newspapers. An awareness of the value of the extensive rail network to the average person during this period explains the IRA reluctance to implement a similar 'military policy' during the War of Independence. Early in the Civil War many trade union and Labour representatives across the country received letters almost identical to the one issued to John Thomas O'Farrell, secretary of the Railway Clerks' Association in August 1922. In summary, railway employees were deemed guilty of aiding and abetting the Provisional/Free State government and were therefore targets. Some rail employees did lose their lives as a result of the conflict. In January 1923 the IRA derailed a train near Liscahane Bridge, outside Ardfert, on the line to Tralee. Their intended target was a train carrying National Army troops, and they were surprised when a freight train rounded the tracks instead. Two railway men, Patrick O'Riordan (fifty) and Daniel Crowley (thirty-six), were killed, having been crushed or scalded as the locomotive careered down an embankment. Attacks on the rail networks increased in tandem with the general escalation of guerrilla violence throughout the country after August 1922. On the less severe end of the spectrum, this involved the severing of signal cables or the cutting of trees onto tracks, a relatively risk-free way for the IRA rank and file in rural parts of the country to contribute to the cause. More serious cases involved digging up tracks to cause derailments (Fig. 10), blowing up bridges and setting fire to train stations. On 3 October 1922 two National Army lieutenants, seated among civilians on a train passing through Ballyhale station in Kilkenny, acted quickly to jettison a bomb that had landed in the carriage. The IRA also held up trains, searched passengers, appropriated post (for intelligence purposes) and commandeered goods. These attacks caused headaches for the fledgling Free State government which was required to pay compensation to the privately owned railway companies, along with recompense to the businesses whose goods were lost in transit. In September 1922 the National Army established a separate unit solely for the protection of railways. Known as the Railway Protection, Repair and Maintenance Corps, and under the command of Col. Charles Russell, it included former rail employees who had lost their jobs due to the closure of lines. National Army outposts were also established close to important bridges and junctions for protection. In addition, improvised armoured carriages were introduced. These were usually rail-borne Lancia cars, which had machine guns to protect the train and passengers from attack. While deeply unpopular, the IRA's 'war on the railways' was, as historian Michael Hopkinson put it, 'the most successful aspect' of its military policy. [Text: Eoin Swithin Walsh / Document: courtesy of Dublin City Library and Archive and the Irish Labour History Society / Sources: Tom Doyle, *The Civil War in Kerry* (Cork, 2008), p. 248; Bernard Share, *In Time of Civil War: The conflict on the Irish railways 1922–23* (Cork, 2006), p. 63; Michael Hopkinson, *Green Against Green, The Irish Civil War* (Dublin, 2004), p. 198]

Fig. 10 (above) Photograph of a train derailed during the Civil War commissioned by Mr J. Larkin of Dunkit, County Kilkenny. [Image: National Library of Ireland, POOLEWP 3094]

Fig. 11 (opposite page) Map showing incidents of IRA attacks on the rail infrastructure in the Free State in January 1923. The map is based on a series of original maps produced by the Railway Protection, Repair and Maintenance Corps. On all lines in this month alone there were almost 200 attacks on the railway infrastructure, including: forty cases where rail lines were damaged or blocked; thirty-five derailments/ambushes/attacks on trains; twenty-five incidents of damage to or destruction of bridges; nineteen raids or attacks on stations, and a further thirteen burnings of stations; twenty-two burnings of, or attempts to damage, signal cabins; eight incidents of damage to permanent ways, and six robberies or attempted robberies. Most of the lines in counties Kerry, Cork and Waterford were closed due to attacks in early 1923. [Source: Railway Protection, Repair and Maintenance Corps maps, Jan. 1923, Maps, Plans & Drawing Collection, Irish Military Archives]

in strikes. Arguing that democracy depended on the Labour presence in Leinster House, Johnson insisted on draining the poisoned chalice. As Tom Foran, president of the ITGWU, predicted, the Labour Party was like 'a model toy [...] during a hurricane'.[36]

Sinn Féin was bitter about what it perceived as the betrayal of James Connolly's legacy. For some republicans it was perplexing that, just as the IRA was moving left, and their enemies were embracing a law-and-order mentality and growing evermore reactionary, Labour was increasingly aligning itself with the Free State. As O'Malley observed, however remiss republicans had been on social issues, Labour would get less from the Treatyites.[37] Sinn Féiners also mistook Labour criticisms of the government for opposition to the regime. Judging Labour to be the underbelly of the Free State and Johnson to be the weak point in Labour, Sinn Féin targeted him personally. The more he denounced the terror against them, the more abusive republicans became of him and his English background. 'It is England's devilish luck', wrote Peadar O'Donnell, 'that at a moment when Irish Labour is faced with a situation of tremendous possibilities, the dominant influence on the [ILPTUC] National Executive should be an Imperialist English mind'.[38] When the Civil War ended, the detention of 12,000 or so republican prisoners kept national feeling on the boil, and families of internees frequently gave Johnson a hard time. A rally in Waterford city in May 1923 turned farcical when he tried to silence hecklers by singing the national anthem. Mercifully, the chairman brought the evening to a close.[39] Labour was beginning to look pathetic.

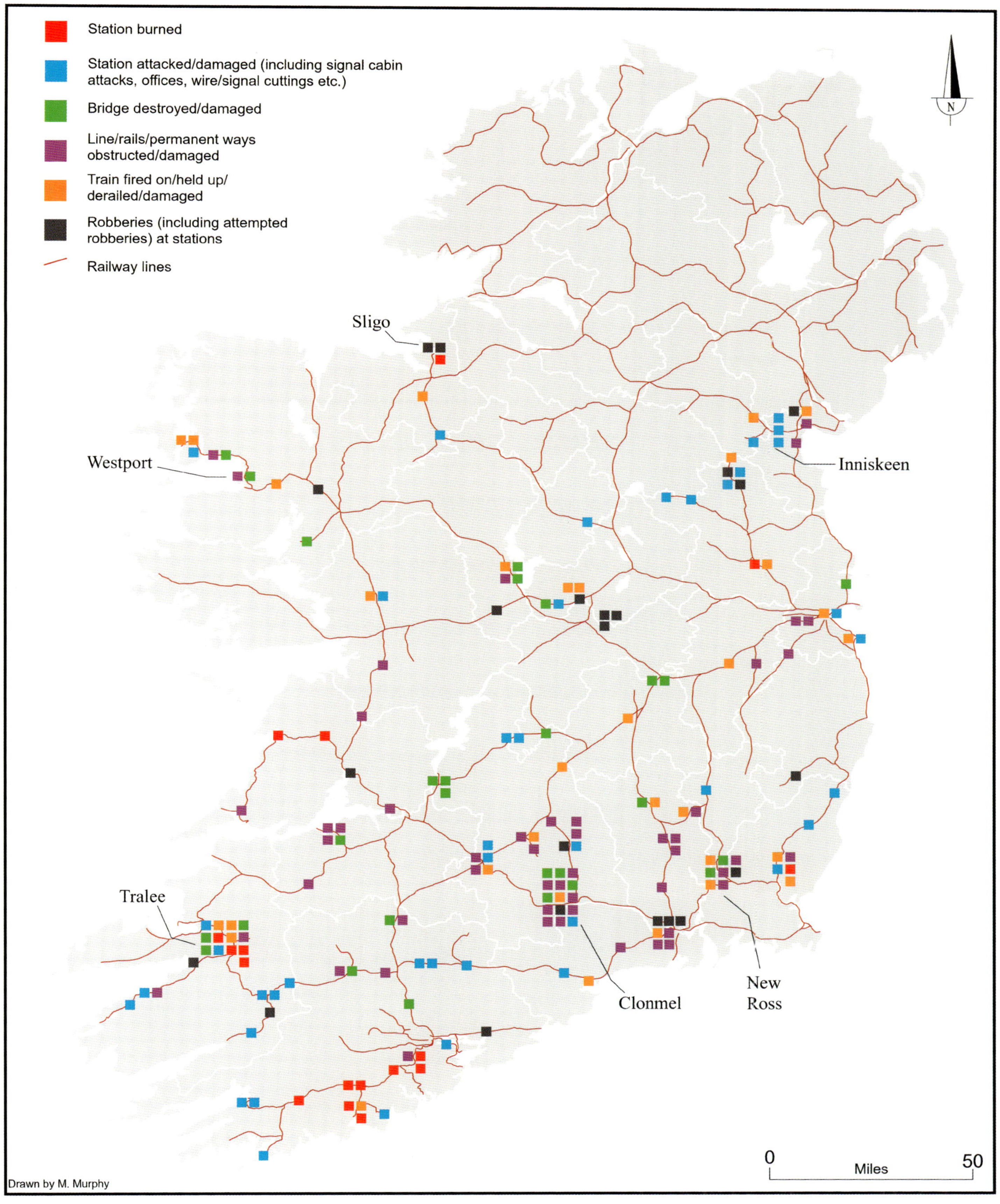
Station burned
Station attacked/damaged (including signal cabin attacks, offices, wire/signal cuttings etc.)
Bridge destroyed/damaged
Line/rails/permanent ways obstructed/damaged
Train fired on/held up/ derailed/damaged
Robberies (including attempted robberies) at stations
Railway lines
N
Sligo
Westport
Inniskeen
Tralee
Clonmel
New Ross
0
Miles
50
Drawn by M. Murphy

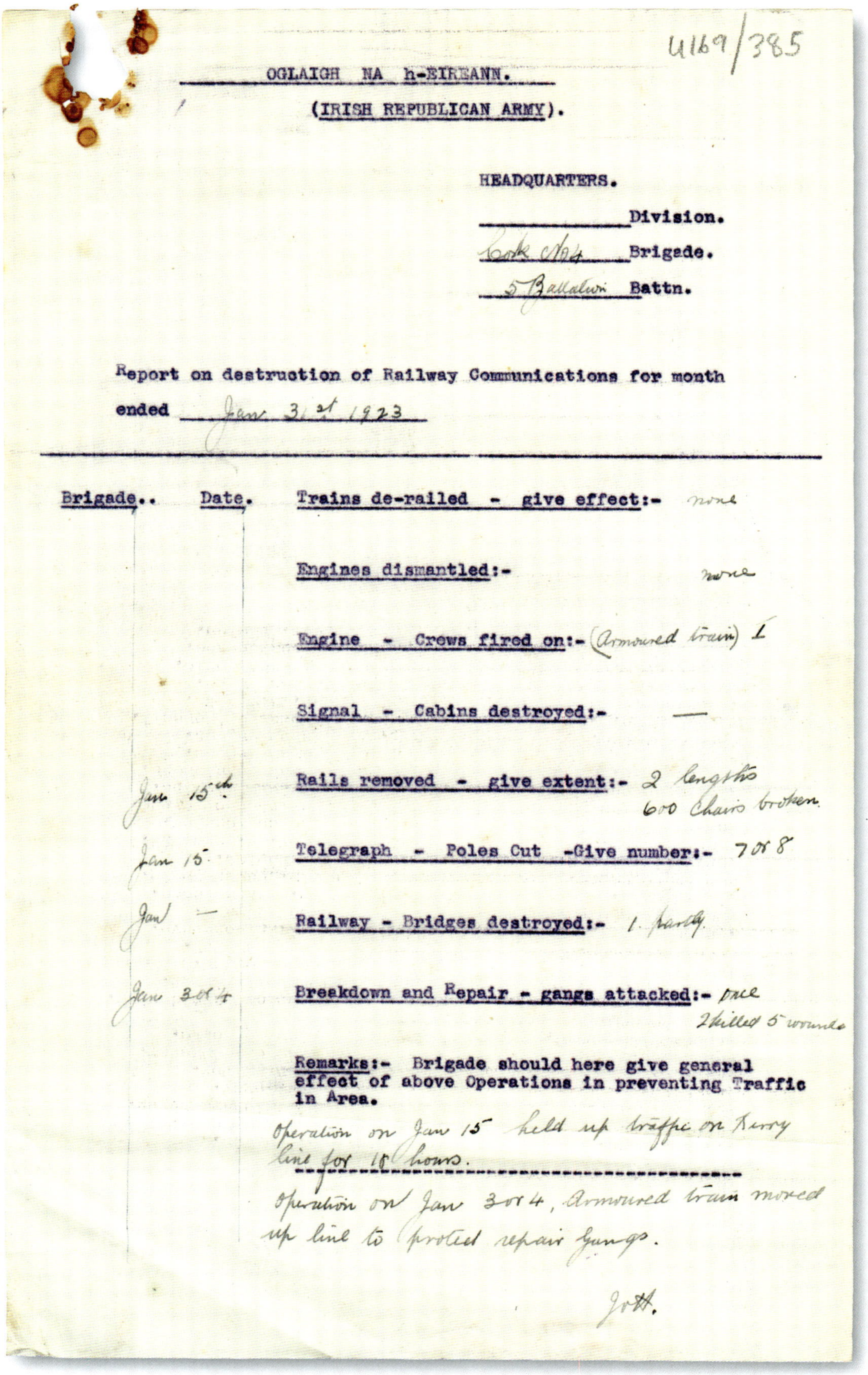

4169/385

OGLAIGH NA h-EIREANN.

(IRISH REPUBLICAN ARMY).

HEADQUARTERS.

_____________ Division.

Cork No 4 Brigade.

5 Battalion Battn.

Report on destruction of Railway Communications for month ended Jan 31st 1923

Brigade..	Date.	
		Trains de-railed - give effect:- none
		Engines dismantled:- none
		Engine - Crews fired on:- (Armoured train) 1
		Signal - Cabins destroyed:- —
	Jan 15th	Rails removed - give extent:- 2 lengths 600 Chairs broken
	Jan 15	Telegraph - Poles Cut -Give number:- 7 or 8
	Jan —	Railway - Bridges destroyed:- 1 partly
	Jan 3 or 4	Breakdown and Repair - gangs attacked:- once 2 killed 5 wounded

Remarks:- Brigade should here give general effect of above Operations in preventing Traffic in Area.

Operation on Jan 15 held up traffic on Kerry line for 10 hours.

Operation on Jan 3 or 4, Armoured train moved up line to protect repair gangs.

Jott.

Fig. 12 A 4th Cork Brigade, 5th Battalion IRA report on the destruction of railway communications for January 1923. [Document: Cork City and County Archives]

Fig. 13 The metaphorical possibilities created by the IRA campaign against the railways were eagerly grasped by pro-Treaty cartoonists. This example is from the front page of *Young Ireland*, 30 September 1922.

Catastrophe

Adding to Labour's woes, Jim Larkin returned from the United States on 30 April 1923. Big Jim had colluded with republicans in America, giving them the impression that he would swing workers behind de Valera once back in Ireland. Instead, conscious of having missed the Easter Rising and the War of Independence, but unable to accept the humility his absence required, Larkin strode boldly to the centre stage. Republicans were appalled to hear him calling for the IRA to surrender its arms. Larkin was not one for patient strategy and was not a well man in the 1920s. The 1913 lockout had turned his egotism to egomania and made him more determined to be his own man. Seeing enemies and rivals on all sides, he refused to work with other organisations such as the CPI, and set about taking back control of 'his' union. In June he split the ITGWU after making a series of random and mendacious allegations of maladministration against the leadership. The split made little impact in the provinces, but in Dublin, especially red Dublin, Larkin had a personal relationship with workers who were hoping he would revive the fortunes of their faltering movement. Two thirds of the Dublin ITGWU, 16,000 workers, joined the Larkinite faction of the union, which became the Workers' Union of Ireland in 1924. If the 1923 split was personal, that in 1924 was ideological. Contrary to popular belief, Larkin did not want a new union. The Workers' Union was founded by his brother Pete and favourite son Young Jim when Jim Senior was en route to Moscow for conferences of the Comintern and its trade union counterpart, the Profintern. It was created as a communist trade union, in affiliation with the Profintern. Over the next thirty years Labour would be plagued by its own civil war.[40]

It was the worst time for an internal crisis. For two years trade unions had been offering dogged resistance to demands for pay cuts, with some success and a few defeats. As the Civil War ended, and with the government restoring order, employers began fingering their knives for a final assault on wage levels. Since early 1923 the government had been redirecting its policy of treating republicanism as nothing more than mindless anarchy; instead it now increasingly referred to it as 'labour irregularism'. The shock troops of the policy were the Special Infantry Corps, recruited to act as 'armed police' in farm strikes to save the army and the Civic Guard (renamed Garda Síochána na hÉireann in early August 1923) from attracting the odium that went with that sort of work.[41] The bosses' 'big push' materialised in July 1923 after a national dock strike over pay cuts. The dockers' action illustrated Labour's lack of unity and strategy as employers had less to lose in lockouts when the ports were at a standstill. By August 1923 about 20,000 trade unionists were locked out or on strike. In Cork, the Employers' Federation fought a dispute with 6,000 workers in building, manufacture, distribution and transport between 21 August and 9 November.[42]

Being in the eye of the storm at least dealt Labour an ace; it could trump the Cabinet's dismissal of republicanism as a cloak for anarchy by raising the spectre of industrial agitation merging with 'irregularism' unless the government agreed to restrain employers. Financial opinion in Britain, which the government was anxious to reassure, believed that republicans might commence a campaign of economic sabotage, aided and abetted by Jim Larkin – just back from the United States – and his communist friends. William T. Cosgrave took seriously a threat by Larkin to prevent the general election, scheduled for August 1923, failing a settlement of strikes. The Cabinet agreed on 1 August to ask employers to postpone wage cuts for three months, during which conferences would be convened under government auspices.[43] It provided a brief and partial respite. By October, Larkin and Labour were begging Cosgrave for government arbitration to effect a general settlement of disputes. Cosgrave could now afford to ignore the pleas.

Abjuring the chance to raise the stakes, Labour had sailed confidently into the hustings with pamphlets entitled *How to Get Houses, How to Reduce the Cost of Living* and *If You Want Your Child to Get a Fair Start in Life*. 'It is certain', predicted the *Voice of Labour*, 'that the Labour Party in the new Dáil will be considerably stronger.'[44] Most observers expected republican candidates to be punished for their lack of a social programme and the wanton destructiveness of the Civil War. On the other hand, there was passionate sympathy for the internees and considerable anger over Free State atrocities. Four Larkinite candidates in Dublin did their best to discredit the party and gleaned a paltry 4,500 votes. Above all, Labour TDs paid the price of their irrelevance to the industrial war. The Dáil party was clipped to fourteen TDs and saw its share of the poll reduced to 10.6 per cent. The end of an era came on 15 December in County Waterford, where 1,500 farm labourers had been on strike against a wage cut since May. The dispute had developed into a miniature civil war. Labour's 'Red Guards' burnt hay ricks and sabotaged creameries. Farmers countered with a

S. McD

D. I/I

I am sure you have the facts all right:

Cause – N. soldiers killed by dump Killarney district; muzzle of gun protruding from dump and when pulled mine exploded.

Alleged effect – Prisoners (8) brought out in early morning to clear away mine near Tralee. 7 prisoners killed, one escaped + 3 soldiers wounded.

It is alleged that the prisoners were beaten + tied together with ropes and the mine then exploded with above result. The mine is alleged to have been placed by N. Soldiers. The escaped prisoner (since dead) is alleged to have made this statement.

It is also said that portion of one of the exploded mines found is apparently belonging to an irregular mine, how true cannot be said.

The effect on the minds of the people was one of horror + detestation and adverse to the Government. The fact of such occurrences are alienating a lot of the public from the Government side, and the elections I imagine will see a good many changes on the ministerial bench; such is opinion of a great many.

Fig. 14 (opposite) Manuscript notes by Thomas Johnson regarding the deaths of seven republican prisoners who were 'beaten and tied together with ropes' around a mine placed and detonated by National Army soldiers in Ballyseedy, County Kerry on 8 March 1923. He is mistaken when he notes that the escaped prisoner (Stephen Fuller), who made a statement about the unofficial reprisal executions, had subsequently died. Also inaccurate is the National Army-sponsored rumour, noted by an incredulous Johnson, that a fragment found at the scene suggested that it was 'an irregular mine'. 'The effect on the minds of the people', finishes the leader of the opposition, who would closely question Richard Mulcahy in the Dáil about the events in Kerry, 'was one of horror and detestation and abuse to the Government'. Responding to Johnson in the Dáil, Mulcahy, the National Army's commander in chief defended the findings of the April 1923 military court of inquiry chaired by officers of the Kerry Command, which cleared the troops of wrongdoing at Countess Bridge, Ballyseedy and Bahaghs. The Labour leader's subsequent demand for a non-military inquiry was rebuffed by a government unwilling to 'give local rumour a wider circulation'. [Document: National Library of Ireland, Thomas Johnson Papers, MS 17140/9 / Sources: *Dáil Debates,* 17 Apr. 1923; Owen O'Shea, *No Middle Path: The Civil War in Kerry* (Dublin, 2003), p. 115]

Fig. 15 (above) Farmers unloading the *SS Cargan* at Davitt's Quay, Dungarvan, County Waterford under the watchful eyes of National Army soldiers during the farm labourers' strike of 1923. Interviewed by Uinseann MacEoin in the 1970s, Frank Edwards, veteran republican and socialist, recalled 'There was another agrarian outbreak, the summer of 1923, after the Civil War had ended. It was a localised civil war, but maybe a more logical one. It was centred in the countryside around Kilmacthomas, between the farm labourers and the big farmers. Houses and hay-barns were burned down. The Free State Army had to convoy the farm crops and stock to the towns.' His words reflect the experience of Waterford city and county in 1923, impacted by not one but two civil wars. The 'second civil war' was initiated in response to the final offer from the Waterford Farmers' Union in the annual pay talks in May 1923. The farmers demanded a reduction in the weekly wage from £38 6*s.* to £30, the abolition of traditional bonuses including the harvest bonus, and an increase in the working week from forty-five hours to fifty-four hours. Even Sir John Keane, chairman of the Waterford Farmers' Union, admitted that 'it is not a generous wage, but it is all that the industry can afford'. The labourers' union, the ITGWU, reacted predictably and a long and bitter strike started immediately. It was distinct from earlier industrial action in Waterford in that, from the beginning, the farmers could rely on government backing and the support of the National Army. Sympathetic action by dockers, shop assistants and other workers who refused to handle the farmers' produce, and the formation of a protection association by urban employers, extended the reach and intensity of the industrial action, which, as it entered its second month, had evolved into 'an outright class conflict'. Virtually every economic sector was torn by strikes, in particular the agricultural sector, bedrock of the economy, but also the transport, building, retail, industry and gas and postal service sectors. The conflict became even more bitter in its final phase between August and December 1923 when tension escalated to include incendiarism, the malicious damage of farm machinery and the retaliatory burning of farm labourers' cottages by a self-styled 'White Guard' of farmers. Finally, in early December 1923, the financial strain on the ITGWU led to the cessation of strike pay, which forced the workers to return to work on their employer's terms. Not all were re-employed. It is estimated that less than half of the 1,600 striking labourers got their jobs back. Edwards, whose brother Jack had been shot while in National Army custody in August 1922, represented those in Waterford who were impacted by both civil wars. Both were prolonged and bitter, and both left their mark on the city and county, politically, economically and socially, for decades afterwards. Every conflict, whether social or political, leaves winners and losers, each with their memories, aspirations and disappointments. The workers lost all the industrial disputes in Waterford city and county in 1923, with lasting consequences for the labour movement there. The defeat of labour in this and the other industrial disputes in Waterford in 1923 left a lasting legacy of bitterness and resentment and seriously impacted the labour movement in the city and county for decades. There can have been very few families in Waterford that were not affected by the two years of turmoil. [Text: Pat McCarthy / Image: courtesy Waterford County Museum, EK363 / Source: Uinseann MacEoin, *Survivors* (Dublin, 1980), p. 4. See also Emmet O'Connor, 'Agrarian Unrest and the Labour Movement in County Waterford 1917–1923', *Saothar,* vol. 6, 1980]

Fig. 16 A detachment of the National Army's Special Infantry Corps providing protection for farmers in County Waterford during the farm labourers' strike in 1923. The seven-month industrial dispute featured violence and intervention by units of the National Army on a scale that remains unprecedented in Irish labour history. What amounted to martial law was introduced in the area most affected by the farm labourers' strike and labourers who broke a curfew could be interned in a makeshift prison camp for weeks. National Army soldiers patrolled the roads at night, guarded farmers while they threshed the corn or unloaded ships with farm feedstuffs when dockers refused to handle such goods. [Text: Pat McCarthy / Original image: National Library of Ireland, POOLEWP 3123, colourised by CentreStage Ltd]

'White Guard'. The government sent in the Special Infantry Corps and admitted that their job was to protect the farmers. Martial law was declared in the affected area on 1 July.[45] O'Brien decided it could bankrupt the union and the strike would have to terminated. As he noted in his memoirs: 'that ended that and we did not try to organize the agricultural labourers afterwards'.[46]

By 1924 the labour movement was battered, divided and demoralised, and the spirit of post-1917 militancy was not even a memory. Trade unionism collapsed in the countryside and contracted severely among unskilled urban workers. The ITGWU had 120,000 members in 1920 and 14,600 in 1930.[47] Labour had known defeat before, but this time it was accompanied by an internal dejection that contributed to a suicidal sectionalism. Membership of the ILPTUC continued to fall until 1929, when it reached 92,000.

Addressing nationalism

Many of the chronic problems that beset the labour movement throughout the twentieth century can be traced to these years. The obvious course for social democrats would have been to oppose an unwanted Treaty, imposed by foreign *force majeure*, by peaceful means. Why did labour have to be so convoluted in addressing nationalism? After decades of mental colonisation in the nineteenth century, trade unions internalised the idea, borrowed from England, that labour and nationalism were dichotomous. Despite Connolly and Larkin, it would always see nationalism more as a problem than an opportunity. It took a backseat in the War of Independence and shied away from demanding a dividend in return for its support for Sinn Féin. It then assumed that the national question would be settled by the Anglo-Irish Treaty, allowing for the emergence of what was termed 'class' but could more accurately be described as 'bread and butter' politics.

The Civil War, and the political cleavage that emerged from it, was seen as an irrational feud over terminology by some two thirds of delegates to the ILPTUC annual congresses. There was no shortage of evidence for arguments that the IRA was fighting a futile war. At the same time, Labour never appreciated the role of British imperialism, or the fact that the national movement was always likely to split over political, cultural and economic relations with Britain. Britain remained the metropole for Ireland up to the 1960s, and a party system based on Anglo-Irish relations was quite rational. Johnson's willingness to sacrifice Labour for constitutional stability would become a repeated alibi in party history, in which, bizarrely, it took pride. Another major question, generated by the industrial war and the 1923 general election, was how the party could be relevant to its affiliated trade unions. Not for the last time, Labour was angry at its betrayal by workers at the ballot box. Yet it never addressed the question of relevance.

For Labour republicans, the ICA, Larkinites and communists, the Civil War was a counter-revolution. Roddy Connolly was prescient in seeing that the outcome of the Anglo-Irish talks in 1921 would split Sinn Féin and that the 'die-hards' would be more amenable to an alliance with the far left. But he underestimated republican reluctance to embrace social radicalism and Moscow's abiding fear of British intelligence getting wind of arms traffic with Ireland. The Comintern's refusal to say 'yea' or 'nay' to the IRA's request for guns was an early example of the contradiction between the demands of the global revolution and the welfare of the Soviet Union and of the subordination of the former to the latter. In Russia, as well as Ireland, the Civil War showed that interests of state prevailed.

CASE STUDY

Agrarian Unrest in Civil War Ireland

Heather Laird

Agrarian unrest in modern Irish history tends to be associated with the late nineteenth century, in particular the Land War of 1879–82. There is a related commonplace assumption that the ensuing series of land purchase acts answered the Irish land question. It is certainly the case that between the Land War and the establishment of the Free State in 1922, an immense change in landownership dramatically transformed rural Ireland. A survey of estates in the 1870s demonstrated that over half the country was owned by less than a thousand landlords.[1] Nine million acres of this land was transferred to its occupiers under the 1903 and 1904 land acts alone.[2] In his 1904 publication, *The Fall of Feudalism in Ireland*, Michael Davitt noted the seismic nature of these land transfers, referring to the 'repossession of the soil' as a 'revolution'.[3] Nevertheless, as a proponent of land nationalisation, Davitt also raised questions about the equitable nature of land acts that focused on purchase rather than redistribution, and seemed primarily aimed at normalising the ownership of land in Ireland from a capitalist perspective.[4]

Rural tensions

Repeated outbreaks of land agitation in the decades following the key land purchase acts indicate that the legislation did not resolve all aspects of the Irish land question. In the immediate aftermath of the land acts of 1903 and 1904, rural tensions focused on the non-residential graziers (also called ranchers) who held land in the grazing areas of the country under the eleven-month system. This type of letting, being for less than a year, was not liable to periodical rent revisions. It suited graziers looking to lease land on a short-term basis for the fattening of cattle, but was resented by small farmers who lacked the capital to outbid them. Thus cattle-driving became a common tactic employed by agitators during the Ranch War of 1906–9.[5] They forcibly removed cattle from the targeted land and either drove them to the grazier's house, placed them on another farmer's land or left them on a road some distance from the land.

In the spring and early summer of 1920 rural unrest became especially pronounced, with police returns of 'agrarian outrages' higher than in any other year since 1882 during the height of the Land War.[6] The dominant form of this new bout of agrarian unrest was the seizure of land. While the farms of small and middling farmers were not guaranteed to be safe, land let out to graziers on the eleven-month system was again particularly targeted. Land under the control of the Congested Districts Board was also seized. The board, which had been established in 1891 in recognition that land purchase acts did little to improve the conditions of those who held

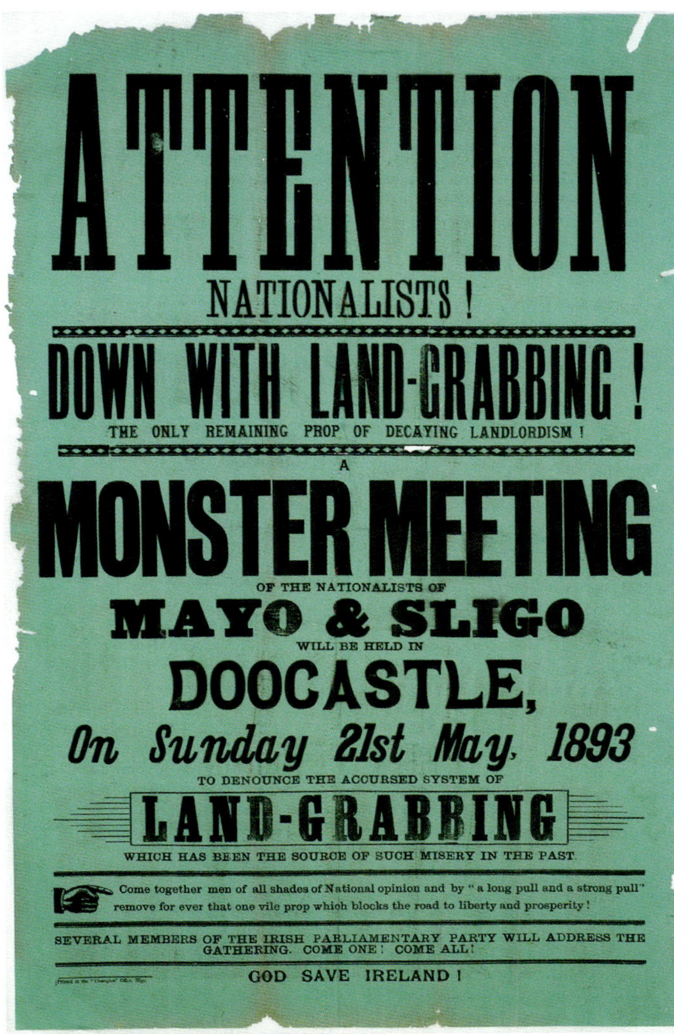

Fig. 1 A poster advertising a monster meeting of nationalists at Doocastle on the Mayo/Sligo border on 21 May 1893 to denounce land-grabbing – 'the only remaining prop of decaying landlordism'. The poster also references the fact that the meeting would be addressed by several members of the Irish Parliamentary Party. One of the basic tactics of the Land League in its agitation against landlordism was to proscribe as public enemies those tenants or 'land grabbers' who would take the land of another evicted tenant. [Document: National Archives of Ireland, CSO/CBS/13585/1. Reproduced by kind permission of the director of the National Archives]

small 'uneconomic' holdings, became the focus of agrarian unrest as it was allowing graziers to stock land already in its possession. Some of the seized land was broken up into holdings for individual farmers, non-inheriting farmers' sons or landless labourers, and some was turned into commons, occasionally referred to as 'soviets'.[7] In addition to longer-standing issues, an immediate context for such land seizures was escalating tensions over resources due to the impact of the First World War on emigration and beef prices. In the west of the country, in particular, an already chronic land hunger that 'peasant proprietorship' itself could not alleviate was exacerbated by wartime restrictions on emigration; increased beef prices further ensured that land was more likely to be let out for commercial grazing than subsistence farming.

Land congestion

The relationship between agrarian agitators and mainstream nationalists had grown increasingly tense in the run-up to and during the War of Independence. In the west land congestion created a dissatisfaction that provided much of the energy for the Anglo-Irish conflict, though participation in the shooting war remained limited.[8] For many within the independence movement the land issue not only distracted from the nationalist project but threatened to derail it. Hence direct action aimed at land distribution was a source of considerable anxiety for both the First Dáil and the ensuing Free State government. To control the situation in early 1920, the First Dáil established special land courts as well as a land commission to fund purchases in congested areas.

Rural unrest remained a significant feature of Civil War Irish society, with the land issue especially divisive at the time. On 22 December 1922, just over two weeks after the Free State was formally established, Patrick Hogan, minister for agriculture, informed key Cabinet members that the 'Land War is very widespread and very serious'. In a memorandum titled 'Seizures of Land', Hogan referred to a notable increase in 'forcible occupation' alongside 'cattle driving', 'the usual knocking of walls', 'seizure of stock' and 'people [...being] shot at'. These incidents, he went on to claim, 'are not isolated but part of an organised campaign' by those who know that 'the "land for the people" is almost as respectable an objective as the "Republic" and would make a much wider appeal'.[9] As suggested by this memorandum, agrarian discontent was viewed by some opponents of the Treaty, most notably Liam Mellows, as a means to mobilise anti-government support, while principal members of the government were hostile to an agitation that they believed was being used to undermine the authority of the Free State.[10] Thus a connection was formed in Civil War Ireland between land seizures and anti-Treaty 'irregularism', and a corresponding link made between the defence of private property rights and the defence of the fledgling state.[11]

Fig. 2 Harvest workers gather barley in stacks, *c.*10 October 1923. As seen below, Irish agricultural work practices relied heavily on farm labourers rather than advanced machinery. Labourers such as these were typically landless and did not have the financial resources to secure their own farms. This image was commissioned by E. Ryan and Sons Ltd, which appears to have been a brewery stores merchant located in Thurles, County Tipperary. [Image: National Library of Ireland, POOLEWP 3135]

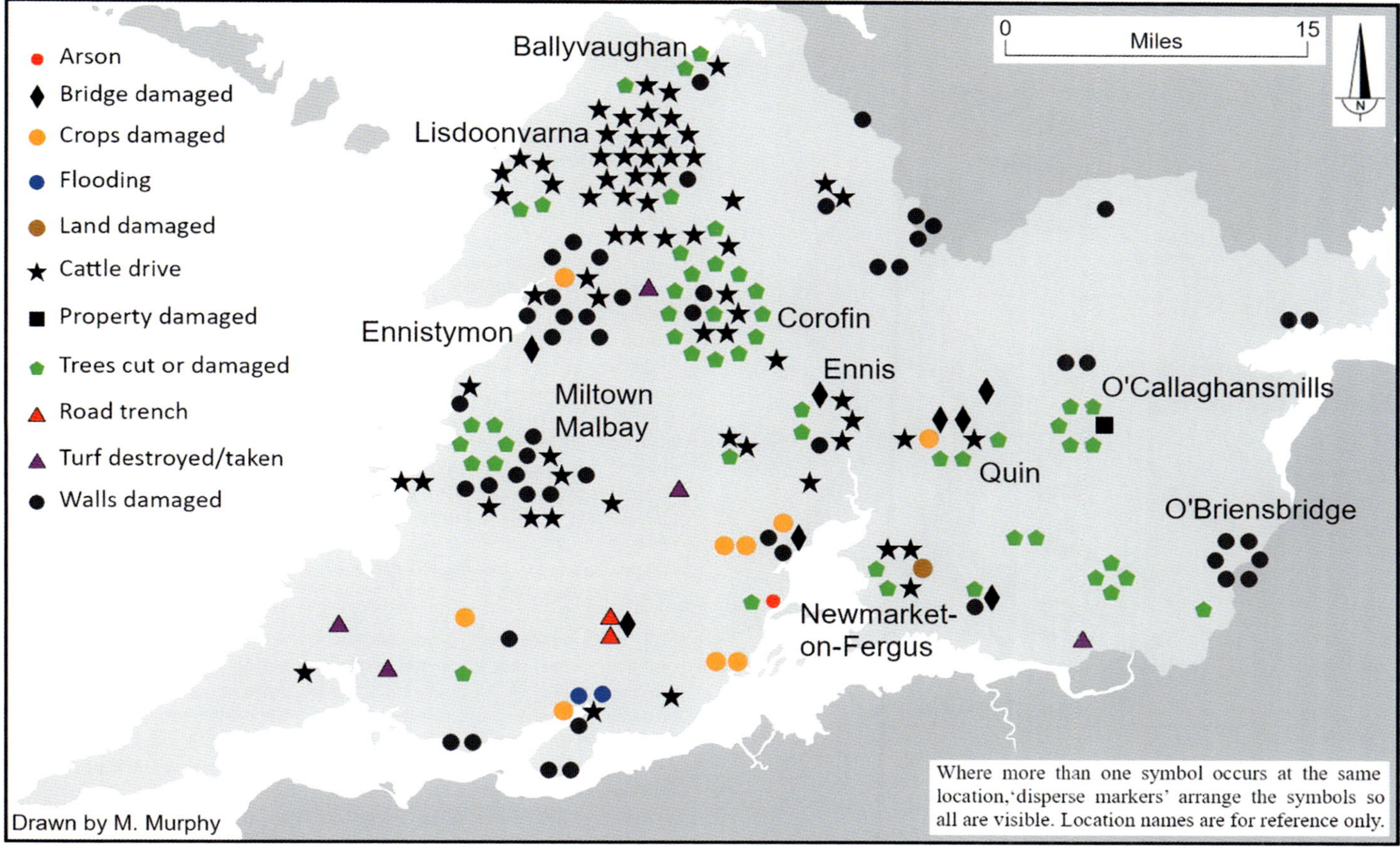

Fig. 3 Map based on civilian compensation claims under the Damage to Property (Compensation) Act 1923 for County Clare. Research by Justin Dolan Stover into the impact of guerrilla warfare on the landscape emphasises the communal disruptions caused by the felling of trees, the (literal) cutting of roads and destruction of walls or ditches, primarily by the IRA. However he also notes the Civil War expansion of 'agrarian sabotage connected to local rivalries, land jealously [*sic*] and unresolved land transfers, as well as the destruction of fences, walls, and earthen boundaries, cattle maiming, and the burning of fields, crops, ricks of turf and farming implements'. This map of Civil War compensation claims in County Clare shows certain common types of damage as well as distinct geographic clusters. County Clare earned a 'black reputation' for agrarianism during the nineteenth century, with David Fitzpatrick remarking that by the First World War, 'The reverberations of the "Land War" were unusually persistent in Clare'. Intense competition for arable land in the Burren, the dominance of strong cattle ranches across the county and the lack of land available for purchase created persistent conflicts over land usage. The county was struck by rural unrest during the Ranch War in 1906–9 and saw a surge of attacks on cattle ranchers in early 1918, when the British government declared Clare a Special Military Area. Though a hotbed of revolutionary violence during the War of Independence, Clare experienced more limited military combat during the Civil War, with Bielenberg and Dorney counting a total of thirty-eight people killed in the county (the lowest fatality rate in Munster). While eastern Clare broadly supported the Free State, the north-western area of the county retained a relatively strong IRA presence. This map shows a revival of cattle driving around the Burren. Long a centre of agrarian unrest, it was also an area where an active IRA had often stymied attempts to assert Free State law and order. Though support for the Free State was strong in east Clare, cattle driving which had been common there in 1918 resumed, particularly around O'Briensbridge. The cutting of trees and trenching of roads was fairly common and usually carried out by the IRA to hinder National Army troop movements. Agrarian conflict is indicated on the map by the destruction of turf, damage to boundary walls and attacks on crops. In such cases those responsible may have been republicans, unaffiliated opportunists or even government supporters. The overlap of social and military conflict is apparent in the county during the Civil War, as it was in many parts of Ireland. [Source: Map data provided by Justin Dolan Stover / See also Justin Dolan Stover, 'Active service and environmental damage in revolutionary Ireland', *Contemporary European History*, vol. 32, Special Issue 4, Nov. 2023, pp. 520–1; David Fitzpatrick, *Politics and Irish Life, 1913–21: Provincial experiences of war and revolution* (Cork, 1998), pp. 2–4]

Coercive measures

To curb agrarian unrest, the Free State government introduced a 1923 land bill focused on redistributive land reform. Coercive measures were also employed, with a specialised unit of the Free State's National Army comprised of approximately 4,000 men established in January 1923 for the purpose. This unit, the Special Infantry Corps, was subsequently described by one of the government's leading ministers, Kevin O'Higgins, as having done 'effective, if "rough and ready" work in stamping [out] agrarian anarchy'.[12] In 1923 the corps, organised into eight battalions and a border unit, arrested at least 173 people for 'agrarian offences'.[13] Reasons recorded for arrest in the military archives include 'land trouble', 'interfering with land other than his own', 'unlawful working in a bog', 'breaking down walls', 'cattle driving', 'maiming of cattle', 'forcible grazing of lands', 'illegal tillage' and 'unlawful possession'.[14] While arrests feature heavily in the Special Infantry Corps Returns and Reports, they were not the main activity of this unit. More commonly the corps simply cleared seized land, sometimes resorting to violence to do so, as O'Higgins's reference to 'rough and ready' work suggests.

Fig. 4 (left) Cartoon by 'Shemus' (Ernest Forbes), titled 'The Toovahara Trotsky', published in the *Freeman's Journal*, 10 May 1923. The 1923 Toovahera (less frequently spelled Toovahara) 'soviet' in north Clare was one of a number of attempts made by landless labourers and small farmers before and during the Civil War to take over large farms and estates and run them in a collective manner. The most well known was the Broadford soviet in Clare, when tenants took over the Going estate and ran it for ten months in 1922. In April 1922 in Toovahera in the vicinity of Crab Island, depicted as 'Grab Island' in the cartoon, herdsmen who had been tending to cattle in large farms owned by farmers from other parts of Clare drove the cattle back to their owners. A Land Co-operative Society was then formed by locals, who rented the land out to neighbours for grazing at a low rent. Similar actions occurred in other districts in the vicinity. The Special Infantry Corps swooped on the area in February 1923 and arrested nineteen of the 'ringleaders', who were interned in Newbridge. The *Freeman's Journal* ran a number of stories under red-scare headlines like 'Reign of Lawlessness' and 'Bolshevicks Work Other People's Farms' in May 1923, based on the mistaken assumption that the soviet was still operational. It was these that inspired the cartoon, which reflects the common Free State trope that 'irregularism' was both synonymous with and a facilitator of lawlessness; it also echoes reports in the paper that implied that the north Clare 'Trotskys' were more interested in self-enrichment than social revolution. [Image: National Library of Ireland, PD 4309 TX 191 /See *Freeman's Journal*, 3, 9, 17 and 25 May 1923]

Fig. 5 (opposite page) Special Infantry Corps unit headquarters and operating areas, July 1923 and border unit strength, September 1923. The rapid evacuation of the South of Ireland by crown forces in early 1922 led to an outbreak of social disorder that caused anxiety within the new government. The uneven deployment and performance of the Civic Guard, which replaced the RIC, combined with surges in agrarianism, labour militancy, illegal distilling and ordinary criminality deepened fears of a social breakdown. One of the government's responses was to create a military police force called the Special Infantry Corps (SIC) in January 1923. With a planned strength of 4,000 soldiers, it was organised into eight battalions with distinct operating areas. Their duties included protecting private property during labour and agrarian disputes, seizing livestock for illegal grazing or in lieu of unpaid debts and overseeing evictions. The average unit size typically numbered between 200 and 300 soldiers. The much larger contingent of 571 stationed at the town hall in Waterford stemmed from the deployment of two separate SIC battalions to the embattled area. It reflected the strong government intervention on behalf of farmers during the Waterford farm labourers' strike in the last seven months of 1923 (see p. 127) A SIC border unit was also created to protect the fourteen posts established by the Free State along the border with Northern Ireland. The strengths and locations of the SIC border units by September 1923 are identified in the map with black circles. Members of the SIC border unit reinforced unarmed customs officials who previously had little control over smugglers, IRA fighters or citizens unwilling to subject themselves to the law of the new state. The SIC ended operations at the close of 1923. |Source: A. Kinsella, 'The Special Infantry Corps', *Irish Sword,* vol. xx, no. 82 (1997), pp. 331–46]

Further coercive measures included the confiscation of stock, the payment of fines and compensation and the debarring of those involved in seizures from future land distribution by the Congested Districts Board.

Given the alignment established towards the end of the nineteenth century between the land movement and Irish nationalism, it is easy to equate the transfer of land that resulted from the land purchase acts with the transfer of ownership of the Irish nation. But this narrative of land and nation – the standard shortened version – contains gaps and silences. It is certainly true that in the late nineteenth century, agrarian agitation was the driving force behind Irish nationalism. In the early twentieth century, however, the radical combination of forces that had placed land at the very centre of nationalist politics had begun to break down. As the independence movement gathered momentum, the land question was increasingly viewed by mainstream nationalists as a damaging social division that was distracting from the more important political issue of capturing and securing the state. Moreover the emphasis placed on containing rural unrest during the Civil War period and the methods employed to do so had long-term repercussions. It ensured that Fine Gael, the Irish political party rooted in support for the Anglo-Irish Treaty, became aligned with the interests of the 'strong' farmer. More broadly, the links formed during the Civil War meant that henceforth securing the Irish state would be synonymous with the defence of private property rights.

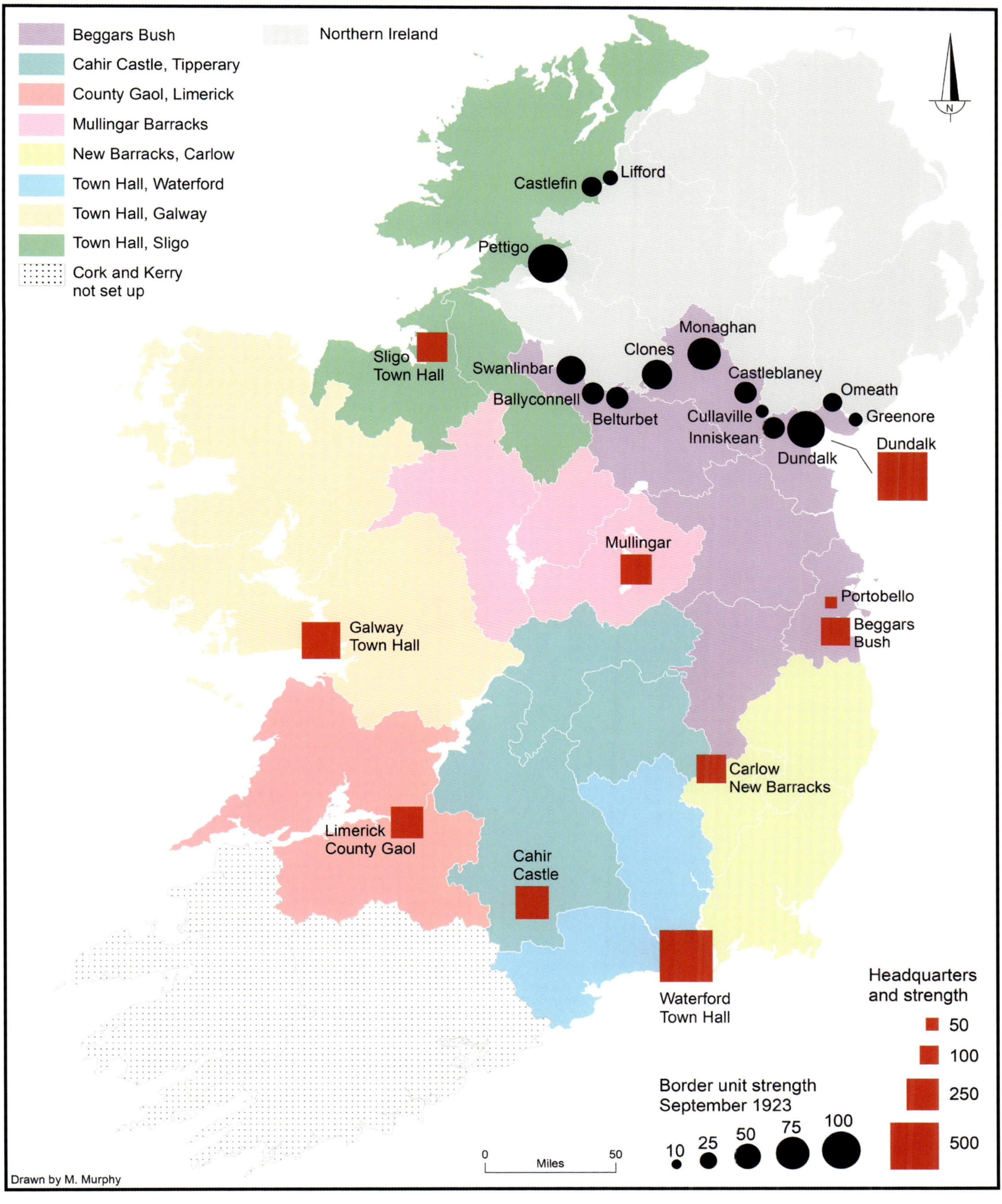

Beggars Bush
Cahir Castle, Tipperary
County Gaol, Limerick
Mullingar Barracks
New Barracks, Carlow
Town Hall, Waterford
Town Hall, Galway
Town Hall, Sligo
Cork and Kerry not set up
Northern Ireland
N
Castlefin
Lifford
Pettigo
Monaghan
Clones
Swanlinbar
Castleblaney
Ballyconnell
Belturbet
Omeath
Cullaville
Greenore
Inniskean
Dundalk
Dundalk
Sligo Town Hall
Mullingar
Portobello
Beggars Bush
Galway Town Hall
Carlow New Barracks
Limerick County Gaol
Cahir Castle
Waterford Town Hall
Headquarters and strength
50
100
250
500
Border unit strength September 1923
10
25
50
75
100
0
Miles
50
Drawn by M. Murphy

The Postal Strike, 1922

Donal Ó Drisceoil

'The Free State Government's attitude towards striking postal workers', wrote Liam Mellows presciently from his prison cell in September 1922, 'makes clear what its attitude towards workers generally will be'. Over 7,000 Irish postal workers, the vast majority of the workforce – organised in the ad hoc United Postal Union, made up of the Irish Postal Union, the Irish Postal Workers' Union and the Irish Post Office Engineering Union – struck on 10 September 1922, the day after the Dáil elected in June 1922 finally met. It was the first major countrywide strike faced by an Irish government, and its reaction was indeed revealing about its attitude to workers' and trade union rights.

In March the Provisional Government had cut the cost-of-living bonus that these workers had been receiving since the First World War, and which had maintained their income at a bare living wage. Another cut was scheduled for September. The Douglas Commission, established by the government to forestall strike action earlier in the year, had recommended in an interim report that further cuts be postponed until a cost-of-living index was established to determine pay levels, and advocated a basic wage raise of 7.5–12.5 per cent to compensate workers for the bonus reduction. The outbreak of the Civil War put the commission on hold and the government effectively ignored the recommendations, pushing through with the bonus cut based on the disputed findings of an interdepartmental cost-of-living committee, and forcing the hand of the unions.

J.J. Walsh, the postmaster-general, saw the strike as a direct challenge to the government's authority in the midst of the Civil War; he later called it a 'stab in the back' and that to 'smash' it would be 'a salutary lesson to the general indiscipline which had

Fig. 1 (opposite page) A group of striking postal workers, September 1922. The placards highlight key issues from the dispute: the employment of 'scab labour', the use of the National Army against the strikers and the high cost of living.

Fig. 2 (left) A handbill issued by the United Postal Union, September 1922, noting the range of penalties imposed on striking postal workers by the government, and asserting the strikers' defiance of intimidation.

Fig. 3 (right) One of a number of handbills issued by the striking postal workers that reference the postal unions' support for the successful April 1920 general strike for the release of the Mountjoy hunger strikers.

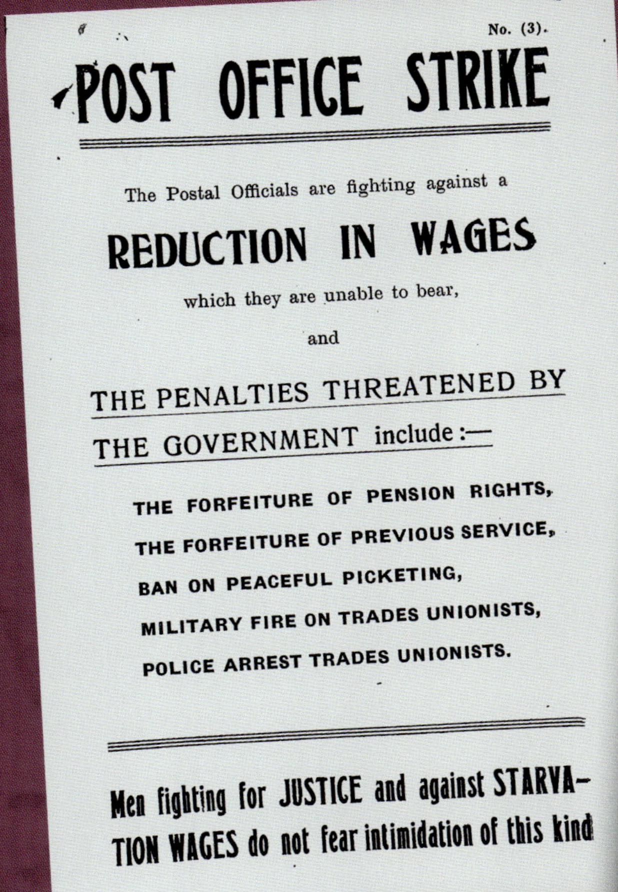

No. (3).

POST OFFICE STRIKE

The Postal Officials are fighting against a

REDUCTION IN WAGES

which they are unable to bear,

and

THE PENALTIES THREATENED BY THE GOVERNMENT include:—

THE FORFEITURE OF PENSION RIGHTS,
THE FORFEITURE OF PREVIOUS SERVICE,
BAN ON PEACEFUL PICKETING,
MILITARY FIRE ON TRADES UNIONISTS,
POLICE ARREST TRADES UNIONISTS.

Men fighting for JUSTICE and against STARVATION WAGES do not fear intimidation of this kind

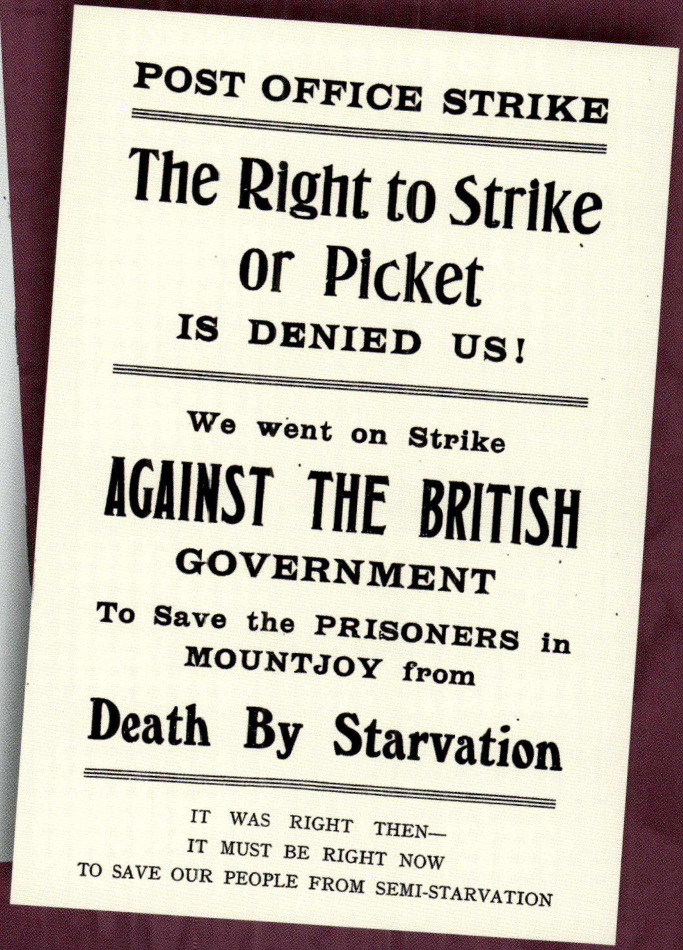

POST OFFICE STRIKE

The Right to Strike or Picket IS DENIED US!

We went on Strike AGAINST THE BRITISH GOVERNMENT To Save the PRISONERS in MOUNTJOY from Death By Starvation

IT WAS RIGHT THEN—
IT MUST BE RIGHT NOW
TO SAVE OUR PEOPLE FROM SEMI-STARVATION

seemed to run riot through the land'. The government's position was that civil servants, including postal workers, had no right to strike. Walsh and Kevin O'Higgins argued that the disruption would be used to its advantage by the IRA.

The workers were warned that if they withdrew their labour, they would forfeit their positions and, if reinstated, would lose pension entitlements from previous service. On the eve of the strike the government announced that picketing would not be permitted and, once it commenced, the police and military were ordered to remove pickets. Shots were fired over the heads of picketers, there were numerous arrests, despite pickets being peaceful, and CID policemen harassed and frequently detained union officials. As the *Voice of Labour* pointed out, 'The government has raised the issue above an ordinary wages dispute—it has raised it to the higher level of the right to strike and the right to picket'.

Some National Army soldiers acted as strike-breakers and protected other 'blacklegs' and 'scabs' who performed the strikers' usual tasks and maintained a skeleton service. The union's strike bulletin carried accounts of unemployed workers being threatened with losing benefits if they refused to blackleg and of republican prisoners being offered release if they were willing to strike-break. On 13 September Labour Party leader Thomas Johnson told Walsh and his colleagues in the Dáil that they were 'laying it down that military can disperse a picket, that military can fire at a picket or over the heads of a picket; that military can use terroristic methods to destroy a body of workers carrying on what I contend to be a legal operation'. Johnson and the leadership of the labour movement, however, demurred from initiating solidarity or sympathetic action, as many rank-and-file trade unionists were demanding.

On 17 September Olive Flood, a striker on picket duty in Dublin, was shot and wounded by a National Army soldier. On 28 September in Limerick fifteen picketers were injured when they were punched with knuckle-dusters and pistol-whipped by soldiers in civilian clothing. The following day the strike ended. Senator James Douglas, who had headed up the commission, persuaded the union that a revived commission would deal with their grievances. The union leaders agreed to call off the strike on condition that the commission would resume and no victimisation of returning workers would occur. Despite a positive spin on the ending of the strike by the union, it had effectively been defeated. The bonus cuts were implemented, the only concession being that they would be spread over three months. The commission's subsequent recommendations of pay rises were resisted by the Department of Finance.

Walsh immediately set about a campaign of victimisation, including carrying out his threat on pensions and considering the strike as a break in service with regard to incremental wage rates. Former strikers were dismissed and demoted, and strike-breakers and non-strikers were promoted. The Irish Postal Union and the Irish Postal Workers' Union had amalgamated as the Post Office

Fig. 4 (right) A handbill condemning a government edict ('ukase' was the term used in Tsarist Russia), issued on the eve of the strike, that banned picketing.

Fig. 5 (above) Members of the Irish postal unions march in Dublin during the postal strike of September 1922.

Workers' Union in 1923. Its general secretary, and later leader of the Labour Party, William Norton, wrote to Walsh in 1924 contrasting the treatment of his members by the British when they struck in support of the release of republican prisoners in 1920 – the stoppage of two days' pay – with the actions of a 'native administration' that showed 'such vindictiveness and such hostility to trade union action'. Postal workers had to wait another decade for the restoration of incremental rates and the resolution of the pension issue, which occurred under the new Fianna Fáil administration. [Images: courtesy of the Irish Labour History Museum / See Gerard Hanley, 'They 'never dared say "boo" when the British were here': the postal strike of 1922 and the Irish Civil War', *Irish Historical Studies*, vol. 6, issue 169, May 2022, and Cathal Brennan, 'The Postal Strike of 1922' at https://www.theirishstory.com/2012/06/08/the-postal-strike-of-1922/]

2

Post Office Strike

The Government Ukase against Trades Unionists.

PEACEFUL PICKETING BANNED

IN THEIR FIGHT AGAINST A

Starvation Wage

POST OFFICE TRADES UNIONISTS HAVE BEEN

Fired on by Military

AND

Arrested by Police

The Public of Dublin will not be on the side of those who deprive their servants of every right but

The Right to Starve

CASE STUDY

Everyday Life in Dublin during the Irish Civil War

Pádraig Yeates

After the first week of hostilities, the Civil War in Dublin city and county may have brought a greater degree of stability and certainty than the period of the Truce that preceded it, which had been characterised by that most confusing and disconcerting of political situations for the general populace: dual power. The ending of the military curfew, disbandment of the Royal Irish Constabulary's Auxiliary Division and withdrawal of British troops to barracks left the citizenry at the mercy not only of competing factions within the IRA, but also of the criminal gangs seeking to fill the power vacuum.

Fig. 1 (right) 'Any day in Dublin', a cartoon by 'Shemus' (Ernest Forbes). The period of the War of Independence had seen a major upsurge in all types of crime. Indeed one of the IRA's tasks had been to try to combat it, through the organisation of a republican police. This type of activity formed a much larger part of the republican movement's remit during the War of Independence than is usually acknowledged. Indeed in 1920 the Volunteer journal *An t-Óglách* complained that some IRA units were spending *too* much time on policing. Though restructured and organised nationwide during the Truce, the republican police were hard-pressed to deal with what was described by a senior figure in the republican police, Simon Donnelly, as a new 'wave of crime'. *An t-Óglách* lamented in February 1922 that the 'criminal elements which exist in every community' were taking advantage of the disturbed situation. In Dublin there were several armed raids of 'amazing audacity' early that year. That city alone would see 479 armed robberies during 1922. In Cork 'large-scale armed robberies became common [...] though they had previously been extremely rare'. Belfast, wracked by violent sectarian conflict, also saw almost 'daily' armed robberies of shops and pubs. Two banks in Sligo were robbed of £13,000 and a bank in Charlestown, County Mayo lost £5,000 to raiders in February alone. There were also 331 raids on post offices between 23 March and 19 April 1922. As the republican split deepened, the pro-Treatyites were eager to place the blame for all of these on the IRA. The reality was generally more complicated. For example, John Cox, a republican policeman, was shot dead during a robbery in Lanesborough, County Longford in April. The raiders, captured in nearby Roscommon, were soldiers of the National Army. Free State personnel, including officers, would feature prominently in all varieties of armed crime during the 1922–3 period. IRA Volunteers also certainly carried out robberies, some of them for personal gain. And non-political criminals remained very active. But it was not until May that republicans endorsed armed robbery as a method of fundraising. On 1 May 1922, £50,000 was taken in a coordinated series of robberies on branches of the Bank of Ireland. That bank was seen as the 'official treasurer of the Treaty party' and the raids justified in order to feed, clothe and arm the anti-Treaty IRA. The robberies themselves, however, had been ordered by a faction of the republican leadership, those in occupation of the Four Courts, rather than the IRA itself. Nevertheless it marked a turning point. There were several clashes during the raids and in Buncrana a young woman, Mary Ellen-Kavanagh, and a girl, Esther Fletcher, were killed in crossfire. Four National Army soldiers also died in a shootout in Donegal later that day. The incidents contributed both to the drift towards war and to the government's determination to associate the anti-Treaty IRA in the public's mind with criminal activity. And crime, of all varieties, with diverse perpetrators, would continue to be a feature of the Civil War and its aftermath. [Text: Brian Hanley / Image: National Library of Ireland, PD 4309 TX 101]

The Dublin Metropolitan Police (DMP) remained in situ but, except for the demoralised G Division, its members suffered from the handicap of being unarmed. The DMP worked as best it could with the republican police and, from December 1921, Emmet Dalton, the IRA's chief liaison officer with the British forces, took effective charge of both bodies until control of the DMP was transferred to the new Provisional Government in April 1922. A new Criminal Investigation Department (CID) was created under the auspices of the National Army and located in Oriel House. Comprised of Collins's loyalists, its main aim was to identify and eliminate anti-Treaty opponents of the new regime.

Escalating crime

Serious crime soared in 1922 as a result. There were 23 murders, 53 attempted murders, 112 cases of malicious wounding, 479 armed robberies and another 234 attacks with intent to rob in Dublin,

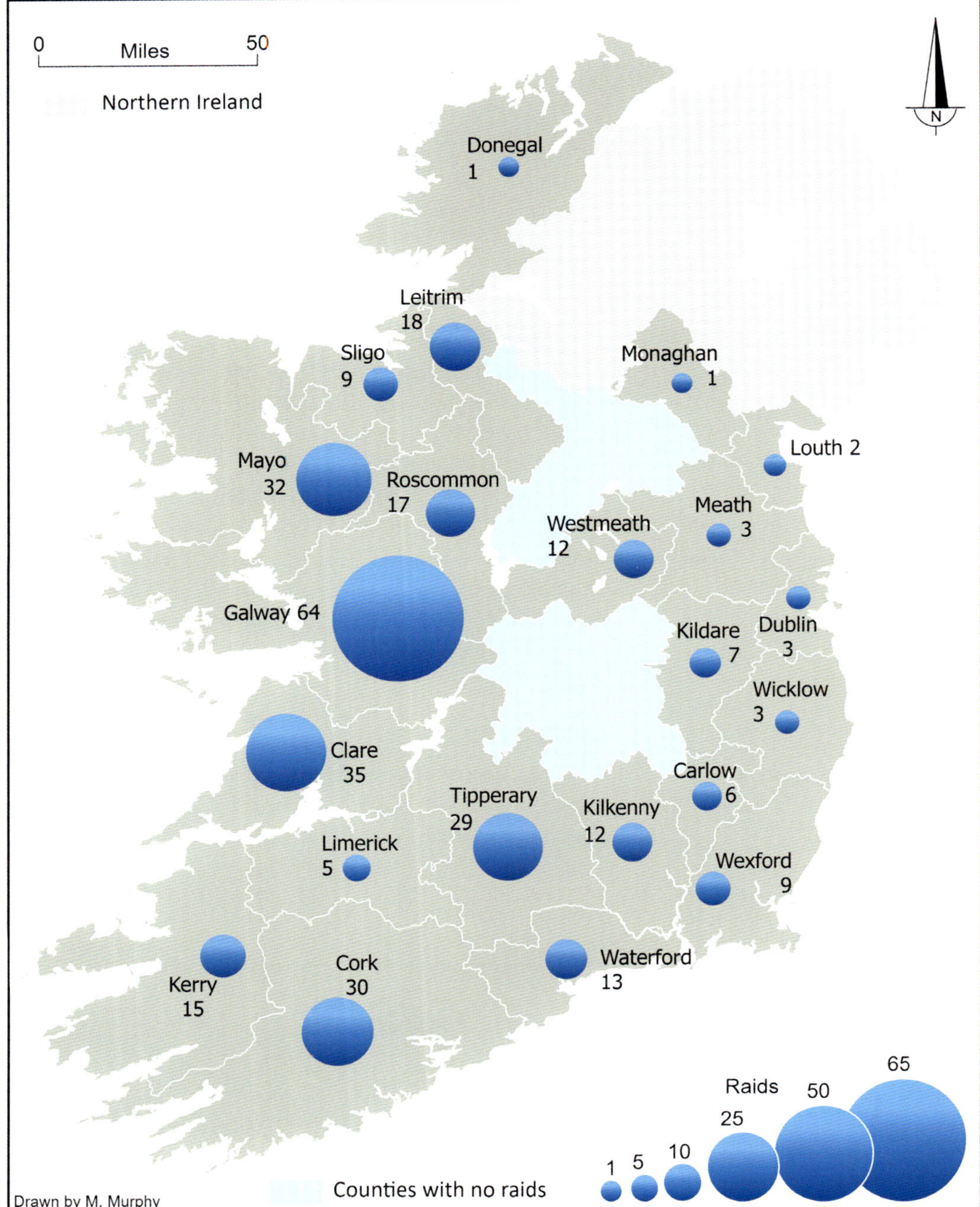

Fig. 2 Map of post office raids, 23 March 1922–19 April 1922. Of the 331 raids carried out during this period, 234 took place over ten days between 29 March and 7 April 1922, with the highest number of raids in Galway (sixty-four), followed by Clare (thirty-five), Mayo (thirty-two), Cork (thirty), Tipperary (twenty-nine), Leitrim (eighteen) and Roscommon (seventeen). When presenting the report on the raids to the Dáil on 26 April 1922, the minister for defence, Richard Mulcahy, emphasised the high number of raids in brigade and divisional areas under the control of sitting TDs, including the fourteen post offices targeted on 7 March within a fifteen-mile radius of Cooraclare in the West Clare Brigade area under pro-Treaty TD Michael Brennan. [Source: *Dáil Debates*, vol. S2, no. 4 (Appendix D), 26 Apr. 1922]

as well as 30 cases of arson and over 900 other serious attacks on property. While major cash robberies from banks attracted the most attention, the vast majority of armed robberies were hold-ups of ordinary citizens. The amounts taken could be minuscule. When two masked gunmen forced their way into Patrick Ryan's home at Benamena Cottages on the Stillorgan Road in County Dublin on the night of 25 January 1922, they found none of the occupants had any money except for Ryan's daughter. She had *9d* in her purse, which the gunmen took.[1]

At the other end of the social scale, countess of Wicklow Alice Howard found herself frequently confined to the house because, as she told friends, 'we cannot take the car out as they are being stopped and stolen every day'.[2] Dalton concurred, declaring that 'a most unprecedented outburst of brigandage [had] swept the whole country'.[3] IRA units were among the worst culprits and in south county Dublin, where Lady Howard lived, a special memorandum had to be issued by the local IRA brigade expressing concern about the number of vehicles being expropriated. In future, units were told, 'seizures shall only be carried out where and when sanctioned by the Brigade O/C. RECEIPTS should be given for all goods commandeered for Army purposes.'[4] Such receipts became as common as banknotes and were issued for goods taken from shops and businesses, money from banks and post offices, and alcohol from pubs and off-licences as well as vehicles. No one was immune.

Fig. 3 Republicans evacuating the Ballast Office on Dublin's Westmoreland Street, which had been occupied by the anti-Treatyites since early May 1922. [Image: Cashman Collection © RTÉ Archives, 0504/066]

Denis Hayes, the Lord Lieutenant's chauffeur, was held up by five Volunteers in Kingstown and the Viceroy's car used for an evening's socialising. If nothing else, the activities of these assorted armed groups garnered support from many terrorised citizens for the pro-Treaty candidates in the June 1922 general election.

The Labour Party also polled well in that general election, after having held its most successful general strike of the revolutionary period on 24 April 1922. While the strike against militarism did little to curb the 'militarists' on either side nationally, the power of organised labour could make itself felt in Dublin. When the anti-Treaty forces took over the Ballast Office commanding O'Connell Bridge, one of the few strategically important buildings occupied in the city, it brought business in Dublin Port to a halt, but they were forced to evacuate after a couple of days when the building was besieged by over a thousand angry dockers.

The continuation of the Belfast boycott by the anti-Treaty forces, in retaliation for 'pogroms', or anti-Catholic violence conducted against the nationalist population in Northern Ireland, also disrupted business. It also represented a direct challenge to the Provisional Government, because Collins agreed to call off the boycott in January 1922 after talks with the new Northern Ireland prime minister, James Craig. The boycott, which the anti-Treaty forces extended to English-based imports, remained popular with much of the population, kept anti-Treaty Volunteers occupied and allowed them to maintain a degree of control of the city. While the policy on seizures was erratic, alcohol and cigarettes were regularly targeted.

Arrest and kidnapping

It was apposite in the circumstances that it was not a high-profile political event, such as the assassination of Sir Henry Wilson, that sparked the Civil War, but the arrest of Leo Henderson, the director of the Belfast boycott, as he attempted to commandeer imported vehicles from the Ferguson garage in Lower Baggot Street on 26 June. Anti-Treaty forces kidnapped J.J. O'Connell, the assistant chief of staff of the new National Army in retaliation and, when they refused to release him, the Provisional Government ordered the attack on the Four Courts, where O'Connell was being held, on 28 June. There followed just over a week of intensive fighting in the north inner city, which was so reminiscent of the Easter Rising that many Dubliners thought, at first, that the British Army had attacked the Four Courts. Among the many local residents trapped by the fighting were my grandmother and father. They lived in a small flat at the rear of a shop on Parnell Street overlooking the dog's lane of Rutland Place.

Fig. 4 (left) A Rolls-Royce armoured car (nicknamed 'The Big Fella'), outside Harry Ferguson's premises on Baggott Street, Dublin following the arrest of IRA commandant Leo Henderson on 26 June 1922. [Image: National Library of Ireland, NPA CIVP6]

Fig. 5 (below) A crowd of Dubliners watching fighting on Sackville (O'Connell) Street during the Battle for Dublin, July 1922. Much of the Civil War's early fighting occurred in urban areas, which resulted in the suspension of businesses, schools and transportation. Curious residents often gravitated to the battle areas to witness proceedings. Here, a crowd gathers on the south side of O'Connell Bridge to watch the fighting. Additional clusters of spectators can be seen across the bridge. Such close proximity to combat was dangerous, and several Dublin residents died observing the Battle for Dublin. [Image: Cashman Collection © RTÉ Archives, 0504/072]

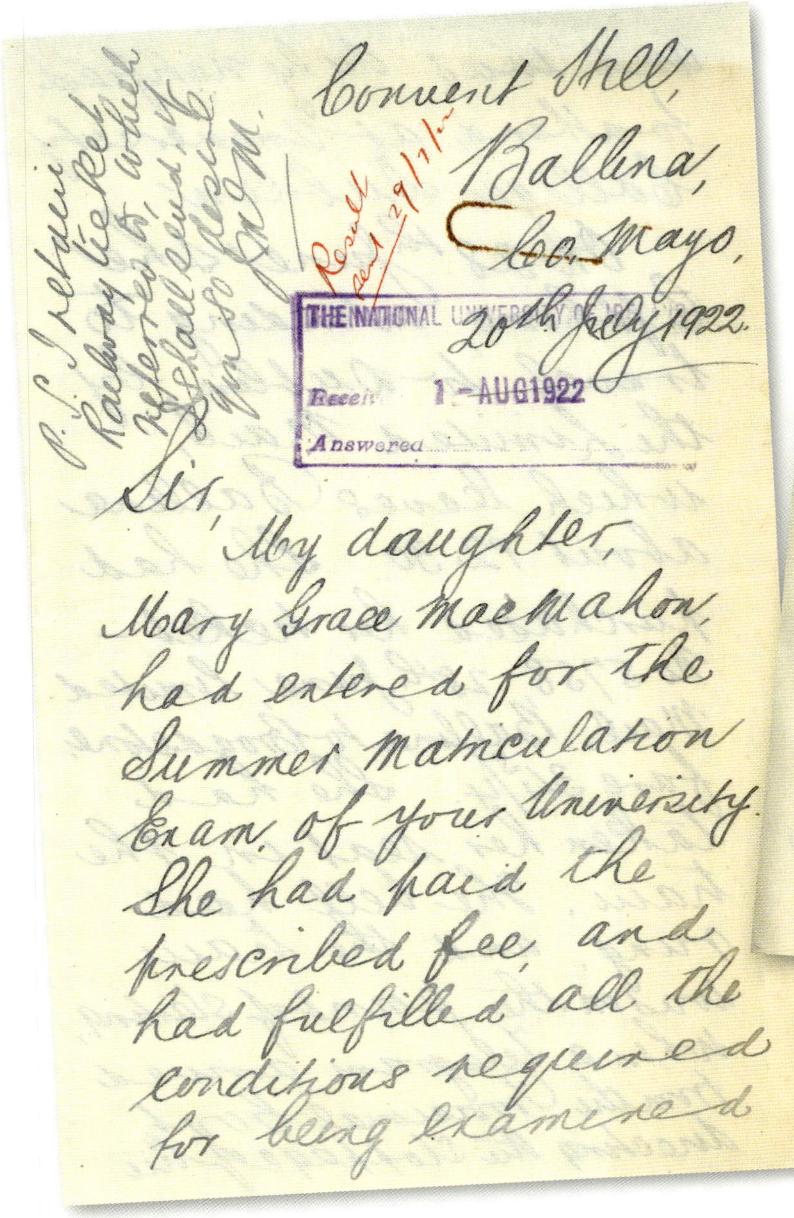

Convent Hill,
Ballina,
Co. Mayo,
20th July 1922.

THE NATIONAL UNIVERSITY OF IRELAND
Received 1 - AUG 1922
Answered ....

Result sent 29/7/22

P.S. I return Railway ticket referred to, which [illegible] J. McM.

Sir,

My daughter, Mary Grace MacMahon, had entered for the Summer Matriculation Exam. of your University. She had paid the prescribed fee, and had fulfilled all the conditions required for being examined and was duly notified to attend at University College Dublin.

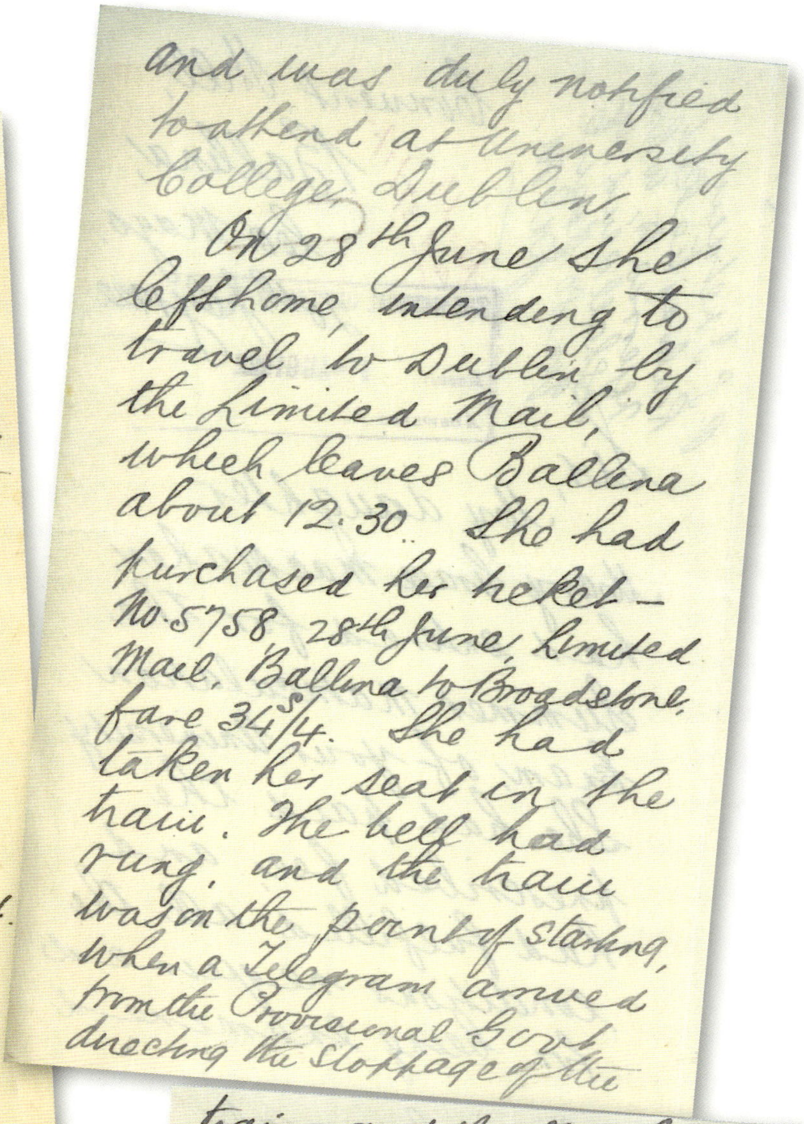

On 28th June she left home, intending to travel to Dublin by the Limited Mail, which leaves Ballina about 12.30. She had purchased her ticket – No. 5758 28th June, Limited Mail, Ballina to Broadstone, fare 34/4. She had taken her seat in the train. The bell had rung, and the train was on the point of starting, when a Telegram arrived from the Provisional Govt. directing the stoppage of the train, and of all other trains till further notice. The passengers had to leave the train. She immediately went to the Post Office to wire you the facts, and to ask your advice. The Telegraph Clerk was counting the words in the message, when orders came to accept no more wires for Dublin. No trains have since left Ballina for Dublin, no Telegrams have been accepted, and, with the exception of one consignment of mails sent by Glasgow boat, no letters have been since despatched from Ballina to Dublin

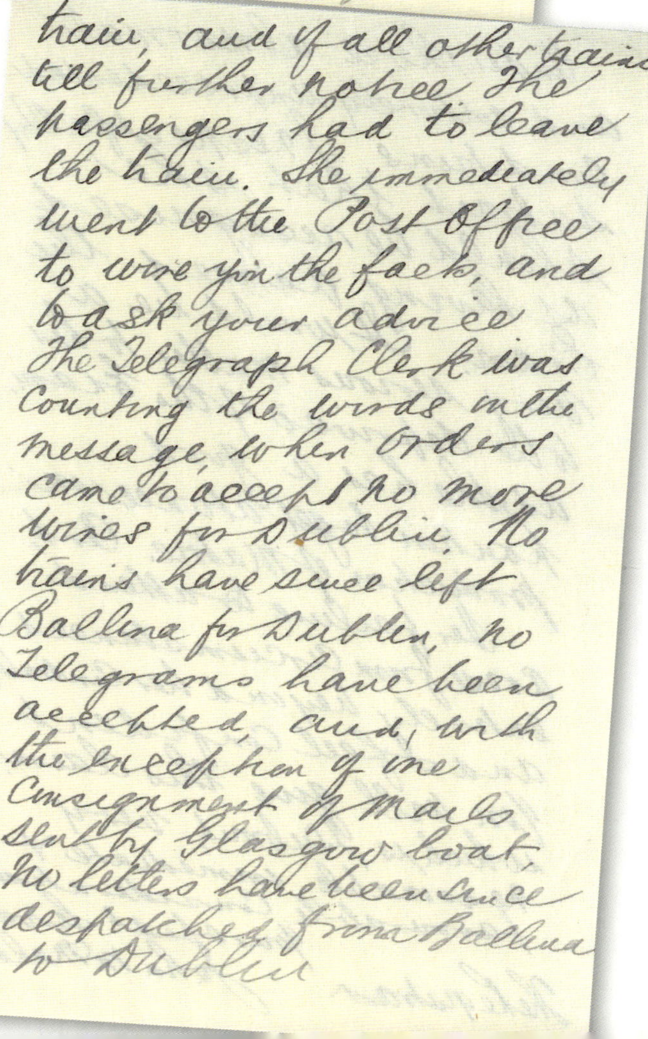

Figs 6–8 (clockwise from top left) The outbreak of the Civil War in Dublin on 28 June forms the backdrop to this letter from a concerned mother writing on behalf of her daughter, Mary Grace MacMahon, from Convent Hill in Ballina. The ripples from events taking place in the heart of the capital in the early hours of 28 June were felt many miles away, causing disruption to the best-laid plans. MacMahon was to attend her matriculation examination in University College Dublin, but events intervened, as detailed by her mother in a letter to the National University of Ireland dated 20 July 1922: 'On 28th June, she [Mary] left home intending to travel to Dublin by the Limerick Mail which leaves Ballina about 12.30. She had purchased her ticket, No. 5758, 28th June, Limerick Mail, Ballina to Broadstone [Broadstone Station in Dublin], fare 34 shillings/4 pence. She had taken her seat in the train. The bell had rung, and the train was on the point of starting, when a telegram arrived from the Provisional Government directing the stoppage of the train, and of all other trains until further notice. The passengers had to leave the train. She immediately went to the Post Office to wire you the facts, and to ask your advice. The Telegraph Clerk was counting the words in the message, when orders to accept no more wires came from Dublin'. Such disruption to rail travel and civilian life would become commonplace throughout the Civil War, with widespread attacks on and destruction of rail infrastructure. [Document: courtesy of the National University of Ireland Archive, and John Foley, retired administration officer, NUI]

The flat provided a partial view of Barry's Hotel on Gardiner Row and, in the summer of 1922, that establishment was the headquarters of Oscar Traynor, brigade commander of the anti-Treaty IRA.

Like many working-class women in that north-east quadrant of the city, my grandmother was a war widow. All of the local shops were closed and residents were at serious risk of being shot if they wandered out looking for staples like milk and bread. As the National Army drove its opponents out of their positions on Sackville Street (O'Connell Street), the Anti-Treaty IRA fell back on Barry's Hotel, pursued by its opponents. The National Army soldiers who took over my granny's flat obviously knew the area well. It gave them an ideal position from which to snipe at Traynor's headquarters. As they had anticipated, their opponents in Barry's assumed that the gunfire was coming from the ruins of the nearby Orange Hall that had been gutted by the anti-Treaty forces a short time earlier. But, after a while, the window of my granny's flat exploded inwards in a shower of shattered glass, wood splinters and brick dust, announcing that the snipers had been discovered. Miraculously, no one was injured. Before they left, the soldiers gave my grandmother their rations to help tide her over until it was safe to go out on the streets again.

Many years later I heard the story from the other side, when an old Irish Citizen Army veteran who had been in Barry's under the command of Constance Markievicz said that she had spotted the real source of the sniping. She ordered the men to aim for the corner of the window in my grandmother's flat that was the source of the problem, telling them to fire only on her command. She said that if the volley did not kill anyone, it should at least blind their opponents. In the event it did neither, but it did stop the sniping.

While the period of intensive fighting in Dublin's city centre was short-lived, its cessation signalled the end of conventional warfare and casual gun law on the streets. The predators soon became the prey, as possession of weapons was made a capital offence.

Fig. 9 Queues for bread supplies at a Dublin city dispensary in 1922. The extent and impact of food shortages during 1922–3 is often neglected in the historiography. The relatively peaceful winter following the Truce of July 1921 did not prevent the food supply crisis that unfolded in the early months of 1922. It was caused by a grave deterioration in economic conditions and unusually high levels of unemployment. The impact was intensified along the Atlantic seaboard due to a reduction in the number of seasonal migratory labourers travelling to work in Britain. Under the dramatic headline, 'Dread story of famine: ghastly state of Connemara', the *Irish Independent* reported in February that people were existing 'on two meals of potatoes that elsewhere would not be fed to pigs'. Irish-American humanitarian aid helped to ameliorate the effects of the food crisis in early 1922 when its Irish conduit, the Irish White Cross, estimated that approximately 100,000 people on the west coast faced starvation. By August it had allocated £20,000 for 'the barest necessities of life – food, clothing and seed'. White Cross aid rendered unnecessary the £1,000 loan for seed potatoes and oats sought in February by the local government minister, William T. Cosgrave, to fend off famine in County Galway. Social campaigner Maud Gonne MacBride publicly demanded a more significant intervention by the Provisional Government in the form of a £200,000 loan to save 'the West from famine'. 'Mr de Valera and Comdt Rory O'Connor', she suggested, indicating the inevitable politicisation of the food crisis, 'would be early subscribers'. Privately, she wrote to Arthur Griffith to describe the distress she had witnessed in County Donegal (Fig. 10). The outbreak of the Civil War sharpened the government's focus on food supply. It was discussed at eighteen Cabinet meetings during the first month of the war A milk shortage was an early consequence of fighting in Dublin, but firm government action secured the city's food supply. They backed the purchase of twenty-five tons of butter from Liverpool and fixed its retail price; they also used the National Army to distribute food in the Marlborough Street area, while food was also distributed from city dispensaries. Rail disruption caused temporary food shortages in many areas, especially in Kerry and west Cork. Coastal locations were supplied by sea, but damaged bridges and IRA raids impeded horse-drawn food supplies to inland towns. When food supplies for Kilkenny city were detained at Waterford port in mid-July, the government directed that the consignment for Kilkenny be supplied from Liverpool via Dublin. The National Army controlled the distribution of flour in Killarney after IRA raids on food convoys in September raised the spectre of famine in the town. Extensive damage to railway lines in July and August also caused prolonged food shortages in Connemara. Three hundred families on Inishbofin island were 'saved from starvation', the *Connacht Tribune* reported in July, only by a charitable delivery of twenty-three tons of flour by sea from Galway. Pro-Treaty propaganda emphasised the government's efforts to relieve the food shortages and cast the IRA as unprincipled 'wreckers' whose campaign of guerrilla warfare and economic sabotage brought economic ruin and famine. [Text: Noel Carolan / Image: part of the Independent Newspapers Ireland/NLI collection, INDH237A / Sources: *Irish Independent*, 10 and 11 Feb.1922; *Report of the Irish White Cross to 31st August, 1922* (New York, 1922), p. 44 and pp. 79–81; Provisional Government Minutes, 5 Apr. 1922 (NAI, TSCH 1/1/2)]

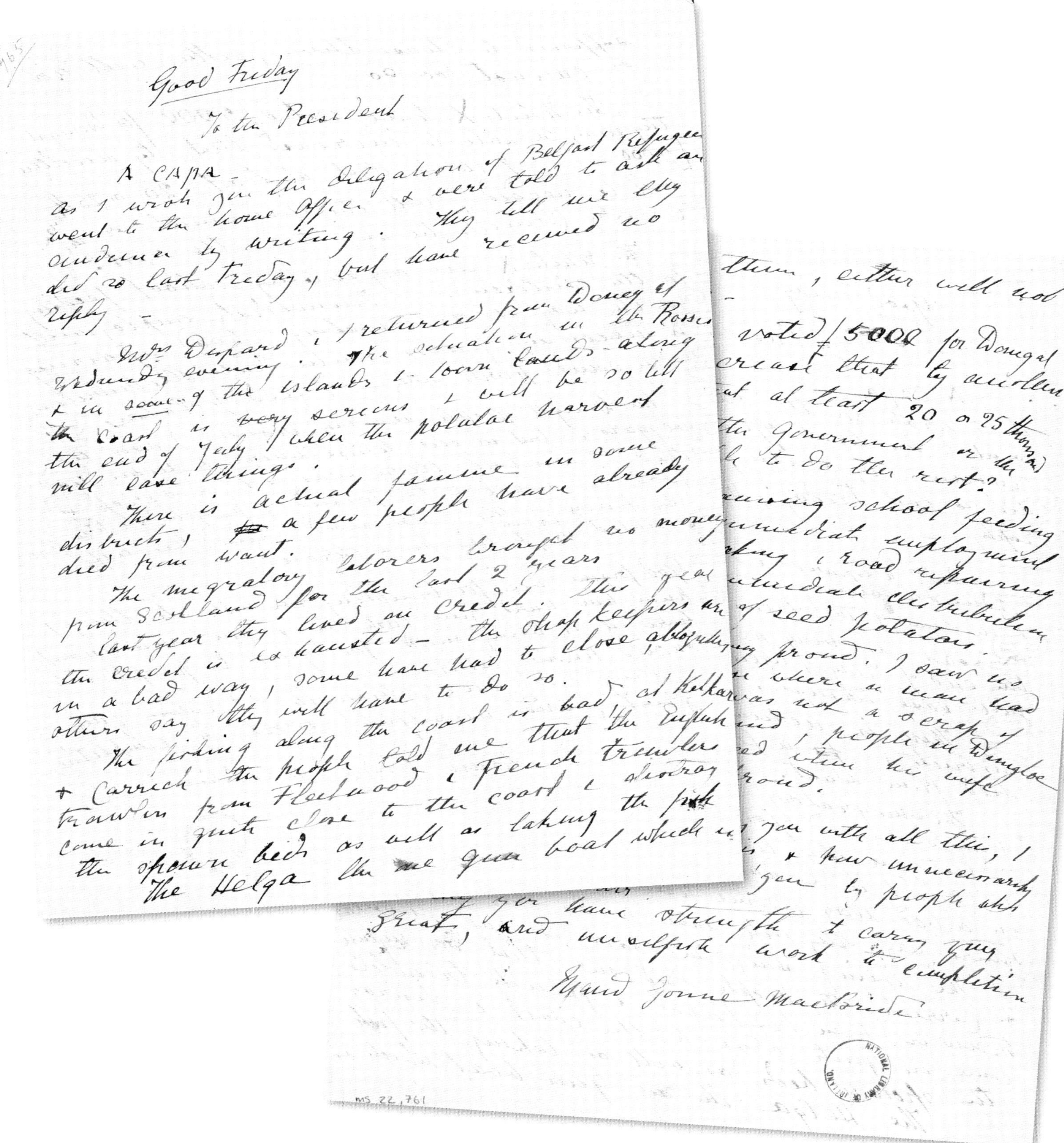

Good Friday

To the President

A CAPA

As I wrote you the delegation of Belfast Refugees went to the Home Office & were told to ask an audience by writing. They tell me they did so last Friday, but have received no reply –

Mrs Despard & I returned from Donegal Wednesday evening. The situation in the Rosses & in some of the islands & down coasts along the coast is very serious & will be so till the end of July when the potatoe harvest will ease things.

There is actual famine in some districts, a few people have already died from want.

The migratory laborers brought no money from Scotland for the last 2 years last year they lived on credit. This year the credit is exhausted – the shop keepers are in a bad way, some have had to close, others say they will have to do so.

The fishing along the coast is bad at Killybegs & Carrick the people told me that the English trawlers from Fleetwood & French trawlers come in quite close to the coast & destroy the spawn beds as well as taking the fish

The Helga the one gun boat which

them, either will not

voted £5000 for Donegal

crease that by another

at least 20 or 25 thousand

the Government or the

to do the rest?

school feeding

immediate employment

& road repairing

immediate distribution of seed potatoes

ground. I saw no

where a man had

was not a scrap of

people in Dungloe

his wife

ground.

you with all this, I

& how unnecessary

you by people who

you have strength to carry your great, and unselfish work to completion

Maud Gonne MacBride

Fig. 10 Letter written by Maud Gonne MacBride to the president of Dáil Éireann, Arthur Griffith, 14 April 1922 to determine whether the government could provide relief for County Donegal. She and Charlotte Despard visited the county in April and found 'an actual famine in some districts'. [Document: National Library of Ireland, Kathleen McKenna Napoli Papers, MS 22,761]

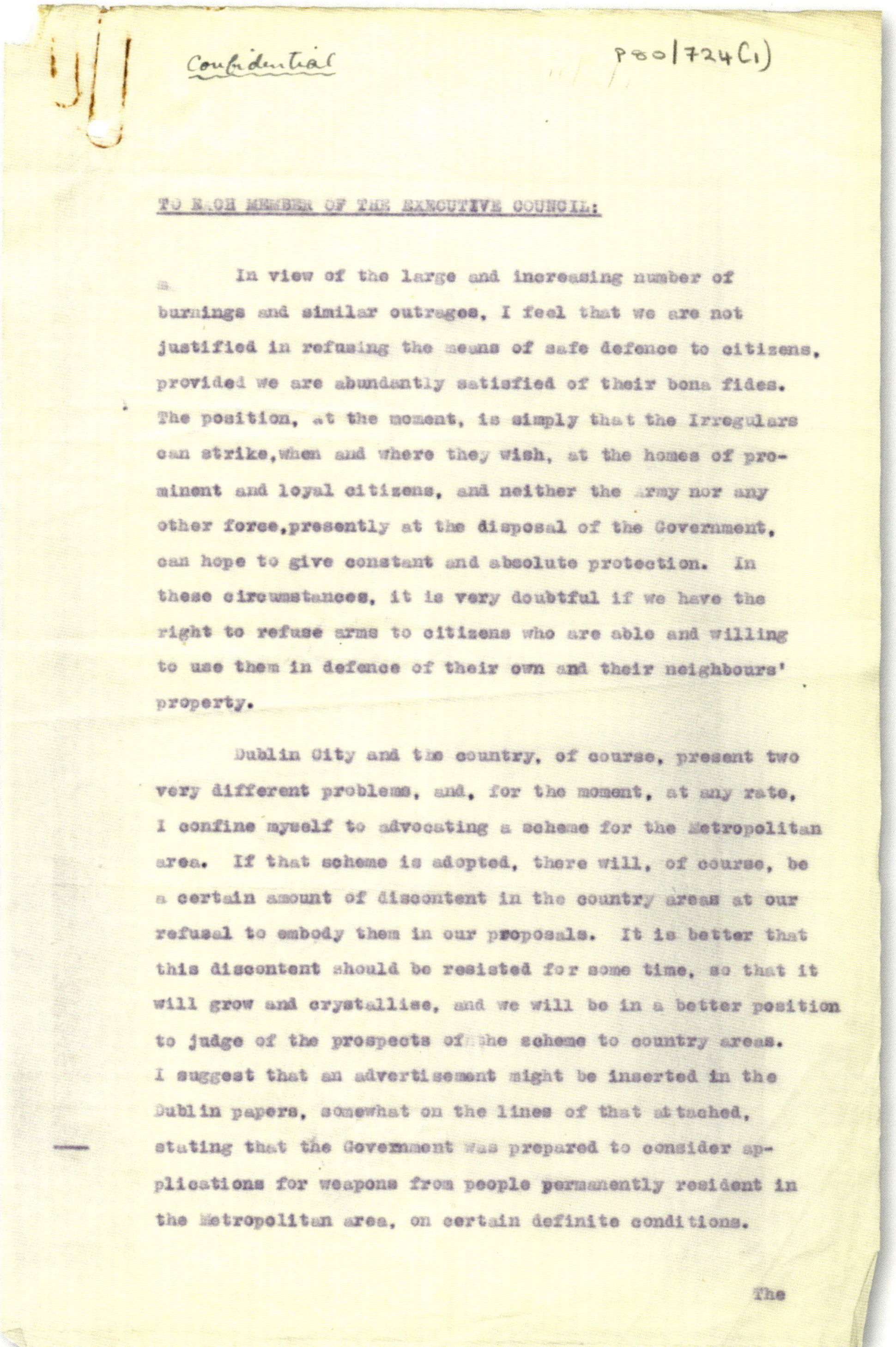

Confidential P80/724(1)

TO EACH MEMBER OF THE EXECUTIVE COUNCIL:

In view of the large and increasing number of burnings and similar outrages, I feel that we are not justified in refusing the means of safe defence to citizens, provided we are abundantly satisfied of their bona fides. The position, at the moment, is simply that the Irregulars can strike, when and where they wish, at the homes of prominent and loyal citizens, and neither the Army nor any other force, presently at the disposal of the Government, can hope to give constant and absolute protection. In these circumstances, it is very doubtful if we have the right to refuse arms to citizens who are able and willing to use them in defence of their own and their neighbours' property.

Dublin City and the country, of course, present two very different problems, and, for the moment, at any rate, I confine myself to advocating a scheme for the Metropolitan area. If that scheme is adopted, there will, of course, be a certain amount of discontent in the country areas at our refusal to embody them in our proposals. It is better that this discontent should be resisted for some time, so that it will grow and crystallise, and we will be in a better position to judge of the prospects of the scheme to country areas. I suggest that an advertisement might be inserted in the Dublin papers, somewhat on the lines of that attached, stating that the Government was prepared to consider applications for weapons from people permanently resident in the Metropolitan area, on certain definite conditions.

The

Fig. 11 The first page of a memorandum, sent by the minister for home affairs, Kevin O'Higgins, to fellow members of the Executive Council in March 1923. He suggests the establishment a self-defence scheme – effectively, the creation of a citizens' militia – for the Dublin area. O'Higgins argued that, 'in view of the large and increasing number of burnings and other outrages' on the part of 'the Irregulars', who could strike 'when and where they wish at the homes of prominent and loyal citizens', the government should supply arms and ammunition to permanent residents who were willing and able to use them in defence of their own and their neighbours' lives and property. The draft newspaper advertisement contained in the memo sets out the conditions attached to the proposed applications for arms, including a deposit and a letter of recommendation from clergy, army officers, TDs and senators, or civil servants. He envisaged a trial in the capital before the scheme was extended to other parts of the country. O'Higgins was the most exercised of all his Cabinet colleagues by what he saw as the spirit of disorder and 'anarchy' unleashed by the IRA, and this scheme was one of several proposals that he put forward to counter it. The ending of the Civil War two months later ensured it was not pursued. [Document: Papers of Desmond and Mabel FitzGerald, UCDA P80/724. Reproduced by kind permission of UCD Archives]

Old regime

Many supporters of the old regime found life in Dublin impossible as they were targeted for retaliation by the anti-Treaty forces. They ranged from figures as prominent as Sir Henry Robinson, the former vice president of the local government board, who lived in Foxrock, to Annie Hole, who ran a boarding house in Lower Mount Street frequented by British Army officers, to Emily Harris, founder of the Red Cross hospital in Dun Laoghaire, to Charles Thompson, who ran a stationery business whose main customers were the British Army and Dublin Castle, to Albert Pennycook, a Protestant foreman at the Inchicore railway works and prominent member of the Orange Order. However the vast majority of Protestants and Unionists left for economic reasons. They were soldiers, policemen and civil servants; followers of the half-crown as much as the Crown.[5]

Economic conditions were grim for those who remained. In Britain employers had already embarked on a series of savage wage cuts epitomised by Black Friday, but the disturbed state of Ireland saw them delay their offensive until it was clear that the Free State would prevail. The last dramatic flourish of labour militancy was the unemployed march through the city on 27 June, just hours before the bombardment of the Four Courts marked the outbreak of the Civil War.

Ironically, the advent of civil war provided a major source of employment for working-class Dubliners. Many who joined the

National Army had served in the British Army during the First World War. This blunted the impact of the post-war recession significantly, at least until the rapid demobilisation in 1924.

Suppressing resistance

The Free State proved far more ferocious in suppressing resistance than the British, who had enjoyed such superiority that the outcome of any military struggle could never be in doubt. Neither was there the same popular support for the anti-Treaty cause as there had been for national independence. Even though brutal acts, such as the execution of three teenage republicans at a quarry in Red Cow for being caught putting up anti-Treaty posters in the city, shocked citizens, the jury still baulked at delivering the murder verdicts demanded by the families against the soldiers involved.

The withdrawal of the British also saw a retreat from social reform. Whereas the secular state continued to expand its reform agenda in Britain in areas such as education, health and social welfare, Catholic social activism filled the vacuum in the new Irish Free State. The Church was respected, even venerated, and its services were available at far less expense to the tax and rate payers. Those most affected were far too weak to mount an effective protest.

Fig. 12 This photograph, first published in the *Irish Independent* on 6 July 1922, features Fr O'Reilly CC Marlborough Street carrying a Red Cross flag and leading evacuating civilians from their homes in the Gardiner Street area to the safety of the model schools. [Image: Cashman Collection © RTÉ Archives, 0504/063]

President of the Executive Council of the Irish Free State, William T. Cosgrave (back seat, wearing bowler hat) at Victoria (now Collins) Barracks, Old Youghal Road, Cork at the conclusion of the Civil War in 1923. [Image: courtesy of the Irish Examiner Archive]

SECTION 4

Propaganda and Legitimisation

The Idealist (to his leader): "Well we've done all the wrecking we could! what next?"
De Valera: "What next! Why, tell the people we are quite prepared to forget the past and—er—take on the job of building it up again!"

Fig. 1 Pro-Treaty cartoon by Louis Dalton, *United Irishman*, 11 August 1923.

CHAPTER 5

Irregulars Versus Slave Staters: Propaganda, censorship and the Irish Civil War

Donal Ó Drisceoil

In August 1923 – as a general election loomed and the dust settled following the formal end of the Civil War three months earlier – the pro-Treaty Cumann na nGaedheal paper, the *United Irishman*, published a striking cartoon by the future playwright and then budding artist, Louis Dalton (Fig. 1). A *Punch*-style simian brute ('The Idealist'), gun in hand, turns to his 'leader', Éamon de Valera, as smoke billows from a ruined landscape, saying, 'we've done all the wrecking we could!', and asks, 'What next?' His Stetson-hatted leader, resembling an American comic-book supervillain, instructs him to 'tell the people we are quite prepared to forget the past and – er – take up the job of building it up again!'. Two standard tropes of pro-Treaty Civil War propaganda (laying the blame on Dev and demonising the 'wreckers' of the anti-Treaty IRA) are present here and would feature in pro-Treaty party propaganda over the following two decades. In the anti-Treaty paper *Éire: The Irish Nation* in the same month, cartoonist Fionnbarr has Cumann na nGaedheal leader, William T. Cosgrave, as the innocent-looking 'Bubbles' from the famous Millais painting (well known from its use in a Pears Soap advertisement), puffing out from his little pipe bubbles of 'Lies', 'Threats', 'Jobs' and 'Bribes' – all familiar accusations against the pro-Treatyites from the recent conflict (Fig. 2).[1]

Thus, the war of words carried on well beyond the end of the shooting war, but it also predated it, commencing as soon as the independence movement split on the Treaty. When de Valera led the fifty-seven anti-Treaty TDs in a walkout from the Dáil on 10 January 1922 in protest at the election of Arthur Griffith as president of the republic, a shouting match ensued that provided a flavour of the bitterness to come. 'Traitors all!' roared Michael Collins, adding that they were 'Deserters from the Irish nation in her hour of trial'. Constance Markievicz shot back with 'Traitors and cowards'; Collins responded with 'Foreigners, traitors, English', as anti-Treaty TDs shouted, 'Up the Republic!'[2] As the process of polarisation developed from January to June 1922, so too did the terminological and discursive rancour. The pro-Treaty writer P.S. O'Hegarty feared where this mud-slinging would lead: 'every person who shouts "traitor" or "renegade" at the opponent loosens a gun in the holster'.[3] The war of words naturally sharpened once the shooting war broke out, when the propaganda of both sides took on a classic belligerent shape and was complemented by censorship. The latter, in pre-war form, had also commenced early in 1922: in the shape of structural censorship on the one hand – whereby

Fig. 2 Anti-Treaty cartoon by 'Fionnbarr', *Éire: The Irish Nation*, 25 August 1923.

Fig. 3 A newsboy with National Army soldiers in County Tipperary, 1923. [Image: Seán Sharkey Collection. Courtesy of Neil Sharkey, Tipperary Studies]

the mainstream media overwhelmingly supported the Treaty and excluded or othered anti-Treaty arguments – and reactive, anti-Treaty 'sledge hammer censorship' on the other.[4]

Media consensus

Of the more than 100 newspapers in the twenty-six counties at the beginning of 1922, only *An Connachtach/The Connachtman* in Sligo, the *Donegal Vindicator* and the *Waterford Standard* took an explicitly anti-Treaty position. These were joined in March 1922 by the newly established *Kerry Leader* in Tralee.[5] How representative this was of public opinion – and to what extent the press followed as much as led public opinion – is difficult to say. There had long been a tendency on the part of local/regional papers, in particular, to reflect 'feeling on the ground' (by following their readers), a phenomenon that led to important shifts in the past, such as that towards a pro-tenant position during the Land War, and from support for First World War recruitment and the Irish Parliamentary Party to an advanced nationalist position after 1916. However, if we accept that at least a third of the electorate (based on election results) in the 1922–3 period was solidly anti-Treaty, one might expect that a larger segment of the media would represent this significant minority position; but it is not that simple. The Irish press was largely conservative and reflective of middle Ireland's relief that dry land had been reached and the turbulence of 'the troubles' might be at an end.

Republicans and radicals believed the press was performing an agenda-setting role on behalf of the pro-Treaty Irish establishment – business, the banks, the Catholic hierarchy, ex-unionists and the property-owning classes in general. Most newspaper proprietors were local or national businessmen, and their general material interests aligned with those of their fellow capitalists. More specifically, they depended on advertising by business and the state, and desired a maintenance of the normality (relatively free-flowing circulation and a restored advertising revenue stream) that had returned since the truce of the previous July. From the Free State perspective, the reason the press backed the Treaty was more straightforward: common sense. Whatever the reasons, the Irish media consensus was overwhelmingly pro-Treaty and subsequently pro-Provisional Government/National Army/Free State. Hostile newspapers were targeted by the anti-Treaty IRA from an early stage, while, on the other side, the *Connachtman* was suppressed by the Provisional Government in July 1922; the *Donegal Vindicator* had its offices attacked in September 1922; and the *Kerry Leader* was put out of business in August 1922 with the arrest and internment of its proprietor and editor, Seán Moynihan.

Dorothy Macardle summed up anti-Treatyite feelings about the Irish media consensus:

> All warnings against the Treaty, all caution as to the dangers latent in it, all opposition to partition, even, seemed flung to the winds. Every effort of the Press was concentrated in stampeding the people into a panic-stricken terror of rejection, a blind clamour for surrender, for peace at any price.[6]

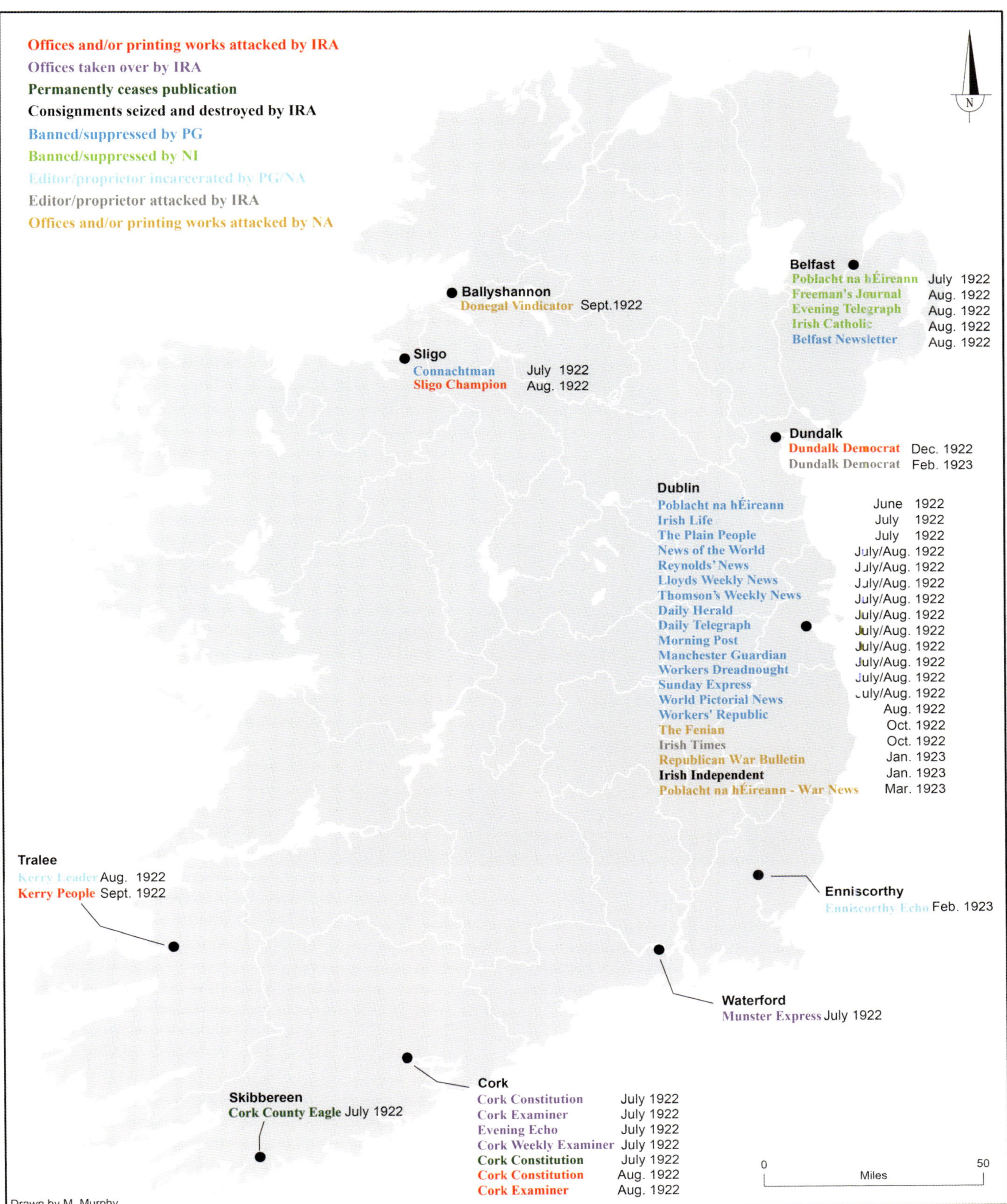

Fig. 4 Map showing key incidents of interference with newspapers in Ireland during the Civil War, June 1922–May 1923. The press fell victim to the Provisional Government, the Northern Ireland government, the IRA and the National Army through censorship, suppression, temporary banning, the destruction of plant, the seizure and burning of consignments and the incarceration of, and attacks on, journalists, editors and proprietors. [Updated version of a map first published in the *Atlas of the Irish Revolution* (CUP, 2017). Map data compiled from multiple sources by Ian Kenneally and Donal Ó Drisceoil]

Fig. 5 Portrait of Frank Gallagher (1893–1962), oil on canvas, by Estella F. Solomons (1920). Cork-born Frank Gallagher began his journalistic career with constitutional-nationalist maverick William O'Brien's *Cork Free Press*, which he edited from 1914 until its demise in 1916. He then moved to the capital and joined the Dublin brigade of the Irish Volunteers and the staff of P.J. Little's republican weekly, *New Ireland*. He became an able propagandist and was prominent in the publicity machine that helped sweep Sinn Féin to victory in the 1918 general election. During the War of Independence, Gallagher was assistant director of publicity and chief compiler of the *Irish Bulletin*, Dáil Éireann's influential propaganda news-sheet, working closely with the stalwarts of republican propaganda, Desmond FitzGerald, Robert Brennan and Erskine Childers. Along with the latter two, he opposed the Treaty and became a dogged propagandist against it. Gallagher was assistant editor to, first, Liam Mellows and then Erskine Childers at *Poblacht na hÉireann*. On the outbreak of the Civil War, Gallagher fought in the battle for Dublin, before moving to publicity work, taking over the editorship of the Dublin edition of the *Poblacht–War News* when Childers went south to Cork. He published a pamphlet, *By What Authority?*, that addressed the question of responsibility for the conflict and argued that the 'overwhelming [...] surrender of national rights' represented by the acceptance of the Treaty made war inevitable. He was arrested in October 1922 and remained in jail until April 1924, having participated in the October–November 1923 hunger strike (he also took part in the 1920 Mountjoy hunger strike). Following a period of freelance journalism, he became de Valera's private secretary and director of publicity for Fianna Fáil in 1927. In 1928 he published *Days of Fear*, his account of the 1920 hunger strike, and a collection of short stories, *The Challenge of the Sentry*, under his *nom de plume*, David Hogan. In 1931 he published a second collection of short stories, *Dark Mountain*, and became first editor of de Valera's daily *Irish Press*, his fresh and radical approach making it an immediate success. He resigned in 1935 and was appointed deputy director of Radio Éireann. In 1939 Gallagher was made head of the Government Information Bureau, a post he held until Fianna Fáil lost office in 1948, though he returned briefly to it in 1951. He was moved to the Department of Health as press officer, and in 1953 published his most successful book (as David Hogan), *The Four Glorious Years*, his account of the War of Independence, which featured the Solomons portrait as a frontispiece. Gallagher became central to the anti-partition campaigns of successive governments of the early-to-mid-1950s, and he published *The Indivisible Island: The story of the partition of Ireland* in 1957. By now he was working at the National Library and contributing regularly to the *Sunday Press*, particularly on the War of Independence and Civil War. A planned biography of de Valera never materialised, but a section on the Treaty written for it was published posthumously as *The Anglo-Irish Treaty* in 1965. [Painting: © The Trustees of the Estate of Estella Solomons. Photograph © National Gallery of Ireland]

POBLACHT NA h-EIREANN.

THE REPUBLIC OF IRELAND.

VOL. 1. NO. 1. DUBLIN, TUESDAY, JANUARY 3, 1922. PRICE 2d

The Terms of Reference.

Peace with Honour.

Message from Cathal Brugha

NINE HOURS BEFORE!

The "Irish Bulletin" of December 5th, 1921.

THE NEXT ISSUE OF THE REPUBLIC OF IRELAND ... On THURSDAY NEXT, JANUARY 5, 1922.

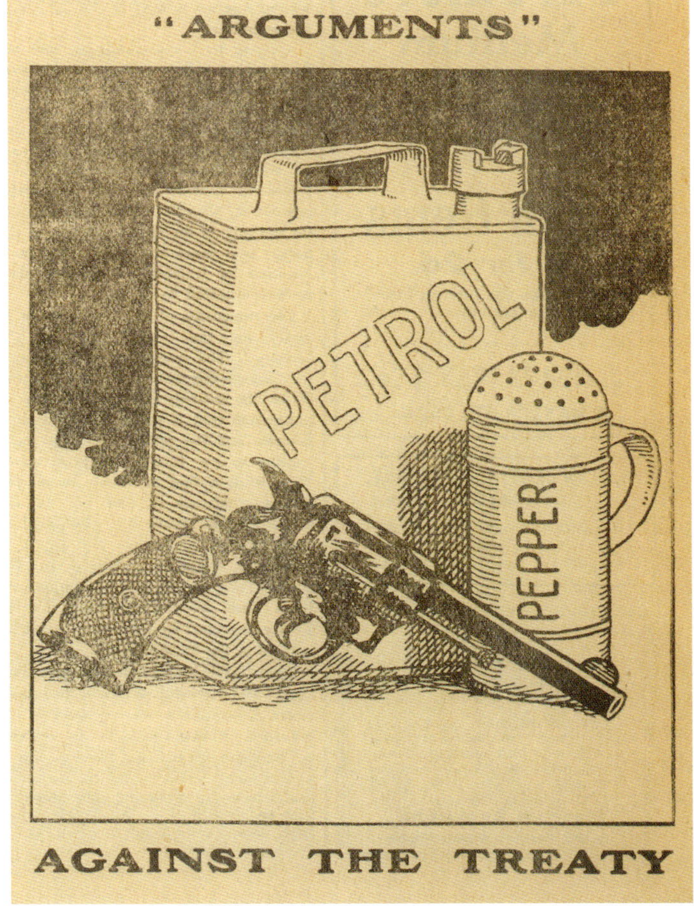

Fig. 6 (top right) Front page of the inaugural issue of the anti-Treaty newspaper *Poblacht na hÉireann/Republic of Ireland*, launched 3 January 1922, in the final week of Dáil Éireann's debates on the Treaty. Arranged around the centrally positioned text of the 1916 Proclamation of the Republic is an article by Countess Markievicz on the Treaty as a 'spiritual defeat'; a piece by her fellow anti-Treaty TD Mary MacSwiney challenging the plenipotentiary powers of the Treaty delegation; an anti-Treaty statement in Irish by the minister for defence, Cathal Brugha; and an article seeking to demonstrate that the signing of the Treaty was a 'sudden and disastrous' policy departure by the Dáil Cabinet. [Source: *Poblacht na hÉireann*, 3 January 1922]

Fig. 7 (bottom right) '"Arguments" Against the Treaty' (gun, petrol, pepper cannister), a pro-Treaty cartoon printed in *Young Ireland*, 25 March 1922.

Tom Garvin has observed that the anti-Treatyites saw the Irish people as being 'intimidated by various tyrannies, in particular the apparatuses of thought control represented by the journalists and the clergy'.[7] Attacking the clergy in response to this perceived state of affairs was not an option for the mostly Catholic Volunteers – although anti-clericalism did emerge in anti-Treaty propaganda, especially after the bishops issued their condemnatory Lenten pastoral in October 1922, in which the hierarchy weighed in ever more heavily behind the Free State, and utilised the propagandist terminology of the Free State authorities, especially the term 'irregulars' to describe the IRA.[8] It was the media, however, that bore the brunt of armed republican reaction, through the targeting and intimidation of journalists and newspapers, and a resort to sledgehammer censorship. Anti-Treaty republicans also responded more constructively to the media imbalance by creating their own media to counter and challenge the pro-Treaty consensus.[9]

Pre-war propaganda

From 3 January 1922 the newly formed republican publicity department produced the weekly *Poblacht na hÉireann/Republic of Ireland* (henceforth, the *Poblacht*), which set out the anti-Treaty position in a restrained and detailed manner, deliberately eschewing abuse and vilification. When some complained in March 1922 that many of its articles were 'too heavy', editor Erskine Childers explained that this was a 'necessary evil', as the paper was 'primarily concerned with explaining an intricate political situation'.[10] Childers had taken over the editorship from Liam Mellows in late February. Frank Gallagher, first editor of Fianna Fáil organ the *Irish Press*, was assistant to both.[11] The *Poblacht* was a weekly refutation in print of the accusations of pro-Treaty propagandists that the anti-Treaty position was irrational, emotional and driven by violence – an attitude epitomised by the *Young Ireland/Éire Óg* cartoon titled '"Arguments" Against the Treaty', which featured simply a revolver, petrol can and pepper cannister (Fig. 7).[12]

The first two issues of the *Poblacht* set out the arguments against the Treaty in advance of the Dáil vote on 7 January. A series featuring a clause-by-clause critical analysis of the Treaty began in the first issue.[13] This was soon published as a pamphlet, as was the paper's comparative analysis of de Valera's alternative Document No. 2 and the Treaty. Once the Treaty vote was lost, the paper trumpeted the

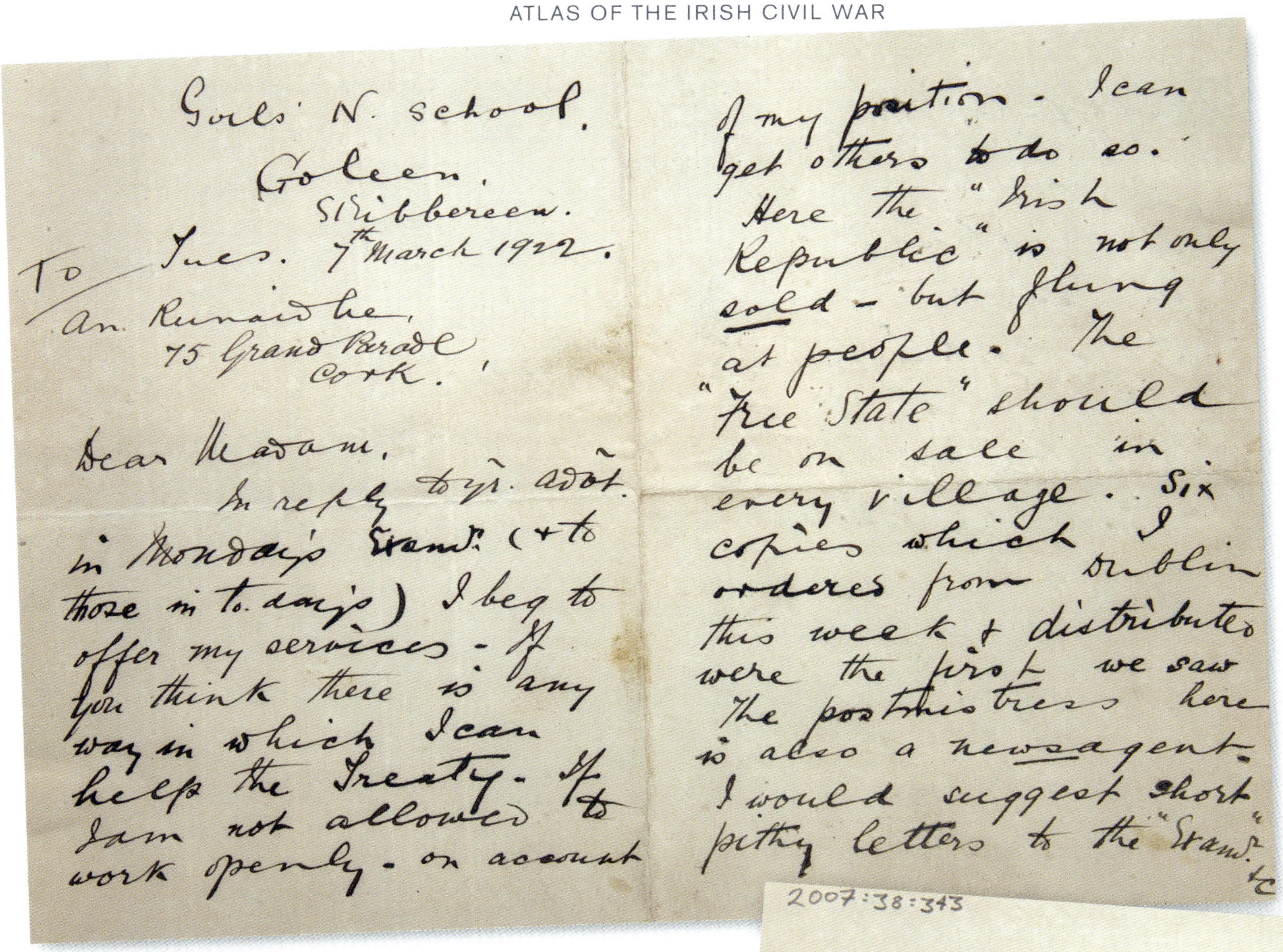

Girls' N. School,
Goleen.
Skibbereen.
Tues. 7th March 1922.

To
An Runaidhe,
75 Grand Parade,
Cork.

Dear Madam,
In reply to yr. advt. in Monday's Stand: (+ to those in to-day's) I beg to offer my services – If you think there is any way in which I can help the Treaty. If I am not allowed to work openly – on account of my position – I can get others to do so. Here the "Irish Republic" is not only sold – but flung at people. The "Free State" should be on sale in every village. Six copies which I ordered from Dublin this week & distributed were the first we saw. The postmistress here is also a newsagent. I would suggest short pithy letters to the "Stand:" &c

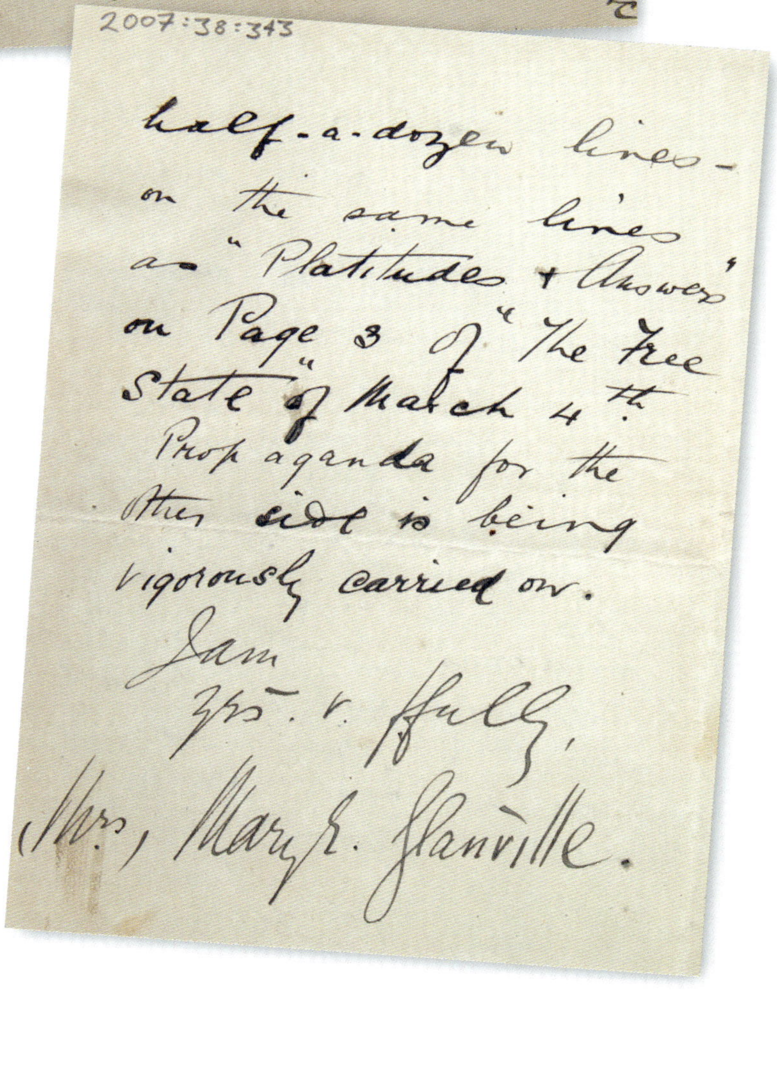

half-a-dozen lines – on the same lines as "Platitudes + Answers" on Page 3 of "The Free State" of March 4th. Propaganda for the other side is being vigorously carried on.

I am
Yrs. v. ffully,
Mrs. Mary E. Glanville.

Fig. 8 Letter from Mary Glanville to the secretary of the central branch of Cumann na mBan, Cork, 7 March 1922. Mary Glanville was a National school teacher in west Cork where, according to the pro-Treaty writer, *Poblacht na hÉireann* was not only sold but 'flung at people'. In this letter dated 7 March 1922, to the secretary of the recently riven central branch of Cumann na mBan in Cork, she writes that 'the *Free State* should be on sale in every village' to counter the influence of local republicans who, according to Glanville's second letter to Lil Conlon on 12 March, had 'hint[ed]' to the local newsagent and postmistress that they would be displeased if she sold it. The second missive also captures the urgency Glanville felt about establishing a local pro-Treaty branch of Cumann na mBan (ultimately Cumann na Saoirse) which, she felt, would 'do splendid work in putting backbone into the timid ones' who were 'afraid to declare openly for the Free State'. [Document: The Conlon Collection, Cork Public Museum]

righteous minority tradition in Irish republicanism: it prominently featured Arthur Griffith's past assertion that 'The Cause of Irish Nationality has always been saved by the Intelligent Minority' (using Griffith's past statements against him was a favourite ploy of anti-Treaty propagandists, mirrored by the other side's utilisation of a range of de Valera's previous utterances). *An Saorstát/The Free State* later mocked these sentiments in its '"Die Hard" Code': 'If the majority of the people are in favour of the Free State, it is not to be accepted for that reason. The minority was right in Easter Week and must therefore be right on every subsequent occasion.'[14]

The *Free State* was launched by the pro-Treaty party in February 1922 as a response to the *Poblacht* and fear that its critiques of the

Treaty and its advocates were beginning to have an effect. Like the *Poblacht*, it was priced at 2*d*, but was often distributed free at public meetings.[15] An article in the first issue argued that the Free State was a de facto republic and represented 'substance' in contrast to the anti-Treaty alternative of 'the shadow of the substance'. 'We want to know', the article asked, 'if a barber's shop is less a barber's shop if it's a Hairdressing Salon?' The paper maintained a constant emphasis on Document No. 2 and how it did not deliver a republic. The Treaty's political opponents – the *Free State*'s principal targets in the early months of 1922 – were 'refugees from reality', 'documentarians', 'formulists and phrase men'. The *Poblacht* maintained its 'responsible' tone, despite frequently criticising key pro-Treaty figures and critiquing their various claims; an early editorial attributed no 'base or cowardly motives' to those who voted for the Treaty, and regarded those who saw it as a stepping stone as 'sincere, though ruinously mistaken'.[16] While a tang of bitterness was increasingly evident as divisions hardened from March 1922, the *Poblacht* resisted the urge to mud-sling much more successfully than the *Free State*, the pages of which revealed the growing frustration of the pro-Treaty elite with the 'galaxy of irreconcilables falsely known as the Republican party'.[17]

From March 1922 Arthur Griffith's *Young Ireland/Éire Óg* featured a series of cartoons that epitomised pro-Treaty arguments and attitudes: the first had St Patrick personifying the Free State, his shamrock depicting 'Fiscal Control', 'Army' and 'Education' as he banishes the snakes of 'Foreign Rule', 'Anglicisation' and 'Terrorism'.[18] In these cartoons, the anti-Treaty position was always synonymous with terrorism, disorder and destruction, while the Treaty was the bridge to freedom or an edifice of stability, security and democracy. The other principal pro-Treaty periodical in the pre-war months was P.S. O'Hegarty's *The Separatist*. While the anti-Treaty press regarded the paper as the mouthpiece of Michael Collins, O'Hegarty was often critical of the pro-Treaty party, mainly for its lack of leadership and for allowing the situation to drift, creating a vacuum that could lead to 'anarchy'. He dismissed Document No. 2 and argued that the separatist position was given away, not when the Treaty was signed, but when de Valera accepted negotiations with the British and the Dáil authorised them.

Sledgehammer censorship

P.S. O'Hegarty's brother, Seán, officer in command of the IRA's Cork No. 1 Brigade, quickly emerged as a scourge of the pro-Treatyites, though he later declared his neutrality in the face of imminent civil war. In early January 1922 he ordered his men to destroy the type for, and all copies they could find of, University College Cork professor Alfred O'Rahilly's pamphlet, *The Case for the Treaty*, because it contained an 'unauthorised' and inaccurate statement about the IRA.[19] On 4 January A.B. Kay, special correspondent of *The Times* (London), was abducted by O'Hegarty's men and forced

Fig. 9 The Linotype and Composing Rooms in the offices of the *Freeman's Journal* in Dublin after they were destroyed on 29 March 1922 by a 200-strong anti-Treaty IRA unit led by Rory O'Connor. The attack followed the paper's publication of a report on the IRA convention of 26 March under the headline 'The Dictators'. Prepared by the pro-Treaty army HQ at Beggars Bush, the report characterised the IRA convention as a mutiny. The paper remained out of circulation for three weeks. [Image: Kilmainham Gaol Archives, 20PO-1A35-20]

Fig. 10 *The Intelligence Man* (Erskine Childers), by Mick O'Dea. Coming from a landed Protestant family in County Wicklow, (Robert) Erskine Childers (1870–1922) was an enigmatic and controversial figure in the Irish independence movement. He was born in London, but largely grew up in Wicklow with his relatives, the Barton family, after his parents died when he was young. Childers was particularly close to his first cousin, Robert Barton. In the nineteenth century, the family's politics were staunchly unionist and British imperialist. Childers served in the British army in the Boer War, while his famous book, *The Riddle of the Sands,* a patriotic spy novel about a German plot to invade England, was published in 1913. Childers and Barton both became supporters of Irish Home Rule, with Childers and his American-born wife Molly (née Osgood) being central figures in the Howth gunrunning in 1914, during which over 1,000 German rifles were landed for the Irish Volunteers aboard Childers's yacht, the *Asgard.* He nevertheless again enlisted in the British forces during the First World War and served in the Royal Navy, the Admiralty and finally in the new Royal Air Force, where he helped to plan a prospective bombing campaign on Germany. However, by 1918 he was reiterating his calls for 'Dominion Home Rule' and in 1919 offered his services to the First Dáil, for which he eventually served as head of propaganda and was elected (unopposed) as a Sinn Féin TD to the Second Dáil in May 1921. By this time he had grown close to Éamon de Valera, but was highly distrusted by Arthur Griffith, who was suspicious of his background in British intelligence. Childers acted as a secretary to the Irish negotiators in the Treaty talks in late 1921; Robert Barton was one of the plenipotentiaries (though he later opposed the Treaty). Childers was adamantly against the clauses in the Treaty that gave the British naval bases in the Irish Free State. He argued fervently that the Treaty did not represent Irish independence or even a path towards it, disputing that it even gave Dominion status in the same manner as Canada. In angry exchanges at the close of the Dáil debates, Arthur Griffith called him 'a damned Englishman' and refused to answer his questions. Childers became editor of the anti-Treaty weekly *Poblacht na hÉireann* in February 1922 and, at the outbreak of the Civil War, produced *Poblacht na hÉireann–War News*, before moving south in July, where he worked on the republican-controlled *Cork Examiner.* Following the capture of Cork by the National Army in August, Childers retreated to west Cork, where he edited *Poblacht na hÉireann–Southern Edition*, produced on a mobile printing press, until October. He was increasingly demonised in the Free State press, which accused him of being responsible for many of the most destructive and deadly actions of the IRA. Two of his comrades in IRA publicity, Frank Gallagher and Frank O'Connor, argued later that this campaign of vilification was deliberately designed to set Childers up for execution. In early November 1922 he made his way back to Wicklow and was arrested in possession of a small hand gun. Sentenced to death by a military court, Childers's legal team argued that, as a civilian, he could not be tried by military courts, but the High Court ruled that the country was in state of war. While his legal team was preparing an appeal, he was executed on 24 November 1922, the fifth man to die in front of Free State firing squads. [Text: John Dorney/ Image: courtesy of An Post / See Andrew Boyle, *The Riddle of Erskine Childers* (London, 1977); John Dorney, '"He Died as a Prince": Erskine Childers, Executed November 1922', https://www.theirishstory.com/2022/11/26/he-died-as-prince-erskine-childers-executed-november-1922/; Anthony Barrett, 'The Media War: Robert Erskine Childers in West Cork', https://www.theirishstory.com/2022/09/13/the-media-war-robert-erskine-childers-in-west-cork/]

to publish a denial that he had interviewed members of the Cork IRA. Newsagents across the country were warned by anti-Treaty IRA units not to stock the *Freeman's Journal* because of a notorious editorial on 5 January headed 'Vanity of Vanities', in which de Valera was accused of having 'not the instinct of an Irishman in his blood' and acting on the advice of Erskine Childers, 'an Englishman who has achieved fame in the British Intelligence Service'. The vilification of Childers was a key element of the propaganda campaign waged by the *Freeman's* and by the Free State side in general. On 10 January 1922 Griffith told Childers in the Dáil that he would not be answerable to 'any damned Englishman in this Assembly', and followed this up in April with detailed accusations, implying that Childers was a British intelligence agent. The *Free State* referred to him as 'Major Erskine Childers D.S.O.' and denounced him as an 'English propagandist'.[20] Such vitriol was indicative of Childers's effectiveness as a propagandist, and also a useful stick with which to hit back at anti-Treaty characterisations of the Free Staters as British puppets. By April the *Free State* was accusing republicans, under the guiding hand of Childers, of adopting 'the whole programme of British methods in Ireland, namely, hypocrisy, lies and terrorism'.[21]

The Cork republicans who had abducted Kay compelled the pro-Treaty *Cork Examiner* to publish a republican proclamation against the settlement on 9 January. Denouncing his opponents' 'Black-and-Tan methods' in the Dáil, Collins argued that the intimidation of the *Examiner* was an illustration of the country's drift towards anarchy and of the urgent need for stable government.[22] In early January the printing presses of the *Nationalist* in Clonmel were badly damaged when it refused to publish an anti-Treaty statement and, from the second week of March, the anti-Treaty

IRA effectively banned circulation of the *Freeman's Journal* in the south and south-west by the seizing and burning of all copies from the Dublin train at the Limerick Junction node. This phase of censorship at gunpoint peaked on 30 March with the destruction of the printing machinery of the *Freeman's*. The context for the attack was the clear split in the IRA that occurred at the army convention of 26 March (banned by the Provisional Government), when the majority voted to repudiate Dáil authority and transfer control to a new executive, which established its headquarters at the Four Courts on 14 April. Under the headline 'The Dictators', the *Freeman's Journal*, the only newspaper to print a report on the convention issued by the pro-Treaty section of the army, characterised it as a mutiny. In response, 200 men, led by Rory O'Connor, entered the paper's Dublin premises and destroyed the printing plant with sledgehammers. The *Freeman's* remained out of circulation for three weeks; on its return on 22 April it carried photographs of the damage, detailed accounts of the destruction, and extracts from American and British newspapers' reactions. The *New York Globe*, for example, argued that 'smashing the *Freeman's Journal* is a confession of moral bankruptcy by the De Valera forces [*sic*] ... The tyrants of the IRA did a black night's work when they applied sledge hammer censorship to an organ of opinion.'

The attack on the *Freeman's* was clearly a public relations own-goal by the anti-Treatyites. It reflected poorly on their democratic claims and general reputation at a time when they were engaged in what was partly a struggle to win over public opinion, including that of the diaspora, especially Irish-America. It was also largely counterproductive, allowing their opponents to cast themselves as a democratic bulwark against 'anarchy' and champions of the liberty of the press (which, conveniently, happened to be overwhelmingly pro-Treaty). When republicans complained about receiving unfair treatment by the newspapers and invoked press freedom during the Civil War, their opponents were able to counterpunch with ease: 'is it fair [...] to dynamite newspaper offices, to drive crow-bars into linotype machines, to sledge-hammer printing presses [...] Verily, the Irregulars have a strange notion of what constitutes the liberty of the Press.'[23]

War of words

Efforts to avert civil war and restore some unity at a military and political level continued against a backdrop of increasing clashes, anti-Treaty IRA threats to newspapers, and widespread seizures. The occupation of the Four Courts and the destruction of the *Freeman's* followed a series of speeches by de Valera in mid-March in which he appeared to threaten civil war – most notoriously, his assertion in Thurles that Volunteers might have to 'wade through Irish blood [...] in order to get Irish freedom'. There was widespread condemnation in the pro-Treaty press, which accused him of 'criminal incitement' to civil war. The war of words intensified, aided by the launch on 9 April of a new anti-Treaty Sunday paper, *Na Daoine Macánta/The Plain People*. The first issue featured a cartoon by Grace Plunkett in which Griffith and Collins sailed the

Fig. 11 'The Free State Ship', a cartoon by Grace Plunkett, featured in the first issue of the anti-Treaty *Plain People*, 9 April 1922. [Image: National Library of Ireland]

good ship *Free State*, flying a Union Jack and constructed of timbers titled 'Ex-RIC', 'Ex-Unionist', 'Job Hunters', 'Oath Breakers' and 'Truce Volunteers'.[24] The following week's editorial challenged 'the people' to either stand by the principles of Easter Week or 'wallow, like Griffith and Collins, in the offal of British Expediency'. The *Plain People* – a 'vituperative and scurrilous' publication, according to the *Free State* – denounced the Treaty as a 'surrender' and attacked the 'prostituted' mainstream press.[25] Like the *Poblacht*, it persistently denied the legitimacy of the Provisional Government, which derived 'its authority from England', not the people. It attacked the Labour leaders who organised the April 1922 general strike against militarism as 'avowed supporters of the slave State', and even added the Catholic hierarchy to the 'avowed enemies of Irish independence'.[26]

The period of the negotiations between de Valera and Collins in May, the resultant agreement to stand a united Sinn Féin panel in the forthcoming general election, and the early run-up to what became known as the 'pact election' on 16 June, was marked by a temporary armistice in the war of words. On 30 May the first cracks in the pact appeared when the *Poblacht* trumpeted pro-Treaty TD Darrell Figgis's 'treachery' in 'plotting' to undermine the agreement by supporting the formation of a pro-Treaty Irish Farmers' Party and encouraging it to run in the election. The encouragement of non-Sinn Féin candidates (farmers, Labour and independents) by the pro-Treaty press; the 'decrepit' state of the electoral register, and the failure to legislate for votes for women over twenty-one; Collins's effective breaking of the pact on the eve of the election; and the delay in the publication of the Free State constitution – denounced by the *Poblacht* as a 'shameful document'– until the morning of the election, were all used by the anti-Treaty side to challenge the pro-Treaty argument that the election results represented the will of the people and amounted to a popular endorsement of the Treaty. The penultimate issue of the *Plain People* argued that, unlike the pro-Treatyites, republicans had refused to dishonour the pact, and the result would have been different if they had. The battle lines were now clearly drawn:

> With the union of the official Slave Staters with the British Imperial farmers, alleged 'Labour' leaders, English Garrison Unionists, and other varieties of 'Independents', the issue for the first time in Ireland is definitely narrowed down to two parties – the loyal subjects [*sic*] of the Irish Republic and its avowed enemies […] On now with the work, military and political, of maintaining the Republic and defending it against all who would overthrow it.[27]

According to the *Free State*, 'Democracy, welling up from the great throbbing heart of the people, has delivered its message in mighty accents', and that message was clear: the people had spoken in favour of the Treaty.

Civil War propaganda and censorship: pro-Treaty

Once the Civil War proper commenced in June, all the publications previously discussed shifted to a war footing ('War Issue', 'War Number', 'War Special'), and new, mostly short-lived, papers appeared on both sides to bolster the propagandist dimension of their respective military efforts. The mainstream press, which fell

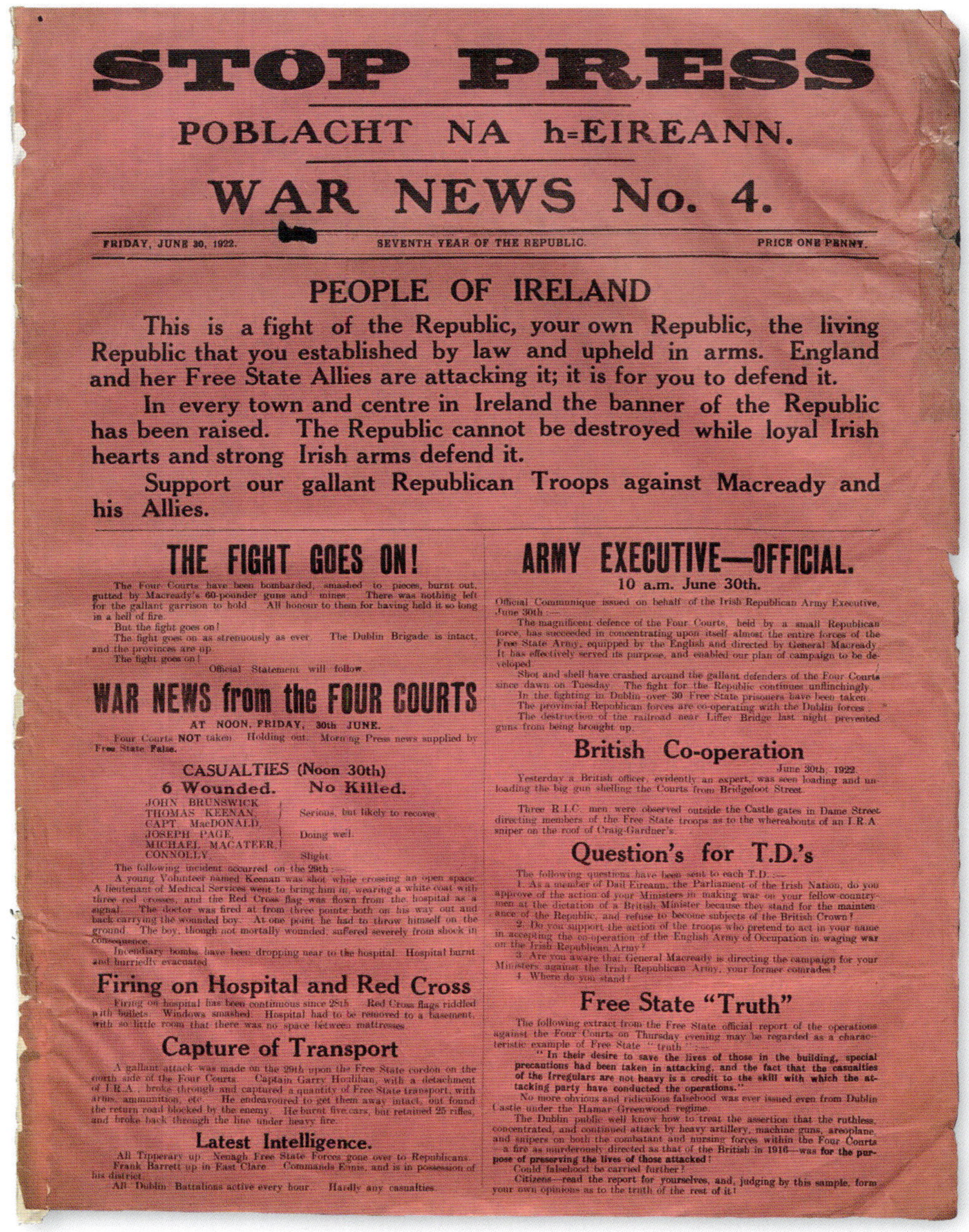

STOP PRESS

POBLACHT NA h-EIREANN.

WAR NEWS No. 4.

FRIDAY, JUNE 30, 1922. SEVENTH YEAR OF THE REPUBLIC. PRICE ONE PENNY.

PEOPLE OF IRELAND

This is a fight of the Republic, your own Republic, the living Republic that you established by law and upheld in arms. England and her Free State Allies are attacking it; it is for you to defend it.

In every town and centre in Ireland the banner of the Republic has been raised. The Republic cannot be destroyed while loyal Irish hearts and strong Irish arms defend it.

Support our gallant Republican Troops against Macready and his Allies.

THE FIGHT GOES ON!

The Four Courts have been bombarded, smashed to pieces, burnt out, gutted by Macready's 60-pounder guns and mines. There was nothing left for the gallant garrison to hold. All honour to them for having held it so long in a hell of fire.

But the fight goes on!

The fight goes on as strenuously as ever. The Dublin Brigade is intact, and the provinces are up.

The fight goes on!

Official Statement will follow.

WAR NEWS from the FOUR COURTS

AT NOON, FRIDAY, 30th JUNE.

Four Courts NOT taken. Holding out. Morning Press news supplied by Free State False.

CASUALTIES (Noon 30th)

6 Wounded. No Killed.

JOHN BRUNSWICK, THOMAS KEENAN, — Serious, but likely to recover.
CAPT. MacDONALD, JOSEPH PAGE, MICHAEL MACATEER, — Doing well.
CONNOLLY, — Slight.

The following incident occurred on the 29th :—

A young Volunteer named Keenan was shot while crossing an open space. A lieutenant of Medical Services went to bring him in, wearing a white coat with three red crosses, and the Red Cross flag was flown from the hospital as a signal. The doctor was fired at from three points both on his way out and back carrying the wounded boy. At one point he had to throw himself on the ground. The boy, though not mortally wounded, suffered severely from shock in consequence.

Incendiary bombs have been dropping near to the hospital. Hospital burnt and hurriedly evacuated.

Firing on Hospital and Red Cross

Firing on hospital has been continuous since 28th. Red Cross flags riddled with bullets. Windows smashed. Hospital had to be removed to a basement, with so little room that there was no space between mattresses.

Capture of Transport

A gallant attack was made on the 29th upon the Free State cordon on the north side of the Four Courts. Captain Garry Houlihan, with a detachment of I.R.A., broke through and captured a quantity of Free State transport, with arms, ammunition, etc. He endeavoured to get them away intact, but found the return road blocked by the enemy. He burnt five cars, but retained 25 rifles, and broke back through the line under heavy fire.

Latest Intelligence.

All Tipperary up. Nenagh Free State Forces gone over to Republicans.

Frank Barrett up in East Clare. Commands Ennis, and is in possession of his district.

All Dublin Battalions active every hour. Hardly any casualties.

ARMY EXECUTIVE—OFFICIAL.

10 a.m. June 30th.

Official Communique issued on behalf of the Irish Republican Army Executive, June 30th :—

The magnificent defence of the Four Courts, held by a small Republican force, has succeeded in concentrating upon itself almost the entire forces of the Free State Army, equipped by the English and directed by General Macready. It has effectively served its purpose, and enabled our plan of campaign to be developed.

Shot and shell have crashed around the gallant defenders of the Four Courts since dawn on Tuesday. The fight for the Republic continues unflinchingly.

In the fighting in Dublin over 30 Free State prisoners have been taken.

The provincial Republican forces are co-operating with the Dublin forces.

The destruction of the railroad near Liffey Bridge last night prevented guns from being brought up.

British Co-operation

June 30th, 1922.

Yesterday a British officer, evidently an expert, was seen loading and unloading the big gun shelling the Courts from Bridgefoot Street.

Three R.I.C. men were observed outside the Castle gates in Dame Street directing members of the Free State troops as to the whereabouts of an I.R.A. sniper on the roof of Craig-Gardner's.

Question's for T.D.'s

The following questions have been sent to each T.D. :—

1. As a member of Dail Eireann, the Parliament of the Irish Nation, do you approve of the action of your Ministers in making war on your fellow-countrymen at the dictation of a British Minister because they stand for the maintenance of the Republic, and refuse to become subjects of the British Crown?

2. Do you support the action of the troops who pretend to act in your name in accepting the co-operation of the English Army of Occupation in waging war on the Irish Republican Army?

3. Are you aware that General Macready is directing the campaign for your Ministers against the Irish Republican Army, your former comrades?

4. Where do you stand?

Free State "Truth"

The following extract from the Free State official report of the operations against the Four Courts on Thursday evening may be regarded as a characteristic example of Free State "truth" :—

"In their desire to save the lives of those in the building, special precautions had been taken in attacking, and the fact that the casualties of the Irregulars are not heavy is a credit to the skill with which the attacking party have conducted the operations."

No more obvious and ridiculous falsehood was ever issued even from Dublin Castle under the Hamar Greenwood regime.

The Dublin public well know how to treat the assertion that the ruthless, concentrated, and continued attack by heavy artillery, machine guns, areoplane, and snipers on both the combatant and nursing forces within the Four Courts —a fire as murderously directed as that of the British in 1916—was **for the purpose of preserving the lives of those attacked**!

Could falsehood be carried further?

Citizens—read the report for yourselves, and, judging by this sample, form your own opinions as to the truth of the rest of it!

Fig. 12 'Stop Press', *Poblacht na hÉireann-War News*, no. 4, 30 June 1922. [Image: reproduced by kind permission of UCD-OFM Partnership, from an original in UCD Special Collections]

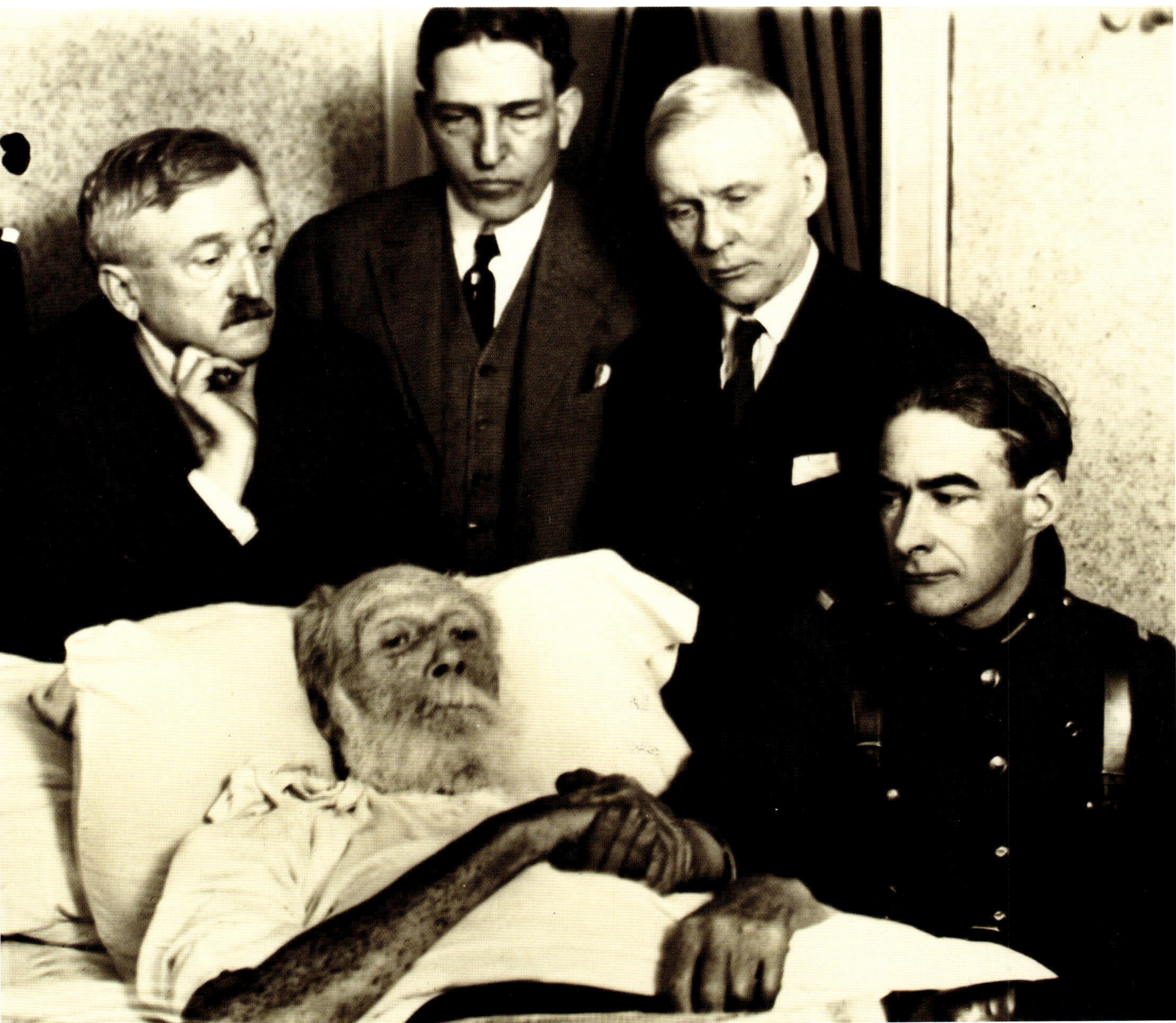

Fig. 13 Piaras Béaslaí (1881–1965), in National Army uniform, at the deathbed of veteran Fenian Richard O'Sullivan Burke in Chicago, April 1922. Béaslaí had been sent to the United States by Michael Collins in March 1922 to publicise the case for the Treaty among Irish-Americans. Paying respects to veteran Fenians like Burke was de rigueur for Irish nationalists on political visits to the United States, and with anti-Treatyites denouncing their opponents as republican apostates, an apparent endorsement from Burke had added resonance. Béaslaí was born in Liverpool to Irish parents and christened Percy Beazley. He learned Irish on summer visits to family in Kerry and joined the Liverpool Gaelic League. He moved to Dublin in 1906 and worked as a journalist on the *Evening Telegraph*. He immersed himself in the Irish-Ireland cultural milieu of the capital, and began using a Gaelicised version of his name. Béaslaí joined the Irish Volunteers on its foundation in 1913 and was also a member of the Irish Republican Brotherhood (IRB). He fought in the 1916 Rising and was jailed in its aftermath. Elected unopposed as TD for Kerry East in the 1918 general election, he became publicity officer for the Dáil government and editor of the IRA newspaper *An tÓglach*. He was elected unopposed for Kerry-Limerick West in the 1921 election and again in June 1922. On the outbreak of the Civil War Béaslaí was ordered to establish a military press censorship at Brunswick Street police station in Dublin. His operation comprised, in his own poetically curt description, 'a temporary department with a temporary staff in an isolated barrack imperfectly equipped'. Due to confusion about payment methods and whether Béaslaí and his censors operated under the embryonic state's military or civilian wing, he received no pay or funding for over two months and maintained the office, including the salaries of his staff of five, out of his own pocket until September 1922. By then, as military victory seemed secure, the censorship was seen as less important by the Provisional Government, and Béaslaí's operation was wound down gradually from October. He returned to Army Publicity, which maintained light-touch regulation on the press over the last months of the war. He worked on his two-volume biography of Collins, which was published in 1926 as *Michael Collins and the Making of a New Ireland*. Béaslaí resigned from the army in 1924, following the so-called army mutiny, and devoted himself to writing plays and criticism in the Irish language, as well as historical articles and reminiscences of the revolutionary period in a variety of newspapers and journals. [Image: National Library of Ireland, Piaras Béaslaí Collection, BEA72 / See Patrick Maume, 'Piaras Béaslaí' at https://www.dib.ie/biography/beaslai-piaras-a0515 and Marie Coleman, 'Biographical note on Piaras Béaslaí', Collection List no. 44, Piaras Béaslaí Papers at https://www.nli.ie/sites/default/files/2022-12/beaslai.pdf]

victim to censorship by both sides, generally reflected the Free State agenda, as delivered through the Provisional Government's publicity department, headed by Desmond FitzGerald, and Piaras Béaslaí's press censorship operation. The final issue of the *Plain People* appeared on 2 July and the *Poblacht* was suppressed in its newspaper format and became a one- or two-page 'stop press' newsletter, renamed *Poblacht na hÉireann–War News*. This continued to be produced regularly until March 1923.[28] On 29 June *An tÓglach* editor Béaslaí established a press censorship office that, despite operating on a shoestring and suffering early teething pains, became very effective.[29] Press telegrams were censored at the Central Telegraph Office, a field censor operated with the National Army, and a censorship of newsreels and photographs relating to the Civil War was temporarily operated by an Irish censor based in London. All British papers and periodicals, and all Irish periodicals were examined, and permits for circulation were issued or withheld depending on whether or not they were deemed to be complying with censorship demands. All British newspapers were initially blocked, but were readmitted over the following weeks, most following the wholesaler Eason's advice that they should avoid 'Anything that would discredit the Provisional Government or exalt the actions of Republicans, or which represents the Provisional Government as acting in the interests of Great Britain or at the suggesting of Great Britain.'[30]

Free State censorship policy was ad hoc in the early days, and it was some weeks before clear guidelines and parameters were set and a level of standardisation achieved, summarised in the following list of instructions prepared for censors in the third week of July:

1 The Army must always be referred to as the 'Irish Army', 'National Army', 'National Forces', 'National Troops' or simply 'The troops'.
2 The Irregulars must not be referred to as 'Executive Forces' nor described as 'Forces' or 'Troops'. They are to be called 'bands' or 'Bodies' or 'Armed men'.
3 Irregular leaders are not to be referred to as of any rank such as 'Commandant' etc. and are not to be called Officers.
4 No news as to the movement of troops is to be published.
5 No news may be published with regard to the movements of newly enrolled members of the Army, movements of food ships or trains, or transport of arms or equipment for Army purposes.
6 Descriptions of a military operation must not be published while the operation is still uncompleted, as for instance, an encircling movement.
7 Articles or letters as to the treatment of Irregular prisoners may not be published.
8 The Censors are not to insert words of their own in any article submitted to them. Their business is to cancel what is objected to. They may, however, propose to substitute words or phrases, such as 'Irregulars' for 'Republicans'; 'fired at' for 'attacked'; 'seized' for 'commandeered'; 'kidnapped by the Irregulars' for 'arrested'; 'enrolled' for 'enlisted'.

Fig. 14 This 1922 cartoon by Countess Markievicz was inspired by her outrage at what she perceived as the Free State government's efforts to suffocate the 'Irregular' Irish Republican Prisoners' Dependants' Fund (IIRPDF). Launched by Cumann na mBan in July 1922 after a Treaty-inspired split in the original Irish Republican Prisoners' Dependants' Fund of 1919–22, the new fund was administered by a central committee. This committee bolstered the fund-raising efforts of local committees organised by Cumann an mBan district councils in collaboration with local IRA officers. Because the Free State authorities were suspicious of the IIRPDF's charitable credentials and convinced that some of the money was being siphoned off for the purchase of arms, its fund-raising was compromised by the 'constant confiscation of collection boxes', the arrest of its members, and the censorship of fundraising appeals to the national press. In the spring of 1923, the refusal of Bishop Daniel Cohalan to permit church-door collections in Cork prompted the IIRPDF executive to publicly protest the campaign of 'persecution' directed by the government and its supporters against the 'purely charitable' fund. In an open letter to the papal legate, Monsignor Salvatore Luzio, in April, the committee listed a litany of offences perpetrated by the agents of the Free State: armed raids on committee headquarters at 6 Harcourt Street in Dublin, the internment of its members, the confiscation of funds and, most reprehensible of all, the seizure of 'parcels of children's clothing, which had been collected for the little ones'. Markievicz turned her artist's pen to a propaganda poster featuring three children clinging plaintively to their young mother, with the caption: 'Will you allow the wives and children of dead + imprisoned Republicans to starve because the Free State Censor Pierce Beasly [*sic*] has suppressed the appeal sent to the daily papers.' It was one of several Civil War sketches in which Markievicz used the trope of woman and children as victims of Free State policies. [Image: National Library of Ireland, PD 3067 TX 1(A)] / See Ann Matthews, *Dissidents: Irish republican women, 1923–1941* (Cork, 2012), pp. 38–40; *Éire: The Irish Nation*, 5 May 1923]

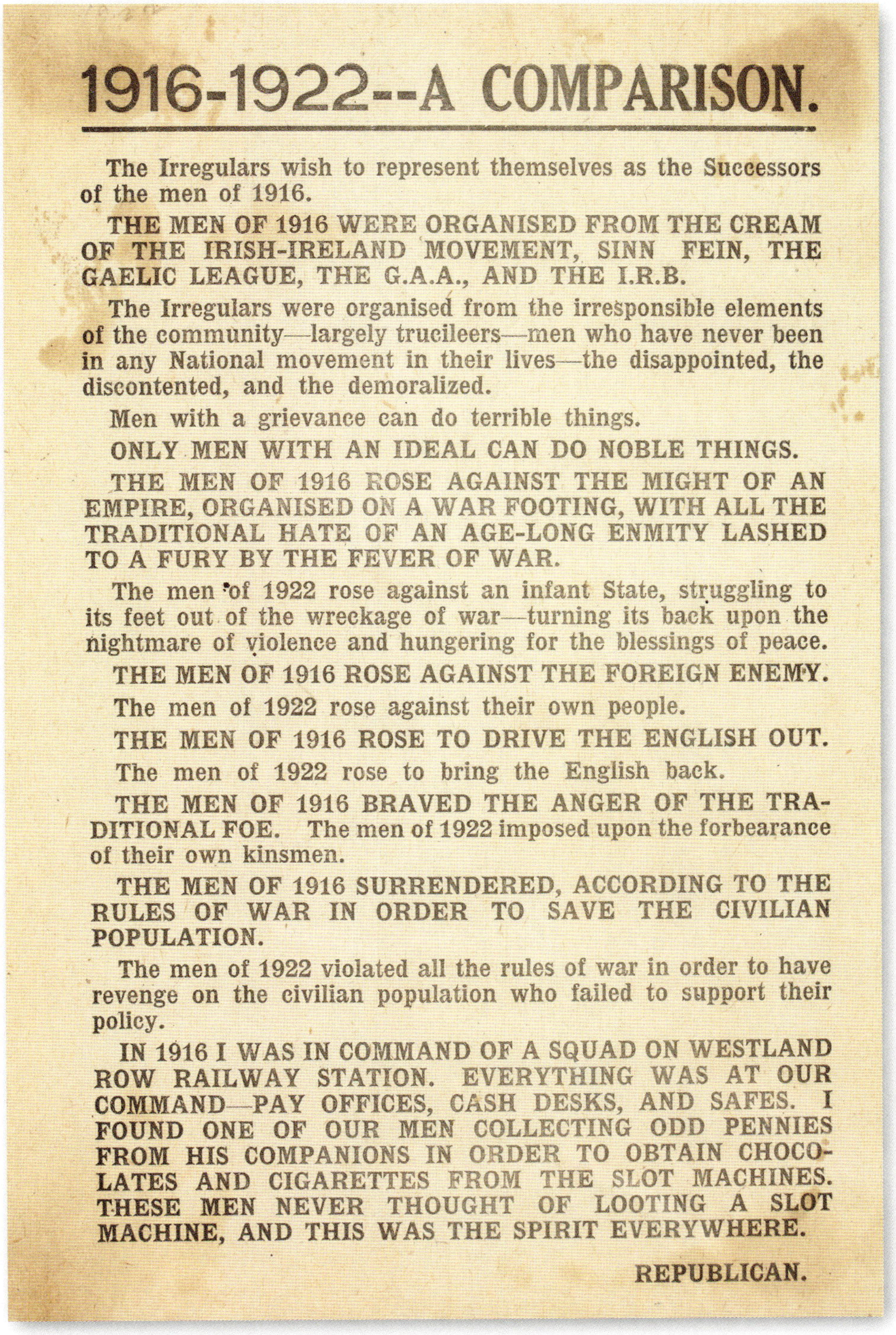

Fig. 15 A pro-Treaty handbill reproducing the text of an article by George A. Lyons in the *Free State*, 29 July 1922, that challenged the anti-Treaty IRA's claim to be the heirs to 'the men of 1916'. The Easter rebels, wrote Lyons offering what he called 'the real comparison', 'were organised from the cream of the Irish-Ireland movement, Sinn Féin, the Gaelic League, the GAA and the IRB', while 'the Irregulars' – 'largely trucileers' represented 'the disappointed, the discontented, and the demoralized' elements of the community. The themes of irresponsibility and unpatriotic, opportunistic ruffianism persisted as a leitmotif of pro-Treaty propaganda to the eve of the general election in August 1923, when the *United Irishman*, successor to Griffith's *Young Ireland*, expressed horror at 'the cruel spectacle of men calling themselves Irishmen casting a shadow upon our patriot dead'. [Document: National Library of Ireland, EPH B116 / Quotation: *United Irishman*, 25 August 1923]

1916-1922--A COMPARISON.

The Irregulars wish to represent themselves as the Successors of the men of 1916.

THE MEN OF 1916 WERE ORGANISED FROM THE CREAM OF THE IRISH-IRELAND MOVEMENT, SINN FEIN, THE GAELIC LEAGUE, THE G.A.A., AND THE I.R.B.

The Irregulars were organised from the irresponsible elements of the community—largely trucileers—men who have never been in any National movement in their lives—the disappointed, the discontented, and the demoralized.

Men with a grievance can do terrible things.

ONLY MEN WITH AN IDEAL CAN DO NOBLE THINGS.

THE MEN OF 1916 ROSE AGAINST THE MIGHT OF AN EMPIRE, ORGANISED ON A WAR FOOTING, WITH ALL THE TRADITIONAL HATE OF AN AGE-LONG ENMITY LASHED TO A FURY BY THE FEVER OF WAR.

The men of 1922 rose against an infant State, struggling to its feet out of the wreckage of war—turning its back upon the nightmare of violence and hungering for the blessings of peace.

THE MEN OF 1916 ROSE AGAINST THE FOREIGN ENEMY.

The men of 1922 rose against their own people.

THE MEN OF 1916 ROSE TO DRIVE THE ENGLISH OUT.

The men of 1922 rose to bring the English back.

THE MEN OF 1916 BRAVED THE ANGER OF THE TRADITIONAL FOE. The men of 1922 imposed upon the forbearance of their own kinsmen.

THE MEN OF 1916 SURRENDERED, ACCORDING TO THE RULES OF WAR IN ORDER TO SAVE THE CIVILIAN POPULATION.

The men of 1922 violated all the rules of war in order to have revenge on the civilian population who failed to support their policy.

IN 1916 I WAS IN COMMAND OF A SQUAD ON WESTLAND ROW RAILWAY STATION. EVERYTHING WAS AT OUR COMMAND—PAY OFFICES, CASH DESKS, AND SAFES. I FOUND ONE OF OUR MEN COLLECTING ODD PENNIES FROM HIS COMPANIONS IN ORDER TO OBTAIN CHOCOLATES AND CIGARETTES FROM THE SLOT MACHINES. THESE MEN NEVER THOUGHT OF LOOTING A SLOT MACHINE, AND THIS WAS THE SPIRIT EVERYWHERE.

REPUBLICAN.

9 Letters, news or articles dealing with proposals for peace or negotiations with Irregulars should not be passed without first submitting them to Chief Censor.

10 The term 'Provisional Government' should not be used. The correct term is 'Irish Government' or simply 'The Government'.

11 All GHQ bulletins issued from here (Censor's office) should bear the date and time of issue.

12 Escapes of prisoners may not be made public.[31]

On the propaganda side, FitzGerald's department maintained pressure on the Dublin dailies to toe the line, and prioritise publicity about 'the campaign of wanton destruction pursued by the Irregulars'.[32] The *Free State* spearheaded the campaign in its nine 'special war numbers'. It was supplemented by *Young Ireland* and two new publications launched by Griffith and edited initially by the *Young Ireland* team of Milroy and Burke: *Truth–War Special*, which ran from 5 July to 22 August, and the Sunday paper *Irish People–War Special* (16 July–22 August).[33] These specialised in large-font, bold statements, containing the familiar dichotomies, catechism-style question and answers, and 'which side are you on?' challenges, e.g. 'The Will of the Nation. Order. Security. Democracy. Protection. Reconstruction Work. National Freedom' (the National Army) or 'The Will of an Armed Minority. Chaos. Looting. Dictatorship. Terrorism. Destruction. Unemployment. National Disaster' (the Irregulars).[34] According to Childers, pro-Treaty propaganda was nothing but 'a tissue of abominable fictions, coined for the most part by salaried Ministerial self-seekers sitting safely in Dublin offices under the shelter of British guns'.[35]

In early July, while O'Hegarty in *The Separatist* was calling for compromise, a ceasefire and negotiations to end the war, *Truth* reflected much more closely the prevailing hardening attitude on the Free State side: 'You cannot compromise with a mad dog. It must be either shot or muzzled.'[36] Both sides issued bulletins that were sent abroad; the Provisional Government's diplomatic representative in Geneva, Michael MacWhite, monitored the continental newspapers and in early August reported that the National Army 'is regarded as most praiseworthy', while 'the irregulars are held to be no better than bandits and brigands'.[37]

A range of social attitudes and snobberies are discernible, as Gavin Foster has shown, in the general war propaganda of the Free Staters. These were already evident before the war began, but came into sharper focus once the gloves were off. In pro-Treaty discourse, those in the anti-Treaty camp were portrayed multifariously as:

> overzealous newcomers to the nationalist cause; peace-threatening 'militarists'; irresponsible youth and reckless hooligans; low status riff-raff; violent criminals; anarchists, radicals, and social malcontents; rural primitives and urban bohemians; deviant intellectuals and illiterate 'yahoos'; as well as un-Irish minorities and sundry 'others'. Although encompassing a seemingly incongruous collection of social elements, the leitmotif of the pro-treaty camp's discursive picture of republican opposition was an implicit emphasis on the latter's essential marginality, otherness, and lack of status [...] Conversely, the pro-treaty camp's self-image was the conceptual opposite of all the social vices, deviances, and worthless qualities attributed to the enemy.[38]

Giving a veneer of credibility to this motley crew, this 'rag, tag and bobtail of society', were the 'renegade Childers' and de Valera, 'warped by vanity and egotism'. 'As the Irregulars themselves are our best arguments for an ordered Ireland', claimed the *Free State,* 'so their publicity is our best propaganda'.[39] Once the situation was 'well in hand from the public and military points of view' in late July, Collins argued that censorship be minimised and, with the long-term future in mind, propaganda toned down: by avoiding 'anything that savours of personal abuse [...] our propaganda will be more telling, and more thoughtful, and much more helpful from a permanent point of view'. Cosgrave disagreed and, with Collins dead within the month, the vitriol continued to flow.[40]

Civil War propaganda and censorship: anti-Treaty

During the Civil War's conventional phase (up to mid-August 1922), when the Free State-censored Dublin newspapers were mainly kept out of, or could not reach, areas in the control of the anti-Treaty IRA, the Provisional Government used an aeroplane to disseminate Free State propaganda to republican-held areas.[41] Newspapers in these areas either gradually went out of business or were censored by the anti-Treatyites and compelled to carry republican war news and general propaganda. In classic war-propagandist style, this emphasised or exaggerated republican victories; challenged Free State military claims and highlighted the enemy's atrocious behaviour; tried to boost republican morale in the face of the National Army's military supremacy and advance; and mourned and praised fallen republican leaders. The pro-Treaty regime was characterised as the product of a coup d'état, and the apostasy, Britishness and venality of the 'Anglo-Free State' 'regime', 'junta' and 'Military Dictatorship', run by discredited 'shoneens', was repeatedly stressed. Most anti-Treaty publications featured 'The Seventh Year of Republic' under their publication dates, emphasising the contention that the anti-Treaty struggle was a defence of the republic of 1916.[42]

From 6 July to 5 August Sean T. O'Kelly edited *Nationality*, a two-page typesheet that featured the standard anti-Treaty propagandist themes and tropes, including the assertion that the IRA was not fighting fellow Irishmen, 'because they are not Irishmen', but 'representatives of British rule in Ireland'.[43] Other republican publications included *The Nation*, *The Fenian*, *The Flame*, *Straight Talk* and the *Republican War Bulletin*. The Communist Party of Ireland's *Workers' Republic* argued for a broadening of the republican struggle to embrace class issues. This was taken up by Liam Mellows in Mountjoy Gaol, whose notes outlining a socialistic policy platform that would attract working-class and small-farmer support were captured and published in the *Irish Independent* under red-scare headlines. A 'Bolshevik' bogeyman was a welcome addition to the pro-Treaty propaganda arsenal. When republican propaganda did engage on a socio-economic level, it was generally a populist discourse that associated support for the Treaty with 'shoneen capitalists', ex-unionist large farmers, jobbery and place-hunting; the Labour Party was an imperialistic sell-out of the ideals of its founder, the republican James Connolly, and the high level of working-class urban recruits to the National Army provoked classist slurs of the type aimed at British army recruits in 1914–18 (though there was some recognition of the economic pressure that led many to join up).[44]

Poblacht na hÉireann–War News continued to be produced in Dublin under severe duress, and was distributed by Cumann na mBan activists as well as by sympathetic newsboys. Women played a central role in republican propaganda efforts. Anna Kelly was responsible for the underground production of *War News*. When the editor, Frank Gallagher, was arrested in October 1922, Kelly took over until her arrest in March 1923. Gallagher had replaced Childers at the end of the battle for Dublin when the latter headed south to the 'Munster Republic'. Robert Brennan oversaw the

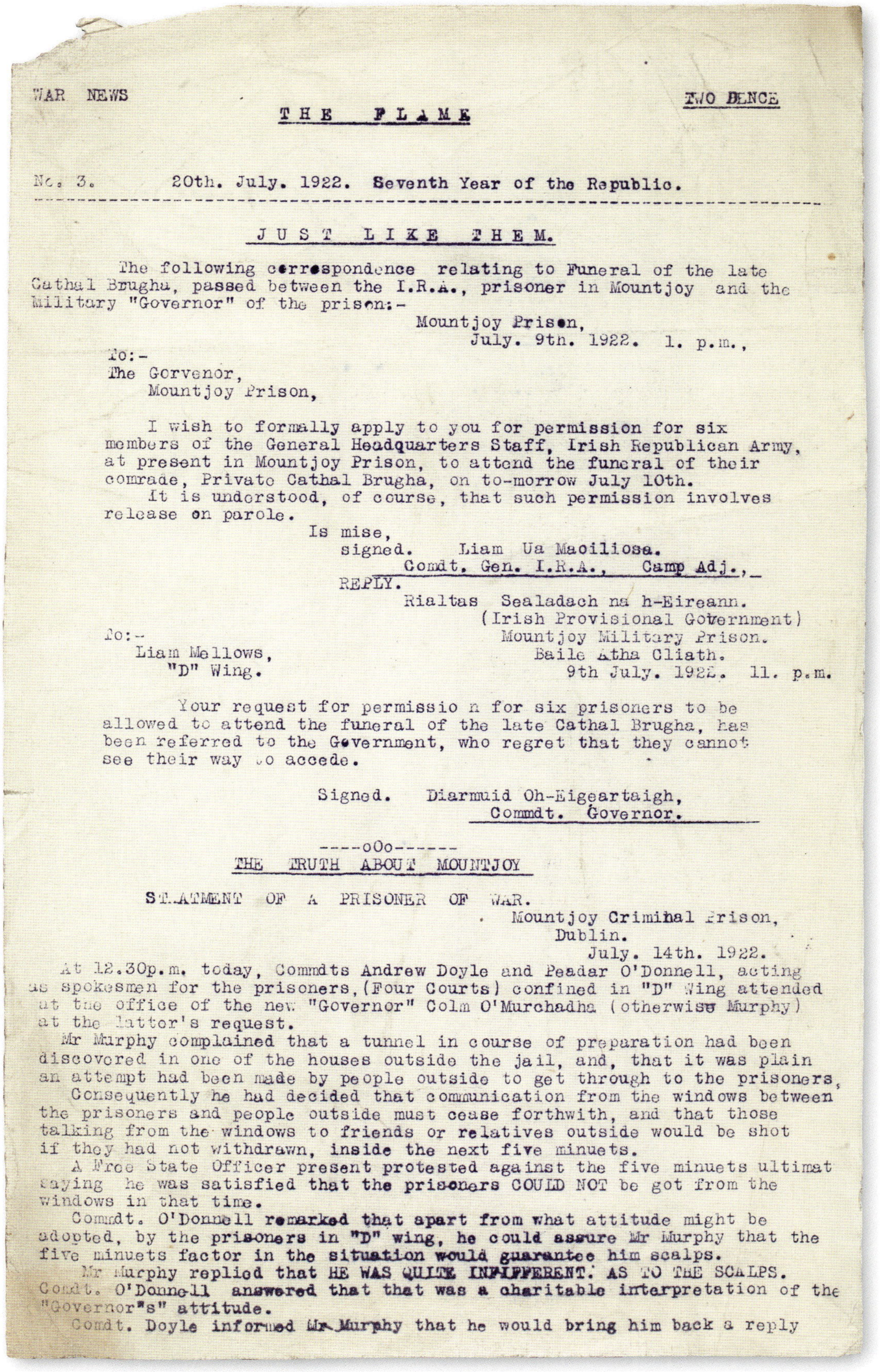

WAR NEWS **THE FLAME** TWO PENCE

No. 3. 20th. July. 1922. Seventh Year of the Republic.

JUST LIKE THEM.

The following correspondence relating to Funeral of the late Cathal Brugha, passed between the I.R.A., prisoner in Mountjoy and the Military "Governor" of the prison:-

Mountjoy Prison,
July. 9th. 1922. 1. p.m.,

To:-
The Gorvenor,
Mountjoy Prison,

I wish to formally apply to you for permission for six members of the General Headquarters Staff, Irish Republican Army, at present in Mountjoy Prison, to attend the funeral of their comrade, Private Cathal Brugha, on to-morrow July 10th.
It is understood, of course, that such permission involves release on parole.

Is mise,
signed. Liam Ua Maoiliosa.
Comdt. Gen. I.R.A., Camp Adj.,

REPLY.

Rialtas Sealadach na h-Eireann.
(Irish Provisional Government)
Mountjoy Military Prison.
Baile Atha Cliath.
9th July. 1922. 11. p.m.

To:-
Liam Mellows,
"D" Wing.

Your request for permissio n for six prisoners to be allowed to attend the funeral of the late Cathal Brugha, has been referred to the Government, who regret that they cannot see their way to accede.

Signed. Diarmuid Oh-Eigeartaigh,
Commdt. Governor.

-----oOo------

THE TRUTH ABOUT MOUNTJOY

STATMENT OF A PRISONER OF WAR.

Mountjoy Criminal Prison,
Dublin.
July. 14th. 1922.

At 12.30p.m. today, Commdts Andrew Doyle and Peadar O'Donnell, acting as spokesmen for the prisoners, (Four Courts) confined in "D" Wing attended at the office of the new "Governor" Colm O'Murchadha (otherwise Murphy) at the latter's request.

Mr Murphy complained that a tunnel in course of preparation had been discovered in one of the houses outside the jail, and, that it was plain an attempt had been made by people outside to get through to the prisoners.

Consequently he had decided that communication from the windows between the prisoners and people outside must cease forthwith, and that those talking from the windows to friends or relatives outside would be shot if they had not withdrawn, inside the next five minuets.

A Free State Officer present protested against the five minuets ultimat saying he was satisfied that the prisoners COULD NOT be got from the windows in that time.

Commdt. O'Donnell remarked that apart from what attitude might be adopted, by the prisoners in "D" wing, he could assure Mr Murphy that the five minuets factor in the situation would guarantee him scalps.

Mr Murphy replied that HE WAS QUITE INDIFFERENT. AS TO THE SCALPS.

Comdt. O'Donnell answered that that was a charitable interpretation of the "Governor"s" attitude.

Comdt. Doyle informed Mr Murphy that he would bring him back a reply

Fig. 16 The third issue of the anti-Treatyite newsletter titled *The Flame–War News*, issued 20 July 1922, 'Seventh Year of the Republic'. [Document: National Library of Ireland, Erskine Childers Papers, MS 48,060/2]

Fig. 17 Anna Kelly (1891–1958). Anna Kelly (née Fitzsimons) was from Ballysadare, County Sligo. She moved to Dublin in *c.* 1910 and worked as a typist for the novelist George Moore and in the publishing firm of Maunsel and Roberts. She joined the Fairview branch of Cumann na mBan in early 1917 and, later that year, joined the office staff at Sinn Féin headquarters on Harcourt Street. She worked as a secretary for Michael Collins, and prepared notes for the inaugural meeting of Dáil Éireann in January 1919 and briefings for foreign correspondents. In late 1919 she became assistant to Robert Brennan and Frank Gallagher in the production of the Dáil's propaganda news-sheet, the *Irish Bulletin*. Always referred to as Miss Fitz or Fitz, her primary task was compiling the lists of atrocities committed by the crown forces. In July 1921 she married fellow Sinn Féin staffer Frank Kelly, who came from Manchester and served with the Kimmage garrison in the 1916 Rising. After the Treaty, she resigned from the Dáil staff and joined Erskine Childers as sub-editor of *Poblacht na hÉireann*. Along with Kevin Ardiff and Kevin O'Carroll, and later Brendan O'Carroll and Dick Saunders, she managed to maintain production of the paper in the most trying circumstances. Following the arrest of Dublin editor Frank Gallagher in October 1922, Kelly took over the reins. She likened the production to that of the *Irish Bulletin*, except the Free State authorities were harder to evade, as 'Everybody knew everybody else'. Kelly was arrested in May 1923 and jailed in Kilmainham. She was released on doctor's advice in July, suffering from a respiratory illness, and immediately threw herself back into propaganda work, helping to start the new *Sinn Féin* weekly in August 1923. Kelly worked as a freelancer in the 1920s before joining de Valera's *Irish Press* on its launch in 1931 as Ireland's first women's page editor. She also wrote features and social columns, and did a number of European assignments. She continued to write for the *Press* to the end, as well as contributing to many other Irish titles. In a tribute following her death, Robert Brennan recalled that 'She hated cant and hypocrisy and pretension [...] She was kindhearted and generous to an amazing degree [...] she was the best and wittiest woman journalist we have had'. The *Irish Times* obituary recalled her 'sharp, salty reviews of social events' and hailed her as being 'in the top rank not merely of women journalists but of journalism'. [Image: Hugh Oram, *The Newspaper Book: A history of newspapers in Ireland 1649–1983* (Dublin, 1983) / See MSP 63744 Anna Christina Kelly, and 'Death of Mrs Anna Kelly: Miss Fitz of Sinn Fein headquarters', *Irish Press*, 16 June 1958]

overall republican publicity operation and Cumann na mBan director of propaganda, Bridget O'Mullane, directed the IRA GHQ's propaganda department until her arrest in November 1922. She edited the *Republican War Bulletin*; organised the countrywide distribution, through Cumann na mBan networks, of bulletins, pamphlets and handbills; and headed up an early-morning 'painting squad' that painted republican slogans on Dublin city-centre walls.[45] In Cork, following its capture by the National Army in August 1922, Cumann na mBan women sold copies of the southern edition of the *Poblacht* from kerbsides.[46]

In the first days of the Civil War a team of republican censors moved into the Cork city-centre offices of the *Cork Examiner* and the unionist daily the *Cork Constitution*, and republican propaganda and opinion pieces were integrated into the newspapers.[47] The importance to the anti-Treatyites of having the republican message wrapped in a mainstream newspaper is illustrated by IRA chief of staff Liam Lynch's letter to his assistant Ernie O'Malley on 13 July: 'Propaganda is playing hell in Dublin and district [...] we are doing our utmost to get *Examiner* paper up along East and if possible to Dublin. Even one copy which will be sent daily should be copied for use in Dublin.'[48] Among the censors installed in the *Examiner* was Michael O'Donovan, who would subsequently find fame as the writer Frank O'Connor. Along with another future literary luminary, Seán O'Faoláin, he worked under the direction of Erskine Childers and Robert Brennan.

On 8 August National Army troops landed in Passage West, signalling the beginning of the end of the republican hold on Cork and its seven-week censorship experiment. As republicans retreated from the city, they destroyed the plant and machinery of both the *Examiner* and the *Constitution*. The latter never returned, but the daily *Examiner* was on the streets in time to mourn Arthur Griffith, who died on 12 August, and was joined by the *Evening Echo* and the *Cork Weekly Examiner* by the time Michael Collins was killed on 22 August. The latter was an early victim of the guerrilla war that had now ensued and would last for another eight months. This phase was marked by a shift towards increased brutality and repression by the post-Griffith/Collins Treatyite leadership, including the adoption of emergency powers and a policy of executions. Childers had headed west from the city and aided by assistants, including O'Connor, Ó Faoláin and the printer Robert Lankford, produced *Poblacht na hEireann–Southern Edition* from 14 August until 25 October 1922, initially from Ballymakeera in west Cork and subsequently on the move in that district. The mobile printing press had been assembled in June by Lankford, who oversaw production in the most trying of circumstances.[49] (Free State politicians and propagandists consistently attributed republican atrocities and acts of sabotage

Fig. 18 Still from 'Battle of the Four Courts', Pathé, issued 3 July 1922. Before the advent of television, the only form of moving-image news available to the general public was the cinema newsreel. The first newsfilm appeared in 1908 and, by the 1920s, these short silent films were firmly established as part of every cinema programme. During the revolutionary period, events in Ireland were regularly covered by the three main newsreel companies in operation, Gaumont, Pathé and Topical Budget, and were usually represented with a distinctly British bias. All three companies covered the shelling of the Four Courts, indicating the importance of the story. The image above depicts troops holding back crowds of adults and children apparently watching the unfolding action. Young boys and girls, many of whom are barefoot, with upturned faces marked by unease and confusion, are pushed aggressively back into the melee by soldiers. The Civil War offered drama and intrigue to the newsreels by way of images of military battles, snipers and tanks, and scenes of gunfire and shelling. These were framed within a broader context of bitter intercommunal strife. Capturing the action was dangerous, and newsreel editors often included self-congratulatory intertitles on scooping the top stories, bringing exclusive pictures to audiences and the bravery of company cameramen, sometimes drawing attention to the processes of filmmaking by describing the daring lengths to which operators went to get as close to the fighting as possible. Priority was often given to the entertainment factor rather than the news values of the items depicted, and sometimes discernible heroes and villains emerged. The Treaty debates had offered the newsreels the opportunity to cover the political rivalry between the 'irreconcilable' Éamon de Valera – as he was described in one Pathé item – and the charismatic Michael Collins, who was, as a signatory of the Treaty, deemed respectable by the newsreels in 1922. The Treaty was depicted as the preferred British solution to the Irish problem and, as signatories, Arthur Griffith and Michael Collins were lauded (with their subsequent deaths represented in particularly melancholic terms). Ideologically, the newsreels appeared to support the pro-Treaty side in their coverage of the Civil War, aided, no doubt, by the Provisional Government's prior censorship of films relating to the politico-military situation from 10 July onwards. A central theme was the damage inflicted on architectural heritage and homes and businesses across the country. In 'Sackville Street in Flames' (issued on 10 July 1922), Pathé's opening intertitle sets the scene for viewers: '£3,000,000 damage and a large number of buildings gutted in final "clean-up" of rebels'. The following shots of storefronts engulfed in fire show billowing smoke filling the sky as evidence of the damage caused, while the language used is reminiscent of comparable items that reported the 'hemming-in' or 'rounding up' of rebels. As well as commercial damage, the newsreels also focused on human suffering through sentimental representations of the displaced, with one intertitle simply and melodramatically stating: 'Homeless!' before cutting to a lingering shot of families outside their homes, some seated on the pavement with their pets and belongings. Contemporary newsreel coverage was consistently informed by a latent propensity to present the Irish as prone to atavistic violence and a willingness to self-destruct in their pursuit of independence. In many ways the imagery of this era with its smoky shots of buildings on fire or in ruins, evictions, military patrols and children playing amid the rubble, encapsulated the same tropes that circulated on television in its coverage of the Troubles almost half a century later. [Text: Ciara Chambers / Image: courtesy of the IFI Irish Film Archive and British Pathé]

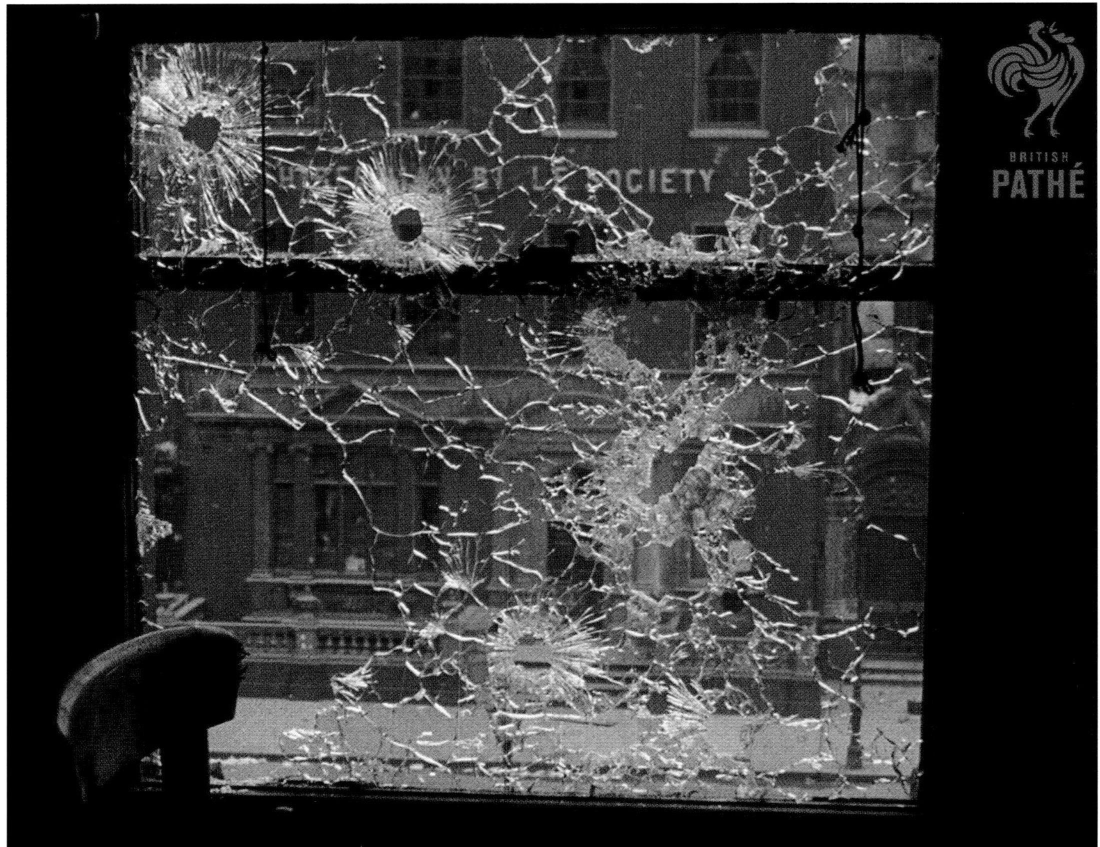

Fig. 19 Detail showing the Hibernian Bible Society through a bullet-riddled window as part of Pathé's coverage of burning buildings on Sackville Street. There were very few instances of local Irish newsreel production, leaving the main coverage of the revolutionary period to British newsreels. These companies were invariably outsiders looking in, often with misapprehension or bewilderment, on Irish affairs. [Text: Ciara Chambers / Image from 'Dublin War Scenes' (Pathé, issued 10 July 1922), Courtesy of the IFI Irish Film Archive and British Pathé]

personally to Childers, as part of a campaign of vilification that both Gallagher and Frank O'Connor were convinced was designed to set him up for execution.)[50] A Scottish edition of the *Poblacht* was published from 26 August until 13 January 1923. A number of other news-sheets also pushed the anti-Treaty message but, in general, republican propaganda lacked coordination and impact, hampered by communications and distribution difficulties. Action against pro-Treaty newspapers continued. On 7 August Liam Lynch ordered divisions to seize and destroy all copies of the *Freeman's*, *Irish Times* and *Irish Independent* found in their districts. On 1 September the last paper still publishing in Kerry, the Tralee-based *Kerry People*, was shut down by republicans who dismantled the printing presses.[51]

Endgame

Having prorogued the parliament elected on 16 June throughout July and August – displaying in the process, according to *The Separatist*, 'as complete [a] disregard for democracy as does the policy of the Irregulars' – the Free State authorities finally convened it on 9 September, in a sure signal of their belief that the war was won. The previous day, Béaslaí informed the Dublin editors that the censorship was being minimised to the 'extremest levels compatible with public safety' and in mid-October Richard Mulcahy announced the official ending of censorship. On 25 October Childers left west Cork and headed to Dublin, his editorship of the southern edition of the *Poblacht* being taken over by Ó Faoláin. Childers was arrested on 10 November and executed two weeks later. The final issue of the *Free State* appeared on 11 November, its circulation figures having fallen so low that it was deemed to have lost all propaganda value. On 6 December 1922 the Irish Free State came into official existence and on 8 December Rory O'Connor, who had led the raid on the *Freeman's* eight months earlier, was executed in Mountjoy Gaol, along with Joe McKelvey, Dick Barrett and the first editor of *Poblacht na hÉireann*, Liam Mellows. Republican morale was severely dented; the executions policy continued, and though sporadic guerrilla actions and occasional clashes occurred until April 1923, the endgame had commenced. Béaslaí returned to Army Publicity, which maintained light-touch regulation on the press over the last months of the war.

In a final Civil War assault on republican propaganda, newsagents with anti-Treaty sympathies across Dublin were raided on 27 February 1923. The following week the machinery and plant used to produce the Dublin *Poblacht* were seized and staff, including the editor, Anna Kelly, were arrested. The only remaining publication representing the anti-Treaty position was *Éire: The Irish Nation*, edited by P.J. Little and published in Glasgow, with contributions from Ó Faoláin, including the first exposure of the atrocious Ballyseedy massacre in March 1923. Military defeat was acknowledged by chief of staff Frank Aiken's dump-arms order of 24 May 1923 and de Valera's accompanying 'Legion of the Rearguard' proclamation.

Conclusion

While further comparative research is needed to back up Gavin Foster's contention that the Irish Civil War 'stands out for the ferocity of the invective and partisan rhetoric that accompanied it', there is little doubt that the crude binaries and bitter animosities produced by the propaganda war continued to exert an influence on Irish politics, media discourse and, arguably, the historiography of the Civil War for many decades afterwards.[52] Joe Lee's suggestion that both sides' respective images of the war had to be subsequently 'burnished and polished, and the fires of hatred stoked, to foster the illusion that fundamental differences remained between the parties' is one possible explanation for its enduring legacy.[53] What is interesting to note in that regard is the extent to which Cumann na nGaedheal/Fine Gael party propaganda continued to be dominated, until the Second World War, by what it presented as the Civil War misdeeds of de Valera and the IRA.[54] De Valera's Fianna Fáil, on the other hand – while always happy to issue reminders about Civil War executions and National Army atrocities – 'moved on' more successfully and foregrounded social and economic factors in its electoral appeals. Once in government from 1932, de Valera adopted Collins's 'stepping stone' and waged a long (constitutional) war against the Treaty settlement that saw it effectively dismantled by 1938.[55] Fianna Fáil's political success was significantly bolstered by the establishment of the *Irish Press* in 1931, which finally brought some balance to the Irish media landscape.

The other dimension of the war of words had arguably an even more enduring and damaging legacy. At a formative historical juncture, both sides embraced censorship with gusto to silence and/or delegitimise their opponents. This illiberal, authoritarian reflex became embedded in the political culture of independent Ireland; allied with the deference of the parties on both sides of the Civil War divide to the Catholic moral agenda, this saw censorship emerge as a defining feature of the new state, much to the detriment of both Irish cultural life and Irish democracy.

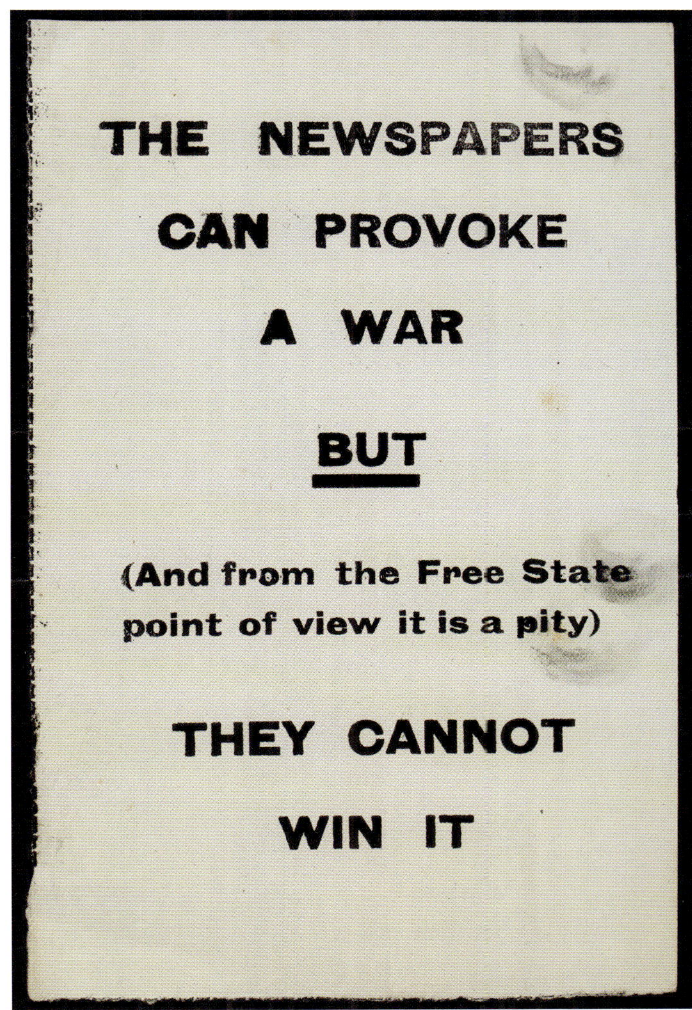

THE NEWSPAPERS

CAN PROVOKE

A WAR

BUT

(And from the Free State point of view it is a pity)

THEY CANNOT

WIN IT

Fig. 20 A handbill from the early days of the Civil War that highlights the significance attached by the anti-Treaty side to the pro-Treaty/Free State press consensus. [Document: National Library of Ireland, Erskine Childers Papers, MS 48,087/1]

The Cartoon War

Donal Ó Drisceoil

Cartoons are an effective and distinctive propaganda weapon and were utilised by both sides before, during and after the Civil War. They were principally used to ridicule and denigrate the other side, individually and collectively, although the pro-Treaty cartoonists had a much greater tendency to boost their own side through valorising and glorifying the Free State and its apparent benefits (e.g. p. 172, Figs 4, 5, 7, 8). While the cartoons were sometimes humorous, they often functioned as straightforward political statements. They mainly featured in the press, but were also used in handbills and posters. Cartoons essentialised and summarised the core themes and tropes of both sides' propaganda. The principal pro-Treaty cartoonist in the mainstream press was Ernest Forbes in the *Freeman's Journal*, who used the pseudonym 'Shemus'. His depiction of de Valera as the puppet of Erskine Childers (Fig. 2), published on 10 February 1922, was particularly controversial in those early days of the war of words. The use of a woman figure – 'Erin' or Mother Ireland – was a standard feature on both sides. In Fig. 3 Forbes has her mourning her fallen leaders, with Collins and Griffith joining the pantheon of Irish heroes on the 'Via Dolorosa'; in Fig. 14, p. 173, she is comforted by a couple of young republicans as the Free State ship sails towards England, while 'Coll' (p. 173, Fig. 17) has her donning an ill-fitting Free State cloak at the direction of the British. *Young Ireland/Éire Óg* was the main pro-Treaty paper that featured cartoons; some were by 'Mórna', but most were unsigned. These were mainly non-humorous depictions of the Treaty/Free State symbolising freedom, progress, stability and prosperity, counterposed to the anti-Treaty alternative of chaos and destruction (see p. 172, Figs 4–6). Grace Plunkett was the principal cartoonist on the other side, her work featuring in the anti-Treaty Sunday paper, the *Plain People*, as well as in the humorous republican-sympathetic monthly *Irish Fun*. The former ceased publication on the outbreak of the Civil War, while censorship forced Plunkett to depoliticise her cartoons in the latter. Her principal focus was on Griffith and Collins, as can be seen in Figs 10–13 (see also p. 153, Fig. 11). Constance Markievicz was also a prolific cartoonist; her work featured in *Republican File* and she produced a series of poster caricatures of prominent pro-Treatyites under the title 'Free State Freaks' (e.g. p. 173, Fig. 16). A twist in the cartoon war was the claim in the pro-Treaty *Free State* on 5 August 1922 that occasional cartoonist for the *Plain People* and *Irish Fun* 'Coll' (see p. 173, Figs 15 and 17) was J.G. Cowell, a former British soldier who had served in Ireland during the War of Independence and, it was implied, was now acting as an agent provocateur. This rhymed with Free State propaganda about Erskine Childers being a British agent; it is never made clear in this curious strand of pro-Treaty thinking how the British were to gain from encouraging the anti-Treatyites in this way. *Irish Fun* welcomed 1923 with a 'neutral' cartoon by Myles Mordaunt (Fig. 1). It did turn out to be a 'scrappy' year, and cartoons featured again in the post-Civil War election of August 1923 (see pp. 150–151, Figs 1 and 2) and were central to the election campaigns of the late 1920s and early 1930s, when Cumann na nGaedheal, in particular, kept on playing the Civil War blame game (see p. 172, Fig. 9).

Clockwise from top:

Fig. 1 *Irish Fun* welcomes the new year, February 1923.

Fig. 2 'Giving him his lines', *Freeman's Journal*, 10 February 1922. [Source: National Library of Ireland, PD 4309 TX 104]

Fig. 3 'Via Dolorosa', *Freeman's Journal*, 25 August 1922. [Source: National Library of Ireland, PD4309TX145]

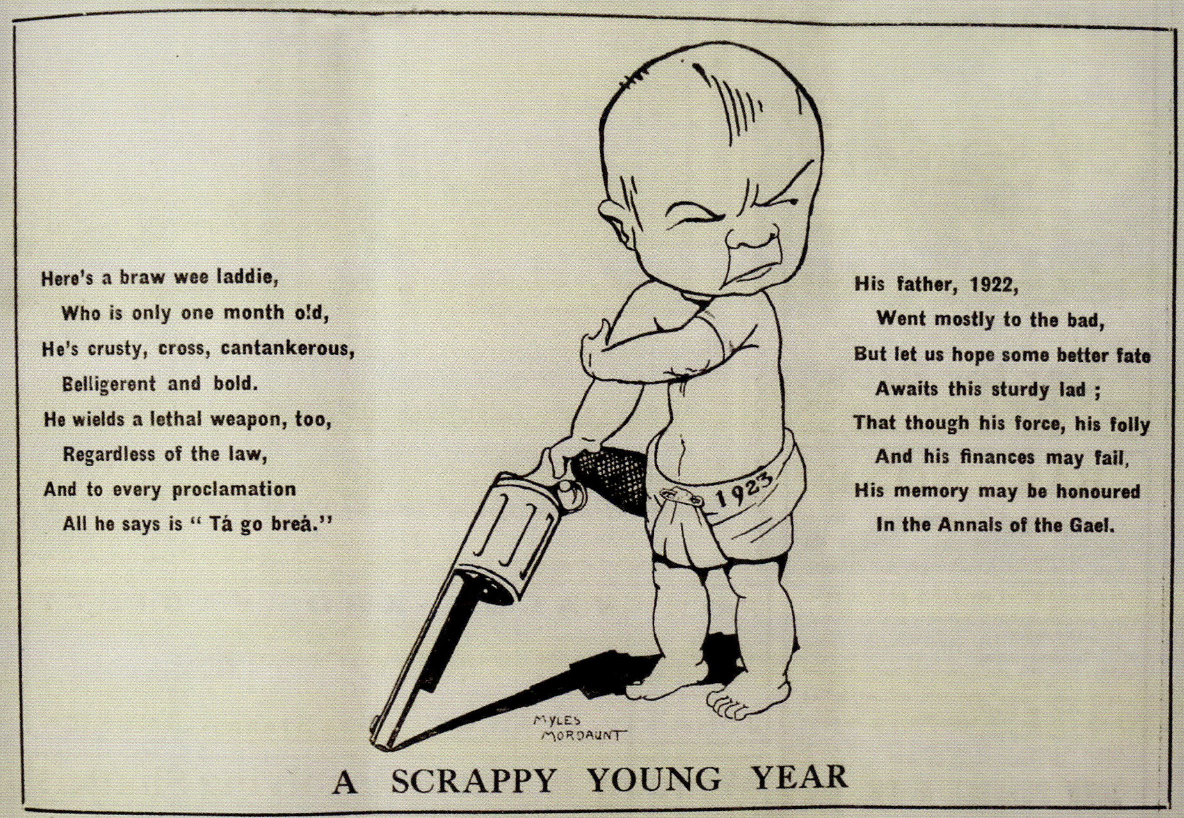

Fig. 4 (left) 'The Deliverer', *Young Ireland*, 18 March 1922.

Fig. 5 (above) 'The Right Road', *Young Ireland*, 29 April 1922. [Source: National Library of Ireland]

Fig. 6 (right) Boy Blowing Bubbles, *Young Ireland*, 5 August 1922. [Source: National Library of Ireland]

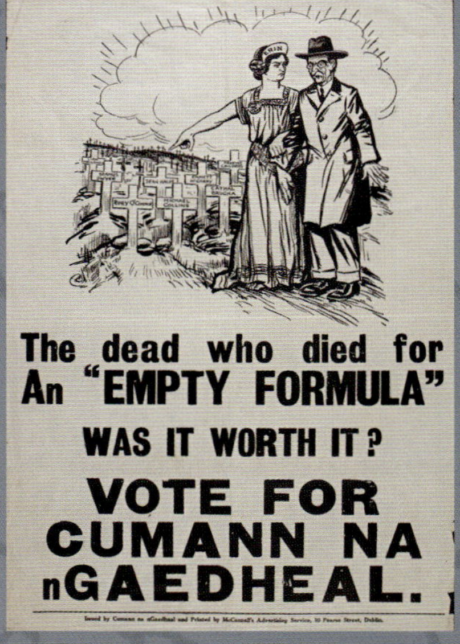

Clockwise from above left:

Fig. 7 'Broken at Last', *Young Ireland*, 16 December 1922. [Source: National Library of Ireland]

Fig. 8 'Gifts for the Nation', *Young Ireland*, 22 December 1922. [Source: National Library of Ireland]

Fig. 9 A Cumann na nGaedheal poster for the 1932 general election. 'Erin' points to the Civil War dead on both sides and asks de Valera if it was worth them dying for an 'empty formula'. In 1927 Fianna Fáil was legally obliged to take the oath if it wanted to partake in parliamentary politics; de Valera described it as 'an empty political formula'. The party abolished the oath when in government in 1933. [Source: National Library of Ireland, EPH F43]

Fig. 10 'The Free Will of the People', *Irish Fun*, May 1922.

Fig. 11 (left) 'In Virtue of our Common Citizenship', *Irish Fun*, May 1922. **Fig. 12** (right) 'The Riddle of the Sands', *Irish Fun*, May 1922.

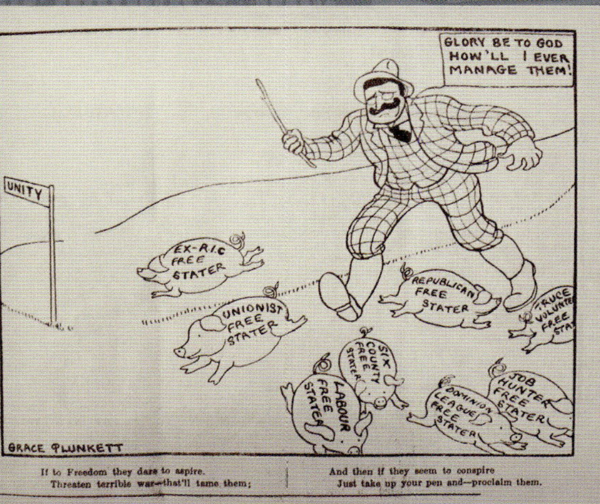

Fig. 13 (left) 'Glory be to God. How'll I ever manage them', *Irish Fun*, May 1922. **Fig. 14** (centre) 'Don't sigh, Mother', *Plain People*, 7 May 1922. **Fig. 15** (right) 'And we have brought back the flag – Arthur Griffith', *Plain People*, 21 May 1922. [Source: National Library of Ireland]

Fig. 16 (bottom left) 'Free State Freaks. No. II: Desmond FitzGerald Liar in Chief to Publicity Department, Slave-State'. [Source: National Library of Ireland, PD 3061 TX]
Fig. 17 (bottom right) 'Empire Productions Ltd', *Irish Fun*, July 1922.

CASE STUDY

Songs of the Irish Civil War

Terry Moylan

To those who follow such things, it sometimes seems as if no event in Ireland, no matter how momentous or trivial, can take place without being promptly described in verse. The writers range from ones who compose a song without ever questioning or changing the lines that first occur to them, to those who agonise over the choice and position of every word. And there is no guarantee that the products of the latter will necessarily be superior to those of the former.

Periods of conflict in Ireland have always provoked lyrical response. Songs of dissent, so-called 'rebel songs', have been written in profusion, in Irish and in English, in response to every episode of military, political or social struggle, and the practice continued during the Civil War. Such material, long dismissed as of no significance, is increasingly gaining scholarly attention for the access it provides to the *mentalité* of a population. Perceptions and emotions not captured in official accounts may be discerned from the literature – popular verse and song – produced, preserved and performed by ordinary people.

Rebel songs

Historically, 'rebel songs' celebrated or lamented leaders and fighters, recorded significant events, or promoted dissident political stances. They were lyrical expressions of resentment or defiance, and were recognised as such by the colonial power in Ireland. Evidence of the suppression of such material may be found in accounts going back to the eighteenth century. In the wake of the 1916 Rising, the performance of Peadar Kearney's 'The Soldiers' Song' was grounds for arrest, as was the purely instrumental performance of the air of John Kells Ingram's 'The Memory of the Dead'. The combatants on both sides of the Civil War were heirs to a centuries-long tradition of nationalist versifying. Although political poems in Irish from earlier centuries are known, H. Halliday Sparling described the song 'The Blackbird', which appeared before the 1715 Jacobite rebellion, as not only the 'first rebel poem', but the first Irish lyric of any kind written in English,[1] and English was the language in which political song became a long-lasting Irish tradition. The United Irishmen were the first to systematically and deliberately use poetry and song as political tools. The four songsters that they published between 1795 and 1803[2] featured over 160 poems (nearly all with an indicated air, so intended to be sung) that established the type of 'rebel songs'. Their example was followed by every campaigning force up to modern times, and the songs produced in each period were not displaced by those of succeeding events, but accumulated as useful exemplars of radical thought. Like artfully designed slogans, rebel songs were created to articulate intuited, perhaps half-formed, beliefs during periods of intense political or social change.

The agrarian campaigns of the Rockites and Whiteboys produced songs such as 'Captain Carder'[3] and John Keegan's 'Bold Captain Rock'.[4] Thomas Davis's 'A Nation Once Again', written in the 1840s, immediately won, and retains, popular approval. T.D. Sullivan's 'God Save Ireland', his response to the hanging of the Manchester Martyrs in 1867, became, for a while, the unofficial anthem of nationalist Ireland. The widespread opposition to the imperialist wars in Africa, and the coincident centenary of the 1798 rebellion, were the sparks for an outpouring of nationalist verse. P.J. McCall's ballads of 1798 – such as 'Boolavogue' and 'Kelly from Killanne' – supplanted in the public mind the songs that had actually circulated during the eighteenth-century rebellion. The cultural revival and rising nationalist consciousness resulted in the emergence of several prolific song-makers, including Peadar Kearney, who penned such enduring songs as 'The Row in the Town', 'Down by the Liffeyside', 'Whack Fol the Diddle'. The enormously prolific Brian O'Higgins wrote hundreds of pieces promoting nationalist consciousness before the Rising, and railing against 'the establishment' after it.

For centuries before the Treaty, England had been the single focus for Irish nationalist invective. The split over the Treaty changed that situation. It might have been expected that both sides would draw on the Irish tradition of political balladry to reflect their respective positions, as they were both inheritors of that tradition, but the record suggests that the anti-Treaty side was by far the more prolific in lyrical responses to conflict. An illustration of this is found in the one-sided response to the events of March 1923 in Kerry. In reprisal for the killing of five National Army soldiers in an IRA trap-mine explosion in Knocknagoshel on 6 March, eight IRA prisoners were killed a day later in a deliberate explosion at Ballyseedy. More reprisal killings were carried out over the following days. During earlier phases of political conflict in Ireland, any of these events might have inspired a ballad or lament. But only songs commemorating the anti-Treaty dead have been found:

At Ballyseedy's steeple view that lies near sweet Tralee
The cowardly Staters laid a mine as you may plainly see

Fig. 1 A romanticised depiction of the meeting of United Irishmen at the Cave Hill, Belfast before Theobald Wolfe Tone's departure for America in June 1795. It imagines the moment when, according to Tone's autobiography, the Belfast radicals swore 'never to desist in our efforts until we had subverted the authority of England over our country and asserted her independence'. The illustration, by John D. Reigh, appeared in the December 1890 edition of the *Shamrock*, a nationalist periodical pitched at younger readers and specialising in patriotic, melodramatic Irish history. Cast primarily in hues of green and gold, the historical scene was unsurprising inspiration for the nationalist illustrator during a period of crisis for the fracturing Irish Parliamentary Party. The male figures are strong and dignified – a counterpoint to the derogatory stock depictions of Irishmen in contemporary British political illustrations – with the epauletted Tone, in heroic attitude beneath an unfurled flag, urging the unified movement onward. Such iconic fare, replete with symbolic resonance and intended to encourage nationalist pride, solidarity and purpose, drew on a deep well of culturally conditioned popular memory. Just as Reigh and his fellow nationalist illustrators were influenced by the balladry of Young Ireland and the heroic depictions of Tone in Victorian melodrama, their 'patriotic visual histories' informed a wealth of commemorative ephemera and a new crop of popular ballads to mark the centenary of 1798. Intended for display in Irish and diasporic homes, the *Shamrock* illustrations, and other nationalist chromolithographs, fired the childhood imaginations of many of what Tom Clarke would call the 'rising generation'. Brian O'Higgins, for one, the Meath-born balladeer, 1916 veteran and anti-Treaty TD, testified to their powerful influence in his youth. Publishing prolifically before 1916 under the Gaelicised pseudonym 'Brian na Banban', his political poetry and ballads married the tropes of traditional patriotic history with early twentieth-century Irish-Irelandism to urge vindication of the republican principles for which Wolfe Tone died. O'Higgins's verses were modelled on the traditional street ballad, pioneered for political purposes by the United Irishmen in the 1790s, and often achieved widespread oral circulation. 'Who is Ireland's Enemy', for example, a popular anti-enlistment poem first published in *Irish Freedom* in 1914, listed what O'Higgins deemed Britain's historic crimes against Ireland and climaxed in a rousing call to arms. He continued to summon the collective memory of Wolfe Tone, 'father of Irish republicanism', during and after the Civil War, casting supporters of the Treaty as traitors to the memory of Ireland's long genealogy of patriot martyrs. [Image: National Library of Ireland, PD Shamrock 1890 December (A) / See also Patrick Maume, 'Keeper of the Flame', *History Ireland*, vol. 27, no. 1, 2019]

Supplement Gratis with Christmas Number of "THE SHAMROCK." December, 1890.

THE CAVE HILL, BELFAST.
Formation of the Society of United Irishmen by Wolfe Tone, Samuel Neilson, and Thomas Russell.

The explosion shook the mountain and was heard for
miles away,
This brutal murder of six men with Tuomey and O'Shea.
(Nora Leahy, 'Tuomey and O'Shea')

Then how the tigers did rejoice they gloated o'er their prey
The sergeant vainly raised his voice they marched him
quick away
The Baranarrig ancient wood the divels did draw near
For how they thirsted for the blood of the Black Smith
Volunteer.
(Anon, 'The Blacksmith Volunteer', Schools Collection)

Contempt and vituperation, once directed at their common enemy, was now aimed by one side against the other.

'Twas traitors vile that damned our isle, and prolonged the
tyrant's sway,
They played the dirty Saxon game, and they're playing it
today.
For filthy English lucre they sold their race and sod,
And played the role that Judas played when he betrayed
his God.
(Anon, 'Jimmy Vaugh – A Memorial Poem')

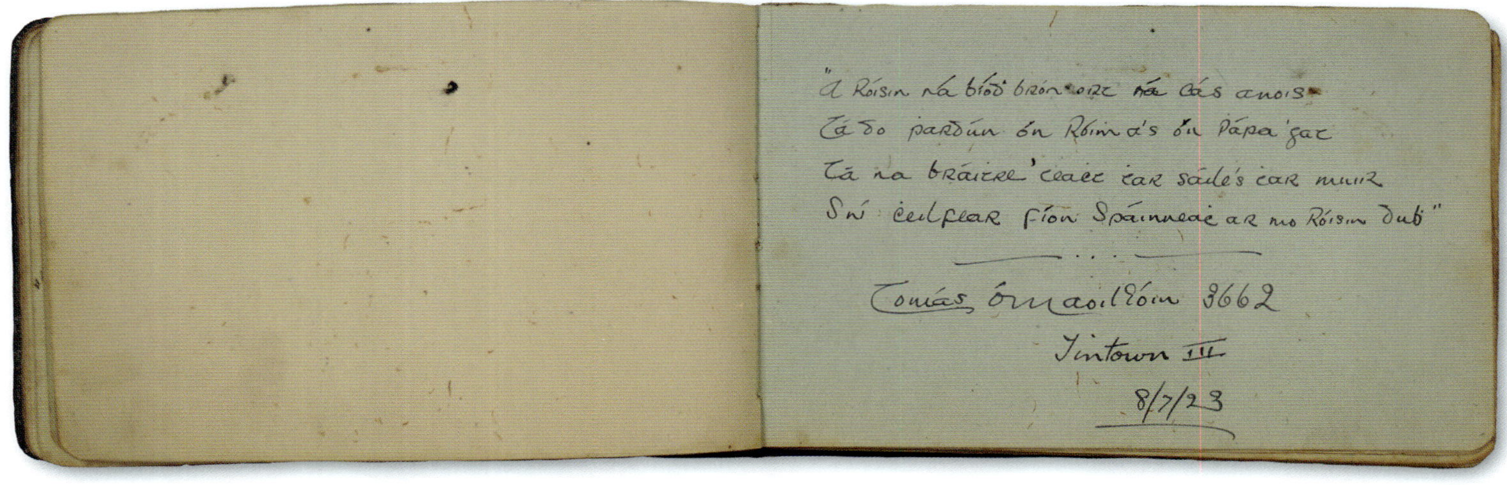

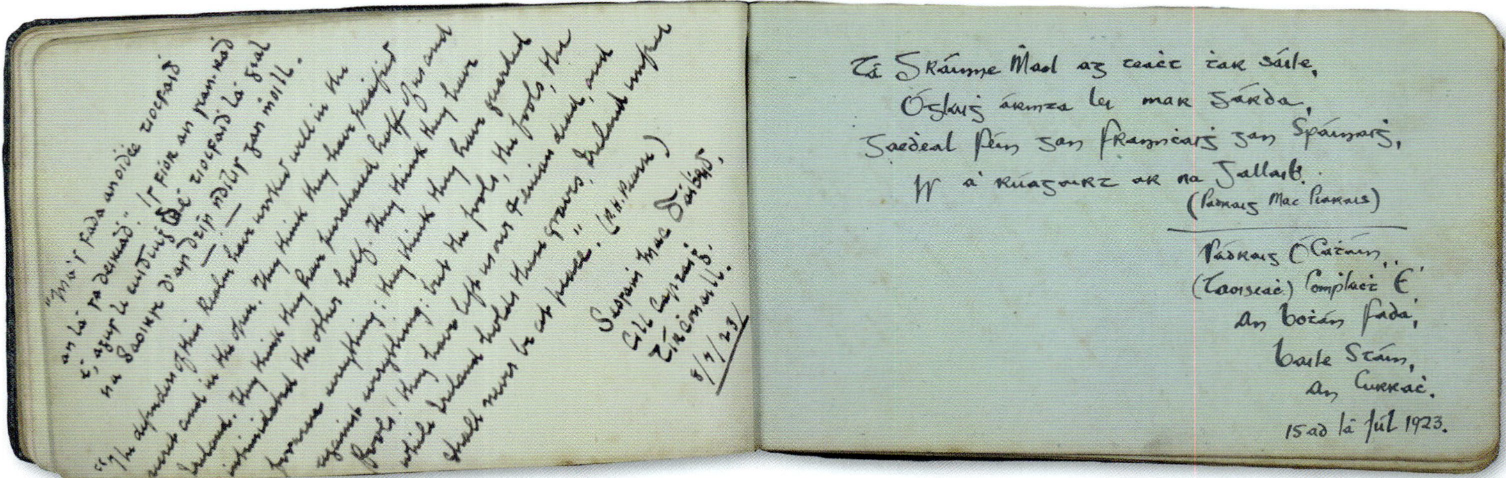

Figs 2 and 3 Pages from Martin McGrath's internment camp autograph book. Extracts from ballads were a common feature of autograph books kept by prisoners and internees in the War of Independence and Civil War eras. Republican belief in the continuity of opposition to the Treaty with the Irish revolutionary tradition is suggested in these transcriptions in the Tintown internment camp autograph book of Martin McGrath, Ballina, in July 1923: (top) Tomás Ó Maoileoin chooses the opening lines of 'Róisín Dubh' (Dark Rosaleen), a ballad that dates back to sixteenth-century Gaelic Ireland, as his entry, and (above) Pádraig Ó Catháin offers lines from Patrick Pearse's version of 'Óró, sé do bheatha abhaile', which he first titled 'Amhrán na nÓglach' (The Volunteers' Song) in 1914, and subsequently called 'An Dord Féinne' (The Fenian or Warrior's Chant). [Image: courtesy of the Jackie Clarke Collection]

> Take it down from the mast, Irish traitors,
> 'Tis the flag we republicans claim.
> (James Ryan, 'Take it down from the mast')

The belief that the attack on the Four Courts on 28 June 1922 had been demanded and supported by Britain inspired a slew of anti-Treaty songs: 'A Four Courts Ditty', 'The Battle of the Four Courts' and 'A Dublin Battle Ditty' (all by 'A.J.B.'), and the anonymous 'When England Gave the Orders' and 'Churchill's Green and Tans'.[5]

> He's in the Four Courts, its walls defending,
> And much I admire his brave cry,
> But the Free Staters to him some shells are sending.
> Where they got them all, sure, it puzzles me.
> (A.J.B., 'The Battle of the Four Courts')

The core conviction in these songs was that being overpowered by a greater force in no way invalidated the principles for which the anti-Treaty IRA had fought. Other songs from the same camp included 'The First Cork Brigade', 'The Drumboe Martyrs', 'In Tipperary of Renown', 'The Belfast Brigade', 'Pat Hartnett' and 'Niall Plunkett O'Boyle'.

The fact that there seems to be no equivalent body of verse from the pro-Treaty side requires an explanation. The late Dublin singer Frank Harte was fond of using the expression 'Those in power write the histories, those who suffer write the songs'. Traditionally, the rebel song was a vehicle for articulating feelings of oppression and injustice, and vocalising such feelings in verse concentrated and sharpened them. The majority who supported and defended the Treaty as an acceptable measure of freedom, those who clearly believed that they were on the right side of history, had no such emotions to vent in song.

Fig. 4 (above) Drawing of a woman with lines from Brian O'Higgins's 1916 ballad, 'The Soldiers of Cumann na mBan', in the autograph book of Martin McGrath of Ballina, Tintown internment camp, the Curragh, 1923. O'Higgins, who was interned in the camp at the time (it is unclear if the entry is by him), was a Sinn Féin TD and prolific author of nationalist verse and ballads. [Image: courtesy of the Jackie Clarke Collection]

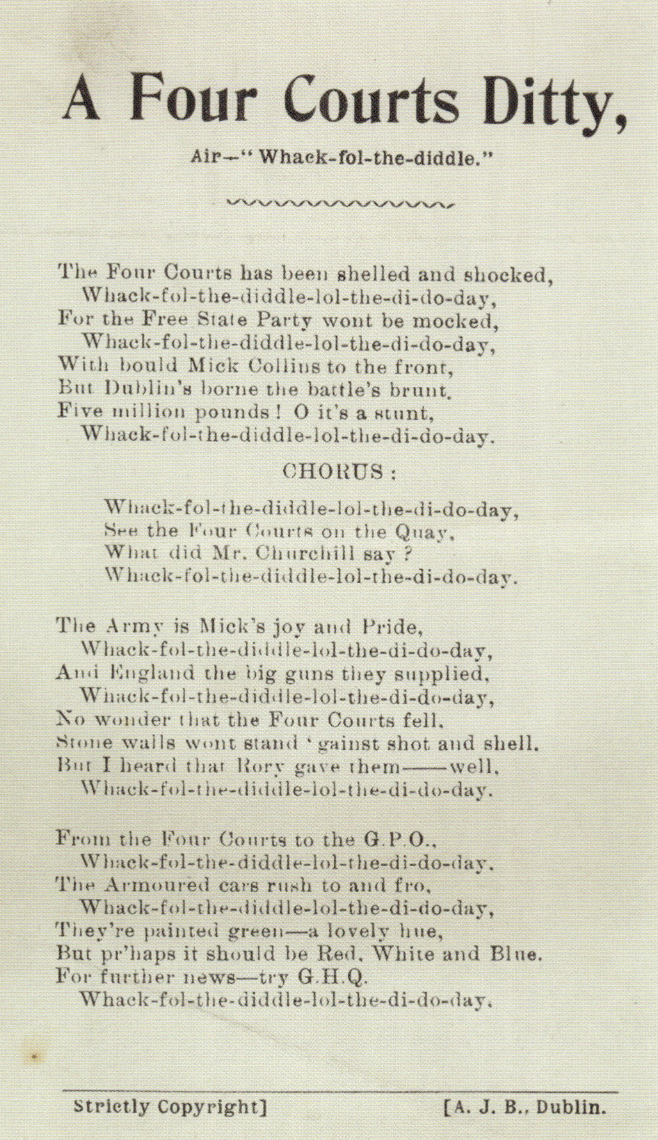

A Four Courts Ditty,

Air—" Whack-fol-the-diddle."

The Four Courts has been shelled and shocked,
  Whack-fol-the-diddle-lol-the-di-do-day,
For the Free State Party wont be mocked,
  Whack-fol-the-diddle-lol-the-di-do-day,
With bould Mick Collins to the front,
But Dublin's borne the battle's brunt.
Five million pounds ! O it's a stunt,
  Whack-fol-the-diddle-lol-the-di-do-day.

CHORUS :

Whack-fol-the-diddle-lol-the-di-do-day,
See the Four Courts on the Quay,
What did Mr. Churchill say ?
Whack-fol-the-diddle-lol-the-di-do-day.

The Army is Mick's joy and Pride,
  Whack-fol-the-diddle-lol-the-di-do-day,
And England the big guns they supplied,
  Whack-fol-the-diddle-lol-the-di-do-day,
No wonder that the Four Courts fell.
Stone walls wont stand 'gainst shot and shell.
But I heard that Rory gave them——well.
  Whack-fol-the-diddle-lol-the-di-do-day.

From the Four Courts to the G.P.O.,
  Whack-fol-the-diddle-lol-the-di-do-day.
The Armoured cars rush to and fro,
  Whack-fol-the-diddle-lol-the-di-do-day,
They're painted green—a lovely hue,
But pr'haps it should be Red, White and Blue.
For further news—try G.H.Q.
  Whack-fol-the-diddle-lol-the-di-do-day.

Strictly Copyright] [A. J. B., Dublin.

Fig. 5 (right) A surprisingly light-hearted ditty on the attack on the anti-Treaty IRA headquarters at the Four Courts, Dublin, 28 June 1922, that marked the official start of the Civil War. 'Bould Mick Collins' was to the front, with Winston Churchill at his back. The Free State doing Britain's bidding is the central theme: 'The Armoured Cars rush to and fro [...]/ They're painted green–a lovely hue/ But pr'haps it should be Red, White and Blue'. [Document: OLS Samuels, box 5, no. 167, The Board of Trinity College Dublin]

Other songs

Uninvolved observers of the events between 1922 and 1923 occasionally expressed their opinions in humorous verse. William Dawson's 'The Lay of Oliver Gogarty'[6] used his subject's name – Oliver St John Gogarty – to comic effect by including it in full, sometimes several times, in all ten verses of his narrative of the attempted murder of the senator. The song is still current among singers; I heard it performed in early 2023. Ned Buckley's cynical 'The Battle of the Bower' records a lengthy exchange of gunfire in Rathmore, County Kerry, which resulted in no casualties:

> But one thing's true, that bullets flew in a dark and deadly shower
> Though none were killed or wounded at the Battle of the Bower.[7]

'The Night Darrell Figgis Lost His Whiskers'[8] recorded an assault on that Treaty supporter with an impeccable nationalist record, during which his flowing beard was forcibly shaved off. The song must have seemed hilarious to some, but not to Figgis's wife Millie, whose suicide in 1924 was partly attributed to the trauma of the attack.

One of the finest pieces about the disastrous consequences of the Civil War was Sigerson Clifford's 'The Ballad of the Tinker's Son'. After sketching the friendship that had developed between a settled boy and a Traveller boy during their schooldays and during their shared participation in the War of Independence, he delivers a shocking blow in the final verses:

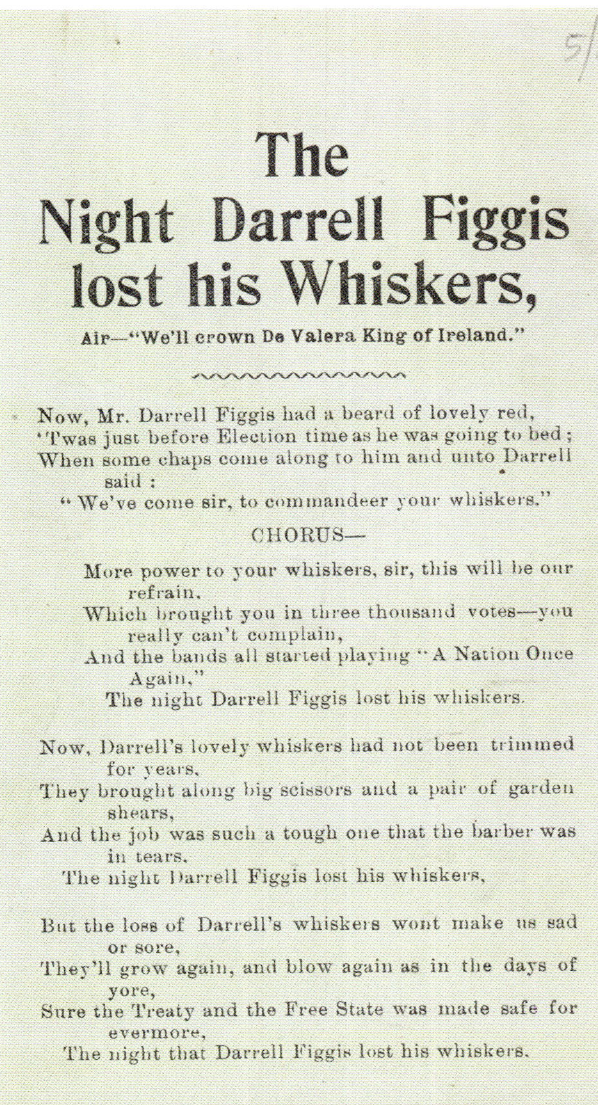

The Night Darrell Figgis lost his Whiskers,

Air—"We'll crown De Valera King of Ireland."

Now, Mr. Darrell Figgis had a beard of lovely red,
'Twas just before Election time as he was going to bed;
When some chaps come along to him and unto Darrell said :
"We've come sir, to commandeer your whiskers."

CHORUS—

More power to your whiskers, sir, this will be our refrain,
Which brought you in three thousand votes—you really can't complain,
And the bands all started playing "A Nation Once Again,"
The night Darrell Figgis lost his whiskers.

Now, Darrell's lovely whiskers had not been trimmed for years,
They brought along big scissors and a pair of garden shears,
And the job was such a tough one that the barber was in tears.
The night Darrell Figgis lost his whiskers,

But the loss of Darrell's whiskers wont make us sad or sore,
They'll grow again, and blow again as in the days of yore,
Sure the Treaty and the Free State was made safe for evermore,
The night that Darrell Figgis lost his whiskers.

Strictly Copyright] [A. J. B., Dublin.

Figs 6 and 7 (left) Humorous ballad celebrating 'The Night Darrell Figgis Lost His Whiskers'. (right) Portrait of Figgis in his cell in Reading Gaol, 1916, by Tom Lalor. Figgis was interned in May 1916 in the aftermath of the Easter Rising, though he had taken no part in the event. He was released in December 1916. A writer, intellectual and colourful activist in the independence movement, Figgis (1882–1925) was well known for his dapper appearance and bright red beard. He had been championed by Arthur Griffith, who valued his intelligence and writing skills, and became one of Sinn Féin's two honorary secretaries in October 1917. Figgis was later secretary of the First Dáil's Commission of Inquiry into Resources and Industries (1919–21). He was a vocal supporter of the Anglo-Irish Treaty and was deputy chairman (but de facto chair) of the committee that drafted the Free State constitution. His opposition to the Collins/de Valera pact before the June 1922 general election and championing of non-Sinn Féin candidates led to his expulsion from the party. On 12 June, four days before the election, three anti-Treaty IRA men, including future Fianna Fáil TD Bob Briscoe, forced their way into the Figgis household and brutally shaved off the famous beard. Briscoe later recalled it as 'a bit of fun'. Figgis had been making 'very detrimental remarks about the IRA' and 'annoyed us with his waspish stings'. According to the attacker, their victim 'squealed like a pig [...] I think he would have been happier had we just cut his throat'. Figgis was a divisive figure and was particularly disliked by Michael Collins. The latter's fiancée, Kitty Kiernan, wrote to him in the aftermath saying she could imagine him 'laughing and enjoying it very much', but noting it was 'a mean thing' to do. Public sympathy helped Figgis to top the poll in Dublin County in the ensuing election, when he stood as an independent, and he was re-elected with a much smaller vote in 1923. He was embroiled in corruption allegations in 1924, the year his estranged wife Millie, who had reportedly not recovered from the trauma of the attack, died by suicide. Figgis had been in a public relationship with a young dance teacher, Rita North, who died of septicaemia following a botched abortion in London in 1925. Figgis died by suicide two days later. [Image: National Library of Ireland: PD FIGG-DA (1) I / Document: OLS Samuels, box 5 no. 87, The Board of Trinity College Dublin / See Robert Briscoe, *For the Life of Me* (Boston, 1958), pp. 158–9; Liam Collins, 'The Short and Tragic Life of an Irish Dandy', *Irish Independent*, 19 February 2012, https://www.independent.ie/life/the-short-and-tragic-life-of-an-irish-dandy/26823069.html; John Crowley et al. (eds), *Atlas of the Irish Revolution* (Cork, 2017), p. 343]

'Tis many a year since he went away
And over the roads the vans
Wheel gaily to horse and cattle fairs
With the O'Briens and the Coffey clans.

The tinker's son should be back again
With the roads and the life he knew,
But I put a bullet through his brain
In nineteen-twenty-two.[9]

Another very fine account of the Civil War, written from the viewpoint of a participant on the anti-Treaty side, but without the vitriol of many of the songs, is Charlie Gilmore's 'The Leggings and the Bandoliers', which beautifully describes the life of fighters, 'on the run', travelling through County Wicklow:

Strange singing reached my straining ears
As the late firelight, flickering, shone
On leggings and on bandoliers ...
And in the morning they were gone.[10]

Both sides did produce laments for fallen leaders. Michael Collins's death was marked in song by Donagh MacDonagh, Padraic Colum and Brendan Behan, along with the anonymous street ballad 'Mournful Lines on the Death of General Michael Collins'.[11] Cathal Brugha was similarly remembered in an anonymous and eponymous street ballad, and the 1916-era 'The Foggy Dew' was adapted to memorialise his death. The line in the original that read 'Oh, had we died by Pearse's side, or fought with Valera too' evolved to 'or fought with Cathal Brugha'.

Locally composed political ballads remained in circulation for

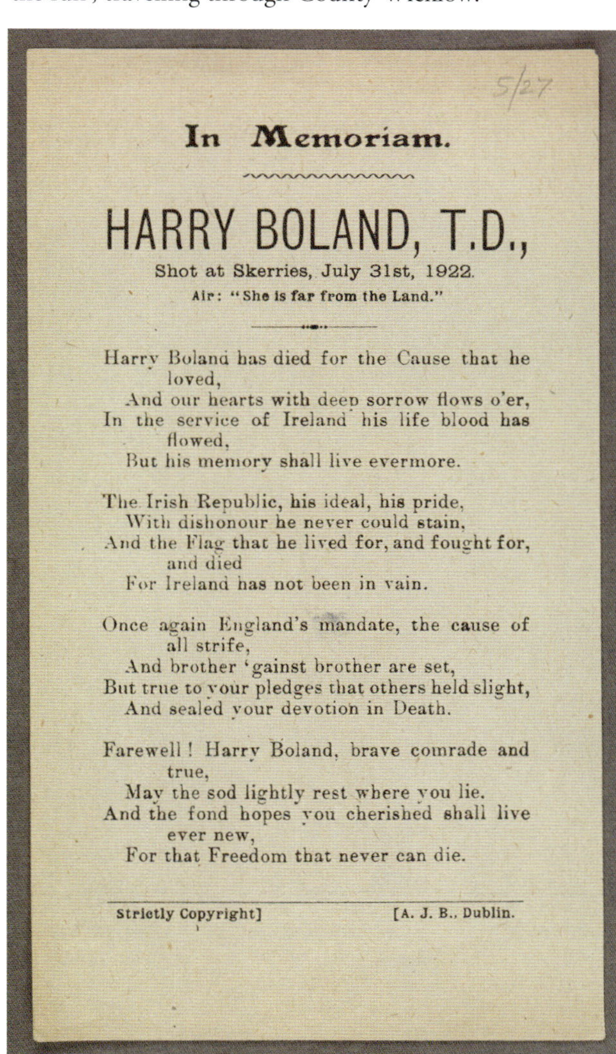

5/27

In Memoriam.

HARRY BOLAND, T.D.,

Shot at Skerries, July 31st, 1922.

Air: "She is far from the Land."

Harry Boland has died for the Cause that he loved,
And our hearts with deep sorrow flows o'er,
In the service of Ireland his life blood has flowed,
But his memory shall live evermore.

The Irish Republic, his ideal, his pride,
With dishonour he never could stain,
And the Flag that he lived for, and fought for, and died
For Ireland has not been in vain.

Once again England's mandate, the cause of all strife,
And brother 'gainst brother are set,
But true to your pledges that others held slight,
And sealed your devotion in Death.

Farewell! Harry Boland, brave comrade and true,
May the sod lightly rest where you lie.
And the fond hopes you cherished shall live ever new,
For that Freedom that never can die.

Strictly Copyright] [A. J. B., Dublin.

Fig. 8 (above left) Song sheet, 'In memoriam: Harry Boland, T.D.' This anonymously authored panegyric marked the death of anti-Treaty TD and prominent Civil War victim Harry Boland. Boland was mortally wounded by National Army soldiers as they tried to arrest him at the Grand Hotel in Skerries, County Dublin on 31 July 1922. He died the following day.

Fig. 9 (above right) Constance Markievicz cartoon depicting 'midnight assassin[s]' of the National Army, who took 'another leaf from the Black-and-Tan book' in the killing of Boland. Republicans depicted the killing of Boland as deliberate (it was asserted by some that he was targeted because he was attempting to broker an end to the conflict with his former close friend Michael Collins), while the Free State authorities claimed the death was the result of Boland resisting arrest. [Document: OLS Samuels, box, 5 no. 27, The Board of Trinity College Dublin/ Image: National Library of Ireland, PD 3076 TX 11(B) / See David Fitzpatrick, *Harry Boland's Irish Revolution* (Cork, 2003)]

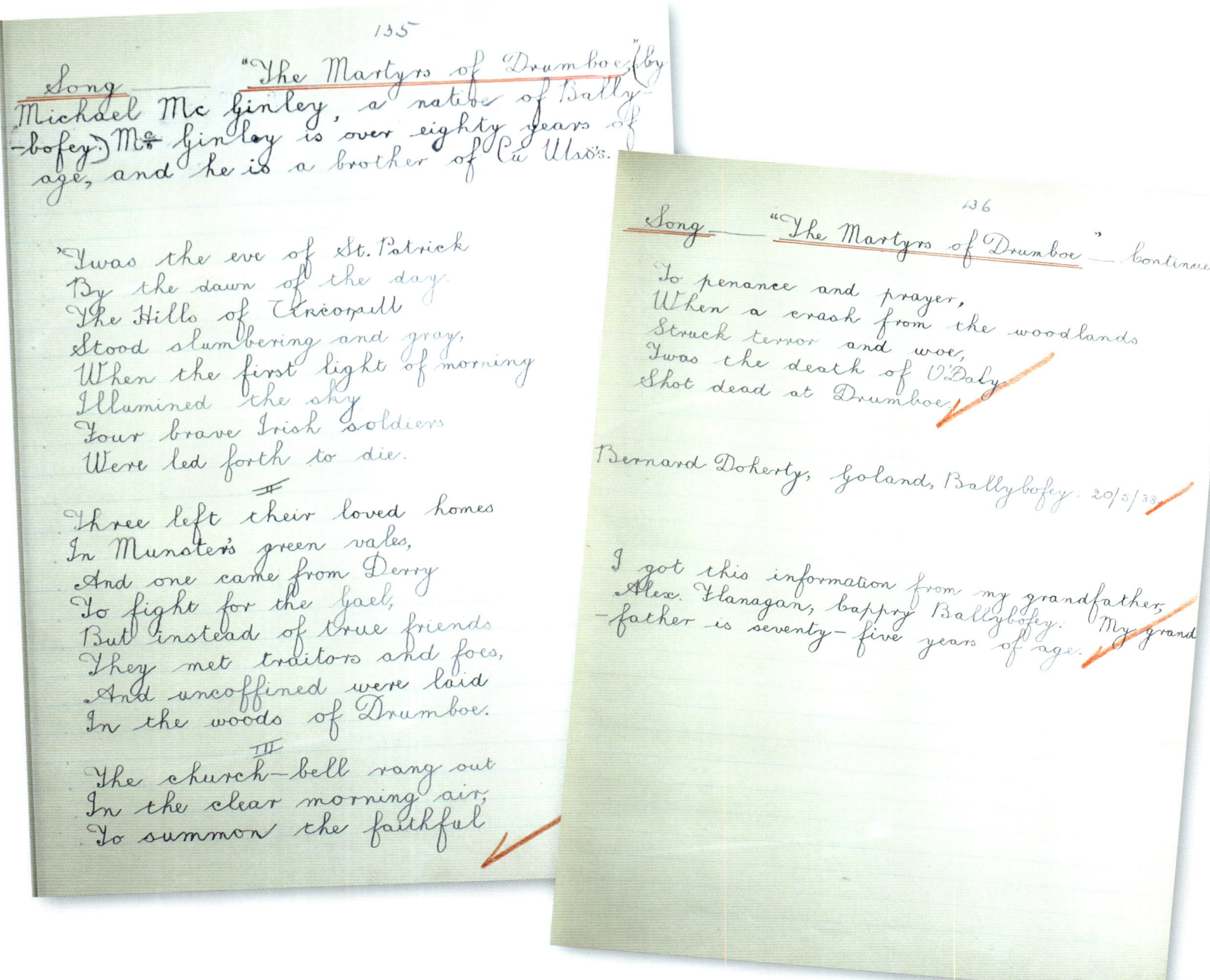

135

Song — "The Martyrs of Drumboe" (by Michael Mc Ginley, a native of Bally-bofey.) Mc Ginley is over eighty years of age, and he is a brother of Cú Uladh's.

'Twas the eve of St. Patrick
By the dawn of the day.
The Hills of Tirconaill
Stood slumbering and gray,
When the first light of morning
Illumined the sky
Four brave Irish soldiers
Were led forth to die.

II

Three left their loved homes
In Munster's green vales,
And one came from Derry
To fight for the Gael,
But instead of true friends
They met traitors and foes,
And uncoffined were laid
In the woods of Drumboe.

III

The church-bell rang out
In the clear morning air,
To summon the faithful

136

Song — "The Martyrs of Drumboe" — continued

To penance and prayer,
When a crash from the woodlands
Struck terror and woe,
'Twas the death of O'Daly
Shot dead at Drumboe.

Bernard Doherty, Goland, Ballybofey. 20/5/38

I got this information from my grandfather Alex. Flanagan, Cappry, Ballybofey. My grand-father is seventy-five years of age.

Fig. 10 The lyrics of the first four verses of the Civil War ballad 'The Martyrs of Drumboe', relayed to Bernard Doherty of Goland, County Donegal by his grandfather Alex Flanagan, aged seventy-five, and transcribed as part of the Irish Folklore Commission's (IFC) Schools Scheme of 1937–39. This valuable archive of oral tradition, generally referred to as Bailiúchán na Scol or the Schools' Collection, was sourced and documented by national school children across the state in an IFC joint initiative with the Department of Education and the Irish National Teachers' Organisation. The ballad was written by Michael (Mick) McGinley (1852–1940) on 14 March 1923 in response to the executions that morning at Drumboe Castle in Donegal of Charlie Daly, Daniel Enright and Tim O'Sullivan from Kerry and Seán Enright from Derry in a reprisal for the killing of a National Army officer. McGinley was from near Glenswilly, County Donegal (he later lived in Ballybofey, but was not 'a native', as suggested by young Bernard). The ballad is also known as 'The Drumboe Martyrs', 'The Woods of Drumboe' and 'Remember Drumboe'. The final verse, not included in this transcription, as remembered by McGinley's daughter Nora Harkin (a significant figure in Irish socialist republican circles from the early 1930s until her death in 2012), runs: 'Let Tír Conaill no more boast of honour or fame / All the waters in the Finn cannot wash out our shame / While the Finn and the Swilly continue to flow / The stain will remain on the name of Drumboe'. Cú Uladh (Peadar Toner Mac Fhionnlaoich (McGinley)), who, as Bernard points out, was Michael's brother, was a noted Irish-language writer and president of the Gaelic League (1922–5 and 1933–40). As well as serving a commemorative function, ballads like 'The Martyrs of Drumboe' played an important role in sustaining and shaping what Guy Beiner describes as the multi-authored 'social memory' of the Irish Civil War. [Images: The National Folklore Collection, UCD / Sources: Turlough O'Riordan, 'Harkin, Nora', *Dictionary of Irish Biography*, https://www.dib.ie/biography/harkin-nora-a9992 - accessed 2 May 2024; Vincent Morley, 'Mac Fhionnlaoich, Peadar Toner', *Dictionary of Irish Biography*, https://www.dib.ie/biography/macfhionnlaoich-peadar-tonermcginleypeter-toner-cu-uladh-a5671 – accessed 2 May 2024; transcription of 'Remember Drumboe' and accompanying note by Nora Harkin, 2000, courtesy of Mary Ahern; Guy Beiner, *Forgetful Remembrance: Social forgetting and vernacular historiography of a rebellion in Ulster* (Oxford, 2018)] generations after the Civil War, and sustained a bitter political partisanship. The song 'The Hills of Sweet Mayo' is typical of the form and is notable for the rare inclusion of an anti-socialist phrase.

> Forget about your Bolshie boy and come along with me,
> We'll both go off together and 'tis happy we will be.
> For what's the use of mourning now for one who's lying low
> With death's cold dew upon his brow on the hills of
> sweet Mayo.
> My own love was a rebel bold, he loved sweet liberty.
> He fought in 1916 to set old Ireland free.
> He fought for Ireland's freedom and never feared the foe,
> But 'twas Free State guns that shot my love on the Hills
> of Sweet Mayo.
> (Anon, 'The Hills of Sweet Mayo')

Other locally composed songs recalled actual events during the hostilities, and fortified attitudes and allegiances in those areas in the wake of the Civil War.

> Four Republican soldiers
> Were dragged from their cells
> Where for months they had suffered
> Wild torments like hell's.
> No mercy was asked
> From their pitiless foe
> And no mercy was shown
> By the thugs at Drumboe.
> (Michael McGinley, 'The Drumboe Martyrs')

Ballads are now considered important sites of memory in their own right that reveal a great deal about the emotional response to events on the ground. The ballad or 'narrative song', as poet Brendan Kennelly referred to it, captures as no other cultural form the relationship between people and place and the immediacy of events that unfolded during a period as tragic as the Civil War.

Fig. 11 Page from the original published version of 'The Foggy Dew'. One of the most famous ballads celebrating the 1916 Rising, 'The Foggy Dew' was written in 1919 by Fr Charles O'Neill. An updated version from the Civil War era replaces de Valera with the most prominent early victim of the conflict, Cathal Brugha – 'Oh, had they died by Pearse's side/ or fought with Cathal Brugha'. [Document: The Irish Traditional Music Archive]

Constructing Identity in the Fledgling State

John Crowley

With the handover of control of the postal system to the Provisional Government at the end of March 1922, the newly appointed postmaster general, J.J. Walsh, lost little time in responding to the challenge of designing stamps that would reflect the cultural identity of the newly founded state. An open competition was organised, and a small number of stamps selected from the competing designs. The first stamp issued by the state priced at 2*d* was designed by James Ingram from Glasnevin in Dublin and controversially featured a borderless map of Ireland (Fig 3). It was released on 6 December 1922. The winning 3*d* stamp, released in March of the following year, was designed by another artist, Lily Williams, and based on the twelfth-century Cross of Cong. It was similar to an earlier design by the same artist issued in 1908 (and in 1916 as in the version used here, Fig. 4) both as a fund-raiser for Arthur Griffith's newly founded Sinn Féin party and as a form of protest against the British administration in Ireland. Griffith made clear the objective of the stamp: 'The Sinn Féin stamp is intended to be affixed to all correspondence of Sinn Féiners as a visible sign that this is Ireland. We recommend it to be placed on the envelope in the opposite corner to that of the revenue (British) stamp. The revenue will carry the correspondence, the Sinn Féin stamp added will spread Sinn Féin propaganda and will help to bring about the one thing Sinn Féin needs to make it win the land from end to end – a daily paper'.* The Hibernia stamp was also issued by Sinn Féin in 1908 (Fig. 5). Griffith was a regular guest at the Williams sisters' literary gatherings at their home in Marlborough Road in Donnybrook, Dublin, and shared Lily's passion for the Irish language and culture. A member of the Five Provinces Gaelic League branch (Craobh na gCúig gCúigí) in Dublin, Williams was a strong advocate of Sinn Féin; however, her separatist beliefs brought her into conflict with her Presbyterian father, who strongly

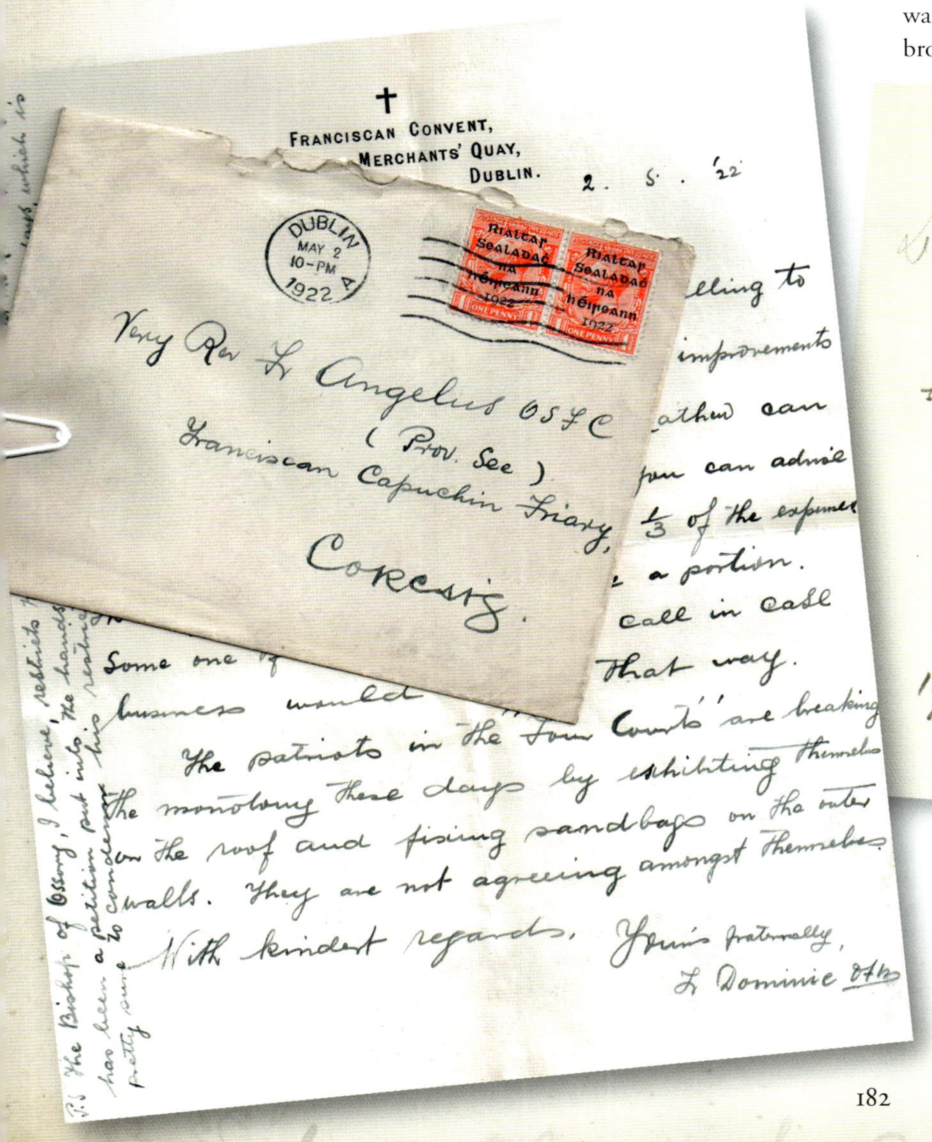

FRANCISCAN CONVENT,
MERCHANTS' QUAY,
DUBLIN. 2. 5. '22

DUBLIN MAY 2 10-PM 1922

Very Rev Fr Angelus OSFC
(Prov. Sec)
Franciscan Capuchin Friary,
Cork

... improvements ... you can advise ... 1/3 of the expense ... a portion. ... call in case ... that way.

The patriots in the Four Courts are breaking the monotony these days by exhibiting themselves on the roof and fixing sandbags on the outer walls. They are not agreeing amongst themselves.

With kindest regards, Yours fraternally,
Fr Dominic OFM Cap

Enclosed is the inscription. It is for a 6d stamp
Excuse the pencil I am in great haste.
Yours
Arthur Griffith

11/3/22

Fig. 1 (left) A letter from Fr Dominic to Fr Angelus Healy OFM Cap. referring to the occupation of the Four Courts in early May 1922, and the covering envelope with a set of British stamps overprinted with 'Rialtas Sealadach na hÉireann 1922'. [Image: courtesy of the Irish Capuchin Archives] **Fig. 2** (right) A note from Arthur Griffith to Lily Williams, 11 March 1922. [Document: National Library of Ireland, MS 5,943/16]

(left to right)
Figs 3, 4 and 5.

supported the union. It is unsurprising, given Griffith's long-term friendship with Williams, that the stamps chosen to represent the fledging Free State would form part of their correspondence (Fig. 2) or, indeed, that a portrait of Griffith would be part of Williams's own artistic output (see p. 28). While the overprinting of British stamps was a quick response by the Provisional Government, it was supplemented by the painting green of imperial red post boxes that displayed the insignia (royal cypher) of the then reigning British monarch George V (1910–36) as well as previous monarchs Queen Victoria (1837–1901) and Edward VII (1901–10). The post box with the Queen Victoria cypher (Fig. 7) is located near Bandon, County Cork, while that displaying the Edward VII cypher is from Bridge Street in Skibbereen, County Cork (Fig. 8). [Stamps, L12a (1916) and L13a (1908), reproduced from the original held by the Department of Special Collections of the Hesburgh Libraries of the University of Notre Dame; An Post Museum and Archive / See also Hilary Pyle, 'Comrades and Friends', *Irish Arts Review*, 2013, vol. 30, no. 2, pp. 114–17; *Griffith quote cited in Sinn Féin propaganda labels 1908–16 - https://rarebooks.nd.edu/digital/stamps/irish/set4L/set4L.html]

Fig. 6 (below right) Pillar box on College Road, Cork city bearing the royal cypher of British monarch George V (1910–36). Just as the stamps carrying the standard head profile of George V were rapidly overprinted with the words Rialtas Sealadach na hÉireann (Provisional Government of Ireland), the newly installed government similarly moved with great alacrity in painting green the existing imperial red post boxes. It was in keeping with a government eager to assert the independence of the fledging state by relegating in the first instance and then removing where possible the symbols of the previous British administration. **Fig. 7** (below centre) **Fig. 8** (below left) [Images: John Crowley]

CASE STUDY

Parliamentary Politics and the Experience of Dáil Éireann during the Irish Civil War

Gary Murphy

Civil wars often revolve around the government's legitimacy to represent the state. Questions about who really speaks for the people and whether governments have the authority to make what their opponents consider to be manifestly wrong decisions become central to the conflict. When a civil war does break out, government opponents generally consider establishing a rival parliament to speak for the 'real' people. On the governing side, maintaining a functioning parliament is often crucial to give the impression both to national and international audiences that, notwithstanding war, the government is able to administer the state and represent its people.

Speaking for the people

All of these issues underpinned the Irish Civil War between June 1922 and May 1923. Not unique to early-twentieth-century Ireland, such matters were also germane to two other conflicts that took place among English-speaking peoples in the mid-1600s and the mid-1800s. The English and American civil wars, waged in much larger geographical territories and with more extensive human involvement, also revolved around the question of who really spoke for the people.

The English Civil War (1642–51) was primarily a series of bloody disputes between supporters of the crown and parliament about how England, Scotland and Ireland should be governed. The bitter American Civil War (1861–5) between supporters of the Union and the Confederacy was caused by the threat to the Union when the southern states seceded. In essence, the war was fought by the northern states to ensure the southern states remained in the Union. The question of the government's authority to act in the name of the state was fundamental to the outbreak of war. Southern politicians claimed northerners had no right to speak for them or their cause, which, in this case, was essentially slavery thinly disguised as states' rights. In England, both Roundheads and Cavaliers, representing parliament and crown respectively, claimed to be the true representatives of the people. While the causes of the English and American civil wars were many, an overriding feature of both was determining who truly represented the common people: Did the crown or parliament in England, and Congress or the president in the United States, have the moral authority to make important decisions on the country's future when society was divided over grave questions of national importance? In England the issues were religion and the conflicting power of the king and parliament. In the United States it was the spread of slavery and the conflicting power of the federal government and individual states.[1] When war broke out in both countries, all sides tried to persuade

Fig. 1 (opposite) Portrait of William Thomas Cosgrave (1880–1965), oil on canvas, by Sir John Lavery (1923). W.T. Cosgrave was the first president of the Executive Council, forerunner of the office of the Taoiseach, and a long-serving TD initially representing Kilkenny North, subsequently Carlow-Kilkenny and later Cork Borough. Born in Dublin in June 1880, he was the son of Thomas and Bridget Cosgrave. The family owned a small pub in one of the city's poorer areas, and Cosgrave left school at sixteen to work in the business. Having attended the first meeting of Sinn Féin, he was elected to Dublin Corporation as a Sinn Féin councillor in 1908, thus beginning his political journey. The conditions he witnessed in Dublin's inner-city influenced his early career, when he marked himself out as a reforming politician, particularly in the area of housing. He was also an effective minister in the revolutionary Dáil, later supporting the 1921 Treaty. Following the deaths of Arthur Griffith and Michael Collins in August 1922, leadership of the pro-Treaty organisation, subsequently Cumann na nGaedheal, and of the Free State fell to him. Though Cosgrave's leadership was in the chairman, rather than chief, mould, Cumann na nGaedheal was commonly referred to as 'the Cosgrave party' by the late 1920s. When the Free State came into formal existence in the midst of civil war on 6 December 1922, he expressed pride in being the 'first man called to preside over the first government'. But his speech at that first meeting was used primarily to criticise the 'mad efforts' of those who challenged the new state's legitimacy. Cosgrave's government embraced the practical task of state building and the statute books in the initial years of independence document a flurry of activity. Though some structures, including the civil service, were retained from British rule, there was much to be decided about how the new state would function. Alongside such practicalities, Cosgrave's government undertook an image-building campaign designed to demonstrate to the international community that the Irish were capable of self-government. Later in life, Ernest Blythe, minister for finance in Cosgrave's government, suggested that Cumann na nGaedheal's greatest achievement was 'getting things going'. By the 1932 general election, however, the government appeared jaded and lacking in fresh ideas as it continued to reference the 1921 Treaty. Cumann na nGaedheal moved to the opposition benches, later becoming part of Fine Gael, a new party intended to rival Fianna Fáil. Eoin O'Duffy, rather than Cosgrave, was chosen as the first president, but O'Duffy, a controversial figure, was soon manoeuvred out of the position. Cosgrave returned to the helm and stayed there until his retirement in 1944. He briefly shared the opposition benches with his son Liam, who was elected in 1943. Liam would go on to become Taoiseach in 1973. While political dynasties have characterised Irish politics, they are the only father and son to have held the office. [Text: Ciara Meehan / Painting: Collection & image © Hugh Lane Gallery]

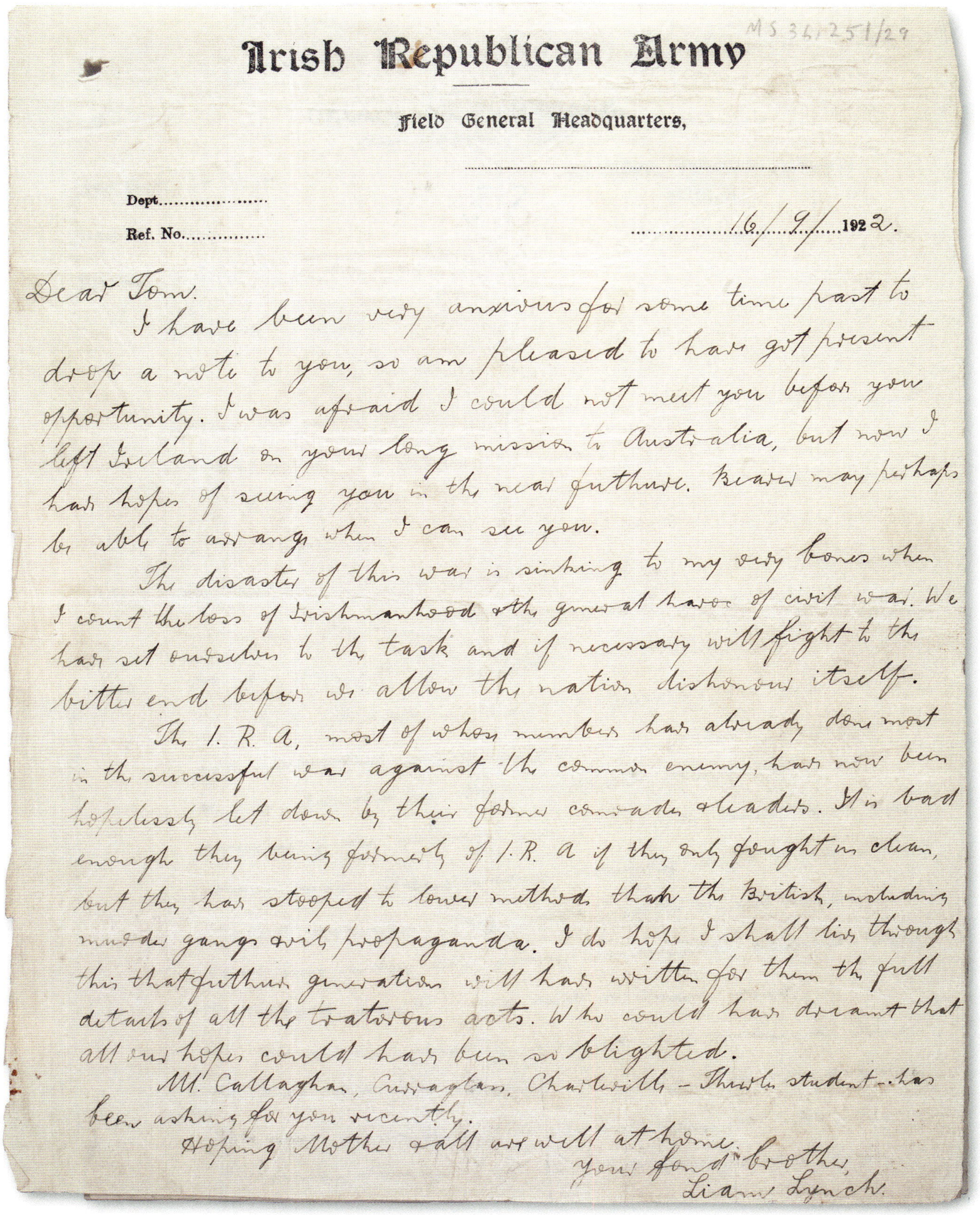

Irish Republican Army

Field General Headquarters,

Dept.

Ref. No.

16/9/1922.

Dear Tom.

I have been very anxious for some time past to drop a note to you, so am pleased to have got present opportunity. I was afraid I could not meet you before you left Ireland on your long mission to Australia, but now I have hopes of seeing you in the near futhure. Beaver may perhaps be able to arrange when I can see you.

The disaster of this war is sinking to my very bones when I count the loss of Irishmanhood & the general havoc of civil war. We have set ourselves to the task and if necessary will fight to the bitter end before we allow the nation dishonour itself.

The I.R.A, most of whose members have already done most in the successful war against the common enemy, have now been hopelessly let down by their former comrades & leaders. It is bad enough they being formerly of I.R.A if they only fought us clean, but they have stooped to lower methods than the British, including murder gangs & vile propaganda. I do hope I shall live through this that futher generations will have written for them the full details of all the traitorous acts. Who could have dreamt that all our hopes could have been so blighted.

Mr. Callaghan, Curraglass, Charleville – Thurles student – has been asking for you recently.

Hoping Mother & all are well at home.

Your fond brother,

Liam Lynch.

Fig. 2 A letter written by Liam Lynch to his brother Tom on 16 September 1922, about the republican commitment to 'fight to the bitter end' for the honour of the nation, despite the disastrous 'loss of Irish manhood' and the 'general havoc of civil war'. [Document: National Library of Ireland, Liam Lynch Papers, 1915–1940, MS 36,251/29] domestic audiences and international opinion that theirs was the righteous and just cause. Ireland in June 1922 was no different.

Legitimising their position

Questions of sovereignty, identity, legitimacy, righteous cause, the authority to make decisions, the mandate to speak for the people, protecting civil society, and gaining the respect of the international community were all central to the Irish Civil War. After the outbreak of war, the battle lines of legitimacy were drawn around parliamentary politics. For pro-Treatyites, it was essential that the Third Dáil, elected on 16 June 1922, would sit and conduct its business like a normal parliament. As far as they were concerned, the Second Dáil had ceased to be a representative body the moment the election result was declared. Conversely, anti-Treaty TDs believed that the undissolved Second Dáil and the IRA executive were the only bodies able to bring about peace.[2] Indeed, fundamental to the IRA position, as articulated by its leader, Liam Lynch, was the idea that peace could only be achieved on the basis of recognising the republic established by the Second Dáil.[3]

The pro-Treatyites intended that the Third Dáil would meet on 30 June, a fortnight after the election, but the Provisional Government's decision to shell the Four Courts on 28 June rendered this impossible. The election results had been issued four days earlier and this was quickly followed by David Lloyd George's ultimatum that continued tolerance of those who had occupied the Four Courts in mid-April would formally violate the Anglo-Irish Treaty and leave the British free to resume military action in Ireland. This was a risk the Provisional Government was not willing to take. The chaos of the first two months of the Civil War resulted in no fewer than four postponements of the first sitting of the new Dáil. It was not until 9 September 1922 that it was eventually convened in Leinster House.

The anti-Treatyite TDs, with the exception of Laurence Ginnell of Westmeath, decided they would not recognise the Third Dáil and boycotted its opening. Éamon de Valera wanted at least one anti-Treaty TD in the Dáil on its first day for publicity purposes and persuaded Ginnell to attend. He repeatedly questioned the assembly's constitutional status, and was forcibly expelled from the chamber after demanding to know whether the parliament was a real Dáil Éireann or a partitionist assembly.[4] Anti-Treatyite fealty to the Second Dáil was as important to legitimising their position as convening the Third Dáil was to the pro-Treatyites. Ginnell, and by extension de Valera, was keen to publicise this on the opening of the new, and in their eyes, illegitimate Dáil.

The first act of the Dáil was to formally elect a new provisional government, whose members immediately signed acceptance of the Treaty, as was mandated by its terms. It also appointed W.T. Cosgrave as president of Dáil Éireann. Now installed, the pro-Treaty government considered the Dáil not just a symbol of legitimacy and sovereignty but as the protector of the Irish people and of civil society. As Cosgrave told the Dáil three days after it was convened, the military actions taken by his government since June were not merely about the security of parliament but 'a formula for the security of the people, of the security of their lives, and the value of the money in the country'.[5] It took that position seriously and, in late September, passed a Special Powers Resolution giving itself the power to impose the death penalty for a variety of offences including the possession of firearms. The resolution was accompanied by an offer of amnesty for those who laid down their arms. Not surprisingly, this was rejected by the anti-Treatyites.

From September 1922 until its dissolution on 9 August 1923, three months after the end of the Civil War, the Third Dáil attempted to run itself as a national legislature with legislation being proposed, debated and then voted on. The Free State government was supported by pro-Treaty Sinn Féin (reformed as Cumann na nGaedheal in April 1923) in parliament, as well as by the Farmers' Party and a number of independents. In the absence of anti-Treaty deputies, the Labour Party assumed the role of responsible opposition. This was a crucial point. Even in times of civil war, governments need an opposition so that they are not portrayed as dictators. As Michael Hayes, Ceann Comhairle in 1922, noted, the seventeen Labour TDs did their best to temper the severities that often accompany civil war and certainly helped maintain parliamentary government in a fledgling state that was trying to find its way in the middle of a war where its very legitimacy was at stake.[6] The minister for defence, Richard Mulcahy, who had succeeded Michael Collins as commander-in-chief of the National Army, attended in uniform, emphasising the government's position that, even during war, parliament was acting on behalf of the people.

Within a week of its opening, the Third Dáil began debating whether to adopt a new constitution for the Irish Free State. The Labour Party leader, Thomas Johnson, questioned the wisdom of ratifying a constitution at all in the middle of raging civil war and suggested that the new state would be better off following Britain in allowing a constitution to develop by custom and usage. But for the government a new country needed a new constitution, and it could not simply wait for an end to war to move ahead. Moreover, there was no clear idea of how and when the war would end and the attitude of the anti-Treatyites to the Dáil when that eventually happened. Within six weeks of its first meeting, the Third Dáil approved the new constitution of the Irish Free State on 25 October 1922, which defined the Oireachtas as comprising the Dáil, the Seanad and the king. From 6 December 1922 it was constituted as Dáil Éireann of the Oireachtas of the Irish Free State.[7]

One of the most controversial actions of the Third Dáil's first month was the passage through the Dáil on 27 September 1922 of emergency legislation known as the Public Safety Bill. On the signature of just two army officers it allowed military courts to impose the death sentence or penal servitude for anyone found guilty of an armed revolt against the government of Saorstát Éireann or certain associated offences. Eighty-one anti-Treaty republicans would be executed as a result of this legislation during the course of the Civil War. It was ultimately succeeded by the Public Safety (Emergency Powers) Act of 1923. In the Dáil Cosgrave declared that the bill intended to show that 'there is a Government prepared to

Fig. 3 Kevin O'Higgins (1892–1927) (left) addressing the Civic Guard at the Phoenix Park Depot, 20 February 1923. 'Theirs was a great mission', the minister of home affairs, Kevin O'Higgins, told the reorganised ranks of the Free State's unarmed police force. They were the 'servants of a democratic, representative government', 'a foundation stone' of 'ordered society'. Described as the 'strong man' of the Free State Executive and known for his hard-headed pragmatism, O'Higgins had little sympathy for anti-Treaty rhetoric that drew on the idealised, abstract republic. 'We would do well', he had asserted during the Treaty debates in December 1921, 'to scrutinise the document not so much in relation to the inscription on our battle standards but rather in relation to our prospects of achieving more'. After re-election in June 1922, O'Higgins's unwavering commitment was to the Irish Free State, which he saw as now mandated by the Irish electorate, the enforcement of constitutional government and, as he told his constituents in June, to 'evolution rather than revolution' to attain our 'political aspirations'. The son of a county coroner who grew up on a sixty-eight-acre farm in Stradbally, County Laois, O'Higgins abandoned an early vocation for the priesthood in favour of a degree in legal and political science in University College Dublin. He joined the Irish Volunteers in 1915 and served five months in prison for anti-recruitment activity in 1918. On his release he took his seat in the First Dáil as Sinn Féin TD for Queen's County (Laois). Decisive, articulate and shrewd, O'Higgins rapidly ascended the ranks of Sinn Féin after 1919 and was appointed minister for economic affairs in Michael Collins's Provisional Government, 'standing', as he wrote, 'amidst the ruins of one administration with the foundations of another not yet laid, and with wild men screaming through the keyhole'. He deployed his skilled polemical pen against those 'wild men' in a series of articles for the *Free State* in the spring of 1922, which he collected for reissue in pamphlet form in January 1923, with an introduction asserting the primacy of the democratic principle (Fig. 4). O'Higgins's biography testifies to complex and divided loyalties among families and communities in revolutionary Ireland. Two of his brothers joined the British army during the First World War and, in December 1922, he was among the Cabinet members that sanctioned the extrajudicial execution of his friend, Rory O'Connor, in reprisal for the IRA assassination of Deputy Seán Hales. Less than a year earlier, O'Connor had delivered the best-man speech at O'Higgins's wedding to Brigid Mary Cole. The 'stern and drastic measure', defended by O'Higgins in the Dáil as 'necessary' if 'the nation [was] to live', is tied inextricably to his legacy, often subsuming his post-Civil War achievements on the domestic and international stages, in consolidating democracy and pushing the boundaries of Ireland's dominion status. Presiding as minister for home affairs over the execution of political prisoners during the Civil War meant that he was reviled by republicans. His father Thomas was killed by the IRA during a raid on his family home in February 1923 and, on 10 July 1927, thirty-five-year-old O'Higgins was fatally wounded by IRA gunmen on his way to Mass in Booterstown. His assassination, as Anne Dolan observes, 'brought back 1923, because in many ways his death was an act of civil war'. [Image: RTÉ Cashman Collection, 0509/069 © RTÉ Archives / See *Irish Independent*, 21 February 1923; *Free State,* 15 April 1922; *Dáil Debates*, vol. 3, 19 December 1921; Anne Dolan, *Commemorating the Irish Civil War: History and memory, 1923–2000* (Cambridge, 2003), p. 33]

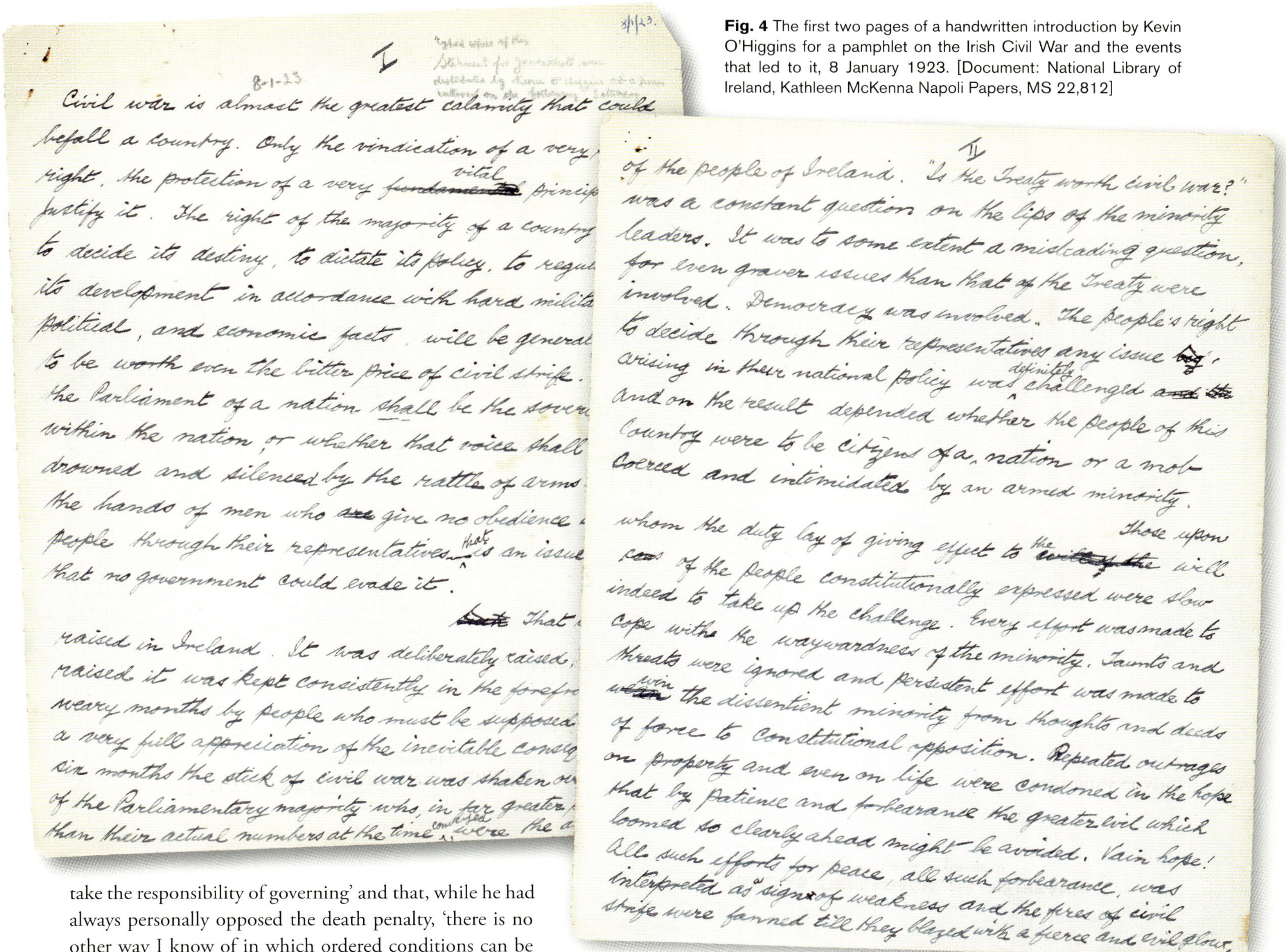
I

8-1-23

8/1/23.

Civil war is almost the greatest calamity that could befall a country. Only the vindication of a very right, the protection of a very ~~fundamental~~ vital principle justify it. The right of the majority of a country to decide its destiny, to dictate its policy, to regu its development in accordance with hard milita political, and economic facts, will be general to be ~~worth~~ even the bitter price of civil strife. the Parliament of a nation shall be the sover within the nation, or whether that voice shall drowned and silenced by the rattle of arms the hands of men who ~~are~~ give no obedience people through their representatives, that is an issue that no government could evade it.

~~Such~~ That raised in Ireland. It was deliberately raised, raised it was kept consistently in the forefro weary months by people who must be supposed a very full appreciation of the inevitable conseq six months the stick of civil war was shaken ov of the Parliamentary majority who, in far greater than their actual numbers at the time combined were the a

IV

of the people of Ireland. "Is the Treaty worth civil war?" was a constant question on the lips of the minority leaders. It was to some extent a misleading question, for even graver issues than that of the Treaty were involved. Democracy was involved. The people's right to decide through their representatives any issue ~~big~~ arising in their national policy was definitely challenged ~~and the~~ and on the result depended whether the people of this Country were to be citizens of a nation or a mob coerced and intimidated by an armed minority.

Those upon whom the duty lay of giving effect to the ~~will of the~~ will of the people constitutionally expressed were slow indeed to take up the challenge. Every effort was made to cope with the waywardness of the minority. Taunts and threats were ignored and persistent effort was made to win the dissentient minority from thoughts and deeds of force to constitutional opposition. Repeated outrages on property and even on life were condoned in the hope that by patience and forbearance the greater evil which loomed so clearly ahead might be avoided. Vain hope! All such efforts for peace, all such forbearance, was interpreted as a sign of weakness and the fires of civil strife were fanned till they blazed with a fierce and evil glow.

Fig. 4 The first two pages of a handwritten introduction by Kevin O'Higgins for a pamphlet on the Irish Civil War and the events that led to it, 8 January 1923. [Document: National Library of Ireland, Kathleen McKenna Napoli Papers, MS 22,812]

take the responsibility of governing' and that, while he had always personally opposed the death penalty, 'there is no other way I know of in which ordered conditions can be restored in this country'.[8]

By the end of 1922 the Dáil had passed four acts, including a critical appropriations measure allowing the Department of Finance to issue funds to all government departments. Throughout 1923, while the intermittent violence of the Civil War continued, the Dáil got on with the business of debating and legislating. Over forty acts were passed before the dissolution of the Third Dáil two weeks before the general election of August 1923. These included acts relating to the censorship of film, army pensions, the enforcement of law, and the adoption of summer time, allowing for Ireland to be an hour ahead of west European time during a certain period of the year. The 1923 Land Act, one of the most important pieces of social legislation in the history of the state, was the final piece of legislation passed by the Third Dáil on its final day. It contributed to the ending of the widespread agrarian turmoil that had characterised the revolutionary period, by allowing the Irish Land Commission to confiscate estates from many landlords or subject them to compulsory-purchase orders, which in turn enabled tenants to buy their own farms.[9]

Opposing the Free State

While the Third Dáil tried to bring some sense of normal governance in the middle of a civil war, the anti-Treatyites not only refused to recognise the legislature but attempted to establish their own republican government in opposition to the Free State. De Valera urged the establishment of a de facto rival government, which the IRA executive approved on 17 October 1922, calling on him to form a presidential government that 'shall preserve inviolate the sacred trust of National Sovereignty and Independence'.[10] De Valera and the IRA viewed the Third Dáil as an illegal assembly because the Second Dáil, which they considered the legitimate parliament of Ireland, had not been officially dissolved. De Valera hoped to rally all anti-Treatyites to his republican government banner and establish a claim to the funds of the republic in the United States in order to purchase badly needed arms for the anti-Treaty cause.

Yet the charade of this emergency republican government was exposed when it failed the crucial legitimacy test. The anti-Treaty deputies had to meet in secret, which they did for the first time on 25 October, the same day the Third Dáil approved the Constitution of the Irish Free State Bill, and constituted themselves as a government. They wielded neither moral nor civil power, the IRA executive directed proceedings, and its minister for defence, Liam Mellows, was in prison and would be executed just six weeks later. (The other ministers were Robert Barton, Seán T. O'Kelly, P.J. Ruttledge and Austin Stack.) De Valera wrote to one of his correspondents that he did 'not care what Republican government is set up so long one as some one is', but his language exposed the pretence of this rival government in exile, which in reality did not exist.[11] His official biographers, Longford and O'Neill, protested that this was an emergency government established as a rival to

Fig. 5 Éamon de Valera's arrest by Free State troops as he addressed an election rally in Ennis on 15 August 1923 was a final humiliation during the most miserable time of his life, highlighting his precipitous fall from political power since the Treaty split. His position as undisputed leader of Irish nationalism had been destroyed in a matter of weeks. Having failed to have his way in the Treaty negotiations, he lost votes at Cabinet and then in the Dáil, leading to his resignation as president in January 1922. Between then and the outbreak of the Civil War, de Valera struggled to reassert his authority, sometimes with inflammatory language (though he always claimed his infamous 'wading through blood' speech was a warning rather than a threat). He did try to prevent the outbreak of civil war, but once fighting began, he signed on as a private in his old unit, the Third Battalion of the Dublin Brigade, convinced his political role was at an end. He was in 'the Block' on O'Connell Street in the opening days of the conflict, and later served as a staff officer in the south, but his role in the actual fighting was limited. His main value to the anti-Treaty side was as a symbol and a spokesman, though it was clear he was not in charge. While de Valera blew hot and cold on republican military prospects, his default position was pessimistic, much to the irritation of Liam Lynch, chief of staff of the anti-Treaty IRA, who dismissed his advice that the conflict should be brought to an early end. De Valera's view on tactics also changed from time to time, sometimes supporting, sometimes opposing Lynch's plans to assassinate pro-Treaty figures in retaliation for the execution of republican prisoners. The reality was that his views did not much matter. Despite this, in October 1922 Lynch agreed to the establishment of a republican 'government' with de Valera at its head. But the IRA executive maintained tight control; recognition depended on the new government sticking to the republican line, while the executive retained final say on any peace deal that might be reached with the Free State. Trust in politics, and in de Valera, remained in short supply. Everything changed when Lynch was killed in April 1923. Once IRA units were ordered to dump arms, de Valera moved quickly to reassert his position, having already laid the groundwork for a new, anti-Treaty Sinn Féin, which contested the August general election. After the Free State government said he would be 'kept on the run', de Valera vowed he would appear in his Clare constituency, 'and nothing but a bullet will stop me'. This is what brought him to Ennis on 15 August and, while not stopped by a bullet, he was imprisoned for almost a year following his arrest. But at least a political path was now coming into a view, with an end to his period of Civil War marginalisation, which had left him 'condemned to view the tragedy here for the last year as through a wall of glass, powerless to intervene effectively'. [Text: David McCullagh / Image: Part of the Independent Newspapers Ireland/NLI Collection, INDH554]

the Provisional Government at least in aspiration, though this was nothing more than post hoc validation for a position that was becoming increasingly hopeless.[12]

As the Civil War continued into the winter of 1922 and early 1923, de Valera became more isolated by Lynch and the republican military command. It was also becoming clear that the republicans, ostracised by the Church and abandoned by a war-weary people who had delivered a mandate to the functioning pro-Treaty parliament, could not win a guerrilla war. On the other hand, the Provisional Government had the support of an increasing amount of the common citizenry who wanted the war to end. The fact that Dáil Éireann was continuing to function was an important factor in that support.

Hope of a peaceful future

After nearly a decade of war and revolution culminating in a bitter and chaotic civil war, most people wanted to get on with normal life. Cosgrave's government, imperfect as it was, promised relative stability.[13] De Valera, who was arrested on an election platform in Ennis on 15 August 1923, spending eleven months in jail, quickly came to realise the importance of participating in parliamentary politics and of Dáil Éireann as the symbol of that politics. In August 1927, less than five years after he challenged the people's right to do wrong, and melodramatically declared that 'victory for the Republic or utter defeat and extermination are now the alternatives', de Valera led forty-four Fianna Fáil TDs into Dáil Éireann.[14] Just four and a half years later, he assumed power as head of a Fianna Fáil government. Democratic mandates are rarely considered by those who wage civil war, convinced as they are by their own righteous cause. Yet, in ultimately recognising Dáil Éireann, de Valera ensured that one of the legacies of the Civil War was acceptance of the primacy of democratic politics and the legitimacy of the state to act on behalf of its people through its parliament. As Michael Hayes pointed out, the Dáil was an institution and was able to overcome those who opposed it.[15] Most famously this included the man who would dominate it as leader of Fianna Fáil for over three decades.

CASE STUDY

The 1923 Land Act

Terence Dooley

On 24 July 1923, a month before the general election, Cumann na nGaedheal passed a Land Act to address the legacy of land questions inherited from the British administration, and also to put an end to the widespread agrarian agitation, fuelled by land hunger, that had come to characterise many parts of the country during the period 1917–23. Patrick Hogan, minister for agriculture, had heeded the mood of the farmer representatives at a land conference held the previous April, who had warned him that 'if the present government did not meet the wishes of the people' in passing legislation favourable to their interests, 'they would put in a government the next time who would'.[1]

Historically, the generous terms – to all sides – of the Wyndham Land Act of 1903 had certainly resulted in a dramatic transfer of land ownership; by the outbreak of the First World War up to 80 per cent of tenanted land had been transferred from landlords to tenant farmers. Historians long argued that this put an end to land questions in Ireland and, until quite recently, avoided any rigorous investigation of the agrarian dimension to the revolutionary period, contending, as summed up by Peter Hart, that 'not only did the Irish Revolution not bring social transformation, there was no socially revolutionary situation in Ireland even in prospect' because 'most farmers owned their farms by 1922'.[2]

Fig. 1 Patrick Hogan (1891–1936), minister for agriculture and architect of the 1923 Land Act. Known for his affability, acumen and sharp parliamentary style, 'Paddy' Hogan hailed from a middle-class Catholic farming family in Kilrickle, County Galway. He was a prize-winning student at University College Dublin, where he first met Kevin O'Higgins, and qualified as a solicitor in 1915 before returning to Galway to establish a practice and help to run the family farm. Unlike his younger brothers, James and Michael, who would forge influential careers in University College Cork and the National Army, he was not a member of the IRA. He did, however, serve time in Ballykinlar Camp during the War of Independence for assisting in the organisation of a Sinn Féin land court in Loughrea. In May 1921 Hogan, the recently elected vice-president of the Irish Farmers' Union, entered the Dáil as Sinn Féin TD for Galway. A 'practical nationalist', he supported the Treaty, and was appointed the Provisional Government's minister for agriculture in February 1922. A surge in agrarian agitation in late 1922, spurred by an agricultural recession and enduring land hunger and facilitated by inadequate local policing, seemed to herald what Hogan feared would be a terrible new 'Land War'. Like the minister for home affairs, Kevin O'Higgins, he attributed land-related disorder to diffuse 'irregularism' with 'a vested interest in chaos'. Hogan supported repressive measures against the agents of land-grabbing, cattle driving and rural property destruction as a prerequisite for his sweeping measure of land reform in 1923. In the post-Civil War Cumann na nGaedheal government, Hogan was committed to agricultural development, which, in a 1924 memo to Cabinet, he deemed 'synonymous with national development'. He introduced legislation to improve the quality and standards of produce and the image of Irish agriculture in export markets. His friend and leading Irish economist of the interwar years, George O'Brien, attributed Hogan's 'greatness' to his willingness to be 'unpopular', his 'imaginative realism, progressive conservatism and courageous consistence'. A key figure in the founding of Fine Gael in 1933, Hogan died prematurely in a motor accident three years later, leaving his wife Mena, erstwhile daughter-in-law of Land League founder Michael Davitt, a widow for a second time. [Image: National Library of Ireland, Kathleen McKenna-Napoli photographic collection, NPA MKN21 / Sources: Hogan to W.T. Cosgrave, 11 January 1923, Richard Mulcahy Papers, P7b/96 (2), UCDA; George O'Brien, 'Patrick Hogan: Minister for agriculture 1922–1932', *Studies: An Irish Quarterly Review*, vol. 25, no. 99 (1936), p. 368; *Irish Times*, 16 July 1936]

A volatile issue

However, that was not the case. Land was, in fact, a volatile issue during 1917–23 and beyond. In 1918 the *Report of the Proceedings of the Irish Convention* estimated that there were just short of 101,000 pending purchases covering an area of 3.3 million acres valued at £23.9 million, undealt with because the British government had stopped land purchase to concentrate its resources on the war effort. Moreover, the former landed elite retained around 2.6 million acres of demesne and untenanted lands.[3] This had created agrarian tensions that came to the fore in the Ranch War of 1908–12, and again towards the end of the First World War.[4] By then, for hundreds of thousands of farmers the most pertinent consideration was not land ownership but farm viability.[5] Their frustrations were shared by the landless agricultural labourers seeking access to land, and the thousands of evicted tenants or their representatives of the Land War era seeking reinstatement.

In the lead-up to the 1918 general election, ascendant Sinn Féin, realising the political capital to be gained in a climate edgy with agrarian grievance, appealed to small farmers and the landless by linking the potential fruits of electoral victory with land redistribution that could only be achieved through compulsory acquisition; they merely exploited the land question in the same way that Parnell's constitutional Irish Parliamentary Party had done during the 1880s. Over the next five years, there was widespread agrarian agitation that gave rise to land-grabbing, often culminating in more extreme violence, including occasional murder, and very often the burning of 'big houses'. The destruction of country mansions, such as Moydrum, County Westmeath, Summerhill, County Meath or Tubberdaly, County Offaly for whatever loose political or military reason, simultaneously ended centuries of landlord presence in an area and provided access to a sizeable amount of productive agricultural land to be potentially divided among locals: in essence, micro social revolutions took place across the country.[6]

Fig. 2 Moydrum Castle, Athlone, County Westmeath. Moydrum Castle was built in the 1750s by the Handcock family, who were granted over 5,000 acres in Westmeath in 1680 under the Cromwellian Act of Settlement, and reimagined by the first Baron Castlemaine, William Handcock, as a Gothic revivalist structure in 1814. The castellated mansion assumed greater potency as a symbol of British power in the heart of Ireland in 1899 when the Fifth Baron Castlemaine, Albert Handcock, a representative peer in the House of Lords, was appointed Lord Lieutenant of Westmeath. While Castlemaine sold more than half of his estate, which had grown to 12,000 acres in extent (located in Westmeath and Roscommon) by the turn of the century, under the Wyndham Land Act of 1903 he retained a sprawling demesne and almost 1,500 acres of untenanted lands. On Sunday 3 July 1921, as a final act in a prolonged cycle of violence and reprisals that began on 20 June with the assassination of Thomas Stanton Lambert, commanding officer of the British army's 13th Infantry Brigade, sixty members of the IRA's Athlone Brigade under Thomas Costello set Moydrum Castle alight. It was targeted, according to IRA Volunteer Frank O'Connor, because the staunchly unionist Castlemaine had 'always opposed anything that was patriotic or Irish national and was really an enemy of Ireland'. However, as Terence Dooley notes, an agrarian dimension to what appeared to be a straightforward counter-reprisal cannot be discounted, given the involvement of Costello, who was the son of a small farmer, in agrarianism in the months before the burning, and the agitation on the Moydrum estate that began shortly afterwards and continued throughout the Civil War. Awarded just over £100,000 in compensation in October 1921, Castlemaine subsequently settled with his family in Wimbledon and sold his 525-acre estate to the Irish Land Commission in 1924. [Image: National Library of Ireland, L_ROY_02940 / Sources: BMH WS 1,309, Frank O'Connor; Paul Hughes, 'Moydrum's Unforgettable Fire', *Westmeath Independent*, 3 July 2021; Terence Dooley, *Burning the Big House* (New Haven, 2023) pp. 112–13 and 143]

The formal introduction of the Land Bill to the Dáil in May 1923 undoubtedly contributed to the ending of civil strife. Some welcomed the legislation as an 'undoing of the conquest of Ireland', a necessary step towards the decolonialisation of the new state. In 1925, as the demand for redistribution gathered momentum, William Sears (Mayo, Cumann na nGaedheal) got to the crux of what the act could mean:

> There are numerous demesnes with Big Houses on them. I hope the Minister is not going to be too tender about dealing with these demesnes. They have been for 500 years in the possession of these landlord families. I think that is long enough for them to have them, and it is time for the people to get them now.[7]

Protecting property rights

However, the more conservative revolutionaries – including the influential Patrick Hogan, minister for agriculture, and Kevin O'Higgins, minister for home affairs, both tellingly from large farming backgrounds – were more politically pragmatic, being determined to put an end to any threat of social revolution and to send out a clear message that property rights had to be protected. In May 1923 O'Higgins made a powerful speech in which he warned anyone who went out 'in the defiance of the law and in defiance of the Parliament to press their claims by their own violence and their own illegalities [that they would] be placed definitely outside the benefits of this Bill'.[8] It had a salutary effect: the politics of land redistribution were now being used to threaten potential enemies of the state. The government could not run the risk of diminishing the credibility of the new state. After all, the funding of the act – estimated at the time to be in the region of £30 million – would be dependent upon British government credit. Hogan told the Dáil: 'No matter how obnoxious a landlord may be personally his legal position as vendor confers on him certain rights which cannot be ignored without running the risk of such diminution of the credit of the nation.'[9] Thus, the aristocracy's lands were not to be expropriated, as more radical revolutionaries might have demanded, but neither were they paid for in cash – payment in land bonds denied the aristocracy the generous terms that had

been available under the 1903 Land Act. More generally, as Vincent Comerford has put it: '[W]ithout a land act that secured structures for the future of land transfer, the Irish Free State in 1923 would have been a much more volatile polity.'[10]

Landlords did not publicly challenge the financial arrangements; their legal representative, Harry Franks, had informed Hogan at the land conference that they were 'prepared to take what they can get now, providing it is anything approaching fair play, rather than take their chance of what they can get from the next parliament'.[11] In the Senate, instead of barking loudly, the aristocratic interest acquiesced, with the exception of Sir John Keane, who 'opposed the basic principle of the bill and […] fought Hogan doggedly on almost every issue', but to little avail, largely because his numerous amendments were not supported by his more lethargic aristocratic colleagues.[12]

The act had two central objectives: the completion of land purchase and the relief of congestion. In relation to the second, the state was given the power, through the Irish Land Commission, to compulsorily acquire demesne and untenanted lands belonging to the former landlord class for redistribution. If they wanted to hold on to these lands, landowners could seek exemption on the grounds that they were providing large-scale employment; that they were rearing thoroughbred animals; or had demesnes with woodlands of historical significance. Exemptions safeguarded great houses including Carton, Abbeyleix and Adare.

The landless – disenfranchised again

When lands were compulsorily acquired, they were then redistributed by the Land Commission to a hierarchy of allottees. Small farmers (congests) living in the vicinity got first preference, followed by tenants or their representatives who had been evicted since 1878, labourers made redundant by the acquisition of estates, and 'any other person or body to whom in the opinion of the Land Commission an advance ought to be made'. The latter was intended to cater for the landless, but it was extremely rare that any land was ever left over to cater for these. They were once again

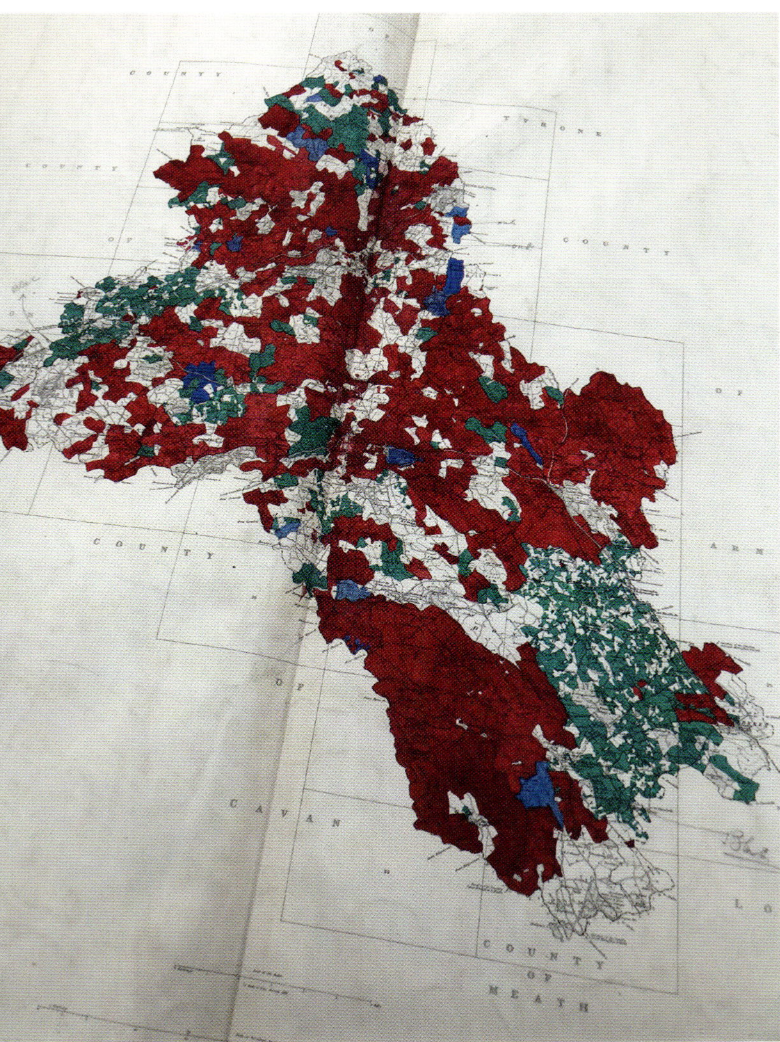

Figs 3 and 4 (left) Irish Land Commission files, Land Commission Records Office, Portlaoise. (right) Colour-coded map of land sales in County Monaghan under British Land Purchase (Ireland) Acts 1881–1903. Between 1880 and 1922, approximately 80 per cent of the land of Ireland was transferred from landlord to tenant, a quiet revolution that followed a noisy and successful Land War. Land was always the big issue in Ireland, from the enormous dispossessions of the seventeenth century onwards. The fact that the problem was partially solved so quickly at the beginning of the twentieth century is both fascinating and problematic. The Land Acts created a rural society of conservative Catholic smallholders with a new-found interest in respectability and sexual probity, both of which bore down most heavily on women, and were ultimately connected to the establishment and maintenance of mother and baby homes. The announcement in March 2024 that the records of the Irish Land Commission, a vast collection spanning the sixteenth to the twentieth centuries, would be transferred to the National Archives was welcome. Many scholars had been urging this course of action over the past thirty years. Their absence has meant that we have not been able to fully understand the creation of the modern state; these records are the last piece of the archival jigsaw relating to the revolutionary period, and what went before and came after it. As Terence Dooley has written, 'post-independence rural Ireland was seething with frustration, local jealousies, bitterness and anger as lands were divided. There is much work to be done on the extent to which the Land Commission, arguably the body with the greatest power to enact revolutionary social change, embraced that potential, or did it simply become another pawn of local élites?' The collection also contains vast amounts of genealogical material in the Fair Rent Registers from the 1880s and 1890s, which are a partial replacement for the 1881 and 1891 census records that were destroyed during the First World War because of a paper shortage. The original deeds to the transferred estates, some going back to the sixteenth century, and a wonderful collection of eighteenth-century leases from the Church Temporalities Commission, are also part of this enormous collection, which merited its own custom-built archival repository at the back of the Land Commission offices on Merrion Square. When the offices were sold in the 1990s, a rescue operation was mounted to prevent the records from being destroyed. The National Archives, with huge input from a young archivist named Oonagh Worke, took in the records in a hurry. They were preserved, only to be made inaccessible. They are now stored in a warehouse in Portlaoise, under the control of the Department of Agriculture. Their transfer to the National Archives will be a huge logistical operation, to be followed by conservation, cataloguing and ultimate release to the public. It is to be hoped that that release will occur at the earliest possible date, perhaps in tranches rather than waiting until everything is done. [Text: Catriona Crowe / Images: courtesy of Terence Dooley / See also Terence Dooley, 'The Irish Land Commission Records, 1881–1992', *History Ireland*, vol. 30, no. 6, November/December 2022]

MAKE IT CLEAR

that the Defeatists speak only for themselves

GIVE FIANNA FÁIL A CLEAR MAJORITY

FODHLA PRINTING CO., LTD., DUBLIN.

disenfranchised, as, indeed, they had been under all previous land legislation.

The 1923 Land Act hastened the end of the longer revolution that had begun with the Land War in 1879. It culminated in the transfer of all tenanted lands from landlords to farmer occupiers, and bolstered by succeeding legislation would result in the almost complete acquisition of demesne and untenanted lands for redistribution in order to tackle congestion. It therefore initiated a social engineering project of historic magnitude carried out under the auspices of the Land Commission, including the migration of thousands of families from congested areas of the west to new farms in the east and midlands.[13]

However, the implementation of the act was not without its critics. Over the decade, the slow and conservative approach taken by the Cumann na nGaedheal government frustrated aggrieved small farmers and other sectors, including IRA rank and file, whose disappointment was eloquently expressed by a Monaghan Volunteer, Tom Carragher:

> During the period of the Truce, the politicians and respectables took over. It was they who interpreted our dream, the dream we fought for. It was they would decide the terms to which we must agree. In the mind of every soldier was a little republic of his own in which he was the hero. But his dream was shattered. The process-server that he once made easy talk to was back in business, the same gripper, the same sheriff with the same old laws while the little hero was back at his plough.[14]

Such frustrations and the continuation of land-related questions would help open the door for Fianna Fáil in 1932. Its Land Act of the following year has its own history to tell.

Fig. 5 (opposite) Fianna Fáil poster for the January 1933 general election. De Valera hoped that the January 1933 general election would deliver a 'clear majority' for the party, which had been governing with Labour Party support since the previous March. The poster depicts Cumann na nGaedheal ministers – their voices wafting into a British government meeting led by the prime minister, Ramsay MacDonald (left) – as 'defeatists' who did not represent the Irish people, as exemplified by their deference to the British on issue of the payment of land annuities. In July 1932 de Valera's new Irish government had withheld the yearly annuities payment of approximately £3 million to the British state. The latter responded by taxing Irish imports, which in turn provoked Irish tariffs on British imports, sparking a six-year 'economic war'. The annuities were a type of mortgage payment, paid each year by Irish tenant farmers against the amounts lent to them by the British government to purchase land from the landlords under the land acts, principally those of 1891, 1903 and 1909. The money was collected by the Irish Land Commission and paid into a Land Purchase Fund established by the British government. Under Article 5 of the Treaty, annuities were included as part of what the Irish Free State would pay to service the UK public debt. In 1923 the Cumann na nGaedheal government agreed to collect the annuities and pay them into the Purchase Fund. The Boundary Agreement of December 1925 released the Free State from its Treaty obligations to service the UK public debt, but the paying-over of collected annuities continued. In March 1926 the Free State government agreed officially with the British that the Irish state would continue to do so, seeing it as a matter of honour and obligation. Later in 1926 a grassroots campaign against the payments was initiated by the socialist republican Peadar O'Donnell in his native Donegal. He saw it as a perfect mobilising issue, combining a material dimension with the national question: 'A tax directly payable to Britain: A tax devoid of any vestige of moral sanction. Refuse this tax, have the people take their stand on that refusal, and you faced the government with a challenge it could not refuse and a fight it could not win. Republicans could roast the Treaty in the fire from this kindling.' The campaign spread countrywide and was taken up by the new Fianna Fáil party, which pledged non-payment in the 1927 general election campaign and again in 1932. Eventually, in 1938, the British accepted a one-off £10 million payment in respect of the remaining annuities. The prime minister, Neville Chamberlain, told de Valera he could go home and 'make a great deal of the fact that the United Kingdom government had agreed to wipe out the Land Annuity payments'. This he did, and the 1938 Anglo-Irish Agreement, which ended the economic war and included the return of the 'Treaty ports', was presented, quite plausibly, as a triumph by Fianna Fáil. [Document: National Library of Ireland, EPH E37 / See Donal Ó Drisceoil, 'When Dev Defaulted: The land annuities dispute, 1926–38', *History Ireland*, vol. 19, no. 3, May/June 2011]

A hearse carrying the remains of General Michael Collins proceeds along St Patrick's Quay, Cork city, 28 August 1922. [Image: courtesy of the Irish Examiner Archive]

SECTION 5

The Dead

CHAPTER 6

Death and Killing in the Irish Civil War

Andy Bielenberg and John Dorney with Hélène O'Keeffe

After the Irish Civil War, it was estimated that in the region of 800 soldiers of the National Army had died between January 1922 and April 1924. Although the government of the nascent state commemorated the deaths of leaders Michael Collins and Arthur Griffith, it was more reticent about commemorating the fallen rank and file who had achieved victory in the conflict.[1] While the republican dead of the 1916 Rising and the War of Independence were subsequently commemorated and listed by the National Graves Association (founded in 1926), the commemoration of those who died in the Civil War was altogether more selective, excluding all National Army deaths. The now outdated *Last Post* listed 404 anti-Treaty fatalities across the thirty-two counties for the years 1922 and 1923.[2] No attempt was made to record and assess civilian fatalities.

Historians initially contributed little to the assessment of fatality levels. Almost half a century after the Irish Civil War, Eoin Neeson's survey conceded that overall fatality figures for the conflict were 'hard to estimate'.[3] He did suggest, however, that almost 600 National Army soldiers had died in July and August 1922 alone (a grossly inflated estimate), and assumed, incorrectly, that anti-Treaty fatalities were even higher. Allowing a death rate of 300 per month for the remainder of the Civil War, Neeson deduced a figure of under 4,000 total fatalities 'for the entire period of the war'. Ronan Fanning assumed that anti-Treaty fatalities were higher still, asserting that military fatalities in the twenty-six counties alone could have reached 4,000 to 5,000.[4] Although Michael Hopkinson concluded quite correctly that Fanning's figures were too high, he maintained that Civil War fatalities were considerably higher than those occurring between the 1916 Rising and the War of Independence, and that anti-Treaty fatalities exceeded those of the National Army. He concluded, in his 2003 contribution to the *Oxford New History of Ireland,* that total fatalities were under 4,000.[5] Such high estimates by the last generation of historians did nothing to dispel the impression that the Irish Civil War was an altogether more traumatic conflict than the War of Independence.

Fig. 1 *Sketch for Pro-Cathedral, Dublin 1922*, by Sir John Lavery. Knighted in 1918 and a recognised society figure in London, Belfast-born artist Lavery was best known for his work as a portraitist. While also noted for his *plein-air* paintings, it was his portraiture that ultimately secured his reputation among the British establishment. Commissioned as an official war artist during the First World War, he never experienced the horrors of the trenches, but was always alive to the significance of history in the making. During the Treaty negotiations in late 1921, Lavery painted portraits of Michael Collins and other members of both negotiating teams, fully aware of how history was unfolding before him. The artist and his American-born wife Hazel, who had opened their South Kensington home to Collins during this time in London, were drawn to the charismatic young leader and, indeed, to Ireland during a tumultuous period in its history. Lavery was again drawn to Collins as subject for his painting in 1922, only this time in the most tragic of circumstances. He was in Dublin in August when he heard that the thirty-one-year-old commander in chief of the National Army had been killed at Béal na Blá in County Cork, and he did not allow the moment to pass without recording it in his own inimitable style. His painting of Collins's body laid out in the mortuary chapel – *Michael Collins, Love of Ireland* – at St Vincent's hospital in Dublin still resonates today. *Love of Ireland* was completed on his return to London and exhibited at the Paris Salon in October 1922. Lavery also painted Collins's funeral Mass in St Mary's Pro-Cathedral in Dublin from a balcony at the back of the church. *Sketch for Pro-Cathedral*, which captures one of the most tragic moments in the Civil War for the pro-Treaty side, draws the eye immediately to Collins's tricolour-draped coffin, bathed in gentle light and positioned before the high altar, a sacred space. The prominence afforded the tricolour in *Love of Ireland* and *Sketch for Pro-Cathedral* demonstrates Lavery's grasp of history and the importance of such symbolism at the birth of the new state. Such paintings also reveal, as Kenneth McConkey points out, his 'innate ability to compose simultaneously, to find the focal point and place it correctly from the start – all led by eye and brain from palette to canvas'. Collins was, and remains, the most iconic victim of the Irish revolution. [Image: courtesy of Gormleys Fine Art / See Kenneth McConkey, *Lavery on Location* (Dublin, 2023) p. 17]

More sober assessments

A new generation of Civil War historians has generated somewhat more sober assessments of its fatal consequences. Bill Kissane suggests that 'over a thousand lives may have been lost in the conflict, but the records do not allow for a precise estimate'.[6] Diarmaid Ferriter's 2021 survey suggested that around 1,300 people lost their lives.[7] In his contribution to the *Cambridge History of Ireland,* Fearghal McGarry alludes to 1,500 deaths, but acknowledges a degree of uncertainty.[8] This project, conducted during the centenary of the Civil War, represents a more systematic investigation. A collaboration between the Schools of History and Geography at University College Cork, it set out to identify and map as many of the fatalities of the Irish Civil War as possible between 28 June

1922 and 24 May 1923.[9] (These have been listed in Section 10 of this book for commemorative purposes.) An additional objective was to tabulate and map the results in order to assess the geography, circumstances and chronology of Civil War fatalities. Data has also been collected, as far as possible, on the age, county of origin, previous service and occupation of the victims.

Killing and death is a central element in warfare and, as such, this research has yielded much new information on the nature of the Irish conflict. Because fatalities are generally better documented than the other physical consequences of political violence (such as woundings, arson, torture and rape), our research results offer a more verifiable measure of violence. Fatalities provide a useful comparison of the temporal and spatial dimensions of violence on the island, while also providing a vital point of comparison with civil wars in other countries.

New sources

The Decade of Commemorations/Centenaries (2012–23) has increased the archival focus on the Irish revolutionary period. The Military Service Pensions Collection (MSPC) and other army service records held at Irish Military Archives have provided a range of new sources on National Army fatalities; sources accessed, for example, by James Langton, who published a pioneering estimate of National Army fatalities in 2019.[10] The MSPC, released online in phases from 2014, has also provided much new data on IRA deaths, so that we now have a range of sources unavailable to previous researchers. Commemorative republican material, including the *Last Post*, was also consulted for this project and a series of important county studies was invaluable in compiling the database. We also carried out a full examination of all death certificates for 1922–3, in addition to assorted compensation files and newspaper records.

This project, which defines the Irish Civil War as an intra-nationalist conflict, focused largely on the twenty-six counties that became the Irish Free State. However, we also examined and mapped conflict deaths in Northern Ireland in the same time frame, though fatalities here followed a very different pattern to those south of the border, peaking in the spring and early summer of 1922 and largely petering out before the start of hostilities in the south. Only

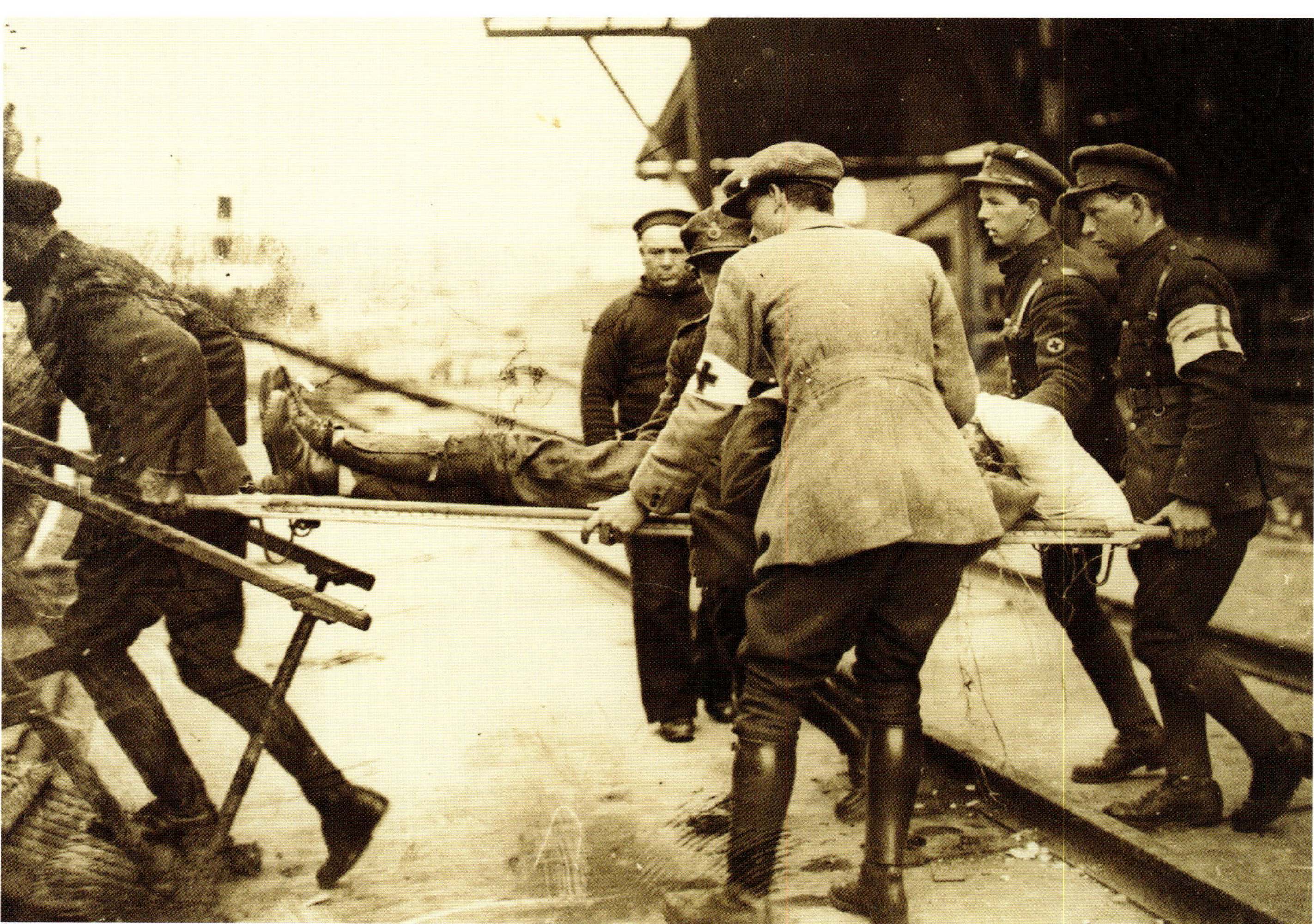

Fig. 2 A soldier wounded after the National Army landing in Passage West, County Cork being conveyed to the base hospital on board the *Lady Wicklow*. [Image: National Library of Ireland, HOG54]

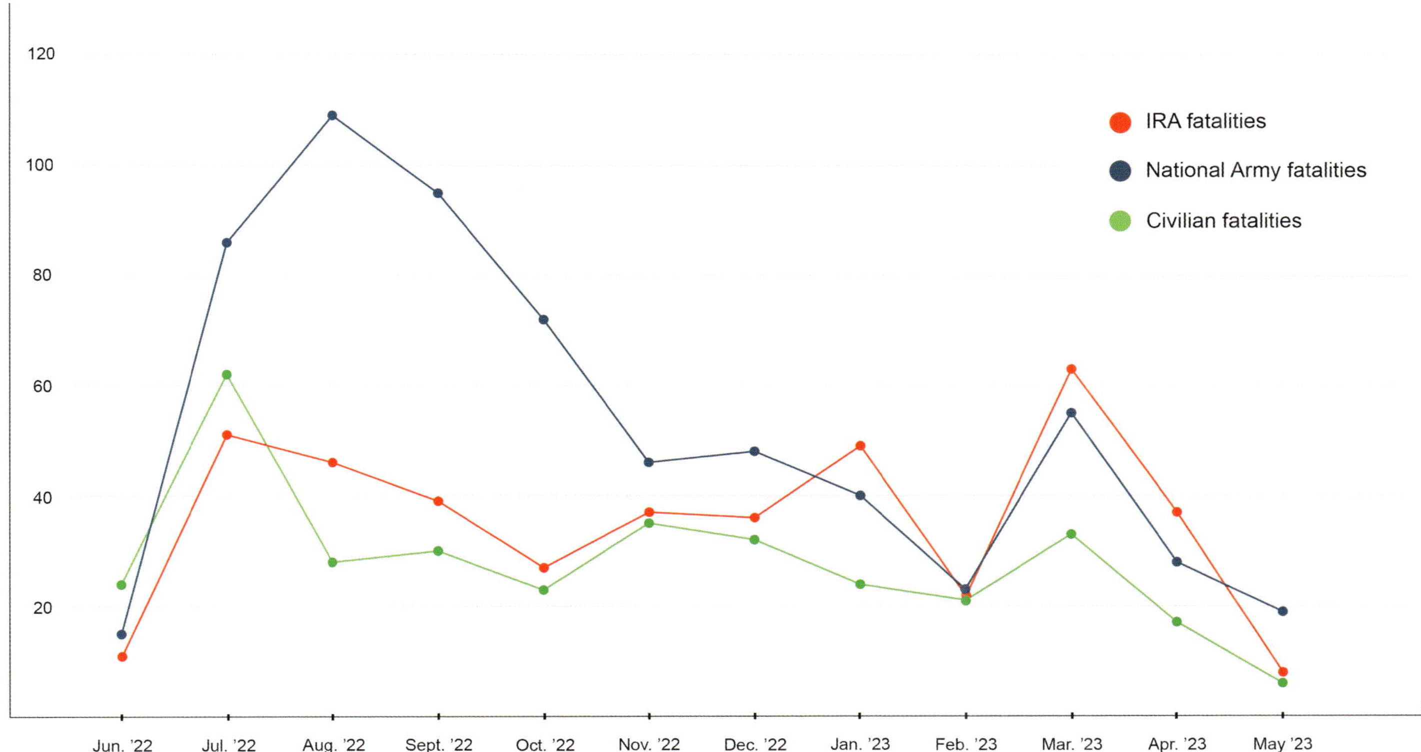

Fig. 3 Line graph showing deaths by month in each category (IRA, National Army and civilian) in the twenty-six counties.

one National Army soldier died in Northern Ireland (from wounds received in the Irish Free State) in the time fame we have examined. Conversely, civilians, who were a minority of victims in the Free State, formed by far the largest category in Northern Ireland. Identifying and listing the fatalities north of the border between 28 June 1922 and 24 May 1923 reinforced the fundamentally different nature of the conflict there.

For methodological purposes, and due to resource and time constraints, it was necessary to impose temporal boundaries on this project. It begins on the date traditionally accepted as marking the beginning of the military conflict, the opening of the bombardment on the Four Courts on 28 June 1922, and concludes on the date of the dump-arms order on 24 May 1923. This excludes the prelude to the Civil War and its aftermath, when there were additional deaths, but this more circumscribed time frame was sufficient to capture, analyse and map the core military history of the conflict. We identified a total of 1,425 violent deaths in the territory of the Free State within this time frame, of whom 648 were pro-Treaty, 438 were anti-Treaty; 335 were civilians and four were members of the crown forces. The death toll rises only slightly to 1,484 when fatalities north of the new border are added.

Chronology

Though there had been deaths due to the Treaty split prior to 28 June 1922, the conflict exploded into open warfare with the attack on the Four Courts, and the months of July and August 1922 marked the peak for total fatalities. The National Army suffered disproportionately in this period because its soldiers were generally attacking republican defensive positions in towns and cities. Anti-Treaty IRA losses were considerably less. Urban combat also proved lethal to civilians, particularly in Dublin, Limerick and Waterford. As a result, this period of a little over two months to the end of August 1922 accounted for almost 34 per cent of civilian fatalities in the twenty-six counties. July 1922 marked the peak month for civilian deaths (sixty-two) during the entire Civil War, while August 1922 marked the peak month for National Army fatalities (109).

While it is often assumed that the end of the so-called 'conventional' phase of the conflict in August 1922 marked the end of major combat in the Civil War, our figures tell another story. Fatalities remained high in the autumn and early winter of 1922 as the IRA, having been driven from fixed positions but not killed or captured in large numbers, resorted to more familiar guerrilla tactics. This period, from September to the end of November 1922 (covering what this project defines as the first guerrilla phase) accounted for over one third of National Army fatalities for the entire conflict (which was marginally higher than the conventional phase). Government forces evidently lost the momentum achieved during the opening phase and pro-Treaty combatant deaths were over double those among the anti-Treaty forces. This was not just in rural contexts; in early September 1922 republicans in County Kerry regained control of the towns of Kenmare and Tarbert, with the former only recovered in December 1922,[11] while such important

Period	Civilians	NA	IRA	Total
Jun.–Aug. 1922	114	210	108	444
Sept.–Nov. 1922	88	214	103	411
Dec. 1922–Feb. 1923	78	111	107	300
Mar.–May 1923	55	102	108	270
Total	335	637	426	1,425

Fig. 4 Table showing the number of fatalities in each category (Civilian, National Army and Irish Republican Army) in each three-month phase during the Civil War in the twenty-six counties. The total figures for each phase in the fourth column include Cumann na mBan, Fianna Éireann, Civic Guard, Citizens' Defence Force, Criminal Investigation Department (CID) and crown forces fatalities.

Period	Civilians %	NA %	IRA %	Total %
Jun.–Aug. 1922	34.0	33.0	25.4	31.2
Sept.–Nov. 1922	26.3	33.6	24.2	28.8
Dec. 1922–Feb. 1923	23.0	17.4	25.1	21
Mar.–May 1923	16.7	16	25.4	19

Fig. 5 Table showing deaths by affiliation in each three-month phase in the twenty-six counties as a percentage of total deaths over the entire conflict in each category. The last column shows the total deaths during each phase as a percentage of total deaths over the entire conflict.

provincial towns as Dundalk, Clifden and Ballina also fell into anti-Treaty hands for much shorter spells. In this period the geographical distribution of violence became more widespread. Cork and Kerry remained centres of violence but were rivalled in terms of casualties by counties such as Tipperary, Wexford, Sligo, Mayo and Louth. Meanwhile, conflict-related deaths in counties Limerick, Waterford and, to a lesser extent, Dublin fell away sharply.

For a variety of reasons, the anti-Treaty IRA war effort could not be maintained. Two thirds of all National Army deaths, and most of their deaths in combat, had already occurred by the end of November 1922. While anti-Treaty fatalities remained numerically steady throughout the conflict, National Army losses began to fall in the winter of 1922. During this period, the growing Free State army began a more aggressive campaign against the guerrillas, whose ranks were progressively depleted, particularly by incarceration. Executions of anti-Treaty prisoners also began in November 1922, with eighteen having been shot by the end of the year, including four republican leaders executed in Mountjoy Gaol on 8 December 1922 in retaliation for the assassination of pro-Treaty TD Seán Hales. In January 1923, for the first time anti-Treaty losses (fifty) exceeded pro-Treaty fatalities (forty), and this remained the case for every subsequent month up to the IRA ceasefire. Though this occurred against a background of an overall reduction in lethal violence, it marked a sea change. Thereafter, there were far fewer National Army deaths in combat, but more republicans died in custody or in official executions.

The fact that executions increased as overall violence declined reflected two important developments. Firstly, the republicans had switched to non-combat tactics such as burning the houses of Free State supporters and the destruction of communications and tax infrastructure. And, secondly, the Free State government's need to bring the war to a speedy conclusion before it bankrupted the state. February 1923 witnessed a pause in executions, an amnesty was offered to anti-Treatyites and there was a marked overall decline in violence. However, the Civil War still had a sting left in its tail. March 1923 proved to be the bloodiest month since September 1922 in terms of total fatalities and the peak month for IRA fatalities. A large proportion of the March victims were the forty-three republican prisoners killed in custody, of whom thirty-two died in 'unofficial' reprisals, most notably in County Kerry, where seventeen prisoners were killed with explosives in retaliation for a booby trap bomb at Knocknagoshel, which claimed the lives of five National Army troops. Additionally, March 1923 saw eleven executions and fifteen assassinations. In total, 58 per cent of anti-Treaty deaths in the final phase of the Civil War (March to May 1923) were either executions or prisoners killed in custody.

Violence abated in April 1923 as IRA units almost everywhere were demoralised and depleted by arrests and perhaps deterred from further activity by the threat of executions. Among the eighty-three fatalities in that month was the IRA chief of staff, Liam Lynch, shot as he was fleeing from a National Army sweep in the Knockmealdown Mountains in County Tipperary.[12] His successor, Frank Aiken, called a ceasefire on 30 April and, in the absence of any viable negotiated settlement, issued an order to 'dump arms' on 24 May 1923. This effectively ended the conflict, though political violence continued long afterwards.

Fig. 6 Thomas Roache, North Mayo Brigade, IRA (1894–1922). Shortly after midnight on Thursday 28 September 1922, IRA man Thomas Roache was arrested by Free State forces on the main street in Ballina, County Mayo. According to a brief notice announcing his death in the pro-government press, twenty-eight-year-old Roache had been 'under the influence of drink' when he was arrested. He was taken to the Central Hotel and placed under guard. When the prisoner tried to disarm one of his guards, reported the *Freeman's Journal*, the weapon discharged, administering a fatal head wound. This early account of the circumstances of Roache's death was contradicted during the inquest on 28 September. Sergeant of the guard, Corporal Moran, painted a picture of calm, even companionability, in the guardroom. They were all 'very friendly', he insisted, and the prisoner and his guards shared tea together by the fire. Hours later, just before 4 a.m., Moran had been startled by the sound of a gunshot coming from the guardroom. He rushed to the scene to discover the 'deceased sitting in a chair'. Further evidence was provided by National Army Private Michael Cannon, who explained that his rifle, which had been lying on a table, accidentally discharged when he went to retrieve it. Private Brett corroborated Cannon's testimony, and the inquest returned a verdict of accidental death. It is impossible to know the truth of events in the Central Hotel over a century ago, but the atmosphere was doubtless charged by the attack on Ballina by republican forces sixteen days before Roache's arrest, and the ambush at Glenamoy on 16 September that claimed the lives of six National Army soldiers. Thomas Roache was not the only republican prisoner killed in National Army custody in Ballina. According to the report in the *Southern Star* on 6 January 1923, Patrick Mahon from Crossmolina was arrested the day before and brought back to barracks. There, a National Army soldier 'pushed him with his rifle', which went off, 'killing Mahon immediately'. Two months later, after the death of republican prisoner Nicholas Corcoran, the coroner regretted that a jury had to be assembled for a third time to pronounce on what appeared to be another tragic accident involving a republican prisoner while in National Army custody. He hoped that, in future, more supervision would be exercised over the soldiers, for 'Ballina garrison was getting an unenviable name in this regard'. [Text: Frank Fagan / Image: reproduced by kind permission of the Roache family, Ballina / Sources: MSPC DP6364, Thomas Roache; *Connaught Telegraph*, 7 October 1922; *Freeman's Journal*, 29 September 1922, 30 March 1922; *Evening Echo*, 30 September 1922; *Western People*, 30 September 1922]

The geography of Civil War fatalities

The map of all fatalities throughout the Civil War across the thirty-two counties reveals a significant concentration of deaths in and around the major urban centres, with Dublin providing the largest single concentration, followed by Cork, Limerick and Tralee. Although all these centres witnessed significant conventional fighting, this was generally short-lived; many were killed in more sporadic confrontations with much smaller numbers of protagonists over the entire span of the Civil War. Apart from being heavily contested, other factors drove up the death toll in these locations. They also retained a significant share of the old British army garrison infrastructure, which included military prisons, where most executions and many deaths in custody took place, and hospitals, where many victims succumbed to their wounds. Garrisons also saw the main concentrations of fatal accidents among the National Army.

Outside these centres, the map highlights secondary concentrations at Dundalk, Waterford city, the Curragh, Athlone, Wexford town, Sligo town and Galway city among others, which shared some of the features that accounted for concentrations in the primary centres. Outside these locales a more diffuse, though notable, pattern of rural killings is apparent in County Kerry, west Cork, south Tipperary and in counties Sligo and Mayo. The great bulk of fatalities took place south of a line taking in Galway, Athlone and Dublin, with lesser concentrations in the west, Dundalk and Belfast.

In absolute numerical terms the Munster counties of Cork, Tipperary, Kerry and Limerick, combined with Dublin, stand out as the primary arenas of the conflict, collectively accounting for 61 per cent of all fatalities in the twenty-six counties. Secondary centres in the west, Sligo, Mayo and Galway, and Wexford, Louth and Kildare in Leinster collectively accounted for an additional 21 per cent. These eleven counties accounted for just over 82 per cent of total fatalities in the Irish Free State area, and the residual were spread over the remaining fifteen quieter counties of the new state. The distribution of fatalities very strongly correlates with areas where the IRA was mostly anti-Treaty. Counties such as Clare and Longford, where the IRA was mostly pro-Treaty, were quiet during the Civil War, despite being relatively violent in 1919–21.

Across the border, Northern Ireland was quieter still for the duration of the Civil War; with the extensive civilian blood-letting on the streets of Belfast earlier in 1922 dwindling dramatically in the months after 28 June 1922, and finally terminating in early October 1922.

1922 = 1923

Is cá bfuil cruaḋ i n-Éirinn
níos mó ná mé:
i ndiaiḋ an ċéad ṁic a
ċráiḋ mo ċroiḋe ?

COMMDT. P. REILLY
Executed Feb. 6, 1923

"If death comes to me swiftly it will be because of my great love for Ireland.
—Columbkille.

VOL. WM. FITZGERALD
Executed Feb. 6, 1923

"For it were better for us to die in battle than to behold the destruction of our nation."
—Machabees.

LIAM LYNCH

"Lord I offer everything Thou askest for Ireland's Resurrection. It is Thy will. Accept our willing sacrifice for our people. May we in dying bring glory to Thy name and honour to our country, that has always been faithful to Thee. God save Ireland. God save, bless and guard the Irish Republic, to live and flourish, and be a model government of Truth and Justice to all nations. May the Liberty of the Irish people shine with Thee, O My God, for ever and ever. Amen."

—*From Terence MacSwiney's Last Prayer.*

VOL. WILLIAM HEALY
Executed March 16, 1923

VOL. McKENZIE-KENNEDY
"Scottie"
Killed in Action Aug. 10, 1922

Fig. 7 A leaflet commemorating five Cork republicans who died during the Civil War. Their photographs are arranged around the text of Terence MacSwiney's last prayer, linking their deaths with his in the same tradition of republican martyrdom. The most prominent of those pictured is the IRA chief of staff, Liam Lynch. Although originally from County Limerick, Lynch made his name as commandant of IRA Cork No. 2 Brigade during the War of Independence, later rising to command of IRA First Southern Division. He was fatally wounded on 10 April 1923 while fleeing from National Army troops in the Knockmealdown Mountains in County Tipperary. Also pictured are three anti-Treaty Volunteers who were executed by the Free State. Twenty-one-year-old William Healy from Donoughmore in Cork was arrested with arms during an attempted arson attack on the Cork city home of Michael Collins's sister, Mary Collins Powell. Interned in Cork male prison, where he was allegedly badly beaten, Healy was executed there on 13 March 1923. It was the only official execution in the city during the Civil War. Michael Fitzgerald from Youghal, County Cork, incorrectly named here as William, was captured at Clashmore, County Waterford, in possession of arms and ammunition. He was not executed on 6 February as the leaflet suggests, but on 25 January 1923 when he and twenty-four-year-old Commandant Patrick O'Reilly, also from Youghal and arrested during the same incident, were shot by firing squad in Waterford. Ian 'Scottie' MacKenzie Kennedy was an IRA Volunteer originally from Inverness in Scotland. He had joined the IRA after moving to Ireland to avoid conscription into the British army during the First World War. Scottie MacKenzie was a celebrated member of the 8th (Ballyvourney) Battalion, Cork No. 1 Brigade, fondly recalled for his study of the Irish language and wearing of Scottish kilts. He was killed in action near Douglas on 9 August 1922 while opposing the advance of pro-Treaty troops on Cork city after their landing at Passage West. [Text: John Dorney / Image: Cork Public Museum]

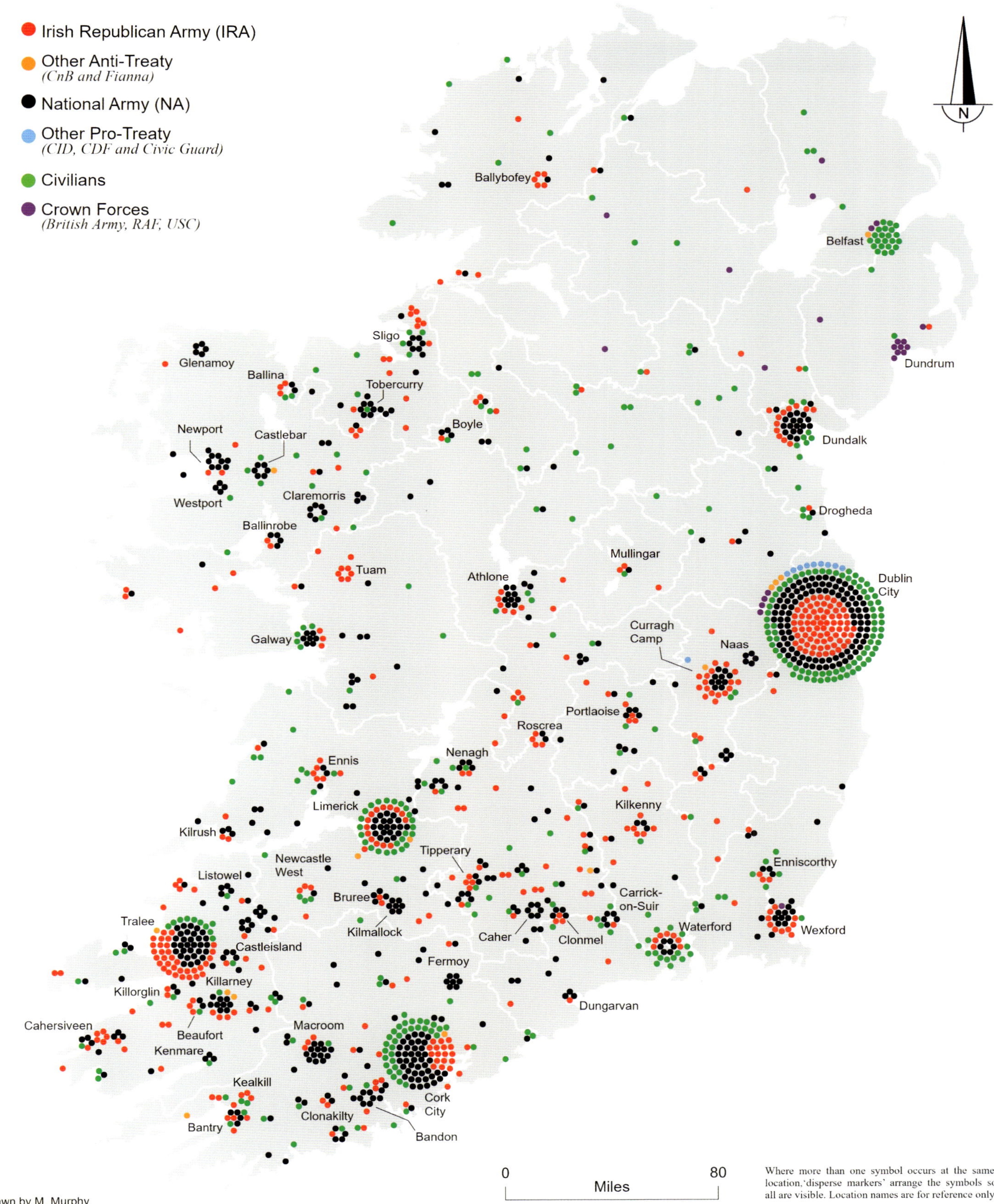

Fig. 8 Map of total fatalities across the thirty-two counties between 28 June 1922 and 24 May 1923.

County Fatality Figures, 28 June 1922–24 May 1923

County	Civilian	Pro-Treaty	Anti-Treaty	Crown Forces	Total
Clare	10	17	10	0	37
Cork	57	107	51	0	215
Kerry	25	88	72	0	185
Limerick	29	43	26	0	98
Tipperary	20	55	37	0	112
Waterford	16	13	10	0	39
Munster	**157**	**323**	**206**	**0**	**686**
Carlow	1	2	5	0	8
Dublin	79	103	74	4	260
Kildare	4	23	21	0	48
Kilkenny	3	8	12	0	23
Laois	4	11	6	0	21
Longford	2	2	0	0	4
Louth	11	21	13	0	45
Meath	2	5	1	0	8
Offaly	3	4	6	0	13
Westmeath	4	14	11	0	29
Wexford	10	23	16	0	49
Wicklow	0	2	4	0	6
Leinster	**123**	**218**	**169**	**4**	**514**
Galway	8	20	17	0	45
Leitrim	6	3	1	0	10
Mayo	13	45	15	0	73
Roscommon	3	6	3	0	12
Sligo	8	21	15	0	44
Connacht	**38**	**95**	**51**	**0**	**184**
Cavan	6	1	1	0	8
Donegal	5	9	10	0	24
Monaghan	6	2	1	0	9
Ulster (Free State)	**17**	**12**	**12**	**0**	**41**
Antrim	27	0	1	4	32
Armagh	3	0	1	1	5
Derry	1	1	1	0	3
Down	1	0	2	10	13
Fermanagh	0	0	0	1	1
Tyrone	3	0	0	2	5
Ulster (Northern Ire.)	**35**	**1**	**5**	**18**	**59**
Total fatalities	**370**	**649**	**443**	**22**	**1,484**

Fig. 9 Table showing fatality numbers for civilians, pro- and anti-Treaty combatants and members of the crown forces in all thirty-two counties between 28 June 1922 and 24 May 1923. Pro-Treaty fatalities included members of the National Army, the Civic Guard, the Citizens' Defence Force and the Criminal Investigation Department. Anti-Treaty fatalities included IRA Volunteers and members of Cumann na mBan and Na Fianna Éireann. The twenty-two crown forces fatalities included members of the British army and the Ulster Special Constabulary, and one member of the Royal Air Force. Twenty-five of the thirty-two fatalities in Antrim during this period occurred in Belfast.

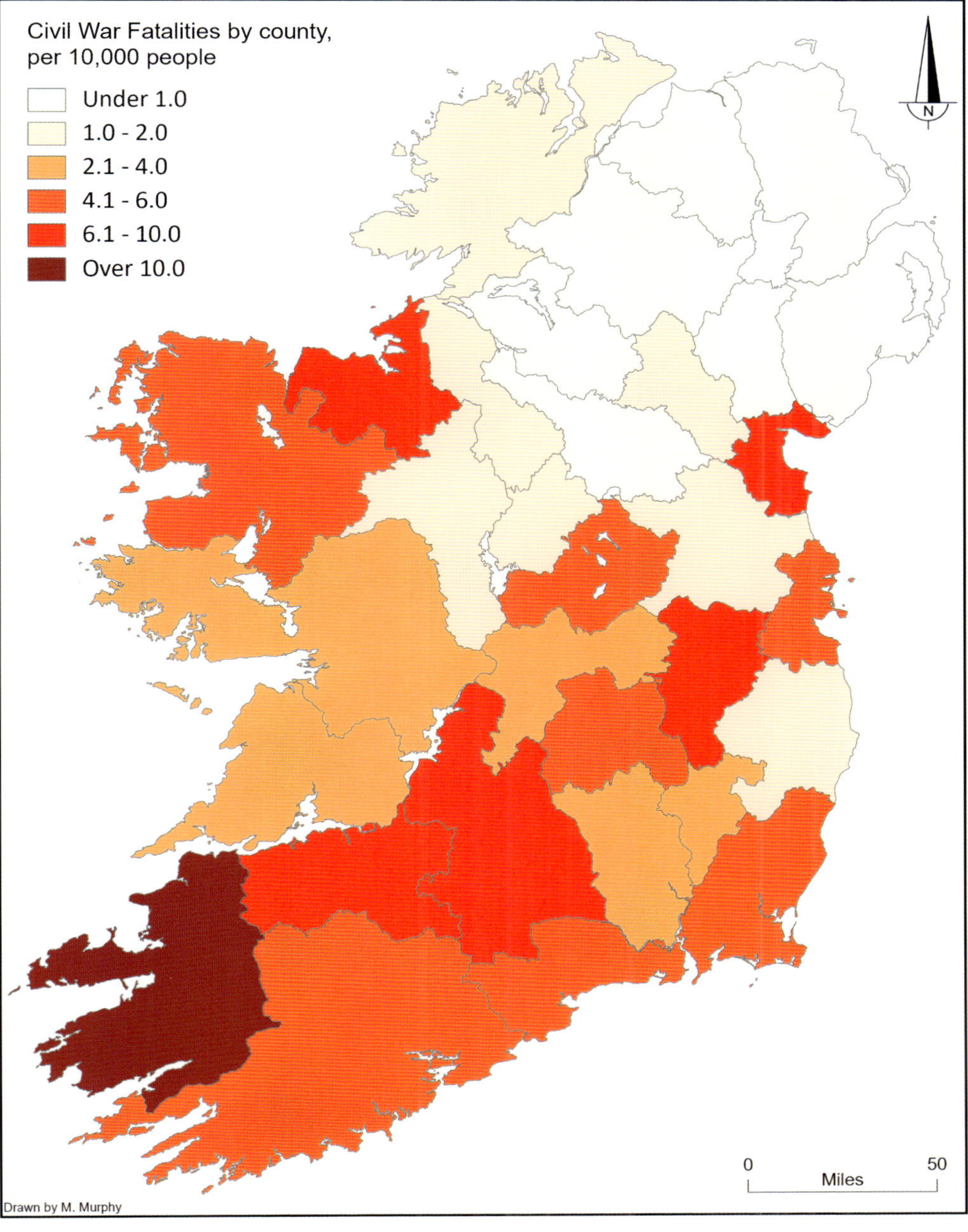

Fig. 10 Map of Civil War fatalities in all thirty-two counties adjusted for population. Fatality levels adjusted for population reveals other aspects of the story. The numbers for Munster are far higher than for the other provinces, demonstrating that the conflict was more intense over a wider geographical area within that province. Kerry is revealed as by far the most violent county in Ireland under this rubric, followed some way behind by Tipperary and Limerick. Cork, on the other hand, was lower than the Munster average, despite having the largest number of fatalities in the province in absolute terms. Although Clare and Waterford were low by Munster standards, Waterford was still higher than the Leinster average. Likewise, Clare was higher than the Connacht average and its fatality profile had more in common with that province. In Leinster, Kildare had by far the highest fatality level when adjusted for population, its garrison status contributing to its relatively high death tally. In Connacht, Sligo had the highest level, followed by Mayo, with Galway coming in below the provincial average. Donegal had the highest level in the nine Ulster counties, but the province overall had far lower levels of fatalities then the rest of the country on both sides of the border, with the six counties of Northern Ireland having a lower fatality level when adjusted for population than all counties. [Text: Andy Bielenberg and John Dorney]

Cause of death

One of the more striking differences between the combatants was the share killed in action. While under 42 per cent of IRA fatalities were killed in combat, the corresponding figure for the National Army was over 60 per cent. This can partially be accounted for by differences in how they fought the war. Conventional offensive action by the National Army in the opening two months of the conflict was costly. The battles for the cities of Dublin, Limerick and Waterford in June–July 1922, and the landings in Cork and Kerry, exacted a high death toll on both sides.

Although the National Army had already achieved military pre-eminence in most urban contexts by the latter part of August 1922, the ambush that led to the death of Michael Collins on 22 August 1922 revealed that the writ of the Provisional Government was only partial in much of rural Ireland. The National Army continued to experience far higher fatality levels in the months from September through November 1922 as the conflict entered its first guerrilla phase. It was exposed to lethal ambushes, which became the dominant cause of fatalities.

The vast majority of deaths, over 90 per cent, were inflicted by gunshot (from rifles, revolvers and machine guns), but explosives, mostly in the form of improvised explosives or 'mines', and to a lesser extent grenades, also featured. Though small in number, these incidents involving explosives could cause large casualties in single incidents. The use of trap mines particularly enraged National Army troops, who viewed their use as involving the cowardly murder of defenceless soldiers, and often led to reprisals, including the worst atrocities committed by the National Army, in Kerry in March 1923.

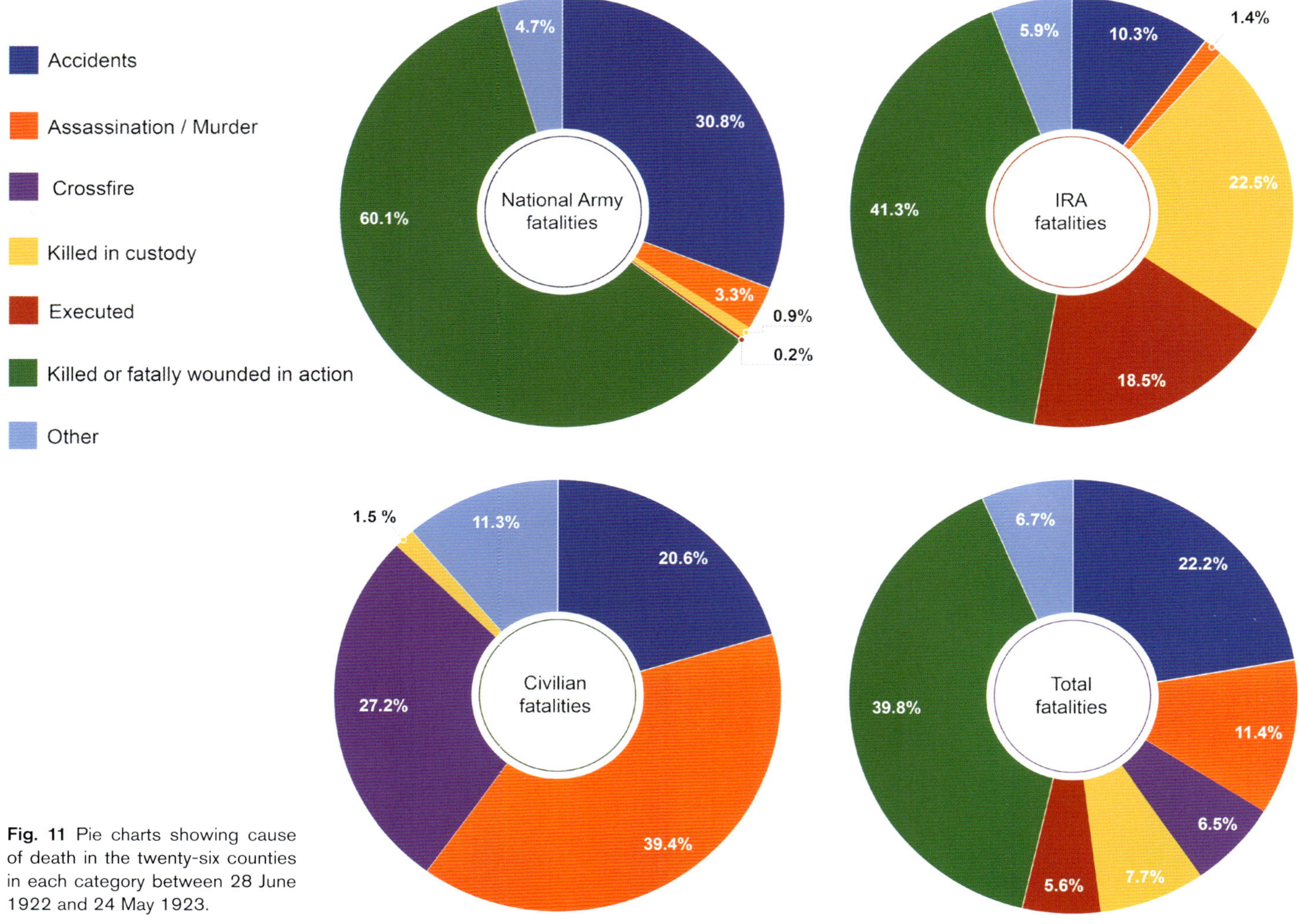

Fig. 11 Pie charts showing cause of death in the twenty-six counties in each category between 28 June 1922 and 24 May 1923.

Apart from combat, most pro-Treaty deaths were the result of accidents, which took an alarmingly high toll on National Army soldiers. Firearms, explosives or motor accidents and 'friendly fire' collectively accounted for almost 31 per cent of pro-Treaty fatalities. These lethal accidents and self-inflicted deaths continued after the dump-arms order of May 1923. It was remarked by an inquiring judge at the Army Inquiry of 1924 that 'in the plots in Glasnevin [cemetery] there are more spaces occupied by persons accidentally shot than by persons actually killed in action'.[13] If he was somewhat mistaken, the prevalence of such incidents is still striking. Nevertheless, the National Army's record of self-inflicted deaths was still well below that of the British army in Ireland in 1919–21.[14]

Anti-Treaty fatalities present quite a different picture. Firstly, the total dead were a little over two thirds of their pro-Treaty opponents. Moreover, if only deaths that occurred in combat were counted, the difference would be starker still, with anti-Treaty losses accounting for only 45 per cent of those of their adversaries. Despite National Army artillery being very important in some engagements in ousting republicans from fortified buildings, it caused a negligible number of deaths among anti-Treaty forces. Furthermore, when faced with overwhelming force, as pro-Treaty sources indignantly reported, the republicans tended to retreat or surrender rather than fight to the end. Indeed, the number of captured republicans, put by the Free State government at 11,500 in April 1923, far exceeded the number killed.[15] Incarceration had a more debilitating impact than death on anti-Treaty forces.

Anti-Treaty IRA Volunteers were less prone to accidents than their opponents, presumably because they had fewer weapons, explosives and transport at their disposal. Nevertheless, just over 10 per cent of IRA fatalities were the result of accidents. The headline figures for republican deaths were that a little over 41 per cent were executed or killed in custody, which greatly shaped republican memory of the conflict. Republicans complained, as Liam Lynch put it, that 'The IRA wishes to fight with clean hands, but the enemy has outraged all the rules of warfare'.[16] While their opponents did not share this view of republican chivalry, we found only twenty-four pro-Treaty soldiers assassinated after being taken prisoner or disarmed, only 3 per cent of the total.

Formal executions began in Dublin in November 1922 and were concentrated there until later in 1922, when government

Fig. 12 Lieutenant Colonel Stephen Mac Eoin of the Irish Defence Forces at the unveiling of a memorial plaque for the National Army soldiers killed in the Ferrycarrig ambush, County Wexford, on 22 October 1922. An inquiry by the mother of one of those soldiers, Private Christopher Kearns, about her deceased son's belongings sparked a series of internal communications within the National Army administration in early 1923. The investigation revealed that Kearns's 'uniform could not have been handed over to his relatives, [because] it was in such a state of blood and dirt' (Fig. 13). Twenty-three-year-old Kearns was one of the four soldiers killed when their vehicle was ambushed enroute to Ferrycarrig, where a small National Army outpost was keeping the bridge open to vehicular traffic. Since the destruction of the main river crossing at Wexford in July 1922, Ferrycarrig Bridge was the primary route connecting the north and south of the county and, because of the isolated nature of the garrison, a frequent target for attacks by the local IRA. In response to these attacks, one of which resulted in the death of Private Edward McAvoy, it was decided to augment the outpost's defences with regular military patrols from Wexford. Little effort was made to stagger them and their predictability made them an easy target for ambush. On the morning of 22 October 1922 a National Army patrol set out from Wexford Military Barracks. As the Lancia car passed under the railway bridge adjacent to Ferrycarrig, it was attacked by the IRA with bombs, rifles and revolver fire. One of the incendiaries exploded in the car, killing Kearns, William Doyle, Peter Behan and Patrick O'Connor outright, and seriously wounding the other four passengers. The local press reported in gruesome detail the most lethal ambush in Wexford since the IRA attack on the National Army in Killurin in July. A witness described how Kearns and his comrades had been wounded so badly that only 'those who knew them intimately' could identify the remains after their arrival at Wexford Barracks. In 1925 the victims' former comrades raised the necessary funds for a simple commemorative Celtic cross at the site of the ambush. When Richard Mulcahy learned of their plans to invite Executive Council president, W.T. Cosgrave, to speak at the summer unveiling ceremony, he moved quickly to disassociate Cumann na nGaedheal from the event. It was all a bit too political, as Anne Dolan writes, 'a ditch in Wexford was no place for a President' and the former commander-in-chief of the National Army was uncomfortable with an official presence at the commemoration of a Civil War loss. The president's attendance, he argued in a letter to prominent Wexford-based Cumann na nGaedheal supporter Kathleen Browne, ran contrary to the government's desire to be fair to all sides of the political spectrum, and perhaps a religious setting would be more appropriate. The Wexford men demurred and purchased a plot at Crosstown Cemetery to commemorate all of Wexford's fallen soldiers. Those who sought to memorialise the dead of Ferrycarrig would have to wait another seventy-seven years. On the centenary of the ambush, during a solemn and dignified ceremony attended by the families of the deceased, Lieutenant Colonel Stephen Mac Eoin unveiled a memorial plaque on the railway bridge. Three months later the plaque was removed under cover of darkness by persons unknown. Even 100 years after the event, the memory of what occurred at Ferrycarrig still proves contentious. [Text: Aaron Ó Maonaigh / Image: courtesy of Gerard Hore / Sources: MSPC 2D/93, Edward McAvoy; *Free Press*, 12 August 1922; Séamus Mac Suain, *County Wexford's Civil War* (Loch Garman, 1995), p. 61; Operations report, 3rd Eastern Division, (nd) October 1922, IMA, CW/OPS/7/1; *Poblacht na hÉireann–War News*, 16 November 1922; South Wexford Brigade IRA, diary of operations, IMA, Brigade Activity Reports, A/65/2/19; *The People*, 25 October 1922; *New Ross Standard*, 27 October 1922; *Enniscorthy Guardian*, 28 October 1922; Anne Dolan, *Commemorating the Irish Civil War: History and memory, 1923–2000* (Cambridge, 2003), p. 122; Richard Mulcahy Letter to Kathleen Browne, 29 May 1925, Mulcahy Papers, P7/B/62 (53–5), UCDA]

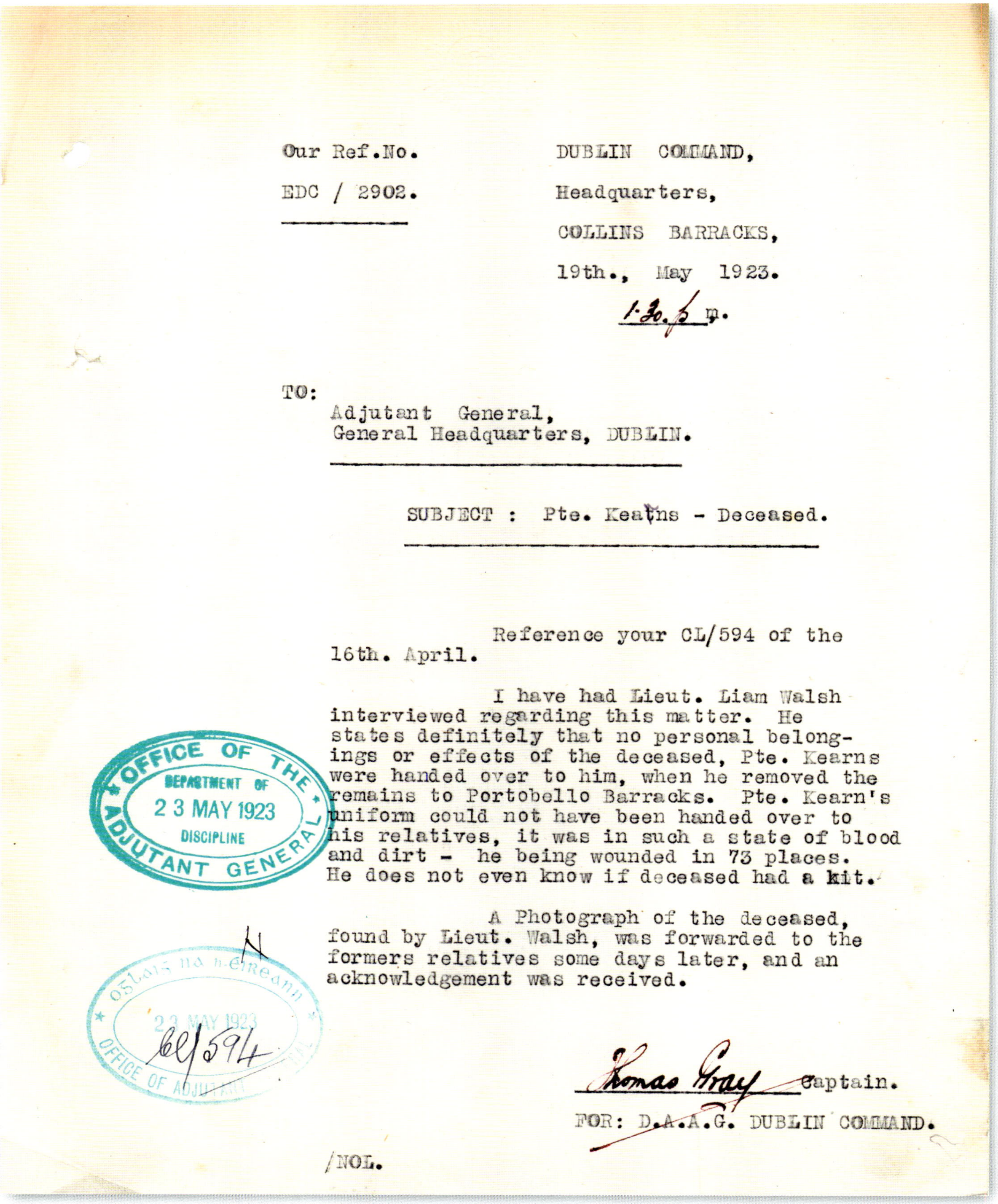

Our Ref.No. DUBLIN COMMAND,
EDC / 2902. Headquarters,
COLLINS BARRACKS,
19th., May 1923.
1.30.p.m.

TO:
Adjutant General,
General Headquarters, DUBLIN.

SUBJECT : Pte. Kearns - Deceased.

OFFICE OF THE ADJUTANT GENERAL
DEPARTMENT OF DISCIPLINE
23 MAY 1923

Reference your CL/594 of the 16th. April.

I have had Lieut. Liam Walsh interviewed regarding this matter. He states definitely that no personal belongings or effects of the deceased, Pte. Kearns were handed over to him, when he removed the remains to Portobello Barracks. Pte. Kearn's uniform could not have been handed over to his relatives, it was in such a state of blood and dirt - he being wounded in 73 places. He does not even know if deceased had a kit.

A Photograph of the deceased, found by Lieut. Walsh, was forwarded to the formers relatives some days later, and an acknowledgement was received.

Óglaigh na h-Éireann
23 MAY 1923
OFFICE OF ADJUTANT
CL/594

Thomas Gray Captain.
FOR: D.A.A.G. DUBLIN COMMAND.

/NOL.

Fig. 13 Letter from the Pension File of National Army soldier Christopher Kearns. [Source: MSPC2D79. Image: courtesy of Military Archives/MSPC Project] policy spread them out across the main garrison towns. As Bill Kissane has argued, the executions were a method of 'broadcasting state power' and logically began at the centre of power in Dublin and were then dispersed around the country, where they also acted to deter guerrilla attacks.[17] We have counted eighty executions by firing squad within the time frame covered. These include two anti-Treaty IRA Volunteers who were shot for armed robbery but disowned by the IRA and therefore not included in the famous memorial figure of seventy-seven executed republicans. It also includes seven National Army soldiers. Six of these were also IRA members, who joined the National Army but deserted during the Civil War and were subsequently captured bearing arms for the anti-Treaty side. One other soldier, however, Gerard Winsley, was executed for 'treachery' in Cork on the orders of General Emmet Dalton in September 1922, having sold arms to the anti-Treaty side.[18]

We have identified at least 109 'unofficial' executions, which were generally carried out by specific groups of pro-Treaty personnel, particularly in units such as the Criminal Investigation Department (CID) and Military Intelligence based in Dublin and the Dublin Guard in Kerry (all three largely officered by former members of Michael Collins's IRA Squad and Intelligence Department). They began in Dublin where Seán Cole and Alf Colley, two Fianna officers abducted and killed in late August 1922, were the first of at least nineteen similar killings in the city before the end of the Civil War.

County Kerry, where the Dublin Guard commander, Paddy O'Daly, succeeded as general officer commanding in early 1923,

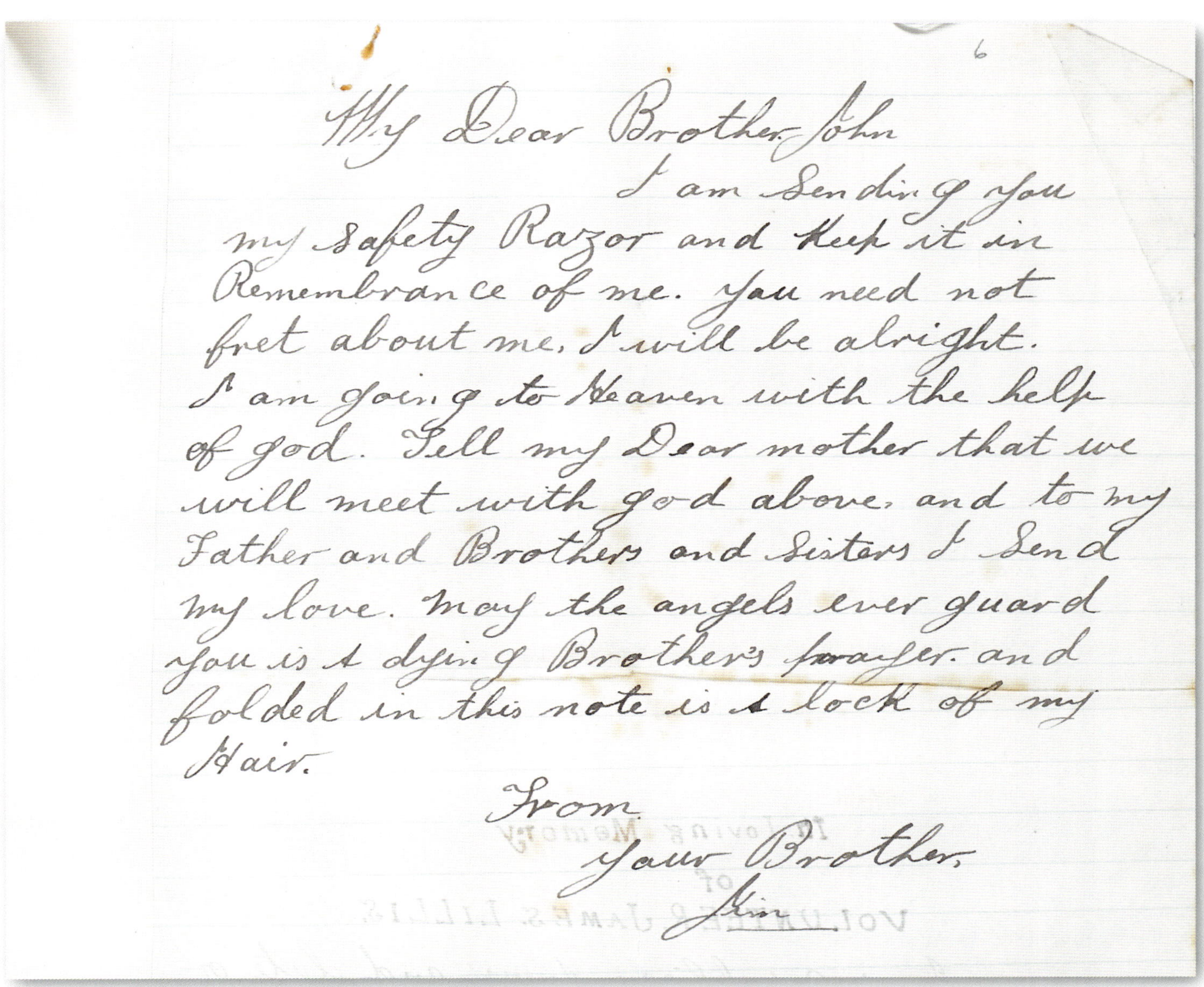

6

My Dear Brother John

I am Sending you my Safety Razor and keep it in Remembrance of me. you need not fret about me, I will be alright. I am going to Heaven with the help of god. Tell my Dear mother that we will meet with god above, and to my Father and Brothers and Sisters I Send my love. may the angels ever guard you is A dying Brother's prayer. and folded in this note is A lock of my Hair.

From
your Brother,
Jim

Fig. 14 Letter from IRA Volunteer James Lillis from Chapel Street, Bagenalstown, County Carlow, to his brother John, written on the eve of his execution at Carlow Barracks on the morning of 15 January 1923. Lillis was one of thirty-four republican prisoners executed by firing squad in January 1923. [Document: National Library of Ireland, MS 3897/6]

Fig. 15 Memorial card for Lieutenant Patrick Carroll, 3rd Western Division IRA. Twenty-four-year-old Carroll of 10 John Street in Sligo town was killed on 20 September 1922. He was one of six members of the North Sligo IRA shot dead by Free State forces on or near Benbulben Mountain in circumstances that still provoke debate a century later. One of nine children born to Bernard and Susan Carroll, he joined the Irish Volunteers in 1917 and, three years later, was battalion engineer with the Sligo Brigade, IRA. An active Volunteer, he participated in one of the most daring and successful operations carried out by the Sligo IRA during the War of Independence. On 28 June 1921 Carroll and several other Volunteers entered Sligo jail and successfully liberated senior republican prisoners Frank O'Beirne, Tom Deignan and Charles Gildea. After the outbreak of civil war, the Sligo IRA abandoned its garrisons in the evacuated Royal Irish Constabulary and military barracks in Sligo town, relocating its headquarters to Rahelly House 10 kilometres (6 miles) to the north. On 13 July 1922, the unit ambushed a convoy of National Army soldiers at Rockwood, County Sligo, killing four and capturing the Rolls Royce armoured car 'Ballinalee', which was called into service on 12 September 1922 when a combined force of republicans from across Sligo and Mayo attacked and captured the Free State garrison in Ballina. Determined to suppress the IRA in north Sligo, the Provisional Government sent large numbers of National Army reinforcements, an armoured car and an 18-pounder gun with the inscription 'McKeon's Own Peacemaker' to the western county. The coordinated assault on the Sligo republicans, now outnumbered by at least ten to one, began in earnest on 18 September 1922 when the National Army advanced on and captured Rahelly House. The republicans retreated to Benbulben Mountain, intending to seek refuge in their cave hideouts. En route to the cave two days later, Brian MacNeill, the divisional adjutant and son of pro-Treaty minister Eoin MacNeill, Brigadier Seamus Devins, Lieutenant Patrick Carroll and Volunteer Joseph Banks were surrounded by National Army troops on King's Mountain and shot, it is alleged, after surrendering. Captain Harry Benson and Volunteer Thomas Langan were subsequently shot dead during a second incident on the same day on nearby Benwiskin Mountain. Collectively, the men became known as 'Sligo's Noble Six'. Except for the Ballyseedy reprisal in Kerry in March 1923, their summary execution in September 1922 represents the largest single killing of prisoners during the Civil War. [Text: Frank Fagan / Image: courtesy of Frank Fagan / Sources: MSPC DP1563, Patrick Carroll; James Bonsall, Marion Dowd and Robert Mulraney, *The Six: The lives and memorialisation of Sligo's Noble Six* (Sligo, 2022), p. 94; *Evening Herald*, 29 June 1921; MSP34REF37329, Frank O'Beirne; MSP34REF22643, Thomas Deignan; MSP34REF30117, Charles Gildea; Michael Farry, *The Aftermath of Revolution: Sligo, 1921–23* (Dublin, 2000), p. 77; Joe McGowan, *Even the Heather Bled* (Sligo, 2021), p. 218]

saw the most brutal pro-Treaty reprisals in March 1923, when seventeen prisoners were blown up at Ballyseedy, Countess Bridge and Cahersiveen. In all, some thirty-six republicans were killed in custody in that county, with another seven formally executed.

Less well known as perpetrators of 'unofficial' reprisals than the Dublin units was the National Army's 1st Western Division. Raised in Clare and Galway, its men were stationed for the first half of the Civil War in County Kerry, where they carried out numerous killings of prisoners. There were, however, other reprisal killings not involving these groups, including the summary execution of six captured republicans on the slopes of Benbulben in Sligo in September 1922. The experience in Cork and Kerry suggests that the key factor in the propensity for reprisals was the presence of outside troops, particularly Dubliners officered by former Collins intelligence operatives. Two reprisal killings in Cork during September 1922 were 'the work of the Squad' and almost provoked a mutiny by locally recruited pro-Treaty troops. General officer commanding Cork, Emmet Dalton, recommended that the Dublin officers responsible be sent away.[19] Reprisals in Cork fell off very sharply after this and the county saw only eight in total, far fewer than neighbouring Kerry. Many reprisals also followed the deaths of well-liked pro-Treaty figures. For instance, reprisal killings in Cork in September 1922 were prompted by the death of former Squad member Tom Kehoe in a mine attack in which six other soldiers were also killed. The March 1923 mine reprisals in Kerry were likewise sparked by the deaths, also in an explosion, of Dublin Guard officers Michael Dunne and Edward Stapleton.

However, there is also evidence of a more calculated policy of targeted killing, particularly in Dublin and Kerry in March and April 1923, designed to terrorise and decapitate anti-Treaty resistance. Those abducted and shot in Dublin during that period included three leaders of IRA active service units. Among the victims of the retaliatory mine explosions in Kerry, the army noted, were 'some of the most inveterate enemies of the government'.[20] A significant number of Civil War combatants died as a result of illness, notably pneumonia and tuberculosis, but we have only counted these where it was formally deemed attributable to service or imprisonment.

Fig. 16 Two women and a child being evacuated during fighting in Dublin in July 1922. [Image: Cashman Collection ©RTÉ Archives, 0504/062]

Civilians

The total number of civilians killed during the period covered in this study, 370 in all thirty-two counties, was far lower than the 817 civilian dead logged by the Dead of the Irish Revolution project for the War of Independence, 1919–21 (up to the Truce).[21] Civilian deaths were concentrated at the start of the war and peaked in July 1922, demonstrating the high cost of urban combat in Dublin, Limerick and Waterford. Just over 60 per cent of the civilian fatalities occurred between June and November 1922, with a progressive decline thereafter.

Almost 47 per cent of the civilians killed in the twenty-six counties were in Munster, with Leinster accounting for slightly less than 37 per cent, and Connacht and the three southern Ulster counties combined accounting for a little over 16 per cent. The fatalities map reveals the concentration in Dublin city (the county with the highest absolute number) and also in Cork city, with lesser concentrations in urban Limerick and Waterford. The fundamentally different pattern evident north of the border reveals that the majority of the far more limited number of victims were civilians (over 59 per cent of the total). One of the few features the fatalities in Northern Ireland shared with those in the South was the significant urban concentration (around Belfast). Civilian deaths across the island followed a significantly different pattern to that of combatants, with a notably wider age range.

Over 27 per cent of civilians were killed in crossfire and over 20 per cent in accidents. Despite the high level of civilian deaths by misadventure, or what might be termed 'collateral damage', almost 40 per cent could be clearly identified as deliberate. Of these, about half occurred in spontaneous encounters between combatants and civilians. The National Army shot many more civilians than the IRA in such cases (fifty as compared to thirteen), usually at checkpoints when civilians 'failed to halt'. A typical IRA shooting of a civilian, by contrast, leaving aside the killing of informers, occurred during night-time raids on houses, usually in search of arms, food or shelter.

This leaves another 20 per cent or so of civilian deaths that were due to targeted assassination or murder. Uncertainty hangs over many civilian killings in the conflict. There were cases where the motives were apparently personal or agrarian rather than political.

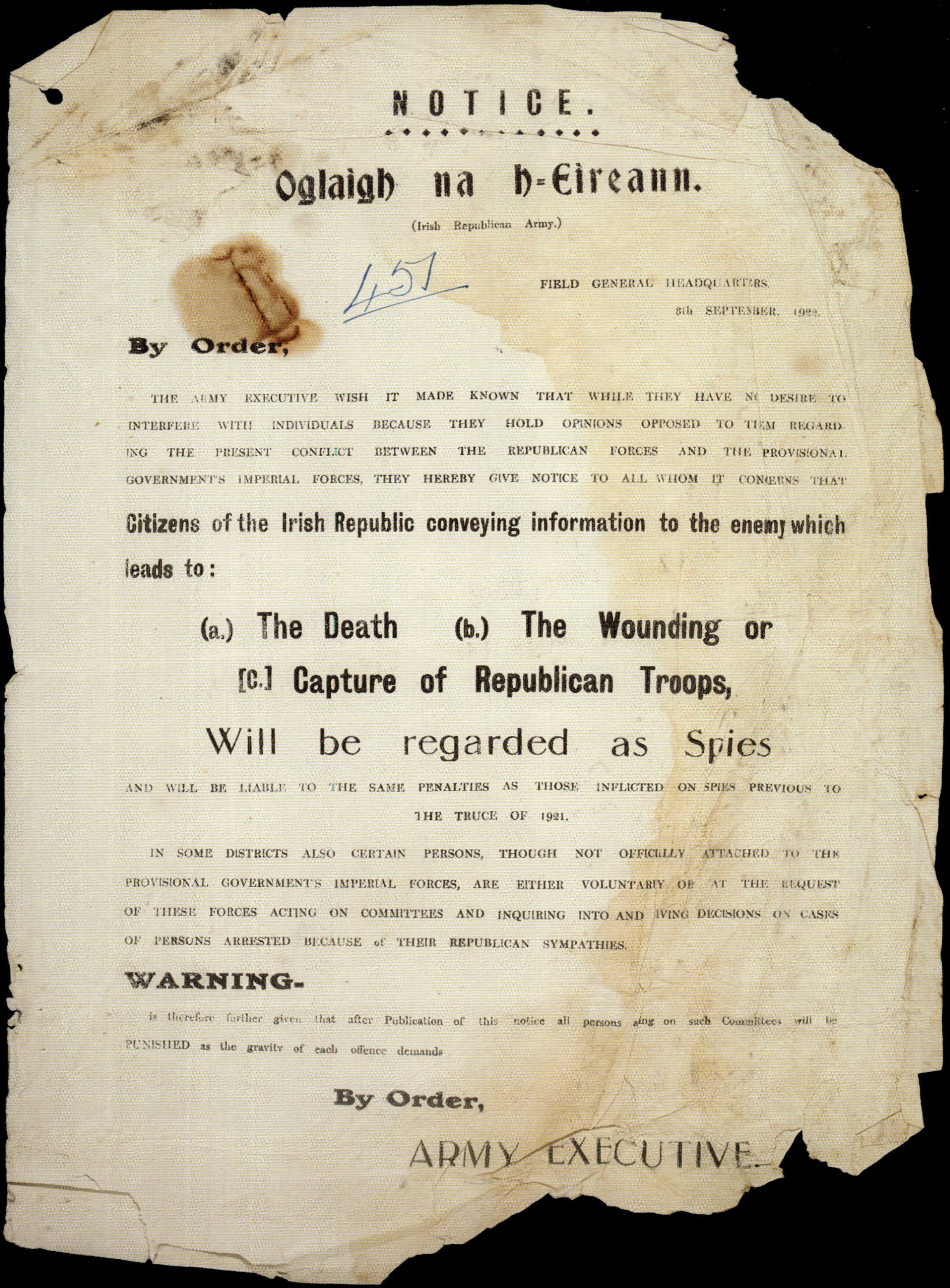

NOTICE.

Oglaigh na h-Eireann.

(Irish Republican Army.)

451

FIELD GENERAL HEADQUARTERS.

8th SEPTEMBER, 1922.

By Order,

THE ARMY EXECUTIVE WISH IT MADE KNOWN THAT WHILE THEY HAVE NO DESIRE TO INTERFERE WITH INDIVIDUALS BECAUSE THEY HOLD OPINIONS OPPOSED TO THEM REGARDING THE PRESENT CONFLICT BETWEEN THE REPUBLICAN FORCES AND THE PROVISIONAL GOVERNMENT'S IMPERIAL FORCES, THEY HEREBY GIVE NOTICE TO ALL WHOM IT CONCERNS THAT

Citizens of the Irish Republic conveying information to the enemy which leads to:

(a.) The Death (b.) The Wounding or [C.] Capture of Republican Troops,

Will be regarded as Spies

AND WILL BE LIABLE TO THE SAME PENALTIES AS THOSE INFLICTED ON SPIES PREVIOUS TO THE TRUCE OF 1921.

IN SOME DISTRICTS ALSO CERTAIN PERSONS, THOUGH NOT OFFICIALLY ATTACHED TO THE PROVISIONAL GOVERNMENT'S IMPERIAL FORCES, ARE EITHER VOLUNTARIY OR AT THE REQUEST OF THESE FORCES ACTING ON COMMITTEES AND INQUIRING INTO AND [G]IVING DECISIONS ON CASES OF PERSONS ARRESTED BECAUSE of THEIR REPUBLICAN SYMPATHIES.

WARNING-

is therefore further given that after Publication of this notice all persons acting on such Committees will be PUNISHED as the gravity of each offence demands

By Order,

ARMY EXECUTIVE.

Fig. 17 Notice issued on 8 September 1922 by IRA GHQ warning that those found providing information to the 'enemy' would be regarded as spies [Document: National Library of Ireland, Ernie O'Malley Papers, MS 10,973/20/1]

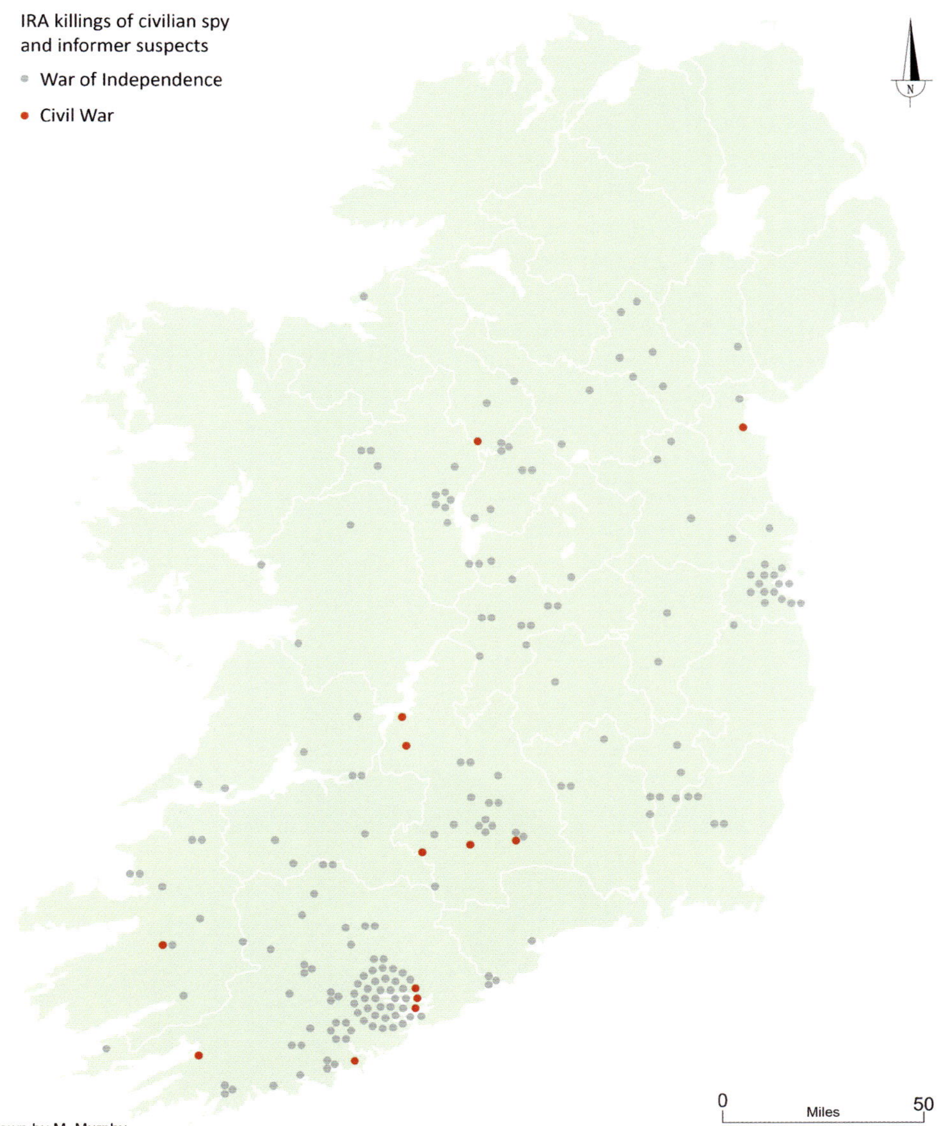

Fig. 18 Civilian spies and informers killed by the IRA during the Irish War of Independence and Civil War. This map shows the locations where 204 alleged civilian spies and informers were killed by the IRA during the Irish War of Independence and Civil War. The most striking aspect of the comparison is the dramatically greater number of alleged spies and informers killed in the War of Independence (191) than during the Civil War (thirteen). This was one of the factors contributing to a lower fatality level among civilians in the latter conflict. The killing of alleged spies appears to have been far more prevalent in Munster than in the other provinces, with Munster accounting for over 55 per cent of all those identified in the War of Independence and almost 85 per cent of the far smaller number killed in the Civil War. County Cork stands out well ahead of all other counties, accounting for almost 39 per cent (seventy-four) of the total in the War of Independence and over 38 per cent (five) of those killed in the Civil War. Other areas where suspects were killed in significant numbers during the War of Independence included Dublin (sixteen), Tipperary (fifteen), Roscommon (ten) and Offaly (eight). In the Civil War, the majority of those killed as alleged spies were in counties Cork and Tipperary (five each). Although it has been claimed that the IRA exploited the War of Independence as an opportunity to conduct a sectarian murder campaign targeting Protestants, three quarters of those killed as alleged British spies in that conflict were Catholic. All the alleged spies executed during the Civil War were Catholic, which discounts anti-Protestant sectarian motives for the killing of those thirteen civilians. Notable in the anti-Treaty IRA's execution of alleged spies between 1922 and 1923 was a change in terminology. The standard wording used on IRA spy labels during the War of Independence, 'Spies and Informers Beware', increasingly changed to 'Spies and Robbers Beware', suggesting a switch in focus from military intelligence to vigilantism. Tellingly, during the Civil War, Frank Henderson, leader of the IRA's Dublin Brigade, sought permission from Ernie O'Malley, commander of the IRA's 1st Eastern Division, to kill members of a 'robber gang – who are possible Free State spies as well'. Assessing the 'guilt' of those killed as spies is a difficult if not impossible task for historians. Between 25–30,000 intelligence files relating to the Civil War were transferred from the Department of Defence to An Garda Síochana in 1927, all of which were destroyed in 1932. In some cases there is strong evidence to suggest those killed had assisted either the British crown forces or the National Army. However, in the case of many killings, no record remains of the evidence on which IRA members based their suspicions of spying. [Text: Pádraig Óg Ó Ruairc and Andy Bielenberg / Sources: Pádraig Óg Ó Ruairc, *Truce: Murder, myth and the last days of the Irish War of Independence* (Cork, 2016), pp. 99–105; Pádraig Óg Ó Ruairc, *The Disappeared: Forced disappearances in Ireland, 1798–1998* (Newbridge, 2024); Cork Fatality Register, 1919–21 (https://www.ucc.ie/en/theirishrevolution/collections/cork-fatality-register); Eunan O'Halpin and Daithí Ó Corráin, *The Dead of the Irish Revolution* (Yale, 2020); Andy Bielenberg and John Dorney, The Irish Civil War Fatalities Project (UCC, 2024) – (https://www.ucc.ie/en/theirishrevolution/irish-civilwar-fatalities-project) / See also John Dorney, *Civil War in Dublin* (Dublin, 2017)]

In some instances bodies were found shot and labelled as informers, but the motives were later traced back to personal and apolitical grievances. Until quite late in the Civil War, IRA general orders laid out explicitly that civilians could not be killed as punishment for providing information to Free State forces.[22] While these orders were eventually rescinded and some civilians were shot as 'spies' by the anti-Treatyites, the thirteen or more killed was dramatically less than during the War of Independence, when at least 191 civilians were executed by the IRA as suspected spies and informers.[23] This was one of the major differences between the two conflicts, and partially accounts for the lower civilian death toll in the Civil War.

This is not to say that civilians were unaffected by the conflict. In reprisal for the government's executions policy, the anti-Treaty leadership ordered attacks on the homes and property of pro-Treaty supporters. A general order issued in December 1922, for instance, declared that 'all Free State supporters are traitors and deserve the latter's stark fate, therefore their houses must be destroyed at once'.[24] Hundreds of houses of government supporters, senators, TDs and military officers were burnt, mostly in the winter of 1922–3, including nearly 200 mansions belonging to the old landed class, many of whom were former unionists. Such property destruction was rarely lethal, as the victims were generally given time to leave. Two exceptional cases were those of Emmet McGarry, the seven-year-old son of pro-Treaty TD Seán McGarry, who died of burns after the family home in Fairview was set alight in December 1922, and Thomas Higgins, the sixty-four-year-old father of government minister Kevin O'Higgins, who was shot dead by an IRA party that had come to burn the family home in Stradbally, County Laois.[25]

Gender, age and social class

Our research provides a useful sample of the social profiles of Civil War fatalities. Firstly, those who died as a result of Civil War violence were overwhelmingly male, with less than 5 per cent being women. Of these, only three, all Cumman na mBan members, were combatants and the remaining sixty-two were civilians. Relatively few elderly people or children were killed.

The typical Civil War fatality was a young adult male. Almost 74 per cent of the National Army dead and just under 82 per cent of republican dead were aged between twenty and thirty-four. The

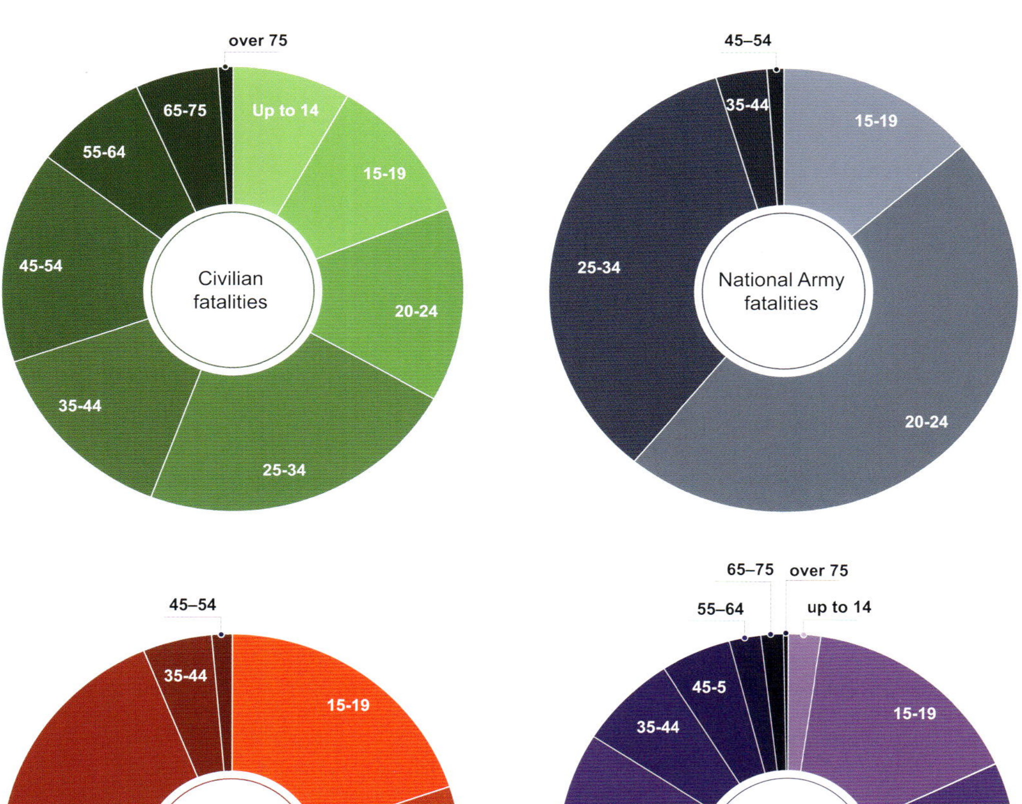

Fig. 19 Three pie charts showing the age profile of the 344 IRA fatalities, 482 National Army fatalities and 307 civilian fatalities in the twenty-six counties where age is known between 28 June 1922 and 24 May 1923. The fourth pie chart shows the age profile of all 1,158 fatalities where age is known, including members of Cumann na mBan, Na Fianna Éireann, the Civic Guard, the Citizens' Defence Force, the Criminal Investigation Department (CID) and the crown forces.

Fig. 20 A National Army soldier with a group of civilians outside a Dublin grocery shop. The children's smiling innocence contrasts with the armed and uniformed figure representative of the steady militarisation of Irish society in the first decades of the twentieth century. The experience of children during the Irish Civil War is a subject long neglected by historians, but there are manifold traces of the physical, emotional and material impact of the eleven-month conflict on their lives. The Military Service Pensions Collection, for example, is an archive of troubled and truncated childhoods, of lives irrevocably changed by the imprisonment or death of a parent, by enforced separation or economic privation. Occasionally, as the new research by Andy Bielenberg and John Dorney demonstrates, the cost for children was more physical, even final. Of the 1,158 fatalities in the twenty-six counties where age is known, twenty-seven (eleven girls and sixteen boys) were under the age of fifteen. The youngest was two-year-old Margaret Byrne, hit by a stray bullet in Dublin on 1 July 1922 and, as the *Irish Times* put it, a particularly 'sad' addition to the list of thirty-two civilian victims of crossfire in the city between 28 June and 6 July. Others, like six-year-old Andrew Barker, who discovered an unexploded bomb by a wall in Bagenalstown, County Carlow on 17 July 1922, succumbed to the perilous detritus of war. Others still, like fifteen-year-old Dublin apprentice William Saunders, shot by National Army soldiers in Dublin on 6 July 1922, were regarded as adult Civil War fatalities because of the narrower definition of childhood in the early twentieth century. For many children from lower socio-economic backgrounds, formal schooling ended at fourteen when they were set out to work. Dan Keating, a fifteen-year-old grocer's apprentice in Tralee when he joined the republican youth organisation Na Fianna Éireann in 1917, recalled being 'caught up' in 'a wave' of martial excitement. Fianna boys served on the anti-Treaty side as messengers, scouts and intelligence gatherers, with nine of its members listed among the Civil War dead. Keating 'graduated' to the IRA at eighteen, a typical route of guerrilla succession. Thirteen per cent of IRA Civil War fatalities were aged between fifteen and nineteen. While the pro-Treaty publicity department condemned the IRA leadership for 'arming children of sixteen years and sending them out to kill', the National Army census taken in mid-November 1922 testifies to the extreme youth of some of its own recruits. Private Con Riordan, for example, who signed up in Tralee on 14 October 1922, was one of twenty-one listed as just fifteen years old. Two other fifteen-year-old recruits, James Byrne, killed in action in Sligo on 3 July 1922, and John Carberry, accidentally shot at Carrick Workhouse in Tipperary on 11 September 1922, were among the 20 per cent of National Army fatalities under the age of nineteen. [Image: courtesy of Dún Laoghaire-Rathdown County Council Library Service / Sources: Dan Keating and Diarmaid Fleming, 'Interview: Last man standing: Dan Keating', *History Ireland*, vol. 16, no. 3, May–June 2008; Irish Army Census Collection, https://census.militaryarchives.ie]

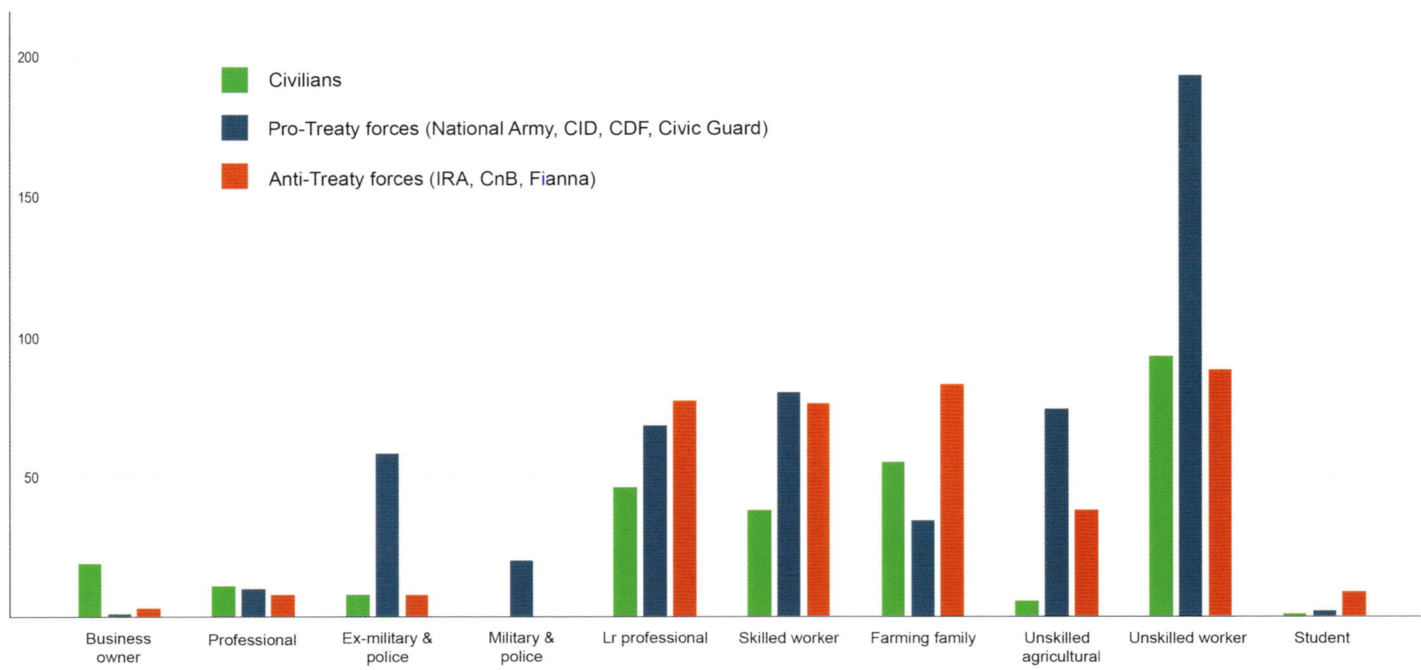

Fig. 21 Bar chart showing the ten categories of employment for civilian, pro- and anti-Treaty fatalities.

Fig. 22 Recruits for National Army. [Image: part of the Independent Newspapers Ireland/NLI Collection, INDH174]

National Army had a somewhat higher number of teenage soldiers killed than the anti-Treaty side.

The occupations of the dead indicate that there were some social differences between the two sides. National Army soldiers were more likely to have lower social status, with almost half of the fatalities recorded as having unskilled occupations, compared to less than one third for anti-Treaty victims. Conversely, there was a higher share of skilled workers, tradesmen and lower professionals (such as clerks, teachers and civil servants) in the IRA. Most striking of all is that over 21 per cent of IRA fatalities were either farmers or their sons, in comparison to under 9 per cent of National Army soldiers. This indicates that the latter recruited primarily from among the urban and rural poor, whereas IRA members came from a broader cross-section of society. This finding corroborates previous research on the social complexion of the IRA by Peter Hart and Michael Farry.[26]

It is not altogether surprising that the majority of the National Army's rank and file were drawn from the unskilled working class, while the IRA was peopled to a greater extent by the skilled working class, farmers and lower professionals. IRA Volunteers joined a mostly unpaid guerrilla army for a range of political and social motives, but rarely for employment. Pro-Treaty IRA members came from similar backgrounds, and many did join the Free State forces out of political conviction, but National Army recruits were generally poor men in need of a steady income. The top echelon of society, the business owners and upper professionals (like doctors, solicitors and higher civil servants), were far better represented among the ranks of the civilian fatalities than belligerents.

Previous service

Part of the anti-Treaty republican narrative of the Civil War is that its volunteer soldiers were overwhelmed by the vast numbers of former British army veterans recruited by the pro-Treaty side. Tom Barry, for example, stated that the recruitment of disbanded British

ANTI-TREATY (IRA, Fianna Éireann, Cumann na mBan)	Numbers	% of Total
Pre-Truce republican service only	306	69.9
Former British service only	9	2.1
Pre-Truce republican and former British service	19	4.3
Unknown/No previous service	104	23.7
Total Anti-Treaty	**438**	**100**

PRO-TREATY (National Army, CID, CDF, Civic Guard)	Numbers	% of Total
Former IRA or Fianna only	162	25
Former British service only	107	16.5
Former IRA and British service	6	0.9
Unknown/No previous service	373	57.6
Total Pro-Treaty	**648**	**100**

Fig. 23 Table showing pre-Civil War service of pro- and anti-Treaty combatant fatalities in the twenty-six counties. 'Republican service' indicates previous service with the IRA, Cumann na mBan, Na Fianna Éireann or the Irish Republican Police (IRP). 'British service' means previous service in the British army, the Royal Air Force, the Royal Navy, the Royal Irish Constabulary, the Dublin Metropolitan Police and, in the case of one IRA member and one National Army soldier, the Australian and Canadian military services, respectively. Among the combatant fatalities, 104 anti-Treatyites and 373 pro-Treatyites are listed as having 'unknown/no previous service'. As previous service was recorded in the military service pension files, this almost always means no previous service. Information on previous service was found for only sixteen of the 335 civilian fatalities: former republican service (3), former British service (12) and former National Army service (1). The sources consulted for civilian fatalities did not often include such details, so it is likely that more may have served in either the British military or police. Those combatants who died during the Civil War represent a small percentage of those who served. Nevertheless, the data here on previous service challenge a number of preconceptions on the conflict, such as the alleged predominance of ex-British servicemen in pro-Treaty ranks and 'trucileers' in anti-Treaty ranks.

A-P.52 1/4/450 Stenning

Kennington Post Office,

Oxford,

Nov. 26th, 1933.

FORM 52 ISSUED 29 NOV .33

The Ministry of Pensions,
Collins Barracks,
Dublin

DEPT. OF DEFENCE RECEIVED 29. NOV 1933 ARMY PENSIONS

Dear Sir,

I wish to apply for the necessary forms in connection with the death of my son Reginald who was executed at Tralee in April 1923.

My son went to Ireland in the Lancashire Regiment espoused the Irish cause, and went out with the boys against the infamous "Black & Tans . He stayed on in the country, and became attached to the Irish Republican Army. He fought with them all during the Civil War until he was captured at Clashmealcon and executed by the Free State Government at the time.

Now, Reginald was my only support , and if he was living today, I would not be in the position which I now find myself.

I shall be thankful therefore if you send me the necessary Pension Forms per return so that I can have them completed and returned you for your kind consideratic

I remain,

Yours faithfully,

E. Stenning

Fig. 24 (opposite) Letter from Edith Stenning, 26 November 1933, seeking the 'necessary form' for an ultimately unsuccessful application for an award under the Army Pensions Acts in respect of the death of her son Reginald Walter Stenning. Several days after the IRA chief of staff, Liam Lynch, was killed in County Tipperary, one of the most dramatic episodes of the conflict unfolded on the rugged cliffs of north Kerry, militarily and symbolically the last line of defence of the Kerry IRA. Trapped in Dunworth's cave on the face of the towering cliff at Clashmealcon, six IRA men were surrounded by the National Army with no means of escape. On 16 April 1923 four soldiers under Lt Henry Pearson descended the treacherous cliff face in an attempt to capture the wanted men. The IRA fired on them: Private James O'Neill was killed instantly, while Pearson was seriously wounded. Two of the IRA men, cousins Thomas McGrath and Patrick O'Shea, decided to swim for it in the dark Atlantic. They were never seen again. Two days into the siege, during which the National Army troops made numerous efforts to extricate the column, IRA leader Timothy 'Aero' Lyons offered his surrender. The rope lowered to aid his ascent was allegedly cut and, as he lay on the rocks below, he was riddled with machine-gun fire. The three surviving IRA Volunteers were taken into custody, sentenced to death and executed at Tralee jail on the morning of 25 April 1923. Facing the firing squad with north Kerry natives Edward Greaney and James McEnery was a mysterious character named in official reports as Reginald Hathaway. Born Reginald Walter Stenning in north London in February 1903, he joined the British army in 1920 and was a member of the East Lancashire Regiment, which was billeted in Tralee during the War of Independence. Stenning, his mother later noted, 'espoused the Irish cause' and deserted the British army in May 1921 to join the Ballyheigue Company of the IRA. Using the alias Reginald Hathaway, or 'Rudge' as he was known to his IRA comrades, he became a member of the flying column led by 'Aero' Lyons. Stenning joined the National Army in 1922 but, in a further remarkable twist, he abandoned his post at Ballymullen Barracks in Tralee to join the anti-Treaty IRA. He was arrested in early 1923 under the name Walter Stephens and, after being released following a commitment not to take up arms against the state, he rejoined his comrades in north Kerry. Within months, Stenning was captured at Clashmealcon and, despite volunteering intelligence that led to the discovery of an arms dump and at least one arrest, he was executed in the barracks where he had twice been billeted as a soldier. His parents, Walter and Edith Stenning, who had not seen him since 1920, applied for a military pension in 1933. Despite interventions from their local vicar and Kerry Fianna Fáil TD Eamonn Kissane the application was rejected on the basis that the Stennings could not prove financial dependency on their son. Reginald Stenning, the man with many aliases and who was a member of three different armies, remains an enigmatic Englishman honoured among the Irish republican dead. [Text: Owen O'Shea / Source: MSPC DP7023, Reginald Walter Stenning. Image courtesy of Military Archives/MSPC Project]

army soldiers into the National Army made it virtually impossible to achieve victory for the anti-Treaty side.[27] Jane Leonard asserts that it was officially estimated that about half of the 55,000 soldiers who fought for the National Army were ex-servicemen. Her own more detailed analysis of the personnel files of the officer corps revealed over 600 veterans of the First World War.[28] The perception of extensive former British army influence was informed by the exaggerations of General Liam Tobin, a leader of the army mutiny in 1924, who claimed 'The army is rotten. [It is] 40 per cent ex-IRA, 10 per cent ex-civilians hostile to the IRA and 50 per cent ex-British army'.[29]

Our data on the previous service of National Army fatalities, however, reveal that only 109 (17 per cent) were recorded as former British army personnel. While these represent a small fraction of the total who served in the National Army, the proportion is in line with Leonard's figures for army officers with First World War service, which, if we take a figure of 3,300 for all officers in the National Army,[30] would imply that ex-servicemen accounted for about 18.2 per cent of the officer corps. It is certainly true that veterans of the British army were actively recruited by the Free State authorities, but our data suggest that a higher share of National Army fatalities, 23 per cent, were ex-IRA or Fianna with pre-Truce service. A far higher share still, some 60 per cent, had no previous affiliation or military service. The latter finding accords better with evidence of poor overall National Army discipline and performance in the Civil War, despite its far superior resources. The share of ex-servicemen in the ranks of the National Army perhaps requires further research.

By contrast, under 5 per cent of the anti-Treaty dead had served in British forces, and most of these also had pre-Truce IRA service. Indeed, 74 per cent of republican fatalities had been members of the IRA, Na Fianna or Cumann na mBan, before the Truce in 1921. These numbers, compiled from military service pension applications, may be slightly inflated by the desire of families to be awarded a larger pension or gratuity, but they do call into question another Civil War propaganda trope: the pro-Treaty charge that most 'irregulars' were opportunistic 'trucileers' who had not fought the British but had joined the IRA only during the safety of the Truce.

County of origin

The origins of those who died in combat also challenge some popular perceptions about the protagonists. On this metric, Dublin again stands out, mainly as it was the National Army's primary recruiting ground. Over three times as many Dublin men died in National Army service as in the IRA, many of them in other counties scattered across the Free State. From this it might be tempting to repeat the narrative that the Civil War represented the conquest of the provinces by a Dublin-recruited army. However, the data complicate this argument significantly. In County Kerry it was indeed the case that more than twice as many local men died in the IRA as in the National Army. In Tipperary and Waterford, locally born republican deaths also outnumbered pro-Treaty ones, though to a lesser extent. In contrast, Corkonians who died in Free State uniform outnumbered those who died for the republican cause, which may not fit popular perceptions. The significance of local recruitment once the National Army had established a foothold across much of the 'Munster Republic' has perhaps been underestimated. The same pattern holds for counties Clare and Limerick.

Outside of Munster, the only Free State counties with a significant death toll, where local anti-Treaty casualties outnumbered those on the pro-Treaty side, were Louth and Wexford. Counties where the IRA was largely pro-Treaty and, as a result, there was little combat during the Civil War – notably Longford and Cavan – saw significant numbers of their sons dying elsewhere in the country in the service of the National Army. Over 100 people from the nine counties of Ulster died in the twenty-six Free State counties in the Civil

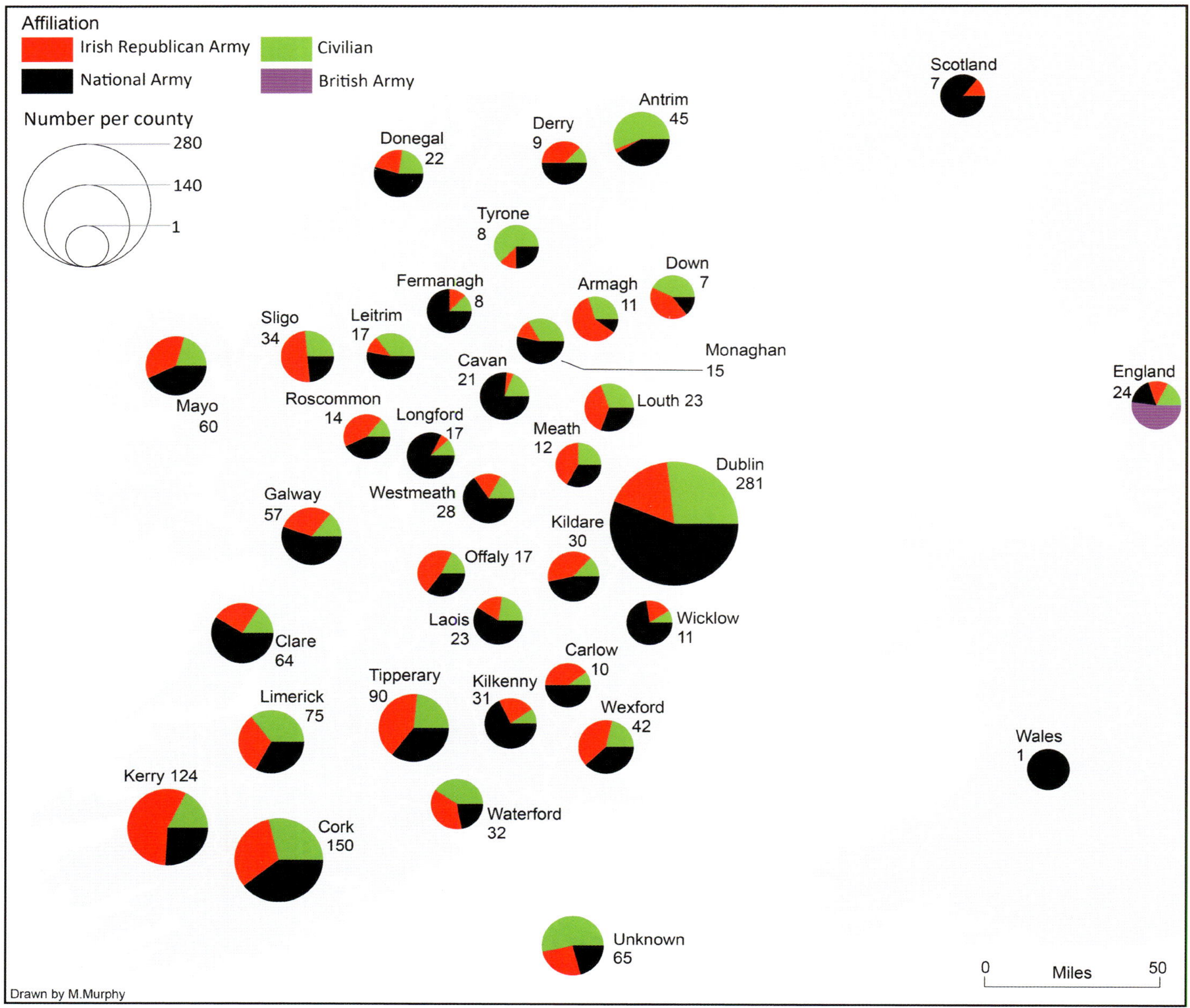

Fig. 25 Map showing the places of origin of all those killed as a result of political violence in the thirty-two counties between 28 June 1922 and 24 May 1923.

War and, again, over three times as many of these died in the pro-Treaty forces as in the IRA. This was due, in part, to the pro-Treaty stance of the Northern IRA divisions, though many Northerners without previous IRA service were also recruited into the National Army, including one whose father was serving as an Ulster Special constable. Armagh (where Frank Aiken's 4th Northern Division took the anti-Treaty side after some prevarication) was the only Ulster county with more anti- than pro-Treaty deaths.

Conclusions

The last phase of the Irish revolutionary period, taking place in 1922–3, bears the name the 'Irish Civil War', a title that perhaps suggests its scale was greater than in fact it was. The intranationalist bloodshed also marked a line of demarcation between the hoped-for all-Ireland republic and the post-1922 reality of two polities on the island. The figures generated here support the conclusion that fatalities between 28 June 1922 and 24 May 1923 were somewhat lower than in the War of Independence. Our total of 1,484 violent deaths on the island (with only fifty-nine in total in Northern Ireland) is well below the figure of 2,176 deaths counted in all thirty-two counties in 1919–21 (up to the Truce) by the Dead of the Irish Revolution project.[31]

Moreover, over 76 per cent of the Civil War fatalities in the twenty-six counties were combatants and less than 24 per cent were civilians. In contrast, civilians made up some 40 per cent of victims of the War of Independence, and nearly 80 per cent if we examine Northern Ireland alone between 1920 and 1922.[32] In terms

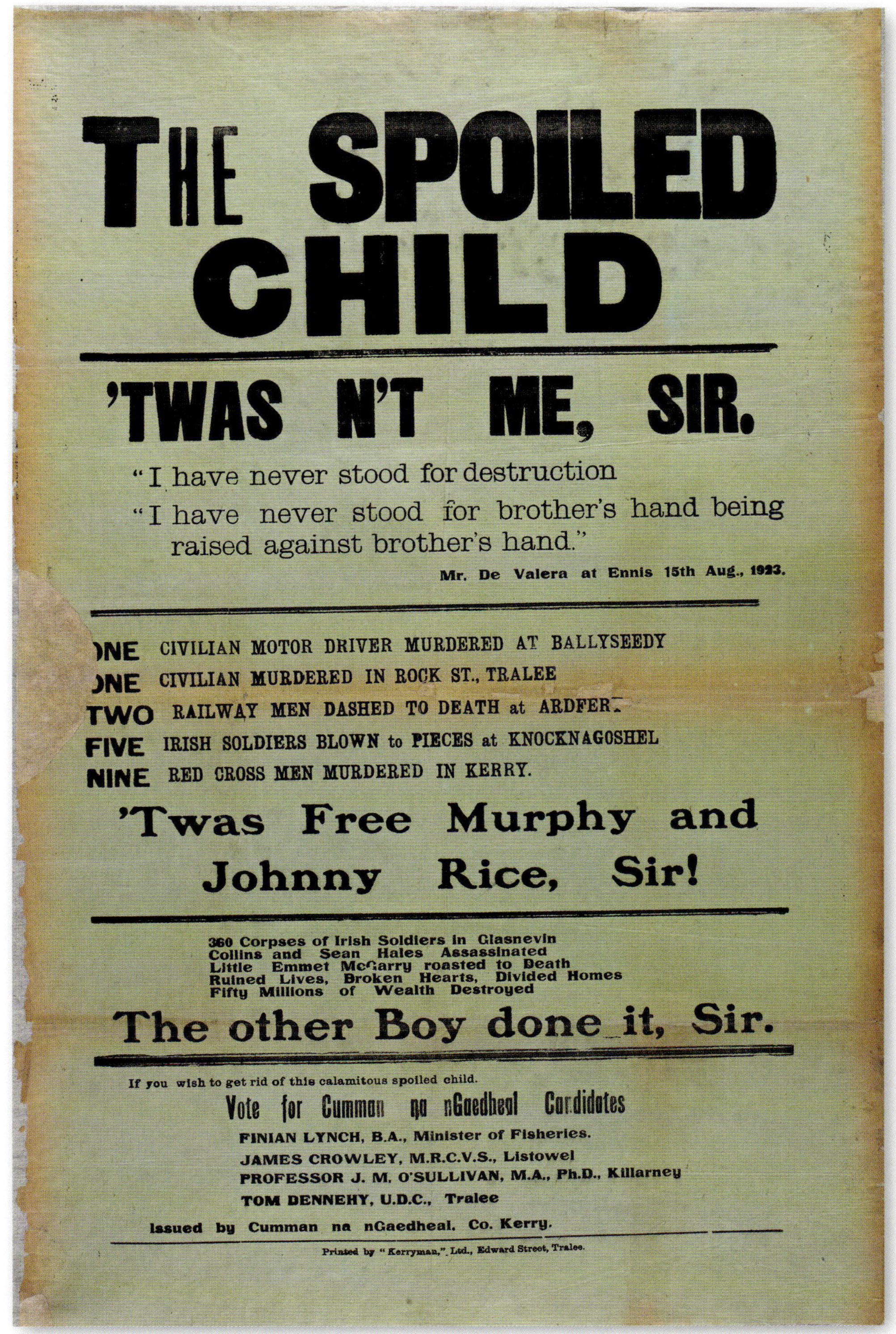

Fig. 26 This 1927 Cumann na nGaedheal election poster reveals that politics in County Kerry were still highly charged by the recent memory of the Civil War. With the entry of Fianna Fáil into the race, the government party was selectively reminding voters of a number of civilian victims of republican attacks. The electorate was also being asked to remember Knocknagoshel (where a trap-mine explosion resulted in five National Army fatalities). Unsurprisingly, no mention is made of the far higher number of reprisal atrocities by the National Army in Kerry, which were undoubtedly the worst in the Civil War in terms of scale. If civil war had been 'politics by other means', evidently things had not entirely returned to normal by 1927. That these specific incidents should be listed in this fashion reveals the extent to which they were at the forefront of public consciousness. While the government had won a decisive military victory in the Civil War, the results of the 1923 general election in the Kerry constituency (where Cumann na nGaedheal received under 33 per cent of the first-preference votes, while Sinn Féin polled over 45 per cent) revealed that the government and its army had not won the battle for 'hearts and minds'. This poster was an attempt to contribute to the reversal of the prevailing outlook. [Text: Andy Bielenberg / Document: National Library of Ireland, EPH G72]

of indiscriminate violence, therefore, the Irish Civil War was by no means more terrible than what had gone before.

Our research provides new insights into the course and conduct of the Civil War and the social profile of the combatants. The chronology of fatalities challenges the idea that the war was all but over after the Provisional Government's offensive in the summer of 1922. Charles Townshend's contention that nearly two thirds of those killed in the Civil War died in the first three months is not supported by our results,[33] which show that just over 43 per cent of fatalities occurred between 28 June 1922 and the end of September 1922. The 'conventional phase' of late June to August did see a peak in total casualties, but the overall level of combatant fatalities also remained high during the first guerrilla phase in the autumn of 1922, which has been a core finding of this project. The National Army suffered by far the majority of fatal casualties in both these phases, which underlines the fact that anti-Treaty guerrillas remained a considerable threat to the Free State well after they had abandoned their positions in towns and cities. It was only after the introduction of executions that losses on both sides began to 'equalise', and by 1923 it was the republicans who were on the back foot, losing more in every month down to the April 1923 ceasefire than their pro-Treaty opponents. Furthermore, the majority of IRA members killed in 1923 did not die in combat but as a result of either formal execution or 'unofficial' execution in custody. This aspect of the latter half of the Civil War gave the republican memory of the conflict its particularly bitter and unforgiving character. Our comparison of the occupational profiles of those who died suggests that the republican 'men of no property' who fought in the Civil War actually had a higher social status than their adversaries in the National Army. The underdog label was certainly electorally advantageous for republicans, particularly from 1932 onwards, but a distinction needs to be made between those who fought on, and those who supported, the different sides.

With this new fatality figure for the Irish Civil War, a realistic estimate for the fatalities of the wider Irish revolution becomes more feasible. Well under 5,000 people lost their lives between 1916 and 1923. The scale of killing in Ireland did not compare remotely to the millions killed in the Russian civil wars or even the short-lived but bloody Finnish Civil War in 1918. The lack of a serious class or ethnic cleavage in the Irish case probably helps account for its relative moderation. It is, nevertheless, worth widening the comparative lens to other parts of western and central Europe. The Irish Civil War alone was apparently bloodier than the political violence prior to the fascist takeover in Italy, where it has been estimated that just under a thousand people were killed in political violence between November 1918 and June 1921, which some scholars see as an outright civil war.[34] In Hungary from mid-1919 to the early 1920s about 5,000 people lost their lives in a civil conflict between 'Reds' and 'Whites'.[35] If allowance is made for the Hungarian population, around two and half times that in the Irish Free State, the death toll per capita appears to be on a par with the Irish Civil War and less than the Irish revolutionary period as a whole. The internal conflict in Upper Silesia, partitioned in 1920 between Germany and Poland, was somewhat bloodier than the Irish Civil War. With a population about a third smaller than that of the Free State, its death toll was calculated as 2,824 by Tim Wilson.[36] It is more the timing and circumstances of the Irish Civil War as the terminal phase in the Irish revolution that provides stronger European parallels than its actual scale. An altogether more representative form of democracy emerged in Ireland in violent circumstances that resonated with a wider wave of democratisation across much of Europe in the violent aftermath of the First World War. Violence in Ireland, however, contributed only a small fraction of the estimated four million deaths across Europe in the multiple conflicts that formed an epilogue to the First World War.[37]

CASE STUDY

The Executions Policy

Seán Enright

By the autumn of 1922 the Civil War was draining the slender resources of the Irish state. This raised serious concerns within the government that the money would run out, that the state would disintegrate, and that Westminster might once again send in British troops. In this scenario, all that had been gained in the War of Independence would be lost. It was in these circumstances that the Provisional Government implemented its executions policy, with a view to ending the war.[1] In late September 1922, the strong pro-Treaty majority in the Dáil passed the Army (Special Powers) Resolution and a proclamation was published in the press. This authorised military courts to try offenders and impose the death penalty for a variety of offences, including carrying arms, attacking the National Army and destroying property.[2]

From the outset, the policy targeted the rank and file among anti-Treaty prisoners. 'Better to take the plain, ordinary case', Kevin O'Higgins told the Dáil in the wake of the first four executions in Kilmainham on 17 November, because 'the country might say, "Oh

Fig. 1 Richard Mulcahy (1886–1971) full-length portrait in uniform at an unidentified outdoor location, *c.* 1922. Mulcahy joined the Irish Volunteers on its foundation. He was second in command at the battle of Ashbourne during the Rising and was subsequently interned at Knutsford and Frongoch. In October 1917 he became director of training and, when IRA GHQ was formed, chief of staff. He played a central role directing the IRA and controlling its conduct during the War of Independence. Following the ratification of the Anglo-Irish Treaty, Mulcahy was simultaneously minister of defence and IRA chief of staff. This blurred the lines between military and civilian governance. He worked assiduously to avoid both the split in the IRA and civil war in early 1922. Following the battle of Dublin (28 June–5 July 1922), Mulcahy personally sanctioned the release of Liam Lynch in what was later judged to be a grievous miscalculation. One of the most critical continuities between Mulcahy's role in the War of Independence and the Civil War was his commitment to army discipline. During the Civil War, the danger of uncontrolled reprisals by a poorly trained National Army threatened control, credibility and morale. On learning of Collins's death, at 3.15 a.m. on 23 August, Mulcahy penned arguably his most important Civil War statement. He exhorted the men of the army to 'Stand calmly by your posts. Bend bravely and undaunted to your work. Let no cruel act of reprisal blemish your bright honour [...]'. By focusing on restraint, Mulcahy showed that he was attuned to the potential for reprisals, which could have unleashed a torrent of uncontrollable, internecine violence. Thereafter, Mulcahy took over as commander in chief of the National Army. His call for restraint in August may seem to jar with his advocacy of the state's executions policy from September onwards. A secret meeting with de Valera on 6 September 1922 hardened Mulcahy's attitude. He later claimed this was when he began to contemplate his executions policy. In advocating a policy of officially sanctioned executions, Mulcahy argued that he was quelling his soldiers' desire for unsanctioned retaliations. On 17 November 1922 Mulcahy told the Dáil that 'Anything that will shock the country into realisation of what a grave thing it is to take human life is justified at the moment.' Erskine Childers's execution a week later began a chain reaction leading to the assassination of Seán Hales on 7 December and the first four reprisal executions the following morning. These death notices were signed by Mulcahy. In 1923 Mulcahy continued to raise the efficiency of the army while progressing the fight in Kerry and other republican strongholds. In defending some of the National Army's worst conduct during the conflict, he prioritised army morale over holding his officers to account. Mulcahy resigned as minister of defence during the army mutiny in 1924. This episode and his conduct initially brought into question but, ultimately, confirmed civilian control over the army. Mulcahy's association with Civil War executions would follow him throughout his political career. He devoted his final years to documenting and chronicling his life. His papers are at UCD Archives. [Text: Conor Mulvagh / Image: National Library of Ireland, Piaras Béaslaí Collection, BEA52 / See Maryann Gialanella Valiulis, *Portrait of a Revolutionary* (Kentucky, 1992); Risteárd Mulcahy, *My Father, the General: Richard Mulcahy and the military history of the revolution* (Dublin, 2009); Ronan Fanning, 'Richard Mulcahy', *Dictionary of Irish Biography*, https://www.dib.ie/biography/mulcahy-richard-a6029]

Miss L. Robinson 3 Eugene St
off Cork St Dublin

4. Oclock A. M. Tuesday
13th March 1923.

Mullingar Military Barracks

My Dearest Dearest Lily

This is the answer to your very kind letter I recived on Sunday, This news may hurt you as I know it will very much, but all I ask of you now is prayer & I have given you the means, Go to Whelan's & they will give you my prayer book with your photos, & other things that are there, you can tell them, also all the lads & Nurse O'Brien all I ask is a prayer from them, Dearest Lily the hour is now 4. A. M. & We have only got 4 hours on this earth, we are Mick & I, to be Executed at 8. A.M. We have seen the priest Fr Kelly & I am very happy, we are to recive Holy communion at Mass at 6.30 here, So I am very happy & Glad to die as a Soldier of the Irish Republic Fr Kelly is to bless our graves, So Lily please pray for my soul & get some Masses said too, & ask the lads to pray for Us. The Staters are to send from here to you my Overcoat, pocket book, £5. note, Photos, & Fr Kelly will send you the pen & this little book, you can keep my Pocket Book, Prayerbook & all the money only send the Cheque & pen & £5 note home with my O'Coat, & you can keep the rest, You can have the whole thing published you know my age & address, my rank was Adj II Batt. III Brigade. II Northern Div I.R.A. I die for the Republic, & also one favour I will ask you to do all you can to console My Dearest Dearest Father, Sisters & Brothers & my wee man I know you will & may God & his Holy Mother bless you. Dearest Lily I was tried last Wednesday week & We heard our sentince last night at 10.30, So the hours are short but we have made our peace with God & are happy, Lily tell my people not to worry about my body they will get it when Ireland has a Republic, console them as best you can, So Now a last & long Good on this earth, dont forget prayer, They can kill our body Dearest but our Spirits still lives Good bye & God bless you Dearest Lily from

yours

Luke. Burke.

Fig. 2 (opposite) Last letter written by Luke Burke to his fiancée, Lily Robinson, 13 March 1923. In the early hours of Tuesday 13 March 1923 in Columb Barracks, Mullingar, two young anti-Treaty IRA officers penned their final letters, reassuring their families that they were proud to die 'as Soldiers of the Republic'. Michael Grealy (sometimes spelled Greally) from Scramogue, County Roscommon and Luke Burke (alias Henry Keenan) from Keady, County Armagh had been arrested, court-martialled and sentenced to death for robbing the Hibernian and Northern Banks in Oldcastle, County Meath on 27 February. The last of seven prisoners executed in Westmeath during the Civil War, they were shot by firing squad at 8 a.m. on 13 March and buried in the grounds of Columb Barracks. While the IRA leadership had initially endorsed the robbing of banks and post offices to fund their campaign, adverse publicity painting the IRA as criminals meant that the practice had been largely abandoned by early 1923. Described officially as 'civilian bank robbers', Grealy and Burke were excluded from the iconic '77, the number of official executions for actions while on active service published in Dorothy Macardle's *The Irish Republic* and enshrined in republican tradition. Several sources suggest that Grealy and Burke, shop assistants in Oldcastle, were active members of the local IRA. Their names, with the designation 'executed while operating within the area', were included in the 'Westmeath Martyrs Roll', read aloud during a large republican commemoration in Mullingar in July 1924. Three months later, on 24 October, their bodies were exhumed and reburied with full military honours. In 1933, however, the Department of Defence rejected pension applications by the families of Grealy and Burke. Writing to a representative of Grealy's mother, the Military Service Pensions Board reported: 'As a result of confidential inquiries made by the Board, they desire me to say that they are satisfied that the deceased Michael Grealy was not engaged in Military Service in Oglaigh na h-Eireann when he was last arrested by Free State Forces'. A similar response was received by the Burke family. Unfortunately, the pension file does not provide further details about the 'confidential inquiries made' into the case. Despite the department's conclusions, one may still question whether Grealy and Burke's activity was entirely unauthorised, or whether the circumstances in Oldcastle were more complicated. While the release of the Military Service Pensions Collection has provided valuable insight into the government's attitudes towards Civil War service, unfortunately they do not answer all questions or fully illuminate the layered reality of IRA operations in the final phase of the conflict. [Text: Jason McKevitt / Image and content is used by permission of Miriam and Hilary Jones, granddaughters of Lily Robinson]

he was killed because he was a leader"'.[3] This policy was pursued relentlessly. With the notable exceptions of Erskine Childers, the Mountjoy executions on 8 December, and the execution of Charles Daly at Drumboe Castle in March 1923, most of the executed prisoners were single men aged in their late teens to mid-twenties, who held no rank in the anti-Treaty IRA. While many senior officers, such as Ernie O'Malley, were captured, execution was usually avoided, and captured anti-Treaty TDs like Austin Stack were likewise spared.

Deterrence

The executions policy was stepped up in January 1923 when thirty-four prisoners were executed across the country.[4] The aim was deterrence through local executions, with firing squads convened in Carlow, Tipperary, Limerick, Dundalk, Athlone, Kerry, Waterford, Maryborough (now Portlaoise) and Offaly. By February 1923 the National Army had the upper hand and was anxious to end the destructive guerrilla warfare. The Army Council further refined the policy of local executions to include reprisal executions, ordering: 'In every case of outrage in any battalion area, three men will be executed.'[5] At this juncture the number of prisoners under sentence of death was rising fast and soon numbered over 400. After an IRA ambush, the National Army often sifted through these sentenced prisoners, selecting for execution men from the area where the ambush took place. Reprisal executions began in March when three prisoners were shot by firing squad in Wexford and four more at Drumboe Castle after an attack on Creeslough barracks in County Donegal. In April six men were executed at Tuam, County Galway, in reprisal for an attack on Headford barracks.

By June 1923 eighty-three prisoners had been executed. Of these only a handful had been convicted of attacks on the National Army. Six were National Army deserters who had taken their rifles and defected to the republicans, and two were executed for destroying railway infrastructure. Most had been convicted of possession of arms, a small number of whom were also convicted of robbery and household burglaries – a reminder, perhaps, that the executions policy was not entirely about suppressing the anti-Treaty faction. It is notable, given that the government's justification for the executions policy was the 'necessity' to stem anti-Treaty militarism, that the last two executions, those of Michael Murphy and Joseph O'Rourke on 30 May 1923, had nothing to do with the Civil War. The pair had robbed a bank without firing their revolvers and were captured while making off on foot. They were both aged eighteen and went to their deaths blindfolded and holding hands.

The case of Erskine Childers

The most significant test of the executions policy came in November 1922 with the capture of Erskine Childers in possession of a pistol. He was convicted by a military court and sentenced to death, but his counsel sought a writ of habeas corpus at the High Court. The fundamental argument was that the military court was not lawful because no statute had been passed and that the only statute regulating possession of arms, the Firearms Act, permitted imprisonment only.[6] Childers's solicitor gathered the names of eight other prisoners under sentence of death and added them to the action. The case came before the Master of the Rolls, Sir Charles O'Connor, and while legal argument continued, the Provisional Government Executive debated the options if the civil court ruling was unfavourable. Some argued for shutting down the courts and immediate execution.[7] Ireland hovered on the brink of rule by junta.

On the final evening of exhausting legal argument at Kings' Inns on 23 November, Sir Charles O'Connor delivered his judgment. After an impassioned protest at the destruction of the Four Courts and the Public Record Office, and the appalling loss of life, he ruled that the jurisdiction of the civil court was 'ousted by the State of War', which Childers himself had 'helped to produce'. The National Army had been charged by the ruling authority to restore order, said the Master of the Rolls, and it was for the army to decide what degree of force was necessary. The court would not intervene. There was more than a hint of undue haste in this

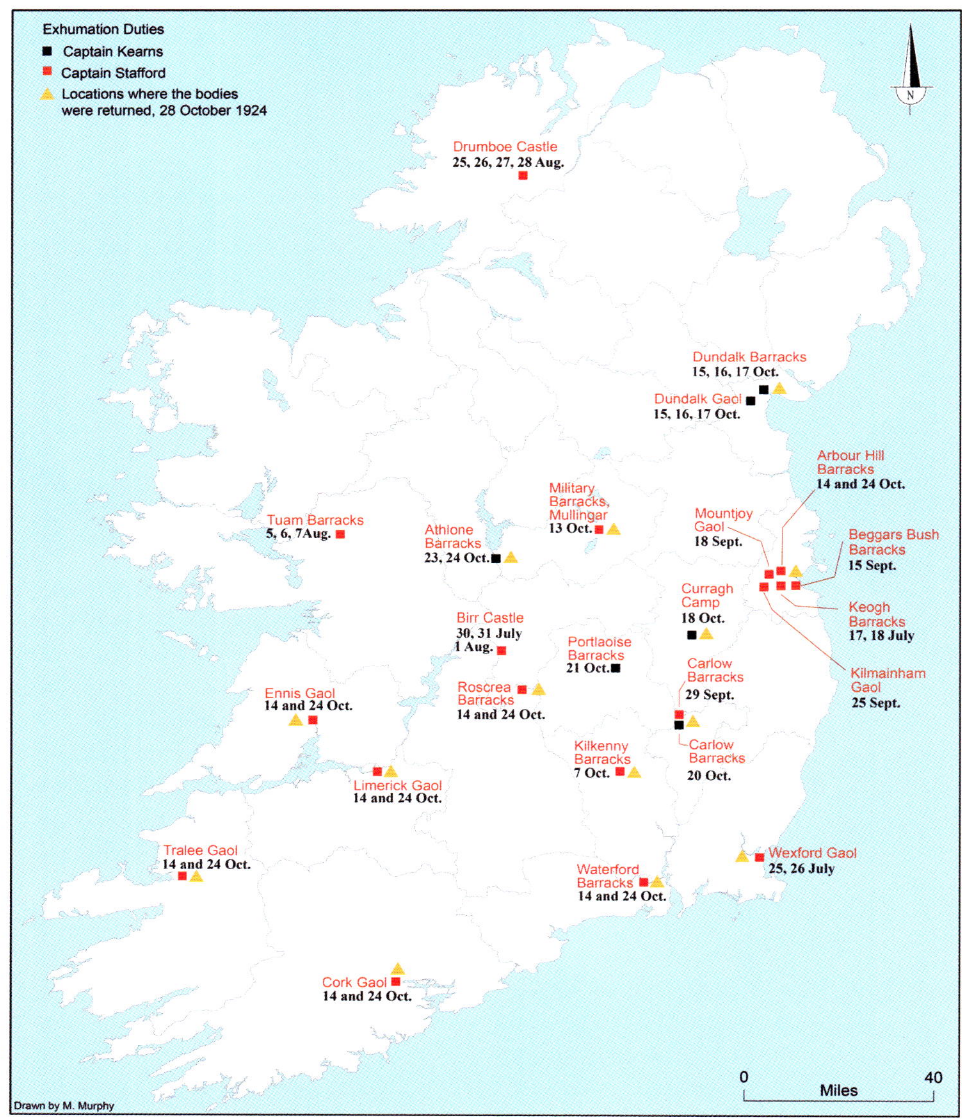

Fig. 3 Map showing a timeline for the exhumations carried out under the supervision of captains Kearns and Stafford of the National Army. Between 17 November 1922 and 30 May 1923, the Provisional/Free State government carried out eighty-one 'official' executions (see Fig. 4). During the Civil War it was government policy to retain the remains of executed men and not hand them over to relations or friends, a policy that prevented funerals from becoming a focal point for those opposed to the Treaty. The government's decision was controversial at the time and it remained a topic of public discussion after the Civil War since the bodies of those executed were still buried on state properties. Following the end of the war, the government ordered a sweeping reduction in the size of the National Army, a decision that led, inadvertently, to renewed public calls for the remains of the executed to be returned to their families. With thousands of soldiers being demobilised, the army had no need for many of the buildings it had occupied during the conflict. It relinquished control of numerous locations around the country, including Tuam Workhouse, which was the site of six executions in April 1923, followed by two more a month later. Before the army departed the workhouse in August 1924, it exhumed the remains of the men buried there, which were then transferred to Athlone's Custume Barracks for reburial. Those events were subsequently reported in the press, resulting in criticism of the government by local Catholic clergy and public bodies, all of which demanded the return of the remains to their families. The government responded by authorising exhumations at all the execution sites across the country. There was a danger, as recognised by W.T. Cosgrave and his Cabinet, that the subsequent hand-over ceremonies could lead to anti-government demonstrations and, in an attempt to avoid such scenes, he ordered the return of all the bodies on a single day. In total eighty-one bodies were handed over: seventy-seven members of the anti-Treaty IRA and four men, often described as 'civilians', who were executed in 1923 after being found guilty of armed robbery. Most of the exhumations occurred between August and October 1924. National Army work parties dug up the graves at the execution sites and encased the remains in new coffins. In some places the remains were then transferred elsewhere: for example, those executed in Donegal were sent to Athlone. Towards the end of that process, the government issued a public notice telling relatives of the executed men to inform the army of their intention to 'claim the remains'. On the day selected for the return of the bodies, 28 October 1924, similar scenes were played out at numerous locations: Athlone, Carlow, Cork, the Curragh, Dublin, Dundalk, Ennis, Kilkenny, Limerick, Mullingar, Roscrea, Tralee, Waterford and Wexford. The largest ceremony was in Athlone, where remains from multiple execution sites were handed over for reburial. Later that week, during the reburials of the executed men, there were clashes between mourners and government forces. The most serious incident occurred at Dundalk's Dowdallshill Cemetery, when soldiers and members of the funeral cortège exchanged gunfire. A civilian, Joseph Hughes, was fatally wounded, becoming another casualty of the conflict that had divided the Irish Free State. [Text: Ian Kenneally / Source: Timothy Breen-Murphy, 'The Government's Executions Policy During the Irish Civil War, 1922–3', unpublished PhD thesis, National University of Ireland, Maynooth, 2010, p. 277]

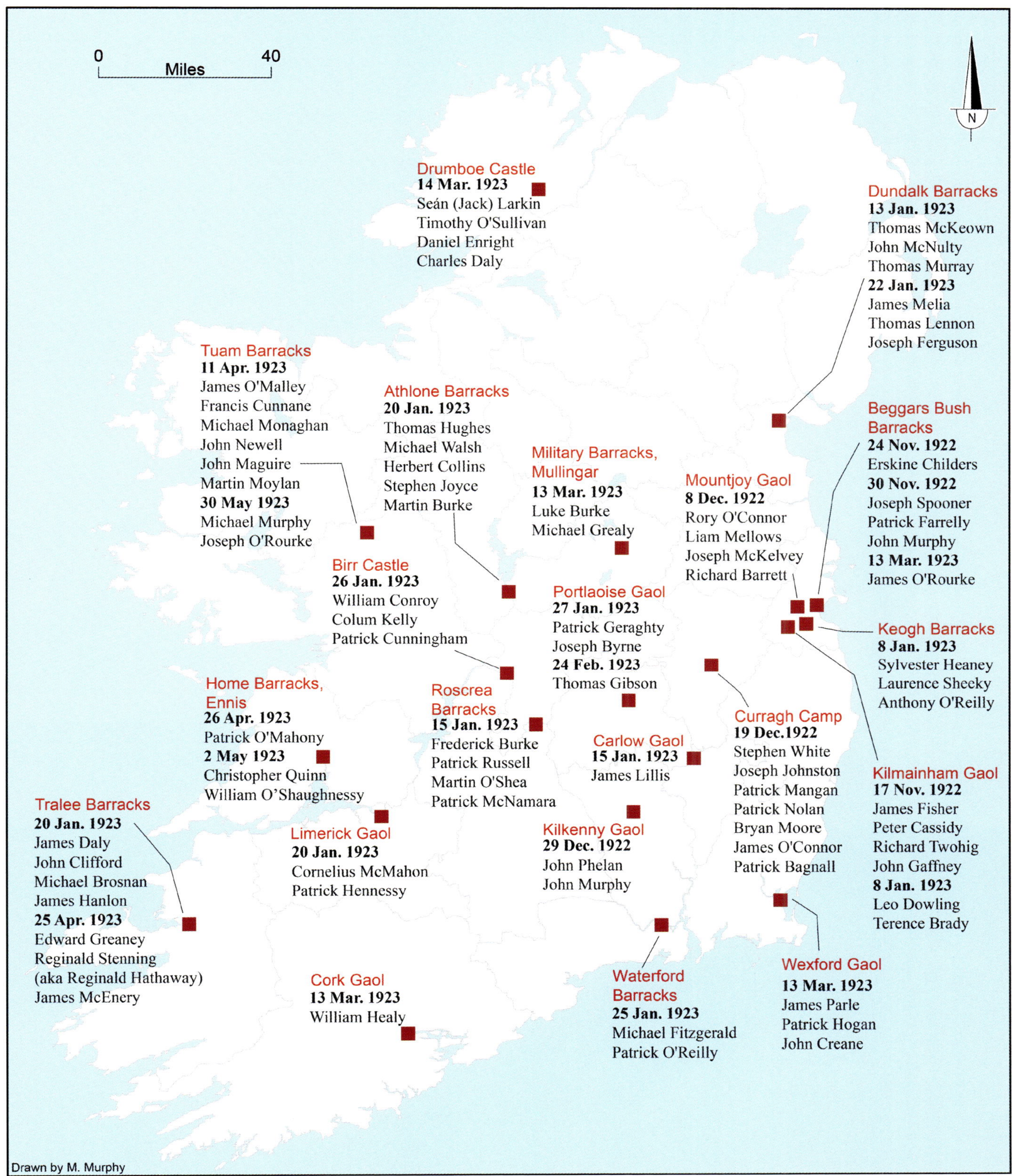

Fig. 4 The eighty-one 'official' executions carried out by the Provisional / Free State Government, 17 November 1922 - 30 May 1923. Two other executions, counted by Seán Enright in *The Irish Civil War: Law, execution and atrocity* (Newbridge, 2019), are not included in the map. National Army soldier Gerard Winsley was executed in Cork city on 1 September 1922, just before the passage of the Army (Special Powers) Resolution and IRA Volunteer Jack Lawlor was executed in Ballyheigue, County Kerry three days before the officially sanctioned trials by military courts began on 3 November. [Updated version of a map first published in the *Atlas of the Irish Revolution* (Cork, 2017) / See also, Andy Bielenberg and John Dorney, The Irish Civil War Fatalities Project (https://www.ucc.ie/en/theirishrevolution/irish-civil-war-fatalities-project)]

high-pressure, high-profile case. O'Connor refused to order a stay of execution pending appeal. He must have known that execution was imminent, and he made his order knowing that counsel was going to the Court of Appeal where another case on the same issue was pending. Hours later Childers was shot by firing squad at Beggars Bush Barracks.

O'Connor's pronouncement that 'the safety and preservation of the people is the highest law' gave the National Army free rein to implement the executions policy, internment without trial and any other measures deemed necessary. And so, *Suprema Lex, salus populi*[8] became the pro-Treaty war cry, used to argue for ever more extreme actions.

The Mountjoy executions, 8 December 1922

IRA chief of staff Liam Lynch responded to the executions on 27 November with a letter to the Ceann Comhairle (speaker) threatening 'very drastic measures' against Dáil deputies who voted for the emergency resolution. Three days later, the IRA issued a general order for operations against the 'enemy', including shooting on sight TDs who supported the 'Murder Bill'. Acting on Lynch's order on 7 December, the IRA killed Seán Hales TD and wounded his parliamentary colleague Pádraig Ó Máille as they left the Ormond Hotel in Dublin. The Executive Council of the newly inaugurated Free State government met that evening and

Fig. 5 The funeral of Captain Thomas Hughes making its way from the old town hall on Northgate Street to Cornamagh Cemetery. Hughes was executed on 20 January 1923 at Custume Barracks, Athlone. [Image: courtesy of Athlone Public Library/Westmeath Library Services]

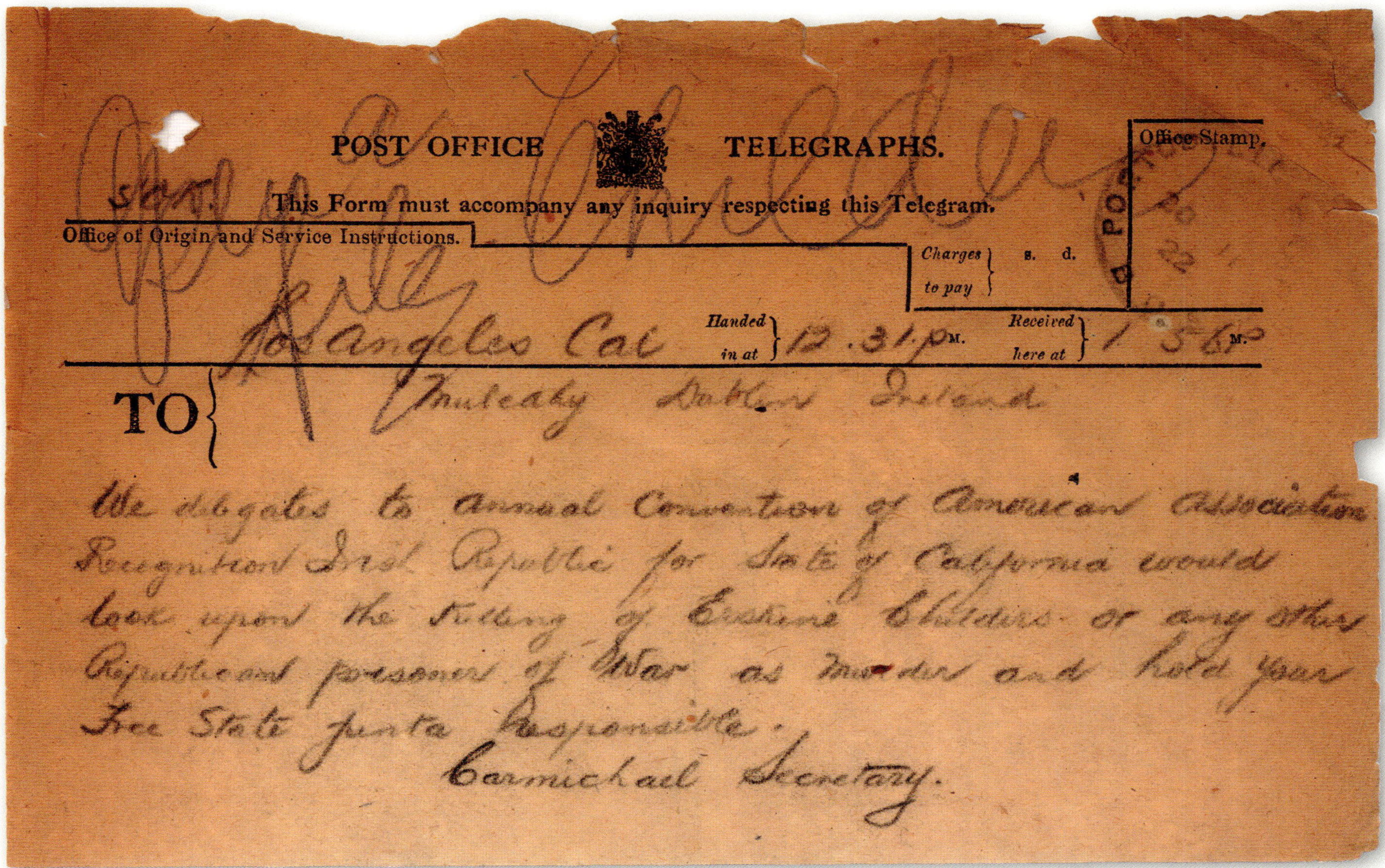

POST OFFICE TELEGRAPHS.

Office Stamp.

This Form must accompany any inquiry respecting this Telegram.

Office of Origin and Service Instructions.

Charges to pay s. d.

Los Angeles Cal

Handed in at 12.31 p.M.

Received here at 1 56 P.M.

TO Mulcahy Dublin Ireland

We delegates to annual Convention of American Association Recognition Irish Republic for State of California would look upon the killing of Erskine Childers or any other Republican prisoner of War as murder and hold your Free State junta responsible.

Carmichael Secretary.

Fig. 6 Telegram from H.E. Carmichael writing on behalf of the American Association for the Recognition of the Irish Republic (AARIR) for the State of California, 20 November 1922. The power and reach of international Irish support organisations like the AARIR faded after the Treaty split. However, these networks did not disappear entirely. They continued to organise protests and demonstrations during the Civil War, such as this telegram from the AARIR state convention following the Free State's execution of Erskine Childers. [Image: courtesy of Military Archives/MSPC Project, DOD/2/15983(A/7627)]

authorised the execution of Rory O'Connor, Liam Mellows, Joe McKelvey and Dick Barrett, who had been in custody at Mountjoy since the fall of the Four Courts. None of these men had been tried or convicted of any offence. O'Higgins defended the executions as the only means of preserving 'representative government', and Richard Mulcahy was adamant that the action was 'a deterrent', but the execution without trial of four high-profile IRA prisoners was fundamentally an act of reprisal.

On the night of the Mountjoy executions, General Richard Mulcahy posted a proclamation in the press announcing trial by army committee for arms offences where there was no factual dispute.[9] The decision about whether there was a factual dispute would, of course, be decided by National Army lawyers. This development facilitated swift trials without rules of evidence. Six weeks later, Mulcahy extended the remit of the army committees and required trial by army committee within forty-eight hours of a prisoner's capture: there were to be no delays.[10] The trial regulations containing protections for prisoners approved by the Dáil during the passage of the Army (Special Powers) Resolution were swept away by the army. After December 1922, prisoners were tried by army committee without defence lawyers or the opportunity to call witnesses. As the war progressed, some were even tried in absentia.[11]

Were the executions lawful?

The first eight executions – those of James Fisher, Peter Cassidy, Richard Twohig and John Gaffney on 17 November, Erskine Childers on 24 November, and Joseph Spooner, Patrick Farrelly and John Murphy on 30 November – were carried out under the terms of the Army (Special Powers) Resolution of September 1922. For reasons of convenience, the Dáil chose to pass a resolution rather than a statute.[12] The resolution had no force of law and so the executions were unlawful. O'Connor, Mellows, McKelvey and Barrett were not tried for any offence, and were executed without judicial process. This contravened Article 70 of the newly enacted Free State Constitution, which guaranteed trial, or at least trial by military court, in times of civil war.[13] It follows that these executions were also unlawful. The trials by army committee after December 1922 also breached the terms of Article 70, which did not permit military tribunals to function unless 'authorised by law'. These tribunals were not 'authorised'. Additionally, the

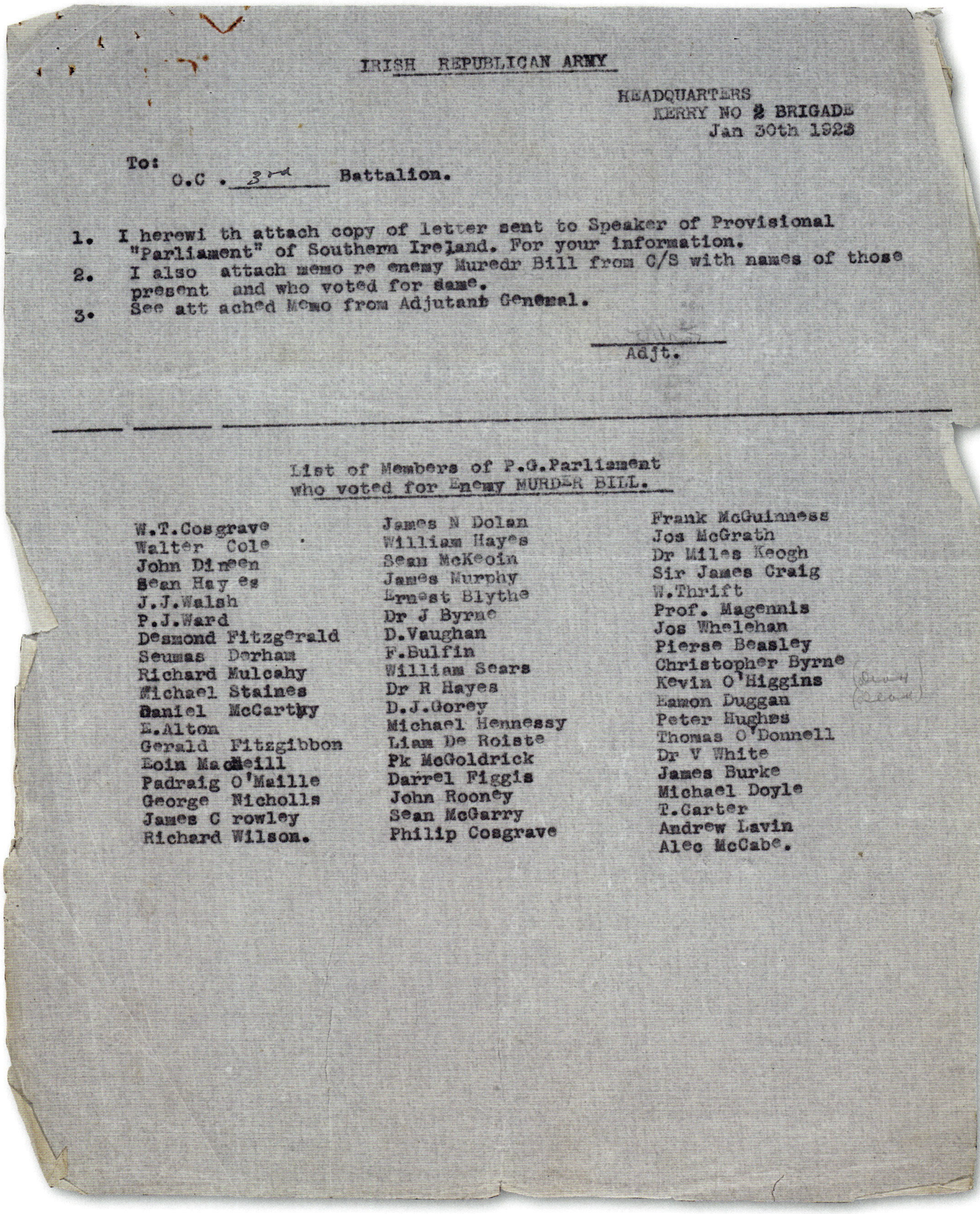

IRISH REPUBLICAN ARMY

HEADQUARTERS
KERRY NO 2 BRIGADE
Jan 30th 1923

To:
O.C . 3rd Battalion.

1. I herewi th attach copy of letter sent to Speaker of Provisional "Parliament" of Southern Ireland. For your information.
2. I also attach memo re enemy Muredr Bill from C/S with names of those present and who voted for same.
3. See att ached Memo from Adjutant General.

Adjt.

List of Members of P.G.Parliament
who voted for Enemy MURDER BILL.

W.T.Cosgrave
Walter Cole
John Dineen
Sean Hay es
J.J.Walsh
P.J.Ward
Desmond Fitzgerald
Seumas Derham
Richard Mulcahy
Michael Staines
Daniel McCarthy
E.Alton
Gerald Fitzgibbon
Eoin MacNeill
Padraig O'Maille
George Nicholls
James C rowley
Richard Wilson.

James N Dolan
William Hayes
Sean McKeoin
James Murphy
Ernest Blythe
Dr J Byrne
D.Vaughan
F.Bulfin
William Sears
Dr R Hayes
D.J.Gorey
Michael Hennessy
Liam De Roiste
Pk McGoldrick
Darrel Figgis
John Rooney
Sean McGarry
Philip Cosgrave

Frank McGuinness
Jos McGrath
Dr Miles Keogh
Sir James Craig
W.Thrift
Prof. Magennis
Jos Whelehan
Pierse Beasley
Christopher Byrne
Kevin O'Higgins
Eamon Duggan
Peter Hughes
Thomas O'Donnell
Dr V White
James Burke
Michael Doyle
T.Carter
Andrew Lavin
Alec McCabe.

Fig. 7 Letter from headquarters, Kerry No. 2 Brigade, IRA, dated 20 January 1923, listing the fifty-four members of the Third Dáil who voted for the 'enemy Murder Bill', and ordering that they be shot on sight. [Document: National Library of Ireland, Ernie O'Malley Papers, MS 10,973/11/55]

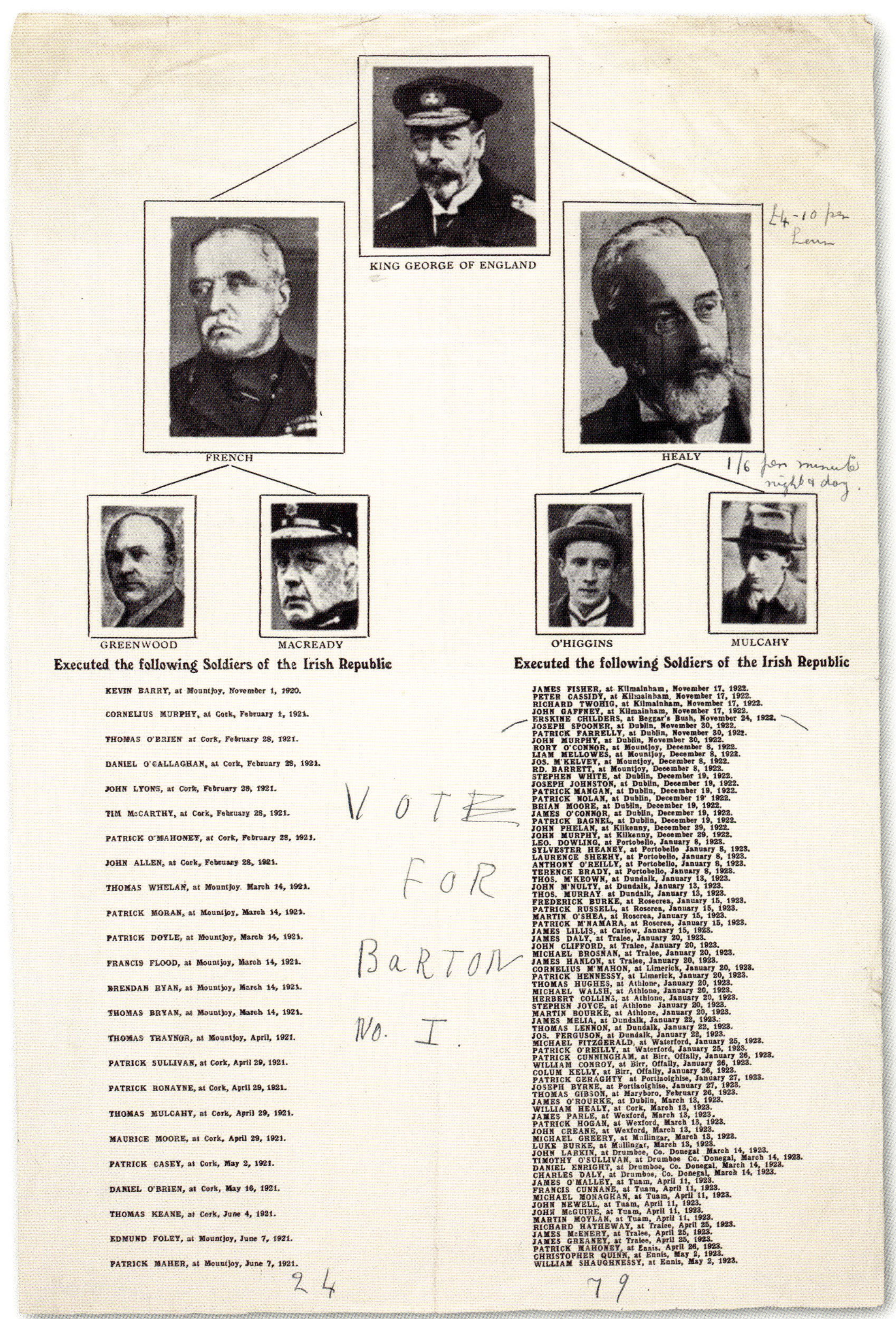

KING GEORGE OF ENGLAND

FRENCH

HEALY

GREENWOOD

MACREADY

O'HIGGINS

MULCAHY

Executed the following Soldiers of the Irish Republic

KEVIN BARRY, at Mountjoy, November 1, 1920.
CORNELIUS MURPHY, at Cork, February 1, 1921.
THOMAS O'BRIEN at Cork, February 28, 1921.
DANIEL O'CALLAGHAN, at Cork, February 28, 1921.
JOHN LYONS, at Cork, February 28, 1921.
TIM McCARTHY, at Cork, February 28, 1921.
PATRICK O'MAHONEY, at Cork, February 28, 1921.
JOHN ALLEN, at Cork, February 28, 1921.
THOMAS WHELAN, at Mountjoy. March 14, 1921.
PATRICK MORAN, at Mountjoy, March 14, 1921.
PATRICK DOYLE, at Mountjoy, March 14, 1921.
FRANCIS FLOOD, at Mountjoy, March 14, 1921.
BRENDAN RYAN, at Mountjoy, March 14, 1921.
THOMAS BRYAN, at Mountjoy, March 14, 1921.
THOMAS TRAYNOR, at Mountjoy, April, 1921.
PATRICK SULLIVAN, at Cork, April 29, 1921.
PATRICK RONAYNE, at Cork, April 29, 1921.
THOMAS MULCAHY, at Cork, April 29, 1921.
MAURICE MOORE, at Cork, April 29, 1921.
PATRICK CASEY, at Cork, May 2, 1921.
DANIEL O'BRIEN, at Cork, May 16, 1921.
THOMAS KEANE, at Cork, June 4, 1921.
EDMUND FOLEY, at Mountjoy, June 7, 1921.
PATRICK MAHER, at Mountjoy, June 7, 1921.

24

Executed the following Soldiers of the Irish Republic

JAMES FISHER, at Kilmainham, November 17, 1922.
PETER CASSIDY, at Kilmainham, November 17, 1922.
RICHARD TWOHIG, at Kilmainham, November 17, 1922.
JOHN GAFFNEY, at Kilmainham, November 17, 1922.
ERSKINE CHILDERS, at Beggar's Bush, November 24, 1922.
JOSEPH SPOONER, at Dublin, November 30, 1922.
PATRICK FARRELLY, at Dublin, November 30, 1922.
JOHN MURPHY, at Dublin, November 30, 1922.
RORY O'CONNOR, at Mountjoy, December 8, 1922.
LIAM MELLOWES, at Mountjoy, December 8, 1922.
JOS. M'KELVEY, at Mountjoy, December 8, 1922.
RD. BARRETT, at Mountjoy, December 8, 1922.
STEPHEN WHITE, at Dublin, December 19, 1922.
JOSEPH JOHNSTON, at Dublin, December 19, 1922.
PATRICK MANGAN, at Dublin, December 19, 1922.
PATRICK NOLAN, at Dublin, December 19' 1922.
BRIAN MOORE, at Dublin, December 19, 1922.
JAMES O'CONNOR, at Dublin, December 19, 1922.
PATRICK BAGNEL, at Dublin, December 19, 1922.
JOHN PHELAN, at Kilkenny, December 29, 1922.
JOHN MURPHY, at Kilkenny, December 29, 1922.
LEO. DOWLING, at Portobello, January 8, 1923.
SYLVESTER HEANEY, at Portobello January 8, 1923.
LAURENCE SHEEHY, at Portobello, January 8, 1923.
ANTHONY O'REILLY, at Portobello, January 8, 1923.
TERENCE BRADY, at Portobello, January 8, 1923.
THOS. M'KEOWN, at Dundalk, January 13, 1923.
JOHN M'NULTY, at Dundalk, January 13, 1923.
THOS. MURRAY at Dundalk, January 13, 1923.
FREDERICK BURKE, at Rosecrea, January 15, 1923.
PATRICK RUSSELL, at Roscrea, January 15, 1923.
MARTIN O'SHEA, at Roscrea, January 15, 1923.
PATRICK M'NAMARA, at Roscrea, January 15, 1923.
JAMES LILLIS, at Carlow, January 15, 1923.
JAMES DALY, at Tralee, January 20, 1923.
JOHN CLIFFORD, at Tralee, January 20, 1923.
MICHAEL BROSNAN, at Tralee, January 20, 1923.
JAMES HANLON, at Tralee, January 20, 1923.
CORNELIUS M'MAHON, at Limerick, January 20, 1923.
PATRICK HENNESSY, at Limerick, January 20, 1923.
THOMAS HUGHES, at Athlone, January 20, 1923.
MICHAEL WALSH, at Athlone, January 20, 1923.
HERBERT COLLINS, at Athlone, January 20, 1923.
STEPHEN JOYCE, at Athlone January 20, 1923.
MARTIN BOURKE, at Athlone, January 20, 1923.
JAMES MELIA, at Dundalk, January 22, 1923.:
THOMAS LENNON, at Dundalk, January 22, 1923.
JOS. FERGUSON, at Dundalk, January 22, 1923.
MICHAEL FITZGERALD, at Waterford, January 25, 1923.
PATRICK O'REILLY, at Waterford, January 25, 1923.
PATRICK CUNNINGHAM, at Birr, Offally, January 26, 1923.
WILLIAM CONROY, at Birr, Offally, January 26, 1923.
COLUM KELLY, at Birr, Offally, January 26, 1923.
PATRICK GERAGHTY at Portlaoighise, January 27, 1923.
JOSEPH BYRNE, at Portlaoighise, January 27, 1923.
THOMAS GIBSON, at Maryboro, February 26, 1923.
JAMES O'ROURKE, at Dublin, March 13, 1923.
WILLIAM HEALY, at Cork, March 13, 1923.
JAMES PARLE, at Wexford, March 13, 1923.
PATRICK HOGAN, at Wexford, March 13, 1923.
JOHN CREANE, at Wexford, March 13, 1923.
MICHAEL GREERY, at Mullingar, March 13, 1923.
LUKE BURKE, at Mullingar, March 13, 1923.
JOHN LARKIN, at Drumboe, Co. Donegal March 14, 1923.
TIMOTHY O'SULLIVAN, at Drumboe Co. Donegal, March 14, 1923.
DANIEL ENRIGHT, at Drumboe, Co. Donegal, March 14, 1923.
CHARLES DALY, at Drumboe, Co. Donegal, March 14, 1923.
JAMES O'MALLEY, at Tuam, April 11, 1923.
FRANCIS CUNNANE, at Tuam, April 11, 1923.
MICHAEL MONAGHAN, at Tuam, April 11, 1923.
JOHN NEWELL, at Tuam, April 11, 1923.
JOHN McGUIRE, at Tuam, April 11, 1923.
MARTIN MOYLAN, at Tuam, April 11, 1923.
RICHARD HATHEWAY, at Tralee, April 25, 1923.
JAMES McENERY, at Tralee, April 25, 1923.
JAMES GREANEY, at Tralee, April 25, 1923.
PATRICK MAHONEY, at Ennis, April 26, 1923.
CHRISTOPHER QUINN, at Ennis, May 2, 1923.
WILLIAM SHAUGHNESSY, at Ennis, May 2, 1923.

79

VOTE FOR BARTON No. I.

Fig. 8 Post-Civil War republican poster/handbill listing executions carried out by the British in 1920–21 and by the Free State in 1922–23. The 'family tree' highlights their direct relationship: John French (Lord Lieutenant, 1918–22), Hamar Greenwood (chief secretary, 1920–22) and General Nevil Macready (GOC of the crown forces in Ireland, 1920–22), on the one hand, and T.M Healy (governor general), Kevin O'Higgins and Richard Mulcahy, on the other, authorised the execution of these 'Soldiers of the Republic' in the name of King George. The scrawled 'Vote for Barton No. 1' relates to the August 1923 general election. Robert Barton TD, a signatory to the Treaty who subsequently opposed it, was a 'Republican' candidate for the Wicklow constituency. He narrowly lost his seat. [Document: National Library of Ireland, EPH D109]

Fig. 9 The Dublin Guards at Beggars Bush Barracks, 4 February 1922. One of the many pressing issues facing the Free State government in the aftermath of the Civil War was the restoration of civilian norms in the criminal justice system. The first jury trials for serious criminal cases took place over a month-long sitting of the Dublin Commission in October and November 1923. The Commission's judge, Chief Justice Thomas F. Molony, presided over a glut of murder cases – eighteen in total – dating as far back as the beginning of the Civil War. Seven men were convicted of murder, four of whom were executed. Though exercising the prerogative of mercy was, by convention, the Cabinet's responsibility, Irish governments after independence rarely strayed from the judge's recommendation in murder cases. Whether a convicted murderer kept their date with the hang house or not was, in effect, left to the discretion of the judiciary. Those who fought on the side of the government during the Civil War could not expect preferential treatment. Between 1922 and 1926 eight serving or former National Army soldiers were sentenced to death for murder, three of whom were executed. The most notorious of these cases was that of Jeremiah Gaffney, standing third from the left in the back row in this photograph. He was hanged at Mountjoy in March 1924 for murdering Thomas Brosnan in Scartaglin, County Kerry, a crime committed the previous December. Gaffney was a serving lieutenant in the National Army when he and a party of soldiers lured Brosnan – an anti-Treaty republican – to his death. Gaffney was probably confident he would get away with it. He threatened to kill his comrades if they said anything and, besides, these were the kinds of killings carried out by the army in Kerry with impunity just a few months earlier. He had been specifically selected to work in the Scartaglin area, where the government's writ was yet to extend. If any case could have been politicised, it was this one. There were reasons why the government might advise a reprieve: Gaffney had an enviable record of involvement with militant republicanism, dating back to his days as a boy in Fianna Éireann, through his active service in the War of Independence and the Civil War. He had been a brave and committed Volunteer since he was a teenager. The government also received letters pleading for mercy from high-profile National Army commanders David Nelligan and Tom Ennis. There were also reasons why they might want the execution to go ahead: the army, by early 1924, was a major headache that needed to be dealt with; Gaffney's case was considered the very week the army mutiny began. Then there was the Kerry factor: if the government was ever to gain the trust of the people of Kerry, then surely they could not be seen to show favour to one of their own. But all of the evidence indicates that these were not decisive factors. In fact, it was a particularly hostile memorandum written by the judge, Mr Justice Jonathan Pim, of the famous Dublin family of Quakers, that sealed Gaffney's fate. Pim advised that the death sentence should go ahead in Gaffney's case. The very same week the Cabinet considered Gaffney's case, it also considered the case of John Ryan, another National Army solidier sentenced to death for murder. This time, Pim pointed out that the crime was not premeditated, and Ryan was reprieved. The same pattern persisted in other similar cases: the Cabinet merely rubber-stamped the judge's recommendation. In some ways this was a powerful expression of justice levied by civilian means. [Text: Liam O'Callaghan / Image: Desmond FitzGerald Photographs, P80/PH/160, reproduced by kind permission of the UCD Archive]

Constitution required that military tribunals should be carried out 'in accordance with the regulations to be prescribed by law'. There were no regulations prescribed by law: only those made by the army. It follows that the trials and executions were unlawful.

In August 1923 the Dáil passed the Indemnity Act to protect all those involved in the executions policy. It did not make what was done lawful, but it prevented any litigation. As to the question of whether the executions policy hastened the end of the Civil War: historians disagree on this, and any conclusion is probably speculative.

A chaotic policy

The result of the Childers case might have changed the course of the executions policy. The Master of the Rolls never regretted his ruling, but he did regret failing to order a stay pending appeal. The legacy of the trial weighed heavily, and he took early retirement. Of the eight prisoners attached to the Childers application, dubbed the 'unknown eight' by the press, none were executed. One was acquitted and three received short terms of imprisonment.[14] The fate of the others reveals the chaotic nature of the executions policy: James Mallin, arrested for possession of a revolver, was spared because he was the son of Irish Citizen Army commander Michael Mallin, executed in 1916.[15] The last two prisoners came from Kerry, where the National Army commander, W.R.E. Murphy, was resolutely against executions and commuted their death sentence. These two Kerry prisoners, P.J. O'Halloran (Ballyheigue) and Pat O'Connor (Causeway), were released after the war and emigrated, part of the diaspora of the defeated.[16] Democratic States are entitled to use force to defend themselves, but there is always a danger that, in times of crisis, steps are taken that may undermine or destroy the democratic institutions they are intended to protect. If the executions were necessary, then they could and should have been carried out within the law. The failure to do so was later used by the defeated faction to make political capital and perpetuate the cycle of violence.

Portobello Barracks Banner

Brian Crowley

On 17 May 1922 troops from the newly formed National Army of the Irish Free State took possession of Portobello Barracks in Rathmines on the southside of Dublin. This was a hugely symbolic event as it was one of the last barracks surrendered to the Provisional Government by the British army under the terms of the Treaty. As they passed through the gates, the soldiers carried aloft a tricolour banner embroidered with the names of nine comrades who had been killed during the War of Independence. The banner, which had been specially commissioned for the occasion from J. Bourke and Sons of Kilkenny, was made from poplin, and all nine names were translated into Irish. When reporting the event on 18 May, the *Freeman's Journal* stated that 'The Banner of the Patriots' added a 'note of poignant impressiveness' to the soldiers' march to Portobello. The banner featured prominently again on 25 May 1922 when a detachment of National Army soldiers from Portobello Barracks marched across the city to St Agatha's church

Fig. 1 (left) Banner of the Patriots. [Image: courtesy of Kilmainham Gaol Museum/ OPW, KMGLM. 20220513_1585M]

Fig. 2 (opposite top) First anniversary Mass for Seán Doyle, member of the Guards IRA, at St Agatha's, North William Street, 25 May 1922. [Image: Courtesy of Kilmainham Gaol Museum/OPW, KMGLM. 2019.0068a]

Fig. 3 (opposite bottom) National Army soldiers enter Portobello Barracks, 17 May 1922. [Image: Cashman Collection ©RTÉ Archives, 0506/017]

on North William Street to attend a memorial Mass for those who had died in the attack on the Custom House the previous year. The name of one of these dead men, Seán Doyle, was among those embroidered on the banner, which was displayed on the altar, facing the seats occupied by the relatives of the dead. The ceremonies in Portobello Barracks and St Agatha's church took place against the backdrop of escalating tensions within the independence movement. In April 1922 forces opposed to the signing of the Anglo-Irish Treaty had seized and occupied the Four Courts in Dublin. Both sides saw themselves as the true guardians of Irish independence, and both regularly invoked the memory of the dead to support their cause. By carrying the banner through the streets of Dublin, the National Army was symbolically asserting its connection with those who had sacrificed their lives in the struggle for independence. The tense stand-off at the Four Courts ended when the National Army attacked the building on 28 June, catalysing a bitter civil war. Tragically, this meant that there were soon more names to add to the banner: Commandant Tom Keogh, a senior National Army officer killed by an IRA mine in Carrigaphooca, near Macroom in County Cork on 16 September 1922, and Captain Michael Dunne, killed on 6 March 1923 in a booby-trap explosion in Knocknagoshel, County Kerry. The final name added to the banner was more unexpected. Denis 'Dinny' Lacey was a hero of the War of Independence in his native Tipperary and a prominent leader of the anti-Treaty IRA. He was shot dead by National Army soldiers while trying to evade capture at Ballydavid, County Tipperary on 18 February 1923. The reason for the name of a casualty from the republican side being included on the banner is not known, but it may have been a gesture of reconciliation or an acknowledgment of the shared losses of the Civil War.

CASE STUDY

The Children and Youth of the Irish Civil War

Sarah-Anne Buckley and Linda Connolly

The reference in the 1916 Proclamation of the Irish Republic to 'cherishing all of the children of the nation equally' was intended to encompass *all citizens*, but it highlights the symbolic significance of childhood to the revolutionaries, and the imagined role of children and young people in realising the ideals of an Irish republic. From the late nineteenth century, focus on youth education for the national cause was clear in the establishment of such groups as the Irish Fireside Club, the Patriotic Children's Treat, St Enda's school (set up by Patrick Pearse) and the Kiddies Scheme. Republican youth organisations were active and visible during the 1916 Easter Rising and the War of Independence, and their example was followed during the Irish Civil War when the membership of Na Fianna Éireann and Clan na Gael Girl Guides gave service on the pro- and anti-Treaty sides.[1] But paramilitary service was only one of many experiences for Irish children and young people during the Irish Civil War.

Fig. 1 Meeting of representatives of Na Fianna Éireann in the Munster area, 6 April 1922, at which they voted to reject the Treaty. The 'pseudo-military' youth organisation, founded by Bulmer Hobson and Constance Markievicz in August 1909 as a 'nationalist counterblast' to the British scouting movement, served as a conduit for the involvement of youth in the Irish revolution. Inculcated with the cult of patriotism, disciplined and trained, Fianna boys participated in the 1916 Rising and the War of Independence as scouts and messengers. Barney Mellows presided over the Fianna Éireann ard fheis on 16 April 1922 at which most delegates 'declared their allegiance to the republic in unqualified terms'. Those members who supported the Treaty, as Marnie Hay writes, quietly left the organisation, many to join the National Army. The reported June 1922 membership of 26,000 began to collapse after the start of the Civil War, as fund-raising was curtailed, senior officers were arrested, and many of its disillusioned members left the movement. The remaining Fianna boys supported the anti-Treaty IRA as intelligence gatherers and dispatch carriers, and several were listed among the Civil War dead. The controversial killings of Fianna officers Alfred Colley and Seán Cole in Dublin in August 1922, seventeen-year-old Bertie Murphy in Killarney in September 1922, and teenagers Eamon Hughes, Brendan Holohan and Joe Rogers at the Red Cow, Dublin in October 1922 are seared particularly deeply on the collective memory of the conflict. [Image: Wickham Family Collection / See: Marnie Hay, *Na Fianna Éireann and the Irish Revolution, 1909–23: Scouting for rebels* (Manchester, 2019)]

Children and youths as victims and survivors

'Wartime childhood', a concept largely neglected in Irish historical studies, refers to how children have experienced and been affected, impaired or injured during, and in the aftermath of, armed conflicts.[2] War affects all areas of children's and young people's lives, including physical and mental health, social relationships within the family and the community, and housing and education. Children and young people also witness and experience trauma through the loss of family members, friends, lovers and neighbours during war, which is an important aspect of the Irish Civil War's enduring legacy and its intergenerational outcomes. Internationally, this has been studied through the lenses of death and injury, sexual violence, family life, migration, resettlement and unmet needs during warfare. In the Irish context Andy Bielenberg and John Dorney's new research indicates that 631 children and young people under the age of twenty-five died in the twenty-six counties during the Irish Civil War[3] (see Chapter 6). Twenty-seven of these fatalities were under the age of fifteen, 183 were aged between fifteen and nineteen, and 421 were aged between twenty and twenty-four. Significantly, those under twenty-five accounted for 54.3 per cent of all fatalities. In relation to gender differences, more males in total were killed in the Civil War, but in the under-twenty-four age group, the proportional percentage of girls and young women killed is significantly higher. Females represent 42 per cent of those killed in the 1–14 age group, 36 per cent of those killed in the 15–19 age group, and 23 per cent of those killed in the 20–24 age group. Of the total fatalities in the 1–24 age group, 33 per cent (103 in total) were female. These figures compare to a total of 19 per cent female civilians killed across all (known) age groups in the Irish Civil War. Young women and girls are an important cohort of casualties and deaths.[4] Archival sources, such as newspapers, family papers, court documents, letters, military service pension applications and first-person accounts, reveal that many other children and young people, including girls and young women, were seriously injured or displaced from their homes, particularly during the urban warfare that characterised the Civil War's conventional phase.

Limerick city provides a case study for this type of violence. The *Irish Times* reported that on 15 August 1922 twelve-year-old Lena Roche was accidentally shot dead at the rear of Mary Street barracks in Limerick.[5] Seven other children were injured on the same night, four seriously, by a bomb thrown by the IRA at a National Army lorry on Edward Street. On 27 September the *Evening Echo* reported nine people wounded, some seriously, as a result of a Mills grenade explosion on Parnell Street. 'Inquiries on the spot' ascertained that when military police asked a National Army soldier outside the railway station to show his pass, he suddenly produced a grenade and pulled the pin. Another soldier 'with commendable presence of mind' snatched it out of his comrade's hand and, amid warning cries, rolled it along the street where it exploded 'with great violence'. Nearly all of those wounded were children. 'Bridie Hannon (thirteen), Parnell Street, both legs; Patrick Quirke (five), Keating's Lane, leg and head (serious); Mary Connolly (ten), Keating's Lane, leg; John O'Leary (thirty-five), Keating's Lane, both legs; Mrs. Lillis, 5 Duggan's Row, right thigh; Bridie Whelan, Parnell Street; Daniel Griffin, 4 Newenham Street, left hip; Ellen Hynes, 4 Upper Mallow Street, both legs, neck (serious); James Smith, 4 Kite's Lane, arm.'

On 11 November 1922 a sixteen-year-old, Dermott O'Callaghan, was 'accidentally wounded' when a soldier's rifle accidentally discharged near Albert Quay. The fatal shooting on Edward Street of Kathleen Hehir, age seventeen, and wounding of Margaret Purtill, a year younger, occurred six weeks later, on Christmas Eve night 1922. A private inquiry by the National Army in New Barracks concluded that Hehir was killed instantly by a shot to the base of the skull. The same bullet grazed Margaret Purtill's face.[6]

The *Cork Examiner* reported another tragedy on 11 October 1922 in County Limerick. Five days earlier, National Army troops operating from Tarbert, County Kerry responded to reports that a band of IRA fighters in Glin had been sniping at passing vessels along the Shannon. By the time the troops reached the village, the IRA, evidently well informed, had fled. The government forces departed after a fruitless hour-long search, and the anti-Treaty forces emerged from their 'fastnesses' in the hills and began firing into Glin, fatally wounding a girl standing at her own doorway. Catherine Hogan died two days later on the eve of her fourteenth birthday. The traumatic

Fig. 2 Photograph, taken from the Mass card of Catherine Hogan, who was wounded in crossfire in Glin, County Limerick on 7 October 1922 and died, two days later, on the eve of her fourteenth birthday. The 'sad occurrence' was recorded for the Schools Collection in 1938 by Tim Joseph Casey of Glin, whose mother was sure it was 'bitterly regretted by the perpetrator'. Catherine Hogan was related, through her paternal grandmother, Margaret Sheehan, to the US president, John F. Kennedy, who visited Limerick just five months before his assassination in November 1963. A plaque in Hogan's memory was erected in the village square by the Glin Historical Society on 9 October 2022. [Image: reproduced with the permission of Tom Donovan and the *Old Limerick Journal* / See Schools' Collection, vol. 480, p. 167, Tim Joseph Casey, Glin, County Limerick, Folklore Collection, UCD] death of a child had a wider impact on the family and community: the family suffered further loss when Catherine's grandmother, Catherine Mangan, died two weeks later, and a pregnant neighbour, Mrs Shaughnessy, who witnessed the shooting from her window across the square, was so traumatised she fell down the stairs and miscarried.[7]

Numerous violent incidents involving babies, children and civilian youth were reported in other parts of the country. In Dublin, for instance, in November 1922, a National Army lorry on its way to Richmond Barracks struck two mothers (and a third woman), throwing two infants from their prams onto the roadway. Mrs McLaughlin and her baby, Patrick, Mrs Mullen and her baby, Norah, and Mrs Devereux were all brought to Meath Hospital where they recovered from the incident.[8] On 19 October 1922 the *Irish Times* reported that two eight-year-old girls were seriously injured on Washington Street in Cork city, where they had been playing, when bombs, thrown by the IRA at National Army troops, exploded.

Death or physical injury is but one measure of the 'wartime childhood'. Many children also experienced the violent trauma of house raids and were often the first ordered to leave during house burnings.[9] Some children and young women were also victims of conflict-related physical and sexual assaults.[10] The *Meath Chronicle* reported on 16 September 1922 that armed and masked men 'proclaiming themselves to be "Irregulars"' had raided the licensed premises of Elizabeth Finegan, Tankardstown'.[11] On 7 October 1922

Fig. 3 A group of children converse with National Army soldiers as they pass through Bruff, County Limerick, July 1922. [Image: National Library of Ireland, HOG124]

Fig. 4 Pro-Treaty cartoon by 'Shemus' (Ernest Forbes), which appeared in the *Freeman's Journal*, 27 July 1922. Using the motif of the popular western to denote the anti-Treaty military campaign, it expertly combines three key themes of pro-Treaty propaganda. The caricature of the 'boy gunman', the 'juvenile lead' in the new production, is intended to ridicule the anti-Treaty IRA for the extreme youth and inexperience of many of its Truce-time recruits ('trucileers'). Forbes also implicitly contrasts what he deems the 'idealist' anti-Treatyites with their pragmatic opponents, and highlights the 'terrorist' actions of the gunmen in the 'wild west and south' of Ireland. [Image: OLS Samuels, box 4, no. 104, The Board of Trinity College Dublin]

Dr Gavin examined Mary Doyle, a seventeen-year-old servant who had reported a rape and second attempted sexual assault by two members of the raiding party (who were named brothers). A subsequent jury trial in Trim circuit court heard that there was not enough evidence to prove the identity of the four raiders. Consequently, the charge of rape against two of the men did not proceed and they were released from Mountjoy Gaol.

A youthful and masculine civil war

Recent studies have shed light on the role of gender and masculinities in the Irish revolution.[12] Young male combatants under twenty-five were very active in the Civil War on both sides and died in larger numbers. Some had fought in the First Word War as 'Teenage Tommies', before joining the pro- or anti-Treaty sides. Combatants were frequently listed as 'youths' in the press and in the courts.[13] In 1923 the *Irish Independent* condemned 'those who put firearms or lethal weapons into the hands of mere schoolboys', for 'beguiling their youth and inexperience by false principles of patriotism'.[14] Youth could also lead to leniency, however, as there are numerous references throughout the period to IRA activists being released 'on account of their youth'.[15]

Youth was often deployed as a metaphor for the national movement itself and celebrated during the War of Independence when flying column members were usually unmarried young men. Like other international conflicts and social movements in the twentieth century, when younger people became politicised, they also become associated with deviant behaviour and 'a lack of home control'.[16] As Colonel Joseph V. Lawless commented in his statement to the Bureau of Military History (BMH), 'the newer national movement represented [to the British authorities] the inevitable turbulence of youth, dangerous, and to be deprecated but not to be taken too seriously'.[17] During and after the Civil War, as Gavin Foster notes, youth featured prominently in pro-Treaty discourse as a way of depicting republicans as immature and irrational.[18] The visibility of the young throughout the revolutionary period was captured in its memory. Many BMH witness accounts, informed by subsequent experience, also contained warnings for younger people in the future to be more cautious.[19] Intergenerational transmission of Civil War memory is traceable in the National Folklore Collection, with children's local knowledge of Civil War events appearing in the Schools' Collection submissions taken in 1937–9. One student contributor reported of his school: 'during the Civil War some of the boys took possession of it and lived in it'.[20]

Given the extreme youth of combatants on both sides, the number of young civilians caught up in the urban warfare, and the many families that suffered bereavement or displacement, children and young people were disproportionally affected by the Irish Civil War. Young women and girls died in far fewer numbers than did young men and boys, but they experienced significant loss, trauma and injury as civilians and activists. Military services pension applications also demonstrated how many young women and men emigrated after the Civil War, invariably disillusioned with the outcome, unable to find employment, socially ostracised and, in some cases, psychologically or physically scarred. The longer-term impact of the Irish Civil War on children and young people in the new state or as part of the diaspora is a story that is just beginning to be told.

Treaty signatory Éamonn Duggan seated with Johanna (Hannie) Collins at the funeral of her brother, Michael Collins, in Dublin, 28 August 1922. [Image: Cashman Collection, ©RTÉ Archives]

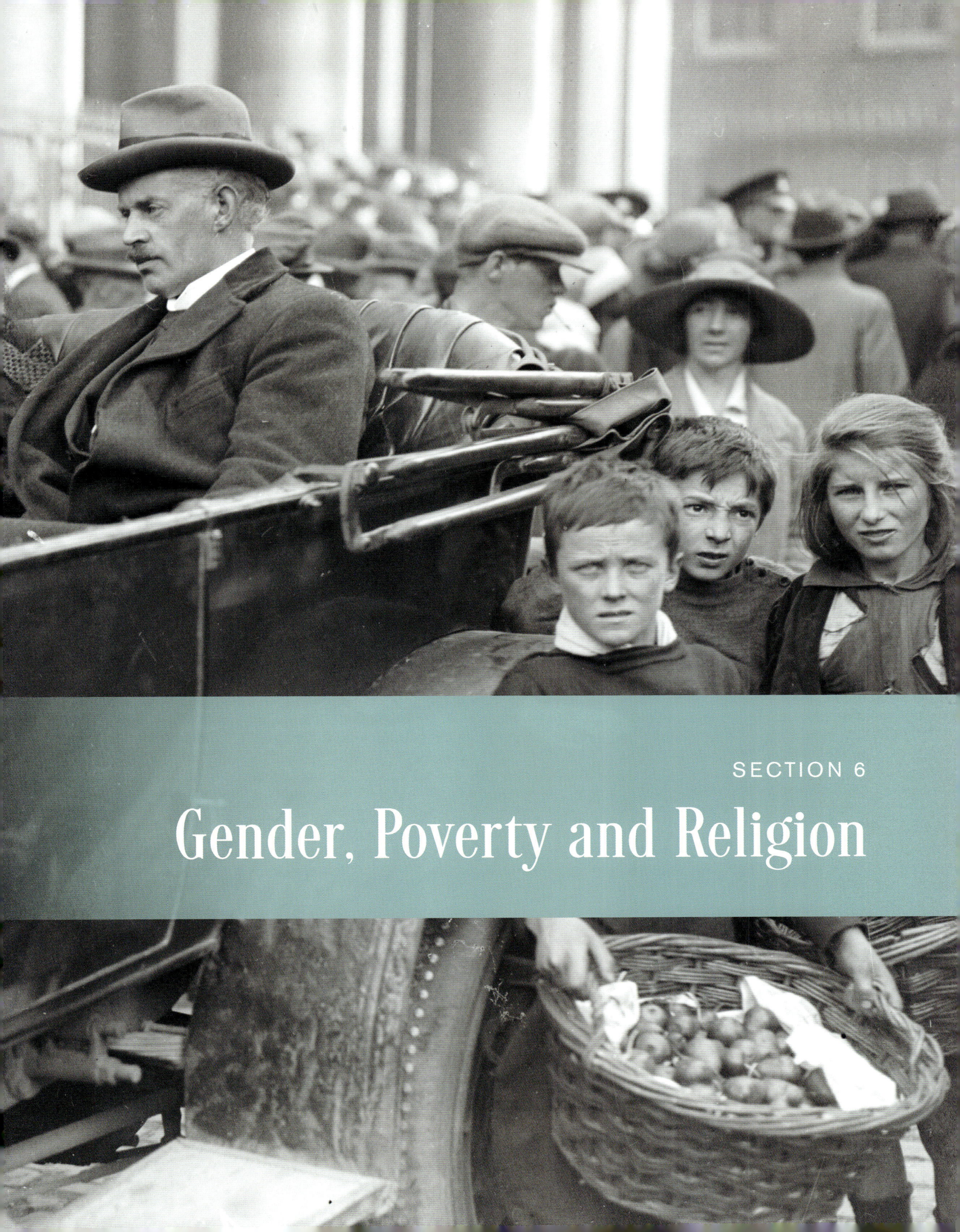

SECTION 6

Gender, Poverty and Religion

CHAPTER 7

The Irish Civil War: Family life, gender and loss

Lindsey Earner-Byrne

Family life was profoundly impacted by the Irish Civil War: every loss, death and injury happened to, and profoundly reshaped, a family. However, the historiographical focus on families has tended to be on the damage done by the ideological split of the war. This is typified by the 'brother against brother' trope, which elides both the gendered dimensions of the violence and grief, and the emotional impact of death and injury on a family. Síobhra Aiken's pioneering study *Spiritual Wounds* raises important questions regarding historians' engagement with the psychological impact of the Civil War, and explores ways survivors processed that trauma through writing.[1] This chapter considers the experiences of those for whom the processing of trauma was often forced to take second place to the immediate needs of survival in the wake of the death or profound injury of a loved one.[2] For some the initial task involved trying to get a clear picture of what had happened to their relative, of where and why their death or injury had occurred, while other families had loved ones returned to them sick, physically and/or mentally injured, sometimes beyond repair. Many of the families diminished and damaged by the Civil War faced an uncertain financial future and paid a high emotional price for the new Free State.

Prolonged violence

The Civil War was part of a continuum of violent conflict. Many families had endured periods of prolonged absence, injury or the deaths of relatives during the First World War,[3] which was followed by the deadly flu pandemic of 1918–1919.[4] Since the 1916 Rising the violence of conflict had often directly involved family homes, which became hiding places, weapons dumps, targets for raids, violent searches, shoot-outs, murder and rape. This continued during the War of Independence, 1919–21, with the *Interim Report of the American Commission on Conditions in Ireland,* for example,

Fig. 1 (left) This photograph was taken on the wedding day of Maria Stenson to Andrew Marren in May 1932, almost a decade after the killing of Maria's brother and Andrew's close friend, IRA Lieutenant Patrick 'Packy' Stenson, by National Army soldiers on 13 March 1923. Staring into the future were five young adults who had survived the brutal revolutionary years to live in a state they had resisted during the Civil War. The Stenson household had been in the eye of the storm since the War of Independence as a safehouse, an arms repository, and a place of unstinting support for any republican requiring refuge. The house was pockmarked with bullets, its windows repeatedly smashed, its furniture 'ransacked' and 'looted', and its residents beaten, traumatised and, in some cases, killed. The Civil War had claimed Maria's brother and father; the latter, she recalled, 'died with grief' shortly after his son's death. The manner of Stenson's death was deeply painful to the family, who believed he had been beaten and shot *after* surrendering to National Army soldiers. Writing in the republican *An Phoblacht* on the fifth anniversary of Packy's death, Andrew Marren described his friend's murder by 'Staters' as 'of callous brutality unrivalled in the Tan days'. Packy, he claimed had been beaten 'unmercifully' with the rifle of one soldier and then 'riddled with bullets in sight of [...] schoolchildren'. Framing the Irish Civil War as 'the great betrayal', Marren recalled how, on the day of Packy's funeral, the Stenson's house, which had been 'a place where boys "on the run"' from the Tans had 'always found a welcome and never wanted for food and shelter', was once 'again raided' and 'the graveyard was packed with spies armed with notebooks and camera'. Contemporary newspaper reports confirm that, after the funeral, which was attended by 'an immense concourse of people of all creeds and classes', 'National troops arrived and held up all the young men' for questioning. Maria was in Cumann na mBan between 1919 and 1923, making the rank of captain in the Ballymote Battalion. Her military service pension application outlines her diverse duties, including dispatch, intelligence/'secret service', election work, the organisation of weekly clubs, first aid and catering for an active service unit, or 'flying column'. Her anti-Treaty activities continued long after the Civil War; for example, her pension application referee, Kathleen Mullen [née Lee], explained: 'The greater part of the IRA leaders stayed regularly in her home for years & were helped with pocket money, cigs etc'. In fact Mullen alleged Maria had been 'beggared' by her ongoing financial support for individual IRA members. Andrew Marren's home was also repeatedly raided during the Civil War and, despite his mother hiding his handgun under her apron, he was detained for his anti-Treaty activities and held between September 1922 and August 1923. Almost ten years after his release and the end of the Civil War, he married Maria. Mrs Stenson transferred the family holding to Maria upon her marriage, and the couple ran the farm. They went on to have a son and a daughter. While Andrew did not appear to have applied for a military pension, Maria applied twice but was not successful until 1956, when, like most of the women who managed to secure a pension, she was awarded a grade E military pension. She received this pension until her husband wrote in November 1978 to inform the army of his wife's passing. [Text: Lyndsey Earner-Byrne / Image: courtesy of Aidan Marren / Sources: MSP34REF64179, Maria Stenson; MSPC/ DP7025, Patrick Stenson; *An Phoblacht,* 13 March 1928; 'Death of Mr Patrick Stenson, Doobeg, Bunninadden', *Roscommon Herald,* 31 March 1923; Military Archives List of Civil War Republican Prisoners, 029 CW/P/01–CW/P/01/02; Frank Fagan, 'Bitter final weeks of Civil War left a dark legacy in May', *Western People*, 26 March 2023, and valuable information generously supplied by Frank Fagan and Maria and Andrew's surviving son, Aidan Marren]

Fig. 2 Wedding of Colonel-Commandant John T. Prout to Limerick native Mary Conba at St John the Evangelist church, Kilkenny city, 12 July 1922. Prout, who was born in Dundrum, County Tipperary and emigrated to the US aged twenty-four in 1904, had a distinguished military career by 1922. Decorated for valour by the French and American governments for his service as an officer in the US 69th Infantry Regiment (the famed 'Fighting 69th') in France during the First World War, he returned to Ireland in 1919, becoming an intelligence and training officer for the IRA. A supporter of the Treaty, Prout was appointed commandant general of the National Army's South-east Division headquartered at Kilkenny military barracks. His wedding, which had been arranged prior to the outbreak of the Civil War, was organised in secret to avoid disruption by the anti-Treaty IRA. Five days later, Prout led his *c*.500-strong column towards Waterford city, the republican stronghold at the east of the virtual defensive boundary of the so-called 'Munster Republic'. The approximately 300-strong IRA garrison (including some Volunteers from Cork No. 1 Brigade) under Pax Whelan could offer little resistance in the face of artillery fire that rained down on IRA positions from Mount Misery above the north bank of the River Suir. Six civilians died during the three-day battle for Waterford city, which fell to Prout's forces on 21 July 1922. Twenty-five-year-old Private Michael Costello, mortally wounded during the National Army advance, was mourned by his parents and twelve siblings. Prout survived the Civil War but was unceremoniously demobilised in 1924. He eventually returned to the US and was a technical advisor on the popular 1940 Hollywood film *The Fighting 69th*, starring Irish-Americans James Cagney and Pat O'Brien. He was buried in the US following his death in 1969. [Image: Museum of the Irish Revolution, in the Michael Cannady Collection / Sources: *Freeman's Journal*, 13 July 1922; *Evening Herald*, 14 July 1922; MSPC 2D33 (Michael Costello); Eoin Swithin Walsh, *Kilkenny: In times of revolution, 1900–1923* (Dublin, 2018), p. 227]

noting the frequency with which 'the sanctity of the family home is violated'.[5] After a brief reprieve between July 1921 and June 1922, during which many celebrated by marrying and starting a family, the country was pitched into a civil war. In the early years of the Irish Free State the level of violence and lawlessness prompted profound anxiety regarding the stability of the family, specifically its moral capacity to withstand the consequences of so many absent men and the engagement of thousands of young people in the violence. This was a period when the day-to-day relationship between the new state and family life was being drawn in small, yet profoundly significant ways in multiple, often hidden, bureaucratic processes.

The Military Service Pensions Collection (MSPC), which emerged out of Irish Army Pensions Acts from 1923, represents the paperwork of one of the most significant of these early bureaucratic exchanges between state and family. As Marie Coleman explained, the 1923 act resulted not only in one of the Irish Free State's first attempts to address the needs of those impacted by the years of violence, but also one of its first welfare initiatives.[6] Section 2 of the act covered extra pensions to married men, while sections 7 and 8 provided for allowances for dependants of deceased officers and soldiers.[7] While these dependants were most often widows and children, the mothers, fathers and siblings of those killed in action or as a result of active service also feature in this archive.[8] In effect, the application process of the Army Pensions Acts represented a site of encounter between families and the state, in which the rules of the game were informed in explicit and implicit ways by the social values of the new state. Qualifying for a pension under the acts, for example, was predicated on notions of legitimate dependency, familial responsibility and morality inherent in the male-breadwinner model.[9] In the most obvious sense the contemporary understanding of the appropriate relationship between gender and dependency meant that wives and mothers were more likely than fathers and sons to be successful in a claim for a dependence pension. Gender conditions were intertwined with ideas of class or rank; for example, a wounded married officer received an extra pension in relation to a son up to the age of eighteen and a daughter up to twenty-one years of age, while for a soldier's children, the gendered age differentials were sixteen and eighteen years of age, respectively.[10] These gendered criteria both recognised and perpetuated an economy that deprived women of the chance of earning a sufficient salary to support themselves, never mind a family.[11] This archive is replete with evidence of the harm done to women by this economic model.

The dependence files are also a microcosm of the gender and social power dynamics of the early twentieth century. It is invariably women appealing to an almost exclusively male cast of actors in the vouching and decision-making roles. The voice of appeal was female, the voice of arbitration and decision-making male. Mothers, wives and sisters made up the cast of 'ordinary voices', while priests/ministers, police and solicitors were the voices of authority, either validating the truth of these women's claims or deciding on whether their stories amounted to qualifying narratives for the purposes of the Pensions Acts. The decisions reflected in this archive were often life-changing for the applicants and their families; thus, this gender dynamic carried with it various risks for women and working-class women, in particular. There are, of course, numerous examples of kindness in this archive, both within the constrained system and the wider community, which tried in various ways to

Fig. 3 A National Army soldier inspecting a cart driven by a woman with a boy passenger. [Image: courtesy of Dún Laoghaire–Rathdown County Council Library Service]

repair itself and help those most injured by the country's transition to independence. However, while establishing whole or partial dependence on a deceased or injured combatant should have been the only criteria of substance, this chapter points to various ways in which the pension process was shaped by particular gendered, class and moral prejudices.

Grieving in the archives

The luxury of grief without counting the cost was one few could afford in 1920s Ireland. For those making an application for a pension or allowance from the state in relation to a dead relative, the first demand was that they translate their grief into an economic narrative of dependency. In the world of administration, families were reduced to relationships between 'applicants' and a 'deceased', bound together in a family economy devoid of sentiment. However, many found a way of expressing their loss and bewilderment, which was often exacerbated by the bureaucracy of death. In January 1923 Catherine Byrne, for example, wrote to Minister for Defence Richard Mulcahy to seek his intervention in her case. Her eldest son, Private James Byrne, had been shot in County Kerry on 13 October 1922, had died later that night in hospital, and had been buried for over three months before she was informed.[12] 'Surely,' she asked 'as my dead child has made the Supreme sacrifice for Ireland the least I might expect is an acknowledgment of his death.'[13] She had been trying to secure certification of his death for weeks but had received no response from the National Army, and had, thus, been forced 'to trouble the Priest who attended poor Jimmie to ask the Doctor for them [certs] which he did'. She explained to Mulcahy:

> Please forgive me troubling you I am sorry as I know you have more than enough to contend with I can get

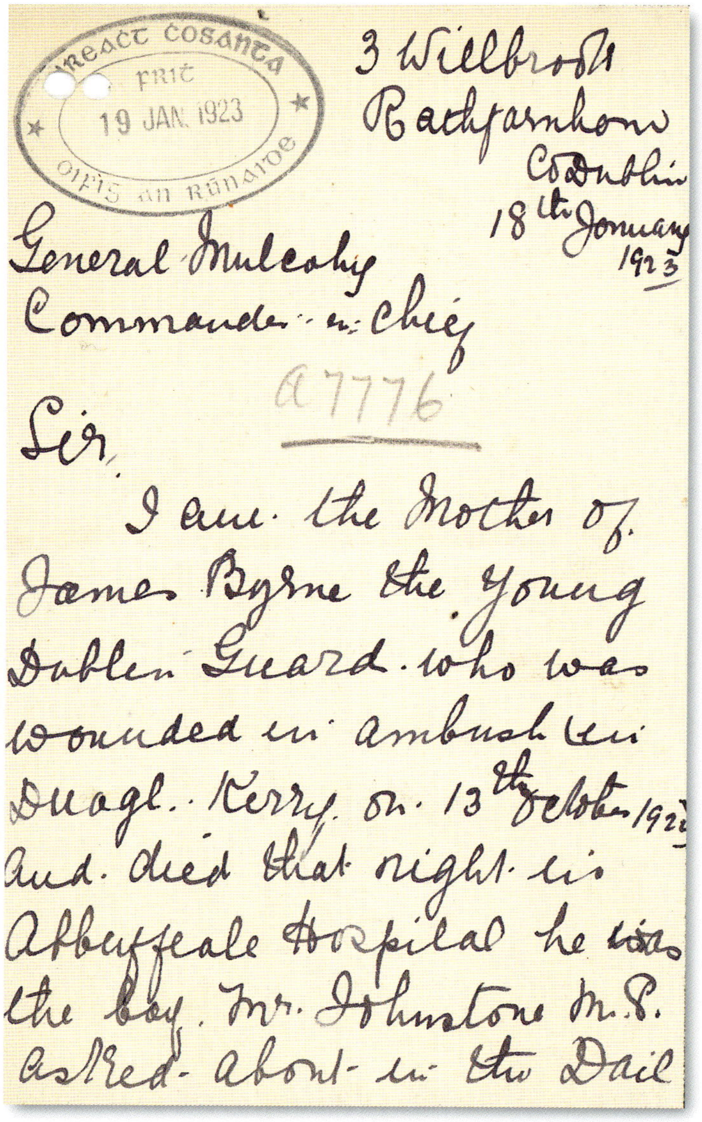

Aireacht Cosanta
Fuair
19 JAN. 1923
Oifig an Rúnaidhe

3 Willbrook
Rathfarnham
Co Dublin
18th January 1923

General Mulcahy
Commander in Chief

A7776

Sir,

I am the Mother of James Byrne the young Dublin Guard who was wounded in ambush in Duagh. Kerry on 13th October 1922 And died that night in Abbeyfeale Hospital he was the boy Mr. Johnstone M.P. asked about in the Dail

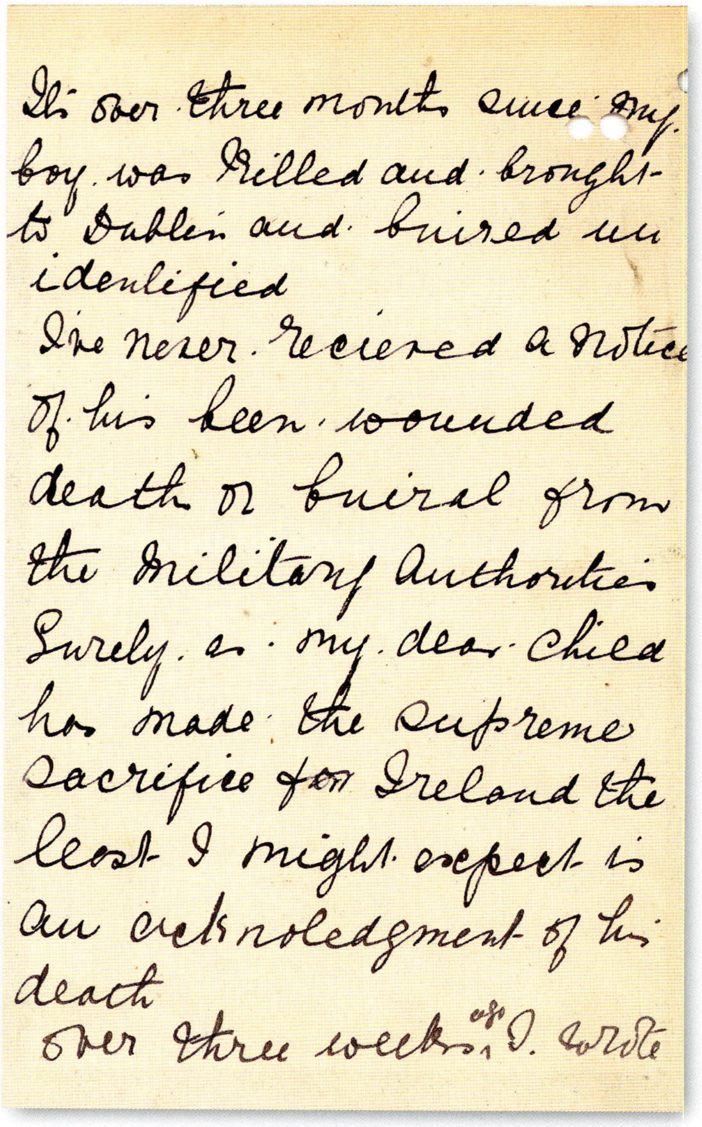

Its over three months since my boy was killed and brought to Dublin and buried un identified

I've never recieved a notice of his been wounded death or burial from the Military Authorities Surely as my dear child has made the supreme sacrifice for Ireland the least I might expect is an acknoledgment of his death

over three weeks ago I wrote

Figs 4–7 (above and opposite page) In this four-page letter to the minister for defence, Richard Mulcahy, dated 18 January 1923, Catherine Byrne appeals for information about her son, James Byrne, who was fatally wounded in an ambush in Duagh, County Kerry on 13 October 1922 and buried 'unidentified' in Dublin. [Source: MSPC2D22. Image: courtesy of Military Archives/MSPC Project]

> no satisfaction from any one else. I am a widow since Jimmie was seven years old he was the eldest of my four children he was only 18 years its breaking my heart I had not the poor Consolation of seeing him or buiring him.[14]

Catherine had been widowed eleven years previously, when she was only twenty-six years of age and, in his teenage years, her son Jimmie had been a key support to her as she raised three other children.[15] While Catherine had managed to work prior to the death of her eldest son in a local laundry, grief had destroyed her health, and she was unable to work since his death. However, because of this previous employment, she could not be considered 'wholly dependent' upon him for the purposes of the 1923 legislation. Thus, a pension was ruled out in her case and only a £60 gratuity was approved. However, on appeal, the army reconsidered and, in making its case to the Department of Finance for an increased gratuity, revealed an awareness that grief and the trauma of not burying her own son had fundamentally broken this woman:

> There is no dispute about the facts [... however] It is represented that the circumstances of the boy's death, the mother's uncertainty as to his fate for months, and the fact that she had not the consolation of being present at his funeral prayed on the applicant's mind to such an extent as to seriously affect her health and render her unable to continue in her employment [...] The boy, seeing that he was the eldest, would naturally be looked to by the mother as her principal support [...] The question is, whether having regard to all the circumstances of the case, (including the circumstances of his death and burial) and [the] low financial position of the mother, you could reconsider the case.[16]

While her gratuity was increased to £100, she was not considered eligible for a pension until 1953 (she had applied again in 1927). Thus, almost thirty years later, Catherine Byrne had to document her loss all over again for another generation of bureaucrats. On this occasion, however, she had to surrender what must have been one of the most precious documents she possessed: a letter written to her sister by the priest who had given her son the last rites as he lay dying on a road in Kerry. Dated 16 December 1922, this letter offers a glimpse of the communal nature of grief in which each

to Captain Stafford for Certificate
of his death as I had him in
Societies he has had not the
Courtesy to answer my letter
I had to trouble the Priest who
attended poor Jimmie to ask
the Doctor for them which he
did
The Priest is Father Harrington
The Presbytery Duagh Kilmorna
Co Kerry and the Dr Dr.
Hartnett Abbeyfeale Co
Limerick
Please forgive me troubling
you I am sorry as I know
you have more than enough

to Contend with I can get no
satisfaction from any one else
I am a widow since Jimmie
was seven years old he was the
eldest of my four children he
was only 18 years
its breaking my heart I had
not the poor Consolation of
seeing him or buiring
him
Again asking you
to forgive me
I am your obedient
Servant
Catherine Byrne

Fig. 8 A priest giving absolution to National Army troops during the Civil War. A devoutly religious man, General Richard Mulcahy was determined to make 'the name of the Irish Soldier a synonym for true manliness, clean living, chivalrous spirit and religious fervour'. Just weeks before the outbreak of civil war, he was soliciting soundings from senior officers, including Michael Collins, Eoin O'Duffy and Liam Lynch – Lynch at that time being firmly ensconced with the anti-Treaty IRA in the Four Courts – on the best methods for incorporating religious observance into the fabric of army life. After the outbreak of the Civil War, Jesuit-led retreats became a conspicuous feature of officer training, with sodalities, confraternities and religious observance strongly fostered. Such work fell under the remit of chaplains, part of Óglaigh na hÉireann (the National Army) since early 1922 with the permission of the hierarchy and, after the outbreak of war, increasingly attached to units and garrisons at the request of local commanders. In late 1922 Mulcahy set about regulating their situation. Following negotiations between the Army Council and the Catholic Church hierarchy, twenty-seven full-time 'chaplains-in-charge' and 'under-chaplains' were appointed. Smaller posts and soldiers of minority denominations were served by 500 'officiating clergymen,' including twelve from the Church of Ireland. The January 1923 reorganisation of the army into nine regional commands necessitated the appointment of supervisory command chaplains. Proposals, however, by a sub-committee of chaplains for the establishment of 'honorary commissions' with 'limited military authority' were deemed unfeasible by the judge advocate general (Cahir Davitt) because of the difficulty in defining 'limited authority' and the fact that it would require an amendment to the Defence Forces (Temporary Provisions) Act 1923. On 13 February 1923 the archbishop of Dublin, Edward Byrne, agreed to the request by the adjutant general, Gearóid O'Sullivan, to make permanent the temporary chaplaincies at Collins Barracks, Portobello Barracks, Beggars Bush Barracks and Wellington Barracks and the appointment of chaplains to Keogh Barracks and St Bricin's military hospital. Fr Francis Gleeson – former British Army Chaplain and subject of the painting *The Last General Absolution of the Munsters at Rue du Bois* – was appointed Dublin command chaplain. Described by the archbishop as 'most zealous and energetic for army work', Fr Eugene Traynor was appointed to Portobello, Fr Pigott to Collins, Fr Richard Casey to Keogh, Fr Dominik Ryan to Wellington, Fr Dermot O'Callaghan to Beggars Bush and Fr William Byrne to St Bricin's. The chaplaincy soon expanded outside Dublin with Fr Patrick Donnelly in the Curragh; Fr Joseph Scannell as Cork command chaplain and Fr John Feely as Athlone command chaplain; Fr Chrysostom in Ennis, County Clare; Fr Edward Harte in Monaghan; and Fr James O'Connor covering the diocese of Kerry. *An tÓglách* reported that 'the Bishops have paid no small tribute of their esteem for our soldiers in the selection of their first chaplains [...] to nurture in our young army that spirit of manly loyalty to God, without which there can never be genuine loyalty to country [... and to ...] help them to become more useful pioneers in a new State'. On 1 November 1923, following a rigorous shortlisting process, the National Army's first head chaplain, Fr Dominik Ryan, was formally appointed. In response to the news O'Sullivan wrote to Byrne that 'the appointment will do much towards securing that Ireland's Defence Forces will be a standard in discipline and behaviour, such as would be a credit to the young army of a Christian state'. [Text: Daniel Ayiotis / Image: National Library of Ireland, HOG137 / See 'Commander-in-Chief: Chaplains. Suggestions re spiritual welfare of national forces. Retreats, sodalities, etc.', IE/MA/DOD/A/7092, Irish Military Archives; *An tÓglach*, 'Our Chaplains', vol. 1, no. 7 (new series), 19 May 1923, p. 18]

seemingly senseless death reminded everyone of the vulnerability of their own family. It also points to the importance of faith and faith leaders in times of crisis. Fr Harrington explained: 'Though mortally wounded [...] I found s perfectly conscious on reaching him. He had little to no difficulty in making his confession, and after giving him absolution, I anointed him & gave him the last blessing.' While the priest did not spare James's loved ones the truth, he imbued his telling with religious significance:

> He was naturally in great pain and said so in my asking him, but you will be glad to learn he never complained or murmured whilst I was with him.

> God rest his soul. He was a dear Good boy, one of the best I have ever met; and I told the people so when denouncing the dastardly murder [...] the following Sunday.

Knowing the significance of a funeral and the role it played in grieving, this priest brought James's family into his church to show them the tears wept in his memory. On that Sunday he had spoken with such conviction about James that 'emotion quite overcame' him, and:

> many of those in church were also in tears [...] Tell his dear mother that she has reason to be proud of James

> for he was an excellent boy as well as a most lovable character, & that I'm sure he is happy. He was quite resigned to die, & gladly forgave those who had so foully done him to death.[17]

James's mother could hardly have missed the biblical references: as with Jesus on the cross, her son forgave those who trespassed against him. In this priest's telling James's death was an opportunity to create a new emotional community in the Free State, one which knew who the 'dastardly' were but also how to forgive them.

Widowed motherhood

For countless families the Civil War represented the first fracturing of their intimate unit, which left them more vulnerable to future loss. Several dependency files end prematurely with the death of a young woman from circumstances exacerbated by the strain of bereavement and its resultant poverty. When Michael Baker was shot dead on 22 March 1923, during a raid on a house in Dún Laoghaire, County Dublin, he had been married for just over two years.[18] His wife Frances was twenty-three years of age and living in one room in a house in Upper Gloucester Street, Dublin, with two children under three years of age.[19] She was awarded an army pension of 17*s* 6*d* per week and an allowance of 8*s* 6*d* per week, per child. However, she struggled so much to keep her children fed and clothed on that sum that, in 1927, she wrote to the army requesting help to find employment.[20] Within a year she was dead of typhoid fever. In September 1928 her father wrote to explain that he and his wife were now caring for their two grandchildren.[21] No one knows how the Baker family would have managed if Michael had survived the Civil War and returned to his family and his job as a barber, but it is highly likely that trying to raise three children alone seriously weakened Frances Baker's health.

3/D/213 43 Upper Glouster Street 6th May 1927

MINISTRY OF ... RECEIVED 9 MAY 1927 DUBLIN ARMY PENSIONS BOARD

To The Paymaster

Dear Sir

would you be so kind as to let me know if You could find me some employment as I find it very difficult to keep the Children in clothes or Bootware as they are going big and are going

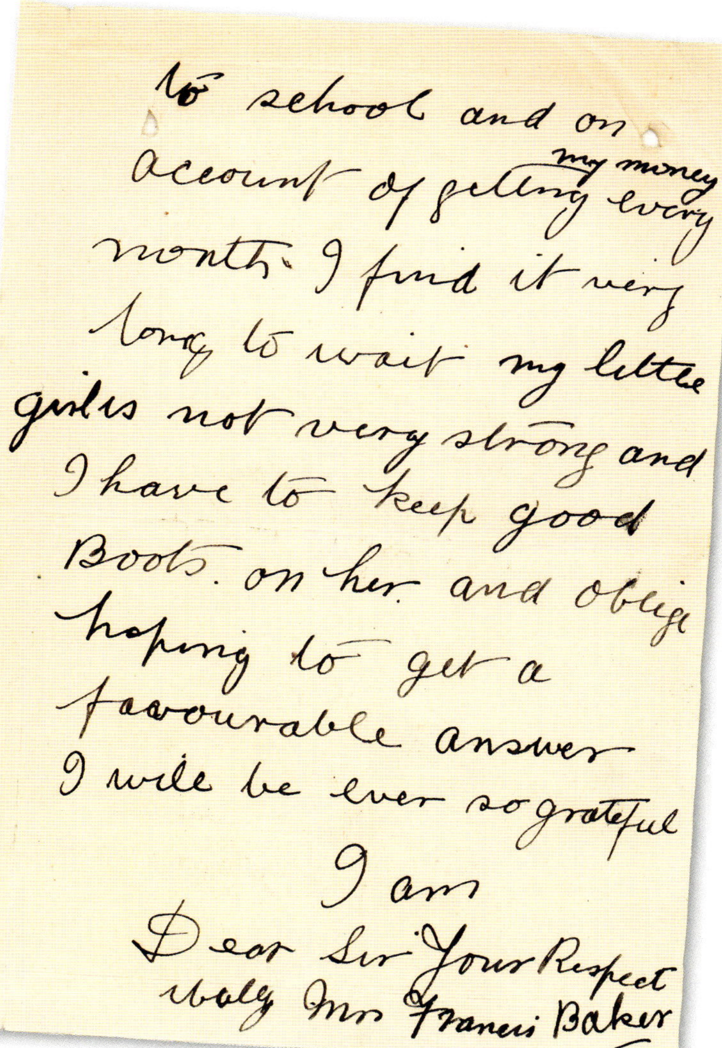

to school and on account of getting my money every month. I find it very long to wait my little girls not very strong and I have to keep good Boots on her and oblige hoping to get a favourable answer I will be ever so grateful

I am

Dear Sir Your Respectubly Mrs Francis Baker

Figs 9 and 10 A letter to the Army Pensions Department from Frances Baker, the twenty-three-year-old widow of National Army soldier Michael J. Baker, who was shot in Dún Laoghaire in March 1923. Written on 6 May 1927 from her single-room accommodation at 43 Upper Gloucester Street, she appeals for assistance in finding employment to provide for her two little girls, one of whom was 'not very strong'. [Source: MSPC3D213. Image: courtesy of Military Archives/MSPC Project]

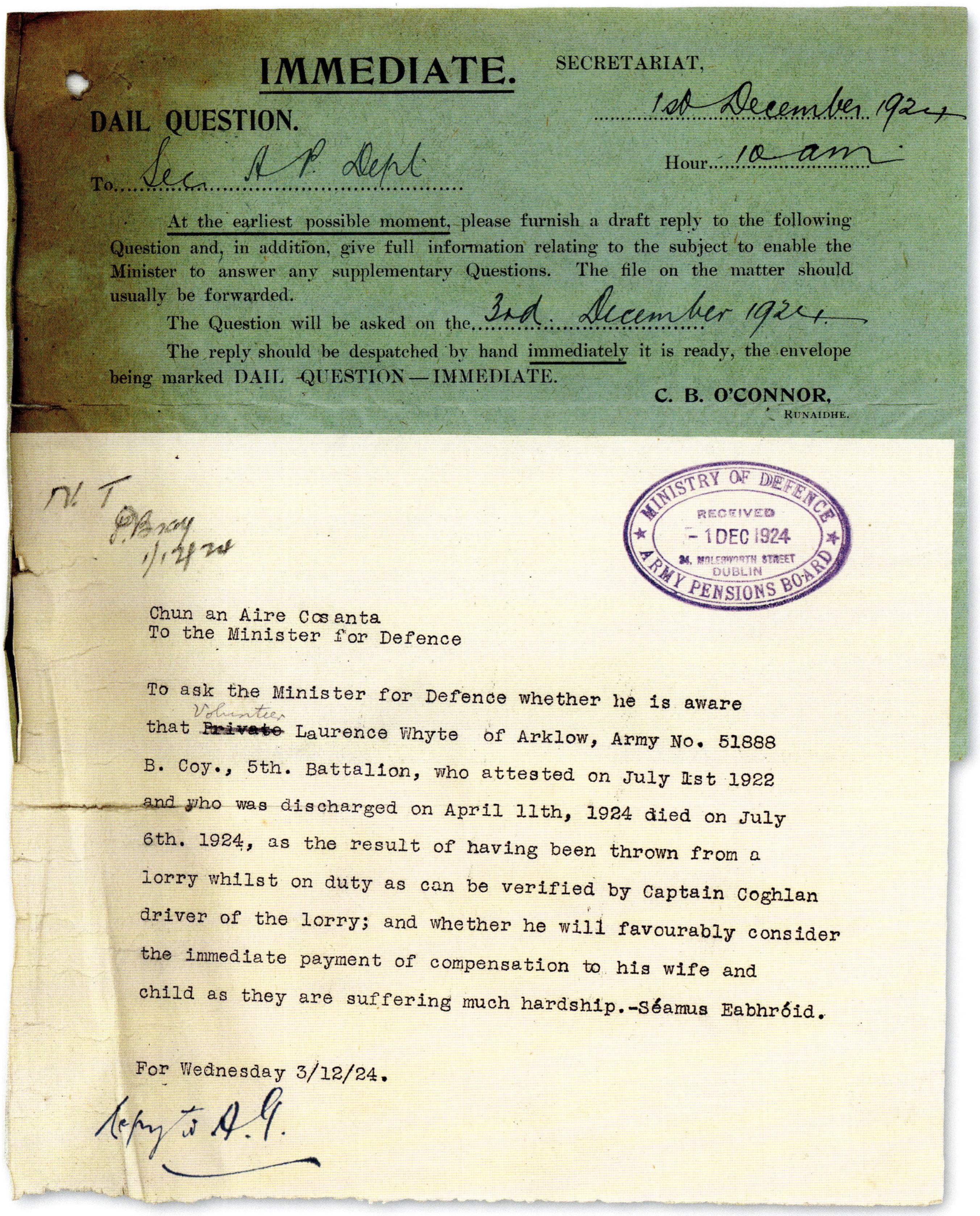

IMMEDIATE. SECRETARIAT,

DAIL QUESTION. 1st December 1924

To Sec. A.P. Dept Hour 10 am

At the earliest possible moment, please furnish a draft reply to the following Question and, in addition, give full information relating to the subject to enable the Minister to answer any supplementary Questions. The file on the matter should usually be forwarded.

The Question will be asked on the 3rd December 1924.

The reply should be despatched by hand immediately it is ready, the envelope being marked DAIL QUESTION—IMMEDIATE.

C. B. O'CONNOR,
RUNAIDHE.

N. T.
P. Bray
1/12/24

MINISTRY OF DEFENCE
RECEIVED
1 DEC 1924
34, MOLESWORTH STREET
DUBLIN
ARMY PENSIONS BOARD

Chun an Aire Cosanta
To the Minister for Defence

To ask the Minister for Defence whether he is aware that ~~Private~~ Volunteer Laurence Whyte of Arklow, Army No. 51888 B. Coy., 5th. Battalion, who attested on July 1st 1922 and who was discharged on April 11th, 1924 died on July 6th. 1924, as the result of having been thrown from a lorry whilst on duty as can be verified by Captain Coghlan driver of the lorry; and whether he will favourably consider the immediate payment of compensation to his wife and child as they are suffering much hardship.-Séamus Eabhróid.

For Wednesday 3/12/24.

Copy to A.G.

Fig. 11 A Dáil question for Minister for Defence Richard Mulcahy prepared by Labour Party TD James (Seamus) Everett on 1 December 1924 relating to 'compensation' for the widow of National Army soldier Laurence Whyte, who was injured in a motor accident on 11 October 1922 and died on 6 July 1924. [Source: MSPC4D74. Image: courtesy of Military Archives/MSPC Project]

The youth of so many of those who fought and died during the Irish Civil War meant that the families left behind were often just at the beginning of what should have been a long journey together. Margaret Whyte's husband died on 6 July 1924, two weeks shy of their first wedding anniversary and a few days before their first child was born.[22] Two years previously, on 11 October 1922, he had fallen from a moving car while on patrol with the National Army.[23] He initially appeared to be suffering from a shoulder injury and shock but, by February 1924, he was in chronic pain and barely able to walk or stand. He was discharged from the army on 11 April 1924 and, that December, his doctor explained to the army's pension board that, as his patient's health deteriorated,

> His wife […] was in a delicate state of health expecting to be confined at a near date and in very poor circumstances. I suggested that he present to the County Home Rathdrum where he died in a state of complete paralysis … I have no doubt that the accident was the original cause of the myelitis, which ended eventually in Paralysis and death.[24]

The following month, the police investigated Margaret Whyte's case, to find that she had no regular employment and no income and had broken up 'her home on the death of her husband and is now living in a room rented […] depending on her people and the St Vincent De Paul Society'.[25] With no decision or word, Seamus Everett TD tabled a Dáil question on her case in April 1925, and wrote to the Army Pensions Department that he was 'strongly of the opinion that [the] case comes under the act and that this Poor woman & child should not be depending upon local Rates for support'.[26] Despite all this, on 9 November 1925 the Pension Board informed her that it had decided her husband's 'death was not attributable to the injury he received in October 1922' and, thus, it was 'regretted that no award' could be made to her.[27]

On 6 December 1925 Margaret Whyte stood in the same church in front of the same priest as she had done in July 1923, and remarried, becoming Mrs Kavanagh.[28] Whether a love match or part of a survival strategy, it proved to be a miscalculation, as within a year her second husband was resident in America.[29] Margaret was persistent and reapplied for an allowance for her daughter under the Army Pensions Act 1927. In that application she explicitly characterised her second marriage as a strategy, explaining 'you will see I am married again in order to obtain a living'.[30] Despite all her efforts, by 1928 the police sent to investigate Margaret's situation noted she was surviving on 'relief from the Co[unty] Board of Health'.[31] On this occasion Margaret was deemed to qualify for a pension but, due to her remarriage, she could receive only an allowance in respect of her late and first husband's daughter, who received 5*s* a week until she turned eighteen in 1942.

Whispers of deep sorrows

The nature of the bureaucratic biographies people supplied when applying for a pension meant that the files often offered only whispers of deeper sorrows or hints at more complex emotional compromises and unorthodox arrangements. Rose Bannon applied for a pension as a result of her son's death in August 1922; the last sentence of the police report on her situation simply noted: 'Her husband went away from her four years ago, and has not been heard of since.'[32] This meant that the death of her only son, two years after her husband's desertion, left her utterly alone with three daughters to raise. Writing in 1927 she reminded the army: 'I have no means

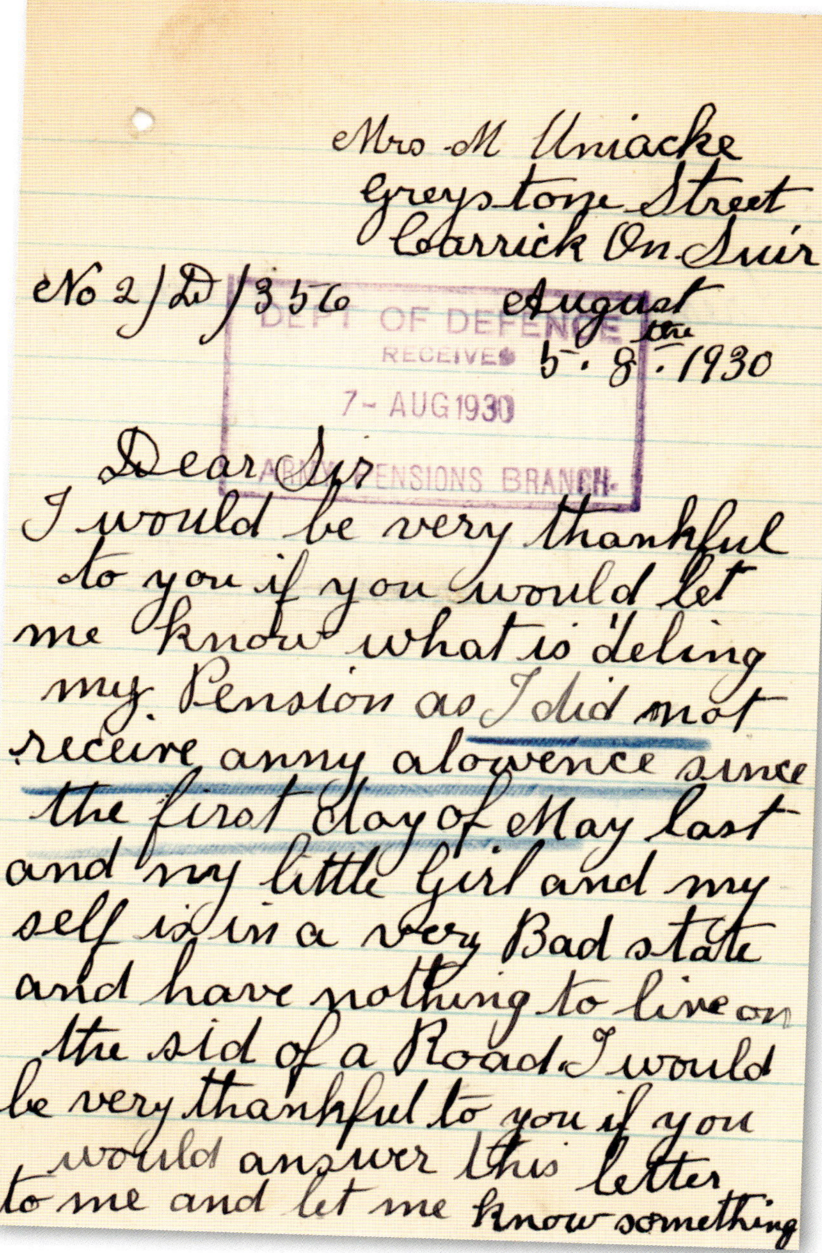

Mrs M Uniacke
Greystone Street
Carrick On Suir
No 2/D/356 August the 5.8.1930

DEPT OF DEFENCE
RECEIVED
7-AUG 1930
ARMY PENSIONS BRANCH

Dear Sir
I would be very thankful to you if you would let me know what is deling my Pension as I did not receive anny alowence since the first day of May last and my little Girl and my self is in a very Bad state and have nothing to live on the sid of a Road I would be very thankful to you if you would answer this letter to me and let me know something

Fig. 12 (right) In this letter dated 5 August 1930, Margaret Uniacke seeks clarification about a delay in the payment of her pension allowance as widow of Thomas Uniacke, who was wounded on 10 August 1922 at the workhouse, Carrick-on-Suir, County Tipperary and died the following day. She and her little girl, she writes, are in 'a very bad state'. [Source: MSCP2D356. Image courtesy of Military Archives/MSPC Project] only my allowance for myself and 3 little girls [...] my one only Boy killed of course my xmas feels very lonely at any time but worse still without means.'[33] Margaret Uniacke, whose husband of six years had been shot after only one day in the National Army, was left, according to the army, 'in very poor circumstances [...] supporting two young children, by her own labour'.[34] The baby son she had six months before her husband's death died in 1928 of measles.[35] Within two years of this bereavement, in May 1930, Margaret's pension was terminated. She wrote several letters throughout that summer requesting clarification as to why she had received neither her pension nor her daughter's allowance, fearing they would have to 'live on the sid[e] of the Road'.[36]

Margaret's case file was virtually silent on the reasons for this judgement. On 17 September 1930, over four months after the termination of her pension, she was informed that 'as a result of reports received in this Department as regards your conduct, the Minister for Defence has decided that you have been guilty of disgraceful conduct within the meaning of section 11 (4) of the [Army Pensions] Act'.[37] Someone had reported her, prompting 'further discreet inquiries made by the local Garda into the case'.[38] While the results of these inquiries are not in the file, their consequences for Margaret and her daughter appear to have been dramatic. In October 1930 a short internal memo referenced the guardianship of her only surviving child, ominously seeking clarification from official records as to 'the Denomination of her late father'.[39] It was state policy to ensure that children placed in either foster or residential care were sent to settings consistent with their faith, which prior to the 1964 Guardianship of Infants Act, was usually determined by the father's faith. That query, and the fact that from that point onwards the child's allowance was paid to the Department of Education, indicate that Margaret's daughter no longer lived with her. The last surviving missive from Margaret came in June 1931, in which she made no reference to her daughter but requested her pension, promising 'for the futer time to Come I will mind myself and to give me a chance for this time'.[40] In response to which, the Department merely repeated the basis for its decision as outlined the year before.[41] The chain of events set in motion by the Civil War had resulted in Margaret losing her husband, a son and, in all likelihood, the guardianship of her daughter.

Contemporaries did have some understanding of the relationship between grief and coping mechanisms, such as alcohol abuse. In December 1922, for example, Fr Flanagan explained to the archbishop of Dublin that one of his parishioners was 'financially at zero' because 'after a long period of abstinence there was a breakdown recently due to the death of her daughter'.[42] The dominant framing remained, however, a moral and relatively punitive one, often informed by class prejudice. In the summer of 1924 Bridget Moloney applied for a pension in relation to her son, who had died on 15 September 1922 while serving in the National Army.[43] The police reported that both her husband and eighteen-year-old son had died in the 'European War'; thus, with the death of her son in the Civil War, she was left with four children at home ranging from six to nineteen years of age.[44]

From the outset the tone of the police report was hostile. It noted that it was 'stated locally' that she was in receipt of weekly payments relating to her husband's drowning in the war, and that she had received a gratuity for her son's death. While the 'applicant denies' these claims, 'she has certainly money to spend freely'. Women whose 'only visible means of support is hawking fish about the district' should not be seen to pay their bills with ease. If the point was to assess her dependence on her son, killed in the service of the state, then the receipt of a once-off gratuity for the death of her husband was irrelevant as it would never have been enough to sustain a large family for long. Similarly, if she had been in receipt of a British army pension for her other deceased son, that was verifiable and should, at worst, have meant that she could only claim 'partial' dependency on her other son. However, the police report's concluding remarks in all likelihood ended any hope she had of acquiring a pension: 'the claimant', it concluded, was 'very much addicted to drink' and had been 'convicted several times during the past twelve months for drunkenness and disorderly behaviour'.[45]

There appears to have been no sense that a life shaped by so much loss might leave some people simply unable, as opposed to unwilling, to cope. Fionnuala Walsh highlights a similar lack of general sympathy for the grief or stress experienced by soldiers' wives during the First World War. She also attributed a particular class dynamic to these narratives.[46] While religious leaders could be advocates for vulnerable women, their immense power could just as easily be used to judge and condemn. On 12 December 1924 Fr Glynn contributed his view on Bridget's case, dismissing her as a 'most degraded character. Drink, Immorality, Foulest invectives, and depraved'. He almost boasted of having had her 'interned in a Borstal Institute' some six years previously, lamenting that, 'by misbehaving', she had been transferred to a 'maternity home'.[47] She was, he claimed, the kind of mother that 'Starves her children and foully abuses those who feed them'. He also denied that she had been dependent on her deceased son. While the army conceded that technically Bridget was entitled to a £50 gratuity, on 24 July 1925 it decided, in light of Fr Glynn's report and the fact that there was no dependency, that 'no award can be made'.[48] If the evidence against Bridget was so robust, one wonders how she managed to retain custody of her children up to that point, particularly when priests and police had the capacity to have children committed to care.[49]

Collectively, the dependence files underscore how the bread-winner model disadvantaged women and how moral judgement compounded that disadvantage. In this universe the 'unmarried mother' had the least social power of all. One letter, written by Miss A. O'Brien in April 1923, remains a testament to the vulnerability of these women. She wrote to inform the army that a recently deceased soldier was the father of her daughter.[50] She was living alone in a room in Dublin with her baby girl: 'I'm left my home through him for the past twelve months, never to be let return, but thanks to my good Mother she gave what kept me going until now otherwise "the Liffey" would have covered me. I got no help from my baby's father RIP I'm sorry to say.'[51] She articulated the social pressure she was under, explaining that, while living with no money and in total

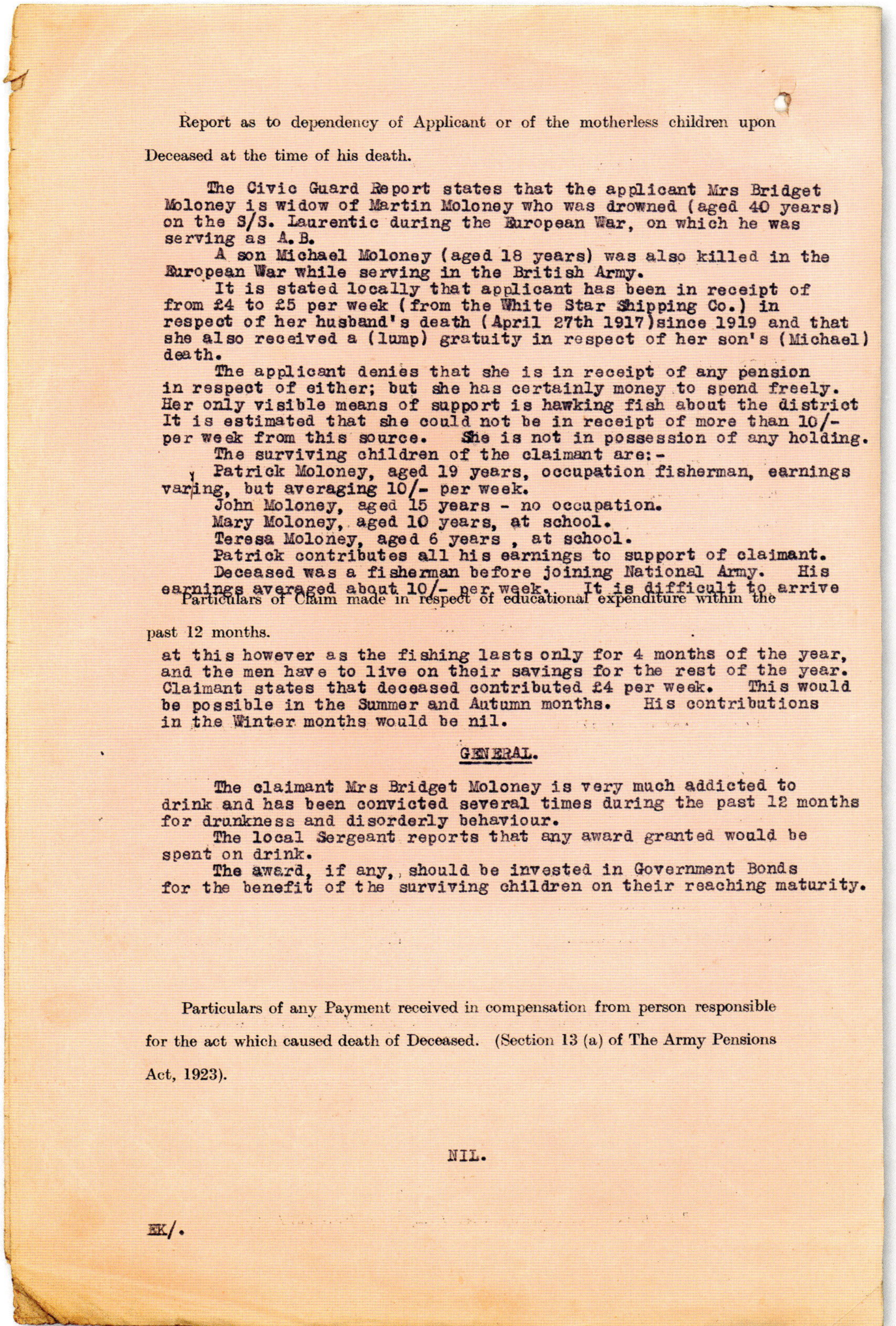

Report as to dependency of Applicant or of the motherless children upon Deceased at the time of his death.

The Civic Guard Report states that the applicant Mrs Bridget Moloney is widow of Martin Moloney who was drowned (aged 40 years) on the S/S. Laurentic during the European War, on which he was serving as A. B.

A son Michael Moloney (aged 18 years) was also killed in the European War while serving in the British Army.

It is stated locally that applicant has been in receipt of from £4 to £5 per week (from the White Star Shipping Co.) in respect of her husband's death (April 27th 1917) since 1919 and that she also received a (lump) gratuity in respect of her son's (Michael) death.

The applicant denies that she is in receipt of any pension in respect of either; but she has certainly money to spend freely. Her only visible means of support is hawking fish about the district It is estimated that she could not be in receipt of more than 10/- per week from this source. She is not in possession of any holding.

The surviving children of the claimant are:-

Patrick Moloney, aged 19 years, occupation fisherman, earnings varying, but averaging 10/- per week.

John Moloney, aged 15 years - no occupation.

Mary Moloney, aged 10 years, at school.

Teresa Moloney, aged 6 years , at school.

Patrick contributes all his earnings to support of claimant.

Deceased was a fisherman before joining National Army. His earnings averaged about 10/- per week. It is difficult to arrive

Particulars of Claim made in respect of educational expenditure within the past 12 months.

at this however as the fishing lasts only for 4 months of the year, and the men have to live on their savings for the rest of the year. Claimant states that deceased contributed £4 per week. This would be possible in the Summer and Autumn months. His contributions in the Winter months would be nil.

GENERAL.

The claimant Mrs Bridget Moloney is very much addicted to drink and has been convicted several times during the past 12 months for drunkness and disorderly behaviour.

The local Sergeant reports that any award granted would be spent on drink.

The award, if any, should be invested in Government Bonds for the benefit of the surviving children on their reaching maturity.

Particulars of any Payment received in compensation from person responsible for the act which caused death of Deceased. (Section 13 (a) of The Army Pensions Act, 1923).

NIL.

EK/.

Fig. 13 Bridget Moloney's Dependants' Allowance of Gratuity AP12 form, *c.*1924, part of her application under the Army Pensions Acts in respect of the death of her son Martin Moloney, who was wounded in Limerick in July 1922 and died on 15 September 1922. The form cites the Civic Guard report, which includes the admonition by the unnamed 'local Sergeant' that 'any award granted would be spent on drink'. [Source: MSPC2D451. Image: courtesy of Military Archives/ MSPC Project] isolation was one thing, 'the hardest of all [was] trying to live under falsehood, & finding words for every question put to you'. She had tried to put her daughter in care, but could not afford the price quoted to her by a home in Drumcondra. So-called rescue homes charged women considerable fees for taking in their children. The Saint Patrick Guild and Rescue Society, for example, was charging women 25*s* per month at the time.[52] She described feeling almost 'insane' since her baby's father's death, and concluded: 'It's a hard cruel world for me, but what you can do for me might lighten a heavy load on a broken heart & a penniless & homeless girl.'[53] There is no evidence that the army either investigated her claim or sought to lighten her burden. The chance of a family such as hers surviving intact in 1920s Ireland was slim, largely because women and their children born outside marriage were not considered to constitute families. In fact, there was a pervasive view that such units undermined the status of 'legitimate' families.

Trauma and the family

For many families the final death of a loved one as a result of the Civil War unfolded slowly before their eyes, entirely reshaping the everyday life and emotional fabric of their family. This was then compounded by having to prove that their loss was attributable to the conflict. In 1933 Nora Murray applied for a pension due to

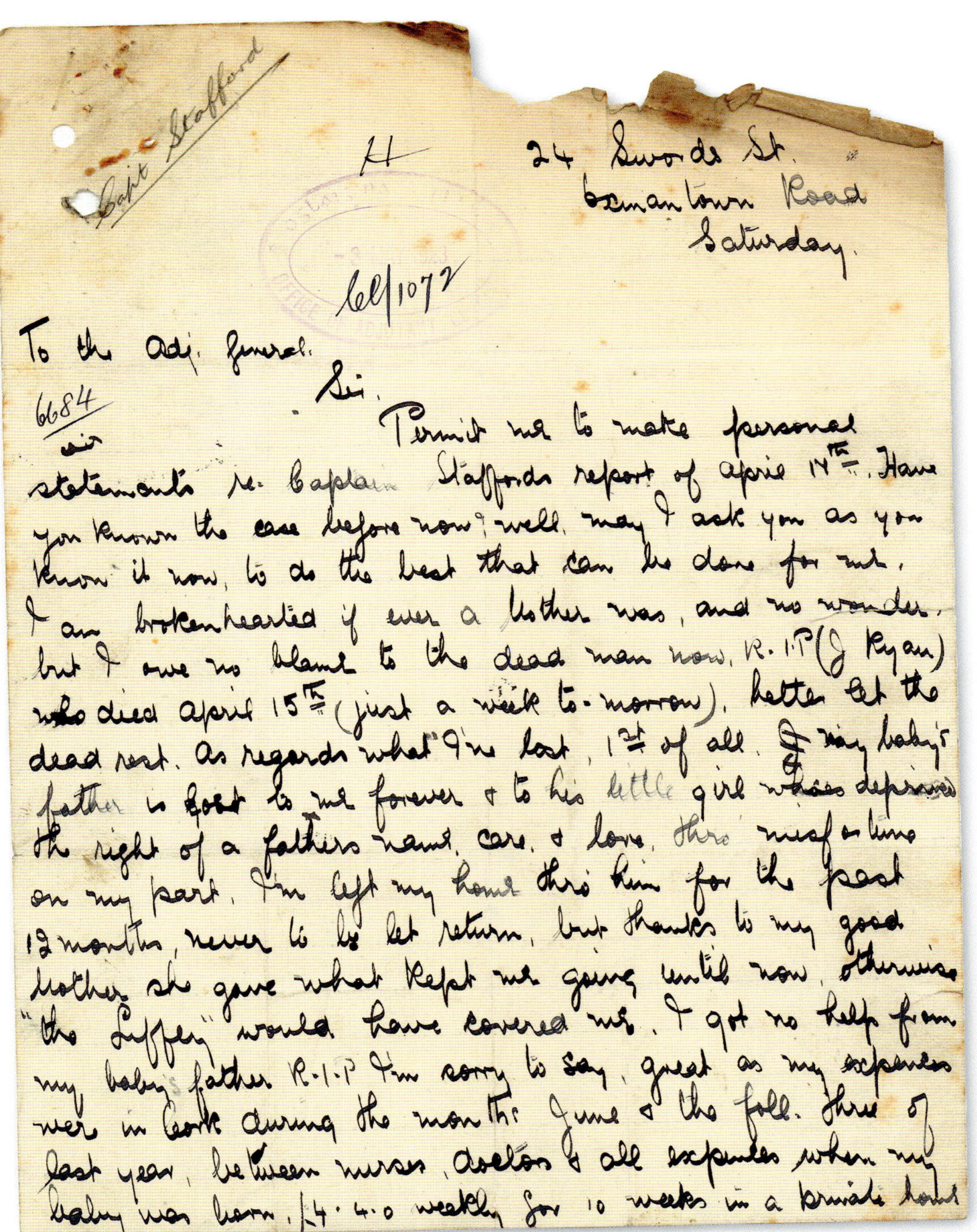

Capt Stafford

H

24 Swords St.
Oxmantown Road
Saturday.

CC/1072

To the Adj. General.

Sir.

6684

Permit me to make personal statements re. Captain Staffords report of April 14th. Have you known the case before now? well, may I ask you as you know it now, to do the best that can be done for me. I am brokenhearted if ever a Mother was, and no wonder. but I owe no blame to the dead man now. R.I.P (J Ryan) who died April 15th (just a week to-morrow). better let the dead rest. As regards what I've lost, 1st of all my baby's father is lost to me forever & to his little girl who's deprived the right of a fathers name, care, & love, thro misfortune on my part. I'm left my home thro him for the past 12 months, never to be let return, but thanks to my good Mother she gave what kept me going until now, otherwise "the Liffey" would have covered me. I got no help from my baby's father R.I.P I'm sorry to say, great as my expenses were in Cork during the months June & the foll. three of last year, between nurses, doctors & all expenses when my baby was born, £4.4.0 weekly for 10 weeks in a private home

Figs 14–16 (left and opposite page) Letter from Miss A. O'Brien to the Department of Defence, Dublin. The accidental death of James Ryan, who was mortally wounded with his own revolver in Bohernacrusha, County Tipperary in mid-April 1923 prompted this appeal from the 'broken-hearted' Miss A. O'Brien to the Department of Defence to do 'the best that can be done for me'. Not only had she lost the father of her baby, who was forever deprived of his 'care and love', but also her home, which she was forced to leave because having a child outside marriage breached the moral code of early twentieth-century Ireland. As Ryan could not come back to 'right his wrong', she was struggling with expenses, isolation, 'delicate health', hopes 'dashed to pieces' and the emotional weight of 'living under a falsehood'. [Source: MSPC3D205. Image: courtesy of Military Archives/MSPC Project] was no small bill. Then again trying to live sinc in a deserted room, with no friend to want me paying 14/- weekly, besides coal & the support of baby & myself in delicate health, & the hardest of all trying to live under falsehood, & finding words for every question put to you. I was told by several to report the matter long ago, but hoping from day to day that he should come back to me, & making right his wrong, but such wasn't my good luck. However I went to see him on Sunday last to see what he had to say (for I knew he'd come with me) at St Bricin's Hospital & just as I was well in (I came) only to find him dead. R.I.P. however, I wish him nothing but Heaven & forgiveness, but may I add that I'm nearly insane, now that I have to face the world pennyless, & I have no position or don't know where to get one & worst of all nobody wants you without money. & I can't live on as I'm living any longer. I've lived in hopes to live this, but now these dashed to pieces, & I'm refused further help at home, therefore I ask you in God's name again to help me. As I am & if I got a position I can't take it, for I have to care & see after my baby now, that is fatherless, & homeless, & soon in poverty, but God is good, & I'll trust in you to do the best you can, & then may you meet a your reward 100 fold. don't refuse me, it takes a lot to repay me for what I have lost, but give me what will keep me & my baby, & let what's lost be lost. I also went to a baby's home in Drumcondra, & the

cheapest a baby would be admitted was 15/- week, first I was told !! so I left it at that hoping on, on, only to meet with still harder knocks. Tis a hard cruel world for me, but what you can do for me might lighten a heavy load on a broken heart & a penniless & homeless girl.

I am,

Very Sincerely Yours,

A. O'Brien.

P.S.

Please don't think I have exaggerated in this letter, what I have said is truth, & bitter truth at that, God help me. & may I further ask to see thro' the matter as soon as possible, & thanking you very much.

AOB.

the death of her daughter Ellen, who had been a Cumann na mBan 'enthusiast who obeyed orders regardless of conditions'.[54] Ellen, known as Nellie to her loved ones, had been imprisoned in Kilmainham Gaol, along with hundreds of other Cumann na mBan women arrested for anti-Treaty activities during the Civil War.[55] When imprisoned, between 13 February and 23 August 1923, she took part in a hunger strike for somewhere between eight and sixteen days.[56] Whether it was the hunger strike, the hardship of imprisonment or work throughout the war carrying dispatches, skipping meals and sleeping in wet clothes, Ellen never recovered from the experience. She was not alone; another Cumann na mBan internee, Polly Cosgrave, described her jail experience as 'written in letters of fire across my brain, never to be effaced'.[57] Ellen's doctor certified that she had been 'very low in health after coming from prison', and 'lingered on between the bed and her room until finally [...] she got a further Haemorrhage from the lungs and died'.[58] Her employer, William Ingle, also testified that she had worked for nine years prior to imprisonment and had 'lost little or no time as a result of illness'. However, she 'returned to the same employment after her release, showing every sign of having been broken in health'.[59] In 1939 Brigid O'Mullane, who had been the commanding officer in Kilmainham, claimed: 'Ellen Murray never seemed to recover after the hunger strike, yet instead of being released was transferred to the North Dublin Union and there detained until sometime in August 1923.'[60] However, Mrs Murray was not deemed to have been dependent on her daughter and was, therefore, awarded a gratuity of £85 in 1940 rather than a pension.[61]

Nellie's mother's grief was obscured in the bureaucratic process, one in which she

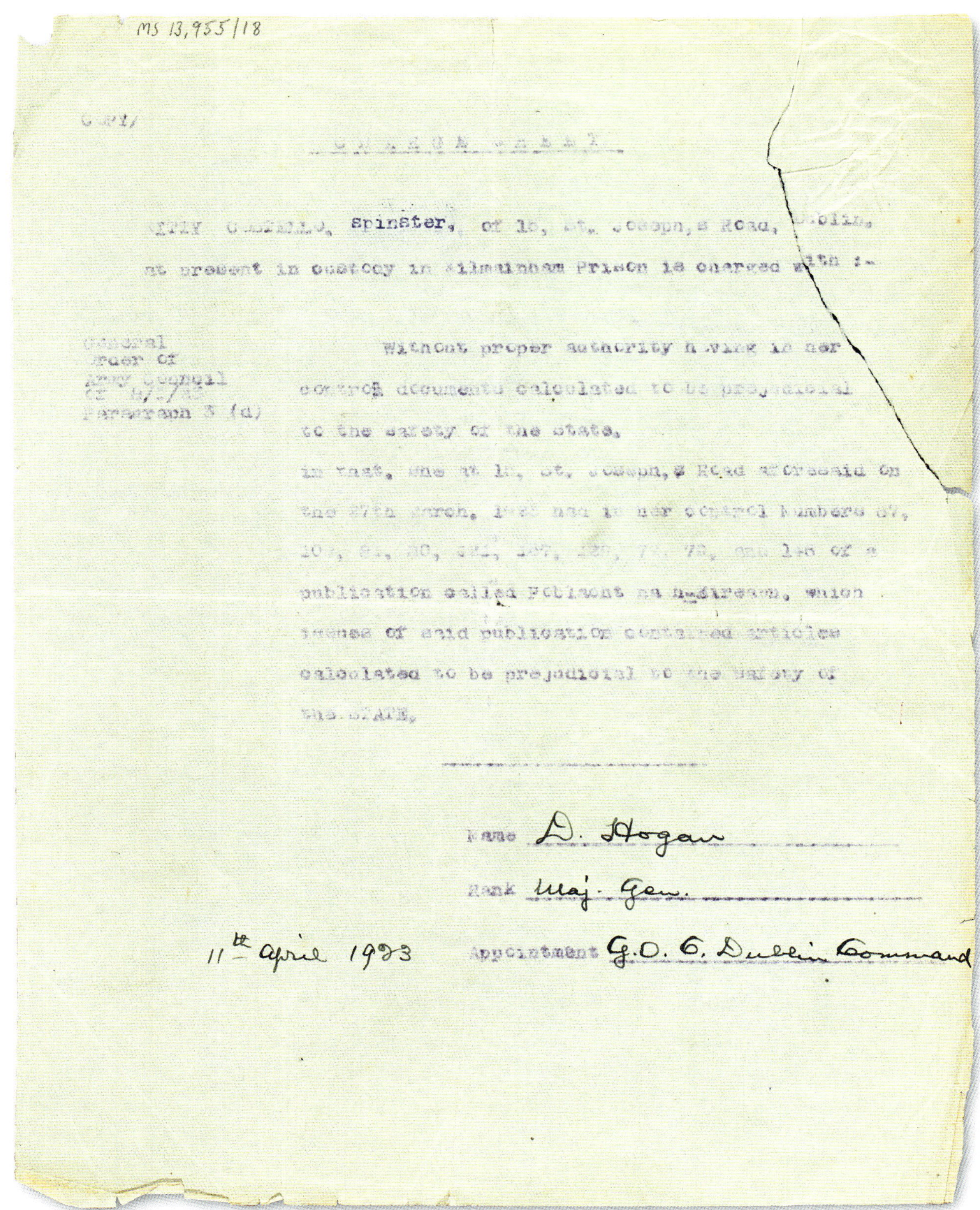

MS 13,955/18

COPY

CHARGE SHEET

KITTY COSTELLO, spinster, of 1[illegible], St. Joseph's Road, Dublin,

at present in custody in Kilmainham Prison is charged with :-

General Order of Army Council of [illegible] Paragraph 3 (d)

Without proper authority having in her control documents calculated to be prejudicial to the safety of the state,

in that, she at 1[illegible], St. Joseph's Road aforesaid on the 27th March, 192[illegible] had in her control numbers [illegible], [illegible] and [illegible] of a publication called Poblacht na hEireann, which issues of said publication contained articles calculated to be prejudicial to the safety of the STATE.

Name D. Hogan

Rank Maj. Gen.

11th April 1923

Appointment G.O.C. Dublin Command

Fig. 17 Charge sheet for Kathleen (Kitty) Costello, signed by Major General Daniel Hogan. It was issued almost a month after her arrest in Dublin on 27 March 1923 for possession of several issues of *Poblacht na hÉireann,* featuring articles deemed 'prejudicial to the safety of the state'. Costello was interned in Kilmainham Gaol, where she immediately went on a hunger strike that continued until her unconditional release on 28 April 1923. Speaking in the Dáil a day earlier in support of Pat McCartan's motion to release the female hunger strikers, Michael Staines TD described Costello's arrest for possession of the republican news-sheet as 'ridiculous'. He charged the government with hypocrisy for allowing its continued circulation and then putting 'a girl into jail and let[ting] her go to death's door before furnishing up the charge'. [Document: National Library of Ireland, William O'Brien (1881–1968) Papers, MS 13,955/18 / *Dáil Debates,* vol. 3, no. 7, 25 April 1923]

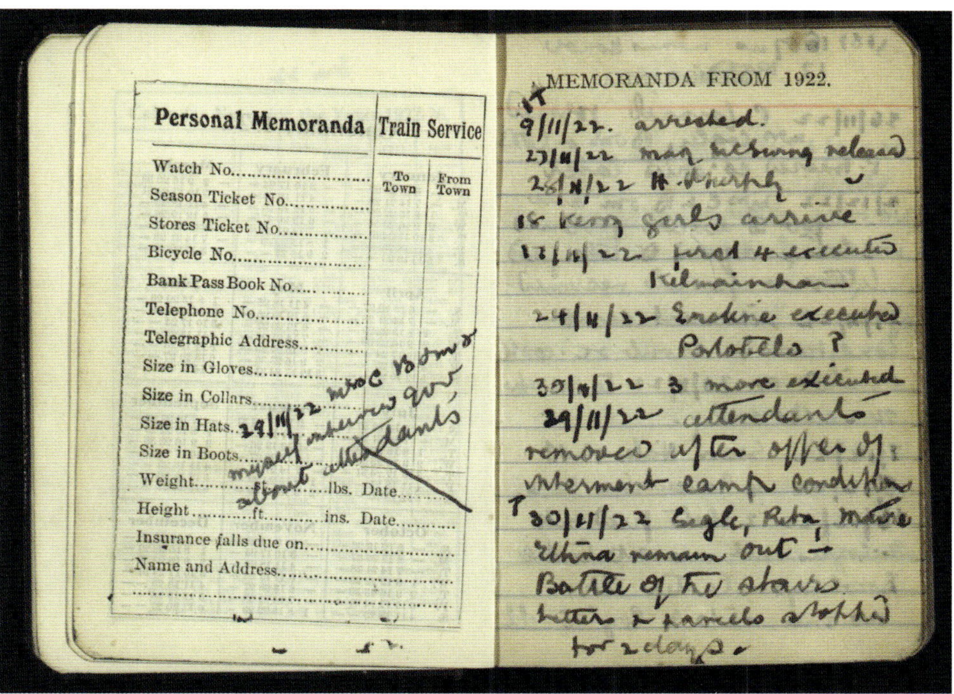

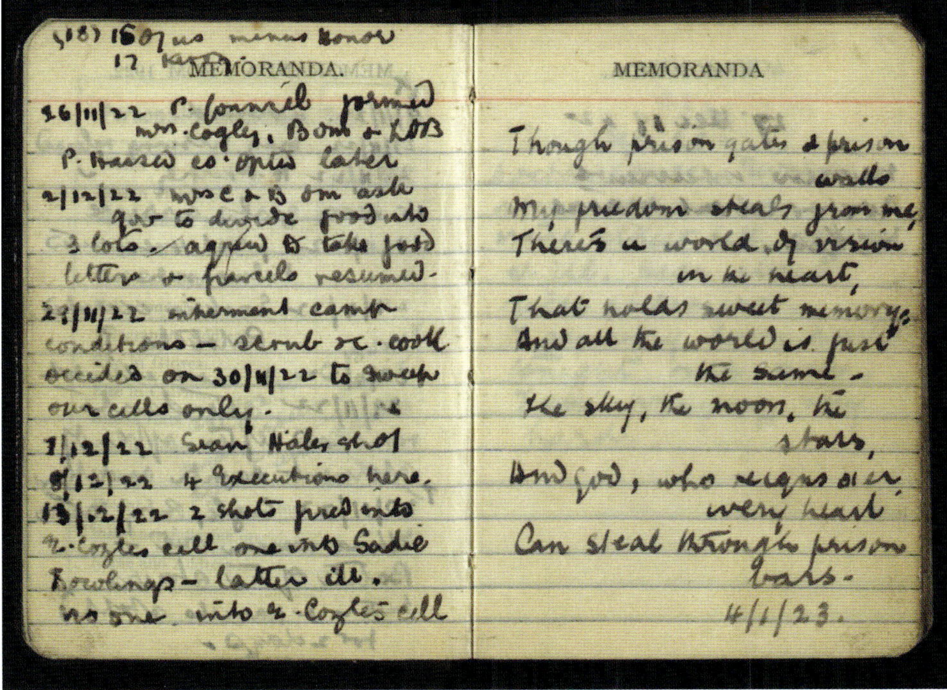

Fig. 18 The first pages of Lily O'Brennan's jail diary in which she provided daily accounts of life in prison between January and February 1923, and then intermittently until July. The opening pages contain a summary of events from her arrest on 9 November until 21 December 1922. Notable entries include the arrival of other prisoners, including '18 Kerry girls' on 28 November, executions and hunger strikes. Also mentioned are the various sanctions imposed on the internees, the formation of the Prisoners' Council, and the 'Battle of the Stairs' on 30 April 1922, when the women prisoners in Kilmainham were forcibly removed to the North Dublin Union. The opening section concludes with a poem composed by O'Brennan on 4 January 1923: 'Though prison gates & prison walls / My freedom steals from me /There's a world of vision in the heart /That holds sweet memory /And all the world is just the same /The sky, the moon, the stars /And God, who reigns o'er [every] heart /Can steal through prison bars.' [Document: Papers of Lily O'Brennan UCDA p13/1. Reproduced by kind permission of UCD Archives. Reproduced by kind permission of UCD Archives]

was obliged to value her loss only in monetary terms. The emotional strain of watching a child waste away over a decade was written between the lines of her pension application. Similarly, Catherine Doherty lived through the slow death of her daughter Margaret, whose assault was uncovered and explored by Linda Connolly.[62] On 31 May 1923 the family home was violently raided by three National Army officers, during which Margaret, the only daughter, was dragged from the house and raped.[63] There were several other rapes related to the Irish Civil War, all occurring in or near the victim's homes, thus directly involving the families, as in the Dohertys case.[64] Mrs Doherty explained that, over the course of the five years between the attack and her death, her daughter 'gradually failed, physically and mentally'.[65] Margaret's father died in August 1928, a mere five months before her.

In 1923 Margaret Doherty was a Cumann na mBan activist, but she was also her mother's main support in the house. Mrs Doherty was paralysed on one side and, thus, relied heavily on her only daughter. While Margaret had never been ill before the night she was raped, from that point onwards she 'was totally incapacitated [...] until death'.[66] While the three doctors who had treated

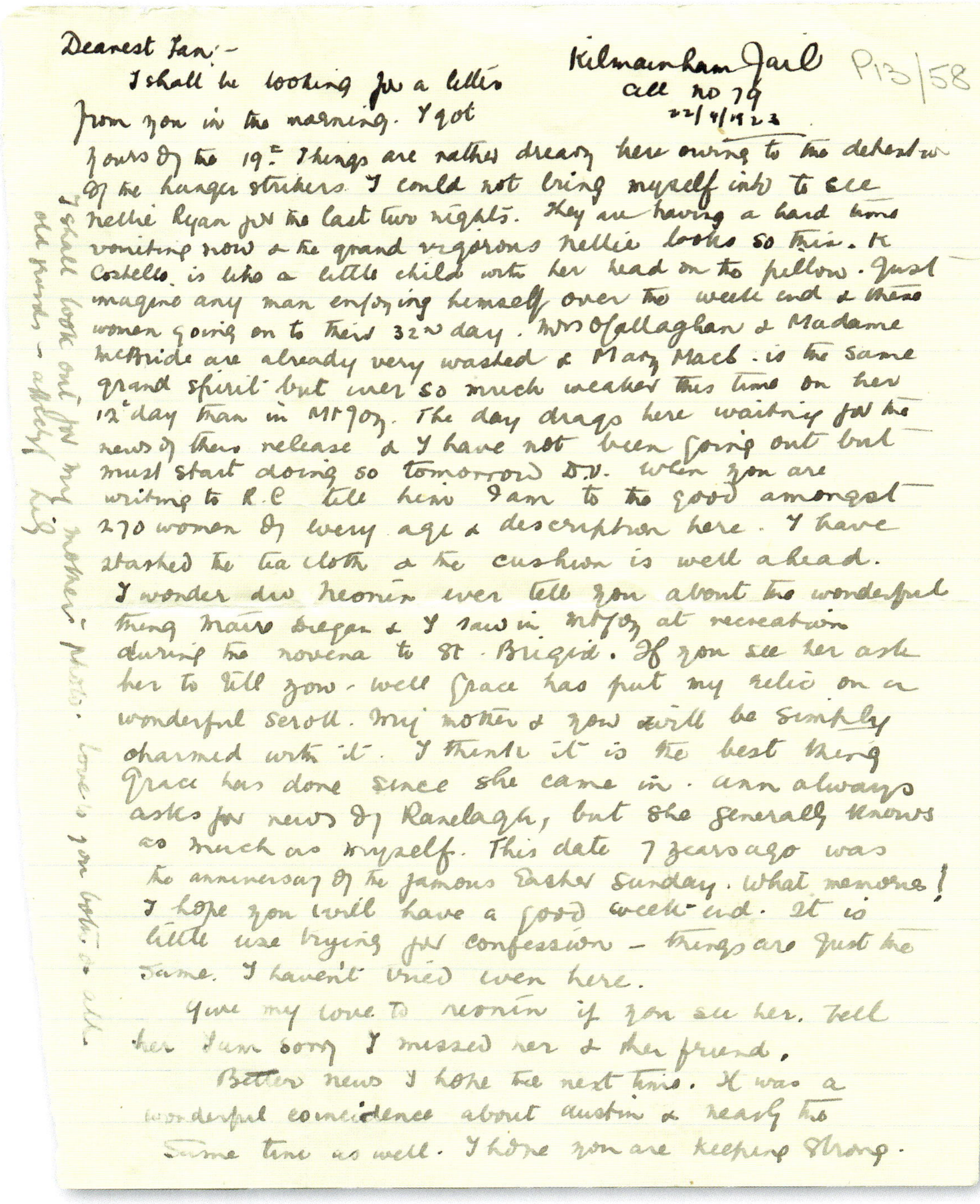

Kilmainham Jail
Cell No 79
22/4/1923

P13/58

Dearest Fan:-

I shall be looking for a letter from you in the morning. I got yours of the 19th. Things are rather dreary here owing to the detention of the hunger strikers. I could not bring myself into to see Nellie Ryan for the last two nights. They are having a hard time vomiting now & the grand vigorous Nellie looks so thin. K Costello is like a little child with her head on the pillow. Just imagine any man enjoying himself over the week end & these women going on to their 32nd day. Mrs O'Callaghan & Madame McBride are already very wasted & Mary MacS. is the same grand spirit but ever so much weaker this time on her 12th day than in Mtjoy. The day drags here waiting for the news of their release & I have not been going out but must start doing so tomorrow D.V. When you are writing to R.C tell him I am to the good amongst 270 women of every age & description here. I have started the tea cloth & the cushion is well ahead. I wonder did Neoinin ever tell you about the wonderful thing Maire Deegan & I saw in Mtjoy at recreation during the novena to St. Brigid. If you see her ask her to tell you - well Grace has put my relic on a wonderful scroll. My mother & you will be simply charmed with it. I think it is the best thing Grace has done since she came in. Ann always asks for news of Ranelagh, but she generally knows as much as myself. This date 7 years ago was the anniversary of the famous Easter Sunday. What memories! I hope you will have a good week-end. It is little use trying for confession - things are just the same. I haven't tried even here.

Give my love to Neoinin if you see her. Tell her I am sorry I missed her & her friend.

Better news I hope the next time. It was a wonderful coincidence about Austin & nearly the same time as well. I hope you are keeping strong.

I shall look out for my mother's photo. Love to you both & all old friends - affecly Lily

Fig. 19 Letter from Elizabeth (Lily) O'Brennan to her sister Fanny (Áine Ceannt), 22 April 1923, reporting on the condition of the female hunger strikers in Kilmainham Gaol. Described by fellow prisoner Margaret Buckley as 'rather diminutive and full of humour', forty-five-year-old Lily O'Brennan, who served over 180 days' internment, was older than many of her fellow prisoners. Sister-in-law to executed leader of the 1916 Rising Éamonn Ceannt, a writer and prominent republican activist in her own right, this was not her first experience of Dublin's 'old bastille'. An early member of Cumann na mBan's central branch in Dublin, she and her sister had been involved in plans for the 1916 Rising, during which she served at Marrowbone Lane Distillery, an outpost of Ceannt's Fourth Dublin Battalion. 'What memories!' she exclaims in her letter written on the seventh anniversary of the 1916 Easter Rising. O'Brennan was one of seventy-seven women interned after Easter Week, after which she devoted her energies to propaganda, commemoration, intelligence work, support for Volunteers' dependants and her membership of the Cumann na mBan executive. She accompanied the plenipotentiaries to London as a member of the secretarial staff in the autumn of 1921, but strongly opposed the resulting Treaty and served on the staff at republican headquarters at 23 Suffolk Street. She was arrested there on 9 November 1922, and interned in Mountjoy before being transferred to Kilmainham after it was made ready for use as a female military prison. Her letter to Áine reveals her distress at the deterioration of Nellie Ryan, who 'looks so thin', Kitty Costello, who 'is like a little child', and Mary MacSwiney, who retained her indomitable spirit despite being very weak. O'Brennan was transferred to the North Dublin Union in May 1923, where she participated in an abortive escape attempt weeks before her release. [Document: Papers of Lily O'Brennan UCDA P13/58. Reproduced by kind permission of UCD Archives / See Bridget Hourican, 'Elizabeth ('Lily') O'Brennan', *Dictionary of Irish Biography*, https://doi.org/10.3318/dib.006449.v1]

Fig. 20 Studio portrait of Lily O'Brennan published in the *Capuchin Annual* (1936), to which she contributed an article about her experiences during the 1916 Rising. [Image: courtesy of the Irish Capuchin Archives]

Margaret struggled to adequately explain her decline, they all agreed the insomnia, loss of appetite, depression and anxiety were a result of 'the hellishly barbaric treatment at the hands of the Free State Soldiers in 1923'.[67] Her death certificate gave no indication of the prolonged trauma that preceded her death in the mental hospital in Castlebar, County Mayo, merely noting that she died at thirty-two years of age on 28 December 1928, of tubercular arthritis.

Despite all the evidence in Mrs Doherty's application, and the particular moral responsibility of the new state for her daughter's death, her two brothers had to write several times over the proceeding four years to push for a decision from the army. In these letters the degree to which the family's life had been marked by the ordeal emerged. In January 1937 the state awarded Mrs Doherty a gratuity of £112 10*s*. However, there was no justice for Margaret or her family. Linda Connolly notes that Margaret Doherty's attack and death 'lived on quietly in the intergenerational memory of her family and community'.[68]

Lived experience

The bureaucratic process of applying for a pension or gratuity resulting from the loss of a loved one demanded particular narratives that were reductive and exhausting for the applicants. However, the files generated as a result of this process yield extraordinary insights into the lived experiences of families in Ireland for much of the twentieth century.[69] The MSPC is a testament to the struggles, strategies and physical and emotional work involved in being a family in Ireland, both before and long after the Civil War had altered the trajectory of their lives. In the process of form-filling, people found ways of documenting how their families functioned, how they loved and, sometimes, how they floundered and maybe failed. Many other voices commented upon and observed those families, often dispassionately, sometimes sympathetically or ungenerously. Thus, despite bureaucracy's best efforts, the army's pension process generated evidence of the spirit, resilience and pain of the vital human relations that underpinned and shaped Irish society and history.

CASE STUDY

Violence against Women during the Irish Civil War

Linda Connolly

Remembering events or periods stained by transgressive violence is very challenging and can evoke strong public reaction, as the botched state proposal to officially commemorate the Royal Irish Constabulary demonstrated in 2020.[1] Anti-colonial memory in the present remains a potent source of protest. Remembering the atrocities of the Irish Civil War is also contentious. A memorial erected at Knocknagoshel, County Kerry in 2013, for instance, to mark the killing of five National Army soldiers on 6 March 1923, was vandalised in 2014 and targeted again in 2017.[2] The onset of the Civil War is usually categorised as starting with the exchange of gunfire between pro- and anti-Treaty forces (presumed to be mostly men) on 28 June 1922. However, another type of conflict-related violence requires broader reflection and analysis – bodily violence and terror targeted at women. For decades, particular forms of gender-based and sexual violence witnessed in many other wars (such as rape, sexual harassment, forced hair cutting/taking and tarring and feathering) were not considered an important feature of the Irish revolution.[3] However, as Louise Ryan, argued in 2000:

> [W]hile acknowledging the limited sources which are available, I believe there is at least sufficient material to begin to reassess the gendered nature of violence during the Irish War of Independence and to seriously reconsider the ways in which sexual violence or the threat of sexual violence may have been deliberately used to intimidate women in the heavily militarized areas of the country.

A new research project I established in 2016, 'Women and the Irish Revolution', continues to discover, research and publish new evidence of sexual and gender-based violence in the Irish Civil War.[4] Detailed documentary research extensively analysing newspapers, state documents, legal papers, trials, military documents, family records, pension applications, compensation claims, etc. is a long-established methodology in sociological and feminist research seeking to analyse and explain wartime violence targeted at women. Such an approach puts the position, experience and treatment of women specifically at the centre of distinct episodes of violence, war and revolution.[5] Gender is an important dynamic of the Irish revolution and of violence that can provide additional insight and an enhanced perspective. The scale of gender-based and sexual violence in Ireland is not atypically small when contextualised in relation to other wars internationally of similar structure, size and duration to the Irish revolution, where women were also subjected to targeted violence. Sexual violence is a feature of all wars and societies throughout time that is frequently shrouded in silence, suppressed and treated with impunity.

A broad spectrum of gender-based violence perpetrated against women, such as the widespread practice of forced hair cutting, bodily searching and destructive house raids, does not fit with any heroic narrative of the period 1919–23. Hair cutting was intended to shame, control and sexually police women who were considered too close to, or intimate with, both crown forces and the IRA. The shame of participating in the systematic taking of women's hair is likewise self-evident and has received less scrutiny. Few IRA veterans of the War of Independence or pro- and anti-Treaty forces in the Civil War have openly discussed or named in first-hand testimonies their own or others' involvement in hair cutting or, indeed, sexual assaults. Yet numerous incidents of hair cutting especially, usually involving large groups of masked local men, are very widely documented (especially in newspaper reports). The IRA very extensively engaged in hair cutting and the associated policing and surveillance of women nationally.

Horrific assault

One particular case of multiple-perpetrator sexual violence, which survived in local public and private memory, has been acknowledged by historians since 2012.[6] The horrific assault of a Protestant woman near Dromineer, County Tipperary in the early hours of 16 June 1922 was allegedly led by four local, anti-Treaty IRA men. The attack on Eileen Mary Warburton Biggs (née Robinson), and her husband Samuel Biggs, documented in detail in an Irish Grants Committee compensation claim of 1926, was reported in contemporary newspapers and referred to by Winston Churchill in the House of Commons.[7] Eileen was erroneously referred to as 'Harriet' Biggs in one newspaper report in 1922, a mistake that has been repeated by historians.

The compensation claim application, signed by Eileen, gives a detailed description of the events on the night in question.[8] It describes how she was locked in a room in her home and was 'outraged' on eight or nine different occasions and severely injured. Her husband Samuel and a house guest were locked in adjoining rooms while the men drank and looted the house. Eileen was found semi-conscious after the ordeal. After a period in hospital

Fig. 1 (left) Eileen Mary Warburton Biggs (née Robinson). Contrary to the suggestion that Eileen Robinson hailed from a 'big house' family in County Tipperary, she was born into a Protestant family in south Dublin on 20 July 1879. Her father, Robert Henry Robinson, from Parsonstown, a colonel in the Royal Army Medical Corps, married Elizabeth ('Bessie') Joyce Coote Leonard in Dublin in September 1871. Robinson served as an army surgeon in Barbados, where Margaret ('Daisy') was born, and in South Africa, where Grace was born. Eileen, Hilda and Robert junior (Robert Harvey St Clair Robinson, a captain in the 5th Royal Dublin Fusiliers) were all born at the family home at Bushfield Avenue, Donnybrook, Dublin. Grace married George Washington Biggs from Bellevue, Borrisokane, County Tipperary in September 1899. Almost twenty years later, in 1918, thirty-nine-year-old Eileen married George's brother, Samuel Dickson Biggs, at Kilbarron church in Borrisokane. Her application for personal-injury compensation states that she was criminally assaulted by armed men 'in IRA uniforms' in the early hours of 16 June 1922. [Image: reproduced with the permission of copyright owner Eleanor Hooker, author of *Where Memory Lies* (Banholt, 2023), supported by a 2021 Markievicz Award / See also Linda Connolly, *Undeservedly Forgotten: Women, war and violence in Ireland, 1919–98* (London, 2025 (forthcoming))]

in Dublin, she and her husband went to England, where she was awarded £6,000 in compensation, a notably large sum for that time. They subsequently returned to Dublin and lived in Monkstown, where Eileen died in 1950, soon after being admitted to St Patrick's Psychiatric Hospital.

The Biggses and Robinsons were military families with officer members of both involved in the Anglo-Boer War and the First World War. Eileen's brother Robert Hervey St Clair Robinson was stationed in Dublin in the British army during the 1916 Rising and is listed as present at the trial of Eoin MacNeill. Other IRA attacks in the Dromineer area, including on Catholics, were reported in the newspapers. In July 1922, for instance, the house of the Trench family (relatives of the Biggses) was visited by the Cloughjordan IRA armed with rifles and revolvers, and a Protestant servant was assaulted. These incidents clearly caused distress and terror in both Protestant and pro-Treaty Catholic households, which undermines the suggestion that sectarianism was the primary motivation for such attacks.

Justice never served

References to the Biggs case and to the chief suspects appear in a number of sources. Some of the alleged members of the group who attacked Eileen, which was said to include brothers and cousins, appeared in Nenagh court, but, due to the intensification of the Civil War, they were never prosecuted. Justice was never served. A century later, local republican men are commemorated heroically on monuments outside the courthouse at Banba Square in Nenagh. In 2019, in contrast, I found Eileen Mary Warburton Biggs buried in an unmarked grave with her sister Hilda V. Robinson in Mount Jerome Cemetery in Dublin. The sense of shame felt by the Biggs and Robinson families is painfully documented in Eileen's compensation claim. Women who were victims of Civil War violence and lived with hidden psychological and physical injuries in its aftermath were not commemorated.

Such crimes were not confined to the IRA, however. In May 2018 I first read the military service pension application of Catherine

Doherty of Currinara, Foxford, County Mayo on behalf of her daughter Margaret, who had died in 1928 in the Castlebar 'mental home'.[9] The pension application submitted in 1933 referred to a 'trial' in the aftermath of an attack (referred to as an 'outrage') on Maggie Doherty by three National Army officers stationed nearby on 27 May 1923. In 2019 I discovered in the Military Archives, Dublin the report on the court of enquiry referred to in the pension application. The detailed file, which documented Maggie Doherty's testimony, revealed that on 25 July three army lieutenants, Waters, Benson and Mulholland, were found 'not guilty' and 'honourably' acquitted of another case of gang rape during the Civil War. The file was subsequently released in conjunction with the Irish Military Archives. It serves as an example of the important role of researchers in this field who work with public archives, opened with the consent and consultation of intergenerational families, to acknowledge and document sexual violence targeted at women.[10]

Margaret (known to her family as Maggie) was born on 2 January 1896 in Foxford.[11] Two of her brothers, Hugh and Willie, actively fought on the anti-Treaty side in the Civil War in north Mayo. The 1933 pension application details Maggie's republican

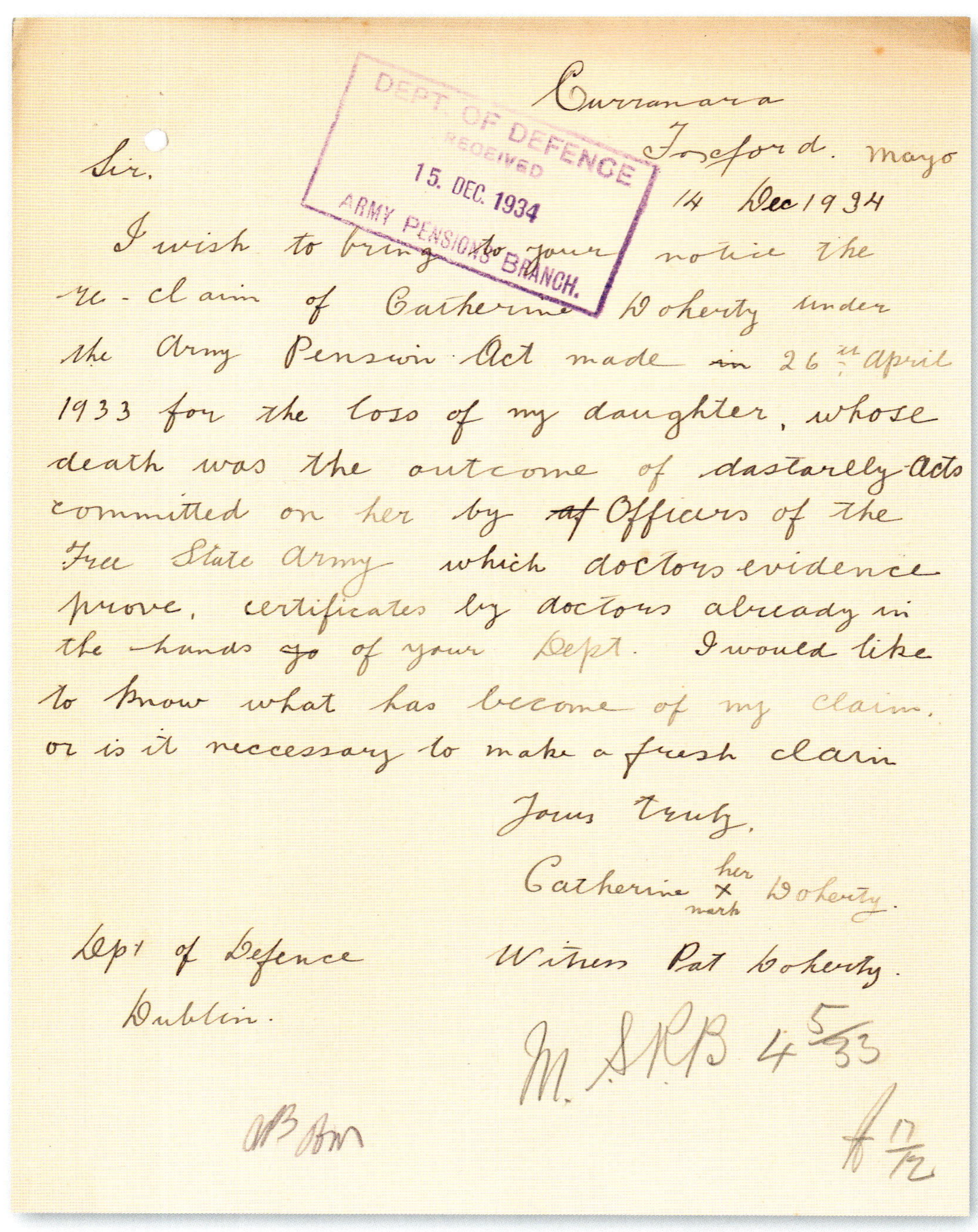

DEPT. OF DEFENCE
RECEIVED
15. DEC. 1934
ARMY PENSIONS BRANCH.

Currinara
Foxford. Mayo
14 Dec 1934

Sir,

I wish to bring to your notice the re-claim of Catherine Doherty under the Army Pension Act made in 26th April 1933 for the loss of my daughter, whose death was the outcome of dastardly acts committed on her by ~~af~~ Officers of the Free State Army which doctors evidence prove, certificates by doctors already in the hands ~~go~~ of your Dept. I would like to know what has become of my claim. or is it neccessary to make a fresh claim

Yours truly,

Catherine her x mark Doherty.

Dept of Defence
Dublin.

Witness Pat Doherty.

Fig. 2 Letter from Catherine Doherty, 14 December 1934. In this letter Catherine Doherty states that the death of her daughter, a Cumann na mBan intelligence officer, Margaret Doherty, 'was the outcome of dastardly acts committed on her by officers of the Free State Army'. She received a partial dependants' gratuity of £112 10*s* in 1937 under the Army Pensions Acts. [Source: MSCPDP2100. Image: courtesy of Military Archives/MSPC Project]

Fig. 3 Margaret (Maggie) Doherty (right) and her mother, Catherine Doherty (née Kneafsey) of Currinara, Foxford, County Mayo. One of the last atrocities of the Civil War left an indelible mark on one young woman from County Mayo. Hidden in the Irish Military Archives for 100 years, the story of Maggie Doherty and the sinister events of May 1923 were first uncovered in 2019 and featured in the 2023 RTÉ radio documentary 'A Dark Night in Foxford'. It was produced by Sarah Blake and Orla Higgins with contributions from Edel Doherty, Tom Doherty, Frank Fagan and Linda Connolly. [Text: Linda Connolly / Image: reproduced with the permission of copyright holder Edel Doherty and the Doherty family/ See 'A Dark Night in Foxford': https://www.rte.ie/radio/doconone/1402773-a-dark-night-in-foxford]

activism in Cumann na mBan from 1920 to 1923, but concentrates on her serious ill health after 1923 due to the incident at the family home. The file documents Catherine Doherty's eventual receipt of a partial dependants' gratuity of £112 10*s* in 1937 under the Army Pensions Acts. According to a letter signed by Maggie's brother (Patrick) on 16 September 1935, a sworn inquiry by 'Officers of the Free State Army' was held into the attack but no further details on this were provided. The pension application clearly indicates that steps were taken in the pursuit of justice and accountability for the atrocity in 1923.

Crucially, these sources also reveal that, by 1933, Maggie had not been forgotten or ostracised by others in her community. Letters of support for the pension application were provided by local doctors, the local headmaster, the Church of Ireland rector, the parish priest and political representatives. It took four years for the pension application to be fully processed, a delay difficult to fathom given the gravity of what had occurred, and the pension was granted on 25 November 1936, just under a year and a half before Catherine died. The act of applying for the pension, however, inscribed in the state's archive an account of what happened to her only daughter. This has served to preserve Maggie's story as an example of trauma history as well as a very uncomfortable aspect of National Army and Civil War violence that has taken many years to be fully acknowledged.

Occluded realities

The extraordinary and tragic story of Margaret Doherty is a powerful reminder of some of the occluded realities of the Irish Civil War. This critical account of sexual violence remained hidden in Irish military archives for almost a century, never referred to by any historian of the period, but Maggie's story lived on quietly in the intergenerational memory of her family and community for almost a century. The long-term sociological impact of the Civil War on individuals, families and communities, long after the gunfire ended, is palpable in the domain of women impacted by such devastating violence. Maggie's death in 1928 was not recorded as one of the killings of the Civil War period, but it was no less the result of political violence. Other similar cases have been revealed in this project. The hidden and uncomfortable histories of women such as Eileen Mary Warburton Biggs, Margaret Doherty, Mary Doyle, Bridget Carolan and others (forthcoming) merit due consideration in a moment of national commemoration and remembrance of a dark and violent episode that touched Irish women as well as men.

Fig. 4 Jack, Catherine, Patrick and Margaret (Maggie) Doherty of Currinara, Foxford, County Mayo. Two of Maggie's brothers, Hugh and Willie, were active in Foxford with the IRA and Maggie was a member of the Foxford branch of Cumann na mBan. [Text: Linda Connolly / Image: reproduced with the permission of copyright holder Edel Doherty and the Doherty family]

Cumann na Saoirse

John Borgonovo

Cumann na mBan was the first republican organisation to openly split over the Anglo-Irish Treaty, which occurred at a convention held on 5 February 1922. A strong majority of its branches, members and leadership rejected the Treaty. Thereafter, what might be called republican Cumann na mBan took a prominent role in the anti-Treaty movement, gradually expanding its role as unarmed guerrilla combatants. However, in April 1922 a smaller but significant number of women formed the pro-Treaty women's organisation Cumann na Saoirse, which remained visible and active throughout the Civil War. Led by former Cumann na mBan leaders Jenny Wyse-Power, Alice Stopford Green, Louise Gavan Duffy and others, Cumann na Saoirse vocally supported the Provisional Government. It appeared strongest in Dublin (seventeen Dublin branches marched at Michael Collins's funeral), but also had branches across the Free State, including an active organisation in Cork city. Prior to the Civil War, Cumann na Saoirse mobilised public support for the pro-Treaty cause via fund-raising, publicity and electioneering. Once the fighting broke out, members organised dances, concerts, travel hostels and railway canteens for National Army troops. They also supplied wounded soldiers with comforts like cigarettes, fruit

Fig. 1 (below) The national executive of Cumann na mBan at its annual convention at the Mansion House in Dublin, 5 February 1922. Cumann na mBan was the first republican group to formally split over the Anglo-Irish Treaty. Most of the organisation's executive opposed the Treaty, but the veteran activist Jenny Wyse-Power (fourth from the left in the front row) led the breakaway pro-Treaty women's organisation Cumann na Saoirse. A number of the Cumann na mBan executive remained hostile to the Free State for decades afterwards. [Image: Papers of Sighle Humphreys, P106/1466. Reproduced by kind permission of UCD Archives]

Fig. 2 (right) Letter from the IRA's Northern and Eastern Command headquarters to Cumann na mBan regarding the latter organisation's contributions to the anti-Treaty campaign. By the autumn of 1922 IRA forces were significantly degraded and increasingly relied on Cumann na mBan for logistical, communications, intelligence and publicity support. This message requests updates regarding various efforts, including intelligence (items 1 and 3), liaising with IRA medical services (item 2) and publicity (item 4). The final question pertains to Cumann na Saoirse and seemingly asks whether the Free State women's organisation is involved in the National Army communications network [Document: National Library of Ireland, Ernie O'Malley Papers, MS 10,973/11/28]

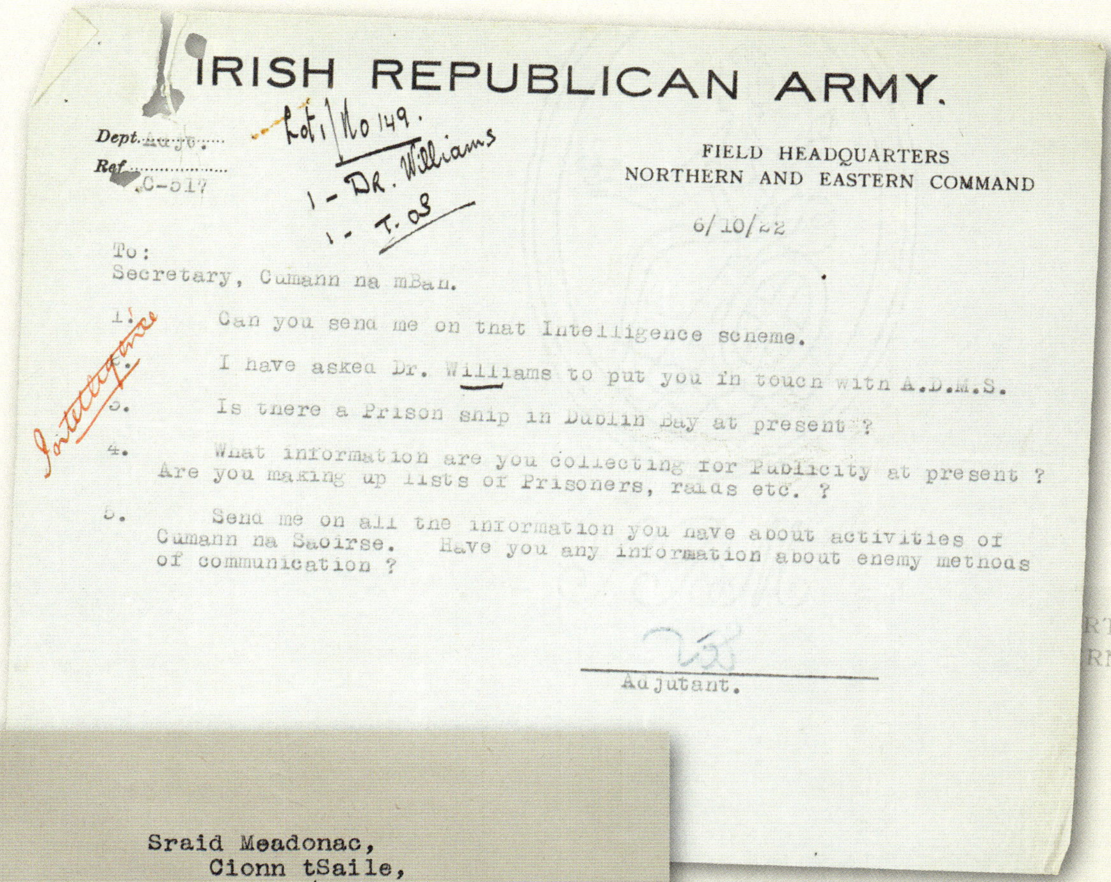

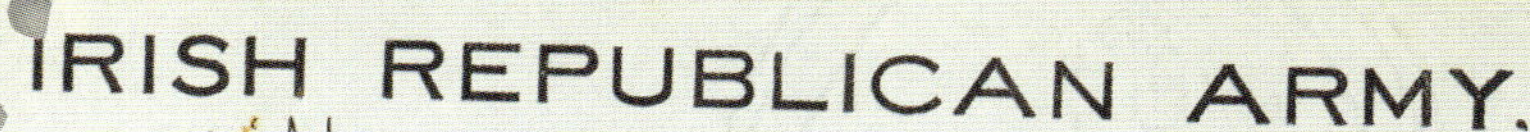

IRISH REPUBLICAN ARMY.

Dept. Adj't.
Ref. C-517

Lot 1 No 149.
1 – Dr. Williams
1 – I.O.

FIELD HEADQUARTERS
NORTHERN AND EASTERN COMMAND

6/10/22

To:
Secretary, Cumann na mBan.

1. Can you send me on that Intelligence scheme.
2. I have asked Dr. Williams to put you in touch with A.D.M.S.
3. Is there a Prison ship in Dublin Bay at present ?
4. What information are you collecting for Publicity at present ? Are you making up lists of Prisoners, raids etc. ?
5. Send me on all the information you have about activities of Cumann na Saoirse. Have you any information about enemy methods of communication ?

Intelligence

Adjutant.

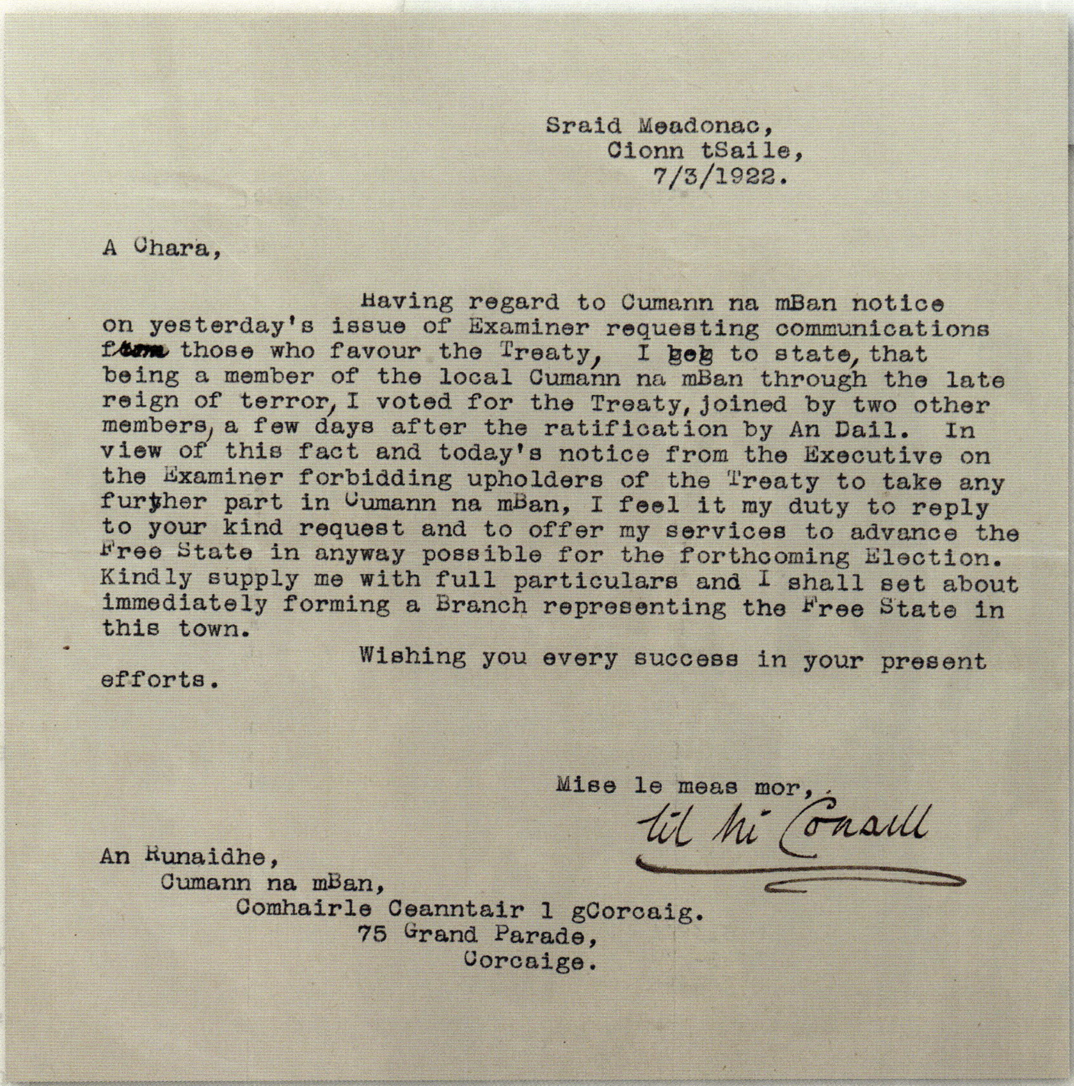

Sraid Meadonac,
Cionn tSaile,
7/3/1922.

A Chara,

Having regard to Cumann na mBan notice on yesterday's issue of Examiner requesting communications from those who favour the Treaty, I beg to state, that being a member of the local Cumann na mBan through the late reign of terror, I voted for the Treaty, joined by two other members, a few days after the ratification by An Dail. In view of this fact and today's notice from the Executive on the Examiner forbidding upholders of the Treaty to take any further part in Cumann na mBan, I feel it my duty to reply to your kind request and to offer my services to advance the Free State in anyway possible for the forthcoming Election. Kindly supply me with full particulars and I shall set about immediately forming a Branch representing the Free State in this town.

Wishing you every success in your present efforts.

Mise le meas mor,
Lil Mi Conaill

An Runaidhe,
Cumann na mBan,
Comhairle Ceanntair 1 gCorcaig.
75 Grand Parade,
Corcaige.

Fig. 3 (left) Letter from Lil Conlon, secretary of Cumann na mBan, Cork District Council, 7 March 1922, announcing her intention to form a pro-Treaty Cumann na mBan branch in Cork. Conlon and other pro-Treaty adherents were particularly visible during Michael Collins's visit to Cork the same month, and helped to organise the pro-Treaty campaign during the June 1922 'Pact' election. [Document: Cork Public Museum]

Cumann na mBan,
Headquarters,
Dublin.

4/4/22.

To Miss May Conlon,

A Chara,

The attention of the Executive of our Cumann na mBan has been directed to the fact that you are making use of the name of our organisation while no longer a member of it, owing to your support of the Free State party.

We beg to point out to you that such ~~action~~ unauthorised use of the name of our organisation is actionable and if you persist in its use we shall seek an injunction in the Republican Court to restrain you.

Is sinne,

[illegible]

Fig. 4 (left) Letter from Cumann na mBan national headquarters to May Conlon, 4 April 1922, threatening to 'seek an injunction in the Republican Court' if the pro-Treaty Cork branch continued to 'make use of the name of our organisation'. Ultimately, the pro-Treaty branches re-formed under the Cumann na Saoirse banner, while anti-Treaty Cumann na mBan in the city retained its national affiliation. A debilitating split between rival leadership factions within the Cork women's organisation began in 1917, was amplified by the Treaty divide in 1922, and continued in various forms for decades afterwards. [Document: Cork Public Museum]

Fig. 5 (below) *Tableau vivant* representing 'Erin and her Daughters', performed for Michael Collins at Cork Opera House on 12 March 1922. As the Provisional Government sought to mobilise support for the Treaty, Michael Collins's March visit to Cork produced warm receptions but also dangerous disruptions by anti-Treaty activists. During a concert at the Cork Opera House held in Collins's honour, members of the anti-Treaty IRA broke into the auditorium balconies, sang the 'Boys of the First Cork Brigade' and 'The Soldiers' Song', and dumped red pepper over the audience. In the words of the *Cork Examiner*, 'the effect was intensely disagreeable and of course disturbed the whole audience.' One of the feature performances was a *tableau vivant* of 'Irish historical incidents' (seen here). A *tableau vivant* (translated to 'living picture') was a popular type of performance in this period, during which stationary and silent actors used costumes and lighting to create memorable images, often of artworks or historical scenes. One of the driving forces of Cumann na Saoirse in Cork was the retired opera soprano Katherine 'Birdie' Conway (known on stage as 'Mademoiselle Eonie Delrita'). From her leadership position in Cumann na mBan's Shandon branch, Conway often organised theatrical and musical performances on behalf of the independence movement and later for the Free State cause. During this episode in the Cork Opera House, even though a couple of revolver shots were fired by anti-Treaty disruptors, in the best show-business tradition the show went on. [Image: Cork Public Museum / See John Borgonovo, *The Battle for Cork, July–August 1922* (Cork, 2011); *Cork Examiner*, 13 March 1922]

Fig. 6 Members of Cumann na Saoirse on the steps of the Cork Courthouse on Sunday 26 August 1923, with William T. Cosgrave, president of the Executive Council, and several other Free State ministers. The visiting dignitaries were in Cork to rally support for Cumann na nGaedheal candidates in the 1923 general election held the next day. May Conlon stands to Cosgrave's right and her sister, Lil, is believed to be four steps behind on the extreme right of the photograph. [Image: Cork Public Museum]

and playing cards. Cumann na Saoirse emphasised feminine tasks traditionally associated with auxiliary organisations rather than paramilitary duties, which were increasingly taken up by their Cumann na mBan counterparts. Cumann na Saoirse, as Margaret Ward pointed out, 'represented the aspirations of the emerging elite, and it looked with horror and distaste on the wild women of Cumann na mBan'. At the same time Cumann na Saoirse members quietly provided military assistance to the National Army, most commonly as searchers of women prisoners and detainees, which led to the organisation being dubbed, as Cal McCarthy has noted, 'Cumann na Searchers' by republicans. Members also occasionally served as intelligence agents and covertly carried messages across IRA lines. Overt pro-Treaty female military service was much less common than in republican Cumann na mBan, and was largely ignored by government propagandists. In keeping with the gendered attitudes/biases of the new state, Cumann na Saoirse service was subsequently denied recognition in the Army Pensions Acts, though Cumann na mBan activism (War of Independence and Civil War) was not. Substantial documentation about Cumann na Saoirse was collected by veteran Lil Conlon, whose *Cumann na mBan and the Women of Ireland, 1913–1925* (Kilkenny, 1969) offered the first substantial study of the republican women's organisation. Conlon challenged anti-Treaty dominance of the Cumann na mBan narrative by asserting pro-Treaty activism throughout the entire 1922–3 period, particularly within her native Cork city. There, debilitating factionalism within the female auxiliary organisation since 1917 likely contributed to the Treaty split, as roughly half of the city members joined Cumann na Saoirse and half remained with republican Cumann na mBan. (In contrast, most IRA volunteers in the city fought on the republican side.) Sniping between the two sides continued intermittently over ensuing decades, and what Lil Conlon described as 'feeling and bitterness' are still palpable in her book written forty-seven years after the Treaty split. [Sources: Margaret Ward, *Unmanageable Revolutionaries: Women in Irish nationalism* (Dublin, 1995); Cal McCarthy, *Cumann na mBan and the Irish Revolution* (Cork, 2007); Ann Matthews, *Dissidents: Irish republican women, 1923–1941* (Cork, 2012); and John Borgonovo, 'Cumann na mBan, Martial Women, and the Irish Civil War, 1922–1923', in Linda Connolly (ed.), *Women and Revolution: Feminism, activism, violence* (Dublin, 2020)]

CASE STUDY

Poor Law Reform in Revolutionary and Independent Ireland

Donnacha Seán Lucey

Welfare reform was a key facet of republicanism and nationalism during the Irish War of Independence, Civil War and early years of the Free State when the Irish poor law and workhouse system was dismantled. While the focus has traditionally been on the political, militaristic and cultural aspects of this highly formative period, closer exploration of poor law reform provides much insight into the social attitudes that underpinned Irish society.

Reform of Ireland's poor law, which included a network of over 130 workhouses, was initiated by the revolutionary Dáil Éireann. Its 1919 Democratic Programme pledged to abolish the 'odious, degrading and foreign' system, and the 1920 Dáil Éireann Commission of Inquiry into Local Government directed local authorities to arrange for the closure and amalgamation of 'evil' workhouses.[1] Motivated by a combination of financial instability brought about by the revolutionary years and a nationalist ideological abhorrence for workhouses, Irish revolutionaries brought an end to the poor law system (outside of Dublin) and created a new layer of county homes, county hospitals and district/cottage hospitals, largely in former workhouses. These reforms were introduced during unprecedented political, social and military upheaval. They were complicated by the enveloping military unrest, and many workhouses were commandeered by the British army, Treatyite and anti-Treatyite forces. Subsequently, twenty-two workhouses were partially or fully destroyed, largely by the IRA in 1920–1 and retreating anti-Treatyites during the Civil War.

The respectable poor

Poor law reform was shaped by deeply ingrained attitudes regarding social class, deservingness, respectability and morality. The rights of the respectable poor and working classes were widely articulated in terms of social integration, community and citizenship. This was evident in June 1923 when W.T. Cosgrave, the first president of the Executive Council of the Irish Free State, stated that the measures were for 'the better relief of the poor and the better care of the sick [... and would] win [...] the confidence of the people'.[2] The reformed poor law system aimed to free local authority provision from the 'taint' of poverty. The success of these reforms varied, and some progress was made in many areas, but the political rhetoric illustrated that poor law reform was framed as symbolic of independence and the legitimacy of the new state.

While workhouses were traditionally synonymous with the horrors of the Great Irish Famine, by the early twentieth century they had emerged as multifunctional institutions that provided ordinary and medical relief. The revolutionary break-up of the poor law led to the closure of workhouses and, with it the removal of long-established local services. In County Galway, for example, prior to independence the county had ten workhouse infirmaries, but after the reforms a single hospital was provided in Galway city and large swathes of the county had limited access to hospital care, leading to calls for the reopening of district hospitals.[3] Medical services for the acute and chronically sick were centralised in newly named county hospitals and homes, while more peripheral district hospitals focused solely on minor and short-term medical treatments. The closure of long-stay beds impacted on remote regions and were often resisted; this was the case in County Kerry where calls were made to reopen wards in the Dingle District Hospital for long-stay patients instead of sending patients to Killarney, located over forty miles away. The self-styled 'oppressed and infirm people of the western seaboard' complained to the local health authorities: 'men and women, Irish speakers born and reared in the stronghold of the Gael have been forcibly ejected from the hospital at Dingle, compelled by brute force to leave their native heath and conveyed to the county home in Killarney'.[4] For these individuals the county home in Killarney was as 'foreign' as the 'British' workhouse. The closure of long-standing institutional services brought harsh realities to the fore.

Harsh attitudes

Reforms also punished or excluded other groups that were at times viewed as undeserving and/or failing to live up to wider social mores. Willingness to enter a workhouse or undertake a workhouse test were previously evidence of need of relief. After the closure of workhouses, reformers feared that an unchecked relief system could lead to immoral welfare dependency, with increased demand on non-institutional relief, now termed home assistance. Work tests were introduced for the able-bodied to demonstrate eligibility for such relief, as a substitute for the former workhouse test, and deterrence – a core poor law principle – remained central to the new relief system. Descriptions of some of the poor as 'lazy', 'riffraff' and 'scum' formed part of the official lexicon in welfare debates throughout revolutionary and early independent Ireland.[5] Harsh attitudes towards many in poverty prevailed throughout this period.

Architecture of containment

Another major aspect of the break-up of the poor law in early independent Ireland, which has been the focus of much modern-day controversy, was the treatment of 'unmarried' mothers and 'illegitimate' children, who often turned to workhouses prior to independence. Revolutionary and independent Ireland established a new system of mother and baby homes, including Bessborough Home – run by the Catholic Sacred Heart of Jesus and Mary congregation – in Cork city, set up by republican administrators during the revolutionary years. Two other Sacred Heart mother and baby homes were later established in Roscrea (1931) and Castlepollard (1936). Other local authority auxiliary mother and baby homes included the Bon Secours Sisters in Tuam, on the grounds of the former workhouse, and Pelletstown Home, the former South Dublin Workhouse school (other mother and baby homes existed but these were less affiliated with local government).[6] These institutions, and to a lesser extent county homes, were part of what has been described as Ireland's 'architecture of containment', where an array of institutions confined, contained and disciplined those who were viewed as immoral.[7]

Competing social, political and cultural attitudes towards poverty and the poor, along with the realities of everyday poverty, shaped a fluctuating welfare and healthcare landscape that could be both harsh and caring. Poor law reform brought to the fore concepts of respectability, social class and deservingness – as much as political allegiance – during this highly formative era.

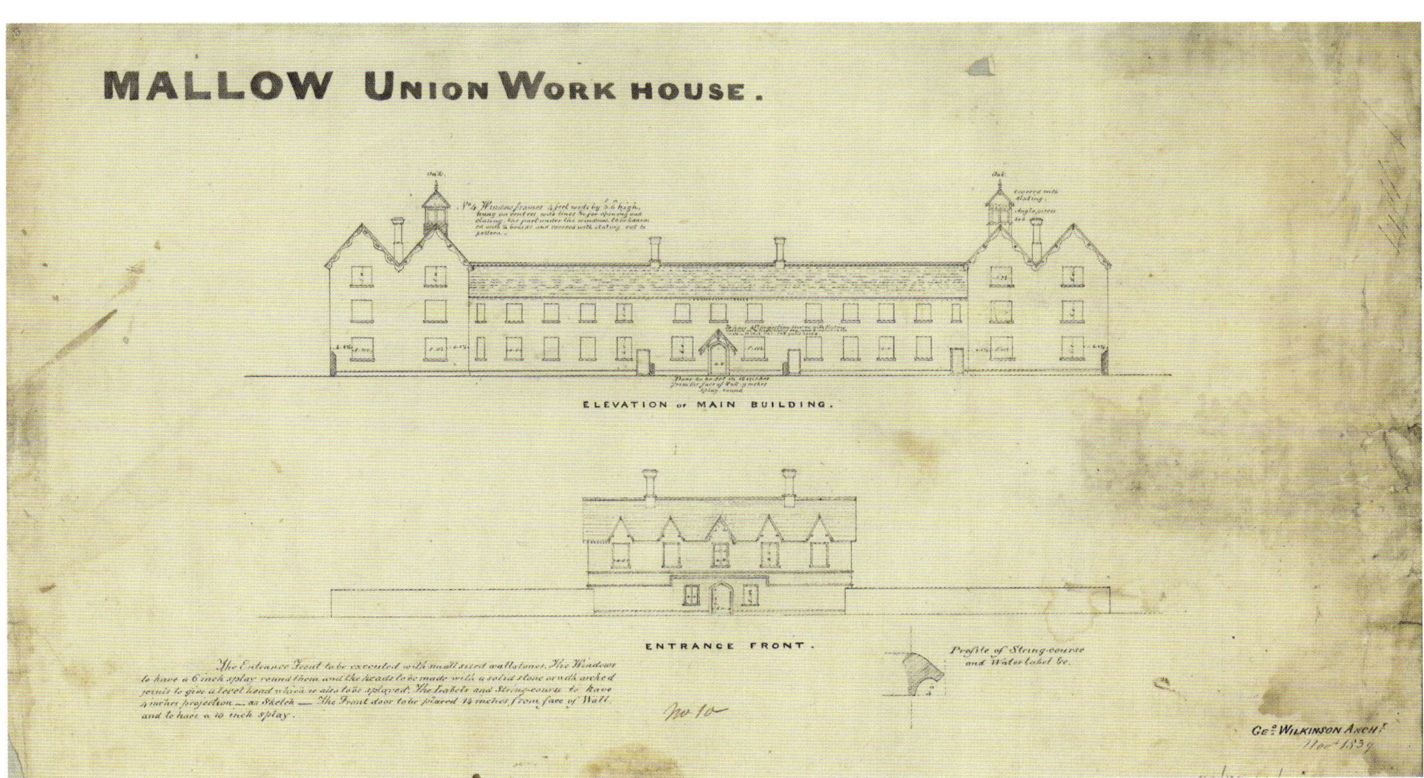

Fig. 1 Hand-drawn elevations of the entrance and main block of the Mallow Union Workhouse, which received its first 'inmates' in 1842. Workhouses were an integral part of the institutional fabric of mid-nineteenth-century Ireland. Following the Irish Poor Law Act (1838), which was modelled on its earlier English equivalent (1834), the country was divided into 130 poor law unions with a workhouse constructed in each union. Conditions in the workhouses were made deliberately harsh to act as a deterrent to those who were regarded by the poor law guardians as the 'idle poor'. Designed by English-born architect George Wilkinson in a familiar cruciform shape, the workhouses were a conspicuous presence in the Irish landscape given their size and extensive footprint. Built to deal with the widespread poverty in Ireland in normal conditions, they were unable to cope with a tragedy on the scale and longevity of the Great Irish Famine (1845–52). As the Famine took its increasing toll, the workhouses became a principal method of providing relief to the starving poor who clamoured at their gates seeking entry. In some cases they also became mass graveyards as overcrowding and the consequent rapid spread of disease caused thousands to perish within their confines. While the memory of the Famine would always be associated with the workhouses, they nonetheless continued to operate until the system was abolished in the Free State by the passing of the Local Government (Temporary Provisions) Act, 1923. During the War of Independence some workhouses were occupied by the British military to serve as barracks and were attacked as such and burned by the IRA, with a small number encountering a similar fate during the Civil War (Fig. 2). Executions were also carried out in Tuam Workhouse in April 1923 by the National Army, which had taken it over in July 1922. During the 1920s many workhouses were converted into county homes, such as Mallow's, which is now a general hospital, but suffering would continue on the site of former workhouses, such as Tuam's, which functioned as a mother and baby home between 1925 and 1961, the tragic consequences of which still reverberate to this day. [Document: Irish Architectural Archive]

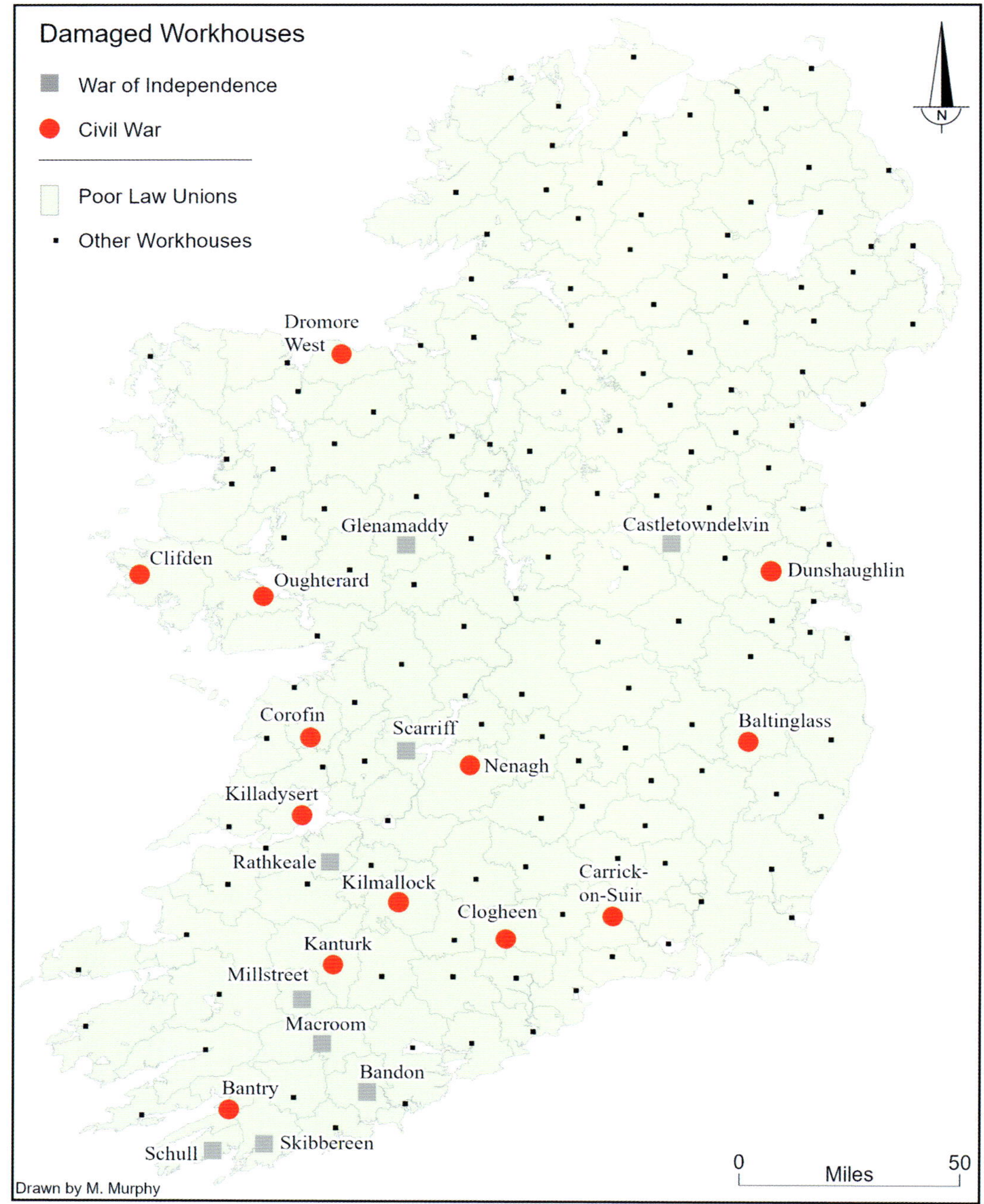

Fig. 2 Workhouses destroyed or partially destroyed during the revolutionary period. During the revolutionary years, twenty-two workhouses were partially or fully destroyed, largely by the IRA in 1920–1 and retreating anti-Treatyites during the Civil War. These burnings were for military purposes to deny opposing forces the use of such buildings as bases. The destruction of these institutions negatively impacted on local welfare and health services. The workhouse system was also dismantled during the Irish revolutionary period and early years of the Irish Free State. Boards of Public Assistance and Boards of Health, based on a county administration, were established in each county, and remaining workhouses were either closed or allocated new roles. In some cases former workhouses were renamed and adopted as county homes, accommodating the long-term chronically sick, elderly, disabled and mentally ill. They were also used frequently as homes for unmarried mothers and their children, and some admitted orphaned and abandoned children. Conditions and standards of care in these mixed institutions were often poor. In 1927, for example, a former clerk of Baltinglass Poor Law Union told the Commission on the Relief of the Sick and Destitute Poor that the county home was 'practically the workhouse in another name'. In several cases former workhouse infirmaries, fever hospitals and other medical facilities were redesignated as county, district, cottage or fever hospitals. These sought to provide for the acute sick. The county schemes were formalised by the Local Government (Temporary Provisions) Act of 1923. [Sources: Donnacha Seán Lucey, *End of the Irish Poor Law? Welfare and healthcare reform in revolutionary and independent Ireland* (Manchester 2015); For reports of individual workhouse burnings, see *Cork Examiner*, 27 May, 25 June 1921, 15 Aug, 30 Aug. 1922; *Kerry People*, 11 June 1921; *Grantham Journal*, 18 June 1921; *Cork Weekly News*, 4 June, 2 July 1921; *Connacht Tribune*, 16 July 1921; *Cork Weekly News,* 2 July 1921; *Freeman's Journal*, 26 Nov. 1921; *Nationalist & Leinster Times*, 8 Apr. 1922; *Galway Observer*, 29 July 1922; *Irish Independent*, 1 Aug. 1922; *Londonderry Sentinel*, 2 Nov. 1922; *Southern Star*, 11 Nov. 1922; *Evening Echo*, 28 Dec. 1922; *Western People*, 27 Jan. 1923; *Meath Chronicle*, 10 Feb. 1923; *Belfast Telegraph*, 9 Feb. 1923; *Westmeath Examiner*, 10 Mar. 1923; *Kerryman*, 30 Aug. 1924; see also www.workhouses.org (accessed 20 Jan. 2024)]

Fig. 3 Ruins of Bahaghs Workhouse, located *c.*4.5 kilometres (c.3 miles) from the town of Cahersiveen in south County Kerry, which served as a temporary place of detention during the Civil War. In the early hours of 12 March 1923, five young republicans were taken from the workhouse and killed – initially shot and then blown up by a land mine – about 1.5 kilometres (1 mile) away on the nearby approach road. The five men – John Sugrue, William Riordan, Dan and Michael Courtney and Eugene Dwyer – had been captured by the National Army on 2 March while attending a wake in Dromod parish near Waterville. Their fate from that point was very much intertwined with the spiralling violence and brutality that marked the Civil War in County Kerry in the first two weeks of March 1923. On 6 March five National Army soldiers had been killed by a trap mine planted by the IRA at Knocknagoshel. Free State forces exacted rapid retribution the following day, killing eight IRA prisoners at Ballyseedy near Tralee by tying them to a landmine that was then detonated, and killing a further five prisoners by the same method at Countess Bridge, Killarney. The atrocity at Bahaghs followed a similar pattern. [Image: John Crowley / See Michael Clifford, 'Cold-blooded Civil War Mass Murders Reverberate around Kerry a Century Later', *Irish Examiner*, 12 Mar. 2023]

The Irish Bishops' Pastoral Letter, 10 October 1922

Gabriel Doherty

While individual bishops spoke out in favour of the Treaty during the course of the debate on its provisions in Dáil Éireann, the Catholic hierarchy as a whole made no public statement prior to the vote in the chamber on Saturday 7 January 1922. Once that decision was announced, however, both individually and collectively they spared no effort in using their authority to mould public opinion in favour of the agreement. Not surprisingly, this pattern of behaviour intensified after the outbreak of the Civil War.

Denial of the sacraments and the penalty of excommunication were, of course, the most potent weapons in the bishops' spiritual arsenal, but they were ones that required careful handling lest they inflict greater damage on the hierarchy that deployed them than on their intended targets. Bearing this in mind, it is an open question as to who suffered the greater long-term damage as a result of the pastoral letter issued in response to the conflict in October 1922.

This was not the first such intervention during these disturbed years (the bishop of Cork had issued an excommunication decree in the aftermath of the burning of the city by British forces in December 1920), nor was it to be the last (the same bishop in November 1923 denied access to any church in the diocese for, and the service of any priest at, the funeral of republican hunger striker Denis Barry). By virtue of its scope as a national decree issued by the hierarchy as a whole, however, this document had a peculiar resonance.

The decree itself was issued on 10 October, following an offer a week earlier of amnesty to its republican adversaries by the Provisional Government, and an appeal for support by that government to the hierarchy the following day. It was a long document and bore clear signs of having been composed at speed, as key passages had to be revised prior to being issued in pamphlet form.

At the heart of the controversy surrounding the edict was its invoking of divine law in support of the proposition that none could justifiably claim 'that the legitimate authority in Ireland just now is not the Dáil or Provisional Government', thereby investing the existing (temporary, unsatisfactory and rather confused) political arrangements with a power almost supernatural in nature. On this basis it decreed that those who opposed the existing political dispensation by illicit means were 'guilty of the gravest sins' and were not to 'be absolved in Confession, nor admitted to Holy Communion' if they persevered 'in such evil courses'. In addition, any priest who even approved of the 'rebellion' was deemed 'guilty of the gravest scandal', and clergy who advocated or encouraged the revolt, publicly or privately, were suspended.

It is doubtful whether the letter had a meaningful effect on the subsequent course of the war, though it did alienate a tiny minority of republicans from the Church altogether. Most simply ignored such perceived dictation as an unwarranted interference in the political realm. Such republicans were generally able to access the sacraments via the network of sympathetic clerics referred to above, whom the bishops were unable to restrain.

There was a significant postscript. In March 1923 (that is, shortly before the end of the war) a legate from Pope Pius XI arrived in Ireland with a brief to gather information. After a fruitless few weeks, during which he was more or less could-shouldered by all parties, most notably by the hierarchy, he returned to Rome with a message that, in effect, the bishops had lost the run of themselves.

Fig. 1 (opposite) *His Eminence Cardinal Logue, 1840–1924*, oil on canvas, by Sir John Lavery (1920). Ordained in December 1866 and appointed bishop of Raphoe in 1879, Donegal-born Michael Logue was influenced by the devastating impact of nineteenth-century emigration on his native county. A moderate nationalist, his primary concerns throughout his long tenure as a member of the Irish hierarchy were the welfare of the Church and the expansion of its influence in Irish society. In December 1887, he was appointed archbishop of Armagh and primate of all Ireland and, six years later, a cardinal. During his early primacy, which coincided with the rise of Irish-Irelandism, he championed campaigns against intemperance, gambling and 'immoral' publications and films in defence of the purity of the Irish Catholic character. Politically, he supported the Home Rule movement, the allied cause during the First World War and, although dismayed by partition, the Anglo-Irish Treaty and its promise of dominion status for Ireland. Logue spent much of the last three years of his life condemning the renewal of violence in the south and sectarian attacks in Northern Ireland, and encouraging his fellow bishops to openly endorse the Treaty and the Free State government. Fiercely opposed to the republican campaign, Logue, a doyen of Catholic conservatism, was particularly disapproving of female participation in 'this wild orgy of violence and destruction'. 'Should this fell spirit spread', wrote Logue in his 1923 Lenten pastoral, 'alas for the future of motherhood in Ireland!'. He courted Vatican support for the Irish bishops' pronouncement on 'irregularism', but was critical of the state's internment and executions policies as a threat to the future peace and stability of the Catholic Free State. [Image: BELUM.U64 © National Museums NI / See also Diarmaid Ferriter, 'Michael Logue', *Dictionary of Irish Biography*, https://doi.org/10.3318/dib.004875.v1; Aisling Walsh, 'Michael Cardinal Logue 1840–1924', *Journal of the Armagh Diocesan Historical Society*, vol. 20, no. 2, 2005]

The response from 'head office' was brutally clear. An anti-Treaty cleric, John Dignan, was appointed to the next diocese that fell vacant, that of Clonfert. It was an unmistakable signal that the partisanship manifested in the pastoral letter had been a serious mistake, one that would not be allowed to be repeated. This sharp rap on the knuckles from on high reminded these princes of the church that even they were not beyond judgement.

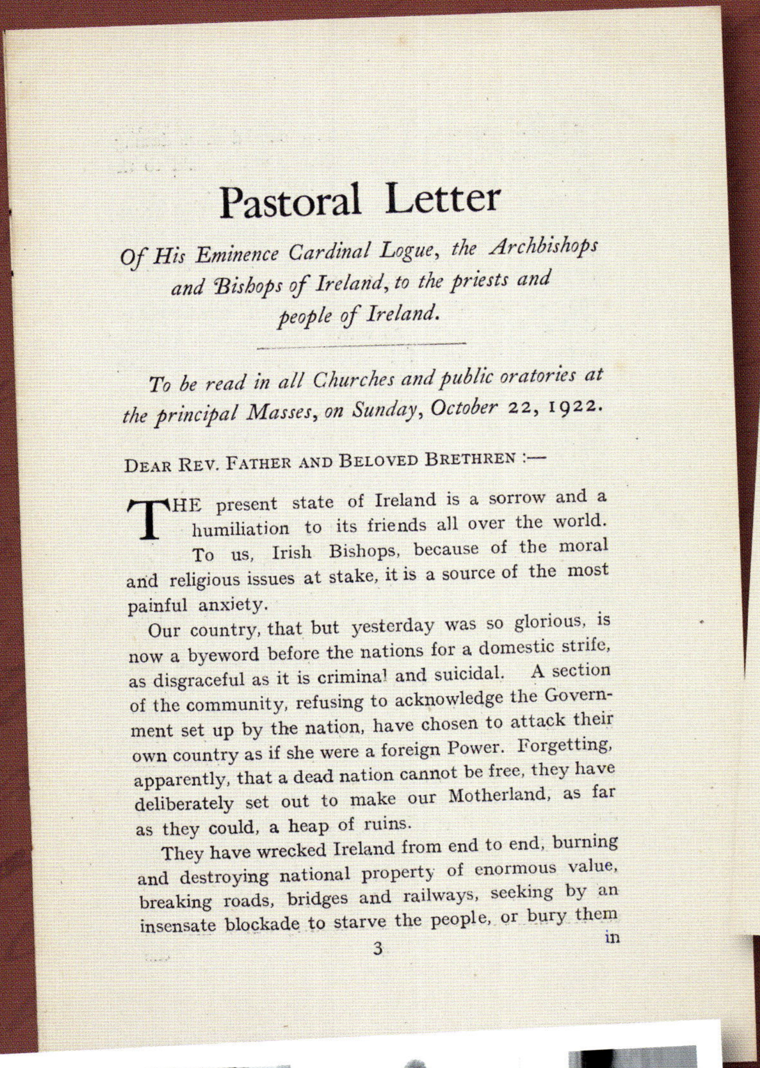

Figs 2 and 3 First two pages of the 'Pastoral Letter of His Eminence Cardinal Logue, the Archbishops and Bishops of Ireland, to the priests and people of Ireland', issued in pamphlet form by Browne and Nolan, Dublin, 1922. [Document: National Library of Ireland: EPH B440]

Pastoral Letter

Of His Eminence Cardinal Logue, the Archbishops and Bishops of Ireland, to the priests and people of Ireland.

To be read in all Churches and public oratories at the principal Masses, on Sunday, October 22, 1922.

Dear Rev. Father and Beloved Brethren :—

The present state of Ireland is a sorrow and a humiliation to its friends all over the world. To us, Irish Bishops, because of the moral and religious issues at stake, it is a source of the most painful anxiety.

Our country, that but yesterday was so glorious, is now a byeword before the nations for a domestic strife, as disgraceful as it is criminal and suicidal. A section of the community, refusing to acknowledge the Government set up by the nation, have chosen to attack their own country as if she were a foreign Power. Forgetting, apparently, that a dead nation cannot be free, they have deliberately set out to make our Motherland, as far as they could, a heap of ruins.

They have wrecked Ireland from end to end, burning and destroying national property of enormous value, breaking roads, bridges and railways, seeking by an insensate blockade to starve the people, or bury them in

3

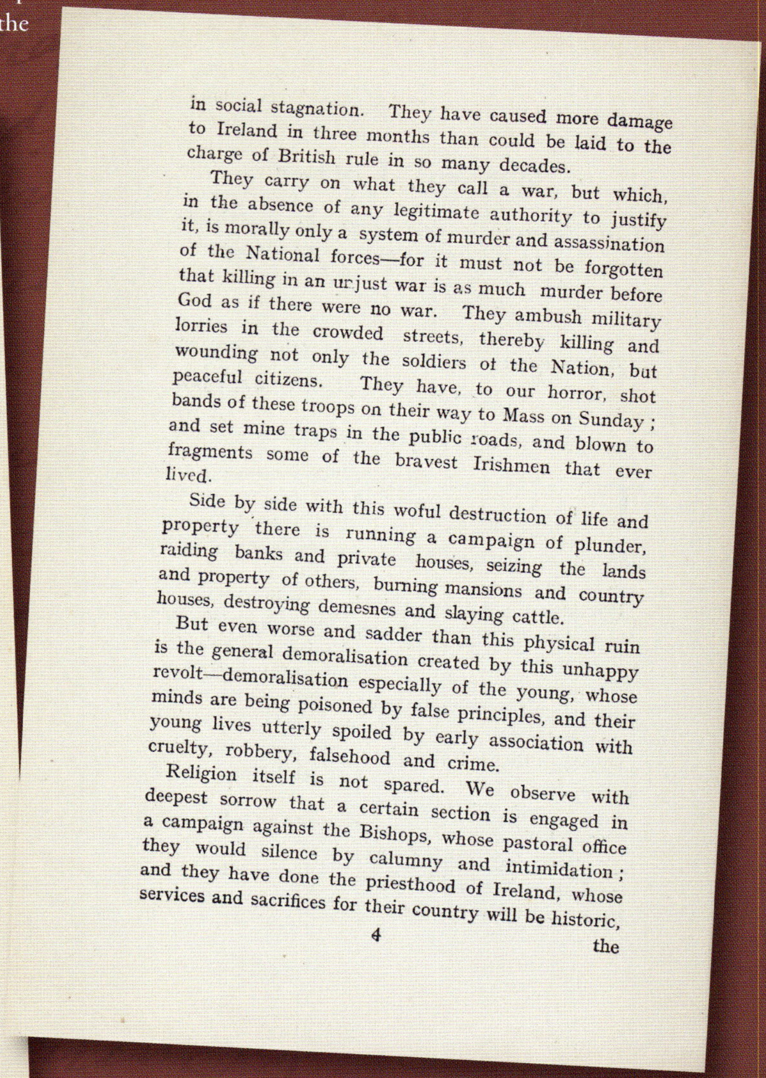

in social stagnation. They have caused more damage to Ireland in three months than could be laid to the charge of British rule in so many decades.

They carry on what they call a war, but which, in the absence of any legitimate authority to justify it, is morally only a system of murder and assassination of the National forces—for it must not be forgotten that killing in an unjust war is as much murder before God as if there were no war. They ambush military lorries in the crowded streets, thereby killing and wounding not only the soldiers of the Nation, but peaceful citizens. They have, to our horror, shot bands of these troops on their way to Mass on Sunday; and set mine traps in the public roads, and blown to fragments some of the bravest Irishmen that ever lived.

Side by side with this woful destruction of life and property there is running a campaign of plunder, raiding banks and private houses, seizing the lands and property of others, burning mansions and country houses, destroying demesnes and slaying cattle.

But even worse and sadder than this physical ruin is the general demoralisation created by this unhappy revolt—demoralisation especially of the young, whose minds are being poisoned by false principles, and their young lives utterly spoiled by early association with cruelty, robbery, falsehood and crime.

Religion itself is not spared. We observe with deepest sorrow that a certain section is engaged in a campaign against the Bishops, whose pastoral office they would silence by calumny and intimidation; and they have done the priesthood of Ireland, whose services and sacrifices for their country will be historic, the

4

Fig. 4 Daniel Cohalan, bishop of Cork 1916–52, being greeted by Irish army officers, Fort Camden, Crosshaven, July 1938. Though Bishop Daniel Cohalan had gained international prominence while presiding over the funeral of Cork republican hunger striker Terence MacSwiney in October 1920, two months later he surprised republicans by issuing an excommunication decree against anyone in his diocese involved in murder, ambushes and kidnappings. In January 1922 the bishop instructed parish priests to celebrate Masses of thanks following the ratification of the Anglo-Irish Treaty, and became a highly vocal supporter of the new Free State regime. Major-General Emmet Dalton noted that Cohalan was among the first callers to his Imperial Hotel headquarters after the National Army captured Cork city in August 1922. Among the bishop's many affronts to his anti-Treaty flock, perhaps the most controversial was his refusal to give a Catholic burial to IRA officer Denis Barry following the latter's death on hunger strike in 1923. That episode led to an angry exchange of letters with anti-Treaty leader Mary MacSwiney, who accused Cohalan of slander. While Bishop Cohalan remained comfortable with the Free State elite, as seen in this 1938 photo, anti-Treaty adherents derided him for years after, sometimes referring to him by the undignified nickname of 'Danny Boy'. [Image: courtesy of the Irish Examiner Archive / See *Cork Examiner*, 13 Dec. 1920]

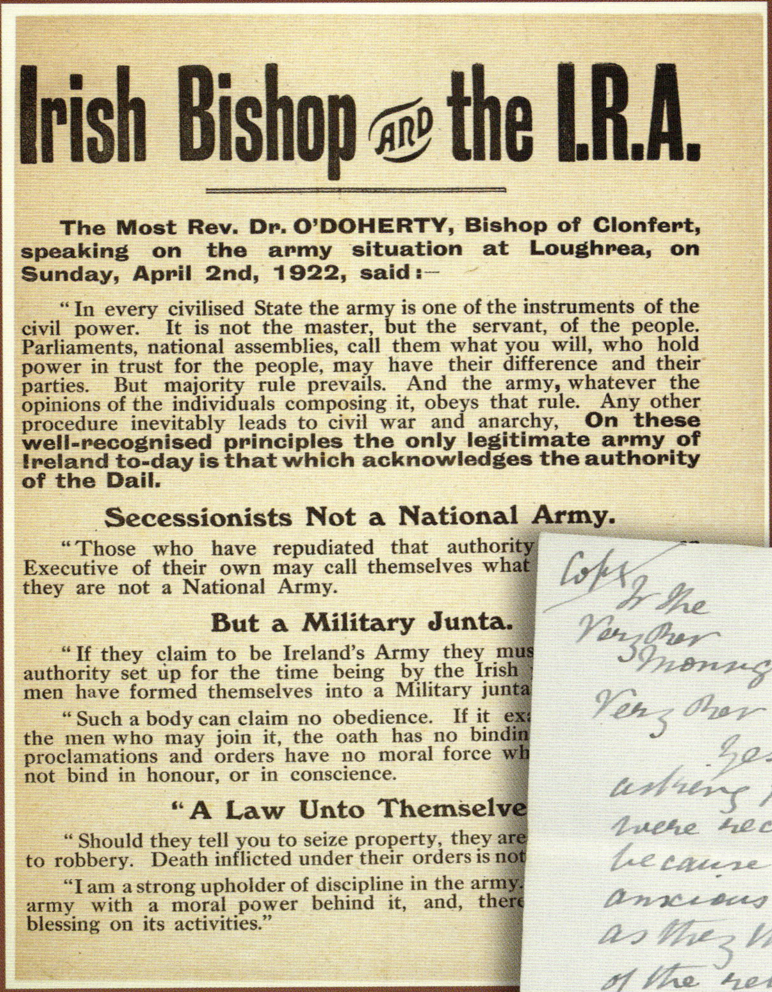

Irish Bishop and the I.R.A.

The Most Rev. Dr. O'DOHERTY, Bishop of Clonfert, speaking on the army situation at Loughrea, on Sunday, April 2nd, 1922, said:—

"In every civilised State the army is one of the instruments of the civil power. It is not the master, but the servant, of the people. Parliaments, national assemblies, call them what you will, who hold power in trust for the people, may have their difference and their parties. But majority rule prevails. And the army, whatever the opinions of the individuals composing it, obeys that rule. Any other procedure inevitably leads to civil war and anarchy. **On these well-recognised principles the only legitimate army of Ireland to-day is that which acknowledges the authority of the Dail.**

Secessionists Not a National Army.

"Those who have repudiated that authority
Executive of their own may call themselves what
they are not a National Army.

But a Military Junta.

"If they claim to be Ireland's Army they mus
authority set up for the time being by the Irish
men have formed themselves into a Military junta

"Such a body can claim no obedience. If it ex
the men who may join it, the oath has no bindin
proclamations and orders have no moral force wh
not bind in honour, or in conscience.

"A Law Unto Themselve

"Should they tell you to seize property, they are
to robbery. Death inflicted under their orders is not

"I am a strong upholder of discipline in the army.
army with a moral power behind it, and, there
blessing on its activities."

Fig. 5 (left) Pro-Treaty handbill quoting the bishop of Clonfert, Dr Thomas O'Doherty, whose sermon at Loughrea on Sunday 2 April 1922 foreshadowed some of the language in the October pastoral. The clergyman, who was a strong supporter of Sinn Féin if not republican violence after he was appointed Ireland's youngest bishop in 1919, was an early supporter of the Treaty. Pro-Treaty propagandists highlighted O'Doherty's distinction between the 'legitimate army' of the state subject to the civil authority and, as such, an instrument of God, and the 'secessionists', the anti-Treaty IRA, whose repudiation of the Dáil's authority divested them of any moral force: 'Death inflicted under their orders is nothing but murder'. [Document: National Library of Ireland, Collection, EPH C99]

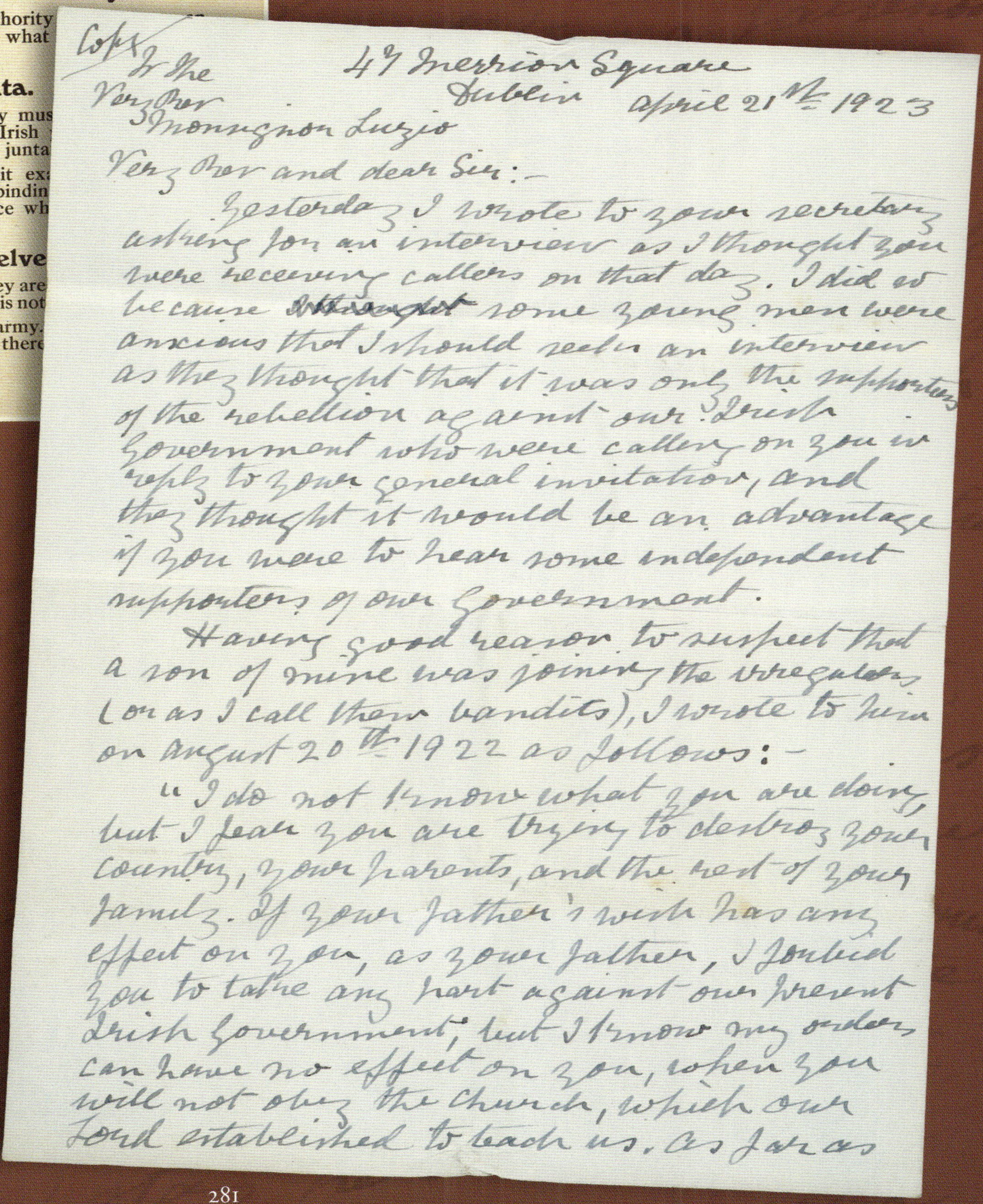

Copy

To the Very Rev
Monsignor Luzio

47 Merrion Square
Dublin April 21st 1923

Very Rev and dear Sir:—

Yesterday I wrote to your secretary asking for an interview as I thought you were receiving callers on that day. I did so because ~~I thought~~ some young men were anxious that I should seek an interview as they thought that it was only the supporters of the rebellion against our Irish Government who were calling on you in reply to your general invitation, and they thought it would be an advantage if you were to hear some independent supporters of our Government.

Having good reason to suspect that a son of mine was joining the irregulars (or as I call them bandits), I wrote to him on August 20th 1922 as follows:—

"I do not know what you are doing, but I fear you are trying to destroy your country, your parents, and the rest of your family. If your father's wish has any effect on you, as your father, I forbid you to take any part against our present Irish Government, but I know my orders can have no effect on you, when you will not obey the Church, which our Lord established to teach us. As far as

Fig. 6 (right) Letter to the papal nuncio, Monsignor Salvatore Luzio, from John Sweetman, a devout and doctrinaire Catholic from County Meath who served a brief and controversial tenure as an anti-Parnellite MP in the 1890s before becoming the enthusiastic patron and erstwhile president of Sinn Féin (1908–11). A wealthy social conservative committed to the unity of the Irish Catholic community, seventy-eight-year-old Sweetman was an outspoken advocate of the Treaty. Writing to the pope's envoy in April 1923 as an independent supporter of 'our own Irish government', he described his distress at the prospect of his son joining the IRA 'bandits'. While his son was eventually dissuaded by his mother, Sweetman was anxious to draw Luzio's attention to the malign influence of some 'mad priests' who convinced many other 'foolish youths' to join the IRA's campaign of violence against 'civilised government'. [Document: National Library of Ireland, Sweetman Family Papers, MS 47, 591 /3]

SECTION 7

Imprisonment

East wing of Kilmainham Gaol.
[Image: courtesy of Kilmainham Gaol Museum/OPW]

Fig. 1 Kilmainham Gaol, Dublin, *c.*1910. [Image: National Library of Ireland, L_CAB_05517] **Fig. 2** (opposite) Large, painted graffiti above the entrance to the '1916 corridor' on the middle floor of Kilmainham Gaol's west wing. It paraphrases the closing lines of 'The Rebel', a poem by Patrick Pearse, who was executed in the Stonebreakers' Yard at Kilmainham on 3 May 1916. The same lines are graffitied on a wall on Corridor 1 on the top floor. [Image: courtesy of Kilmainham Gaol Museum/OPW]

CHAPTER 8

Graffiti and Geographies of the Women of Kilmainham Gaol during the Irish Civil War

Laura McAtackney

Kilmainham Gaol is one of the most iconic sites associated with the revolutionary period in Ireland. This is due to its role not only in containing many of those involved in various facets of the conflict but also its continued material presence that has allowed it to become a national heritage monument. One of the most fascinating, extant material traces located at Kilmainham Gaol is its extensive graffiti assemblages that cover many walls of the prison, especially notable in the older west wing.

The graffiti assemblages primarily date to the Civil War (1922–3), which was also the prison's last period of operation as a site of incarceration. A smaller number can be dated to the War of Independence (1919–21), while there are also a few individual examples and small assemblages that predate that period. Women held in prison for various periods between 1922 and 1923 were the primary creators of the most noticeable and long-standing graffiti assemblages. The extant graffiti assemblages from Kilmainham Gaol

– primarily in the west wing but also in the extensively renovated east wing, basements and administrative areas – and the adjoining courthouse were recorded as part of an Irish Research Council (IRC)-funded project (2012–5).[1] There are many interpretative angles one could take on graffiti assemblages, including drawing out the women's relationships with the Free State, the prison guards, the Irish language and Irish history. But this chapter will explore what they can tell us about the geography of the Irish Civil War from the perspective of women graffiti creators who were incarcerated there in 1922 and 1923.

The chapter begins with a short section on Kilmainham Gaol before focusing on the graffiti, including how academics have used and interpreted graffiti through various disciplinary lenses to tell us about its creators and the societies they belonged to. This will be followed by a discussion of the graffiti recording project's aims, methodology and details on the assemblages located at Kilmainham Gaol. The chapter concludes with thematic approaches to the assemblages, especially those from the west wing. In particular, it explores the gendered geographies of incarceration during the Civil War, including the enduring emphasis on the women's external organisation and loyalties, and the prison walls' role in maintaining links between the women in their post-incarceration lives.

Kilmainham Gaol

Kilmainham Gaol is now considered an iconic heritage site in Ireland because of its connection to the so-called 'revolutionary period' as reremembered and reconfigured through the Decade of Centenaries (2012–23). While we primarily associate the site with the Easter Rising and the fate of its leaders in 1916, Kilmainham's connection to political imprisonment dates back to its inception as Dublin County Gaol in 1796.[2] It quickly became associated with the imprisonment of United Irishmen members after their

Figs 3 and 4 (left) Volunteers clearing the east wing of Kilmainham Gaol in 1960. (right) Volunteers clearing one of the overgrown yards in Kilmainham Gaol in 1960. On 9 June 1958 Dublin engineer Lorcan Leonard wrote to Seán Dowling, the IRA's director of organisation during the Civil War and chairman of the Old IRA in the 1950s, seeking support for a voluntary restoration project. Dowling supported Leonard's plan to form a committee 'to save Kilmainham Jail from the ravishes of time and the indifference of the politicians'. Within eighteen months the committee had submitted its restoration plan to Minister for Finance, James Ryan, and the Fianna Fáil government agreed to a five-year lease of the jail (at a nominal rent) to a board of trustees. On Saturday 21 May 1960 the keys to Kilmainham were handed over to the trustees and the army of volunteers began the mammoth task of meeting the committee's aim of preserving and maintaining the jail as a monument 'to the gallant dead, and the still living patriots who were imprisoned there'. By October the workers had put 9,000 voluntary hours into the restoration project, over 200,000 tons of debris had been removed and, in early 1961, donations were forthcoming to support the 'patriotic work' of the newly incorporated Kilmainham Jail Restoration Society. On 10 April 1966 the Kilmainham Jail Historical Museum was officially opened by the president of Ireland, Éamon de Valera, who had served time in its cells in 1916 and 1923–4. To preserve the 'old dungeon fortress', he told the assembled crowd, was 'not to continue bitterness' but to 'inspire our people and make them remember the great efforts that were made through the centuries to preserve this nation'. [Image: courtesy of Kilmainham Gaol Museum/OPW / See also Niamh O'Sullivan, *Every Dark Hour: A history of Kilmainham Jail* (Dublin, 2007); Rory O'Dwyer, 'Kilmainham Jail: From abandonment to restoration', *Dublin Historical Record*, vol. 63, no. 1, spring 2010]

failed rebellion in 1798. Because of its defensive capabilities, the jail became the main incarceration centre for every insurrection and communal revolutionary act in Ireland from the Act of Union (1801) until its closure in 1924. Kilmainham's association with political imprisonment means that the majority of individuals seen as integral to the struggle for Irish independence – through both constitutional and violent routes – have had some physical association with the site. In the case of especially high-profile leaders, such as Charles Stewart Parnell and Countess Markievicz, we can even pinpoint the cells they were held in, thus emphasising the site's material connections to Irish history.

Kilmainham Gaol's status has also been ensured by what has happened to the site since it closed in 1924. Though the prison stopped operating as a place of incarceration after the Civil War, it materially persisted through many decades of dereliction and unofficial usages, which will be discussed below. In 1960 the Kilmainham Jail Restoration Society (KJRS) was formed, primarily by ex-political prisoners. It was permitted by the Irish government to restore the site in time for the fiftieth anniversary of the Easter Rising in 1966.[3] The decisions the KJRS made then, and in the decades until the site came under state management in 1986, have greatly shaped the buildings we visit as researchers and visitors today.[4] This extends beyond our understanding of how the buildings functioned, but also to how we view imprisonment as a tool of not only colonial oppression but of subversion and resistance as well. In its current state Kilmainham Gaol is not only a symbol of revolutionary Ireland but is also an evolving material entity that must take into account recent and historical material and immaterial changes that both permit and restrict us from uncovering the past experiences and realities of imprisonment.[5] While we can visit the main buildings of the jail, many of its auxiliary structures were torn down during restoration, creating a very different experience of the prison compound. This concentration on the cellular structures has altered how visitors understand it.

Another key restriction is the extent and focus of the 'restoration' undertaken to prepare the site for opening to the public for commemorative purposes. Once the buildings were made physically sound and the clearing of decades of accumulated debris and degradation from all parts of the prison was completed, restoration took the form of interventions with the material environment to revert to the jail's state prior to 1921.[6] Due to a reluctance to discuss the still divisive Civil War, a conscious decision was made not only to exclude mention of it from the interpretation of the site, but to actively conceal it. This included the thorough whitewashing of walls in the communal 'circle' area of the east wing, which had retained a substantial proportion of political cartoons, murals and texts from the prison's Civil War inhabitants, despite the decades of dereliction. Inside the east wing cells, plaster was chipped from the walls with an efficiency that is almost admirable. Of the 111 rooms (mainly cells) on the wing, all but seventeen were thoroughly de-plastered during the restoration period. The remnants of the walls often remain as rubble, still piled into the centre of cell floors to the present day. With the graffiti in the west wing largely untouched by well-meaning restorers unconcerned with its appearance, this assemblage was the focus of the IRC-funded recording and interpretation exercise that began in 2012.

Recording graffiti

Until the Decade of Centenaries, one of the most significant exclusions from our understandings of the revolutionary period was a thorough appreciation of the role of women as individuals and as collective actors. While this oversight has been largely addressed thanks to the work primarily of women academics who have added to our understandings of their myriad roles, the graffiti at Kilmainham Gaol brings its own insights.[7] The graffiti assemblages have been known about for a long time and were the subject of a 2016 book highlighting the most prominent and visually impressive elements.[8] But the graffiti had never been systematically recorded before 2012. At that time I embarked on a three-year recording exercise that followed a rigorous methodology. It included systematic movement around the structure, using different forms of photographic recording, including static and moving lighting, as well as the absence of light. Interestingly, while graffiti-recording exercises are increasingly prominent in material-focused disciplines like archaeology, there is infrequent discussion of their methodology. In this case the chosen methodological approach allowed for controlled replication of the same actions across the basic recording unit of the site, which for a prison was the cell. While recording was also completed in hallways, stairwells and other spaces, the focus fell on the cells because they were the basic containment unit for the prisoners. Each cell was approached to search the surfaces most likely to contain graffiti. These were primarily the walls; very few floors remained from the Civil War period due to dereliction, while the roofs were either too high for prisoners to have reached unaided or had been replaced. On entering the cell, recording commenced on the wall to the left of the entrance door and moved clockwise across the wall, photographically recording each wall both with a lighting source and without one. I then moved from the top left to the bottom right of the wall to record every individual piece/group of graffiti with lighting and without as made sense. The location of each piece was plotted and its description was noted at the time of recording. There was little to no graffiti over the height of two metres and virtually no examples close to the floor (one exception was a note in Sighle Humphreys's cell indicating where a tunnel had been started in the basement under the west wing). Evidently, the majority of the graffiti was made to be seen, rather than as an illicit or hidden phenomenon.

The role of lighting was important. Many graffiti examples were pencil drawings largely hidden to the naked eye by the cell's darkness, or subsequently covered by light layers of whitewash that were either greatly degraded or made semi-transparent by water infiltration or the artificial lighting used during recordings. Alternatively, there was also a rich range of engraved graffiti that was intentionally made to be seen, owing to its placement close to windows. This meant the graffiti could either be seen or concealed

Fig. 5 A small piece of pencil text in Sighle Humphreys's cell in Kilmainham's west wing that reads: 'Tunnel begun in basement of laundry, inside door at left, may be of use to successors, good luck, S'. Humphreys was the only daughter of Mary Ellen (Nell) O'Rahilly, sister of Irish Volunteer leader Michael J. O'Rahilly (The O'Rahilly), who was killed in Moore Street on Friday of Easter Week 1916. Sighle Humphreys was studying in Paris at the outbreak of the War of Independence in 1919, but on her return served as Cumann na mBan organiser in County Kerry. According to IRA Assistant Chief of Staff Ernie O'Malley, twenty-three-year-old Humphreys was 'a very active member of Cumann na mBan' during the Civil War. She engaged in propaganda work – daubing Dublin's walls with republican slogans – attended the wounded, located safehouses, carried dispatches and, 'dressed in uniform, she attended burials of our boys at the Republican Plot in Glasnevin'. She was arrested with her mother and aunt Nancy (Madame) O'Rahilly in the aftermath of O'Malley's dramatic capture at their home at 36 Ailesbury Road on 4 November 1922. Humphreys was interned for more than a year, first in Mountjoy, later in Kilmainham – where, as Margaret Buckley wrote, 'the time-honoured idea of digging a tunnel took root' – and, finally, in the North Dublin Union (NDU). Far from a being docile prisoner, she suffered three months of solitary confinement in Mountjoy for her 'defiant attitude' and a thirty-one-day hunger strike before her release from the NDU on 29 November 1923. In the years after the Civil War, Humphreys, an increasingly committed socialist republican, was a leading Cumann na mBan activist in Dublin, pioneering the sale of the Easter Lily (a fund-raising effort and an anti-imperialist challenge to the commemorative poppy), protesting against public expressions of Free State 'West Britonism' on Armistice Day and spearheading the 'Ghosts' campaign to influence juries in political cases, for which she served two terms in Mountjoy between 1926 and 1928. An executive member of the short-lived socialist republican groups Saor Éire and, later, the Republican Congress in the early 1930s, she was one of the first women to appear before the military tribunals convened under Cumann na nGaedheal's 'red-scare'-facilitated 1931 Public Safety Act. Though broadly supportive of Fianna Fáil's protectionist policies in the 1930s, Humphreys became disillusioned by de Valera's increasingly repressive measures against militant republicans, dedicating herself to the welfare of prisoners and their dependants. She married prominent IRA activist and *An Phoblacht* editor Donal O'Donoghue in 1935 and the couple was active in Clann na Poblachta in the 1940s and 1950s. Humphreys, who in 1923 graffitied on her Kilmainham wall the words 'Men and Measures may come and go / but principles are eternal', remained a committed republican and language activist until her death on 14 March 1994. [Image: Courtesy of Kilmainham Gaol Museum/OPW / Quotations, Ernie O'Malley, *The Singing Flame* (Dublin, 1992), p. 174; Margaret Buckley, *The Jangle of the Keys* (Dublin, 1938); See also Patrick Maume, *Dictionary of Irish Biography*, 'Sighle Humphreys', https://doi.org/10.3318/dib.004157.v2]

depending on the placement of lighting sources. In many cases both engraved and drawn graffiti intermingled. While the aim of the project was to locate graffiti related to women prisoners from the Civil War, in reality it was not always possible to identify the creator of every assemblage or precisely when it was created. This meant that, at an early stage, any graffiti that appeared to predate the work of the KJRS was included in the recording, as well as some sporadic post-1960 graffiti up to the present day. In total over 10,000 separate photographs of graffiti were taken, first of the west wing and later of the east wing, the administrative areas and the adjoining courthouse. The graffiti included examples created by female prisoners, male prisoners (primarily from the revolutionary period, but also earlier), British soldiers (from 1914–21) and subsequent visitors to the site (from 1924 onwards).

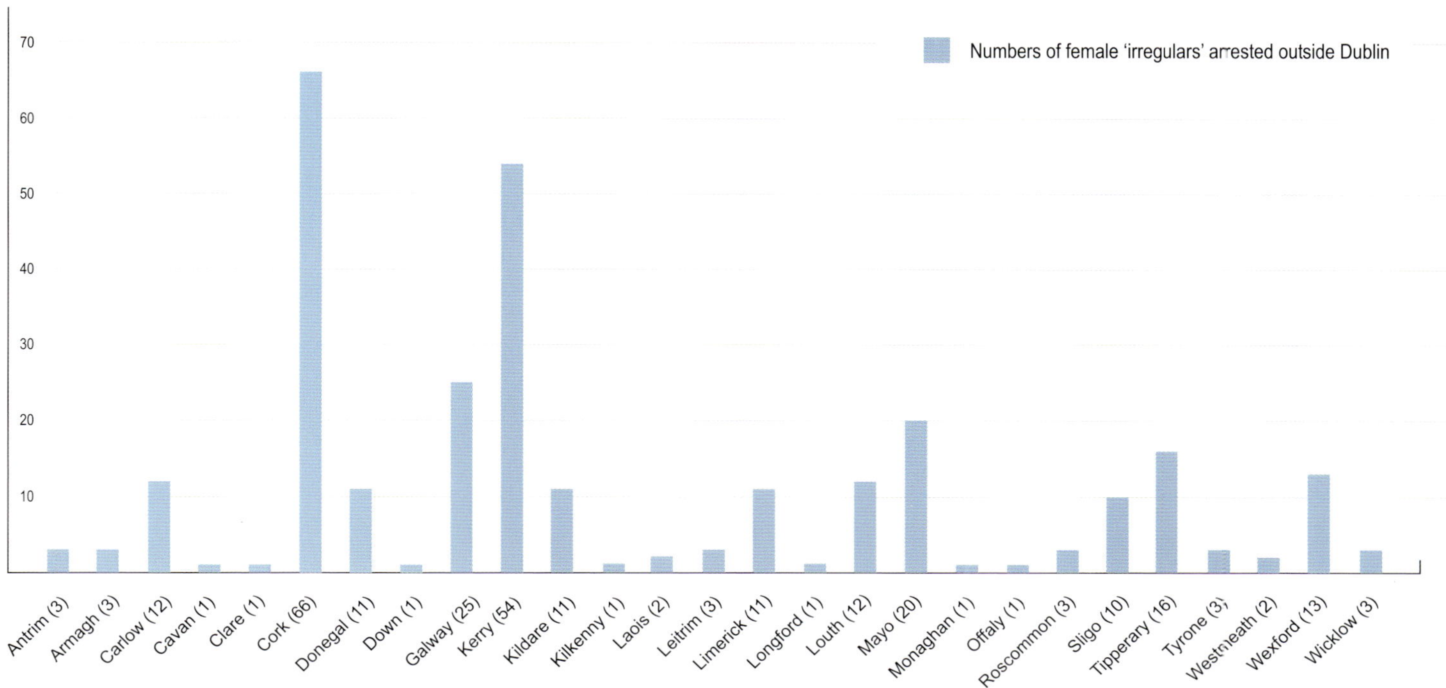

Fig. 6 Numbers of female 'irregulars' arrested at different locations outside Dublin. [Compiled by Ann Matthews / Source: AGP Ledgers, Irish Military Archives, Dublin]

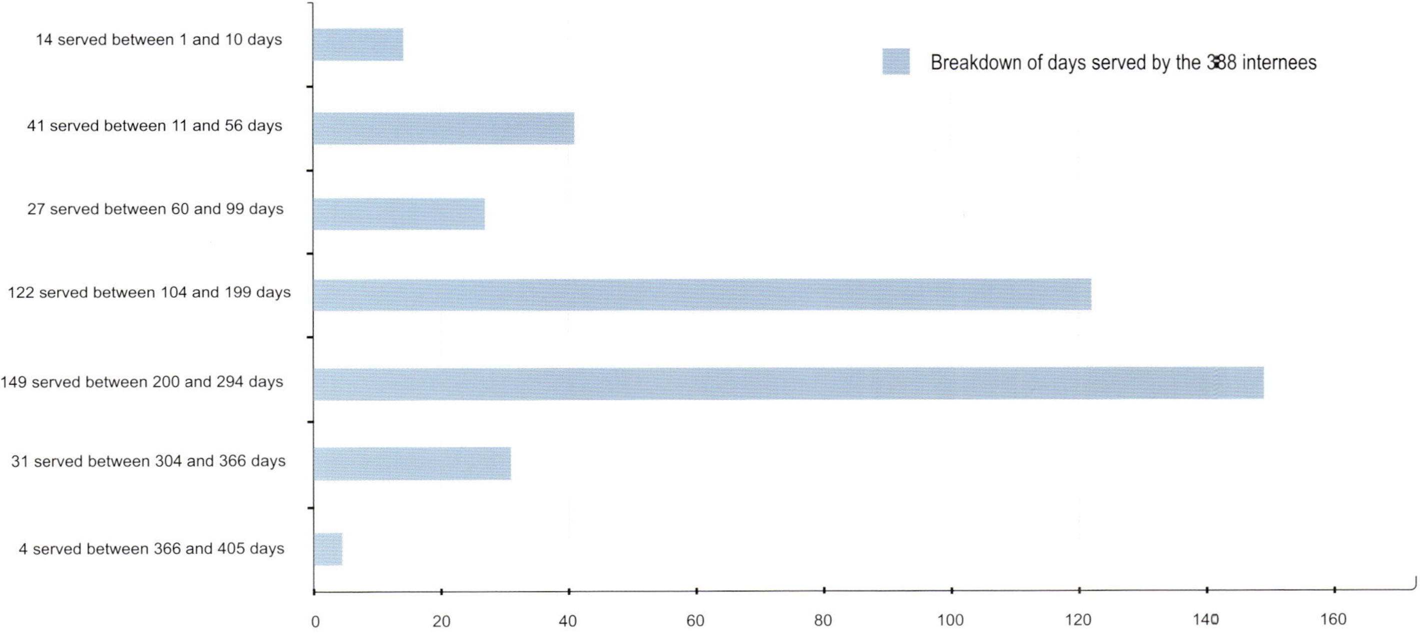

Fig. 7 Breakdown of days served by the 388 female republicans interned between September 1922 and November 1923. Members of Cumann na mBan comprised less than half the female prison population. [Compiled by Ann Matthews / Source: Prisoners Ledgers Military Archives; Ann Matthews, *Dissidents: Irish republican women 1923–1941* (Cork, 2012)]

As mentioned previously, the graffiti remnants dated to the final months of the Civil War are especially complete on the walls of the older west wing of Kilmainham Gaol, but it appeared that there was targeted whitewashing, especially of graffiti related to Civil War executions and partition. In all locations there were issues with sporadic whitewashing and the impact of dereliction. Later graffiti intrusions also affected the ability to trace, read and record all the graffiti. But what remains is extensive, complete and diverse enough to provide fascinating insights into the lives and experiences of the jail's last inhabitants. Any analysis of the graffiti must be based on theorised understandings of what such a source can tell us about the creator and the space they have graffitied.

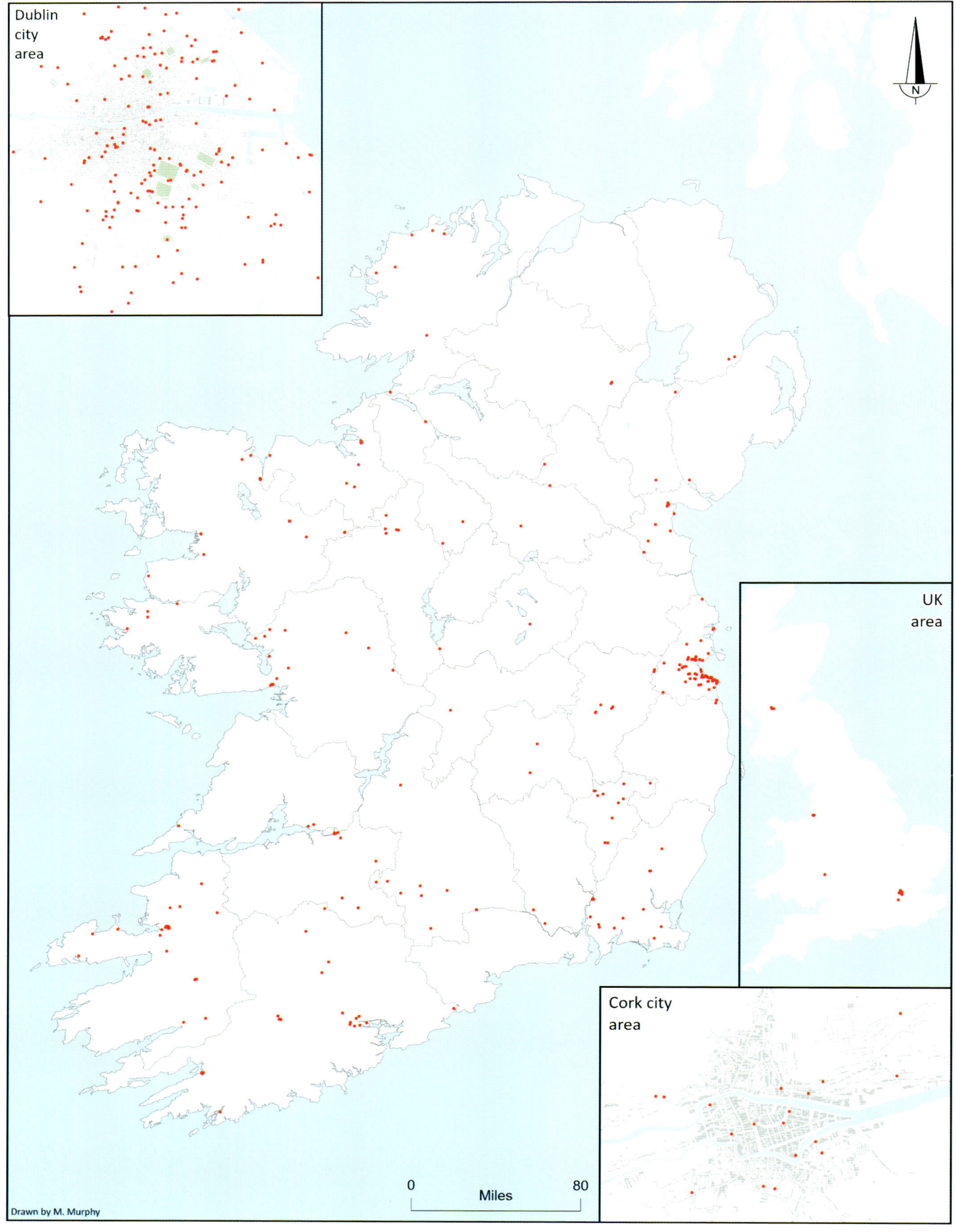
Dublin
city
area
UK
area
Cork city
area
0
Miles
80
N
Drawn by M. Murphy

Fig. 8 (opposite) Map showing the places of arrest of the 636 women arrested by Free State authorities between September 1922 and November 1923. In mid-1922 anti-Treaty republicans threatened to oppose by arms the legitimately elected Irish Free State government. This culminated in a eleven-month civil war that descended into ferocious bloodletting on all sides and financially shattered the new state. To stabilise the new state, in late September 1922 the Irish Free State government introduced the Army (Special Powers) Resolution, which enabled military law to be applied to the civilian population. A special Prisoners Department was organised within the office of the adjutant general (PDAG) at the Free State army headquarters. The government appointed Colonel C. Costello, director of intelligence, as officer in command (O/C) of the department. During the period July 1922 to early 1924, the PDAG kept detailed accounts on the arrests of all female and male internees. Under the Public Safety Acts 1922–3, the military arrested 636 women and, of this number, 388 were interned. The remaining women were released without charge because they signed a document called the 'form of undertaking' (FU). The FU stated: 'I beg to state that I have not taken part in the warfare against the Free State and that I have no intention of doing so.' Some of the 388 internees also signed the FU to secure an early release. However, this figure is difficult to ascertain because of the intimidation surrounding the issue within and outside the prisons. This was also the case within the male prison population. The number arrested in Dublin city and county represented 51 per cent (325) of the total number (636) of women arrested. This 51 per cent includes twenty-five deportees from Britain and nine women arrested at the Suffolk Street headquarters of Cumann na Poblachta, the republican party founded by Seán T. O'Kelly in early 1922. Regarding the deportees, on 11 March 1923 the British authorities rounded up 111 men and twenty-five women and transported them to the North Wall in Dublin. The PDAG described this group as 'persons engaged in a conspiracy to supply the irregulars with warlike material to support the campaign of destruction in Ireland'. On 12 March 1923 the deportees were handed over to the Irish military authorities. The cluster of arrests in Dublin does not indicate that they resided there. Dublin was central to all levels of anti-Treaty activity, and many female supporters travelled from rural Ireland 'on the run' because they worked as couriers, kept arms dumps, and supported attacks on the Free State army by supplying primed arms and ammunition to the IRA. According to one Cumann na mBan member from County Wexford, some of the women were even engaged in boiling the tar for the practice of tarring and feathering. The remaining 49 per cent, who were arrested outside the capital, are tracked in the bar chart (Fig. 6). The 338 women interned were never held concurrently. They served various periods of time from one to 405 days, in Mountjoy, Kilmainham and the North Dublin jails. Some were incarcerated at different times in the three locations. The graph (Fig. 7) shows the numbers interned and the length of their internments. [Text: Ann Matthews / Sources: Civil War [Prisoners] Ledgers, Irish Military Archives, Dublin, CW/OPS/07/03, CW/p/01/01, CW/p/04/06, CW/p/05/01, CW/p/05/07-09, CW/p/06/01, CW/p/06/01/03, CW/p/06/02-04; Ann Matthews, *Dissidents: Irish republican women 1923–1941* (Cork, 2012), Appendix 1, pp. 257–86; Eithne Coyle O'Donnell Papers, UCD Archive, pp. 61/4 8pp]

Interpreting graffiti

Graffiti studies have been growing since they first began in the 1970s, and are increasingly sophisticated in how they interpret the recent past. Graffiti analysis is not simply a means to retrieve and record individual text and images but also to reconstruct spatial and temporal realities. Traditionally, graffiti studies have been the preserve of the social sciences, especially sociology, and have been linked to analyses of male identity and criminality in particular.[9] This perception of graffiti as an illicit activity was initially related to its role in urban American street culture, especially to large-scale tags added to degraded buildings by gangs of young, disaffected men from marginalised communities. In the last decade, more materialised approaches to graffiti have developed, such as *Wild Signs*, the edited volume by Jeff Oliver and Tim Neal.[10] In this volume Kirsty Owen's research on medieval church graffiti reveals more nuanced understandings of who creates graffiti and why in historic buildings.[11] Her call to move beyond the analysis of graffiti as 'an inconvenient defacement rather than an informative cultural production' has greatly helped the study of the Kilmainham Gaol graffiti. In contrast to traditional views of graffiti, these assemblages have been explored as creations by women political prisoners from all social backgrounds and for myriad reasons to articulate their existence and their enduring political status as prisoners of the Irish Free State. In the context of a state institution – especially a 'hard' institution such as a prison – there is much we can infer beyond the textual and visual content. This includes the creators' relationships with authority and transgression, claims of ownership of space, and connections between the various forced and voluntary inhabitants. The rest of this chapter will explore a number of themes related to geographical and spatial aspects of the graffiti.

Geographies of gendered incarceration

The spatial patterns of Kilmainham Gaol graffiti hint at the power dynamics and communal relationships negotiated within the structure. For instance, the prisoners' ability to create large, detailed and openly viewable graffiti throughout cells, corridors and stairwells, seemingly without deterrent, clearly indicates the prison authorities' lack of control over their activities. There are numerous examples of graffiti appearing in corridors and stairwells – often defiant, accusatory and even threatening of the Free State authorities – that remain in place. Caricatures of prison personnel located at the entrance to the top floors of the west wing were clearly positioned to be seen by the prison officers. During the long period when the prison contained ODCs (ordinary decent criminals), records show a small number of prisoners charged with creating graffiti, reflecting a previous policy of careful control of graffiti creation. In the time of the Civil War, however, political prisoners had officially sanctioned access to pencils and paints to decorate their cells. They also used a glue-like substance to attach postcards to their cell walls; this remains visible through the outline of frames and a small number of the cards that remain in situ. An especially telling source illustrates the prison's material riches during this period. The register of parcels held in the Irish Military Archives from the period includes entries for 'paints, [...] pencils, pens' and implements required for creating graffiti.[12] The resultant graffiti included large slogans on well-lit walls, over doorways and in corridors, as well as more typical illicit graffiti traditionally studied by sociologists, which was hidden or secreted in unseen corners.

Some cells had more graffiti than others, and some were more personalised than others. This reflected the occupants' differing desires to make their cell more aesthetically pleasing, or to perform their role as protesting political prisoners, or to meekly serve their

In Memoriam.

Padraic	Pearse.
Thomas	McDonagh
Thomas	Clarke.
Joseph	Plunkett.
William	Pearse.
Eamonn	Daly.
Michael	O'Hanrahan.
John	McBride.
Thomas	Ceannt.
Sean	Heuston.
Con	Colbert.
Michael	Mallin.
Eamonn	Ceannt.
James.	Connolly.
Sean	McDermott
Roger	Casement.

Kilmainham
April 24th 1923

Play

The Singer.
by
Padraig Pearse

Characters.

MacDara.	The Singer	Mary McSwiney
Colm.	his brother	Sighle Bowen.
Maire ní Fhiannachta:	Mother	Hanna O Connor.
Sighle:		Maureen Power.
Maolsheachlainn	a Schoolmaster	Lily O Brennan
Cuimin Conna.		Nellie Fennell.
Diarmuid of the Bridges		Mrs Kirwan

At the end of the Play – Hanna O Connor will speak Pearse's Poem
The Mother

The Soldiers Song

Programme of Commemoration.

held by Republican Women Prisoners of War in Kilmainham on April 23.1923.
The seventh Anniversary of the Proclamation of the Irish Republic.

9. a.m.
Requiem Mass for the men executed in 1916

3 p.m.
Procession to the place of Execution
Placing of Laurel Wreath by Mrs Joseph Plunkett.
Rosary recited in Irish.

In the Prison Compound.
Unfurling of the Tricolour
Hymn "Faith of our Fathers"
"Speeches:
"Kilmainham in 1916." Lily O Brennan
"Joseph Plunkett" Mrs J. Plunkett
"The Proclamation of the Republic" Nora Connolly O'Brien.
The Republican Oath

Concert and Play.
7. p.m.

Song.	"The Battle Hymn"	Countess Markievicz. Kathleen O Carroll
Poem	"Treason" Joseph Plunkett	Mrs Kirwan.
Song	"They are Calling" James Connolly	Kathleen O Carroll
Poem	"Renunciation"	Padraig Pearse. Lily O Brennan.
Song	"The Foggy Dew"	Katty Murphy.
Poem	"The Fool"	Padraig Pearse. Iseult Stewart.
Song	"The Sound of the Trumpet"	Hanna O Connor.
Recitation	"McDonagh's Address to the Jury."	Maire O Halloran.
Song	"The Dublin Brigade"	D. Barry
Song	"The Wayfarers"	Padraig Pearse. Nora C. O'Brien
Poem	"Lux Perpetua Luceat Eis" Fr Brown.	D. Macardle.
Song	"Wrap the Green Flag"	K. O Carroll, H. O Connor, D. Barry, K. Murphy.

Fig. 9 (opposite) A programme, handmade by Nan Hogan, for the commemorative events organised by Kilmainham's women prisoners to mark the seventh anniversary of the 1916 Rising on 24 April 1923. After an early requiem Mass for the sixteen men executed in 1916, the women prisoners marched in a solemn procession to the Stonebreakers' Yard where Joseph Plunkett's widow, Grace Gifford Plunkett, placed a laurel wreath; Lily O'Brennan, who occupied the cell in which her brother-in-law Éamonn Ceannt had been held in 1916, delivered a speech, and James Connolly's daughter, Nora, read the Proclamation of the Republic. In the evening the prisoners attended a concert of poetry and songs and a performance of Patrick Pearse's play *The Singer*. Writing from Kilmainham a day later, Dorothy Macardle claimed: 'We were not altogether unfortunate to be in this prison on April 24 [...] it was good to be prisoners where the men of 1916 were prisoners and to know that it was because we had been faithful to their deed and would not waste their sacrifice that we were here.' [Document: courtesy of Kilmainham Gaol Museum/OPW / Quotation: *Éire: The Irish Nation*, 12 May 1923]

time. Over 100 individual portraits were located throughout the west wing during the recording exercise, but the vast majority were only viewable at close distance, and very few had any indications of who they were intended to represent. There were a small number of cells in the west wing that had images on such a scale that they aesthetically impacted the cells, including a few completed pictorial landscapes. Two cells in particular stand out. On the top floor of the west wing, Brigid O'Mullane's cell featured large slogans painted on the walls, including text from a Terence MacSwiney play and Celtic-style designs framing the window and the doorway. The paint colours were still evident, as was a pencil signature also below the MacSwiney quotation, identifying the artist as Brigid and dating the work to '1922–1923'. The identification of O'Mullane appeared to have been added after the prison was closed. Sighle Humphreys's cell was on the middle floor of the west wing and it likewise contained a number of slogans, including a large painted image of the Cumann na mBan insignia along with other painted images. It also contained one of the only pieces of graffiti located close to the floor, which provided evidence of a tunnel started in the basement, a revelation also included in a small piece of text found in another cell on that floor.

In such a context graffiti transcends its typical interpretation as an essentially secretive and even criminal activity. Instead, in Kilmainham it can be interpreted as openly subversive and intrinsic to the arsenal of resistance of the political prisoner. In this respect such graffiti is deeply meaningful to both the creator and their intended audience.[13] Such an argument is confirmed by one of the most common graffiti forms located on the walls: prisoners' personal details, such as name, address and prison record. Such details create what Eleanor Casella calls prisoner 'testimonies', which personalise

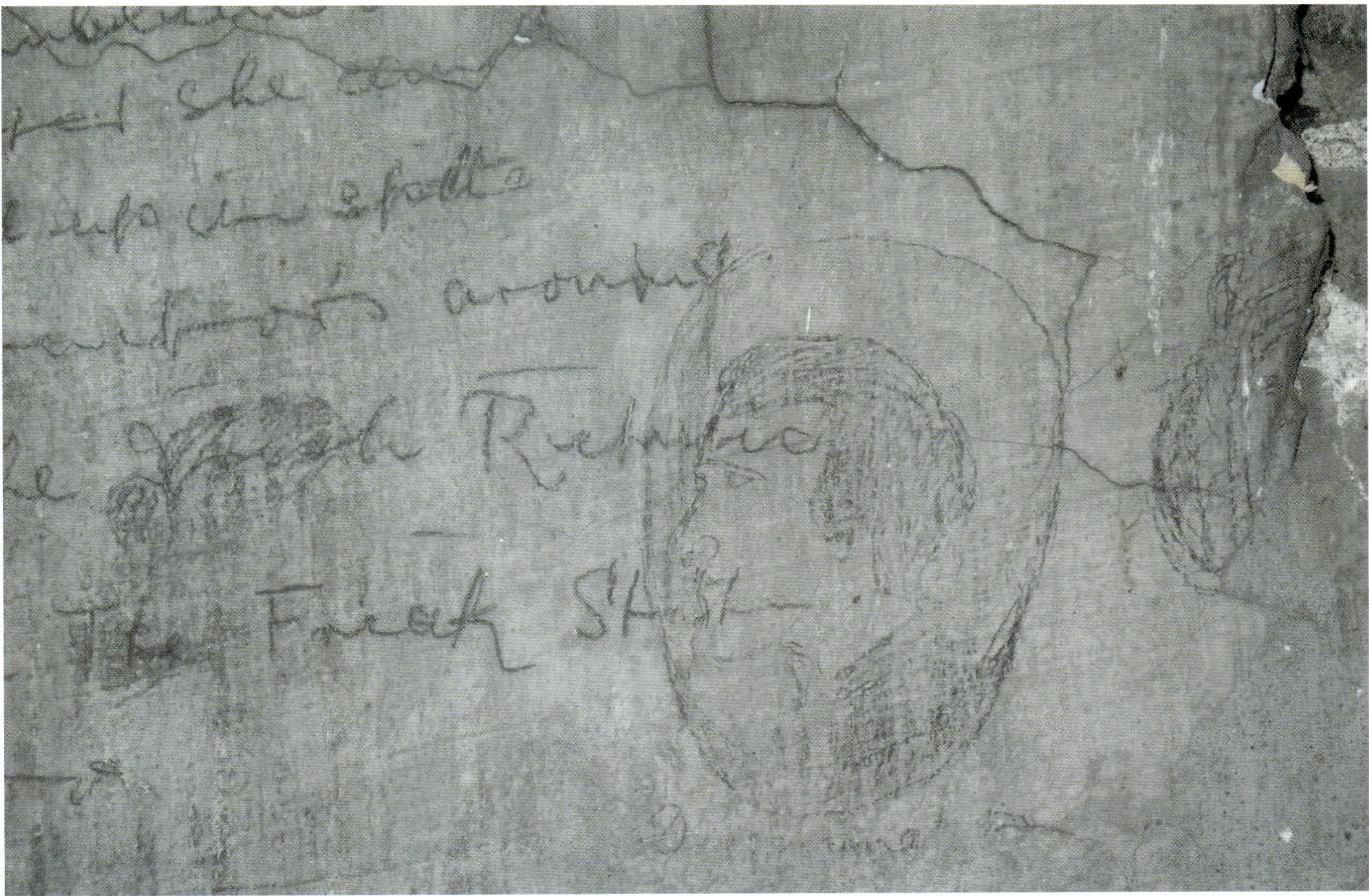

Fig. 10 Portrait of an unknown male in a cell in the west wing of Kilmainham Gaol. Located in a relatively shaded area of a wall close to a window, the portrait, fainter than the text that partially covers it, is not obvious to the naked eye. It was only revealed in photographs taken during the graffiti-recording process. [Image: courtesy of Laura McAtackney]

I.R.
1923.
"A FEW MEN FAITHFUL
AND
A DEATHLESS DREAM."
BRIGID O'MULLANE
PRISONER HERE

Fig. 11 (opposite top) The graffiti in Brigid O'Mullane's cell on the top floor of the west wing of Kilmainham Gaol is one of several that invokes Terence MacSwiney, the Volunteer leader and republican lord mayor of Cork, who died after a seventy-four-day hunger strike in London's Brixton Prison in October 1920. This well-preserved example quotes from 'The Prophesy of Fionn', first published in 1918 in MacSwiney's poetry collection *Battle Cries*. The speaker, Fionn Mac Cumhaill of Celtic legend, promises his retreating Fianna warriors that the bravery of the 'hero-dreamers' would be remembered. Their triumphant failure would 'strike slave souls to fire' and inspire 'a few men faithful and a deathless dream' to triumph over 'tyrannies'. [Image: courtesy of Kilmainham Gaol Museum/OPW]

Fig. 12 (opposite bottom) The Cumann na mBan insignia features in a number of cells, like this prominent, monumental example in a cell on Corridor 1 of the top floor. Most, but not all, of the female prisoners transferred to Kilmainham Gaol after it was opened as 'a prison for suspect women' in February 1923 were members of the anti-Treaty women's auxiliary organisation. Cumann na mBan members were active before June 1922 as propagandists and political organisers, but after the fighting began they proved particularly valuable to the IRA's military campaign in the realms of communications, intelligence, medical care and logistics. They also provided assistance to the dependants of republican prisoners, and were a visible and subversive presence at protest meetings and republican funerals. Incomplete Military Service Pensions Collection returns suggest that during the Civil War the organisation had roughly 18,000 members, or an estimated 70 per cent of its War of Independence strength. Cumann na mBan was healthiest in the urban areas of Dublin, Cork and Limerick and in the counties that provided the most sustained opposition to the Free State, such as Kerry, Tipperary, Mayo and Wexford. Unlike the British administration during the War of Independence that rarely arrested women, the Free State authorities, aware of their value, detained almost ten times as many during the Civil War. Once interned, as Sinéad McCoole notes, the Cumann na mBan women imposed their own structure, 'forming a Prisoners' Council with commanding officers, quartermasters and adjutants' who 'made depositions to the Governor on behalf of the prisoners' and 'arranged classes in reading, writing and basic mathematics, Irish language and culture, Latin and 'intermediate French"'. [Image: courtesy of Kilmainham Gaol Museum/OPW / See John Borgonovo, 'Cumann na mBan in the Civil War', in John Crowley, Donal Ó Drisceoil, Mike Murphy and John Borgonovo (eds), *Atlas of the Irish Revolution*, (Cork, 2017), pp. 698–702; Sinéad McCoole, '"The Mainstay of the Trouble": The imprisonment of 'suspect women' during the Civil War', 'The Civil War Project', RTÉ (2023) https://www.rte.ie/history/liam-deasy/2022/1206/1340347-the-mainstay-of-the-trouble-imprisonment-of-suspect-women/]

their environment and ensure their time was literally written on the walls.[14] Far from imprisonment being shameful for the prisoner, graffiti played a significant role in publicly performing their political status and presencing their internment. Its analysis also allows us to better understand the prisoners' sensory experiences of place.

External connections and enduring loyalties

Two of the most common forms of graffiti found in Kilmainham Gaol articulate the enduring external networks and loyalties of the imprisoned women. They most commonly took physical form in two ways: (1) reference to the places (primarily counties) they came from; (2) geographical references of pre- and post-imprisonment belonging. Mentions of prisoners' counties of origin materialises in a number of ways, including large slogans such as 'Up Dublin' or insults to other counties – most commonly involving Dublin and Kerry. These slogans tended to be painted in large text across walls and were not usually associated with named individuals. Rather, they were slogans that indicated enduring connections from outside to inside the prison walls – including the county-based geographic nature of the prisoners' organisation in Cumann na mBan. Localised geographies were also represented and connected to individual cells, especially in the east wing. Although the cellular nature of the prison was intended to separate prisoners, during the revolutionary period prisoners were allowed relatively free association across their wings. They decided which cells to occupy and with whom to share them. It is evident that groups of prisoners from counties further away from Dublin – particularly Kerry and Donegal – created cellular 'homes' that contained women solely from that county and even more localised places within the county. For example, one west-wing cell had text above the door referencing 'Dungloe' in Donegal. Not all of those cellular 'homes' directly name their county, as some mentioned prominent (often male) combatants identified with that locale from either historical or contemporary contexts, such as Dan Breen of Tipperary.

Fig. 13 An example of place-specific graffiti over a cell door in the east wing of Kilmainham Gaol. [Image: courtesy of Kilmainham Gaol Museum/OPW]

Ms 17,141/11

Irish Labour Party
& Trade Union Congress
MAY 1923

COPY.

Kilmainham Jail,
May 1st 1923.

A Chara,

I wish to bring the following facts to your notice, and I request that you will give them all possible publicity.

On April 30th our Prisoners' Council received notice from the Deputy Governor of the Jail that 81 of us would be removed that night to the North Dublin Union. On this date Miss McSweeney and Mrs O'Callaghan had been 20 days on hunger-strike. A large number of ~~yx~~ prisoners had already been taken away from their wing, and we foresaw that when we were removed the two hunger-strikers would be left all alone in this Jail at the mercy of their captors. So we refused to go until they were released. We considered this course of action absolutely necessary on account of the treatment received by previous hunger-strikers.

At 9 p.m. we were informed by the Deputy Governor that if we persisted in our refusal we would be removed by force.

At 10.20 p.m. Mrs O'Callaghan was released, leaving Miss McSweeney alone.

At midnight a large force of C.I.D. and F.S. soldiers rushed into the compound and up to the top landing where the prisoners were. They caught hold of each girl in turn, kicking, beating and dragging them along the landing to the top of the iron staircase. Down this they threw them in some cases, and dragged them in others. Several prisoners - notably Mrs Gordon of Dublin - were dragged to the foot of the stairs by their hair, and along the stone floor to the door. Others were dragged by the feet, their heads beating each iron-bound step. One girl - a cousin of Liam Lynch - had her hand badly bitten Many girls fainted, and were carried away in a condition of collapse. There was no Doctor in the building- and only one nurse on duty- and as her time was mainly devoted to Miss McSweeney, no medical attention could be hadd The language and behaviour of these men surpasses description, and the effect on Miss McSweeney of the cries and moans of the injured girls, and the shouts of the men may be imagined.

This torture went on from 12.5 a.m. Then the soldiers were called off, having taken about 70 girls, and leaving many of those behind in a condition of collapse.

I testify on my word of honour that all I have said is true without exaggeration.

You may use my signature, which I append.

ANNIE HOGAN,
Cratloe, Co. Clare.

P.S. I may also add that as lights were turned out at midnight, we had to submit to the added terror of darkness, except for the light of the moon through the glass roof, and the candles on the alter

Extract from a note, enclosed with above.

" I cannot give you any adequate idea of what we went through lasttnight. We can hardly believe it ourselves. Of course we did not see any of the girls after they were dragged away, but we heard - through a soldier - that one girl's leg was broken. We cannot confirm this until we reach the Union. It was the murder gang from Oriel House and Portobello" ....

" We are wondering what we have to face to-night" If Miss McSweeney is not released we shall have to go through the same performance"

Fig. 14 (above) The title page from the prison autograph book of Annie (Nan) Hogan. [Image: courtesy of Kilmainham Gaol Museum/OPW]

Fig. 15 (left) Copy of a letter from Annie Hogan to Labour Party leader Thomas Johnson, 1 May 1923. Annie (Nan) Hogan, from Cratloe, County Clare, qualified as a teacher in 1908. She spent several years in England before returning to Ireland in 1914, after which she rose through the ranks of Cumann na mBan to assume a leadership role in east Clare during the War of Independence. She transported guns, carried dispatches, gathered intelligence, and offered her home as headquarters for the IRA East Clare Brigade. Hogan fiercely opposed the Treaty and was active under Madge Daly's command during the Battle for Limerick in July 1922. She was arrested in February 1923 while waiting to assist prisoners who were foiled in their escape attempt from Limerick jail. From Kilmainham Gaol, where she shared a cell with Grace Gifford, she was moved to write to the leader of the Labour Party about the brutal treatment of women prisoners during their forcible removal to the North Dublin Union on 30 April. Publication of details of what Hogan called 'the torture' at Kilmainham led to MacSwiney's release after nineteen days on hunger strike on 1 May. Thirty-seven-year-old Hogan was released on 4 July 1923 'in a very emaciated state' after a second hunger strike in the North Dublin Union. She died on 29 June 1924, just four months after her marriage to Tim Foley in Cratloe. [Document: National Library of Ireland, Thomas Johnson Papers, MS 17,141/11/ See Mary McAuliffe, 'Nan Hogan: A revolutionary life', https://www.rte.ie/history/the-silent-civil-war]

Fig. 16 Mary MacSwiney (left) at Hotel St Regis, New York, December 1920. In her speech during the Treaty debates, MacSwiney (1872–1942) spoke for two hours and thirty-five minutes, longer than the contributions of the five plenipotentiaries combined. Her avowal of an inflexible stance on the evils of compromise was indelibly formed by the experience of watching her brother Terence die on hunger strike in Brixton Prison in October 1920. She witnessed an intimate act of self-sacrifice that bound her to a belief that her task was to continue her brother's fidelity to a separatist republic. She is pictured here in December 1920 with Terence MacSwiney's widow, Muriel, prior to their departure for Washington to testify before the American Commission on Conditions in Ireland in December 1920. Mary MacSwiney's compelling testimony saw her emerge as a strong political voice. She left Washington on 16 December 1920 to conduct a tour of the United States under the auspices of the American Association for the Recognition of the Irish Republic. Taking de Valera's place 'in leading the bond drive' was at his special request, as MacSwiney reminded him in July 1921. While in America she was elected unopposed to the Second Dáil, one of four representatives for Cork city. MacSwiney was imprisoned four times during the Civil War: in Mountjoy in November 1922, and briefly in Kilmainham in mid-February 1923 when she was arrested at the reopening of the Sinn Féin offices in Suffolk Street. She was rearrested on 29 March and released again on 1 April. Her brief incarceration did not dampen her willingness to address an anti-Treaty meeting two days later outside the General Post Office in Dublin. According to the *Belfast Newsletter*, she was joined at the meeting by other 'wild women', among whom were Countess Plunkett and Mrs Pearse. On 12 April 1923 she was taken into custody for the fourth time, en route to Mitchelstown, County Cork for Liam Lynch's funeral. MacSwiney endured two gruelling and high-profile hunger strikes during the Civil War: in November 1922 and again in April 1923. The authorities grappled with how to respond to a female prisoner on hunger strike, especially one with such a republican pedigree. The government's problems were heightened during her November hunger strike when Annie MacSwiney began to fast outside the walls of Mountjoy Gaol in protest at being refused entry to see her sister. In November, and again during her April imprisonment, MacSwiney conducted a detailed correspondence with the archbishop of Dublin, Edward Byrne. Referring to the Bishops' Joint Pastoral of 10 October 1922, she excoriated him for denying her the 'consolation' of Holy Communion that was granted to her brother in Brixton Prison. In the context of the gender roles of the period, MacSwiney's strident political voice saw her represented by the pro-Treaty side as a difficult female who did not know her place. No republican man was caricatured as she was. The *Belfast Newsletter* on 26 June 1923 described her as falling on those with whom she disagreed 'with every tooth bared, drops of clotted venom suspended from every outstretched fang'. This vitriol was, however, testament to the political centrality of MacSwiney, as was the fact that de Valera chose to confide in her, in a very intimate political correspondence, his deepest unease about the course of the Civil War. [Text: Leeann Lane / Image: National Library of Ireland, NPA POLF150]

This geographic connection is more noticeable when examining Kilmainham Gaol autograph books, which were booklets of signatures passed among the women prisoners while they were incarcerated (many can be found in the Kilmainham Gaol archive). From these I was able to connect extant graffiti to 242 individual women prisoners. One third of those names were associated with a geographical location. This indicates that the women prisoners deeply connected their personal identities to their external origins and prior associations. Of course, not all prisoners added their names, but a significant portion of the estimated 600 women imprisoned during the Civil War left some textual trace of their presence.[15] As one might expect, the most represented county was Dublin, with 116 of the 161 examples explicitly referencing the capital city or county. The next highest was Kerry with twenty-five examples, and then Cork with seventeen. Generally, places with high participation in the Civil War or those that were deeply affected by the preceding War of Independence were well represented, along with some outliers. Donegal was the seventh-highest number on the county list, with ten examples. It was also the outlier in terms of the province of Ulster, as Cavan and Tyrone had two examples each, Antrim and Armagh a solitary example, and Derry, Down, Fermanagh and Monaghan were completely absent. However, given the prominence of Donegal Cumann na mBan members, such as Eithne Coyle, one might understand their relatively high number of references, which mainly came from the one cell that housed women from Dungloe. Indeed, the lack of northern representation is hardly surprising because of partition and the possibility that some of the women may have relocated across the border and affiliated to their adopted county. A number of absences was also interesting. Very few high-profile women prisoners, such as Countess Markievicz or Mary MacSwiney, added their names to the walls, although some may have taken part in their decoration (including Sighle Humphreys, whose cell was discussed above). There was also no reference connected to the Irish diaspora. Extradited women from London, Glasgow and Manchester wrote both their names and origin place in numerous autograph books, but left no extant graffiti on the jail walls.

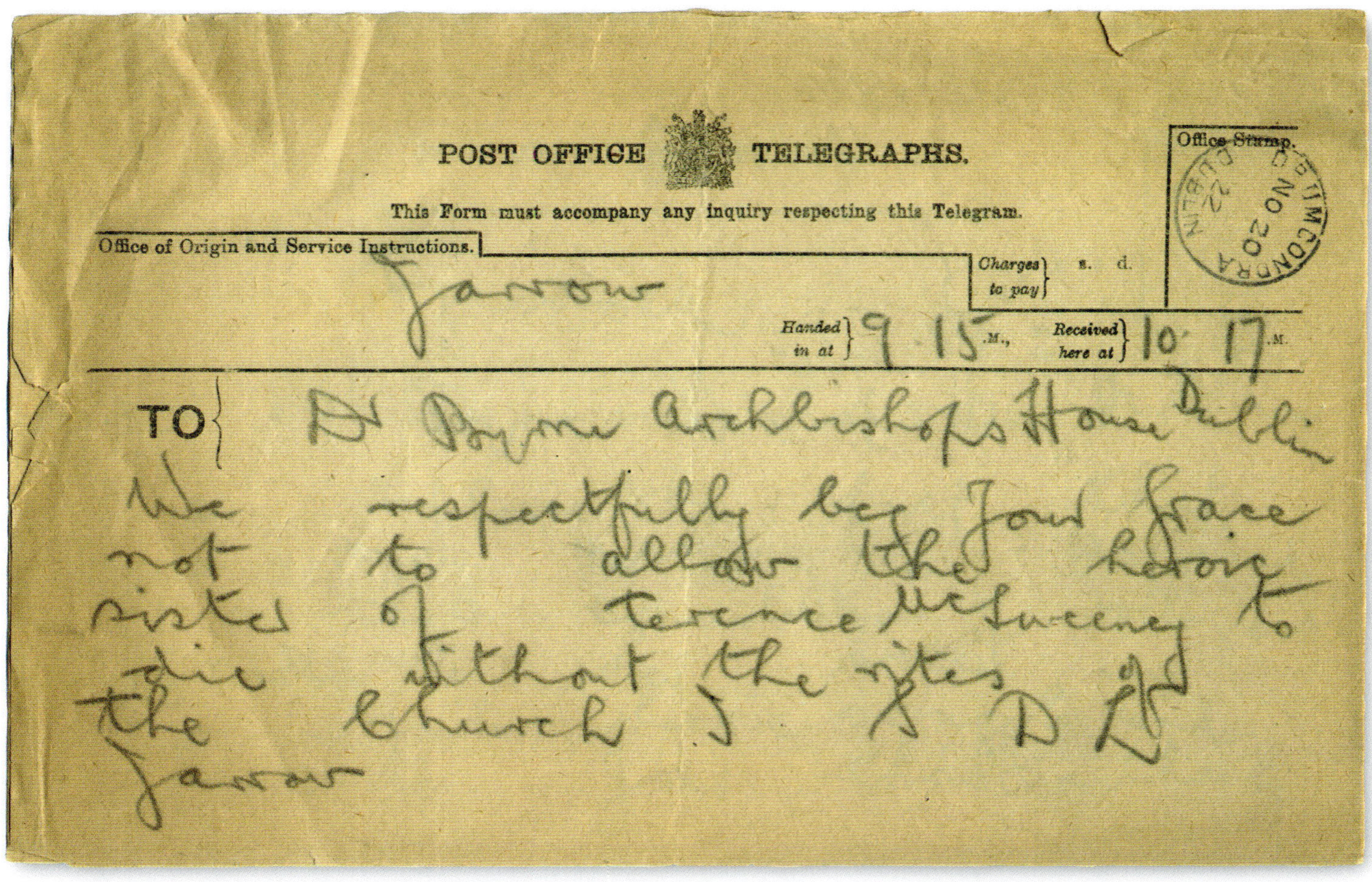
POST OFFICE TELEGRAPHS.

This Form must accompany any inquiry respecting this Telegram.

Office of Origin and Service Instructions. Jarrow

Charges to pay s. d.

Office Stamp.

Handed in at 9 15 .M., Received here at 10 17 .M.

TO Dr Byrne Archbishops House Dublin

We respectfully beg Your Grace not to allow the heroic sister of Terence McSwiney to die without the rites of the Church I S D L Jarrow

Fig. 17 Telegram dated 20 November 1922 from the Irish Self Determination League, Jarrow Branch, pleading with Archbishop Byrne to not let Mary MacSwiney die without 'the rites of the Church'. [Document: courtesy of the Dublin Diocesan Archives]

Post-incarceration graffiti

Kilmainham Gaol officially ceased operating in early 1924 following the Civil War, and was officially decommissioned as an active prison in 1929.[16] After the Civil War it endured a long period of official abandonment and dereliction that ensured material alterations to the site well prior to its conversion into a heritage site in the 1960s. This period of abandonment is important. It shows that value changes are strongly tied to temporality, which is evident when the pain of the Civil War needed to subside before a site could be interpreted and presented for the public. But a lack of official function did not mean that Kilmainham Gaol was unvisited or forgotten. Visits to the site were officially allowed and facilitated, and the material remains reveal that various interactions and material changes were ongoing. Rory O'Dwyer recounts how, in the period from 1924 to 1960, there were many half-hearted or unsuccessful attempts to plan, and finance, Kilmainham Gaol's 'future' uses.[17] The year 1938 was especially busy in terms of publicly recorded and semi-official interactions with the site.[18] Of particular note was 14 March, when a trip into Kilmainham was organised by the executive committee of Cumann na mBan. The *Irish Press* described how 'crowds of members and their friends visited the jail and spent the afternoon in visiting theirs or their old friends' old cells, or in increasing their knowledge of the place as a whole'.[19] The surviving structures retain what Laurent Olivier called 'material memory' of these post-war activities, particularly the eighteen graffiti examples created in the west wing during 1938.[20] Of particular note is the fact that women created the majority of these and placed them in publicly accessible places (often in the middle of cell walls or on the surrounds of interior cell doors) in order to be seen. There are eight extant examples located in two adjoining cells on the top floor of the west wing. They include the names of the women who visited Kilmainham Gaol during the March 1938 Cumann na mBan visit, while also providing detailed and personal information regarding their connection to this place. Two examples can be exemplified, and they are attributed to Lillie Gleeson and Peg Quinn:

> *Arrested by CID 20th March / Lillie Gleeson 228 / Political prisoner / Visited 12th March 1938 / Up B Wing / Up Barry's Hotel*

> *Arrested by CID 1923 / 20th March 1923 / Peg Quinn 10229 Political Prisoner / Visited 12th March 1938 / Up B Wing / Barry's Hotel*

Fig. 18 Éamon de Valera with supporters visiting the dangerously dilapidated Kilmainham Gaol, 19 June 1938, two days after the snap general election that returned a majority Fianna Fáil government. The open day, one of several in 1938, was a fund-raising event organised by the Easter Week Men's Association. The Taoiseach, accompanied by Tánaiste Seán T. O'Kelly and five other government ministers, was received by a guard of honour of 1916 veterans. The press reported how 'a huge throng followed the ministerial party through the gloomy corridors – paths trodden by generations of Irish patriots' and noted the Taoiseach's moment of silent contemplation in the yard where the leaders of the Easter Rising were executed. Unmentioned in news reports was de Valera's second term of imprisonment in Kilmainham after his arrest in Ennis in August 1923. Released in July 1924, he was Kilmainham Gaol's last prisoner. [Image: courtesy of Kilmainham Gaol Museum/OPW / See *Irish Independent,* 20 June 1938, *Leitrim Observer*, 25 June 1938]

Such graffiti is significant because it is not intended to simply vandalise or fill space. The text is spatially and temporally specific, listing identifiable and specific information about ex-prisoners' names, prisoner numbers, political status, date of arrest and even the unofficial name of the cell in which they were housed. By this process these women effectively materialised themselves back into the material structures of Kilmainham Gaol. Although individual motives cannot be categorically stated, societal context seems important. By 1938 anti-Free State republicans had been marginalised from the state's political life, but retained virtually uncontested ownership of the public memory of revolutionary nationalism.[21] By creating this graffiti on their collective visit to Kilmainham Gaol, these women left their presence at the place most meaningful to their experiences. They simultaneously engraved their enduring existence into the walls as they were being marginalised in the public and political sphere. Niamh O'Sullivan has written about the importance of this official visit to the women because it allowed them to share their experiences with friends and family and to claim political imprisonment as a form of Civil War active service. O'Sullivan argues that the women felt that 'their arduous participation should count for something'.[22] The graffiti shows the women took direct action as a response to the national amnesia about their wartime contributions.

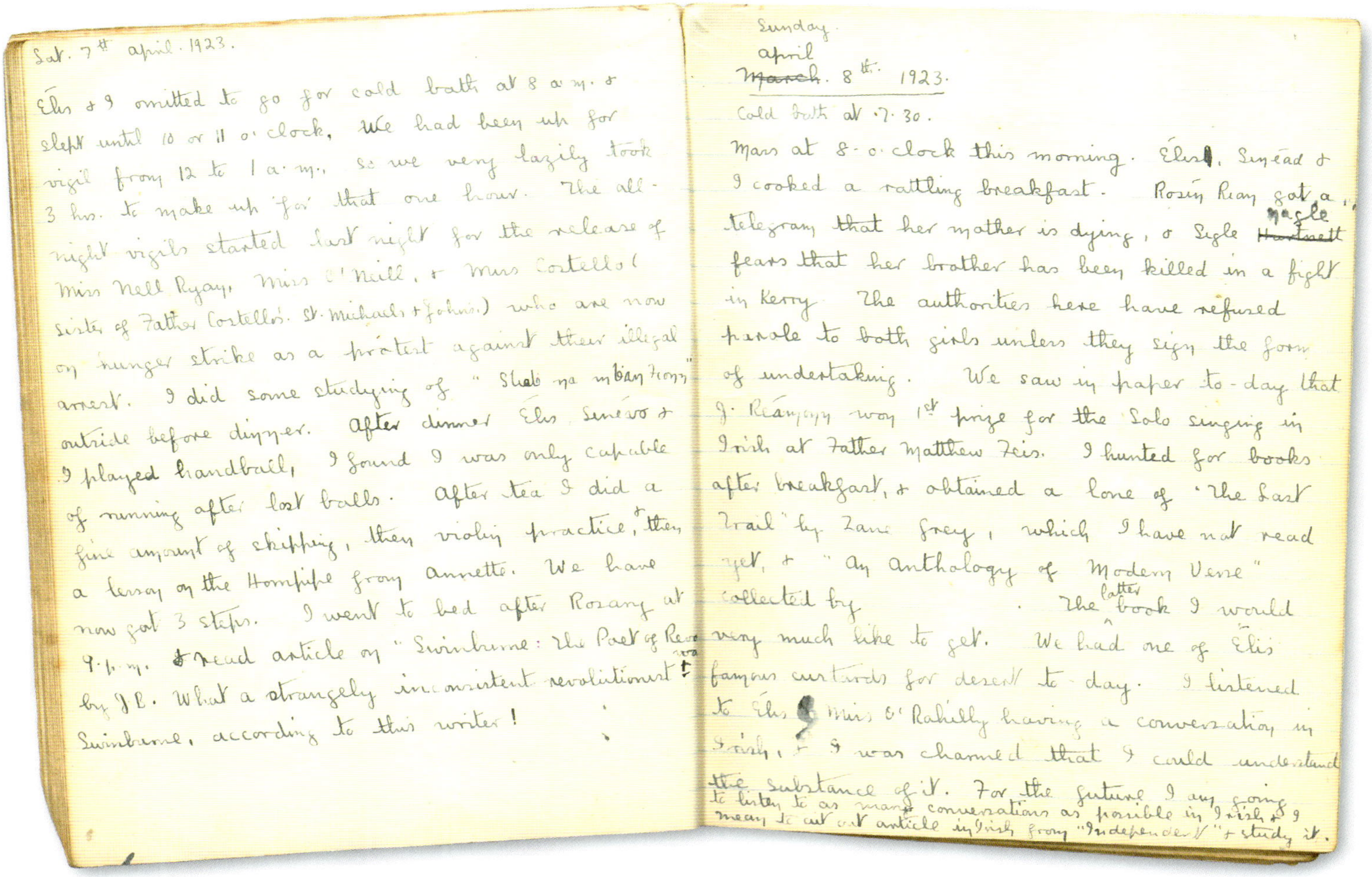

Sat. 7th April. 1923.

Elis & I omitted to go for cold bath at 8 a.m. & slept until 10 or 11 o'clock. We had been up for vigil from 12 to 1 a.m., so we very lazily took 3 hrs. to make up for that one hour. The all-night vigils started last night for the release of Miss Nell Ryan, Miss O'Neill, & Miss Costello (sister of Father Costello's. St. Michael's & John's) who are now on hunger strike as a protest against their illegal arrest. I did some studying of "Shab na mBan [illegible]" outside before dinner. After dinner Elis, Sinéad & I played handball, I found I was only capable of running after lost balls. After tea I did a fine amount of skipping, then violin practice, then a lesson on the Hornpipe from Annette. We have now got 3 steps. I went to bed after Rosary at 9 p.m. & read article on "Swinburne: The Poet of Revolt" by J.L. What a strangely inconsistent revolutionist was Swinburne, according to this writer!

Sunday.
April
~~March~~. 8th. 1923.
Cold bath at 7.30.

Mass at 8 o'clock this morning. Elis, Sinéad & I cooked a rattling breakfast. Rosin Ryan got a telegram that her mother is dying, & Sighle ~~[illegible]~~ Nagle fears that her brother has been killed in a fight in Kerry. The authorities here have refused parole to both girls unless they sign the form of undertaking. We saw in paper to-day that J. Ryan won 1st prize for the Solo singing in Irish at Father Matthew Feis. I hunted for books after breakfast, & obtained a loan of 'The Last Trail' by Zane Grey, which I have not read yet, & "An Anthology of Modern Verse" collected by . The latter book I would very much like to get. We had one of Elis' famous custards for desert to-day. I listened to Elis & Miss O'Rahilly having a conversation in Irish, & I was charmed that I could understand the substance of it. For the future I am going to listen to as many conversations as possible in Irish, & I mean to cut out article in Irish from "Independent" & study it.

Fig. 19 Pages from the Civil War diary (March–June 1923) of Maura Redmond. Redmond was a member of the Ranelagh branch of Cumann na mBan who lived in the Portobello area of Dublin. She kept a record of her experiences of internment during the Civil War, which she initially spent in Kilmainham Gaol and subsequently in the North Dublin Union. Not all the days in the diary are filled in and pages have been removed, but what remains provides a glimpse into the routine of prison life and the individual and collective responses to the prison regime. There is a sense of putting down time, but there is also a real sense of the resilience and passions that motivated women like Redmond. Just as the individual cells and prison yards were physical sites of resistance as represented by the graffiti, Redmond's diary, with its references to activism, hunger strikes and the violence perpetrated by prison authorities, also bears witness to a determination to endure and overcome. Like many of her contemporaries, Redmond spoke little to her family of her Civil War activism, and they were surprised to discover the diary after her death in March 1990. It included a short entry made in 1938 when she revisited the jail: 'It was strange to walk through Kilmainham Jail again after a lapse of 15 years [...] I gaze around & see that time has not effaced the names of some of the calls. "Tara's Hall", "An Daingean". "The West's Awake" etc. still exhibit the poetic & rebel sentiments of the inhabitants'. [Document: Kilmainham Gaol Museum/OPW / See Derek J. Byrne, *Maura Redmond: An Irish Civil War prison diary* (2021), p. 105]

Conclusion

The Civil War graffiti at Kilmainham Gaol was primarily created by women prisoners. Its scale, size and frequency indicates that the walls, cells and corridors were not only part of a repressive place of incarceration, but were consciously reconfigured by the women to exercise their agency for active resistance. Such seemingly ephemeral 'mark-making' survived not only long-term dereliction but also the process of 'restoration' and heritagisation of the jail.[23] As such, the graffiti is a remarkable source that allows us to explore the often-overlooked materialised experiences of this period. It is also a substantial enough assemblage to reveal why graffiti should not simply be reduced to recording text and images. By taking a geographically-informed approach to recording and analysing these substantial assemblages, we can move beyond the individualised nature of graffiti. In the case of Kilmainham Gaol, the graffiti reveals enduring details about the realities of women's experiences, relationships, external connections and memories of their incarceration.

CASE STUDY

Irish Civil War Imprisonment, Humanitarianism and the Red Cross

Lia Brazil

On the eve of the Civil War, internment facilities in Ireland were limited. In January 1922 the Prisons Board had informed the Provisional Government that it could accommodate just 647 women and 2,038 men, yet at the height of the Civil War almost 12,000 men and almost 400 women were interned. This mass detention of anti-Treaty associates inevitably led to overcrowding, which, alongside claims of unhygienic conditions, meagre rations and torture, became a focal point for prisoner relatives and anti-Treaty supporters. Led by women such as Maud Gonne MacBride and Charlotte Despard through the Women Prisoners' Defence League, these campaigns adopted humanitarian and international legal rhetoric. They directed their appeals towards Geneva and the International Committee of the Red Cross (ICRC).[1]

Founded in 1862 by the Swiss businessman Henri Dunant after experiencing the devastation of the 1859 Battle of Solferino, the ICRC held a mandate under the 1864 and 1906 Geneva Conventions to protect medical volunteers assisting the wounded during battle.[2] During the First World War, delegates from the organisation inspected detention conditions for prisoners of war throughout Europe, under the terms of the Hague Conventions. In the turmoil of revolutions after the war, the ICRC voted in 1921 to further extend its remit to include advocacy on behalf of all prisoners during internal conflicts, civil wars and rebellions.[3]

The first appeal to the ICRC during the Irish Civil War emanated from the Mater Misericordiae Hospital in Belfast in the summer of 1922. Fighting in the city led to a forty-minute attack on the hospital and the distressed mother superior paged an emergency mayday to Geneva. In the aftermath of the attack, the ICRC recommended the formation of an independent Irish Red Cross society and sent its guidelines on the treatment of prisoners to Dublin. However, the Free State did not formally accede to the Geneva or Hague Conventions, while an Irish Red Cross Society was not established until 1939.[4]

Instead, the idea of establishing an Irish Red Cross society was taken up by Éamon de Valera and members of the Women Prisoners' Defence League. Appeals on behalf of Irish prisoners to Geneva increased throughout the autumn of 1922, culminating, in December 1922, in a visit by Dr Kathleen Lynn and Kathleen O'Brennan to the ICRC headquarters in Geneva. Armed with lists of detained men and details of ill-treatment and torture, they argued that the Provisional Government was acting in contravention of the 1921 Geneva Conventions, likely referring to the 1921 resolution. The two women urged the ICRC to investigate prison conditions in Ireland and to issue an 'exposé' as a 'moral force'.

After months of back and forth, the Red Cross delegation arrived in Dublin on 16 April 1923 to an 'agreeable, if slightly frosty', reception.[5] It was informed by Desmond FitzGerald, the minister for external affairs, that the situation in Ireland was not a war but a police operation. However, FitzGerald agreed to a 'technical' investigation of prison sites on the condition that the delegate, Rodolphe Haccius, could not speak to any prisoners. Haccius was a veteran with the Red Cross who had made visits to almost 200 political detainees in Budapest in 1919. He drew from this expertise in Ireland.

Between 18 and 25 April Haccius visited three internment camps, at Newbridge, Tintown (the Curragh) and Gormanston, as well as Mountjoy Gaol in Dublin. Unable to converse with the detained, his reports focused on elements of the prison visible to him – like bedding, sanitation facilities, correspondence, medical provisions and rations. Although conditions in the women's prisons had formed part of the appeals to the Red Cross, Haccius did not visit Kilmainham Gaol, where 300 women were held and where a hunger strike was ongoing. Instead, he was shown the vacant site at North Dublin Union, which he described as spacious with plentiful facilities.[6]

Overall, Haccius concluded that the 'serious accusations' made by republicans were unfounded, and that the prisoners, while not officially considered prisoners of war, were housed and treated in accordance with the 'general principles' of prisoner-of-war treatment in international law.

When the report appeared in the *Revue Internationale de Croix-Roux* in July 1923 it was lauded by the *Freeman's Journal* as 'sane, balanced and moderate in tone', while excerpts were read in the Dáil by the National Army commander in chief, Richard Mulcahy. Republicans countered the report with long editorials on conditions in prison and testimonies about alleged torture and ill-treatment, even as the Red Cross visit was taking place. Leopold Kerney, the republican envoy in Paris, drew attention to a note

COMITÉ INTERNATIONAL DE LA CROIX-ROUGE

CR.22.84.
GA/HC.

GENÈVE, le 12 Février 1923.
1, Promenade du Pin

La Comtesse de Gabriac

29 rue François 1er
Paris.

Madame,

J'ai l'honneur de vous accuser réception de votre lettre du 5 courant et de ses deux annexes.

Ainsi que je vous l'ai expliqué à Paris, le Comité International de la Croix- Rouge s'est depuis longtemps efforcé d'organiser une Société de la Croix- Rouge en Irlande.

Malheureusement, la situation politique de l'Irlande - le refus des républicains de reconnaitre le gouvernement régulier de l'État libre - la continuation de la guerre civile, rendent toute intervention de notre part très délicate. Notre Comité doit, en effet, soigneusement éviter d'avoir l'air de prendre parti dans des luttes politiques.

Veuillez croire, Madame, à ma respectueuse considération

G. Ador.

Président du Comité International de la Croix- Rouge
(G. Ador)

Fig. 1 (opposite) Letter from Gustave Ador, president of the International Committee of the Red Cross, to Countess de Gabriac, 12 February 1923. Appeals for intervention in Ireland reached the International Committee of the Red Cross (ICRC) from multiple sources. On 4 February 1923 Countess de Gabriac met with Gustave Ador, president of the ICRC, in Paris. The following day she sent Ador documents on the situation in Ireland, including a newspaper interview with de Valera, statements by the republican envoy in Paris, and a statement presented by the Women Prisoners Defence League to the US Congress. In this letter Ador gently refuses de Gabriac's requests for a Red Cross delegation to be sent to Ireland to investigate prison conditions. He writes that the political situation in Ireland made intervention on the part of the ICRC appear difficult, as the ICRC must 'carefully avoid appearing to take sides in political struggles'. By 1918 impartiality was already one of the key principles of the ICRC, though in practice its members often sided with liberal, internationalist politics, particularly against the threat of Bolshevism. De Gabriac's letter indicated that she very clearly took sides in the struggle, in favour of the republicans, or 'true patriots'. Despite her French title, Fanny de Gabriac was a Californian heiress with Irish heritage. Her grandfather, Richard B. Connolly, emigrated from Cork to New York in 1826, where he became a Tammany Hall Democrat, senator and comptroller. These familial ties had prompted a previous effort by Gabriac's nephew, Gavin Arthur, to prevent the execution of Erskine Childers. Arthur invoked his grandfather, US president Chester A. Arthur, and claimed he had 'no personal interest in Irish affairs other than those of humanity'. Yet, like de Gabriac, he was evidently sympathetic towards the republican cause. Both professed high hopes in the 'great ideal for which the Red Cross stands' – hopes that were surely dashed by Ador's clear reluctance for the Red Cross to investigate in Ireland. [Text: Lia Brazil / Document: National Library of Ireland, Ceannt and O'Brennan Papers, MS 41,522/4/9]

Fig 2 (below) Children in Dublin in 1922, dressed as members of the Red Cross. [Image: Part of the Independent Newspapers Ireland/NLI Collection, INDH211]

in Haccius's draft report explaining that he was unable to talk to prisoners, which had been removed from the final text published by the ICRC.

Disquiet about the report continued during the summer. In the Dáil George Gavan Duffy questioned the veracity of the ICRC report, and asked whether the local councils could perform another, more impartial inquiry. Dublin Metropolitan Council had been refused access to prisons and barracks for an inquiry the previous October. But W.T. Cosgrave argued that allegations against the prisons were 'false and malicious propaganda', suggesting that their conditions were preferable to that in lodging houses throughout Dublin.

The visit from the ICRC delegates and ensuing report allowed the Free State government to deflect criticism from its internment policy as it tightened its controls. Despite the April 1923 ceasefire, over 10,000 republicans remained interned. As well as humanitarian challenges, they mounted campaigns under domestic legislation for the right to trial under habeas corpus. To justify the continuation of internment, the government drafted new emergency legislation, the Public Safety (Emergency Powers) Act 1923. Effective from 1 August 1923, it provided for the continued detention of unsentenced prisoners whose release would be considered a 'danger to public safety'.[7] Faced with seemingly endless internment, republican women again travelled to Geneva demanding a revision of Haccius's report. Though the veteran delegate asked his superiors for the opportunity to return to Ireland, the ICRC refused, not willing to become further involved in Irish affairs.

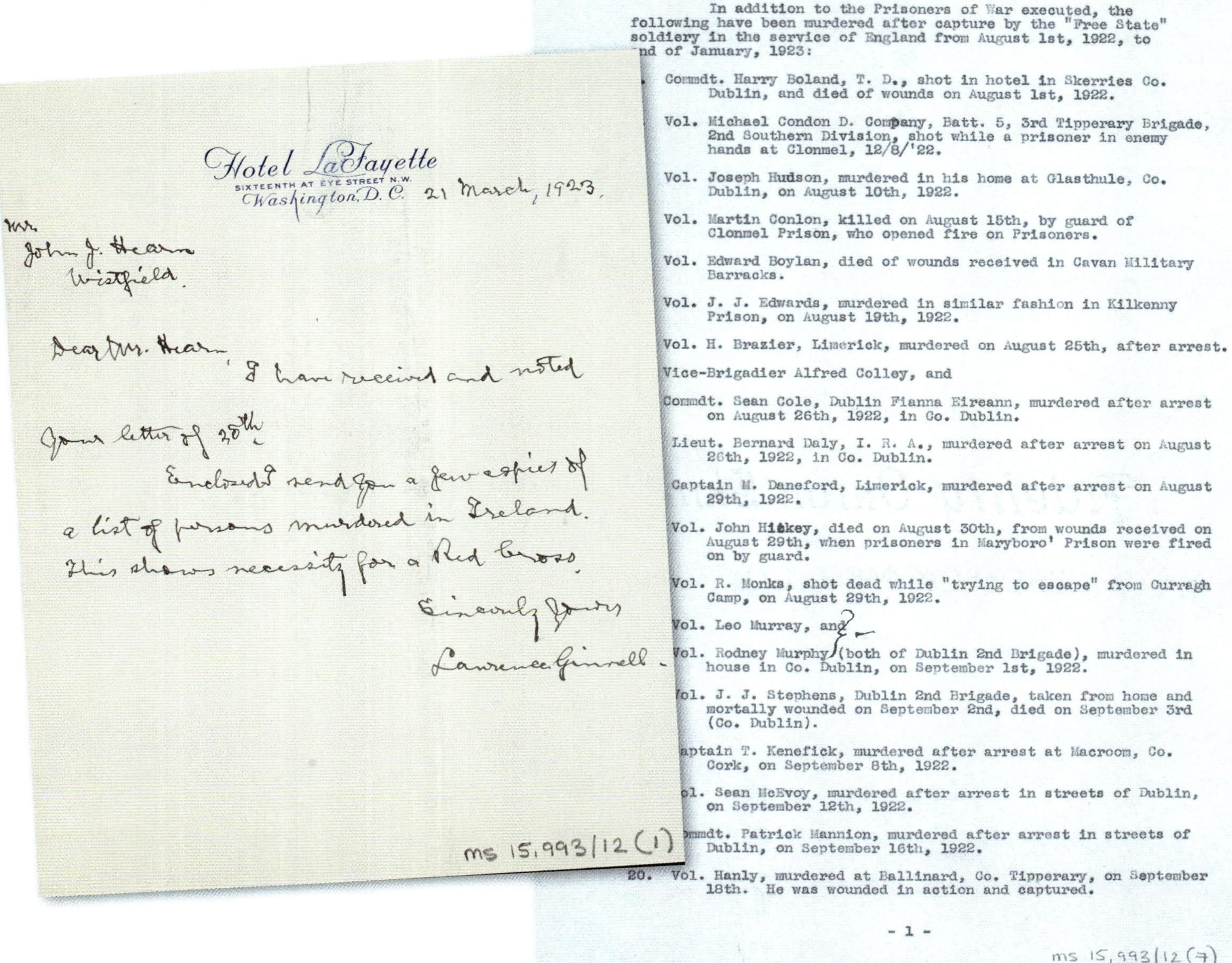

Hotel LaFayette
SIXTEENTH AT EYE STREET N.W.
Washington, D. C. 21 March, 1923.

Mr.
John J. Hearn
Westfield.

Dear Mr. Hearn,
I have received and noted your letter of 20th.
Enclosed I send you a few copies of a list of persons murdered in Ireland. This shows necessity for a Red Cross.
Sincerely yours
Lawrence Ginnell.

ms 15,993/12 (1)

In addition to the Prisoners of War executed, the following have been murdered after capture by the "Free State" soldiery in the service of England from August 1st, 1922, to end of January, 1923:

Commdt. Harry Boland, T. D., shot in hotel in Skerries Co. Dublin, and died of wounds on August 1st, 1922.

Vol. Michael Condon D. Company, Batt. 5, 3rd Tipperary Brigade, 2nd Southern Division, shot while a prisoner in enemy hands at Clonmel, 12/8/'22.

Vol. Joseph Hudson, murdered in his home at Glasthule, Co. Dublin, on August 10th, 1922.

Vol. Martin Conlon, killed on August 15th, by guard of Clonmel Prison, who opened fire on Prisoners.

Vol. Edward Boylan, died of wounds received in Cavan Military Barracks.

Vol. J. J. Edwards, murdered in similar fashion in Kilkenny Prison, on August 19th, 1922.

Vol. H. Brazier, Limerick, murdered on August 25th, after arrest.

Vice-Brigadier Alfred Colley, and

Commdt. Sean Cole, Dublin Fianna Eireann, murdered after arrest on August 26th, 1922, in Co. Dublin.

Lieut. Bernard Daly, I. R. A., murdered after arrest on August 26th, 1922, in Co. Dublin.

Captain M. Daneford, Limerick, murdered after arrest on August 29th, 1922.

Vol. John Hickey, died on August 30th, from wounds received on August 29th, when prisoners in Maryboro' Prison were fired on by guard.

Vol. R. Monks, shot dead while "trying to escape" from Curragh Camp, on August 29th, 1922.

Vol. Leo Murray, and

Vol. Rodney Murphy (both of Dublin 2nd Brigade), murdered in house in Co. Dublin, on September 1st, 1922.

Vol. J. J. Stephens, Dublin 2nd Brigade, taken from home and mortally wounded on September 2nd, died on September 3rd (Co. Dublin).

Captain T. Kenefick, murdered after arrest at Macroom, Co. Cork, on September 8th, 1922.

Vol. Sean McEvoy, murdered after arrest in streets of Dublin, on September 12th, 1922.

Commdt. Patrick Mannion, murdered after arrest in streets of Dublin, on September 16th, 1922.

20. Vol. Hanly, murdered at Ballinard, Co. Tipperary, on September 18th. He was wounded in action and captured.

- 1 -

ms 15,993/12 (7)

Fig. 3 Letter dated 21 March 1923 from Laurence Ginnell, the chief republican envoy to the United States, to John J. Hearn of the American Association for the Recognition of the Irish Republic (AARIR). Enclosed was a list of the names, ranks and, in most cases, the circumstances of death of fifty-two republicans 'unofficially' executed by Free State forces between August 1922 and January 1923 (the first page of which is reproduced here). Its purpose, as Ginnell explained, was to show 'the necessity for a Red Cross' in Ireland. County Westmeath-born Ginnell – a protégé of Michael Davitt and John Dillon – had been one of the few TDs elected to the First Dáil in 1918 with any real parliamentary experience. He was already a qualified barrister and an accomplished writer in 1898 when he became assistant secretary of William O'Brien's grassroots agrarian organisation, the United Irish League. Eight years later, fifty-four-year-old Ginnell began his parliamentary career as representative for Westmeath North, quickly earning a reputation in the House of Commons for tempestuousness and radicalism, particularly in relation to land reform. He was arrested in December 1907 for his advocacy of cattle driving during the 'ranch war' and served the first of several terms of 'imprisonment for Ireland' before 1921 that would severely affect his health. Ginnell's public criticism of the Irish Parliamentary Party led to his expulsion in 1910, but he retained his seat as a vocal independent, with an international profile, before becoming the only sitting MP to join the reconstituted Sinn Féin. After a brief tenure as the First Dáil's director of propaganda, and a year in Chicago in a Dáil consular role, Ginnell was dispatched in July 1921 as republican envoy to Argentina. He took the anti-Treaty side in 1922 and returned to Ireland in time to retain his seat in the June election and attended the inaugural meeting of the Third Dáil. He was forcibly ejected for his intentionally disruptive questioning of the assembly's constitutional status. As anti-Treaty representative in the United States, Ginnell, who Paul Hughes has described as 'one of the truly global figures of the Irish Revolution', worked with the AARIR to further the republican cause. He died suddenly of heart failure at Washington's Hotel Lafayette on 17 April 1923, less than a month after penning this hastily written cover letter to Hearn. 'Remarkably', Hughes notes, 'for a man whose political career began as a functionary in the Parnell-era Irish National League (1885), Ginnell ended life among the most zealous of anti-Treaty republicans'. [Document: National Library of Ireland, John J. Hearn Papers, MS 15,993/12 / See Paul Hughes, 'Laurence Ginnell (1852–1923), one of the truly global figures of the Irish revolution', *History Ireland*, vol. 31, no. 3, May–June 2003, pp. 38–41]

THE MOUNTJOY HOTEL

Menu Card

BREAKFAST

1 Pint of Tea
8oz. Bread
¾oz. Butter
1lb. of Stirabout
½ pint of Milk

DINNER

4oz. Meat, served with Broth
1 lb. of Potatoes
4oz. of Cabbage
4oz. of Bread

FRIDAY DINNER

4oz. of Bread
1lb. of Potatoes
1 Pint Vegetable Soup
2oz. plain boiled Rice
1 Pint of Milk

SUPPER

1 Pint of Tea or Cocoa
8oz. of Bread
¾oz. of Butter
½ Pint of Milk

Smoking Allowed, also Music and Card Playing

Details of Meals of the Members of the COMMON PEOPLE thrown out of Employment by the callous Military tactics of the Guests are not available.

Fig. 4 Pro-Treaty Handbill, 1923, referencing the popular satirical republican ballad 'The Mountjoy Hotel', penned in 1918 by Phil O'Neill ('Sliabh Rua'). The wide-scale arrest and detention of thousands of republicans after the introduction of the Army (Special Powers) Resolution in September 1922 led to inevitable overcrowding at internment centres like Dublin's Mountjoy Gaol. Anti-Treaty propagandists highlighted reports of inadequate and insanitary prison conditions and of 'unclean' and meagre food rations. Pro-Treaty propagandists, like the author of this handbill, sought to undermine the republican campaign by highlighting the findings of the International Committee of the Red Cross (ICRC) delegation's prison enquiry of April 1923. Rodolphe Haccius found, for example, that the kitchens at Tintown internment camp in the Curragh were 'well run' and the food provisions 'amply sufficient' and had 'no complaints to register concerning the food, medical care or treatment' provided to the 700 prisoners at Mountjoy. (The second clause of that sentence – 'not having been authorised to question internees' – was omitted from the published ICRC report of July 1923.) Appended to Haccius's report on Mountjoy was a detailed listing of the prisoners' daily food rations, reproduced almost exactly as a 'menu card' on this pro-Treaty handbill. The swipe at republican militants is driven home in the final line, which condemns the destructive tactics of those well-catered-for 'guests' at the 'Mountjoy Hotel' for causing deprivation among civilians. [Document: National Library of Ireland, EPH B178 / Quotations: Typescript reports from Rodolphe A. Haccius, ICRC, Eoin O'Duffy Papers, 19 April 1923 and 25 April 1923, MS 48,283/2/2 and MS 48,283/2/4, NLI]

The Prison Autograph Book of Seán Sharkey

John Crowley

Figs 1–5. Seán Sharkey's Autograph Book, Tintown No. 3, the Curragh, 1923, a collection of autographs, messages and sketches by prisoners held at the internment camp. Autograph books were quite common in such camps and provide a glimpse into the shared experiences of prison life. They were also an integral part of the material culture of internment camps like Tintown. Seán (Jack/John) Sharkey was born in Clonmel, County Tipperary in 1900, the son of a local jeweller. Initially educated in Clonmel, he transferred to Ratcliffe College in Leicester at the age of twelve with the objective of joining the Indian Civil Service. He later moved to London, to St Joseph's De la Salle College, before returning to his home place in 1918 where he became involved in Sinn Féin during the 1918 general election, lending his support to successful candidate Pierce McCann. He then joined his father's jewellery business rather than return to London and became active in the independence struggle with the Irish Volunteers, A Company, 4th Battalion (later part of the 5th Battalion), South Tipperary Brigade. As he admitted in his statement to the Bureau of Military History, 'it was then unusual in Clonmel at any rate for businessmen's sons to be associated with the Volunteer movement'. At the end of 1919 he was appointed intelligence officer for the company, taking part in arms raids and local ambushes, such as that 'near John Allsop's cottage about two miles from Clonmel on the road to Lisronagh'. Keen on photography, Sharkey carried a camera with him throughout 1919 and 1921, taking photographs of Tipperary Lawn Tennis Club for instance at the request of Ernie O'Malley: 'After the 2nd Southern Division was formed in May or June 1921, O'Malley, who was the Divisional O/C., asked me to get him some good photographs of the lawn tennis club in Clonmel. This club was frequented by British army officers and officers of the RIC, so I presumed he had in mind some plan such as capturing a number of them there. I took the photographs and gave them to him, but nothing came of it.' During the Civil War Sharkey was interned in Tintown in County Kildare. The lengthy delay in releasing prisoners following the order to dump arms in May 1923 and the ending of the Civil War was a source of deep frustration among the many thousands who went on hunger strike, in 1923. At its height there were over 7,500 prisoners on hunger strike with the vast majority – over 5,200 – in camps in County Kildare, including Tintown. The strike ended following the deaths of Cork Volunteer Denis Barry (interned in Newbridge) on 20 November at the Curragh Military Hospital and Cavan-born Andy Sullivan (interned in Mountjoy) on 23 November.

[Images: Seán Sharkey Collection, courtesy of Neil Sharkey, Tipperary Studies, Tipperary County Council / Quotations: BMH WS 1,100, John Sharkey]

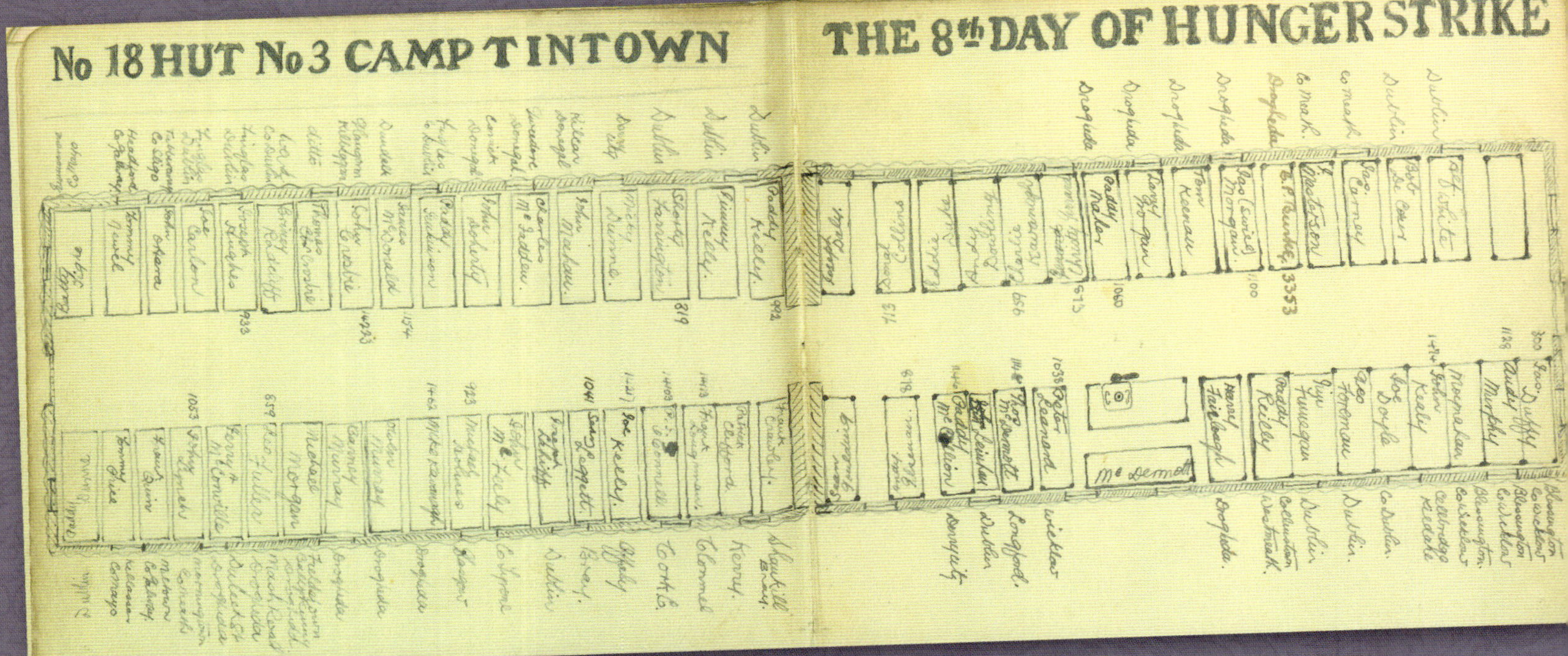

Tintown
No 3.
2nd Dec 1923.

Hugh Cully
Drogheda.
Co Louth

And the Moon shines
Bright to Night,
Along the SLANEY

Keeping Watch
above
The Hero's that are
SLEEPING

ON the Bank's of the
SLANEY far away,

Tintown Camp
The Curragh
19/10/23

Hungerstrike for unconditional release commenced last night at 12 o'clock. The watchword is: "Freedom or Death". Should it be the former please God we shall live to see it applied to Ireland or perish in our efforts to raise her among the nations of the earth; should it be the latter then we shall only follow the countless thousands of Irish martyrs who sacrificed their lives that the nation might live. Let us remember the immortal lines:

"There's yet a world where souls are free
Where tyrants taint not nature's bliss,
If only death its opening be
Ah! who would live a slave in this?"

Mire
Do Dearbhráthair na cúise
Eamonn MacBlorcaig

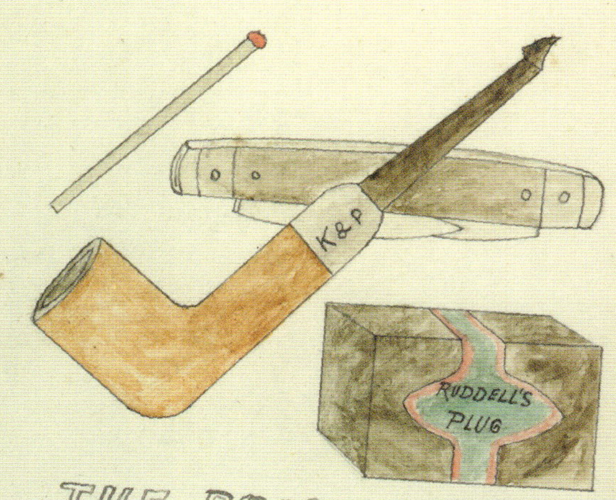

CASE STUDY

'Freedom or the Grave': The mass hunger strike of October–November 1923

Hélène O'Keeffe

On 1 November 1923 at her home in leafy Glasnevin, Marion O'Malley folded the Sinn Féin *Daily Sheet* and began composing a letter to the minister for defence, Richard Mulcahy. Still mourning the death of her seventeen-year-old-son Charlie, killed fighting the National Army in Dublin on 3 July 1922, and having never fully come to terms with her sons' militant republicanism, she had been moved to extreme anger by the news-sheet's profile of Ernie O'Malley as a paragon of resolve and self-sacrifice during the ongoing mass hunger strike.[1] Brothers Cecil and Patrick were reportedly 'very weak' in an internment camp in the Curragh, but of most concern to her was the depiction of her second-eldest son Ernie, a senior IRA officer and Sinn Féin TD, 'lying at deaths [*sic*] door' in Kilmainham Gaol.[2] 'Sudden collapse in his case', she reminded Mulcahy, would be especially dangerous given the multiple gunshot wounds he received during his dramatic capture twelve months before.[3] Her final admonition reflected her deep-seated anger at her sons' treatment: 'I warn you solemnly that if my sons die, I shall take steps to have you indicted in their murder'.

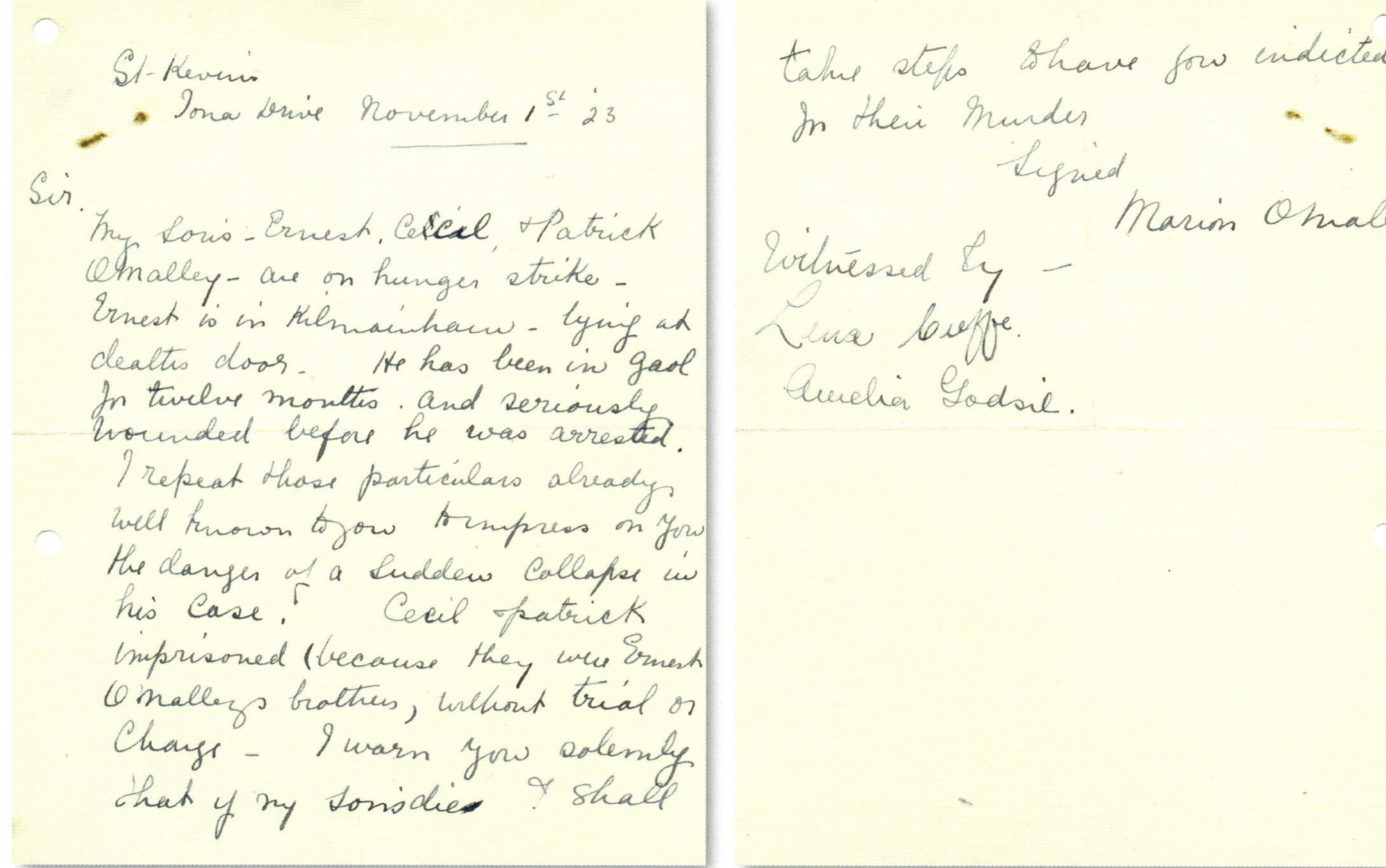

St-Kevins
Iona Drive November 1st 23

Sir.
My Sons - Ernest, Cecil, & Patrick O'Malley - are on hunger strike - Ernest is in Kilmainham - lying at deaths door. He has been in gaol for twelve months. and seriously wounded before he was arrested. I repeat those particulars already well known to you to impress on you the danger of a Sudden Collapse in his Case. Cecil & patrick imprisoned (because they were Ernest O'Malley's brothers, without trial or Charge - I warn you solemnly that if my sons die I shall take steps to have you indicted In their Murder

Signed
Marion O'Malley

Witnessed by -
Lena Keeffe.
Amelia Godsil.

Fig. 1 Original handwritten letter, dated 1 November 1923, from Marion O'Malley to Minister for Defence Richard Mulcahy, in which she states that should any of her three imprisoned sons die, she would 'take steps to have you indicted in their murder'. [Document: Ernie O'Malley Papers P17a/289. Reproduced by kind permission of UCD Archives]

"Truth on their lips and Courage in their hearts."

SINN FEIN HEAD QUARTERS, 23 SUFFOLK STREET.

DAILY SHEET.

No. 3. 27th OCTOBER, 1923. PRICE 1d.

ALL-IRELAND HUNGER-STRIKE.

TINTOWN No. 3 CAMP.

In our last edition we gave you an account of the brutal removal to Tintown No. 2 Camp in open lorries of the Mountjoy prisoners who were on Hunger Strike for seven days.

On the same day, 19th October, at 7 p.m., fifty-two men to Tintown No. 3 Camp, already seven days on Hunger Strike, were removed from "A" Wing, Mountjoy. They were driven to Broadstone, poorly clad, in open lorries, and when at Broadstone they were kept for about an hour in the open before they were removed to the train. When they got to the Curragh they were kept in the train famished with the cold for over three hours. They were then put into lorries and kept another hour in the open air before being driven to Tintown No. 3 Camp. The whole party were in a pitiable plight from cold and exposure. At the Camp they were again kept in the open air for another hour before they were shifted into a hut, into which most of the men had to be carried at 4 a.m.

The doctors also in this Camp will not treat any man "who refuses food."

Hot water was cut off from the strikers for three days.

The men are so weak they are confined to bed practically all day. The sanitary conditions are deplorable, and the men are now too weak to clean huts and remove refuse. Several are housed in stables and suffer intensely from cold. There are no stoves or heating apparatus of any kind. Purgatives supplied are totally insufficient.

A large number of boys from 16 to 20 insisted on joining the Hunger Strike. Men over 50 have done the same.

The Authorities who were inclined, like Mr. Cosgrave, to believe this Strike was a hoax, now realise their mistake when the gravity of the danger is apparent. The men stand firm. They are fighting against fearful odds for what should be every man's birthright—Freedom. If you would realize the conditions of these Camps, go down to the trains and watch for the haggard, tattered men who stumble on to the platforms. These are the released prisoners. Penniless they arrive to find penury before them, wife and children, in many cases, on the rates, having been deprived of the earnings of their rightful bread-winners.

The Authorities who think they can cope with the unemployment consequent on the demobilization of the Free State Army by keeping our men in jail lest they should compete with their quondam soldiers, should remember that economic problems are not so easily solved.

In this Camp, Brian O'Higgins, T.D., Clare, who has been in delicate health since his imprisonment, is also on Hunger Strike.

TINTOWN No. 2 CAMP.

In the above Camp, Jack O'Brien, of Minard, Dingle, a boy of 16, who was arrested last February while attending the National School, is on Hunger Strike. Since his arrest his health, always delicate, has become worse. This child is hardly a danger to the public. He also has been served with a Detention Certificate, which entitles his jailors to keep him.

Irish fathers and mothers, ye who gather your boys and girls comfortably round your sides at night, do you ever think of the Jack O'Briens' who also have parents with feelings like yours?

Perhaps such facts have not until lately come to the ears of the Clergy? We will assume they have not. We have been taught to believe they loved Ireland and her children and would feign believe it still. Yet, until to-day their voice has been silent. Sligo sends us the first gleam of hope. We have received the following wire:—

"Reverend Canon Butler, as deputy for His Lordship Dr. Coyne, of Sligo, pledged his solemn word to Republican Deputation, who waited on him to-day, that none of the Hunger Strikers will be let die."

Fig. 2 The 27 October 1923 edition of the Sinn Féin bulletin *Daily Sheet*, which chronicled the mass hunger strike in the autumn of 1923. Like the IRA executive, Sinn Féin was supportive of the prison protest, and anxious to maximise the propaganda potential of an 'All-Ireland Hunger-Strike'. This edition updates its readers on efforts by the prison authorities to divide the hardcore of strikers in Mountjoy and distribute them among the camps outside Dublin. It also highlights the poor conditions in Tintown and the doctors' refusal on ethical grounds to treat the hunger strikers. Despite the writer's enthusiasm about the participation of 'men over 50' and a 'large number of boys from 16 to 20', such vulnerable cohorts would have been excluded had the prisoners followed the advice of the IRA executive in August 1923. This propagandist also deftly ascribes the government's refusal to release the Civil War prisoners to concerns that they would compete for employment with the thousands of newly demobilised National Army soldiers. [Document: National Library of Ireland, Thomas Johnson Papers, MS 17,141/17]

Prisoners of conscience

In August 1923 the electorate had entrusted Mulcahy, and the other members of W.T. Cosgrave's renamed pro-Treaty party, Cumann na nGaedheal, with the formidable task of post-Civil War state building. The fourth Dáil, convened without the forty-four abstentionist Sinn Féin TDs on 19 September, was committed to maintaining the delicate peace achieved in May, reinforcing its legitimacy and consolidating power in the nascent state. Of the approximately 12,000 republicans in Free State prisons and internment camps in July 1923, more than 2,000 rank-and-file IRA members had been gradually released because of their relative unimportance or their willingness to sign an undertaking renouncing anti-government militarism.[4] The continued detention of the remaining prisoners under the new Public Safety Act was an effective deterrent to the resumption of violence by the IRA, which had dumped but not surrendered its arms at Frank Aiken's call.[5] For those still behind bars in the wake of a militarily ceded Civil War, resort to hunger strike was a way to register their opposition to the 'illegitimate' Free State and its chiefs, to challenge the steady criminalisation of political prisoners, and to demand unconditional release. But the largest hunger strike in Irish history was not a carefully planned prison protest. Rather, it was initiated spontaneously by 300 men in Mountjoy's D wing, frustrated by their prolonged incarceration in the overcrowded, badly ventilated Victorian prison. The decision to deploy the 'final weapon of passive resistance' was inspired by the republican tradition of hunger striking.[6] It was also influenced by

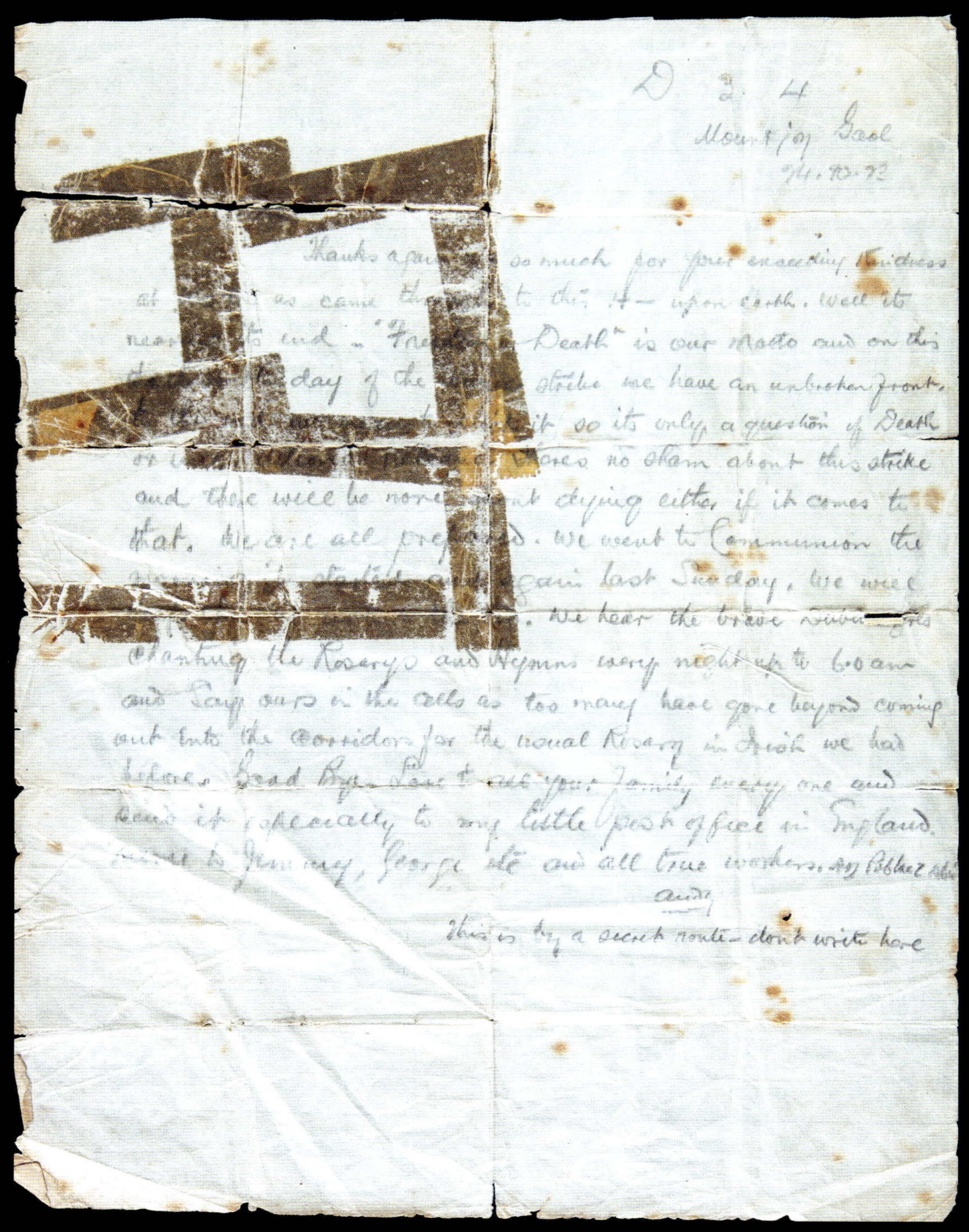

D 2 4
Mountjoy Gaol
24.10.23

Thanks again [illegible] so much for your exceeding kindness at [illegible] as came through to this H— upon earth. Well its near [illegible] to end. "Freedom [illegible] Death" is our Motto and on this [illegible] day of the [illegible] strike we have an unbroken front. [illegible] it so its only a question of Death or [illegible] theres no sham about this strike and there will be none about dying either if it comes to that. We are all prepared. We went to Communion the [illegible] again last Sunday. We will [illegible]. We hear the brave Dublin girls chanting the Rosarys and Hymns every night up to 6.0 am and Say ours in the cells as too many have gone beyond coming out into the Corridors for the usual Rosary in Irish we had before. Good Bye Love to all your family every one and send it especially to my little post office in England. [illegible] to Jimmy, George etc and all true workers. [illegible]

Andy

this is by a secret route – dont write here

Fig. 3 A prison letter written from D wing in Mountjoy Gaol on 24 October 1923 by Andrew (Andy) O'Sullivan and delivered 'by a secret route' to his friend Kattie. It was the eleventh day of O'Sullivan's fatal forty-day hunger strike in the prison he describes as 'H -[ell] on earth'; however, his unwavering resolve to 'stick it' is clear in the letter. Likewise palpable is the writer's devout Catholicism. Like the other strikers, he received Communion on Sundays and was buoyed by prayer and the nightly ritual 'chanting of Rosarys [*sic*] and Hymns' by the 'brave Dublin girls' outside the prison walls. The strikers said prayers in their cells, he explained, 'as too many have gone beyond coming out into the Corridors for the usual Rosary in Irish'. Forty-one-year-old O'Sullivan died on 22 November 1923 in St Bricin's Military Hospital, Dublin. An instructor and inspector with over ten years' experience in the Department of Agriculture and Technical Instruction in Mallow, O'Sullivan had served as an ordinary IRA Volunteer in the Cork No. 4 Brigade during the War of Independence. However, during the Civil War the IRA leveraged his civil service expertise by making him the 1st Southern Division acting officer in charge of civil administration. While operating in Cork city in July and early August 1922, O'Sullivan implemented several imaginative and highly effective republican fund-raising strategies. These included the interdiction of Free State customs duties in the Cork Custom House, and the levying of unpaid income taxes upon the city's largest merchants. In roughly a month O'Sullivan raised over £100,000 for the anti-Treaty cause and provoked consternation among government leaders Michael Collins and William T. Cosgrave. [Document: courtesy of Cork Public Museum / See John Borgonovo, 'Civil Administration and Economic Endowments in the Munster Republic's "Real Capital", July–August 1922', *Éire-Ireland*, vol. 58, nos 3 & 4, pp. 9–34]

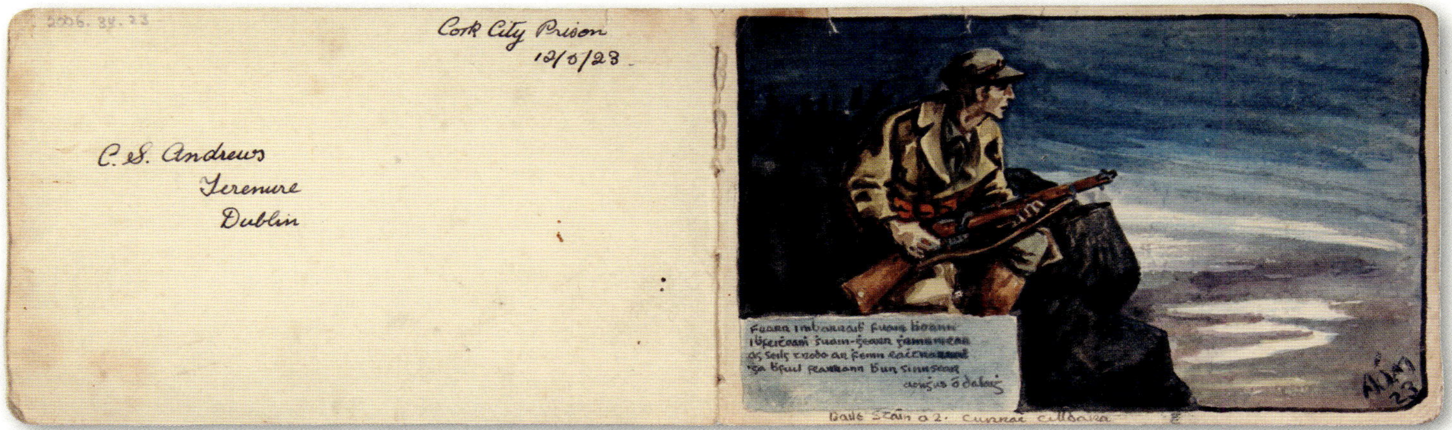

Fig. 4 A page from a prison autograph book that belonged to Jim Hurley, future bursar of University College Cork. It was in his possession while he was imprisoned in the Curragh during the Civil War. The image on the right is a drawing by a fellow inmate and the opposite page shows the signature of Todd Andrews, who served as an adjutant to Liam Lynch during the closing phases of the Civil War. He went on to become a highly successful civil servant and a senior figure in Fianna Fáil. [Image: courtesy of Cork Public Museum]

the unexpected 27.5 per cent share of electoral support for Sinn Féin in the August 1923 general election, and the concessions granted to the women Civil War hunger strikers, such as the indomitable Mary MacSwiney.[7] The mass hunger strike began in Mountjoy at midnight on 13 October 1923 and spread sporadically and without coordination or instruction to other sites of detention. As striker Peadar O'Donnell put it simply: 'No one was ordered on to it, but then no one felt they could stay off it'.[8] The IRA leadership on the outside was latterly supportive, even though the prisoners' councils ignored Aiken's August advice to select a small, reliable cohort of participants if they resorted to hunger strike. Éamon de Valera, imprisoned in Arbour Hill since August and more pragmatic about the political currency of republican self-sacrifice in the post-Civil War context, remained aloof.

After ten days Mountjoy hunger strikers had been joined by internees in the sprawling Tintown camp in the Curragh; Hare Park; Gormanstown Camp; Newbridge Barracks; Kilkenny, Dundalk and Cork jails; and fifty-one women prisoners in the North Dublin Union. Some prisoners in Tralee, Castlebar and aboard the prison ship *Argenta* in Belfast would soon follow suit. The surge of enrolment was exhilarating, but an uncoordinated mass protest involving a reported 8,000 prisoners at its peak on 24 October was entirely unsustainable.[9] The success of hunger strike as a moral tactic depends on a willingness to pursue it to the end, an imperative summed up in the Mountjoy prisoners' manifesto with Terence MacSwiney's phrase: 'Freedom or the Grave'.[10] Many of the 1923 hunger strikers had bowed to peer pressure or were swept up by what Peadar O'Donnell called 'a sort of moral conscription'.[11] Curragh internee Frank O'Connor testified to how his refusal to join led to his ostracisation by fellow prisoners.[12] Ernie O'Malley's inner turmoil at the prospect of an 'unsoldierly death', and his doubts about his own stamina and the strategic value of hunger strike – an increasingly 'obsolete weapon' since Terence MacSwiney was allowed to die in Brixton Prison in 1920 – are laid bare in his Civil War memoir.[13] His unwillingness to exempt himself when younger men were prepared to die, and his fidelity to the republican 'doctrine of triumph through endurance', proved the stronger impulses in the autumn of 1923.[14] Cavan-born IRA intelligence officer Andy O'Sullivan was likewise committed, writing zealously to his friend Kattie on the eleventh day of his fast of the 'unbroken front' in Mountjoy. 'To the end we mean to stick it, so its [*sic*] only a question of death or unconditional release'.[15]

In most cases, the reality of extreme depravation quickly eroded the thin layers of resolve. Todd Andrews noted the mounting strain in the Curragh as more and more strikers peeled off: 'Men felt that in abandoning the strike they were guilty of weakness. Human nature being what it is, they resented those who continued to hold out'.[16] Morale was also sapped by the government's continued commitment to the phased release of prisoners who signed the pledge, and by the absence of the cross-sectional public support that had buoyed the hunger strikers in Mountjoy in April 1920. Enduring censorship precluded sympathetic media coverage, and the Catholic Church was overtly hostile to the recalcitrant republican prisoners. By mid-November only a hard core of roughly 200 prisoners was still refusing food. Petitions, resolutions, letters like Marion O'Malley's and the efforts of the prisoners' release campaign fell on deaf ministerial ears. Mulcahy, for instance, dismissed a telegram from Cork County Council recommending a general amnesty with the question: 'are our people or prisoners to be our first consideration?'[17]

Refusing to yield

Cosgrave's government refused to yield to the prisoners' absolutist demands, unwilling to undermine hard-line decisions made during the Civil War. Indeed, the president of the Executive Council considered offering 'grace', a sign of weakness, and rubbished comparisons between Terence MacSwiney's celebrated, self-sacrificial resistance to 'illegitimate' British rule in 1920 and the contemporary strikers, who challenged the legitimate, democratically mandated government of the Free State. Cosgrave and his ministers remained

Fig. 5 Dan Breen throwing in the ball at the replay of the 1920 All-Ireland football final (cancelled in the aftermath of Bloody Sunday), which took place in Croke Park on 11 June 1922. Tensions within sporting bodies like the Gaelic Athletic Association (GAA) during and after the Civil War reflected wider political divisions. Several 'legacy issues' impacted the GAA well after Frank Aiken's May 1923 dump-arms order, not least the continued detention behind bars and barbed wire of a large number of republican internees. During the 1923 general election campaign, government candidates, who framed the prisoner question as a test of their will to govern, supported continued detention, while their republican opponents demanded the swift release of Civil War internees. Unsurprisingly, the issue was particularly contentious in Cork city and county, which remained a hotbed of republican sentiment long after its military eclipse, and had a disproportionate share of the prisoner population. The GAA in that county, long a well spring of advanced nationalism, suffered disproportionately from the enforced absence of large numbers of young men. The mass hunger strike by republican prisoners from mid-October 1923 raised the stakes and struck a particular cord within the Gaelic games fraternity in Cork. Three years earlier, in the autumn of 1920, the Cork County Board had called a halt to all games organised under its auspices in support of the hunger strikes of Terence MacSwiney in Brixton Prison and the local prisoners in Cork men's jail. It had resumed its activities, reluctantly, given its anti-Treaty stance, in early 1922. The arrest and detention during the Civil War of the board secretary, Pádraig O'Keeffe, and chairman, Seán Murphy (the former released after eight months in April 1923, and the latter detained until 1924), added a personal dimension for their fellow board members. The issue came to a head between late October and mid-November 1923. In response to a Sinn Féin executive circular requesting that all clubs cease playing in protest at the continued detention of republicans, the Sarsfield club did not fulfil a fixture on 28 October. The decision provoked rebuke from the acting chair at the subsequent board meeting, but the collective sympathies of the club delegates were clear in their decision to back Sarsfields and not confirm dates for any club fixtures in the immediate future. The stakes were raised significantly a week later on the night of 3–4 November when the goalposts at Sarsfield's pitch at Rivertown were torn down, and the 'home' of Gaelic games in the city, the Cork Athletic Grounds (on the site of the modern Páirc Uí Chaoimh), effectively destroyed. The four dressing rooms were burned to the ground, the reserved stand was partially burned, the goalposts sawn in half, the pitch dug up, and the nets cut, rendering the facility redundant for three months. Attacks were also made on other sporting grounds in the city on the same night, with the goalposts at Turner's Cross soccer pitch and Mardyke rugby ground removed. The death on 20 November of the popular Cork hurler, former county board member and republican hunger striker Denis Barry heightened tensions further still, all the more so because of the controversies that followed his death (notably the government's initial refusal to release his body to his relatives for burial in his native county, and the denial by the bishop of Cork, Daniel Cohalan, of a church or the services of a clergyman for Barry's funeral). The board's decision to send a wreath to the Barry family, and to be represented in the cortège that made its way to the republican plot in St Finbarr's cemetery, was a principled indication to authorities of both Church and state that the Gaelic games fraternity in the county would not readily bow the knee on this most sensitive of topics. [Text: Gabriel Doherty / Image: RTÉ Cashman Collection, 0506/056, © RTÉ Archives]

steadfast and silent when two prisoners succumbed to the effects of more than thirty-five days on hunger strike. Denis Barry died of heart failure at Curragh Hospital on 20 November 1923, followed two days later by Mountjoy prisoner Andy O'Sullivan. Mary MacSwiney delivered a short oration at Barry's grave, located close to her brother's in the republican plot at St Finbarr's Cemetery in their native Cork city. She must have been keenly aware that day, when the doors of Cork's churches were closed to the mourners, of the inconsistency of the Catholic bishop of Cork, Daniel Cohalan. Three years after attending Terence MacSwiney's bedside, presiding at his funeral, and eulogising his political 'martyrdom', Cohalan denounced hunger strikes like Mary MacSwiney's as sinful acts of suicide, and denied Denis Barry Christian burial rites in his diocese.

An intervention by Cardinal Michael Logue, however, proved influential in bringing the pyrrhic protest to a close. Architect of the bishop's pastoral of October 1922 that ensured that many republican prisoners were refused the sacraments, Logue was an unexpected advocate for compromise. In a letter read aloud at Masses in his archdiocese of Armagh on 18 November 1923, he appealed to the hunger strikers to abandon the 'dangerous and unlawful expedient', while urging the government to release the remaining, 'untried and unconvicted' prisoners.[18] The cardinal's new conciliatory attitude was doubtless influenced by the Vatican's disapproval of the Irish hierarchy's staunchly pro-Treaty attitude. Logue's visit to the strike leadership in Kilmainham Gaol also eased its decision to call off the faltering protest after forty-one days. On 23 November Michael Kilroy, officer commanding the prisoners in Kilmainham, announced that he had accepted the cardinal's guidance to cease on humanitarian grounds. Tomás Derrig and David Robinson were dispatched to the other prisons to relay the decision.

The weeks before Christmas 1923 saw the phased release of all women prisoners and most of the men – the final stages, the government claimed, of a process begun six months before and, as such, reflective of the futility of the republican last stand. But the requirement to 'sign the form' was quietly abandoned and the swift pace of releases spoke of an official urgency to clear the prisons. 'We were flattened', Sighle Humphreys recalled after her liberation from the North Dublin Union in November. 'We felt the Irish public had forgotten us. The tinted trappings of our fight were hanging like rags about us'.[19] The republican roll of honour suggests that there were at least six more male victims of the forty-one-day fast in late 1923 and early 1924, and, as testified to by so many doctors' letters in the military service pensions files, many more would suffer long-term physical and psychological effects.[20] High value prisoners like Ernie O'Malley were retained until the summer of 1924 when the government made the judicious decision to declare a general amnesty. Released on 16 July 1924, Éamon de Valera was Kilmainham's Gaol's last prisoner. Within two decades, the Fianna Fáil taoiseach, whose wartime Emergency Powers Act precipitated a new era of hunger striking by IRA internees, would face the ire of a new generation of letter writers.[21]

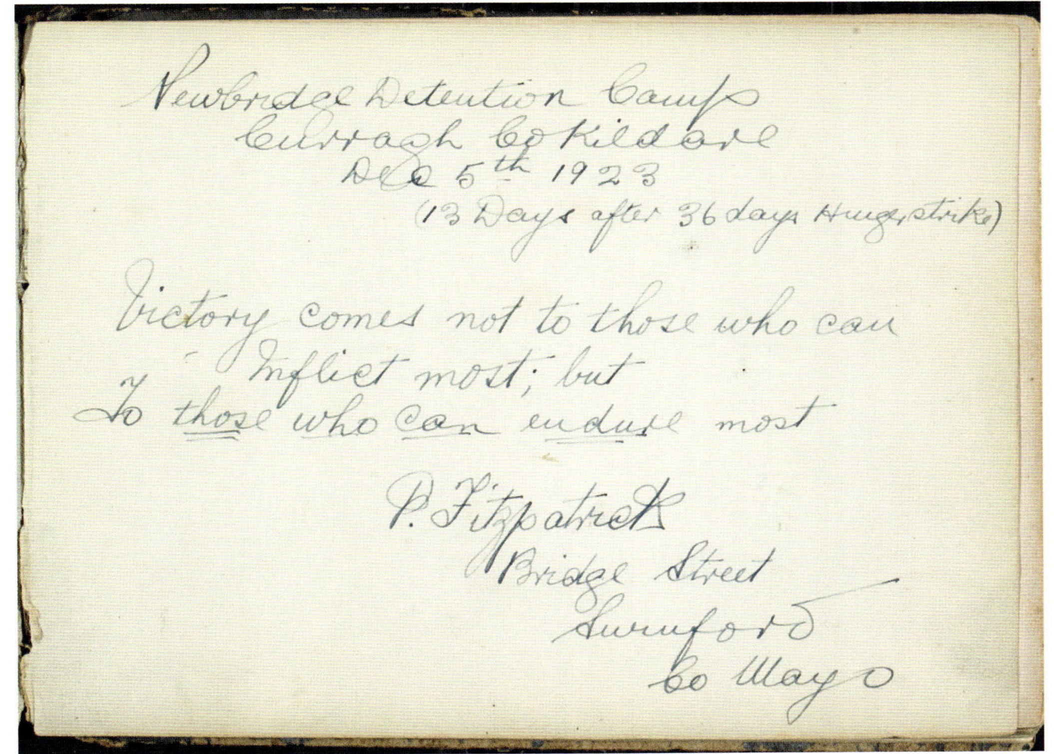

Newbridge Detention Camp
Curragh Co Kildare
Dec 5th 1923
(13 Days after 36 days Hunger strike)

Victory comes not to those who can
inflict most; but
to those who can endure most

P. Fitzpatrick
Bridge Street
Swinford
Co Mayo

Fig. 6 A page from an autograph book belonging to a prisoner in Newbridge internment camp in 1923. The dedication on the autograph book's first page reads: 'In loving memory of Denis Barry (of Cork) who died on hunger-strike in Newbridge Camp 20th November 1923. RIP'. This entry, dated 5 December 1923, was made by Cork-born IRA officer Patrick Fitzpatrick of Swinford, County Mayo thirteen days after his thirty-six-day hunger strike. Despite the cessation of the strike without any concessions from the Free State government, Fitzpatrick remained defiant, paraphrasing the famous line from Terence MacSwiney's address to Cork Corporation on his inauguration as lord mayor in 1920: 'It is not those who can inflict the most but those who can suffer the most who will conquer [...] Those whose faith is strong will endure to the end and triumph'. [Image: National Library of Ireland, MS 42,236 / Information about Patrick Fitzpatrick supplied by Ann Leydon, Charlestown, County Mayo]

John Devoy (right) and Desmond FitzGerald at Cobh, County Cork in July 1924. [Image: part of the Independent Newspapers Ireland/ NLI Collection, INDH357]

SECTION 8

Global Connections

Fig. 1 Éamon de Valera, 'President of the Irish Republic', accompanied by the briefcase-carrying Harry Boland, Sinn Féin TD and Irish Republican Brotherhood envoy, leading a parade of American dignitaries around the New York City Polo Grounds, 31 October 1920. Over 40,000 (mainly Irish-American) supporters attended this last great meeting of de Valera's eighteen-month American tour. It was organised to protest the death of Terence MacSwiney in Brixton Prison six days earlier, following his seventy-four-day hunger strike. [Image: National Library of Ireland, NPA POLF148]

CHAPTER 9

Divided Allies: Irish-America responds to the Irish Civil War

Michael Doorley

The role of the United States in Ireland's Civil War can be seen through the lens of a broader Irish-American relationship with Irish nationalist movements during the revolutionary period (1912–23). This relationship was not always an easy one given that the objectives of Irish-American nationalism and Irish nationalism frequently diverged. By the time of the outbreak of the Civil War in the summer of 1922, the Irish-American nationalist movement was already a deeply divided force. These divisions were born of a bitter dispute between Judge Daniel Cohalan, leader of the New York-based Friends of Irish Freedom, and Éamon de Valera, president of Sinn Féin, during the latter's eighteen-month mission to the US in 1919–20.

To some extent Irish-American divisions over the Treaty and Civil War mirrored this earlier split, but other factors also played a role in determining attitudes towards the conflict in Ireland. Many Irish-Americans, bewildered and appalled by reports of armed clashes between erstwhile comrades, strove to adopt a neutral stance. Others made fruitless efforts to mediate between the warring parties. Meanwhile, in Ireland, each side in the Civil War looked towards its respective Irish-American allies for continued assistance, though in radically different ways.

The Irish-American split of 1920

In order to assess the impact of the Civil War on Irish-America, it is necessary to outline the complex relationship between Irish nationalism and its Irish-American counterpart during the revolutionary period. Historically, nationalists in Ireland looked to the large Irish diaspora in the US for both financial assistance and diplomatic support. It has been estimated that by 1900 almost five million Americans were either first- or second-generation Irish, a number that exceeded the contemporary population of Ireland.[1] While not all Irish-Americans took an interest in Irish politics, significant numbers did, particularly during times of political turmoil. In turn, Irish nationalists of all political persuasions saw Irish-American help as vital to their respective campaigns.

For much of the late nineteenth and early twentieth centuries, Clan na Gael, led by the old Fenian rebel John Devoy, was the voice of Irish-American revolutionary nationalism. The Clan worked closely with the Irish Republican Brotherhood (IRB) in Ireland and saw the establishment of an Irish republic as its key objective. The founding of the *Gaelic American* newspaper in 1903, with Devoy as editor, gave the Clan a public voice, but with its secret membership, passwords and rituals, the organisation did not attract mass support. In the years before the First World War, when Home Rule seemed inevitable, John Redmond's United Irish League of America (UILA) was in the ascendant.[2]

Friends of Irish Freedom

This situation changed in 1914 following Redmond's declaration of support for Britain's war effort. Even the *Irish World,* which had trumpeted the cause of Home Rule and John Redmond before the war, briskly withdrew its support. In March 1916, at an Irish Race Convention in New York, the Clan formed a new broad-based organisation, the Friends of Irish Freedom (FOIF), designed to appeal to Redmond's disillusioned supporters in America and cultivate a united Irish-American front in support of Irish republican ideals. The FOIF was backed by both the *Irish World* and the *Gaelic American* newspapers and drew support from all sections of Irish-American society.[3]

FOIF leader and Devoy's close ally, Justice Daniel Cohalan, had been chairman of the Clan in New York prior to his appointment as a New York State Supreme Court justice in 1911. A high-profile public figure in comparison to the more reclusive Devoy, Cohalan had close links with the Tammany Hall Democratic Party political machine in New York and with senior members of Congress. He was also well respected by leading members of the Catholic hierarchy, such as Cardinal William O'Connell of Boston and Cardinal James Gibbons of Baltimore.[4] From the outset the FOIF pledged itself to 'encourage and assist any movement that will tend to bring about the national independence of Ireland'.[5] However, the movement also had specifically American objectives, which proved a source of conflict with nationalists from Ireland in later years. Both Cohalan and Devoy sought to counter what they perceived as a pro-British movement in the United States because it was detrimental to Irish-American interests, and in 1916 fiercely opposed the prospect of American involvement in the First World War on Britain's side. The campaign was rendered redundant by US entry into the war in April 1917, and Coholan, facing media accusations of treason because of his links with Germany prior to the 1916 Rising, adopted a low profile and professed his allegiance to the American flag. Irish-Americans had always prided themselves on loyalty to America at war and were wary of allegations of disloyalty. Even verbal attacks on Britain, now America's ally, could be construed as attacks on America itself. As a result many FOIF branches ceased operation for the duration of the war.[6]

This stance rankled with some FOIF and Clan members such as Joe McGarrity, the powerful Clan leader in Philadelphia, and many newly arrived Irish nationalists also felt that Irish objectives, such as the campaign against British conscription in Ireland, should take precedence over Irish-American fears about appearing disloyal to the American nation. These so-called Irish exiles, including Sinn Féin 'envoy' Patrick McCartan, Liam Mellows, who had fought in the 1916 Rising, Hanna Sheehy Skeffington and Nora Connolly, a daughter of the executed James Connolly, supported a new organisation led by Irish-American poet and singer Peter Golden known as the Irish Progressive League (IPL).

The IPL took a more radical stance on the Irish question, especially in its campaign of protest against British conscription in Ireland. Not all Irish nationalists in America supported this approach. The 1916 veteran Diarmuid Lynch, who became national secretary of the FOIF in 1918, argued that Irish-American disunity played into the hands of anti-Irish elements in the United States. While Lynch pleaded for 'discipline and 'obedience', Liam Mellows,

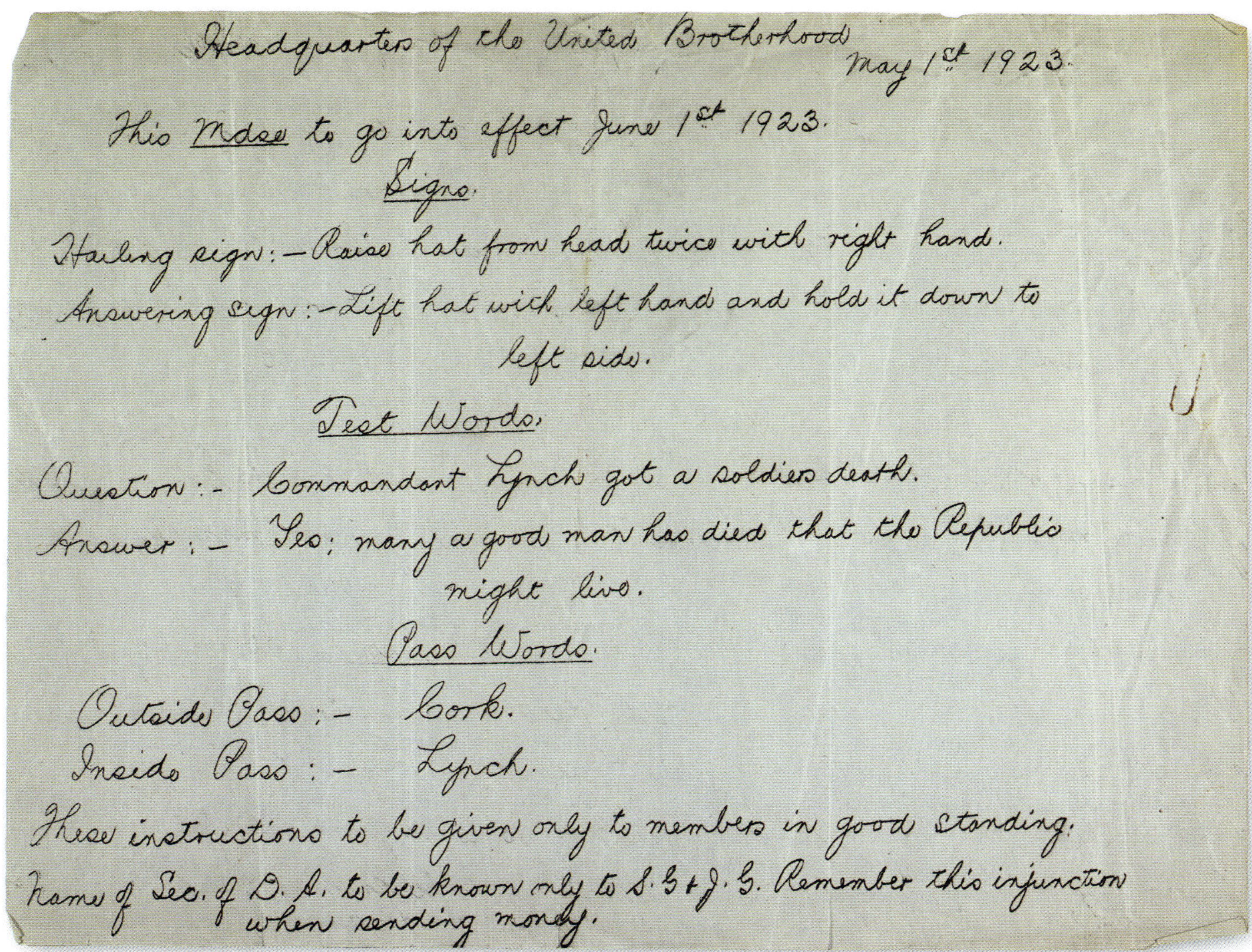

Headquarters of the United Brotherhood May 1st 1923.

This Mdse to go into effect June 1st 1923.

Signs.

Hailing sign:—Raise hat from head twice with right hand.

Answering sign:—Lift hat with left hand and hold it down to left side.

Test Words.

Question:— Commandant Lynch got a soldiers death.

Answer:— Yes; many a good man has died that the Republic might live.

Pass Words.

Outside Pass:— Cork.

Inside Pass:— Lynch.

These instructions to be given only to members in good standing.

Name of Sec. of D. A. to be known only to S. G + J. G. Remember this injunction when sending money.

Fig. 2 A list of instructions for circulation 'to members in good standing' of Clan na Gael in May 1923. Clan na Gael was the clandestine Irish-American sister organisation of the secretive Irish Republican Brotherhood. The impact of the death of the anti-Treaty IRA chief of staff, Liam Lynch, on 10 April 1923 is clear in the organisation's choice of 'test words' and 'pass words'. [Document: National Library of Ireland, Joseph McGarrity Papers, MS 17,655/6/2]

MS 41,511/1/4

This Is To Certify That

Willard De Lue

having declared acceptance of the National Constitution of the

Friends of Irish Freedom

and paid the national membership fee of $1.00 for the current year is hereby accredited a member of this organization.

Diarmuid Lynch

NATIONAL SECRETARY

Date OCT 23 1919

1776

1916

Fig. 3 Willard de Lue's Friends of Irish Freedom (FOIF) membership card signed by the national secretary, Diarmuid Lynch. The decorative Celtic border, the representation of Ireland's four provinces, and the profiles of George Washington and Patrick Pearse identified the cardholder as a member of the Irish-American organisation devoted to the realisation of a thirty-two-county Irish republic. During his eighteen-month mission to America, the republic's self-styled 'President', Éamon de Valera, frequently compared Ireland's independence campaign to America's successful revolutionary war against Britain (1775–83). Cork-born Diarmuid Lynch, the effective FOIF national secretary, who helped to swell the organisation's membership and coffers after his appointment in 1918, had first emigrated to the United States in 1896. He became an American citizen and was active in Irish-American nationalist circles for twelve years before returning to Ireland, where he became a member of the supreme council of the clandestine Irish Republican Brotherhood (IRB). He was aide-de-camp to James Connolly in the GPO during the 1916 Easter Rising, and was perhaps the most senior IRB participant to escape execution. Following his release in 1917, he resumed his IRB leadership and became Sinn Féin's food controller during a campaign to prevent food exports to Britain. This triggered his 1918 arrest and deportation to the United States where he was elected in absentia as TD for Cork South-East in the December 1918 general election. Lynch's role as FOIF national secretary brought him into public conflict with de Valera (his 'chief'), prompting his resignation as Dáil deputy in August 1920. It was a decision, Lynch told his Cork constituents, which allowed him the freedom to continue his 'efforts for the recognition of the Irish republic on the lines which long and practical experience in America have shown me to be for the best interest of the Irish cause'. From the 1920 split in the FOIF, the American Association for the Recognition of the Irish Republic was born. Its membership card replicated the Celtic iconography adorning that of the FOIF, but replaced Washington's profile with Benjamin Franklin's, and Pearse's with de Valera's. [Document: National Library of Ireland, Joseph McGarrity Papers / Source: MS 41,511/1/4; *Freeman's Journal*, 20 August 1920. See also Eileen McGough, *Diarmuid Lynch: a forgotten Irish patriot* (Cork, 2013)]

who joined the *Gaelic American* staff, tried to defend the work of the IPL. In a letter to Golden he complained that 'the gang', meaning Cohalan and Devoy, 'opposed and sabotaged' IPL efforts 'by threats and underhand means'.[7] Given that the United States was itself conscripting its young men to fight on Britain's side, the IPL campaign made little headway. Nevertheless, these tensions between the more America-focused leadership of the FOIF and the more Ireland-orientated IPL were a portent of deep post-war divisions.

Once the war ended, a sense of unity within the Irish-American nationalist movement once again prevailed, at least in public. In February 1919 over 5,000 delegates representing various Irish nationalist organisations including the IPL and the Ancient Order of Hibernians (AOH) attended an Irish Race Convention organised by the FOIF in Philadelphia. Presided over by Cardinal James Gibbons of Baltimore, the Convention's main resolution called upon the post-war Peace Conference, then meeting in Paris,

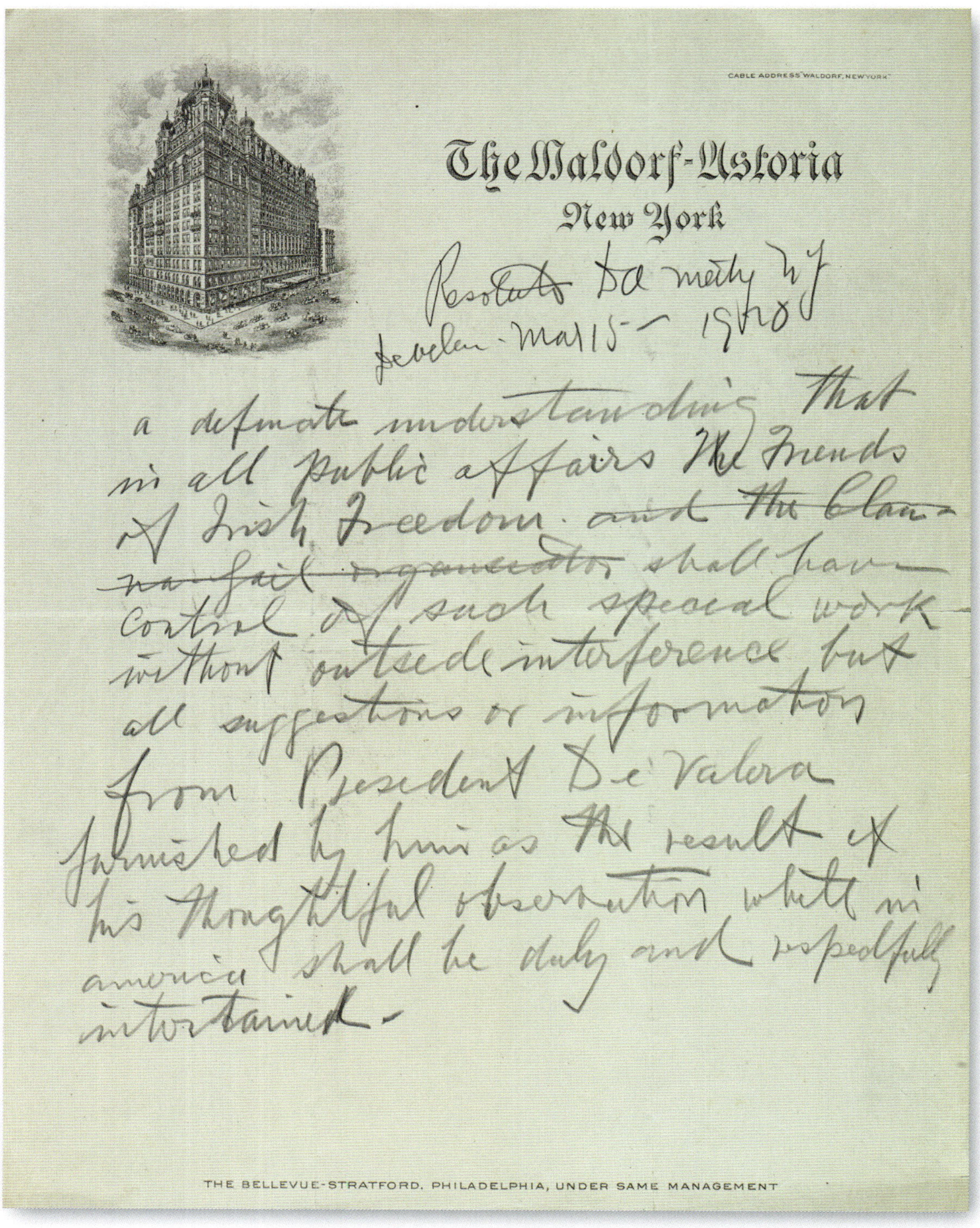

CABLE ADDRESS "WALDORF, NEW YORK"

The Waldorf-Astoria
New York

Resolution Da meeting NY
DeValera - Mar 15 - 1920

a definate understanding that in all public affairs the Friends of Irish Freedom. ~~and the Clan na Gael organization~~ shall have control of such special work without outside interference but all suggestions or information from President De Valera furnished by him as the result of his thoughtful observation while in america shall be duly and respectfully entertained -

THE BELLEVUE-STRATFORD, PHILADELPHIA, UNDER SAME MANAGEMENT

Fig. 4 Draft resolution hastily written by Philadelphia's Joseph McGarrity (1874–1940), 15 March 1920, amid deteriorating relations between Éamon de Valera and Friends of Irish Freedom (FOIF) leaders Judge Cohalan and John Devoy. McGarrity sought a 'definite understanding' that 'President de Valera' would not interfere directly in the work of the Irish-American organisation, but 'any suggestions or information furnished by him as a result of his thoughtful observation while in America' would be 'duly and respectfully entertained'. Tyrone-born McGarrity emigrated to America in 1892 when he was eighteen years old. Settling in Philadelphia, he built a successful career in the wholesale wine and liquor business. After his appointment to the national executive of Clan na Gael in 1912, he channelled his time, energies and considerable wealth into the Irish-American movement dedicated to securing an Irish republic by force of arms. After the FOIF split in 1920, McGarrity and his *Irish Press* newspaper remained resolutely loyal to de Valera and the Irish-controlled American Association for the Recognition of the Irish Republic. After some initial vacillation on the Treaty, and an effort during a brief trip to Ireland in February 1922 to reconcile the opposing sides, McGarrity adopted an anti-Treaty stance. As leader of Clan na Gael he continued to support republican militancy in Ireland during and after the Civil War. His relationship with de Valera, however, deteriorated in 1927 when the leader of Fianna Fáil took the oath of allegiance to enter the Dáil, and shattered in 1936 when de Valera's government proclaimed the IRA as an illegal organisation. [Document: National Library of Ireland, Joseph McGarrity Papers, MS 17,521/17] to apply President Wilson's principle of self-determination for small nations specifically to the question of Ireland. But behind the scenes, tensions emerged. Irish envoy Patrick McCartan, supported by Joe McGarrity, argued that 'self-determination' was too vague and that the resolution needed to be more explicit in its call for American recognition of an Irish republic.[8]

Simmering tensions

In the end Cohalan's view that the call for Irish self-determination had more chance of being accepted by the American political establishment prevailed. The simmering tensions were fuelled by the arrival in the United States in June 1919 of the Sinn Féin president, Éamon de Valera. The 'Irish President', as he was described in the American media, argued publicly that a powerful Irish-American political lobby could persuade the American government to recognise the Irish republic and that this, in turn, would put pressure on the British government to accede to Irish republican demands. He also sought to raise funds for the Irish struggle at home, a policy adopted by many previous Irish nationalist visitors to the United States.[9] With considerable help from the FOIF, de Valera's fund-raising campaign raised over $5 million in a bond-certificate drive. Some of these funds were dispatched to Ireland, but approximately $2.5 million remained in US banks at the conclusion of the Irish War of Independence in 1921. The ownership of this fund would later be subject to much legal wrangling.[10]

There were also key Congressional resolutions passed in favour of Irish self-determination. One of the most important of these included a resolution in the Senate introduced by Cohalan's ally, Republican Senator William Borah of Idaho, which called on the American delegation then attending the Paris Peace Conference to secure a hearing for an Irish delegation led by de Valera. Passed by sixty votes to one, with thirty-five senators abstaining, the resolution also expressed sympathy for Irish self-determination. President Wilson, anxious to maintain good relations with Britain, ignored these resolutions, but their passing underlined the power of the Irish lobby in Congress at this time.[11]

Perhaps inevitably, de Valera and Cohalan clashed over a number of key policies. Cohalan and Devoy opposed Wilson's proposed post-war League of Nations, fearing that membership would draw the United States into a war to protect the 'territorial integrity' of the British Empire. FOIF funds and resources were channelled into an FOIF campaign against the League. In contrast, de Valera believed that a 'real' League of Nations could be used to protect small, independent countries like Ireland. Unlike Cohalan and Devoy, who were vehemently opposed to Wilson, de Valera also wanted to pursue a more bipartisan policy towards the two main American political parties.[12] As president of Sinn Féin, de Valera believed that he should control the direction of the Irish nationalist movement in the US. Cohalan, with the support of John Devoy and the majority of the FOIF leadership, rejected this view. If the movement was seen to be under the direction of Ireland, according to Cohalan, this would undermine its effectiveness in American eyes and would play into the hands of nativist critics who argued that the Irish were loyal to a foreign leader rather than to the United States.[13]

Public split

The two sides splintered publicly at the Republican National Convention in Chicago in June 1920. Cohalan drew on his influence with the Republican Party to engineer the passing of a policy plank in favour of self-determination for Ireland. This was promptly disavowed by de Valera, who arrived with a separate delegation and insisted on a resolution seeking recognition of an Irish republic. Ultimately, a confused Republican Party resolution committee rejected both resolutions, claiming that since the Irish did not seem to know what they wanted, it would disregard Ireland completely during its deliberations.[14]

Each side blamed the other for the debacle. After his efforts to reduce Devoy and Cohalan's power within the FOIF failed, de Valera severed the links between Sinn Féin and the FOIF in the United States. His assistant in the US, Harry Boland, also formally broke ties between the IRB in Ireland and the American Clan in October 1920. In a statement to the press he claimed that the reluctant split would endure 'until such time as the will of the members of the executive becomes operative and not the will of Justice Cohalan'.[15] It is important to note that, during his struggle with Cohalan and Devoy, de Valera had the full backing of the Sinn Féin leadership in Dublin.

Predictably, the bitter split within the Irish-American movement led to the emergence of new organisations led by de Valera loyalists. Joe McGarrity established Reorganised Clan na Gael and, prior to his departure for Ireland in December 1920, de Valera founded the American Association for the Recognition of the Irish Republic (AARIR). Edward L. Doheny, an American oil tycoon and nephew of Young Irelander Michael Doheny, became its leader.[16] The Irish Progressive League, enduringly critical of Devoy and Cohalan, merged with the AARIR, and Peter Golden became national secretary of the new organisation, which drew many disaffected FOIF members into its ranks. Most senior officers stayed loyal to Cohalan. However, the FOIF was now a much weakened force and membership had fallen to approximately 20,000 in 1921. In contrast, membership of the AARIR reached an estimated 700,000 across the United States.[17]

Devoy's *Gaelic American* continued to support the FOIF and blamed de Valera for destroying the unity of the Irish-American organisation at such a crucial time in Ireland's history. In the aftermath of the split, a *Gaelic American* editorial lamented: 'No better work for Ireland was ever done in living memory and yet those who did it are treated as the enemies of Ireland.'[18] In contrast, the *Irish World* supported the AARIR and de Valera's position. Yet this conflict between the two newspapers did not extend to any policy differences on the War of Independence. Both staunchly supported the IRA's campaign against crown forces in Ireland.

Fig. 5 This striking photograph of (l-r) Éamon de Valera, Michael Collins and Harry Boland first appeared in the *Irish Independent*'s coverage of the Sinn Féin ard fheis on 22 February 1922. The caption read: 'They were brothers there that day', a quote from a speech delivered by de Valera at the event. The photograph captures a smiling trio enjoying the moment, with Boland a gleeful centre of attention and affection. Boland's unique position as close friend to the polar-opposite personalities of Collins and de Valera marked him out as a powerful unifying and energising force in the republican movement. Having spent time together in prison following the 1916 Rising, Boland's devotion to de Valera was never more apparent than during de Valera's tour of America from June 1919 to November 1920. As official envoy of both the Dáil and the Irish Republican Brotherhood Supreme Council, Boland prepared the ground for de Valera's tour, the primary aim of which was to gain recognition for the 'Irish Republic' and to raise funds to support the newly established Dáil. In addition to devising their travel and speaking schedules and navigating the choppy waters of rival 'pro-Irish' American bodies, Boland organised secret consignments of arms for Ireland (including a massive shipment of Thompson sub-machine guns, seized by US authorities in New Jersey). He also made overtures to Indian nationalists in an effort to form a global movement against the British Empire. Boland served as de Valera's intermediary during direct negotiations with David Lloyd George in the summer of 1921 but was dispatched back to the United States prior to the Treaty negotiations. He would reject the resulting agreement in the Dáil on 7 January 1922 as the 'very negation of all that for which we have fought. It is the first time in the history of our country that a body of representative Irishmen has ever suggested that the sovereignty of this nation should be signed away'. Boland subsequently brokered a pact between the two sides prior to the 1922 general election, but it failed to prevent the descent into civil war. At the outbreak of fighting, he returned to the IRA and served as quartermaster of the Dublin Brigade. His comment at the time – 'Can you imagine me on the run from Mick Collins? It is ludicrous' – conveys some of the incredulity felt by many close friends turned enemies. Within a month he was killed by Free State forces in contested circumstances in Skerries. Three weeks later Collins was shot dead by anti-Treaty Volunteers at Béal na Blá, leaving de Valera, the tall, reserved onlooker in the photograph, as the only one of the three friends alive to pursue their shared aim of achieving an Irish republic. [Text: John FitzGerald / Image: part of the Independent Newspapers Ireland/NLI Collection, INDH54]

Fig. 6 'Gentle womanly loving loyal generous Harry – Harry strong and Harry brave.' Éamon de Valera's poignant expression of grief in this letter is remarkable for its deep affection for his lost friend and comrade. 'I feel I am privileged as one to whom Harry was more than a brother [...] When my time comes, Harry more than all others I want to meet you.' The letter has survived through the sequential care of its recipient, Harry Boland's mother Kate (née Woods), Harry's sister Kathleen (later O'Donovan) and his niece Fionnuala Crowley (née O'Donovan), whose family trust deposited it at University College Cork in 2022. A glimpse of Collins's grief at Boland's death is afforded in a letter to Kitty Kiernan in which he says: 'Last night I passed Vincent's hospital and saw a small crowd outside. My mind went into him lying dead there and I thought of the times together, and whatever good there is in any wish of mine, he certainly had it [...] I'd send a wreath but I suppose they'd return it torn up.' [Text: John FitzGerald / Document: Kathleen Boland Collection, UCC, IE BL/PC/KB]

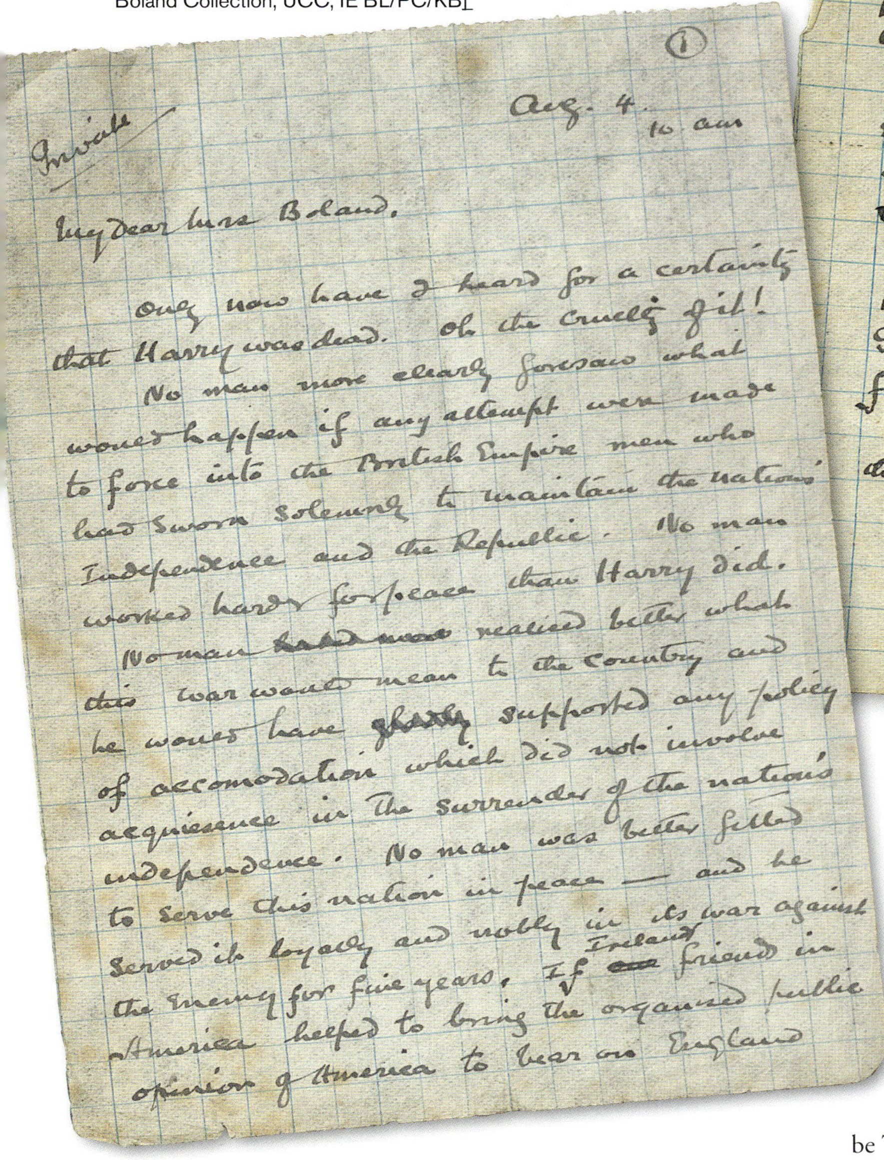

Irish-America and the Anglo-Irish Treaty

In December 1921, news of the Treaty settlement offering dominion status with some form of permanent partition reached the United States. The *Irish World*, de Valera's stalwart supporter during his feud with the FOIF, bitterly opposed the measure on constitutional grounds. Anticipating the Dáil vote on the Treaty on 7 January 1922, a front-page headline read: 'Fate of Republic in the Balance'. Another strident headline in the same issue declared that 'The issue of the Absolute Independence of the Irish Nation or the Abandonment of it to the position of a Province of the British Empire is placed before Dáil Éireann'.[19] Unambiguous about identities of the defenders and enemies of the republic, another headline stated: 'De Valera and Those Acting with Him Loyal to Their Oath of Allegiance to the Irish Republic – No Compromise Possible – Ratification of the Griffithian Treaty of Surrender Would be Treason to the Heroic Dead Who Died That Ireland Might Be Free of Foreign Rule'.[20]

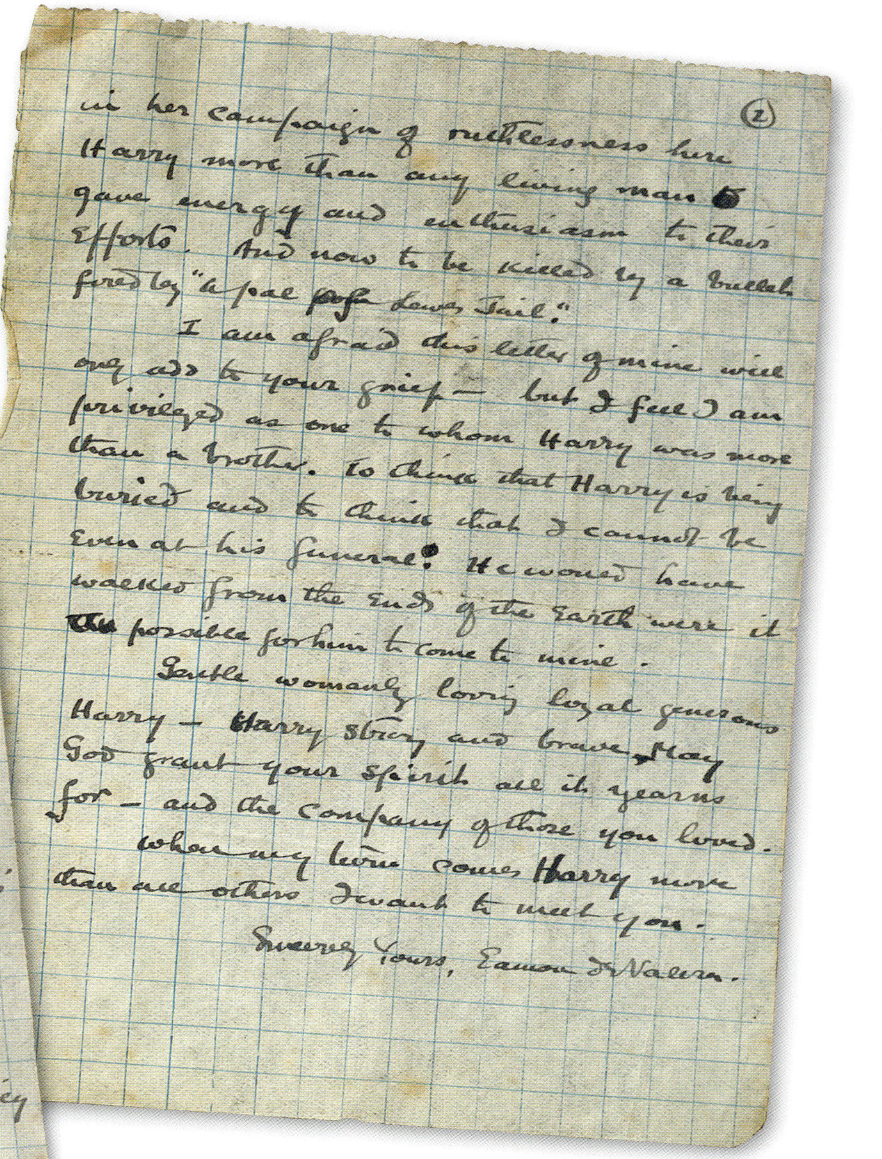

The FOIF was also initially critical of the Treaty. On 8 December National Secretary Diarmuid Lynch issued a press statement dismissive of its provisions: 'With Irish coastal fortifications under British control [...] with an Ireland swearing allegiance to a foreign King, the use of the term "Irish Free State" is an insult to the dead who died fighting for an independent Irish Republic.'[21]

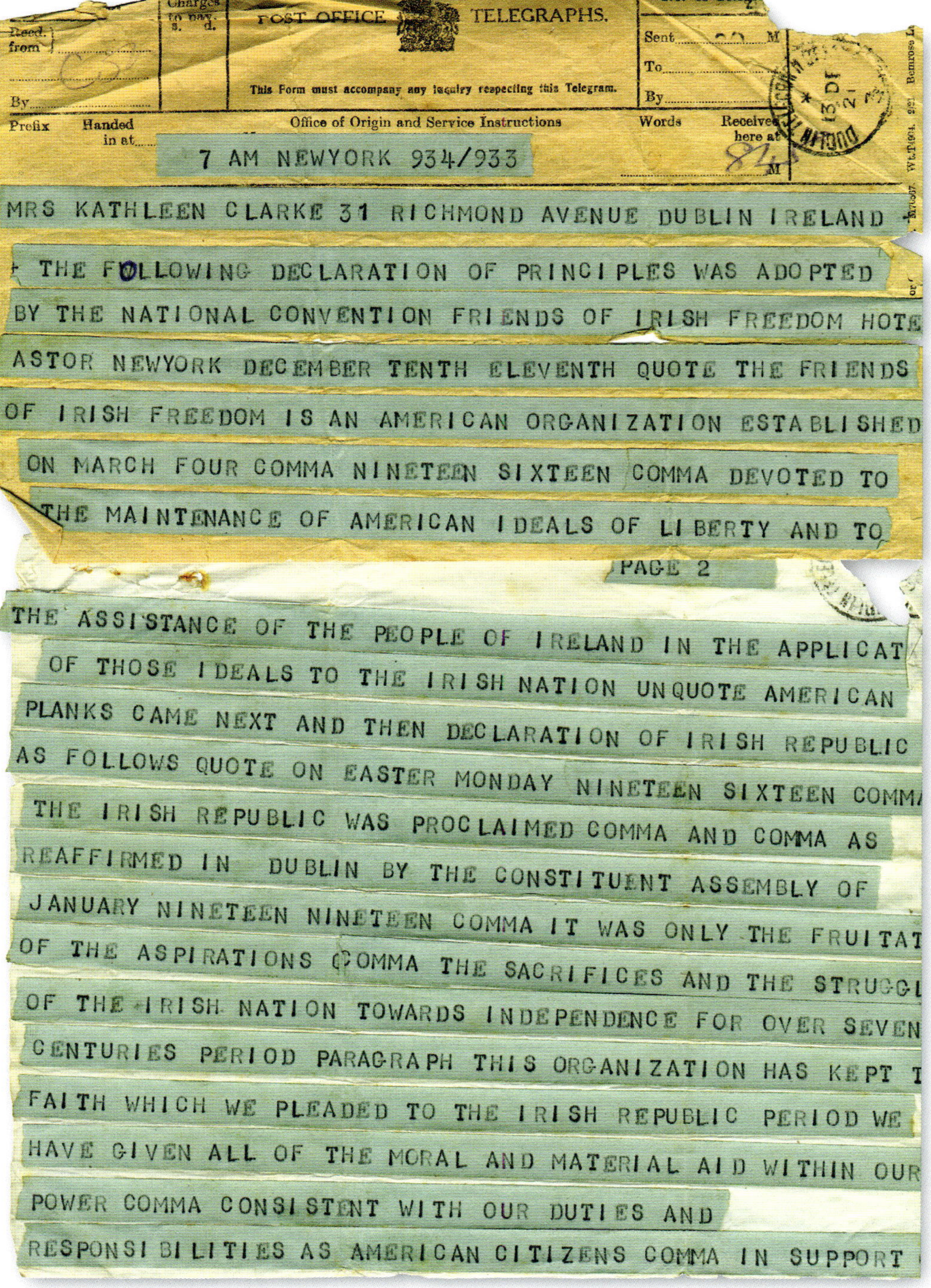

POST OFFICE TELEGRAPHS.

This Form must accompany any inquiry respecting this Telegram.

Office of Origin and Service Instructions

7 AM NEWYORK 934/933

MRS KATHLEEN CLARKE 31 RICHMOND AVENUE DUBLIN IRELAND
THE FOLLOWING DECLARATION OF PRINCIPLES WAS ADOPTED
BY THE NATIONAL CONVENTION FRIENDS OF IRISH FREEDOM HOTE
ASTOR NEWYORK DECEMBER TENTH ELEVENTH QUOTE THE FRIENDS
OF IRISH FREEDOM IS AN AMERICAN ORGANIZATION ESTABLISHED
ON MARCH FOUR COMMA NINETEEN SIXTEEN COMMA DEVOTED TO
THE MAINTENANCE OF AMERICAN IDEALS OF LIBERTY AND TO

PAGE 2

THE ASSISTANCE OF THE PEOPLE OF IRELAND IN THE APPLICAT
OF THOSE IDEALS TO THE IRISH NATION UNQUOTE AMERICAN
PLANKS CAME NEXT AND THEN DECLARATION OF IRISH REPUBLIC
AS FOLLOWS QUOTE ON EASTER MONDAY NINETEEN SIXTEEN COMM
THE IRISH REPUBLIC WAS PROCLAIMED COMMA AND COMMA AS
REAFFIRMED IN DUBLIN BY THE CONSTITUENT ASSEMBLY OF
JANUARY NINETEEN NINETEEN COMMA IT WAS ONLY THE FRUITAT
OF THE ASPIRATIONS COMMA THE SACRIFICES AND THE STRUGGL
OF THE IRISH NATION TOWARDS INDEPENDENCE FOR OVER SEVEN
CENTURIES PERIOD PARAGRAPH THIS ORGANIZATION HAS KEPT T
FAITH WHICH WE PLEADED TO THE IRISH REPUBLIC PERIOD WE
HAVE GIVEN ALL OF THE MORAL AND MATERIAL AID WITHIN OUR
POWER COMMA CONSISTENT WITH OUR DUTIES AND
RESPONSIBILITIES AS AMERICAN CITIZENS COMMA IN SUPPORT

Fig. 7 First page of telegram from Diarmaid Lynch to Kathleen Clarke, Sinn Féin TD and widow of executed leader of the 1916 Rising Tom Clarke, 13 December 1921. This long telegram conveyed details of the Declaration of Principles adopted by the National Convention of the Friends of Irish Freedom at the Hotel Astor in New York two days before. With the 'American ideals of liberty' at its heart, the declaration dealt first with American planks, including the Friends of Irish Freedom's opposition to the League of Nations, before committing to its continued 'moral and material support' to those in Ireland 'who carry forward the fight for complete National Independence'. The declaration echoed Lynch's press statement of 8 December denouncing the Treaty. [Image: courtesy of Adams Auctioneers]

Early FOIF opposition did not necessarily mean a sudden shift in support for de Valera. Indeed, the *Gaelic American* upbraided the anti-Treaty Sinn Féin leader, arguing that his blunderings during his mission to the United States had made such a compromise inevitable.[22] In the wake of a Dáil vote in support of the agreement, the FOIF adopted a more positive attitude towards the Treaty. On 22 January a meeting of the FOIF National Council recorded in its minutes the following statement: 'We as American citizens of Irish blood will do nothing to interfere with or obstruct any plans the result of which is to take the English army out of Ireland and put the powers of Government – limited and constricted though they be – into the hands of Irishmen.'[23] In a letter to Michael Collins in February, John Devoy, representing his wing of the now divided Clan na Gael, wrote: 'Although they remain Republicans, our best men, under existing conditions, favour giving the Free State a chance to do what it can for Ireland.'[24]

Given the about-face by the FOIF and the Clan's approach to the Treaty, the question must be asked: Was Cohalan's and Devoy's support for the Treaty influenced by the fact that de Valera opposed it? Some Irish officials in the United States at that time thought

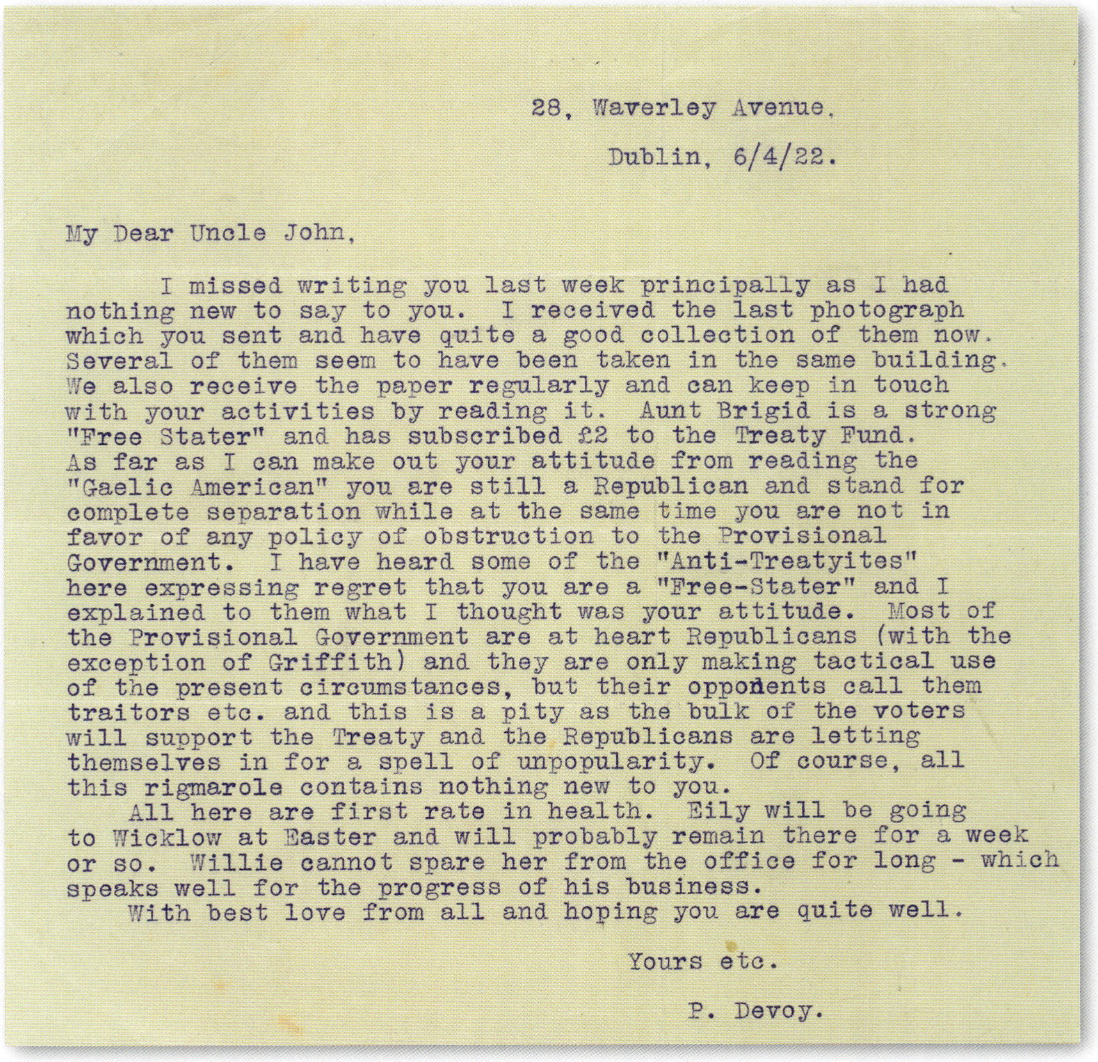

Fig. 8 Writing affectionately to John Devoy from Dublin on 6 April 1922, Peter Devoy shares his impressions, gleaned from his avid readership of the *Gaelic American*, of his uncle's stance on the Treaty. Though some 'anti-Treatyites' were convinced that John Devoy was a 'Free Stater', Peter knew that his uncle was 'still a Republican' but unwilling to support 'any policy of obstruction of the Provisional Government'. [Document: National Library of Ireland, John Devoy Papers, MS 18,004/9/13]

28, Waverley Avenue,

Dublin, 6/4/22.

My Dear Uncle John,

I missed writing you last week principally as I had nothing new to say to you. I received the last photograph which you sent and have quite a good collection of them now. Several of them seem to have been taken in the same building. We also receive the paper regularly and can keep in touch with your activities by reading it. Aunt Brigid is a strong "Free Stater" and has subscribed £2 to the Treaty Fund. As far as I can make out your attitude from reading the "Gaelic American" you are still a Republican and stand for complete separation while at the same time you are not in favor of any policy of obstruction to the Provisional Government. I have heard some of the "Anti-Treatyites" here expressing regret that you are a "Free-Stater" and I explained to them what I thought was your attitude. Most of the Provisional Government are at heart Republicans (with the exception of Griffith) and they are only making tactical use of the present circumstances, but their opponents call them traitors etc. and this is a pity as the bulk of the voters will support the Treaty and the Republicans are letting themselves in for a spell of unpopularity. Of course, all this rigmarole contains nothing new to you.

All here are first rate in health. Eily will be going to Wicklow at Easter and will probably remain there for a week or so. Willie cannot spare her from the office for long - which speaks well for the progress of his business.

With best love from all and hoping you are quite well.

Yours etc.

P. Devoy.

so. In March 1922 the newly established Provisional Government entrusted Dennis McCullough with the impossible task of trying to 'make peace' between the bitterly opposed Irish-American nationalist organisations. During this mission McCullough worked closely with Professor Timothy A. Smiddy, the Provisional Government's envoy to the United States.[25] In his report to Dublin McCullough argued that Cohalan's and Devoy's support for the Treaty was

> founded more on hate of de Valera than on love for those who are opposed to him – if de Valera was on the other side, they would be loudest against it – and because there is too large an element of selfishness in their purpose, I would advise no direct affiliations with them from home for the present anyhow.[26]

Certainly, de Valera's opposition to the Treaty in Ireland would have made support for the measure easier for Cohalan and Devoy. Yet there were other more fundamental factors at play. In the first instance, the Treaty had been approved by the Dáil and endorsed by business organisations, the Irish labour movement and the Catholic Church in Ireland. Support for the Treaty also extended to the Catholic Church in America, of which Cohalan was a devout member.[27]

An American lens

Cohalan, who had always viewed developments in Ireland through an American lens, would also have been acting contrary to his political instincts by opposing the measure. Most American opinion, including that of the media and political class, supported the Treaty, a point conceded by Harry Boland in the Dáil on 7 January and confirmed by Joseph Connolly, the Dáil's consul general in New York in his report to the Department of Foreign Affairs in Dublin on 16 January.[28]

Michael Laffan has described the Treaty divide in Ireland as one between 'purists' and 'pragmatists'.[29] A similar analogy could be used to describe attitudes in the United States. Cohalan and Devoy had already demonstrated their pragmatic attitude towards the achievement of an Irish republic at the Irish Race Convention in February 1919 and at the Republican Party Convention in June 1920.

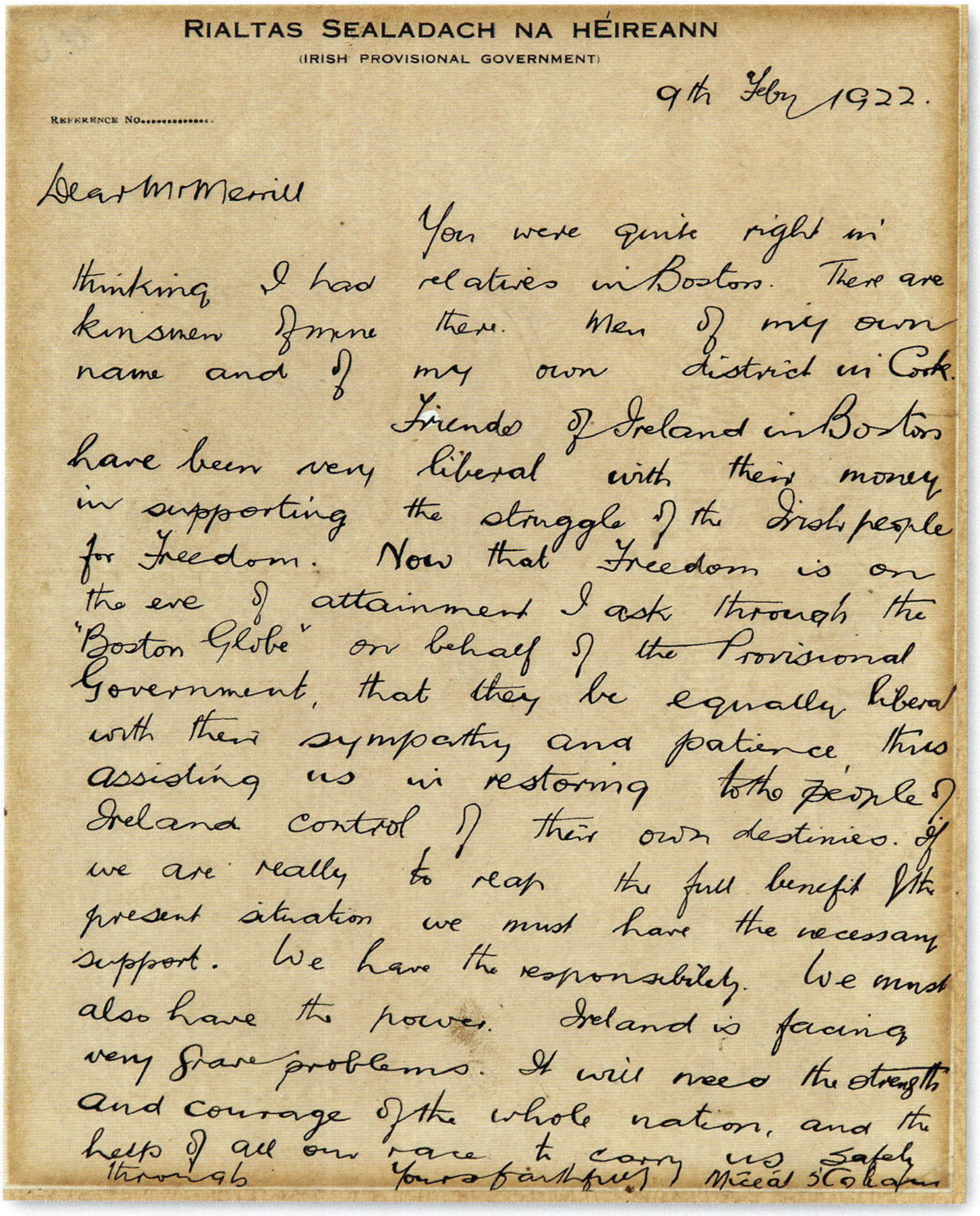

RIALTAS SEALADACH NA hÉIREANN
(IRISH PROVISIONAL GOVERNMENT)

REFERENCE NO..............

9th Feby 1922.

Dear Mr Merrill

You were quite right in thinking I had relatives in Boston. There are kinsmen of mine there. Men of my own name and of my own district in Cork.

Friends of Ireland in Boston have been very liberal with their money in supporting the struggle of the Irish people for Freedom. Now that Freedom is on the eve of attainment I ask through the "Boston Globe" on behalf of the Provisional Government, that they be equally liberal with their sympathy and patience, thus assisting us in restoring to the people of Ireland control of their own destinies. If we are really to reap the full benefit of the present situation we must have the necessary support. We have the responsibility. We must also have the power. Ireland is facing very grave problems. It will need the strength and courage of the whole nation, and the help of all our race to carry us safely through

Yours faithfully Mícéal Ó Coileáin

Fig. 9 Letter, with extracts intended for publication, from Michael Collins to Mr Merrill (probably Samuel Merrill), a journalist at the *Boston Globe*, 9 February 1922. Beginning by asserting his personal connections to Boston, and acknowledging the liberal support for the Irish freedom struggle in that city, the chairman of the Provisional Government appeals for the 'sympathy and patience' of Irish nationals abroad while power was consolidated and freedom secured under the terms of the Treaty. [Image: courtesy of Adams Auctioneers]

In both these instances, a declaration in favour of self-determination was considered more practically beneficial to Ireland than a call for an Irish republic, which would, in any case, have faced rejection. Yet this support was not unqualified. Both Cohalan and Devoy still saw an Irish republic as the end result of such a compromise. In March 1922, in a letter of instruction to the Boston FOIF leader Matthew Cummings, Cohalan insisted that, while he preferred Collins to de Valera, he would not unequivocally endorse the Free State:

> I hope that you make it clear in anything that you say that while the Free State is regarded as a step forward on the road to independence, it is only that, and not in any sense an end in itself, or an achievement about which there will be any enthusiasm, if the result is going to be only to tie Ireland more closely to England.[30]

The leadership of the AARIR was also pragmatic about the Treaty. Shortly after news of the deal reached the United States, Edward L. Doheny announced that 'he was delighted with the results of the Irish peace negotiations'.[31] The AARIR executive later endorsed this position but, due to divisions among the leadership, retracted its support for the Treaty in February 1922 and pledged allegiance to de Valera and the Irish republic. This reversal led to an exodus of many of the rank and file, with membership falling to 75,000 in

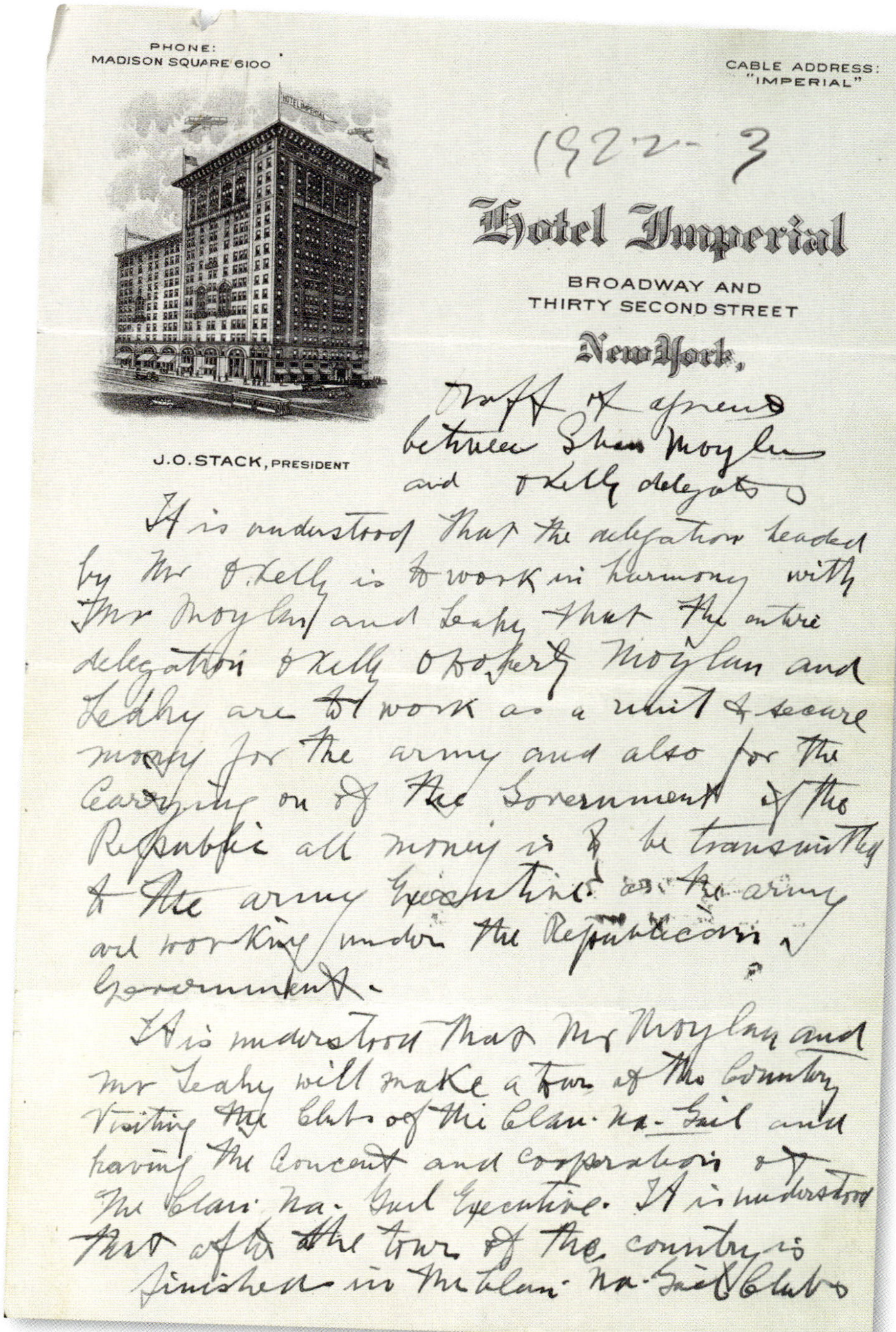

PHONE:
MADISON SQUARE 6100

CABLE ADDRESS:
"IMPERIAL"

1922-3

Hotel Imperial

BROADWAY AND
THIRTY SECOND STREET

New York,

J.O. STACK, PRESIDENT

Draft of agreement
between Sean Moylan
and O'Kelly delegation

It is understood that the delegation headed by Mr O'Kelly is to work in harmony with Mr Moylan and Leahy that the entire delegation O'Kelly O'Doherty Moylan and Leahy are to work as a unit & secure money for the army and also for the carrying on of the Government of the Republic all money is to be transmitted to the army Executive as the army are working under the Republican Government.

It is understood that Mr Moylan and Mr Leahy will make a tour of the country visiting the Clubs of the Clan-na-Gael and having the consent and cooperation of the Clan-na-Gael Executive. It is understood that after the tour of the country is finished in the Clan-na-Gael Clubs

Fig. 10 First page of an undated draft commitment by Joseph McGarrity on behalf of the Reorganised Clan na Gael to support the efforts of Seán Moylan, a senior leader of the IRA, during his mission to the United States. Moylan was despatched to the US in the autumn of 1922 to raise funds for the IRA and the newly formed 'republican government'. He was joined by anti-Treaty Sinn Féin representatives J.J. O'Kelly ('Sceilg') and Joseph O'Doherty, as well as the IRA's Cork No. 1 Brigade leader, Mick Leahy, who was a trained ship's engineer with arms smuggling experience. [Document: National Library of Ireland, Joseph McGarrity Papers, MS 17,654/4/6]

1922 and further declining in the years that followed. Doheny resigned and was replaced as leader in May 1922 by James E. 'Red' Murray, a left-wing senator and labour lawyer from Butte, Montana, a resolutely Irish-American city.[32]

While the majority of Irish-Americans supported the Treaty, the remaining AARIR members were among a substantial and vocal minority who continued to oppose it. Other voices of opposition, many of whom were first-generation Irish, included McGarrity's Reorganised Clan na Gael and the *Irish World* newspaper.

Arrival of two delegations

The existence of pro- and anti-Treaty factions in the United States did not go unnoticed in Ireland. Both sides of the Treaty divide recognised the importance of an American support base and funding stream, particularly with the impending elections in June. In May 1922 two rival delegations arrived in the United States on the same ship from Ireland. All had served the Irish cause in some capacity during the War of Independence and it was felt that the record of service against British forces would appeal to Irish-Americans. Yet the simultaneous arrival of the two delegations caused some unease. As Francis Carroll points out, 'both groups began touring the country, denouncing their opponents in Ireland with all the malice and vituperation previously reserved for the British government'.[33]

The Provisional Government delegation, representing the pro-Treaty side, included James O'Mara, previously involved in American fund-raising, and 1916 veteran Piaras Béaslaí, who later served as a publicity director for the IRA. The anti-Treaty delegation included Austin Stack, another 1916 veteran, and John J. O'Kelly, president of the Gaelic League and minister of education in the Second Dáil. Kathleen Barry and Countess Constance Markievicz arrived on a later ship. Barry had served as a judge in the republican courts and was a sister of Kevin Barry, a young IRA Volunteer executed by the British during the War of Independence.[34] American newspapers were particularly interested in Markievicz, described by the *Irish World* as Ireland's 'Joan of Arc', who began her US lecture tour in April 1922.[35] From the Anglo-Irish Gore-Booth family, Markievicz had married Polish Count Casimir Dunin-Markievicz in 1900, but later turned her back on her ascendancy background in favour of radical activism in a range of socialist and feminist organisations. She participated in the Easter Rising as an Irish Citizen Army officer and was the first female MP elected to the British House of Commons in 1918. In line with Sinn Féin policy, she did not take up her seat. Avidly anti-Treaty, Markievicz showed little restraint during her American speaking tour in her criticism of the Treaty, describing Michael Collins and Arthur Griffith as 'traitors' to

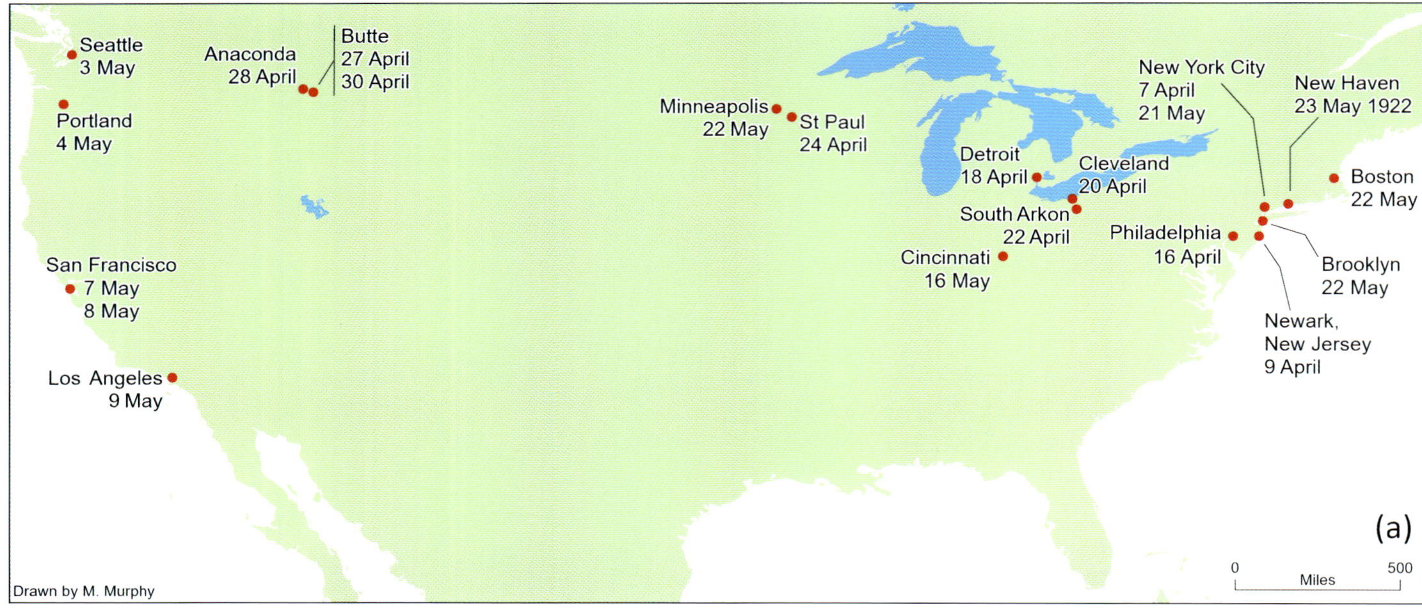

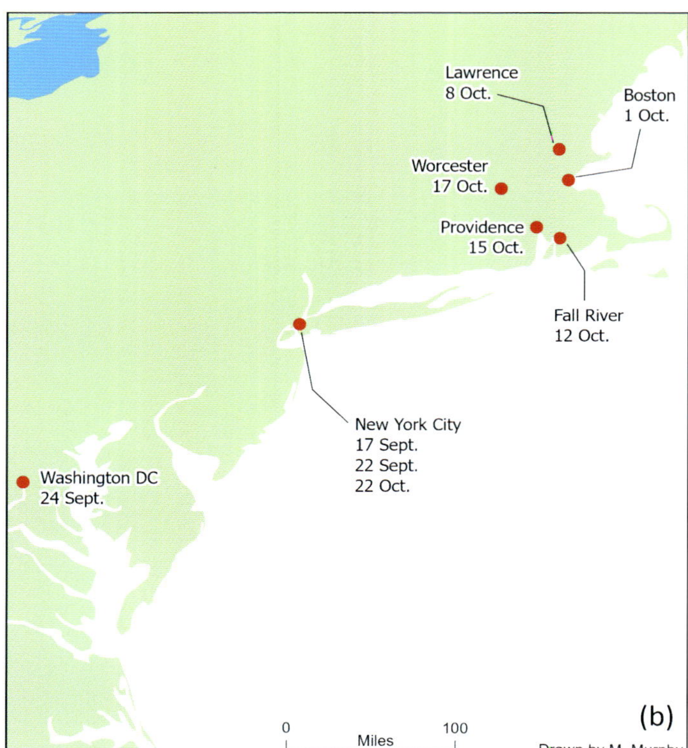

Figs 11 (a–c) Anti-Treaty republican speaking tours of the United States, 1922–3. The mobilisation of Irish-America, first under the Friends of Irish Freedom and later by the American Association for the Recognition of the Irish Republic (AARIR), created a mass movement in the United States. The Treaty split saw AARIR membership and financial support plummet, though the organisation still managed to generate fund-raising and propaganda opportunities, as seen during three separate anti-Treaty republican speaking tours of the United States in 1922–3. All were fronted by female republicans, who were experienced public performers. The first tour occurred in April and May 1922 before fighting broke out, and was headlined by Constance Markievicz, one of the republicans' best-known and most effective speakers (Fig. 11a, top). She was accompanied for most of it by Cumann na mBan leaders Kathleen Boland and Kathleen Barry, and the Gaelic League president, J.J. O'Kelly (anti-Treaty Sinn Féin TD Austin Stack also joined briefly). The national tour publicised the anti-Treaty position and secured funds for its political campaign during visits to the American north-east, a couple of stops in the Midwest, and a swing along the west coast. Perhaps the most enthusiastic reception was provided in Butte and Anaconda, Montana by militant copper miners, who cheered Markievicz's uncompromising message and criticism of local working conditions. The tour was cut short in mid-May by the announcement of the 'Pact' general election to be held in Ireland on 16 June. Markievicz was needed at home to contest her parliamentary seat.

The second tour was undertaken by Muriel MacSwiney, the widow of Terence MacSwiney (Fig. 11b, left). She was another global republican figure, who had been well received during a short visit to the United States just after her husband's death on hunger strike in late 1920. MacSwiney was joined by Nancy Kearns, a nurse with extensive IRA service. (As Gerri O'Neill points out, the Military Service Pensions Board later recognised Kearns as an IRA officer rather than as a Cumann na mBan member.) Kearns had made national headlines in 1920 when she was arrested in her native County Sligo driving a carload of rifles, and achieved even more notoriety following her spectacular escape from Mountjoy Gaol in October 1921. Both Kearns and Muriel MacSwiney served with anti-Treaty forces during the Battle for Dublin, before travelling to New York in September 1922 to raise money for the Irish Republican Prisoners' Dependants Fund. They spoke at a series of meetings in New York and New England, although these were significantly smaller events than those addressed by republican emissaries in 1920 and 1921. The tour was sidetracked by news from Ireland that Muriel's sister-in-law Mary MacSwiney had gone on hunger strike following her imprisonment. In response, Muriel MacSwiney helped picket the British embassy in Washington DC, and was arrested with a number of female AARIR members. The charges were eventually dropped, though they may have contributed to a health collapse that required MacSwiney to abandon the tour (her fragile health may help explain the presence of the nurse Linda Kearns on the tour). She returned to Ireland in November, but was replaced by Hanna Sheehy Skeffington and Kathleen Boland

By this stage Sheehy Skeffington, Boland and Kearns all had extensive public-speaking experience in the United States (Sheehy Skeffington undertook a national tour there during 1917–18). Their extensive tour lasted from November 1922 until early May 1923 (Fig. 11c, opposite top). The three women occasionally addressed different meetings to cover more ground, as they appeared across New England, the Midwest and the west coast. They continued to fly the anti-Treaty flag, even as the republican war effort collapsed. Joanne Mooney Eichacker reports that Sheehy Skeffington, Boland and Kearns raised $123,000 during the tour, helping at least to refill some of the depleted republican coffers. [Source: Joanne Mooney Eichacker, *Irish Republican Women in America: Lecture tours 1916–1923* (Dublin, 2003); Gerri O'Neill, 'Private Lives and Public Personas: female participation in the IRA during Ireland's War of Independence, 1919–1921', unpublished PhD thesis, Dublin City University, 2019]

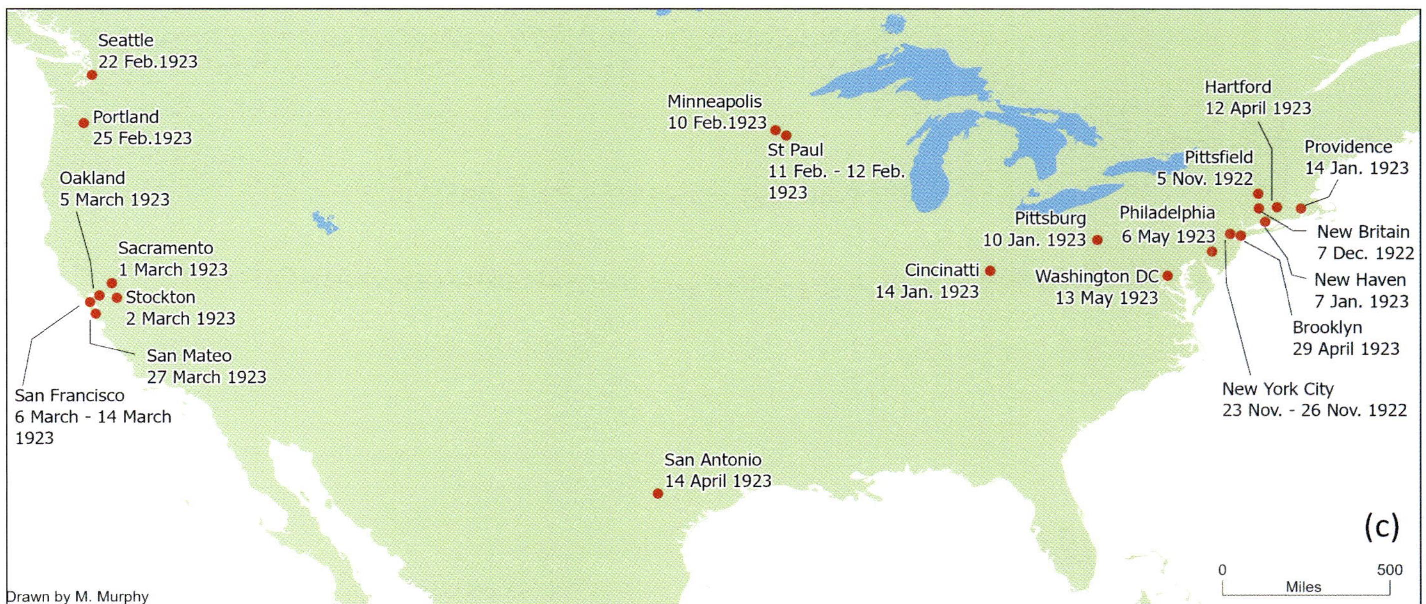

the Irish cause.[36] Both delegations wanted to put their respective arguments on the Treaty to the American people and raise money for the forthcoming election in Ireland.[37] The latter objective was more important to the anti-Treaty side, which, unlike its pro-Treaty rivals, did not have the resources of the state behind it.

Ignoring McCullough's earlier advice not to take sides in the Irish-American split, the pro-Treaty delegation actively sought the help of the FOIF. In this regard it had the full approval of Michael Collins who, in a letter to Devoy, apologised for Boland's action in severing the ties between the IRB and the Clan, and assured him that his 'good opinion is of concern to us here'.[38] The *Gaelic American* heavily endorsed the pro-Treaty position and adopted a most critical attitude towards de Valera. When the pro-Treaty side gained an overall majority of seats in the Dáil in the June 1922 election, Devoy's *Gaelic American* gloated at de Valera's defeat, but warned, in a reference to the recent civil war in Mexico, that 'routed in elections he seeks by Mexican methods to overcome the decision of the people by force'.[39]

In turn the anti-Treaty delegation worked closely with the AARIR. On 13 May 1922 the front page of the *Irish World* was devoted to the AARIR National Convention held a week earlier at the Wardman Park hotel in Washington. The convention heard a message from de Valera declaring that: 'Until the unity and sovereignty of the Irish Nation are recognized, the fight for Irish independence will continue. The surest path and the path of least sacrifice is the road of the Republic.' To cheering crowds, 'envoy' Austin Stack denounced members of the Dáil who had voted for the Treaty and declared: 'The Irish Republic will never be allowed to die.'[40]

Fig. 12 (right) Advertisement for the 16 April 1922 anniversary celebration of the Easter Rising in Philadelphia with speakers including Constance Markievicz, Austin Stack and Kathleen Barry. [Document: National Library of Ireland, Joseph McGarrity Papers, MS 17,654/6/11]

answered 6/6/22

Hotel Waldorf Astoria
New York
May 1922

My dear Stashou, I have just received your letter forwarded to me from Ireland via New York to this place. St Paul's it is called, & its on the Mississippi in the wilds of Minnesota, I am on a tour visiting all our Irish centres in the U.S.

I never wrote to you because I was afraid of compromising you but I sent you many messages by Eva. She gave me yours. Do you remember you wrote her asking for some articles of apparel? I was getting them for you & my daughter in law when I was again shut up. You know I've had a pretty stiff time of it, about 3 years & a half, & some of it was awful. I did what I could to help you & I think that some of the people whom I got to intercede for you may have been a little help. I did not know how it was with you for a long time, ~~but~~ & when I first heard I could find out nothing. Father just mentioned that you were locked up for no reason. Some of poor "Mixer's" old friends found out all about you for me & have been doing all they could

Fig. 13 First page of a letter from Constance Markievicz to Stanislaw Dunin Markievicz, May 1922. From the city of St Paul, in 'the wilds of Minnesota', in late April 1922, Constance Markievicz stole a moment to respond to a letter from her stepson, Stanislaw. She was anxious to reassure him that, on belatedly hearing of his incarceration by Bolsheviks in Russia, she had made every effort to secure his release, including prevailing upon her old comrade, the imprisoned socialist Jim Larkin. Continuing the correspondence on the train to Butte, Montana through the unfamiliar 'wild and rugged landscape' where 'real cowboys' rounded up cattle on the open range, she mused that when 'things get fixed up right in Ireland', there would be work for multilingual men like Stanislaw. Son of Polish nobleman and artist Casimir Dunin-Markievicz who married Constance Gore-Booth in 1900, Stanislaw had spent part of his peripatetic childhood in pre-revolutionary Dublin, where his stepmother, increasingly estranged from her ascendancy background, had embraced the radical cross-currents of Bohemianism, socialism, feminism and advanced nationalism. Markievicz was second in command to Irish Citizen Army officer Michael Mallin during the 1916 Rising – a role celebrated and romanticised in the publicity for her American speaking tour six years later when she was hailed as 'Ireland's greatest military leader since Queen Maeve' (Fig. 12). Cumann na mBan president, recognised spokesperson for labour and a member of the Sinn Féin executive by 1917, Markievicz was serving a term in London's Holloway Prison as one of the 'German Plot' prisoners when she was returned as Sinn Féin candidate for Dublin's St Patrick's Division in the 1918 general election. A zealous, if often absent, minister for labour in the underground Dáil, she furiously opposed the Treaty as anathema to 'the Workers' Republic for which Connolly died'. Markievicz joined the anti-Treaty delegation at the Irish Race Convention in Paris in February 1922, and in April departed for America with Kathleen Barry. The 'Countess', who lost her parliamentary seat in the June election, took up a sniper's gun in the Hammon Hotel during the Battle for Dublin, and regularly turned her classically trained artist's pen against those she regarded as the Treatyite agents of British imperialism. One of the most evocative of her 1922 cartoons depicted the abduction and killing in August of Alfred Colley and Seán Cole, senior officers in the republican youth organisation Na Fianna Éireann, that she had co-founded with Bulmer Hobson in 1909. Having spent most of the Civil War period in Britain engaged in underground propaganda work, the newly elected abstentionist member of the Third Dáil joined fellow republican prisoners on hunger strike after her arrest in November 1923. 'Madame' remained a committed and vocal post-Civil War republican, severing ties with Cumann na mBan in 1926 to join the newly established Fianna Fáil party. By then, her long political activism and many terms of imprisonment had taken their toll, and she died on 15 July 1927 aged fifty-nine in a public ward at St Patrick Dun's hospital in Dublin. [Document: National Library of Ireland, MS 13,778/1/1 / See *Dáil Debates*, vol. T, no. 10, 3 January 1922.See also Senia Pašeta, 'Constance Georgine Markievicz', *Dictionary of Irish Biography*, https://www.dib.ie/biography/markievicz-constance-georgine-a5452]

Fig. 14 (right) Cablegram from Michael Collins to Boston's John J. Hearn, a key figure in the American Association for the Recognition of the Irish Republic, 16 March 1922, emphasising the importance of avoiding 'division among Irishmen in America'. [Document: National Library of Ireland, John J. Hearn Papers, MS 15,992/5]

Fig. 15 (below) Page from transcribed notes taken in shorthand by D. McManus of a speech made by Tralee-born Austin Stack (1879–1929) at the Mayflower Theatre, Providence, Rhode Island, 20 March 1922. Éamon de Valera had declined an invitation to speak to the Massachusetts branch of the American Association for the Recognition of the Irish Republic (AARIR), but selected uncompromising republicans Stack and Valentia islander John Joseph O'Kelly ('Sceilg') to represent him. De Valera became president of Cumann na Poblachta, which was formally established in March prior to the US visit, with Stack as one of the vice-presidents. The visit to the United States was seen by the new organisation as a significant opportunity to raise funds 'for the preservation of the Republic'. Stack and 'Sceilg' were joined by Fr Michael O'Flanagan, who was already in the US, and later in April by Kathleen Barry and Constance Markievicz. Stack was an inveterate opponent of the terms of the Treaty and anything that threatened the republic that he had sworn allegiance to. The Mayflower Theatre was one of many venues in the American North East states where he made the case for the republic. Not noted for his oratory, Stack honed his own effective style of delivery during a busy itinerary that saw him make speeches in Atlantic City, Jersey City, Saratoga, Stanford and Syracuse, among other places. Early in his speech in Providence, as with many of his speeches, Stack established his Fenian and republican credentials before proceeding to criticise those who had signed the Treaty. He made it clear that there could be no dishonouring of those like Pearse who had given their lives for the republic: 'we are told today that those men died that we might become members of the British Empire. I say it is a lie'. With an election imminent in his homeland, he then proceeded to attack the 'British' electoral register, which he argued was denying votes to young men and women who had endured much during the struggle for independence. However, Stack reminded his audience that there was still time for the principled among those who supported the Treaty to act. They 'have the framing of the Irish constitution in their hands, [they] can frame a constitution making a Republic of Ireland. The most honourable of them can do it'. When the delegation returned to Ireland in May, over $80,000 had been raised in support of Cumann na Poblachta. [Document: National Library of Ireland, Austin Stack Papers, MS 17,088.4 / See J. Anthony Gaughan, *Austin Stack, Portrait of a separatist* (Dublin, 1977), pp. 194–200]

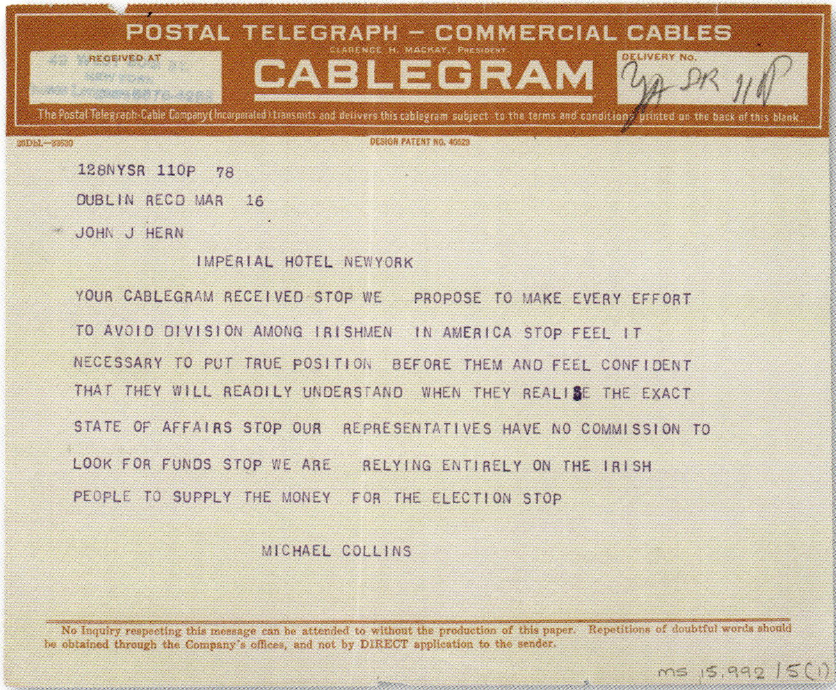

POSTAL TELEGRAPH – COMMERCIAL CABLES

CLARENCE H. MACKAY, PRESIDENT

RECEIVED AT

CABLEGRAM

DELIVERY No.

The Postal Telegraph-Cable Company (Incorporated) transmits and delivers this cablegram subject to the terms and conditions printed on the back of this blank.

DESIGN PATENT NO. 40529

128NYSR 110P 78

DUBLIN RECD MAR 16

JOHN J HERN

IMPERIAL HOTEL NEWYORK

YOUR CABLEGRAM RECEIVED STOP WE PROPOSE TO MAKE EVERY EFFORT TO AVOID DIVISION AMONG IRISHMEN IN AMERICA STOP FEEL IT NECESSARY TO PUT TRUE POSITION BEFORE THEM AND FEEL CONFIDENT THAT THEY WILL READILY UNDERSTAND WHEN THEY REALISE THE EXACT STATE OF AFFAIRS STOP OUR REPRESENTATIVES HAVE NO COMMISSION TO LOOK FOR FUNDS STOP WE ARE RELYING ENTIRELY ON THE IRISH PEOPLE TO SUPPLY THE MONEY FOR THE ELECTION STOP

MICHAEL COLLINS

No Inquiry respecting this message can be attended to without the production of this paper. Repetitions of doubtful words should be obtained through the Company's offices, and not by DIRECT application to the sender.

MS 15,992 / 5(1)

13

someof them were wounded in the conflict for us.

And so you have it. That the young men of Ireland and the young women of Ireland, the people who won the war, have no voice whatever in the coming election.

We say that an election held without giving them a voice-- an election held without the evacuation of every Tommy out of the country, will be null and void.

But all the same, we don't care. We are game, as you found us. We will fight this election, if necessary, on the present register. But we want to make our protest heard: that any decision come to will be null and void.

But even without that protest it would be null and void anyway. Why? Because the young men of Ireland will make it null and void very quick.

Any way, I fear I am detaining you too long. There is only one more point, and that is this.

We want unity and peace in Ireland. (Applause) That isn't a little point by the way. But it is an important point. We do really want peace and unity in Ireland, and it can be had. And it can be had in this way. The men who have the framing of the Irish Constitution, in their hands, can frame a Con-stitution making a Republic of Ireland. (Applause)

The most honorable of them can do it.

They can say it will be a breach of contract with England. Because if you believe they have Canadian status, although Canada today flies -- like the Irish Free State will fly -- the Union Jack in the corner of her flag, and although Canada

Irish-America reacts to the Civil War

The outbreak of the Civil War in June 1922 was greeted with revulsion by most Irish-Americans, and there were some attempts to bring about a reconciliation between the two sides. William Maloney, de Valera's loyal supporter in 1920, and former FOIF president Rev. Peter Magennis travelled to Ireland to meet with representatives of the Free State and republican forces, but they failed to negotiate a truce. Diarmuid Lynch, FOIF national secretary, who travelled to Ireland in a private capacity to attempt to broker peace, also failed.[41]

The AARIR became embroiled in a leadership crisis over how the organisation should respond to the Civil War. Newly appointed President James Murray wanted to use the AARIR to demand a reconciliation between both sides. This proposal was rejected by the executive, and Murray resigned to be replaced by John F. Finerty, a Chicago lawyer who had worked as de Valera's legal counsel during the bond drive.[42]

The anti-Treaty side attracted some American sympathy as a result of the visits of Hanna Sheehy Skeffington and Muriel MacSwiney, whose husband, the republican lord mayor of Cork

Fig. 16 (above) (l-r) Linda Kearns, Hanna Sheehy Skeffington and Kathleen Boland, posing in the snow in Massachusetts around Christmas 1922. [Image: Kathleen Boland Archive, UCC]

Fig. 17 (right) Studio portrait of Kathleen Boland (1889–1954). In her witness statement for the Bureau of Military History, transcribed in September 1951, Kathleen Boland declares her identity as 'Sister of the late Harry Boland' and states at the outset that she was reared 'in the national tradition'. Her family's republican credentials were strong. Her father James, a trade union organiser and prominent leader in both the Irish Republican Brotherhood and the Gaelic Athletic Association, was also a friend of Parnell's. From an early age Kathleen assisted in storing arms at the family home in Marino Crescent, Clontarf, Dublin, including weapons used in the Easter Rising of 1916, which she personally helped to smuggle to Gilbey's wine depot in Fairview – an outpost for the second battalion of the Irish Volunteers. She joined Cumann na mBan after the Rising and, with her mother, 'hosted' several fugitive republicans – including Seán Treacy and Seamus Robinson, exhausted on their return from an ambush at Soloheadbeg in January 1919 – at their home in Clontarf. While brother Harry was in America during the War of Independence, Kathleen worked in his tailor's shop at Middle Abbey Street, Dublin, where she secretly kept a ready supply of arms and gelignite, accessible via a number of disguised recesses at the rear of the premises. She worked closely with Michael Collins from her base in Middle Abbey Street in organising secret meetings and holding money used by the IRA's director of intelligence 'for various purposes', including the purchase of arms. She reveals candidly in her statement that, while Collins held 'no personal appeal for me as a man', he was 'a Trojan worker and kept everyone up to the mark'. She also recalled an angry and upset Harry Boland returning home after a heated exchange with Collins during the Christmas recess in the Treaty debates. Her account of her last hours with the fatally wounded Harry in August 1922 includes his moving reply to her question about who had shot him: 'The only thing I'll say is that it was a friend of my own that was in prison with me that fired the shot. I'll never tell the name and don't try to find out. I forgive him and want no reprisals.' After Harry's death Kathleen toured America as a representative of the Prisoners' Dependants' Fund. Accompanied by Linda Kearns and Hanna Sheehy Skeffington, she visited over two dozen states in twelve months, collecting what she described as 'an awful lot of money'. In 1923 Kathleen married Seán O'Donovan from Clonakilty, a veterinary surgeon who was to become a founding member of Fianna Fáil and serve as a member of Seanad Éireann. Like many women of her time, Kathleen spoke little in later life of her role in 'national activities' and, despite her achievements, she was never properly recognised for her important contribution to the republican cause. [Text: John Fitzgerald / Image: Kathleen Boland Collection, UCC]

Fig. 18 Postcard sent by Kathleen Boland from San Diego to her imprisoned fiancé Seán O'Donovan. [Image: Kathleen Boland Archive, UCC)

Terence MacSwiney, had died in a widely publicised hunger strike in October 1920. The high-profile female emissaries embarked on separate fund-raising tours, facilitated by the AARIR and the Clan, for imprisoned Irish republican soldiers and their dependants.[43] The AARIR faced some opposition by supporters of the Free State. In Baltimore, much to John F. Finerty's frustration, Archbishop Curley denied the AARIR the use of Catholic halls for MacSwiney's speech.[44] While, in comparison to de Valera's bond drive in 1920, these fund-raising efforts had only limited success, their propaganda value nonetheless caused Smiddy deep concern. In a report to Dublin he described Skeffington as 'one of the most active of publicists in the U.S.A. for the irregulars'.[45] Throughout the Civil War she also contributed articles to the *Irish World*, which continued its verbal attacks on the Irish Free State. Many of its headlines and vivid, front-page cartoons accused what it termed 'the Irish Freak State' of acting on the orders of the British to destroy the Irish republic.

The anti-Treaty side in Ireland desperately needed finance and looked longingly at the vast amounts of unspent bond-drive funds in American banks. Given his legal background, Finerty became involved in a struggle to obtain these funds, which he, with other republicans, rightly argued belonged to the Irish republic. In August 1922 Smiddy obtained an injunction from an American court which effectively froze the funds, preventing either side from making withdrawals.[46] This affected the anti-Treaty side far more than the Free State, which had superior resources at its disposal.

Blaming de Valera

The FOIF leadership, including Cohalan and Devoy, who fully backed the Free State in the conflict, redoubled its support for the pro-Treaty side after the death of Michael Collins in an ambush at Béal na Blá in west Cork in August 1922. Judge Cohalan wrote a moving tribute to Collins for *Pearsons' Magazine*, which highlighted de Valera's part in the conflict:

> Shot down in his early thirties at the very moment of victory he has left behind him an inheritance that will steady and stabilize his people and make them with iron resolution put out the last fitful flashes of that flame of insensate fury with which the malignant vanity of de Valera has scourged a long-suffering people.[47]

The *Gaelic American* was constant in its support for the pro-Treaty side. After the killing of pro-Treaty TD Seán Hales on 7 December 1922, the newspaper supported the reprisal executions of four republican prisoners, including Liam Mellows, in Mountjoy. Under the headline 'Executions to Protect Nation's Life', the paper explained that such actions were 'vital to the existence of the nation' and a necessary response to 'a definite plan to decapitate the nation by extermination of the Government and Parliament'.[48] De Valera had limited influence on the anti-Treaty IRA after June 1922, but the *Gaelic American* tended to exaggerate his role in the conflict. In a bitter editorial in September 1922, Devoy claimed that: 'He [de Valera] is a monster which must be punished for his crimes. Eliminate him and the trouble will soon end.'[49]

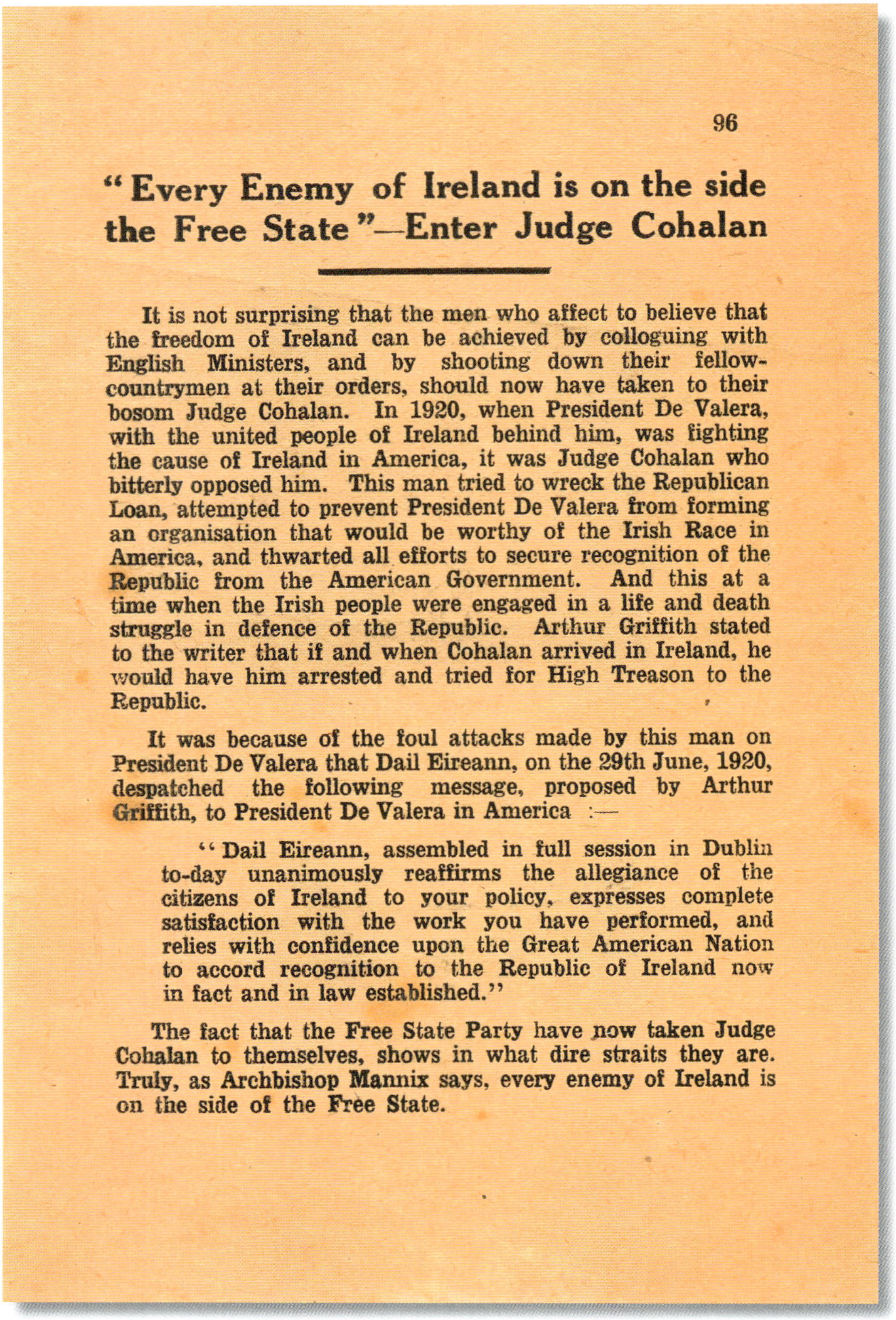

96

"Every Enemy of Ireland is on the side the Free State"—Enter Judge Cohalan

It is not surprising that the men who affect to believe that the freedom of Ireland can be achieved by colloguing with English Ministers, and by shooting down their fellow-countrymen at their orders, should now have taken to their bosom Judge Cohalan. In 1920, when President De Valera, with the united people of Ireland behind him, was fighting the cause of Ireland in America, it was Judge Cohalan who bitterly opposed him. This man tried to wreck the Republican Loan, attempted to prevent President De Valera from forming an organisation that would be worthy of the Irish Race in America, and thwarted all efforts to secure recognition of the Republic from the American Government. And this at a time when the Irish people were engaged in a life and death struggle in defence of the Republic. Arthur Griffith stated to the writer that if and when Cohalan arrived in Ireland, he would have him arrested and tried for High Treason to the Republic.

It was because of the foul attacks made by this man on President De Valera that Dail Eireann, on the 29th June, 1920, despatched the following message, proposed by Arthur Griffith, to President De Valera in America :—

> "Dail Eireann, assembled in full session in Dublin to-day unanimously reaffirms the allegiance of the citizens of Ireland to your policy, expresses complete satisfaction with the work you have performed, and relies with confidence upon the Great American Nation to accord recognition to the Republic of Ireland now in fact and in law established."

The fact that the Free State Party have now taken Judge Cohalan to themselves, shows in what dire straits they are. Truly, as Archbishop Mannix says, every enemy of Ireland is on the side of the Free State.

Fig. 19 Anti-Treaty handbill referencing Judge Daniel Cohalan. While still a New York Supreme Court justice, second-generation Irish-American and Friends of Irish Freedom leader, Judge Daniel Cohalan, travelled to Ireland in 1923 to support the electioneering efforts of William T. Cosgrave's pro-Treaty Cumann na nGaedheal party. He accompanied Cosgrave on an election tour of the country, during which they travelled in a small aircraft. In this anti-Treaty handbill Cohalan's support for the Free State was noted by the Sinn Féin opposition party, which also recalled his earlier clash with de Valera in 1920. The title of the handbill is drawn from a speech made by anti-Treaty Australian Archbishop Daniel Mannix in Melbourne on St Patrick's Day in 1923. [Text: Michael Doorley / Document: courtesy of Kilmainham Gaol Museum/OPW KMGLM-21NO-1K54-28]

Republican seizure of the Irish consulate

The Irish Civil War in the United States was generally fought in newspaper headlines, speeches and at public meetings. While there is no recorded violence between the two sides, the threat was ever present. On the morning of 27 December 1922, for example, an anti-Treaty group led by Sinn Féin TD Laurence Ginnell seized the Irish consulate on Nassau Street in Lower Manhattan. Ginnell was accompanied by IRA man Robert Briscoe, then 'on the run' in the United States, Jim Finerty and other AARIR members. According to Briscoe's memoir and Smiddy's reports to Dublin, they intended to secure a list of American bond-certificate holders who could then be persuaded to claim back the money for the anti-Treaty side.[50] In the event no such list was found, but Ginnell still argued that the office properly belonged to the Irish republic.

Unsurprisingly, neither Smiddy nor the Irish government's newly appointed trade representative Lindsay Crawford recognised Ginnell's claim. Both sides agreed to avoid using force until the issue was resolved, but an ensuing stand-off lasted several days. During this period the anti-Treatyites in the Irish consulate were joined by Muriel MacSwiney and another activist, Gertrude Corles, who undoubtedly welcomed the wide coverage of the incident by the US press.[51] Finally, on 30 December, Smiddy produced a receipt for the rent of the building. Facing arrest for trespassing, the republican group reluctantly withdrew. In his report to Desmond FitzGerald, minister for external affairs in Dublin, Smiddy emphasised the legal support of Judge Cohalan in his efforts to eject the 'intruders'.[52]

Fig. 20 John Devoy with Irish Free State dignitaries (l–r) Richard Mulcahy, Diarmaid O'Hegarty, Harry Cunningham, Mary Collins Powell (sister of Michael Collins), John Devoy, General Michael Brennan and the minister for external affairs, Desmond FitzGerald. In July-August 1924 Kildare-born veteran Fenian John Devoy made his first visit to Ireland since a clandestine trip during the Land War in 1879. After the Civil War Devoy's newspaper *The Gaelic American* and the Friends of Irish Freedom (FOIF) became increasingly critical of what they described as the 'reactionary' tendencies of the Cosgrave administration and its economic overdependence on Britain. It also objected strenuously to the Free State's application to join the League of Nations, an organisation that the FOIF had violently opposed in 1920, contributing to the split with de Valera and the American Association for Recognition of the Irish Republic. In April 1924 the FOIF sent funds to Joe McGrath's 'National Group' of nine TDs who had withdrawn from the governing Cumann na nGaedheal party in protest at its handling of the Irish army mutiny of March 1924. President of the Executive Council of the Irish Free State William T. Cosgrave was aware of this but made every effort to conciliate John Devoy during his visit to Ireland to attend the inaugural Aonach Tailteann. The pro-Treaty government seized the opportunity afforded by Devoy's visit to present the new Irish state as a living link with the Fenian struggle for Irish nationhood in the previous century. [Text: Michael Doorley / Image: courtesy of Kilmainham Gaol Museum/OPW KMGLM-20PO-1A58-10]

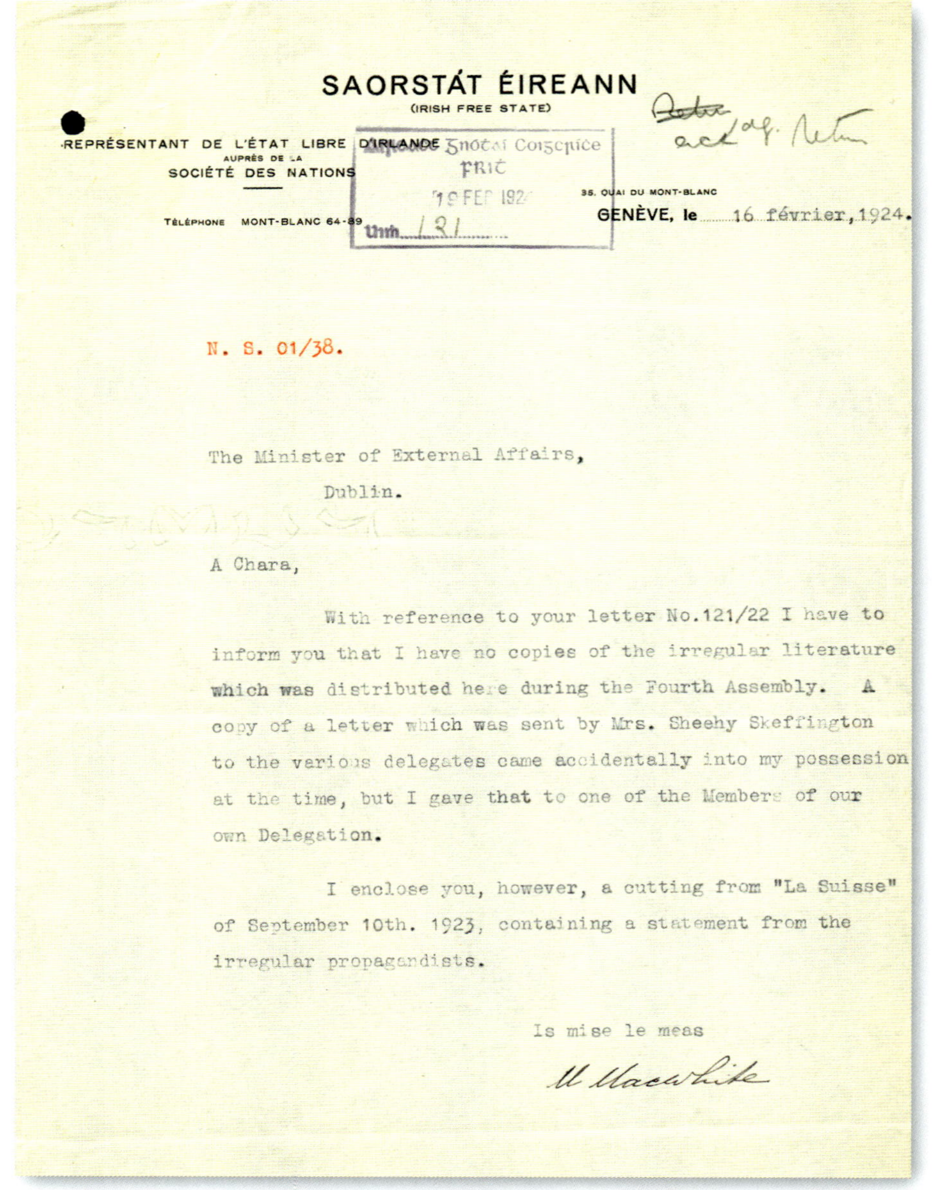

SAORSTÁT ÉIREANN
(IRISH FREE STATE)

REPRÉSENTANT DE L'ÉTAT LIBRE D'IRLANDE
AUPRÈS DE LA
SOCIÉTÉ DES NATIONS

TÉLÉPHONE MONT-BLANC 64-89

35, QUAI DU MONT-BLANC
GENÈVE, le 16 février, 1924.

N. S. 01/38.

The Minister of External Affairs,
Dublin.

A Chara,

With reference to your letter No.121/22 I have to inform you that I have no copies of the irregular literature which was distributed here during the Fourth Assembly. A copy of a letter which was sent by Mrs. Sheehy Skeffington to the various delegates came accidentally into my possession at the time, but I gave that to one of the Members of our own Delegation.

I enclose you, however, a cutting from "La Suisse" of September 10th. 1923, containing a statement from the irregular propagandists.

Is mise le meas

M MacWhite

Fig. 21 Letter from Michael MacWhite to Desmond FitzGerald, 16 February 1924. This letter from MacWhite, the Cork-born former French Legionnaire, who was now the Irish permanent delegate to the League of Nations to the Irish Free State's minister for external affairs, reveals an overseas echo of the Civil War that had ended the previous year. It concerns the activities of 'Irregular propagandists' in Geneva during the Fourth Assembly of the League of Nations, which the Irish Free State had first attended on 10 September 1923. Both the author and the subject of his correspondence, feminist and republican activist Hanna Sheehy Skeffington, were playing roles akin to those they had played during the revolution. Sheehy Skeffington, whose pacifist husband Francis was shot without trial by the British during the Easter Rising, had embarked on publicity and fund-raising tours of the United States in 1917–18 and 1922–3, while the Francophone MacWhite was a member of the First Dáil Éireann's mission to Paris in early 1919, tasked with lobbying the post-war peace conference to recognise Irish independence. In the first half of 1922 the pro-Treaty faction needed to build up a new foreign service, partly to counter anti-Treaty – or, as MacWhite later had it, 'Irregular' – propaganda. An instinct for international lobbying and activism, both inside and outside the Irish diaspora, was ingrained within the culture of the independence movement and survived the Treaty split. Many of those who had represented the Dáil abroad and subsequently opposed the Treaty devoted their energies to opposing the Provisional Government and the nascent Free State. The pro-Treaty authorities took a great interest in their activities; they were especially concerned with support for the anti-Treaty cause within the diaspora communities of the United States and Britain, and were also aware that their own actions, such as the policy of executions, could have detrimental consequences in countries such as France. In general they sought to justify their policies and to counter the overseas activities of their opponents. To that end they requested that they be kept abreast of those activities by their own international representatives. The letter reproduced here was not the first of its kind: just after Christmas 1922 MacWhite had reported back to Dublin on the purported activities of a republican messenger in Lausanne attempting to facilitate links between anti-Treaty forces and the Russian Bolsheviks. After the end of the Civil War the ideological conflict over the Treaty continued internationally as both the new Irish Free State and its opponents sought to challenge or affirm the Treaty's legitimacy overseas, and to denounce or defend their actions during and after the Civil War. The physical Civil War ended in May 1923; the propaganda war, as hinted at in MacWhite's letter, continued both at home and abroad throughout the 1920s and beyond. [Text: John Gibney / Document: National Archives, DFA/1/LN/28. Reproduced by kind permission of the Director of the National Archives]

There is no doubt that Smiddy feared further republican action, and security at his Washington office was stepped up. He also hired six private detectives to monitor the activities of Briscoe, who he described as a 'great intriguer'. In a memo to Dublin, Smiddy also pleaded for more financial assistance to establish a well-organised secret service to counter republican plots against him and other supporters of the Free State in the United States:

> I have learned from inside sources that an attempt was contemplated, after the execution of Mellows, on the lives of Geddis [*sic*] [Sir Aukland Geddes, British Ambassador in Washington], the Representative of the Irish Free State in Washington [Smiddy himself] and Judge Colohan [*sic*] [Daniel Cohalan], and that attempts will be made to carry out their intention should de Valera be shot. They will not succeed in getting away with action of this kind in America as easily as they are, unfortunately, doing in Ireland.[53]

In his communications to his superiors in Dublin, Smiddy referred to possible collusion between republican anti-Treaty 'irregulars' and 'reds' in New York. This was a common theme in his reports and in his work as an Irish envoy in the United States.[54] While little evidence exists for such claims, these allegations during the so-called 'Red Scare' of the early 1920s must have influenced American opinion. Unlike de Valera's mission in 1919–20, the anti-Treaty side had little support in Congress or from the Catholic Church in America. While some prominent American figures supported de Valera, and AARIR meetings could always count on the participation of individual priests, this did not match the level of clerical support for the pro-Treaty side.

End of conflict

After the conflict ended in 1923, each side looked to its allies in America for support. Many in the defeated republican ranks, unable to find work in Ireland, emigrated to the United States. This was frowned upon by some anti-Treaty IRA leaders, who complained that those who emigrated were 'playing the enemy's game', but there was little they could do to prevent the exodus.[55] While some immigrants severed their links with republican politics, others joined the declining ranks of McGarrity's Clan na Gael or the AARIR. Brian Hanley estimates a 1929 AARIR membership of just 1,722 across the US, and this may have further fallen in depression-era America. The republican paper *An Phoblacht* had only 100 American subscribers in 1932.[56]

Meanwhile, de Valera continued to engage in fund-raising trips to the United States. After a New York court ordered that the bond monies should be released to the subscribers in 1927, de Valera offered the bond holders shares in his new company, the Irish Press Corporation, which was registered in Delaware. These funds helped to launch the *Irish Press* newspaper in Dublin and did much to further the aims of de Valera's new Fianna Fáil party.[57]

Having secured victory, the Free State government was not interested in fund-raising. Instead, it sought American diplomatic support to enhance the political legitimacy of the new Irish state. This goal received a boost in 1924 when the United States recognised Timothy Smiddy as the Free State's first minister plenipotentiary in

Fig. 22 American Association for the Recognition of the Irish Republic (AARIR) demonstration in Washington, 3 October 1925. Richard Mulcahy served as commander in chief of the National Army after the death of Michael Collins in August 1922. During his tenure as army leader, eighty-one anti-Treaty prisoners were executed. In 1925 he represented the Free State government at an Inter-Parliamentary Union meeting in the United States, where he encountered demonstrations against his visit by members of the AARIR. The protestors' placards recall his Irish Civil War record and describe him as the 'Benedict Arnold of Ireland'. The organisation, which had acted as a support group for the anti-Treaty side during the Civil War, was in decline by 1925 but, as this photograph suggests, it could still muster protests against visiting Free State dignitaries. [Text: Michael Doorley / Image: Library of Congress Prints and Photographs Division Washington, LC-F8- 37603 [P&P]]

Washington. As Carroll points out, the Irish Free State was the first British dominion to be given diplomatic recognition by the United States. This did much to convince international and domestic audiences that Ireland was an independent country, though still a member of the Commonwealth.[58]

The Irish-American response to the Civil War was undoubtedly influenced by the bitter, earlier split in the Irish nationalist movement in the United States. Yet while memories of that earlier conflict shaped the respective responses to the Treaty and provided useful ammunition for both sides, there were other more fundamental factors at play, namely, the overwhelming public and press support for the Treaty, public revulsion at the fratricidal conflict in Ireland, and the absence of support for the anti-Treaty side in Congress and among the influential Catholic hierarchy in America. Ultimately, all Irish-American organisations and nationalist parties in Ireland had to contend with a declining American interest in Ireland and the general sense that, after the end of the Civil War, the Irish question had finally been settled.[59] In an interview with the *Cork Examiner* in 1926, during one of his many visits to his summer home at Glandore in west Cork, Cohalan remarked that Ireland had 'completely disappeared from the newspapers and in a large way from the public thought of America'.[60] Of course, the Civil War was not forgotten in Ireland and the bitter legacy of the conflict cast a long shadow for many decades to come.[61]

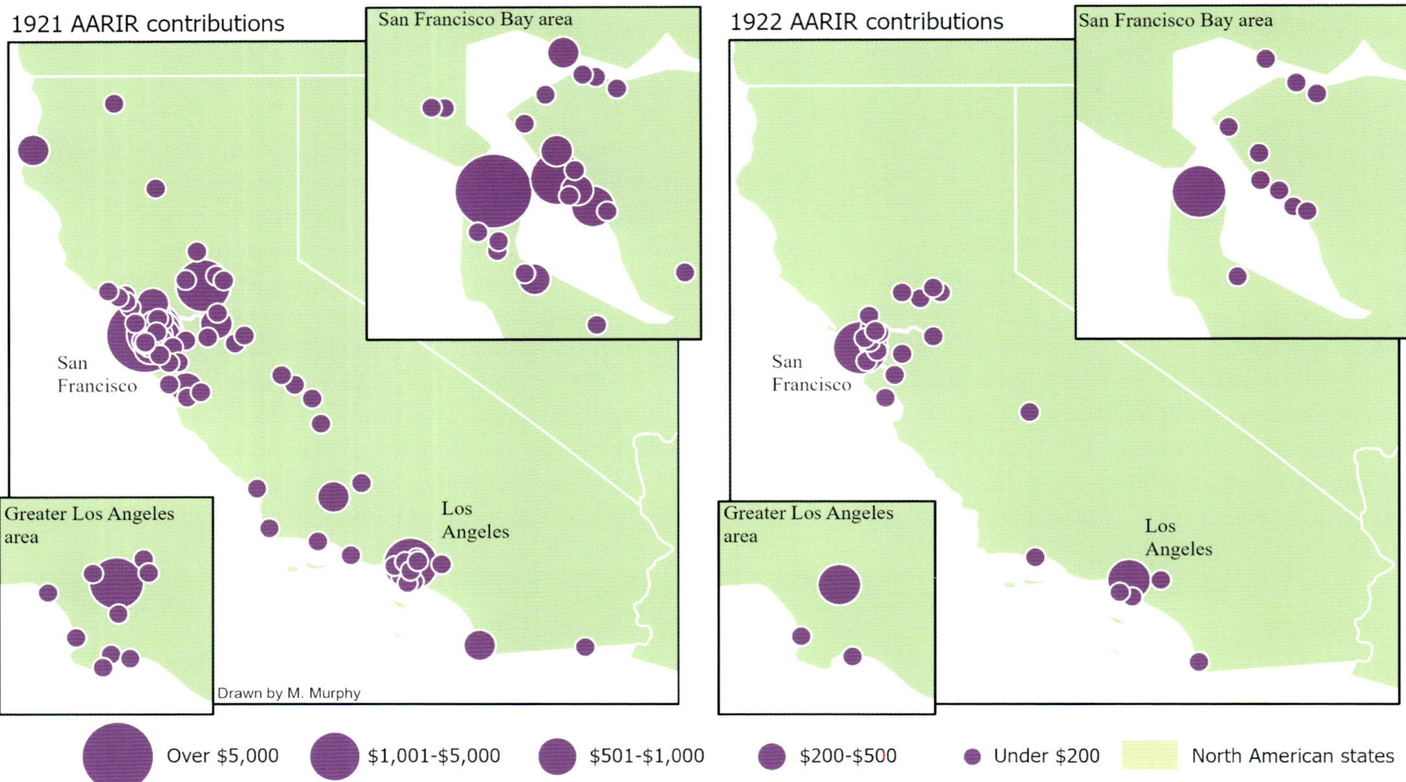

Fig. 23 (left) The Californian branches of the AARIR active in 1921 and (right) in 1922. The American Association for the Recognition of the Irish Republic (AARIR) was a mass movement of (primarily) Irish-Americans in support of Irish independence. Directly controlled by emissaries of Dáil Éireann, the AARIR raised funds for various Irish republican initiatives and waged a propaganda campaign to secure American support for Irish independence. One of its most effective state organisations was in California, which was dominated by its highly active San Francisco branches. By the summer of 1921 the AARIR in California numbered 174 branches in sixty-five different towns and cities, with roughly 35,000 members. San Francisco alone accounted for sixty-six branches and 23,880 members. By that time the Irish-American diaspora was highly mobilised and responding with increasing urgency to the violent British counter-insurgency campaign in Ireland. The map on the left shows active California AARIR branches in 1921, along with their paid affiliation fees raised from membership dues. The map on the right shows the active branches in 1922, as Civil War loomed in Ireland. Though the AARIR opposed the Anglo-Irish Treaty, the split had cataclysmic effects for the American organisation. In California the AARIR lost over half of its branches (from 174 to eighty-two) between 1921 and 1922. Membership fees dropped even more precipitously, from $21,906 in 1921 to $3,066 in 1922, or just 14 per cent of the 1921 total. Similar collapses were apparent nationally. The end of British state violence in Ireland, ambiguity over the Treaty's implications for independence, and wariness at taking sides in a civil war between Irish nationalists, caused many AARIR members to drop out of the movement. While it continued to function throughout the Civil War and even into the 1930s, the AARIR no longer carried the same political weight. Darragh Gannon's work on a similar Irish republican support group in Great Britain, the Irish Self Determination League (see *Conflict, Diaspora, and Empire: Irish nationalism in Britain, 1912–1922* (Cambridge: 2023), shows the same kind of membership collapse during the Civil War, an outcome that seems to have been largely replicated elsewhere among the politically organised Irish global diaspora. [Source: AARIR State of California, Office of the State Secretary Detailed Statement of Cash Receipts 1 January 1921 to 4 January 1923, Fr York Papers, Bancroft Library, University of California]

CASE STUDY

Unfinished Business in Post-Civil War Ireland: The repatriation of Fr Albert Bibby and Fr Dominic O'Connor

John Borgonovo

Two members of the Irish Capuchin Franciscan Friars religious order, Fr Albert Bibby and Fr Dominic O'Connor, were closely associated with the republican movement from 1916 to 1923. After the 1916 Rising, the Dublin-based Bibby attended several rebel leaders before their execution. Father Dominic was the IRA's Cork No. 1 Brigade chaplain during the War of Independence, and became internationally known for ministering to the assassinated Cork lord mayor Tomás MacCurtain and his successor, Terence MacSwiney, during the latter's fatal hunger strike in 1920. O'Connor gained further notoriety after he was convicted by a British military court in 1921 and served a year in prison. Both Bibby and O'Connor rejected the Anglo-Irish Treaty and, at the outset of the Civil War, joined the IRA's Four Courts garrison. During the opening phase of fighting, the two priests were highly visible and active chaplains attached to the republican forces.

In late 1922 Capuchin authorities dispatched Father Dominic to the far reaches of the western United States, almost certainly because of his anti-Treaty activism. Dominic was assigned to the remote Baker diocese in the high desert of eastern Oregon, which was administered by the Capuchins. In early 1924 Father Albert, already in poor health, was transferred to the Capuchin's mission at Santa Inez near Santa Barbara, California. He died within months of his arrival and was buried there. Dominic remained in the United States, and in 1935 died and was buried in Bend, Oregon. Both priests told their friends that they wished Ireland to be their final resting place.

Fig. 1 Copy of a pencil sketch of Fr Dominic O'Connor OFM Cap. (1883–1935), a British army chaplain in Salonika during the First World War, and chaplain to the IRA in Cork during the War of Independence and in Dublin during the Civil War. The artist is thought to have been Kathleen Shackleton (1884–961), the Dublin-born, Montreal-based journalist and illustrator and sister of the Antarctic explorer, Ernest Shackleton. [Image: courtesy of the Irish Capuchin Archives]

Initial inquiries

Shortly after Father Dominic's death, his former Cork city IRA colleagues made inquiries about repatriating his remains. The Cork effort included mainly anti-Treaty veterans but was spearheaded by Neutral IRA leaders Florrie O'Donoghue and Seán O'Hegarty and their close friend and brother of Dominic, Joe O'Connor, a leading IRA officer during the Civil War. All had been excommunicated by their local bishop, Daniel Cohalan (initially in 1920 and subsequently in 1922; O'Donoghue and O'Hegarty did not

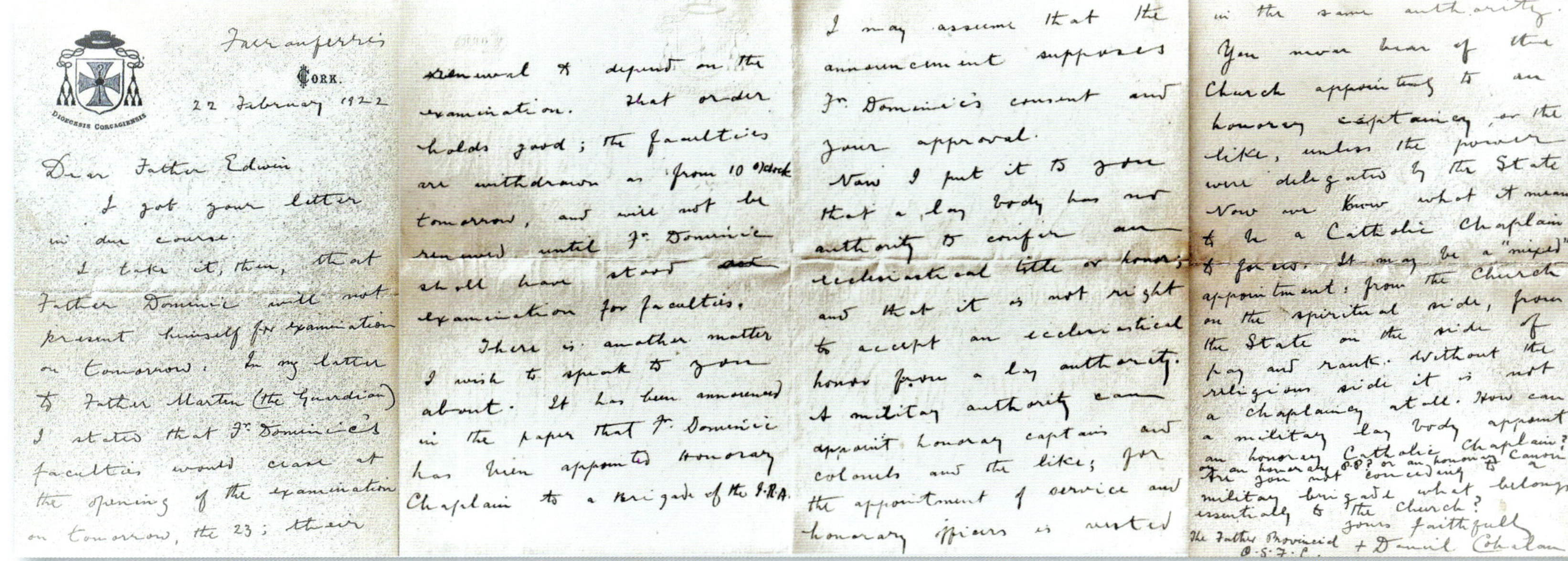

Farranferris
CORK.
22 February 1922

Dioecesis Corcagiensis

Dear Father Edwin

I got your letter in due course.

I take it, then, that Father Dominic will not present himself for examination on tomorrow. In my letter to Father Martin (the Guardian) I stated that Fr Dominic's faculties would cease at the opening of the examination on tomorrow, the 23; their renewal to depend on the examination. That order holds good; the faculties are withdrawn as from 10 o'clock tomorrow, and will not be renewed until Fr Dominic shall have stood examination for faculties.

There is another matter I wish to speak to you about. It has been announced in the paper that Fr Dominic has been appointed Honorary Chaplain to a brigade of the I.R.A. I may assume that the announcement supposes Fr Dominic's consent and your approval. Now I put it to you that a lay body has no authority to confer an ecclesiastical title or honour, and that it is not right to accept an ecclesiastical honor from a lay authority. A military authority can appoint honorary captains and colonels and the like; for the appointment of service and honorary officers is vested in the same authority. You never hear of the Church appointing to an honorary captaincy, or the like, unless the power were delegated by the State. Now we know what it means to be a Catholic Chaplain to forces. It may be a "mixed" appointment: from the Church on the spiritual side, from the State on the side of pay and rank. Without the religious side it is not a chaplaincy at all. How can a military lay body appoint an honorary Catholic Chaplain? an honorary D.D.? or an honorary Canon? Are you not conceding to a military brigade what belongs essentially to the Church?

Yours faithfully
+ Daniel Cohalan

The Father Provincial
O.S.F.C.

Fig. 2 Letter from Daniel Cohalan, Catholic bishop of Cork 1916–52, to Fr Edwin Fitzgibbon OFM Cap., provincial minister, 22 February 1922. Cohalan expresses his displeasure at learning of Fr Dominic's appointment as chaplain to the IRA's 1st Southern Division: 'Now I put it to you that a lay body has no authority to confer an ecclesiastical title or honour … Are you now conceding to a military brigade what belongs essentially to the Church?' Tension between the bishop and Fr Dominic spiked in December 1920 after Bishop Cohalan excommunicated IRA fighters in the Cork No. 1 Brigade. In response Fr Dominic had instructed the Volunteers to ignore the order, and 'let the boys keep going to Mass and Confession as usual'. Cohalan had his vengeance the following year, after Fr Dominic was released from prison in Britain. The bishop immediately ordered Dominic to submit to a theology examination given by Cohalan himself or face suspension of his priestly faculties, noting that Dominic had not had an opportunity to study theology in jail (Dominic held an advanced degree in theology from the University of Louvain). Through his Capuchin superior, Fr Dominic asked for a postponement, citing the 'degrading and cruel treatment he suffered these past 13 or 14 months'. Bishop Cohalan, however, was unmoved and suspended Fr Dominic from saying Mass or hearing confession in the Cork diocese. In this letter the bishop added insult to injury by criticising Fr Dominic for accepting the IRA chaplain commission announced in the press the previous day. [Image: courtesy of the Irish Capuchin Archives]

fall under the 1922 order), which added another complicating layer to their efforts to retrieve their exiled comrade. In 1930, during an unsuccessful petition to the papal nuncio in Ireland to revoke Bishop Cohalan's 1920 excommunication of IRA fighters, O'Hegarty and O'Donoghue made their feelings clear: 'the men are now scattered […] but wherever they are and under whatever conditions they live, over all our heads hovers the nightmare horror of this decree of excommunication: tarnishing our honour, besmirching our motives, a challenge to our historical justification, a menace to the salvation of our souls'. It can be assumed that they and their colleagues shared similar feelings about the Irish bishops' 1922 excommunication decree during the Civil War.

Rebuffed by the Irish government

The efforts to repatriate both Dominic and Albert stalled during the Second World War, but gathered momentum afterwards. In the early 1950s, after consultations between Dublin and Rome, the Capuchin authorities agreed to authorise the reburial of both priests in Ireland if the return was sanctioned by the Irish government and the ceremony was not overtly political. The Capuchins did not want to reignite the Treaty split or have the return exploited politically by the contemporary IRA. By now the Cork Father Dominic Committee had asked Dublin IRA veterans to form a Father Albert repatriation committee, to combine efforts and facilitate two reburials. The Father Albert committee was comprised of both pro- and anti-Treaty veterans of the Dublin Old IRA and was led by Fianna Fáil TD Oscar Traynor. After consulting with the O'Connor and Bibby families, the two committees asked Ireland's President Seán T. O'Kelly to sanction the reburials, a permission that the Capuchin authorities required. While O'Kelly was privately supportive, he deferred the decision to the government of the day – an inter-party government with John A. Costello of Fine Gael as Taoiseach. Costello's Cabinet rejected the repatriation, possibly at the request of Fine Gael minister Richard Mulcahy. The two committees decided to quietly accept the rebuff and wait until Fianna Fáil eventually returned to power.

American rivals

About this time, an Old IRA repatriation committee was established in the United States to finance and organise the American end of the initiative. However, the American end was muddled by the activities of two rival repatriation committees established independently by individual republicans from within New York City's Irish-American community. The two unauthorised committees caused consternation in Ireland because they were unconnected to the more thorough and methodical Irish committees, emphasised the priests' Civil War service, confused Irish-Americans by issuing duplicate public appeals, and alarmed the Capuchin authorities in Dublin with aggressive and incendiary overtures. Of particular concern was the committee led by Charles Tiernan, which tried to liaise with the republican-affiliated National Graves Association in Dublin and was well disposed towards the contemporary IRA. To rein in the American committees and organise the American leg of the repatriation, the Cork committee turned to yet another former comrade, city IRA veteran Connie Neenan, who had remained active in Irish-American republican circles from his base in New York. Beyond his ability to mobilise IRA veterans of the 1919–23 period in the United States, Neenan could also steer the initiative clear of the two rival repatriation committees. At Florrie O'Donoghue's request, Neenan used his contacts among the Old IRA and New York Irish communities to isolate the rival American committees and stymie their fund-raising, going as far as arranging for the influential *Irish World* newspaper to refuse to carry the American committees' financial appeals.

Approval at last

The repatriation effort accelerated following Fianna Fáil's return to government in 1957. Florrie O'Donoghue quickly met with the new Taoiseach, Éamon de Valera, to secure government approval for the reburials. A major potential complication had arisen with the IRA's border campaign in 1957, which produced massive public funerals for the slain IRA Volunteers Seán South and Fergal O'Hanlon, and the introduction of internment of IRA suspects in July. Amid a tense cross-border environment, de Valera was particularly wary of any exploitation of the Fathers Dominic and Albert reburial by the American repatriation committee led by Charles Tiernan. O'Donoghue assured de Valera that Tiernan would not be involved, and ultimately received de Valera's blessing, albeit with a pointed parting instruction that O'Donoghue ensure 'the transfer was carried out in a dignified manner'.

Repatriation costs in Ireland were to be paid by the Father Dominic and Father Albert committees, which raised funds within the IRA veterans' community, thereby maintaining a degree of control. At the direction of the Capuchin provincial general, Irish fund-raising circulars omitted reference to the Civil War, mentioning only the priests' service in the 1916–21 conflict. Anticipating opposition from Archbishop John Charles McQuaid to the reburial of Father Albert in Dublin, the groups secured permission to bury both priests in the Capuchin monastery in Rochestown, just outside Cork city. In the United States, what might be called the 'official' Father Dominic and Albert committee arranged its end of proceedings and raised funds to finance the exhumation of the corpses, new coffins and transportation back to Ireland. Members of the Irish diaspora were visible at every stage of the process, from the different priests who accompanied and prayed over the remains, to the morticians who placed the corpses in new coffins, and to the Waterford Crystal agents who liaised with TWA airlines for the final flight from San Francisco to Shannon airport.

Fig. 3 Postcard print of Fr Dominic O'Connor OFM Cap. (seated at the front, second from the left) with a group of republicans at Fairpost, California on St Patrick's Day, 17 March 1923. The remote community of Fairpost, straddling the California/Oregon border, at that time accommodated logging, mining, and cattle and sheep ranching. This group of Irish sheep ranchers hailed primarily from Kiskeam/Newmarket in County Cork. According to the Military Service Pensions Collection, at least twenty IRA veterans from that part of north Cork found themselves in Oregon by 1935, most of them around Lake County. This isolated high-desert location on Oregon's southern border was over 300 miles from Fr Dominic's first parish in Baker, and is a ghost town today. [Image: courtesy of the Irish Capuchin Archives]

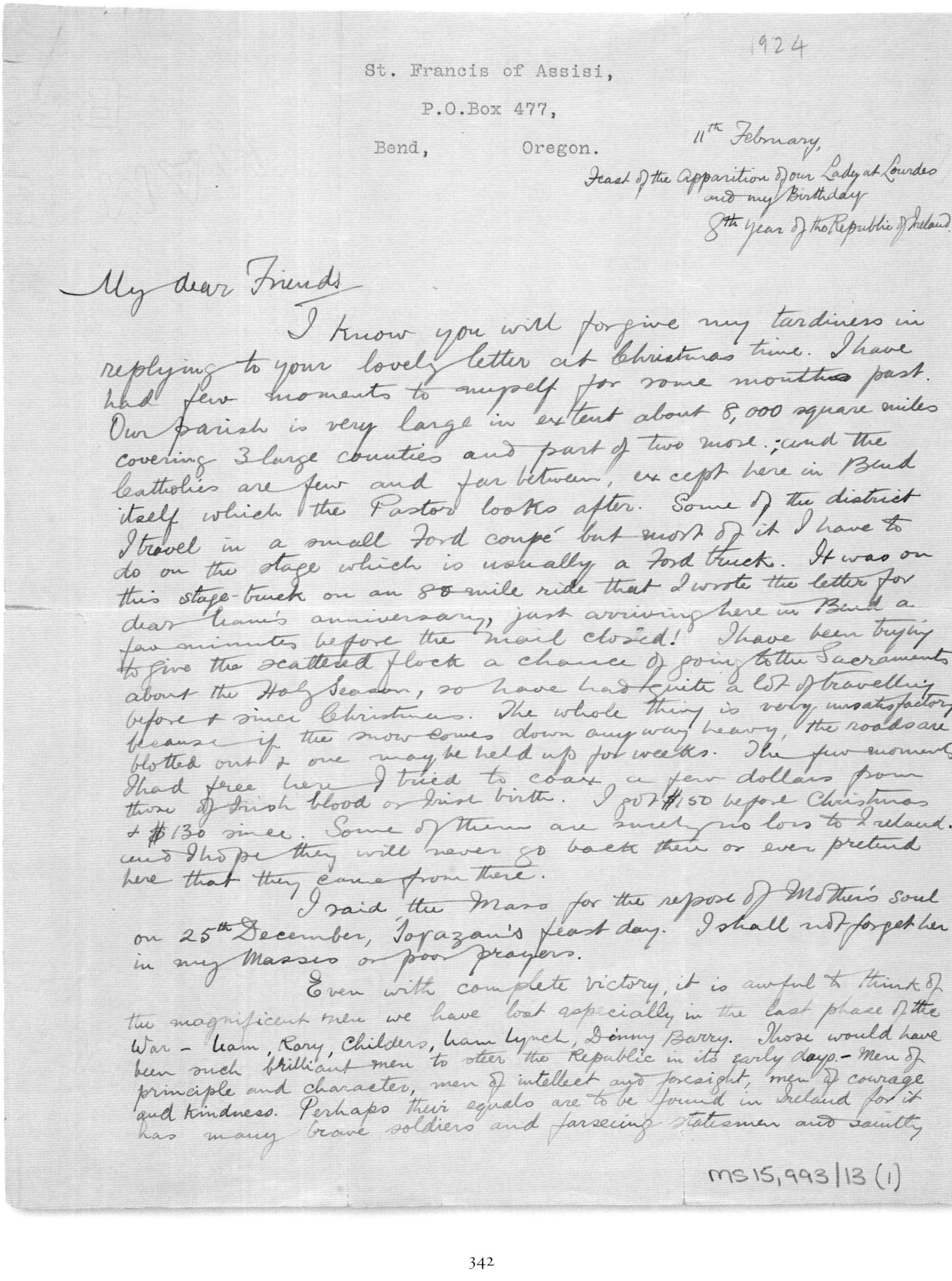

1924

St. Francis of Assisi,

P.O.Box 477,

Bend, Oregon.

11th February,
Feast of the Apparition of our Lady at Lourdes
and my Birthday
8th Year of the Republic of Ireland.

My dear Friends

I know you will forgive my tardiness in replying to your lovely letter at Christmas time. I have had few moments to myself for some months past. Our parish is very large in extent about 8,000 square miles covering 3 large counties and part of two more; and the Catholics are few and far between, except here in Bend itself which the Pastor looks after. Some of the district I travel in a small Ford coupé but most of it I have to do on the stage which is usually a Ford truck. It was on this stage-truck on an 80 mile ride that I wrote the letter for dear Liam's anniversary, just arriving here in Bend a few minutes before the mail closed! I have been trying to give the scattered flock a chance of going to the Sacraments about the Holy Season, so have had quite a lot of travelling before & since Christmas. The whole thing is very unsatisfactory because if the snow comes down any way heavy, the roads are blotted out & one may be held up for weeks. The few moments I had free here I tried to coax a few dollars from those of Irish blood or Irish birth. I got $150 before Christmas & $130 since. Some of them are surely no loss to Ireland and I hope they will never go back there or ever pretend here that they came from there.

I said the Mass for the repose of Mother's soul on 25th December, Tojazan's feast day. I shall not forget her in my Masses or poor prayers.

Even with complete victory, it is awful to think of the magnificent men we have lost especially in the last phase of the War – Liam, Rory, Childers, Liam Lynch, Denny Barry. Those would have been such brilliant men to steer the Republic in its early days. – Men of principle and character, men of intellect and foresight, men of courage and kindness. Perhaps their equals are to be found in Ireland for it has many brave soldiers and farseeing statesmen and saintly

Fig. 4 (opposite) First page of a letter from Fr Dominic O'Connor OFM. Cap. to John J. Hearn of the American Association for the Recognition of the Irish Republic, 11 February 1924. In this two-page letter, Fr Dominic gives a sense of the vastness of his Oregon parish, which extended to 'about 8,000 square miles covering 3 large counties and part of two more', and the difficulties involved in travelling large distances to minister to his 'scattered flock'. Cork-born O'Connor, who was ordained on 17 March 1906 in the Capuchin friary in Kilkenny, was, as this letter attests, a committed republican. He was arrested at the Capuchin friary in Dublin's Church Street in 1921 and sentenced to five-years' imprisonment, during which he befriended republican internees Ernie O'Malley and Pádraig Ó Caoimh. Released in the wake of Dáil's approval of the Treaty in January 1922, he was present with Fr Albert Biddy at the Four Courts when it was bombarded by the National Army on 28 June 1922. In this letter to Hearn, he explained that his suggestion that the republicans should engage in military action before June had been 'turned down solely because they would precipitate "civil war"' and that 'it was only after the first days of firing on the Four Courts that Rory [O'Connor] realised how low the Free Traitor crowd had fallen'. The priest lamented the loss during the Civil War of Liam Mellows, Liam Lynch, Erskine Childers and Rory O'Connor, who would 'have been such brilliant men to steer the Republic in its early days'. 'Ireland', he wrote, 'will be lonely whenever I get a chance of going back, my best friends in the grave'. However, the 'Army and the Government of the Republic have stood the test and have preferred suffering and death to denial of principle, truth with hunger to falsehood and wealth'. He finishes with the hope that he might live to see the 'sight of Ireland's freedom' and 'die on the bosom of my mother Éire'. Fr Dominic died on 17 October 1935 in Bend, Oregon, and was buried there, 'on a sweet and gentle slope amid the tall pines'. [Document: National Library of Ireland, John J. Hearn Papers, MS 15,993/13]

Fig. 5 (below) The remains of Fathers Albert and Dominic after their arrival at Shannon airport, 13 June 1958. Taoiseach Éamon de Valera can be seen with his hat removed, standing behind the Old IRA honour guard. To de Valera's left – two across – in the second row stands Old IRA leader Florrie O'Donoghue (directly behind the hatted man standing at an angle just in front of the coffins). While the Old IRA organised the repatriation, the Capuchin friars were given prominence and the authority to issue invitations to the proceedings. This was done to reduce Civil War tensions, as the Capuchins and the government (and preceding governments) did not want the repatriation to become a divisive 'partisan spectacle'. At the airport, honour guards met the coffins representing the Cork Old IRA, Dublin Old IRA and the Four Courts garrison, one of the few distinctly Civil War 'Old IRA' veterans' groups. [Image: courtesy of the Irish Examiner Archive and the Irish Capuchin Archives]

Avoiding a 'partisan spectacle'

Old IRA organisers carefully planned the repatriation ceremonies. To avoid 'creating a partisan spectacle' that would inflame Civil War political divisions, the committees deliberately structured the proceedings as 'entirely religious'. The Capuchins led the various processions, memorial Masses (one in Shannon and one in Cork city) and a reburial ceremony within the Capuchin monastery at Rochestown, which omitted any speeches by attending political leaders. The Capuchin order issued just three formal invitations to the main memorial Mass in Cork city: to President Seán T. O'Kelly, Taoiseach Éamon de Valera and Fine Gael opposition leader John A. Costello. Acting in the spirit of the Old IRA's political ecumenism, all three agreed to attend. No other invitations were issued, though organisers made it clear that anyone wishing to attend was welcome. The Irish repatriation committees acted quietly in the background throughout to minimise overt political displays. Tensions were still apparent, however, as indicated by the absence of the former IRA chief of staff and leader of Fine Gael, Richard Mulcahy, and a call for a boycott of the proceedings by the son of the assassinated Cork lord mayor Tomás MacCurtain, Tomás Óg, who was at the time interned by de Valera's government for IRA activity.

Home at last

The repatriations themselves occurred over multiple days in June 1958. The two coffins arrived at Shannon airport, and were met by Capuchin priests, the O'Connor and Bibby families, and different Old IRA committees, as well as by de Valera. The remains were then processed from Shannon through Limerick city, Croom, Charleville, Buttevant, Mallow and Cork city. At every stop hundreds of elderly IRA and Cumann na mBan veterans paraded with the coffins along streets lined with tens of thousands of respectful onlookers. Civic groups, including trade unions, GAA clubs and public bodies also processed, displaying local unity that crossed political (and Treaty) boundaries. The Irish media celebrated the proceedings and seemed particularly struck by the remarkable public attendance and the countless aged revolutionaries accompanying the two exiled priests on their final journey.

Fr Dominic O'Connor and Fr Albert Bibby, part of what Gavin Foster and Brian Hanley have termed the anti-Treaty 'wild geese', had been returned to their native soil at last. Their repatriation also seemingly ended the IRA veterans' own moral exile following the Catholic Church's Civil War excommunications of 1922. In a thank-you note to their donors after the event, the American repatriation committee announced that 'the humiliation of the 1922–1923 incidents was at last wiped out'. By creating such an evocative public ceremony so many years after the Civil War, the Old IRA organisers had reasserted themselves as respectable patriots and good Catholics, decades after both identities had been called into question.

[See John Borgonovo, 'The Exile and Repatriation of Father Dominic O'Connor (OFM Capuchin), 1922–58', *Éire-Ireland*, vol. 52, nos 3 & 4, fall/winter 2017, pp. 122–56]

Fig. 6 The cortège with the remains of Fathers Albert Bibby and Dominic O'Connor leaving Shannon airport. The coffins were driven from Shannon through Limerick city, Croom, Charleville, Buttevant, Mallow and Cork city. Behind the hearse, cars carried the Taoiseach's party, representatives of the Capuchin religious order, the O'Connor and Bibby families, and the Old IRA delegations. Outside each town and city, hundreds of local IRA and Cumann na mBan veterans met the procession and slowly marched the coffins through the streets. At each stop the cortège was also joined by local elected bodies, trade unions, GAA clubs and other associations, as silent crowds lined the route. A newspaper reported that 'whole towns followed the friars from the town's edge and out into the surrounding country'. After the cortege passed through Cork city centre, it eventually arrived at the Capuchin Holy Trinity church, where an evening rosary was recited. Thousands viewed the coffins that night. The next day government officials, civic groups and IRA and Cumann na mBan veterans packed the memorial Mass. Another procession took the coffins from the city centre to the Capuchin monastery in the suburb of Rochestown, where the two priests were buried. Massive crowds numbering in the tens of thousands witnessed the different legs of the repatriation procession or joined its various ceremonies. An *Irish Press* newspaper headline captured the mass public participation: 'The war was long over, but the people remembered'. [Image: courtesy of the Irish Examiner Archive and the Irish Capuchin Archives]

CASE STUDY

'This Great Institution for Peace': How Ireland joined the League of Nations in 1923

Michael Kennedy

On 10 September 1923 a milestone event in the history of Irish foreign policy took place. On that date, amid much international interest, newly independent Ireland joined the League of Nations. The League was a multilateral organisation created by the post-First World War Paris Peace Conference. It came directly out of US President Woodrow Wilson's 'Fourteen Points' for the post-war world. Based in Geneva, its formation was a direct response to the First World War. Its goal was to ensure that never again would there be such a devastating global conflict. It proposed a system of collective security, global disarmament and the rule of international law as tools for a peaceful world order.

For Ireland, known from 1922 to 1937 as the Irish Free State under the terms of the 1921 Anglo-Irish Treaty, the League had an added significance. Ireland's desire for membership was shaped by the wish to have an independent voice in world affairs, one distinctly separate from Britain, and perhaps thus to influence the course of international relations. Ireland's achieving League membership was a complicated diplomatic manoeuvre illustrating the difficulties facing a new state on the world stage. The quest for membership had been part of Dáil Éireann foreign policy and was implicit in the 21 January 1919 Declaration of Independence and in the subsequent Message to the Free Nations of the World. However, the first practical steps for membership began three years later, on 9 January 1922, when Ireland's representative in Geneva, Michael MacWhite, inquired from the League's Secretariat how the Irish Free State's Provisional Government might apply for League membership.

Caution

Aware of the deepening split in Ireland over the Treaty and of how the Dáil Éireann Department of Foreign Affairs had itself split over its terms, the League secretary general, Sir Eric Drummond, checked that MacWhite was the genuine representative of the Irish government. He specifically noted the need to be cautious in the circumstances of the split. The Dáil Éireann administration was not recognised internationally and thus could not seek admission for Ireland to the League. The Irish Free State created through the 1921 Treaty was in a different position. Once it was officially in existence, an event which would occur on 6 December 1922, it could apply to join the League. Until then it could not because the Provisional Government of January to December 1922 had no international capacity and no responsibility for the conduct of Ireland's foreign policy. The other dominions – Canada, South Africa, Australia and New Zealand – were already members. During the Treaty negotiations Britain's prime minister, David Lloyd George, had made it clear that Britain would support Irish membership of the League as soon as the Irish Free State's constitution was enacted.

The Provisional Government had no international remit and could not make decisions on matters of external relations. The question, following the establishment of the Provisional Government in January 1922, was when, not if, Ireland would apply. Sir Eric supported Ireland's admission and proposed membership at the September 1922 meeting of the League's Assembly. He played down the need to have the Irish Free State's constitution ratified and in full operation, and thus for the state to legally exist in international law, before admission could be considered. MacWhite suggested waiting until after 6 December 1922, the date the Provisional Government would dissolve and the Irish Free State would come into existence as a self-governing dominion. It was all to do with timing and when Ireland would have an appropriate level of international sovereignty to successfully apply. Senior League Secretariat officials had a wider perspective on Irish membership. They hoped an Irish application might convince the isolationist United States to join the League. MacWhite agreed. He considered Ireland could act as an independent force at Geneva.

'Too evident for argument'

In the first half of 1922 the chairman of the Provisional Government, Michael Collins, and Dáil Éireann minister for foreign affairs, George Gavan Duffy, also anticipated Ireland's joining the League. Gavan Duffy thought the case for membership 'too evident for argument'.[1] The outbreak of civil war in June 1922 did not dampen Gavan Duffy's enthusiasm. Collins overruled him, citing the internal situation in Ireland and anti-League feeling in the United States. MacWhite still hoped Ireland might enter the League in 1922. Membership would give a positive international image of

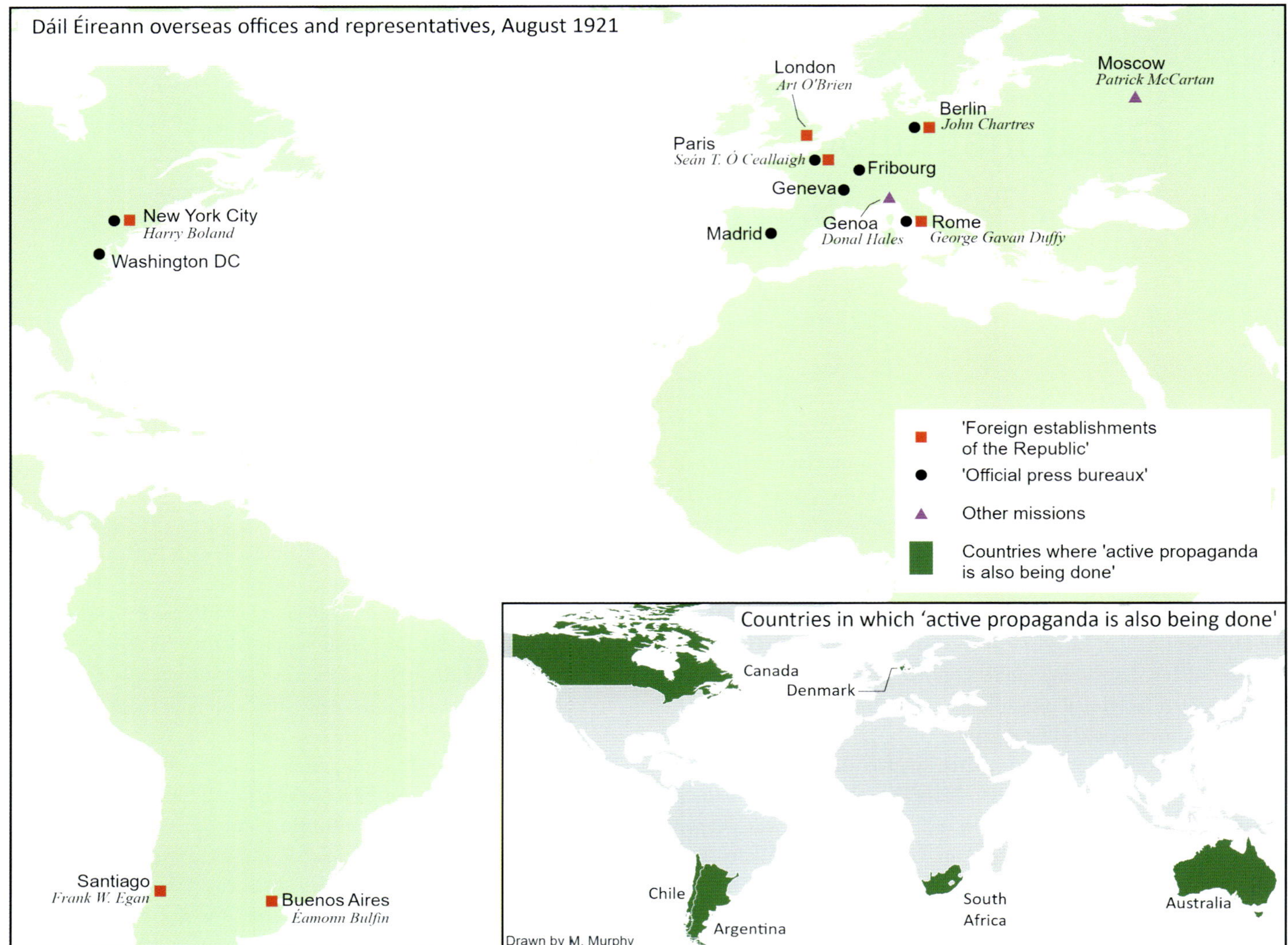

Fig. 1 Map of Dáil Éireann's overseas offices and representatives, August 1921. In early 1919 the first Dáil Éireann pressed its claim to Irish independence on the post-war peace conference assembled in Paris, and sent a delegation led by Seán T. Ó Ceallaigh to the French capital to lobby the victorious allies. The Irish claim was never recognised, but the Dáil realised the propaganda value of the exercise and subsequently established and maintained an international network of emissaries to generate sympathy and support for the Irish cause overseas. According to Robert Brennan, who eventually served as 'undersecretary' of the Dáil's Department of Foreign Affairs, 'none of them was afforded official recognition' but, in the countries where they operated, their function was 'to make known our cause for independence, to expose the methods of the British government in Ireland and to set up and maintain contact with as many representatives of foreign countries as they could'. They were also tasked with attempting to influence public opinion through 'elected representatives' and 'through publicity in the newspapers and magazines'. In addition 'there were special missions for the purchase of arms, particularly in England and Germany'. The designations of the Dáil's representatives, and the circumstances in which they operated, could vary dramatically, but they gave the independence movement an international profile. By August 1921 there was, or had been, a republican presence of some kind in the United States, UK, France, Switzerland, Canada, Denmark, Argentina, Chile, Australia, South Africa, Germany, Russia and Italy. This de facto diplomatic service comprised a diverse range of individuals: some were recruited by virtue of their linguistic skills (like Máire O'Brien in Spain) or their place of residence (like Donal Hales, of the famed Cork republican family, in Genoa). Alongside those formally working for the Dáil, dozens of others (especially Irish clerics) assisted in unofficial capacities. Other international initiatives included Éamon de Valera's eighteen-month fund-raising and publicity tour of the United States in 1919–20, and an unsuccessful attempt to reach out to the Bolsheviks via the Tyrone-born doctor Patrick McCartan, who spent a six-month sojourn in Russia in 1920–1. Figures such as Art O'Brien of the Irish Self-Determination League of Great Britain also facilitated the logistics of the Treaty negotiations in London between October and December 1921. This overseas network fractured following the signing of the Treaty. The outbreak of the Civil War in June 1922 meant that the Provisional (and subsequently Free State) government had to deal with anti-Treaty activism and propaganda in Europe and America, often carried out by veterans with pre-truce service. Many of the pro-Treaty members of the Dáil's pre-Civil War foreign service continued their careers as part of the first generation of post-independence diplomats. Others took the opposite path and, during the Civil War, sought to challenge the pro-Treaty government overseas by the same means with which they had challenged the British prior to 1922. [Text: John Gibney / Quotations: BMH WS 790, Robert Brennan / Source: Department of Foreign Affairs report, 10 August 1921, NA DE/4/4/2, published in Ronan Fanning, Michael Kennedy, Dermot Keogh and Eunan O'Halpin (eds), *Documents on Irish Foreign Policy vol. 1: 1919–1922* (Dublin, 1998)]

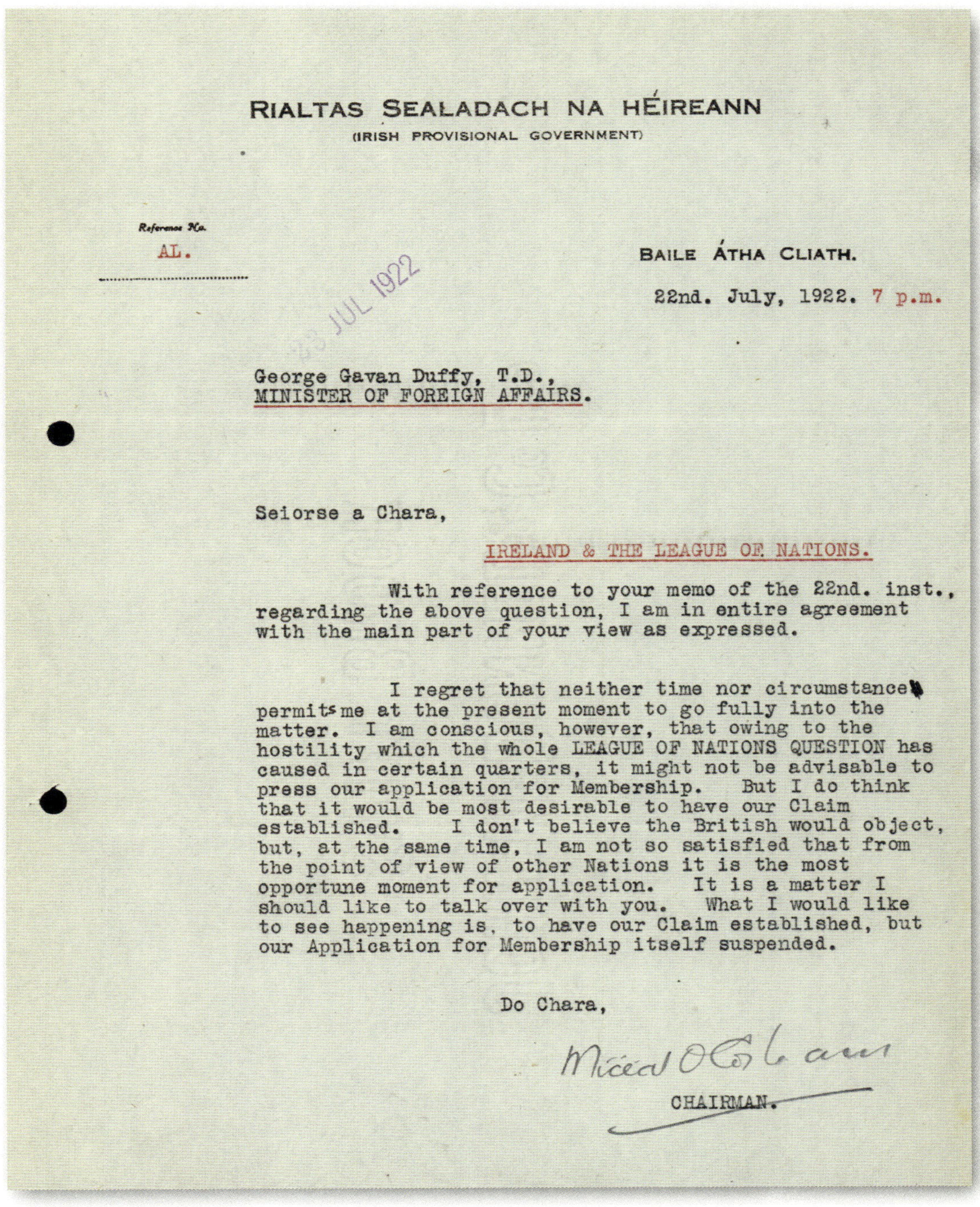

RIALTAS SEALADACH NA HÉIREANN
(IRISH PROVISIONAL GOVERNMENT)

Reference No. AL.

BAILE ÁTHA CLIATH.

22nd. July, 1922. 7 p.m.

23 JUL 1922

George Gavan Duffy, T.D.,
MINISTER OF FOREIGN AFFAIRS.

Seiorse a Chara,

IRELAND & THE LEAGUE OF NATIONS.

With reference to your memo of the 22nd. inst., regarding the above question, I am in entire agreement with the main part of your view as expressed.

I regret that neither time nor circumstances permits me at the present moment to go fully into the matter. I am conscious, however, that owing to the hostility which the whole LEAGUE OF NATIONS QUESTION has caused in certain quarters, it might not be advisable to press our application for Membership. But I do think that it would be most desirable to have our Claim established. I don't believe the British would object, but, at the same time, I am not so satisfied that from the point of view of other Nations it is the most opportune moment for application. It is a matter I should like to talk over with you. What I would like to see happening is, to have our Claim established, but our Application for Membership itself suspended.

Do Chara,

Mícéal Ó Coileáin

CHAIRMAN.

Fig. 2 Letter from Michael Collins to George Gavan Duffy, 22 July 1922. The British government made it clear during the Anglo-Irish Treaty negotiations that it would be in favour of the Irish Free State applying for League of Nations membership. Writing as chairman of the Provisional Government of the Irish Free State one month before his death, Michael Collins queried whether the new state should pursue League of Nations membership in summer 1922. Sent to the Dáil Éireann minister for foreign affairs, George Gavan Duffy, who had submitted to Collins a memorandum on League membership the same day in July 1922 in which he made the assumption that membership was already agreed, Collins's reply cites opposition in 'certain quarters' to League of Nations membership. This was a reference to anti-League hostility among elements of the Irish-American diaspora (particularly Judge Daniel Cohalan, John Devoy and the Friends of Irish Freedom organisation). He also mentions 'the point of view of other nations', referring to possible wariness towards the Irish Free State's League membership by some of its members following the outbreak of civil war in Ireland on 28 May 1922. Collins was in favour of Ireland joining the League of Nations but wished it to occur at a more appropriate time. [Text: Michael Kennedy / Source: National Archives, DFA/1/LN/258/2. Reproduced by kind permission of the Director of the National Archives]

the nascent Irish Free State and show how the Treaty gave Ireland full statehood. MacWhite also recognised that the League could assist following any British default on the Treaty. Irish officials often conjectured on how the League might intervene in British–Irish relations, in particular over the Boundary Commission, but through the 1920s and 1930s British–Irish relations were dealt with on the Dublin–London axis.

In September 1922 Gavan Duffy's successor, Desmond FitzGerald, with the backing of a vote in Dáil Éireann, held off applying for League membership. MacWhite noted the resulting general disappointment in the Secretariat. FitzGerald knew that the Provisional Government could not apply on behalf of the future Irish Free State and that membership was impossible until after 6 December 1922. All changed after 6 December 1922 once the Irish Free State existed as an internationally recognised self-governing state. On 20 March 1923 the Executive Council, basing its decision on the September 1922 Dáil vote, gave the go-ahead for application for League membership. FitzGerald sent a short formal letter of application on 17 April 1923 to Sir Eric Drummond. In its English translation it referred initially to the Free State of Ireland and made no reference to Ireland's dominion status. MacWhite reported that his letter was enthusiastically welcomed in Geneva. MacWhite and Drummond set the date of Ireland's admission as September 1923, during the League's Fourth Assembly.

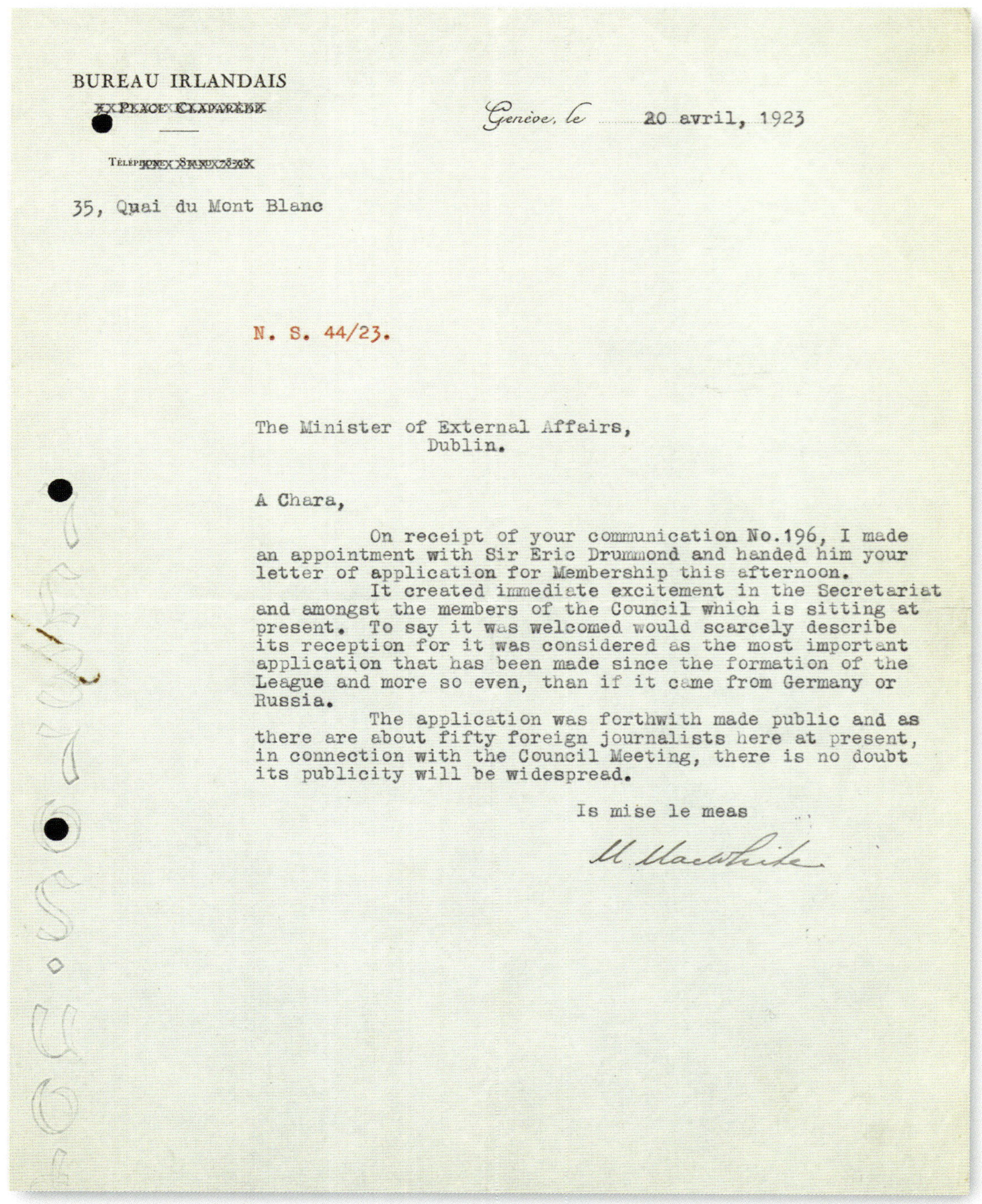

BUREAU IRLANDAIS

Genève, le 20 avril, 1923

35, Quai du Mont Blanc

N. S. 44/23.

The Minister of External Affairs,
Dublin.

A Chara,

On receipt of your communication No.196, I made an appointment with Sir Eric Drummond and handed him your letter of application for Membership this afternoon.

It created immediate excitement in the Secretariat and amongst the members of the Council which is sitting at present. To say it was welcomed would scarcely describe its reception for it was considered as the most important application that has been made since the formation of the League and more so even, than if it came from Germany or Russia.

The application was forthwith made public and as there are about fifty foreign journalists here at present, in connection with the Council Meeting, there is no doubt its publicity will be widespread.

Is mise le meas

M. MacWhite

Fig. 3 Letter from Ireland's permanent delegate to the League of Nations, Michael MacWhite, to the minister for external affairs, Desmond FitzGerald, 20 April 1923. MacWhite captures the 'immediate excitement' in the League of Nations Secretariat and among members of the League's Council caused by Ireland applying for League of Nations membership in April 1923. MacWhite forwarded the view that Ireland's application was 'the most important application which has been made since the formation of the League'. The League's Secretariat had been expecting an application from Ireland since early 1922, but the interim status of the Provisional Government, and in particular its lack of a remit in external relations, prevented an application until the official establishment of the Free State in December 1922. [Text: Michael Kennedy / Document: National Archives, DFA/26/102/2. Reproduced by kind permission of the Director of the National Archives]

Suddenly there were hitches. First, the Senate in Dublin questioned whether the Executive Council could apply for League membership without the approval of the Oireachtas. Then the League Secretariat queried the size of Ireland's military forces, which were greatly expanded due to the Civil War. It sought clarification on whether, due to its level of militarisation, the Irish Free State was in conformity concerning disarmament with the terms of the League's Covenant.

An August 1923 act of the Oireachtas, the League of Nations (Guarantee) Act, allowed the Senate to debate League membership and give its approval of the Executive Council's action, while also placing control of the Irish Free State's foreign policy firmly under the remit of the Executive Council. The act also placed in law that Ireland would accept League recommendations on the size of the state's military forces. FitzGerald backed this up with a despatch to Sir Eric Drummond. The League authorities were satisfied and the Irish Free State's road to League membership was open.

Unanimous vote

Led by the president of the Executive Council, W.T. Cosgrave, a high-profile delegation departed for Geneva on 29 August 1923. Seeking to show Ireland's independence, their travel documents

Fig. 4 The first Irish Free State delegation to the League of Nations, attending its Fourth Assembly in Geneva, September 1923. Seated (l–r): Hugh Kennedy (attorney general), William T. Cosgrave (president of the Executive Council), Eoin MacNeill (minister for education). Standing (l–r): Michael MacWhite (permanent representative of Ireland to the League of Nations), Desmond FitzGerald (minister for external affairs), Marquis MacSwiney of Mashonaglas (substitute delegate), Kevin O'Sheil (assistant legal adviser), Ormond Grattan Esmond TD (delegate), Diarmaid O'Hegarty (Cabinet secretary), Gearóid McGann (secretary to the president of the Executive Council). [Text: Michael Kennedy / Image: National Archives, DFA/Early/League of Nations/258 (1). Reproduced by kind permission of the Director of the National Archives]

were in Irish, they used the Irish forms of their names, and communicated in French, Irish and only finally in English. Following the unanimous vote of the League's Assembly, at 11.00 a.m. on Monday 10 September 1923 Ireland was admitted to the League of Nations. Amid resounding applause, Cosgrave, FitzGerald and fellow delegate Eoin MacNeill took Ireland's seats in the Assembly Hall. Addressing the Assembly, Cosgrave began in Irish, and moved to English, concluding that Ireland 'resolved to play her part' in making 'this great institution for peace as complete and efficient as possible'.[2] Writing to his wife Agnes, MacNeill considered League membership gave 'international recognition that Ireland is a sovereign independent state'.[3] Not a year independent, Ireland had confirmed its place among the nations. Support for membership was not unanimous, and anti-Treaty and republican activists protested vocally though with limited impact at Geneva and internationally at the Irish Free State's actions at Geneva.

Many of the smaller states in the League hoped Ireland would take an active position in the Assembly. As delegation member Kevin O'Shiel put it: 'They welcomed us as yet a further useful addition to their class, the class of the little nations, and saw in our entry the prospects of one more vote against the designs and potency of the big powers'.[4]

The League of Nations was the first international organisation joined by Ireland after independence. MacWhite knew that, through membership, Ireland had 'entered into the domain of international affairs and definitely broken down the isolation wall which caused her to be known on the Continent as an "island behind an island". Henceforward, she is a part of the European comity'.[5] The registration of the Anglo-Irish Treaty at the League of Nations in July 1924, despite some British protest, was a further step in this direction as, through it, the League recognised Ireland's ability to negotiate and sign treaties with other states, something Britain contended a dominion could not do.

Ireland remained a member until the League was dissolved in 1947. The League's third, and last, secretary general was the Irish diplomat Seán Lester. Seconded from the Department of External Affairs to the League Secretariat in 1934, Lester served as the League's high commissioner in Danzig (today Gdansk) to 1937. He said in 1932 of the League that it was Ireland's 'official point of contact with about sixty nations, where we stand on an equal footing with all, where, more than anywhere else, our influence, independence of view, and continuous, solid work can bring prestige to our country'.[6]

Fig. 5 President of the Executive Council and minister for external affairs, Éamon de Valera, speaking on the League of Nations' radio station Radio Nations during a broadcast to the United States in September 1935. While at times in the late 1910s and early 1920s equivocal towards the League of Nations, citing it as an organisation of great and imperial powers and thus an unsuitable organisation for small states to join, on taking office in 1932 de Valera showed himself to be a firm supporter of the League of Nations as a forum for small states seeking to stabilise the anarchic world order. During the final year of Ireland's 1930–3 three-year temporary term on the League's Council, de Valera chaired its sessions and was president of the League's Assembly. He remained a supporter of the League of Nations up until its collapse in the later 1930s. [Text: Michael Kennedy / Image: National Archives, DFA/1/LN/120. Reproduced by kind permission of the Director of the National Archives]

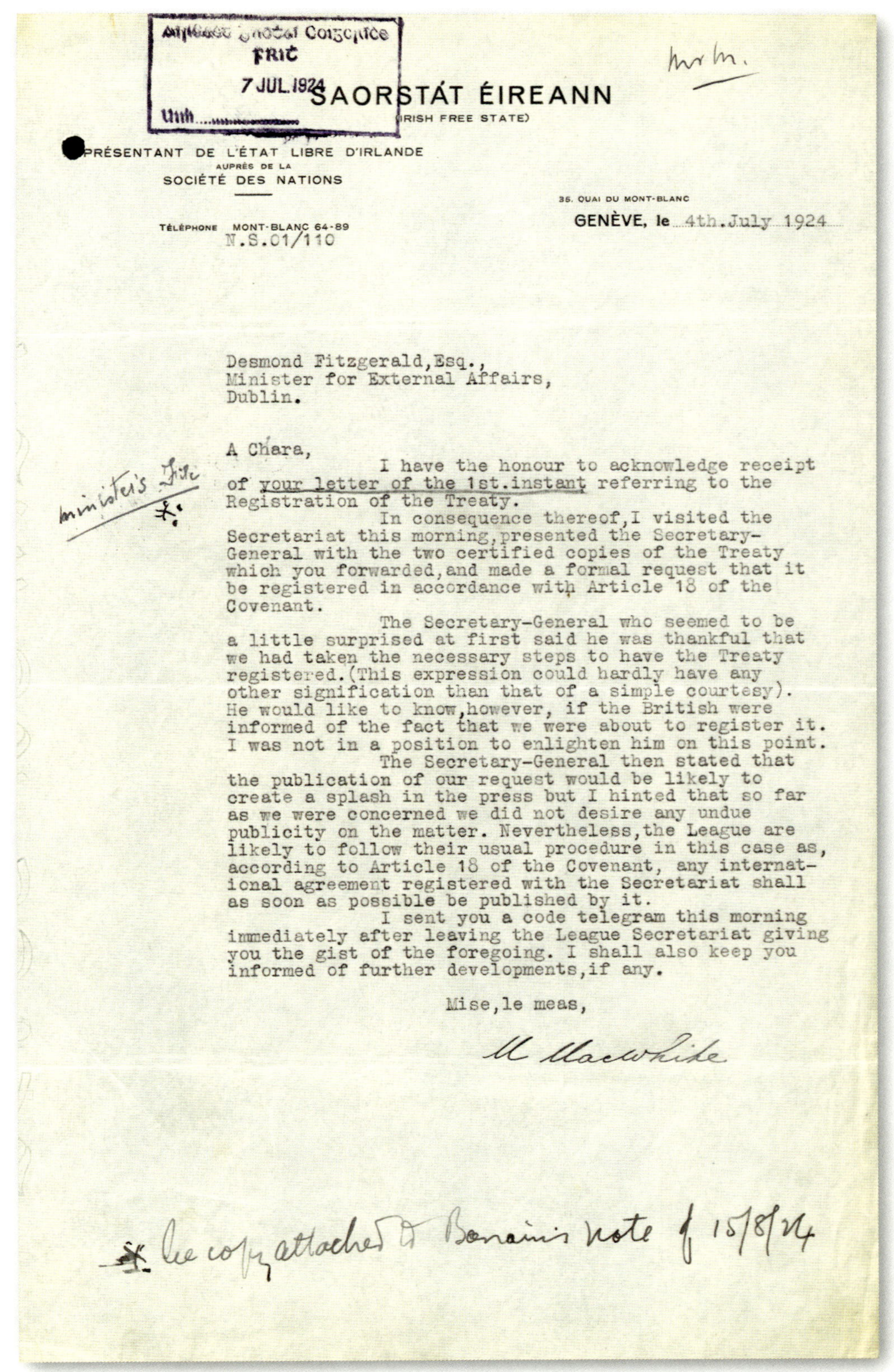
7 JUL 1924

SAORSTÁT ÉIREANN
(IRISH FREE STATE)

REPRÉSENTANT DE L'ÉTAT LIBRE D'IRLANDE
AUPRÈS DE LA
SOCIÉTÉ DES NATIONS

35, QUAI DU MONT-BLANC
GENÈVE, le 4th.July 1924

TÉLÉPHONE MONT-BLANC 64-89
N.S.01/110

Desmond Fitzgerald,Esq.,
Minister for External Affairs,
Dublin.

A Chara,

I have the honour to acknowledge receipt of your letter of the 1st.instant referring to the Registration of the Treaty.

In consequence thereof,I visited the Secretariat this morning,presented the Secretary-General with the two certified copies of the Treaty which you forwarded,and made a formal request that it be registered in accordance with Article 18 of the Covenant.

The Secretary-General who seemed to be a little surprised at first said he was thankful that we had taken the necessary steps to have the Treaty registered.(This expression could hardly have any other signification than that of a simple courtesy). He would like to know,however, if the British were informed of the fact that we were about to register it. I was not in a position to enlighten him on this point.

The Secretary-General then stated that the publication of our request would be likely to create a splash in the press but I hinted that so far as we were concerned we did not desire any undue publicity on the matter. Nevertheless,the League are likely to follow their usual procedure in this case as, according to Article 18 of the Covenant, any international agreement registered with the Secretariat shall as soon as possible be published by it.

I sent you a code telegram this morning immediately after leaving the League Secretariat giving you the gist of the foregoing. I shall also keep you informed of further developments,if any.

Mise,le meas,

M MacWhite

Fig. 6 Michael MacWhite to Minister for External Affairs, Desmond FitzGerald regarding the registration of the Anglo-Irish Treaty as a treaty with the League of Nations, 4 July 1924. On first impressions, Michael MacWhite's July 1924 act of registering the 1921 Anglo-Irish Treaty at the League of Nations might appear rather legalistic. In fact it was a bold move by Dublin in Anglo-Irish relations. The League Secretariat's acceptance of the Anglo-Irish Treaty as an international agreement was a further blow against Britain's argument that it alone represented the dominions in international relations and that relations between the dominions and between Britain and the dominions were internal imperial affairs. London made a weak protest to the League, but the registration stood. Dublin had created another precedent that showed the growing international stature of the dominions and of the Irish Free State in particular. [Text: Michael Kennedy / Document: National Archives, DFA/6/417/105/2. Reproduced by kind permission of the Director of the National Archives]

The unveiling of the memorial to Seán Hales, the pro-Treaty TD assassinated on 7 December 1922, in Bank Place (now Seán Hales Place), Bandon, County Cork on 19 January 1930. [Image: courtesy of the Irish Examiner Archive]

SECTION 9

Legacies

ONE PROMISE
THAT HOGAN WILL KEEP—

"You did not think that we would execute Irishmen. We did,—
and we will bloody well execute again!"

—Mr. HOGAN (Free State Minister for Agriculture)
speaking at Crossmolina, Mayo, 10/11/24.

—IF YOU VOTE FOR THE
FREE STATE

CHAPTER 10

The Irish Civil War Legacy: Ireland in the 1920s and 1930s

Fearghal McGarry

> As a young politician in Leinster House, I recall my shock at the white-hot hate with which that terrible episode had marked their lives. The trigger words were 'seventy-seven', 'Ballyseedy', 'Dick and Joe', and, above all, 'The Treaty' and 'damn good bargain'. The raised tiers of the Dáil chamber would become filled with shouting, gesticulating, clamouring, suddenly angry men.
>
> Noel Browne

The Civil War shaped inter-war Ireland in important ways. Most obviously, its legacy structured party political divisions during this era and long beyond it. Cumann na nGaedheal was formed in 1923 as the party of pro-Treaty Sinn Féiners. Fianna Fáil, founded in 1926, emerged from the ranks of anti-Treaty Sinn Féin. Both parties defined their aims and identity in relation to the Treaty and the Civil War it brought about. Cumann na nGaedheal set out to prove that the Treaty could, as Michael Collins had claimed, provide a stepping stone to full independence. Fianna Fáil aimed to achieve the sovereignty that Éamon de Valera had insisted was possible in 1921. Each attributed moral responsibility for the Civil War to the other, ensuring that minor differences over how best to advance Irish sovereignty became invested with intense emotional and ideological significance. Consequently, inter-war political discourse was shaped by the bitterness of Civil War enmities. Treatyites depicted their opponents as wreckers, criminals, IRA fellow-travellers, even Bolshevists. Anti-Treatyites portrayed Cumann na nGaedheal as traitors and imperialists. Even by the late 1940s, the

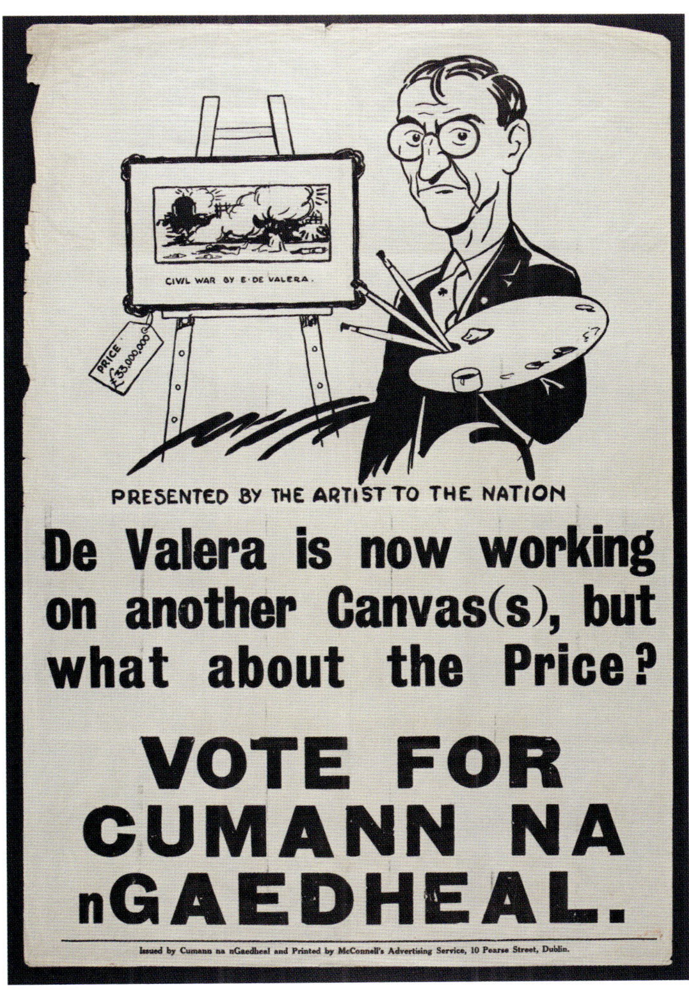

Fig. 1 (opposite) This 1927 republican election poster concentrates on the figure of Patrick Hogan, Cumann na nGaedheal's minister for agriculture since 1922. The university-educated Galway landowner was never popular with republicans, not only because of his apparent disdain for revolutionary shibboleths, but also on foot of his membership of the Cabinet that sanctioned the Civil War executions. Recalling the iconic 'seventy-seven' was a keynote of republican electioneering just five years later. In this striking example the blood-stained Hogan stands at the foreground of a corpse-strewn landscape, marked with memorial crosses and surveyed by two laughing Free State soldiers. The grotesque imagery, recalling the government's past coercive measures and portending more, is reinforced with reference to a typically unapologetic speech by Hogan in November 1924, in which he stated: 'You did not think that we would execute Irishmen. We did, and we will bloody well execute again!'. [Document: National Library of Ireland, EPH E213 / See Jason Knirck, *Afterimage of the Revolution: Cumann Na nGaedheal and Irish politics, 1922–1932* (Wisconsin, 2014), p. 27]

Fig. 2 (right) Cumann na nGaedheal election poster, 1932. The Civil War featured heavily in Cumann na nGaedheal's 1932 election materials, many of which stressed de Valera's alleged responsibility for the bitter conflict. In this unambiguous example, the Fianna Fáil leader is depicted as the creator of the costly canvas titled 'Civil War'. Captioned 'Presented by the Artist to the Nation. De Valera is now working on another Canvas(s), but what about the Price?'. [Document: National Library of Ireland, EPH F38] 'savage, angry and bitter recriminations about the civil war' could shock the socialist TD Noel Browne on entering the Dáil.[1]

If Free State politics represented the continuation of the Civil War through other means, the outcome of this conflict was ambiguous. It is true that Fianna Fáil rapidly dismantled the Treaty settlement after its election in 1932, so much so that it had created an essentially sovereign state by the end of the decade, as Ireland's neutral status during the Second World War demonstrated to the world. On the other hand this achievement highlighted how Collins had been right to argue that the Treaty would enable full independence – rather than permanently confining the Free State within the British Empire as anti-Treatyites had feared. Moreover the Ireland that Éamon de Valera created – neither unified nor a republic – remained more rooted in the Treaty than Fianna Fáil could comfortably acknowledge. This is why Ireland is one of few modern states without an independence day to mark its establishment.

So far, so familiar: the impact of the Civil War on Free State politics has long been evident. Indeed it suited both parties to accentuate the conflict's significance as a means of unifying the broad – and potentially incoherent – electoral coalitions mobilised by each during the 1920s and 1930s, and to defuse criticism of any seemingly inconsistent political initiatives. As well as exploring the divisive impact of the Civil War, this chapter will consider how the trope of Civil War bitterness obscured more complex aspects of the conflict's legacy. It does so by addressing questions that cut across the binary divisions that characterised Free State politics. Why did some supporters and opponents of the Treaty come to criticise the development of their own political traditions after the Civil War? Did 'Civil War politics' mask a consensus on social issues that, from our present-day perspective, may seem more significant than differences over the new state's constitutional status? To what extent was this conservative consensus reinforced by the Civil War?

Fig. 3 Photograph of the pro- and anti-Treaty members of the Sinn Féin standing committee at Dublin's Mansion House, 21 February 1922. Front row (l–r): Áine Ceannt, Éamonn Duggan, Kathleen Lynn, Arthur Griffith, Éamon de Valera, Michael Collins, Harry Boland, Hanna Sheehy Skeffington. Middle row (l–r): Jennie Wyse Power, George Lyons, Darrell Figgis, George Murnaghan, Austin Stack, Thomas Dillon. Back row (l–r): Sean Milroy, Walter Cole, Seán Mac Caoilte, Henry O'Hanrahan, Pádraig (Paudeen) O'Keeffe. The Collins–de Valera electoral pact was announced, after a series of army-inspired peace moves, at the same venue on 20 May 1922. The pact was intended to maintain Sinn Féin party unity and facilitate an unimpeded general election in June. Pro- and anti-Treaty Sinn Féin would be represented in proportion to the respective existing strengths in the Dáil through an agreed joint panel of candidates on the ballot. The central issue of the campaign was intended to be unity of the independence movement, instead of public ratification of the Anglo-Irish Treaty. Once the pact panel was victorious, a reunified Sinn Féin would form a 'coalition cabinet' to navigate the crisis. The pact, however, was violated in dramatic fashion by Michael Collins in Cork the evening before the polls opened. On a campaign platform, Collins told supporters to vote for 'the candidate you think best of' rather than those listed on the pact ticket. Because the election was held under the proportional representation system, voting for Sinn Féin candidates based on the Treaty issue became an inevitability (see p. xxi). With its hand strengthened by the overwhelming polling preference for its candidates, the pro-Treaty wing became much less interested in forming a coalition government. Little progress had been made towards implementing the terms of the pact when fighting broke out in Dublin twelve days later. [Image: part of the Independent Newspapers Ireland/NLI Collection, INDH45]

State building

Any attempt to assess the legacy of the Civil War raises a counterfactual question: what if it had not taken place? The emergence, throughout the first six months of 1922, of various peace initiatives demonstrated how many republicans believed that divisions over the Treaty could be constrained within constitutional parameters. The most significant of these were an attempt to devise a republican constitution, and an electoral pact intended to enable pro- and anti-Treaty republicans to form a coalition government. How might the Irish Free State have developed had such an initiative proven successful? Its evolution towards full independence would certainly have been more rapid. 'Once the Treaty split set in', Charles Townshend has recently noted: 'it was clear the Britain did not want it to end in a peaceful accommodation. That, the government feared, would mean a republic.'[2]

How might relations between North and South have differed had the Civil War not occurred? Prior to June 1922 pro- and anti-Treaty republicans drew on a shared anti-partitionism, and a genuine desire to protect Northern Catholics from loyalist violence, by supporting several initiatives that also usefully served to postpone the threat of Civil War in the South. Among the first victims of the Irish Civil War, therefore, were Northern Catholics who found themselves abruptly abandoned by Southern republicans. Until the Civil War broke out, the unionist government in Belfast had been under immense pressure from Dublin, London and its own alienated minority. At a stroke, the Civil War removed the internal and external threats to Northern Ireland's security. Cross-border IRA raids came to an end, while Northern republicans fled South to enlist in the National Army or sit out the conflict in the Curragh. Abandonment by Southern republicans diminished the already limited power of Northern nationalists. The Civil War,

Fig. 4 (left) Cover of the souvenir programme for a public meeting in Birmingham in January 1949 organised by the Anti-Partition of Ireland League of Great Britain. This meeting was one of many addressed by Fianna Fáil leader Éamon de Valera during his worldwide anti-partition campaign, which began in New York a month after his electoral defeat in February 1948, and included appearances in America, New Zealand, Australia, India and Great Britain. Fianna Fáil was strongly associated with anti-partitionism since its foundation in 1926, but the party implemented no realistic policies in pursuit of its self-proclaimed 'first political objective': a thirty-two county republic. While in opposition before 1932, party resources were focused on securing a republican government in the twenty-six counties. Thereafter successive Fianna Fáil governments implemented social and economic policy reforms, dismantled Ireland's constitutional links with Great Britain and, in 1937, introduced a new Irish constitution. Despite the territorial claim to Northern Ireland in Article 3 of *Bunreacht na hÉireann*, and sustained rhetorical attacks on the 'illegality' of partition and the 'unnatural boundary' with Northern Ireland, de Valera's party failed to formulate any realistic or official long-term Northern policy during the inter-war period. The different wartime experiences of neutral Éire and Northern Ireland served only to reinforce the border between North and South, and confirm for the British government and her wartime ally, America, the strategic importance of a British military presence in Ireland in the event of a future war. Resorting to anti-partitionism in this new postwar context, de Valera maintained that, while there was no immediate solution, a Fianna Fáil government represented the best chance – when circumstances allowed – of achieving Irish unity. De Valera's international campaign was a political failure. Recycling decades-old rhetoric casting Ireland as the victim of British injustice merely highlighted his party's inability to foster a new approach to partition. The campaign also reinforced Ulster unionism's mistrust of the Irish government; highlighted the American government's lack of interest in helping to end partition; and confirmed for the British government that Irish unity was unattainable without the support of a majority of Northern Irish citizens. Preaching the injustice of partition to British and American audiences proved particularly futile. As Aldous Huxley put it, 'the propagandist is a man who canalises an already existing stream. In a land where there is no water, he digs in vain.' If anything, de Valera's campaign spurred Taoiseach John A. Costello, leader of the first inter-party government, to play the 'green card' to counteract the perception that Fianna Fáil was the sole custodian of the aspiration for Irish unity. Westminster's response to the introduction of the Republic of Ireland Act in 1948 was to give the Stormont government a veto over reunification, under the terms of the Ireland Act of 1949. Significantly, de Valera abandoned what would be his last anti-partition propaganda campaign in June 1950. On Fianna Fáil's return to government in May 1951, de Valera dismantled the anti-partition apparatus in Ireland and abroad. Thereafter his party replaced anti-partitionism with a new policy of 'persuasion'. Aimed directly at encouraging cross-border cooperation between Dublin and Belfast, particularly on economic matters, Fianna Fáil promoted a more 'practical' Northern Ireland policy. Privately, de Valera admitted that 'a more realistic attitude' to partition was required. [Text: Stephen Kelly / Image: private collection / See Stephen Kelly, *Fianna Fáil, Partition and Northern Ireland, 1926–1971* (Newbridge, 2013)]

Ronan Fanning notes, 'had the dramatic, albeit indirect, effect of stabilising the Northern Ireland settlement'.[3] Policies implemented by the Free State after Collins's death, notably the government's decision to drop non-recognition of Northern Ireland, reinforced this sense of abandonment.

The legacy of the Civil War was clearly not confined to the state in which it was fought. One of its first consequences was to allow Ulster unionists to secure greater control over what they regarded as their territory. In contrast to the Provisional Government, which was held by Britain to a strict implementation of the Treaty's terms, James Craig's government could ruthlessly unpick basic safeguards of Britain's partition settlement. It emboldened Craig, for example, to face down the British government's objections to his proposal to strengthen unionist domination by abolishing proportional representation in local elections in September 1922. We will never know how – in the absence of a civil war – a less divided, demoralised and weak Free State would have engaged with the Boundary Commission, or whether a less isolated Northern nationalist community would have witnessed the same exodus of activists as occurred in 1922.

An imperial settlement

Turning south, how did the Civil War shape the development of the Irish Free State? The destruction and expense of the conflict set the new state back in many respects. Speaking after his election as president of the Executive Council in December 1922, William T. Cosgrave complained of 'Twelve months which had been wasted in resisting the mad efforts of those who [...] took up arms in order that they might, by violence and tyranny, wrench from the people what they had won.'[4] But the Treatyite regime's illegitimacy in the

Fig. 5 Actors in Celtic dress, accompanied by Irish wolfhounds, at the opening ceremony of Aonach Tailteann, the Tailteann Games, in 1924. The Tailteann Games were staged in August 1924. An Irish version of the Olympics, reputedly last held on the eve of the twelfth-century Anglo-Norman intervention in Ireland, this new iteration was intended to fuse Ireland's pre-colonial Celtic past with the image of a modern, functioning state that the Cumann na nGaedheal government wanted to project. More than 5,000 entrants competed for 1,000 medals across twenty-three different categories over sixteen days. Alongside the sporting events, there were competitions for painting, poetry, literature and Irish dancing, among others. Competitors were drawn not only from Irish citizens and the diaspora, but also from the community of international athletes. Johnny Weissmuller – later of *Tarzan* fame – travelled to the Free State after competing in the Paris Olympics where he had taken gold in swimming for the United States, a feat he would repeat in the Tailteann Games. He was joined by other Olympic competitors. The presence of some of the biggest sporting names lent prestige to the event and brought the attention of international journalists. *The Times*, *New York Times* and *Sydney Morning Herald* were among those newspapers that reported on the proceedings. Held so soon after the end of the Civil War and at a time of great financial strain, reviving the Tailteann Games was a gamble. The visionary behind the project was J.J. Walsh, minister for posts and telegraphs and a legendary GAA organiser. Before the transfer of power was even complete he requested money to renovate Croke Park, which would be the site of the opening ceremony and a key location for many of the competitions (see Fig. 6). Strategically constructing and projecting an identity would be a hallmark of the government's approach to state building. Alongside priorities like membership of the League of Nations, the Tailteann Games was intended to demonstrate to international onlookers that the Free State was a functioning, independent state, capable of self-government. As Walsh later put it, the festival would have 'satisfied [visitors] that the people of Ireland were capable of one common great effort to re-establish this old nation once again on its feet'. Culture did not trump politics, however, and Éamon de Valera called on his supporters to boycott the games. Although some republicans were in attendance, they never officially endorsed the state-sponsored event. Nonetheless international journalists heralded the games a great success, while the *Irish Times* speculated that they may have represented the 'most important psychological moment in the history of the Free State'. The games were held again in 1928 but, by then, they had served their political purpose and they were subsequently wound down by the new Fianna Fáil government after the 1932 staging. [Text: Ciara Meehan / Image: part of the Independent Newspapers Ireland/NLI collection, INDH524]

eyes of a substantial minority of its citizens presented as great a problem for Cosgrave as the destruction of infrastructure. Having only reluctantly accepted the Treaty, Cumann na nGaedheal politicians increasingly felt compelled to talk up what was, in effect, an imperial settlement. The Treaty, Cosgrave insisted in his first speech to the Dáil after the establishment of the Irish Free State, would allow the people 'to conduct their affairs as they shall declare right without interference, not to say domination, by any other authority whatsoever on this earth'.[5] They had joined not the empire but the Commonwealth: a 'free partnership, in which all are equal'. Unveiling the Cenotaph outside Leinster House in August 1923, Cosgrave similarly emphasised the freedom secured by the Treaty: 'The tragedy of the death of Arthur Griffith and Michael Collins lies in the blindness of the living who do not see, or refuse to see, the stupendous fact of the liberation these two men brought to pass.'[6]

These assertions rang hollow for many, including some who had reluctantly accepted the Treaty. In his inaugural speech as leader of the opposition, the Labour Party's Tom Johnson protested the necessity for an oath to the British monarch, an imposition that contradicted Cosgrave's depiction of dominion status as representing equal partnership:

> We recognise the 'Oath of Allegiance' as a formality, a condition of Membership of the Legislature, implying no obligation other than the ordinary obligation of every person who accepts the privileges of citizenship [...] The terms of the Treaty [...] are accepted by us, as they are accepted by the people generally, under protest, having been imposed upon Ireland by the threat of superior force, and were not freely determined by the people of Ireland or their representatives.[7]

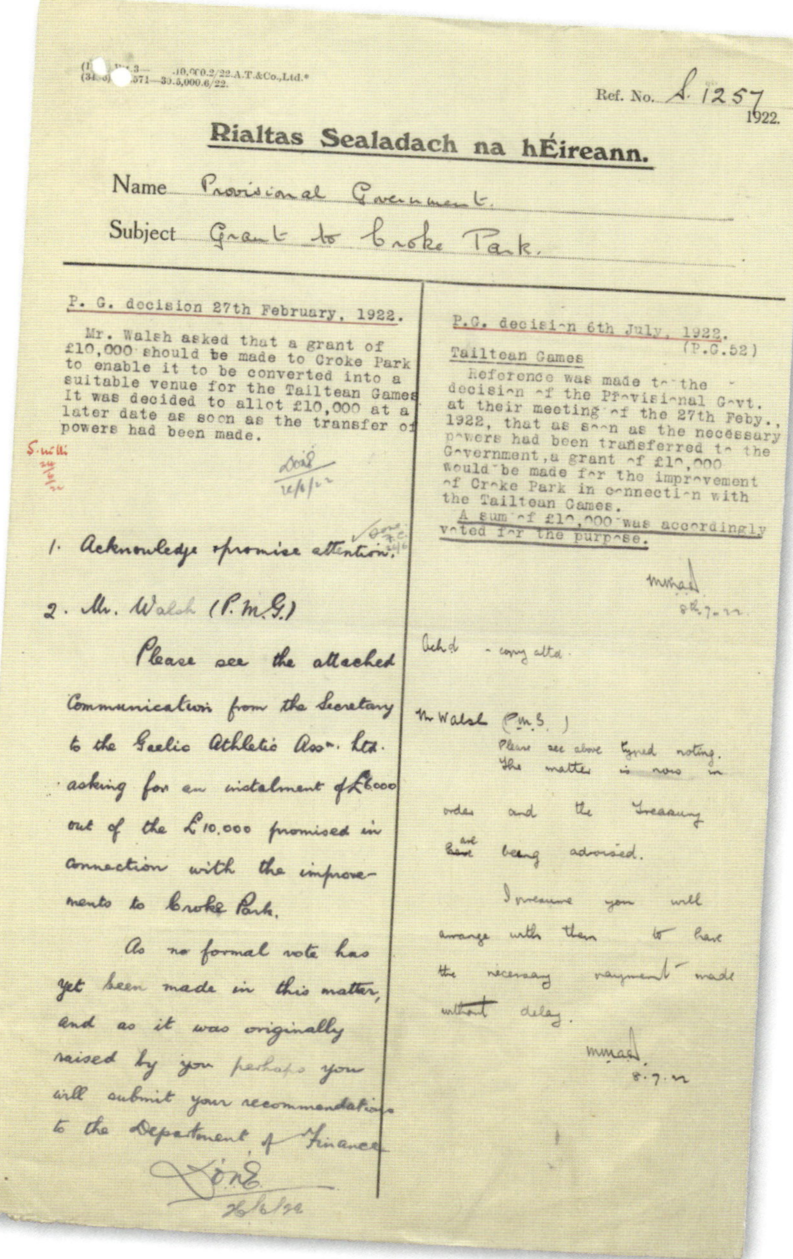

Ref. No. S. 1257
1922.

Rialtas Sealadach na hÉireann.

Name Provisional Government.

Subject Grant to Croke Park.

P. G. decision 27th February, 1922.

Mr. Walsh asked that a grant of £10,000 should be made to Croke Park to enable it to be converted into a suitable venue for the Tailtean Games. It was decided to allot £10,000 at a later date as soon as the transfer of powers had been made.

1. Acknowledge & promise attention.

2. Mr. Walsh (P.M.G.)

Please see the attached Communication from the Secretary to the Gaelic Athletic Assn. Ltd. asking for an instalment of £6000 out of the £10,000 promised in connection with the improvements to Croke Park.

As no formal vote has yet been made in this matter, and as it was originally raised by you perhaps you will submit your recommendations to the Department of Finance

P.G. decision 6th July, 1922. (P.G.52)

Tailtean Games

Reference was made to the decision of the Provisional Govt. at their meeting of the 27th Feby., 1922, that as soon as the necessary powers had been transferred to the Government, a grant of £10,000 would be made for the improvement of Croke Park in connection with the Tailtean Games.

A sum of £10,000 was accordingly voted for the purpose.

8.7.22

Mr Walsh (P.M.G.)

Please see above typed noting. The matter is now in order and the Treasury are being advised.

I presume you will arrange with them to have the necessary payment made without delay.

8.7.22

Fig. 6 1922 Provisional Government memo allocating £10,000 for renovations to Croke Park to stage the Tailteann Games. [Document: National Archives of Ireland, FIN_1_741_0001. Reproduced by kind permission of the Director of the National Archives]

Cosgrave was right to argue that the Free State was rooted in a measure of self-government that was substantial, popular and – as events over the next decade would demonstrate – capable of evolving towards greater sovereignty. But its great weakness was that it fell short of the Republic for which separatists had fought. Moreover, because Fianna Fáil dedicated itself to dismantling the Treaty, Cumann na nGaedheal developed a political identity as its defenders. This allowed Fianna Fáil to position itself as the party dedicated to Irish sovereignty, a goal that was shared across the Civil War divide. The emergence of 'Civil War politics' ensured that dislike of the settlement, as articulated by many reluctant Treatyites at the time of the split, was overlooked, as was the extent to which much bitter debate over the Treaty reflected the 'intense party divisions' that subsequently developed during the 1920s and 1930s.[8]

The role of the Treaty split in structuring party politics in the new state ensured that Fianna Fáil's rapid success in undoing the settlement after its election provoked bitter resentment from Cumann na nGaedheal, as evidenced by the following exchange during a debate on the government's bill to remove the oath of allegiance in 1933:

> **The President [de Valera]**: The Treaty originated and eventuated directly in the destruction of a State here which was established with the full approval and consent of the Irish people and maintained with their consent. That was at that time unconstitutionally disestablished. I do not want to go back into particular incidents. We know of them. The Pact was broken and we got into a Civil War [...]

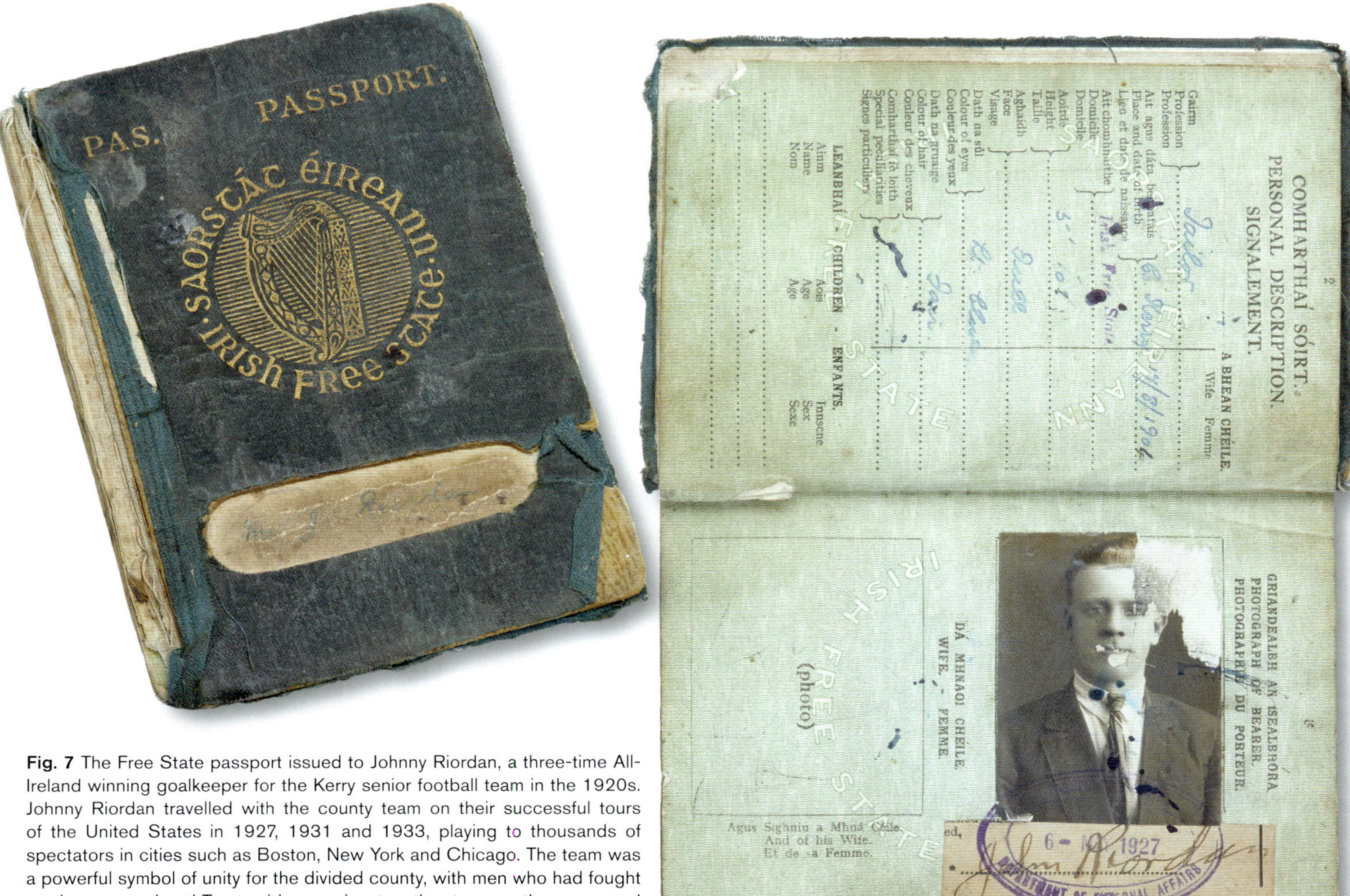

Fig. 7 The Free State passport issued to Johnny Riordan, a three-time All-Ireland winning goalkeeper for the Kerry senior football team in the 1920s. Johnny Riordan travelled with the county team on their successful tours of the United States in 1927, 1931 and 1933, playing to thousands of spectators in cities such as Boston, New York and Chicago. The team was a powerful symbol of unity for the divided county, with men who had fought on the pro- and anti-Treaty sides coming together to wear the green and gold of Kerry. Riordan's passport identified him as a 'citizen of the Irish Free State and the British Commonwealth of Nations'. From 1924 Irish passports were issued with this designation, much to the chagrin of the British government. The Anglo-Irish Treaty had provided for common citizenship in the British Commonwealth and an oath of fidelity to the Crown, but William T. Cosgrave's Cumann na nGaedheal government worked hard in the wake of the Civil War to assert the Free State's distinctive nationhood by pursuing an independent foreign policy. Its earliest efforts in this regard included registering the Treaty with the League of Nations in 1924 and the establishment of international diplomatic legations. In 1930 the British and Free State governments accepted a compromise solution identifying the passport bearer as 'His Majesty's subject of the Irish Free State and the British Commonwealth of Nations'. De Valera's constitution of 1937 changed the name of the state to Éire or Ireland, and in 1939 the Irish government unilaterally dropped all references to the king; the bearer of an Irish passport was now simply a citizen of Ireland / Éire. [Text: Helen O'Carroll / Image: courtesy of Kerry County Museum and Neustock Media]

> **Mr. Cosgrave**: There was no necessity to take an oath between September and December, 1922.
> **The President**: There was a civil war begun by the members on the opposite benches during that time.
> **Mr. Cosgrave**: You began it, and we ended it.
> **The President**: No, we did not. You began it. We are ending it here to-day, thank God. (Applause in public gallery.) [...] We are ending this civil war and the causes of this civil war.[9]

The opposition's irritation at de Valera's disingenuous claim that the Civil War was brought about by the oath of allegiance was understandable. Less so was its vote to retain one of the most despised elements of the settlement imposed by Britain on the grounds that its removal would constitute 'a breach of the Treaty'. It seems unlikely that Collins would have led Cumann na nGaedheal down the same ideological cul-de-sac of 'rigorous implementation', to borrow a phrase from the impasse over Brexit, that saw Cosgrave describe the quashing of the Boundary Commission in 1925 as 'a damn good bargain' rather than a setback for Treatyite aspirations for reunification.[10]

A challenge to democracy?

The legacy of the Civil War embittered Irish politics, but did it present a challenge to democracy? In some respects. For instance the Dáil remained half empty until 1927 as Fianna Fáil deputies refused to sit in an 'illegitimate' parliament. And this abstentionism

Fig. 8 (left) President William T. Cosgrave delivering an oration at the Cenotaph to Michael Collins and Arthur Griffith on Leinster Lawn, 1927. The hastily constructed makeshift memorial of cement-covered wood and plaster that cost the penurious Free State government just £5,000 was triumphally unveiled after a military parade in August 1923. By the following December it was already showing signs of deterioration, the painted bronze effigies of the fallen leaders flaking, but Cosgrave's administration failed to replace it with the promised more permanent memorial. Such neglect and diminishing numbers at the official commemorations in the mid-1920s was reflective, perhaps, of the difficulty of reconciling the idealism embodied by Collins and Griffith with the realities of post-Civil War Ireland. As the fruits of compromise became more evident, Anne Dolan writes, the Cenotaph became 'a shrine to what [the government] had failed to achieve'. Alternatively, Bill Kissane has suggested that the Cumann na nGaedheal government had achieved its Civil War aims and the Free State's enduring government institutions were a more important and lasting monument to their victory. Cosgrave's government did turn to the Cenotaph after the assassination of Minister for Justice Kevin O'Higgins in 1927. The annual Cenotaph ceremony was expanded to include O'Higgins, and a plaque in his honour was added a year later. The official commemoration was abandoned when Fianna Fáil came to office in 1932. However the increasingly decrepit monument was the focal point for the Blueshirt 'march of the nation against Fianna Fáil' in August 1933, illustrating the potency of such Civil War memory even a decade later. The Cenotaph stayed in place until de Valera approved designs for its replacement in 1939. Work on a new memorial was vetoed by the Department of Defence during the Second World War, but in 1950 a sixty-foot granite obelisk enclosed by railings was erected without ceremony on Leinster Lawn. The Cenotaph, described by David Fitzpatrick as a 'chronicle of embarrassment' and by Anne Dolan as the 'elephant on Leinster Lawn', represented the ambiguities and contradictions inherent in Civil War remembrance (or forgetting). [Image: An tÓglách Glass Plate Negative Collection, Military Archives, IE-MA-GPN-023-021 / See Anne Dolan, *Commemorating the Irish Civil War: History and memory, 1923–2000* (Cambridge, 2006); David Fitzpatrick, 'Commemoration in the Irish Free State: A chronicle of embarrassment', in Ian MacBride (ed.), *History and Memory in Modern Ireland* (Cambridge, 2001), p. 38]

Fig. 9 (right) A coloured postcard of the Griffith-Collins Cenotaph, Leinster Lawn, Dublin. [Image: National Library of Ireland, NPA DOCG59]

was seen by Cumann na nGaedheal as condoning the persistence of anti-Treaty violence, the most dramatic example being the assassination of Kevin O'Higgins by rogue IRA men in 1927. The addition of a third plaque to the Cenotaph to commemorate O'Higgins, a temporal conflation implicitly assigning some of the responsibility for this crime to Fianna Fáil, symbolised how this murder was intentionally framed 'as an act of civil war'.[11]

But the legacy of the Civil War also reinforced the stability of democracy in the Free State, which became one of the few post-war 'successor states' to sustain liberal democracy throughout the inter-war era. The Dáil's broad-based two-party system, for example, contrasted with that of most other new states, where parliamentary politics fractured along class, ethnic and sectional lines. In the Czech parliament, for instance, fourteen parties were returned in 1920; in Poland, thirty-one parties were represented by 1926.[12] Civil War political alignments, which persisted long after the bitter memory of the Civil War itself, contributed to the stability of the Irish political system. The price paid for this stability was a lack of ideological diversity. In particular, as was also the case north of the border, the continued pre-eminence of the 'national question' stymied political alternatives. The Labour Party's success in winning over 21 per cent of first-preference votes cast in 1922, the same proportion as won by anti-Treaty Sinn Féin, proved a false dawn in terms of the emergence of class divisions in Irish politics.

The Civil War reinforced the conservatism of the new regime in other ways. Kevin O'Higgins's much-quoted recollection dramatically conveys the scale of the crisis faced by his Cabinet in 1922:

> there was no State and no organized forces. The Provisional Government was simply eight young men in the City Hall

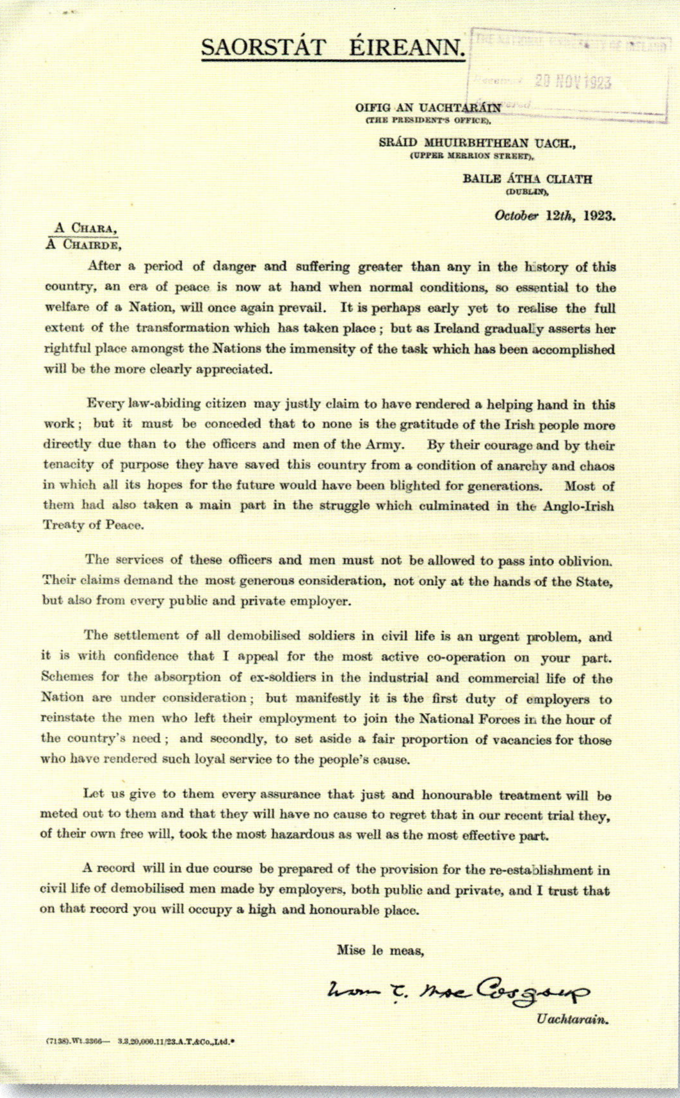

SAORSTÁT ÉIREANN.

OIFIG AN UACHTARÁIN
(THE PRESIDENT'S OFFICE),

SRÁID MHUIRBHTHEAN UACH.,
(UPPER MERRION STREET),

BAILE ÁTHA CLIATH
(DUBLIN),

October 12th, 1923.

A CHARA,
A CHAIRDE,

After a period of danger and suffering greater than any in the history of this country, an era of peace is now at hand when normal conditions, so essential to the welfare of a Nation, will once again prevail. It is perhaps early yet to realise the full extent of the transformation which has taken place; but as Ireland gradually asserts her rightful place amongst the Nations the immensity of the task which has been accomplished will be the more clearly appreciated.

Every law-abiding citizen may justly claim to have rendered a helping hand in this work; but it must be conceded that to none is the gratitude of the Irish people more directly due than to the officers and men of the Army. By their courage and by their tenacity of purpose they have saved this country from a condition of anarchy and chaos in which all its hopes for the future would have been blighted for generations. Most of them had also taken a main part in the struggle which culminated in the Anglo-Irish Treaty of Peace.

The services of these officers and men must not be allowed to pass into oblivion. Their claims demand the most generous consideration, not only at the hands of the State, but also from every public and private employer.

The settlement of all demobilised soldiers in civil life is an urgent problem, and it is with confidence that I appeal for the most active co-operation on your part. Schemes for the absorption of ex-soldiers in the industrial and commercial life of the Nation are under consideration; but manifestly it is the first duty of employers to reinstate the men who left their employment to join the National Forces in the hour of the country's need; and secondly, to set aside a fair proportion of vacancies for those who have rendered such loyal service to the people's cause.

Let us give to them every assurance that just and honourable treatment will be meted out to them and that they will have no cause to regret that in our recent trial they, of their own free will, took the most hazardous as well as the most effective part.

A record will in due course be prepared of the provision for the re-establishment in civil life of demobilised men made by employers, both public and private, and I trust that on that record you will occupy a high and honourable place.

Mise le meas,

Liam T. MacCosgair

Uachtarain.

(7138).Wt.3366— 3.3.20,000.11/23.A.T.&Co.,Ltd.*

Fig. 10 (left) Letter from William T. Cosgrave, president of the Executive Council of the Free State government, to public and private employers appealing to them to prioritise the reinstatement and employment of demobilised National Army soldiers, 12 October 1923. The need to drastically downsize and reform the army after the Civil War was a major challenge for the government, not least in terms of finding employment for former soldiers during an economic recession. Beyond the government's moral obligation to the defenders of the nascent Free State, it was also aware of the political danger posed by widespread unemployment among ex-servicemen, which had already been demonstrated among First World War veteran populations in countries across Europe. Indeed dissatisfaction with the government's policies in relation to army reform led to the 'army mutiny' of March 1924. [Document: courtesy of the National University of Ireland Archive, and John Foley, retired administration officer, NUI]

Fig. 11 (opposite) Map showing the ranks and locations of officers who resigned during the 'army mutiny' of 1924. The demobilisation of the National Army following the end of the Civil War produced profound discontent within the service and a crisis over government control over the military, which resulted in events known as the army mutiny. The mutiny had adherents in places as far apart as Athlone and Tralee but at its core was a coterie of Dublin officers with impressive fighting records. Most had served in Michael Collins's IRA 'Squad' and Intelligence Department during the War of Independence, and in the Dublin Guard, Military Intelligence or the Criminal Investigation Department (CID) detective unit in Oriel House during the Civil War. Led by former Army Director of Intelligence Liam Tobin and his deputy Charlie Dalton, the mutineers of 1924 had been ousted from top commands in the army in late 1922 by Minister for Defence Richard Mulcahy and senior generals on the Army Council. This was in part because Tobin and Dalton had proved ineffective as heads of intelligence, but it also reflected dangerous factionalism within the army's leadership. Members of Tobin's circle were pushed into subordinate administrative jobs without real authority. Mulcahy and his loyal generals replaced them with men they could trust, often members of the Irish Republican Brotherhood (IRB), a secret organisation led by senior generals on the Army Council loyal to Mulcahy. In response to the demotions, 'Tobin's crowd', as they became known in the army, formed their own faction, the Irish Republican Army Organisation (IRAO), which emphasised their pre-Civil War service under Michael Collins. They enjoyed the tacit backing of Minister for Labour Joe McGrath, who was the former head of the CID. Rivalry between the two factions (the Army Council's IRB and Tobin's IRAO) came to a head in late 1923 and early 1924 when the army radically cut its Civil War strength of over 55,000 down to under 10,000 troops. Few of the IRAO's disgruntled officers were retained in the regular army, causing the IRAO to warn the government to halt the demobilisation, retain its members in positions of authority and fire the Army Council, headed by Mulcahy. They also insisted that the government purge the army of former British Army officers and make clearer progress towards Michael Collins's ideal of an all-Ireland Republic. In March 1924 the army head of intelligence, General Michael J. Costello, having listened to Tobin and Dalton's telephone calls, concluded that they were planning a military coup, including the assassination of government ministers. After consulting with Mulcahy, the Army Council ordered the arrest of the head mutineers at Devlin's public house on Dublin's Parnell Street. Shots were exchanged, some of the mutineers were arrested and others went on the run. About fifty National Army officers who were set to be demobilised seized weapons and abandoned their posts. About another fifty mid-ranked officers subsequently resigned. For a few days there was considerable anxiety across the country, but the army leadership quickly regained control of the situation without serious bloodshed. The affair was not an unequivocal victory for Mulcahy's faction, however. Since 1918 the senior leadership of the IRA and subsequent National Army had resisted close civilian supervision, including efforts to discipline problematic officers during the Civil War. Mulcahy and the Army Council had launched the Parnell Street raid and subsequent raids without notifying the civilian Executive Council. When the government learned of the IRAO raids and the extent of the IRB's influence among the army's top generals, it pardoned the mutineers and demanded the resignation of Mulcahy and the Army Council. Mulcahy and his generals accepted their dismissal without threats of violence, thereby enshrining the Free State's civilian control over the military for the first time. [Text: John Dorney / Sources: 'List of officers who resigned owing to crisis', 1924, MS 51,230/1/8, NLI; *Freeman's Journal*, 3 Apr. 1924]

> standing amidst the ruins of one administration, with the foundations of another not yet laid, and with wild men screaming through the keyhole. No police force was functioning through the country, no system of justice was operating, the wheels of administration hung idle battered out of recognition by the clash of rival jurisdictions.[13]

How did this chaos impact on the development of the Free State? In seeking to restore order, Treatyite politicians had to choose between creating new forms of administration, adapting existing British structures or building on innovative republican institutions that had emerged during the War of Independence. This dilemma was exemplified by Dublin Castle's administration, which was staffed by 21,000 civil servants. At the time of the Treaty the Dáil government, organised in departments that reported to elected ministers, appeared more modern than the ramshackle, hierarchical Dublin Castle structure administered by unaccountable political appointees. Dáil departments, such as Local Government and External Affairs, were regarded as effective, while republican courts

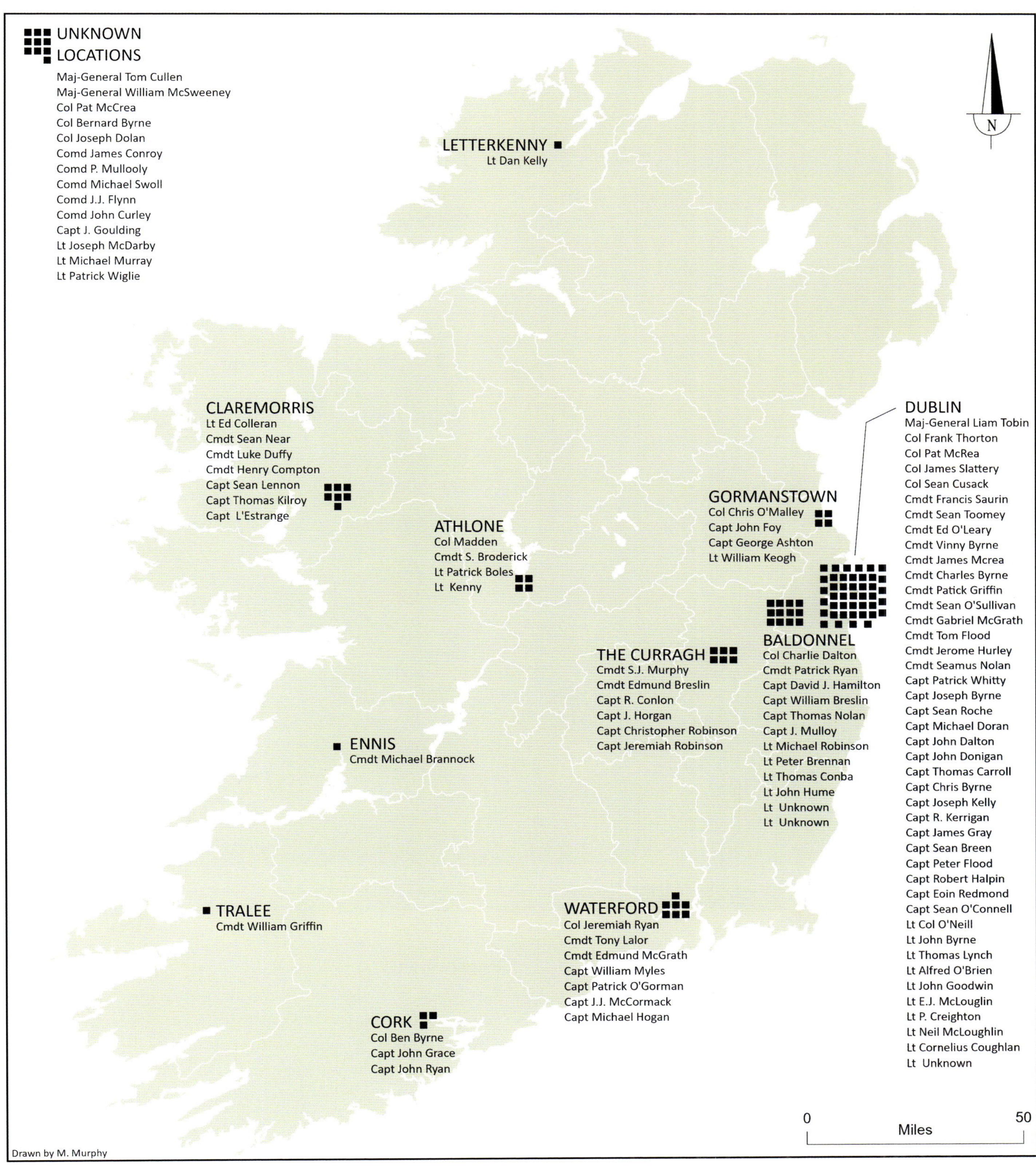

had been largely accepted by the public. 'As late as June 1922', notes Martin Maguire, 'the Provisional Government, regarding the inherited civil service with suspicion, was still planning a process by which the Dáil administration would take over and assimilate the Castle civil service.'[14]

The existential crisis faced by the state frustrated plans to integrate the existing civil service into more suitable Irish administrative structures. Whereas divisions over the Treaty had paralysed the existing Dáil institutions, Dublin Castle's comparatively apolitical civil service accepted the new state's authority. Consequently, as

Fig. 12 Minister for Defence Richard Mulcahy (left) with Major General J.J. 'Ginger' O'Connell (centre) and General Tom Ennis at a flag raising ceremony at Beggars Bush Barracks, Dublin soon after its handover to the Provisional Government on 1 February 1922. [Image: National Library of Ireland, HOGW 183]

Maguire observed, 'Plans to construct a completely new apparatus were abandoned and the civil service of the Dáil was assimilated into the old Castle administration; the reverse of what was originally intended.' That government was administered by the same people performing the same tasks in much the same way as before, David Fitzpatrick suggests, 'virtually eliminated the chance of radical structural change' after independence.[15] As did the political instincts of most government ministers. Although this Cabinet was always likely to have pursued conservative policies, the destabilising impact of the Civil War contributed to its notorious parsimony. The conflict, which cost an estimated £50 million, necessitated the creation of a vast, poorly disciplined and expensive National Army. As late as 1927 defence spending and compensation costs continued to absorb one third of state expenditure.

Repression

The Civil War also reinforced the Provisional Government's authoritarian inclinations. On 27 September 1922, as the National Army struggled to suppress the anti-Treaty IRA's costly and destructive guerrilla war campaign, the Dáil voted to introduce emergency powers, establishing military tribunals with the power to impose the death penalty. Inaccurately described as the Public Safety Act, this draconian measure was authorised by a resolution rather than legislation. Only in August 1923, when the Irish Free State passed an act indemnifying itself for its actions during the Civil War, were its emergency powers legalised. This ostensible technicality illustrates an authoritarianism long overlooked by historians who, partly in response to a subsequent republican threat to the Irish state during the Troubles, identified the

Fig. 13 *Paddy O'Daly* (1888–1957), oil on canvas by Seán Keating (1955). In April 1955 the artist Seán Keating presented a portrait to Dublin's Municipal Gallery. It depicted General Paddy O'Daly, a leading member of the Dublin IRA during the War of Independence. In the painting O'Daly, wearing a trench coat, stares into the distance by a table on which sits a Mauser pistol, a weapon much favoured by his old comrades. It is hard to tell from his expression whether the past weighs heavily on O'Daly; certainly the most controversial aspects of his career went unmentioned when the portrait was unveiled. Nor did they feature in any of the obituaries when O'Daly died two years later. But O'Daly was responsible for some of the worst atrocities of the Civil War. Born in Dublin during 1888, he followed his two brothers into separatist politics, through the Gaelic Athletic Association (GAA) and later the Irish Republican Brotherhood (IRB). A carpenter by trade, he was an early recruit to both the Irish Volunteers and Na Fianna Éireann. On Easter Monday 1916 O'Daly led the attack on the Magazine Fort in the Phoenix Park. Later in the week he was wounded. Jailed several times, during 1919 he helped organise a breakout from Mountjoy Gaol. That year he became an early member of Michael Collins's 'Squad' and thereafter played a central role in the IRA's war in Dublin, personally taking part in the killing of policemen and suspected informers. In May 1921 he became overall commander of the combined 'Squad' and Dublin Brigade active service units, the Dublin Guard. A strong supporter of Collins, O'Daly was a key figure in the organisation of the new National Army. In June 1922 he commanded the Dublin Guard during the attack on anti-Treaty headquarters in the Four Courts. Following the fighting in Dublin, he led a seaborne landing of National Army forces at Fenit in County Kerry. From an early stage troops under his command brutalised prisoners and killed unarmed men. The nature of this response was very much shaped by O'Daly. In January 1923 he was promoted to general and appointed GOC (general officer commanding) of the region. Ill-treatment of prisoners, killings of captured men and brutal retaliations for losses suffered in IRA attacks became routine. The worst atrocities occurred in March 1923 following the killing of five soldiers by an IRA mine; two of the men were Dublin Guard veterans, which enraged O'Daly. Seventeen republican prisoners were killed in retaliation, eight of them at Ballyseedy. O'Daly himself then presided over the military court of inquiry that exonerated his men. Though hostilities ended in May, O'Daly took part in a brutal and highly controversial assault on two young women in Kenmare the following month. Though supported again by the army leadership, O'Daly's behaviour worried some in government and ultimately, he resigned his commission in 1924. O'Daly was one of a number of 'Squad' veterans who committed war crimes during the Civil War. Their behaviour says much about the brutalising impact of violence, but also shows that they perceived their elite status and the patronage of Michael Collins gave them leeway to behave as they wished. [Text: Brian Hanley / Collection and image © Hugh Lane Gallery]

Free State government with the defence of law and order and democracy.[16]

This authoritarianism was largely rooted in the threat to the state posed by republican violence. On 7 December, the day after the inauguration of the Irish Free State, the Treatyite deputy Seán Hales was killed by the IRA as he made his way to the Dáil. Meeting in emergency session, the Cabinet agreed, as one of its first acts of government, to execute four internees held in Mountjoy Gaol. This grim reprisal epitomised the intimacy of the split and the consequent bitterness of its legacy. One of those executed, Rory O'Connor, had served as best man for Kevin O'Higgins, the government minister who confirmed his death sentence. The IRA avenged O'Connor the following year by killing Kevin O'Higgins's father, Thomas, in front of his wife and daughter and burning down the family home. O'Higgins's assassination would follow in 1927.

There was no legal basis for the execution in Mountjoy of O'Connor, Mellows, Barrett and McKelvey. Treatyite politicians were frank about their rationale, one minister describing it as 'an act of counter-terror'. 'Ultimately, all government is based on force', Kevin O'Higgins informed the Dáil on 8 December, and 'must meet force with greater force if it is to survive'. The only way to safeguard the state, William T. Cosgrave asserted, was to strike 'terror' into its enemies. Following the Emergency Powers resolution, eighty-one republicans were officially executed by the state. These killings were accompanied by further unauthorised murders, including an infamous cycle of reprisals in Kerry, sparked by the killing of five National Army soldiers, which resulted in the killing of seventeen anti-Treaty IRA men in horrific circumstances.

These killings formed part of a wider pattern of state terror that commenced in August 1922 when National Army intelligence officers and Criminal Intelligence Department detectives – some previously associated with Collins's 'Squad' – began to abduct, torture and murder anti-Treaty republicans. The killings, in which senior army officers were implicated, continued beyond the Civil War, demonstrating how a minority of revolutionaries had become inured to shocking forms of violence. The brutal methods that had so effectively undermined British power during the Irish revolution led to the creation of two Irish states whose survival rested on their ability to use the same means to impose their authority on recalcitrant minorities.

Illegality

Only recently have politicians across the Civil War divide acknowledged the illegality of the state's conduct. In 2011 Fine Gael minister (and subsequently taoiseach), Leo Varadkar, told the Dáil that 'people killed without trial' by Cosgrave's government 'were murdered'.[17] Shortly before their centenary, Taoiseach Micheál Martin described the Mountjoy Gaol executions as 'murder by any definition'.[18] In marked contrast, there was little public criticism of state executions at the time, indicating considerable acceptance of the need for draconian measures.

Fig. 14 Cartoon by Constance Markievicz depicting the personified Ireland, 'Hibernia', in chains. The message of this anti-Treatyite cartoon is that the Free State government used a combination of armed force, moral force, political dissemblance and propaganda to ensure that Ireland remained a slave to British imperialism. The uniformed 'Carey Collins' (a reference to the notorious Fenian traitor James Carey) holds a gun to Hibernia's head, demanding that she swear allegiance to the British king; Cosgrave, the clown, declares that talk of freedom was just 'an awful joke'; Desmond FitzGerald, the 'faker', levels tired accusations about de Valera's Spanish heritage, while the dismissive bishop, representative of the Catholic Church, oversees the enslavement. [Image: National Library of Ireland, PD 3064 TX -A]

In addition to press censorship by the state, one reason for the lack of protest was the vociferous support of the Catholic Church, the most important body of opinion in Ireland, for the Provisional Government. In October 1922 the hierarchy issued a pastoral condemning anti-Treaty violence:

> The present state of Ireland is a sorrow and a humiliation to its friends all over the world. To us, Irish Bishops, because of the moral and religious issues at stake, it is a source of the most painful anxiety. Our country, that but yesterday was so glorious, is now a byword before the nations for a domestic strife, as disgraceful as it is criminal and suicidal.

Fig. 15 Cumann na nGaedheal election poster, 1932. This is one of a series of striking election posters produced by Cumann na nGaedheal for the general elections in 1927 and 1932, which aimed at denigrating Fianna Fáil from a variety of angles, often related to the Civil War. This 1932 poster was part of the attempt to tar de Valera's party with the red-scare brush, due to its historical association with the IRA and de Valera's early support for the party. The IRA had increasing associations with the Communist International in the late 1920s, and in 1931 adopted a socialist party platform in the form of Saor Éire. This provoked a Church–state backlash and a red scare. Introducing coercion legislation on 16 October 1931, William T. Cosgrave referred to a conspiracy by republican and 'Communistic' groups to overthrow the state, and identified Saor Éire as 'a new element of danger [...] We believe that the new patriotism based on Muscovite teachings with a sugar coating of Irish extremism is completely alien to Irish tradition'. On Sunday 18 October a joint pastoral from the Irish Catholic bishops was read out in all Irish churches. It described Saor Éire as 'frankly Communistic', declared it and the IRA 'sinful and irreligious' and pronounced that no Catholic could lawfully be a member of those organisations. The bishops called for solutions to the country's social and economic problems that were 'in accordance with the traditions of Catholic Ireland', the very solutions that Fianna Fáil was about to offer the electorate. De Valera had reassured Cardinal MacRory of this at a private meeting and had reiterated his party's adherence to Catholic principles and rejection of communism during the debates on the new legislation. Although state repression succeeded in neutralising most radical opposition by the end of 1931, the government and its supporters continued to fan the flames of the red scare, hoping that it would provide enough heat to burn off the political challenge of Fianna Fáil. Cosgrave dissolved the Dáil in January 1932 and called an early general election. Cumann na nGaedheal had decided to go to the country eight months early, before the economic situation deteriorated any further, and to take advantage of what Minister Patrick McGilligan described as 'the Irregular and Bolshie situation'. While the government stressed the communist/subversive threat and Fianna Fáil's part in it, de Valera's party had been working successfully since the 1927 elections to neutralise the fears of the elites in Irish society, while developing an electorally fruitful programme, based on 'our own traditional attitude to life, a solution that is Irish and Catholic' and designed to appeal to as broad a constituency as possible. [Image: National Library of Ireland, EPH F54 / See Donal Ó Drisceoil, 'The Irregular and Bolshie situation': Republicanism and communism, 1921–36', in Fearghal McGarry (ed.), *Republicanism in Modern Ireland* (Dublin, 2003)]

> [...] even worse and sadder than this physical ruin is the general demoralisation created by this unhappy revolt – demoralisation especially of the young, whose minds are being poisoned by false principles, and their young lives utterly spoiled by early association with cruelty, robbery, falsehood and crime.[19]

The pastoral was explicit in its support for 'the legitimate Government', describing the anti-Treaty IRA as 'irregulars' (a Treatyite propaganda term). It accused anti-Treaty republicans of an 'immoral usurpation [...] of the people's rights', threatening them with excommunication. The pastoral was timed to support the government's adoption of emergency powers although the bishops, as Patrick Murray noted, 'could scarcely have foreseen what spiritual and moral problems they would encounter' when the state executions commenced several weeks later.[20] Crucially for the Provisional Government though, the bishops confined their unease about the state's unlawful killings, including the Mountjoy executions, to private appeals to Cosgrave rather than public statements of disapproval.[21]

This alliance between Church and state cast a long shadow. The joint pastoral enabled the bishops, who had been largely silent about republican violence since the Easter Rising, to reassert their traditional role as the moral arbiters within Irish society. For the clergy, as Brian Heffernan observed, 'the foundation of the Irish Free State in 1922 was equivalent to the reaching of dry ground again'.[22] While any independent Irish state was always likely to defer to Catholic interests, the repudiation of the Treaty by a substantial republican minority created a crisis of legitimacy that deepened the new state's dependence on ecclesiastical support. Church and government leaders responded to the chaos of 1922 by linking the political authority of the state with the moral authority of the Church, reinforcing a mutually beneficial relationship. Revealingly, the bishops' next joint pastoral was occasioned by the 1931 Public Safety Act. This emergency legislation was prompted by a Cumann na nGaedheal-orchestrated 'red scare', which alleged that an alliance between communists and republicans threatened a return to civil war. The threat to morality posed by the spectre of communism justified what would otherwise have been seen as an inappropriate clerical intervention in politics, just as the Church's intervention in the Civil War had been justified by 'the moral and religious issues at stake'.

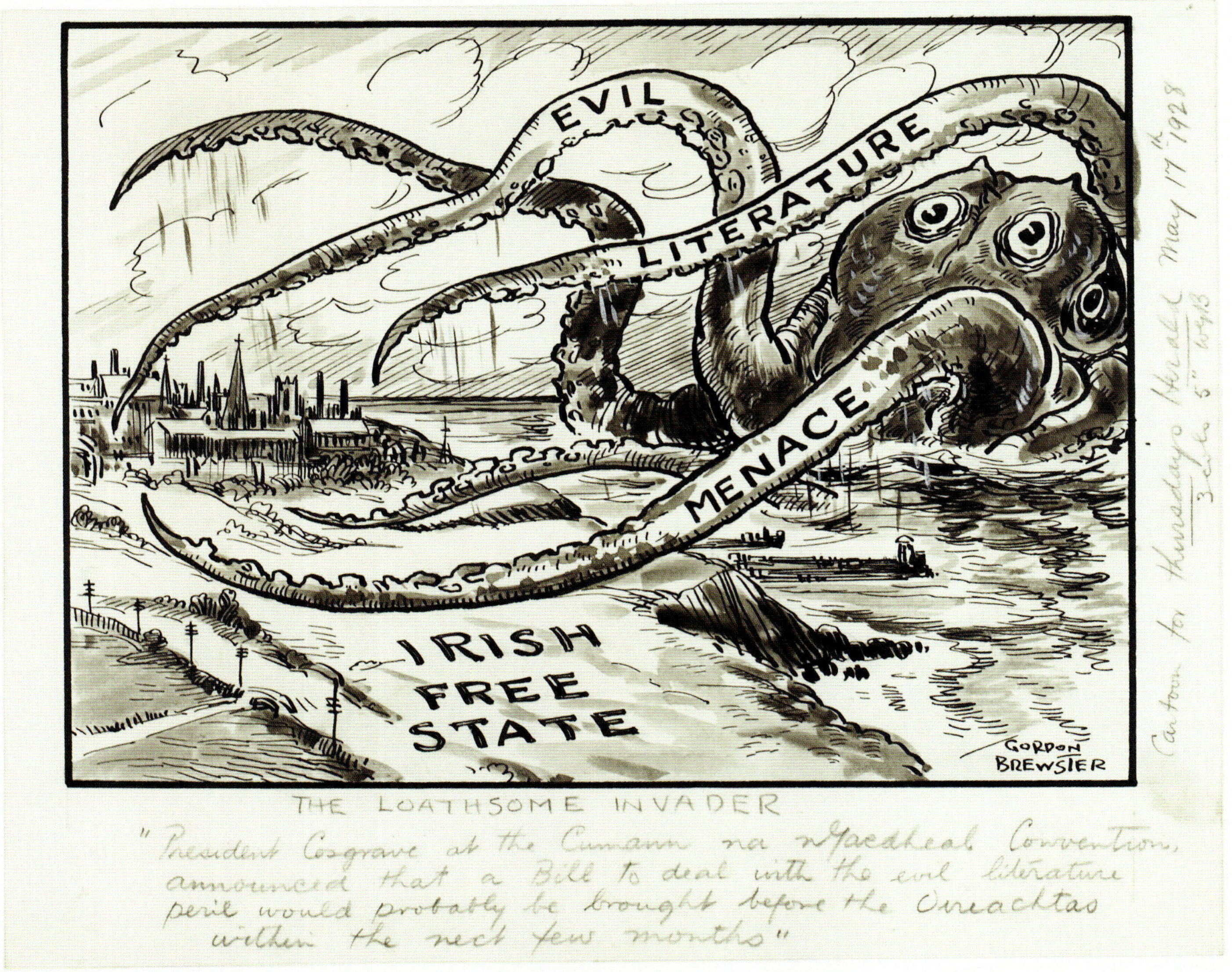

Fig. 16 'The Loathsome Invader' by Gordon Brewster, published in the *Evening Herald*, 17 May 1928. Brewster (1889–1946) was an editorial cartoonist for the Irish Independent group of newspapers. His work also appeared in the Christian Brothers publication, *Our Boys*, and he provided artwork for a number of Catholic Truth Society of Ireland (CTSI) publications. In a series of cartoons like this one, Brewster supported the vigorous campaign – in which both the Christian Brothers and CTSI played leading roles – for the introduction of censorship of publications legislation to complement the Censorship of Films Act 1923. An initially reluctant Kevin O'Higgins, as minister for home affairs, established the Committee on Evil Literature (CEL) in 1926 to consider the need for censorship of publications. The committee's report, delivered in January 1927, effectively endorsed the main thrust of the recommendations of the Catholic Action groups that dominated submissions to it: it recommended the establishment of a censorship system whereby a government-appointed board could prohibit publications deemed indecent or obscene or which advocated contraception and abortion. Catholic Actionists maintained pressure on the government to legislate in line with the CEL report throughout 1927 and 1928, and this cartoon relates to William T. Cosgrave's promise at the Cumann na nGaedheal conference in May 1928 that a censorship bill was imminent. The previous month Fianna Fáil had officially decided to support the implementation of the CEL's recommendations, thus increasing the pressure on a dithering government. The difficulty in finding a suitable formula had contributed to the delay, as did the death of O'Higgins and the political turmoil of 1927, including two general elections. The bill was finally brought before the Dáil for a formal first reading on 19 July 1928, the day before the summer recess, by O'Higgins's successor James Fitzgerald-Kenney. It broadly reflected the recommendations of the CEL, putting forward a scheme for post-publication censorship to be carried out by the minister for justice based on the recommendations of a board of five, nominated by the minister. Months of parliamentary and media debate followed, as attempts were made to ameliorate the dangers perceived to be inherent in the scheme; among the amendments accepted by the Oireachtas was the addition of a proviso that books would be banned only if they were 'in their general tendency indecent and obscene' and the specification that the board should take into account a book's 'literary, artistic, scientific or historic merit or importance' and 'the class of reader' the book might reasonably be expected to have. The scope of the bill was also extended to periodical publications that devoted 'an unduly large proportion of space to the publication of sensational matter relating to crime'. The Censorship of Publications Act 1929 became operative on 16 July 1929, though the first Censorship of Publications Board was not convened until February 1930. Over the following decades successive boards, dominated by Catholic Actionists, waged war on modern literature, banning thousands of books often on the basis of a single passage and largely ignoring the provisos about 'general tendency' and 'merit'. [Image: National Library of Ireland, Gordon Brewster Cartoon Collection, PD 2199 TX 192]

If the legacy of Civil War violence heightened clerical anxieties about immorality, it also strengthened the authoritarian inclinations of Cumann na nGaedheal, which reflected a similar pessimism about the character of the Irish people for whom independence had been achieved. The alliance between the two most powerful institutions in the state encompassed more than the policing of anti-Treaty republicanism. The extent of republican opposition to the new state saw the government emphasise its Catholic values as a means of establishing its legitimacy. The resulting Church–state nexus was a product not merely of opportunism but of the genuine psychological impact of the Civil War. In his classic polemic, *The Victory of Sinn Féin*, P.S. O'Hegarty reflected a mindset of despair shared by many Treatyite writers:

> We adopted political assassination as a principle; we devised the ambush; we encouraged women to forget their sex and play at gunmen; we turned the whole thoughts and passions of a generation upon blood and revenge and death; we placed gunmen, mostly half-educated and totally inexperienced, as dictators with powers of life and death over large areas. We derided the Moral Law, and said that there was no other law but the law of force.[23]

O'Hegarty placed most of the blame for the resulting 'complete moral collapse' on opponents of the Treaty: 'The Irregulars drove patriotism and honesty and morality out of Ireland. They fouled the wells which had kept us clean, and made the task of saving Ireland tenfold harder.'

Such pessimism was shared by the bishops. The Civil War, Deirdre McMahon has observed, had 'profound psychological consequences' for the Church, which was shocked by the bitter hostility of republicans following their denunciation by the bishops:

> the bishops' pastorals were full of gloomy, doom-laden pronouncements about the inherent sinfulness of the people and the need for constant vigilance against threatening influences which might corrupt them. The picture of a triumphalist Catholic Church in post-independence Ireland has now been set in stone but on closer examination this triumphalism was deceptive. The Church was, in fact, deeply insecure about its role in a new State that had been born out of violence, a violence, moreover, which had revealed how volatile and unstable its flock could be.[24]

This anxiety helps to explain the emphasis on respectability after independence. This often centred on a moralistic discourse about women whose culpability for Civil War hatreds was a feature of the reactionary Free State literature of disillusionment associated with writers such as O'Hegarty. The corollary of the archbishop of Tuam's belief that 'the future of the country is bound up with the dignity and purity of the women of Ireland' was the need to discipline women who fell short of these exacting standards.[25] This mentality helps to explain the establishment of a legislative framework aimed at policing the behaviour and bodies of women and other suspect or marginalised groups. It also helps to explain the prevalence of moral panics about popular entertainment, communism and sinfulness in a society that remained deeply conservative. This ethos contributed to a repressive consensus that disfigured Irish society, underpinning the cultures of hypocrisy, containment and concealment that prevailed until recent years.

Moral consensus

In Ken Loach's influential 2006 film, *The Wind that Shakes the Barley*, the Civil War is portrayed as marking a wrong turn that saw British rule replaced by a reactionary alliance between the Catholic Church and Treatyite politicians. Crucially, though, the moral consensus that shaped post-independence Ireland was shared by politicians across the Treaty divide, as is evidenced by the bipartisan willingness to cede influence over health, education, welfare and other spheres of the state to clerical authority. The power of this consensus rested not just on top-down Church–state authority but on popular support for the idea of Ireland as a Catholic nation with a unique spiritual destiny. Rather than strengthening anti-clericalism within anti-Treaty politics, the Church's denunciation of republicans during the Civil War prompted de Valera to accentuate Fianna Fáil's Catholicism after it won power. Ostentatious displays of piety included the installation of a large crucifix in the Dáil, the suspension of sittings on Holy Days and enthusiasm for the 1932 Eucharistic Congress. De Valera's efforts to enshrine a repressive Catholic morality in the ethos and practices of the state surpassed those of Cosgrave, as is evidenced by the ceding of a 'special position' to the Catholic Church and the emphasis on the place of women within the home in his 1937 constitution.

As such measures indicate, the Free State was characterised by the weakness of liberal and radical impulses – including secularism, feminism and socialism – that had been evident during the revolutionary period. The aggressive subordination of 'certain kinds of liberation' to 'the national project of restabilization (and clericalization)' resulted in a stunted civil society, and a coarsening of Irish culture epitomised by a literary censorship characterised by George Russell as 'moral infantilism'.[26] Like O'Hegarty, intellectuals such as Russell attributed this development, in part, to the legacy of the Irish revolution, which saw the ideals of the cultural revival displaced by a preoccupation with physical force. Writing two months before the end of the Civil War, he drew a link between the 'abstract plane' on which debates on the Treaty centred and the failure to develop a constructive and pragmatic vision of independence:

> Our spiritual, cultural and intellectual life has not changed for the better. If anything, it has retrograded. Nothing beautiful in the mind has found freer development [...] The mass of people in the country continue to think as they did before the revolution [...] The Free State came

Fig. 17 (above) Photograph of the papal legate Cardinal Lorenzo Lauri arriving in Dublin for the Eucharistic Congress, 1932. Lauri was officially welcomed by Éamon de Valera, Fianna Fáil leader and, since March 1932, head of the new minority government. The thirty-first Eucharistic Congress, held in Dublin over five sunny days in late June 1932, was an organisational triumph and clear announcement, as Terence Brown notes, that Ireland had 'appropriately taken its place among the Catholic nations of the earth'. The scale of the event itself, the impressive line-up of international ecclesiastical dignitaries and the vast attendance at the high mass in the Phoenix Park – at which a papal message was broadcast using the most modern technology – were powerful expressions of national pride and progress. It was also an opportunity, a decade after the end of the Civil War, for Church and state to emphasise a Catholic unity that transcended Civil War enmities. Visiting journalists were struck by the scale of participation from across Ireland and the decorating efforts of the denizens of even Dublin's poorest areas. The new president of the Executive Council maintained a high profile throughout the public proceedings, consolidating his position, emphasising his Catholic credentials and courting the hierarchy while also demonstrating his commitment to the pursuit of sovereignty by publicly snubbing the governor general, James McNeill. The king's representative in the Free State, a post created by the Treaty, had been prominent at events celebrating the centenary of Catholic Emancipation hosted by the Cumann na nGaedheal government in 1929. Three years later he was not even invited to the state reception at Dublin Castle to welcome the papal legate. He resigned in 1933 and was replaced by Domhnall Ua Buachalla, who was complicit in de Valera's moves to downgrade the position before it was finally abolished by the Constitution Amendment Act in 1936. For the Catholic Church, as Diarmaid Ferriter writes, the intense public piety and communal devotion in June 1932 helped narrow 'the ground available to those who wanted to promote radicalism or protest'. At a time of international upheaval and economic uncertainty, 'religion was presented as providing security in a dangerous world'. Such Catholic triumphalism, however, thoroughly embraced at every level in the Free State, also served to further alienate Northern Ireland's Protestant unionist population and helped to consolidate partition. [Image: part of the Independent Newspapers Ireland/NLI Collection, INDH2140 / See Diarmaid Ferriter, 'Pope and Ceremony: How the 1932 congress melded Church and state', *Irish Times*, 2 June 2012; Terence Brown, 'Culture and Society', in *Atlas of the Irish Revolution* (Cork, 2017)]

Fig. 18 A house decorated for the Eucharistic Congress: commissioned by Mr M. Quinn, 37 Green Street, Waterford. [Image: National Library of Ireland, POOLEWP 3922]

> into being with popular feeling stagnant. Why was this? Seven years of sensation had dulled the heart and made it insensitive. If a Republic were proclaimed in Ireland next year or the year after, would there be any more exultation?[27]

The writer, veteran and nemesis of 'Irish puritanism and ignorance' Seán O'Faoláin also linked the Free State's philistinism to the legacy of the revolution. He attributed its excessive censorship to the influence of 'a fanatical minority maggot-bred by the decay of national morale during the years following the Civil War, a time when the Catholic Church was felt, feared and courted on all sides as the dominant power'.[28]

Politics of Irish Civil War memory

One response to the psychological demoralisation brought about by the Civil War was to abandon previous loyalties. Some supporters and opponents of the Treaty came to express criticism, dissent or disillusionment about the development of their own political traditions after the Civil War. As noted earlier, Cumann na nGaedheal claimed in 1932 that Fianna Fáil's election would return Ireland to the chaos of Civil War. This did not prove a successful electoral strategy, but it did reflect genuine Treatyite fears, particularly within the police and army. Consequently, Fianna Fáil's election prompted not just rumours of a coup, centring on Garda Commissioner Eoin O'Duffy, but also the rise of the Army Comrades' Association, which was founded to defend the interests of National Army veterans who feared victimisation by the new government. The Blueshirts, as they would become known, were a product of Civil War tensions as well as the concerns of a rural elite about de Valera's agrarian policies. O'Duffy emerged as the new movement's leader following his dismissal as commissioner (which was viewed by Treatyites as an act of political vindictiveness by de Valera).

There was a significant Civil War dimension to the activism and appeal of the Blueshirts, whose propagandists depicted O'Duffy as embodying 'the spirit of Michael Collins'.[29] O'Duffy also drew heavily on the cult of Collins. The Blueshirts, he declared,

> are doing the work for which Collins and O'Higgins gave their lives. While we uphold the ideas of these great leaders we remain, under God, the only true custodians of the national tradition of our people, the only true guardians of Ireland's historic cause [...]. If we die, it will be as guardians of the cause for which Collins was a martyr.

Whereas Cumann na nGaedheal, wary of identifying loyalty to the state with a narrow Treatyite affiliation, had largely neglected to commemorate its Civil War dead, O'Duffy had no compunction about stoking partisan hatreds. The incident that finally led de Valera to ban the Blueshirts as a threat to democracy was its 'March on Dublin' in August 1933. The destination of this parade, which some feared was intended to emulate the infamous 'March on Rome' that saw Mussolini seize power, was the Cenotaph commemorating Griffith, Collins and O'Higgins. Under O'Duffy's leadership, Civil War sites of memory became venues for fascistic rallies where Blueshirts gave the raised-arm salute. At Béal na Blá, Blueshirts were urged to 'Remember the words of Collins – "If I fall, you have O'Duffy".'

Such commemoration aimed not merely to instrumentalise the memory of the Civil War but also to identify the Blueshirts with the militarist republican tradition associated with Collins: it represented, therefore, an implicit critique of Cumann na nGaedheal's moderate nationalism. Ernest Blythe, one of that party's most enthusiastic Blueshirt supporters, described the movement as 'the authentic successors to the Volunteers'. After the former Blueshirt organisation merged with Cumann na nGaedheal to form Fine Gael under his presidency in 1933, O'Duffy sought to wrest the leadership of Irish nationalism from Fianna Fáil. Declaring that Fine Gael would 'not play second fiddle to anybody in the matter of Nationality', he asserted that his party's 'prevailing motive will be nationalism'.

The resulting tensions between O'Duffy's Anglophobic anti-partitionism and the moderate Commonwealth politics of former Cumann na nGaedheal leaders, tensions that had previously surfaced during the mid-1920s 'army mutiny' and boundary crisis, were central to the split that occurred within Fine Gael in the summer of 1934. Although the Blueshirts quickly imploded (due in no small part to O'Duffy's ineptitude), their initial popularity indicates resentment among grassroots Treatyites about the ease with which Cumann na nGaedheal had reconciled itself to membership of the British Empire. After O'Duffy broke with Fine Gael he was quick to denounce 'the pan-British party of the Free State', even claiming to have resigned 'because he was not prepared to lead the League of Youth with the Union Jack tied to his neck'. The Blueshirt leader articulated an uncharacteristically insightful critique of Fine Gael's political vision:

> Fine Gael say they are the Treaty party. May I ask which Treaty? You could hardly recognise it now. Many of its main provisions are already gone, and I do not think any party will ever attempt to restore them. If acceptance of the Treaty position means renunciation of the teachings of Parnell and Pearse, of Griffith and Collins, then away with it [...] few in the Free State are enthusiastic over the status the Treaty gives us.

The belated acceptance of these harsh truths by his former colleagues helps to explain how it was Fine Gael that ultimately proclaimed the Republic in 1949.

Similar tensions can be identified on the other side of the Civil War divide as de Valera's success in using constitutional means to dismantle the Treaty increasingly called into question the purpose of the IRA. Militant republicans understood their role as continuing the struggle that had been defeated in the Civil

War: that is, overthrowing the Treatyite government to restore the Republic. Partition was a secondary consideration for the inter-war IRA. Although Fianna Fáil had benefited from IRA support in the 1932 general election, its outcome created an existential crisis for physical-force republicans. As the IRA's chief of staff conceded, 'nobody visualized a Free State which Republicans were not supposed to attack'.[30] The IRA's refusal to concede the legitimacy of the Southern state, and to disavow violent means, inevitably led to a parting of ways with the Fianna Fáil government.

'self-crazed by abstractions'

For some, including a militant minority who remained loyal to the IRA, the Civil War intensified commitment to the anti-Treaty cause but, for many veterans, its sterile legacy led to disengagement from an increasingly solipsistic tradition. Writing from Gormanstown internment camp during the Civil War, Frank O'Connor repudiated martyrdom, complaining that mythical abstractions generated 'a tedious morality'.[31] His fellow Cork writer and Civil War veteran, Seán O'Faoláin, recollected his growing unease with the casuistry underpinning de Valera's opposition to the Treaty. 'We were all idealists, self-crazed by abstractions, lost in the labyrinths of the

Fig. 19 Richard Mulcahy TD delivering the oration at Béal na Blá, August 1932, the tenth anniversary of Michael Collins's death. From the first anniversary of the fatal Civil War ambush in 1923, the highly charged annual commemoration spoke more to contemporary politics and divergent political identities than faithful remembrance of the 'lost leader'. In 1932, when Fianna Fáil's electoral victory stoked fears of resurgent republican militancy, the right-wing Army Comrades' Association (ACA) was a vocal and muscular presence at the west Cork ceremony. Formed by ex-National Army members in the same year to protect Cumann na nGaedheal party meetings against IRA intimidation, the ACA, later the National Guard (known colloquially as the Blueshirts), developed between 1933 and 1935 under the leadership of Eoin O'Duffy into a more generalised fascistic anti-republican and anti-communist movement that often clashed violently with the IRA along Civil War lines. They also led a renewed campaign against the payment of land annuities and the impact on large cattle farmers of the 'Economic War' and Fianna Fáil's land policies. Speaking at Béal na Blá in 1932, Mulcahy drew explicit links between the ACA and Collins as defenders of the institutions of state from a 'tyrannical body'. It was a theme later seized upon and expounded by O'Duffy, who frequently cast the Blueshirts as the direct inheritors of Collins's legacy and true custodians of the national tradition. In 1933 the government banned the procession to Béal na Blá. A month later, the Blueshirts merged with the National Centre Party and Cumann an nGaedheal to form Fine Gael. O'Duffy returned to Cork as leader of the new pro-Treaty party in August 1934, a month before he was forced to resign because of his bellicosity and advocacy of illegal methods. Two years later O'Duffy used the commemorative platform to announce the formation of the ill-fated Irish Brigade to support General Franco in the Spanish Civil War. [Image: courtesy of the Irish Examiner Archive, Ref. 963A / See *Cork Examiner*, 22 Aug. 1932]

Fig. 20 Portrait of Seán O'Faoláin (1900–1991) by Howard Coster (1930s). The Cork-born man of letters, O'Faoláin was a major cultural figure of independent Ireland. He was the author of seven books of short stories, five novels, five biographies, one play, five travel books, three books of criticism, multiple articles in Irish and international magazines and journals and an autobiography, *Vive Moi!* (1963). He was also editor of the legendary *Bell* magazine (1940–6). O'Faoláin was a prominent opponent of Irish literary censorship; his first short-story collection *Midsummer Night Madness* (1932) and first novel *Bird Alone* (1936) were both banned by the Censorship of Publications Board. In 1918–21, he was a member of the IRA's University Company (UCC), but was involved in no military engagements; the same applied in the Civil War, when he was engaged in bombmaking and publicity on the republican side. His application for a military service pension was rejected on the grounds that there was 'not any element of military service' in his record. He regarded the Treaty as a 'base betrayal' and instinctively took the anti-Treaty side. He launched a short-lived republican monthly titled *An Long* (The Ship) in May 1922. Having initially helped out in bombmaking, O'Faoláin joined the team of republican censors at the *Cork Examiner* at the outset of the Civil War and was appointed director of publicity for the 1st Southern Division. He rejoined the munitions staff in west Cork following the evacuation of the city and took over editorship of the *Poblacht na hEireann–Southern Edition* following the departure of Erskine Childers in October 1922. He continued to work on publicity and propaganda as the war drew to a close, including his exposure of the Ballyseedy massacre in *Éire: the Irish nation*. From August 1923 until the end of that year he acted as director of publicity for the republican movement, after which he 'retired'. He had lost his job as an educational representative for Talbot Press and the Educational Company of Ireland due to his activities, so he returned to UCC to work for a Master's degree and 'to lick my wounds'. Many years later, writing about the Treaty and Civil War, O'Faoláin remembered that, while he stood vaguely then for the 'historical Underdog–for Wolfe Tone's "men of no property"', he had no clear idea of what each side actually represented: 'If some visible, human alternatives had been imaginatively put before us, it might have been different – a choice, say between slavery and antislavery [...] or between socialism and capitalism, or between privilege and equality, even between clerical domination and secular rule, even between such urgent ideas [had they been then urgent] as freedom of speech and state censorship [...] No such polarities presented themselves to us [...]'. In terms of the 'realists' versus 'idealists' polarity, he reflected that 'our realists said goodbye to too many of their feelings. I cannot say that we idealists said goodbye to our sense of realism, because, alas, if we had any worthy of the name I saw but little sign of it in those disheartening days of civil war' (*Vive Moi!: An autobiography* (London, 1993 edn), pp. 149–50). [Image: National Portrait Gallery, UK / See Maurice Harmon, *Sean O'Faolain: A life* (London, 1988) and Military Service Pensions Collection: Seán O'Faoláin, MSP49115]

dreams to which we had retreated.'[32] The Civil War, he claimed, 'woke us up from the mesmerism of the romantic dream'.[33]

O'Faoláin recalled with disgust de Valera's decision to swear an oath to the British monarch as an 'empty formula' in 1927: 'From that day to this I have never trusted any politician anywhere.' De Valera's further descent from the planes of republican purism intensified his disillusionment:

> Within five years his party was in office. They stayed in office for sixteen stolid years, during which they not only stolidly refused to declare Ireland their Republic but, when opposed in arms by the old and young irreconcilables, gave them the same treatment that they had got from the original Irish Free State Government. They imprisoned them, executed them, and let them die on hunger strike.[34]

Noting the irony that Fine Gael had declared the Republic in 1948, O'Faoláin recorded – just as George Russell had predicted in 1923 – that

> the Republican ideal, if it had ever meant anything visible or touchable, any vision of life as men might actually live it or hope to live it, had lost all its content. Every foreign government acknowledged it, the Church blessed it, the people huzzahed for it, and perhaps some dead bones may have stirred to hear the cannons salute the tardy arrival of a stillborn child. It has made no least difference to life in Ireland.[35]

Reckoning

Although the legacy of the Civil War structured the political divisions of the 1920s and 1930s, O'Faoláin's assessment of its bathetic denouement raises the question of its importance in terms of everyday life. Anne Dolan has suggested that the 'sense that the State lived in the shadow of its revolution, that its political life was defined by the Civil War divide, underestimates the intensity of bread and butter politics from the very outset'.[36] Beyond the performative discourse of electoral politics, there is considerable evidence that – even among politically engaged veterans – the impact of its legacy can be questioned. For instance many in the IRA did not choose a side in the Civil War, while the largest section of 1916 GPO veterans remained neutral.[37]

If the bitterness of Free State politics was an obvious consequence of the Civil War, a less visible, but perhaps more significant, aspect of the conflict's legacy was the ability of former veterans to manage – if not necessarily reconcile – its divisions. The Military Service Pensions Collection contains many applications by veterans who were supported by referees from the opposing side of the Civil War divide. Among the most notable examples is that of Charles Dalton. In 1941, while he was being treated in St Patrick's Hospital, Dalton's wife Theresa submitted an application for a disability pension on his behalf. A doctor who examined Dalton for the pension board reported:

> He has delusions of being shot, executed and that all around are in conspiracy to kill him. He hears voices urging his destruction and his whole delusional state is definitely linked up with his previous military experiences. In my opinion such experiences this man has had during military service and particularly his own active part have preyed on his mind and conscience so that in the following years he has gradually lost his reason.[38]

The psychological consequences of joining Collins's 'Squad' while still a teenage schoolboy must have been considerable, but omitted from Dalton's file was any explicit reference to the potential impact of his actions after the War of Independence when he had participated in a campaign of abduction, torture and murder of anti-Treaty republicans, some as young as sixteen. Strikingly, Dalton's application was supported by a five-page hand-written letter to his wife from the minister for supplies (and later taoiseach), Seán Lemass, who attested to Dalton's hysteria following his involvement in the assassination of four British agents during Bloody Sunday.[39] Lemass's willingness to support a former comrade who had not only fought with the opposing side in the Civil War but had also been implicated in a 'murder gang' responsible for a campaign that claimed the life of his own brother, Noel, in horrific circumstances, demonstrates how some veterans could prioritise compassion for former comrades over the desire for retribution.

Managing Irish Civil War animosities

The survival of democracy throughout the inter-war years points to a similar capacity to manage Civil War animosities. The actions of governments on both sides of the divide were characterised by comparative restraint. In contrast, in Spain 50,000 republicans were executed by Franco's regime in the aftermath of the Spanish Civil War, while many more continued to be imprisoned or discriminated against decades after the conflict.[40] In Finland, which had a population similar to Ireland but endured a far more vicious civil war, 76,000 of those on the losing side were tried after the conflict, resulting in 68,000 convictions for treason and 113 executions. Civil war hatreds 'continued to translate into violence for years to come', with 226 killings taking place in Finland between 1918 and 1921.[41] In contrast, the losing side in the Irish Civil War were reintegrated into Irish society rather than demonised as an alien threat to the nation.[42] One reason for this was that both sides in Ireland subscribed to the same values, whereas republicans in Spain and Finland were depicted as Russian-backed 'Reds'. Another was the self-interested decision by the Free State authorities to introduce acts of indemnity and amnesty in 1923 and 1924, which ensured that there would be no retribution for the crimes of the Civil War: 'The consensus that marked Ireland out as one of the few European states born in the broad post-First World War settlement to survive the upheavals of the next twenty years was based on a decision not to settle accounts.'[43]

Perhaps then the hatreds of the Civil War have received too much attention from historians. Any emotional history of that conflict must also consider 'what put this place back together again', as Anne Dolan has observed. 'The stitching, for so many reasons, can be as important as the tear.'[44] Family histories record ruptures healed, as well as the better-known stories of divisions that endured. Reviewing a memoir by Máire Mhac an tSaoi, whose father Seán MacEntee took the anti-Treaty side (and later served as tánaiste), Garret FitzGerald (a future taoiseach) recorded how the friendship between his father's family and the MacEntees survived the Civil War:

> In the early stages of that tragic conflict, when my father and his colleagues were under fire in Government Buildings from Republicans, and Sean MacEntee was besieged by the Free State army in what is now the Gresham Hotel, my republican mother and Margaret MacEntee took turns at bringing their children to stay the night in each other's houses on either side of Marlborough Road.[45]

Barely a year after republicans were released from internment, Margaret MacEntee became godmother to Garret. His father, Desmond FitzGerald, then minister for external affairs, presented Seán MacEntee with a passport, enabling him to leave the country rather than face return to the internment camp from which he had secured temporary release. Garret's final meeting with Seán MacEntee occurred in the mid-1980s when the latter, aged ninety-four, lay on his deathbed: 'I was deeply moved that he asked to see me, to tell me how much I had been loved by Margaret – a love that I warmly reciprocated – and to talk of his regret that the Civil War had happened.'

CASE STUDY

Veterans, Memorialisation and the Old IRA Movement in Post-Civil War Ireland

John Borgonovo

The Irish Civil War cast a long shadow over the entire revolutionary period. Decades later, veterans of the Irish War of Independence coalesced in 'Old IRA' fraternal groups around the country. This 'Old IRA movement' often deployed the memory of the Anglo-Irish War not just to commemorate fallen comrades or to protect their own self-interests, but also to reunify the separatist community and challenge earlier efforts to delegitimise the republican struggle.[1]

Early veterans' associations

Immediately after the First World War, ex-servicemen's associations were highly visible in Ireland and Britain.[2] War veterans demanded government assistance as a right rather than a privilege, and lobbied for state-financed housing, employment, job training and medical treatment. In Ireland, three different ex-soldier groups were politically active from 1919 to 1921 and fielded dozens of candidates in the 1920 local elections (few were elected).[3] When the largely apolitical British Legion emerged in the early 1920s, Irish ex-servicemen's associations evolved into fraternal bodies committed to protecting veterans' benefits provided by the British government.[4] Although continuing to participate in First World War commemorations for several decades, ex-servicemen as a self-organised political entity slowly faded from Irish public life.

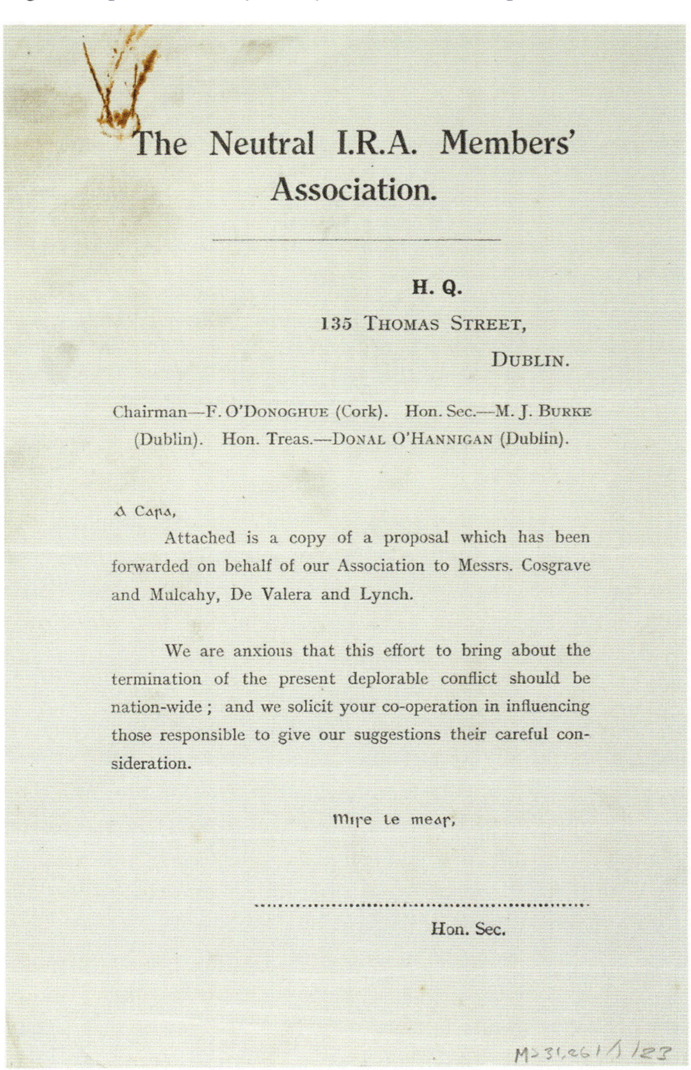

The Neutral I.R.A. Members' Association.

H. Q.
135 Thomas Street,
Dublin.

Chairman—F. O'Donoghue (Cork). Hon. Sec.—M. J. Burke (Dublin). Hon. Treas.—Donal O'Hannigan (Dublin).

A Cara,

Attached is a copy of a proposal which has been forwarded on behalf of our Association to Messrs. Cosgrave and Mulcahy, De Valera and Lynch.

We are anxious that this effort to bring about the termination of the present deplorable conflict should be nation-wide; and we solicit your co-operation in influencing those responsible to give our suggestions their careful consideration.

Mise le meas,

....

Hon. Sec.

Fig. 1 Cover letter for peace proposals issued by the Neutral IRA in February 1923. In late 1922 as the Civil War entered its guerrilla phase, thousands of IRA veterans who had abstained from the fighting but largely opposed the Anglo-Irish Treaty joined the 'Neutral IRA Members' Association'. Headed by Florence 'Florrie' O'Donoghue, the former adjutant-general of the anti-Treaty IRA, the group ultimately claimed 20,000 members and several high-profile veterans of the War of Independence. For several months, the Neutral IRA sought to bridge the Civil War divide and reunite the independence movement. It announced its adherence to two principles: '(1) the sovereignty of the Irish nation is inalienable and indefeasible. (2) All power in Ireland legislative, executive, and judicial is derived from the people of Ireland, and they alone can decide upon its exercise.' The group sought to bring about a ceasefire, to be followed by a free and fair election to form a new government. Anti-Treaty deputies refusing to take the oath of allegiance would be allowed voting rights in the Oireachtas should they agree to abstain from armed resistance to the government. Neither the government nor the IRA was open to this option. Bill Kissane notes that William T. Cosgrave told a Neutral IRA delegation that it would mean 'that the people who roast children, burst watermains, murder our men, will have to get a constitutional position in the state'. Having failed in its primary mission, the Neutral IRA wound down in late 1923. Several of its leaders, however, re-emerged decades later in the Old IRA veterans' movement and again tried to reunify their War of Independence comrades. [Document: National Library of Ireland, Florence O'Donoghue Papers, MS 31,261/1/23 / See 'Documents relating to Old IRA Members and the Neutral IRA Members' Association', MS 31,261, Florrie O'Donoghue Papers, National Library of Ireland; Bill Kissane, *The Politics of the Irish Civil War* (Oxford, 2005), pp. 138–41]

Fig. 2 At Seán Hales Place in Bandon, County Cork stands a life-size statue dedicated to the memory of Brigadier-General Seán Hales. It was unveiled on 19 January 1930, at what was then Bank Place, by Éamonn Duggan, a signatory of the Treaty and parliamentary secretary to William T. Cosgrave, president of the Executive Council. The dedication acknowledged Hales's contribution as 'Volunteer, soldier, statesman and patriot' and recognised 'his services to the cause of Irish freedom'. Among those present at the unveiling were his sister Madge and three of his four brothers – Tom, Robert and William – who fought for the anti-Treaty side during the Civil War. The family bonds, fortified between 1913 and 1921 when six of the nine Hales siblings were active in the independence movement, were sundered by the signing of the Anglo-Irish Treaty. Tom, the youngest brother, had been the first to join the Irish Volunteers in 1913, followed by Seán, Robert and William. Together, they founded the Ballinadee Company in 1915. Seán, Robert and William were interned after the 1916 Easter Rising. When the Volunteers were reorganised in 1917, Tom, who took charge of the Bandon Battalion, was succeeded by Seán as officer commanding Ballinadee. Further reorganisation in 1919 saw Seán take the leadership of the Bandon Battalion, and William the captaincy of Ballinadee Company, when the youngest Hales brother was elected leader of the 3rd West Cork Brigade. As well as leading attacks against the crown forces in west Cork during the War of Independence, Seán cut his political teeth as a member of the rural district council, and presided at sittings of the republican courts. The family was deeply affected by the arrest and torture of Tom Hales and his quartermaster Pat Harte by British intelligence officers in late July 1920 and by the burning of the family home in Knocknacurra by crown forces in March 1921. Seán, William and Robert, members of the 3rd West Cork Brigade flying column, were forced to go on the run in 1920, while Madge was involved in efforts to secure an arms shipment, organised in part by her brother Donal in Italy. In June 1921 newly elected TD Seán Hales oversaw the kidnapping of the earl of Bandon and the destruction of Castle Bernard. Seán and Madge were the only members of the Hales family to support the Treaty, but, despite their political differences, the eldest and youngest Hales brothers never publicly criticised each other. During his ill-fated tour of west Cork in August 1922, Michael Collins stopped in Bandon and met with Seán Hales, now brigadier-general in the National Army. As Seán warned his commander-in-chief that many roads were impassable, he was unaware that his brother Tom was overseeing preparations for the ambush at Béal na Blá. By November, Tom, William and Robert were interned and on 7 December, forty-two-year-old Seán Hales was assassinated by members of the IRA on Ormonde Quay on his way to Dáil Éireann. In 1925 the Seán Hales Memorial Committee was established. A public subscription received funds from home and abroad. The memorial, commemorating a respected figure in the struggle for independence and a prominent family who straddled both sides of the Civil War divide, helped to unite a divided community. [Text: Liz Gillis / Image: John Crowley]

Similar organisation of War of Independence veterans was absent during the Civil War period, with two exceptions. The Neutral IRA was initiated by senior Cork city IRA veterans Florrie O'Donoghue and Seán O'Hegarty. It limited its membership to those with IRA service during the War of Independence and sought to end the Civil War fighting.[5] By early 1923 the Neutral IRA claimed 20,000 members, but failed in its central goal of facilitating the anti-Treaty movement's transition from armed rebellion to parliamentary representation in Dáil Eireann.[6] The organisation ultimately wound down later in 1923, though several Neutral IRA members would reemerge in the Old IRA movement.

Within the National Army, disgruntled officers who lost out during demobilisation at the end of the Civil War formed their own Old IRA veterans' organisation. Led by former members of Michael Collins's 'Squad', they sought to use their War of Independence prestige to compel the Free State government to halt the downsizing of the National Army. Those efforts culminated in the 1924 'army mutiny', which ended many careers and established firm civil control over the military in the new state.[7] A number of those dismissed officers, including leaders Liam Tobin and Frank Thornton, reappeared in 1928 with a new Old IRA association, Clan na nGaedheal.[8] It limited membership to veterans who had served in the War of Independence, regardless of their stance during the Civil War, and included prominent anti-Treaty Dublin IRA veterans who had served alongside 'Squad' members from 1916 to 1921. Clan na nGaedheal claimed to be 'non-party and non-political', but the group generally supported Fianna Fáil's challenge to the Anglo-Irish Treaty after the party came to power in 1932. Clann na nGaedheal participated in Easter Rising commemorations with anti-Treaty republicans and urged former colleagues to 'forget all feuds'.[9] The organisation remained primarily Dublin-based and faded later in the 1930s, though some of its leaders were later active in veterans' unity organisations.[10]

A more dynamic and problematic Civil War veterans' group appeared in 1932. The Army Comrades' Association (ACA) was formed by National Army ex-soldiers just before their Civil War opponents in Fianna Fáil formed their first government.[11] Within six months, the ACA leadership included senior Cumann na nGaedheal political figures such as Dr T.F. O'Higgins, General Richard

Fig. 3 National Army soldiers bearing the coffin of Brigadier-General Seán Hales led by Bishop Daniel Cohalan, following the requiem mass at St Mary and St Anne's Cathedral (North Cathedral) in Cork city on 11 December 1922. Hales's remains were later buried in St Mary's Cemetery, Innishannon, County Cork. Despite their deep-seated differences on the Treaty and the circumstances of Seán's assassination, the Hales family managed to maintain lines of communication during the Civil War. Following Seán's killing, the family publicly registered in the pages of the *Cork Examiner* their 'horror and disgust' at the executions of Liam Mellows, Rory O'Connor, Richard (Dick) Barrett and Joseph McKelvey that were carried out in reprisal. While their father Robert died soon after, broken by his son's killing, the family was united in the aftermath of the Civil War in their efforts to commemorate Seán in his own place. [Image: National Library of Ireland, Hogan-Wilson Collection, HOGW7]

Mulcahy and General Seán MacEoin. By 1933 the ACA advocated anti-communism, opposition to Fianna Fáil and protection of Cumann na Gaedheal political speech. As Mike Cronin notes, within seventeen months, 'the Association had transformed itself from a benevolent group protecting the interests of ex-army men, into a shirted and increasingly involved political group'.[12] That same year the recently fired Garda commissioner Eoin O'Duffy (a prominent IRA and National Army veteran) assumed leadership of the group, opened membership to non-veterans, changed the name to the National Guard and adopted fascistic uniforms and salutes. O'Duffy and his 'Blueshirts' resembled fascist war veterans' groups active in central Europe during the same period.

Within the anti-Treaty movement, any potential veterans' organisation was compromised by the refusal of many republicans to recognise the Irish Free State, even after Fianna Fáil took power. For those veterans, continued membership in, or support for, the IRA grew more problematic when the government suppressed the militant republican organisation in 1936.[13] Other ruptures in that decade included the de facto split of 1934 that saw the formation of the socialist Republican Congress and later when much of the Civil War generation opposed the IRA's 1939 bombing campaign in Great Britain and left the organisation.[14] Gavin Foster has urged historians to be aware of cleavages 'within the anti-Treaty tradition', and noted that such internal competition required careful navigation by those veterans' groups.[15] The Civil War division among veterans was not a simple binary between pro- and anti-Treaty followers, but had additional fractures that were often amplified geographically and temporally.

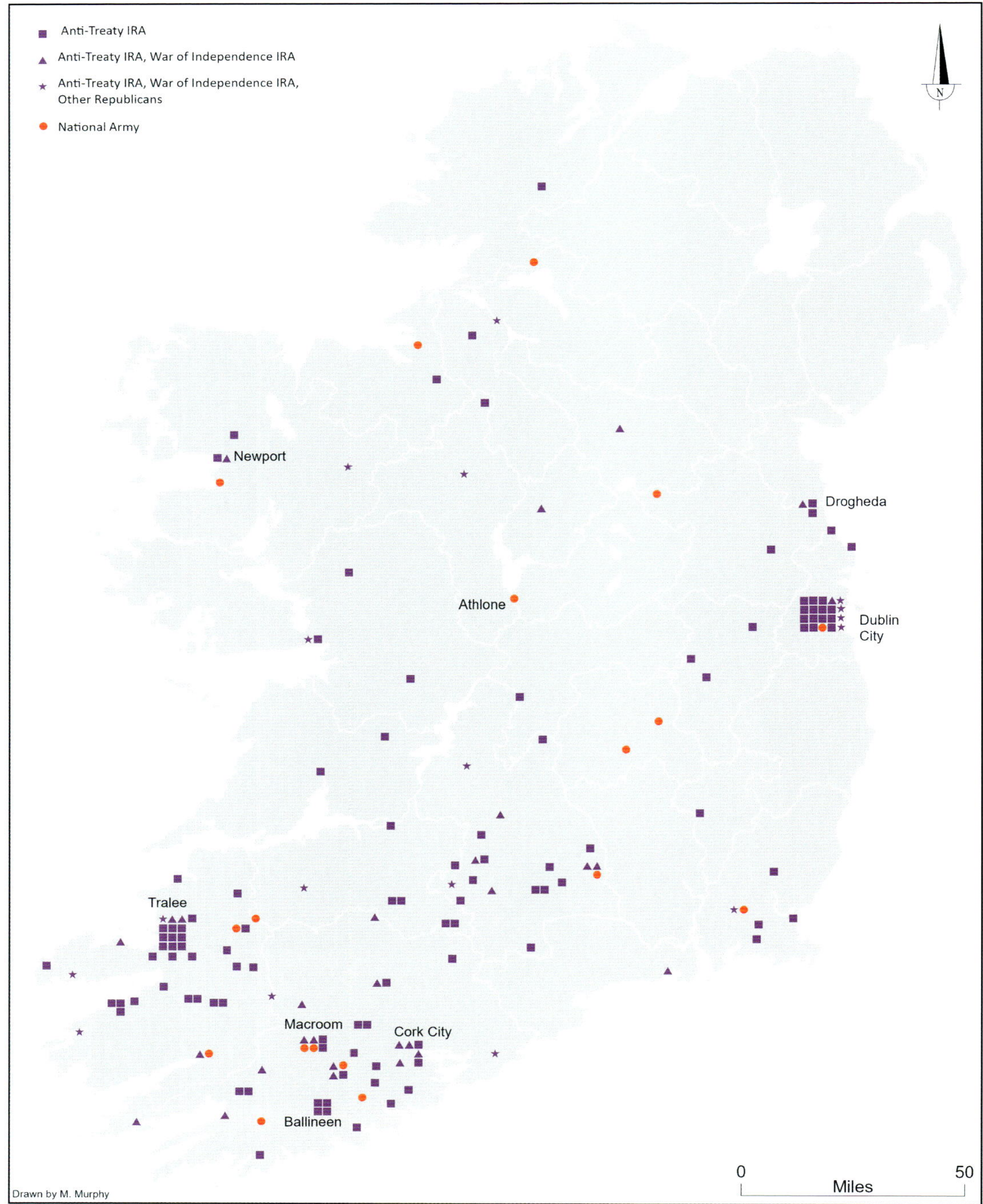

Fig. 4 Map identifying the locations of 172 Civil War memorials. A feature of Irish Civil War memory is the localised memorialisation of the republican dead. These memorials range from elaborate public monuments dedicated to the dead of specific IRA units, to simple crosses and wall plaques commemorating the deaths of individuals. Most often they were erected by republican veterans or family members, with some notable exceptions. This map, based on data collected by historian and surveyor Tony McGrath, focuses primarily on roadside memorials and publicly accessible monuments, and represents the findings of ongoing research into Irish memorialisation in public spaces. The relative scarcity of National Army memorials is clear, a disparity examined by Anne Dolan in her 2006 book *Commemorating the Irish Civil War: History and memory, 1923–2000.* McGrath's memorial data also highlights the different sites of conflict during the Irish Civil War (such as south Munster) and can be read alongside Andy Bielenberg and John Dorney's fatalities data in Chapter 6, particularly in relation to anti-Treaty IRA losses. Perhaps most interestingly, the map identifies twenty-nine IRA memorials which name both IRA War of Independence and IRA Civil War dead. A further seventeen combine IRA Civil War dead with other republican 'martyrs' beyond the War of Independence, including those associated with the 1798 Rebellion, the Fenian Rising of 1867, and the 1916 Easter Rising. Thus, adherents to the anti-Treaty cause colonised popular memory of patriotic sacrifice, linking Civil War republican resistance with conflicts more broadly accepted and legitimised in the eyes of the public. However, some of those latter memorials also include the names of republicans killed in IRA campaigns that took place well after 1923, which reveals the ongoing weaponisation of memory by successive republican activists in Ireland. To date, McGrath has located and mapped 390 war memorials of all kinds in Ireland, as well as a substantial number of Famine memorials, road traffic fatality crosses, holy wells, and other groupings, which can be found at his website 'Reading the Signs': https://readingthesigns.weebly.com. [Map data provided by Tony McGrath]

Fig. 5 President Seán T. O'Kelly leading the procession of Old IRA members at the October 1952 unveiling of the East Limerick Brigade memorial in Bruff, County Limerick. [Image: courtesy of Limerick Archives]

The Old IRA movement

In 1934 Fianna Fáil expanded military service pensions to include veterans of the War of Independence and Civil War who had not served in the National Army. The new pension scheme required reliable records to ascertain claims of active military service during the 1916–23 period. As the IRA was organised geographically (individual units aligned to designated areas), the Military Service Pensions Board asked leading veterans to establish local committees of knowledgeable ex-officers to assemble membership and leadership lists.[16] These veterans' committees (both for IRA and Cumann na mBan units) worked closely with pension officials and undertook extensive consultation with former comrades to determine precise roles and positions. Pension applications also required service testimonials from fellow veterans. This entire process often generated collaboration between veterans who took different stances on the Treaty (pro-, anti- and neutral). It also seemed to encourage the formation of more formal fraternal 'Old Comrades' groups at the county and brigade level, which are visible within Military Service Pensions Collection correspondence.[17]

In 1937 a new national veterans' organisation emphasised unity based on the 1916 Proclamation and welcomed anyone with past military service from 1916 to 1923 (including Cumann na mBan). The National Association of Old IRA was led by Liam Deasy, a senior anti-Treaty IRA officer during the Civil War, who had controversially appealed for an IRA ceasefire following his capture in January 1923. Among the organisation's leadership were Cork city anti-Treaty IRA veterans who had advocated IRA reunification just before the Civil War, prominent members of the Neutral IRA and Dublin leaders of Clan na nGaedheal.[18] Most of these figures assumed leading roles in Old IRA initiatives in the decades that followed. The National Association of Old IRA welcomed members from all political parties, but in reality most of its leadership supported Fianna Fáil. The organisation advocated changes to the military service pensions system, but also attempted to organise an all-Ireland campaign to end partition. Anti-partitionism remained a core political belief among veterans' groups over several decades and was often expressed in clear terms. While some historians have emphasised the disillusionment of members of the revolutionary generation, a far more common position was continued support for unfettered Irish sovereignty and the reunification of the island.

The fusion of IRA veterans accelerated during the Second World War, particularly after Germany defeated France in June 1940. In response to the government's warnings of imminent danger and the need for defence forces recruits, thousands of IRA veterans rallied to the flag. In several cities and towns, groups of IRA veterans marched en masse to the nearest recruiting station to enlist, publicly demonstrating newfound national unity.[19] In south Tipperary one former officer declared 'all who were in the

Fig. 6 Memorial plaque unveiled in 1948 at the former site of the Cork Men's Gaol, University College Cork (UCC). In the decades following the Civil War republican memorialisation was often used to emphasise the unity of the separatist movement during the War of Independence and promote reconciliation among IRA veterans who had split over the Treaty. The Cork Men's Gaol was an important site of resistance from 1919 to 1923, and included a mass grave of thirteen IRA prisoners who were executed in 1921 and buried in the old jail exercise yard. In 1948 an IRA monument was built inside the jail grounds with a memorial plaque placed on the exterior wall (and thus visible to pedestrians). This initiative was organised by local IRA veterans rather than a government body, thus allowing the participation of former anti-Treaty comrades who still did not recognise the legitimacy of the independent state. Fund-raising for the monument and plaque foregrounded those executed in 1921 and buried on the jail grounds. However both memorials also included the names of two Civil War republicans who died in the jail in 1923 – one by execution and the other shot dead by a National Army sentry. The unveiling souvenir programme described all the men as having 'died in the service of the Irish Republic', a diplomatic wording that included the two anti-Treaty fatalities without directly insulting pro-Treaty supporters. Similar subtle inclusions of Civil War dead are visible on War of Independence memorials across Munster, which were also typically organised by 'Old IRA' veteran groups. The university memorial required careful mediation between the veterans' memorial committee, the university and the Irish government, which resulted in the handing over of the prison site to UCC. The Old IRA committee specifically thanked the college president, Alfred O'Rahilly, for his cooperation. Politically active in the independence movement, O'Rahilly was a prominent supporter of the Anglo-Irish Treaty and a Cumann na nGaedheal TD in 1923–4. His direct participation gave symbolic as well as practical assistance to the memorialisation effort. The wall plaque was designed by sculptor Seamus Murphy, whose oeuvre also included busts of Constance Markievicz and Jeremiah O'Donovan Rossa and an elaborate obelisk in Midleton (County Cork) dedicated to local IRA members 'who gave their lives to the Irish Republic'. Though Murphy possessed strong anti-Treaty connections, his ecumenism when it came to commissions is apparent in his bust of Michael Collins in National Army uniform located in Cork's Fitzgerald's Park. [Image: John Crowley]

fight for freedom from 1916 to the cease-fire, apart from the side they took after the truce, should unite in this emergency and put themselves at the disposal of the government'.[20] Within the defence forces, a similar mitigation of Civil War divisions was apparent in the enlistment of numerous prominent anti-Treaty leaders, and the establishment of the Local Defence Force's celebrated 26th Battalion, comprised of IRA veterans from 1916–21.[21]

Memorialisation

Following the war's end and the passage of the Republic of Ireland Act in 1948, veterans increasingly took on more public roles, particularly in the memorialisation of the War of Independence dead. Such efforts, implicitly and occasionally explicitly acknowledging Civil War divisions, were often intended to bridge them. The new attitude was expressed at the unveiling of an IRA memorial to the dead of the East Limerick Brigade in Bruff during 1952. The Old IRA organising committee included numerous pro-Treaty members of the brigade, who paraded with their anti-Treaty colleagues at the unveiling attended by President Seán T. O'Kelly. The Irish president praised their decision 'to sink all the differences and animosities that have kept them in different camps since 1922'.[22]

Scores of similar memorials and monuments to the war dead were erected by IRA veteran organisations (with significant non-veteran support) across the country during the 1950s.[23] By establishing memorial fund-raising committees under the Old IRA banner, veterans controlled the placement of individual monuments, the wording of inscriptions, the inclusion or exclusion of named fatalities and the organisation of subscriptions and unveiling ceremonies. This allowed them to carefully navigate local cleavages, some of which had persisted for decades and were invisible to outsiders. The monuments were not erected with government financing, though they frequently enjoyed the support of local government bodies, which often included IRA veterans. While space does not allow for a discussion of Cumann na mBan veterans, it will be noted that republican women typically were visible during the unveiling of such monuments though they do not appear to have been as directly involved in their planning as Old IRA veterans.[24]

Memorialisation varied from commemorating the deaths of individuals at the site where they were killed to unit memorials listing members who died on active service. Some, but not all, of the unit memorials included anti-Treaty republican fatalities but excluded National Army ones.[25] In such cases the wording of the inscription typically avoided direct mention of the Civil War, using more general phrases such as 'died for Ireland' or 'in defence of the republic'. The style ranged from simple plaques and markers to more elaborate obelisks, Celtic crosses and IRA fighter figurine statues. As such, they resembled First World War monuments and memorials erected in Northern Ireland, Britain and, indeed, throughout Europe.[26] An exception was the lack of Old IRA memorialisation inside Catholic churches, which differed from the First World War tradition in the Church of Ireland.[27] Ireland's Catholic churches excluded First World War memorials as well, though they were relatively common in Catholic churches across Europe. Therefore it would appear the Irish Catholic Church considered such memorials as political and thus to be avoided.

In her study of Civil War commemoration, Anne Dolan linked the Old IRA's construction of memorials to similar commemorations in other countries by aging war veterans, as a 'plea to posterity before death'. Facing their own mortality, Dolan argued, the veterans 'wanted their stories told, their comrades remembered'.[28] This was undoubtedly a feature of IRA veterans' memorialisation efforts, but memory of the Irish Civil War added another dimension. At a ceremony marking an IRA memorial in Tullamore during 1953, it was observed that the statue had been erected fourteen years previously but never officially unveiled. The reason was, 'the unveiling was deliberately delayed until men who had taken opposite sides in the disastrous Civil War of thirty years ago could be persuaded to stand at its limestone base and honour the illustrious dead'.[29] At such ceremonies, the powerful symbolism of former Civil War enemies standing silently together or marching in military formation was obvious to observers at the time.

The Old IRA movement appealed to veterans who wanted to put the shame, trauma and regret of the Civil War behind them. Anti-Treaty 'irregulars' (to use that pejorative term) had their respectability questioned and masculinity undermined by Free State propaganda throughout the Civil War and suffered the moral shame of excommunication by the Catholic Church. Pro-Treaty veterans had been deemed sell-outs, pro-British and opportunists by anti-Treaty diehards.[30] Neutral IRA veterans were, in some ways, held in contempt by both sides. The Old IRA movement provided veterans with the opportunity to reclaim their status as patriots dedicated to the national cause. Indeed these veterans (IRA and Cumann na mBan) would feature prominently in the triumphant national pageantry that surrounded the fiftieth anniversary of the Easter Rising in 1966.[31] By that time the Civil War's long shadow had at last started to recede.

KEATING.

'Night's Candles are Burnt Out', by Seán Keating (1929)

Éimear O'Connor

Just as *An Allegory* (cover image) symbolised Seán Keating's call for post-Civil War peace, *Night's Candles are Burnt Out*, completed some five years later, presents a metaphor of the artist's vision for Ireland's future. The painting is an amalgam of various oil sketches made while onsite at Ardnacrusha, otherwise, the 'Shannon Scheme' in County Limerick, where a vast engineering project was taking place that would provide hydro-powered electricity, and thus light and power, to post-Civil War Ireland. Keating, always interested in painting emerging history, was enamoured of the project from which New Ireland's modernity would derive. Akin to *An Allegory*, much of the action in *Night's Candles* takes place in a stage-like setting across the foreground of the work. An expensively well-dressed businessman seemingly accepts the genuflection of his less sophisticated gun-toting compatriot. To their left the stage Irish 'Paddy whack' drinks himself off his feet, while his seated companion may be suffering the ill-effects of imbibing. A young man shines an oil lamp at a skeleton hanging from a crane in the background, a reference, perhaps, to the death of Old Ireland, while in the right foreground, a priest sits doggedly reading by candlelight, in spite of the modernisation taking place around him, thereby giving rise to the title of the work. To the right a couple stand pointing over the new dam and, implicitly, towards the future. The couple are Seán and May Keating, with their first child, Michael, who was born in 1927. Just as she did in *An Allegory*, May is holding the future, but this time it is a vision of the family future; their son, Justin, was born in January 1930. Indeed Keating's vision for his family's future, and that of the New Ireland, bathed in sunlight and electric light, was captured in the title of the painting, which is a quote from William Shakespeare's *Romeo and Juliet*: 'Night's candles have burned out, and jocund day stands tiptoe on the misty mountaintops.' Called 'the problem painting of the year' by a critic visiting the Royal Academy Exhibition in 1929, Keating's own words best describe his intended meaning: 'The title suggests that the dawn has come, when the dim candlelight of surviving medievalism in Ireland is fading before the rising sun of scientific progress, exemplified by the Shannon electricity works'. *Night's Candles are Burnt Out* was shown in the Carnegie Institute in Pittsburgh in 1929 and in the Walker Gallery Liverpool in 1930, followed by an exhibition in Oldham in 1931. The painting was purchased by Gallery Oldham, which specialises in collection works focused on social history, in 1931. [Painting: image courtesy of Bridgeman Images, © Estate of Seán Keating, IVARO Dublin, 2023 / Sources: Seán Keating, *The Sphere* (London, 1931). See also Éimear O'Connor, *Seán Keating and the ESB: Enlightenment and legacy* (Dublin, 2012), pp. 45–7, catalogue for the eponymous exhibition of the ESB collection of works by Seán Keating at the RHA, curated by Dr Éimear O'Connor]

Fig. 1 A National Army soldier searching a suspect in Dublin in 1922. [Image: Cashman Collection © RTÉ Archives, 0504/057]

CHAPTER 11

'Befitting Emblems of Adversity': Temporality and disruption in Irish Civil War poetry

Ailbhe McDaid

> the problem after any revolution is what to do with your
> gunmen as old Billyum found out in Oirland
>
> in the Senate, Bedad! or before then
> Your gunmen thread on moi drreams
>
> Ezra Pound[1]

Ezra Pound's lines on the Irish Civil War, laced as they are with sarcasm, recognise a very real predicament of literary representation in the aftermath of violent conflict. Written across six decades, the chaotic, looping structure and allusive content of Pound's *Cantos* takes in much of the rapid destabilisation of the early twentieth century. Canto 80, contained within *The Pisan Cantos* (1948) from which Pound's commentary on Yeats's poetic challenge is taken, was mostly composed after the Second World War and draws widely on a number of European war circumstances, including the Irish revolution. By linking the political and poetic problems posed by revolution, Pound demonstrates that the impact of violence on the foundling state is not limited to the designated period of war itself. The absolutism of Pound's opening lines ('the problem after any revolution is') wavers under the uncertainty of timelines in the second clause of the phrase ('or before then'). The arrival of gunmen into the final sentence, which manipulates a well-known line from Yeats's 'He Wishes for the Cloths of Heaven' (1899), threatens the sincerity and stability of literary representation more profoundly again. Yeats's own letters from the period recognise the particular challenge of civil war division: writing in October 1922, he muses 'Perhaps there is nothing so dangerous to a modern state, when politics take the place of theology, as a bunch of martyrs. A bunch of martyrs (1916) were the bomb and we are living in the explosion.'[2] While 'the bomb' was unarguably poetically generative for Yeats, 'the explosion' and its repercussions brought about a different kind of aesthetic productiveness, which can be read along local and universal lines.

The uncertainty of Yeats's *Meditations in Time of a Civil War* is both specific to the Irish context and indicative of the wider Modernist period. Kate McLoughlin's *Authoring War: The literary representation of war from the Iliad to Iraq* describes the 'inherently anxiogenic' quality of writing about and out of conflict – resulting in a body of literature that both induces and is induced from anxiety.[3] In her extensive study of war literature, McLoughlin suggests categories of representation for different conflicts, proposing that 'the First World War's natural form was the lyric poem, that the Second World War's was the epic novel, that the Vietnam War's was the movie, that the Iraq Wars' may well turn out to be the blog'.[4] While the Western limitations of McLoughlin's lens are self-evident, these categorisations prompt the question of whether other conflicts might be similarly defined along genre lines. The relatively limited critical scholarship on the literature of the Irish Civil War has proposed a Modernist approach with sub-themes within particular writers' works that might collectively form a canon of civil war literature. Síobhra Aiken's field-altering research on published and unpublished narratives of the troubled period introduced important questions of literary practice, publishing policies and political preference into these canonical conversations.[5]

One of the most significant of these sub-themes is temporality: that is, how time is understood and experienced individually and collectively, as well as how time is manipulated within a literary text. This is particularly relevant in the context of the Decade of Centenaries that sought to impose decisive points of initiation and conclusion on a period that, as numerous scholars have observed, has a much more fluid legacy. Defining the boundary dates of historical events is less of a concern for literary interpretation, because war timelines as depicted in literature 'often elude the usual models for organizing time such as linearity, punctuality and periodicity'; that is to say, war resonates 'beyond the here and now'.[6] In this way the literature of the Irish Civil War registers both the impact and the aftershock of Yeats's 'bomb' *and* its 'explosion'. A century of civil war writing has produced a body of work that reinscribes the 'catastrophe's experiential and imaginative limits'.[7] As this chapter demonstrates, the experience of time during civil war is fraught and contested; furthermore the representation of

Fig. 2 Members of St John Ambulance Brigade hold a damaged clock found among the debris in Sackville (O'Connell) Street in the wake of the Battle for Dublin, 28 June–5 July 1922. [Image: part of the Independent Newspapers Ireland/NLI Collection, INDH202]

time in the poetry of civil war is often subversive, questioning the premise of the 'mutually constitutive relationship between time and the nation'.[8] This chapter offers an exploration of how notions of time and temporality are used by Irish poets in representing the Civil War, thereby building on work by Allen, Aiken, Meaney, Ní Bheacháin and others in identifying the specific aesthetics of Irish conflict literature.[9]

'[A]nnihilation/ and realisation': Negotiating time in a literature of war

Imperial literatures historically embrace an energy of invigoration, such as that encapsulated in Ernest Hemingway's excitable observation that '[war] groups the maximum of material and speeds up the action and brings out all sorts of stuff that normally you have to wait a lifetime to get'.[10] Contrastingly, Rob Nixon's concept of 'slow violence' challenges that trope of war as a sudden outbreak, instead arguing that conflict is experienced by many in post-colonial contexts as a more insidious and flattening phenomenon.[11] This concept of flatness is well established in the literature of the Irish Free State: Lawrence McCaffrey argues that 'disillusionment and frustration are the dominant themes in post-revolutionary Irish writing' in contrast to the 'preceding generation of writers [who] lived in a period of excitement and national enthusiasm'.[12] Likewise, Frank Shovlin suggests that 'the writers of post-independence Ireland were busy adjusting to the difficulties and disappointments of their new reality'.[13] For Gerardine Meaney the gendered dynamics of the emergent nation deliver an 'exhausted discontent' for women writers, while Lucy Collins notes that post-independence writing was often concerned with the increasing cultural isolation of the Free State.[14] This body of scholarship also indicates how time is punctured in conflict literatures. In the Irish case, this occurs by collapsing civil war tensions into the residue of the preceding years of revolution and armed struggle against British forces. Síobhra Aiken traces the origins of this 'wide-spread blurring of chronologies' to Dorothy Macardle's collection *Earthbound and Other Supernatural Stories*, written while Macardle was imprisoned in Kilmainham Gaol during the Civil War. By renaming the story 'The Prisoner 1798–1923' as simply 'The Prisoner', Macardle could 'superficially, at least, evade the Civil War'.[15]

Manipulation of these timelines is integral to the poetry of the Irish Civil War. The representative challenges to which Pound's question alludes ('what to do with your gunmen') certainly preoccupied Yeats in his 'Meditations in a Time of Civil War', written when he was a senator and, as such, 'messily imbricated with the contingency of contemporary events'.[16] Like other Modernist writers of the period, he was preoccupied with a commitment to 'present futures' wherein present action is considered in terms of its implications in time to come. Having 'fed the heart on fantasies', Yeats nevertheless proposes that his generation might 'take our greatness with our bitterness'. In doing so, he sources a future in which a project of nation-building can begin, albeit in an 'empty nest'. In 'Meditations' Yeats sees the past firmly in the service of the future, a future that he sees as potentially reconciling individual, personal and political rhetoric. These tensions speak to familiar Yeatsian tropes and demonstrate the intensity of his poetic

Fig. 3 Senator, poet and Nobel laureate William Butler Yeats (1865–1939), bespectacled and holding his academic robe, in the second row from the back, stands among a group of foreign diplomats and Free State dignitaries outside 19 Dawson Street, 1924. Yeats was chair of the representative committee that secured their attendance at the opening of the Tailteann Games in the summer of 1924. In the first two weeks of August thousands of competitors and tens of thousands of spectators packed venues around Dublin for a series of events intended to celebrate and showcase Ireland's sporting and cultural prowess. The photograph – which features in the front row members of what the *Catholic Bulletin* dubbed the 'New Ascendancy', Eoin O'Duffy, William T. Cosgrave, Kevin O'Higgins, Desmond FitzGerald and Hugh Kennedy – was taken just over seven months after Yeats had received the Nobel Prize in Literature. It was an honour that the poet considered 'part of Europe's welcome to the Free State', while the establishment *Irish Times* claimed it as a 'national as well as a personal triumph'. Writing to artist Edmund Dulac in February 1923, Yeats was clearly optimistic about the future of the arts in post-independence Ireland: 'The psychological moment has come, for Dublin is reviving after the Civil War, and self-government is creating a little stir of excitement. People are trying to found a new society. Politicians want to be artistic, and artistic people to meet politicians, and so on.' Disillusionment would follow after the introduction of the Censorship of Films Act in 1923 by the same politicians and a Church-supported campaign against 'evil literature' – a campaign that prompted Ezra Pound's rejection of Yeats's invitation to attend the Tailteann Games as 'a Guest of the Nation'. In 1928 the text of the Censorship of Publications Bill was published on the same day as the Tailteann Games literary awards were announced. The latter represented the nearest the Free State came to recognising its writers, and Yeats was in correspondence with the government about it providing the basis for a state-supported Irish academy of letters. The 1928 winners included Yeats himself for poetry (*The Tower*). According to the *Irish Statesman*'s assistant editor, James Good, the simultaneous publication was a symbolically significant statement about the trajectory of the government's cultural policy, such as it was. The project to establish a state-recognised representative body of Irish writers, he wrote, 'had been blown sky-high by the Censorship of Publications Bill'. [Image: National Library of Ireland, HOG100 / See *Irish Times*, 15 Nov. 1923; R.F. Foster, *W.B. Yeats: A Life II: The arch poet, 1915–1939* (Oxford, 2003), pp. 254 and 263; Nicholas Allen, 'Free Statement: Censorship and the *Irish Statesman*', in Fran Brearton and Eamonn Hughes (eds), *Last Before America: Irish and American writing* (Belfast, 2001), p. 85]

engagement with the Civil War, as well the extent to which the intimacy of the conflict impacted his own ideological development. Yeats was atypical in this regard. It was far more usual, as Lucy Collins observes, for poets of the period, and after, to write occasionally about the war in allusive and elusive works.[17] The remainder of this chapter considers a selection of those occasional poems, poems that offer negotiations and manipulation of time as integral to addressing the Civil War.

'How long since? /Long till?': Coming to terms with time after the Irish Civil War

Thomas MacGreevy's 'Autumn 1922' is very firmly in a Modernist vein of 'present futures'. Beyond its title, the poem eschews any direct reference to action, or any explicit attempts at the representation of violence; rather it reaches for the essence of a moment at the outset of the Civil War. A short poem, just three lines long, it offers very little in terms of consolation:

> The sun burns out,
> The world withers,
> And time grows afraid of the triumph of time.

The sense of apprehension here is clear in the phrase 'grows afraid' through which the reader is made to understand that something worse lies ahead. The 'pictorialist poetics' on display (depicting a burned out, withered landscape) embody an 'aesthetics of waste' that connects with other war poetries (MacGreevy served in the First World War) as well as with the wider sense of depletion perceptible in poems of the period.[18] And yet, like Yeats's 'Meditations', 'Autumn 1922' sees a pathway through the wreckage to a future, albeit one to be met with dread. The final line reminds the reader of the relentless march of modernity: even while the 'world withers', time progresses. The crucial line stating 'the triumph of time' over 'time' embeds intimate conflict at the poem's core, bringing a distinctive civil war dimension that recognises the similarities between two entities.

The hot energy of engagement yields to a slow degradation in the withering of the world of MacGreevy's civil war poem, until fear ultimately prevails. The slippage between winning and defeat here speaks very directly to a civil war context, where 'winners' and 'losers' are indistinguishable in a post-conflict society that has lost its ideals in the pursuit of a pyrrhic victory.

Moving to the other end of the Modernist poetic spectrum, MacGreevy's only extended sequential poem 'Crón Tráth na nDéithe' (1929) is clearly indebted to T.S. Eliot's *The Wasteland* (1922) and to Joyce's mythic recasting of Dublin in *Ulysses* (1920). The poem's title literally translates as 'the twilight of the gods' and offers an Irish equivalent to the Norse term *ragnarok*. When first published, however, in the Modernist magazine *Transition*, 'Crón Tráth na nDéithe' was entitled 'School of [...] Easter Saturday Night (Free State)' and that time stamp is retained at the conclusion of the poem.[19] The date is significant: 'On 29–30 April 1923, the seventh calendar anniversary of Easter Sunday 1916, the republican forces in the Civil War declared a cease-fire and ordered those still in the field to dump arms, thus effectively ending the war.'[20] The timelines fold in upon each other here. Over the course of the poem, Easter 1916 collapses forward into Easter Saturday 1923. Inspired by the 'cataclysmic events' in Ireland, the poem's final title reflects MacGreevy's immersion in Modernist aesthetics as well as his commitment to myth-making in response to the recent revolutionary events.[21] In prefacing the poem with two epigraphs – one Biblical, 'How is the faithful city become a harlot' (taken from Isaiah 1.21) and one from the folk tradition, 'Her ghosts wheel the barrow' (from the ballad 'Molly Malone') – MacGreevy invokes a fallen Dublin in the aftermath of civil strife. The unfinished Biblical quotation leaves unspoken the post-conflict context – 'righteousness lodged in it; but now murderers' – while MacGreevy's specific invocation of the ghosts of the popular folk song centres the haunted atmosphere of Dublin city on this night drive on Easter Saturday 1923.

The fragmenting effect of war is made clear by the speaker who admonishes '[y]ou cannot pick up the / pieces' of the preceding seven years of conflict. The melting, uncertain timeframes of war are evoked in the poem as well:

> Nineteen-sixteen perhaps,
> Or fierce, frightened Black-and-Tans
>
> Rain, rain ...
>
> Wrecks wetly mouldering under rain,
> Everywhere.

A recurring trope of the wheel of time in the opening section picks up on Molly Malone's ghost of the epilogue, as 'heavy turning wheels' propel 'the dark-and-light-engulfing box' as it '[w]heels through the wetness'. These revolutions gesture towards the political slippages that occur during and after civil wars:

> Britannia indeed is not gone
> But the red, red rose
> Withers into its mossy coat.

Once again the collapsing distinctions here between foe and friend pick up the uncertainty between victory and defeat in 'Autumn 1922', before settling into an uncomfortable space of 'annihilation / and realisation' – an apt summary of the legacy of civil war.

Described by Beckett as 'the darkest [...] in this small volume of [...] intensely personal verse', 'Crón Tráth na nDéithe' exemplifies what many contemporaneous works on the period strive for: it collapses the distinctive time periods that define historical specificity, and therefore creates a literary atmosphere that can be directly linked to the uncertainty of civil war circumstances.[22] The difficulty of unpicking historical periodicity was also cultivated by other poets, including Austin Clarke in 'The Lost Heifer'

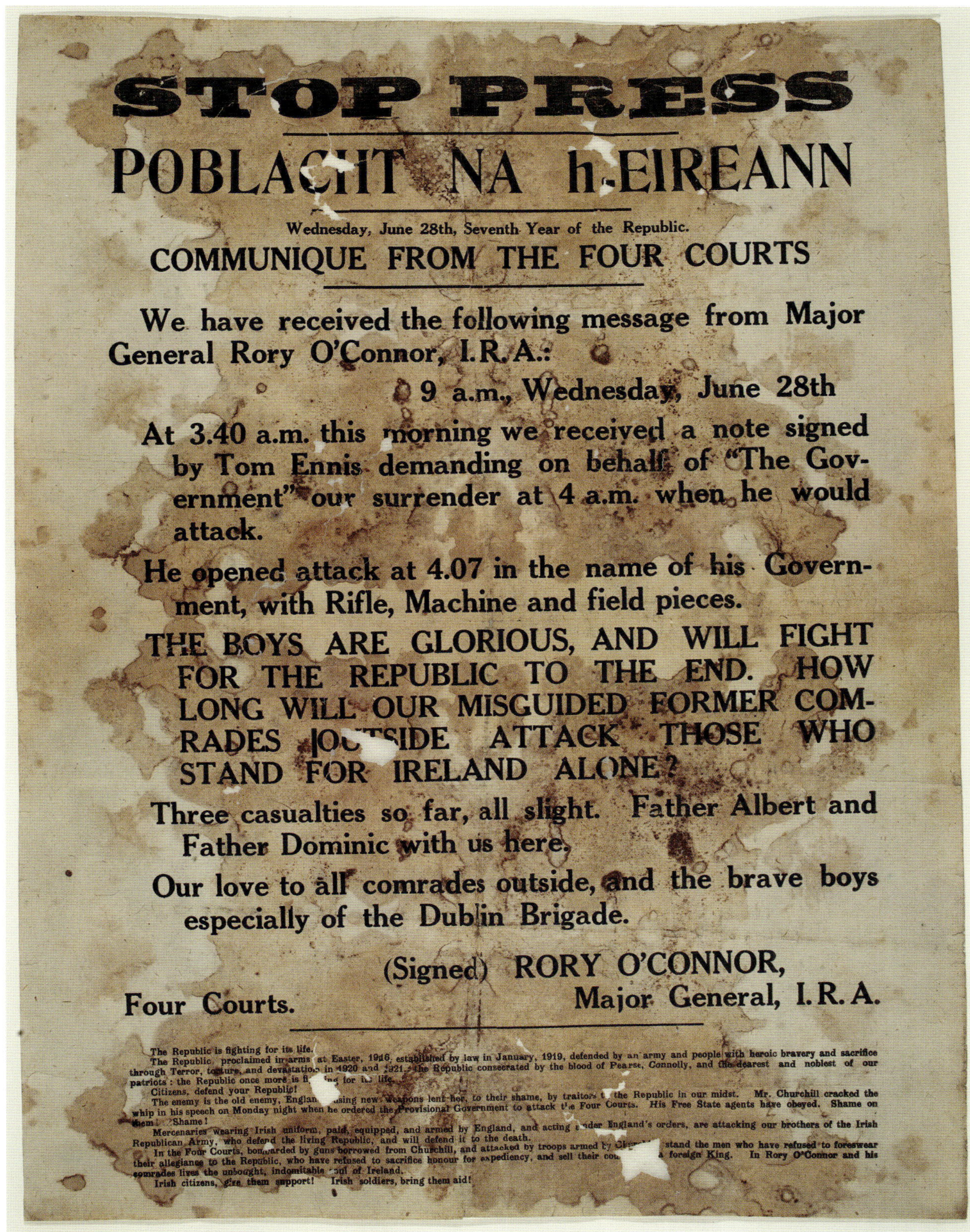

STOP PRESS

POBLACHT NA h-EIREANN

Wednesday, June 28th, Seventh Year of the Republic.

COMMUNIQUE FROM THE FOUR COURTS

We have received the following message from Major General Rory O'Connor, I.R.A.:

9 a.m., Wednesday, June 28th

At 3.40 a.m. this morning we received a note signed by Tom Ennis demanding on behalf of "The Government" our surrender at 4 a.m. when he would attack.

He opened attack at 4.07 in the name of his Government, with Rifle, Machine and field pieces.

THE BOYS ARE GLORIOUS, AND WILL FIGHT FOR THE REPUBLIC TO THE END. HOW LONG WILL OUR MISGUIDED FORMER COMRADES OUTSIDE ATTACK THOSE WHO STAND FOR IRELAND ALONE?

Three casualties so far, all slight. Father Albert and Father Dominic with us here.

Our love to all comrades outside, and the brave boys especially of the Dublin Brigade.

(Signed) RORY O'CONNOR,
Major General, I.R.A.

Four Courts.

The Republic is fighting for its life.

The Republic proclaimed in arms at Easter, 1916, established by law in January, 1919, defended by an army and people with heroic bravery and sacrifice through Terror, torture, and devastation in 1920 and 1921, the Republic consecrated by the blood of Pearse, Connolly, and the dearest and noblest of our patriots: the Republic once more is fi[illegible]ing for its life.

Citizens, defend your Republic!

The enemy is the old enemy, Englan[illegible] using new weapons lent her, to their shame, by traitors t[illegible] the Republic in our midst. Mr. Churchill cracked the whip in his speech on Monday night when he ordered the Provisional Government to attack the Four Courts. His Free State agents have obeyed. Shame on them! Shame!

Mercenaries wearing Irish uniform, paid, equipped, and armed by England, and acting [illegible]nder England's orders, are attacking our brothers of the Irish Republican Army, who defend the living Republic, and will defend it to the death.

In the Four Courts, bombarded by guns borrowed from Churchill, and attacked by troops armed by [illegible] stand the men who have refused to foreswear their allegiance to the Republic, who have refused to sacrifice honour for expediency, and sell their cou[illegible] a foreign King. In Rory O'Connor and his comrades lives the unbought, indomitable [illegible]oul of Ireland.

Irish citizens, give them support! Irish soldiers, bring them aid!

Fig. 4 'Stop Press', *Poblacht na hÉireann*, 28 June, 'Seventh Year of the Republic'. In republican propaganda dates were often recorded in relation to the number of years since the proclaiming of the republic on 24 April 1916. Therefore June 1922 marked the 'Seventh Year' since that foundational event. Evoking the French revolutionary calendar, it was a simple but effective method of reinforcing for their 'misguided former comrades' continuity with the republican movement of 1916–21, and the immutability of the declared republic to which the IRA had sworn allegiance in 1919. So ingrained was this temporal measurement in the republican calendar that anti-Treaty TD Laurence Ginnell used it as the title for his 1923 publication *The Seventh Year of the Republic: A defence of Erskine Childers.* [Document: National Library of Ireland, EPH E813]

Fig. 5 Irish poet, playwright and novelist, Austin Clarke, photographed near St Stephen's Green, Dublin in 1967. [Image: *RTÉ Guide* © RTÉ Archives, 2040/088]

Fig. 6 Letter from Austin Clarke (1896–1974) to Noel Kavanagh, honorary secretary of the Yeats Association, 14 September 1966. In this letter Austin Clarke declines Kavanagh's invitation to recite poetry at the unveiling of the Yeats memorial by sculptor Henry Moore in St Stephen's Green, Dublin. The principal reason for his refusal was his unwillingness to share a public platform with 'politicians' because of the executions and atrocities committed during the Civil War and the later repression of militant republicans by Fianna Fáil governments. In a year that marked the fiftieth anniversary of the Easter Rising, the Civil War and its fallout still loomed large in Clarke's thinking. While he eventually relented and participated in the unveiling, performed by Taoiseach Jack Lynch in October 1967, his initial response was a measure of his deep-seated disillusionment with the conservative values of the Irish state and what he regarded as an all-powerful Catholic Church. Born in Dublin, Clarke was educated by the Jesuits at Belvedere College, Dublin and briefly in Mungret College in Limerick. A first-class scholar, he succeeded the executed 1916 leader Thomas MacDonagh as an assistant lecturer in English at University College Dublin (UCD), but his time in UCD was short lived, as was his first marriage to Lia Cummins. He later worked in England as a literary reviewer, before returning permanently to Dublin in 1937. Drawing on mythology and history, and inspired by the metres of medieval Irish verse, Clarke carved a career not only as a distinguished poet but also as a playwright, novelist, reviewer and broadcaster. Challenging the rigid Catholicism of his upbringing and the doctrinaire faith embraced so wholeheartedly by the new Irish state was a familiar theme in his work, as was his abhorrence of censorship. His novel *A Bright Temptation* was banned in 1932 and, in that year, he was a founding member, with Yeats, of the Irish Academy of Letters, which opposed the operations of the Censorship of Publications Board; he served as the academy's president from 1952 to 1954. By the 1960s his literary status was such that he was considered the natural successor to Yeats as a 'national' poet despite a significant hiatus in his career when he did not publish any poetry. [Document: Sybil Le Broquy Papers, courtesy of Bruce Stewart and Ricorso / See Mary Shine Thompson, *Austin Clarke Papers*, National Library of Ireland, 2003, p. 9]

Bridge House,
Templeogue,
Dublin 14.
14th September, '66

Noel Kavanagh, Esq.,
Hon. Secretary,
The Yeats Association.

Dear Mr. Kavanagh,

Thank you for your letter.
Ever since the Civil War and the executions, hangings, atrocities, then and later, I have avoided all contact with politicians. I would not wish, therefore, to be connected, directly or indirectly, with any Association in which they take part. I am sorry that your Society has not been kept to writers and sympathisers.

Yours sincerely,

A Clarke

(published 1936), which deliberately divorces itself from an explicit point in time through its elusive subject and imagery. However Clarke's accompanying note states it was '[w]ritten during a period when our national idealism suffered eclipse', a comment that picks up the perception of slow and all-encompassing ideological damage beyond the physical destruction of the revolutionary period.[23] The act of writing the poem is itself a political gesture, of course. While evidence of Clarke's own involvement in republican politics is patchy, his deliberate cultivation of Gaelic modes was, in his own aesthetic and despite ridicule from others, a rhetorically republican declaration. The range of his poetic concerns is also essentially republican – addressing Catholicism and conservatism as anathema to the possibilities of a fully realised Irish Republic. Fryatt suggests that Clarke's is 'largely a poetry of reaction and representation, not of political engagement [and] Clarke's inactive support for the Republican cause in the Civil War is similarly reflexive'.[24]

This reflexivity is highlighted in the contrast between Clarke and MacGreevy's Civil War poems. Where MacGreevy destabilises poetic cohesion by moving through the wreckage of the city streets, 'The Lost Heifer' demonstrates an 'achieved stillness' that stands outside time.[25] Yet both poems reach for the common code of collapsing time. In Clarke's poem, this is sourced by moving beyond the immediate moments of crisis to find a point of stability. The poem's allegorical allusions to the Jacobean 'droimeann donn dílis' and the *aisling* tradition merge with more Modernist and Imagistic impulses to deliver a 'strange little weather poem' that refuses explicit allusion and yet delivers distinctive emergent civil war poetics.[26] Clarke's characteristically disrupted sentences place the desired objects of 'The Lost Heifer' almost beyond reach in

Fig. 7 (right and below) 'The Lost Heifer', a mural by Garreth Joyce, commissioned by Michael Collins House/Cork County Council as part of the Decade of Centenaries Programme, 2022. Painted in Croppy Park in Clonakilty, County Cork as an emotional but 'apolitical' response to the Civil War, each of the mural's six panels illustrates a line from Austin Clarke's 1936 poem 'The Lost Heifer'. It follows the elusive heifer, symbolic of the unattainable ideal of Irish sovereignty, lost in the dark mists of the countryside, before emerging briefly into the optimistic sunshine of the early revolutionary period and disappearing again into the dark rain of the Civil War. [Image: courtesy of the artist, Garreth Joyce]

Fig. 8 Portrait of Alice Milligan (1866–1953) by Estella Frances Solomons, oil on canvas, 1918. Milligan, from near Omagh, County Tyrone, had been a significant figure in the advanced nationalist/cultural revivalist milieu of the late nineteenth and early twentieth centuries. A poet, playwright and novelist, she co-edited *Shan Van Vocht* (1896–9) with Anna Johnston, which featured writings by figures like Douglas Hyde and James Connolly. The journal championed the Gaelic League and the 1798 centenary celebrations, among other nationalist causes. Eleven of her plays were staged by the Irish Literary Theatre, the Gaelic League and the advanced nationalist-feminist organisation Inghinidhe na hÉireann, of which she was a member. From 1904 to 1909 Milligan worked as a Gaelic League organiser. Due to family commitments, she subsequently gradually drifted from the mainstream of Irish nationalist, feminist and cultural activism, though she continued to write and remained committed to the cause of Irish freedom. She opposed the Treaty but despaired at the tragedy of the Civil War. In the poem 'Til Ferdia Came', published in December 1922, she invokes Irish myth and presents Ireland as the mother of two warring sons: 'Two brothers, pledged to Ireland's righting, In severed ranks were sternly fighting, In cause opposed.' The poem mourns prominent Civil War victims on both sides – 'I think of Collins in the West, The life blood clotted on his breast' – but reveals its sympathies: 'My grief for Childers, Boland too, And, oh, unconquered Cathal Brugha, When reeling through the lurid flame / Still armed, defiant you came.' This portrait was painted by Estella Solomons, one of many she completed of Irish revolutionaries. A member of Cumann na mBan in Dublin during both the War of Independence and the Civil War, Solomons opened her studio to republican activists and remained closely connected to the country's cultural and political elite throughout her life. [Image: © The Trustees of the Estate of Estella Solomons, courtesy of National Museums NI, Ulster Museum Collection / See Catherine Morris, *Alice Milligan and the Irish Cultural Revival* (Dublin, 2013) and Henry Mangan (ed.), *Poems by Alice Milligan* (Dublin, 1954)]

narrative terms, such as 'the last honey by the water / that no hive can find'. This unattainability recalls MacGreevy's 'annihilation / and realisation', which Clarke locates through the cultivation of that which was once known but has now become elusive. Counterpointing MacGreevy's gritty urbanity, Clarke's imagery is resolutely rural, using the weather to accelerate the temporal shift of the poem. The 'gap of the pure cold wind / [a]nd the watery hazes of the hazel' facilitate the imaginative turn to the symbolic heifer in the first stanza, while a brief 'drenching' of light enables her to wander 'again' in the second. She remains, however, beyond the speaker's grasp, rendered almost imperceptible in the shifting weather of 'mist becoming rain'. The *aisling* elements of the poem have been widely analysed, as has Clarke's use of the 'Irish mode', which, as John Goodby suggests, 'involves establishing an interplay of styles in which Revival and neo-Revival effects are constantly undermined'.[27] This technique of 'undermining', in the context of civil war poetics, leads to the same point of uncertainty as MacGreevy's speaker, asking 'How long since? / Long till?'

Other poems responding to the Civil War foreground this negotiation with timelines and timeframes. The practice of including a timestamp (a date indicating the point of composition) functions as a kind of legitimising practice, which confers

Fig. 9 *Boreen: Mícheál* (2022), oil, mixed media on tarpaulin, part of Hughie O'Donoghue's installation *Original Sins*, which was hosted in the Shaw Room of the National Gallery of Ireland in 2022 to mark the Decade of Centenaries. A great deal of O'Donoghue's historical work is concerned with the nature of memory and identity and different ways of excavating and seeing the past. Growing up in Manchester to Irish parents, O'Donoghue was always aware of his dual heritage and that sense of Irishness and Britishness frames his exploration of the six historical figures – St Deirbhile, Anglo-Saxon King Wuffa, Aoife MacMurrough, William the Conqueror, Emily Davison and Michael Collins – that comprise *Original Sins*. Responding to Daniel Maclise's painting *The Marriage of Aoife and Strongbow*, which is on permanent display in the Shaw Room, each of the large-scale portraits that comprise *Original Sins* challenges the viewer to look at Irish and British history in ever more complicated and amplified ways. It is not surprising, then, that O'Donoghue was drawn to Collins as a revolutionary figure who influenced the course of both Irish and British history. [Image: courtesy of the artist, Hughie O'Donoghue]

historical authority on a poem. This contrived authority is then steadily defrayed by challenging the stability of time within the world of the poem itself. Alice Milligan's *Till Ferdia Came* comes with the subtitling note '(Written during a time of civil strife in Ireland 1922–23)' and applies a conventional Revivalist mythical approach to the brutalities of the Civil War by invoking the death of Ferdia from *An Táin Bó Cualigne* as an analogy for the death of Michael Collins during 'these sad days of blood and tears'.[28] In an entirely different register, Louis MacNeice's 'Canto XVI' in *Autumn Journal* (composed in 1938) has the reader both within and outside of time in his recollection of the anticipation of the Civil War and partition:

> And I remember, when I was little, the fear
> Bandied among the servants
> That Casement would land at the pier
> With a sword and a horde of rebels;
> And how we used to expect, at a later date,
> When the wind blew from the west, the noise of shooting
> Starting in the evening at eight
> In Belfast in the York Street district

The intermingling of precision and vagueness in the collapsing tenses of the phrase '[a]nd how we used to expect, at a later date' contrasts with the absolutism of time and place as the line concludes 'at eight / [i]n Belfast in the York Street district'. The 'dialectical poetics' of *Autumn Journal* navigate imminent war and his own relationship with Ireland and England, but in the sequence 'The Closing Album' (1939) – MacNeice tackles the detail of the Irish Civil War within his larger concerns about the coming global conflict.[29] The city of Dublin itself, 'historic with guns and vermin', manipulates time in the sequence ('You give me time for thought / [a]nd by a juggler's trick / [y]ou poise the toppling hour') while, as Maria Johnston notes, the rhythm of the poetic line 'reprises the pulsating, three-beat metre of Yeats's "Easter 1916"'.[30]

Denis Devlin's elegiac 'Tomb of Michael Collins' was published in 1956. It recounts his recollection of hearing of the assassination of Collins while simultaneously recreating immediacy through memory.[31] Devlin's poetic self-consciousness around his fashioning of a hero from a distance is evident, stating as he does the effects of time on notions of truth, and on the capacity to reckon with the 'voracious fathers [who] bore him down'. Devlin's indictment of the past marks a new phase in the evolution of twentieth-century civil war poetry, whereupon direct responses begin to tremble under the weight of elapsed time: 'But what I was is one thing, what I remember / Another thing, how memory becomes knowledge –'. By 1967, and Eavan Boland's 'Yeats in Civil War', the specifics of the conflict have faded in favour of the essence of poetic resilience that Boland seeks out in her return to Yeats's 'Meditations'. The opening stanza implicitly invokes multiple historical periods in Irish history ('middle age' offers Middle Ages; sandalled 'pilgrim'; 'Norman keep'), as a means of blurring historicity even while naming the titular event:

> In middle age you exchanged the sandals
> Of a pilgrim for a Norman keep
> In Galway. Civil war started, vandals
> Sacked your country, made off with your sleep.

These enfolding timelines situate the Civil War in a longer process of Irish historical progress, in generations of barter and robbery rather than a specific (and recent) political crisis during which Yeats's poetic imagination and politics were subjected to intense pressures. For Boland,[32] the triumph of Yeats' Civil War work is the transcendence of the brutalities of the time in which he wrote:

> Somehow you arranged your escape
> Aboard a spirit-ship which every day
> Hoisted sail out of fire and rape,
> And on that ship your mind was stowaway.

In Boland's poem, packed with Yeatsian allusions, it is a time from which to turn away. She never mentions the specifics of the context beyond the detached detail that '[c]ivil war started'. Notably, however, the war is never cited as ending. The legacy of the period is implied in the penultimate line '[y]ou are its sum, struggling to survive—'. The em dash as a punctuation mark suggests that the 'struggle[e] to survive' continues. While Boland's poem ends on a 'reprieve', it captures the contradictions of the period and of its subsequent representations that sought, through blurred timelines, to invoke while simultaneously obscuring the Civil War.

The shock of its disturbance: Troubling time in commemoration

> It is the essence of culture that, in contrast to the natural course of things, the past does not pass; that is, the past does not simply disappear. Fixed in the memory of the culture, it achieves [...] duration. The memory of a culture is designed not only to be a repository of texts, but it also has a certain generative mechanism. A culture connected to its past through its memory not only generates its future, but it generates its past as well.[33]

According to memory theorist Aleida Assmann, the 'commemorative turn' in the Irish context is part of a wider phenomenon that marks a shift in our 'cultural temporal order'.[34] In this reshuffling of how we register and value time, 'the focus has shifted from present futures to present pasts'.[35] While a huge amount of scholarship now exists on commemorative practices, tracing the evolution of Civil War poetry during the Decade of Centenaries can reveal how commissioned and self-produced works influenced the cultural imaginary of a period. In tracing fictional responses to the Civil War across the century, Aiken suggests that the recent proliferation of popular novels is 'a gauge of public interest in the muffled memory of Civil War'.[36] A survey of poetry publishing between 2012

Fig. 10 Portrait of Dublin-born poet Eavan Boland (1944–2020) by Debbie Chapman, oil on canvas, 2021. This portrait was commissioned as part of Druid Theatre's production of 'Boland: Journey of a poet'. It was painted onstage during the performances, which were live streamed around the world. The interrogation of history always loomed large in the writings of Boland and the poem 'Yeats in Civil War' is an early example of her search for meaning in historical events, in this case preferring to situate Yeats's Civil War not in the narrow moment but in terms of the broader sweep of history. The crafting or writing of history was a constant theme in her work, where she sought to include the experiences and voices of women that had previously been forgotten, ignored or excluded from the accepted historical narrative. Boland fought all her life for that distinctive voice to be heard, hence her preoccupation with the meaning of what Colm Tóibín (2021) refers to as the 'erasures and ambiguous textures' of the past. From her collection *Outside History* published by Carcanet Press in 1990 to the posthumously published *The Historians*, Boland recognised the stories 'that needed to be told'. A winner of numerous poetry awards, Boland was also a highly respected teacher at Stanford University. She was also a founding member of the feminist press Arlen House where, as Alan Hayes points out, 'she helped create and shape a place and a space for so many female voices previously ignored and unwelcome'. Boland ranks as one of Ireland's finest modern poets. [Image © Debbie Chapman, 2023 / See Colm Tóibín, 'When silence is broken', in *Boland: Journey of a poet* (Druid Programme, 2021) and Alan Hayes, 'Remembering Eavan Boland on Nollaig na mBan - a leading feminist light', *Irish Times*, 6 Jan. 2023]

Fig. 11 (top left and bottom left) *Elizabeth Dunne*, by Joshua Griffith. This two-piece illustration, a combination of traditional and digital drawing, focuses on the life and experiences of Elizabeth Dunne during the Civil War. Dunne joined the Killarney branch of Cumann na mBan in 1917 and, during the War of Independence and Civil War periods, provided food and first aid to IRA Volunteers and prisoners, carried dispatches, arms and ammunition, and was involved in fund-raising and propaganda work. On the night of 8 September 1922 she was one of six women, described by the *Irish Independent* as having 'sympathy with the Irregulars', who were dragged from their beds by 'armed and masked' National Army soldiers. The raiders stripped the women and 'painted their bodies green'. As her unsuccessful application for a military service pension attests, the trauma of this violent humiliation and a subsequent cerebral haemorrhage left her mute, disconnected and ultimately overwhelmed by the world that had silenced her: 'I wish to state that since the Black and Tan and Civil Wars my nerves are broken down. I have lost my speech altogether for some time and cannot speak well yet, and I attribute this to what I have done and gone through during the above wars.' The diptych depicts Dunne, her mouth held just beneath the tensioned surface, while she languishes below. It formed part of the 'Mise, le Meas' project, a collaboration between visual media students from MTU Kerry campus and Kerry College, inspired by the lived experience of local people during the Civil War, particularly the largely untold stories of remarkable women such as Elizabeth Dunne, Mollie O'Shea and the Power sisters from Tralee. The artworks on display at the 'Mise, le Meas' exhibition in Siamsa Tíre, Tralee during the Kerry Civil War Conference in March 2023 represented diverse visual responses to letters sent and received during that tumultuous period in County Kerry. [Text: Joshua Griffith / Image: courtesy of the artist, Joshua Griffith / Sources: *Irish Independent*, 14 Sept. 1922; MSPC/34/REF57075, Elizabeth Dunne]

Fig. 12 (opposite page) 'Special Topics in Commemoration Studies: The Kerry Archives', by Victoria Kennefick, written in response to a commission by UCD Library, Poetry Ireland and the Arts Council of Northern Ireland as part of *Poetry as Commemoration*, an initiative supported by the Department of Tourism, Culture, Arts, Gaeltacht, Sport and Media, under the Decade of Centenaries 2012–23 programme. [Poem reproduced with the permission of the poet, Victoria Kennefick]

and 2023 produces a similar uptick, although Civil War poems tend to be published as individual poems in larger collections, and linked to themes of memory, family and retrieval of hidden narratives. Historical events have been extensively reimagined, especially by women poets. The focus has shifted away from the political and towards the domestic, moving into private space and time, and to intimate griefs and betrayal.[37] Martina Evans, for example, explores the intimacies of female relationships in her 2019 collection *Now We Can Talk Openly About the Men* via a prose poem/dramatic monologue set in the contexts of pre- and post-Civil War.[38] Evans's previous collection *Facing the Public* offers a deconstruction of canonical narratives of the period by engaging directly with quotations from Ernest O'Malley's *On Another Man's Wound* as well as detailing events of the War of Independence.[39] Leanne O'Sullivan's 'Safe House' is a powerful but non-conflict-specific evocation of family tragedy held within a national grief.[40] Beyond the opening line – '[w]hen they were beginning to build a country' – the poem employs that characteristically blurred chronology that indicts no political entity and sites a collective trauma in the depravations experienced during the protracted conflicts of the period.

> There was never a map that could lead back to
> or out of that place, foreknown or imagined,

'Special Topics in Commemoration Studies: The Kerry Archives'

by Victoria Kennefick

Not coffins, but boxes
neat and small enough
to be lined up
in chronological order
on the desk upstairs
in Kerry Library.

The paper inside
each one, burnt
with age, emits a bitter
smell that turns
sweet when exposed
to air. Pages

as fragile as skin,
as thin. Words
and letters typed, scrawled,
printed,
shaped by a very
careful child's hand

pile up. So many
leaflets, postcards,
and copybooks,
labelled *exercise books*,
where students practice
remembering

for those who do not
wish to. Blood turned
blue and black instead
along horizontal lines
moving forward. Divided
into sections, these accounts

are numbered, with mistakes
crossed out but still
visible as the eye moves
over each page, names
and dates (re)arranged,
a repository of pain.

SECTION 1

(a) Collected by __________, as told by _________ and __________, and other members of the __________ family.
(b) Song given to __________ by her mother _________.
(c) __________ gave the following song to her daughter _________.
(d) The following account of _________ incidents was given to __________ of _________ by __________.
(e) As recorded by _________ in conversation with _________.
(f) __________ gave the following information to _________.
(g) __________ got the following information from _________.
(h) Told by _________ to __________.
(i) Told to _________ by __________.
(j) Collected by _________ as told by __________, __________ and other members of the __________ family.

SECTION 2

We were often out   at night   blocking roads   knocking bridges

SECTION 3

Sad is the story in Kerry today ~~*They beat them up and cut off their hair*~~ *To this day he is stone deaf in both ears   Uisce faoi thalamh* ~~*They used the pump to wash off the blood*~~ *No means whatsoever   A complete wreck, unfit for any work   Hopelessly insane   Neurasthenic* ~~*No middle path*~~ *We are near starving*

SECTION 4

What in God's Holy name am I to do? / What in God's name am I supposed to do?

SECTION 5

One pile for receipts   one for pension books   another for begging letters
Do I fit the eligibility criteria?   One relative gets a pension, the other doesn't
I am an encumbrance to myself and everyone   Even in death hounded and tortured by bureaucracy
It is money that kills   the paper   the lack of   paper   the papers

SECTION 6

I can't think of any more because I am getting old

SECTION 7

I have been given advice: The B__________ M__________ is unavoidable but I must avoid it.

I avoid it.

SECTION 8

I become increasingly alert. There are monuments everywhere. I drive past them too quickly.

SECTION 9

I cannot get the phrase *war of friends* out of my head.

SECTION 10

Group work for Secondary School History students to promote co-operative learning when studying the War of Independence Irish Civil War:

1. Imagine you were there, what would you do?
2. Write a letter to one of the participants/witnesses/soldiers/civilians outlining your thoughts on the events. What advice would you give them?
3. What side of the conflict would you be on? Give reasons for your answer.
4. Quantify and discuss individual/family/generational/ancestral trauma in your own life.
5. Compare and contrast this trauma to others you know.
6. Make a timeline.
7. Construct a poster.
8. Draw a diagram.
9. Write a poem.
10. Haven't we all suffered enough?

When I pack up the boxes
one elderly page slashes my finger.
I am terrified it will bleed over everything
so work quickly to reseal that which cannot be
contained. I had been so careful to memorise
the placement of each piece;
I have certainly gotten it wrong
but healing allows for a wound.

where the furze, the dark-rooted vetch, turned
over and over with the old ground and disappeared.

Other occasional poems, in collections by Eiléan Ní Chuilleanáin, Paula Meehan, Eleanor Hooker and Vona Groarke, similarly court this imprecision around timelines and historical periods, while concentrating on restoring the narratives of those left out of the historical record. This is facilitated by foregrounding personal testimony and lyric subjectivity and resists explicit political assertion. The specifics of the Civil War remain peripheral to a shared poetic commitment to resituating marginal stories within the larger thrust of historical and literary representation.

That emphasis on the unseen and unregistered is perceptible in a commissioned collection entitled *Grief's Broken Bow*, published by Salvage Press and facilitated by the *Poetry as Commemoration* project, funded by the Department of Tourism, Culture, Arts, Gaeltacht, Sport and Media, under the Decade of Centenaries 2012–23 programme.[41] Ten prominent Irish poets were invited to respond to an archival item relating to the Civil War and the War of Independence. The difficulty in delineating periods of conflict is again evident here, and acknowledged by some of the poets who employ the aesthetics of temporal manipulation seen in earlier Civil War works. Stephen Sexton's 'The Head of a Man' was inspired by the charred fragments of *Pleadings Made to the Law Exchequer, 1773*, one of the many records destroyed during the attack on the Four Courts in June 1922.[42] Currently on display in the National Library of Ireland, the unreadable artefact becomes for Sexton a symbol of the irretrievability of the period:

Then among the final years of the horse,
cannon are horse-drawn along the river
into position at the edge of June.

In the last throes of the era of horsepower and on the periphery of the month, the arrangement of artillery on the banks of the river seems almost anachronistic – not because the act is dated, necessarily, but because time is so uncertain here. The object is transformed, not into confetti of the recorded past but rather into a 'new species of vellum and ink' in an act of permanent transubstantiation. In place of the original book, we are left with a monstrous creature, analogous perhaps of the British state in 'shock [at] its disturbance' or perhaps of the emergent Free State, 'tattooed with all that remains legible' from its centuries under the needle.

'Haven't we all suffered enough?': Required witnessing

Other contributors to *Grief's Broken Bow* meditate on the nature of commemoration itself. As scholars of memory theory argue, much of what is said and done about century-old events are mediated acts of remembering and forgetting.[43] Indeed the act of commissioning is a deliberate memory act which, in turn, exerts a literary and cultural influence. Victoria Kennefick's 'Special Topics in Commemoration Studies: The Kerry Archives' addresses the implications of prescriptive memory through formal experimentation as well as narrative meditation. Divided into ten sections, the poem is laid out across two columns which can be read either horizontally or vertically, thereby producing two different narratives. This narrative instability conveyed on the page speaks to broader debates about accepted historical narratives – which stories are accepted and relayed and which stories remain unheard. In the opening unnumbered section, the narrative of the poem reiterates the act of commissioned commemoration with careful enjambment, as 'students practice / remembering / for those who do not / wish to'. As 'names and dates' are '(re)arranged', the vulnerability of the past to present manipulation is made explicit. Subsequent sections of the poem approximate an exam paper, with section 1 offering a fill-in-the-blanks exercise and section 10 comprising detailed instructions for 'Secondary School History students', all of which contribute to the sense of artificiality cultivated by Kennefick. This self-reflexivity is punctured, however, with interjections from the archive in what appear to be direct quotations from the papers under consideration.[44] Italicised phrases pierce the ironic detachment of the poem, including sentence fragments crossed out:

> *Sad is the story in Kerry today* ~~*They beat them up and cut*~~
> ~~*off their hair*~~ *To this day he is stone*
> *deaf in both ears Uisce faoi thalamh* ~~*They used the pump*~~
> ~~*to wash off the blood*~~ *No means*
> *whatsoever A complete wreck, unfit for any work*
> *Hopelessly insane Neurasthenic* ~~*No middle*~~
> ~~*path*~~ *We are near starving*

'Special Topics in Commemoration Studies: The Kerry Archives' concludes with a reflection on the responsibility of the poet in trying to makes sense of the archival material, and how, as poetic witness, to cope with the legacy of trauma. In many ways it is a poetic exploration of Anne Dolan's observation that,

> [u]sually someone has to tell us about violence; they have to speak it or write it, put words on it, describe it, bear some kind of witness to it even by their silence. But some narrators are preferred to others, some listened to more readily and easily, and the same voices are returned to again and again.[45]

In opening the archival boxes, described as 'not coffins', the poet commits to listening, and takes on a responsibility to its contents and its authors. 'I cannot get the phrase *war of friends* out of my head', section 9 laments, and yet the final unnumbered section is urgent in its desire 'quickly to reseal that which cannot be / contained'. In approaching the Irish Civil War, even from the distance of a century and through the prism of a highly stylised poem, the threat of 'a wound' remains intense.

The poetry of the Irish Civil War is underpinned by a shared rhetoric of temporal instability. This is realised in early responses from participants and observers in the register of shock, and in later engagements via more self-conscious deliberations on historical memory. The range of formal responses documented here suggests that the theme of the Civil War requires poetic innovation to contain and transform the raw and, at times, damaging realities of the period. Focusing on the fluctuations of time as a crucial element of the formal and representative strategies in Civil War poetry is one mode of reading poetry of this period and beyond. It is an interpretative lens that accommodates shifting sociocultural, political and literary pressures and values at various times during the last century. Still the Civil War troubles contemporary Irish poetry; but to return to Yeats's original poetic response, there remains '[y]et no clear fact to be discerned'.

The Poet in a Time of Civil War

Theo Dorgan

A realist in his own way, also one deeply attracted to power, W.B. Yeats saw in the infant Free State an opportunity to retain some of the power he felt was the prerogative of his class. He saw in the new state, with its inherently authoritarian nature, its ruthless prosecution of the Civil War, a vehicle for the implementation of his vision of rule by the best. Yeats was in thrall to a naive governing idea; that the nation, any nation it seems, should be 'controlled by highly trained intellects'. In short, the cultural revolutionary was a political reactionary.

He was a senator appointed by a government that executed eighty-one anti-Treaty prisoners, most in reprisal for republican attacks on Free State forces and without any semblance of a fair trial. About this barbarism, he made no public complaint. At a time when anti-government elements were putting bullets through his windows in Merrion Square, the poet had been in London, vainly attempting to find support for a reformulated oath that would resolve the impasse in the terms of the Treaty; but this was a solo effort, made with no reference to the Free State government and without its authority.

One might expect, in the light of all this, a more public support of the new government than the senator seemed prepared to make. Equally, despite 'Easter 1916', with its qualified salute to the architects of the declared Republic, he might have been expected to condemn unequivocally the irredentists who claimed to be the direct lineal inheritors of that Republic's authority. In fact, for whatever opaque reasons, Yeats markedly refrained from public comment on the bitter struggle between them, even though he clearly stood by the state in which he was such an anomalous senator.

In his long poem sequence, *Meditations in Time of Civil War*, only two stanzas, section V, 'The Road at my Door', and section VI, 'The Stare's Nest by my Window', deal directly with the Civil War, and in curiously equalising terms. We find in section V 'An affable irregular […] cracking jokes of civil war' and 'A brown Lieutenant and his men / Half dressed in national uniform' – both 'affable' and 'half-dressed' suggest bemused dismissiveness, as if none of this is either real or important. The poet, uninvolved, can 'turn towards my chamber, caught / In the cold snows of a dream'.

Only in section VI, 'The Stare's Nest by my Window', does he allow the brute reality of the living day break into his lofty preoccupations and prompt direct comment:

> A barricade of stone or of wood;
> Some fourteen days of civil war;
> Last night they trundled down the road
> The dead young soldier in his blood [...]
>
> We had fed the heart on fantasies,
> The heart's grown brutal from the fare;
> more substance in our enmities
> than in our love [. . .]

But he turns away again. There is a call for vengeance on murderers in the next and final section, but it is the murderers of Jacques de Molay who draw down the curse – de Molay, the last grand master of the Knights Templar, was burned at the stake in 1314. In the end, the youth who admired the Fenian O'Leary, the honoured senator of a native Irish government, finds that 'The abstract joy, / the half-read wisdom of daemonic images' must 'Suffice the ageing man as once the growing boy'.

The stare's nest

The bees build in the crevices
Of loosening masonry, and there
The mother birds bring grubs & flies.
My wall is loosening; honey bees
Come build in the empty house of the stare

We are closed in & the key turned
On our uncertainty. Somewhere
A man is killed or a house burned
Yet no clear fact to be discerned
(Come build in the empty house of the stare)
A barricade of stone or of wood;
Some fourteen days of civil war:
Last night they trundled down the road
That dead young soldier in his blood.
Come build in the empty house of the stare.

WBY
July 14 1922

Fig. 1 (opposite) (l–r) Mr Justice Wylie, Senator W.B. Yeats, Sir John Irwin, Sir Henry McGloughlin and director of the Aontach Tailteann, J.J. Walsh, at the opening of the 1924 Tailteann Games. [Image: part of the Independent Newspapers Ireland/NLI Collection]

Fig. 2 (top right) 'The Stare's Nest', a unique bronze by Meath-based sculptor Orla de Brí. It was first exhibited in 2021 at the Hamilton Gallery as part of an exhibition by 125 invited artists thematically drawing upon W.B. Yeats's *Meditations in Time of Civil War.* [Image: reproduced with the permission of the artist, Orla de Brí]

Fig. 3 (right) A manuscript copy of 'The Stare's Nest by my Window' dated 14 July 1922 and printed in W.B. Yeats, *Seven Poems and a Fragment* (Dublin, 1922). [Image: courtesy of Stuart A. Rose Manuscript, Archives, and Rare Book Library, Emory University]

CHAPTER 12

The Historiography of the Irish Civil War

Diarmaid Ferriter

On a Friday night in November 1968, Dublin teenager Gene Kerrigan was watching the *Late Late Show* on RTÉ, the public broadcaster's popular entertainment and chat show. A guest on the programme was the Australian historian, Calton Younger, who was there to talk about his new book on the Irish Civil War. Kerrigan was in for a rude awakening. 'I watched, slightly puzzled at first, then more than a little agitated', he recalled. 'What civil war? I had lately turned nineteen, five years out of school, making my way in the world, and I'd just discovered that there had been a civil war in my country only twenty-six years before I was born.' It prompted Kerrigan to dig out his old primary school history textbook, James Carty's *Junior History of Ireland*, the version published in 1959, which celebrated the 1916 martyrs and then proceeded to the Treaty negotiated between the British government and Sinn Féin representatives in late 1921. That was it: 'there ended the lesson', Kerrigan remembered: 'there wasn't a single word in the book or in my schooling about the bloodshed that led from the Treaty and the split which created the dominant political culture of the decades that followed'.[1] Kerrigan went on to become a dogged and distinguished journalist and this experience of 1968 imbued him with a scepticism about the reliability of establishment narratives: 'since discovering the missing civil war I have never totally believed the official version of anything.'[2]

That Calton Younger featured on the *Late Late Show* was indicative of the interest generated by an outsider's take on the Civil War. A native of Victoria and educated in Melbourne, Younger served with the Royal Australian Air Force (RAAF) during the Second World War and spent three years as a prisoner of war, which left him with 'an abhorrence of oppression [...] an understanding of freedom' and 'an unsentimental compassion for those in difficulties'.[3] He clearly admired the Irish revolutionary generation as brave, but also referred to them as 'fanatical' and 'ruthless' in their idealism. The book made a claim to be a balanced account. While acknowledging that, as a middle-aged man, 'I plump for law

Fig. 1 (opposite) A studio portrait of Máire Comerford taken in the United States in 1924. Comerford was born in Wicklow in 1893, raised in Wexford and died at her home in Sandyford, County Dublin in 1982. Living on the fringes of the gentry, her upbringing was happy and carefree, if financially precarious. Radicalised after witnessing the 1916 Rising during a trip to Dublin, she joined Cumann na mBan, Sinn Féin and the Gaelic League. In 1919 she moved to Dublin to work for the nationalist historian, Alice Stopford Green. In this highly charged political house on St Stephen's Green, Comerford became immersed in republican politics and, during the War of Independence, travelled all over Dublin and across the county, mostly by bicycle – moving arms, carrying dispatches, finding safe houses, researching atrocities and working assiduously for an Irish Republic. Following the ratification of the Treaty in 1921, Cumann na mBan voted decisively against the Articles of Agreement and some, like Comerford, became active combatants in the Civil War. They were also able and daredevil propagandists, beginning with the Heads Up Campaign (January–June 1922), composing, printing and posting pithy, uncompromising republican messages of dissent all over Dublin. By June 1922 Comerford was in the Four Courts, one of the few women present for the bombardment by Free State forces. Following the surrender, she joined the fighting in and around O'Connell Street. Based at the Hamman Hotel, she careered around the city in an ambulance and cycled through the fighting to deliver dispatches. It is not surprising that in 1923 the *Daily Mail* described her as the most daring woman working for the republican cause. In January 1923, she was actively working to bring an end to the Free State executions and was involved in an IRA plan to kidnap the head of the new Irish Free State, William T. Cosgrave, when she was caught, arrested and sentenced to prison. Máire escaped in May but was rearrested a month later and sent to Kilmainham Gaol, where she went on hunger strike. She was released after twenty-seven days and carried out on a stretcher. By August 1923 Comerford was in Cork, the chief republican election organiser for the entire county, a task she described as herculean in her revolutionary period memoir, *On Dangerous Ground*. At the behest of Éamon de Valera, she set sail for America on a false passport (Fig. 2) arriving in New York in late 1923. During a nine-month tour of the big cities and smaller towns of east-coast America, Comerford spoke at rallies and organised fund-raising events for republican prisoners in Ireland. Her letters home during this period highlight the increasing sense of defeat and disillusionment felt by republicans following the end of the Civil War. Comerford returned to a poverty-stricken existence in Ireland, running a small poultry farm in Wexford for almost a decade. Her journalistic career began in 1935 when she became editor of the women's page in the *Irish Press*. For the remainder of her life, Máire worked as a journalist and historical researcher and remained a committed republican and activist. She was involved in numerous republican activities, including a campaign of jury intimidation, with related seditious publication and bill posting in the late 1920s and 1930s. Her focus turned to the North in 1969, when she befriended and supported a new generation of republicans. Máire Comerford was also a staunch advocate for republican prisoners and their dependants right up to her death in 1982. She devoted the latter part of her life to writing her memoir of the revolutionary period, finally published by the Lilliput Press in 2021, and to compiling and sharing the contents of her extensive archive, now held in Boston College. [Text: Hilary Dully / Image: courtesy of the Comerford family and Boston College]

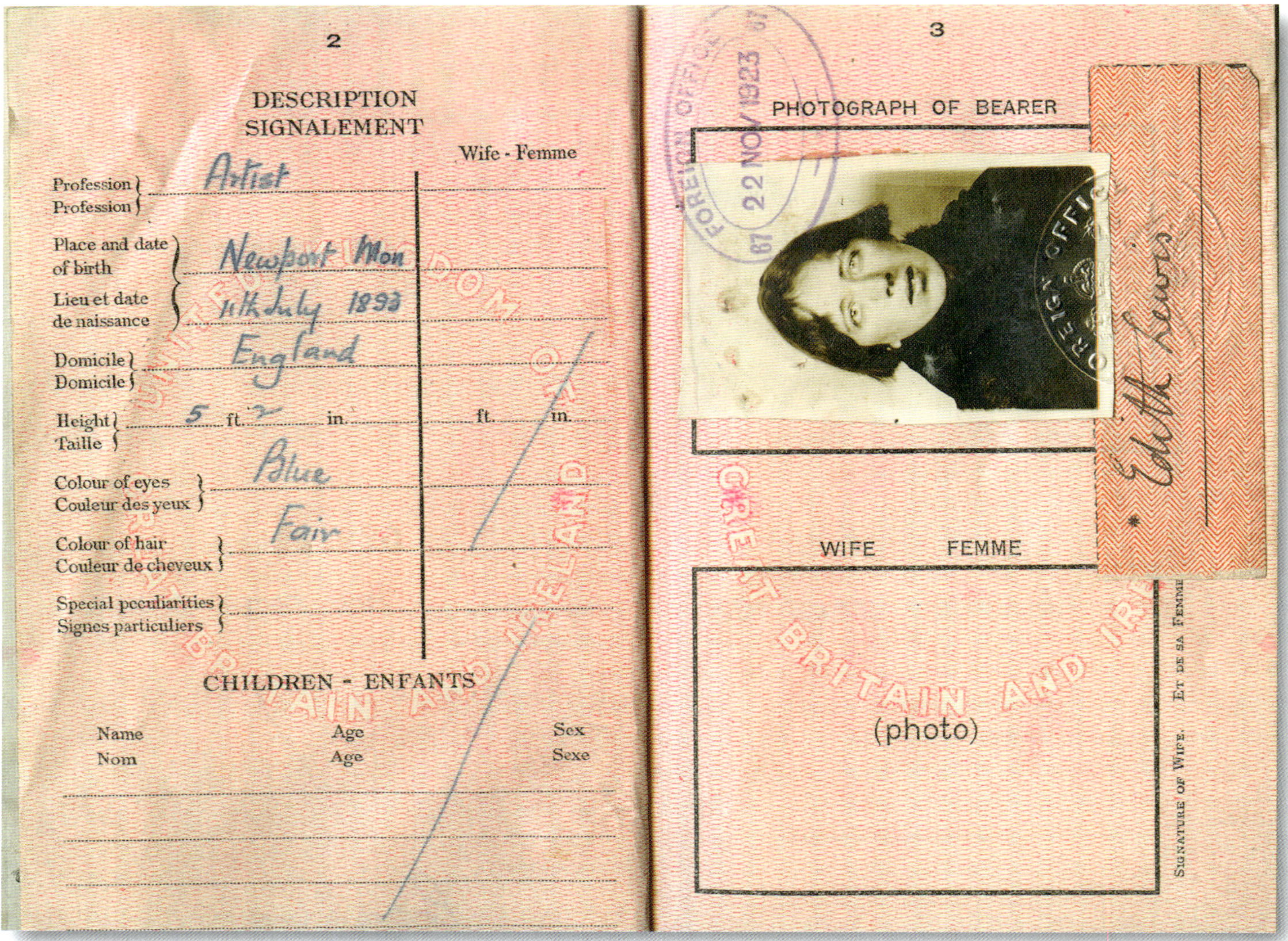

2

DESCRIPTION
SIGNALEMENT

		Wife - Femme
Profession / Profession	Artist	
Place and date of birth / Lieu et date de naissance	Newport Mon 11th July 1893	
Domicile / Domicile	England	
Height / Taille	5 ft. 2 in.	ft. in.
Colour of eyes / Couleur des yeux	Blue	
Colour of hair / Couleur de cheveux	Fair	
Special peculiarities / Signes particuliers		

CHILDREN - ENFANTS

Name / Nom	Age / Age	Sex / Sexe

3

PHOTOGRAPH OF BEARER

FOREIGN OFFICE 22 NOV 1923

Edith Lewis

WIFE FEMME

(photo)

Signature of Wife. Et de sa Femme.

Fig. 2 A false passport issued to Máire Comerford under the name 'Edith Lewis' and used for her American trip in 1923–4. [Image: courtesy of the Comerford family]

and order and respect for majority rule, I haven't lost my feeling for those young men who could not bring themselves to relinquish, at any cost, the ideal of an Irish republic.'[4] Younger was also able to speak to Civil War veterans including Seán Mac Eoin, Emmet Dalton, Tom Barry, Peadar O'Donnell and a 'splendid' Dan Breen.[5] None of those individuals would have been known for their coyness or lack of trenchancy. Likewise, when Michael Laffan was researching the politics of Sinn Féin as a young historian in the late 1960s, he interviewed Máire Comerford, Michael Hayes, Éamon de Valera, Seán MacEntee and Richard Mulcahy. Significantly, all these individuals' private papers ended up in the University College Dublin (UCD) Archives, ensuring a richly documented overview of various aspects of the Civil War from both sides.[6]

These experiences from the late 1960s are a reminder that, alongside reticence and elisions, there were always those willing to write and talk about the Civil War and seek to have their versions of the conflict recorded. There is little doubt that many preferred silence, a preference memorably summed up by retired taoiseach and Civil War veteran Seán Lemass when responding to journalist Michael Mills in 1969: 'Terrible things were done by both sides [...] I'd prefer not to talk about it.'[7] But there were parallel streams of direct and indirect Civil War narratives.

'controversies that best lie buried'

Degrees of discomfort and nervousness about the subject were hardly surprising. In 1967, Taoiseach Jack Lynch told historian, journalist and novelist Eoin Neeson that even if Britain opened state papers from 1922, the Irish government would not, because access 'might well stir domestic controversies that best lie buried'.[8] Nonetheless Neeson, whose father Seán and mother Geraldine were active anti-Treatyites, published his bestselling history *The Civil War in Ireland* in 1966. Neeson did not hide his anti-Treaty bias, but his book was also widely regarded as a lucid and relatively objective account, though Terry Clavin noted, 'its anti-treaty slant elicited a gracious rebuttal from surviving civil war protagonist Ernest Blythe'.[9] Clearly, some military and political veterans of the period still felt it incumbent on them to fight the history wars.

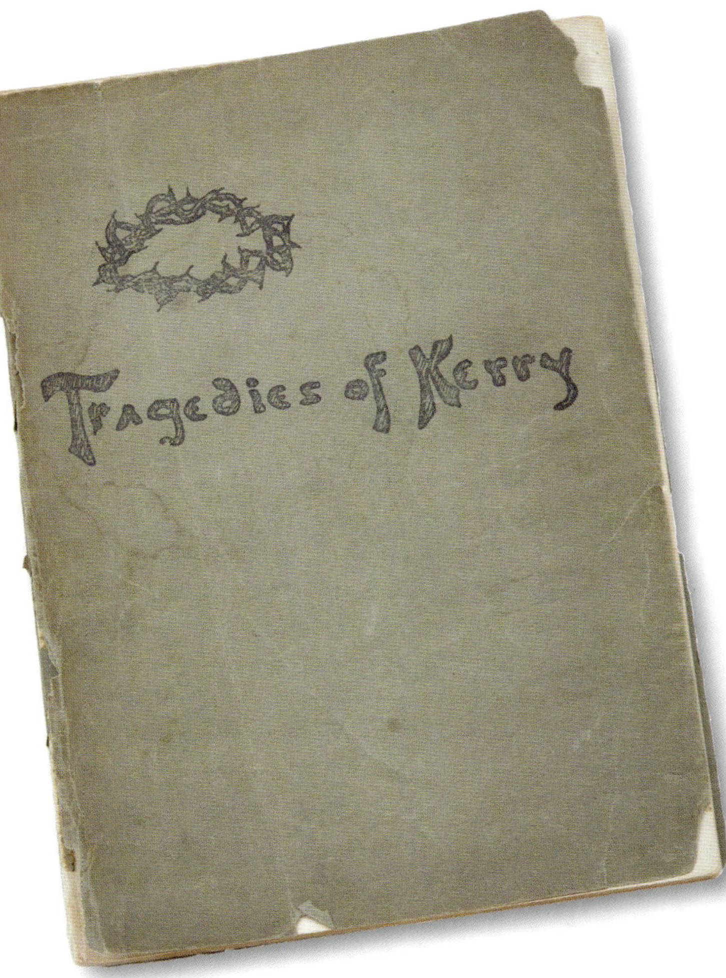

Those history wars had waged for decades. Walter Alison Phillips, a unionist appalled by the recent upheavals, came early to the task of writing its history, producing *The Revolution in Ireland, 1906–23* in 1923 while, in his own words, 'the embers of civil war were still glowing in Southern Ireland'.[10] The following year Dorothy Macardle, a leading republican propagandist who served six months in jail, portrayed Free State soldiers and officials as morally reprehensible in *Tragedies of Kerry*, her account of Civil War atrocities during the vicious final phase of the conflict in that county.

Early Civil War publications are a reminder that we need to be careful of blanket assertions about silence and avoidance; in one sense they are 'imagined silences', though it is also important to acknowledge the testimony of those children of veterans who have highlighted their parents' unwillingness to talk about it.[11] As Síobhra Aiken explains in her 2021 book *Spiritual Wounds*, veterans found ways to address the conflict and its legacy, sometimes indirectly and sometimes through fiction. Aiken's book has been described as 'a riposte to the idea that, after the Irish Civil War, nobody wanted to talk about it'.[12] She argues that 'The many voices that broke

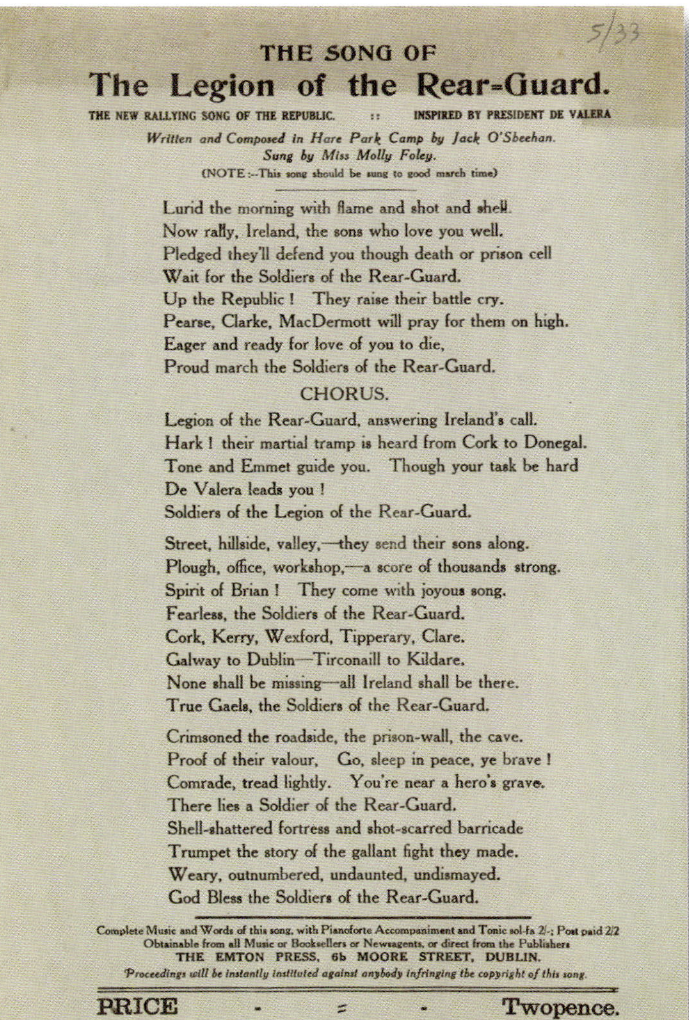

5/33

THE SONG OF

The Legion of the Rear-Guard.

THE NEW RALLYING SONG OF THE REPUBLIC. :: INSPIRED BY PRESIDENT DE VALERA

Written and Composed in Hare Park Camp by Jack O'Sheehan.
Sung by Miss Molly Foley.

(NOTE :--This song should be sung to good march time)

Lurid the morning with flame and shot and shell.
Now rally, Ireland, the sons who love you well.
Pledged they'll defend you though death or prison cell
Wait for the Soldiers of the Rear-Guard.
Up the Republic ! They raise their battle cry.
Pearse, Clarke, MacDermott will pray for them on high.
Eager and ready for love of you to die,
Proud march the Soldiers of the Rear-Guard.

CHORUS.

Legion of the Rear-Guard, answering Ireland's call.
Hark ! their martial tramp is heard from Cork to Donegal.
Tone and Emmet guide you. Though your task be hard
De Valera leads you !
Soldiers of the Legion of the Rear-Guard.

Street, hillside, valley,—they send their sons along.
Plough, office, workshop,—a score of thousands strong.
Spirit of Brian ! They come with joyous song.
Fearless, the Soldiers of the Rear-Guard.
Cork, Kerry, Wexford, Tipperary, Clare.
Galway to Dublin—Tirconaill to Kildare.
None shall be missing—all Ireland shall be there.
True Gaels, the Soldiers of the Rear-Guard.

Crimsoned the roadside, the prison-wall, the cave.
Proof of their valour, Go, sleep in peace, ye brave !
Comrade, tread lightly. You're near a hero's grave.
There lies a Soldier of the Rear-Guard.
Shell-shattered fortress and shot-scarred barricade
Trumpet the story of the gallant fight they made.
Weary, outnumbered, undaunted, undismayed.
God Bless the Soldiers of the Rear-Guard.

Complete Music and Words of this song, with Pianoforte Accompaniment and Tonic sol-fa 2/-; Post paid 2/2
Obtainable from all Music or Booksellers or Newsagents, or direct from the Publishers
THE EMTON PRESS, 6b MOORE STREET, DUBLIN.
Proceedings will be instantly instituted against anybody infringing the copyright of this song.

PRICE - = - Twopence.

Fig. 3 (above) The original cover of Dorothy Macardle's *Tragedies of Kerry* (Dublin, 1924). The slim volume, reprinted numerous times, was a powerful work of republican propaganda, documenting events and giving emotive accounts of the killing of unarmed republicans by Free State forces in the south-western county. [Image: Kerry County Museum and Neustock Media]

Fig. 4 (right) 'The Song of the Legion of the Rear-Guard', by Jack O'Sheehan. Both the title of Jack Carty's 1934 testimonial novel set in Wexford during the Civil War and Jack O'Sheehan's political ballad composed during his internment in Hare Park eleven years earlier invoke Éamon de Valera's proclamation to the IRA issued in conjunction with Frank Aiken's ceasefire order on 24 May 1923. The nominal leader of the anti-Treaty forces directed the 'Soldiers of Liberty, Legion of the Rearguard' to temporarily cede military victory to 'those who ha[d] destroyed the Republic'. O'Sheehan's 'rallying song' is clearly a response to de Valera's assertion that once the Irish people, exhausted after 'seven years of intense efforts', recovered and rallied again to the standard, 'your place will be once more as of old with the vanguard'. The martial lyrics conjure a formidable, resurgent force, drawn from all counties and classes, led by de Valera and inspired and endorsed by republican martyrs – Theobald Wolfe Tone, Robert Emmet, Patrick Pearse, Thomas Clarke and Seán Mac Diarmada. The tone changes in the final verse which, in the republican tradition, urges remembrance of those who fought and died during the Civil War. Performed to stirring effect at Fianna Fáil rallies in the 1930s, the rousing chorus places the Civil War in a centuries-old tradition culminating, inevitably, in de Valera's leadership. In contrast, as Síobhra Aiken notes, Carty's novel, a blend of fiction and memoir, underscored 'the psychological devastation to family life in civil war' and offered 'a solemn alternative to more glorified accounts of revolutionary activity'. [Document: OLS Samuels box 5 no.33. The Board of Trinity College Dublin / See Richard Parfitt, *Musical Culture and the Spirit of Irish Nationalism, 1848–1972* (New York, 2019), p. 104; Síobhra Aiken, *Spiritual Wounds: Trauma, testimony and the Irish Civil War* (Dublin, 2022), p. 47]

PEADOR ODONNELL

Fig. 5 Portrait of Peadar O'Donnell (1893–1986) by Harry Kernoff RHA (1934). In the introduction to the 1966 edition of his Civil War memoir *The Gates Flew Open* (1932), O'Donnell noted that its portrayal of the conflict between the Mountjoy prisoners and the chaplains, who refused them the sacraments following the condemnatory bishops' pastoral of October 1922, was what gained it the most attention. He had previously and controversially broached the same subject in fictional form in *The Knife* (1930), which was condemned in the press and from the pulpit; a flavour can be gleaned from the utterance of one prisoner that the 'anti-Christs in Maynooth made a new religion to back the Treaty'. O'Donnell had moved from being a trade union organiser to the ranks of the IRA in 1919. He saw the Treaty as a sell-out of the revolution by the Irish middle class and was part of the anti-Treaty IRA executive that occupied the Four Courts in April 1922. He was imprisoned after the fall of the Four Courts. O'Donnell was close to the first Communist Party of Ireland and, with other left-wing prisoners in Mountjoy, encouraged Liam Mellows to pen his 'Notes', outlining a socialistic policy platform for republicans. Following Mellows's execution, O'Donnell was moved to the Curragh and then to Finner Camp in County Donegal. There, in solitary confinement, he ruminated on the nature and form of the next republican mobilisation and made a crucial decision: 'I know that I know the insides of the minds of the mass of the folk in rural Ireland: my thoughts are distilled out of their lives. Therefore, it is not my task to say anything new but to put words on what is in confused ferment in their minds.' A seed was planted that flowered into a writing career that saw him publish seven novels, one play, three autobiographical accounts and millions of words of campaigning journalism. He was transferred back to Mountjoy in August 1923 and was elected as a TD in the general election later that month. After partaking in the mass hunger strike that October–November, he was transferred back to the Curragh, from where he escaped with the aid of a sympathetic guard in March 1924. He married Lile O'Donel, a Cumann na mBan activist with whom he had been liaising on communications while incarcerated. Lile's independent wealth meant O'Donnell could devote himself to a life of full-time writing and activism. He helped to pull the IRA to the left in the late 1920s, and was a lynchpin in a range of campaigns and organisations that involved a high level of IRA–communist cooperation. He edited the IRA's *An Phoblacht*, which he used to promote the agitation against the land annuities that he spearheaded (see p. 197). A Church–state backlash saw the collapse of the IRA–communist nexus, and O'Donnell left in 1934 to help form the short-lived Republican Congress. He founded the legendary *Bell* magazine in 1940 and, in the postwar years, was accepted as the 'grand old man' of the Irish left and patron saint of progressive causes and campaigns, such as opposition to the US war in Vietnam, the Campaign for Nuclear Disarmament and the Irish Anti-Apartheid Movement. [Source: © The Trustees of the Estate of Harry Kernoff / Image: courtesy of whytes.com / See Donal Ó Drisceoil, *Peadar O'Donnell* (Cork, 2001)]

the silence can no longer be overlooked. Civil wars engender vibrant bodies of competing discourses.'[13] One such example, Francis Carty's *Legion of the Rearguard*, was a bestseller after its publication in 1934; Francis (a brother of James Carty, mentioned above) had spent a month on hunger strike during the Civil War.[14]

Yet censorship of literature inspired by the Civil War was also an issue: the state's Irish language publishing company, An Gúm, refused to publish Seosamh Mac Grianna's novel *An Druma Mór* in the 1930s. Mac Grianna had also been interned as an anti-Treaty republican and the publishers were concerned that his novel, based on ruptures between Catholic nationalists and republicans in Donegal, could revitalise Civil War tensions. Mac Grianna's book was not published until 1969. Síobhra Aiken also identifies an 'unwillingness' among 'the architects of official memory – journalists, historians, politicians, to listen to the testimony of civil war veterans'.[15] What emerges from her research is 'the simultaneous desire to forget and the inability to stop remembering'.[16]

Constructing and curating narratives

Memoirs were also published, including Peadar O'Donnell's Civil War prison memoir *The Gates Flew Open*, in which he insisted that 'it is no longer of any importance who took what side in that period [...] the interest should shift towards the study of the play of social forces that went into the making of the crisis of the Treaty', an invitation historians were slow to embrace.[17] Leading Civil War era politicians were careful to curate selective narratives. Historian Patrick Murray has detailed Éamon de Valera's preoccupation with the verdict of history, his need to keep his reputation in constant repair and an anxiety to influence the interpretation of his political activity and discourse. His effort to police the evolving public presentation of his career, wrote Murray, was,

> not a foible of old age but the settled practice of a lifetime. He consciously developed the mythopoeic significance of his career in order to emphasise his unique contribution to history along with his probity, consistency and sound judgement. There was also the obsessive, recurring focus upon a particular set of episodes in which he was the central participant.[18]

De Valera actively engaged in 'his parallel role as supervisor of those accommodating historians whose function it was to interpret this history in terms favourable to him'. He would have been happy with Dorothy Macardle's *The Irish Republic*. While the book unashamedly promoted the anti-Treaty (and de Valera's) stance, it was much more than that. As Leeann Lane has shown, a decade of research underpinned it but, given Macardle's bias, the era's political polarisation and de Valera's visage gracing the cover, it became primarily associated with his contested stature.[19] In contrasting republican morality with the violence and brutality of British and Free State soldiers, 'her binary was deeply flawed' and in that sense she was 'a politician and propagandist before she was a historian'. She was selective in the documents she used, parroted de Valera's stated reasons for not attending the Treaty negotiations and suggested his 'fatal flaw' was his strength of principle.[20]

The following decade the 'Fighting Stories' series reflected an urgency to document the experiences of revolutionary veterans, with the narratives driven 'by the men who made' the revolution happen. Four books appeared between 1947 and 1949: *Rebel Cork's Fighting Story*, *Kerry's Fighting Story*, *Limerick's Fighting Story* and *Dublin's Fighting Story*. These accounts, focusing on experiences in some of the most active counties during the War of Independence, were dramatically described as 'gripping episodes' and 'more graphic than anything written of the late war zones'. They were valuable contemporary accounts, and also designed, as was stated in the preface to *Dublin's Fighting Story*, to 'preserve in the hearts of the younger generation that love of country and devotion to its interests which distinguished the men whose doings are related within'. According to Brian Ó Conchubhair, editor of editions republished in the early twenty-first century, it was also clear there was no question of straying beyond 1921 to cover the Civil War;

Fig. 6 Éamon de Valera, with the author examining a copy of Dorothy Macardle's *The Irish Republic* (1937), for which he wrote the foreword. Irish academic historians showed little interest in the Irish revolution during the decades that followed the 1916–23 period. A number of intellectual republican veterans filled the breach, including Dorothy Macardle. Though historians have emphasised the anti-British and anti-Treaty politics of its author, *The Irish Republic* was a significant historical narrative that captured the major events of the revolutionary period in an accessible style. Macardle built a distinguished record as a republican activist during the War of Independence and Civil War, particularly in the realm of propaganda. She was imprisoned for six months in 1922–3 and underwent a week-long hunger strike. Afterwards she continued her writing career, as a journalist, novelist and historian. [Image: Press Photographs of Éamon de Valera (1882–1975), UCD Archives P150/PH/3664/6. Reproduced by kind permission of UCD-OFM Partnership]

it was apparently still too soon to attempt public memory of that event.[21] Irish language writers, however, continued to probe the conflict, including Colm Ó Labhra in his 1955 account *Trodairí na Treas Briogáide*, which details the activities of the 3rd Tipperary Brigade, though it was published under a penname.[22]

'economic root to the fight'

Ernie O'Malley's *On Another Man's Wound,* published in 1936, focused on his experiences during the War of Independence. He subsequently worked on his Civil War memoir, *The Singing Flame,* though this was not published until 1978, over twenty years after his death. O'Malley took aim at the comfortable bourgeoisie and their betrayal of the authentic spirit of liberation; those he perceived as 'determined to defend this Free State of theirs which had been handed them on a platter cooked *a l'imperiale* [...] there was an economic root to the fight' and the real spirit of freedom was 'deep down in the soil and with the poor of the cities'.[23] Liam Deasy's *Brother Against Brother* was another posthumous account, published over twenty years after his death in 1974. Deasy argued that state executions prolonged the war, but was frank in admitting various shades of militancy among anti-Treaty republicans, and in wondering whether public support for the IRA in numerous parts of the country existed only 'because of who we were or because of our success in earlier times'.[24]

The Troubles in Northern Ireland from 1969 prompted much more robust assertions about the extent of the problematic legacies created by the violence of the 1916–23 period. The work of F.S.L. Lyons, including *Ireland Since the Famine*, revealed scepticism about eulogising the giants of the republican pantheon ('unfortunately for

Fig. 7 (top) Two transcribed pages of Ernie O'Malley's interview with Liam Manahan (1878–1972), IRA leader from Ballylanders, County Limerick. O'Malley begins writing on the page on the right-hand side and continues on the left. [Image: O'Malley Notebooks, P17b/106,117. Reproduced by kind permission of UCD Archives]

Fig. 8 Two head and shoulders photographs of Ernie O'Malley (1921). Ernie O'Malley (1897–1957) is best known for his evocative Irish War of Independence memoir, *On Another Man's Wound*, but he also produced key sources for Irish Civil War historians. After earning an impressive 'fighting' record as a roving IRA organiser during 1919–21, O'Malley emerged as an influential leader of the anti-Treaty forces in 1922. At the opening of hostilities he took over command of the besieged Four Courts complex, and later in 1922 commanded all IRA forces in Leinster and Ulster. Having been captured at his Donnybrook (Dublin) hideout after a fierce gunbattle in which he was wounded nine times (and killed a National Army soldier), O'Malley remained in prison until his postwar release in 1924. Until his death O'Malley exhibited an enduring fascination with the Civil War through his various projects, including his posthumous Civil War memoir, *The Singing Flame*. During the 1940s and 1950s, he conducted roughly 450 interviews with prominent IRA veterans around the country and documented their Civil War (and War of Independence) memories (Fig. 7). During these transcribed conversations O'Malley displayed particular interest in aspects of the conflict he must have found troubling, including the machinations of the Irish Republican Brotherhood, Liam Deasy's 'surrender document' and the torture and killings of republican prisoners. Housed in the University College Dublin Archives, the 'O'Malley interviews' are a valuable resource for historians, and six different collections of interviews have been published (the Irish Manuscripts Commission intends to publish all of his interview notebooks). In addition, in 1991 Richard English edited a collection of Ernie O'Malley's prisoner letters (*Prisoners: The Civil War letters of Ernie O'Malley*), while Anne Dolan and Cormac O'Malley in 2007 produced a lengthy volume of O'Malley's Civil War military correspondence (*No Surrender Here: The Civil War papers of Ernie O'Malley, 1922–1924*). O'Malley's voluminous writings, both during and long after the Civil War, continue to generate interest decades after his death. [Image: Papers of Professor F.X. Martin, P189/400. Reproduced by kind permission of UCD Archives] them, it was a republic which was more invisible than indivisible and the sincere and moving idealism with which its champions sought to evoke it roused little echo in a war weary country'). Lyons, however, was also balanced and at times reticent, pointing out that it was still too early, in the absence of sufficient source material, to arrive at a 'mature judgement' about individual attitudes.[25]

British shadows and threats

Approaching the fiftieth anniversary of the conflict, for some the Civil War was still seen through the prism of the careers of Michael Collins and Éamon de Valera. That period witnessed the publication of Margery Forester's biography of Collins, *The Lost Leader*, the title trading on the endurance of regret for what might have been (Collins, ever resolute, had 'an intense sense of loyalty coupled with a seemingly paradoxical habit of independent action.'[26]). The authorised biography of de Valera by T.P. O'Neill and the earl of Longford (Frank Pakenham) also involved an overly laudatory assessment: 'de Valera submitted all his actions to a criterion which was at once intellectual and moral'.[27]

In 1979 Michael Laffan welcomed what he regarded as accounts of the revolutionary period that 'superseded' the nationalist propaganda of Macardle's *The Irish Republic* and a new tone that was 'sceptical and unideological'.[28] But he later observed: 'for decades historians of modern Ireland have avoided the Civil War, viewing it with apparent distaste and embarrassment'.[29] That was rectified in 1988 with the publication of Michael Hopkinson's *Green Against Green: The Irish Civil War*. Tom Garvin hailed its appearance, suggesting 'Hopkinson has finally broken the taboo on research into this crucial event in Irish political history and has given us the first full-length, archive-based history of the Irish Civil War'. It skilfully exploited newly available archival material, including collections from UCD, the National Library of Ireland, the Public Record Office in London and the State Paper Office in Dublin. Hopkinson approached these new sources 'in a thorough and rigorous fashion', according to Garvin. 'While he is ready to praise and more frequently to criticise, his tone is always detached and his judgements fair.' The great strength of the book lay in its analysis of the military conduct of the war and its regional variations and, as Hopkinson observed, he was 'often forced to describe chaos'.[30] He also contended that it was untenable to 'impose a pattern to the events which conveniently forgets how reactive, confused and unplanned actual developments were on both sides'.[31]

Approaching the seventy-fifth anniversary of the Civil War in 1997, Tom Garvin was keen to present it as a battle between democrats and dictators in his book *1922: The birth of Irish democracy*. He argued that 'moderate and realistic' nation-builders had triumphed over militant republicans contemptuous of 'democratic principles of legitimacy'. The pro-Treaty leaders were 'unconditional democrats and they killed people for the nascent Irish democracy that they saw menaced by the anti-Treatyites' who saw the Republic as a 'transcendental, moral entity'.[32] This was a trenchant distortion; John Regan's *The Irish Counter-Revolution 1921–1936* argued that the

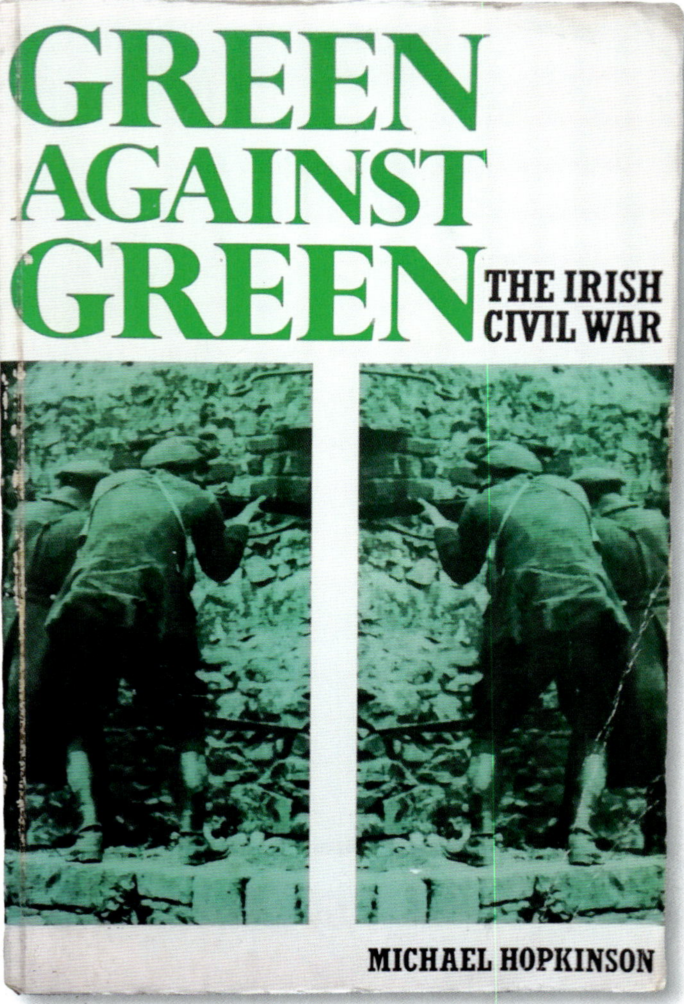

Fig. 9 The cover of Michael Hopkinson's *Green Against Green: The Irish Civil War* (1988). While the Irish Civil War was the subject of full-length histories written by Eoin Neeson and Calton Younger in the 1960s, the first extended academic historical treatment was completed by Michael Hopkinson in his 1988 landmark, *Green Against Green: The Irish Civil War*. Using British state archival sources opened in the 1970s and numerous private collections in Ireland, Hopkinson produced a sweeping narrative of the military conflict that managed to be both rigorous and fair. He also broke what historian Tom Garvin called 'the taboo on research into this crucial event in Irish political history'. [Image: reproduced with the permission of Gill Books / Source: *Irish Times*, 17 Sept. 2016]

issue of democratic will was more complicated and compromised by British shadows and threats. To brand opponents of the Treaty as fundamentally anti-democratic, Regan wrote, 'demands the exclusion of British coercion as a force for change in 1922 [...] the threat of British violence [...] is fundamental to understanding the nature of both treatyite and anti-treatyite politics in post-revolutionary Ireland'.[33] As the Civil War clouds gathered, Winston Churchill, who had little desire to return to what he called 'that hideous bog of reprisals from which we have saved ourselves', suggested Britain would have to consider resuming 'full liberty of action'. Regan argues that neither side of the divide in Ireland had a monopoly on democratic virtue, meaning 'no bi-polar model, not even with modifications for the Civil War, can adequately do justice

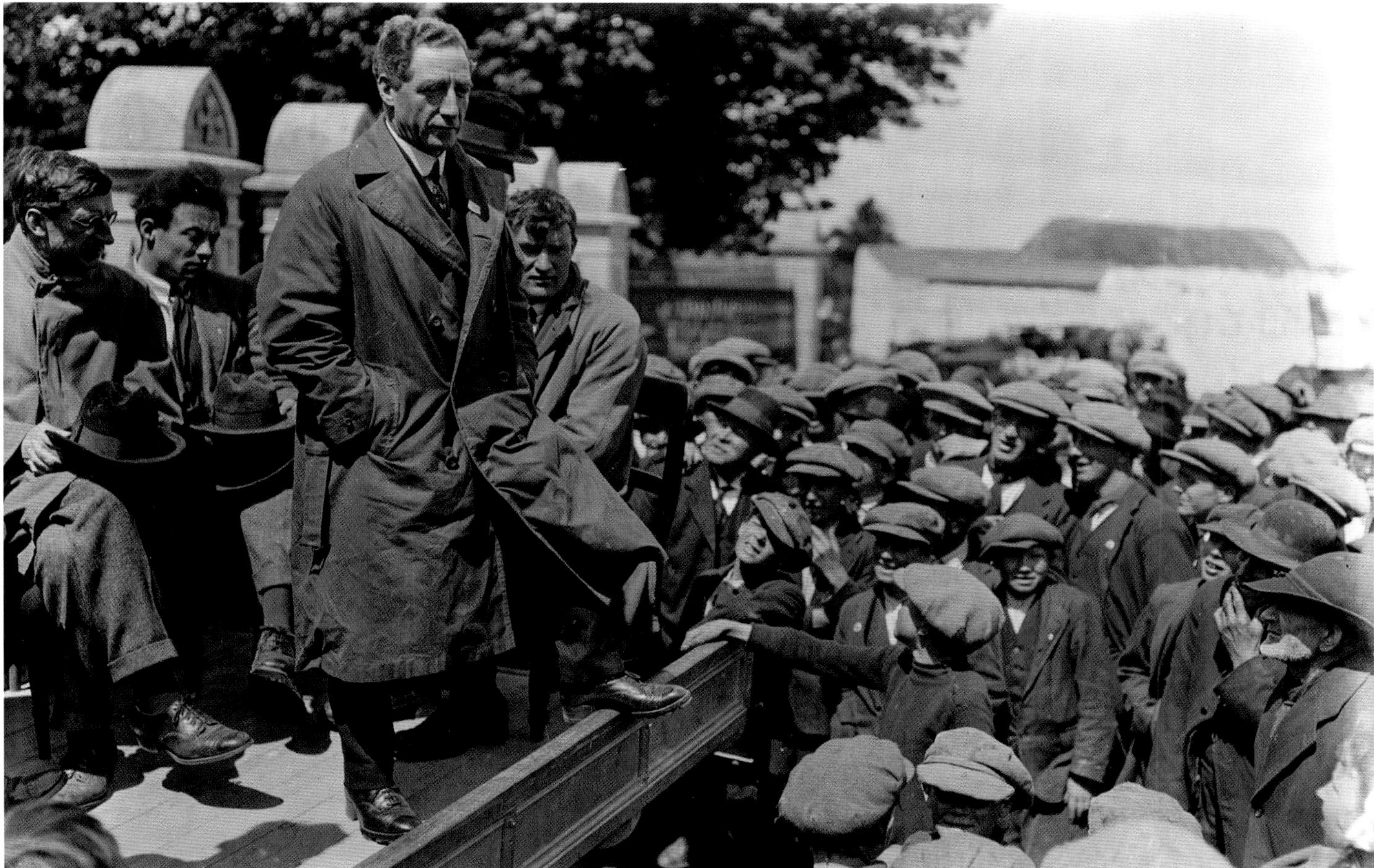

Fig. 10 Cathal Brugha at an election rally in Mooncoin, County Kilkenny on 13 June 1922. Cathal Brugha fought and died in a civil war that he tried to prevent and was that conflict's first high-profile fatality in early July 1922. A celebrated survivor of the 1916 Rising, despite multiple gunshot wounds, Brugha was a crucial figure in the post-Rising reorganisation of the Volunteers and Sinn Féin, speaker at the first sitting of Dáil Éireann and minister for defence in the underground government during the War of Independence. He was a passionate and acerbic opponent of the Anglo-Irish Treaty, which he regarded as the undoing of his lifework – the pursuit of an Irish republic. As Ó Corráin and Hanley argue in *Cathal Brugha: 'an indomitable spirit'*, he was no simplistic militant or extremist. In the six months prior to the June 1922 general election, he had two principal objectives. The first was to convince the Irish public that they should be citizens of a republic rather than subjects of a British dominion. The second was to prevent the Treaty split culminating in civil war, a prospect that was abhorrent to Brugha, who had tried unsuccessfully to restrain bellicose republicans at the IRA convention in March–April 1922. He repeatedly called for nationalist unity. For example at a ceremony in County Waterford he insisted that 'Every effort should be made to achieve unity and maintain it, and almost any concession short of a sacrifice of principle should be made in that direction.' For this reason, Brugha subsequently allowed his name to go forward on the national coalition panel in the five-seat Waterford–Tipperary East constituency at the 1922 election. On 13 June he addressed supporters in Mooncoin (where he was photographed for the last time before his death), Carrick-on-Suir and Clonmel, telling his audience that while he continued to disagree with 'friends on the opposite side', he did not 'say that they were absolutely wrong'. Brugha retained his Dáil seat, but the decisiveness of the election result was a shattering blow to republicans. Nevertheless that the guns of war remained silent offered some solace. The situation changed decisively for Brugha when he learned that borrowed British artillery had been used by the National Army against the anti-Treaty forces in the Four Courts. On 29 June he bid farewell to his wife, Caitlín, and six young children to re-enlist in the IRA as a private. Brugha soon found himself in command of a diminished garrison in a block of buildings on the eastern side of O'Connell Street. Linda Kearns, a member of Cumann na mBan, was certain that Brugha did not intend to surrender and asked if he was 'acting wisely in going to his death'. He replied: 'Civil War is so serious that my death may bring its seriousness home to the Irish people. I feel that if it put a stop to the Civil War, it would be a death worthwhile.' Brugha died on 7 July in the Mater Hospital, having been fatally wounded two days before. While his premature death did not end or shorten the Civil War, it demonstrated a fidelity to the Irish republic. For Brugha, that was sacrosanct – a holy mission for which he was willing to make the ultimate sacrifice. [Text: Daithí Ó Corráin and Gerard Hanley / Image: National Library of Ireland, Poole K 402_001 / Sources: *Tipperary Star*, 11 Mar. 1922; *Waterford News and Star*, 16 June 1922; Linda McWhinney (BMH WS 404, p. 20) / See also Daithí Ó Corráin and Gerard Hanley, *Cathal Brugha: 'an indomitable spirit'* (Dublin, 2022)]

to the complexities of the divided revolutionary Sinn Féin party or the ongoing revolutionary situation in 1922'.[34]

In 2005 Bill Kissane, in *The Politics of the Irish Civil War*, also questioned the democrat versus dictator paradigm, highlighting the issue of coercion within the empire as he simultaneously re-evaluated the wider issue of the roots of Irish democratic culture. The Provisional Government's pursuit of the war without democratic sanction had been widely criticised at the time but the war also culminated in a stable democratic system, suggesting the attachment to democratic culture was deep rooted and predated the Treaty. 'So the vista of a heroic elite forcing democratic values down the throat of a recalcitrant society', wrote Kissane, 'should

Fig. 11 Main Street, Dunmanway, the site of a series of civilian shootings on 27 April 1922. The killing of thirteen west Cork Protestants by the IRA during late April 1922 still resonates over a century later. Following the fatal shooting of an IRA officer in Ballygroman House, near Ovens, County Cork during a confusing nocturnal affray, the three male, Protestant residents were secretly killed by the IRA. Over the next three nights unidentified IRA assailants shot dead ten more male Protestants in the greater Dunmanway/Bandon Valley area, while other Protestants escaped attempted assassination. The killings were condemned in Dorothy Macardle's 1937 monograph *The Irish Republic* and well remembered in west Cork, but were introduced to a new audience by Peter Hart's 1998 study, *The IRA and Its Enemies*. He cited the episode as evidence of sectarianism at the heart of the IRA's campaign in Cork. A 2014 journal article by Andy Bielenberg and John Borgonovo acknowledged the sectarianism of the Bandon Valley killings, but challenged Hart's wider analysis of the event as the culmination of a general sectarian campaign against Cork Protestants throughout the revolution. Historians have generally (though not unanimously) accepted the 2014 interpretation, but it has triggered criticism of its proponents by elements of the Irish media who wish to view the 'Bandon Valley Massacre' as an exemplar of the sectarianism of the republican revolution (1916–23) writ large, viewed retrospectively as a cause of sectarianism in Northern Ireland from 1969 to 1996 (while largely ignoring the far greater number of sectarian killings in Belfast in 1920–22). Although the scholarly debate about the 'Bandon Valley Massacre' has largely ceased, public disputes about the nature of the Bandon Valley killings will likely continue so long as sectarianism remains an element of contemporary Northern Ireland politics. [Image: National Library of Ireland, L_ROY_10976 / See Andy Bielenberg and John Borgonovo, '"Something in the nature of a massacre": The Bandon Valley killings revisited', *Éire-Ireland*, vol. 49, issues 3 & 4, Fall/Winter, 2014, pp. 7–59]

not be taken at face value.'[35] The legal basis for executions by the state was the subject of a specialist study by Seán Enright. It dwelt on the eighty-three executed between 1 September 1922 and 1 June 1923, including those executed 'without trial for acts committed by others' at a time when the 1922 constitution 'guaranteed life, liberty, freedom of conscience and due process or at least trial by military court'.[36]

New biographies of prominent Civil War political leaders rectified a long-standing neglect. Owen McGee observed that Arthur Griffith 'took umbrage' at attempts to label him ideologically but, in looking at the span of his full life, there needs to be an appreciation 'of the debates upon the concept of the nation-state that existed internationally throughout his lifetime'. As contributor to, and mediator of, those debates, as well as being the founder of Sinn Féin, Griffith, as Harry Boland put it, 'made us all'.[37] Boland also died during the Civil War, one of its most high-profile casualties, and the assessment of his life by David Fitzpatrick is another reminder of the danger of simplistic labels. Fitzpatrick concluded that Boland was 'at once a dictator, an elitist, a populist and a democrat [...] whether we consider that he was driven by a laudable conviction in the inalienable rights of nations or a grotesque delusion, the sincerity of his struggle cannot be impugned'.[38] Also on the anti-Treaty side was Cathal Brugha, whose contested legacy has been revisited by Daithí Ó Corráin and Gerard Hanley, while Gerard Shannon reassessed the life and legacy of Liam Lynch.[39]

Sectarianism

The theme of sectarianism during the Civil War era has led to contested scholarship, particularly relating to the months preceding the outbreak of the war: Peter Hart looked closely and controversially at sectarianism in his book *The IRA and Its Enemies: Violence and community in Cork, 1916–1923*, promoting a rancorous historiographical dispute. His most contentious assertions centred on the killing of thirteen Protestants in west Cork over three nights in April 1922 (apparently in response to the fatal shooting of an IRA officer) that sparked the flight of numerous Protestants from the area. Hart argued that communal conflict, and even 'ethnic cleansing', were at the heart of the revolution: 'Protestants had become fair game because they were seen as outsiders and enemies, not just by the IRA but by a large segment of the Catholic population as well.'[40] But he also maintained, in a separate study, 'Republican organisations were officially non-sectarian and this played an important part in dampening down southern ethnic violence, though the IRA were its main practitioners.'[41] Hart also acknowledged that 'Behind the killings lay a jumble of individual histories and possible motives. In the end, however, the fact of the victims' religion is inescapable. These men were shot because they were Protestants.' He also observed, however, 'many of these men had been marked out as enemies [of the IRA] long before April 1922'.[42] Narratives more sympathetic to the republicans have honed in on the idea that those killed were slain spies. Allegations of 'mass murder' in Cork during this period have thus been disputed and the reliability of contrasting accounts contested: supposition, rumour and various possibilities have stitched themselves into competing sermons. What is clear, as Andy Bielenberg and John Borgonovo have shown, is that some IRA members were intent on acting without sanction from their supposed leaders; sectarianism (not divorced from what was happening in Ulster), lust for revenge and anticipation of renewed conflict combined to create a lethal turmoil and a shameful chapter in the history of the period. What happened in west Cork was not, however, representative of a co-ordinated or widespread strategy.[43]

Transformative period

The research space opened up by witness accounts, personal testimony and other archival material in the early twenty-first century was transformative, especially as so much became available online. Particularly notable was the 2003 release of the Bureau of Military History (BMH) interviews (the result of a state-sponsored oral history project conducted in the 1940s and 1950s to collect testimony from men and women involved in the revolutionary period 1913–21) and the beginning of the release of the Military Service Pensions Collection (generated by applications from veterans of the groups active from 1913 to 1923) were particularly notable. Collectively, the scale of the sources underlined the veracity of the assertion made by Peter Hart: that Ireland is a great laboratory for the study of revolution because 'Ireland's is quite possibly the best documented revolution in modern history'.[44]

Despite the official chronological cut-off point of the Truce of July 1921 for the BMH testimonies, Eve Morrison has noted that 'statements and documents dealing with the Civil War were accepted almost from the beginning. About seventeen percent of the statements covering the period after 1917 discuss the Civil War, though not always in much detail.'[45]

The efforts of Ernie O'Malley, given oxygen through the publishing projects of his son Cormac, a remarkably determined keeper of his father's literary and historical flame, ensured that the anti-Treaty perspective was also well documented. From the late 1940s O'Malley interviewed almost 500 veterans, including many who did not make statements to the BMH. Those have been transcribed and published by numerous historians. The 'Men Will Talk to Me' series encompasses veteran interviews from the IRA's Northern Division, west Cork and counties Clare, Kerry, Galway and Mayo. Gavin Foster suggests that O'Malley's interviews can be seen as 'a shadow project or counter-archive to the government's efforts, highlighting the revolutionary activities of primarily anti-Treaty Volunteers who, often for political reasons, did not participate in the state's efforts to (rather selectively) historicise and commemorate its revolutionary origins'. 'Moreover', writes Foster, 'the candid conversations collected by O'Malley provide an almost inverse focus on the traumatising 1922–3 conflict [...] O'Malley's interviews often provide explicit and chilling details of a wider range of extra-judicial murder and almost casual brutality against prisoners.'[46]

Another important transformation in the historiography was the challenging of the 'men who made it' narrative or the 'brother against brother' framework. Many historians built on the pioneering work of Margaret Ward, who had noted in *Unmanageable Revolutionaries: Women and Irish nationalism* the determination to keep women out of the fighting: 'at no stage were [women] accepted as equal members'.[47] Thirty years later there was much interest in the fate and correspondence of interned and imprisoned women, seen in Ann Matthew's *Dissidents* (2012); but preceding that there were numerous studies of the broader social, cultural, educational and religious contexts relating to the status of women, for example in Senia Pašeta's *Before the Revolution: Nationalism, social change and Ireland's Catholic elite, 1872–1922* (1999). There was also a determination by Ward and others to document the women's own voices as seen with *In Their Own Voice, Women and Irish Nationalism* (1995). These books are a reminder of the inaccuracy of blanket assertions about Irish women being 'written out of history'. As Mary McAuliffe noted in 2020, 'the last four decades have seen an upsurge of interest in and research and writing on women's experience and involvement in the revolutionary decade'.[48]

This was also reflected in the focus on women active in Cumann na mBan and their later battles for military service pensions. As Marie Coleman explains, 'a strict demarcation between the less regarded work of Cumann na mBan and that of providing military support for the IRA informed the attitude of pension assessors'. Dangerous work such as transferring rifles was summarily dismissed as 'routine work' and 'to succeed in obtaining a pension they had

50/APB/2127.

STATEMENT OF MISS SARAH SHEEHY.

I am 35 years of age. I joined Cumann na mBan in 1917. "A" Co. Tralee. In 1917 I was doing prop aganda work. I also removed arms two or 3 times from the home of the Captain of the Volunteer Coy. In 1918 and 1919 I was engaged in propaganda, collecting funds for Volunteers, arranging dances, etc. In the summer of 1920 after the arrival of the Tans, I was engaged in removing arms and intercepting arms in the town of Tralee on several occasions. There was an attack in Tralee Town one November night 1920. I carried verbal despatches in the Boherbee district of the town. I was out all night that night. I did not sleep at home for 2 weeks after. I used to scout the roads outside the town up to about 12 o'clock and stop in farmers houses around. Some nights we had dances in the houses. From that time up to the Truce I was engaged in the shifting of arms, observation duty, etc. I wasn't out at night. I slept at my own house. In August 1922 I left my job to take part in the Civil War. I was directly attached to Brigade H.Q., at Ashe Hill and Knocknane, for Humphrey Murphy. I carried despatches every day to and from Tralee on foot, a total journey of 14 miles, sometimes twice a day. I hardly ever slept at home during the Civil War. I slept in neighbours' houses. I continued on until May 1924. I was never sick in my life before that. I broke down in 1924. I got a nervous breakdown. I was attended by Dr. Coffey, Tralee, and Dr. Shanahan, Farranfore. I felt sick for about 3 months before I gave up. I was 6 weeks under the Doctors care. I went back to work sometime in New Year 1925. I got sick again in 1925. Dr. Coffey attended me for a couple of weeks. I got abscesses and was run down. I went to U.S.A. in 1928. I broke down when I got there and attended a Doctor all the time. I was there. I returned in 1932. I was engaged as a lady's companion in U.S.A. The work was not hard. I went back to U.S.A. in September 1932 and returned March 1933. I went again in May 1935 and returned in October that year. I have done no work since, not even house work. I went to Dr. Quinlan sometime in 1933 or 1934. He examined my heart and advised me to stay at home. I was insured in the Slainte Insurance Co. I do not know my number. I attribute my breakdown to my activities during the Civil War. I had to do very hard work, not suitable to a woman at all. walking and cycling long distances against time, etc. I was held up at night several times by Free State Soldiers. After the Ballyseedy Mine tragedy I was one of the party that gathered the remains of the dead - bodies, brains, clothes. I was often with an ambush party and caught in cross fire. There was an ambush practically every day for the first 3 months of the Civil War.

SIGNED: Sarah Sheehy

WITNESS: [illegible signature]

ST. BRICIN'S HOSPITAL,
DUBLIN.

7th December, 1937.

Fig. 12 (opposite) Statement by Sarah Sheehy, 7 December 1937, in support of her claim for a disability pension following a nervous breakdown in 1924, that she attributed to her active service with Cumann na mBan in Kerry, 1922–4. The Military Service Pension Collection (MSPC) is a major primary source for any researcher of the Civil War in Ireland but also for anyone interested in the nature of civil wars more generally. The MSPC is versatile and dense, inviting a range of approaches to the study of its content. The reader can focus on localities and microhistories or use the vast archive as a source for discerning wider trends that provide a more nuanced national picture. Most file series contain valuable factual data, be it membership strengths of the IRA or information about operations during the revolutionary period. The IRA, Cumann na mBan and Fianna Éireann Nominal Rolls afford a solid basis to compare organisational strengths between the War of Independence and the start of the Civil War. The brigade activity reports contain details of many IRA operations conducted against the National Army during the Civil War. Individual pension applications are extremely valuable sources for examining different aspects of the Civil War in Ireland. Chronologically, the first military service applications were those of the National Army veterans (24SP series) claiming for their Easter Rising, War of Independence and Civil War service. If personal accounts remain limited in that particular series, statements by men and women in pensions claims lodged under the Military Service Pensions Act 1934 are more expansive, due to the body of evidence requested by the referee and his advisory committee. From the files, it is clear that Civil War tensions and divisions were exacerbated by the pension legislation that regulated the award of pensions. Those who died during the Civil War are represented in the MSPC through the claims of their relatives. The archival material associated with the dependants' claims is of the utmost interest, as it provides an abundance of personal information about the composition and living circumstances of families, as well as the life of the deceased. The MSPC contains files relating to over a thousand Civil War fatalities (pro- and anti-Treaty, who died between 28 June 1922 and 31 December 1924) as well as files relating to seventy-four men executed as a result of their service with anti-Treaty forces, including three departmental files created in the context of Erskine Childers's arrest, his execution and its aftermath. The Civil War in Kerry, for instance, is well documented: more than 200 individuals claimed in respect of 157 fatalities in the county (84 National Army members and 73 IRA members). While the MSPC contains evidence relating to the epicentres of Civil War violence, its greatest strength lies in its potential to provide a wider picture of each pivotal event and of the conflict as a whole: the files offer social, political and military context, details of the protagonists and evidence of the aftershocks. Some material affords a sense of immediacy, while other files reveal the broader impact of war on individuals and families, on those standing at the periphery of those epicentres. The trauma endured by the survivors of violence is also discernible in the MSPC. The files relating to Joseph O'Brien, for example, who survived the explosion at Knocknagoshel (6 March 1923) or Stephen Fuller, the sole survivor of the 'Ballyseedy Massacre' (7 March 1923), describe their life-altering wounds, and the testimony of the women, including Sarah Sheehy, who 'gathered the remains of the dead' following the atrocity at Ballyseedy reveal deep psychological scars. The collection also allows for the investigation of emigration trends among many thousands of young men and women on the 'losing side' who left the country in the aftermath of the Civil War. The MSPC is made of tens of thousands of files and each constitutes a snapshot of an individual's life, with their own history and circumstances. This continues to remind us of the unique capacity of the archives to let us see what is on the margins of what we think we know. [Text: Cécile Chemin / Source: MSP34REF56706 Sarah Sheehy / Image: courtesy of Military Archives/ MSPC Project]

FARRANFORE,
CO. KERRY.

April 22. 1938.

This is to certify that I have this day examined Miss Sarah Sheehy. I find she has softening of first heart sound in the mitral area, accentuation of second sound in aortic area, together with palpitation.

She suffers from severe nervous prostration amounting to that of a nervous wreck. She is getting progressively worse. I attended her for a period in January of this year after examination before Pensions Board. She was in a shocking condition of nerves. Only for heavy dosage of luminal she certainly would have lost her mental balance. I knew her previous to 1924 to be an active healthy girl. Now she is absolutely unfit to earn a living.

Edmond R. Shanahan M.B., B.Ch. B.A.O.

Fig. 13 (above) Letter from Dr Edmund Shanahan, Farranfore, 22 April 1938, to the Army Pensions Board. Dr Shanahan's report focuses on Sarah Sheehy's 'shocking' mental and physical condition, which, he asserts, made her wholly unfit for work. Despite his diagnosis of 'severe nervous prostration amounting to that of a nervous wreck', the Army Pensions Board contended that her state amounted to only 60 per cent disablement, 20 per cent less than the minimum requirement for a disability pension. Her condition continued to deteriorate and, after another medical assessment, she was eventually awarded a special allowance. Notably, the vocabulary used in the doctor's letter is similar to that used to describe veterans of the First World War who were suffering from shell-shock and cardiac diseases. [Source: MSP34REF56706, Sarah Sheehy / Image: courtesy of Military Archives/ MSPC Project] to prove that they had transgressed gender norms'. There were five grades of pension, A–E, but women were confined to the two lower grades of D and E on the grounds that, in the words of Minister for Defence Frank Aiken in 1934, 'their responsibilities were not as great' as those of the IRA.[49] But as Claire McGing points out, Cumann na mBan 'undertook most of the republican propaganda responsibilities' during the Civil War when they also 'assumed more overtly military and thus less gendered duties'; at least 400 of them were incarcerated compared to about fifty during the War of Independence. On the back of these efforts and activities, writes McGing, the contention that women were 'too inflexible, bitter and emotional for politics' took hold; they were 'practically unsexed' according to P.S. O'Hegarty.[50]

Cultural taboo

Some women were also subjected to sexual assault, as evidenced by the horrific gang rape of Protestant woman Eileen Biggs in Dromineer, County Tipperary in June 1922, a case detailed by Gemma Clark and Linda Connolly. Biggs was a young married woman from the Protestant landowning class, who described how 'I was outraged by different men in turn, one after the other [...] I believe I was outraged altogether on 8 or 9 different occasions.'[51] The rape devastated the family for decades and Eileen ended up in psychiatric care: 'we cannot hold up our heads amongst friends and acquaintances', she said afterwards.[52] Clarke explains that some women suffered 'serious and traumatising interpersonal violence – often on account of their gender', but there were cultural and religious restraints that militated against 'the need for sexual violence as warfare'.[53] Linda Connolly, however, suggests, 'the issue of whether such violence was unequivocally or exceptionally "rare" in Ireland's Civil War is considered an issue that requires much more in-depth research, understanding, and contextualization in Irish historical studies'.[54]

The centenary of the Civil War also resulted in the publication of the long-neglected memoir of Máire Comerford, *On Dangerous Ground*. An incomplete version had been deposited in the UCD Archives in the 1970s and there were other parts of it in her own archive. Her intention was that it would be published in her lifetime. Editor Hilary Dully chose not to retrospectively contextualise the text but instead preserve the 'authenticity of Máire's voice in the telling of her story'.[55] That voice was righteous about the Civil War; by the time she found herself in the Four Courts in June 1922: 'I was in a place where there was no need for argument, and among people whose unanimity was like a distilled spirit of highest concentration.'[56]

Also relevant was the long-term impact the Civil War had on the status of women; the new state for women, according to Margaret Ward, was 'a far cry' from the idealism of revolutionary promise. She quotes the memorable summing up by Sheila Humphreys of the bleak new Free State dawn for female republican activists: 'We were flattened. We felt the Irish public had forgotten us. The tinted trappings of our fight were hanging like rags about us.'[57]

Fig. 14 (opposite) Map showing the Sack of Ballyconnell, County Cavan, 6 February 1923, by the Arigna column of the IRA. The attack on the town resulted in the killing of William Ryan, a shop assistant at the local hardware shop and Seán McGrath, a teacher. The owner of the hardware shop, William Owens, also suffered grave injuries in the attack. The IRA column was intent on revenge for the killing of one of its own men, Michael Cull, by a National Army officer during a raid on the same hardware shop the previous month. The killings that took place in the town were condemned by leading government figures, including the minister for defence, Richard Mulcahy, who described the actions of the column as 'a particular type of madness', and the minister for justice, Kevin O'Higgins, who called the killings 'the most unnatural thing that has happened since this unnatural strife began' (McGarty, p. 126). The events in Ballyconnell are now well documented by John Dorney, Patrick McGarty and Dermot McMonagle. Similar research conducted across the country has allowed for a more comprehensive and in-depth picture to emerge of not only the military conflict itself and the lives lost – combatants and civilians – but also the wider socio-economic impact of the war on specific localities. *The Irish Revolution* county series (of which McGarty's study of Leitrim is a part), edited by Mary Ann Lyons and Daithí Ó Corráin, has been an important vehicle in underlining the value of local and regional research. In examining the spatial as well as the temporal, such studies have facilitated a much more fine-grained and nuanced understanding of the Civil War and its impact. [Source for map: Dermot McMonagle, Patrick McGarty and John Dorney / See Patrick McGarty, *The Irish Revolution 1912–23: Leitrim* (Dublin, 2020), pp. 124–7 and John Dorney, 'The Tragedies of Ballyconnell', *The Irish Story*, https://www.theirishstory.com/2014/06/19/the-tragedies-of-ballyconnell]

Local perspectives

Numerous local studies of the Civil War have underlined its regional dynamics and various of its turning points, including Michael Fewer's *The Battle for the Four Courts* (2018), focusing on the initial fighting in Dublin and incorporating the destruction of the Public Record Office. John Dorney has dissected the conflict in Dublin, combining minute attention to detail with a focus on lawlessness and extrajudicial killings, hallmarks of a conflict that was 'intensely local and at the same time national'.[58] Padraig Yeates's trilogy of historical overviews of Dublin city during the revolution, including *The City in Civil War*, reminds us that many of the victims of violent events were civilians with divided loyalties. Yeates's research of contemporary newspapers and private archives offers a multitude of perspectives on the political, military and administrative concerns of an elite involved in governance, but his book is also filled with the struggles of ordinary people living their lives during extraordinary political and economic upheaval. His Civil War study concludes with 'the abolition of three of Dublin's great institutions: the city council, the South Dublin Union and the Dublin Metropolitan Police'.[59]

John Borgonovo looked specifically at *The Battle for Cork* in 2011, the outcome of which suggested the appetite of former comrades to fight each other was dulled. But it was not just about the military environment; there had been strikes and soviets in the city in the Spring of 1922 and class tensions were paramount.[60] Owen O' Shea has examined the conflict in detail in Kerry, the county where the final, brutal phase of the war was most acute, with a particular attention given to the personal testimonies of the combatants, but also the speed with which the conflict shifted to the electoral arena.[61] Kerry is also the focus of Fergal Keane's

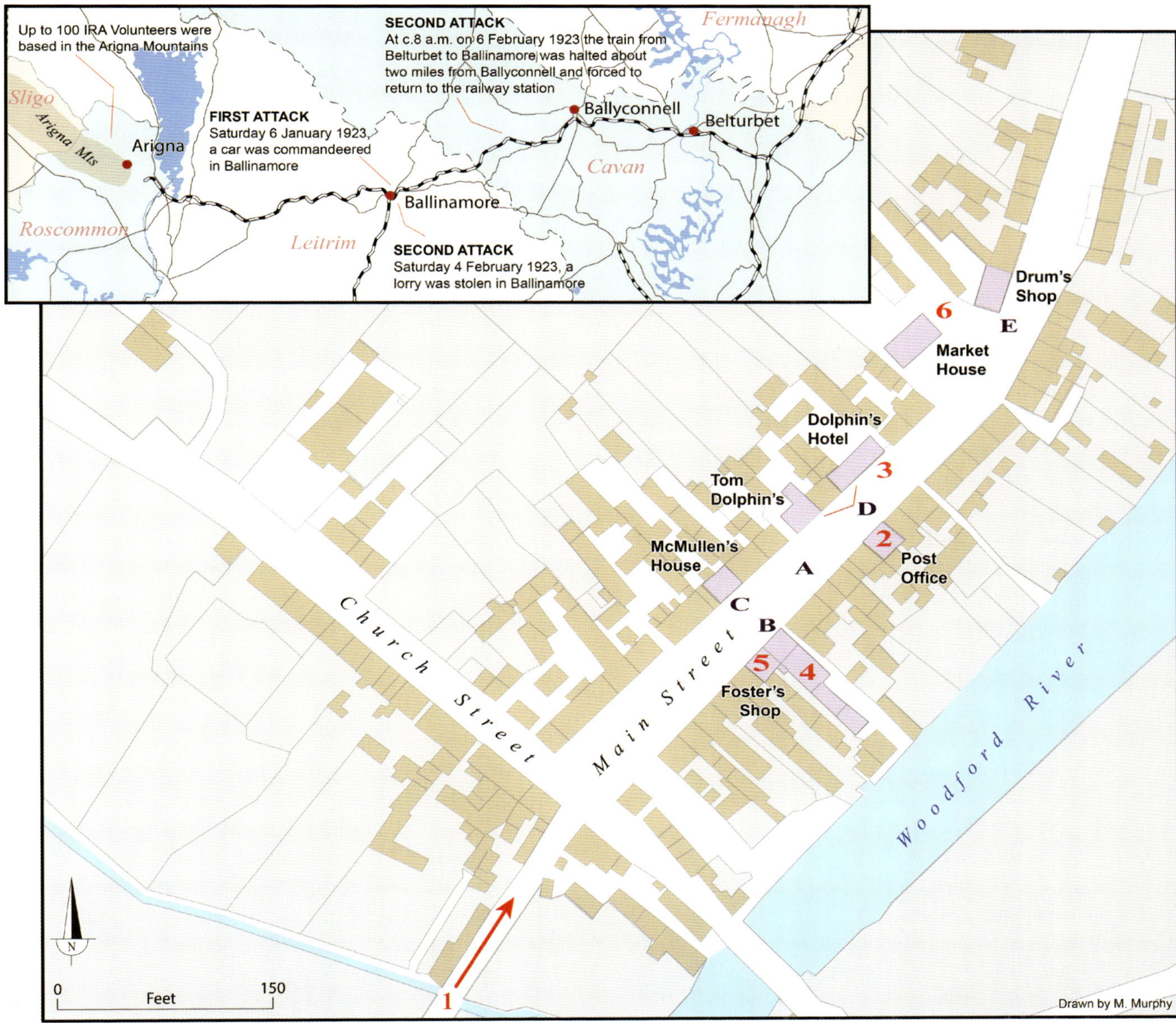

IRA attacks on Ballyconnell, County Cavan, 1923

FIRST ATTACK: Saturday 6 January 1923

1. Two IRA Volunteers commandeered a car and driver in Ballinamore and proceeded to Ballyconnell.
2. At *c.*1.30 p.m. the two men entered the post office asking for cash and military correspondence, and then dismantled the phone system. The assistant went looking for the postmistress, Annie Crawfield (her sister).
3. On hearing the commotion in the post office, Annie went out the back to Dolphin's Hotel and alerted two National Army officers, Frank Dolphin and J.F. Kellegher.
4. Meanwhile the raiders had moved onto Foster's hardware shop co-owned by Willie Owens. One of the shop assistants on duty was named Ryan. After emptying the till, Michael Cull and his companion opened the shop safe, just as the armed Dolphin and Kellegher entered. The raiders made their escape from the shop and exchanged fire with the two soldiers in the street. Cull was preparing to throw a Mills bomb when he was struck by a bullet and died instantly.
5. A local doctor who examined the body noted that the dead Cull still held the Mills bomb in his hand. The other raider, although injured, made his getaway in the waiting car.

SECOND ATTACK: Tuesday 6 February 1923

A. At 8:00 a.m. a group of about fifty well-armed IRA Volunteers travelling in two motor vehicles and carrying two machine guns arrived in town. They disabled the post office telephone exchange and moved through the town, visiting numerous shops and seizing goods.
B. At Foster's hardware shop they took shop assistant William Ryan out onto the street, apparently connecting him to the death of Cull the previous month. The shop proprietor Willie Owens was also taken outside. They then set fire to the Foster's premises.
C. Ryan was shot multiple times, stumbled across the street to McMullen's front door, and died. Owens was shot in the thigh but survived.
D. The IRA party moved up Main Street, bombed Thomas Dolphin's shop and burned Dolphin's Hotel. The windows of Ulster Bank were broken and £200 was taken. Other premises in the town were looted.
E. The raiders also visited a shop owned by the Drum family, and its adjoining residence. Assorted family members were being held at gunpoint when their lodger, twenty-four-year-old Irish teacher Seán McGrath, entered the home and was shot. He died later that afternoon. After controlling the town for over thirty minutes, the IRA Volunteers remounted their vehicles and headed back towards the Arigna Hills.

family memoir *Wounds*, meditating on the consequences of an 'accumulating local viciousness' and its aftermath, also drawing on the Military Service Pensions Collection.[62] Distinct county perspectives have also been produced in the Four Courts Press series, 'The Irish Revolution, 1912–23' edited by Mary Ann Lyons and Daithí Ó Corráin. Geographical variance and nuance also emerged as a key theme from the Civil War section of the 2017 *Atlas of the Irish Revolution*.[63]

Disillusioned and impoverished

One of the most interesting strands of Civil War historiography has involved looking at the social and economic elements; in 1996 Conor Kostick made the point that, for all the focus on the conservative outcome of the revolution, the violence did at times prompt 'popular militancy that raised the prospect of a deeply radical upheaval' in the North and South; including, for example, a six-week occupation of the Waterford gas works.[64] Two more recent studies also stand out: Gavin Foster's *The Irish Civil War and Society* and Gemma Clark's *Everyday Violence in the Irish Civil War*. Social status was a key component of friction, and there was bilious sermonising from the pro-Treaty side about misguided republican youth, 'foolish young men', 'young hot bloods' and the 'attraction of the wild life'. These characterisations dovetailed with the lambasting of the women deemed to be neurotic and hysterical. Foster noted that the use of other insults such as 'city scum', 'corner boys', 'brigands' and 'blackguards' to describe those in arms against the Treaty suggested deeper snobberies and a 'degree of internal colonisation'.[65] The Free State's ministers and (paid) soldiers were accused of self-seeking materialism (Cosgrave was on an annual salary of £2,500, his ministers £1,700), in contrast to the self-sacrifice of the unpaid republicans.

A related theme was republican emigrants – a 'lost legion', according to writer Frank O'Connor. Gavin Foster points out that roughly 220,000 people left the Free State for the United States in the 1920s and another estimated 185,000 relocated to the British dominions or Great Britain; the Civil War disillusioned and impoverished were part of a very broad exodus.[66] Gemma Clark explores the economic impact, class, sectarianism and sexual crime and emphasises the value of the local study in understanding a war in which violence was not the sole preserve of armed combatants; 'intra-community conflicts over land and religion' also raged, with a need to understand 'the form, function and symbolism of the violent act'.[67]

Given what Calton Younger had maintained in 1968 about empathy, it is interesting that more recent accounts have also stressed the importance of giving sufficient weight to the emotional charge of 1922–3 and the need to 'bring the war back' to those who fought it, recognising that, in the words of Brian Hanley, 'any balanced discussion of terror in twentieth-century Ireland must identify all of its origins and agencies, not just those which conform to our own opinions and prejudices'.[68]

Important gaps remain; research efforts are ongoing to match the accuracy now given to the figures for the War of Independence dead.[69] But there has been serious, thoughtful engagement with the aftermath and commemoration of the war, most skilfully in Anne Dolan's *Commemorating the Irish Civil War*, reflecting on 'the memory of civil war' at a time when 'no one else has even bothered to count the lives it claimed'.[70] It is also about memories that are 'assumed, distorted, misunderstood'. The shame felt that things descended to the point they did and the fact that the Irish democratic culture predated the Civil War combined to act as a salve of sorts. Dolan suggested 'although there could be no forgetting, there was a will to forget […] the end had been reached; there was no need to reminisce about the means'.[71] That attitude facilitated a speedy political recovery, though the trauma experienced and internalised has yet to be fully aired and is likely to be central to future accounts of the impact of the conflict.

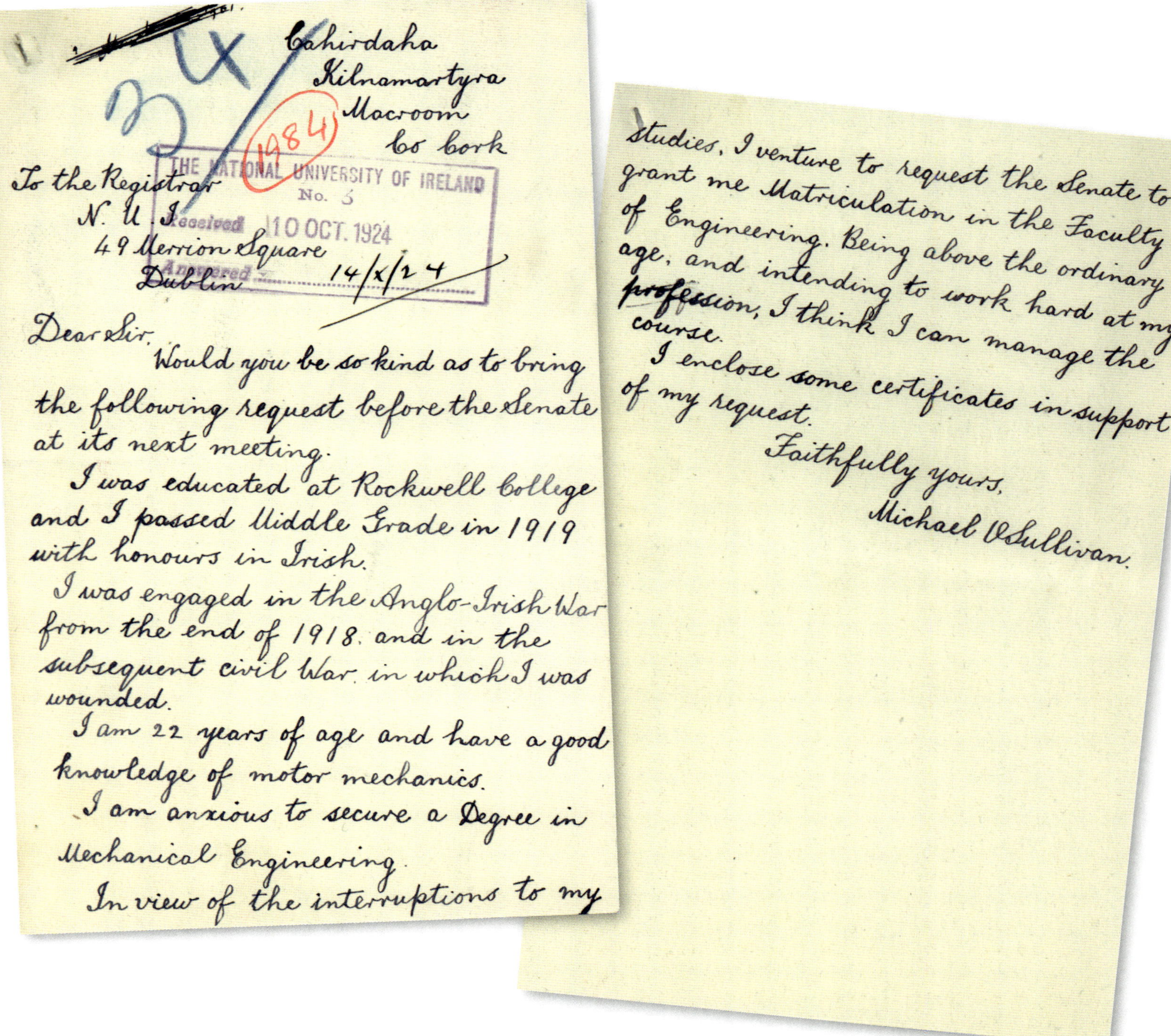

Cahirdaha
Kilnamartyra
Macroom
Co Cork

To the Registrar
N. U. I.
49 Merrion Square
Dublin

THE NATIONAL UNIVERSITY OF IRELAND
No. 3
Received 10 OCT. 1924
Answered

(1984)

14/x/24

Dear Sir,

Would you be so kind as to bring the following request before the Senate at its next meeting.

I was educated at Rockwell College and I passed Middle Grade in 1919 with honours in Irish.

I was engaged in the Anglo-Irish War from the end of 1918. and in the subsequent civil War. in which I was wounded.

I am 22 years of age and have a good knowledge of motor mechanics.

I am anxious to secure a Degree in Mechanical Engineering.

In view of the interruptions to my studies, I venture to request the Senate to grant me Matriculation in the Faculty of Engineering. Being above the ordinary age, and intending to work hard at my ~~profession~~, I think I can manage the course.

I enclose some certificates in support of my request.

Faithfully yours,
Michael O'Sullivan.

Fig. 15 Letter from twenty-two-year-old Michael O'Sullivan, Cahirdaha, Kilnamartyra, Macroom, County Cork to the Registrar of the National University of Ireland. O'Sullivan asks that his request for an exemption from matriculation in the University College Cork (UCC) Faculty of Mechanical Engineering be brought before the next meeting of the NUI Senate. He outlines how his studies were interrupted because he was 'engaged in the Anglo-Irish War from the end of 1918 and in the subsequent civil war in which [he] was wounded'. O'Sullivan and his brother Patrick of Kilnamartyra were both UCC students who became highly active in the IRA. Patrick commanded the 8th (Ballyvourney) Battalion in the Cork No. 1 Brigade, one of the most prominent fighting units in mid-Cork, and Michael served alongside him throughout 1919–23. Both brothers participated in multiple ambushes, raids and other actions during both the War of Independence and Civil War. While Patrick completed his medical studies at UCC a few years after the Civil War and practised medicine for over forty years, Michael never resumed his studies. Writing under the name Micheál Ó Súilleabháin in 1965, he published a popular memoir of his revolutionary experiences, *Where the Mountainy Men have Sown: War and peace in rebel Cork in the turbulent years, 1916–1921*. Like many anti-Treaty IRA authors, he limited his remembrances to the war against the British, and excluded the Civil War. [Document: courtesy of the National University of Ireland Archive, and John Foley, retired administration officer, NUI]

Dorothy Macardle: 'an unlikely republican'

Leeann Lane

Dorothy Macardle (1889–1958), daughter of Thomas Callan Macardle, owner of Macardle Moore Brewery, Dundalk, was an unlikely republican. A university graduate, she was living in Stratford-upon-Avon in 1916, immersed not in Irish revolutionary politics but in the literature of Shakespeare. Returning to Ireland in 1917, her Irish 'awakening' came with her involvement in the Irish theatre movement, meeting Constance Markievicz and Maud Gonne, moving politically and assuming an advanced nationalist position. In 1952 Macardle recalled how, on 8 November 1922, she was 'suddenly translated from the position of lecturer in Alexandra College to that of a military prisoner in Mountjoy Jail'. In arresting women such as Macardle who did not have a previous history of incarceration, the pro-Treaty side showed an understanding that republican women posed a direct threat to the establishment of the Irish Free State. During her six-month incarceration in Mountjoy, Kilmainham and, briefly, in the North Dublin Union, Macardle's republican persona evolved. She maintained a jail journal in which she detailed the common experiences of female republican prisoners grappling with damp, unsanitary and overcrowded conditions and the constant threat of violence by prison officials. Macardle likened

A Message From Mountjoy.

....

<u>To the People of Ireland.</u>

We, the sixteen women of the Republic who share Miss Mac Swiney's
imprisonment in Mountjoy, send out to the men and women of Ireland a
most urgent and vehement appeal.
Miss Mac Swiney has now fasted for eleven days, denied the
sacraments which were her brother's consolation. Her thoughts have been
all for Ireland and for our welfare here. Patient and loving she has
struggled to hide her suffering from us. But to-day a terrible change
has come. Exhaustion has set in; she is scarcely able to speak. We
know, as do all who ever knew her, that she will persist to the end, and
we know that the end is near. Our hearts are breaking, but here we a
helpless. We can do nothing but pray.
What effort, what danger, what sacrifice is it not worth, to save
for Ireland so noble a life as this? What is it not worth to save
Ireland from the ineffaceable shame of having, through cowardice or inaction, allowed Terence Mac Swiney's sister to die in an Irish gaol?
He gave his life willingly, a prisoner in the hands of the
English enemy. Mary Mac Swiney is a prisoner in the hands of Irishmen.
No one, friend or enemy, needs to be told what Miss Mac Swiney's
protest means. As Ireland, physically weak but spiritually inconquerable,
withstood the brute force of an Empire, so this great woman, in prison
and helpless, challenges with her dauntless will the force that would
give Ireland over for ever to the domination of a foreign power.
Whichever way the struggle ends, victory will be with her who
can endure so much and with the cause for which she is going to her
agony, joyous if her death will bring back her fellow-countrymen to
their ideals and make them brothers-in-arms again.
She is one of the people's representatives. Let the people of
Ireland see that the crime of her death be not perpetrated against them.
Irishman and women, will you allow the sister of Terence Mac Swiney
to die for you in an Irish gaol.

(Signed)

Nel Bean Mhic Amhlaoibh.
D. Cogley.
Lili Ni Bhraonain.
Kathleen Devaney.
Rita Birmingham.
Cecilia Gallagher.
Dorothy Macardle.
Sighle Nic Amhlaoibh.
Brighid Ni Mhaolain.
Esther Davis.
Caitlin Ni Chearbhaill.
Maire McKee.
K. Doody.
T. O'Connell.
S. Dowling.
Maire Deegan.

the oppressive physical space of the prison to a form of living death for the inmates. Adopting certain signifiers of what it was to be an Irish republican – involvement in 1916, familial connections to republicanism and previous jail experience – Macardle believed that she did not measure up to fellow prisoners such as Nora Connolly and Mary MacSwiney. When she entered Mountjoy in November 1922, the female wing of the prison reverberated with discussion of MacSwiney's hunger strike, which she had begun immediately on her arrest on 4 November. Macardle believed that imprisonment would accord her republican credentials, but she feared having to engage in hunger strike. After much inner questioning, she did participate in the week-long hunger strike in Kilmainham beginning on 23 March, declaring in *The Irish Republic* (1937) that the right to send and receive letters were 'essentials of political treatment'. Released in May 1923, the inferiority she had felt due to the lack of a fully developed republican past vis-à-vis her fellow prisoners had been eliminated by her jail sacrifice. She was determined to deploy her intellectual and literary skills in the service of the republic yet to be established. Her prison experience attuned her to the value of propaganda and the way a prisoner and his or her treatment could be utilised as a tool in the war of words. The Civil War prison experience, both her own and that of her comrades, was presented by her as a new instalment of the Anglo-Irish story. The depravity of the English was, in many respects, surpassed for Macardle by the cowardice of those who accepted the Irish Free State as a solution to the Irish national question. The way those who accepted the Treaty had betrayed their former comrades forms the theme of her poem 'Captivity', written in Kilmainham Gaol in 1923.

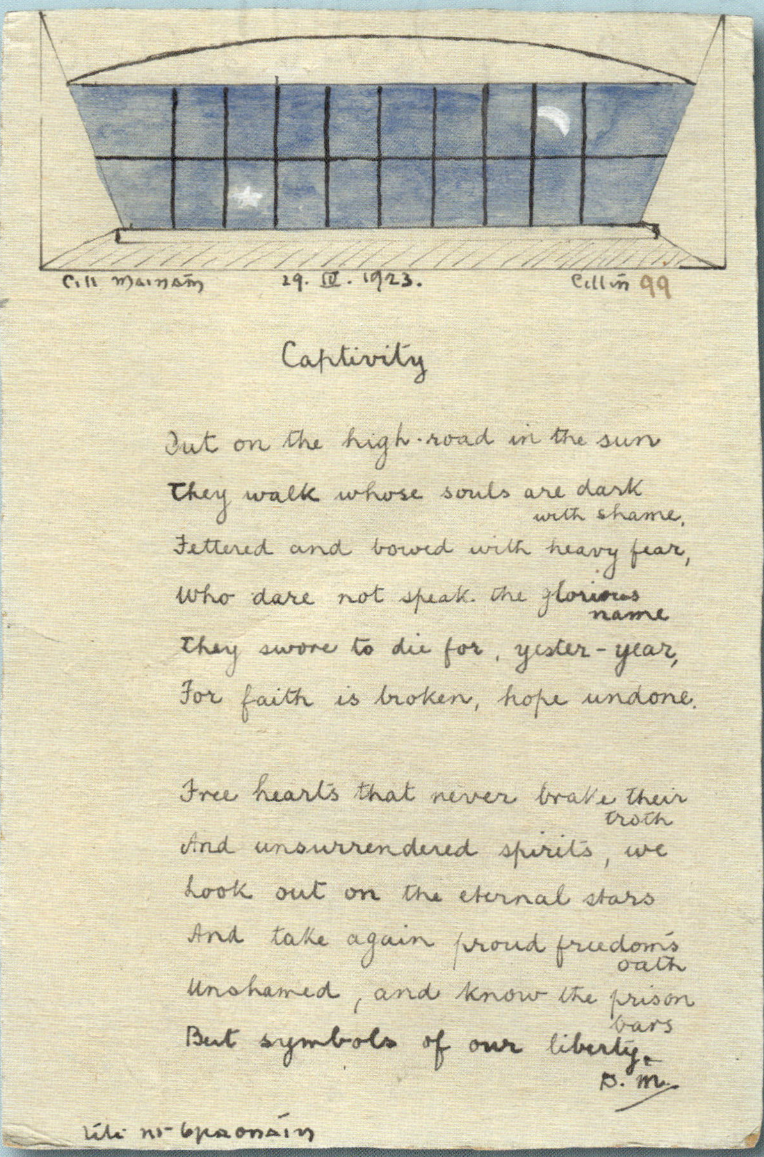

Cill Maiġnain 29. IV. 1923. Cillín 99

Captivity

Out on the high-road in the sun
They walk whose souls are dark with shame,
Fettered and bowed with heavy fear,
Who dare not speak the glorious name
They swore to die for, yester-year,
For faith is broken, hope undone.

Free hearts that never brake their troth
And unsurrendered spirits, we
Look out on the eternal stars
And take again proud freedom's oath
Unshamed, and know the prison bars
But symbols of our liberty.

D. M.

Lili ní-Ḃraonáin

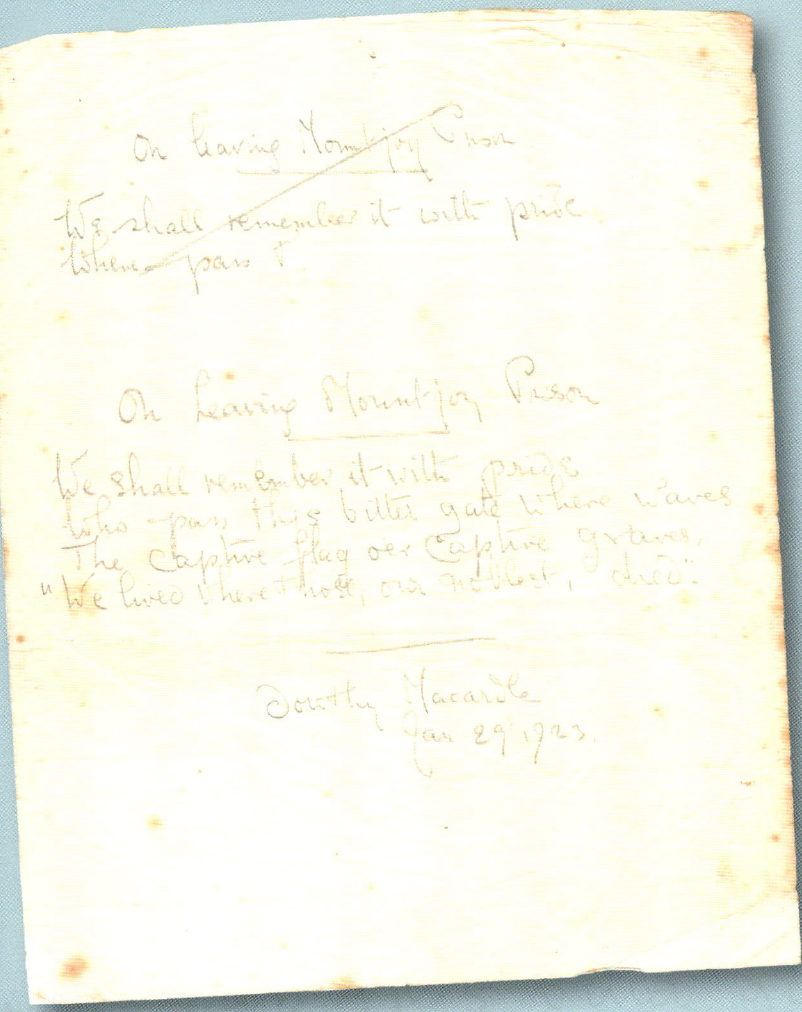

~~On Leaving Mountjoy Prison~~

~~We shall remember it with pride~~
~~Where pass~~

On Leaving Mountjoy Prison

We shall remember it with pride
Who pass this bitter gate where waves
The captive flag oer captive graves
"We lived there those, our noblest, died."

Dorothy Macardle
Jan 29 1923.

Fig. 1 (opposite page) Typed carbon copy of an appeal on behalf of the hunger striker Mary MacSwiney, signed by, among others, Lily O'Brennan and Dorothy Macardle. [Document: courtesy of Kilmainham Gaol Museum / OPW, 20MS-1B42-06]

Fig. 2 (left) 'On Leaving Mountjoy Prison', poem written in pencil by Dorothy Macardle, 29 January 1923. [Document: courtesy of Kilmainham Gaol Museum / OPW, 20MS-1B32-29]

Fig. 3 (above, right) 'Captivity', poem written by Dorothy Macardle while a prisoner in Kilmainham Gaol during the Civil War. It was copied and illustrated by her fellow prisoner, Lily O'Brennan on 29 April 1923. [Document: courtesy of Kilmainham Gaol Museum / OPW, 2019.0057]

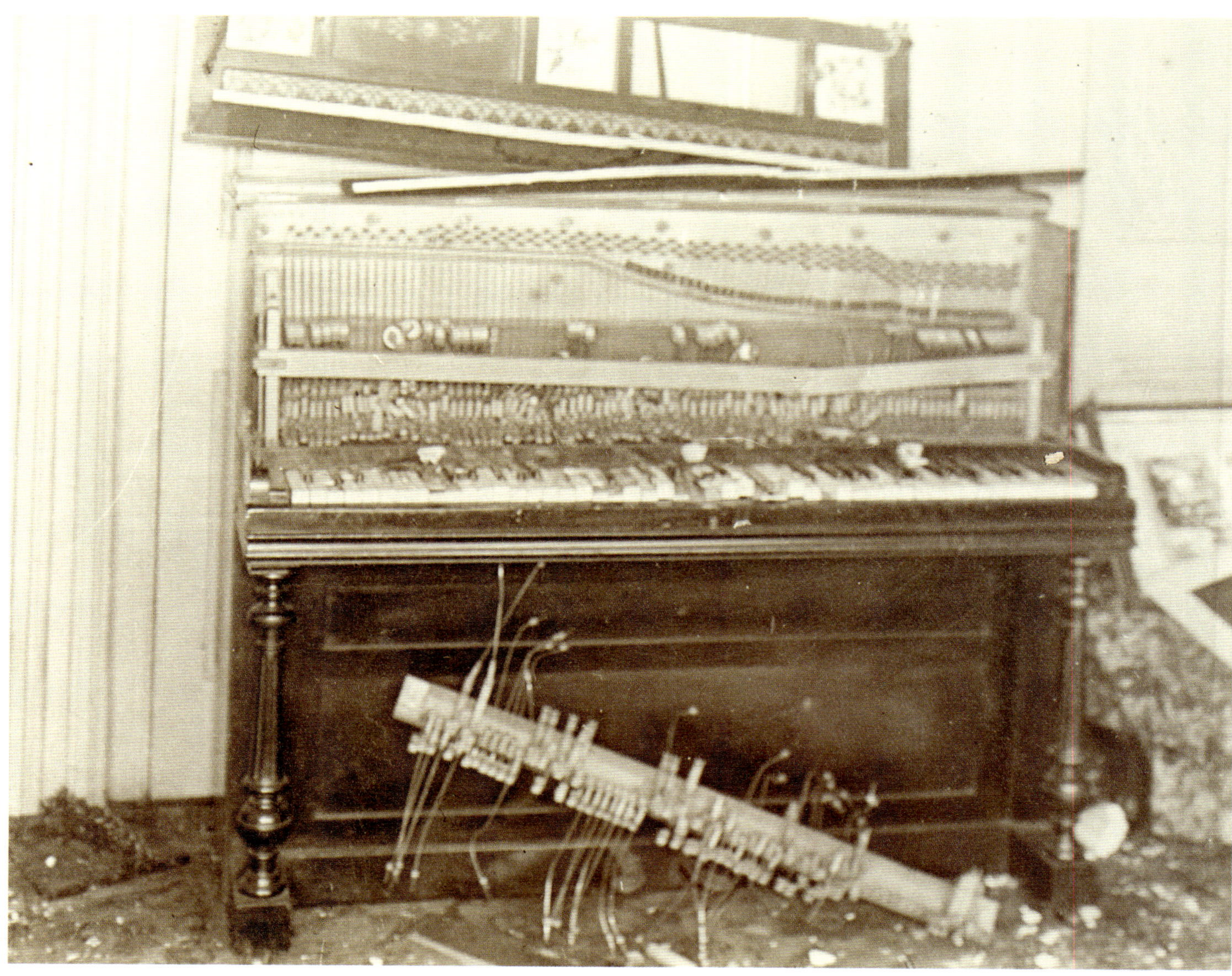

Fig. 1 The silent piano at Áine Ceannt's home on Oakley Road, Ranelagh, Dublin damaged during a National Army raid in 1922. Widow of musician, Irish Volunteer leader and executed signatory of the 1916 proclamation, Éamonn Ceannt, and a prominent cultural and political separatist in her own right, Áine Ceannt suffered a series of violent domestic raids between 1916 and 1923. The first occurred during Easter Week when she and her ten-year-old son, Rónán, having abandoned their home in Dolphin's Barn for the relative safety of the suburbs, returned to find the doors and windows smashed and their belongings ransacked. Elected Cumann na mBan vice-president and co-opted onto the Sinn Féin national executive in 1917, Ceannt was also an executive member of the Irish National Aid and Volunteers' Dependants' Fund, a vehicle for the distribution of both aid and propaganda, and a focal point for republican coherence and reorganisation in the wake of the Rising. New responsibilities emerged in 1920 for the indefatigable Ceannt, when she was elected vice-chairman of Rathmines Urban District Council and deputy vice-chairman of the Dublin Board of Guardians. She also assumed the roles of district justice in the Dáil Courts, and arbitrator for Dáil Éireann's labour department in wage disputes between employers and employees, which demanded difficult and often dangerous nationwide travel in the midst war. Despite her own prominence and that of her fellow 'Easter Widows' in political, propaganda and philanthropic roles, it was often their symbolic status as living representatives of Ireland's republican martyrs that motivated destructive raids by agents of the British and the Free State governments. During the Civil War, anti-Treaty propagandists sought to highlight the apparent continuity between the 'reign of terror' presided over by Crown forces in 1919–21 and what they dubbed the 'new terror' under the Free State 'military junta'. Republican news-sheets reserved particular outrage for the 'sacrilegious' military raids, the desecration of 'holy places', conducted by former comrades on the homes of Áine Ceannt, Michael J. O'Rahilly's widow, Nancy and former TD and mother of the executed Pearse brothers, Margaret Pearse. The Ceannt home was subjected to a series of destructive raids by 'men in mufti' in the Spring of 1923, just over a year after Ceannt had presided at the Cumann na mBan convention, that voted overwhelmingly against the Treaty. During the same period she was preoccupied with her stewardship of the orphan care committee of the Irish White Cross, which met for the first time on 6 February 1922. Dedicated and determined, with an innate sense of civic duty, Ceannt was much more than simply a figurehead widow for the tradition of republican martyrdom: she was foremost among those women activists who channelled Irish volunteerism and social activism into the underground charitable networks that did so much to sustain of the republican movement and help the innocent victims of political violence. [Image: National Library of Ireland, Ceannt and O'Brennan Papers, NPA CEA81 / See BMH WS, 264 (Áine Ceannt); Anti-Treaty handbill, 'The New Terror', Irish Capuchin Archives, IE CA IR-1/7/3/4/5; Áine Ceannt to Lily O'Brennan, 25 Feb. 1922, Lily O'Brennan Papers, P13/34, UCDA; Frances Clarke, 'Áine Ceannt', *Dictionary of Irish Biography*, https://www.dib.ie/biography/ceannt-aine-a1580; Mary Gallagher, *Éamonn Ceannt: 16 Lives* (Dublin, 2014) p. 316]

CHAPTER 13

Historians and the 'Silence' of the Irish Civil War: Some comparative perspectives

Síobhra Aiken

Revolutionaries, politicians and commentators alike lamented the split over the Anglo-Irish Treaty, with many attempting to prevent 'the *unspeakable* horror' of the Civil War that was to come. For many, the spectre of civil conflict defied language: the terror was regarded as 'indescribable' and communities and families were left in an 'unimaginable state of disorder'. In early 1924 the *Irish Independent* even reported the events had repressed musical expression across Ireland: 'during the conditions of the last year when the madness of civil war and domestic tragedy had the people in its grip, song became silent'.[1]

This emphasis on silence is often evident in discourses surrounding events that are particularly devastating. The concerns expressed in 1924 about the cessations of song directly mirror contentions following the Irish Famine that 'níl ceol in aon áit ná suim ina dhéanamh' (there is no music anywhere nor desire to make it). Similar language shrouds the events of the First World War, as gravestones carry inscriptions such as: 'A sorrow too deep for words'. After the Spanish Civil War (1936–9), people 'would put a finger to their lips and look from side to side' when later asked about the war years. Auschwitz survivor Primo Levi contended that language was inadequate to bear witness to the extremities of the Holocaust: 'la nostra lingua manca di parole per esprimere questa offesa, la demolizione di un uomo' (our language lacks words to express this offence, the demolition of a man).[2]

However in all of the contexts mentioned above, scholars have cautioned against any overly literal interpretations of such

Fig. 2 Áine Ceannt (second from the right) with Kathleen Clarke (far left), Nancy O'Rahilly and chairman James H. Webb at a meeting of the council of the Irish White Cross children's committee. The Irish White Cross (IWC) was established in 1921 as an Irish conduit for American humanitarian aid and to collect and distribute its own funds at parish level in a country where there was little welfare provision for the 'innocent' victims of political violence. The White Cross also acted as a platform to highlight British state violence, particularly when directed against Irish civilians. In 1922 Ceannt was appointed secretary of its orphan care committee which, in the aftermath of the Civil War, expanded its remit to incorporate the dependants of those killed during that conflict and during the 1916 Rising. From April 1922 to January 1925 it allocated relief payments to 723 children in Ireland. Ceannt resigned from both Sinn Féin and Cumann na mBan in 1925 to focus on her work with the committee, which continued as the Children's Relief Association following the dissolution of the IWC in 1928. [Image: National Library of Ireland, Ceannt and O'Brennan Papers, NPA CEA99 / See also Lia Brazil and Melanie Oppenheimer 'Saving 'Ireland's children': Voluntary action, gender, humanitarianism, and the Irish White Cross, 1921–1947', *Women's History Review*, 31:7 (2022)]

assertions of silence. In many cases researchers who have pushed against established tropes of 'unspeakability' have been able to uncover previously occluded voices that call these perceived silences into question.[3] Since the 1980s scholars of the Irish Famine have highlighted that statements as to the impossibility of speech were often no more than rhetorical flourishes and that the events of the Famine in fact generated a wealth of literature in Ireland and abroad. Historians of the First World War, too, have long cautioned against the normalisation of assertions of the 'unspeakable' and suggest that such veiled language actually serves to domesticate the 'nastiness' of war. Meanwhile various historians of the Spanish Civil War, including Santos Juliá, have been arguing since the 1990s that 'es sencillamente absurdo seguir hablando de olvido y de silence cuando resulta imposible moverse entre las montañas de papel crecidas desde el 18 de julio de 1936' (it is simply absurd to continue talking about oblivion and silence when it is impossible to move among the mountains of paper that have grown since 18 July 1936).[4]

Debates continue to wage regarding the perceived silence following the Holocaust. There remains a strong view that the liberation of the concentration camps was followed by an initial period of 'traumatic' latency and that survivor stories only began to emerge in earnest after the Eichmann trial in Jerusalem in 1961. Ongoing scholarship on early Holocaust remembrance challenges this perception, however, and sets out to highlight that 'the world was gifted a plenitude of information about the horrors that had so recently occurred in Europe'. For example, in her 2009 study, Hasia R. Diner offers a particularly bold critique of her fellow historians for perpetuating the view that the American Jewish community was largely silent on the Holocaust and attributes this misconception to 'slipshod scholarship that put ideology over evidence'.[5]

Yet despite such vibrant international debates, it is still widely assumed – in both academic study and popular discourse – that the events of the Irish Civil War were shrouded in an almost total silence. This chapter considers the 'silence' of the Irish Civil War as a historiographical construct in light of scholarship in other comparative and international contexts – responding, thus, to recent scholarship on the 'global' Irish revolution that highlights the merits of comparative approaches in understanding Ireland's revolutionary period.[6] In particular the chapter considers how the Irish Civil War continues to be viewed through a popular psychoanalytic lens – or 'lay trauma theory' perspective – and how the perhaps unconscious use of such frameworks has resulted not only in the occlusion of numerous sources relating to the Civil War, but also in the selective (mis)reading of historical evidence to support the conventional view that 'trauma' is characterised by an initial period of silence and repression that is followed by a belated response. Further this chapter cautions that the persistent endorsement of post-Civil War silence risks privileging an elite-focused, depoliticised and singular understanding of the legacy of the conflict. The fact that these received wisdoms have been largely unquestioned is also indicative, perhaps, of what Caoimhe Nic Dháibhéid refers to as the 'historiographical peacefulness' that has characterised writing about the Irish revolution during the decade of commemorations.[7]

The silent Irish Civil War

A reconsideration of the 'silence' of the Irish Civil War does not deny that the history of the conflict, like most historical episodes, is characterised by 'relative silences and selective memories'. The Civil War left a profound legacy. It caused divisions in families and communities, and many advocated for the forgetting of these contentious events for the sake of political stability and to protect subsequent generations from social fallouts. Memoirs, school textbooks and history books covered the 'heartening and inspiring' revolutionary period of 1916–21, but left out the 'best-forgotten' Civil War that followed in 1922. The centrality of this legacy of silence is evident in the titles of family memoirs, novels, and television documentaries: *A Woven Silence*, *The Silence of the Glasshouse*, *The Silent Civil War*.[8]

Nevertheless the confidence with which the totality of this silence is endorsed in empirically driven historical scholarship is deserving of scrutiny. Leading scholars in the fields of history, sociology and literature casually refer to 'the conspiracy of silence', 'that collective silence' and 'traumatised silence', with many of the belief that there was a 'knowledge deficit' about the conflict that has only recently been redressed thanks to the availability of major state archives such as the Bureau of Military History and Military Service Pensions Collection.[9] The advice issued in 2018 by the government-appointed Expert Advisory Group on Centenary Commemorations is particularly striking in both its acceptance and defence of Civil War silence: 'There was nothing ignoble in the many silences that followed the Irish Civil War – they were a better alternative to simplistic, polarised narratives and myth-making. *With time*, those silences can be replaced by meaningful engagements with a difficult and traumatic time' (my emphasis).[10] Two features stand out from this statement that merit further discussion here: first, the foregrounding of the virtues of silence and, second, the endorsement of popular conceptions of trauma as a means to assess the legacy of the Civil War and its possible resolution. Both narratives are firmly established within public and academic discourses of the period and are central to understanding how the codes of silence around the Irish Civil War have been constructed and maintained.

The virtues of silence

The idea that silence was a *better* response to the horrors of the Civil War is not necessarily a new idea. This celebration of the virtues of silence, and even the weaponisation of forgetting, was a dominant feature of Irish political debate for much of the twentieth century. From the immediate aftermath of the conflict, political figures and former revolutionaries not only promoted forgetting for the sake of the common good, but also chastised their opponents for their perceived unwillingness to 'let sleeping dogs lie'. Many veterans,

MINISTRY OF DEFENCE
22 JUL. 1924
34, MOLESWORTH STREET
ARMY PENSIONS BOARD

Ref. No. 3/D/57.

Lissycurrig,
Causeway,
Co Kerry. 19/7/24.

The Army Finance Officer,
Army Pensions Branch,
Ministry of Defence,
34 Molesworth Street,
Dublin.

Sir,

In a communication dated 17. 4. 1924 you state that the Army Pensions board were pleased to grant me "£30 gratuity payable in one sum" in respect of the death of my son. I have been since expecting that you would inform me that some further allowance would be granted to me, for I refused to believe that you would estimate the life of a young Irishman as of less value than an Irish terrier for which I have often seen larger Compensation awarded.

I am informed that the friends of

Fig. 3 Letter from Margaret O'Connor to the Army Finance Officer, 19 July 1924, seeking gratuity under the Army Pensions Act 1923 in relation to the death of her son at Knocknagoshel, County Kerry, 6 March 1923. Eighteen-year-old Private Laurence O'Connor from Causeway was one of eight National Army soldiers lured by false intelligence to investigate a supposed IRA arms dump. As they moved the rocks placed around a concealed trap-mine, it exploded, killing five of the soldiers instantly and seriously injuring a sixth. Events at Knocknagoshel triggered a series of brutal National Army killings of IRA prisoners at Ballyseedy, Countess Bridge near Killarney and Bahaghs near Cahersiveen, earning March 1923 the title 'Terror Month', and forging a bitter legacy of recrimination in the south-western county. Margaret O'Connor's personal grief and deep frustration is clear in her admonition of the bureaucrats who, in offering a meagre gratuity of £30, seemed to 'estimate the life of a young Irishman as of less value than an Irish terrier'. Documents like this one in the extraordinarily valuable Military Service Pensions Collection, released in phases from 2014, have contributed significantly to our understanding of not only the military history of the Civil War, but also the often occluded lived experience of internecine violence and its bitter aftermath. Civil War scholarship, however, has only belatedly begun to engage with the 'unofficial archives' – the oral histories, unpublished memoirs, folklore and intergenerational family memory – which challenge the traditionally accepted pervasiveness of a post-Civil War 'traumatised silence'. They offer the potential, if treated carefully, to yield new insights into the conflict, its fraught afterlife and, as Anne Dolan noted, the ways that a community 'however hardened by its hatreds, puts itself back together again' in the wake of civil war. [Source: MSPC 3D75, Laurence O'Connor / Image: courtesy of Military Archives/MSPC Project / See Síobhra Aiken, 'The Silence and the Silence Breakers of the Irish Civil War, 1922–2022', *Éire-Ireland*, vol. 57, nos 1–2 (Spring/Summer 2022), p. 286; Anne Dolan, 'Reply to an Address by Taoiseach Micheál Martin', 30 Nov. 2002, https://www.ria.ie/news/publications-ireland-1922/taoiseach-micheal-martin-addresses-royal-irish-academy]

like political figure Pádraic Ó Máille, were critical of the pro-Treaty government for 'keeping alive passions and hatreds', contending that 'those who suffered most in the Civil War are the least bitter and they were the first to show signs that they were prepared to forgive and forget'.[11]

The government party, for its part, also prided itself on its commitment to tight-lippedness. William T. Cosgrave, leader of Cumann na nGaedheal, argued in 1928 that 'there was no use in discussing the starting of the civil war [...] What good purpose would be served – what good would it do for the future of the country?' Nevertheless Cumann na nGaedheal came in for criticism by the anti-Treaty party, Fianna Fáil, who gained power in 1932 and accused their opponents of trying to 'revive memories of things better forgotten'. Meanwhile the Labour Party criticised both Civil War parties in the 1930s for doing nothing 'but talk about the responsibility of the civil war [...] They should forget the past and look to the future.' These virtuosity wars waged for decades: Seán MacBride, leader of Clann na Poblachta, denounced Fianna Fáil in 1954 for 'keeping alive this bitter intolerance' and for handing down 'this unnatural bitterness to the new generation'. There were similar squabbles at a community level too. Through to the 1960s, local councillors continued to argue over who was most committed to honourable silence regarding the years 1922–3: 'It is you who are not forgetting the civil war[!].'[12]

Fig. 4 (opposite page) Portrait of Seán MacBride (1904–88), pastel, by Harry Kernoff RHA (1958). Born in Paris in January 1904, MacBride was the son of Maud Gonne and John MacBride, the former a convert to nationalism and later to Catholicism and a prominent social and political activist, the latter a member of the Irish Republican Brotherhood and hero of the Irish Brigade in the Second Boer War. Their marriage did not last, dissolving rapidly and publicly during a protracted and bitter divorce case. Seán MacBride was imbued from a young age with his mother's conviction that Britain was culpable for a great deal of the historic injustices and suffering in Ireland. She intended to return to Ireland to enrol him in Patrick Pearse's St Enda's School, but the outbreak of the First World War intervened. The subsequent execution of John MacBride for his part in the 1916 Rising prompted a return to Dublin, where Maude Gonne assumed the public and subversive role of 'Easter Widow' and where the memory and reputation of John MacBride was redeemed in the eyes of his effectively estranged twelve-year-old son. Maude Gonne's arrest and internment in 1918 weighed heavily on the increasingly strong-willed MacBride who, despite his youth, was determined to play his part in the revolutionary struggle. In early 1920 while studying law and agriculture at University College Dublin, he left Na Fianna Éireann to join B Company, of Dublin's 3rd Battalion, IRA. Having impressed Michael Collins during the struggle in Dublin, he joined IRA GHQ staff and was assigned various roles, including gun-running during the Truce period and the carrying of dispatches for the plenipotentiaries during the Treaty negotiations in London. Within six months he was a member of the surrendering anti-Treaty IRA garrison after the shelling of the Four Courts. He was imprisoned in Mountjoy, where he spent most of the Civil War, before escaping in October 1923 while being relocated to Kilmainham. Evading recapture, he maintained his IRA activism and his trenchant opposition to the pro-Treaty government. When the Free State minister for justice, Kevin O'Higgins, was assassinated near his home in Booterstown, County Dublin in July 1927, MacBride was charged with his murder, later changed to 'suspicion of murder' under the Public Safety Act, and later again to 'suspicion of conspiracy'. In a letter dated 23 September 1927 Maud Gonne MacBride wrote to the Labour Party leader, Thomas Johnson (who had lost his seat in the general election a week earlier), laying bare the circumstances of her son's arrest, the draconian nature of the legislation and the charges brought against him under different acts: 'If this is the law in Ireland, one must feel ashamed of being Irish' (Fig. 5). MacBride was later released and resumed his prominent role in the IRA, becoming chief of staff for a brief period in 1936 before resigning in 1937 and pursuing a successful legal career. He was a founding member of a new republican political party, Clann na Poblachta, in 1946 and served as its leader, becoming minister for external affairs in the first inter-party government (1948–51). In 1954 MacBride castigated Fianna Fáil in the Dáil for stoking the flames of an 'unnatural bitterness' in relation to the Civil War and keeping it alive for a 'new generation'. Yet in 1948 his own party had refused to enter coalition with a Fine Gael party led by Richard Mulcahy because of his role in the executions policy during the Civil War. MacBride retired from Irish politics in 1961 and became a major international figure in the areas of peace and justice. A founding member of Amnesty International, he was awarded the Nobel Peace Prize in 1974 and the Lenin Peace Prize in 1975. [Image: courtesy of Whytes Auctioneers and the Kernoff family; Letter: National Library of Ireland, MS 17,242/14 / See also Caoimhe Nic Dháibhéid, *Seán MacBride: A republican life 1904–1946* (Liverpool, 2011), p. 37]

Fig. 5 (below) Letter from Maud Gonne MacBride to Labour leader Thomas Johnson, 23 September 1927, regarding Seán MacBride's arrest for the murder of Kevin O'Higgins and his treatment in prison. [Document: National Library of Ireland, Thomas Johnson Papers, MS 17,242/14]

ROEBUCK HOUSE,
CLONSKEIGH,

23rd September, 1927.

A Chara,

(1) On the morning of the August 24th Sean MacBride was arrested, without warrant, at his home by Sergeant O'Driscoll and some twelve plain-clothes policemen brandishing revolvers, he was verbally charged under an old Act 1848 with the murder of Mr. O'Higgins.

~~Ten~~ 12 other republicans have already been arrested under this Act and charged with this murder by Superintendent Ennis without a shadow of evidence being produced and after imprisoning them for periods varying from 10 days to 3 weeks they were released without compensation.

(2) Sean was able to establish by direct evidence and documents that prior to and at the date of the murder he was out of Ireland on business of the Firm for which he is Managing Director and the only result of this was that Superintendent Ennis formally re-arrested him at the police station and changed the charge to suspicion of murder under the Public Safety Act, which precludes the production of evidence it being impossible to bring evidence of what is in the mind of a policeman.

(3) On the 25th August Sean MacBride was tried before District Judge Little who refused to remand him under the Public Safety Act for a crime which was prior to the existance of the Act and in Court Superintendent Ennis changed the charge back to the murder charge under the 1848 Act and obtained a remand in custody for 8 days.

(4) In Mountjoy Sean was submitted to several identification parades where naturally he was not identified and Superintendent Ennis again shifted the charge back to the Public Safety Act one, of suspicion, and on 31st August he was again brought before Judge Little who acquitted him and declared it would be against his conscience as a magistrate to remand Sean MacBride under the Public Safety Act.

On the Court charge sheet the two charges are entered, that of murder under the 1848 Act and that of suspicion of murder under the Public Safety Act and at the bottom of this charge sheet is written "Discharged, informations refused".

(5) On leaving the Court Sean MacBride was immediately re-arrested by Superintendent Ennis who charged him under the old Act

with the murder and he was once more lodged in the verminous filth of the Bridewell, again the following day he was brought before Judge Little and charged under the '48 Act and again remanded for 8 days to Mountjoy.

In the meantime the Free State Attorney General obtained from Judge Hanna in the High Court an Order of Certiorari to quash Judge Little's acquittal of Sean MacBride and a Mandamus to oblige him to do what in open Court he had said his conscience as a magistrate would not allow him to do.

(6) So for the sixth time the charge against Sean MacBride was changed and he was remanded by Judge Little for 7 days under the Public Safety Act on the suspicion of Superintendent Ennis that he had been engaged in the murder of Mr. O'Higgins.

On the 13th September the day before the expiration of the last remand the Governor of Mountjoy informed Sean MacBride that he had received an order of internment for him for 2 months signed by Richard Mulcahy, Minister of Local Government and Public Health, and that the charge was changed from suspicion of murder to suspicion of conspiracy.

(7) In Mountjoy Sean MacBride is locked in a tiny cell 22 hours out of 24, deprived of everything - not even allowed a pencil or note-book for study, while his business is being ruined by his enforced absence.

If this is the Law in Ireland one must feel ashamed of being Irish.

Is mise,

Maud Gonne MacBride

Fig. 6 The National Army monument at Glasnevin Cemetery. In 1922 and 1923, Dublin's Glasnevin Cemetery hosted many funerals of National Army soldiers. Some were grand national affairs, most notably that of the National Army commander-in-chief, Michael Collins, killed in Cork in August 1922, whose tricolour-draped coffin was transported on an artillery carriage in a huge military procession from central Dublin. Described by the pro-Treaty press as a 'pageant of sorrow' even greater than Parnell's, it was carefully planned by the Provisional Government to reinforce its popular legitimacy by recalling traditional nationalist political funerals. Political, military and clerical dignitaries were present at Collins's graveside, where Richard Mulcahy's oration was followed by volleys of rifle fire over the grave. Most of the funerals for pro-Treaty soldiers, however, were low-key events with minimal ceremony. Because so few graves were individually marked, the Cumann na nGaedheal government could not provide an exact number of how many soldiers were buried in Glasnevin. Estimates ranged from 115 to 189 in the aftermath of the Civil War and later reports alluded to as many as 214. The National Army plot remained unmarked for many years – an indication of the shortage of state funds in the wake of the Civil War, but also of the marked reticence of the winning side to commemorate those who died in its forces. Finally, in 1957 a plaque was placed on the spot, marking it as the resting place of the 'deceased officers and men of Óglaigh na hÉireann', but it was not until 1968 that a monument featuring the soldiers' names was commissioned. This was largely the result of lobbying for a permanent monument to fallen Irish Army soldiers by the comrades and families of soldiers who died on United Nations service in the Congo. It was thus only by association with less politically uncomfortable Irish military casualties that the names of the National Army's Civil War dead were inscribed on limestone tablets; even then, it is unlikely that those 183 names covered all of the soldiers buried there. Of those recorded on the National Army memorial, 113 were privates, 48 NCOs and 22 officers, the most senior of whom was Colonel Commandant Thomas Mandeville, killed, along with Captain Michael Vaughan, on Leeson Street in Dublin on the first day of the Civil War, 28 June 1922. Most of the soldiers, 128 out of 183, were from Dublin, about half of whom died in the province of Munster. The next largest place of origin after Dublin was Belfast, birthplace of twelve of the men on Glasnevin monument. Unlikely to be commemorated in their home city due to hostility of both the Northern government and the republican movement, Belfast-born National Army casualties were often buried in Dublin. Of the 179 cases where cause of death can be discerned, 96 were killed by enemy fire, 58 died in accidents and another 25 due to illness. The Glasnevin National Army memorial was rededicated in August 2023, and remains a relatively rare example of the memorialisation of the National Army's Civil War dead. [Text: John Dorney / Image: John Crowley / See Anne Dolan, *Commemorating the Irish Civil War: History and memory* (Cambridge, 2006)]

This lauding of silence also marks historical writing on the period, with historians passing favourable judgement on the personal decisions of (certain) political figures to shirk away from discussing the Civil War. This is implied, perhaps, in J.J. Lee's word choice when he notes that some former revolutionaries 'suppressed their feelings in the interest of the national good', while others 'would miss no opportunity to lacerate the wounds'. R.F. Foster is more overt in contending that 'for politicians, scrupulous silence about the past is sometimes the right course'. Tom Garvin claims that the 'conspiracy of silence' following the Civil War was upheld for 'the best of all possible reasons'. Eunan O'Halpin associates the decision of politicians not to draw attention to Civil War tragedies affecting their political opponents with a 'fundamental decency in Irish political discourse'. Anne Dolan, while criticising the failure of the pro-Treaty government to honour its own war dead, also points to the virtues of silence: 'Silence was better than hypocrisy. Silence was also better than disgust.'[13]

There are, of course, valid arguments for the benefits of forgetting in post-Civil War society. Bill Kissane suggests that the 'even-handed neglect' of Civil War commemoration on the part of the Cumann na nGaedheal government avoided the more divisive victory commemorations evident in the aftermath of other twentieth-century European civil wars.[14] In Francoist Spain the dominant commemorative paradigm was to vigorously commemorate the feats and losses of the nationalist side while actively repressing the republican side through both physical violence (such as execution or imprisonment) and social control (through denial of employment and economic security).[15] Meanwhile, in Finland, the triumphant commemoration of the winning side (the Whites) effectively eclipsed public recollection of the experiences and sufferings of the losing side (the Reds) for decades.[16] Nevertheless the persistent view on the part of Irish historians that the silence of the Irish Civil War was 'entirely understandable'[17] risks presenting a one-sided official narrative that fails to accommodate the multiplicity of responses generated by the contentious events of the Civil War: responses that involved not only silence, but also silence-breaking.

The longevity of Irish Civil War 'trauma'

The second striking feature of the advice of the government-appointed board of historians is its evidence of the widespread use of popular psychoanalytic theories to understand the legacy of the Civil War. Jeffrey C. Alexander refers to this set of beliefs as 'lay trauma theory' and traces its development to the aftermath of the First World War.[18] According to such theories, the repression of Civil War memory is read as a symptom of its 'traumatic' nature and this repression of memory is seen as possibly reversible at some point in the future. The implication here is that the pent-up pain of the Civil War will resurface after a sufficient period of time (Freud referred to this as 'the period of latency'), after which the supposedly traumatic legacy of the conflict can be expressed and even resolved.

The seeds of these popular psychoanalytic ideas around the longevity of the conflict's legacy were sown *even before* the Civil War erupted. When pro- and anti-Treaty leaders met in May 1922 to avert the outbreak of hostilities, they warned the conflict would be so detrimental that it would 'leave Ireland broken for generations'.[19] Numerous commentators have since supported this assumption that deferral (or belatedness) is at the core of the trauma of the Civil War, and that its legacy will thus only be properly reconciled at a point of time in the future. Dan Breen asserted in

Fig. 7 Funeral cortege passing through Sackville Street (O'Connell Street) on the way to Glasnevin for the burial of Michael Collins. [Image: part of the Independent Newspapers Ireland/NLI Collection, INDH303]

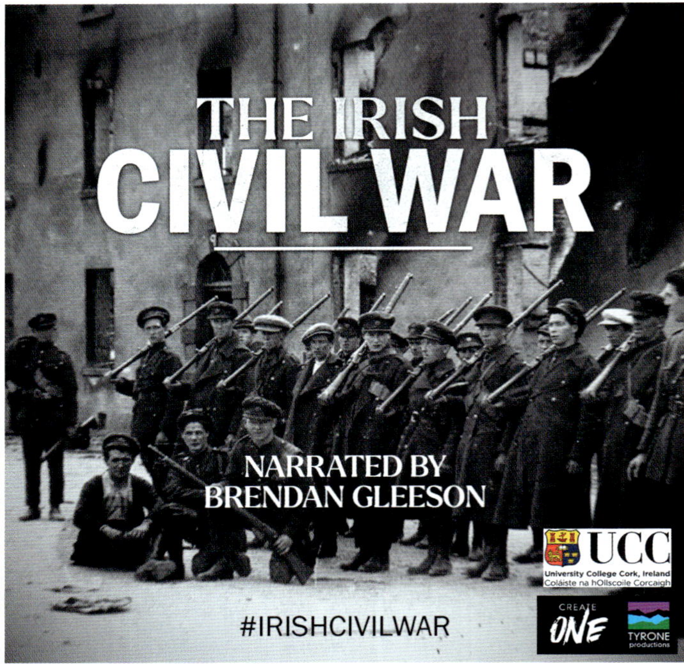

Fig. 8 Promotional poster for the 2022 documentary *The Irish Civil War.* One of the principal aims of the three-part RTÉ documentary series, first broadcast in 2022, was to examine the violent events that marked the founding of the state and the bitter animosities that flowed from it. A joint production of RTÉ and University College Cork (in collaboration with the Atlas of the Irish Revolution Project), the series attracted a wide national and international audience. By drawing on the most recent scholarship, it allowed for a fuller understanding of and engagement with the causes, nature and legacy of the conflict. [Image: courtesy of Tyrone Productions and Create One / Background image: National Army soldiers, Sarsfield Barracks 1922, courtesy of Dr Matthew Potter, Limerick Museum 1990.0234.14]

1954, as a Fianna Fáil TD, that 'the time had *not yet* come when an impartial judgement could be made' (my emphasis) on the Civil War. Historian F.S.L. Lyons famously commented in 1971 that the Civil War was 'an episode which has burned so deep into the heart and mind of Ireland that it is *not yet* possible for the historian to approach it with the detailed knowledge or the objectivity which it deserves and sooner or later must have' (my emphasis). This is reflected in Townshend's contention that, although sources were no longer lacking for studying the Civil War, 'Objectivity may *still* be more difficult to achieve' (my emphasis), while Diarmaid Ferriter, in 2022, claimed 'we have *not yet* reached an era of mature Civil War commemoration' (my emphasis).[20]

This temporal narrative of closure can also be evoked in an affirmative sense. While it is regularly asserted that Civil War tensions have *not yet* been resolved (as above), the *end* of Civil War hostilities is also frequently heralded. Frank Thornton of the short-lived Clann na nGaedheal party claimed in 1934 that '*today* as far as the civil war combatants were concerned, bitterness did not exist' (my emphasis). Garret FitzGerald pinpointed the late 1930s as the time when Civil War 'animosities' ceased, a time when the children of revolutionary veterans attended university together. Fianna Fáil Taoiseach Jack Lynch sent Irish Army representation to the Michael Collins commemoration in Béal na Blá in 1972, and was celebrated in newspaper editorials as the 'leader who *finally* healed the Civil War divide' (my emphasis). The 2022 RTÉ documentary, *The Irish Civil War*, directed by Ruán Magan, celebrates the idea that 'the animosities of the Civil War are, *at last*, being consigned to history' (my emphasis), while the National Museum of Ireland's 2020 exhibition 'Exploring the Irish Wars 1919–23' refers to the 'long-lasting schism in Irish society, which is *only now* being healed' (my emphasis).[21]

While these two narratives have existed side by side for decades, both endorse a Freudian conception of a prolonged period of stasis following the initial traumatic event, whether that period be defined, as in the present model ('today', 'at last', 'finally', 'only now'), or undefined and finite, as in the future-orientated model ('with time', 'not yet'). Thus, even though the historiography of the Irish revolutionary period remains strongly wedded to empirical methods, by not critically engaging with the unacknowledged influence of 'lay trauma theory' on perceptions of the Civil War, historians risk placing their empirical evidence into a 'lay trauma theory' framework without recognising the limitations of such lens of analysis.

The limitations of the psychoanalytic model

What are the risks associated with reading history through such psychoanalytic models? Lindsay Janssen cautions in the context of studies of the Irish Famine that the use of 'lay trauma theory' can result in 'singular interpretations' of historical events, as the trauma purportedly endured by a society is treated like the trauma experienced by an individual.[22] Indeed the Irish population has been casually referred to as 'a traumatised society' following the Civil War, while Kissane, taking a more affirmative position, likens Irish society to a patient who is treated after a psychotic episode, arguing that the 'Irish quickly returned to their narrative core' following the Civil War.[23] What emerges here, potentially, is a homogeneous picture of post-Civil War society that downplays the significant variety of responses exhibited by those who have been exposed to traumatic events.

Another potential risk of applying popular ideas of trauma to historical understanding – as addressed by Jo Labanyi in regards to the Spanish Civil War – is that the emphasis on the psychological mechanisms of repression (and possible subsequent processing) can deflect from the 'political explanations' that either prohibit or facilitate the production of remembrance in postwar life. The silence and silence-breaking of Irish revolutionaries is always informed by the various political, social, socio-economic and gender forces that characterised the production of memory at specific historical moments. Equally, popular ideas of trauma can too readily equate trauma with powerlessness and victimhood, thus overlooking the frequent collapsing of victim–perpetrator–bystander models and failing to see that silence can function as an assertion of agency as much as a symptom of anguish. Radhika Mohanram highlights that women's silence could serve as a 'mute protest of the condition of citizenship' in post-partition India, a phenomenon that resonates with the mute protest of revolutionaries who refused to engage with state commemorative projects.[24]

Fig. 9 This commemorative stamp, issued by An Post in 2022, to mark the centenary of the beginning of the Irish Civil War, features the painting *Commencement of Hostilities* by Clare-born artist, Mick O'Dea, a past president of the Royal Hibernian Academy (RHA) and member of Aosdána. The Irish revolutionary period has figured prominently in the work of O'Dea, who since childhood has been interested in Irish history. As an eight-year-old growing up in Ennis, he was attracted to the pageantry surrounding the fiftieth anniversary of the 1916 Rising. Living in the premises of a family-owned public house also introduced him to the art and power of storytelling that has been a constant thread in his development as an artist – both as a sculptor and as a painter. Narrative has been an essential ingredient in his signature paintings from portraiture to landscapes, to his rendering of historical events such as the 1916 Rising, the War of Independence and the Irish Civil War. His critically acclaimed 1916 exhibition *The Foggy Dew* was hosted by the RHA at Ely Place in Dublin in the early months of 2016, and featured paintings of significant sites of memory associated with the Rising as well as sculptural installations such as *The Britannia*. The exhibition was praised by art critic Cristín Leach for 'its thorough, intelligent and highly successful artistic interrogation of the origins of Irish independence'. An earlier exhibition on the Civil War, *The Split*, which was hosted by the Kevin Kavanagh Gallery in Dublin, also relied on O'Dea's hallmark mining of historical photographs to provide the viewer with new ways of comprehending the tumultuous and tragic events of the period. *Commencement of Hostilities* is another example of O'Dea's grasp of the layering of history, his excavation of memory and the mutability of the commemorative process. [Image: courtesy of An Post / See Cristín Leach, '21st Century Ireland in 21 Artworks: *The Britannia*', https://www.rte.ie/culture/2017/0914/904833-the-britannia/]

Finally, and most crucially, perhaps, the use of psychoanalytic models to understand historical episodes can lead to a view that commemorative practice should and can support social healing and reconciliation. Niall Ó Ciosáin warned in 1996 that the idea that recovering and remembering the Famine was 'beneficial' placed 'inordinate expectations on historians and researchers, since it makes them largely responsible for the process'. Nevertheless this discourse has been replicated in subsequent state commemorations, with the idea of 'reconciliation' being placed 'at the heart of the State's commemorative programme for 2022'.[25]

Reconciliation, though, is 'a contested idea and practice'. Since Ó Ciosáin's comments in 1996, numerous international studies have questioned the consensual belief that remembrance of the past can somehow improve and even heal society in the present. In fact in the volume *Reconciliation After Civil Wars: Global perspectives,* Paul Quigley cautions that the noble goal of post-conflict reconciliation can often translate into a 'continuation of civil war by other means' and that reconciliation itself becomes 'the object and state of ongoing struggle, a political weapon deployed to shape the outcomes and meanings of war'. Moreover the insistence on the potential psychological benefits of historical work feeds into what Lea David refers to as 'moral remembrance', whereby supposedly correct ways of remembrance are mandated for moving beyond societal trauma. Thus, in the case of the Irish Civil War, calls are made again and again for its 'proper' remembrance, ranging from pleas by politicians in the early decades of the state that we must 'forget the Civil War', to republican graffiti reading 'Remember the 77' (a reference to the anti-Treatyites executed during the Civil War), to appeals during the centenary commemorations to 'find a way to ethically remember' the conflict.[26]

A 'relative' knowledge deficit

An effect of lay trauma perspectives is the belief that the Civil War, by virtue of its traumatic nature, is subject to a paucity of source material. The Irish Civil War has been associated with a 'knowledge deficit', with many of the view that the memory of the Civil War 'remained submerged between the earlier war of independence and the recent Northern Irish conflict'.[27]

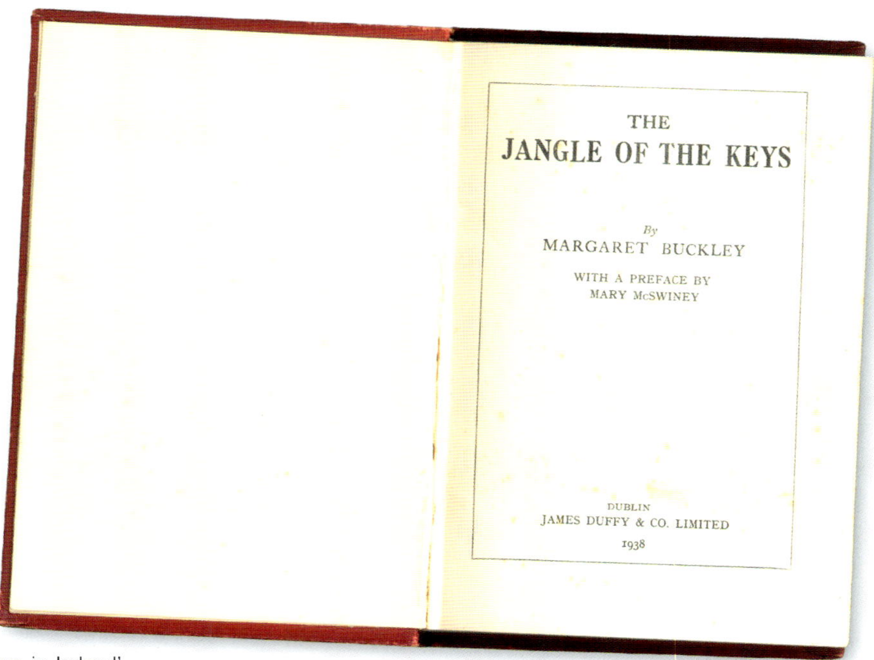

Fig. 10 Margaret Buckley's 1938 prison memoir, *The Jangle of the Keys*, chronicles her nine-month internment in Mountjoy, the North Dublin Union and Kilmainham Gaol in 1923. Born Margaret Goulding in Cork in 1879, she was radicalised two decades later through her involvement in cultural nationalist organisations, including the radical Cork Celtic Literary Society, which one contemporary quipped 'was more revolutionary than literary'. She served as president of the Cork branch of Inghinidhe na hÉireann, and was closely associated with Cork's radical separatist elite, including Tomás MacCurtain, Liam de Róiste, Seán O'Hegarty and Terence and Mary MacSwiney, who would gain prominence a decade later. In 1906 she moved with her husband, Patrick Buckley, to Dublin, where she became involved in the Irish trade union movement and, after the 1916 Rising, was an active member of Sinn Féin. A judge in the Dáil courts during the War of Independence, Buckley opposed the Treaty and joined the Women's Prisoners' Defence League before her arrest on 6 January 1923. Her frank and evocative memoir captures the often brutal treatment of the female internees, their idealism, discipline and defiance, and the physical and psychological impact of imprisonment. Prefacing the book, Mary MacSwiney emphasised its value as a corrective to what she deemed the unreliable 'records of the history of the past twenty years in Ireland'. Republicans like Ernie O'Malley and Peadar O'Donnell published their first-person full-length prison memoirs in the same decade but, due to the challenges experienced by many female chroniclers in finding a publisher for non-fiction, Buckley's was a pioneering female perspective in that genre. As Síobhra Aiken notes, however, testimonial fiction, the more typical literary vehicle for female veterans, did allow them to 'take ownership of wartime trauma' and counter 'the widespread stereotyping of female revolutionaries in men's fiction'. As president of a peripheral Sinn Féin party in 1937, Buckley was a vocal critic of de Valera's draft constitution, which, she memorably insisted, treated 'the women of the country as half-wits'. She continued to publish articles and stories as 'Margaret Lee' in the decades that followed, many of which criticised the treatment of women and the poor in de Valera's Ireland. She died at her home in Glasnevin on 24 July 1962 and was buried at St Finbarr's Cemetery in Cork. [Image: Kilmainham Gaol Museum/ OPW / See Frances Clarke, 'Margaret (Goulding) Buckley', *Dictionary of Irish Biography*, https://doi.org/10.3318/dib.001101.v1; *Irish Independent*, 30 June 1937; Síobhra Aiken, *Spiritual Wounds: Trauma, testimony and the Irish Civil War* (Dublin, 2023), pp. 103 and 158]

Like many of these discourses, the characterisation of the Civil War as an absence within the commemorative landscape can be traced back to early commentary. For example the editor of the *Irish Book Lover* lamented in 1929 that 'the pictorial and other literature dealing with the civil conflict of 1922–1923 should be much more difficult to procure than that relating to the Rising of 16'.[28] This view was echoed by journalist Eoin Neeson in his 1966 study, in which he regretted that 'official documents of the Civil War are generally incomplete, unattainable or have been destroyed. Though some authorities may claim otherwise, there is no complete and reliable collection of Civil War documents available up to now.' In 1988 historian Michael Hopkinson also acknowledged the 'lack of state archival material' and was particularly sharp in his criticism of both the Dublin and Stormont governments in this regard.[29]

There is an irony in this perception: how can the Civil War be associated with a 'knowledge deficit' given that this period in Irish history is widely considered the 'best-documented modern revolution in the world'? As Peter Hart argued in his study *The I.R.A. at War, 1916–1923*, there is no shortage of materials, from police, military, church and IRA records to newspapers, to the many personal recollections, diaries and letters housed in both family and state archives. Yet, paradoxically, the wealth of documentation relating to the Easter Rising and later struggle for independence (1919–21) might explain the general view that there is an 'incomplete' body of material regarding the period 1922–3.[30]

Indeed what comparative perspectives suggest is that supposed silences are almost always *relative*. The idea that the two decades following the Holocaust were characterised by silence must be understood in relation to the preponderance of representations that began to emerge from the 1990s. Thus the perceived silence of the Civil War exists because the memory of the Civil War was 'displaced' by the memorialisation of the 1916 Rising and subsequent struggle for independence. The silence exists in revolutionary memoirs that end suddenly in 1921, in veteran interviews that gloss over the Civil War and in the *relative* lack of songs regarding the Civil War period given that 'the old English–Irish polarity was no longer there to be exposed'.[31]

Yet if the question of *relativity* is removed, it emerges that the events of the Civil War nevertheless produced a wealth of representations in numerous forms, including popular histories, novels, diaries, plays, poetry and films. The proliferation of narratives may even be an anticipated outcome of civil war: Elisa Adami, writing of the Lebanese civil wars, suggests that '[a]midst enforced collective amnesia, public censorship and the maddening proliferation of competing versions, the task of fashioning historical narratives becomes all the [more] urgent as it is contentious'.[32]

The very idea that there was a silence surrounding the Civil War actually generated attempts to preserve the Civil War's overshadowed memory. The debates on the pages of the *Irish Book Lover* in 1929 are a case in point. After the editor expressed his concern that it was *more* difficult to attain documentation regarding the 1922–3 conflict than the earlier period, a number of readers wrote to the journal listing various Civil War publications. The editor subsequently committed himself to compiling a bibliography of the 'Literature of the Revolt', which included details of the many underground periodicals produced during the Civil War. Concerns about a drastic lack of material thus proved to be less warranted than initially assumed. Indeed, by 1931, commentators could remark that 'the Civil War seems to inspire more literature than its forerunner and we wonder why', while literary critics complained about the publication of 'civil war novels to a formula' and quipped about the lack of originality of such writings: 'but we have heard it in all the novels about the Irish civil war'.[33]

Nevertheless the initial concerns of the editor of the *Irish Book Lover* are so ingrained to this day that these popular, and even bestselling, books have been utterly neglected by both historians and literary scholars alike. These include different forms of life writing, from autobiographical novels and short stories to confessional poetry (as addressed in my study *Spiritual Wounds: Trauma, testimony and the Irish Civil War*). These insider autobiographical works emerged alongside imaginative evocations of the period by outside observers, such as the writings of French novelist Étiennette Beuque, Danish writer Nis Petersen, English-born novelist Kathleen Pawle or Irish-American Constantine FitzGibbon, whose 1969 novel *High Heroic* controversially portrayed Michael Collins in bed with a prostitute.[34] There is no shortage of popular representations by subsequent generations either, be that in the form of popular fiction, memoirs or other creative outputs. If anything, the assumed silence around the conflict has produced a remarkable (anti)tradition, as generation after generation have set out to shatter a perceived silence, often unaware of the lineage of silence-breakers to which they belong.[35]

How, then, can 'the notion of a virtual conspiracy of silence' still be, in Gavin Foster's words, the 'most common assumption about the period's memory legacy'?[36] In many ways the idea of silence is self-perpetuating, as the persistent idea of the 'traumatic silence' around the conflict has discouraged scholars from looking at the available materials, much of which has been hidden for decades in plain sight. But, equally, the 'silence' of the Civil War casts a light on the hierarchies that remain in academic study, highlighting prevailing views on what constitutes 'authentic' source material according to often narrowly defined disciplinary boundaries.

Where one looks: Authentic sources

Famine scholars have also noted that the perception of silence around the events of the 1840s was reinforced by the exclusion of popular source material. Margaret Kelleher, for example, argued in her 1997 study that the 'extent to which Irish literature contains references to the famine depends, very simply, on where one looks'. In the context of the Irish Civil War, it is clear where historians tend to look. Indeed historians who see the Civil War as 'Ireland's Great Silence' are often not referring to an actual lack of source material, but rather to the perceived lack of official records enabling 'dispassionate' analysis and 'detached' study, criteria commonly seen as the hallmark of historical writing on the Civil War. Neeson, for example, lamented the lack of 'official documents' available to him when writing his 1966 study, commenting that, although he was able to draw on published diaries, letters and personal recollections, these were 'obviously lacking the stamp of authority desirable for the recounting of controversial events'. When Younger published his 1968 study *The Irish Civil War*, it was telling that journalist Robert Kee commented that 'professional historians' might be disappointed by 'its dependence on oral testimony often delivered more than 40 years after the event'. Meanwhile Ferriter celebrates the opening of the Military Service Pensions Collection in *Between Two Hells* and suggests that 'historians are *now* in a position to investigate' (my emphasis) the 'personal trauma' and 'long, long reach' of the Civil War. Popular sources (including oral evidence, as explored by Gavin Foster) have thus been neglected in favour of 'official' archival sources, which are seen to better enable the historical profession in their pursuit of the 'noble dream' of objectivity.[37]

Literary scholars also tend to privilege established sources over popular writings, and accordingly have tended to view the decades following the Civil War as a time of disillusionment and cultural repression. James M. Cahalan, writing in the 1980s, postulated that 'Irish writers, like the Irish people as a whole, were slow in recovering from the divisive and disastrous Civil War of 1922–23'. Enda Longley contended in the early 1990s that the 'Civil War has not yet fully emerged from a traumatised silence', evoking as evidence the many participants who refused to speak of it. In 2021 R.F. Foster suggested that 'Creative literature inspired by the civil war [...] remains scanty', citing W.B. Yeats as 'the signal exception' to such silence. That many popular writings are overlooked in such an assumption mirrors other post-civil war situations: for example, it was believed in the 1950s that Spanish novelists had always avoided the Spanish Civil War, despite the almost 100 novels dealing with the period that had been published by that point.[38]

The adherence to the idea of silence among Irish literary scholars is all the more intriguing given that earlier considerations of the literature of the Irish revolution reached no such conclusions. Indeed Peter Costello argued in his 1977 study *The Heart Grown Brutal: The Irish revolution in literature from Parnell to the death of Yeats, 1891–1939* that 'to think of the Civil War as a failure of imagination would be wrong. It was quite the otherwise.' Perceptions of literary representations of the Civil War nevertheless remain inflected by popular ideas of trauma's latency. For example Emer Nolan suggests that there was a period of silence following the staging of Seán O'Casey's *Juno and the Paycock* in 1924 and that 'Other *key* works directly concerned with the Civil War appeared much later' (my emphasis). Here the idea of a period of societal repression following the establishment of the Free State essentially eclipses consideration of popular literature, reinforcing instead the established literary canon that conveniently supports the official preference for Civil War silence. While Yeats has been cited as the 'signal exception' to Civil War silence, the avid readers of bestselling

FORWARD

This is not a history; nor is it the story of a Movement; nor of martyrs - nor of heros: it is a tale of plain people caught in the mad whirl of revolution. I have not tried to write about leaders - history records them - I have merely written a straightforward story of the rank and file, and I have tried to show, what Secret Societies, firebrand leaders, and blind patriotism, can do to men, and to a Nation.

The story is coarse in parts, for which I am sorry, but this is unembellished realism. All the incidents related are true, ~~although they did not occur in the sequence recorded~~ the entire story being based on a series of true incidents, which have come within the author's personal experience.

While all the characters have been drawn from real life, they are purely ficticious, and no offence, directly or indirectly, is meant towards any living being.

FIONN O'MALLEY.

TELEGRAMS:
"IVERNA," PICCY LONDON.
TELEPHONE:
REGENT 4716.
Please reply to
The Secretary,
and quote No.

éıre

HIGH COMMISSIONER FOR IRELAND,
33-37 REGENT STREET,
LONDON, S.W.1.

21st August, 1947.

Dear Sir,

Referring to my recent call and to my conversation with Mr. Kissane, I now enclose the original manuscript of my novel, "Jackets Green". A glance through the manuscript will show that in parts it is not identical with the published work. This is due to the fact that when a clear copy was made I was dissatisfied with certain parts and, in fact, practically re-wrote the first chapter. Nevertheless the enclosed manuscript is the original, marked indelibly by the labour pains of creation! It has survived much bombing during the bombardment of London 1940/45, and indeed had quite an adventurous career in London during the war. It is with great pleasure that I now offer the manuscript as a gift to the National Library of Ireland and I feel honoured at its acceptance.

Yours faithfully,

Patrick Mulloy

PATRICK MULLOY.

The Librarian,
National Library of Ireland,
Kildare Street,
Dublin.

Fig. 11 (left) Unpublished foreword to *Jackets Green*, the 1936 novel by Fionn O'Malley (Patrick Mulloy). **Fig. 12** (right) Cover letter written by Mulloy to accompany his donation of the original manuscript to the National Library of Ireland in August 1947. The testimonial novel by London-based civil servant and National Army veteran Patrick Mulloy follows three young men whose friendship, formed in a prison camp during the War of Independence, is sundered by brutal civil war. It was briefly a Dublin bestseller before falling foul of the Censorship of Publications Board because of its graphic portrayals of physical and sexual violence. As one unforgiving *Irish Press* reviewer put it, 'as the story develops, the tragedy becomes grimmer and grimmer, sour and cynical [...] incidents of a horrible nature crowd on thickly. Shootings, burnings, third-degree methods, drunken orgies, scenes in brothels, men blown to bits pass across nightmare pages'. But Mulloy had never intended to write a romantic or heroic history. Rather, as he put it in his (unpublished) foreword, it was a tale of frustrated hopes, of 'unembellished realism', of 'plain people caught in the mad whirl of revolution'. It was a cautionary tale, dedicated to 'the rank and file, of every National Movement, and every Secret Society in every country in the world, to remind them, that many a path of glory leads to a graveyard of human souls'. The historical value of this example of what Siobhra Aiken describes as 'literary witnessing' lies in the 'foregrounding of experience effaced from official remembrance'. [Documents: National Library of Ireland, MS 2142 / See *Irish Press*, 10 Mar. 1936; Siobhra Aiken, *Spiritual Wounds: Trauma, testimony and the Irish Civil War* (Dublin, 2023), p. 34]

popular novels like former Free State soldier Patrick Mulloy's *Jackets Green* or Cumann na mBan activist Annie M.P. Smithson's *The Marriage of Nurse Harding*, or audiences at successful plays like A.P. Fanning's *Vigil*, might have a different view.[39]

There is also a tendency to view events that are deemed traumatic as ghostly presences on the fringes of creative works rather than as central thematic concerns. Writing in 2003, Terry Eagleton suggested that the Famine had 'inspired surprisingly little imaginative writing' and that this historical episode emerges as 'no more than a dim resonance' in the works of Joyce and Yeats. Eagleton's view has since been challenged by scholars, who have unpacked the many literary legacies of the Famine, including in the writings of Joyce and Yeats. Yet this idea of looming shadows endures. For example Gerardine Meaney contends that fiction regarding the revolutionary period tends 'to approach big historical events obliquely' and mentions that the Civil War appears as 'an ominous shadow at the edge of the story in the work of [Frank] O'Connor, [Liam] O'Flaherty, and [Rosamond] Jacob'.[40] While Jacob's novel *Troubled House* evokes the Civil War indirectly through a father–son fratricide plot, it is not as easy to characterise the conflict as a mere shadow in the works of O'Connor and O'Flaherty. Both wrote significant works directly referring to the events of 1922–3: O'Connor addressed the split in autobiographical writings and short stories (including in the celebrated collection *Guests of the Nation*), while O'Flaherty's banned 1933 novel, *The Martyr*, is set in Kerry during the Civil War.

Another key way that assumed silences are maintained is through what Alan Rosen refers to in the context of the Holocaust as an

Fig. 13 Portrait of writer Liam O'Flaherty (1896–1984) by Harry Kernoff (1936). O'Flaherty's native Inis Mór, one of the Aran Islands, forms the backdrop. On 18 January 1922, two days after the formation of the Provisional Government, young Communist Party of Ireland (CPI) member and chair of the Dublin Council of the Unemployed, Liam O'Flaherty, led over 100 unemployed workers in occupying the Rotunda concert hall in central Dublin, over which they raised the red flag. The O'Flaherty-penned 'Manifesto to Citizens of Dublin' was fly-posted across the city. Making no mention of the Treaty, it denounced the 'apathy of the ruling class' and the 'tyranny of capitalism', which left 30,000 Dubliners unemployed and driven to criminality to feed their families. Many, like O'Flaherty himself, had fought in the First World War, while others had been active in the War of Independence. The council demanded 'work for the workless' and 'maintenance until work is procured'. The occupation lasted four days. It came under attack from Catholic Action mobs and was defended by both the Dublin Metropolitan Police and the IRA. The occupation ended after negotiations between the latter and the CPI, whose leader Roddy Connolly, son of James, privately saw the occupation as a pointless stunt. The CPI joined the anti-Treaty IRA in the Battle for Dublin in the first days of the Civil War, though the nature of O'Flaherty's involvement is unclear. He fled to London after the fall of the Four Courts, where he published his first short story in 1923. Entitled 'The Sniper', it is set during the battle for Dublin and is a classic 'brother against brother' tale of the conflict. The first of his sixteen novels, *Thy Neighbour's Wife*, was also published in 1923. Although best known as a novelist, O'Flaherty has won most literary plaudits for his short stories. He returned to Ireland in 1924, and found fame with his 1925 novel, *The Informer*, which was made into an Academy Award-winning film by John Ford in 1935. O'Flaherty was the first Irish writer to be banned by the notorious Censorship of Publications Board when *The House of Gold* was prohibited in 1930. Five of his novels were banned by the board, including *The Martyr* (1933), which is set in Kerry during the Civil War. It was not prohibited for political reasons, but for being 'indecent and obscene'. 'In my work', wrote O'Flaherty in 1932, 'I have been forced in honesty to hold up a mirror to life as I found it in my country [...] So a censorship has been imposed upon my work [...] imported literature which is the product of Irish genius is seized [...] as dangerous contraband'. He moved to the United States in the 1930s, and returned to Ireland after the Second World War, where he remained until his death. [Image: courtesy of Sothebys and the Kernoff family / See Mike Milotte, 'When Communists Took Over the Rotunda to Fight for Dublin's Unemployed', *Irish Times*, 22 Jan. 2022 and 'Liam O'Flaherty' at the 'Ricorso' digital resource on Irish writers: http://www.ricorso.net/rx/az-data/index.htm]

Fig. 14 Photograph showing Noel Lemass (standing, in uniform, third from the right) at a bazaar in the Mansion House in Dublin in about 1915. Noel Lemass (1897–1923) was born in Capel Street in Dublin's city centre. Along with his younger brother Seán, he joined the Irish Volunteers in 1915. He was wounded during the 1916 Rising and captured on Marlborough Street and imprisoned. In the aftermath of the Rising, he managed to secure employment as an apprentice engineer with the Great Southern Railways company, spending time in Cork before returning to take a job with Dublin Corporation. Lemass was active in the War of Independence, and, in October 1919, he was arrested for his IRA activities – the first of numerous jailings. He took the anti-Treaty side in the Civil War and was captured in Glencullen in south County Dublin during the 'Night of the Bridges' (5–6 August 1922) when the IRA was foiled in its efforts to destroy road and railway infrastructure around Dublin city (Fig. 15). Lemass was interned but escaped from Gormanstown Camp in County Meath in September 1922. After a period in England he returned to Dublin but was seized on 3 July 1923 on Exchequer Street in the city. The abduction controversially took place after the IRA ceasefire in late April and the order to dump arms in May. An early appeal by his parents in the *Freeman's Journal* for any information on their missing son achieved little. Over three months elapsed before his mutilated body was found in the Dublin Mountains. No one was ever convicted of his killing. The brutal circumstance of Lemass's death is something his brother Seán – a founder of the Fianna Fáil party in 1926 and future taoiseach – rarely spoke about in public. A memorial to Captain Noel Lemass was unveiled in 1935 at the site where his body was found. [Image: Papers of Fr Senan Moynihan OFM Cap. (1900–70), courtesy of the Irish Capuchin Archives / See 'Noel Lemass (1897–1923) in the MSPC', Military Service Pensions Collection Blog Post, 2 July 2023, https://militarypensions.wordpress.com/2023/07/03/noel-lemass-1897-1923-in-the-mspc/; see also Ronan McGreevy, 'Who killed Noel Lemass, the brother of former Taoiseach Seán Lemass, in 1923?', *Irish Times*, 2 May 2023]

'idiom of discovery', as writings are marketed for their use of 'fresh materials' and 'newly available sources'. A rather intriguing trope in this vein is the frequent heralding of Irish Civil War writing as the 'first' such publication, essentially denying the existence of previous works. Colm Ó Labhra's *Trodairí na Treas Briogáide* (1955) has been celebrated for being 'an chéad leabhar a chuimsigh an cogadh cathartha ina léamh ar chogadh na saoirse' (the first book that included the civil war in its reading of the war of independence). Neeson's *The Civil War in Ireland* was advertised on its publication in 1966 as the 'First Documented Book Published On Hitherto Unspeakable War'. Michael Hopkinson's 1988 study, *Green Against Green*, was welcomed as the 'first dispassionate analysis of the civil war based on documentary evidence'. *The Irish Civil War* (1998) by Tim Pat Coogan and George Morrison was said to offer US audiences 'for the first time an overview of this rift'. Meanwhile Mark O'Sullivan's 1994 novel *Melody for Nora* has been celebrated as one of 'the first Irish novels' to grapple with the complexities of the Civil War. Thus the idea that there was a silence around the Civil War is consistently reinforced even in the face of the silence being broken.[41]

Personifications of silence

Questions can also be asked about the subjectivity of some of the evidence used to support Civil War silence. One of the most common ways this silence is illustrated is through reference to the many leading male figures who were reticent on the topic. For example Ferriter supports the view that silence was a legacy of the

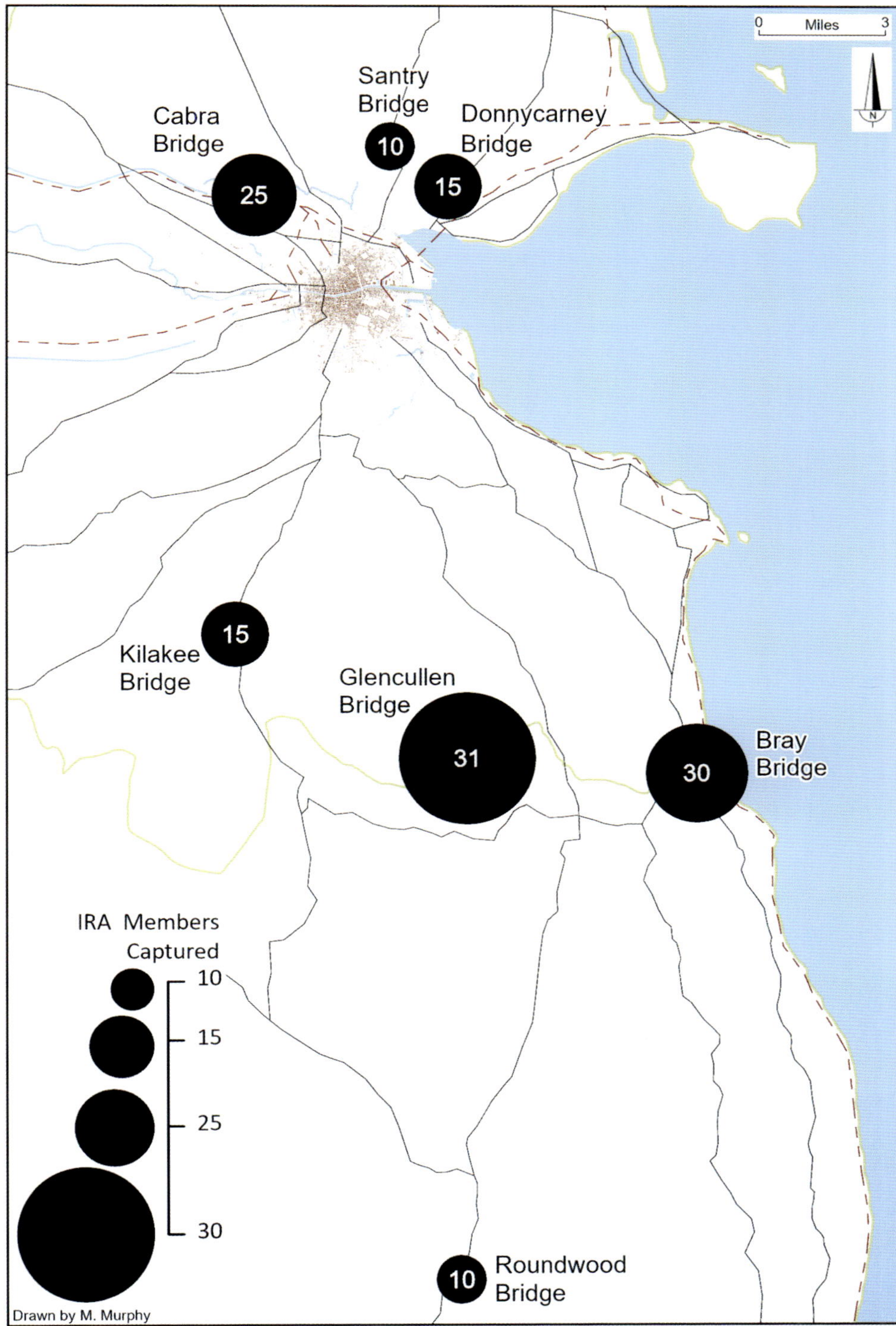

Fig. 15 'The Night of the Bridges', 5-6 August 1922: map showing the locations at which IRA members who were attempting to destroy bridges around Dublin were captured. The Dublin IRA was trying to disrupt the Provisional Government's ongoing efforts to secure the anti-Treaty heartland in south Munster. The Dublin anti-Treatyites had just regrouped after their shattering defeat in early July when they received orders from the IRA chief of staff, Liam Lynch, to destroy all the bridges leading into and out of the city. There was some dissension at a meeting of the Dublin IRA leadership. The risks of mobilising so many guerrillas (around 250, only some of whom could be armed) at one time and concentrated in a few locations were obvious. Nevertheless, as one reluctant IRA quartermaster, Laurence Nugent, conceded, the order 'had to be carried out'. The IRA prepared by creating several caches of explosives and gathering hundreds of picks, which the National Army reported had mysteriously gone missing in the capital. Disastrously for the anti-Treatyites, the plan was compromised. National Army intelligence chiefs Liam Tobin and Charles Dalton learned of a planned IRA meeting in the south Dublin suburb of Rathfarnham where intelligence officer Liam Clarke was captured. He was carrying a map of the bridges targeted for destruction on the night of 5–6 August. IRA battalions 1 and 2 were tasked with destroying bridges at Cabra, Santry, Donnycarney, Raheny and several other locations in the rural area north of the city. To the south, battalions 3 and 4 would cut the links between Dublin and the Wicklow mountains at Kilakee, Glencullen, Enniskerry and as far south as Roundwood. Most were taken by surprise when their work on the 'Night of the Bridges' was disrupted by parties of heavily armed National Army troops, some accompanied by armoured cars. Frank Henderson, commander of the 2nd Battalion in the north side of the city, recorded that they were 'attacked on both flanks by British and F.S. [Free State] troops who were cooperating'. The allegation of British involvement, which occurs numerous times in Henderson's account, is not supported in National Army reports. It is plausible, however, as the most experienced and motivated pro-Treaty troops had left Dublin for the south by August 1922, and a garrison of 6,000 British Army troops remained in the city until December. Whatever the composition of their forces, pro-Treaty troops rounded up most of the anti-Treaty parties with little resistance. Only two anti-Treatyites and no National Army soldiers were wounded. Charlie Dalton reported to National Army command: 'In nearly every case the Irregulars were found in the act of tearing up bridges. 104 were captured [...] [and] practically no damage was done in North County Dublin.' At least another fifty were captured in south County Dublin and more in follow up raids. The National Army recorded taking 187 prisoners in Dublin between 5 and 13 August 1922. The 'Night of the Bridges' not only failed to disrupt the National Army's seizure of the south of Ireland, it also almost crippled what remained of the anti-Treaty IRA in Dublin. [Text: John Dorney / Source: John Dorney, *The Civil War in Dublin: The fight for the Irish capital, 1922–1924* (Dublin, 2017)]

Civil War that 'was not necessarily ignoble' with reference to Fianna Fáil Taoiseach Seán Lemass, who was reluctant to revisit the war in interviews with journalists, including the brutal killing of his brother Noel by pro-Treaty soldiers on 3 July 1923. R.F. Foster evokes political figure Robert Barton who 'never discussed the civil war', while Dolan refers to the 'silence of Stephen Fuller' before asking 'does civil war, by its very nature, demand silence?'[42]

The reticence of these public figures is certainly notable, highlighting what Eunan O'Halpin refers to as a culture of 'male

Fig. 16 Shirt worn by Stephen Fuller at the 'Ballyseedy Massacre'. Fuller was the sole survivor of the 'massacre' at Ballyseedy, County Kerry on 7 March 1923 when nine IRA prisoners were tied together around a land mine that was then detonated by National Army troops. Fuller was blown clear and managed to make his way to a nearby house, from where he was taken to a dug-out and attended to by Dr Shanahan of Farranfore. The injured man was then moved to the house of a well-known republican family, the Dalys in Knockaneacoolteen, where he was sheltered for several days before being moved to another safe house. The shirt was left behind in Knockaneacoolteen, where it remained until it came into the care of Kerry County Museum in 2023. It is clearly badly damaged, particularly on the right-hand side where Fuller seems to have taken the main force of the blast. On the back are numerous small holes, consistent with Dr Shanahan's account that dozens of small pieces of grit were embedded under the skin of his back. This was later confirmed by an x-ray taken in Peamount Sanitorium in 1933 while Fuller was being treated for TB. When Fuller was brought to the Daly house, the shirt was not only torn but blackened and bloody. So why keep it? It is tempting to say that it was kept as a kind of sacred relic, but the story is more layered than that. As the family grappled with the enormity of what happened in Ballyseedy, their first instinct was to keep the shirt as evidence. Within a week, the Dalys had their own tragedy to deal with, having received word that one of their sons, Charlie, had been executed by a Free State firing squad in Dromboe, County Donegal. Active in the Northern counties since 1921, Charlie was captured in Donegal in November 1922, tried by military court, sentenced to death in January 1923 and executed on 14 March. Fuller's shirt was put away. It was not a conscious effort to banish the horror of Ballyseedy, but the act of a grieving family unsure of what else to do with it. As the years passed it took on a terrible significance for Nancy, one of the younger members of the Daly family, as a tangible link to a deeply troubling time. She was a child in 1920 when British soldiers burned the family home and one of her sisters died of TB around the same time. Stephen Fuller's arrival just a few years later was closely followed by the news of her brother's execution. For her, all these traumatic events became wrapped up in the shirt, with its bloodstains, rips and tears. As an adult in the 1940s she felt compelled to wash it, perhaps symbolically trying to wash the past clean. The shirt was again put away, although never forgotten and often spoken about within the family circle. It is an object that connects the viewer directly with two families, the Fullers and the Dalys, and the traumas they endured. [Text: Helen O'Carroll / Image: courtesy of Kerry County Museum and Neustock Media]

reticence' about personal loss that was the norm both in Ireland and elsewhere among this generation.[43] Even so, silence was not the only response to the Civil War among the political elite. One could equally point to the many political figures who found themselves 'shouting, gesticulating, clamouring' in the Dáil when the words '77', 'Ballyseedy', 'Dick and Joe' or 'the Treaty' were mentioned.[44] Moreover the evocation of male reticence to illustrate Civil War silence only gives one side of the story, given that leading women activists were much less likely to subscribe to the 'honourable' silence for which their male counterparts were praised. Indeed a key dimension of female political rhetoric during this period was the public evocation of loss, as evident in the emotive contributions of female politicians during the Treaty debates and the 'culture of eye-witness' that was employed widely, particularly in the diaspora, to tug at heartstrings and increase fund-raising efforts.[45]

The cited reticence of certain public figures was not necessarily uninterrupted either. In this regard, Stephen Fuller is an interesting example. On the one hand Fuller followed the lead of many leading figures and, during his career as a Fianna Fáil TD, apparently did not address his Civil War experience and most notably his experience as the sole survivor of the atrocity in Ballyseedy in March 1923, a reprisal attack – for the killing of five National Army soldiers in an explosion at Knocknagoshel – during which nine anti-Treatyites were tied to a mine that was detonated. However the assertions that Fuller never spoke of the 'event publicly until the 1960s' and that he 'shunned interviews' are untrue.[46] Fuller give a statement about his survival just weeks after the event; his testimony was circulated widely during the spring of 1923 in republican papers including the *Daily Bulletin* and *Éire:*

> We were brought to Ballyseedy Cross or thereabouts. We were all placed round a log of timber on the road and tied together with a big rope. Our hands were then tied together and our ankles, and another rope was tied around our knees. We were then told that we were to be blown to atoms as a reprisal [...] Then the explosion

> occurred and I remember no more. I was blown away to some distance and my clothes were blown off me. I then escaped through the field.[47]

Fuller's testimony subsequently generated numerous representations of the atrocity among anti-Treaty republicans, from Dorothy Macardle's *Tragedies of Kerry* in 1924, to poems and songs like Liam Mac Gabhann's 'The Message of the Banshee', to the play *Ballyseedy* by Dónal O'Keefe, which was serialised in *An Phoblacht* from 1933.[48]

Moreover the suggestion that Fuller 'shunned media interviews' does not hold. As Owen O'Shea's research highlights, when Fuller made his debut television appearance in 1981 as part of Robert Kee's BBC documentary series *Ireland – A Television History,* he told a reporter for *The Kerryman* that 'I am surprised that I have not been interviewed before.' Fuller attributed the delay to the fact that 'it was a job done by Irishmen' rather than by the Black and Tans, but also quipped that 'RTÉ should have done it long ago.'[49] Fuller's case underlines the extent to which the 'silence' is as much about an unwillingness to listen as an unwillingness to speak. And while Fuller might be evoked to personify Civil War silence, could he not also be considered one of the key silence-breakers to emerge from this period, without whom the realities of what happened at Ballyseedy would never be known?

Comparative and transnational approaches

The global turn within scholarship of the Irish revolution highlights the merits of comparative and transnational approaches in understanding Ireland's past. This chapter suggests that such comparative approaches are also helpful for understanding the legacy of silence and trauma associated with the Irish Civil War, a legacy that has much in common with the popular psychoanalytic discourses surrounding other devastating events such as the Irish Famine, the First World War, the Spanish Civil War and the Holocaust. This psychoanalytically influenced lens on the events of the Civil War was evident during, and even before, the conflict erupted, but what is remarkable in the Irish context is that these models have been largely unquestioned over the last 100 years. The blind spots of these approaches come into sharp relief when assessed in comparative terms. Generalisations can emerge as personal trauma and societal trauma are equated. The agency of historical actors risks being downplayed as the political factors underpinning silence and silence-breaking are obscured by a tendency to conflate trauma with distress and powerlessness. Equally, the idea that historical remembrance can unproblematically redress social cleavages can lead to the mandating of 'proper' forms of remembrance (which, in the case of the Irish Civil War, is also reflected in a tendency among historians and public commentators to praise honourable silence on the topic).

One of the key effects of these psychoanalytically informed perspectives is the tendency to assume that the shock of traumatic events results in cultural stagnancy, leading to a dearth of source material for the study of the difficult episode. In many contexts, these preconceptions obscure the *relative* body of material that is available despite (or even because of) the contentious legacies of these events. The idea that silence was the default response to the Irish Civil War has nevertheless discouraged scholars from investigating the material that does exist. When sources regarding the Civil War are discussed, they have been dismissed or misread to satisfy the established viewpoint, or they are treated as exceptional discoveries, which in turn perpetuates the belief that there was a silence. The maintenance of the idea of Civil War silence has also been achieved by the privileging of official and canonical source material, through the corresponding neglect of popular and oral forms of remembrance, and through the selective foregrounding of the experiences of certain male public figures. The reconsideration of the 'silence' of the Irish Civil War demands not just revisiting the writing of the conflict of 1922–3, but also a reassessment of the values and priorities that have characterised historical writing for much of the past century.

Seán O'Casey and the Irish Civil War

Paul O'Brien

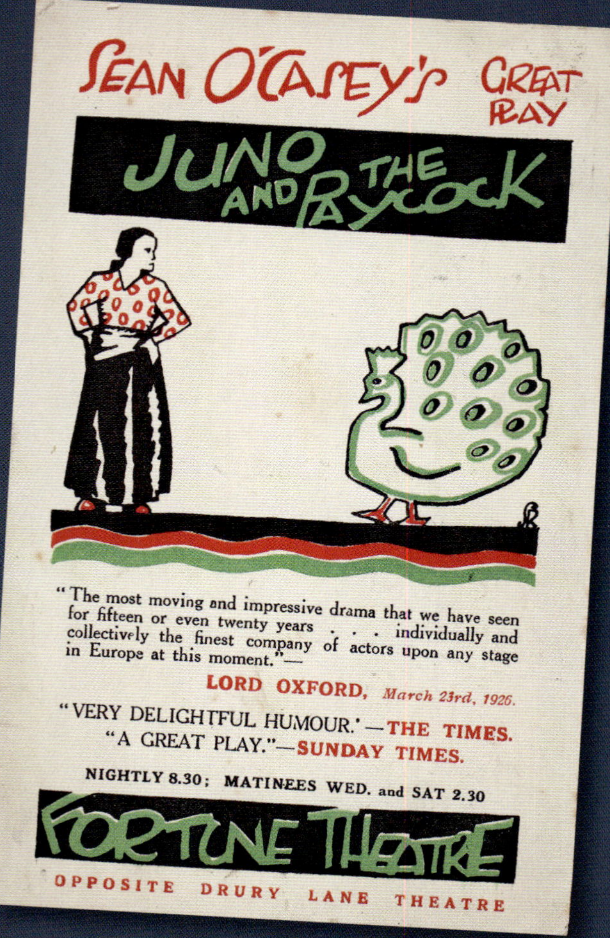

Despite his differences with Sinn Féin on the issue of class politics during the War of Independence, Seán O'Casey was clear about which side he was on. This was not the time to shout about the differences between Labour and Sinn Féin; he had lost that battle, and all he could do was add his voice to those calling for a more radical outcome. In January 1918 he wrote a Sinn Féin election ballad, 'Hurrah for Ireland and Sinn Féin', but his offer of a pamphlet, *England's Atrocities in Ireland*, was not taken up by his publisher. In the three Dublin plays, written between 1922 and 1926, he set out to deconstruct the prevailing narrative of heroic sacrifice that was devoid of any social or economic significance. He asked a question in these plays; who was the new freedom for, and what class would shape the new state? During the Civil War, his sympathies were with the republican forces and against the Free State army, whom he referred to as the 'Green and Tans', but this did not compromise his criticism of the anti-Treaty position. O'Casey argued for other possibilities during the Civil War, a point he makes very forcefully in his 1923 one-act play, *Kathleen Listens In*, which focused on the social and political shortcomings of the Free State. His regard for the anti-Treaty side is evident in this Swiftian-style fantasy. He sent it to the Abbey for consideration, but the script was returned a week later with a note saying; 'it is too definite a piece of propaganda for us to do it'. O'Casey subsequently resurrected the script, updating and rewriting it to take account of the political situation in the months following the end of the Civil War. He submitted the revised script to the Abbey, and it premiered in October 1923.

His most considered response to the Civil War is *Juno and the Paycock*, which is set during those terrible events and first produced at the Abbey in 1924. The audience during that first production would have contained many ex-combatants from both sides of the Civil War divide. The play is structured around the Boyle family, and the family as a metaphor for the disintegration of the state is clearly implied. The dominant theme of *Juno and the Paycock* is one of betrayal. Johnny Boyle, a republican, betrays his comrade, Tancred, who is abducted and shot by the Free State forces. Johnny is seized by his former comrades and executed for his treachery. In the midst of the Civil War, Captain Boyle says, 'we've nothing to do with these things one way or the other', but the unfolding tragedy that affects the Boyle family undermines that position. O'Casey portrays the tension between the desires of ordinary people to live in peace and the real world of civil war and strife intruding into their lives, for what O'Casey came to consider a meaningless and futile conflict.

In the aftermath of the Civil War O'Casey questioned the distinction between the two positions that led to the Civil War and wondered what it was actually about: 'For Document No. 2! Not to abolish poverty. No; just for a spate of words that Alice in Wonderland wouldn't understand' that divided family and friends. Despite this criticism, O'Casey never wavered in his support for a united Irish republic. He was invited to speak at a meeting to commemorate the 1916 Rising in London in 1940, and could always be relied upon to write for an Irish republican newspaper if requested. [Sources: Paul O'Brien, *Seán O'Casey: Political activist and writer* (Cork, 2023), p. 109; Robert Goode Hogan and Richard Burnham, *The Years of O'Casey 1921–1926: A documentary history* (Delaware, 1992), p. 240; Sean O'Casey, *Letters*, vol. 1 (New York, 1975), p. 101; Sean O'Casey, *Juno and the Paycock* (London, 1925), p. 71; Sean O'Casey. *Autobiographies*, vol. 4 (London, 1972), p. 96]

Fig. 1 (opposite top) Postcard advertising Seán O'Casey's *Juno and the Paycock* at the Fortune Theatre, London, March 1926. [Image: National Library of Ireland, EPH A205]

Fig. 2 (opposite bottom) Seán O'Casey and a policeman outside the Fortune Theatre, on Drury Street, London, March 1926. [Image: National Library of Ireland, NPA SOC]

Fig. 3 (right) A page from a draft of Act 1, *Juno and the Paycock*, with manuscript amendments by Seán O'Casey, c. 1923. The scene features Mary Boyle, daughter of the 'Captain' Jack Boyle, the eponymous Juno who dubs her husband, the 'Paycock' for his unproductive, if often poetic posturing, and Mary's suitor, Jerry Devine, another resident of the Dublin tenement. According to O'Casey's stage directions, Devine is 'about twenty-five, well set, active and earnest. He is a type, becoming very common now in the Labour Movement, of a mind knowing enough to make the mass of his associates, who know less, a power, and too little to broaden that power for the benefit of all'. O'Casey's annotation to the naturalistic dialogue indicates his dissatisfaction with Jerry's appeal to Mary's recollection of happier times. But the ambitious Mary, who reads Ibsen and sees education as an escape from poverty, is more attracted to schoolteacher and theosophist, Charlie Bentham. He appears more worldly and sophisticated than Jerry but, like the other male characters, he abandons the pregnant Mary at the play's tragic end. O'Casey's trade union sympathies are reflected in his characterisation of Jerry, the aspirant trade union secretary, and Mary, who is on strike, because 'a principle's a principle', but the play is essentially a tragicomedy that underscores the very human inheritance of political violence. As Juno puts it in a memorable allusion to W.B. Yeats's 'Easter 1916', when she learns of the death of her 'Irregular'-turned-informer son, 'Take away our hearts of stone and leave us with hearts o'flesh'. [Document: National Library of Ireland, MS 50,080/2]

Fig. 4 (below) Aaron Monaghan and Caitríona Ennis in *Juno and the Paycock*, staged as part of the acclaimed DruidO'Casey production (2023), when a company of eighteen actors directed by Garry Hynes, performed Seán O'Casey's 'Dublin trilogy' – *The Plough and the Stars*, *The Shadow of a Gunman* and *Juno and the Paycock*, in chronological sequence, in one day. [Image: Ros Kavanagh]

Juno And The Paycock. 13

Jerry-
The bitther word agen , Mary.

Mary-
You wont allow me to be friendly with you; if I thry, you deliberately misundherstand it.

Jerry-
I didnt I always misundherstand it; you were ofen delighted to to have the arms of Jerry around you.

Mary-
If you go on talkin like this, Jerry Devine, youll make me hate you !

Jerry-
Well, let it be either a weddin or a wake ! Listen, Mary, I'm standin for the Secretaryship of our Union. Theres only one opposin me; I'm popular with all the men, an a good speaker-all are sayin that I'll get elected.

Mary-
Well ?

Jerry-
The job's worth three hundred an fifty pounds a year, Mary. You an I could live nice an eosily on that;it would lift you out o this place an-

Mary-
I havent time to listen to you now-I have to go.

(She is going out when Jerry bars the way.)

Jerry(Appealingly)
Mary, whats come over you with me for the last few weeks ? You hardly speak to me, an then only a word with a face o bittherness on it. Have you forgotten, Mary, all the happy evenins ~~that were as sweet as the scented hawthorn that sheltered the sides o the road~~, as ~~we sauntehred through the country ?~~ we spent, an all the gentle things we said to each other whenever we went saunterin thro' the country.

Mary-
Thats all over now. When you get your new job, Jerry, you wont be long findin a girl far betther than I am for your sweetheart.

Jerry-
Never, never, Mary ! No matther what happens youll always be the same to me.

Mary-
I must be off; please let me go, Jerry.

Jerry

This index, compiled by Andy Bielenberg and John Dorney for the Irish Civil War Fatalities Project and presented in chronological order, is a record of the 1,484 victims of political violence in Ireland that have so far been documented between 28 June 1922 and 24 May 1923. It lists 649 members of the pro-Treaty forces, which included the National Army (NA), the Civic Guard, the Citizens' Defence Force (CDF) and the Criminal Investigation Department (CID). It also names 443 anti-Treaty combatants, including members of the Irish Republican Army (IRA), Cumann na mBan (CnamB) and Na Fianna Éireann; 370 civilians and 22 members of the crown forces, including the British Army, the Ulster Special Constabulary (USC) and one member of the Royal Air Force (RAF). Each entry includes the name, age and affiliation of the fatality as well as the location and date of their death. An analysis of the causes of death, the age and social profiles of the victims and the geographical and temporal patterns of violence during the Civil War can be found in Chapter 6 of this volume. The wide variety of sources consulted to compile the index are listed in the bibliography on pp. 481–3. Supported by the Government of Ireland under the Decade of Centenaries Programme 2023, the Irish Civil War Fatalities Index is the first comprehensive attempt to enumerate and list all of the fatalities of the Irish Civil War of 1922–3. [Image: crowds in Cork city, August 1922. National Library of Ireland, HOGW 92]

SECTION 10

Irish Civil War Fatalities Index

Name	Location	County	Date	Affiliation	Age
Joseph Considine	Jervis Street Hospital	Dublin	28/06/1922	IRA	20
Thomas Wall	Richmond Hospital	Dublin	28/06/1922	IRA	17
William Clarke	North Great George's Street	Dublin	28/06/1922	Fianna	
William Doyle	Jervis Street Hospital	Dublin	28/06/1922	IRA	22
Thomas Mandeville	Baggot Street Hospital	Dublin	28/06/1922	NA	46
Michael Vaughan	Saint Vincent's Hospital	Dublin	28/06/1922	NA	25
Patrick Cosgrave	Richmond Hospital	Dublin	28/06/1922	Civilian	14
Margaret Kelly	Jervis Street Hospital	Dublin	28/06/1922	Civilian	43
Arthur McKeever	Jervis Street Hospital	Dublin	28/06/1922	Civilian	24
Thomas Fitzgerald	Mercer's Hospital	Dublin	28/06/1922	Civilian	15
Laurence Frier	Mercer's Hospital	Dublin	28/06/1922	Civilian	20
James Hurley	Jervis Street Hospital	Dublin	28/06/1922	Civilian	29
Michael Keogh	Jervis Street Hospital	Dublin	28/06/1922	Civilian	46
James Shine	Richmond Hospital	Dublin	28/06/1922	Civilian	77
William Cooke McAllistair	Meath Hospital	Dublin	28/06/1922	Civilian	36
William Boardman	Jervis Street Hospital	Dublin	28/06/1922	Civilian	20
Robert Perkins	Mater Hospital	Dublin	28/06/1922	Civilian	30
John Healy	Richmond Hospital	Dublin	28/06/1922	Civilian	25
Elizabeth Gorman	Jervis Street Hospital	Dublin	28/06/1922	Civilian	54
Patrick Ormonde	Benburb Street	Dublin	28/06/1922	Civilian	
John Moran	Kilkenny Military Barracks	Kilkenny	28/06/1922	NA	23
Jack Lynch	Cottage Hospital, Drogheda	Louth	28/06/1922	NA	
John O'Mahoney	Jervis Street Hospital	Dublin	29/06/1922	IRA	
Matthew Tompkins	Mater Hospital	Dublin	29/06/1922	IRA	21
John Monks	Clondalkin	Dublin	29/06/1922	IRA	
George Walsh	Richmond Hospital	Dublin	29/06/1922	NA	32
Patrick McGarry	Mater Hospital	Dublin	29/06/1922	NA	21
James Walsh	Four Courts	Dublin	29/06/1922	NA	26
Patrick Walsh	Richmond Hospital	Dublin	29/06/1922	NA	
Patrick Lowe	Mater Hospital	Dublin	29/06/1922	NA	24
Michael Curtin	Richmond Hospital	Dublin	29/06/1922	NA	21
Patrick Connolly	Killosery, north County Dublin	Dublin	29/06/1922	Civilian	
John William Murphy	Richmond Hospital	Dublin	29/06/1922	Civilian	26
William Byrne	Richmond Hospital	Dublin	29/06/1922	Civilian	34
Patrick White	Richmond Hospital	Dublin	29/06/1922	Civilian	19
Alexander Taylor	King George V Hospital	Dublin	29/06/1922	British Army	21
Francis Jackson	Dame Street/Cecilia Street	Dublin	29/06/1922	IRA	22
William Leech	Millmount Barracks, Drogheda	Louth	29/06/1922	IRA	
William Moran	Kiltimagh	Mayo	29/06/1922	IRA	20
James Connolly	Finner Camp, Ballyshannon	Donegal	30/06/1922	IRA	34
Sean Cusack	Richmond Hospital	Dublin	30/06/1922	IRA	19

Name	Location	County	Date	Affiliation	Age
James George Walsh	Richmond Hospital	Dublin	30/06/1922	NA	
Thomas Hogan	Jervis Street Hospital	Dublin	30/06/1922	NA	22
Michael McGrath	Four Courts	Dublin	30/06/1922	NA	
John Lewis	Parnell Street	Dublin	30/06/1922	NA	23
Rosaline Dora Harrison	Meath Hospital	Dublin	30/06/1922	Civilian	27
Thomas Daly	Jervis Street Hospital	Dublin	30/06/1922	Civilian	45
Sarah Richardson	Mark Street	Dublin	30/06/1922	Civilian	63
Hannah McGowan	Jervis Street Hospital	Dublin	30/06/1922	Civilian	42
John Doran	Jervis Street Hospital	Dublin	30/06/1922	Civilian	27
Stanley Rogers	King George V Hospital	Dublin	30/06/1922	RAF	21
Edward Sheehy	Workhouse, Listowel	Kerry	30/06/1922	NA	21
Hanna O'Meara	Pearse Street, Nenagh	Tipperary	30/06/1922	Civilian	47
William Frazer	Newtownhamilton	Armagh	30/06/1922	USC	
Casey	Curragh Military Hospital	Kildare	July 1922	NA	
Thomas Markey	Jervis Street Hospital	Dublin	01/07/1922	IRA	25
David Bain	Richmond Hospital	Dublin	01/07/1922	NA	25
Richard Reid	Jervis Street Hospital	Dublin	01/07/1922	NA	22
Daniel Brennan	Jervis Street Hospital	Dublin	01/07/1922	NA	19
John Banbrick	St Michael's Hospital, Dun Laoghaire	Dublin	01/07/1922	Civilian	56
Margaret Byrne	Doctor Steeven's Hospital	Dublin	01/07/1922	Civilian	2
Edward Dwan	Mater Hospital	Dublin	01/07/1922	Civilian	15
Patrick Meehan	Mater Hospital	Dublin	01/07/1922	Civilian	24
John McGowan	Vincent's Hospital	Dublin	02/07/1922	IRA	22
Joseph Stewart	Jervis Street Hospital	Dublin	02/07/1922	NA	22
Luke Condron	Meath Hospital	Dublin	02/07/1922	NA	27
William O'Connor	Arran Quay	Dublin	02/07/1922	Civilian	29
James Kealy	County Infirmary, Portlaoise	Laois	02/07/1922	NA	24
Shelly	Boyle	Roscommon	02/07/1922	NA	30
Michael Dockery	Boyle Workhouse, Boyle	Roscommon	02/07/1922	NA	34
Charles O'Malley	Jervis Street Hospital	Dublin	03/07/1922	IRA	18
Mabel Lynn	Jervis Street Hospital	Dublin	03/07/1922	Civilian	24
Thomas Prendergast	Blindwell, Foxhall	Galway	03/07/1922	IRA	19
James Tracy	Raheen	Galway	03/07/1922	Civilian	23
James Byrne	Sligo Jail	Sligo	03/07/1922	NA	15
Terence Byrne	Castle Street, Nenagh	Tipperary	03/07/1922	NA	22
Patrick McCarthy	Nursing Home, Clancoole, Bandon	Cork	04/07/1922	IRA	22
William Brennan	Jervis Street Hospital	Dublin	04/07/1922	NA	23
Kathleen Dowling	Jervis Street Hospital	Dublin	04/07/1922	Civilian	25
Henry Hynes	Jervis Street Hospital	Dublin	04/07/1922	Civilian	41
Alice Slowey	Fair Street, Drogheda	Louth	04/07/1922	Civilian	21
John Blaney	Ferbane, Offaly	Offaly	04/07/1922	NA	22

Name	Location	County	Date	Affiliation	Age
Arthur Mitchel	Ulster Bank, High Street, Tullamore	Offaly	04/07/1922	Civilian	59
Patrick McDermott	Markree Castle, Collooney	Sligo	04/07/1922	NA	29
Martin Flannelly	Gurteen	Sligo	04/07/1922	IRA	24
James Roche	Newtownbarrry	Wexford	04/07/1922	IRA	21
Joseph Hurzon	Mater Hospital, Belfast	Antrim	04/07/1922	Fianna	15
James Mooney	Unity Street, Belfast	Antrim	04/07/1922	Civilian	70
Joseph Sweeny	County Infirmary, Carlow	Carlow	05/07/1922	IRA	20
John Fitzsimons	Meath Hospital	Dublin	05/07/1922	NA	23
Leo Walpole	Mercer's Hospital	Dublin	05/07/1922	Civilian	31
Sylvester Shepard	Rosetown, Ballitore	Kildare	05/07/1922	IRA	22
Laurence Sweeney	Rosetown, Ballitore	Kildare	05/07/1922	IRA	
William Galbraith	Abbeyleix	Laois	05/07/1922	Civilian	8
Thomas Ruane	County Infirmary, Castlebar	Mayo	05/07/1922	NA	29
George McDermott	Curraghtown, Navan	Meath	05/07/1922	IRA	34
Maurice Spillane	Friary Lane, Enniscorthy	Wexford	05/07/1922	IRA	20
Joseph Hammill	Blessington	Wicklow	05/07/1922	IRA	
Mary Semple	Ardgowan Street, Belfast	Antrim	05/07/1922	Civilian	25
John Keenan	Vicar Street	Dublin	06/07/1922	NA	22
James Clarke	Jervis Street Hospital	Dublin	06/07/1922	Civilian	29
William Saunders	Mater Hospital	Dublin	06/07/1922	Civilian	15
Christopher McGlynn	Abbeyleix	Laois	06/07/1922	NA	22
John Nolan	Curraghtown, Navan	Meath	06/07/1922	NA	23
James Kivlehan	County Infirmary, Sligo	Sligo	06/07/1922	Civilian	66
Patrick English	Longford Pass, Thurles	Tipperary	06/07/1922	IRA	
Cathal Brugha	Mater Hospital	Dublin	07/07/1922	IRA	47
Patrick Smyth	Saint Vincent's Hospital	Dublin	07/07/1922	NA	22
John Dunne	Taylor's pub, Swords	Dublin	07/07/1922	NA	22
John McGrath	Doctor Steeven's Hospital	Dublin	07/07/1922	Civilian	14
Francis Kearns	Roxborough, Kilchreest, Loughrea	Galway	07/07/1922	IRA	19
Michael Hynes	Military barracks, Ballinrobe	Mayo	07/07/1922	IRA	23
Francis Balfe	Ballytrasna	Roscommon	07/07/1922	NA	26
Ellen Nolan	Boyle	Roscommon	07/07/1922	Civilian	50
James McNamee	Mullingar Courthouse, Mullingar	Westmeath	07/07/1922	NA	23
Matthew Pender	County Home, Enniscorthy	Wexford	07/07/1922	NA	27
George Hawden	Killduff	Cavan	08/07/1922	Civilian	
Patrick Malone	O'Brien's Bridge	Clare	08/07/1922	NA	20
Patrick Doyle	Crooksling, Brittas	Dublin	08/07/1922	NA	18
John Joseph Byrne	Meath Hospital	Dublin	08/07/1922	NA	31
Gerald O'Connor	Roxborough, Gort	Galway	08/07/1922	NA	
Patrick Walsh	Bohermore, Galway city	Galway	08/07/1922	NA	18
Joseph Donnellan	Bohermore, Galway city	Galway	08/07/1922	IRA	25

NAME	LOCATION	COUNTY	DATE	AFFILIATION	AGE
Patrick Murphy	Drogheda Workhouse	Louth	08/07/1922	Civilian	48
Thomas Murphy	Emly	Tipperary	08/07/1922	NA	
Patrick Connolly	Monck Street, Wexford	Wexford	08/07/1922	IRA	23
Frank McAleer	Argyle Street, Belfast	Antrim	08/07/1922	Civilian	
Peter McManus	Carrigmore	Tyrone	08/07/1922	Civilian	
Francis Dolan	Rosafaraghan, Ferbane	Offaly	09/07/1922	IRA	26
Andrew Smith	Rathmore	Antrim	09/07/1922	Civilian	
Anthony Walsh	Kilakee House, Rathfarnham	Dublin	10/07/1922	Civilian	27
Laurence Bradley	Limerick city	Limerick	10/07/1922	NA	
Charles McGinley	Lifford Infirmary	Donegal	11/07/1922	NA	23
John Sweeney	Drumkeen	Donegal	11/07/1922	NA	22
John Connolly	Tullaghan	Donegal	11/07/1922	IRA	18
Thomas O'Brien	Saint John's Hospital, Limerick	Limerick	11/07/1922	NA	19
Thomas Sheerin	County Infirmary	Sligo	11/07/1922	IRA	33
Patrick O'Brien	County Home, Enniscorthy	Wexford	11/07/1922	IRA	23
Harry Little	Bramcote Street, Belfast	Antrim	11/07/1922	Civilian	35
Thomas Cochrane	Banbridge Infirmary	Down	11/07/1922	USC	
Thomas O'Reilly	Coolcarrigan	Kildare	12/07/1922	IRA	28
Denis Dwyer	Capard House, Rosenallis	Laois	12/07/1922	IRA	22
Patrick Stapleton	Saint John's Hospital, Limerick	Limerick	13/07/1922	NA	24
John Kennedy	Military Hospital, Limerick	Limerick	13/07/1922	Civilian	36
Sean Adair	Dooney Rock	Sligo	13/07/1922	NA	20
Patrick Callaghan	Dooney Rock	Sligo	13/07/1922	NA	
John Farrell	Dooney Rock	Sligo	13/07/1922	NA	
Robert Boyd	Belfast	Antrim	13/07/1922	Civilian	
Peter Francis Cahill	Thomas Davis Street, Cork city	Cork	14/07/1922	Fianna	11
John O'Sullivan	Knoppoge, Mastergeehy, Killarney	Kerry	14/07/1922	IRA	
Mary Cadden	Barringtons Hospital, Limerick	Limerick	14/07/1922	Civilian	19
Michael Kavanagh	Lansdowne, Limerick	Limerick	14/07/1922	Civilian	55
Patrick Walsh	Barracks, Maam	Mayo	14/07/1922	IRA	
John Brett	Tobercurry Hospital	Sligo	14/07/1922	IRA	22
John Furlong	Rahealty, Ballyduff	Tipperary	14/07/1922	NA	
John Francis Cusick	Military Hospital, Custume Barracks, Athlone	Westmeath	14/07/1922	NA	26
William Browne	Londonderry Infirmary	Derry	14/07/1922	NA	
T. Lynch	Bellanagh	Cavan	15/07/1922	Civilian	
John O'Connor	Clooneyogan, Lahinch	Clare	15/07/1922	Civilian	49
Stephen Roughan	Ennis Hospital, Ennis	Clare	15/07/1922	Civilian	20
John O'Connor	Clonyogan, Ennistymon	Clare	15/07/1922	Civilian	49
Patrick Greaney	Gort	Galway	15/07/1922	NA	24
Percy Tweedle	Saint John's Hospital, Limerick	Limerick	15/07/1922	NA	

Name	Location	County	Date	Affiliation	Age
Michael Moynihan	Saint John's Hospital, Limerick	Limerick	15/07/1922	Fianna	19
Michael Minahan	Saint John's Hospital, Limerick	Limerick	15/07/1922	Civilian	19
John Sweeney	County Infirmary	Sligo	15/07/1922	NA	18
Patrick O'Dea	Kilrush Hospital, Kilrush	Clare	16/07/1922	IRA	18
Timothy Murphy	Kilmallock	Limerick	16/07/1922	NA	
James Ambrose	Ballyquirke, Newcastle, Limerick	Limerick	16/07/1922	Civilian	40
Daniel King	Ballyquirke, Newcastle, Limerick	Limerick	16/07/1922	Civilian	40
John Campbell	Anne Street Barracks, Dundalk	Louth	16/07/1922	IRA	23
John Murphy	Templeshannon, Enniscorthy	Wexford	16/07/1922	Civilian	17
Andrew Baker	Hospital, Bagnalstown	Carlow	17/07/1922	Civilian	6
Sean O'Halloran	Ennis Hospital	Clare	17/07/1922	IRA	21
Martin Rooney	Coshla Athenry	Galway	17/07/1922	NA	
Joseph McEnery	Limerick Docks, Limerick	Limerick	17/07/1922	NA	
Patrick Cummins	City Home and Hospital, Limerick	Limerick	17/07/1922	NA	
Patrick O'Mahoney	Saint John's Hospital, Limerick	Limerick	17/07/1922	IRA	20
Philip Giblin	County Infirmary, Sligo	Sligo	17/07/1922	Civilian	20
Henry Giblin	County Infirmary, Sligo	Sligo	17/07/1922	Civilian	15
William O'Sullivan	Mercy Hospital, Cork city	Cork	18/07/1922	IRA	20
Margaret Ryan	Doctor Steeven's Hospital	Dublin	18/07/1922	Civilian	22
Andrew Hickey	Grange, Longford Bridge, Ballingoola	Limerick	18/07/1922	NA	
Bridget O'Brien	Bank Place, Limerick	Limerick	18/07/1922	Civilian	18
Thomas Hartigan	Mater Hospital	Dublin	19/07/1922	NA	18
Patrick Hanley	County Jail, Limerick	Limerick	19/07/1922	NA	22
Ellen Windrum	Saint John's Hospital, Limerick	Limerick	19/07/1922	Civilian	51
John Nunan	Saint John's Hospital, Limerick	Limerick	19/07/1922	Civilian	52
William Long	County Hospital, Waterford	Waterford	19/07/1922	Civilian	40
John Duane	Olaf Street, Waterford	Waterford	19/07/1922	Civilian	35
William Phillips	Killaloe	Clare	20/07/1922	NA	24
Patrick Farnan	Mater Hospital	Dublin	20/07/1922	IRA	24
Margaret King	Dolphin's Barn	Dublin	20/07/1922	Civilian	18
Patrick Burke	Cregaclare	Galway	20/07/1922	NA	
Peter Roche	Naas Military, Hospital	Kildare	20/07/1922	NA	24
William Conroy	Kilmallock	Limerick	20/07/1922	NA	
Edward Wallace	Roches Street, Limerick	Limerick	20/07/1922	Civilian	57
John Flynn	Ferrybank, Waterford	Waterford	20/07/1922	Civilian	8
Peter O'Neill	Doctor Steeven's Hospital	Dublin	21/07/1922	Civilian	32
Timothy Hanniffy	Cregaclare	Galway	21/07/1922	NA	
Martin Brennan	Galway Hospital	Galway	21/07/1922	NA	
William Dunworth	Tullbrackey, Bruff	Limerick	21/07/1922	Civilian	56
James O'Leary	The Crescent, Limerick	Limerick	21/07/1922	Civilian	
William Howlett	Waterford city	Waterford	21/07/1922	NA	22

Name	Location	County	Date	Affiliation	Age
Mary Hennessy	Lower Sion Row, Waterford	Waterford	21/07/1922	Civilian	8
Thomas O'Connor	Beggars Bush Barracks	Dublin	22/07/1922	NA	20
James McGrath	County Hospital, Waterford	Waterford	22/07/1922	IRA	40
Patrick Hutchinson	County Hospital, Waterford	Waterford	22/07/1922	Civilian	40
Emily De Courcy	County and City Infirmary, Waterford	Waterford	22/07/1922	Civilian	10
John Martin	Mountjoy Prison	Dublin	23/07/1922	NA	16
Arthur Richardson	Angler's Rest, Strawberry Beds	Dublin	23/07/1922	Civilian	36
John Tobin	Angler's Rest, Strawberry Beds	Dublin	23/07/1922	Civilian	25
John 'Jack' Jordan	Castlegar	Galway	23/07/1922	NA	19
Leslie Edmonds	Castlegar	Galway	23/07/1922	Civilian	
Jeremiah Burke	Ballymullen, Tralee	Kerry	23/07/1922	Civilian	
Denis O'Mahony	Thomastown	Limerick	23/07/1922	NA	
Patrick Brady	Waterford city	Waterford	23/07/1922	IRA	
Mary Connolly	Edenappa, Jonesborough	Armagh	23/07/1922	Civilian	20
Margaret Moore	Edenappa, Jonesborough	Armagh	23/07/1922	Civilian	12
Patrick O'Hara	Jervis Street Hospital	Dublin	24/07/1922	NA	26
Michael Callaghan	County and City Infirmary, Waterford	Waterford	24/07/1922	Civilian	22
Maurice Quirke	Killurin	Wexford	24/07/1922	NA	23
Thomas McMahon	Killurin	Wexford	24/07/1922	NA	40
Daniel O'Neill	Rosbrien, Limerick	Limerick	25/07/1922	NA	
Patrick Naughton	Saint John's Hospital, Limerick	Limerick	25/07/1922	IRA	25
Edward Boylan	Military Hospital, Clones	Monaghan	25/07/1922	IRA	21
William O'Hara	Castlerea	Roscommon	25/07/1922	NA	
Ellen McDonagh	County Infirmary, Sligo	Sligo	25/07/1922	Civilian	36
James Scanlan	Lignagillew, Glenties	Donegal	26/07/1922	NA	27
Daniel Harkin	Lifford Infirmary	Donegal	26/07/1922	IRA	22
Henry Stainsfield	Richmond Barracks	Dublin	26/07/1922	British Army	19
Cornelius Sullivan	Ballingaddie, Kilmallock	Limerick	26/07/1922	NA	
Patrick Murphy	Bruree	Limerick	26/07/1922	NA	31
John Quirke	Ballingaddie, Kilmallock	Limerick	26/07/1922	NA	
Patrick Foran	Limerick city	Limerick	26/07/1922	IRA	20
Thomas Power	Ballingaddie, Kilmallock	Limerick	26/07/1922	NA	
Alfred Divine	Lignagillew, Glenties	Donegal	27/07/1922	NA	24
Michael Campion	Saint Vincent's Hospital	Dublin	27/07/1922	NA	17
William Harrington	Barringtons Hospital, Limerick	Limerick	27/07/1922	IRA	23
David Sugenor	Smithfield Barracks, Belfast	Antrim	27/07/1922	USC	
Louisa Whelan	Letterkenny	Donegal	28/07/1922	Civilian	3
Margaret Hegarty	Lower Bridge Street	Dublin	28/07/1922	Civilian	24
Patrick Walsh	Cornamona, Clonbur	Galway	28/07/1922	IRA	23
Austin McCurtin	Tonduff, Raheen	Laois	28/07/1922	NA	23
John Collison	Portlaoise	Laois	28/07/1922	NA	32

Name	Location	County	Date	Affiliation	Age
Thomas Grace	Tonduff	Laois	28/07/1922	NA	32
Daniel O'Mahony	Bruree	Limerick	28/07/1922	NA	
Patrick Carey	Bruree	Limerick	28/07/1922	NA	
Daniel Murphy	Kilmallock	Limerick	28/07/1922	IRA	
Catherine Sexton	Saint John's Hospital, Limerick	Limerick	28/07/1922	Civilian	60
John McCaffrey	Louth County infirmary, Dundalk	Louth	28/07/1922	NA	
John Deasy	Broclagh Newport	Mayo	28/07/1922	NA	21
Frederick Greydon	Newport	Mayo	28/07/1922	NA	22
Edward Hegarty	Broclagh Newport	Mayo	28/07/1922	IRA	
James O'Meara	District Hospital, Tipperary	Tipperary	28/07/1922	IRA	22
Jeremiah Riggs	Kingswell	Tipperary	28/07/1922	IRA	
Patrick Butler	Kingswell	Tipperary	28/07/1922	IRA	32
Seamus Quirke	Golden	Tipperary	28/07/1922	IRA	19
Mary Gaffney	Bishopscourt, Waterford	Waterford	28/07/1922	Civilian	54
Patrick Kinsella	Thurles Hospital	Tipperary	29/07/1922	NA	21
Michael O'Haire	Donaskeigh	Tipperary	29/07/1922	NA	
John McIntyre	Eatons Cottages, Henry Street, Tipperary town	Tipperary	29/07/1922	NA	19
Thomas Kennedy	Golden	Tipperary	29/07/1922	IRA	20
Patrick McGivern	Old Lodge Road, Belfast	Antrim	29/07/1922	Civilian	
Dominic Wilson	Desertmartin	Derry	29/07/1922	IRA	28
James O'Donovan	Garretstown Road, Ballinspittle	Cork	30/07/1922	Civilian	23
Samuel Oakes	Blackmill Street, Kilkenny city	Kilkenny	30/07/1922	IRA	21
William Spillane	Ashford, Broadford	Limerick	30/07/1922	IRA	21
Julia French	Bansha, Road Bank Place, Tipperary	Tipperary	30/07/1922	Civilian	7
Patrick Deehan	Custume Barracks, Athlone	Westmeath	30/07/1922	NA	16
Patrick Concannon	Ardrahan	Galway	31/07/1922	NA	
John McSweeney	Ennis Hospital	Clare	August 1922	IRA	24
Henry (Harry) Boland	Vincent's Hospital	Dublin	01/08/1922	IRA	35
Peter Traynor	Killaster	Roscommon	01/08/1922	NA	
Thomas Brown	Clonderlaw Bridge, Kilrush	Clare	02/08/1922	NA	25
Muriel Bruton	Mercer's Hospital	Dublin	02/08/1922	Civilian	19
William Carson	County Infirmary, Tralee	Kerry	02/08/1922	NA	20
Michael Farrell	Pembroke Street, Tralee	Kerry	02/08/1922	NA	
Frederick Gillespie	Rock Street-Pembroke Street, Tralee	Kerry	02/08/1922	NA	24
Patrick Harding	Pembroke Street, Tralee	Kerry	02/08/1922	NA	19
John Kenny	Fenit	Kerry	02/08/1922	NA	19
Thomas Larkin	Castle Street, Tralee	Kerry	02/08/1922	NA	
Edward O'Connor	Ballyseedy	Kerry	02/08/1922	NA	22
James O'Connor	Rock Street-Pembroke Street, Tralee	Kerry	02/08/1922	NA	17
Patrick O'Reilly	Rock Street, Tralee	Kerry	02/08/1922	NA	22

Name	Location	County	Date	Affiliation	Age
Thomas Flynn	The Spa, Seafield, Tralee	Kerry	02/08/1922	IRA	
John O'Sullivan	Sammy's Rock, Oysterhall	Kerry	02/08/1922	IRA	
Michael Ryle	Ballycarty	Kerry	02/08/1922	Fianna	19
Patrick Murphy	Killonery, Piltown	Kilkenny	02/08/1922	NA	22
John Fitzpatrick	Acragor	Laois	02/08/1922	Civilian	32
Henry Meaney	Patrickswell	Limerick	02/08/1922	IRA	31
Michael Skelly	Callow, Swinford	Mayo	02/08/1922	NA	
Joseph Traynor	Callow, Swinford	Mayo	02/08/1922	NA	21
Patrick Quinn	Kilfenora, Tralee	Kerry	03/08/1922	NA	23
Richard O'Neill	County Infirmary, Limerick	Limerick	03/08/1922	Civilian	50
John McGahern	Military Barracks, Tobercurry	Sligo	03/08/1922	NA	
James Magee	Tobercurry	Sligo	03/08/1922	NA	
Christina Howard	County Infirmary, Cashel	Tipperary	03/08/1922	Civilian	22
Hyacinth Darcy	Mercer's Hospital	Dublin	04/08/1922	Civilian	34
Robert Barry	Kilmallock Hill, Kilmallock	Limerick	04/08/1922	NA	17
Maurice McCarthy	Bruff Barracks	Limerick	04/08/1922	NA	
Charles O'Hanlon	Bruree	Limerick	04/08/1922	IRA	17
Margaret Ada Hartney	Adare Manor Hotel, Adare	Limerick	04/08/1922	CnamB	
Patrick Moran	Kilkeeran, Ballinrobe	Mayo	04/08/1922	IRA	19
Christopher McCann	Military Barracks, Bannagher	Offaly	04/08/1922	NA	26
Patrick O'Dea	Kilrush	Clare	05/08/1922	NA	32
Brian Houlihan	Dysert, Farranfore	Kerry	05/08/1922	NA	29
Michael Purcell	Ballymacthomas, Ballycarty	Kerry	05/08/1922	NA	
Daniel McEnery	Newcastlewest	Limerick	05/08/1922	IRA	
John Doyle	County Hospital, Waterford	Waterford	05/08/1922	IRA	22
Samuel Hayes	Newtownards Road, Belfast	Antrim	05/08/1922	USC	17
Patrick O'Hanlon	Ballybough Bridge	Dublin	06/08/1922	NA	22
Francis Norton	Churchtown, Carrick on Suir	Tipperary	06/08/1922	IRA	
Joseph Hudson	Saint Michael's Hospital, Dun Laoghaire	Dublin	07/08/1922	IRA	19
Denis O'Dwyer	Newcastlewest	Limerick	07/08/1922	IRA	23
Edward O'Dwyer	Newcastlewest	Limerick	07/08/1922	IRA	20
John Lavery	Louth County Infirmary, Dundalk	Louth	07/08/1922	NA	23
Patrick McCluskey	County Infirmary, Monaghan	Monaghan	07/08/1922	Civilian	11
James Gavigan	Rochestown	Cork	08/08/1922	NA	21
Patrick Maguire	Passage West	Cork	08/08/1922	NA	25
Thomas Mahony	Blarney	Cork	08/08/1922	NA	20
Frederick McKenna	Passage West	Cork	08/08/1922	NA	18
Gerald McKenna	Passage West	Cork	08/08/1922	NA	16
William Nevin	Passage West	Cork	08/08/1922	NA	38
Christopher O'Toole	Rochestown	Cork	08/08/1922	NA	43

Name	Location	County	Date	Affiliation	Age
Patrick Perry	Rochestown	Cork	08/08/1922	NA	24
Henry Quinn	Passage West	Cork	08/08/1922	NA	18
Denis Coffey	Kinsale	Cork	08/08/1922	IRA	29
Jeremiah Hourigan	Rochestown	Cork	08/08/1922	IRA	36
John Kennedy	Jervis Street Hospital	Dublin	08/08/1922	NA	23
Peter McGarrity	Jervis Street Hospital	Dublin	08/08/1922	NA	
Edward Coughlan	Jervis Street Hospital	Dublin	08/08/1922	NA	18
Patrick Whelan	Mater Hospital	Dublin	08/08/1922	Civilian	31
Patrick McGuigan	Queens Road, Belfast	Antrim	08/08/1922	Civilian	31
John Curley	Rochestown	Cork	09/08/1922	NA	32
James Madden	Lynch's Cross, Rochestown	Cork	09/08/1922	NA	26
Ian MacKenzie Kennedy	Ballincurrig, Douglas	Cork	09/08/1922	IRA	22
James Moloney	Belmont Cross, Rochestown	Cork	09/08/1922	IRA	19
Patrick Phelan	Brittas Castle, Clonaslee	Laois	09/08/1922	IRA	19
John Kelly	Powerstown, Ballyvaughan	Tipperary	09/08/1922	NA	
Edward McAvoy	Ferrycarrig	Wexford	09/08/1922	NA	27
Patrick Corcoran	South Infirmary	Cork	10/08/1922	NA	20
John O'Gorman	Ennis Hospital	Clare	11/08/1922	IRA	24
Christopher Olden	South Infirmary	Cork	11/08/1922	IRA	20
William Purdy	Abbeyfeale	Limerick	11/08/1922	NA	
James Duffy	The Mall, Castlebar	Mayo	11/08/1922	NA	26
Thomas Uniake	Carrick Workhouse	Tipperary	11/08/1922	NA	27
Alexander Hamilton	Downpatrick Infirmary	Down	11/08/1922	USC	
Unidentified	Victoria Barracks, Cork city	Cork	12/08/1922	Civilian	
Michael Swift	Clooncastle	Galway	12/08/1922	NA	23
John Quayne	Beaufort	Kerry	12/08/1922	NA	19
Patrick Moran	Ballina Union Hospital, Ballina	Mayo	12/08/1922	NA	23
Kate Morrisey	Carrick	Tipperary	12/08/1922	Civilian	37
Mrs O'Donnell-Byrne	Carrick	Tipperary	12/08/1922	Civilian	
William O'Donnell-Byrne	Carrick	Tipperary	12/08/1922	Civilian	
Martin Egan	Kilrush District Hospital	Clare	13/08/1922	NA	
Timothy Hayes	Saint John's Hospital, Limerick	Limerick	13/08/1922	IRA	20
John Hogan	Saint John's Hospital, Limerick	Limerick	13/08/1922	IRA	19
Michael Condon	Clonmel Town Hall, Clonmel	Tipperary	13/08/1922	IRA	
Edward Maher	Urlingford Barracks	Kilkenny	14/08/1922	NA	26
Nellis Duggan	Barringtons Hospital, Limerick	Limerick	14/08/1922	Civilian	7
Peter Duffy	Louth County Infirmary, Dundalk	Louth	14/08/1922	NA	23
Frank Byrne	Louth County Infirmary, Dundalk	Louth	14/08/1922	NA	
Patrick Donnelly	Military Barracks, Dundalk	Louth	14/08/1922	NA	
Patrick McGowan	Military Barracks, Dundalk	Louth	14/08/1922	NA	
Patrick McKenna	Dundalk Prison, Dundalk	Louth	14/08/1922	IRA	

NAME	LOCATION	COUNTY	DATE	AFFILIATION	AGE
James Nolan	Kenyon Street, Nenagh	Tipperary	14/08/1922	IRA	32
John Dobbyn	Lay Lodge, Kilmacthomas	Waterford	14/08/1922	IRA	24
Albert Ross	Ballymena Barracks	Antrim	14/08/1922	USC	
John O'Keeffe	Rochestown, Mullinavat	Kilkenny	15/08/1922	Civilian	34
Lena Roche	Mary Street, Limerick	Limerick	15/08/1922	Civilian	12
Patrick McBreen	Church Street, Dundalk	Louth	15/08/1922	NA	27
Patrick Keogh	Oberstown	Meath	15/08/1922	NA	22
Edward O'Brien	Barrack Street, Shortcourse, Waterford	Waterford	15/08/1922	NA	22
Thomas Greenfield	Randalstown	Antrim	15/08/1922	USC	
Joseph McEvoy	Clonmult	Cork	16/08/1922	NA	
Patrick Mullen	Mater Hospital	Dublin	16/08/1922	IRA	22
Michael O'Driscoll	Ballinknockae, Kilgubban	Kerry	16/08/1922	Civilian	47
James Moloney	Hospital, Listowel	Kerry	16/08/1922	Civilian	22
James McEvoy	Louth County Infirmary, Dundalk	Louth	16/08/1922	Civilian	48
Cornelius Roche	Woodrooffe, Clonmel	Tipperary	16/08/1922	NA	
Daniel Fogarty	Woodrooffe, Clonmel	Tipperary	16/08/1922	NA	
Joseph Bergin	Woodrooffe, Clonmel	Tipperary	16/08/1922	NA	
Cecil Fitzgerald	Innisfallen, Killarney	Kerry	17/08/1922	NA	19
Joseph O'Meara	Innisfallen, Killarney	Kerry	17/08/1922	NA	
Bernard Gaughran	Louth County Infirmary, Dundalk	Louth	17/08/1922	Civilian	48
Thomas Moore	Castlebar	Mayo	17/08/1922	NA	
Michael Costello	County Infirmary, Waterford	Waterford	17/08/1922	NA	
Patrick Breen	Kildorrery	Cork	18/08/1922	NA	19
Jeremiah McDonald	Tawnies, Clonakilty	Cork	18/08/1922	NA	38
Anna Curtin	Greenhall, Bridgeland East, Rathcormack	Cork	18/08/1922	Civilian	23
James Byrne	Adelaide Hospital	Dublin	18/08/1922	IRA	23
John Lydon	County Infirmary, Tralee	Kerry	18/08/1922	NA	25
Peter Devlin	Louth County Infirmary, Dundalk	Louth	18/08/1922	NA	25
Patrick Behan	Saint Vincent's Hospital	Dublin	19/08/1922	NA	17
Sean Edwards	Kikenny Jail, Kilkenny city	Kilkenny	19/08/1922	IRA	23
Christopher Hynes	Bruree, Kilmallock	Limerick	19/08/1922	NA	
John Butler	Ryan Lock, Plassy	Limerick	19/08/1922	IRA	26
Thomas Gillanders	Monaghan Court House	Monaghan	19/08/1922	NA	26
Edward Grace	Mullinahone	Tipperary	19/08/1922	NA	18
Edward Cregan	Curraghs, Kanturk	Cork	20/08/1922	NA	22
Daniel McCarthy	Rochestown, Douglas	Cork	20/08/1922	IRA	
Stephen Coakley	Ballinrobe	Mayo	20/08/1922	NA	
William John Doherty	Claremorris Military Hospital	Mayo	20/08/1922	NA	22
Peter Kenny	Blessington	Wicklow	20/08/1922	NA	24
Hugh Cotter	Falls Road, Belfast	Antrim	20/08/1922	Civilian	12

NAME	LOCATION	COUNTY	DATE	AFFILIATION	AGE
Patrick Comber	Ennis Hospital	Clare	21/08/1922	NA	30
Patrick Burns	Ballincollig	Cork	21/08/1922	IRA	40
Thomas Clougherty	County Infirmary, Tralee	Kerry	21/08/1922	NA	18
Frank Byrne	Castlecomer	Kilkenny	21/08/1922	IRA	21
Michael McSweeney	Barringtons Hospital, Limerick	Limerick	21/08/1922	Civilian	32
John O'Shea	Saint John's Hospital, Limerick	Limerick	21/08/1922	Civilian	25
Michael Finnegan	Redmondstown, Clonmel	Tipperary	21/08/1922	NA	24
Daniel Kane	Sallygap	Wicklow	21/08/1922	IRA	20
Patrick Kelly	William's Hotel, Kilrush	Clare	22/08/1922	NA	
Michael Collins	Béal na Blá	Cork	22/08/1922	NA	32
William Levingstone Cooke	Old Blackrock Road, Cork city	Cork	22/08/1922	Civilian	57
Thomas Drummond	Bon Secours Home, Tralee	Kerry	22/08/1922	IRA	25
Michael Daly	Castleisland	Kerry	23/08/1922	NA	29
Thomas 'Denny' Woods	Basin, Tralee	Kerry	23/08/1922	NA	
Edward O'Neill	Naas County Hospital	Kildare	23/08/1922	NA	
John Beatty	Basin, Tralee	Kerry	24/08/1922	NA	
John Galworthy	Ballymullen Barracks	Kerry	24/08/1922	NA	
Timothy McMahon	Moyderwell, Ballymullen, Tralee	Kerry	25/08/1922	NA	
Harry Brazier	GSWR yard, railway station, Limerick	Limerick	25/08/1922	IRA	21
Michael Bannon	Tobercurry	Sligo	25/08/1922	NA	
Sean McCormack	Glasson. Athlone	Westmeath	25/08/1922	NA	16
Patrick Murtagh	Dispensary Doctor's Clinic, Glancy	Westmeath	25/08/1922	Civilian	42
Sean Cole	Yellow Lane, Whitehall	Dublin	26/08/1922	Fianna	19
Alfred Colley	Yellow Lane, Whitehall	Dublin	26/08/1922	Fianna	20
Bernard Daly	Saint Dolough's, Swords	Dublin	26/08/1922	IRA	
Patrick Fagan	Meath Hospital	Dublin	26/08/1922	Civilian	28
Patrick Sheehan	Waterville	Kerry	26/08/1922	NA	
Thomas Tiernan	Ballyhaunis	Mayo	26/08/1922	NA	
Jeremiah O'Callaghan	Bushfield, Nenagh	Tipperary	26/08/1922	NA	
Michael McInerney	Ballywilliam, Nenagh	Tipperary	26/08/1922	NA	
Cyril Lee	Clondrohid, Macroom	Cork	27/08/1922	NA	26
Hugh Thornton	Clonakilty	Cork	27/08/1922	NA	25
Jeremiah O'Callaghan	Mallow Military Barracks	Cork	27/08/1922	Civilian	30
John Cullen	Mater Hospital	Dublin	27/08/1922	Civilian	31
Michael Roche	Military Hospital, Tralee	Kerry	27/08/1922	NA	
Sean Moriarty	Ballonagh Convent, Tralee	Kerry	27/08/1922	IRA	29
Charles Sullivan	County Infirmary, Castlebar	Mayo	27/08/1922	NA	23
David O'Shea	Workhouse Hospital, Nenagh	Tipperary	27/08/1922	NA	23
Thomas White	Wexford Military Barracks, Wexford	Wexford	27/08/1922	NA	19
John Joe Murray	Saint Vincent's Hospital	Dublin	28/08/1922	CID	28
John Jones	Upper Merrion Street	Dublin	28/08/1922	Civilian	48

Name	Location	County	Date	Affiliation	Age
Timothy Patrick James Burke	Castlemaine Railway Bridge, Castlemaine	Kerry	28/08/1922	NA	26
Edward O'Connor	Quills Cross, Ballyseedy	Kerry	28/08/1922	NA	
Patrick Keating	Kilrush District Hospital	Clare	29/08/1922	IRA	30
John Hourihan	Bantry	Cork	29/08/1922	NA	24
Denis McCarthy	Barrack Street	Cork	29/08/1922	NA	22
Patrick Cooney	William Street, Bantry	Cork	29/08/1922	IRA	25
Michael Crowley	William Street, Bantry	Cork	29/08/1922	IRA	23
Gibbs Ross	William Street, Bantry	Cork	29/08/1922	IRA	30
Donal McCarthy	William Street, Bantry	Cork	29/08/1922	IRA	20
Michael Danford	Clino, Ballysimon, Limerick	Limerick	29/08/1922	IRA	26
Matthew Cullen	Bunaterin, Blueball	Offaly	29/08/1922	NA	31
Edward Donoghue	Birr Workhouse, Birr	Offaly	29/08/1922	Civilian	12
Richard Cantwell	Redmondstown	Tipperary	29/08/1922	NA	23
Peter Mullan	Crumlin Road, Belfast	Antrim	29/08/1922	Civilian	65
Albert Cottle	Watergrasshill	Cork	30/08/1922	NA	21
Richard Storey	Islandbridge	Dublin	30/08/1922	British Army	20
Patrick Hickey	Portlaoise Prison	Laois	30/08/1922	IRA	21
Joseph Hudson	District Hospital, Fermoy	Cork	31/08/1922	NA	25
Richard Monks	The Curragh	Kildare	31/08/1922	IRA	35
James Alfred Hayes	Military Hospital, Custume Barracks, Athlone	Westmeath	31/08/1922	NA	20
Nicholas Ward	Watergrasshill	Cork	01/09/1922	NA	23
John Winsely	Cork County Male Prison	Cork	01/09/1922	NA	30
Edward Leo Murray	Newpark Lodge, Stillorgan	Dublin	01/09/1922	IRA	18
Charles Joachim 'Rodney' Murphy	Newpark Lodge, Stillorgan	Dublin	01/09/1922	IRA	22
Michael Rouse	Richmond Hospital	Dublin	01/09/1922	IRA	22
John Doyle	Baldonnell Aerodrome	Dublin	01/09/1922	NA	25
Michael Walsh	Barnaderg, Tuam	Galway	01/09/1922	NA	29
George Higgins	Ballymacarrett, Belfast	Antrim	01/09/1922	Civilian	38
Michael Behan	Grand Parade	Cork	02/09/1922	NA	
Thomas Conway	Grand Parade, City Club	Cork	02/09/1922	NA	
Francis Neary	Gurteenroe, near Macroom	Cork	02/09/1922	NA	22
John O'Leary	Gurteenroe, near Macroom	Cork	02/09/1922	NA	21
Robert Hempenstall	Newcastlewest	Limerick	02/09/1922	NA	25
James Meegan	The Workhouse, Dundalk	Louth	02/09/1922	IRA	30
Alexander O'Neill	County and City Infirmary, Waterford	Waterford	02/09/1922	NA	
Evelyn Bell	Lisnaskea	Fermanagh	02/09/1922	British Army	25
James Murray	Mercy Hospital, Cork city	Cork	03/09/1922	NA	23
Jeremiah Coleman	Keysers Hill, Cork city	Cork	03/09/1922	Civilian	34

Name	Location	County	Date	Affiliation	Age
John Joe Stephens	Red Cow Lane, Inchicore	Dublin	03/09/1922	IRA	28
Michael Arthur	Castleconnell	Limerick	03/09/1922	NA	
Charles McNamara	Castleconnell	Limerick	03/09/1922	Civilian	25
Christopher O'Neill	County and City Infirmary, Waterford	Waterford	03/09/1922	NA	20
James Minahan	Clarecastle	Clare	04/09/1922	NA	
Daniel Shinnick	Glennacurrane, Mitchelstown	Cork	04/09/1922	IRA	
Charles Roarty	Drumboe Castle	Donegal	04/09/1922	NA	19
William Somers	Capel Street	Dublin	04/09/1922	IRA	19
Clement Cooper	Araghmoon, Aughatubrid, Cahirciveen	Kerry	04/09/1922	NA	21
John Donoghue	Oghermog	Kerry	04/09/1922	NA	23
Joseph Murray	Louth County Infirmary, Dundalk	Louth	04/09/1922	NA	28
Catherine Walsh	Bakehouse Lane, Waterford	Waterford	04/09/1922	Civilian	66
Richard Kearns	Mercy Hospital, Cork city	Cork	05/09/1922	NA	26
Thomas Butler	Mercer's Hospital	Dublin	05/09/1922	NA	23
Thomas Kavanagh	Military Hospital, Killarney	Kerry	05/09/1922	NA	23
William Maddigan	City Home and Hospital, Limerick	Limerick	05/09/1922	Civilian	36
John O'Leary	Louth County Infirmary, Dundalk	Louth	05/09/1922	Civilian	
Patrick McCabe	National Army Barracks, Carrickmacross	Monaghan	05/09/1922	NA	
John Howlett	Fethard	Tipperary	05/09/1922	NA	18
Patrick Byrne	Cashel	Tipperary	05/09/1922	NA	24
Patrick Crowley	Bantry Hospital	Cork	06/09/1922	Civilian	56
C. Falley	Ballyhaunis	Mayo	06/09/1922	NA	
Unidentified	Firville, Coolehane, Macroom	Cork	07/09/1922	IRA	
George Fahy	Athenry	Galway	07/09/1922	NA	39
Joseph Smyth	Athboy Barracks, Athboy	Meath	07/09/1922	NA	25
John Hanly	Cuckoo Hill, Derrygrath, Clonmel	Tipperary	07/09/1922	NA	
Timothy Kenefick	Nadrid, Coachford	Cork	08/09/1922	IRA	27
Joachim Kirwan	Buncranna Military Barracks, Buncranna	Donegal	08/09/1922	NA	21
Thomas Lyne	Kilinane, Tralee	Kerry	08/09/1922	Civilian	40
Joseph Lawlor	Ballinrobe	Sligo	08/09/1922	NA	
Paul Geoghegan	Beltra	Sligo	08/09/1922	IRA	
John O'Connor	Kenmare	Kerry	09/09/1922	NA	26
Thomas O'Connor	Kenmare	Kerry	09/09/1922	NA	20
Michael McCaffery	Military Barracks, Tobercurry	Sligo	09/09/1922	NA	22
Michael Heffernan	Knockura, Drangan	Tipperary	09/09/1922	IRA	
Margaret Downey	Jervis Street Hospital	Dublin	10/09/1922	Civilian	75
Thomas Brennan	Ballinacourt, Bansha	Tipperary	10/09/1922	Civilian	45
John Lyden	Blennerville	Kerry	11/09/1922	NA	29
Michael Magee	Castleisland	Kerry	11/09/1922	NA	

Name	Location	County	Date	Affiliation	Age
John Carberry	Carrick Workhouse	Tipperary	11/09/1922	NA	15
Patrick Murphy	Mercy Hospital, Cork city	Cork	12/09/1922	IRA	28
Sean McEvoy	Adelaide Hospital	Dublin	12/09/1922	IRA	21
Constance Tynan	Bridge Street, Ballina	Mayo	12/09/1922	Civilian	22
Malachy Geraghty	Medical Dispensary, Ballina	Mayo	12/09/1922	Civilian	
Hugh Smith Brownlow	Killagan Crossroads	Antrim	12/09/1922	Civilian	34
James Spratt	Westmorland Road, Belfast	Antrim	12/09/1922	Civilian	
Margaret Kavanagh	Seabrook House, East Wall	Dublin	13/09/1922	Civilian	75
John Durcan	Ballymote	Sligo	13/09/1922	IRA	23
Edward Gething	Ballyrobin Bridge, Grange	Tipperary	13/09/1922	NA	
John Walker	Little George Street, Belfast	Antrim	13/09/1922	Civilian	18
James McCann	Mercy Hospital, Cork city	Cork	14/09/1922	NA	21
James Yates	Mercy Hospital, Cork city	Cork	14/09/1922	NA	
John O'Brien	Knockarourke, Donoughmore	Cork	14/09/1922	IRA	21
Edward Williams	North Infirmary, Cork city	Cork	14/09/1922	Civilian	18
Henry O'Reilly	Ordinance Survey Office, Phoenix Park	Dublin	14/09/1922	NA	19
Michael Joseph Ring	Bunnyconnellan, Drumsheen, Ox Mountains	Mayo	14/09/1922	NA	32
Thomas Ingham	Mullany's Cross, Ox Mountains	Mayo	14/09/1922	NA	
Louisa Cannon	Cullingtree Road, Belfast	Antrim	14/09/1922	Civilian	30
James McNamara	Jervis Street Hospital	Dublin	15/09/1922	NA	27
James Cornelius O'Rourke	Jervis Street Hospital	Dublin	15/09/1922	Civilian	60
Martin Moloney	St Joseph's, City Home and Hospital, Limerick	Limerick	15/09/1922	NA	19
Edward Tuite	Oldcastle Barracks, Oldcastle	Meath	15/09/1922	Civilian	33
Raphael Conway	Carrigaphooca Bridge, Macroom	Cork	16/09/1922	NA	22
Thomas Keogh	Carrigaphooca Bridge, Macroom	Cork	16/09/1922	NA	23
Thomas Manning	Carrigaphooca Bridge, Macroom	Cork	16/09/1922	NA	26
William Murphy	Carrigaphooca Bridge, Macroom	Cork	16/09/1922	NA	22
Daniel O'Brien	Carrigaphooca Bridge, Macroom	Cork	16/09/1922	NA	25
Patrick O'Rourke	Carrigaphooca Bridge, Macroom	Cork	16/09/1922	NA	23
John Riordan	Carrigaphooca Bridge, Macroom	Cork	16/09/1922	NA	22
Denis Creedon	Mercy Hospital, Cork city	Cork	16/09/1922	IRA	32
James Buckley	Carrigaphooka, Macroom	Cork	16/09/1922	IRA	46
John Moloney	Beaufort	Kerry	16/09/1922	NA	20
James Dolan	Leitrim County Infirmary, Carrick on Shannon	Leitrim	16/09/1922	NA	32
Patrick Naughton	Rathkeale Army Barracks, Rathkeale	Limerick	16/09/1922	NA	21
Sean Higgins	Glenamoy	Mayo	16/09/1922	NA	
Patrick Bray	Glenamoy	Mayo	16/09/1922	NA	
William Gill	Glenamoy	Mayo	16/09/1922	NA	

Name	Location	County	Date	Affiliation	Age
Thomas Healy	Glenamoy	Mayo	16/09/1922	NA	
Edward Crabbe	Glenamoy, Belderrig	Mayo	16/09/1922	NA	22
Thomas Rawl	Ballina Union Hospital, Ballina	Mayo	16/09/1922	NA	
John Clarke		Cork	17/09/1922	NA	
Patrick Mannion	Mount Street Bridge	Dublin	17/09/1922	IRA	22
Anthony Deane	Oriel House, Westland Row	Dublin	17/09/1922	CID	27
John Tyrrell	G.S. Hospital, Blackrock	Dublin	17/09/1922	Civilian	10
Patrick Brady	Saint Vincent's Hospital	Dublin	17/09/1922	Civilian	50
Patrick Power	Rock Street, Tralee	Kerry	17/09/1922	Civilian	35
Terence Kane	County Infirmary, Portlaoise	Laois	17/09/1922	NA	46
Christopher Nunan	Barringtons Hospital, Limerick	Limerick	17/09/1922	Civilian	15
John Lynn	Boher Cross Bushfield, Nenagh	Tipperary	17/09/1922	NA	
John Moore	Workhouse Hospital, Nenagh	Tipperary	17/09/1922	NA	20
Patrick Keogh	Workhouse Hospital, Nenagh	Tipperary	17/09/1922	NA	
Thomas Hayes	Boher	Tipperary	17/09/1922	IRA	16
James McCloskey	Marine Street, Belfast	Antrim	17/09/1922	Civilian	
Jane Rafferty	New Andrew Street, Belfast	Antrim	17/09/1922	Civilian	40
William Kinsella	Great George's Street south, Belfast	Antrim	17/09/1922	Civilian	
Thomas McCullough-Costello	Great George's Street south, Belfast	Antrim	17/09/1922	Civilian	
Bernard Gray	Coachford	Cork	18/09/1922	NA	17
Francis Derham	Harcourt Street Railway Station	Dublin	18/09/1922	NA	17
Thomas Bolton	Rathangan Barracks	Kildare	18/09/1922	Civic Guard	26
Andrew Walsh	Rahilly, Benbulben	Sligo	18/09/1922	NA	19
David O'Sullivan	Aherla, Crookstown	Cork	19/09/1922	NA	
Frances Haynes	Mercy Hospital, Cork city	Cork	19/09/1922	Civilian	73
Charles Flynn	William Street, Limerick	Limerick	19/09/1922	NA	
Matthew Hayes	Union Hospital, Tipperary	Tipperary	19/09/1922	NA	
Cornelius Hanley	Ballinard, Donaskeigh	Tipperary	19/09/1922	IRA	
Michael Cleary	Crory, Ferns	Wexford	19/09/1922	Civilian	34
John Murphy	Nursing home, Fitzgerald St., Tralee	Kerry	20/09/1922	NA	
Margaret Collins	Grangemore, Brannockstown	Kildare	20/09/1922	Civilian	18
Patrick Seery	Coolanarney, Blueball	Offaly	20/09/1922	IRA	
Brian MacNeill	Benbulben	Sligo	20/09/1922	IRA	22
Joseph Banks	Lislahelly, Benbulben	Sligo	20/09/1922	IRA	17
Patrick Carroll	Lislahelly, Benbulben	Sligo	20/09/1922	IRA	24
Seamus Devins	Lislahelly, Benbulben	Sligo	20/09/1922	IRA	48
Thomas Langan	Ardnaglass Upper, Benbulben	Sligo	20/09/1922	IRA	23
Henry Benson	Ardnaglass Upper, Benbulben	Sligo	20/09/1922	IRA	23
Robert O'Sullivan	Kinsale	Cork	21/09/1922	NA	20
Daniel Hannan	Military Hospital, Killarney	Kerry	21/09/1922	NA	28
Edward Mulvany	Mercy Hospital, Cork city	Cork	22/09/1922	NA	30

NAME	LOCATION	COUNTY	DATE	AFFILIATION	AGE
Jeremiah Collins	Derrycreigh Mountain	Cork	22/09/1922	Civilian	43
James Kennedy	Saint Vincent's Hospital	Dublin	22/09/1922	NA	28
William Warren	Howth Tower, Howth	Dublin	22/09/1922	NA	19
Joseph Guinan	Bushfield	Tipperary	22/09/1922	NA	20
Michael Neville	Killester Cemetery	Dublin	23/09/1922	IRA	22
Matthew M'Grath	Listowel	Kerry	23/09/1922	NA	
William Barrett	Cordal Mullin	Kerry	23/09/1922	IRA	21
Jeremiah Hanifin	Knockreigh, Milltown, Killarney	Kerry	23/09/1922	Civilian	52
Owen Sherlock	Mounthamilton, Ardee Road, Dundalk	Louth	23/09/1922	NA	20
Michael Downes	Kilmihill	Clare	24/09/1922	NA	
Jeremiah Long	Myrtleville, Crosshaven	Cork	24/09/1922	IRA	
Patrick Mangan	Cork Gaol	Cork	24/09/1922	IRA	
Charles Eastwood	Mercer Hospital	Dublin	24/09/1922	Civic Guard	19
Jack Lohan	Kileen, Galway	Galway	24/09/1922	IRA	22
John Looney	Killorglin Barracks	Kerry	24/09/1922	NA	20
John Dennehy	Bunbane, Cahirciveen	Kerry	24/09/1922	Civilian	45
John Riordan	Waterville	Kerry	24/09/1922	Civilian	67
John McGuigan	Belfast	Antrim	24/09/1922	Civilian	4
Denis Herlihy	Millstreet District Hospital	Cork	25/09/1922	Civilian	50
Bernard Murphy	Cork Military Barracks, Old Youghal Rd	Cork	25/09/1922	NA	40
Michael Considine	Ennistymon Hospital	Clare	26/09/1922	NA	27
Patrick O'Brien	Amiens Street	Dublin	26/09/1922	NA	27
Edward Searls	Innishannon	Cork	27/09/1922	NA	25
Daniel Lehane	Langford Street, Killorglin	Kerry	27/09/1922	NA	25
John Martin	Military Hospital, Killarney	Kerry	27/09/1922	NA	24
Bartholomew Murphy	Military Hospital, Killarney	Kerry	27/09/1922	Fianna	17
Con Looney	Church Corner, Killorglin	Kerry	27/09/1922	IRA	23
Patrick Murphy	Killorglin	Kerry	27/09/1922	IRA	
Patrick O'Malley	Altymount Street, Westport	Mayo	27/09/1922	NA	22
Patrick Walsh	Irishtown, Claremorris	Mayo	27/09/1922	IRA	
Thomas Murray	Lismore Castle	Waterford	27/09/1922	NA	
Sean O'Donoghue	Dublin Hill	Cork	28/09/1922	IRA	24
William Stafford	Richmond Hospital	Dublin	28/09/1922	NA	
Thomas Raoche	Central Hotel, Ballina	Mayo	28/09/1922	IRA	27
Edward Noone	Rathmore	Kerry	29/09/1922	NA	25
Denis O'Connor	County Infirmary, Tralee	Kerry	29/09/1922	NA	
Peter Farrell	Drogheda Workhouse	Louth	29/09/1922	Civilian	57
Patrick Cosgrave	Doctor Steeven's Hospital	Dublin	30/09/1922	Civilian	60
Cornelius O'Shea	County Infirmary, Tralee	Kerry	30/09/1922	NA	20

Name	Location	County	Date	Affiliation	Age
John Galvin	Ballyseedy Castle, Ballyseedy	Kerry	30/09/1922	IRA	28
Francis Johnston	Priestown, Drogheda	Louth	30/09/1922	Civilian	45
William Purcell	Templemore Barracks	Tipperary	30/09/1922	NA	16
James Torpey	Carrickbeg, Carrick	Tipperary	30/09/1922	IRA	19
Henry McAuley	Herbert Street, Belfast	Antrim	30/09/1922	Civilian	
James Dunne	Dungarvan Hospital, Dungarvan	Waterford	October 1922	NA	32
John O'Brien	Tiermaclane, Ennis	Clare	01/10/1922	Civilian	
Stephen Diviney	Athenry	Galway	01/10/1922	NA	24
Stephen Donovan	Inchigeela	Cork	02/10/1922	NA	a 'youth'
Joseph Walsh	Woodroofe	Tipperary	02/10/1922	NA	25
Thomas Brownrigg	Woodroofe	Tipperary	02/10/1922	NA	
Ignatious Redmond	The Kiln, Ballinavocran	Wexford	02/10/1922	NA	25
Daniel O'Callaghan	Masseytown, Macroom	Cork	03/10/1922	Civilian	65
Jeremiah Keating	Union Hospital, Caherciveen	Kerry	03/10/1922	IRA	
Michael Hayes	Lissanisky, Upton	Cork	04/10/1922	IRA	18
Daniel O'Sullivan	Upton	Cork	04/10/1922	IRA	
Patrick Pierse	Upton	Cork	04/10/1922	IRA	25
Jeremiah Holland	Kealkil	Cork	04/10/1922	Civilian	48
Patrick Byrne	Dunmanway Hospital	Cork	05/10/1922	NA	26
John Harford	Grand Parade	Cork	05/10/1922	NA	17
Daniel Hanlon	Knockboy, Carrignavar	Cork	05/10/1922	Civilian	36
Patrick Byrne	Knockboy, Carrignavar	Cork	05/10/1922	Civilian	36
Mary Sherlock	Mater Hospital, Belfast	Antrim	05/10/1922	Civilian	44
Michael Keane	Tullycrine, Kilrush	Clare	06/10/1922	NA	29
Daniel O'Donovan	Timoleague	Cork	06/10/1922	IRA	33
Catherine Hogan	Glin, Listowel	Limerick	06/10/1922	Civilian	13
Bernard Brannigan	Anne Street Barracks, Dundalk	Louth	06/10/1922	Civilian	23
Michael Meagher	Glenmore Latteragh, Thurles	Tipperary	06/10/1922	IRA	
Edwin (Eamon) Hughes	Red Cow quarry, Clondalkin	Dublin	07/10/1922	IRA	17
Brendan Holohan	Red Cow quarry, Clondalkin	Dublin	07/10/1922	IRA	17
Joseph Rogers	Red Cow quarry, Clondalkin	Dublin	07/10/1922	IRA	16
Myles Broughan	Lismore Castle	Waterford	07/10/1922	NA	
Sean Hunter	Gormanstown Army Camp, Gormanstown	Meath	08/10/1922	NA	24
Julia Molloy	Oaklands, New Ross	Wexford	08/10/1922	Civilian	45
Terence Watters	Carcaclogher, Keady	Armagh	08/10/1922	IRA	20
Thomas Reddington	County Infirmary, Longford	Longford	09/10/1922	NA	37
Charles Kearns	The Mall	Cork	09/10/1922	NA	
William Moore	Carmen Hall, Stillorgan	Dublin	09/10/1922	Civilian	50
James Rourke	County Infirmary, Portlaoise	Laois	09/10/1922	Civilian	22
Sean Halpin	Ravensdale	Louth	09/10/1922	IRA	19

NAME	LOCATION	COUNTY	DATE	AFFILIATION	AGE
Peadar Breslin	Mater Hospital	Dublin	10/10/1922	IRA	28
John Gaffney	Mountjoy Prison	Dublin	10/10/1922	NA	20
James Kearns	Mountjoy Prison	Dublin	10/10/1922	NA	27
James Gallagher	Mater Hospital	Dublin	10/10/1922	NA	24
John Killeen	Bridge Street, Ballinrobe	Mayo	10/10/1922	NA	25
Christopher Murphy	Griffinstown, Killucan	Westmeath	10/10/1922	IRA	17
Peter Doyle	Main Street, Enniscorthy	Wexford	10/10/1922	NA	29
Kenny	Kilmurray	Clare	11/10/1922	NA	
Joseph Claffey	Bandon	Cork	11/10/1922	NA	
Richard Noonan	Cork Male Prison	Cork	11/10/1922	IRA	18
John Burns	Macroom	Cork	12/10/1922	NA	
Annie Philips	Water Street, Longford	Longford	12/10/1922	Civilian	25
John Kelly	Loughbraddy, Castleblaney	Monaghan	12/10/1922	Civilian	28
Patrick Hayes	Clonmel Hospital	Tipperary	12/10/1922	NA	
John Coonan	Glen of Aherlow	Tipperary	12/10/1922	NA	
John Murray	Custume Barracks, Athlone	Westmeath	12/10/1922	NA	
Patrick Clancy	North Infirmary, Cork city	Cork	13/10/1922	Civilian	31
Matthew MacNamara	County Home, Loughrea	Galway	13/10/1922	NA	29
Timothy Goggin	Fenit Pier	Kerry	13/10/1922	NA	22
John Young	Rathmore	Kerry	13/10/1922	NA	21
James Byrne	Abbeyfeale Hospital	Limerick	13/10/1922	NA	
Francis McWeeney	Dowra	Cavan	14/10/1922	NA	33
Christopher Guerin	Kildysart Barracks	Clare	14/10/1922	NA	26
Andrew Furlong	Jervis Street Hospital	Dublin	14/10/1922	NA	31
John Gilligan	County Infirmary, Tralee	Kerry	14/10/1922	NA	21
Joseph Dooley	Dungarvan Hospital	Waterford	14/10/1922	NA	26
Jeremiah Driscoll	Bantry	Cork	16/10/1922	NA	18
James O'Callaghan	Monaniny, Rahan, Mallow	Cork	16/10/1922	IRA	21
James O'Callaghan	Killavullen	Cork	16/10/1922	IRA	20
Patrick Walsh	Gerald Griffin Street, Hillgrove Lane	Cork	16/10/1922	Civilian	25
Victor Meaney	Castleconnell	Limerick	16/10/1922	Civilian	26
Patrick Tiquin	Rathcabin, Ratheabhain	Tipperary	16/10/1922	NA	26
Patrick Frieze	Lough Veagh House, Churchill	Donegal	17/10/1922	IRA	28
Michael Coffey	Workhouse, Dingle	Kerry	17/10/1922	Civilian	35
Patrick Collins	Louth County Infirmary, Dundalk	Louth	17/10/1922	NA	19
James Sullivan	Rathmore	Kerry	18/10/1922	Civilian	42
Patrick Quigley	Kilmanagh	Kilkenny	18/10/1922	NA	22
Thomas O'Dea	Kilmanagh	Kilkenny	18/10/1922	IRA	24
Thomas Doyle	County Home, Enniscorthy	Wexford	18/10/1922	NA	27
Thomas Allen	Friary Place, Enniscorthy	Wexford	18/10/1922	Civilian	35
Robert Dixon	Wexford Military Barracks, Wexford	Wexford	18/10/1922	NA	19

Name	Location	County	Date	Affiliation	Age
Sean O'Sullivan	Mater Hospital	Dublin	19/10/1922	NA	16
Michael Bailey	Naas Road	Kildare	19/10/1922	NA	23
John Brown	Duagh	Kerry	20/10/1922	NA	28
William Myles	Tonevane, Curraheen	Kerry	20/10/1922	IRA	
John McGivney	Louth County Infirmary, Dundalk	Louth	20/10/1922	NA	28
James Mulrennan	Military Hospital, Boyle	Roscommon	20/10/1922	IRA	33
Samuel Holmes	Baronscourt	Tyrone	20/10/1922	USC	22
James Marum	Mercy Hospital, Cork city	Cork	21/10/1922	NA	37
Edward Horne	Galbally	Limerick	21/10/1922	NA	25
Thomas Maher	New Ross	Wexford	21/10/1922	Civilian	62
William Jordan	Alfred Street, Derry	Derry	21/10/1922	Civilian	78
Daniel O'Halloran	Carrigaloe, Cobh	Cork	22/10/1922	IRA	34
Michael Mahony	Mercy Hospital, Cork city	Cork	22/10/1922	NA	
John Corcoran	Military Hospital, Killarney	Kerry	22/10/1922	NA	32
James Burke	Cashel	Tipperary	22/10/1922	NA	
Laurence Phelan	Millstreet, Dungarvan	Waterford	22/10/1922	NA	
Patrick Foley	Dungarvan Hospital	Waterford	22/10/1922	NA	
Peter Behan	Ferrycarrig	Wexford	22/10/1922	NA	26
Patrick O'Connor	Ferrycarrig	Wexford	22/10/1922	NA	26
William Doyle	Ferrycarrig	Wexford	22/10/1922	NA	21
Christopher Kearns	Ferrycarrig	Wexford	22/10/1922	NA	23
Ellen Gallagher	Mercy Hospital, Cork city	Cork	23/10/1922	Civilian	8
Thomas O'Shea	Curragh Camp	Kildare	23/10/1922	NA	46
Joseph Hanrahan	Saint John's Hospital, Limerick	Limerick	23/10/1922	NA	22
Nevin Jackson	Ardee	Louth	23/10/1922	Civilian	25
Alexander Gardner	Teeshin, Ballymena	Antrim	23/10/1922	Civilian	24
Nicholas Tobin	Mater Hospital	Dublin	24/10/1922	NA	23
Daniel Nagle	Tralee County Hospital	Kerry	24/10/1922	NA	19
Edward Byrne	Graney	Kildare	24/10/1922	NA	16
James Murphy	Graney	Kildare	24/10/1922	NA	41
Patrick Allison	Graney	Kildare	24/10/1922	NA	31
Thomas Kavanagh	Michael Barracks, Cork city	Cork	25/10/1922	NA	20
William Cox	Workhouse, Midleton	Cork	25/10/1922	IRA	22
Joseph Gilchrist	Ballyrobert, Ardfert	Kerry	25/10/1922	NA	
Michael Ahern	Beaufort House	Kerry	25/10/1922	IRA	
David Nolan	Mercy Hospital, Cork city	Cork	26/10/1922	Civilian	52
Joseph O'Riordan	Mercer's Hospital	Dublin	26/10/1922	NA	20
Patrick Dalton	Donohill	Tipperary	26/10/1922	IRA	
Daniel Sullivan	Curragh Hill, Clonakilty	Cork	27/10/1922	NA	19
Daniel Nevin	Mungret Street, Limerick	Limerick	27/10/1922	NA	38
James Foley	Dock Road, Limerick	Limerick	27/10/1922	IRA	36

Name	Location	County	Date	Affiliation	Age
James Hunt	County Infirmary, Carlow	Carlow	28/10/1922	NA	22
Peter Byrne	Buttevant	Cork	28/10/1922	NA	18
Edward Kavanagh	Jervis Street Hospital	Dublin	29/10/1922	NA	
Thomas Connelly	Clifden Wireless Station	Galway	29/10/1922	NA	
Thomas James	Clifden Wireless Station	Galway	29/10/1922	IRA	22
Jeremiah Sullivan	Cork Female Prison	Cork	30/10/1922	NA	17
John Bagot	Goig, Castleconell	Limerick	30/10/1922	IRA	32
James Cullinan	Tullassa, Ennis	Clare	31/10/1922	Civilian	40
Daniel Dennehy	Monard viaduct	Cork	31/10/1922	NA	19
John Lawlor	Saint James Cemetery, Ballyheigue	Kerry	31/10/1922	IRA	
Joseph Martin	Curragh Camp	Kildare	31/10/1922	NA	20
Ms Grant	Ballyvaughan Post Office	Clare	01/11/1922	Civilian	
Patrick Morrison	Clifden Wireless Station	Galway	01/11/1922	IRA	20
John Cadogan	Military Hospital, Killarney	Kerry	01/11/1922	NA	25
Nora O'Leary	Killarney Hospital	Kerry	01/11/1922	CnamB	37
Francis Power	Lissonfield House, Rathmines	Dublin	02/11/1922	IRA	22
Michael O'Sullivan	Knockanes, Headford, Barraduff	Kerry	02/11/1922	IRA	
James Cleary	Cahir	Tipperary	02/11/1922	Civilian	43
Francis Crampton	Sallins Railway Station	Kildare	03/11/1922	NA	26
Patrick Mulrennan	Curragh Military Hospital	Kildare	03/11/1922	IRA	30
John Mulchrone	Brockagh, Aughagowla	Mayo	03/11/1922	IRA	24
Michael Keane	Shragh, Moyasta	Clare	04/11/1922	IRA	22
Thomas Gallagher	Ballineen	Cork	04/11/1922	NA	18
Michael Woods	Military Hospital, Bandon	Cork	04/11/1922	NA	22
John Howell	Enniskeane	Cork	04/11/1922	IRA	30
Timothy/Tadhg O'Leary	Ballineen	Cork	04/11/1922	IRA	24
Samuel Jones	Hospital, Youghal	Cork	04/11/1922	Civilian	15
James Lacy	Grattan Street, Youghal	Cork	04/11/1922	Civilian	41
Peter McCartney	City of Dublin Hospital	Dublin	04/11/1922	NA	23
Patrick Conroy	Blennerville	Kerry	04/11/1922	NA	
James Boyle	Louth County Infirmary, Dundalk	Louth	04/11/1922	NA	24
Peter Treanor	Rockmarshall	Louth	04/11/1922	NA	41
Christopher Caffrey	County Infirmary, Navan	Meath	04/11/1922	NA	29
Michael Sadlier	New Inn, Cashel	Tipperary	04/11/1922	IRA	26
Patrick Kennedy	Portroe, Barbe Harbour, Nenagh	Tipperary	04/11/1922	Civilian	25
Michael Twohig	Shanaknock, Drishane, Millstreet	Cork	05/11/1922	IRA	
John Doyle	Templeogue	Dublin	05/11/1922	IRA	23
Matthew Hunt	Powelsboro, Tobercurry	Sligo	05/11/1922	NA	50
James O'Connor	Powelsboro, Tobercurry	Sligo	05/11/1922	NA	27
James McPartland	Powelsboro, Tobercurry	Sligo	05/11/1922	Civilian	27
Christopher McKeon	Main Street, Moate	Westmeath	05/11/1922	IRA	28

Name	Location	County	Date	Affiliation	Age
Patrick Duff	Belfast	Antrim	05/11/1922	Civilian	
Michael Buckley	Limerick Prison, Limerick	Limerick	06/11/1922	Civilian	38
Frank Scanlon	Cloonacool	Sligo	06/11/1922	Civilian	41
Andrew Hogan	Bandon Hospital	Cork	07/11/1922	NA	30
William Ahern	Curragheen Road, Cork city	Cork	07/11/1922	Civilian	20
Jeremiah McKenna	Hospital, Tralee	Kerry	07/11/1922	Civilian	26
James Spain	Meath Hospital	Dublin	08/11/1922	IRA	21
Thomas Murphy	Wellington Barracks, South Circular Road	Dublin	08/11/1922	NA	20
John O'Callaghan	Cahirciveen	Kerry	09/11/1922	NA	
Frank Cregan	District Hospital, Fermoy	Cork	10/11/1922	NA	20
James Murphy	North Infirmary, Cork city	Cork	10/11/1922	Civilian	25
Helena Barry	Mercy Hospital, Cork city	Cork	11/11/1922	Civilian	26
Frederick Weatherup	Mater Hospital	Dublin	11/11/1922	NA	23
Michael Cronin	Goulane, Rathmore	Kerry	11/11/1922	Civilian	14
George Dowd	Westport Barracks, Westport	Mayo	12/11/1922	NA	23
James Martin	Drumreery Arva	Cavan	13/11/1922	Civilian	21
Daniel Griffin	North Infirmary, Cork city	Cork	13/11/1922	Civilian	28
Eileen O'Driscoll	Brookhill, Riverstown	Cork	13/11/1922	Civilian	3
Mary Egan	Newtownshandrum	Cork	13/11/1922	Civilian	24
Samuel Webb	Ulverton Road, Dalkey	Dublin	13/11/1922	NA	19
Henry Manning	Ulverton Road, Dalkey	Dublin	13/11/1922	Civilian	43
Lillie Bennet	Jervis Street Hospital	Dublin	13/11/1922	Civilian	17
Mary McKenna	Milltown	Kerry	13/11/1922	Civilian	
George Reidy	Abbeyfeale Military Barracks	Limerick	13/11/1922	NA	
Charles Boyce	Michael Street, Waterford	Waterford	13/11/1922	Civilian	24
John Cronin	Rathduff	Cork	14/11/1922	NA	19
Joseph Ryan	River Shannon, Drumshambo	Leitrim	14/11/1922	IRA	
Henry Phelan	Mullinahone	Tipperary	14/11/1922	Civic Guard	21
William Cronin	Bandon Hospital, Bandon	Cork	15/11/1922	NA	24
David Mulhall	Patrick Dunn Hospital	Dublin	15/11/1922	Civilian	15
William Woulahan	Bandon	Cork	16/11/1922	NA	33
John Lunny	Mullins, Ballyshannon	Donegal	16/11/1922	IRA	26
Peter Hogan	Aughnagan Bridge	Wexford	16/11/1922	NA	22
John White	Dungannon Hospital	Tyrone	16/11/1922	USC	29
Patrick Duggan	Glengarriff	Cork	17/11/1922	IRA	20
James Fisher	Kilmainham Gaol	Dublin	17/11/1922	IRA	18
Peter Cassidy	Kilmainham Gaol	Dublin	17/11/1922	IRA	19
Richard Twohig	Kilmainham Gaol	Dublin	17/11/1922	IRA	21
John Gaffney	Kilmainham Gaol	Dublin	17/11/1922	IRA	21
Michael Flynn	Derrymore Bridge, Derrymore	Kerry	17/11/1922	IRA	28

Name	Location	County	Date	Affiliation	Age
John Casey	Castlegregory	Kerry	17/11/1922	Civilian	59
Thomas Manifold	Killaloe	Clare	18/11/1922	NA	34
Patrick Egan	Blackhorse Bridge, Inchicore	Dublin	18/11/1922	IRA	20
Thomas Maguire	Blackhorse Bridge, Inchicore	Dublin	18/11/1922	IRA	23
Bernard Curtis	Blackhorse Bridge, Inchicore	Dublin	18/11/1922	IRA	20
Phillip Gilgunn	Saint Vincent's Hospital	Dublin	18/11/1922	IRA	23
Peter Cummins	Mater Hospital	Dublin	18/11/1922	Civilian	28
James Hayes	Silverfort Moyglass	Tipperary	18/11/1922	IRA	
John Powell	Shalee Cross	Tipperary	18/11/1922	Civilian	
Margaret Kerrigan	Tyrone County Hospital	Tyrone	18/11/1922	Civilian	20
Thomas Whelan	Doctor Steeven's Hospital	Dublin	19/11/1922	IRA	22
John Foley	Jervis Street Hospital	Dublin	19/11/1922	NA	21
John Crosbie	Richmond Hospital	Dublin	19/11/1922	Civilian	22
Aeneas Lane	Knockcoolkeare, Mount Collins, Abbeyfeale	Limerick	19/11/1922	IRA	34
Daniel Desmond	Devonshire Street, Mulgrave Road	Cork	20/11/1922	NA	19
Margaret Daly	Mulgrave Road, Cork city	Cork	20/11/1922	Civilian	24
John Devoy	Saint Vincent's Hospital	Dublin	20/11/1922	NA	19
Arthur Keogh	Lacka, Shinrone	Offaly	20/11/1922	IRA	22
James Doyle	Ulverton Road, Dalkey	Dublin	22/11/1922	NA	21
Henry Stringer	Between Millstreet and Kanturk	Cork	23/11/1922	NA	
Bernard Conaty	Louth County Infirmary, Dundalk	Louth	23/11/1922	NA	22
Thomas McCann	Ballyvolane	Cork	24/11/1922	NA	47
Erskine Childers	Beggars Bush Barracks	Dublin	24/11/1922	IRA	52
Thomas Davis	Ardee Military Barracks, Ardee	Louth	24/11/1922	NA	23
Patrick Murphy	Newport	Mayo	24/11/1922	NA	45
Joseph Ruddy	Newport	Mayo	24/11/1922	NA	30
Austin Woods	Seaview, Newport	Mayo	24/11/1922	NA	18
Patrick McEllin	Kilbride, Newport	Mayo	24/11/1922	NA	26
George Brophy	Donegall, Clonmel	Tipperary	24/11/1922	Civilian	49
Patrick Healy	Kanturk	Cork	25/11/1922	IRA	30
James Delaney	Warren Lane, Cork city	Cork	25/11/1922	Civilian	32
Michael Joseph Walsh	Newport	Mayo	25/11/1922	NA	24
Felix Murray	Mountdevlin	Roscommon	25/11/1922	Civilian	36
William Merriman	South Main Street, Wexford	Wexford	25/11/1922	Civilian	25
John Walsh	North Infirmary	Cork	26/11/1922	NA	21
Daniel O'Meara	Mercy Hospital, Cork city	Cork	26/11/1922	Civilian	30
William 'Kruger' Graham	Saint Vincent's Hospital	Dublin	26/11/1922	IRA	22
Donald Murray	Mercer's Hospital	Dublin	26/11/1922	Civilian	19
Michael Casey	County Infirmary, Tralee	Kerry	26/11/1922	NA	18
William Williamson	Crossbarry	Cork	27/11/1922	NA	

Name	Location	County	Date	Affiliation	Age
Christopher Grehan	Saint Vincent's Hospital	Dublin	27/11/1922	NA	24
Francis Mullen	Lixnaw	Kerry	27/11/1922	NA	
Patrick McClean	County Infirmary, Castlebar	Mayo	28/11/1922	Civilian	22
Patrick Griffin	Johns Street, Kilkenny city	Kilkenny	29/11/1922	Civilian	47
Michael McGrade	Claremorris Hospital, Claremorris	Mayo	29/11/1922	NA	
William Buckley	Mercy Hospital, Cork city	Cork	30/11/1922	IRA	32
Joseph Spooner	Beggars Bush Barracks	Dublin	30/11/1922	IRA	
Patrick Farrelly	Beggars Bush Barracks	Dublin	30/11/1922	IRA	
John Murphy	Beggars Bush Barracks	Dublin	30/11/1922	IRA	19
Patrick Lynch	Moyrish, The Glen, Ballinskelligs	Kerry	30/11/1922	IRA	37
Thomas Walsh	Saint John's Hospital	Limerick	30/11/1922	NA	25
Matthew Brennan	Quarryfield	Sligo	30/11/1922	NA	22
James Clarke	Quarryfield	Sligo	30/11/1922	NA	19
Joseph Moran	Between Leixlip and Maynooth	Kildare	01/12/1922	NA	36
Charles Gyles	Louth County Infirmary, Dundalk	Louth	01/12/1922	NA	24
Thomas Doyle	Ryland's Cross, Clohamon	Wexford	01/12/1922	NA	33
Daniel O'Leary	Dunmanway Hospital	Cork	02/12/1922	NA	24
William Joyce	Kilmilkin	Galway	02/12/1922	NA	
Patrick Cormack	Johnstown	Kilkenny	02/12/1922	IRA	26
Francis McGarron	Drumshambo	Leitrim	02/12/1922	Civilian	
John Dooley	Wexford Hospital	Wexford	02/12/1922	NA	19
George McGlynn	Ballyvourney	Cork	03/12/1922	NA	
William Brosnan	Main Street, Castleisland	Kerry	03/12/1922	IRA	26
John Carter	Westport	Mayo	03/12/1922	NA	
Martin Joyce	Glenbeg West, Maamtrasna	Mayo	03/12/1922	Civilian	23
Thomas Leahy	Cahir Barracks	Tipperary	03/12/1922	NA	19
Patrick Bennett	Bawndonnell, Slievenamon	Tipperary	03/12/1922	IRA	
E. Butler	Bawndonnell, Slievenamon	Tipperary	03/12/1922	IRA	
Angela Bridgeman	Meath Hospital	Dublin	04/12/1922	Civilian	23
Myles Carroll	Shean Myshall	Carlow	05/12/1922	IRA	26
Thomas Nolan	Killeen, Ballymakeera	Cork	05/12/1922	NA	24
Jeremiah Casey	Gortnalicky, Macroom	Cork	05/12/1922	IRA	19
Cornelius O'Leary	Ballymakeera	Cork	05/12/1922	Civilian	45
John Moyles	Ballyhaunis	Mayo	05/12/1922	NA	21
John Aylward	Richmond Hospital	Dublin	06/12/1922	NA	22
Seamus O'Toole	Curragh Camp	Kildare	06/12/1922	IRA	27
Daniel Hurley	Mercy Hospital, Cork city	Cork	07/12/1922	NA	25
William McNeice	Mercy Hospital, Cork city	Cork	07/12/1922	NA	24
Seán Hales	Jervis Street Hospital	Dublin	07/12/1922	NA	42
Annie Cardwell	Beatty Park, Celbridge	Kildare	07/12/1922	Civilian	18
Hugh O'Donnell	Ballintubber, Kilfinane	Limerick	07/12/1922	IRA	19

Name	Location	County	Date	Affiliation	Age
Charles McCaffrey	Fermoy	Cork	08/12/1922	NA	
George Dease	Kealkil	Cork	08/12/1922	IRA	
John Dwyer	Droumacappal, Kealkil	Cork	08/12/1922	IRA	
Rory O'Connor	Mountjoy Gaol	Dublin	08/12/1922	IRA	39
Liam Mellows	Mountjoy Gaol	Dublin	08/12/1922	IRA	30
Joseph McKelvey	Mountjoy Gaol	Dublin	08/12/1922	IRA	24
Richard Barrett	Mountjoy Gaol	Dublin	08/12/1922	IRA	32
William Harrington	The Rink, Basin Road, Tralee	Kerry	08/12/1922	IRA	23
John Carey	Doorlusbeg, Doolass, Granagh	Limerick	08/12/1922	NA	
James Skeffington	Sligo	Sligo	09/12/1922	NA	32
Peter Gilsenan	Carrick on Suir	Tipperary	09/12/1922	NA	21
James Gardiner	Carrick on Suir	Tipperary	09/12/1922	NA	
James Malone	Fair Hill, Cork city	Cork	10/12/1922	Civilian	31
Ernest Allen	Mercer's Hospital	Dublin	10/12/1922	NA	17
Emmet McGarry	Temple Street Hospital	Dublin	10/12/1922	Civilian	7
James Guinane	Saint John's Hospital, Limerick	Limerick	10/12/1922	NA	23
Thomas Mooney	Mercy Hospital, Cork city	Cork	11/12/1922	NA	20
Hugh Gallagher	Drumboe Castle	Donegal	11/12/1922	IRA	22
Thomas Fitzpatrick	Curragh Camp	Kildare	11/12/1922	Civilian	61
Sean Riordan	Coolbrook, Ballingarry	Tipperary	11/12/1922	IRA	
Carson Dennison	Drumkeeran	Leitrim	12/12/1922	Civilian	74
Thomas Henry Dennison	Drumkeeran	Leitrim	12/12/1922	Civilian	29
Edward Kilroy	Charlestown	Mayo	12/12/1922	IRA	27
John Travers	Youghal	Cork	13/12/1922	NA	16
Thomas Behan	The Curragh	Kildare	13/12/1922	IRA	32
Robert Mullins	Portobello Barracks	Dublin	14/12/1922	Civilian	40
John McGolderick	Custume Barracks, Athlone	Westmeath	14/12/1922	NA	25
Laurence Galvin	District Hospital, Fermoy	Cork	15/12/1922	NA	26
James Roche	O'Leary's Pub, Passage	Cork	15/12/1922	Civilian	38
Thomas Fagan	Jervis Street Hospital	Dublin	15/12/1922	NA	18
Eric Wolfe	Ringnanean, Kinsale	Cork	16/12/1922	Civilian	31
Matthew Ferguson	Military Hospital, Killarney	Kerry	16/12/1922	NA	21
Thomas Walshe	Doctor Steeven's Hospital	Dublin	17/12/1922	NA	28
Patrick Mullhall	Dingle	Kerry	17/12/1922	NA	19
John Keogh	Johnstown	Kildare	17/12/1922	NA	22
John O'Shea	County and City Infirmary, Waterford	Waterford	17/12/1922	Civilian	38
Maryanne Higgins	The Green, Fethard	Tipperary	18/12/1922	Civilian	69
Patrick Martin	Carrick	Tipperary	18/12/1922	Civilian	26
Michael Nagle	Mercy Hospital, Cork city	Cork	19/12/1922	Civilian	55
John Sullivan	Ballihilow, Leap	Cork	19/12/1922	Civilian	'young boy'
Patrick Bagnall	The Curragh	Kildare	19/12/1922	IRA	19

Name	Location	County	Date	Affiliation	Age
Patrick Mangan	The Curragh	Kildare	19/12/1922	IRA	22
Joseph Johnston	The Curragh	Kildare	19/12/1922	IRA	18
Bryan Moore	The Curragh	Kildare	19/12/1922	IRA	28
Patrick Nolan	The Curragh	Kildare	19/12/1922	IRA	20
Stephen White	The Curragh	Kildare	19/12/1922	IRA	19
James O'Connor	The Curragh	Kildare	19/12/1922	IRA	19
Patrick White	Portlaoise Court, House	Laois	19/12/1922	NA	21
James Kenna	Gorey	Wexford	19/12/1922	NA	36
Catherine Feehely	Mercy Hospital, Cork city	Cork	20/12/1922	Civilian	28
Seamus Dwyer	Lower Rathmines Road	Dublin	20/12/1922	CDF	37
Francis Moy	Glassagh, Cloghan	Donegal	21/12/1922	Civilian	25
Jeremiah Desmond	Mercy Hospital, Cork city	Cork	22/12/1922	NA	19
James Ryan	Mitchelstown	Cork	22/12/1922	NA	30
Robert Baylor	Mercy Hospital, Cork city	Cork	22/12/1922	Civilian	55
Patrick Fitzgerald	Granby Road/Dorset Street	Dublin	22/12/1922	NA	38
Frederick Lidwell	Kilkenny Military Barracks	Kilkenny	22/12/1922	NA	22
Charles O'Donnell	Ballyhaise	Cavan	23/12/1922	Civilian	27
Samuel Crawford	Strawhill, Monkstown	Cork	23/12/1922	NA	
Connell McBride	Carrick, Deerbybeg	Donegal	23/12/1922	Civilian	70
Kathleen Hehir	Edward Street, Limerick	Limerick	23/12/1922	Civilian	17
Thomas Hastings	Barringtons Hospital, Limerick	Limerick	23/12/1922	Civilian	48
James Murphy	Clones	Monaghan	23/12/1922	Civilian	21
John O'Farrell	Carlow Military Barracks, Carlow	Carlow	24/12/1922	NA	27
Thomas Ganley		Galway	24/12/1922	IRA	
William Lombard	Naas	Kildare	24/12/1922	NA	23
Edward Burke	Urlingford	Kilkenny	24/12/1922	Civilian	19
James Haire	Flowerhill, Lisburn	Antrim	24/12/1922	Civilian	19
James Byrne	Whitegate	Cork	25/12/1922	IRA	40
John Gallagher	Ballymacadden	Donegal	25/12/1922	Civilian	23
John Foran	Mater Hospital	Dublin	25/12/1922	NA	19
Michael McDonald	Ring, Clonakilty	Cork	26/12/1922	NA	
Tom Lane	Ring, Clonakilty	Cork	26/12/1922	IRA	
James Mangan	Kilbacan, Killarney	Kerry	26/12/1922	Civilian	19
Charles James Tucker	Midland & Great Western Railway Station, Athlone	Westmeath	26/12/1922	NA	19
Francis Lalor	Orwell Road, Rathgar	Dublin	28/12/1922	IRA	
Patrick Slyne	Mater Hospital	Dublin	28/12/1922	Civilian	60
John Newsome	The Curragh	Kildare	28/12/1922	NA	19
Michael Ryan	Curragh Military Hospital	Kildare	28/12/1922	IRA	21
Patrick Mahon	Ballina	Mayo	28/12/1922	IRA	31
Michael Morris	Kyle	Wexford	28/12/1922	IRA	23

NAME	LOCATION	COUNTY	DATE	AFFILIATION	AGE
Matthew Daly	Mater Hospital	Dublin	29/12/1922	CID	28
Henry McLoughlin	Castlegregory	Kerry	29/12/1922	NA	
John Talty	Castlegregory	Kerry	29/12/1922	NA	
John Phelan	Kilkenny Military Barracks	Kilkenny	29/12/1922	IRA	32
John Murphy	Kilkenny Military Barracks	Kilkenny	29/12/1922	IRA	22
Thomas Connolly	Limerick	Limerick	29/12/1922	NA	30
John Doyle	Castlebellingham	Louth	29/12/1922	Civilian	36
Matthew Leavy	Mercer's Hospital	Dublin	30/12/1922	NA	27
Hugh O'Donnell	Priorland, Dundalk	Louth	30/12/1922	IRA	26
Michael Downey	Pearsons Bridge, Bantry	Cork	31/12/1922	Civilian	20
Thomas McEvoy	Graney Cross, Castledermot	Kildare	01/01/1923	NA	18
Pierse Murphy	Doyle Street, Waterford	Waterford	01/01/1923	Civilian	33
Thomas Cullen	County and City Infirmary, Waterford	Waterford	02/01/1923	Civilian	33
Patrick Acton	Clonaheen	Laois	03/01/1923	NA	20
Myles Cahill	Leitrim County Infirmary, Carrick on Shannon	Leitrim	03/01/1923	NA	33
William Hogan	Silvermines, Nenagh	Tipperary	03/01/1923	NA	21
Edward Snoddy	Thornville, Palatine	Carlow	05/01/1923	IRA	19
Jeremiah Mahony	Carnegie Library, Millstreet	Cork	05/01/1923	NA	51
Robert Tobin	Courthouse Street, Cork city	Cork	05/01/1923	Civilian	32
Michael Cull	Ballyconnell Post Office, Ballyconnell	Cavan	06/01/1923	IRA	26
James Caffrey	Fermoy	Cork	06/01/1923	NA	
Denis Coakley	Skibbereen	Cork	06/01/1923	NA	33
Thomas Flannery	Portobello Barracks	Dublin	06/01/1923	IRA	23
John Ryan	Coolbawn, Castleconell	Limerick	06/01/1923	NA	
Christopher Sweeney	Labour Exchange, O'Connell Street	Waterford	06/01/1923	NA	19
Adelaide Kinney	Belfast	Antrim	07/01/1923	Civilian	
Leo Dowling	Kilmainham Gaol	Dublin	08/01/1923	IRA	21
Sylvester Heaney	Kehoe Barracks	Dublin	08/01/1923	IRA	22
Laurence Sheeky	Kehoe Barracks	Dublin	08/01/1923	IRA	20
Anthony Reilly	Kehoe Barracks	Dublin	08/01/1923	IRA	22
Terence Brady	Kilmainham Gaol	Dublin	08/01/1923	IRA	20
Michael Clancy	Curraghmore Bridge	Galway	08/01/1923	IRA	23
Martin Fahy	Curraghmore Bridge	Galway	08/01/1923	Civilian	29
Andrew Quinn	Curraghmore Bridge	Galway	08/01/1923	Civilian	34
John Fahy	Cloughallagh, Aughrim, Ballinasloe	Galway	08/01/1923	Civilian	26
Daniel Doherty	Curragh Military Hospital	Kildare	08/01/1923	NA	22
John Ivory	Crooke, Passage East	Waterford	08/01/1923	Civilian	20
Ellen Weir	Cullybackey	Antrim	08/01/1923	Civilian	22
Walter Joyce	Saint Bride's Hospital, Galway	Galway	09/01/1923	Civilian	57
Martin Breen	Limerick Road, Roseboro, Tipperary	Tipperary	10/01/1923	IRA	

Name	Location	County	Date	Affiliation	Age
Cornelius McCarthy	Spencerstown	Wexford	10/01/1923	IRA	24
Bernard Radford	County Home, Wexford	Wexford	10/01/1923	IRA	23
Patrick Lynch	Curragh Military Hospital	Kildare	12/01/1923	NA	24
Mr Fitten	Quilty Railway Station	Clare	13/01/1923	Civilian	
James Stapleton	Granby Road/Dorset Street	Dublin	13/01/1923	Civilian	65
Thomas Murray	Dundalk Prison, Dundalk	Louth	13/01/1923	IRA	
Thomas McKeown	Dundalk Prison, Dundalk	Louth	13/01/1923	IRA	
John McNulty	Dundalk Prison, Dundalk	Louth	13/01/1923	IRA	
Patrick McCarthy	Rathea, Ballyhorgan	Kerry	14/01/1923	NA	23
James Lillis	Carlow Jail, Carlow	Carlow	15/01/1923	IRA	22
Patrick Butler	County Infirmary, Castlebar	Mayo	15/01/1923	NA	21
James Higgins	Claremorris Hospital, Claremorris	Mayo	15/01/1923	NA	25
William Fitzgerald	Commons, Ballingarry	Tipperary	15/01/1923	NA	28
Frederick Bourke	Castle Barracks, Roscrea	Tipperary	15/01/1923	IRA	
Martin O'Shea	Castle Barracks, Roscrea	Tipperary	15/01/1923	IRA	22
Patrick Russell	Castle Barracks, Roscrea	Tipperary	15/01/1923	IRA	26
Patrick McNamara	Castle Barracks, Roscrea	Tipperary	15/01/1923	IRA	22
Unidentified	Galtee Mountains	Tipperary	15/01/1923	Civilian	
William Winnery	Bastion Street, Athlone	Westmeath	15/01/1923	NA	16
Patrick Nugent	Kilmihil	Clare	16/01/1923	NA	
Thomas Martin	Saint Vincent's Hospital	Dublin	16/01/1923	NA	19
Michael Mullins	Ballingarry	Tipperary	16/01/1923	NA	22
John Kelly	Kilfeacle, Golden	Tipperary	16/01/1923	NA	22
Joseph Tubridy	Kilkee Barracks	Clare	17/01/1923	NA	
Robert Nash	Portobello Barracks	Dublin	17/01/1923	NA	
Patrick O'Riordan	GSWR, Liscahane, Ardfert	Kerry	17/01/1923	Civilian	50
Daniel Crowley	County Infirmary, Tralee	Kerry	17/01/1923	Civilian	36
Christopher Farrell	Claremorris	Mayo	17/01/1923	Civilian	50
Patrick Geraghty	Kilfeacle, Golden	Tipperary	17/01/1923	NA	23
John Coombs	Goolds Cross Railway Station	Tipperary	17/01/1923	Civilian	50
Patrick Conlon	Moygrehan	Westmeath	17/01/1923	Civilian	59
James Bonner	Rock Barracks, Ballyshannon	Donegal	18/01/1923	NA	23
George Gorman	Saint Bricin's Hospital	Dublin	18/01/1923	NA	23
Patrick White	The Curragh	Kildare	18/01/1923	NA	23
John Doyle	Knocklong Railway Station	Limerick	18/01/1923	NA	20
John Nealon	Derreens, Barnatra, Ballina	Mayo	18/01/1923	IRA	
James Blaney	Downpatrick	Down	18/01/1923	IRA	19
Henry Pomeroy	Mercy Hospital, Cork city	Cork	19/01/1923	NA	41
Leo Francis Beahan	Saint Vincent's Hospital	Dublin	20/01/1923	NA	20
James Hanlon	Ballymullen Gaol, Tralee	Kerry	20/01/1923	IRA	25
Michael Brosnan	Ballymullen Gaol, Tralee	Kerry	20/01/1923	IRA	28

Name	Location	County	Date	Affiliation	Age
John Clifford	Ballymullen Gaol, Tralee	Kerry	20/01/1923	IRA	22
James Daly	Ballymullen Gaol, Tralee	Kerry	20/01/1923	IRA	25
Patrick Hennessy	Limerick Prison, Limerick	Limerick	20/01/1923	IRA	29
Cornelius McMahon	Limerick Prison, Limerick	Limerick	20/01/1923	IRA	28
Thomas Neary	Military Hospital Custume Barracks, Athlone	Westmeath	20/01/1923	IRA	21
Thomas Hughes	Custume Barracks, Athlone	Westmeath	20/01/1923	IRA	21
Herbert Collins	Custume Barracks, Athlone	Westmeath	20/01/1923	IRA	23
Michael Walsh	Custume Barracks, Athlone	Westmeath	20/01/1923	IRA	26
Martin Burke	Custume Barracks, Athlone	Westmeath	20/01/1923	IRA	25
Stephen Joyce	Custume Barracks, Athlone	Westmeath	20/01/1923	IRA	29
Samuel Hamilton Hinton	Fitzwilliam Nursing Home, Upper Pembroke Street	Dublin	21/01/1923	Civilian	44
Eugene Fitzgerald	Ballymullen Barracks, Tralee	Kerry	22/01/1923	IRA	20
Joseph Ferguson	Dundalk Military Barracks, Dundalk	Louth	22/01/1923	IRA	27
James Melia	Dundalk Military Barracks, Dundalk	Louth	22/01/1923	IRA	20
Thomas Lennon	Dundalk Military Barracks, Dundalk	Louth	22/01/1923	IRA	19
Richard Bertles	Low Street, Ballymore	Westmeath	22/01/1923	IRA	31
James McGovern	Castlemaine Barracks	Kerry	23/01/1923	NA	19
Daniel Daly	County Infirmary, Tralee	Kerry	23/01/1923	IRA	38
Joseph Foster	Nine Mile House	Tipperary	23/01/1923	NA	
George Cruise	Tullamalen Churchyard, Clonmel	Tipperary	23/01/1923	NA	20
James Kennedy	Tullamalen Churchyard, Clonmel	Tipperary	23/01/1923	NA	23
Michael Ryan	Aherlow	Tipperary	23/01/1923	NA	35
Michael Cullen	County Home, Enniscorthy	Wexford	23/01/1923	Civilian	56
Patrick Murphy	Mater Hospital	Dublin	24/01/1923	IRA	
Jerome O'Reilly	Darrary, Clonakilty	Cork	25/01/1923	Civilian	
Michael Rock	Caherciveen	Kerry	25/01/1923	NA	27
Daniel Foley	Curragh Military Hospital	Kildare	25/01/1923	Fianna	20
Patrick McGinty	Malranny Barracks	Mayo	25/01/1923	NA	28
Michael Fitzgerald	Waterford Barracks, Waterford	Waterford	25/01/1923	IRA	24
Patrick O'Reilly	Waterford Barracks, Waterford	Waterford	25/01/1923	IRA	24
Thomas Browne	Claremorris Hospital, Claremorris	Mayo	26/01/1923	NA	38
William Conroy	Birr Castle, Birr	Offaly	26/01/1923	IRA	18
Patrick Cunningham	Birr Castle, Birr	Offaly	26/01/1923	IRA	20
Colum Kelly	Birr Castle, Birr	Offaly	26/01/1923	IRA	22
Martin Leonard	Tobercurry	Sligo	26/01/1923	NA	22
William McGowan	Phoenix Park	Dublin	27/01/1923	Civilian	24
Patrick Coye	Feale's Bridge, Kilmaniheen, Brosna	Kerry	27/01/1923	NA	30
Denis O'Connor	Meen, Tooreenmore	Kerry	27/01/1923	IRA	20
Andrew Power	Kilkenny Jail	Kilkenny	27/01/1923	IRA	24

Name	Location	County	Date	Affiliation	Age
Patrick Geraghty	Portlaoise Prison	Laois	27/01/1923	IRA	27
Joseph Byrne	Portlaoise Prison	Laois	27/01/1923	IRA	24
Robert Fuller	County Infirmary, Limerick	Limerick	27/01/1923	Civilian	26
Thomas Prendiville	Castleisland Barracks, Main Street, Castleisland	Kerry	28/01/1923	Civilian	48
Charles Burke	County Home, Wexford	Wexford	29/01/1923	NA	24
Patrick O'Boyle	Arigna	Leitrim	31/01/1923	Civilian	31
Alice Ryan	County and City Infirmary, Waterford	Waterford	31/01/1923	Civilian	17
Patrick Sheridan	Bessbrook	Armagh	31/01/1923	Civilian	45
Patrick Barcoe	Shankill, Paulstown	Kilkenny	02/02/1923	IRA	18
Patrick Murray	Farranlough, Newcestown	Cork	04/02/1923	IRA	22
Charles O'Leary	Farnalough, Newcestown	Cork	04/02/1923	Civilian	18
Michael Egan	Mater Hospital, Eccles Street	Dublin	04/02/1923	Civilian	19
Michael McSweeney	Shrone, Rathmore	Kerry	04/02/1923	IRA	17
A.H. Hunt	Dundrum	Down	04/02/1923	British Army	19
A. Howe	Dundrum	Down	04/02/1923	British Army	21
Richard Wollard	Dundrum	Down	04/02/1923	British Army	22
J.E. Bellingham	Dundrum	Down	04/02/1923	British Army	20
A. Dellbridge	Dundrum	Down	04/02/1923	British Army	
Alfred Longley	Dundrum	Down	04/02/1923	British Army	23
A. Hyndman	Dundrum	Down	04/02/1923	British Army	23
Robert Lowey	Dundrum	Down	04/02/1923	Civilian	17
W.H. Broom	Dundrum	Down	04/02/1923	British Army	
James Nolan	Mercy Hospital, Cork city	Cork	05/02/1923	NA	22
George King	Meath Hospital	Dublin	05/02/1923	IRA	26
Elizabeth Walsh	Jervis Street Hospital	Dublin	05/02/1923	Civilian	18
Michael Raleigh	Kings Island	Limerick	05/02/1923	NA	36
Sean McGrath	Ballyconnell	Cavan	06/02/1923	Civilian	23
William Ryan	Ballyconnell	Cavan	06/02/1923	Civilian	21
James Molloy	Curragh Military Hospital	Kildare	06/02/1923	NA	31
Thomas Roche	Moanleane, Newcastlewest, Limerick	Limerick	06/02/1923	Civilian	32
Martin McGuinn	Curry	Sligo	06/02/1923	IRA	
Murphy	Bantry	Cork	07/02/1923	IRA	
Michael Cussack	Mercy Hospital, Cork city	Cork	07/02/1923	Civilian	48
Thomas Higgins	Timogue, Stradbally	Laois	07/02/1923	Civilian	64
Owen Cashin	Ballingarry	Tipperary	07/02/1923	Civilian	41
James McCarthy	The Faythe	Wexford	07/02/1923	NA	22
James Brennan	Jervis Street Hospital	Dublin	08/02/1923	NA	28
Michael Moloney	Poleberry	Waterford	09/02/1923	IRA	19
Thomas Walsh	Poleberry	Waterford	09/02/1923	IRA	25
Albert O'Brien	Lemeneigh, Corofin	Clare	10/02/1923	Civilian	25

Name	Location	County	Date	Affiliation	Age
Unidentified body	Kilmaley Burial Ground, Kilmaley	Clare	10/02/1923	Civilian	
John Gallagher	Dunfanaghy, Knockastolar	Donegal	10/02/1923	Civilian	47
Thomas Slattery	Dromulton, Scartaglin	Kerry	11/02/1923	NA	
John O'Grady	Gladstone Street, Clonmel	Tipperary	11/02/1923	Civilian	18
John Finlay	Leabeg, Ballycumber	Offaly	12/02/1923	Civilian	26
Ellen Hayes	Tracton Park, Montenotte, Cork city	Cork	13/02/1923	Civilian	17
James O'Connor	Carrahane, Ardfert	Kerry	13/02/1923	IRA	19
Michael Sinnott	Carrahane, Ardfert	Kerry	13/02/1923	IRA	18
Denis Minogue	Ballineen	Cork	14/02/1923	NA	27
Thomas Moran	Saint Bricin's Hospital	Dublin	14/02/1923	NA	19
Thomas Burke	Jervis Street Hospital	Dublin	14/02/1923	NA	21
Laurence Cunningham	Mercy Hospital, Cork city	Cork	15/02/1923	IRA	28
Thomas Goff	Beltra	Sligo	15/02/1923	IRA	22
Michael Aherne	Castledonavan	Cork	16/02/1923	NA	21
Henry Breheny	Coolaney	Sligo	16/02/1923	IRA	
Michael Gorman	Albert Quay, Victoria Road, Cork city	Cork	17/02/1923	Civilian	42
Jeremiah Nunan	Thomastown	Limerick	17/02/1923	IRA	27
James Saint John	Bawnlea, Kilcooley, Thurles	Tipperary	17/02/1923	IRA	
Patrick Harford	Cork Military Barracks, Old Youghal Road	Cork	18/02/1923	NA	20
Thomas O'Sullivan	Caherquinn, Ballyferriter	Kerry	18/02/1923	IRA	22
Patrick Kilkelly	Claremorris Hospital, Claremorris	Mayo	18/02/1923	NA	28
William McGrath	Aherlow	Tipperary	18/02/1923	NA	
Denis Lacey	Ballydrehid, Cahir	Tipperary	18/02/1923	IRA	
Edmund Quirke	Ashgrove, Bansha	Tipperary	18/02/1923	Civilian	10
David Lehane	Lee Barracks, Macroom	Cork	19/02/1923	NA	22
Patrick MacDonagh	Saint Vincent's Hospital, Tipperary	Tipperary	19/02/1923	IRA	24
Andrew Callaghan	Saint Bricin's Hospital	Dublin	20/02/1923	NA	18
William Crolly	Doctor Steeven's Hospital	Dublin	20/02/1923	Civilian	36
John Francis Manning	Military Hospital, Custume Barracks, Athlone	Westmeath	21/02/1923	NA	21
Nicholas Williamson	Hollybank Road, Drumcondra	Dublin	22/02/1923	CDF	20
William Collins	Greenbeg, Newport	Mayo	22/02/1923	NA	21
Joseph McCurley	Saint Bricin's Hospital	Dublin	23/02/1923	NA	22
Agnes Keogh	Jervis Street Hospital	Dublin	23/02/1923	Civilian	16
John Campbell	Louth County Infirmary, Dundalk	Louth	23/02/1923	NA	23
John Desmond	Mercy Hospital, Cork city	Cork	24/02/1923	Civilian	22
Anabell Carson	Mater Hospital	Dublin	24/02/1923	Civilian	68
John Ryan	Brosna	Kerry	24/02/1923	NA	24
John Conway	Rathass, Tralee	Kerry	24/02/1923	IRA	26
Thomas Gibson	Portlaoise Barracks	Laois	24/02/1923	IRA	23

Name	Location	County	Date	Affiliation	Age
Rose Anne Nelson	Tullywhisker, Sion Mills	Tyrone	24/02/1923	Civilian	17
Denis Galvin	Mercy Hospital, Cork city	Cork	25/02/1923	NA	28
James Finlay	Chapelizod	Dublin	25/02/1923	NA	
Eugene McQuaid	Newport	Mayo	26/02/1923	NA	23
James Cull	Giddown, Arigna	Roscommon	27/02/1923	IRA	23
Patrick Tymon	Giddown, Arigna	Roscommon	27/02/1923	IRA	21
John Savage	Tralee Hospital, Tralee	Kerry	01/03/1923	IRA	
John Gunning	Roscrea Military Barracks	Tipperary	01/03/1923	NA	35
John Kelly	Barraduff	Kerry	02/03/1923	NA	
Patrick Byrne	Roscrea Military Barracks	Tipperary	02/03/1923	NA	26
Thomas McGrath	Clerihan	Tipperary	02/03/1923	NA	28
Patrick William Gleeson	Townfield, Cloughjordan	Tipperary	02/03/1923	IRA	29
Laurence Power	Pouldrew	Waterford	02/03/1923	Civilian	23
John Sheerin	Saint John's Hospital, Limerick	Limerick	03/03/1923	Civilian	65
John Hornick	Palace East	Wexford	03/03/1923	Civilian	25
Margaret Hornick	Palace East	Wexford	03/03/1923	Civilian	12
Patrick Gallagher	Curragh Military Hospital	Kildare	04/03/1923	IRA	22
Peter Clune	Bandon Military Hospital	Cork	05/03/1923	NA	
William Healy	Gurrane, Cahirciveen	Kerry	05/03/1923	NA	19
Timothy O'Shea	Gurrane, Cahirciveen	Kerry	05/03/1923	NA	
Jeremiah Quane	Gurrane, Cahirciveen	Kerry	05/03/1923	NA	27
Daniel Clifford	Gurrane	Kerry	05/03/1923	IRA	28
Joseph Ryan	Kilworth	Cork	06/03/1923	NA	19
Michael Dunne	Knocknagoshel	Kerry	06/03/1923	NA	25
Michael Galvin	Knocknagoshel	Kerry	06/03/1923	NA	23
Laurence O'Connor	Knocknagoshel	Kerry	06/03/1923	NA	18
Patrick O'Connor	Knocknagoshel	Kerry	06/03/1923	NA	32
Edward Stapleton	Knocknagoshel	Kerry	06/03/1923	NA	30
John Sullivan	Cahirquinn, Ballyferriter	Kerry	06/03/1923	IRA	
Denis Horgan	County Infirmary, Tralee	Kerry	06/03/1923	Civilian	56
William Newcombe	The Three Jolly Pidgeons Pub, The Pigeons	Westmeath	06/03/1923	NA	17
Willam Kelly	Parkgate Street Barracks	Dublin	07/03/1923	NA	18
Louis Connolly	Baldonnell Aerodrome	Dublin	07/03/1923	NA	
Patrick Kelly	Jervis Street Hospital	Dublin	07/03/1923	CID	22
George Fitzhenry	Mercer's Hospital	Dublin	07/03/1923	Civilian	67
Christopher McGrane	Barraduff	Kerry	07/03/1923	NA	19
James Walsh	Ballyseedy Cross	Kerry	07/03/1923	IRA	33
George O'Shea	Ballyseedy Cross	Kerry	07/03/1923	IRA	25
Timothy Tuomey	Ballyseedy Cross	Kerry	07/03/1923	IRA	21
Patrick Hartnett	Ballyseedy Cross	Kerry	07/03/1923	IRA	24

Name	Location	County	Date	Affiliation	Age
Patrick Buckley	Ballyseedy Cross	Kerry	07/03/1923	IRA	32
John Daly	Ballyseedy Cross	Kerry	07/03/1923	IRA	
Michael O'Connell	Ballyseedy Cross	Kerry	07/03/1923	IRA	
Stephen Buckley	Countess Bridge	Kerry	07/03/1923	IRA	31
Timothy Murphy	Countess Bridge	Kerry	07/03/1923	IRA	27
Daniel O'Donoghue	Countess Bridge	Kerry	07/03/1923	IRA	22
Jeremiah O'Donoghue	Countess Bridge	Kerry	07/03/1923	IRA	
John O'Connor	Ballyseedy Cross	Kerry	07/03/1923	IRA	
James Moran	Glenhest, Newport	Mayo	07/03/1923	IRA	25
Edward Cowman	County Home, Enniscorthy	Wexford	07/03/1923	IRA	24
P. Scannell	Mallow	Cork	08/03/1923	Civilian	60
James Taylor	Ballyseedy Cross	Kerry	08/03/1923	IRA	
Patrick Carney	Casmir Road, Harold's Cross	Dublin	09/03/1923	Civilian	40
Gerald Comerford	Holy Stone, Inistioge	Kilkenny	09/03/1923	NA	23
Samuel Atkinson	County Infirmary, Monaghan	Monaghan	09/03/1923	Civilian	53
Michael Hickey	St Patrick's Bridge, Cork city	Cork	10/03/1923	Civilian	25
Bernard Cannon	National Army Barracks, Creeslough	Donegal	10/03/1923	NA	25
Frank O'Donohoe	Curragh Military Hospital	Kildare	10/03/1923	IRA	21
Thomas Mealey	Ballyragget	Kilkenny	10/03/1923	IRA	19
Joseph Mangan	Workhouse Hospital, Nenagh	Tipperary	10/03/1923	IRA	24
Thomas Greehy	Kilwatermoy, Tallow	Waterford	10/03/1923	IRA	
Frank Grady	Mountain Stage, Glenbeigh	Kerry	11/03/1923	IRA	27
Tadgh Keating	County Infirmary, Tralee	Kerry	11/03/1923	IRA	
Richard Duggan	County and City Infirmary, Waterford	Waterford	11/03/1923	NA	23
John Carroll	Saint Bricin's Hospital	Dublin	12/03/1923	NA	19
Michael Courtney	Bahaghs, Caherciveen	Kerry	12/03/1923	IRA	21
Eugene Dwyer	Bahaghs, Caherciveen	Kerry	12/03/1923	IRA	24
Daniel Shea	Bahaghs, Caherciveen	Kerry	12/03/1923	IRA	
William Riordan	Bahaghs, Caherciveen	Kerry	12/03/1923	IRA	29
John Sugrue	Bahaghs, Caherciveen	Kerry	12/03/1923	IRA	21
Patrick McMahon	New Docks, Limerick	Limerick	12/03/1923	NA	22
William Connolly	Mount Pleasant, Dundalk	Louth	12/03/1923	NA	24
Patrick McCormack	Cashel	Tipperary	12/03/1923	NA	
William Healy	Cork Male Prison	Cork	13/03/1923	IRA	21
Michael Higgins	Ballycrenane, Midleton	Cork	13/03/1923	Civilian	20
James O'Rourke	Beggars Bush Barracks	Dublin	13/03/1923	IRA	
Hugh Haughton	Meath Hospital	Dublin	13/03/1923	Civilian	18
James Currane	Waterville	Kerry	13/03/1923	Civilian	14
Henry Spelman	Bunnacrana, Sandyhill	Sligo	13/03/1923	NA	32
Patrick Stenson	Bunnacrana, Curry	Sligo	13/03/1923	IRA	
Michael Grealy	Miltary Barracks, Mullingar	Westmeath	13/03/1923	IRA	27

NAME	LOCATION	COUNTY	DATE	AFFILIATION	AGE
Luke Burke	Military Barracks, Mullingar	Westmeath	13/03/1923	IRA	26
James Parle	Wexford Jail	Wexford	13/03/1923	IRA	25
John Creane	Wexford Jail	Wexford	13/03/1923	IRA	18
Patrick Hogan	Wexford Jail	Wexford	13/03/1923	IRA	22
Sean Larkin	Drumboe Castle	Donegal	14/03/1923	IRA	26
Timothy O'Sullivan	Drumboe Castle	Donegal	14/03/1923	IRA	24
Daniel Enright	Drumboe Castle	Donegal	14/03/1923	IRA	21
Charles Daly	Drumboe Castle	Donegal	14/03/1923	IRA	26
Donal McGuinness	Glengarriffe Place	Dublin	14/03/1923	NA	28
Henry Kavanagh	Meath Hospital	Dublin	14/03/1923	NA	23
Michael Cleary	The Hospital, Listowel	Kerry	14/03/1923	NA	24
Alfred Glynn	Listowel	Kerry	14/03/1923	NA	27
Daniel Sugrue	Great Southern Hotel, Killarney	Kerry	14/03/1923	NA	38
Daniel Connor	Lislibane, Killorglin	Kerry	14/03/1923	Civilian	30
John Walsh	County Infirmary, Kilkenny city	Kilkenny	14/03/1923	IRA	23
John Nolan	Bride Street	Dublin	15/03/1923	NA	29
Peter Cassidy	Galway Central Hospital, Galway	Galway	15/03/1923	Civilian	50
John Kevins	Carnahone, Beaufort	Kerry	15/03/1923	IRA	30
Michael Brown	Windgap	Kilkenny	15/03/1923	NA	21
Nicholas Corcoran	Ballina Union Hospital	Mayo	15/03/1923	IRA	20
Michael Henry	Cloonrow, Uralaur	Mayo	15/03/1923	Civilian	50
James Ben McCarthy	Derryginagh, Lough Bofinna	Cork	16/03/1923	Civilian	17
Charles Cooper	Saint Vincent's Hospital	Dublin	16/03/1923	CDF	26
John Murphy	Tullywood, Mount Temple	Westmeath	16/03/1923	Civilian	25
John Monahan	Manlinstown, Mullingar	Westmeath	16/03/1923	Civilian	67
Henry O'Reilly	Cottage Hospital, Arklow	Wicklow	16/03/1923	NA	30
John Little	Saint Bricin's Hospital	Dublin	17/03/1923	NA	18
Patrick Coyle	Ellison Street, Castlebar	Mayo	17/03/1923	NA	23
Henry Conlon	Upper Barracks, Arigna	Roscommon	17/03/1923	NA	25
Michael Patrick Muldoon	Mohill	Leitrim	18/03/1923	Civilian	31
Edward Fitzgerald	Ballinamuck	Longford	18/03/1923	NA	26
Patrick Hogan	Workhouse Hospital, Nenagh	Tipperary	19/03/1923	Civilian	43
William Beale	South Infirmary, Cork city	Cork	20/03/1923	Civilian	51
Richard Doherty	Curragh Camp	Kildare	20/03/1923	NA	18
Daniel Bell	Portarlington Railway Station	Laois	20/03/1923	NA	40
Rose Hamill	Ballinfuill, Barronstown, Dundalk	Louth	20/03/1923	Civilian	8
Edward Gethings	Ballybranis, The Still	Wexford	20/03/1923	Civilian	
Jeremiah Casey	Beaufort House, Beaufort	Kerry	21/03/1923	IRA	23
Michael Baker	Saint Michael's Hospital, Dun Laoghaire	Dublin	22/03/1923	NA	26
Margaret Fitzpatrick	Aughnafin, Mostrim	Longford	22/03/1923	Civilian	80

NAME	LOCATION	COUNTY	DATE	AFFILIATION	AGE
Owen McGuinness	Annascue	Monaghan	22/03/1923	Civilian	53
Thomas O'Leary	Mercer's Hospital	Dublin	23/03/1923	IRA	22
Patrick O'Brien	Jervis Street Hospital	Dublin	23/03/1923	IRA	25
Bernard McGuill	Saint Bricin's Hospital	Dublin	23/03/1923	Civilian	30
Daniel Murphy	Ballyduff, Moonbannvin, Knocknagoshel	Kerry	23/03/1923	IRA	31
John Lacey	Ballyboggan, Kyle	Wexford	23/03/1923	IRA	24
Denis Leacy	Ballyboggan, Kyle	Wexford	23/03/1923	IRA	22
John O'Connor	Ballyboggan, Kyle	Wexford	23/03/1923	IRA	34
Martin Nolan	Ballyboggan, Kyle	Wexford	23/03/1923	IRA	25
William Walsh	Mater Hospital	Dublin	24/03/1923	IRA	38
Denis O'Sullivan	Kenmare	Kerry	24/03/1923	Civilian	11
William Barrett	County Infirmary, Castlebar	Mayo	24/03/1923	Fianna	16
Edward O'Gorman	Kyle's Cross, Adamstown	Wexford	24/03/1923	NA	24
Thomas Jones	Kyle's Cross, Adamstown	Wexford	24/03/1923	NA	26
Patrick Horan	Kyle's Cross, Adamstown	Wexford	24/03/1923	NA	25
Cornelius Driscoll	Bandon	Cork	25/03/1923	NA	19
Cornelius Hayes	Newtownsandes	Kerry	25/03/1923	NA	
Daniel Robert McCarthy	Ballymullen Barracks	Kerry	25/03/1923	IRA	
Daniel Spencer	Durrow Barracks	Laois	25/03/1923	NA	19
Michael Furlong	Old Court, Adamstown	Wexford	25/03/1923	IRA	20
Christopher Reddan	Gurtheen, Ennis	Clare	26/03/1923	Civilian	18
James McManus	Curragh Military Hospital	Kildare	26/03/1923	NA	30
Nicholas Whelan	Kilgarvan Bridge, Athlone	Westmeath	26/03/1923	NA	22
William Johnson	Theatre Royal, Hawkins Street	Dublin	27/03/1923	CDF	31
John Pender	Saint Bricin's Hospital	Dublin	27/03/1923	NA	21
James Walsh	Mount Falvey	Kerry	27/03/1923	IRA	
Patrick Gallagher	Grallagh	Mayo	27/03/1923	Civilian	22
John Sheehy	Foilduff	Tipperary	27/03/1923	IRA	27
Matthew Ryan	Foilduff	Tipperary	27/03/1923	IRA	30
Bernard O'Brien	Mercy Hospital, Cork city	Cork	28/03/1923	NA	
George Copeland	Sneem, Kenmare	Kerry	28/03/1923	NA	24
John Fleming	Workhouse Road, Tralee	Kerry	28/03/1923	IRA	29
Michael Mulvehill	Ballinrobe Barracks, Ballinrobe	Mayo	28/03/1923	NA	19
Daniel O'Leary	Drimoleague	Cork	29/03/1923	Civilian	
Robert Bonfield	Clondalkin	Dublin	29/03/1923	IRA	20
Patrick Shea	Ballyclare, Caragh, Caragh Bridge	Kerry	30/03/1923	Civilian	47
Owen O'Brien	Curragh Military Hospital	Kildare	30/03/1923	IRA	
Michael O'Shea	Killorglin	Kerry	31/03/1923	Civilian	
James Taylor	Waterstown House, Glasson	Westmeath	31/03/1923	NA	22
Thomas Draper	Military Hospital, Custume Barracks,	Westmeath	31/03/1923	NA	22

NAME	LOCATION	COUNTY	DATE	AFFILIATION	AGE
	Athlone				
Martin Daly	Ballybinaby	Louth	01/04/1923	NA	22
Bernard Morris	Ballybinaby	Louth	01/04/1923	IRA	23
John Fahy	County Hospital, Castlebar	Mayo	01/04/1923	Civilian	22
John O'Dea	Lisvernane, Aherlow	Tipperary	01/04/1923	NA	
Jeremiah Kiely	Lisvernane, Aherlow	Tipperary	01/04/1923	IRA	
John Flynn	Bandon	Cork	02/04/1923	NA	19
Michael O'Brien	Bandon	Cork	02/04/1923	NA	27
Catherine McGuinness	Cairns, Dromore West	Sligo	02/04/1923	Civilian	76
Christopher Breslin	Cabra Road	Dublin	03/04/1923	IRA	25
James Kiernan	Cabra Road	Dublin	03/04/1923	IRA	
John Hannon	Ardreigh	Kildare	03/04/1923	Civilian	68
Jeremiah Lyons	Clonmel Military Barracks	Tipperary	03/04/1923	IRA	24
Martin O'Loughlin	Saint Bricin's Hospital	Dublin	04/04/1923	NA	26
John Higgins	Headford	Galway	06/04/1923	IRA	30
George Nagle	Derrynafeana, Glencar	Kerry	06/04/1923	IRA	21
William O'Connor	Gortmaloon, Glencar	Kerry	06/04/1923	IRA	24
Eugene Crowley	Saint Patrick's Hospital	Cork	07/04/1923	IRA	27
Michael Barry	Midleton Hospital	Cork	07/04/1923	Civilian	
Bridget Geoghegan	Greagh	Monaghan	07/04/1923	Civilian	62
Thomas Keane	County Hospital, Tullamore	Offaly	07/04/1923	NA	26
Margaret Dunne	Drumlave, Adrigole	Cork	08/04/1923	CnamB	27
James Hunt	Timoleague	Cork	08/04/1923	Civilian	12
Thomas Keane	Headford	Galway	08/04/1923	NA	
James Lyons	Renmore Barracks, Galway	Galway	08/04/1923	NA	21
James Mahony	Bantry	Cork	09/04/1923	NA	32
John Carty	Renmore Barracks, Galway	Galway	09/04/1923	NA	22
John Cravan	Mountbellew	Galway	09/04/1923	Civilian	45
Elmer Loftus	Nursing home, Mary Street, New Ross	Wexford	09/04/1923	NA	28
Martin Moloney	Ennistymon Hospital	Clare	10/04/1923	IRA	21
Michael Hanlon	North Wall	Dublin	10/04/1923	NA	28
John MacSweeney	City Home and Hospital, Limerick	Limerick	10/04/1923	IRA	40
Liam Lynch	Saint Joseph's Hospital, Clonmel	Tipperary	10/04/1923	IRA	32
James O'Malley	Military Barracks, Tuam	Galway	11/04/1923	IRA	28
John Newell	Military Barracks, Tuam	Galway	11/04/1923	IRA	28
Michael Monaghan	Military Barracks, Tuam	Galway	11/04/1923	IRA	30
Martin Moylan	Military Barracks, Tuam	Galway	11/04/1923	IRA	22
Francis Cunnane	Military Barracks, Tuam	Galway	11/04/1923	IRA	24
John Maguire	Military Barracks, Tuam	Galway	11/04/1923	IRA	20
Thomas Keating	Dungarvan Hospital	Waterford	11/04/1923	IRA	29
John Linnane	Duagh, Kilmorna	Kerry	13/04/1923	IRA	

Name	Location	County	Date	Affiliation	Age
John Moore	Mooney's public house, Manor Kilbride	Wicklow	13/04/1923	IRA	30
James Manley	Phoenix Park	Dublin	14/04/1923	Civilian	52
Timothy McCarthy	Meencheala, Abbeyfeale, Dromtrasna South	Limerick	14/04/1923	NA	26
James Ryan	Saint Bricin's Hospital	Dublin	15/04/1923	NA	22
William Kelly	Curragh Military Hospital	Kildare	15/04/1923	IRA	28
James O'Neill	Clashmealcon Caves	Kerry	16/04/1923	NA	18
John Monaghan	Kells	Meath	16/04/1923	Civilian	
Edwin Williams	Ballinphull, Dromore West	Sligo	16/04/1923	Civilian	23
Edward Somers	Castleblake, Rosegreen	Tipperary	16/04/1923	IRA	33
Theo English	Castleblake, Rosegreen	Tipperary	16/04/1923	IRA	23
Denis Kelly	Kealkil	Cork	17/04/1923	IRA	25
James Tierney	Mater Hospital	Dublin	17/04/1923	IRA	24
Thomas McGrath	Clashmealcon Caves	Kerry	17/04/1923	IRA	22
Patrick O'Shea	Clashmealcon Caves	Kerry	17/04/1923	IRA	23
Henry Pierson	Strand Street, Tralee	Kerry	18/04/1923	NA	30
Jeremiah Daly	Bandon Union Hospital	Cork	19/04/1923	Civilian	48
Joseph O'Dare	Saint Bricin's Hospital	Dublin	19/04/1923	NA	24
Timothy Lyons	Clashmealcon Caves	Kerry	19/04/1923	IRA	
Timothy Shea	Brackloon, Tahilla	Kerry	19/04/1923	IRA	25
James Egan	Callan Hospital	Kilkenny	19/04/1923	IRA	26
Christopher Smith	Saint John's Hospital, Limerick	Limerick	19/04/1923	NA	
Andrew Mooney	Tobercurry	Sligo	20/04/1923	NA	16
Stephen Canty	Carmody Street, Ennis	Clare	21/04/1923	NA	21
William Murphy	Mercy Hospital, Cork city	Cork	21/04/1923	Civilian	42
Martin Hogan	Grace Park Road	Dublin	21/04/1923	IRA	32
John Melvin	Curryane, Swinford	Mayo	22/04/1923	Civilian	30
John McGeehin	Ballina	Mayo	22/04/1923	Civilian	
Patrick Shalley	Bealnamulla, Creagh	Roscommon	22/04/1923	Civilian	50
James Delaney	Kiltimagh	Mayo	23/04/1923	NA	24
Patrick Kennedy	Saint Bricin's Hospital	Dublin	24/04/1923	NA	22
James Corrigan	Union Workhouse, Ballybot	Down	24/04/1923	IRA	22
Michael Behan	Currow, Castleisland	Kerry	25/04/1923	NA	
Edward Greaney	Ballymullen Gaol, Tralee	Kerry	25/04/1923	IRA	25
Reginald Stenning, aka Hathaway	Ballymullen Gaol, Tralee	Kerry	25/04/1923	IRA	23
James McEnery	Ballymullen Gaol, Tralee	Kerry	25/04/1923	IRA	28
James Montgomery	Monasterevin	Kildare	25/04/1923	NA	26
John Gannon	Derryfore, Ballyroan, Abbeyleix	Laois	25/04/1923	NA	26
Patrick O'Mahony	Home Barracks, Ennis	Clare	26/04/1923	IRA	25
John Cribbon	Annascaul	Kerry	26/04/1923	NA	20

Name	Location	County	Date	Affiliation	Age
James Hogan	Telephone Exchange, Cecil Street, Limerick	Limerick	26/04/1923	NA	18
Peter McNicholas	Murneen, Kiltimagh	Mayo	26/04/1923	Civilian	31
Charles Byrne	Knock, Ballymurphy	Carlow	27/04/1923	IRA	23
Alex Williams	Castletown Station	Kerry	27/04/1923	NA	25
Michael Reynolds	Clooneagh, Dromod	Leitrim	30/04/1923	Civilian	69
Michael Monahan	Mallow South Railway Station	Cork	01/05/1923	NA	38
Cyril Hogan	Cahir Barracks, Nenagh	Tipperary	01/05/1923	NA	19
Christopher Quinn	Home Barracks, Ennis	Clare	02/05/1923	IRA	19
William O'Shaughnessy	Home Barracks, Ennis	Clare	02/05/1923	IRA	18
Peter Bracken	Saint Bricin's Hospital	Dublin	02/05/1923	NA	23
Thomas Steenson	Kenmare	Kerry	03/05/1923	NA	
Brian Brady	Clew Bay	Mayo	03/05/1923	NA	19
Joseph Brady	Westport Barracks, Westport	Mayo	03/05/1923	NA	34
John Duggan	Carrigleagh, Macroom	Cork	04/05/1923	NA	17
Thomas Fitzgerald	Loo Bridge, Killarney	Kerry	04/05/1923	NA	23
James O'Keeffe	Kilkenny Military Barracks	Kilkenny	04/05/1923	NA	21
Michael McGrath	Curragh Military Hospital	Kildare	05/05/1923	IRA	33
Patrick Gallagher	County Infirmary, Castlebar	Mayo	05/05/1923	Civilian	19
Michael King	Galway Court House, Galway city	Galway	06/05/1923	NA	19
Bernard McDonnell	Aghagower, Westport	Mayo	06/05/1923	Civilian	72
Michael Brabstone	Goatsbridge, Ardfinnan, Clonmel	Tipperary	06/05/1923	NA	28
Francis McGinley	Saint Bricin's Hospital	Dublin	08/05/1923	NA	24
Cornelius Cotter	Dunmanway Union Hospital	Cork	13/05/1923	Civilian	40
John McGinley	Eccles Street	Dublin	13/05/1923	Civilian	24
Thomas Devenney	National Army Barracks, Dungloe	Donegal	14/05/1923	NA	24
Neil Boyle	Knocknadruce, Blessington	Wicklow	15/05/1923	IRA	27
Edward Flahive	Ballycarthy, Tralee	Kerry	16/05/1923	Civilian	25
Michael Candy	Littleton, Moycarkey	Tipperary	16/05/1923	Civilian	24
Bartley Walsh	Kilkerrin, Carna	Galway	17/05/1923	IRA	28
Gerald Kane	Claremorris Barracks	Mayo	17/05/1923	NA	19
James Conway	Clancy Street, Fermoy	Cork	18/05/1923	NA	23
Patrick Keville	Currycramp, Dromod	Leitrim	19/05/1923	NA	27
Michael Condon	Coolcour, Macroom	Cork	20/05/1923	NA	27
Philip Coleman	Saint Bricin's Hospital	Dublin	20/05/1923	NA	23
Thomas McNicholas	Woodfield	Mayo	20/05/1923	IRA	27
Sean Quinn	Saint Bricin's Hospital	Dublin	22/05/1923	IRA	22
Michael Neary	Saint Michael's Hospital, Dun Laoghaire	Dublin	24/05/1923	IRA	24
Hugh McMenamin	Midland Great Western Railway Station	Sligo	24/05/1923	NA	18

Irish Civil War Fatalities Index
By Andy Bielenberg and John Dorney

Primary Sources

General Registry Office
Central Death Registry

Irish Military Archives
Bureau of Military History (BMH)
Civil War Operations Reports (IE/MA/CW/OPS)
Department of Defence papers (IE/MA/DOD)
Military Intelligence and Press Analysis Collection (MIPR-02-42)
Military Service Pensions Collection (MSPC)
National Army Roll of Honour
Reports to the Executive Council (IE/MA-CREC)

National Archives of Ireland
Coroners' Court Inquests (NAI FC/1D/)
Department of Finance files (NAI/FIN)
Department of Justice files (NAI/JUS)
Dublin Coroners' Registration 1922

Pearse Street Library Dublin
Dean's Grange Cemetery Records

University College Dublin Archives Department
C.S. 'Todd' Andrews Papers (IE/UCDAD/P91)
Moss Twomey Papers (IE/UCDAD/P69
Richard Mulcahy Papers (IE/UCDAD/P7)

Secondary Sources

Abbott, Richard, *Police Casualties in Ireland, 1919–1922* (Cork, 2019)
Aiken, Síobhra (ed.), *The Men Will Talk to Me: Ernie O'Malley's interviews with the Northern divisions* (Newbridge, 2018)
Andrews, C.S., *Dublin Made Me* (Dublin, 2001)
Anon., *Eleven Galway Martyrs: The story of the republican soldiers of the Second Western Division, IRA, executed at Tuam and Athlone in 1923* (1985)
Bielenberg, Andy and Pádraig Óg Ó Ruairc, 'Shallow Graves: Documenting and assessing IRA disappearances during the Irish revolution, 1919–1923', *Small Wars & Insurgencies*, vol. 32, no. 4–5 (2021), pp. 619–41
Brady, James, *With the Sixth Battalion: South County Dublin and the War of Independence 1919–21* (Dublin, 2020)
Burke, John, *The Irish revolution, 1912–23: Roscommon* (Dublin, 2021)
Clark, Gemma, *Everyday Violence in the Irish Civil War* (Cambridge 2014)
Cogan, Edward, *Unsettled Territory: The 5th Battalion, Meath Brigade in north Meath, 1917–1921* (Meath, 2022)
Coleman, Marie, *County Longford and the Irish Revolution* (Dublin 2006)

Connolly, Linda, 'Women and the Civil War in Limerick', in Sean Gannon (ed.), *The Inevitable Conflict: Essays on the Civil War in Limerick* (Limerick, 2023)
Corrigan, Mario and James Durney, *A Timeline of the Civil War in County Kildare, 1922–24* (Kildare, 2022)
Dodd, Conor, *Casualties of Conflict: Fatalities of the War of Independence and Civil War in Glasnevin Cemetery* (Cork, 2023)
Dooley, Terence, *The Irish Revolution, 1912–23: Monaghan* (Dublin, 2017)
Doyle, Kieran and Alan O'Rourke (eds), '*Monuments to our Past': Understanding the revolutionary period and commemoration in Cork 1914–1923* (Cork 2021)
Doyle, Tom, *The Civil War in Kerry* (Cork, 2008)
Durney, James, *The Civil War in Kildare* (Cork, 2011)
Farry, Michael, *The Aftermath of Revolution: Sligo 1921–23* (Dublin, 2000)
Fitzpatrick, Billy, *'Rebel Aghada': The untold story of an east Cork parish, 1798–1923* (Dublin, 2021)
Galway Sinn Féin Commemorations Committee, *Galway Republican Roll of Honour, 1916–1940* (Gaillimh, 2023)
Grant, Adrian, *The Irish Revolution, 1912–1923: Derry* (Dublin, 2018)
Hall, Donal, *The Irish Revolution, 1912–23: Louth* (Dublin, 2019)
Keane, Barry, *Cork's Revolutionary Dead, 1916–1923* (Cork, 2017)
Langton, James, *The Forgotten Fallen: National army soldiers who died in the Civil War* (Dublin, 2019)
Mac Suain, Séamus, *County Wexford's Civil War* (Loch Garman, 1995)
Lawlor, Pearse, *The Outrages 1920–1922: The IRA and the Ulster Special Constabulary in the border campaign* (Cork, 2012)
Magill, Christopher, *Political Conflict in East Ulster, 1920–22: Revolution and reprisal* (Suffolk, 2020)
Marnane, Dennis and Mary Guinan Darmody, *The Civil War in County Tipperary* (Dayton, 2021)
Martin, Mal, 'Civil War in Drogheda', in Donal Hall and Martin Maguire (eds), *County Louth and Irish Revolution, 1912–1923* (Newbridge, 2017)
McConway, Philip, 'Offaly and the Civil War Executions', *Offaly Tribune,* 26 December 2007
McGarty, Patrick, *The Irish Revolution, 1912–23: Leitrim* (Dublin, 2020)
McNamara, Conor, *The Independence Struggle in County Galway: A research guide, 1916–1923* (Galway, 2023)
McCarthy, Patrick, *The Irish Revolution, 1912–23: Waterford* (Dublin, 2015)
Murphy, Séamus, 'Carlow Brigade IRA Roll of Honour, 1916–1924', *Carloviana*, vol. 52 (2003), pp. 36–42
National Graves Association, *The Last Post* (Dublin, 1976)
Newcastle West Historical Journal, no. 3, 2002
O'Callaghan, John, *The Battle for Kilmallock* (Newbridge, 2011)
Ó Corráin, Daithí, *Cathal Brugha: An indomitable spirit* (Dublin, 2022)
Ó Duibhir, Liam, *Donegal and the Civil War: The untold story* (Cork, 2011)
Ó Maonaigh, Aaron, 'Wexford's Civil War Dead: A statistical survey', *The Past: Organ of the Uí Cinsealaigh Historical Society*, vol. 34 (2020), pp. 89–109
Ó Ruairc, Pádraig Óg, *Blood on the Banner* (Cork, 2009)
O'Shea, Owen, *No Middle Path: The Civil War in Kerry* (Newbridge, 2022)
Ó Súilleabháin, Cormac, *Leitrim's Republican Story, 1900–2000* (Béal an Átha Mór, 2019)
Owens, Henry, '*Neath an Irish Sky: Roscommon's republican dead* (Roscommon, 2022)
Power, Christopher, *Lives Cut Short: The casualties of the 1916–1923 period associated with Carlow* (Carlow, 2022)
Power, Joe, *Clare and the Civil War* (Dublin, 2020)
Price, Dominic, *The Flame and the Candle: War in Mayo, 1919–1924* (Dublin, 2012)
Swithin Walsh, Eoin, *Kilkenny in Times of Revolution, 1900–1923* (Newbridge, 2018)

Online Sources

Breen Murphy, Timothy, 'The Government Executions Policy During the Irish Civil War 1922–23', unpublished PhD thesis, Maynooth University, 2010, https://mural.maynoothuniversity.ie/4069/1/The_Government's_Executions_Policy_During_the_Irish_Civil_War_1922_-_1923_(Breen_Murphy_-_62129007).pdf
Dáil Debates, https://www.oireachtas.ie/en/debates/find/?debateType=dail
Death Certificates, Civil Records, irishgenealogy.ie
Find a Grave, https://www.findagrave.com/memorial/199664900/patrick-butler
McConway, Philip, 'Offaly and the Civil War executions', in *Offaly Heritage*, vol. 5, https://www.offalyhistory.com/wp-content/uploads/2008/01/5_civil_war.pdf

McKenna, Michael, 'Who was Seamus Dwyer?' The Irish Story, https://www.theirishstory.com/2013/09/02/who-was-seamus-dwyer/

O Maonaigh, Aaron, 'Civil War Casualties in County Wicklow', The Irish Story, https://www.theirishstory.com/2021/11/22/civil-war-casualties-in-county-wicklow-1922-1923/

Third Tipperary Brigade Roll of Honour, https://thirdtippbrigade.ie/knowledge-base/third-tipperary-brigade-ira-roll-of-honour

Cork Fatality Register, 1919–23, https://www.ucc.ie/en/theirishrevolution/collections/cork-fatality-register/

Westmeath County Council Blog, 'Civil War in Glasson', http://www.westmeathcoco.ie/en/ourservices/planning/conservationheritage/decadeofcentenariesblog/civilwaringlassonparttwo.html

Newspapers

Anglo Celt
Army Bulletin
Belfast Newsletter
Connaught Telegraph
Derry Journal
Evening Echo
Evening Herald
The Fenian
Fermanagh Herald
Freeman's Journal
Irish Independent
The Irish Times
Kerry People
Kildare Observer
Limerick Chronicle
Munster Express
Nationalist and Leinster Times
Nationalist and Munster Advertiser
Nenagh Guardian
Northern Standard
Poblacht na hÉireann
The Republican War Bulletin
Southern Star
Tipperary Star
Western People
Westmeath Independent
Wicklow People

Notes

Abbreviations

BMH WS	Bureau of Military History Witness Statement, Irish Military Archives, Dublin
CCCA	Cork City and County Archives
CÓFLA	Cardinal Ó Fiach Library and Archive, Armagh
HC Deb.	House of Commons Debates
HL Deb.	House of Lords Debates
IMA	Irish Military Archives, Dublin
MSPC	Military Service Pensions Collection, Irish Military Archives, Dublin
NAI	National Archives of Ireland, Dublin
NAUK	National Archives UK, Kew, London
NLI	National Library of Ireland, Dublin
PRONI	Public Records Office of Northern Ireland
RGASPI	Russian State Archive for Social and Political History, Moscow
TCD	Trinity College Dublin
UCDA	University College Dublin Archives

Introduction

1 Gavin Foster, 'Patterns of Irish Civil War Memory in Later-generation Oral Histories', *Contemporary European History*, vol. 32, no. 4 (May 2023), pp. 1–14.
2 Ronan Fanning, *Fatal Path: British government and Irish revolution, 1910–1922* (London, 2013), p. 252.
3 Confusion about duplicate ministries and their respective powers and the contested legitimacy of the Provisional Government also contributed to the general disorder in the country in the wake of the British evacuation. The question was further complicated by the fact that, even though Lloyd George's government recognised the temporary administration, it had no legal authority until the Irish Free State (Agreement) Bill, the measure to enact the Treaty, was finally passed by the British parliament on 31 March 1922.
4 BMH WS 1043, Colonel Joseph V. Lawless, IMA.
5 Cited in Fanning, *Fatal Path*, p. 262.
6 BMH WS 0802, Seán Prendergast, IMA.
7 *Éire – The Irish Nation*, 24 February 1923.
8 'The Responsibility', a statement issued by the Publicity Department, IRA, and addressed to each Teachta Dáil Éireann, on 7 September 1922, MS 17,141/5, NLI.
9 *United Irishman*, 25 August 1923.
10 Cited in John Borgonovo, *Florence and Josephine O'Donoghue's War of Independence: A destiny that shapes our ends* (Dublin, 2006), appendix, p. 200.
11 See Gary Murphy, 'Case Study: Parliamentary politics and the experience of Dáil Éireann during the Irish Civil War', p. 190.
12 *Cork Examiner*, 6 December 1922.
13 Heather Laird, 'Case Study: Agrarian unrest in Civil War Ireland', p. 130.
14 Gavin Foster, 'No "Wild Geese" this time"? IRA emigration after the Irish Civil War', *Éire-Ireland*, vol. 47, nos 1–2 (spring/summer 2012), pp. 94–122.
15 Anne Dolan, 'Politics, Economy and Society in the Irish Free State, 1922–1939', in Thomas Bartlett (ed.), *The Cambridge History of Ireland Volume 4: 1880 to the present* (Cambridge, 2018), p. 324.
16 Ibid.
17 Gerard Hanley, *Workers, Politics and Labour Relations in Independent Ireland, 1922–46* (Dublin, 2024), p. 59.
18 Síobhra Aiken, 'The Silence and the Silence Breakers of the Irish Civil War, 1922–2022', *Éire-Ireland*, vol. 57, nos 1–2 (spring/summer 2022), p. 286.
19 Idem., *Spiritual Wounds: Trauma, testimony, and the Irish Civil War* (Newbridge, 2022).
20 See, for example, 'The Men Will Talk to Me', a series of interviews conducted by Ernie O'Malley, such as *The Men Will Talk to Me: Galway interviews by Ernie O'Malley*, eds. Cormac K.H. O'Malley and Cormac Ó Comhraí (Cork, 2013).
21 Interview with Máire Brugha (née MacSwiney), 2009, Fleischmann Oral History Collection, irishlifeandlore.com.
22 Pierre Nora, 'Between Memory and History: Les lieux de mémoire', *Representations*, no. 26 (spring 1989), p. 9.
23 The Irish Civil War Fatalities Project, published in April 2024 and funded by the government of Ireland under the 2023 Decade of Centenaries Programme, enumerated and mapped all of the civilian and combatant fatalities in the thirty-two counties between 28 June 1922 and 24 May 1923. The full index of fatalities and an interactive map providing additional information on the ages, occupations, places of origin and previous service of the 1,484 fatalities is publicly accessible at https://www.ucc.ie/en/theirishrevolution/irish-civil-war-fatalities-project/. The findings are also presented in Chapter 6 in this volume, and the full index of fatalities is included in Section 10.
24 President Michael D. Higgins (ed.), *Machnamh 100: President of Ireland centenary reflections, volume 2* (Dublin, 2023), p. 29.
25 Liam de Róiste Diary, 29 June 1922, U271/A/1, CCCA.
26 Keynote address by Taoiseach Micheál Martin at the National Conference on the Irish Civil War, University College Cork, 15 June 2002, https://www.gov.ie/en/speech/e55aa-speech-by-taoiseach-micheal-martin-td-at-the-national-civil-war-conference (accessed 14 April 2024).
27 Since the publication of the *Atlas of the Irish Revolution* (eds John Crowley, Donal Ó Drisceoil, Mike Murphy and John Borgonovo (Cork, 2017)) the interdisciplinary, UCC-based research and editorial team has coordinated a series of exhibitions, public lectures, digital history projects, educational resources, conferences and two three-part television documentary series. These public outreach and engagement projects showcased existing and ongoing map-based research by the interdisciplinary Atlas of the Irish Revolution research team and a range of invited contributors.

SECTION 1: BEFORE THE WAR

Chapter 1 – The Treaty and the Irish Civil War: British perspectives

1 The recent historiography on the Irish Civil War includes Anne Dolan, *Commemorating the Irish Civil War: History and memory 1923–2000* (Cambridge, 2003); Bill Kissane, *The Politics of the Irish Civil War* (Oxford, 2007); Gemma Clark, *Everyday Violence in the Irish Civil War* (Cambridge, 2014); Pádraig Yeates, *A City in Civil War: Dublin, 1921–24* (Dublin, 2015); Diarmaid Ferriter, *Between Two Hells: The Irish Civil War* (London, 2021). For British perspectives, see Theodore Hoppen, *Governing Hibernia: British politicians and Ireland* (Oxford, 2016); William Sheehan, *British Voices of the Irish War of Independence: The words of British servicemen in Ireland, 1918–1921* (London, 2007). D.G. Boyce's *Englishmen and Irish Troubles: British public opinion and the making of Irish policy, 1918–1922* (London, 1972) only covers the Civil War briefly in its epilogue. Kevin Matthews's book *Fatal Influence: The impact of Ireland on British politics, 1920–25* (Dublin, 2004) is the most comprehensive current study of the Irish Civil War's impact on politics in Britain.
2 John D. Fair, 'The Anglo-Irish Treaty of 1921: Unionist aspects of the peace', *Journal of British Studies*, vol. 12, no. 1 (1972), p. 144.
3 Ivan Gibbons, 'The Anglo-Irish Treaty 1921: The response of the British Parliamentary Labour Party and the Labour press', *Labour History Review*, vol. 76, no. 1 (2011), pp. 1–15.
4 Ibid., p. 2.
5 Keiko Inoue, 'Dáil Propaganda and the Irish Self-Determination League of Great Britain during the Anglo-Irish War', *Irish Studies Review*, vol. 6, no. 1 (1998), p. 48.
6 The current historiography includes: David Fitzpatrick, 'The Irish in Britain, 1871–1921', in W.E. Vaughan (ed.), *A New History of Ireland, VI: Ireland under the Union, 1870–1921* (Oxford, 1996), pp. 653–702; John Hutchinson and Alan O'Day, 'The Gaelic Revival in London, 1900–22: Limits of ethnic identity', in Roger Swift and Sheridan Gilley (eds), *The Irish in Victorian Britain: The local dimension* (Dublin, 1999), pp. 254–76; Darragh Gannon, *Conflict, Diaspora and Empire: Irish nationalism in Britain, 1912–22* (Cambridge, 2023); Peter Hart, '"Operations Abroad": The IRA in Britain, 1919–23', in *English Historical Review*, no. cxv (2000), pp. 71–102, all of which focus on the period up to 1922. Two exceptions, which also cover the Civil War, are: Gerard Noonan, *The IRA in Britain, 1919–1923: 'In the heart of enemy lines'* (Liverpool,

2014), and Keiko Inoue, 'Political Activity of the Irish in Britain 1919–1925', unpublished PhD thesis, Trinity College, 2008.

7 Gannon, *Conflict, Diaspora and Empire*, p. 6.

8 Niamh Brennan, 'A Political Minefield: Southern loyalists, the Irish Grants Committee and the British government, 1922–31', *Irish Historical Studies*, vol. xxx, no. 119 (1997), p. 406.

9 Clark, *Everyday Violence in the Irish Civil War*, p. 98.

10 Paul Bew, *Churchill and Ireland* (Oxford, 2016)

11 Ruth Dudley Edwards, 'Harmsworth, Alfred Charles William', *Dictionary of Irish Biography*, https://doi.org/10.3318/dib.003809.v1 (accessed 15 February 2023).

12 Ibid.

13 David Torrance, 'How Parliament Approved the Anglo-Irish Treaty', https://constitution-unit.com/2021/12/06/how-parliament-approved-the-anglo-irish-treaty/ (accessed 15 February 2023).

14 David Torrance, 'The Anglo-Irish Treaty, 1921', House of Commons Library briefing paper, p. 23, chrome-extension://efaidnbmnnnibp cajpcglclefindmkaj/ https://researchbriefings.files.parliament.uk/documents/CBP-9260/CBP-9260.pdf (accessed 29 September 2023).

15 Heather Jones, *For King and Country: The British monarchy and the First World War* (Cambridge, 2021).

16 *HC Deb.*, fifth series, vol. 149, col. 347, and Address in Reply to His Majesty's Most Gracious Speech, *HL Deb.*, vol. 48, col. 145, 16 December 1921.

17 For Gretton's effort, see *HC Deb.*, 16 December 1921, fifth series, vol. 149, cols 305–6.

18 Address in Reply to His Majesty's Most Gracious Speech, *HL Deb.*, vol. 48, col. 135.

19 David Torrance, 'How Parliament Approved the Anglo-Irish Treaty', https://constitution-unit.com/2021/12/06/how-parliament-approved-the-anglo-irish-treaty/ (accessed 15 February 2023); 'King's Speech', *HC Deb.*, fifth series, vol. 149, col. 5, 14 December 1921.

20 *Dáil Debates*, vol. T, no. 15, 7 January 1922.

21 Jones, *For King and Country*, p. 274.

22 Churchill, *HC Deb.*, fifth series, vol. 155, col. 1701, 26 June 1922.

23 Jones, *For King and Country*, p. 279.

24 *Dáil Debates*, vol. T, no. 15, 7 January 1922.

25 Churchill, *HC Deb. 2*, fifth series, vol. 155, col. 1700, 6 June 1922.

26 *Dáil Debates*, vol. T, no. 15, 7 January 1922.

27 R.J.Q. Adams, *Bonar Law* (London, 1999), p. 315.

28 Parliamentary Archives, David Lloyd George Papers, 22 June 1922, LG/F/10/6/4, PA.

29 War Office memorandum, 25 July 1922, CAB 24/138/28, NAUK.

30 Ibid.

31 Ibid.

32 Churchill, *HC Deb.*, fifth series, vol. 155, col. 1701, 26 June 1922.

33 Minute by Thomas Jones, 6 January 1923, BL/114/1/18, Bonar Law Papers, PA.

34 Alison Martin, 'Michael Collins and the British Press', *History Ireland*, vol. 29, no. 4 (July/August 2020), https://www.historyireland.com/michael-collins-and-the-british-press (accessed 24 October 2022).

35 Michael Kinnear, *The Fall of Lloyd George: The political crisis of 1922* (London, 1973); Thomas Jones, *A Whitehall Diary, Vol. 1, 1916–1925*, ed. Keith Middlemas (London, 1969), and idem., vol. 3, *Ireland, 1918–25*, ed. Keith Middlemas (London, 1971); Kenneth O. Morgan, *Consensus and Disunity: The Lloyd George coalition government, 1918–1922* (Oxford, 1979).

36 Adams, *Bonar Law*, p. 335.

37 Irish Free State Constitution Bill, *HC Deb.*, fifth series, vol. 159, col. 331, 27 November 1922.

38 Ibid.

39 Ibid., cols 359–60.

40 Ibid., col. 329, 332–3.

41 Deborah Lavin, *From Empire to International Commonwealth: A biography of Lionel Curtis* (Oxford, 1995), p. 181.

42 Irish Free State Constitution Bill, *HC Deb.*, fifth series, vol. 159, col. 332, 27 November 1922.

43 Ibid., col. 359.

44 Ibid., col. 341.

45 *HC Deb.*, fifth series, vol. 159, col. 88530, November 1922.

46 Ibid.

47 Col. Gretton, Irish Free State Constitution Bill, *HC Deb.*, fifth series, vol. 159, col. 341, 27 November 1922.

48 *HC Deb.*, fifth series, vol. 161, col. 2244, 19 March 1923.

49 *HC Deb.*, fifth series, vol. 161, col. 1158, 12 March 1923.

50 *The Nation*, 25 October 1922, cited in Kissane, *Politics of the Irish Civil War*, p. 65.

51 Adams, *Bonar Law*, pp. 340, 358.

52 'The Carlton Club Meeting and the Fall of the Lloyd George Coalition in October 1922', Lord Lexden (website), https://www.alistairlexden.org.uk/news/carlton-club-meeting-and-fall-lloyd-george-coalition-october-1922 (accessed 24 October 2022).

53 Winston Churchill, *Great Contemporaries* (London, 1941), p. 290.

Case Study – The Treaty Debates and the Irish Civil War

1 Gavin Foster, *The Irish Civil War and Society: Politics, class and conflict* (Basingstoke, 2015), p. 4.

2 Michael Laffan, *The Resurrection of Ireland: The Sinn Féin party, 1916–1923* (Cambridge, 2012), p. 350.

3 Liam Weeks, Slava Jankin Mikhaylov, Alex Herzog, Mícheál Ó Fathartaigh and Hannah Bechara, 'It's Only Words? Analysing the roots of the Irish party system using historical parliamentary debates', *Parliamentary Affairs*, vol. 76, no. 4 (October 2023), pp. 836–56.

4 Mícheál Ó Fathartaigh and Liam Weeks, *Birth of a State: The Anglo-Irish Treaty* (Dublin, 2021), p. 103.

5 *Dáil Debates*, vol. T, no. 14, 6 January 1922, p. 298.

6 Ibid., vol. S2, no. 3, 2 March 1922, pp. 190–1.

Case Study – Military Dress and the Irish Civil War

1 'I.R.A. March into Beggar's Bush', *Irish Times*, 2 February 1922, p. 2.

2 'Ireland's Army', *Freeman's Journal*, 27 January 1922, p. 5.

3 Ibid.

4 'Uniforms for Irish Army', *Evening Herald*, 27 January 1922, p. 2.

5 'Ireland's Army', *Freeman's Journal*, 27 January 2022, p. 5. For details of the National Army uniform, see Gerry White and Brendan O'Shea, *Irish Volunteer Soldier, 1913–23* (London, 2003).

6 'Army Orders', *An t-Óglach*, 27 May 1922, p. 7.

7 See Department of Defence (DoD) 2/48608; DoD-2-22696, NAI.

8 'The People's Army', *An t-Óglach*, 25 April 1922, p. 15.

9 See Jane Tynan and Lisa Godson (eds), *Uniform: Clothing and discipline in the modern world* (London, 2019).

10 DoD A/07535.

11 DoD A/7684. See also *Dáil Debates*, vol. 1, no. 3, 1 December 1922; *Dáil Debates*, vol. 3, no. 24, 8 June 1923.

12 For example, 'Important Captures', *Cork Examiner*, 14 September 1922, p. 5; 'Captures in Many Parts', *Irish Independent*, 4 October 1922, p. 7.

13 Ernie O'Malley, *The Singing Flame* (Dublin, 1978), pp. 179–80.

14 Ibid., p. 147.

15 Ernie O'Malley, *On Another Man's Wound* (London, 1961 [1936]), p. 77; 'Looting Post Office', *Cork Examiner*, 21 February 1923, p. 4. See also 'Dublin Raiding Peril', *Irish Independent*, 14 October 1922, p. 9.

16 O'Malley, *Singing Flame*, p. 152.

SECTION 2: THE WAR IN THE PROVINCES

Chapter 2 – The Irish Civil War in Provincial Ireland: Landscapes, communities and localised conflict

1 Donal Ó Drisceoil, 'Irish Newspapers, the Treaty and the Civil War', in John Crowley, Donal Ó Drisceoil, Mike Murphy and John Borgonovo (eds), *Atlas of the Irish Revolution* (Cork, 2017), pp. 661–4.

2 Michael Hopkinson, *Green against Green: The Irish Civil War*, 1st edn (Dublin, 1988), pp. 34–46, 58–69.

3 John Borgonovo, 'IRA Conventions', in Crowley, et al. (eds), *Atlas of the Irish Revolution*, pp. 670–4.

4 John Borgonovo, 'Defending the Republic: The IRA field army and the Civil War's conventional phase', in Darragh Gannon and Fearghal McGarry (eds), *Ireland 1922: Independence, partition, civil war* (Dublin, 2022), pp. 9–34.

5 For details of the battles in County Limerick, see Pádraig Óg Ó Ruairc, *The Battle for Limerick City* (Cork, 2010), and John O'Callaghan, *The Battle for Kilmallock* (Cork, 2011). For Waterford, see Pat McCarthy, *The Irish Revolution, 1912–23: Waterford* (Dublin, 2015).

6 Gavin Foster, *The Irish Civil War and Society: Politics, class, and conflict* (Basingstoke, 2015), pp. 22–57.

7 Bielenberg and Dorney divide the guerrilla period into three phases, which is also a logical delineation.

8 John Borgonovo, 'Cumann na mBan, Martial Women and the Irish Civil War, 1922–1923', in Linda Connolly (ed.), *Women and the Irish Revolution: Feminism, activism, violence* (Dublin, 2020), pp. 68–84. See also Ann Matthews, *Dissidents: Irish republican women, 1923–1941* (Cork, 2012); Cal McCarthy, *Cumann na mBan and the Irish Revolution* (Cork, 2007); Margaret Ward, *Unmanageable Revolutionaries: Women in Irish nationalism* (London, 1995).

9 John Regan, *The Irish Counter-revolution, 1921–36* (Dublin, 1999), p. 102.

10 For a more detailed discussion of the National Army during the Civil War, see Eoin Kinsella, *The Irish Defence Forces, 1922–2022* (Dublin, 2023).

11 For easy access to the 12–13 November 1922 army census, see Military Archives, https://www.militaryarchives.ie/collections/online-collections/irish-army-census-collection-12-november-1922-13-november-1922 (accessed 14 August 2023).

12 Gemma Clark, *Everyday Violence in the Irish Civil War* (Cambridge, 2014).

13 Linda Connolly, 'Sexual Violence in the Irish Civil War: A forgotten war crime?', *Women's History Review*, vol. 30, no. 1 (2021), pp. 126–43; Linda Connolly, 'Towards Further Understanding of Violence Experienced by Women in the Irish Revolution', in Connolly (ed.), *Women and the Irish Revolution*, pp. 103–28. See also Susan Byrne, '"Keeping Company with the Enemy": Gender and sexual violence against women during the Irish War of Independence and Civil War, 1919–1923', *Women's History Review*, vol. 30, no. 1 (2021), pp. 108–25.

14 See John Borgonovo, '"Another Flake of the Hammer": The torture of republican prisoners, narratives and discourses of the Irish revolutionary period', unpublished paper, 'Violent Contexts: Ireland and the Wider World' conference, University College Cork, 1 April 2016. There is ample evidence of this mistreatment in the Ernie O'Malley interviews at University College Dublin Archives and in the Military Service Pensions Collection in the Irish Military Archives.

15 John Dorney, *The Civil War in Dublin: The fight for the Irish capital, 1922–1924* (Dublin, 2017).

16 Marion Dowd, 'Caves, Guerrilla Warfare and the Irish Revolution', in Crowley, et al. (eds), *Atlas of the Irish Revolution*, pp. 722–4. In the same publication, see the map of maritime events during the Civil War, p. 709. See also John Borgonovo, 'The Heritage of the Revolution: Coastal legacies', in Robert Devoy, Val Cummins, Barry Brunt, Darius Bartlett and Sarah Kandrot (eds), *The Coastal Atlas of Ireland* (Cork, 2021), pp. 314–18.

17 Charles Townshend, *The Republic: The fight for Irish independence* (London, 2013), pp. 438–41.

18 For details on Cumann na mBan and Civil War propaganda, see Borgonovo, 'Cumann na mBan, Martial Women and the Irish Civil War, 1922–1923'.

19 Gareth Prendergast, 'Clear-Hold-(Re)Build: An examination of the Irish Civil War', unpublished PhD thesis, University College Cork, 2022.

20 For a brief discussion, see Peter Rigney, 'Railways: Campaign of destruction', in Crowley, et al. (eds), *Atlas of the Irish Revolution*, pp. 688–9. For a more complete study, see Bernard Share, *In Time of Civil War: The conflict on the Irish railways, 1922–23* (Cork, 2006).

21 For a broader view on the subject, see Brian Hanley, *Republicanism, Crime and Paramilitary Policing in Ireland, 1916–2020* (Cork, 2022). For ordinary criminality in Cork city during the Civil War, see John Borgonovo, 'Civil Administration and Economic Endowments in the Munster Republic's "Real Capital", July–August 1922', *Éire-Ireland*, vol. 58, nos 3–4 (fall/winter 2023), pp. 9–34.

22 Brian McCarthy, *Civic Guard Mutiny* (Cork, 2012).

23 Conor Brady, *Guardians of the Peace: The early years of the Irish police force* (Dublin, 2022), pp. 73–100.

24 James Donnelly Jr, 'A New Ranch War? Cattle driving and agrarian disorder, 1922–23', *Éire-Ireland*, vol. 58, nos 3–4 (fall/winter 2023), pp. 174–223.

25 Heather Laird, '"Agrarian Anarchy": Containing the Land War', in Gannon and McGarry (eds), *Ireland 1922*, pp. 317–22.

26 Foster, *Irish Civil War and Society*, pp. 130–42. See also Anthony Kinsella, 'The Special Infantry Corps', *Irish Sword: The Journal of the Military History Society of Ireland*, vol. 20, no. 82 (winter 1997), pp. 331–45.

27 Foster, *Irish Civil War and Society*, p. 130.

28 Ibid., pp. 134–5.

29 For a comprehensive study of Civil War executions, see Seán Enright, *The Irish Civil War: Law, execution and atrocity* (Newbridge, 2019).

Case Study – Graffiti at Ash Hill Towers

1 We are very grateful to Nicole and Simon Johnson for facilitating access to record the graffiti and to the Irish Research Council for funding this project under the COALESCE scheme (2022/533). For further work on graffiti of this period, see inter alia, Laura McAtackney, 'Graffiti Revelations and the Changing Meanings of Kilmainham Gaol in (Post)Colonial Ireland', *International Journal of Historical Archaeology*, vol. xx, no. 3 (2016), pp. 492–505. Elsewhere, graffiti of the period remains unrecorded and in danger of being lost – for example, in the holding cells of Kanturk courthouse, currently in a state of serious disrepair: *Irish Examiner*, 22 July 2023.

2 Thomas Toomey, *The War of Independence in Limerick, 1912–1921* (Castletroy, 2010), p. 400; Ernie O'Malley, officer-commanding IRA 2nd Southern Division, notebook (copy) entry, 2 June 1921, BMH-CD-053-2, Bureau of Military History Contemporary Documents.

3 John O'Callaghan, *The Battle for Kilmallock* (Cork, 2011), pp. 62–3. For a colourful picture of life inside the IRA headquarters, see the account by IRA publicity officer Michael O'Donovan (later the writer Frank O'Connor) in his autobiographical volume, Frank O'Connor, *An Only Child* (London, 1964), pp. 215–16.

4 IRA Kilfinane Company Nominal Roll, RO 129, MSPC, IMA; Kilmallock Petty Sessions Court Order Book, 1920, NAI.

5 See IRA and Cumann na mBan nominal rolls RO and CMB series in the Military Service Pensions Collection, available on the Irish Military Archives website.

6 Anti-Treaty IRA Table of Medical Personnel and Hospitals, 5 August 1922, RO 26, MSPC, IMA.

7 The likelihood of him being at Ash Hill Towers *after* the National Army's arrival is strengthened by his not being discharged from the British army until late July 1922. Our thanks to Jean Prendergast, Royal Munster Fusiliers Association, for assistance with Martin Duhig's British army service records.

8 Irish Army Census Records, IMA, https://www.militaryarchives.ie/en/collections/online-collections/irish-army-census-collection-12-november-1922-13-november-1922 (accessed 13 June 2023).

9 Terence Dooley, *Burning the Big House: The story of the Irish country house in time of war and revolution* (New Haven, CT, 2022); James S. Donnelly Jr, 'Big House Burnings in County Cork during the Irish Revolution, 1920–21', *Éire-Ireland*, vol. 18, nos 3–4 (2012), pp. 141–97.

Case Study – 'Small House' Burnings during the Irish Civil War: A County Kilkenny case study

1 Gemma Clark, *Everyday Violence in the Irish Civil War* (Cambridge, 2014), *passim*.

2 MSPC 34/44960, Mary Teehan-Foley, IMA.

3 Ibid.; MSPC 34/60441, Mary Stallard/O'Kelly, IMA; FIN/COMP/2/10/324, Bridget Teehan, NAI; *Kilkenny People*, 24 March 1923.

4 *Cork Examiner* 6 April 1923; *Kilkenny People*, 6 April 1923.

5 *Cork Examiner* 6 April 1923; *Kilkenny People*, 6 April 1923; FIN/COMP/2/10/78, James Walsh, NAI.

6 FIN/COMP/2/10/317, Mary Walsh, NAI.

Case Study – Tormore: The strategic use of a cave dugout during Sligo's Civil War

1 Audio recording conducted by Niall Delaney with Chris Branley (Ocean FM, 2014). Part of this recording was included in a radio documentary, *Sligo's Noble Six*, first aired on Ocean FM in 2015. Recording kindly provided by Niall Delaney.

2 Ernie O'Malley Notebooks, P17a/119, UCDA: Divisional HQ Dispatches of 3rd Western Division, August 1922–March 1923, UCDA; MSPC A/29, Brigade Activity Report of 1st Brigade, 3rd Western Division, IMA.

3 James Bonsall, Marion Dowd and Robert Mulraney, *The Six. The lives and memorialisation of Sligo's Noble Six* (Sligo, 2022).

4 Scanlon, Ernie O'Malley Notebooks, P17b/133, UCDA.

5 *Derry Journal*, 27 September 1922.

6 Marion Dowd, Robert Mulraney and James Bonsall, *An Irish Civil War Dugout: Tormore Cave, County Sligo: Archaeology, history, memory* (Oxford, 2024).

7 Video and audio recording of Chris Brandley conducted by Michael McDowell for television documentary, *A Lost Son* (RTÉ, 2012), dir. Angela Sammon, first aired 10 December 2012. Transcript kindly provided by Angela Sammon.

8 Uinseann MacEoin, *Survivors* (Dublin, 1980), p. 412.

9 Fr Seán McManus, interview with Robert Mulraney, 12 December 2022.

Chapter 3 – Civil Conflict in Ireland, 1922–3: Political violence and the consolidation of Northern Ireland

1 Jonathan Bardon, *A History of Ulster* (Belfast, 2001), pp. 445–8.
2 Adrian Grant, 'Anticipating Partition in Derry', in Caoimhe Nic Dháibhéid, Marie Coleman and Paul Bew (eds), *Northern Ireland, 1921–2021: Centenary historical perspectives* (Belfast, 2022), p. 15.
3 James A. Cousins, *Without a Dog's Chance: The nationalists of Northern Ireland and the Irish Boundary Commission, 1920–25* (Newbridge, 2020), pp. 324–5.
4 Richard Murphy, 'Walter Long and the Making of the Government of Ireland Act, 1919–20', *Irish Historical Studies*, vol. 25, no. 97 (1986), pp. 82–96.
5 Patrick Buckland, *Irish Unionism 2: Ulster Unionism and the origins of Northern Ireland, 1886–1922* (Dublin, 1973), pp. 117–21.
6 Bill Kissane, *The Politics of the Irish Civil War* (Oxford, 2005), p. 44.
7 Conor McCabe, 'The Irish Labour Party and the 1920 Local Elections', *Saothar*, vol. 35 (2010), pp. 7–20.
8 *HC Deb.*, vol. 114, cols 99–183, 24 March 1919.
9 Fergal McCluskey, *The Irish Revolution, 1912–23: Tyrone* (Dublin, 2014), p. 105.
10 Adrian Grant, *The Irish Revolution, 1912–23: Derry* (Dublin, 2018), p. 126.
11 Ibid., p. 94.
12 Ibid., pp. 98–103.
13 Alan F. Parkinson, *Belfast's Unholy War: The troubles of the 1920s* (Dublin, 2004).
14 Adrian Grant, 'The Uneasy Relationship Between Unionists and the RIC', RTÉ 'Brainstorm', 24 June 2020, https://www.rte.ie/brainstorm/2020/0623/1149128-unionists-ric-ireland/.
15 Grant, *Derry*, pp. 99–100.
16 Michael Farrell, *Arming the Protestants: The formation of the Ulster Special Constabulary and the Royal Ulster Constabulary, 1920–27* (London, 1983), pp. 23–9.
17 Transcript of interview with Thomas J. Kelly, 18 April 1967, CÓFLA, Fr Louis O'Kane Collection (LOK) LOK.IV.B.06; interview with Thomas Morris, 30 October 1967, CÓFLA, LOK.IV.A.09; Breaches of the Truce, County Londonderry, Drilling and Camps, September 1921, CO 904/154, NAUK.
18 Transcript of interview with Thomas J. Kelly, 18 April 1967, CÓFLA, LOK.IV.B.06.
19 Truce Liaison Officer, Derry to Intelligence Office, Belfast, 10 October 1921; District Inspector Magherafelt to County Inspector Derry, 11 October 1921, CO 904/154, NAUK.
20 Robert Lynch, *The Northern IRA and the Early Years of Partition, 1920–22* (Dublin, 2006), pp. 116–7.
21 Grant, *Derry*, pp. 122–3.
22 Terence Dooley, *The Irish Revolution, 1912–23: Monaghan* (Dublin, 2017), p. 103.
23 Lynch, *Northern IRA*, pp. 100–5, 116.
24 Michael Hopkinson, 'The Craig-Collins Pacts of 1922: Two attempted reforms of the Northern Ireland government', *Irish Historical Studies*, vol. 27, no. 106 (1990), pp. 146–9.
25 Robert Lynch, 'The Clones Affray, 1922: Massacre or invasion?' *History Ireland*, vol. 12, no. 3 (2004), pp. 33–7.
26 Lynch, *Northern IRA*, pp. 107–15.
27 Parkinson, *Belfast's Unholy War*, pp. 241–56.
28 Tim Wilson, '"The most terrible assassination that has yet stained the name of Belfast": The McMahon murders in context', *Irish Historical Studies*, vol. 37, no. 145 (2010), pp. 83–106.
29 Lynch, *Northern IRA*, pp. 136–7.
30 Grant, *Derry*, p. 134.
31 Robert Lynch, 'Donegal and the Joint-IRA Northern Offensive, May–November 1922', *Irish Historical Studies*, vol. 35, no. 138 (2006), p. 189; divisional commissioner, fortnightly reports, 16 May 1922, HA/5/152, PRONI; McCluskey, *Tyrone*, p. 122.
32 Divisional commissioner, fortnightly reports, 16 May 1922, HA/5/152, PRONI; *Derry Journal*, 5 May 1922.
33 Interview with Tom Morris, 30 October 1967, CÓFLA, LOK.IV.A.09; transcript of interview with Thomas J. Kelly, 18 April 1967, CÓFLA, LOK.IV.B.06.
34 *Derry Journal*, 5 May 1922.
35 Divisional commissioner, fortnightly reports, 16 May 1922, HA/5/152, PRONI.
36 *Derry Journal*, 5 May 1922.
37 Lynch, 'Donegal and the Joint-IRA Northern Offensive', p. 189.
38 BMH WS 1741, p. 235, Michael O'Donaghue, IMA; Patrick [?] to John McAleer, 30 March 1938, CÓFLA, LOK.I.A.07; *Derry Journal*, 5 May 1922; Liam Ó Duibhir, *Donegal and the Civil War: The untold story* (Cork, 2011), pp. 102–3.
39 Ó Duibhir, *Donegal and the Civil War*, pp. 104–5; Kieran Glennon, *From Pogrom to Civil War: Tom Glennon and the Belfast IRA* (Cork, 2013), pp. 156–67.
40 Pauric Travers, *The Irish Revolution, 1912–23: Donegal* (Dublin, 2022), pp. 128–9.
41 Transcript of interview with Barney Young [n.d.], CÓFLA, LOK.I.B.17.
42 Harry Clark to Norman Stronge, 30 March 1922 in Wallace Clark, *Guns in Ulster* (Belfast, 1967), pp. 55–6.
43 Pearse Lawlor, *The Outrages: The IRA and the Ulster Special Constabulary in the border campaign* (Cork, 2011), pp. 270–2; *Derry Journal*, 8 May 1922.
44 Transcript of interview with Roddy O'Kane, 16 July 1966, CÓFLA, LOK.I.B.11; interview with Thomas O'Neill, 8 September 1967, CÓFLA, LOK.I.A.09.
45 Lawlor, *The Outrages*, pp. 281–3.
46 Divisional commissioner, fortnightly reports, 16 May 1922, HA/5/152, PRONI; Clark, *Guns in Ulster*, p. 67.
47 Lynch, *Northern IRA*, pp. 153–4.
48 Sarah Campbell, '"A Cold House for Catholics"? The consolidation of the Northern Ireland state in the 1920s', in Mel Farrell, Jason Knirck and Ciara Meehan (eds), *A Formative Decade: Ireland in the 1920s* (Newbridge, 2015), pp. 204–5.
49 Margaret O'Callaghan, 'A Border Vignette: The Belleek–Pettigo events of June 1922', in Nic Dháibhéid, Coleman and Bew (eds), *Northern Ireland, 1921–2021*, pp. 62–70.
50 Denise Kleinrichert, *Republican Internment and the Prison Ship* Argenta, *1922* (Dublin, 2001), pp. 182–3, 337–68; unnamed [probably Rory Graham] to Miss Seeton concerning conditions on the *Argenta*, 13 March 1924, CÓFLA, LOK.III.F.06.
51 Lynch, 'Donegal and the Joint-IRA Northern Offensive', p. 199.
52 Travers, *Donegal*, pp. 128–9.
53 Grant, *Derry*, p. 138.
54 BMH WS 693, Patrick Maguire, p. 15, IMA; John Lafferty to [Peter Hughes] Minister for Defence, 12 April 1927, MSPC W24SP6369, IMA.
55 Lynch, *Northern IRA*, pp. 191–7.
56 John Lafferty to [Peter Hughes] Minister for Defence, 12 April 1927, MSPC WS24SP6369, IMA.
57 A.M. Gallagher, *Majority Minority Review 2: Employment, unemployment and religion in Northern Ireland* (Coleraine, 1991), section 2; Susannah Riordan, 'Politics, Economy, Society: Northern Ireland, 1920–1939', in Thomas Bartlett (ed.), *The Cambridge History of Ireland: Volume 4, 1880 to the present* (Cambridge, 2018), p. 318.
58 Farrell, *Arming the Protestants*, p. 29.
59 Conall Parr, 'Expelled from the Yard and the Tribe: The "rotten Prods" of 1920 and their political legacies', *Studi Irlandesi*, vol. 11 (2021), pp. 299–321.
60 Eamon Phoenix, *Northern Nationalism: Nationalist politics, partition and the Catholic minority in Northern Ireland, 1890–1940* (Belfast, 1994), pp. 258–9.
61 John O'Brien, *Discrimination in Northern Ireland, 1920–1939: Myth or reality?* (Newcastle, 2010), pp. 7–18.
62 Inspector General RUC to unknown, 9 October 1922, HA/32/1/168, PRONI.
63 City Commissioner, Derry to Inspector General RUC, Belfast, 23 February 1923, HA/32/1/168, PRONI.
64 District Inspector Belfast to Secretary, Ministry for Home Affairs, 31 January 1923, HA/32/1/168, PRONI.

Case Study – Protestants and the Irish Civil War

1 See, for example, *Dundalk Democrat*, 4 September 1920; *Irish Times*, 9, 23 August, 25, 30 September 1920; unknown author, *The Voice of the Protestant Church in Ireland* (*c.*1922), p. 2.
2 *Church of Ireland Gazette*, 6 January 1922.
3 Andy Bielenberg, 'Exodus: The emigration of Southern Irish Protestants during the Irish War of Independence and the Civil War', *Past & Present*, vol. cciix (2013), pp. 210–11.
4 See *Freeman's Journal*, 12 May 1922; Dublin *Evening Mail*, 12 May 1922; *Gaelic Churchman*, June 1922.
5 See Conor Morrissey, *Protestant Nationalists in Ireland, 1900–1923* (Cambridge, 2019), ch. 8.

6 Saorstát Éireann, *Census of Population 1926*, vol. iii (Religions and birthplaces) (Dublin, 1929), p. 1.
7 For recent writing on this topic, see, for example, Bielenberg, 'Exodus'; David Fitzpatrick, 'Protestant Depopulation and the Irish Revolution', *Irish Historical Studies*, vol. xxxviii (2013), pp. 643–70; Enda Delaney, *Demography, State and Society: Irish migration to Britain, 1921–1971* (Liverpool, 2000), pp. 69–83.
8 See, for example, Marie Coleman, 'Protestant Depopulation in County Longford during the Irish Revolution, 1911–1926', *English Historical Review*, vol. cxxxv (2020), pp. 932–77.
9 *Church of Ireland Gazette*, 18 May 1923.

SECTION 3: LABOUR, LAND AND EVERYDAY LIFE

Chapter 4 – 'What the hell do they want a republic for?' Labour, the left and the Irish Civil War

1 Emmet O'Connor, *Reds and the Green: Ireland, Russia, and the Communist Internationals, 1919–43* (Dublin, 2004), pp. 66–70.
2 Borodin to the ECCI [Executive Committee of the Communist International], interview with delegates from the Irish party, 15 July 1922, 495/89/13–6/23, RGASPI.
3 For membership figures, see Donal Nevin (ed.), *Trade Union Century* (Cork, 1994), p. 433.
4 'The Ministry of Labour in the First Dáil', *Saothar: Iris Ráithiúil na Roinne Saothair*, vol. iii (spring 1969), pp. 1–23; Dáil Éireann Papers, 1–4, Cabinet minutes, 11 January 1922, NAI.
5 James Meenan, *The Irish Economy since 1922* (Liverpool, 1971), pp. 71, 91; J.D. Clarkson, *Labour and Nationalism in Ireland* (New York, 1925), pp. 441–2.
6 Emmet O'Connor, *Big Jim Larkin: Hero or wrecker?* (Dublin, 2015), p. 200.
7 Gavin Foster, *The Irish Civil War and Society: Politics, class, and conflict* (Basingstoke, 2015). For a recent local study, see Kieran McNulty, 'Class, Gender, and Civil War Politics in Kerry, 1921 to 1923', in Francis Devine and Fearghal MacBhloscaidh (eds), *Bread Not Profits: Provincial working class politics during the Irish revolution* (Dublin, 2022), pp. 161–76; Bill Kissane, *The Politics of the Irish Civil War* (Oxford, 2005) is excellent on mentalities but, like the literature generally, undervalues the role of Labour and the CPI.
8 T.A. Jackson, *Ireland Her Own* (New York), p. 413.
9 ILPTUC, *Report* (1922), p. 22.
10 J. Anthony Gaughan, *Thomas Johnson* (Dublin, 1980), p. 195.
11 ILPTUC, *Report* (1922), pp. 19–21.
12 Ibid., pp. 57–87.
13 Gaughan, *Thomas Johnson*, p. 198; ILPTUC, *Report* (1922), pp. 44–5, 52.
14 Letter from William O'Brien, 10 January 1922, Ernie O'Malley Papers, P17a/161, UCDA.
15 *Voice of Labour*, 29 April 1922; Report of the CPI [Communist Party of Ireland] to the ECCI, October 1921–October 1922, 495/89/16–62, RGASPI.
16 R.M. Fox, *The Irish Citizen Army* (Dublin, 1944), pp. 211–26; Frank Robbins, *Under the Starry Plough: Recollections of the Irish Citizen Army* (Dublin, 1977), pp. 232–4.
17 *Workers' Republic*, 18–25 March 1922; Report of the CPI to the ECCI, October 1921–October 1922, 495/89/16–64/79, RGASPI.
18 Mike Milotte, *Communism in Modern Ireland: The pursuit of the workers' republic since 1916* (Dublin, 1984), p. 59; *Workers' Republic*, 1 April 1922.
19 ILPTUC, *Report* (1922), pp. 28–30; Arthur Mitchell, *Labour in Irish Politics, 1890–1930* (Dublin, 1974), pp. 156–7.
20 O'Connor, *Big Jim Larkin*, p. 202.
21 William O'Brien, *Forth the Banners Go: Reminiscences of William O'Brien* (Dublin, 1969), pp. 220–1.
22 Report to the Comintern on the Irish party, R. Connolly, Berlin, 12 April 1922, 5/3/581–9/17, RGASPI.
23 C. Desmond Greaves, *Liam Mellows and the Irish Revolution* (London, 1971), pp. 313–14.
24 Report of the CPI to the ECCI, October 1921–October 1922, 495/89/16–40/145, RGASPI.
25 Lynch to Acting Assistant Chief of Staff, 25 July 1922, Ernie O'Malley Papers, P17/a/60, UCDA.
26 Report of staff meeting, Field GHQ, 27 July 1922, Ernie O'Malley Papers, P17a/15, UCDA; Report of staff meeting, 1 August 1922, Ernie O'Malley Papers, P17a/16, UCDA.
27 J.T. Murphy, *New Horizons* (London, 1941), pp. 184–6.
28 Connolly to Luise, 22 August 1922, 495/89/12–36, RGASPI.
29 Captured documents, O'Malley to O/C 1st Southern Division, 9 September 1922, IMA; O'Malley to Lynch, 3 September 1922, Ernie O'Malley Papers, lot 3, P17/a/56, UCDA.
30 O'Malley to Lynch, 24 August 1922, Ernie O'Malley Papers, P17/a/55, UCDA; TÓD [Tomás Ó Deirg] to O'Brien, 3 August 1922, William O'Brien Papers, 13957, NLI.
31 ILPTUC, *Report* (1922), pp. 39, 156.
32 Kissane, *Politics of the Irish Civil War*, pp. 158–9.
33 The latest contribution to the hagiography is FÓRSA, *Seeking No Honours: Tom Johnson, 1872–1963, Marie Johnson, 1874–1974* (Dublin, 2022).
34 Denis Gwynn, *The Irish Free State, 1922–1927* (London, 1928), pp. 92, 193.
35 Mitchell, *Labour in Irish Politics*, pp. 171–81.
36 ITUC, *Annual Report* (1922), p. 86.
37 O'Malley to Lynch, 24 September 1922, Ernie O'Malley Papers, P17a/57, UCDA.
38 *Workers' Republic*, 26 August 1922; on O'Donnell, see Donal Ó Drisceoil, *Peadar O'Donnell* (Cork, 2001).
39 *Munster Express*, 2 June 1923.
40 Emmet O'Connor, *A Labour History of Ireland* (Dublin, 2011), pp. 130–8.
41 Richard Mulcahy Papers, P7/B/321–22, UCDA.
42 Luke Dineen, 'Class War in Cork: The Cork general lockout of 1923', *Saothar*, vol. 46 (2021), pp. 93–106.
43 O'Connor, *Big Jim Larkin*, pp. 223–4.
44 *Voice of Labour*, 25 August 1923.
45 *Freeman's Journal*, 2 June 1923; *Dáil Éireann*, vol. 3, 1409–12, 31 May 1923; John Dorney, 'Rough and Ready Work', The Irish Story, 15 October 2015, https://www.theirishstory.com/2015/10/15/rough-and-ready-work-the-special-infantry-corps (accessed 15 July 2021).
46 O'Brien, *Forth the Banners Go*, p. 113.
47 Francis Devine, *Organising History: A centenary of SIPTU, 1909–2009* (Dublin, 2010), p. 1005.

Case Study – Agrarian Unrest in Civil War Ireland

1 See W.E. Vaughan, *Landlords and Tenants in Ireland, 1848–1904* (Dundalk, 1994), p. 5.
2 See ibid., p. 40.
3 Michael Davitt, *The Fall of Feudalism in Ireland: Or the story of the Land League revolution* (London, 1904), pp. xii–xiii.
4 See, for example, Michael Davitt, 'The Irish Social Problem', *Today*, vol. 4 (April 1884), pp. 241–55. This 'normalisation' took the form of strengthening absolute property rights that had been undermined by previous land acts, most notably the 1881 land act, which placed considerable emphasis on tenant rights.
5 For further information on the Ranch War, see Patrick Cosgrove, 'The Ranch War, *c.*1906–09', in John Crowley, Donal Ó Drisceoil, Mike Murphy and John Borgonovo (eds), *Atlas of the Irish Revolution* (Cork, 2017), pp. 81–4.
6 See Paul Bew, 'Sinn Féin, Agrarian Radicalism and the War of Independence, 1919–1921', in D.G. Boyce (ed.), *The Revolution in Ireland, 1879–1923* (Basingstoke and London, 1988), p. 266, fn. 31. In this footnote, Bew refers to a return of 'Agrarian Outrages' that gives a total of 822 for the period 1 January 1920 to 1 June 1920, and a total of 175 'Outrages' for the same period in 1919.
7 A 1,000-acre farm in County Clare belonging to H.V. McNamara, which was seized and used collectively by at least thirty-seven small farmers and fishermen, is an example of one such commons.
8 For an overview of agrarian unrest in the west of Ireland during the War of Independence, see Tony Varley, 'Land, Revolution and Counter-revolution in the West', in Crowley, et al. (eds), *Atlas of the Irish Revolution*, pp. 495–6.
9 Patrick Hogan, Memorandum: seizures of land, 22 December 1922, DoD A.07869, IMA.
10 For an overview of the differences between the 'official' anti-Treaty agrarian policy and the policy pursued by the Free State, see C. Desmond Greaves, *Liam Mellows and the Irish Revolution* (Belfast, [1971]; 2004), pp. 313–4.
11 See Gavin Foster, *The Irish Civil War and Society: Politics, class, and conflict* (Basingstoke, 2015), pp. 117–21, 130–4.
12 Letter from Kevin O'Higgins to the army inquiry committee, 12 May 1924, Papers of the Army Inquiry Committee, IE.MA.AMTY.03.055, IMA.
13 Anthony Kinsella, 'The Special Infantry Corps', *Irish Sword*, vol. 20, no. 82

(winter 1997), p. 343. The *Atlas of the Irish Revolution* includes three maps based on information about the Special Infantry Corps contained in this article by Kinsella. See Crowley, et al. (eds), *Atlas of the Irish Revolution*, pp. 668–9. See also Foster, *Irish Civil War and Society*, pp. 135–41.

14 Special Infantry Corps Returns and Reports, CW.P.02.02.02, IMA.

Case Study – Everyday Life in Dublin during the Irish Civil War

1 Jim Herlihy, *The Dublin Metropolitan Police: A short history and genealogical guide* (Dublin, 2001), pp. 186–7; Dublin Metropolitan Police, Bi-weekly Precis of Reports of Important Occurrences in the DMP Area, 1921–2, IMA.
2 Lady Alice Howard's Diary, 27 January 1922, MS 3,625, NLI.
3 Truce Reports (LE/4), IMA.
4 'RECEIPTS' is capitalised in the original order (CD6/48/1, IMA).
5 David Fitzpatrick, 'Protestant Depopulation and the Irish Revolution', *Irish Historical Studies*, vol. 38, no. 152 (November 2013).

SECTION 4: PROPAGANDA AND LEGITIMISATION

Chapter 5 – Irregulars Versus Slave Staters: Propaganda, censorship and the Irish Civil War

1 *United Irishman*, 11 August 1923 and *Éire*, 25 August 1923. Dalton later changed the format of his surname to D'Alton. The pro-Treaty *Young Ireland* had earlier featured the bubble motif on 5 August 1922 (See Fig. 6, p. 172). a young IRA man sits on a can of petrol, blowing bubbles labelled 'Terrorism', 'Documentary Republic' and 'The Shadow' from his revolver (5 August 1922).
2 *Irish Times*, 11 January 1922. According to the *Irish Independent*, Collins said, 'Deserters all' and 'Foreigners, English' (the *Freeman's Journal* likewise). The *Evening Herald* had Collins shouting, 'Deserters all' and 'Foreigners, traitors, English.'
3 *The Separatist*, 18 February 1922.
4 'Sledge hammer censorship' was the term used by the *New York Globe* to describe the anti-Treaty IRA destruction of the *Freeman's Journal* plant on 30 March 1922.
5 The four main dailies in the North – the unionist *Belfast Telegraph*, *Belfast Newsletter* and *Northern Whig* and the nationalist, Devlinite *Irish News* – were less concerned with the Treaty *per se* than the developing violence in the North in the first half of 1922. The *Irish News* was critically supportive of the settlement, while the unionist papers warmed to an agreement that divided their opponents. The majority of Ulster's nationalist weeklies were also broadly pro-Treaty. A majority of the Northern IRA was either pro-Treaty or neutral.
6 Dorothy Macardle, *The Irish Republic* (Dublin, 1951), p. 624.
7 Tom Garvin, *1922: The birth of Irish democracy* (Dublin, 2005), p. 134.
8 On a couple of isolated occasions, however, shots were fired in the direction of prominent pro-Treaty priests. See Patrick Murray, *Oracles of God: The Roman Catholic Church and Irish politics, 1922–37* (Dublin, 2000), p. 52.
9 Among the nationalist periodicals still in circulation, only P.J. Little's *New Ireland* opposed the Treaty. A short-lived Republican monthly titled *An Long* (The Ship) was launched by Seán O'Faoláin in Cork in May 1922. Only three issues were produced. It was revived temporarily as *An Long–War News* in October 1922.
10 *Poblacht na hÉireann* committee, minutes, 14 March 1922, 10050/491–2, Frank Gallagher Papers, TCD. Note: presumably for typesetting reasons, *Éireann* appeared on the masthead without a *fada* on the *E*.
11 Frank Gallagher, Self-penned Biographical Note, Frank Gallagher Papers, Ms 18,374 (12), NLI.
12 *Young Ireland*, 25 March 1922.
13 The first issue was on 3 January, with an additional issue on 5 January in advance of the Treaty vote. The paper was weekly from then on.
14 *Poblacht*, 3, 5, 10, 17 January 1922, and *Free State*, 13 May 1922.
15 Ciara Meehan, 'The Propaganda War Over the Anglo-Irish Treaty', in Darragh Gannon and Fearghal McGarry (eds), *Ireland 1922: Independence, partition, civil war* (Dublin, 2022), p. 72.
16 *Poblacht*, 14 February and 10 January 1922.
17 18 March 1922.
18 18 March 1922. The paper was edited by long-time Griffith associate and Liverpool Irish Republican Brotherhood man J.J. Burke, and pro-Treaty TD Seán Milroy.
19 *Cork Constitution*, 3 January 1922.
20 Childers had been awarded a Distinguished Service Order (DSO) in 1916 for his wartime services with the British armed forces.
21 8 April 1922.
22 *Dáil Debates*, vol. 3, col. 392, 10 January 1922. The accusation that the other side was using Black and Tan methods became commonplace in the propaganda of both sides during the Civil War.
23 *Truth*, 22 August 1922.
24 Anti-Treaty cartoons by Plunkett also appeared in the humorous monthly *Irish Fun* in May and June, many of which were better and more hard-hitting than those that appeared in the *Plain People* (see this *Atlas*, pp. 172–3).
25 *Plain People*, 16 April 1922.
26 Ibid., 20 April 1922.
27 *Plain People*, 25 June 1922.
28 The final issue of *Plain People* featured a proclamation from the IRA executive in the Four Courts – issued 'amidst the roar of guns and rattling of rifles – the guns of England attacking, and the rifles of the gallant I.R.A. defending your Republic' – and warning readers against the 'foul, false and malicious libels' produced by 'the King of England's Own', especially the 'despicable Desmond Fitzgerald'.
29 See Donal Ó Drisceoil, 'Sledgehammers and Blue Pencils: Censorship, suppression and the Irish regional press, 1914–23', in Ian Kenneally and James T. O'Donnell (eds), *The Irish Regional Press, 1892–2012* (Dublin, 2018) and John Horgan, 'In the Firing Line: Censorship, the Civil War in Ireland, and its aftermath', *New Hibernia Review*, vol. 22, no. 4 (winter 2018).
30 Memoranda on Censorship, Piaras Béaslaí Papers, Ms 33,915/9, NLI; L.M. Cullen, *Eason & Son: A history* (Dublin, 1989), p. 215.
31 'General Instructions', July 1922, Desmond Fitzgerald Papers, P80/282/12/2, UCDA.
32 Provisional Government Minutes, 26 July 1922, NAI.
33 Milroy took over as sole editor when Burke joined the National Army in mid July. *Truth* and *Irish People* ceased publication following the death of Griffith. *Young Ireland* ceased publication in January 1923 following the winding up of Griffith's estate. It was replaced by the Milroy-edited *United Irishman* in February 1923.
34 *Irish People*, 13 August 1922. The internal army paper, *An t-Óglach*, was registered as a newspaper and sold to the public from 24 June 1922. It specialised in valorising the National Army and traducing the 'terrorist Dictators' and 'swashbuckling and revolver-twirling terrorists' of the anti-Treaty IRA.
35 Letter to *Poblacht na hÉireann–War News*, 15 August 1922.
36 8 August 1922.
37 MacWhite report, 1 August 1922, DFA, ES box 8, file 55, NAI.
38 Gavin Foster, *The Irish Civil War and Society: Politics, class and conflict* (Basingstoke, 2015), p. 49. In chapter 2, Foster provides extensive examples from a trawl of pro-Treaty propaganda.
39 *Free State*, 8, 22 and 29 July 1922.
40 Collins to Fitzgerald, 26 July, Collins to Cosgrave, 25 July, and Cosgrave to Collins, 26 July 1922, DT S1394, NAI.
41 Provisional Government 'Decisions', 4–20 July 1922, D/T S1394, NAI.
42 Analogies between 1916 and 1922 were repeatedly drawn by anti-Treaty propagandists in July 1922, and repeatedly refuted by their opponents.
43 8 July 1922.
44 See Foster, *Irish Civil War and Society*, ch. 3.
45 MSP63744, Anna Christina Kelly and MSP1178, Brigid O'Mullane, IMA.
46 Anthony Barrett, 'The Media War: Robert Erskine Childers in west Cork', https://www.theirishstory.com/2022/09/13/the-media-war-robert-erskine-childers-in-west-cork (accessed 2 June 2023).
47 The *Evening Echo* and *Weekly Examiner* were also controlled by the republicans.
48 Lynch to O'Malley, 13 July 1922, in Cormac O'Malley and Anne Dolan (eds), *'No Surrender Here!' The Civil War papers of Ernie O'Malley, 1922–1924* (Dublin, 2007), p. 51.
49 MSP31293, Robert Lankford (sometimes, Langford) and Sylvester Clarke, 'With Childers in the South', *Irish Press* 'Christmas Number', 1932. See Anthony Barrett, 'The Media War: Robert Erskine Childers in west Cork', https://www.theirishstory.com/2022/09/13/the-media-war-robert-erskine-childers-in-west-cork, for a detailed account.
50 Frank O'Connor, *An Only Child* (London, 1961), p. 232, and Frank Gallagher,

'Erskine Childers: A study in serenity', *Ireland-American Review*, vol. 1, no. 2 (1938–9), pp. 197–200.

51 Lynch to O/Cs all divisions, 7 August 1922, in O'Malley and Dolan (eds), *'No Surrender Here!'*, p. 524; Lynch to O'Malley, 12 September 1922, and O'Malley to Moloney, 13 September 1922, in ibid., pp. 174, 180; *Freeman's Journal*, 2 September 1922. O'Malley recalled in his Civil War memoir that 'I had been instructed by Liam Lynch to capture and execute the editors of the *Irish Independent* and the *Irish Times*, but I did not carry out his order' (O'Malley, *Singing Flame*, p. 175). However, in early October, shots were fired into the home of *Irish Times* editor John Healy (Siobhán Jones, 'Southern Irish Unionism: Press and politics, 1860–1960', unpublished PhD thesis, UCC, 2005, p. 261).

52 Gavin Foster writes of 'a widespread tendency to reduce the complexities of allegiances and the tumult and chaos of the period to seductively simple binaries in which the pro-Treaty side predictably emerges as the clear moral victor over intransigent republicanism'. Along with John Regan (*The Irish Counter-revolution, 1921–1936* (Dublin, 1999)) and Bill Kissane (*The Politics of the Irish Civil War* (Oxford, 2007)), he argues against the 'reductive "democrats-versus-dictators" models' that dominated the historiography for so long ('In the Shadow of the Split: Writing the Irish Civil War', *Field Day Review*, vol. 2 (2006), p. 296). Kissane attributes to P.S. O'Hegarty's 'instant history', *The Victory of Sinn Féin* (Dublin, 1924), a formative influence on the subsequent pro-Treaty historiographical consensus (pp. 206–8).

53 J.J. Lee, *Ireland, 1912–1985: Politics and society* (Cambridge, 1989), p. 69.

54 The continuing existence of the IRA, which rowed in behind de Valera's new constitutional republican party until the relationship broke down irretrievably in the mid 1930s, was a pertinent factor here.

55 The fundamental exception was the failure to end partition, which, though not the creation of the Treaty, was intrinsic to it.

Case Study – Songs of the Irish Civil War

1 H. Halliday Sparling, *Irish Minstrelsy* (London, 1888).

2 The songsters were entitled *Paddy's Resource* (three editions), and *The Harp of Erin*. They included original compositions and items recycled from British radical publications.

3 George Petrie, *Ancient Music of Ireland* (Dublin, 1855), p. 100.

4 Sandie Purcell, *New Songs from Old Stories* (Dublin, 2023), p. 20.

5 For these and others, see Terry Moylan, *The Indignant Muse* (Lilliput Press, 2016).

6 Ibid.

7 Ibid.

8 Ibid.

9 Ibid. This was written as a poem, but the singer Tim Dennehy has put an air to it and recorded it.

10 Ibid.

11 Colm O Lochlainn, *More Irish Street Ballads* (Dublin, 1965).

Case Study – Parliamentary Politics and the Experience of Dáil Éireann during the Irish Civil War

1 On the English Civil War, see Anna Keay, *The Restless Republic: Britain without a crown* (London, 2022). The best one-volume account of the American Civil War remains James C. McPherson, *Battle Cry of Freedom: The Civil War era* (Oxford, 2003).

2 See Bill Kissane, 'Explaining the Intractability of the Irish Civil War', *Civil Wars*, vol.3, no.2, Summer, 2000, pp. 65–88, at p. 70.

3 On Lynch, see Gerard Shannon, *Liam Lynch: To declare a republic* (Dublin, 2023).

4 Bill Kissane, *The Politics of the Irish Civil War* (Oxford, 2005), p. 86. See also entry for Ginnell in the *Dictionary of Irish Biography* at https://www.dib.ie/biography/ginnell-laurence-a3488.

5 Cosgrave is quoted in Bill Kissane, 'Civil Society Under Strain: Intermediary organisations and the Irish Civil War', *Irish Political Studies*, vol. 15 (2000), pp. 1–23, at p. 2.

6 Michael Hayes, 'Dáil Éireann and the Irish Civil War', *Studies*, vol. 58, no. 229 (spring 1969), pp. 1–23, at p. 20.

7 For the 1922 constitution, see Laura Cahillane, *Drafting the Irish Free State Constitution* (Manchester, 2016).

8 Michael Laffan, *Judging W.T. Cosgrave* (Dublin, 2014), p. 120.

9 On the 1923 Land Act, see Terence Dooley and Tony McCarthy, 'The 1923 Land Act: Some new perspectives', in Mel Farrell, Jason Knirck and Ciara Meehan (eds), *A Formative Decade: Ireland in the 1920s* (Newbridge, 2015).

10 The Earl of Longford and Thomas P. O'Neill, *Éamon de Valera* (London, 1970), p. 2000. See also Kissane, *Politics of the Irish Civil War*, p. 90.

11 Ronan Fanning, *Éamon de Valera: A will to power* (London, 2015), p. 139.

12 Longford and O'Neill, *Éamon de Valera*, pp. 200–3.

13 See, for instance, Diarmaid Ferriter, *Between Two Hells: The Irish Civil War* (London, 2021), ch. 12.

14 Eoin Neeson, *The Civil War: 1922–23* (Dublin, 1989).

15 Hayes, 'Dáil Éireann and the Irish Civil War', p. 23.

Case Study – The 1923 Land Act

1 Patrick Hogan, Report on the Land Purchase and Arrears Conference, 10–11 April 1923, 17 April 1923, P24/174, Ernest Blythe Papers, UCDA.

2 Peter Hart, 'Defining the Irish Revolution', in Joost Augusteijn (ed.), *The Irish Revolution, 1913–23* (Basingstoke, 2002), p. 27.

3 *Return of Untenanted Lands in Rural Districts, Distinguishing Demesnes on Which There Is a Mansion …*, Parliamentary Papers, HC, 1906, c.177.

4 Terence Dooley, *Burning the Big House: The story of the Irish country house in a time of war and revolution* (New Haven and London, 2022), pp. 79–90.

5 In 1917, there were almost 226,500 farms below fifteen acres in 1917, which was almost 40 per cent of the total number of farms in the country (*Agricultural Statistics for Ireland with Detailed Report for 1917*, cmnd 1316, Parliamentary Papers, HC, 1921, lxi. 135, p. xiv).

6 Dooley, *Burning the Big House*, pp. 93–164.

7 *Dáil Debates*, vol. 12, no. 10, 17 June 1925, p. 1143.

8 Ibid., vol. 3, no. 17, 28 May 1923, pp. 1161–2.

9 Ibid., p. 1165.

10 Vincent Comerford, 'Why There Had to be a Land Act in 1923', in 'The Last Land War', *Farming Independent* supplement, 8 August 2023, p. 5.

11 Patrick Hogan to W.T. Cosgrave, 18 April 1923, D/T S 3192, NAI.

12 Quoted in Joseph Sheehan, 'Land Purchase Policy in Ireland 1917–23: From the Irish Convention to the 1923 Land Act', MA thesis, Maynooth University, 1993, p. 135.

13 Terence Dooley, *'The Land for the People': The land question in independent Ireland* (Dublin, 2004), pp. 132–55.

14 Witness statement, Tom Carragher, Marron Papers, Monaghan County Museum.

SECTION 5: THE DEAD

Chapter 6 – Death and Killing in the Irish Civil War

1 *Dáil Éireann Parliamentary Debates Official Report* (Dublin, 1924), vol. 7, p. 193; Anne Dolan, *Commemorating the Irish Civil War: History and memory, 1923–2000* (Cambridge, 2003).

2 National Graves Association, *The Last Post: The details and stories of the republican dead, 1913–1975* (Dublin, 1976); David Fitzpatrick, *The Two Irelands, 1912–1939* (Oxford, 1998), p. 252, fn. 29.

3 Eoin Neeson, *The Civil War in Ireland, 1922–23* (Cork, 1969), p. 291.

4 Ronan Fanning, *Independent Ireland* (Dublin, 1983), p. 39.

5 Michael Hopkinson, *Green against Green: The Irish Civil War*, 2nd edn (Dublin, 2004), p. 272. Michael Hopkinson, 'Civil War and Aftermath, 1922–4', in J.R. Hill (ed.), *A New History of Ireland, 1921–1984* (Oxford, 2003), p. 54.

6 Bill Kissane, *The Politics of the Irish Civil War* (Oxford, 2005), p. 1.

7 Diarmaid Ferriter, *Between Two Hells: The Irish Civil War* (London, 2021), p. 2.

8 Fearghal McGarry, 'Revolution, 1916–1923', in Thomas Bartlett (ed.), *The Cambridge History of Ireland* (Cambridge, 2018), vol. iv, p. 291.

9 The research and public engagement project was funded by the Department of Tourism, Culture, Arts, Gaeltacht, Sport and Media under the Government of Ireland Decade of Centenaries Programme, 2023. A wide range of sources were consulted to create the database of fatalities, including a series of county level studies by Coleman, Doyle, Durney, Farry, Hall, Keane, McNamara, Marnane and Guinan, McCarthy, Ó Duibhir, Ó Ruairc, Power, Swithin, Price, Ó Maonaigh, McConway, Bielenberg and Donnelly. More fully cited in the bibliography on pp. 481–3, these works have marked an important step forward in the last decade and a half in identifying fatalities at a regional level.

10 James Langton, *The Forgotten Fallen, National Army Soldiers Killed in Action in Civil War* (Dublin, 2019).

11 Owen O'Shea, *No Middle Path: The Civil War in Kerry* (Dublin, 2022), p. 39.

12 Gerard Shannon, *Liam Lynch: To declare a republic* (Dublin, 2023), p. 261.
13 Army Mutiny Papers, AMTY.03-07, IMA.
14 According to data from the Dead of the Irish Revolution project, 44 per cent of the British army's deaths were due to accident or 'misadventure'. Eunan O'Halpin and Daithí Ó Corráin, *The Dead of the Irish Revolution* (Yale, 2020), pp. 11, 544.
15 For the figure of anti-Treaty prisoners, see Red Cross report from Ireland, TAOIS/1369, box 3, NAI.
16 P150/1749, Éamon de Valera Papers, UCDA.
17 Bill Kissane 'The Geographical Spread of State Executions during the Irish Civil War, 1922–23', *Social Science History*, vol. 45, no. 1 (2021), pp. 165–86.
18 Seán Enright, *The Irish Civil War: Law, execution and atrocity* (Newbridge, 2019), pp. 22, 45.
19 Seán Boyne, *Emmet Dalton: Somme soldier, Irish general, film pioneer* (Newbridge, 2016), pp. 262–3.
20 Intelligence reports, Kerry Command, 14 March, cw/ops/08/08, IMA.
21 O'Halpin and Ó Corráin, *Dead of the Irish Revolution*, p. 544.
22 IRA general orders, 8 August 1922, P69/2, Moss Twomey Papers, UCDA.
23 O'Halpin and Ó Corráin, *Dead of the Irish Revolution*, p. 15.
24 Liam Lynch, IRA general orders, 9 December 1922, P67/2, Moss Twomey Papers, UCDA.
25 Gemma Clark, *Everyday Violence in the Irish Civil War* (Cambridge, 2014), pp. 70, 194.
26 Peter Hart, *The IRA at War, 1916–1923* (Oxford, 2003), pp. 126–30; Michael Farry, *The Aftermath of Revolution: Sligo, 1921–23* (Dublin, 2000) pp. 115–30.
27 Kenneth Griffin and Timothy O'Grady, *Curious Journey: An oral history of Ireland's unfinished revolution* (Cork, 1998), pp. 299–300.
28 Jane Leonard, 'Survivors', in John Horne (ed.), *Our War: Ireland and the Great War* (Dublin, 2008), p. 219.
29 Richard Mulcahy Papers, P7/B/195, UCDA. Later, in 1927, Cooper (an ex-unionist TD and ex-serviceman) claimed in the Dáil with some pride that 'It is, I believe, a fact that that 50 per cent of the members of the National Army were men who served in the British army'. (Paul Taylor, *Heroes or Traitors? Experiences of Southern Irish soldiers returning from the Great War, 1919–39* (Liverpool, 2015), p. 210.)
30 J.J. Lee, *Ireland, 1912–1985: Politics and society* (Cambridge, 1989), p. 96. The advantages of previous combat experience and training for officers can be seen in particular in the tactical success of the sea landings in Munster in August 1922 (see Boyne, *Emmet Dalton*, pp. 127–50).
31 O'Halpin and Ó Corráin, *The Dead of the Irish Revolution*, p. 544.
32 Ibid.; for Northern Ireland, specifically Belfast, see Kieran Glennon, 'The Dead of the Belfast Pogrom: Counting the cost of the revolutionary period, 1920–22', The Irish Story, 27 October 2020, https://www.theirishstory.com/2020/10/27/the-dead-of-the-belfast-pogrom-counting-the-cost-of-the-revolutionary-period-1920-22 (accessed 1 March 2024).
33 Charles Townshend, *The Republic: The fight for Irish independence* (London, 2013), pp. 428–9.
34 Matteo Millan, 'The Institutionalisation of "Squadrismo"': Disciplining paramilitary violence in the Italian fascist dictatorship', *Contemporary European History*, vol. 22, no. 4 (November 2013), p. 556.
35 Robert Gerwarth, *The Vanquished: Why the First World War failed to end, 1917–1923* (London, 2017), p. 139.
36 Tim Wilson, *Frontiers of Violence, Conflict and Identity in Ulster and Upper Silesia, 1918–1922* (Oxford, 2010), pp. 5, 19.
37 Gearóid Barry, 'Ireland and the "End of European Crisis," 1923–24', in Elaine Callinan, Mel Farrell, Thomas Tormey (eds), *Vying for Victory: The 1923 general election in the Irish Free State* (Dublin, 2023), p. 111.

Case Study – The Executions Policy

1 For an analysis of the origins of the execution policy, see Seán Enright, *Law, execution and atrocity* (Newbridge, 2022). Also, John Dorney, *The Civil War in Dublin: The fight for the Irish capital, 1922–24* (Dublin, 2017).
2 *Iris Oifigiúil*, 31 October 1922, IMA.
3 *Dáil Debates*, vol. 1, no. 30, 17 November 1922.
4 IE/MA/HS/A0770, IMA.
5 Decision of Army Council, 12 February 1923, Richard Mulcahy Papers, P/7/B/178, UCDA.
6 Firearms Act, 10–11 Geo V., ch. 43.
7 BMH WS 939, Ernest Blythe, pp. 190–2, IMA.
8 *R (Childers) v The Officer Commanding the Troops, Portobello Barracks, in the County of Dublin, and Adjutant General of the Forces of the Irish Provisional Government* [1923] IR 5.
9 Proclamation, 7 December 1922. See DoD/A/07266, IMA. Published in *Irish Times*, 8 December 1922.
10 Internal National Army order, issued by General Mulcahy, 27 January 1923, IMA.
11 Cahir Davitt, then judge advocate general, records the trial in absence of Martin Byrne for the murder of Dr Thomas Higgins. See BMH WS 1,751, Justice Cahir Davitt, p. 45, IMA. The tenor of his accounts suggests that trial in absentia had become usual.
12 Legal advice of Hugh Kennedy KC, P/7/B/142, Richard Mulcahy Papers, UCDA. In short, the Dáil had power to pass legislation but it needed the signature of the king. Cosgrave and his Cabinet decided to pass a resolution instead, presumably to avoid the embarrassment of enlisting the aid of the king in executing anti-Treaty prisoners.
13 The Constitution of the Irish Free State (Saorstat Éireann) Act No. 1 of 1922.
14 Joseph O'Toole and Daniel Regan received eighteen months. Michael Geraghty from Longford was acquitted and released. Patrick Healy from Longford was sentenced to twelve months. Henry Casey from Dublin received five years' penal servitude. See IE/MA/CW//02/02/23, IMA.
15 BMH WS 1,751, Justice Cahir Davitt, IMA. According to Davitt, this was the only reason for Mallon escaping the death penalty.
16 Bryan MacMahon, *Ballyheigue in Arms: Portrait of a Kerry parish, 1914–23* (Ballyheigue, 2023), p. 130.

Case Study – The Children and Youth of the Irish Civil War

1 Marnie Hay, *Na Fianna Éireann and the Irish Revolution, 1909–23* (Manchester, 2021).
2 Wartime childhood has been studied extensively in relation to much larger European wars. See for instance: Irena Grudzińska-Gross and Jan Tomasz Gross (eds), *War Through Children's Eyes: The Soviet occupation of Poland and the deportation, 1939–1941* (Stanford, 1981). Exceptions to this in Irish historical studies include Caoimhe Nic Dháibhéid, 'National Orphans: Trauma, emotions and experiences of the children of the 1916 Easter Rising martyrs', *Journal of British Studies*, vol. 62 (July 2023), pp. 687–712; Caoimhe Nic Dháibhéid, 'Schooling the National Orphans: The education of the children of the Easter Rising leaders', *The Journal of the History of Childhood and Youth*, vol. 9, no. 2 (2016), pp. 261–76; Roy Foster, *Vivid Faces: The revolutionary generation in Ireland, 1890–1923* (London, 2014); Joe Duffy, *Children of the Rising: The Untold Story of the Young Lives Lost during Easter 1916* (Dublin, 2015), which explored the deaths of forty children who died during Easter week.
3 See Chapter 6, Andy Bielenberg and John Dorney, 'Death and Killing in the Irish Civil War'. Of the three Cumann na mBan fatalities recorded by Bielenberg and Dorney, just one was in the 25–34 age range, the second was in the 35–44 age range and the age of the third is unknown. Two hundred and sixty-eight deaths are 'age unknown' out of a recorded total of 1,425 fatalities. To date, the twenty-seven children under the age of fifteen who died in the Irish Civil War (recovered in Bielenberg and Dorney, 2024) have not been commemorated in a public monument or in an other context.
4 Of all fatalities for all age cohorts in Bielenberg and Dorney's (Chapter 6) study, 95.4 per cent were male. Of the 307 civilian fatalities in the twenty-six counties between 28 June 1922 and 24 May 1923 where age is known, there were eleven female and fifteen male fatalities in the 0–14 (inclusive) age category, twelve female and twenty-one male fatalities in the 15–19 (inclusive) age category, and ten female and thirty-three male fatalities in the 20–24 (inclusive) age category. In terms of combatants, there was also one (male) Fianna fatality in the 0–14 age range, and five Fianna, one Civic Guard and one British army fatality (male) in the 0–19 age range.
5 See Linda Connolly, 'Women and the Civil War in Limerick: Trauma, injury and loss', in Seán William Gannon (ed.), *The Inevitable Conflict: Essays on the Civil War in County Limerick* (Limerick, 2022), pp. 47–58.
6 *Cork Examiner*, 27 December 1922.
7 Tom Donovan, 'The Tragic Shooting of Catherine Mary Hogan during the Irish Civil War', *Old Limerick Journal*, winter 2022, p. 59.
8 *Irish Times*, 18 November 1922.
9 'Mr Gordon Campbell's house burned. Children ordered out', *Irish Times*, 23 December 1922.
10 Further examples will be outlined in Linda Connolly, *Undeservedly Forgotten: Women, war and violence in Ireland, 1919–98* (London, 2025, forthcoming).

11 *Meath Chronicle*, 16 September 1922. See Linda Connolly, 'Gender, Punishment and Violence in Ireland's Revolution 1919–23', in Lyndsey Black, Louise Brangan and Deirdre Healy (eds), *Histories of Punishment and Social Control in Ireland* (London, 2022), pp. 207–24.
12 Jennifer Redmond, 'Masculinities in Revolutionary and Post-revolutionary Ireland', *Irish Studies Review*, vol. 29, no. 2 (2021), pp. 131–41.
13 *Derry Journal*, 21 July 1922.
14 *Irish Independent*, 12 February 1923.
15 For example, see BMH WS 428, Thomas Devine, IMA.
16 *Cork Examiner*, 8 March 1932.
17 BMH WS 1043, Colonel Joseph V. Lawless, IMA.
18 Gavin Foster, *The Irish Civil War and Society: Politics, class and conflict* (Basingstoke, 2015), p. 44.
19 BMH WS 1087, Patrick Mullooly, IMA.
20 For a discussion of the Schools' Collection, see Caoimhe Nic Lochlainn, '"A Work of National Importance": Child–adult dynamics in Bailiúchán Na Scol/ The Schools' Collection, 1937–1939', *Journal of the History of Childhood and Youth*, vol. 9, no. 2 (2016), pp. 203–11. For examples of Civil War memory, see Schools' Collection, vol. 0166, p. 040; vol. 0468, p. 021; vol. 0166, p. 040.

SECTION 6: GENDER, POVERTY AND RELIGION

Chapter 7 – The Irish Civil War: Family life, gender and loss

1 Síobhra Aiken, *Spiritual Wounds: Trauma, testimony & the Irish Civil War* (Newbridge, 2022).
2 For a good exploration of violence during this period, see Gemma Clark, *Everyday Violence in the Irish Civil War* (Cambridge, 2014).
3 See Fionnuala Walsh, *Irish Women and the Great War* (Cambridge, 2020).
4 Caitriona Foley, *The Last Irish Plague: The great flu epidemic in Ireland, 1918–1919* (Dublin, 2012) and Ida Milne, *Stacking the Coffins: Influenza, war and revolution in Ireland, 1918–19* (Manchester, 2018).
5 *The American Commission on Conditions in Ireland: Interim report* (London, 1921), p. 52.
6 For a contextual analysis of this legislation, see Marie Coleman, 'Military Service Pensions for Veterans of the Irish Revolution, 1916–1923', *War in History*, vol. 20, no. 2 (2013), pp. 201–21.
7 Army Pensions Act 1923, sections 2, 7, 8. See https://www.irishstatutebook.ie/eli/1923/act/26/enacted/en/html.
8 I am grateful to Cécile Gordon and Leanne Ledwidge for assistance in relation to these dependants' files.
9 This was similar for the separation allowances and pensions paid to the wives of soldiers during the First World War. See Walsh, *Irish Women and the Great War*, pp. 87–113.
10 Army Pensions Act 1923, section 2(2). See https://www.irishstatutebook.ie/eli/1923/act/26/section/2/enacted/en/html#sec2.
11 This was not unique to Ireland, but was part of a wider Western European understanding of the breadwinner model. See also Janis Lomas, '"Delicate Duties": Issues of class and respectability in government policy towards the wives and widows of British soldiers in the era of the Great War', *Women's History Review*, vol. 9, no. 1 (2000), pp. 123–47, at 127.
12 It appears there was confusion as to his identity due to the state of his body and how common his name was. See T. Gorman, Army Finance Officer to Secretary, Department of Finance, 3 September 1925, MSPC 2D22, James Byrne, IMA.
13 Catherine Byrne to Department of Defence, 18 January 1923, MSPC 2D22, James Byrne, IMA.
14 Ibid. Please note an effort has been made to retain the typographical character of all primary sources quoted in this essay, including errors.
15 Information supplied by Catherine Byrne on her A.P.5 form, MSPC 2D22, James Byrne, IMA.
16 A three-page memo was prepared for the minister on Mrs Byrne's case, *c.* July 1926.
17 Fr Harrington, The Presbytery, Duagh, Kilmorna, County Kerry, 12 December 1922.
18 They married on 2 November 1920. See MSPC 3D213, Michael J. Baker, IMA.
19 Information supplied by the superintendent, C Division, Fitzgibbon Street Station, 21 May 1924.
20 Mrs Baker, 43 Upper Gloucester Street to Army Pensions Department, 6 May 1927.
21 Michael Eastwood, 43 Gloucester Street, Upper Dublin to Department of Defence, 28 September 1932.
22 They married on 25 July 1923. MSPC 4D74, Laurence Whyte, IMA.
23 See ex-Captain Coughlan's account of the accident dated 23 May 1925.
24 Dr A.T. Byrne to Army Pension Board, 17 December 1924.
25 Widow's Allowance or Gratuity, Army Pensions Act, 1923, A.P.15 form, dependency report provided by M. Leahy, chief superintendent, Bri Chualann, Dublin and Arklow, 15 January 1925.
26 Memo marked and underscored in red: 'Dail Question, Very Urgent.' Letter from Mr Seamus Everett TD to Army Pensions Department, 21 April 1925.
27 J.J. Horgan, Army Finance Office to Margaret Whyte, Arklow, 9 November 1925.
28 Remarriage was not uncommon; see, for example, MSPC 3D79, John Mahony, IMA, whose wife remarried within months of his death.
29 Margaret and the police confirmed he had emigrated. Garda Divisional Office, Bray, report, 13 July 1928.
30 Mrs Margaret Kavanagh, Abby Street, Arklow to Department of Defence, 13 February 1928.
31 Garda Divisional Office, Bray, report, 13 July 1928.
32 Thomas Duffy, Garda Síochana, Mullingar, report, 1923, 29 February 1924.
33 Mrs Rose Bannon, Athlone to Department of Defence, 14 December 1927. She was awarded 15*s* per week from May 1924, and £180 per annum from 1 January 1953.
34 Southern Command HQ, Michael [Collins] Barracks, Cork to Adjutant General, GHQ, 5 June 1924. MSPC 2D356, Thomas Uniacke, IMA.
35 He was born on 18 February 1922 and died on 24 November 1928.
36 Surviving letters from her requesting clarification are dated 4 June 1930, 2 July 1930, 5 August 1930, 8 August 1930, 5 September 1930, 2 October 1930, 15 October 1930, 1 June 1931.
37 Department of Defence to Margaret Uniacke, 17 September 1930.
38 The Commissioner, An Garda Síochána, Dublin to Department of Defence, 3 July 1930.
39 Memo dated 10 October 1930.
40 Mrs Uniacke to Department of Defence, 1 June 1931.
41 Department of Defence to Mrs Uniacke, 9 June 1931.
42 Fr John Flanagan, Pro-Cathedral, Dublin to Archbishop Edward Byrne, Drumcondra, Dublin, 4 December 1922, Dublin Diocesan Archives, AB 7 Charity Cases, box 1.
43 See MSPC 2D451, Martin Moloney, IMA.
44 Bridget Moloney's Dependants' Allowance of Gratuity A.P.12. form, *c.* 1924.
45 Ibid.
46 Walsh, *Irish Women and the Great War*, p. 110.
47 Fr Glynn, Miltown Malbay, County Clare to Department of Defence, 12 December 1924.
48 Memo re. Mrs Moloney, 24 July 1925.
49 On how morality informed the treatment of women during the First World War, see Walsh, *Irish Women and the Great War*, pp. 97–124; Sarah-Anne Buckley, *The Cruelty Man: Child welfare, the NSPCC and the state in Ireland, 1889–1956* (Manchester, 2017).
50 MSPC 3D205, James Ryan, IMA.
51 Miss O'Brien, Cremantown Road, Dublin to Department of Defence, *c.* April 1923.
52 L. Earner-Byrne, 'The Rape of Mary M.: A microhistory of sexual and moral redemption in 1920s Ireland', *Journal of the History of Sexuality*, vol. 24, no. 1 (January 2015), pp. 75–98, at p. 94.
53 Miss A. O'Brien to Department of Defence.
54 Testimonial from D. O'Donovan, IRA, Youghal, Cork, 21 May 1938. MSPC DP5995, Ellen Murray, IMA.
55 Marie Coleman, 'Compensation Claims and Women's Experience of Violence and Loss in Revolutionary Ireland, 1921–23', in Linda Connolly (ed.), *Women and the Irish Revolution, 1917–1923: Feminism, activism, violence* (Dublin, 2020), pp. 129–47; Cal McCarthy, *Cumann na mBan and the Irish Revolution* (Cork, 2007); Margaret Ward, 'From Marginality and Militancy: Cumann na mBan, 1914–1936', in Austen Morgan and Bob Purdie (eds), *Ireland: Divided nation, divided class* (London, 1980), pp. 96–110.
56 Various witnesses in the file give different timespans for this hunger strike.
57 Letter from Polly Cosgrave to Bridie Halpin on NDU paper, 19 July 1923, Kilmainham Gaol Archive, OBJ0027 (cited in Aiken, *Spiritual Wounds*, p. 232).

58 Thomas Blake, 22 St Patrick's Hill, Cork, 24 July 1935.
59 J.M. Ingle, leather merchant, Parliament Street, Cork, 23 December 1937.
60 Brigid O'Mullane, 20 Harcourt Street, Dublin to Military Service Registration Board, Dublin, 15 June 1939.
61 She received a subsequent gratuity of £50 in 1942.
62 For a detailed exploration of this case, see Linda Connolly, 'Sexual Violence in the Irish Civil War: A forgotten war crime?' *Women's History Review*, vol. 30, no. 1 (2021), pp. 126–43. For further discussion of the Doherty case, see Linda Connolly, 'Sexual Violence and the Irish Revolution: An inconvenient truth?', *History Ireland*, vol. 27, no. 6 (November/December 2019), and idem., 'Sexual Violence a Dark Secret of the War of Independence and Civil War', *Irish Times*, 10 January 2019.
63 MSPC DP2100, Margaret Doherty, IMA. For a detailed exploration of this case, see Connolly, 'Sexual Violence in the Irish Civil War', pp. 126–43.
64 See Connolly, 'Sexual Violence in the Irish Civil War'; Clark, *Everyday Violence in the Irish Civil War*, pp. 186–93; Susan Byrne, 'Keeping Company with the Enemy': Gender and sexual violence against women during the Irish War of Independence and Civil War, 1919–1923', *Women's History Review* (2020), pp. 108–25; Earner-Byrne, 'The Rape of Mary M'; Robert Lynch, 'Explaining the Altnaveigh Massacre', *Éire-Ireland*, vol. 45, nos 3–4 (fall/winter 2010), pp. 184–210; Mary McAuliffe, '22 May 1922. The Forcible Hair Cutting of the Cullen Sisters of Keenaghan, Co. Tyrone: Gendered violence against women', in Darragh Gannon and Fearghal McGarry (eds), *Ireland 1922* (Dublin, 2022), pp. 136–9.
65 Description on Catherine Doherty's Army Pension Act, 1932 A.P.52 form, April 1933.
66 Ibid.
67 Dr Hardy/Henry[?], The Bungalow, Foxford, County Mayo, 18 April 1933.
68 Connolly, 'Sexual Violence in the Irish Civil War', p. 136.
69 Some files remained active into the 1990s.

Case Study – Violence against Women during the Irish Civil War

1 *Irish Times*, 6, 7, 9, 10 January 2020.
2 *Kerryman*, 2 April 2014; *Irish Times*, 21 August 2017.
3 Louise Ryan made a groundbreaking contribution to the Irish literature with her 2000 article, '"Drunken Tans": Representations of sex and violence in the Anglo-Irish War (1919–1921)', *Feminist Review*, no. 66 (2000), pp. 73–94.
4 Women and the Irish Revolution, funded by the Irish Research Council, Decade of Centenaries, New Foundations Grant.
5 Linda Connolly, 'The "Decade of Centenaries": Commemoration, controversies, gender, and "trending"', *Estudios Irlandeses*, no. 17 (2022), pp. 173–7; idem., 'Ethical Commemoration, Women, violence and the Irish Revolution, 1919–23', in Michael D. Higgins (ed.), *Machnamh 100: President of Ireland Centenary Reflections, Volume I* (Dublin, 2021); idem., 'Towards a Further Understanding of the Violence Experienced by Women in the Irish Revolution', in Linda Connolly (ed.), *Women and the Irish Revolution: Feminism, activism, violence* (Dublin, 2020); idem., 'Sexual Violence in the Irish Civil War: A forgotten war crime?', *Women's History Review*, vol. 30, no. 1 (2021), pp. 126–43; idem., 'Towards a Fuller Understanding of the Violence Experienced by Women in the Irish Revolution', Maynooth Social Sciences Institute working paper, 2019; idem., 'Sexual Violence and the Irish Revolution: An inconvenient truth?', *History Ireland*, vol. 27, no. 6 (November–December 2019), pp. 34–8.
6 Pádraig Yeates, *A City in Turmoil – Dublin, 1919–1921: The War of Independence* (Dublin, 2012).
7 The case is documented at length in Connolly, 'Towards a Further Understanding of the Violence Experienced by Women in the Irish Revolution'; and Connolly, 'Sexual Violence in the Irish Civil War'.
8 Mrs E.M.W. Biggs, Irish Grants Commission, CO 762/4/8, NAUK. Thank you to John Dorney, Pádraig Yeates and Pádraig Óg Ó Ruairc for sharing documents.
9 MSPC DP2100, Margaret Doherty, IMA.
10 Doherty family members also cooperated with, and participated in, a 2023 radio documentary on the case: 'A Dark Night in Foxford', RTÉ *Documentary on One* (2023; episode 3).
11 Details of this episode can be found in Connolly, 'Sexual Violence in the Irish Civil War'.

Case Study – Poor Law Reform in Revolutionary and Independent Ireland

1 BMH WS 501, T.J. McArdle, secretary, Department of Local Government, 1919–21, IMA.
2 Committee of Inquiry, Charles H. O'Connor (chairman), *Report on the Commission of the Relief of the Sick and Destitute Poor, Including the Insane Poor* (Dublin, 1927), p. 18.
3 Ibid., p. 30.
4 Board Meeting, 12 June 1924, Kerry Board of Health and Public Assistance/A/2, Minute Book, Kerry County Library.
5 Donnacha Seán Lucey, *The End of the Irish Poor Law? Welfare and healthcare reform in revolutionary and independent Ireland* (Manchester, 2015), pp. 48, 55, 129.
6 Committee of Inquiry, *Report of the Commission on the Relief of the Sick and Destitute Poor*, pp. 69, 89.
7 James M. Smith, *Ireland's Magdalen Laundries and the Nation's Architecture of Containment* (Manchester, 2007); Eoin O'Sullivan and Ian O'Donnell (eds), *Coercive Confinement in Ireland: Patients, prisoners and penitents* (Manchester, 2012), pp. x, 7.

SECTION 7: IMPRISONMENT

Chapter 8 – Graffiti and Geographies of the Women of Kilmainham Gaol during the Irish Civil War

1 'Following the Fighters? Female political imprisonment in early 20th century Ireland', funded by the Irish Research Council in collaboration with the Office of Public Works; Dr Laura McAtackney, PI. For details, see the project website: https://kilmainhamgaolgraffiti.com.
2 Pat Cooke, *A History of Kilmainham Gaol* (Dublin, 1998), p. 1.
3 Rory O'Dwyer, *The Bastille of Ireland: Kilmainham Gaol: From ruin to restoration* (Dublin, 2010), pp. 41–2.
4 Cooke, *History of Kilmainham Gaol*, p. 39.
5 Laura McAtackney, 'Material and Intangible Interventions as Future-making Heritage at Kilmainham Gaol, Dublin', *Journal of Contemporary Archaeology*, vol. 1, no. 1 (2019), pp. 120–35.
6 O'Dwyer, *Bastille of Ireland*, p. 36.
7 Margaret Ward, *Unmanageable Revolutionaries* (Dublin, 2021); Mary McAuliffe, *Margaret Skinnider* (Dublin, 2020); Sinéad McCoole, *Guns and Chiffon: Women revolutionaries and Kilmainham Gaol, 1916–1923* (Dublin, 1997); Senia Pašeta, *Irish Nationalist Women, 1900–1918* (Cambridge, 2012); Linda Connolly (ed.), *Women and the Irish Revolution: Feminism, activism, violence* (Dublin, 2020).
8 Niamh O'Sullivan, *Written in Stone: The graffiti in Kilmainham Jail* (Dublin, 2016).
9 Jeff Farrell, *Crimes of Style: Urban graffiti and the politics of criminality* (London, 1993).
10 Jeff Oliver and Tim Neal (eds), *Wild Signs: Graffiti in archaeology and history* (Oxford, 2010).
11 Kirsty Owen, 'Traces of Presence and Pleading: Approaches to the study of graffiti at Tewkesbury Abbey', in Oliver and Neal (eds), *Wild Signs*, pp. 35–46.
12 CW/P/05/02, Civil War Internment Collection, IMA.
13 Ursula Frederick and Annie Clark, 'Signs of the Times: Archaeological approaches to historical and contemporary graffiti', *Australian Archaeology*, vol. 78, no. 1 (2014), pp. 93–9; Samuel Merrill and Hans Hack, 'Exploring Hidden Narratives: Conscript graffiti at the former military base of Kummersdorf', *Journal of Social Archaeology*, vol. 13 (2013), pp. 101–21.
14 E.C. Casella, 'Written on the Walls: Inmate graffiti within places of confinement', in A.M. Beisaw and J.G. Gibb (eds), *The Archaeology of Institutional Life* (Tuscaloosa, 2009).
15 Ann Matthews, *Dissident: Irish republican women, 1923–1941* (Cork, 2012).
16 O'Dwyer, *Bastille of Ireland*, p. 13.
17 Ibid., pp. 16–39.
18 Ibid., pp. 22–4.
19 Ibid., p. 22.
20 Laurent Olivier, *The Dark Abyss of Time: Archaeology and memory* (Lanham, MD, 2011).
21 Anne Dolan, *Commemorating the Irish Civil War: History and memory, 1923–2000* (Cambridge, 2003), p. 152.
22 O'Sullivan, *Written in Stone*, p. 70.
23 Frederick and Clark, 'Signs of the Times', p. 54.

Case Study – Irish Civil War Imprisonment, Humanitarianism and the Red Cross

1 Archives of the Comité international de la Croix-Rouge, Geneva, CICR 22/84.
2 For the history of the Red Cross, see John Hutchinson, *Champions of Charity: War and the rise of the Red Cross* (Boulder, CO, 1996); David Forsythe, *The Humanitarians: The International Committee of the Red Cross* (Cambridge, 2005).
3 Kimberly Lowe, 'Humanitarianism and National Sovereignty: Red Cross intervention on behalf of political prisoners in Soviet Russia, 1921–3', *Journal of Contemporary History*, vol. 49, no. 4 (2014), pp. 652–74.
4 Shane Lowe, *A History of the Irish Red Cross* (Dublin, 2019).
5 André Durand, *History of the International Committee of the Red Cross: From Sarajevo to Hiroshima* (Geneva, 1984), pp. 226–9.
6 Haccius's reports can be found at the National Library of Ireland. See NLI MS 48,283/2/1–5.
7 On emergency legislation, imprisonment and the Free State, see Seán McConville, *Irish Political Prisoners, 1920–1962: Pilgrimage of desolation*, 1st edn (London, 2014), pp. 167–274; Seosamh Ó Longaigh, *Emergency Law in Independent Ireland, 1922–1948* (Dublin, 2006).

Case Study – 'Freedom or the Grave': The mass hunger strike of October–November 1923

1 Marion Malley (who adopted the *O* in her surname after 1922) had lost two sons by 1923. Frank Malley, an officer in the British army, was killed in east Africa, and seventeen-year-old anti-Treaty Volunteer, Charlie, in Dublin in the first week of the Civil War. See David Lloyd, 'On Republican Reading: Ernie O'Malley, Irish intellectual', in Cormac K.H. O'Malley, *Modern Ireland and Revolution: Ernie O'Malley in context* (Dublin, 2016), p. 86.
2 'Ernie O'Malley, TD', *Daily Sheet*, 31 October 1923.
3 Marion O'Malley to Richard Mulcahy, 1 November 1923, P17a/289, Ernie O'Malley Papers, UCDA.
4 Seán McConville puts the number of Civil War 'military captives' in July 1923 at 11,989 (Seán McConville, *Irish Political Prisoners, 1920–1962: Pilgrimage of desolation*, 1st edn (London, 2014), p. 212.
5 The Public Safety Act that came into effect in August 1923 enabled the government to proclaim a state of emergency and continue the use of internment.
6 Handbill, 'Freedom or the Grave. The Final Hunger Strike', October 1923, MS 17,141/19, Thomas Johnson Papers, NLI.
7 Gavin Foster, *The Irish Civil War and Society* (Basingstoke, 2015), p. 154. Mary MacSwiney's brother, Terence MacSwiney, IRA leader and Sinn Féin lord mayor of Cork, died under an international media spotlight after seventy-four days on hunger strike in October 1920. He was invoked frequently during the 1923 protest as the embodiment of the republican tenets of self-sacrifice, defiant passive resistance and triumphant failure.
8 Uinseann MacEoin, *Survivors* (Dublin, 1980), p. 31.
9 Estimates of the numbers on hunger strike in different detention centres and at different times in October and November 1923 vary significantly between republican and government sources.
10 *Sinn Féin*, 27 October 1923.
11 Cormac Moore, John Dorney and Leeann Lane, '100 Years since Final Act of Civil War', *Morning Ireland*, RTÉ Radio 1, 6 October 1923, https://www.rte.ie/radio/radio1/clips/22305586/; James Healy, 'The Civil War Hunger-strike: October 1923', *Studies: An Irish Quarterly Review*, vol. 71, no. 283 (autumn 1982), p. 216; Peadar O'Donnell, *The Gates Flew Open* (Cork, 1966), p. 85.
12 Michael Hopkinson, *Green against Green: The Irish Civil War*, 2nd edn (Dublin, 2004), p. 488.
13 Ernie O'Malley, *The Singing Flame* (Dublin, 1978), p. 250.
14 Seán McConville, *Irish Political Prisoners, 1848–1922: Theatres of war* (London, 2003), p. 755.
15 Andy O'Sullivan to 'Kattie', Mountjoy Gaol, 24 October 1923, 1D28.6, Cork Public Museum.
16 C.S. Andrews, *Dublin Made Me* (Cork, 1979), p. 301.
17 *Irish Times*, 10 November 1923.
18 Letter reproduced in *Cork Examiner*, 19 November 1923.
19 MacEoin, *Survivors*, p. 374.
20 John Dorney, *The Civil War in Dublin: The fight for the Irish capital, 1922–1924* (Newbridge, 2017), p. 266.
21 Kevin Grant, *Last Weapons: Hunger strikes and fasts in the British Empire, 1890–1948* (California, 2019), p. 95.

SECTION 8: GLOBAL CONNECTIONS

Chapter 9 – Divided Allies: Irish-America responds to the Irish Civil War

1 Kevin Kenny, *The American Irish: A history* (Edinburgh, 2000), p. 131.
2 Michael Doorley, *Irish-American Diaspora Nationalism: The Friends of Irish Freedom, 1916–1935* (Dublin, 2005), pp. 27–30.
3 Ibid., p. 37.
4 Michael Doorley, *Justice Daniel Cohalan: 1865–1946: American patriot and Irish-American nationalist* (Cork, 2019), pp. 2, 112.
5 Doorley, *Irish-American Diaspora Nationalism*, p. 38.
6 Doorley, *Justice Daniel Cohalan*, p. 99.
7 Quoted in Doorley, *Irish-American Diaspora Nationalism*, p. 79. See also Liam Mellows to Peter Golden, 8 August 1918, Golden Papers, MS 13141, NLI.
8 Doorley, *Justice Daniel Cohalan*, pp. 115–6.
9 David McCullagh, *De Valera, Volume 1: Rise, 1882–1932* (Dublin, 2017), pp. 162–8.
10 Francis Carroll, *Money for Ireland: Finance, diplomacy, politics and the First Dáil Éireann loans, 1919–1936* (Westport, 2002), pp. 33–44.
11 Doorley, *Justice Daniel Cohalan*, p. 121.
12 De Valera to Arthur Griffith, 9 July 1919, P150/727, Éamon de Valera Papers, UCDA.
13 Resolution of the national council of the Friends of Irish Freedom, reprinted in *Gaelic American*, 8 November 1919. See also Doorley, *Justice Daniel Cohalan*, pp. 150–1.
14 Doorley, *Justice Daniel Cohalan*, p. 152.
15 Press release, 22 October 1922, McGarrity Papers, MS17445, NLI.
16 Francis Carroll, 'American Association for the Recognition of the Irish Republic (AARIR)', in Michael F. Funchion (ed.), *Irish-American Voluntary Organizations* (Westport, CT, 1983), p. 10.
17 Doorley, *Irish-American Diaspora Nationalism*, p. 135; Carroll, 'American Association for the Recognition of the Irish Republic', p. 10.
18 *Gaelic American*, 30 October 1920.
19 *Irish World*, 7 January 1922.
20 Ibid.
21 *New York Times*, 8 December 1921.
22 *Gaelic American*, 17 December 1921. See also Francis Carroll, *America and the Making of an Independent Ireland* (New York, 2021), p. 147.
23 Minutes of the National Council of the FOIF, 22 January 1922, Friends of Irish Freedom Papers, American Irish Historical Society.
24 Devoy to Collins, 16 February 1922, quoted in Carroll, *America and the Making of an Independent Ireland*, p. 147.
25 Troy D. Davis, 'Irish Americans and the Treaty: The view from the Irish Free State, *New Hibernia Review*, vol. 18, no. 2 (summer 2014), p. 87.
26 McCullough to Gavan Duffy, 8 May 1922, *Documents of Irish Foreign Policy*, vol. 1, no. 282, www.difp.ie.
27 Doorley, *Justice Daniel Cohalan*, pp. 165.
28 *Dáil Éireann Debates*, vol. T, no. 15, 7 January 1922; Joseph Connolly to Department of Foreign Affairs (Dublin), 16 January 1922, *Documents of Irish Foreign Policy*, vol. 1, no. 222, www.difp.ie.
29 Michael Laffan, *The Resurrection of Ireland: The Sinn Féin party, 1916–1923* (Cambridge, 2006), pp. 350, 360.
30 Daniel Cohalan to Matthew Cummings, 13 March 1922, fl. 19, box 13, Cohalan Papers, American Irish Historical Society.
31 Carroll, *America and the Making of an Independent Ireland*, p. 146.
32 Carroll, 'American Association for the Recognition of the Irish Republic', pp. 9–12; see also American Association for the Recognition of the Irish Republic Membership Figures, July 1925, P104/2520 (55), Frank Aiken Papers, UCDA.
33 Carroll, *America and the Making of an Independent Ireland*, p. 148.
34 Joanne Mooney Eichacker, *Irish Republican Women in America: Lecture tours, 1916–1925* (Dublin, 2003), p. 141.
35 *Irish World*, 15 April 1922.
36 *New York Times*, 8 April 1922.
37 Carroll, *America and the Making of an Independent Ireland*, p. 148.
38 Collins to Devoy, February 1922, cited in Terry Golway, *John Devoy and America's Fight for Ireland's Freedom* (New York, 1998), p. 302; Michael Collins to Devoy, 2 March 1922, MS18001 (14), Devoy Papers, NLI.
39 *Gaelic American*, 8 July 1922.
40 *Irish World*, 13 May 1922.
41 Eileen McGough, *Diarmuid Lynch: A forgotten Irish patriot* (Cork, 2013), p. 158.
42 Carroll, 'American Association for the Recognition of the Irish Republic', p. 11.
43 Carroll, *America and the Making of an Independent Ireland*, p. 150.

44 Eichacker, *Irish Republican Women in America*, p. 160.
45 *Documents of Irish Foreign Policy*, vol. 11, document 69, Smiddy to Fitzgerald, 20 April 1923.
46 John Gibney, '27 December 1922. The Occupation of the Irish Consulate, New York', RTÉ Century Ireland, https://www.rte.ie/centuryireland/index.php/articles/27-december-1922-the-occupation-of-the-irish-consulate-new-york#notes (accessed 10 March 2023).
47 *Pearson's Magazine*, September 1922.
48 *Gaelic American*, 30 December 1922.
49 Ibid., 2 September 1922.
50 Gibney, 'Occupation of the Irish Consulate, New York'; Robert Briscoe, *For the Life of Me* (Boston, 1958), p. 198.
51 Gibney, 'Occupation of the Irish Consulate, New York'; *New York Times*, 31 December 1922.
52 *Documents of Irish Foreign Policy*, vol. 11, document 14, Smiddy to Fitzgerald, 6 January 1923.
53 Ibid., vol. 11, document 13, Smiddy to Fitzgerald, 6 January 1923.
54 Davis, 'Irish Americans and the Treaty', p. 91.
55 Quoted in Brian Hanley, *The IRA, 1926–1936* (Dublin, 2002), p. 161; see also Gavin Foster, 'Locating the "Lost Legion": IRA emigration and settlement after the Civil War', in John Crowley, Donal Ó Drisceoil, Mike Murphy and John Borgonovo (eds), *Atlas of the Irish Revolution* (Cork, 2017), pp. 741–7.
56 Hanley, *The IRA*, p. 164; according to IRA leader Moss Twomey, republican immigrants from Ireland helped to sustain the Clan in America, which numbered 5,000 in 1927. However, as Hanley's figures suggest, membership was still falling. An Timithire, Clan na Gael, 20 May 1927, P69/183 (47), Moss Twomey Papers, UCDA.
57 McCullagh, *De Valera*, pp. 397–9.
58 Carroll, *America and the Making of an Independent Ireland*, p. 158.
59 Bernadette Whelan, *United States Foreign Policy and Ireland, 1913–1929* (Dublin, 2006), p. 466.
60 *Cork Examiner*, 28 July 1926.
61 The research reported in this chapter was supported by the Royal Irish Academy.

Case Study – 'This Great Institution for Peace': How Ireland joined the League of Nations in 1923

1 *Documents of Irish Foreign Policy*, vol. 1, no. 299, www.difp.ie.
2 Ibid., vol. 1, no. 118.
3 Ibid., vol. 2, no. 120.
4 Ibid., vol. 3, no. 135.
5 Ibid., vol. 3, no. 161.
6 Ibid., vol. 4, no. 114.

SECTION 9: LEGACIES

Chapter 10 – The Irish Civil War Legacy: Ireland in the 1920s and 1930s

1 Noel Browne, *Against the Tide* (Dublin, 1986), p. 228.
2 Charles Townshend, 'Britain and the Irish Civil War', in Tommy Graham, Brian Hanley, Darragh Gannon and Grace O'Keeffe (eds), *The Split: From Treaty to civil war, 1921–23* (Dublin, 2021), p. 48.
3 Ronan Fanning, *Fatal Path: British government and Irish revolution, 1910–1922* (London, 2013), p. 337.
4 *Dáil Debates*, vol. 2, no. 1, 6 December 1922.
5 Ibid.
6 Quoted in Deaglán de Bréadun, 'At Leinster House, a Historically Significant Monument Lies Overlooked', *Dublin Inquirer*, 26 August 2020 (https://dublininquirer.com/2020/08/26/at-leinster-house-a-historically-significant-monument-lies-overlooked/).
7 *Dáil Debates*, vol. 2, no. 1, 6 December 1922.
8 Brian Hanley, 'The End of Civil War Politics?', in Graham, et al. (eds), *The Split*, p. 99.
9 *Dáil Debates*, vol. 47, no. 4, 3 May 1933.
10 Cormac Moore, *Birth of the Border: The impact of partition in Ireland* (Dublin, 2019), p. 82. In terms of his broader cultural and economic outlook, however, there is little to support the contemporary perception of Collins as a more modern or progressive figure than de Valera. See, for example, Michael Collins, *The Path to Freedom* (Dublin, 1968).
11 Anne Dolan, *Commemorating the Irish Civil War: History and memory, 1923–2000* (Cambridge, 2003), p. 37.
12 Anne Dolan, 'Politics, Economy and Society in the Irish Free State, 1922–1939', in Thomas Bartlett (ed.), *The Cambridge History of Ireland: Volume iv: 1880 to the present* (Cambridge, 2018), p. 343.
13 Terence de Vere White, *Kevin O'Higgins* (Tralee, 1966), p. 84.
14 Martin Maguire, 'The "Surrender" of Dublin Castle. Administering Ireland', in Darragh Gannon and Fearghal McGarry (eds), *Ireland 1922: Independence, partition, civil war* (Dublin, 2022), p. 18.
15 David Fitzpatrick, *The Two Irelands, 1912–1939* (Oxford, 1996), p. 157.
16 Darragh Gannon and Fearghal McGarry, 'Remembering 1922', in Gannon and McGarry (eds), *Ireland 1922*, pp. xxxvii–xxxviii.
17 Diarmaid Ferriter, *Between Two Hells: The Irish Civil War* (London, 2021), p. 242.
18 Ronan McGreevy, 'Execution of Four Prisoners by Free State Government Was "Murder"', *Irish Times*, 2 December 2022.
19 *Freeman's Journal*, 11 October 1922.
20 Patrick Murray, *Oracles of God: The Roman Catholic Church and Irish politics, 1922–1937* (Dublin, 2000), pp. 75, 81.
21 Michael Laffan, *Judging W.T. Cosgrave* (Dublin, 2014), p. 122.
22 Brian Heffernan, *Freedom and the Fifth Commandment: Catholic priests and political violence in Ireland, 1919–21* (Manchester, 2014), p. 33.
23 P.S. O'Hegarty, *The Victory of Sinn Féin* (Dublin, 2015), pp. 38, 91.
24 Deirdre McMahon, 'The Politician: A reassessment', *Studies: An Irish Quarterly Review*, vol. 87, no. 348 (1998), p. 346.
25 *Irish Independent*, 12 May 1925.
26 R.F. Foster, *Vivid Faces: The revolutionary generation in Ireland, 1890–1923* (London, 2014), p. 117; Daniel Mulhall, 'George Russell: A literary witness to Irish history', *History Ireland*, vol. 25, no. 4 (2017), pp. 35–6.
27 George Russell, 'Lessons of Revolution', *Studies: An Irish Quarterly Review*, vol. 12, no. 45 (1923), p. 2.
28 Seán O'Faoláin, *Vive Moi! An autobiography* (London, 1993), p. 170.
29 Quoted in Fearghal McGarry, *Eoin O'Duffy: A self-made hero* (Oxford, 2005), p. 234. Subsequent references are from the same source.
30 Moss Twomey, quoted in Brian Hanley, *The IRA, 1926–1936* (Dublin, 2002), p. 129.
31 Quoted in Ferriter, *Between Two Hells*, p. 114.
32 O'Faoláin, *Vive Moi!*, p. 170.
33 Seán O'Faoláin, '1916–1941: Tradition and creation', *The Bell*, vol. 2, no. 1 (1941), p. 11, cited in Dolan, *Commemorating the Irish Civil War*, p. 149.
34 O'Faoláin, *Vive Moi!*, pp. 171–2.
35 Ibid., p. 172.
36 Dolan, 'Irish Free State', p. 343.
37 Jimmy Wren, *The GPO Garrison Easter Week 1916: A biographical dictionary* (Dublin, 2015), p. 389.
38 Dr Harry Lee Parker, 6 September 1941, MSPC 24SP1153 Charles Dalton, IMA. See also Anne Dolan, 'The Killing of Teenagers Eamonn Hughes, Brendan Holohan and Joseph Rogers. Trauma and the legacy of violence', in Gannon and McGarry (eds), *Ireland 1922*, pp. 267–71.
39 Seán Lemass to Theresa Dalton, 12 May 1941, MSPC 24SP1153 Charles Dalton, IMA
40 Julius Ruiz, 'Seventy Years On: Historians and repression during and after the Spanish Civil War', *Journal of Contemporary History*, vol. 44, no. 3 (2009), pp. 449–72.
41 Pertti Haapala and Marko Tikka, 'Revolution, Civil War and Terror in Finland in 1918', in Robert Gerwarth and John Horne (eds), *War in Peace: Paramilitary violence in Europe after the Great War* (Oxford, 2012), p. 82.
42 Bill Kissane, *The Politics of the Irish Civil War* (Oxford, 2005), p. 239.
43 Maurice Walsh, *Bitter Freedom: Ireland in a revolutionary world, 1918–1923* (London, 2015), p. 427.
44 Dolan, 'Irish Free State', p. 345; Anne Dolan, quoted by Micheál Martin, address, Foundation of the Irish Free State conference, UCD, 2 December 1922, https://www.gov.ie/en/speech/7f202-the-taoiseachs-address-at-the-academic-conference-on-the-centenary-of-the-establishment-of-the-irish-free-state/.
45 Garret FitzGerald, 'No Mean Era', *Irish Times*, 15 November 2003.

Case Study – Veterans, Memorialisation and the Old IRA Movement in Post-Civil War Ireland

1 The term 'the Old IRA movement' first appeared in John Borgonovo, 'The Exile and Repatriation of Father Dominic O'Connor (OFM Capuchin), 1922–58', *Éire-Ireland*, vol. 52, nos 3–4 (fall/winter 2017), pp. 122–56.

2 John Borgonovo, 'Revolution, Ex-servicemen, and the Cork Branch of the National Federation of Discharged and Demobilised Sailors and Soldiers, 1918–21', in David Swift and Oliver Wilkinson (eds), *Veterans of the First World War: Ex-servicemen and ex-servicewomen in post-war Britain and Ireland* (London, 2019); David Swift and Oliver Wilkinson, 'The Deep Roots of the British Legion: The emergence of First World War veterans' organisations', in Swift and Oliver (eds), *Veterans of the First World War*; Niall Barr, *The Lion and the Poppy: British veterans, politics, and society, 1921–1938* (London, 2005); Robert Gerwarth and John Horne, *War in Peace: Paramilitary violence in Europe after the Great War* (Oxford, 2013).

3 Borgonovo, 'Revolution, Ex-servicemen, and the Cork Branch of the National Federation of Discharged and Demobilised Sailors and Soldiers'.

4 Paul Taylor, *Heroes or Traitors: Experiences of Southern Irish soldiers returning from the Great War, 1919–1939* (Liverpool, 2015).

5 Bill Kissane, *The Politics of the Irish Civil War* (Oxford, 2005), pp. 138–41.

6 Ibid., p. 146.

7 Maryann Gialanella Valius, *Almost a Rebellion: The Irish army mutiny of 1924* (Cork, 1985).

8 Brian Hanley, *The IRA, 1926–1936* (Dublin, 2002), pp. 110–13.

9 *Kerry News*, 10 May 1933.

10 *Irish Press*, 11 March 1935; Hanley, *The IRA*, p. 112.

11 Mike Cronin, *The Blueshirts and Irish Politics* (Dublin, 1997); Maurice Manning, *The Blueshirts* (Dublin, 1970).

12 Cronin, *Blueshirts and Irish Politics*, p. 20.

13 Hanley, *The IRA*, pp. 110–13.

14 Donal Ó Drisceoil, 'The "Irregular and Bolshie Situation": Republicanism and communism, 1921–36', in Fearghal McGarry (ed.), *Republicanism in Modern Ireland* (Dublin, 2003).

15 Gavin Foster, 'Glashmealcon Caves: Civil War history and memory under siege in north Kerry', *Éire-Ireland*, vol. 58, nos 3–4 (fall/winter 2023), pp. 250–94.

16 Patrick Brennan, 'Origins, Scope, and Content of the Collection', in Catriona Crowe (ed.), *Guide to the Military Service (1916–1923) Pensions Collection* (Dublin, 2012), pp. 14–43.

17 For examples in the Nominal Rolls collection, see the County Cork Old IRA Men's Association, 14 April 1937, MSPC RO-27, IMA; Cork No. 2 Brigade Old IRA Men's Association, 12 December 1936; the County Clare Old IRA Men's Federation, 24 April 1935, MSPC RO-214, IMA; the Southeast Galway Brigade Association, 21 December 1936, MSPC RO-194, IMA; Kerry No. 2 Brigade IRA Old Comrades' Association, 26 December 1936 MSPC RO-102, IMA; for military archives for the Association of the Old Cumann na mBan, see Nominal Rolls, South Wexford Brigade Cumann na mBan, MSPC CMB-127, IMA.

18 National Association of Old IRA Convention Programme, 20–21 March 1937, MS 31,270-2-5, NLI; Conventional Programme, 3 September 1938, MS 31, 270-2-21, NLI. The Cork veterans included Tom Crofts and Joe O'Connor; Florrie O'Donoghue (also from Cork city) and George Lennon were senior figures in the Neutral IRA; and the Clan na nGaedheal figures included the Dublin veterans Frank Thornton and Simon Donnelly.

19 *Irish Independent*, 1 June 1940; *Irish Press*, 4, 6 June 1940; *Cork Examiner*, 5 June 1940; *Mayo News*, 8 June 1940; *Southern Star*, 8 June 1940; *Sligo Champion*, 8 June 1940; *National and Munster Advertiser*, 8 June 1940; *Kerry News*, 10 June 1940.

20 *Nationalist and Munster Advertiser*, 5 June 1940.

21 Terry Reilly, 'The FCA, 1946–2005', *History Ireland*, vol. 19, no. 4 (January–August 2011), pp. 38–41.

22 *Irish Press*, 13 October 1952.

23 For examples, see the Kilkenny Old IRA Brigade monument at Dunnaggin, *Cork Examiner*, 1 July 1950; the memorial at Nadd, County Cork, *Cork Examiner*, 23 March 1951; the 3rd Tipperary Brigade memorial, *Tipperary Star*, 9 February 1952; the Cavan memorial, *Anglo-Celt*, 23 October 1954; the Southwest Donegal Old IRA memorial at Carrick, *Donegal Democrat*, 6 April 1951; the Ardee memorial in Louth, *Drogheda Independent*, 14 July 1951; the Athlone memorial, *Westmeath Independent*, 1 August 1951; the Ballylanders memorial in Limerick, *Nationalist and Munster Advertiser*, 12 December 1953; and the West Limerick Brigade memorial at Newcastle West, *Limerick Leader*, 22 January 1955.

24 While there were Old Cumann na mBan organisations, they were not as common as Old IRA organisations.

25 Anne Dolan, *Commemorating the Irish Civil War: History and memory, 1923–2000* (Cambridge, 2003), p. 137; Gavin Foster, 'Remembering and Forgetting in Public and Private: Reflections on the dualities of Irish Civil War memory in the "Decade of Commemoration"', *Journal of the Old Athlone Society*, vol. 3, no. 10 (2015), pp. 31–50.

26 Nuala Johnson, *Ireland, the Great War, and the Geography of Remembrance* (Cambridge, 2003); Catherine Switzer, *Unionists and the Great War: Commemoration in the North of Ireland in 1914–1939* (Dublin, 2007); Jay Winter, *Sites of Memory, Sites of Mourning: The Great War in European cultural history* (Cambridge, 1995). This chapter does not address utilitarian memorials, such as stadiums or parks named after patriotic figures.

27 Heather Jones, 'Church of Ireland Great War Remembrance in the South of Ireland: A personal reflection', in John Horne and Edward Madigan (eds), *Towards Commemoration: Ireland in war and revolution, 1912–1923* (Dublin, 2013), pp. 74–82. For a fascinating comparison of war memorials at a county level, see Kieran Doyle and Alan O'Rourke, *Monuments to Our Past: Understanding commemoration and the revolutionary period in Cork, 1914–23* (Cork, 2021). There are a couple of examples of republican memorials in Catholic churches, though they are atypical.

28 Dolan, *Commemorating the Irish Civil War*, p. 81.

29 *Westmeath Independence*, 9 May 1953.

30 Gavin Foster, *The Irish Civil War and Society: Politics, class, and conflict* (Basingstoke, 2015), pp. 22–82.

31 Roisín Higgins, *Transforming 1916: Meaning, memory, and the fiftieth anniversary of the Easter Rising* (Cork, 2012), pp. 36–40, 49–54; Mary Daly, 'Less a Commemoration of the Actual Achievements of the Men of 1916', in Mary Daly and Margaret O'Callaghan (eds), *1916 in 1966: Commemorating the Easter Rising* (Dublin, 2007), pp. 18–25.

Chapter 11 – 'Befitting Emblems of Adversity': Temporality and disruption in Irish Civil War poetry

1 Ezra Pound, *Collected Poems* (London, 2002).

2 W.B. Yeats, *The Letters of W B. Yeats*, ed. Allan Wade (London, 1954), p. 690.

3 Kate McLaughlin, *Authoring War: The literary representation of war from the Iliad to Iraq* (Cambridge, 2011), p. 6.

4 Ibid., p. 10.

5 Nicholas Allen, *Modernism and the Irish Civil War* (Cambridge, 2009); Lauren Arrington, 'Irish Modernism and its Legacies', in Richard Bourke and Ian McBride (eds), *The Princeton History of Modern Ireland* (Princeton & Oxford, 2016); Luke Gibbons, *Joyce and the Irish Revolution* (Chicago, 2023); James McNaughton, *Beckett and the Politics of Aftermath* (Oxford, 2018); Síobhra Aiken, *Spiritual Wounds: Trauma, testimony and the Irish Civil War* (Newbridge, 2022).

6 Mary Favret, *War at a Distance* (Princeton, 2010), p. 11.

7 Lyndsey Stonebridge, *The Judicial Imagination: Writing after Nuremberg* (Edinburgh, 2011), p. 5.

8 Ibid.

9 Nicholas Allen, *Modernism and the Irish Civil War* (Cambridge, 2009); Aiken, *Spiritual Wounds*; see also Síobhra Aiken 'The Silence and the Silence-breakers of the Irish Civil War, 1922–2022', *Éire-Ireland*, vol. 57, nos 1–2 (spring/summer 2022), pp. 260–88; Gerardine Meaney, 'Fiction, 1922–1960', in Heather Ingman and Clíona Ó Gallchóir (eds), *A History of Modern Irish Women's Writing* (Cambridge, 2018), pp. 187–203; Caoilfhionn Ní Bheacháin, 'Seeing Ghosts: Gothic discourses and state formation', *Éire-Ireland*, vol. 47 (2012), pp. 37–63; Ailbhe McDaid, '"It was a smoke dream": Affective aesthetics in women's literature of the Irish Civil War', *Humanities*, vol. 11, no. 4 (2022), p. 102.

10 Ernest Hemingway, *Selected Letters, 1917–1961*, ed. Carlos Baker (London, 1981), p. 176.

11 Rob Nixon, *Slow Violence and the Environmentalism of the Poor* (Cambridge, MA, 2013).

12 Lawrence J. McCaffrey, 'Trends in Post-revolutionary Irish Literature', *College English*, vol. 18, no. 1 (1956), pp. 26–30, https://doi.org/10.2307/372766, at 27, 30.

13 Frank Shovlin, 'Was *The Bell* Modernist?', in Gregory Castle and Patrick Bixby (eds), *A History of Irish Modernism* (Cambridge, 2019), pp. 364–78.

14 Meaney, 'Fiction, 1922–1960'; Lucy Collins, 'The Loss of the Irish Woman Poet 1930–50', in Paul Fagan, John Greaney and Tamara Radak (eds), *Irish Modernisms* (London, 2022), pp. 43–56, at 45.

15 Aiken, 'The Silence and the Silence-breakers', p. 267.
16 Lee M. Jenkins, 'Atlantic Triangle: Stevens, Yeats, Eliot in time of war Ireland', *Wallace Stevens Journal*, vol. 42, no. 1 (2018), pp. 17–30, doi:10.1353/wsj.2018.0002; see also Elizabeth Cullingford, 'How Jacques Molay Got Up the Tower: Yeats and the Irish Civil War', *ELH*, vol. 50, no. 4 (winter 1983), pp. 763–89.
17 Collins, 'The Loss of the Irish Woman Poet 1930–50', pp. 43–56, at 45.
18 Karen Elizabeth Brown, 'The Pictorialist Poetry of Thomas MacGreevy and the Aesthetics of Waste', *Études britanniques contemporaines*, vol. 43, 2012, pp. 27–42.
19 *Transition*, vol. 18 (Nov. 1929); see also Lauren Arrington, 'Finding His Voice: Newly discovered poems by Thomas MacGreevy', *Times Literary Supplement*.
20 Susan Schreibman, *Collected Poems of Thomas MacGreevy, An Annotated Edition* (Dublin, 1991), p. 122.
21 Lauren Arrington, 'Irish Modernism and its Legacies', in Richard Bourke and Ian McBride (eds), *The Princeton History of Modern Ireland* (Princeton & Oxford, 2016); see also Timothy P. Martin, *Joyce and Wagner. A study of influence* (Cambridge, 1991).
22 Samuel Beckett, 'Foreword', in Thomas Dillon Redshaw (ed.), *Collected Poems* (Dublin, 1971).
23 Austin Clarke, Accompanying Note to 'The Lost Heifer', *Collected Poems* (Manchester: Carcanet, 2008), p. 543.
24 Kit Fryatt, *Austin Clarke* (Aberdeen, 2020), p. 13.
25 Maurice Harmon, *Austin Clarke* (Dublin, 1989), p. 44.
26 Seán Lucy, 'The Poetry of Austin Clarke', *The Canadian Journal of Irish Studies*, vol. 9, no. 1 (1983), pp. 5–21, at 8.
27 John Goodby, 'The Poetry of Austin Clarke', in Matthew Campbell (ed.), *The Cambridge Companion to Contemporary Irish Poetry* (Cambridge, 2003), pp. 21–41.
28 Alice Milligan, 'Till Ferdia Came', in Henry Mangan (ed.), *Poems by Alice Milligan* (Dublin, 1954), pp. 189–93.
29 C.D. Blanton, *Epic Negation: The dialectical poetics of late modernism* (New York, 2015).
30 Maria Johnston, 'A Poem for Ireland: Thinking through "Dublin"', https://mariajohnstondotcom.wordpress.com/2015/02/02/a-poem-for-ireland-writing-dublin/.
31 Denis Devlin, 'The Tomb of Michael Collins', *The Sewanee Review*, vol. 64, no. 4 (1956), pp. 597–9; see also Karl O'Hanlon, 'The Case for Irish Modernism: Denis Devlin at the League of Nations and 1930s international broadcasting.' *Modernism/Modernity*, vol. 28, no. 1, pp. 157–80.
32 Eavan Boland, 'Yeats in Civil War', in *New Territory* (Dublin, 1967).
33 Yuri Lotman and Boris Ušpenskij, quoted in Aleida Assman (ed.), *Is Time Out of Joint? On the Rise and Fall of the Modern Time Regime*, trans. Sarah Clift (Ithaca, NY, 2020), pp. 217–8.
34 Assman, *Is Time Out of Joint?*, p. 17.
35 Andreas Huyssen, 'Present Pasts: Media, politics, amnesia', *Public Culture*, vol. 12, no. 1 (winter 2000), p. 21.
36 Aiken, 'The Silence and the Silence-breakers', p. 286.
37 Much earlier, and in a different genre, the domestic and the political were merged by Frank O'Connor relaying the intimate depravities of the War of Independence in 'Guests of the Nation'. Maeve Brennan's short story 'The Day We Got Our Own Back' offers a depiction of the indignities of the Civil War period through the eyes of a child; Brennan was the daughter of revolutionaries and Anti-Treatyites Robert and Úna Brennan. See Ailbhe McDaid, '"As large in my childhood as the Catholic Church and the fight for Irish freedom": Legacies of witnessed conflict in Maeve Brennan's Cherryfield Avenue stories', *New Hibernia Review*, vol. 23, no. 4 (winter/geimhreadh 2019), pp. 79–99.
38 Martina Evans, *Now We Can Talk Openly About the Men* (Manchester, 2019).
39 Martina Evans, *Facing the Public* (Manchester, 2009). See also: Ailbhe McDaid, '"When we've licked the wounds of history": Literary representations of women's experiences of the War of Independence and Civil War', in Linda Connolly (ed.), *Women and the Irish Revolution, 1917–1923: Feminism, activism, violence* (Dublin, 2020), pp. 183–97.
40 Leanne O'Sullivan, *The Mining Road* (Northumberland, 2013).
41 https://www.poetryascommemoration.ie/.
42 https://www.nationalarchives.ie/article/july-document-of-the-month/.
43 See Anne Dolan, *Commemorating the Irish Civil War: History and memory, 1923–2000* (Cambridge, 2003), p. 200; see also Guy Beiner, 'Probing the Boundaries of Irish Memory: From postmemory to prememory and back', *Irish Historical Studies*, vol. 39, no. 154 (2014), pp. 296–307.
44 The following note is offered: 'Inspired by the Papers of Michael McElligott and the Papers of Con Casey held in The Kerry Archives'.
45 Anne Dolan, 'Death in the Archives: Witnessing war in Ireland, 1919–1921', *Past and Present*, vol. 253, no. 1 (November 2021), pp. 271–300, doi:10.1093/pastj/gtab003.

Chapter 12 – The Historiography of the Irish Civil War

1 Gene Kerrigan, *Another Country: Growing up in 1950s Ireland* (Dublin, 1998), pp. 163–7.
2 Ibid.
3 Diarmaid Ferriter, *A Nation and Not a Rabble: The Irish revolution* (London, 2015), p. 55.
4 Calton Younger, *Ireland's Civil War* (London, 1968), p. vi.
5 Ibid., p. vii.
6 Michael Laffan, *The Resurrection of Ireland: The Sinn Féin party, 1916–1923* (Cambridge, 1999), p. xi.
7 John Horgan, *Seán Lemass: The enigmatic patriot* (Dublin, 1997), p. 28.
8 Ferriter, *A Nation and Not a Rabble*, p. 61.
9 Terry Clavin, 'Neeson, Eoin Francis', *Dictionary of Irish Biography*, https://www.dib.ie/biography/neeson-eoin-francis-a9988.
10 Walter Alison Phillips, *The Revolution in Ireland, 1906–23*, 2nd edn (London, 1926), p. v.
11 Diarmaid Ferriter, *Between Two Hells: The Irish Civil War* (London, 2021), p. 13, and Ferriter, *A Nation and Not a Rabble*, p. 25.
12 *Irish Times*, 30 December 2022.
13 Síobhra Aiken, *Spiritual Wounds: Trauma, testimony and the Irish Civil War* (Newbridge, 2022), pp. 7–18.
14 Ibid.
15 Ibid., pp. 2–3.
16 Ibid., p. 19.
17 Peadar O'Donnell, *The Gates Flew Open: An Irish Civil War prison diary* (Cork, 2013), pp. 132–57.
18 Patrick Murray, 'Obsessive Historian: Eamon de Valera and the policing of his reputation', *Proceedings of the Royal Irish Academy*, 101 C (2001), pp. 37–65.
19 Dorothy Macardle, *The Irish Republic* (London, 1937); Leeann Lane, *Dorothy Macardle* (Dublin, 2019), pp. 170–89.
20 Lane, *Dorothy Macardle*, pp. 170–89.
21 Brian Ó Conchubhair (ed.), *Dublin's Fighting Story, 1916–21: Told by the men who made it* (Cork, 2009; first published 1948), p. 10.
22 Síobhra Aiken, 'Contesting the Silence: Irish language writers on the Civil War', *Irish Times*, 10 May 2022.
23 Ernie O'Malley, *The Singing Flame* (Dublin, 1978), pp. 220, 286.
24 Liam Deasy, *Brother against Brother* (Cork, 1982), pp. 100–11.
25 F.S.L. Lyons, *Ireland since the Famine* (London, 1989), pp. 462–3.
26 Margery Forester, *Michael Collins: The lost leader* (London, 1971), p. 279.
27 T.P. O'Neill and Lord Longford, *Eamon de Valera* (Dublin, 1970), p. 463.
28 Michael Laffan, 'New Variations on an Old Theme: Recent works on Irish history, 1914–1922', *Stair, Journal of the HTAI* [History Teachers' Association of Ireland], vol. 2 (1979), pp. 11–13.
29 Michael Laffan, review of Michael Hopkinson, *Green against Green: The Irish Civil War*, 1st edn (Dublin, 1988), *Irish Historical Studies*, vol. 28, no. 111 (May 1993), pp. 335–6.
30 Ibid.; Tom Garvin, review of Michael Hopkinson, *Green against Green: The Irish Civil War*, 1st edn (Dublin, 1988), *Irish Literary Supplement* (fall 1989), p. 41.
31 Michael Hopkinson, *Green against Green: The Irish Civil War*, 1st edn (Dublin, 1988), p. xi.
32 Tom Garvin, *1922: The birth of Irish democracy* (Dublin, 1996), pp. 142–3.
33 John Regan, *The Irish Counter-revolution, 1921–1936: Treatyite settlement and politics in independent Ireland* (Dublin, 2001), p. 377.
34 Ibid., p. 380.
35 Bill Kissane, *The Politics of the Irish Civil War* (Oxford, 2005), p. 97.
36 Seán Enright, *The Irish Civil War: Law, execution and atrocity* (Newbridge, 2019), p. 54.
37 Owen McGee, *Arthur Griffith* (Newbridge, 2015) pp. 8, 344–6. See also Colum Kenny, *The Enigma of Arthur Griffith* (Newbridge, 2020).
38 David Fitzpatrick, *Harry Boland's Irish Revolution* (Cork, 2003), pp. 326–7.
39 Daithí Ó Corráin and Gerard Hanley, *Cathal Brugha: An indomitable spirit*

(Dublin, 2022), and Gerard Shannon, *Liam Lynch: To declare a republic* (Newbridge, 2023).

40 Peter Hart, *The IRA and Its Enemies: Violence and community in Cork, 1916–1923* (London, 1998), p. 290.

41 Peter Hart, *The IRA at War, 1916–1923* (Oxford, 2003), p. 22.

42 Hart, *IRA and Its Enemies*, pp. 286–8.

43 Gerard Murphy, *The Year of Disappearances: Political killings in Cork, 1921–1921* (Dublin, 2010), and Andy Bielenberg, John Borgonovo and James S. Donnelly Jr, '"Something of the nature of a massacre": The Bandon Valley killings revisited', *Éire-Ireland*, vol. 49, nos 3–4 (fall/winter 2014), pp. 7–59.

44 Peter Hart, 'The Social Structure of the IRA, 1916–23', *Historical Journal*, vol. 42, no. 1 (March 1999), pp. 207–31.

45 Eve Morrison, 'Bureau of Military History Witness Statements as Sources for the Irish Revolution', www.militaryarchives.ie/collections/online-collections/bureau-of-military-history-1913–1921/wp-content/uploads/2019/06/Bureau_of_Military_witness_statements-as_sources-for_the_Irish-Revolution.pdf.

46 Ibid.

47 Margaret Ward, *Unmanageable Revolutionaries: Women and Irish nationalism* (London, 1995), p. 2.

48 Mary McAuliffe, 'The Homefront as Battlefront: Women's experience of violence and loss in revolutionary Ireland, 1921–23', in Linda Connolly (ed.), *Women and the Irish Revolution* (Kildare, 2020), pp. 164–83.

49 Marie Coleman, 'Compensation Claims and Women's Experience of Violence and Loss in Revolutionary Ireland, 1921–23', in Connolly (ed.), *Women and the Irish Revolution*, pp. 129–48.

50 Claire McGing, 'Women's Political Representation in Dáil Éireann in Revolutionary and Post-revolutionary Ireland', in Connolly (ed.), *Women and the Irish Revolution*, pp. 85–103.

51 Gemma Clark, *Everyday Violence in the Irish Civil War* (Cambridge, 2014), pp. 86–93.

52 Linda Connolly, 'Sexual Violence and the Irish Revolution: An inconvenient truth?', *History Ireland*, vol. 27, no. 6 (November/December 2019), pp. 34–8.

53 Ibid.

54 Linda Connolly, 'Sexual Violence in the Irish Civil War: A forgotten war crime?', *Women's History Review*, vol. 30, no. 1 (2021), pp. 126–43.

55 Máire Comerford, *On Dangerous Ground: A memoir of the Irish revolution*, ed. Hilary Dully (Dublin, 2021), p. viii.

56 Ibid., p. 258.

57 Ward, *Unmanageable Revolutionaries*, pp. 197–8.

58 John Dorney, *The Civil War in Dublin: The fight for the Irish capital, 1922–1924* (Dublin, 2017), p. 2.

59 Pádraig Yeates, *A City in Civil War: Dublin, 1921–1924* (Dublin, 2015), p. xi.

60 John Borgonovo, *The Battle for Cork: July–August 1922* (Cork, 2011).

61 Owen O'Shea, *No Middle Path: The Civil War in Kerry* (Newbridge, 2022).

62 Fergal Keane, *Wounds: A memoir of war & love* (London, 2017), pp. 216–46.

63 John Crowley, Donal Ó Drisceoil, Mike Murphy and John Borgonovo (eds), *Atlas of the Irish Revolution* (Cork, 2017), pp. 694–732.

64 Conor Kostick, *Revolution in Ireland: Popular militancy, 1917–1923* (London, 1996), pp. 1, 190.

65 Gavin Foster, *The Irish Civil War and Society: Politics, class and conflict* (Basingstoke, 2015), pp. 57–61.

66 Ibid., p. 205, and Gavin Foster, 'Locating the "Lost Legion": IRA emigration and settlement after the Civil War', in Crowley, et al. (eds), *Atlas of the Irish Revolution*, pp. 741–7.

67 Clark, 'Violence against Women', and idem., *Everyday Violence in the Irish Civil War*, pp. 6–8.

68 Brian Hanley, 'Terror in Twentieth-century Ireland', in David Fitzpatrick (ed.), *Terror in Ireland, 1916–23* (Dublin, 2012), pp. 10–26.

69 Eunan O'Halpin and Daithí Ó Corráin, *The Dead of the Irish Revolution* (New Haven, CT, 2020).

70 Anne Dolan, *Commemorating the Irish Civil War: History and memory, 1923–2000* (Cambridge, 2003), p. 1.

71 Ibid., p. 200.

Chapter 13 – Historians and the 'Silence' of the Irish Civil War: Some comparative perspectives

1 *Irish Independent*, 24 January 1924; *Donegal Democrat*, 3 February 1922; *Irish Examiner*, 12 September 1922; *Belfast Newsletter*, 5 November 1923.

2 'Amhrán an Ghorta', in Cormac Ó Grada, *An Drochshaol: Béaloideas agus amhráin* (Dublin, 1994), p. 73; Paul Fussell, *The Great War and Modern Memory* (Oxford, 2013), p. 77; Carles Santacana i Torres, cited in Michael Richards, *Un tiempo de silencio: La guerra civil y la cultura de la represión en la España de Franco, 1936–1945* (Barcelona, 1999), p. 113; Primo Levi, *Se questo è un uomo* (Turin, 1992), p. 23.

3 See Guy Beiner, *Forgetful Remembrance: Social forgetting and vernacular historiography of a rebellion in Ulster* (Oxford, 2018).

4 Niall Ó Ciosáin, 'Was There "Silence" About the Famine?', *Irish Studies Review*, vol. 4, no. 13 (December 1995), pp. 7–10; Kelleher, *The Feminization of Famine: Expressions of the inexpressible?* (Durham, NC, 1997); Fussell, *Great War and Modern Memory*, p. 170. Jay Winter, *War beyond Words: Languages of remembrance from the Great War to the present* (Cambridge, 2017); Santos Juliá, 'De "guerra contra el invasor" a "guerra fratricida"', in Santos Juliá and Julián Casanova (eds), *Víctimas de la Guerra Civil* (Temas de Hoy, 1999), p. 49.

5 David Cesarani, 'Introduction', in David Cesarani and Eric J. Sundquist (eds), *After the Holocaust: Challenging the myth of silence* (New York, 2011), p. 2; Hasia R. Diner, *We Remember with Reverence and Love: American Jews and the myth of silence after the Holocaust, 1945–1962* (New York, 2010), p. 7.

6 See Enda Delaney and Fearghal McGarry, 'Introduction: A global history of the Irish revolution', *Irish Historical Studies*, vol. 44, no. 165 (May 2020), pp. 1–10.

7 Caoimhe Nic Dháibhéid, 'Historians and the Decade of Centenaries in Modern Ireland', *Contemporary European History*, vol. 32, no. 1 (February 2023), p. 26.

8 Ó Ciosáin, 'Was There "Silence" About the Famine?', p. 9; terms used by Fr Aloysius Travers, Bureau of Military History Witness Statement 200, pp. 18–19; Felicity Hayes-McCoy, *A Woven Silence* (Dublin, 2015); Martin Malone, *The Silence of the Glasshouse* (Dublin, 2008); *The Silent Civil War* (Scratch Films for RTÉ, 2023), dir. Maurice Sweeney, aired 26 April 2023.

9 Tom Garvin, *Judging Lemass: The measure of the man* (Dublin, 2009), p. 187; Charles Townshend, *The Republic: The fight for Irish independence, 1918–1923* (London, 2013), p. 450; Edna Longley, *The Living Stream: Literature & revisionism in Ireland* (Northumberland, 1994), p. 81.

10 'Decade of Centenaries Programme Phase 2: 2018–2023: Guidance from the Expert Advisory Group on Commemorations', *Irish Museums Association*, 12 July 2018, p. 5.

11 Ó Máille initially supported the Treaty and was elected for Cumann na nGaedheal in 1923. He later founded the short-lived party Clann Éireann, before joining Fianna Fáil in 1927. *Connacht Tribune*, 2 February 1929.

12 *Irish Independent*, 10 March 1928; *Dáil Debates*, vol. 50, no. 7, 7 February 1934; *Irish Examiner*, 17 August 1936, 3 May 1954; *Corkman*, 23 August 1969.

13 J.J. Lee, *Ireland, 1912–1985: Politics and society* (Cambridge, 1989), p. 68; R.F. Foster, *The Irish Story: Telling tales and making it up in Ireland* (Oxford, 2002), p. 234.; Tom Garvin, 'The Aftermath of the Irish Civil War', speech at St Columban's College, 20 October 1997, http://meathpeacegroup.org/wp/1997/10/; Eunan O'Halpin, 'Personal Loss and the "Trauma of Internal War": The cases of W.T. Cosgrave and Seán Lemass', in Melania Terrazas Gallego (ed.), *Trauma and Identity in Contemporary Irish Culture* (Bern, 2020), p. 176; Anne Dolan, *Commemorating the Irish Civil War: History and memory, 1923–2000* (Cambridge, 2003), p. 200.

14 Bill Kissane, review of Anne Dolan, *Commemorating the Irish Civil War: History and memory, 1923–2000* (Cambridge, 2003), *Field Day Review*, vol. 2 (2006), p. 339.

15 For example, see Fernando Martínez López and Miguel Gómez Oliver, 'Political Responsibilities in Franco's Spain: Recovering the memory of economic repression and social control in Andalusia, 1936–45', in Aurora G. Morcillo (ed.), *Memory and Cultural History of the Spanish Civil War: Realms of oblivion* (Leiden, 2014), pp. 111–45.

16 For example, see Anne Heimo and Ulla-Maija Peltonen, 'Memories and Histories, Public and Private after the Finnish Civil War', in Katharine Hodgkin and Susannah Radstone (eds), *Memory, History, Nation: Contested pasts* (New York, 2005), pp. 42–56.

17 Gabriel Doherty, 'Foreword', in Pádraig Óg Ó Ruairc, *The Battle for Limerick City* (Cork, 2010), p. 12.

18 Jeffrey C. Alexander, *Trauma: A social theory* (Cambridge, 2013), p. 7.

19 *Nenagh News*, 6 May 1922.

20 *Irish Independent*, 5 February 1954; F.S.L. Lyons, *Ireland since the Famine* (London, 1971), p. 460; Townshend, *The Republic*; Diarmaid Ferriter, 'We Have Not Yet Reached an Era of Mature Civil War Commemoration', *Irish Times*, 9 December 2022.

21 *Irish Press*, 22 October 1934; *Irish Times*, 13 November 2008; *Evening Herald*,

3 June 1972; *The Irish Civil War*, episode 3 (51'58") (Create One/Wonderland and Tyrone Productions for RTÉ, 2022), dir. Ruán Magan, aired 13 December 2022; *Bitter Divisions* (exhibition), 2 November 2020, National Museum of Ireland, https://www.museum.ie/en-IE/Collections-Research/Art-and-Industry-Collections/Exploring-the-Irish-Wars,-1919–1923/Bitter-Divisions.

22 Lindsay Janssen, 'From Silence to Plenty: The Famine in early twentieth-century periodical fiction', *Éire-Ireland*, vol. 54, no. 3 (2019), p. 141.

23 Bill Kissane, 'On the Shock of Civil War: Cultural trauma and national identity in Finland and Ireland', *Nations and Nationalism*, vol. 26, no. 1 (2020), p. 34.

24 Jo Labanyi, 'Memory and Modernity in Democratic Spain: The difficulty of coming to terms with the Spanish Civil War', *Poetics Today*, vol. 28, no. 1 (March 2007), p. 109; Radhika Mohanram, 'Gendered Spectre', *Cultural Studies*, vol. 25, no. 6 (1 November 2011), p. 927.

25 Ciosáin, 'Was There "Silence" About the Famine?', p. 9; Maurice Manning, 'Context from the Chair of the Expert Advisory Group (EAG) on Centenary Commemorations', *Decade of Centenaries, 2012–2023: 2022 programme*, p. 4.

26 Paul Quigley, 'Reconciliation: Civil war by other means', in Paul Quigley and James Hawdon (eds), *Reconciliation After Civil Wars: Global perspectives* (New York, 2018), p. 2; Lea David, *The Past Can't Heal Us* (Cambridge, 2020), p. 1; see Dr Noël Browne's opposition to calls by Taoiseach Seán Lemass to forget the Civil War, *Dáil Debates*, vol. 191, no. 2, 5 July 1961; *Irish Press*, 10 July 1933; Michael D. Higgins, 'An Opportunity for Ethical Remembering', *Irish Times*, 10 May 2022.

27 Townshend, *The Republic*, p. 450; Bill Kissane, 'A Nation Once Again?', in idem. (ed.), *After Civil War: Division, reconstruction, and reconciliation in contemporary Europe* (Philadelphia, PA, 2014), p. 53.

28 'Current Commentary', *Irish Book Lover*, November/December 1929, p. 45.

29 Eoin Neeson, *The Civil War in Ireland, 1922–23* (Cork, 1966), p. 11; Michael Hopkinson, *Green against Green: The Irish Civil War*, 1st edn (Dublin, 1988), p. xi.

30 Peter Hart, *The I.R.A. at War, 1916–1923* (Oxford, 2005), p. 30.

31 James M. Cahalan, *Great Hatred, Little Room: The Irish historical novel* (Syracuse, NY, 1983), p. 42.

32 Elisa Adami, 'The Truth of Fiction: Some stories of the Lebanese civil wars', in Karine Deslandes, Fabrice Mourlon and Bruno Tribout (eds), *Civil War and Narrative: Testimony, historiography, memory* (Cham, Switzerland, 2017), p. 110.

33 P.C. Trimble, 'A Current Commentary (announcing Frank O'Connor's *Guests of the Nation*)', *Irish Book Lover*, July/August 1931, p. 112; *Irish Press*, 10 June 1936, p. 6; Ida Bachmann, review of Nis Petersen, *Spildt Mælk* (Copenhagen, 1934), *Books Abroad*, vol. 10, no. 3 (summer 1936), p. 300.

34 Étiennette Beuque, *L'Holocauste: Roman* (Valencia, 1937); Nis Petersen, *Spildt mælk* (Copenhagen, 1934); Kathleen Pawle, *We in Captivity* (New York, 1936); Constantine FitzGibbon, *High Heroic* (New York, 1969).

35 See Síobhra Aiken, 'The Silence and the Silence Breakers of the Irish Civil War, 1922–2022', *Éire-Ireland*, vol. 57, no. 1 (2022), pp. 260–88.

36 Gavin Foster, 'Collective Trauma: War inherited an awkward place in history', *Irish Examiner*, 13 June 2022.

37 Kelleher, *Feminization of Famine*, p. 4; Doherty, 'Foreword', p. 13; *Irish Examiner*, 23 June 1966; *Observer*, 17 November 1968; Diarmaid Ferriter, *Between Two Hells: The Irish Civil War* (London, 2021), p. 11. For consideration of oral histories, see Gavin Foster, 'Patterns of Irish Civil War Memory in Later-generation Oral Histories', *Contemporary European History*, vol. 32, no. 4 (May 2023), pp. 1–14.

38 Cahalan, *Great Hatred, Little Room*, p. 110; Edna Longley, 'The Rising, the Somme and Irish Memory', in Máirín Ní Dhonnchadha and Theo Dorgan (eds), *Revising the Rising* (Derry, 1991), p. 43; R.F. Foster, 'W.B. Yeats in Thoor Ballylee: Meditating in time of Civil War', in Gannon and McGarry (eds), *Ireland 1922*, p. 127; Gareth Thomas, *The Novel of the Spanish Civil War (1936–1975)* (Cambridge, 1990), p. 3.

39 Peter Costello, *The Heart Grown Brutal: The Irish revolution in literature from Parnell to the death of Yeats, 1891–1939* (Dublin, 1977), p. 193; Emer Nolan, 'Irish Culture's Remarkable Response to the Political Turmoil from 1891 to 1922', *Irish Times*, 10 May 2022; Patrick Mulloy, *Jackets Green* (London, 1936); Annie M.P. Smithson, *The Marriage of Nurse Harding* (Dublin, 1935); A.P. Fanning, *Vigil: A play in one act* (Birr, 1933).

40 Terry Eagleton, 'Another Country', review of Joseph O'Connor, *Star of the Sea* (London, 2002), *Guardian*, 25 January 2003; Gerardine Meaney, 'Best Fiction of the Irish War of Independence', *Irish Times*, 30 May 2021.

41 Alan Rosen, '"We know very little in America": David Boder and un-belated testimony', in Cesarani and Sundquist (eds), *After the Holocaust*; D. Ó Maol Blagaide, 'In principio erat verbu', *An tUltach*, vol. 90, no. 1 (January 2013), p. 17; *Munster Express*, 24 June 1966; Eunan O'Halpin, 'A Savage Chaos', *Irish Review*, no. 6 (1989), p. 147; John L. Murphy, review of Tim Pat Coogan and George Morrison, *The Irish Civil War* (Boulder, CO, 1998), *New Hibernia Review*, vol. 3, no. 2 (samhradh/summer 1999), pp. 158–9; Pádraic Whyte, *Irish Childhoods: Children's fiction and Irish history* (Newcastle, 2011), p. 27.

42 Ferriter, *Between Two Hells*, p. 13; Roy Foster, 'Remembering 1798', in Ian McBride (ed.), *History and Memory in Modern Ireland* (Cambridge, 2001), p. 93; Dolan, *Commemorating the Irish Civil War*, p. 4.

43 O'Halpin, 'Personal Loss and the "Trauma of Internal War"', p. 162.

44 Noel Browne, *Against the Tide* (Dublin, 1986), p. 228.

45 Jason K. Knirck, *Women of the Dáil: Gender, republicanism and the Anglo-Irish Treaty* (Kildare, 2006); Dianne Hall, 'Irish Republican Women in Australia: Kathleen Barry and Linda Kearns's tour in 1924–5', *Irish Historical Studies*, vol. 43, no. 163 (May 2019), pp. 73–93, Síobhra Aiken, '"Sinn Féin permits … in the heels of their shoes": Cumann na mBan emigrants and transatlantic revolutionary exchange', *Irish Historical Studies*, vol. 44, no. 165 (May 2020), pp. 106–30.

46 Dolan, *Commemorating the Irish Civil War*, p. 4; Ferriter, *Between Two Hells*, p. 206; Townshend, *The Republic*, p. 450.

47 *Daily Bulletin*, 22 March 1923; *Éire*, 7 April 1923.

48 Dorothy Macardle, *Tragedies of Kerry, 1922–1923* (Dublin, 1924); Liam Mac Gabhann, 'The Message of the Banshee', *Kerry News*, 10 March 1926, p. 1; Dónal O'Keeffe, 'Drama of Ballyseedy', *An Phoblacht*, 16 December 1933–10 February 1934.

49 For further discussion, see Owen O'Shea, *No Middle Path: The Civil War in Kerry* (Dublin, 2023), p. 4; *Kerryman*, 26 December 1980.

Index

ROYAL HOSPIT
PROPOSED CONVERSION INTO

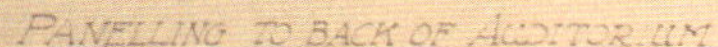

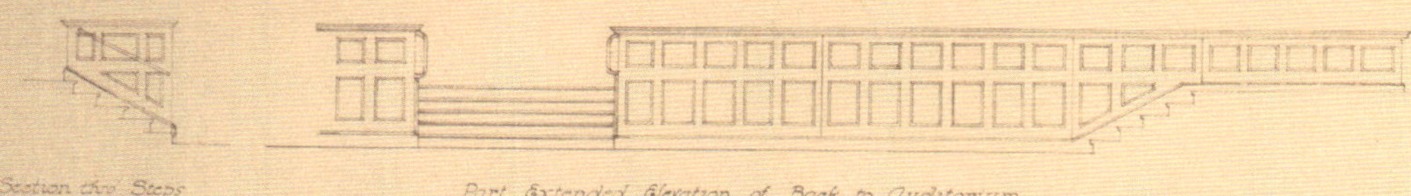

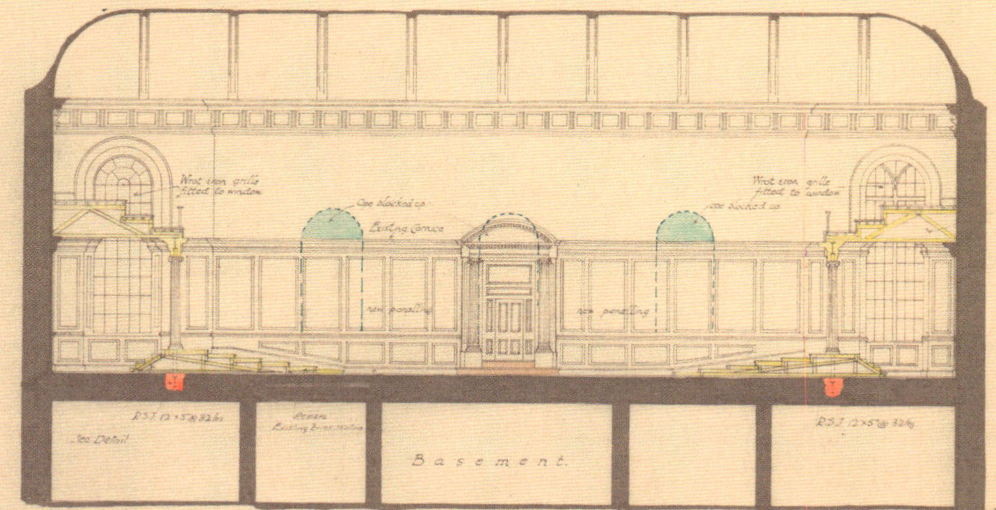

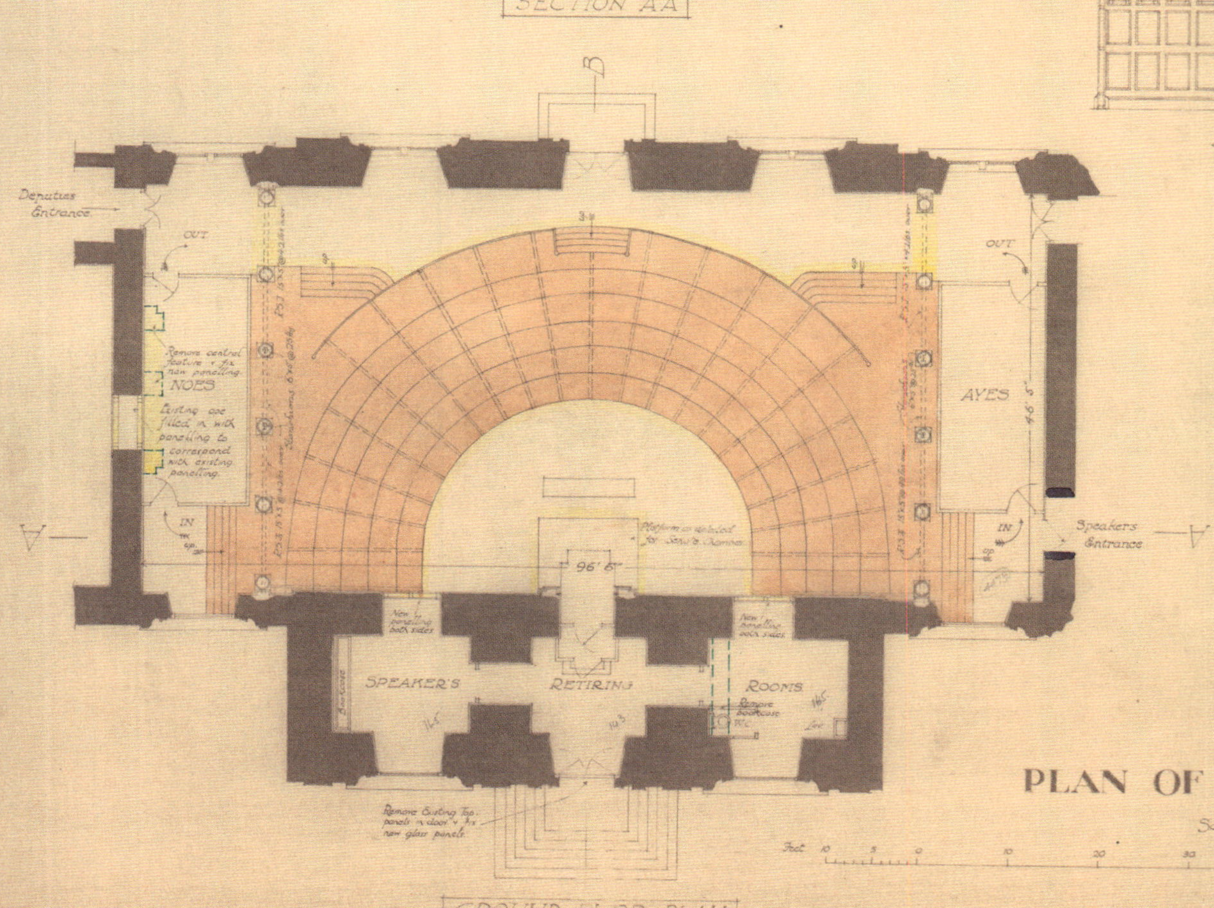

Royal Hospital Kilmainham: proposed conversion into the Houses of the Oireachtas (1923), pen and ink on linen-backed paper. In the early years of the Irish Free State, the site for a new parliament – the Oireachtas – had to be identified. This was not a straightforward decision. Rather than building a costly new structure, the Office of Public Works considered three existing sites for renovation: Leinster House, Dublin Castle and the Royal Hospital Kilmainham. All three sites were closely associated with British rule. In fact, the Royal Hospital was still home to a number of retired soldiers. While detailed plans were drawn up to transform the building into the Irish house of parliament, Leinster House, which was used as a temporary home initially from September 1922, became the permanent site following the purchase of the building by the state in 1924. [Document: Oireachtas Plans, Dáil Chamber, 1923, National Archives, OPW/5/HC/3/11/ Plan 5. Reproduced by kind permission of the director of the National Archives]